The Princeton Review
PrincetonReview.com

The Best Northeastern Colleges

212 Select Schools to Consider

By Robert Franek,
Tom Meltzer, Christopher Maier,
Julie Doherty, Erik Olson, Eric Owens,
Michael Palumbo, and Marissa Pareles

Random House, Inc.
New York

The Princeton Review, Inc.
2315 Broadway
New York, NY 10024
E-mail: bookeditor@review.com

ISBN 978-0-375-42873-9

VP, Publisher: Robert Franek
Editors: Seamus Mullarkey, Adam Davis, Laura Braswell
Executive Director, Print Production: Scott Harris
Senior Production Editor: M. Tighe Wall

Printed in the United States of America.

9 8 7 6 5 4 3 2 1

FOREWORD

Every year, about two million high school graduates go to college. To make sure they end up at the *right* school, they spend several billion dollars on the admissions process. This money pays for countless admissions officers and counselors, a bunch of standardized tests (and preparation for them), and many books similar to—but not as good as—this one.

It's so expensive because most admissions professionals have a thing about being in control. As a group, colleges resist almost every attempt to standardize or otherwise simplify the process. Admissions officers want you to believe that every admissions decision that they render occurs within systems of weights, measures, and deliberations that are far too complex for you to comprehend. They shudder at the notion of having to respond to students and their parents in down-to-earth language that might reveal the arbitrary nature of a huge percentage of the admissions and denials that they issue during each cycle. That would be admitting that good luck and circumstance play a major part in many successful applications. So, in flight from public accountability, they make the process a lot more mysterious than it needs to be.

Even the most straightforward colleges hide information you would want to know about the way they'll evaluate your application: What grades and SAT scores are they looking for? Exactly how much do extracurricular activities count? What percentage of the aid that they give out is in loans and what percentage is in grants?

We couldn't get answers to these questions from many colleges. In fact, we couldn't get answers to *any* questions from some schools. Others who supplied this information to us for earlier editions of this guide have since decided that they never should have in the first place. After all, knowledge is power.

Colleges seem to have the time and money to create beautiful brochures that generally show that all college classes are held under a tree on a beautiful day. Why not just tell you what sort of students they're looking for and what factors they'll use to consider your application?

Until the schools demystify the admissions process, this book is your best bet. It's not a phone book containing every fact about every college in the country; it's not a memoir written by a few graduates describing their favorite dining halls or professors. We've given you the facts you'll need to apply to the best schools in the Northeast. And we've gathered information from hundreds of college administrators and tens of thousands of college students to help you make a smart decision about which school to attend.

One note: We don't talk a lot about majors. This is because most high school students really don't know what they want to major in—and the ones who do almost always change their minds by the beginning of junior year. Choosing a school because of the reputation of a single department is often a terrible idea.

If you're interested in learning about majors and the colleges that offer them, pick up our *Guide to College Majors* or visit our website, PrincetonReview.com, where we explain majors and list the colleges that offer them.

As complicated and difficult as the admissions process is, we think you'll love college itself—especially at the schools listed in this book.

Good luck in your search.

John Katzman
March 2008

ACKNOWLEDGMENTS

A special thank you goes to our authors, Tom Meltzer, Michael Palumbo, Christopher Maier, Julie Doherty, Erik Olson, Marissa Pareles, and Eric Owens for their dedication in sifting through tens of thousands of surveys to produce the essence of each school profiled. Very special thanks go to Seamus Mullarkey, Adam Davis, and Laura Braswell for their editorial commitment and vision. They met the challenges of this book head on; I am grateful for their thoughtful and careful reading. Thanks also to Jennifer Little and Lisa Marie Rovito for their meticulous work on this book.

A warm and special thank you goes to our Student Survey Manager Jen Adams who works exceptionally well with school administrators and students alike. Jen is in the trenches every day, and her spirit never wavers.

My continued thanks go to our data collection pros, Ben Zelevansky and David Soto, for collecting the statistical data that appear with each college profile. An additional thank you goes to Ben Zelevansky for smoothly transferring all that data to this book.

The enormousness of this project and its deadline constraints could not have been realized without the calm presence of our production team, Scott Harris, Executive Director of Print Production; M. Tighe Wall, Senior Production Editor. Their focus, unconditional dedication, and careful eyes continue to inspire and impress me. They deserve great thanks for their flexible schedules and uncompromising efficiency.

Robert Franek
Publisher
Lead Author—The Best Northeastern Colleges:
212 Select Schools to Consider

CONTENTS

...So Much More Online!

More Guidance...

- Find school matches with Counselor-O-Matic
- Explore majors with the click of the mouse
- Advice on everything from raising test scores to career planning
- Help with selecting a summer program, a study abroad program, or finding an internship
- Get the inside scoop of scholarships and financial aid

More Information...

- Articles on college life for students and parents alike
- Our College Hopes & Worries Survey
- Detailed profiles for hundreds of colleges help you find the school that is right for you
- Dozens of Top 20 ranking lists based on our student surveys. Categories include schools with "Best Classroom Experience," "Dorms Like Palaces"/"Dorms Like Dungeons," "Most Beautiful Campus," "Best Athletic Facilities" and tons more!

More Good Stuff...

- Discover other Princeton Review titles that will help you ace the big test or find your best fit college
- Discuss issues with your peers on our discussion board
- Info on grad, med, business, and law schools
- And much, much more!

PrincetonReview.com

PART 1: INTRODUCTION

GETTING INTO THE BEST NORTHEASTERN COLLEGES

This is a guide to the Northeast's 212 most academically outstanding institutions, so it's no surprise that many of them may be selective in their admissions. If you're like any one of the 2,000,000 (and growing!) high school students who apply to college each year, you're probably wondering what admissions officers at these schools are looking for in an applicant. What exactly does it take to get into a selective college? To be sure, high grades in challenging courses are just the beginning. To get into most of the colleges in this book, you will need to:

- Earn high grades.

- Enroll in challenging courses.

- Prepare for the SAT or the ACT, and SAT Subject Tests.

- Polish your writing skills.

- Plan ahead for those letters of recommendation you'll need by establishing great relationships with your teachers and advisors.

- Focus on activities, community service, and/or after-school or summer employment that show commitment over a long period of time and allow you to demonstrate leadership skills.

Here's a brief primer in what you should be doing year by year in high school to prepare yourself for admission to *your* "best fit" college. For a detailed guide on how you can make the most of your high school years and segue those experiences into a successful college application, check out our new book: *The Road to College: The High School Student's Guide to Discovering Your Passion, Getting Involved, and Getting Admitted*. Pick it up at PrincetonReview.com/bookstore.

FRESHMAN YEAR

It's easier to finish well in high school if you start off that way. Concentrate on your studies and work hard to earn good grades. Get to know your teachers and ask for their help if you are having trouble in a subject (or even if you just really enjoy it and want to learn more): They'll most certainly want to help you do your best. Odds are, there is an honor roll at your school: Make it a goal to get on it. And if your grades are so good that you qualify for membership in the National Honor Society, pat yourself on the back and don't think twice about accepting the invitation to join.

Make it a point to meet your guidance counselor to begin thinking about colleges you may be interested in and courses and admission tests they require. Also work on building your vocabulary to get an early start on prepping for the SAT and ACT. Sign up for the Princeton Review's Vocab Minute on PrincetonReview.com.

READ A GOOD BOOK!

Your vocabulary and reading skills are key to doing well on the SAT and ACT. You can do some early prep for both tests by reading good books. Here are some fiction and non-fiction books we love by great authors you may not have encountered before.

- *The Curious Incident of the Dog in the Night-Time: A Novel* by Mark Haddon

- *A Heartbreaking Work of Staggering Genius* by Dave Eggers

- *Life of Pi* by Yann Martel

- *Reading Lolita in Tehran* by Azar Nafisi

- *White Teeth* by Zadie Smith

For extra practice building your vocabulary, check out our *Word Smart* books. Full of mnemonic tricks, they make learning even the toughest vocabulary a breeze.

SOPHOMORE YEAR

As a sophomore, you'll need to stay focused on your studies. You'll also want to choose one or more extracurriculars that interest you. Admissions officers look favorably on involvement in student government, student newspaper, varsity sports, and community service. But don't overload your schedule with activities just to rack up a long list of extracurriculars that you hope will impress admissions officers. Colleges would much rather see you focus on a few worthwhile extracurriculars than divide your time among a bunch of different activities that you're not passionate about. If you didn't earn strong grades during your freshman year, start doing so this year. Scope out the Advanced Placement course offerings at your school. You'll want to sign up for as many AP courses as you can reasonably take, starting in your junior year. Admissions officers will want to see that you've earned high grades in challenging classes. Our test-prep series, *Cracking the AP*, can help give you a leg up on passing the AP exams and gaining college credit while in high school.

Your sophomore year is when you'll have an opportunity to take the PSAT. Given every October, the PSAT is a shortened version of the SAT. It is used to predict how well students may do on the SAT, and it determines eligibility for National Merit Scholarships. While your PSAT scores won't count until you retake the test in your junior year, you should approach this as a test run for the real thing. Check out our book, *Cracking the PSAT/NMSQT* for more info. It has two full-length practice tests and tips on how to score your best on the test.

What Should You Do This Summer?

Ahhh, summer. The possibilities seem endless. You can get a job, intern, travel, study, volunteer, or do nothing at all. Our Princeton Review book, The Road to College, also has great suggestions for summer projects. Here are a few ideas to get you started:

- **Go to College**: No, not for real. However, you can participate in summer programs at colleges and universities at home and abroad. Programs can focus on anything from academics (stretch your brain by taking an intensive science or language course) to sports to admissions guidance. This is also a great opportunity to explore college life firsthand, especially if you get to stay in a dorm.

- **Prep for the PSAT, SAT, or ACT**: So maybe it's not quite as adventurous as trekking around Patagonia for the summer or as cool as learning to slam dunk at basketball camp, but hey, there's nothing adventurous or cool about being rejected from your top-choice college because of unimpressive test scores. Plus, you'll be ahead of the game if you can return to school with much of your PSAT, SAT, and ACT preparation behind you.

- **Research Scholarships:** College is expensive. While you should never rule out a school based on cost, the more scholarship money you can secure beforehand, the more college options you will have. You'll find loads of info on financial aid and scholarships (including a scholarship search tool) on our site, PrincetonReview.com.

Junior Year

You'll start the year off by taking the PSAT in October. High PSAT scores in your junior year will qualify you for the National Merit Scholarship competition. To become a finalist, you also need great grades and a recommendation from your school.

Make sure your grades are high this year. When colleges look at your transcripts they put a heavy emphasis on junior year grades. Decisions are made before admissions officers see your second-semester senior-year grades, and possibly before they see your first-semester senior-year grades! It's critical that your junior-year grades are solid.

During your junior year, you'll probably take the SAT or ACT test for the first time. Most colleges require scores from one of these tests for admission and/or scholarship award decisions. Plan to spend 3–12 weeks preparing for the tests. The SAT is comprised of Math, Critical Reading, and Writing sections. Colleges will see your individual section scores and your composite score, but generally they'll be most concerned with your composite score.

More and more students are opting to take the ACT in addition to, or instead of, the SAT. Most colleges accept the ACT in lieu of the SAT. The ACT has an English, Reading, Math, and Science section, plus the optional Writing section. (Some schools require the essay, so be sure to ask before you take the test.) One great advantage of the ACT is that you can take the test several times and choose what scores to send. If you take the SAT several times, all your scores are sent to the colleges. If you're not sure which test to take, first make sure that all the schools to which you're applying accept both tests. If your chosen schools do accept both scores, visit PrincetonReview.com to take a free assessment test that will help you identify whether the ACT or SAT is better for you.

Most highly selective colleges also require you to take three SAT Subject Tests in addition to the SAT or ACT. If you have SAT Subject Tests to take, plan now. You can't take the SAT and SAT Subject Tests on the same day. The Princeton Review can help with all the standardized tests you will need to take throughout high school. Log on to PrincetonReview.com for more info about our classes and study guides.

Also take time during your junior year to research colleges, and, if possible, visit schools high on your "hopes" list. When researching colleges, you'll want to consider a variety of factors besides whether or not you can get in, including location, school size, majors or programs offered that interest you, and cost and availability of financial aid. It helps to visit schools because it's the best way to learn whether a school may be right for you. If you can schedule an interview with an admissions officer during your visit, it may help him or her discover how right *you may be* for the school. The Princeton Review book, *Guide to College Visits,* offers plenty of tips on how you can make the most of your college visits, plus it has profiles of more than 370 popular colleges with tips on how to get there, where to stay, and what to do on campus.

SENIOR YEAR

It's time to get serious about pulling everything together for your applications. Deadlines will vary from school to school, and you will have a lot to keep track of, so make checklists of what's due when. If you're not happy with your previous SAT scores, you should take the October SAT. If you still need to take any SAT Subject Tests, now's the time.

If you have found the school of your dreams and you're happy with your grades and test scores, consider filing an Early Decision application. Many selective colleges commit more than half of their admissions spots to Early Decision applicants. To take this route, you must file your application in early November. By mid-December, you'll find out whether you got in—but there's a catch. If you're accepted Early Decision to a college, you must withdraw all applications to other colleges. This means that your financial aid offer might be hard to negotiate, so be prepared to take what you get.

Regardless of which route you decide to take, have a backup plan. Make sure you apply to at least one safety school—one that you feel confident you can get into and afford. Another option is to apply Early Decision at one school, but apply to other colleges during the regular decision period in the event that you are rejected from the early decision college.

FINANCIAL AID 101

All students applying for financial aid (including federal, state, and institutional need-based aid), need to complete the FAFSA (Free Application for Federal Student Aid) form. The form is available in high schools in December, but you can't submit it until January. You may also need to complete the CSS/PROFILE form, state aid forms, and any additional forms provided by the colleges. The Princeton Review's Paying for College Without Going Broke explains how the financial aid process works and how to maximize your eligibility for aid. It is the only annually-updated guide that gives line-by-line strategies for completing the FAFSA, which is particularly complicated and crucial. The FASFA is the need analysis document used to determine your "EFC" (Expected Family Contribution)—the amount of money the family is expected to ante up toward the cost of college.

When you ask teachers to write recommendations for you, give them everything they need. Tell them your application deadline and include a stamped, addressed envelope, or directions on how to submit the recommendation online, and be sure to send them a thank-you note after you know the recommendation was turned in. Your essay, on the other hand, is the one part of your application you have total control over. Don't repeat information from other parts of your application. And by all means, proofread! You'll find tips from admissions officers on what they look for (and what peeves them the most) about college applicants' essays in our book, *College Essays That Made a Difference*.

In March/April, colleges will send you a decision from the admissions office regarding your admission or rejection. If you are admitted (and you applied for financial aid) you'll also receive a decision from the financial aid office detailing your aid award package. The decision from the financial aid office can sometimes be appealed. The decision from the admissions office is almost always final. If you are wait-listed, don't lose hope. Write a letter to the college expressing how much you'd still like to attend the school and include an update on your recent activities. When colleges admit students from wait lists, they almost always give preference to students who have made it clear that they really want to attend.

It's important to wait until you've heard from all of the colleges you've applied to before making your final choice. May 1 is when you'll need to commit to the lucky college that will have you in its freshman class. We know how exciting but stressful that decision can be. If you're having a difficult time choosing between two colleges, try to visit each of them one more time. Can you imagine yourself walking around that campus, building a life in that community, and establishing friendships with those people? Finally, decide and be happy. Don't forget to thank your recommenders and tell them where you'll be going to school. Some of the best times of your life await!

How and Why We Produce This Book

This book is modeled after our bestselling guidebook, the *Best 368 Colleges*. When we published the first edition of *Best Colleges* in 1992, there was a void in the world of college guides (hard to believe, but true!). No publication provided college applicants with statistical data from colleges that covered academics, admissions, financial aid, and student demographics along with narrative descriptions of the schools *based on comprehensive surveys of students attending them*. Of course, academic rankings of colleges had been around for some time. They named the best schools on hierarchical lists, from 1 to 200 and upwards, some in tiers. Their criteria factored in such matters as faculty salaries, alumni giving, and peer reviews (i.e. what college administrators thought of the schools that, in many cases, they competed with for students). But no one was polling students at these terrific colleges about their experiences on campus—both inside and outside the classroom. We created our first *Best Colleges* guide to address that void. It was born out of one very obvious omission in college guide publishing and two very deep convictions we held then and hold even more strongly today:

- **One:** The key question for students and parents researching colleges shouldn't be *"What college is best, academically?"* The thing is, it's not hard to find academically great schools in this country. (There are hundreds of them, and many of them are concentrated in the Northeast.) The key question—and one that is truly tough to answer—is *"What is the best college for me?"*

- **Two:** We believe the best way for students and parents to know if a school is right—and ultimately best—for them is to visit it. Travel to the campus, get inside a dorm, audit a class, browse the town, and—most importantly—talk to students attending the school. In the end it's the school's customers—its students—who are the real experts about the college. Only they can give you the most candid and informed feedback on what life is really like on the campus.

Fueled by these convictions, we worked to create a guide that would help people who couldn't always get to the campus nonetheless get in-depth campus feedback to find the schools best for them. We culled an initial list of 250 academically great schools, based on our own college knowledge and input we got from 50 independent college counselors. We gathered institutional data from those schools and we surveyed 30,000 students attending them (about 120 per campus on average). We wrote the school profiles featured in the book, incorporating extensive quotes from surveyed students, and we included in the book more than 60 ranking lists of top 20 schools in various categories based on our surveys of students at the schools. In short, we designed a college guide that did something no other guide had done: It brought the opinions of a huge number of students at the nation's top colleges to readers' doorsteps.

The success of *Best Colleges* prompted us to publish the first edition of *Best Northeastern Colleges* in 2003. Our goal was to raise awareness of academically excellent but lesser-known colleges for those looking to study within the Northeastern United States. Many of the schools within these pages are nationally competitive institutions of higher learning; we therefore also include profiles of them in the *Best 368 Colleges*. An important difference between this book and the *Best 368 Colleges*, however, is that we do not include any ranking lists.

But why are some of the outstanding schools in this book *not* included in *Best 368 Colleges*? For one or both of two possible reasons. First, it may be because—at this time—they have a regional, rather than a national, focus. That is, they draw their students primarily from the state in which they are located or from bordering states. A second possible reason is that—again, at this time—they have not met the rigorous standards for inclusion in *Best 368 Colleges*. Is that

meant as a snub to the schools that didn't make it into *Best 368 Colleges*? Absolutely not. There are more than 3,500 institutions of higher learning in the United States, and the *Best 368 Colleges* profiles the top 10 percent, academically, of those schools. *Best Northeastern Colleges*, on the other hand, offers student opinion-driven information on all of the top colleges in eleven states and the District of Columbia. The 11 states are: Connecticut, Delaware, Maine, Maryland, Massachusetts, New Hampshire, New Jersey, New York, Pennsylvania, Rhode Island, and Vermont.

To determine which schools will be included in each edition, we don't use mathematical calculations or formulas. Instead we rely on a wide range of quantitative and qualitative input. Every year we collect data from nearly 2,000 colleges for our *Complete Book of Colleges* and our web-based profiles of schools. We visit colleges and meet with scores of admissions officers and college presidents. We talk with hundreds of high school counselors, parents, and students. Colleges also submit information to us requesting consideration for inclusion in the book. As a result, we are able to maintain a constantly evolving list of colleges to consider adding to each new edition of the book. Any college we add to the guide, however, must agree to allow its students to complete our anonymous student survey. (Sometimes a college's administrative protocols will not allow it to participate in our student survey; this has caused some academically outstanding schools to be absent from the guide.) Finally, we work to ensure that our book features a wide representation of colleges by environment, character, and type. It includes public and private schools, historically black colleges and universities, men's and women's colleges, science- and technology-focused institutions, nontraditional colleges, highly selective schools, and some with virtually open-door admissions policies.

Our student survey for the book is a mammoth undertaking. In the early years, our surveys were conducted on campuses and on paper, but the launch several years ago of our online survey (http://survey.review.com), has made it possible for students to complete a survey anytime and anywhere. In fact, 99 percent of our student surveys are now completed online. A few schools prefer the old-fashioned paper survey route; in those instances we work with the administration to hire a campus representative (usually a student) to set up shop in one or more highly-trafficked areas of the campus where students can stop and fill out the survey.

Each school in *Best Northeastern Colleges* is surveyed *at least* once every three years. The reality is that unless there's been some grand upheaval or administrative change on campus, there's little change in student opinion from one year to the next; shifts only tend to emerge in a third or fourth year (as surveyed students leave or matriculate). Thus, each year we target a third of the campuses in the book for resurveying. We resurvey colleges more often than that if colleges request it (and we can accommodate the request) or if we believe it is warranted for one reason or another. Online surveys submitted by students outside of a school's normal survey cycle and independent of any solicitation on our part are factored into the subsequent year's ratings calculations. In that respect, our surveying is a continuous process.

All colleges and universities whose students we plan to survey are notified about the survey through our administrative contacts at the schools. We depend upon them for assistance either in notifying the student body about the availability of the online survey via e-mail or, if the school opts for a paper version of the survey, in identifying common, high-traffic areas on campus at which to survey. The survey has more than 90 questions divided into four sections: "About Yourself," "Your School's Academics/Administration," "Students," and "Life at Your School." We ask about all sorts of things, from "How many out-of-class hours do you spend studying each day?" to "How do you rate your campus food?" Most questions offer students a five-point grid on which to indicate their answer choices (headers may range from "Excellent" to "Awful"). Eight questions offer students the opportunity to expand on their answers with narrative comment. These essay-type responses are the sources of the student quotations that appear in the school profiles.

Once the surveys have been completed and responses stored in our database, every college is given a score (similar to a grade point average) for its students' answers to each question. This score enables us to compare students' responses to a particular question from one college to the next. We use these scores as an underlying data point in our calculation of the ratings that appear in the profile headers and "Stats" section. Once we have the student survey information in hand, we write the college profiles. Student quotations in each profile are chosen because they represent the sentiments expressed by the majority of survey respondents from the college; or, they illustrate one side or another of a mixed bag of student opinion, in which case there will also appear a counterpoint within the text. We do not select quotes for their extreme nature, humor, or unique perspective.

Our survey is qualitative and anecdotal rather than quantitative. In order to guard against producing a write-up that's off the mark for any particular college, we send our administrative contact at each school a copy of the profile we intend to publish prior to its publication date, with ample opportunity to respond with corrections, comments, and/or outright objections. In every case in which we receive requests for changes, we take careful measures to review the school's suggestions against the student survey data we collected and to make appropriate changes when warranted.

For this year's edition, on average, we surveyed 300 students per campus, though that number varies depending on the size of the student population. Whether the number of students we survey at a particular school is 100 or 1,000, on the whole we have found their opinions to be remarkably consistent over the years. What is most compelling to us about how representative our survey findings are is this: We ask students who take the survey—after they have completed it—to review the information we published about their school in the previous edition of our book and to grade us on its accuracy and validity. Year after year we've gotten high marks: This year, 81 percent of students said we were *right on.*

All of the institutions in this guide are academically terrific in our opinion. Not every college will appeal to every student, but that is the beauty of it. These are all very different schools with many different and wonderful things to offer.

We hope you will use this book as a starting point (it will certainly give you a snapshot of what life is like at these schools) but not as the final word on any one school. Check out other resources. Visit as many colleges as you can. Talk to students at those colleges—ask what they love and what bothers them most about their schools. Finally, *form your own opinions* about the colleges you are considering. At the end of the day, it's what *you* think about the schools that matters most, and that will enable you to answer that all-important question: *"Which college is best for me?"*

How This Book Is Organized

Each of the colleges and universities in this book has its own two-page profile. To make it easier to find and compare information about the schools, we've used the same profile format for every school. Look at the sample pages below:

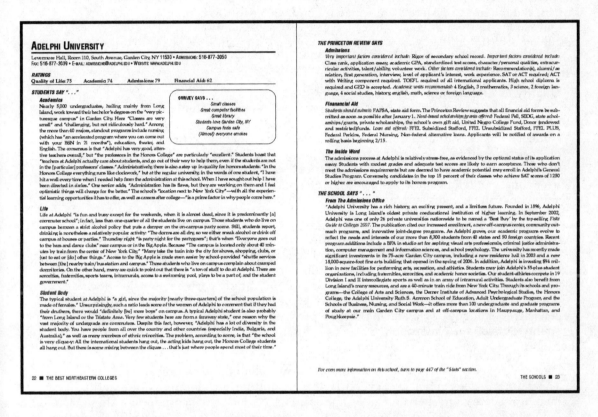

Each spread has several components. First, at the very top of the profile you will see the school's address, telephone and fax numbers for its admissions office, the telephone number for its financial aid office, and its website and/or e-mail address. Next, you will find the school's ratings in four categories: Quality of Life, Academics, Admissions Selectivity, and Financial Aid. We compile the ratings based on the results from our student surveys and/or institutional data we collect from school administrators. These ratings are on a scale of 60–99 If a 60* (60 with an asterisk) appears as any rating for any school, it means that the school reported so few of the rating's underlying data points by our deadline that we were unable to calculate an accurate rating for it. In such cases the reader is advised to follow up with the school about the specific measures the rating takes into account. Be advised that because the Admissions Selectivity Rating is a factor in the computation that produces the Academic Rating, a school that has **60*** (60 with an asterisk) as its Admissions Selectivity Rating will have an Academic Rating that is lower than it should be. Also bear in mind that each rating places each college on a continuum for purposes of comparing colleges within *this edition only*. Since our ratings computations may

change from year to year, it is invalid to compare the ratings in this edition to those that appear in any prior or future edition.

The profile header is followed by a "Survey Says . . ." bubble and "Academics," "Life," and "Student Body" sections, which are based primarily from student survey responses for that particular college. Then comes the "Admissions" section, which includes information on how the school's admissions office weighs the different components of your application; followed by the "Inside Word" on admissions, academics, life, or demographics at that school; "Financial Aid" application pointers; and an institution-authored message under the title "From the Admissions Office." Finally, at the end of the profile is the page number on which the school's statistical data appears. Here's an explanation of each profile section:

Contact Information
Includes the school's address, admissions phone and fax numbers, financial aid phone number, admissions e-mail address, and website.

Quality of Life Rating
On a scale of 60–99, this rating is a measure of how happy students are with their lives outside the classroom. To compile this rating, we weighed several factors, all based on students' answers to questions on our survey. They included the students' assessments of: their overall happiness; the beauty, safety, and location of the campus; comfort of dorms; quality of food; ease of getting around campus and dealing with administrators; friendliness of fellow students; and the interaction of different student types on campus and within the greater community.

Academic Rating
On a scale of 60–99, this rating is a measure of how hard students work at the school and how much they get back for their efforts. The rating is based on results from our surveys of students and institutional data we collect from administrators. Factors weighed included how many hours students reported that they study each day outside of class, and the quality of students the school attracts as measured by admissions statistics. We also considered students' assessments of their professors' teaching abilities and of their accessibility outside the classroom.

Admissions Selectivity Rating
On a scale of 60–99, this rating is a measure of how competitive admission is at the school. This rating is determined by several factors, including the class rank of entering freshmen, test scores, and percentage of applicants accepted. By incorporating these factors (and a few others), our admissions selectivity rating adjusts for "self-selecting" applicant pools. The University of Chicago, for example, has a very high admissions selectivity rating, even though it admits a surprisingly large proportion of its applicants. This is because Chicago's applicant pool is self-selecting; that is, nearly all the school's applicants are exceptional students.

Financial Aid Rating
On a scale of 60–99, this rating is a measure of the financial aid the school awards and how satisfied students are with the aid they receive. It is based on school-reported data on financial aid and students' responses to the survey question, "If you receive financial aid, how satisfied are you with your financial aid package?"

Survey Says . . .
Our "Survey Says" list, located under the ratings on each school's two-page spread, is based entirely on the results of our student surveys. In other words, the items on this list

are based on the opinions of the students we surveyed at those schools (*not* on any quantitative analysis of library size, endowment, etc.). These items reveal popular or unpopular trends on campus for the purpose of providing a snapshot of life on *that campus only*. The appearance of a Survey Says item in the sidebar for a particular school does *not* reflect the popularity of that item relative to its popularity amongst the student bodies at other schools. Some of the terms that appear on the Survey Says list are not entirely self-explanatory; these terms are defined below.

Different types of students interact: We asked students whether students from different class and ethnic backgrounds interacted frequently and easily. When students' collective response is "yes," the heading "Different types of students interact" appears on the list. When the collective student response indicates there are not many interactions between different students from different class and ethnic backgrounds, the phrase "Students are cliquish" appears on the list.

No one cheats: We asked students how prevalent cheating is at their school. If students reported cheating to be rare, the term "No one cheats" shows up on the list.

Students are happy: This category reflects student responses to the question "Overall, how happy are you?"

Students are very religious *or* **Students aren't religious:** We asked students how religious students are at their school. Their responses are reflected in this category.

Diverse student types on campus: We asked students whether their student body is made up of a variety of ethnic groups. This category reflects their answers to this question. This heading shows up as "Diversity lacking on campus" or "Diverse student types on campus." It does not reflect any institutional data on this subject.

Students get along with local community: This category reflects student responses to a question concerning how well the student body gets along with residents of the college town or community.

Career services are great: New to the book last year, this category reflects student opinion on the quality of career/job placement services on campus. This heading shows up as "Career services are great."

Academics, Life, and Student Body

This section shares the straight-from-the-campus feedback we get from the school's most important customers: The attending students. The section summarizes the opinions of freshman through seniors we've surveyed and it includes direct quotes from scores of those students. When appropriate, it also incorporates statistics provided by the schools. The Academics section describes how hard students work and how satisfied they are with the education they are getting. It also often tells you which programs or academic departments students rated most favorably and how professors interact with students. Student opinion regarding administrative departments also works its way into this section. The Life section describes life outside the classroom and addresses questions ranging from "How comfortable are the dorms?" to "How popular are fraternities and sororities?" In this section, students describe what they do for entertainment both on-campus and off, providing a clear picture of the social environment at their particular school. The Student Body section will give you the lowdown on the types of students the school attracts and how the students view the level of interaction among various groups, including those of different ethnic, socioeconomic, and religious backgrounds. All quotations in these

sections are from students' responses to open-ended questions on our survey. We select quotations based on the accuracy with which they reflect overall student opinion about the school as conveyed in the survey results.

Admissions
This section lets you know which aspects of your application are most important to the admissions officers at the school. It also lists the high school curricular prerequisites for applicants, which standardized tests (if any) are required, and special information about the school's admissions process (e.g., Do minority students and legacies, for example, receive special consideration? Are there any unusual application requirements for applicants to special programs?).

The Inside Word
This section gives you the inside scoop on what it takes to gain admission to the school. It reflects our own insights about each school's admissions process and acceptance trends. (We visit scores of colleges each year and talk with hundreds of admissions officers in order to glean this info.) It also incorporates information from institutional data we collect and our surveys over the years of students at the school.

Financial Aid
Here you'll found out what you need to know about the financial aid process at the school, namely what forms you need and what types of merit-based aid and loans are available. Information about need-based aid is contained in the financial aid sidebar. This section includes specific deadline dates for submission of materials as reported by the colleges. We strongly encourage students seeking financial aid to file all forms—federal, state, and institutional—carefully, fully, and on time. Check out our annually-updated book, *Paying for College Without Going Broke*, for advice on completing the forms and strategies for getting the most financial aid possible.

From the Admissions Office
This section is the school's chance to speak directly to you about the key things they would like you to know about their institution. For schools that did not respond to our invitation to supply text for this space, we excerpted an appropriate passage from the school's catalog, web site, or other admissions literature. For this section, we also invited schools to submit a brief paragraph explaining their admissions policies regarding the SAT (especially the Writing portion of the exam) and the SAT Subject Tests. We are pleased that nearly every school took this opportunity to clarify its policies as we know there has been some student and parent confusion about how these scores are evaluated for admission.

For More Information
We refer you to the page number in our school statistics section where you can find detailed statistical information for the particular school you're reading about.

SCHOOL STATISTICS

This section, located in the back of the book, contains various statistics culled from our student surveys and from questionnaires school administrators fill out. Keep in mind that not every category will appear for every school, since in some cases the information is not reported or not applicable.

ADELPHI UNIVERSITY

CAMPUS LIFE

Fire Safety Rating	TK
Green Rating	TK
Type of school	private
Environment	metropolis

STUDENTS

Total undergrad enrollment	4,973
% male/female	28/72
% from out of state	8
% from public high school	75
% live on campus	23
% in (# of) fraternities	7 (2)
% in (# of) sororities	4 (5)
% African American	14
% Asian	6
% Caucasian	50
% Hispanic	8
% international	4
# of countries represented	56

ACADEMICS

Calendar	semester
Profs interesting rating	TK
Profs accessible rating	TK
Student/faculty ratio	9:1
Most common reg class size	20–29 students
Most common lab size	10–19 students

MOST POPULAR MAJORS
education
nursing, other
business/commerce

SELECTIVITY

# of applicants	6,165
% of applicants accepted	69
% of acceptees attending	21

FRESHMAN PROFILE

Range SAT Critical Reading	480–590
Range SAT Math	490–590
Range SAT Writing	480–580
Range ACT Composite	20–24
Minimum paper TOEFL	550
Minimum computer TOEFL	213
Average HS GPA	3.3
% graduated top 10% of class	19.7
% graduated top 25% of class	47.6
% graduated top 50% of class	85.6

DEADLINES

Early action

Deadline	12/1
Notification	12/31
Notification	rolling
Nonfall registration?	yes

FINANCIAL FACTS

Annual tuition	$21,000
Room and board	$9,900
Required fees	$1,200
Books and supplies	$1,000
% frosh rec. need-based scholarship or grant aid	58
% UG rec. need-based scholarship or grant aid	54
% frosh rec. non-need-based scholarship or grant aid	34
% UG rec. non-need-based scholarship or grant aid	33
% frosh rec. need-based self-help aid	60
% UG rec. need-based self-help aid	57
% frosh rec. athletic scholarships	2
% UG rec. athletic scholarships	1
% frosh rec. any financial aid	93
% UG rec. any financial aid	88

If a school has completed ea   do), the headings will appear in the following order:

Fire Safety Rating
On a scale of 60–99, this ratin   w well prepared a school is to prevent or respond to campus fires, specifi   esidence halls.

We asked schools several questions about their efforts to ensure fire safety for campus residents. We developed the questions in consultation with the Center for Campus Fire Safety (www.campusfire.org). Each school's responses to eight questions were considered when calculating its Fire Safety Rating. They cover:

1. The percentage of student housing sleeping rooms protected by an automatic fire sprinkler system with a fire sprinkler head located in the individual sleeping rooms.

2. The percentage of student housing sleeping rooms equipped with a smoke detector connected to a supervised fire alarm system.

3. The number of malicious fire alarms that occur in student housing per year.

4. The number of unwanted fire alarms that occur in student housing per year.

5. The banning of certain hazardous items and activities in residence halls, like candles, smoking, halogen lamps, etc.

6. The percentage of student housing fire alarm systems that, if activated, result in a signal being transmitted to a monitored location, where security investigates before notifying the fire department.

7. The percentage of student housing fire alarm systems that, if activated, result in a signal being transmitted immediately to a continuously monitored location which can then immediately notify the fire department to initiate a response.

8. How often fire safety rules-compliance inspections are conducted each year.

Schools that did not report answers to any of the questions receive a Fire Safety Rating of 60* (60 with an asterisk). The schools have an opportunity to update their fire safety data every year and will have their fire safety ratings recalculated and published annually. You can also find Fire Safety Ratings for the *Best Northeastern Colleges* (and several additional schools) in our *Complete Book of Colleges, 2009 Edition.*

Green Rating

We asked all the schools we collect data from annually to answer a number of questions that evaluate the comprehensive measure of their performance as an environmentally aware and responsible institution. The questions were developed in consultation with ecoAmerica, a research and partnership-based environmental nonprofit that convened an expert committee to design this comprehensive rating system, and cover: 1) whether students have a campus quality of life that is both healthy and sustainable; 2) how well a school is preparing students not only for employment in the clean energy economy of the 21st century, but also for citizenship in a world now defined by environmental challenges; and 3) how environmentally responsible a school's policies are.

Each school's responses to ten questions were considered when calculating its Green Rating. They cover:

1. The percentage of food expenditures that go toward local, organic, or otherwise environmentally preferable food.

2. Whether the school offers programs including free bus passes, universal access transit passes, bike sharing/renting, car sharing, carpool parking, vanpooling, or guaranteed rides home to encourage alternatives to single-passenger automobile use for students.

3. Whether the school has a formal committee with participation from students that is devoted to advancing sustainability on campus.

4. Whether new buildings are required to be LEED Silver certified or comparable.

5. The schools overall waste diversion rate.

6. Whether the school has an environmental studies major, minor or concentration.

7. Whether the school has an 'environmental literacy' requirement.

8. Whether a school has produced a publicly available greenhouse gas emissions inventory and adopted a climate action plan consistent with 80% greenhouse gas reductions by 2050 targets.

9. What percentage of the school's energy consumption, including heating/cooling and electrical, is derived from renewable resources (this definition included 'green tags' but not nuclear or large scale hydro power)

10. Whether the school employs a dedicated full-time (or full-time equivalent) sustainability officer.

Colleges that did not supply answers to a sufficient number of the green campus questions for us to fairly compare them to other colleges receive a Green Rating of 60*. The schools have an opportunity to update their green data every year and will have their green ratings re-calculated and published annually.

Affiliation
Any religious order with which the school is affiliated.

Environment
Whether the campus is located in an urban, suburban, or rural setting.

Total undergrad enrollment
The total number of degree-seeking undergraduates who attend the school.

"% male/female" through "# countries represented"
Demographic information about the full-time undergraduate student body, including male-to-female ratio, ethnicity, and the number of countries represented by the student body. Also included are the percentages of the student body who are from out of state, attended a public high school, live on campus, and belong to Greek organizations.

Calendar
The school's schedule of academic terms. A "semester" schedule has two long terms, usually starting in September and January. A "trimester" schedule has three terms, one usually beginning before Christmas and two after. A "quarterly" schedule has four terms, which go by very quickly: the entire term, including exams, usually lasts only nine or ten weeks. A "4-1-4" schedule is like a semester schedule, but with a month-long term in between the fall and spring semesters. (Similarly, a 4-4-1 has a short term following two longer semesters.) When a school's academic calendar doesn't match any of these traditional schedules, we note that by saying "other." For schools that have "other" as their calendar, it is best to call the admissions office for details.

Student/faculty ratio
The ratio of full-time undergraduate instructional faculty members to all undergraduates.

Profs interesting rating
On a scale of 60–99, this rating is based on levels of surveyed students' agreement or disagreement with the statement: "Your instructors are good teachers."

Profs accessible rating
On a scale of 60–99, this rating is based on levels of surveyed students' agreement or dis-agreement with the statement: "Your instructors are accessible outside the classroom."

% profs teaching UG courses
This category reports the percentage of professors who teach undergraduates and distin-guishes between faculty who teach and faculty who focus solely on research.

% classes taught by TAs
This category reports the percentage of classes that are taught by TAs (teaching assis-tants) instead of regular faculty. Many universities that offer graduate programs use graduate students as teaching assistants. They teach undergraduate courses, primarily at the introductory level.

Most common lab size; Most common regular class size
Institutionally-reported figures of the most commonly occurring class size for regular courses and for labs/discussion sections.

Most popular majors
The three majors with the highest enrollments at the school.

% of applicants accepted
The percentage of applicants to whom the school offered admission.

% of acceptees attending
The percentage of those who were accepted who eventually enrolled.

 # accepting a place on wait list
The number of students who decided to take a place on the wait list when offered this option.

% admitted from wait list
The percentage of applicants who opted to take a place on the wait list and were subse-quently offered admission. These figures will vary tremendously from college to college, and should be a consideration when deciding whether to accept a place on a college's wait list.

# of early decision applicants
The number of students who applied under the college's early decision or early action plan.

% accepted early decision
The percentage of early decision or early action applicants who were admitted under this plan. By the nature of these plans, the vast majority who are admitted ultimately enroll. (See the early decision/action description that follows in this section for more detail.)

Range/Average SAT Verbal, Range/Average SAT Math, Range/Average SAT Writing
The average and the middle 50 percent range of test scores for entering freshmen. Don't be discouraged from applying to the school of your choice even if your combined SAT scores are 80 or even 120 points below the average, because you may still have a chance of getting in. Remember that many schools value other aspects of your application (e.g., your grades, how good a match you make with the school) more heavily than test scores.

Minimum TOEFL
The minimum test score necessary for entering freshmen who are required to take the TOEFL (Test of English as a Foreign Language). Most schools will require all international students or non-native English speakers to take the TOEFL in order to be considered for admission.

Average HS GPA
The average grade point average of entering freshman. We report this on a scale of 1.0–4.0 (occasionally colleges report averages on a 100 scale, in which case we report those figures). This is one of the key factors in college admissions.

% graduated top 10%, top 25%, top 50% of class
Of those students for whom class rank was reported, the percentage of entering freshmen who ranked in the top tenth, quarter, and half of their high school classes.

Early decision/action deadlines
The deadline for submission of application materials under the early decision or early action plan.

Early decision, early action, priority, and regular admission deadlines
The dates by which all materials must be postmarked (we'd suggest "received in the office") in order to be considered for admission under each particular admissions option/ cycle for matriculation in the fall term.

Early decision, early action, priority, and regular admission notification
The dates by which you can expect a decision on your application under each admissions option/cycle.

Nonfall registration
Some schools will allow incoming students to matriculate at times other than the fall term, which is the traditional beginning of the academic calendar year. Other schools will allow you to register for classes only if you can begin in the fall term. A simple "yes" or "no" in this category indicates the school's policy on nonfall registration.

Annual in-state tuition
The tuition at the school, or for public colleges, the cost of tuition for a resident of the school's state. Usually much lower than out-of-state tuition for state-supported public schools.

Annual out-of-state tuition
For public colleges, the tuition for a nonresident of the school's state. This entry appears only for public colleges, since tuition at private colleges is generally the same regardless of state of residence.

Room & board
Estimated annual room and board costs.

Books and supplies
Estimated annual cost of necessary textbooks and/or supplies.

% frosh receiving need-based aid
The percentage of all degree-seeking freshmen who applied for financial aid, were determined to have financial need, and received any sort of aid, need-based or otherwise.

% UG receiving need-based aid

The percentage of all degree-seeking undergrads who applied for financial aid, were determined to have financial need, and received any sort of aid, need-based or otherwise.

Nota Bene: The statistical data reported in this book, unless otherwise noted, was collected from the profiled colleges from the fall of 2007 through the summer of 2008. In some cases, we were unable to publish the most recent data because schools did not report the necessary statistics to us in time, despite our repeated outreach efforts. Because the enrollment and financial statistics, as well as application and financial aid deadlines, fluctuate from one year to another, we recommend that you check with the schools to make sure you have the most current information before applying.

To all of our readers, we welcome your feedback on how we can continue to improve this guide. We hope you will share with us your comments, questions, comments, and suggestions. Please contact us at Editorial Department, Princeton Review Books, 2315 Broadway, New York, NY 10024, or e-mail us at bookeditor@review.com. Good luck!

GLOSSARY

ACT: Like the SAT but less tricky—the ACT tests stuff you actually learned in the classroom. Most schools accept either SAT or ACT scores; if you consistently get blown away by the SAT, consider taking the ACT instead of (or in addition to) the SAT.

APs: Advanced Placement courses are essentially college-level courses offered in various high schools that culminate in the Advanced Placement Examinations each May. Students who obtain a minimum score on their AP exams may be awarded college credit or placement out of intro-level courses in the subject area. Excellent deal, no matter how you cut it!

College-prep curriculum: 16 to 18 academic credits (each credit equals a full year of a high school course), usually including: 4 years of English, 3 to 4 years of social studies, and at least 2 years each of science, mathematics, and foreign language.

Common Application: A general application form used by nearly 300 colleges and universities. Students who complete the Common Application save on time and mental frenzy, but may be required to submit application supplements to schools.

Core curriculum: Students at schools with core curricula must take a number of required courses, usually in such subjects as world history, Western civilization, writing skills, and fundamental math and science.

CSS/Financial Aid PROFILE: The College Scholarship Service PROFILE, an optional financial aid form required by some colleges in addition to the FAFSA.

Direct Lender: Direct Lending schools participate in the Direct Lending Program (see "Direct Loan Program").

Direct Loan Program: With this federal educational loan program, funds are lent directly by the U.S. Government through the school's financial aid office, with no need of a private lender such as a bank. If the college only participates in the (William D. Ford) Direct Loan Program, the borrower must obtain any Stafford, PLUS, or GradPLUS loan through this program, though one can use a private alternative loan program for any additional non-federal funding.

Distribution or general education requirements: Students at schools with distribution requirements must take a number of courses in various subject areas, such as foreign language, humanities, natural science, and social science. Distribution requirements do not specify which courses you must take, only which types of courses.

Early Decision/Early Action: Early decision is generally for students for whom the school is a first choice. The applicant commits to attending the school if admitted; in return, the school renders an early decision, usually in December or January. Early action is similar to early decision, but less binding; applicants need not commit to attending the school and in some cases may apply early action to more than one school. Early decision and early action policies of a few of the most selective colleges in the country have changed quite dramatically recently. It's a good idea to call the school and get full details if you plan to pursue one of these options.

FAFSA: Stands for the Free Application for Federal Student Aid. This is a financial aid need analysis form written by the U.S. Department of Education. This form is required for virtually all students applying to colleges for financial aid. Some colleges also require that applicants complete other aid application forms (such as the CSS/Financial Aid PROFILE or the college's own form) to be considered for financial aid.

Greek system, Greeks: Fraternities and sororities.

Humanities: The branches of knowledge concerned with human art and culture. These include such disciplines as art history, drama, English, foreign languages, music, philosophy, and religion.

Merit-based grant: A scholarship (not necessarily covering the full cost of tuition) given to students because of some special talent or attribute. Artists, athletes, community leaders, and academically outstanding applicants are typical recipients.

Natural sciences: The branches of knowledge concerned with the rational study of the universe using the rules or laws of natural order. These include such disciplines as astronomy, biology, chemistry, genetics, geology, mathematics, physics, and zoology.

Need-based grant: A scholarship (not necessarily covering the full cost of tuition) given to students because they would otherwise be unable to afford college. Student need is determined on the basis of the FAFSA. Some schools also require the CSS PROFILE and/or institutional applications to determine a student's need.

Priority deadline: Some schools will list a deadline for admission and/or financial aid as a "priority deadline," meaning that while they will accept applications after that date, all applications received prior to the deadline are assured of getting the most thorough, and potentially more generous, appraisal possible.

RA: Residence assistant (or residential advisor). Someone, usually an upperclassman or graduate student, who supervises a floor or section of a dorm, usually in return for free room and board. RAs are responsible for enforcing the drinking and noise rules.

SAT: A college entrance exam required by many schools; most schools will accept either the ACT or the SAT.

SAT Subject Tests: Subject-specific exams administered by the Educational Testing Service (the same folks who do the SAT). These tests are required by some, but not all, colleges.

Social sciences: The branches of knowledge which emphasize the use of the scientific method in the study of the human aspects of the world. These include such disciplines as anthropology, economics, geography, history, international studies, political science, psychology, and sociology.

Work-study: A federally-funded financial aid program that provides assistance to students by subsidizing their wages for on-campus and off-campus jobs. Eligibility is based on need.

PART 2

THE SCHOOLS

ADELPHI UNIVERSITY

Levermore Hall, Room 110, South Avenue, Garden City, NY 11530 • ADMISSIONS: 516-877-3050
FAX: 516-877-3039 • E-MAIL: ADMISSIONS@ADELPHI.EDU • WEBSITE: WWW.ADELPHI.EDU

RATINGS
Quality of Life: 75   Academic: 74   Admissions: 79   Financial Aid: 62

STUDENTS SAY ". . ."

Academics

> SURVEY SAYS . . .
> *Small classes*
> *Great computer facilities*
> *Great library*
> *Students love Garden City, NY*
> *Campus feels safe*
> *(Almost) everyone smokes*

Nearly 5,000 undergraduates, hailing mainly from Long Island, work toward their bachelor's degrees on the "very picturesque campus" in Garden City. Here "Classes are very small" and "challenging, but not ridiculously hard." Among the more than 40 majors, standout programs include nursing (which has "an accelerated program where you can come out with your BSN in 21 months"), education, theater, and English. The consensus is that "Adelphi has very good, attentive teachers overall," but "the professors in the Honors College" are particularly "excellent." Students boast that "teachers at Adelphi actually care about students, and go out of their way to help them, even if the students are not in the [particular] professors' classes." Administratively, there is also a step up in quality for honors students: "In the Honors College everything runs like clockwork," but at the regular university, in the words of one student, "I have hit a wall every time when I needed help from the administration at this school. When I have sought out help I have been directed in circles." One senior adds, "Administration has its flaws, but they are working on them and I feel optimistic things will change for the better." The school's "location next to New York City"—with all the experiential learning opportunities it has to offer, as well as careers after college—"is a prime factor in why people come here."

Life

Life at Adelphi "is fun and busy except for the weekends, when it is almost dead, since it is predominantly [a] commuter school"; in fact, less than one-quarter of all the students live on campus. Those students who do live on campus bemoan a strict alcohol policy that puts a damper on the on-campus party scene. Still, students report, drinking is nonetheless a relatively popular activity: "The dorms are all dry, so we either sneak alcohol or drink off campus at houses or parties." Thursday night "is party night for the partygoers"; that's when "Everyone goes out to the bars and dance clubs" near campus or in the Big Apple. Because "The campus is located only about 40 minutes by train from the center of New York City," "Many take the train into the city for shows, shopping, clubs, or just to eat or [do] other things." Access to the Big Apple is made even easier by school-provided "shuttle services between [the] nearby train/bus station and campus." Those students who live on campus complain about cramped dormitories. On the other hand, many are quick to point out that there is "a ton of stuff to do at Adelphi. There are sororities, fraternities, sports teams, intramurals, access to a swimming pool, plays to be a part of, and the student government."

Student Body

The typical student at Adelphi is "a girl, since the majority [nearly three-quarters] of the school population is made of females." Unsurprisingly, such a ratio leads some of the women of Adelphi to comment that if they had their druthers, there would "definitely [be] more boys" on campus. A typical Adelphi student is also probably "from Long Island or the Tristate Area. Very few students here are from a faraway state," one reason why the vast majority of undergrads are commuters. Despite this fact, however, "Adelphi has a lot of diversity in the student body. You have people from all over the country and other countries (especially India, Bulgaria, and Australia)," as well as many members of ethnic minorities. The problem, according to some, is that "the school is very clique-y: All the international students hang out, the acting kids hang out, the Honors College students all hang out. But there is some mixing between the cliques . . . that's just where people spend most of their time."

THE PRINCETON REVIEW SAYS

Admissions

Very important factors considered include: Rigor of secondary school record. *Important factors considered include:* Class rank, application essay, academic GPA, standardized test scores, character/personal qualities, extracurricular activities, talent/ability, volunteer work. *Other factors considered include:* Recommendation(s), alumni/ae relation, first generation, interview, level of applicant's interest, work experience. SAT or ACT required; ACT with Writing component required. TOEFL required of all international applicants. High school diploma is required and GED is accepted. *Academic units recommended:* 4 English, 3 mathematics, 3 science, 2 foreign language, 4 social studies, history, english, math, science or foreign language.

Finanancial Aid

Students should submit: FAFSA, state aid form. The Princeton Review suggests that all financial aid forms be submitted as soon as possible after January 1. *Need-based scholarships/grants offered:* Federal Pell, SEOG, state scholarships/grants, private scholarships, the school's own gift aid, United Negro College Fund, Donor (endowed and restricted)funds. *Loan aid offered:* FFEL Subsidized Stafford, FFEL Unsubsidized Stafford, FFEL PLUS, Federal Perkins, Federal Nursing, Non-federal alternative loans. Applicants will be notified of awards on a rolling basis beginning 2/15.

The Inside Word

The admissions process at Adelphi is relatively stress-free, as evidenced by the optional status of its application essay. Students with modest grades and adequate test scores are likely to earn acceptance. Those who don't meet the admissions requirements but are deemed to have academic potential may enroll in Adelphi's General Studies Program. Conversely, candidates in the top 15 percent of their classes who achieve SAT scores of 1250 or higher are encouraged to apply to its honors program.

THE SCHOOL SAYS " . . . "

From The Admissions Office

"Adelphi University has a rich history, an exciting present, and a limitless future. Founded in 1896, Adelphi University is Long Island's oldest private coeducational institution of higher learning. In September 2002, Adelphi was one of only 26 private universities nationwide to be named a 'Best Buy' by the top-selling *Fiske Guide to Colleges 2007*. The publication cited our increased enrollment, a new off-campus center, community outreach programs, and innovative joint-degree programs. As Adelphi grows, our academic programs evolve to reflect the needs and interests of our more than 8,300 students from 40 states and 50 foreign countries. Recent program additions include a BFA in studio art for aspiring visual arts professionals, criminal justice administration, computer management and information sciences, and school psychology. The university has recently made significant investments in its 75-acre Garden City campus, including a new residence hall in 2003 and a new 18,000-square-foot fine arts building that opened in the spring of 2006. In addition, Adelphi is investing $94 million in new facilities for performing arts, recreation, and athletics. Students may join Adelphi's 55-plus student organizations, including fraternities, sororities, and academic honor societies. Our student-athletes compete in 19 Division I and II intercollegiate sports as well as in an array of intramural activities. Students also benefit from Long Island's many resources, and are a 40-minute train ride from New York City. Through its schools and programs—the College of Arts and Sciences, the Derner Institute of Advanced Psychological Studies, the Honors College, the Adelphi University Ruth S. Ammon School of Education, Adult Undergraduate Program, and the Schools of Business, Nursing, and Social Work—it offers more than 100 undergraduate and graduate programs of study at our main Garden City campus and at off-campus locations in Hauppauge, Manhattan, and Poughkeepsie."

For even more information on this school, turn to page 447 of the "Stats" section.

ALBRIGHT COLLEGE

PO Box 15234, Thirteenth and Bern Streets, Reading, PA 19612-5234 • Admissions: 800-252-1856
Fax: 610-921-7294 • E-mail: admissions@albright@.edu • Website: www.albright.edu

RATINGS
Quality of Life: 66   Academic: 82   Admissions: 80   Financial Aid: 76

STUDENTS SAY ". . ."

Academics

Albright College's motto is "A different way of thinking," and students tell us that it's not just an empty slogan. Rather, this principle "is truly evident, in a positive way, in all aspects" of an Albright education "including the academic options, clubs and organizations, campus living, and social aspects." Interdisciplinary study is central to Albright's academic philosophy; one junior majoring in sociology tells us that "I have been able to relate theater and sociology within the same semester, which is something I could have never pictured before." Students thrive or fail here to the extent that they can embrace the Albright approach. Those who love it appreciate "the interdisciplinary nature of each class" and insist that "if you come to Albright and come to believe in Albright's principles, you will have the opportunity to exceed any imaginable expectations in social life, academics, athletics, and any other endeavor that you wish to be a part of." Those who don't may conclude that "Albright costs at least twice what a state school does and doesn't offer anything more than you would find at a state school," although to do so they'd have to ignore the "small classes where you can feel comfortable answering or asking questions." Most classes are "discussion- rather than lecture-based, which makes for a much better learning environment!" Albright also boasts "great facilities. The new gym, the Shumo Center, is state of the art, and now Albright is making renovations on other buildings that will make the campus even better."

Life

Life at Albright "is relaxing and fun," with students focused on schoolwork during the week and on the "plenty of things to do on and around campus" on the weekends. This includes "'experience events' that the school sets up," which can be "anything from comedians to educational lectures to plays. You have to attend sixteen experience events by the end of your sophomore year." Other options include "Greek life (date parties, formals, philanthropic activities), athletics, shopping (mall, outlets, King of Prussia, which is about 60 minutes from campus), reading Phillies and Royals games" and taking advantage of "sports recreation facilities nearby (rock climbing, laser tag, water parks, mini golf)." Also, "The college actually plans trips to locations that are further than we want to drive, like New York City. There are always things going on in Philadelphia, and if you want to go, you can find others who want to, too." Despite all these options, "there is quite a bit of alcohol on campus, although there's plenty to do for those who don't want to drink." While some city folks may find life here a bit to slow, many here believe that "you will not be bored unless you allow yourself to be."

Student Body

Albright's academic approach attracts students who "value being unique and following your own path. We are able to fit together, because we respect and reward individuality." Most are "very involved and full of school spirit," and "everyone is very open and friendly," but "there are still many cliques." These include "the Greeks, the artists, the jocks and cheerleaders, the 'gangstas,' the Asians, and the shy folk. The cliques are most apparent in the cafeteria, however outside of the dining hall all the groups do mesh and interact." Undergrads here tend to be "either really career-minded or really socially-minded." Socially-minded men take note: "females outnumber males" by a substantial margin.

Admissions

Very important factors considered include: Rigor of secondary school record. *Important factors considered include:* Class rank, application essay, academic GPA, recommendation(s), standardized test scores, character/personal qualities. *Other factors considered include:* Alumni/ae relation, extracurricular activities, talent/ability, volunteer work, work experience. SAT or ACT required; high school diploma is required and GED is accepted. *Academic units required:* 4 English, 2 mathematics, 3 science, (1 science labs), 2 foreign language, 2 social studies, 1 history, 2 academic electives. *Academic units recommended:* 4 English, 3 mathematics, 4 science, (2 science labs), 3 foreign language, 2 social studies, 2 history, 2 academic electives.

Finanancial Aid

Students should submit: FAFSA. The Princeton Review suggests that all financial aid forms be submitted as soon as possible after January 1. *Need-based scholarships/grants offered:* Federal Pell, SEOG, state scholarships/grants, private scholarships, the school's own gift aid. *Loan aid offered:* FFEL Subsidized Stafford, FFEL Unsubsidized Stafford, FFEL PLUS, Federal Perkins, private educational loans. Applicants will be notified of awards on a rolling basis beginning 2/14. Federal Work-Study Program available. Institutional employment available. Off-campus job opportunities are good.

The Inside Word

Albright is a small school with a 70+ percent acceptance rate, so you can expect a close, sympathetic reading of your application here. Admissions officers are looking for reasons to accept you. Give them that reason. Counter poor test scores or mediocre high school grades with a killer essay, enthusiastic recommendations, and a list of extracurricular experiences that promises you will contribute something of value to the Albright campus community.

THE SCHOOL SAYS " . . . "

From The Admissions Office

"**Academics:** Founded in 1856, Albright College is recognized as a national leader in interdisciplinary study. Nearly half of our students opt for combined or interdisciplinary majors . . . while still graduating in 4 years. Last year, students chose 143 different combinations of majors—from art/biology and psychology/business to education/theater and sociology/Latin American studies. But whether students select one major or combine fields, Albright's faculty work closely with students to create experiences that reflect individual talents, interests, and career goals.

"**Atmosphere**: Albright College is renowned for its openness and warmth. Students who visit Albright rate it as one of the friendliest small liberal arts colleges anywhere. Albright students have a strong sense of community based on friendliness, tolerance, and mutual support. These are the common ties that bind the community and make Albright an easy place for students to be heard and have an impact.

"**Outcomes:** An Albright education is designed to help students develop their individual voices and visions and become skilled problem solvers and communicators. Albright graduates leave with the knowledge, skills, and confidence to succeed.

"**Location:** The Albright campus is located 1 hour west of Philadelphia in a tree-lined suburb of Reading, Pennsylvania, a metropolitan area of 250,000.

"**Scholarships and Financial Aid:** Albright is pledged to help make its education affordable. This is evident in Albright's inclusion in Barron's *Best Buys in College Education* and in our generous need-based financial aid awards and numerous merit scholarships (ranging from $5,000 per year to full tuition)."

For even more information on this school, turn to page 447 of the "Stats" section.

ALFRED UNIVERSITY

Alumni Hall, One Saxon Drive, Alfred, NY 14802-1205 • Admissions: 607-871-2115
Fax: 607-871-2198 • Financial Aid: 607-871-2159 • E-mail: admwww@alfred.edu • Website: www.alfred.edu

RATINGS
Quality of Life: 78   Academic: 82   Admissions: 78   Financial Aid: 86

STUDENTS SAY "..."

> **SURVEY SAYS . . .**
> *Large classes*
> *Great library*
> *Frats and sororities are unpopular*
> *or nonexistent*
> *Lots of beer drinking*

Academics
Alfred University is best known for its unique and prestigious glass engineering, ceramic arts, and ceramic engineering programs ("the best in the nation," students insist). These programs' reputations are well earned, but they occasionally overshadow AU's many other assets, according to undergrads here; as one student points out, "Alfred offers tons of majors and minors within four different undergraduate schools (Art School, Engineering School, College of Liberal Arts and Sciences, and the College of Business)," and the school does a good job of "integrating the four very distinct schools into one cohesive whole, so you can make friends from absolutely every conceivable background while pursuing any course of study." Engineering is among the school's hallmark disciplines, attracting nearly one in seven undergraduates; business studies are nearly as popular. AU offers its breadth of academic options on an intimate scale; explains one undergrad, "The size of the school is a strength. Because the school is so small, students have chances that they might never have had at other schools. Some of the best friends I have made here are upperclassmen whom I probably would not have met had I gone to a larger school. In such a small school, everyone also has the chance to make his or her voice heard in a way that probably cannot happen at larger schools."

Life
Alfred University is located "in the middle of nowhere" in "the one-stoplight town" of Alfred, New York. "If the Student Activities Board does not provide it, it does not happen," warns one student. Undergrads fill their spare time with "over one hundred clubs and organizations" and "crazy stuff" like "snow sculptures and secret sledding (we have snow more often than not)." Students here "are very forward thinking," so many "try to get internships and co-ops during their undergraduate years." Otherwise, there's always the "multiple events and programs each week, especially on the weekends," sponsored by Student Activities, which are "very well-publicized and have great attendance." Such events include "movies, lectures, comedy acts, music shows, art shows, and plays." Low-key activities such as group dinners, watching DVDs, and video gaming are also quite popular. As one student sums up the situation, "Life is quiet for those who like it quiet, but it also offers something for everybody." Party nights "are pretty popular," and "a lot of students from both schools"—Alfred State College, located across the street, and Alfred University—"go out to a party and drink."

Student Body
"There really is no typical student at Alfred" because the "wide variety of majors and minors...attracts such a wide variety of students." The predominant note is "a mix of engineers and art students" (they make up about 40 percent of the student body) with "a smattering of other majors" across a broad range of disciplines, business and psychology most prominent among them. Students report that the population is "polarized among the art school, the liberal arts school, and the business school. Everybody seems to fit in somewhere, though." Engineers and artists tend toward the outer edges of the bell curve, so it's not surprising that "The school is made up of crazies of every variety. If you're a freak in high school, you will fit right in at Alfred. We have everything from people who will fall over themselves to discuss postmodernism to people who make chain mail bikinis." Most here "are from small towns, although there is also a proportionally high percentage of study abroad students."

THE PRINCETON REVIEW SAYS

Admissions

Very important factors considered include: Class rank, recommendation(s), rigor of secondary school record, character/personal qualities, extracurricular activities. *Important factors considered include:* Application essay, standardized test scores, volunteer work, work experience. *Other factors considered include:* Interview, talent/ability, SAT or ACT required; TOEFL required of all international applicants. High school diploma is required and GED is accepted. *Academic units required:* 4 English, 2 mathematics, 2 science, (2 science labs), 2 social studies. *Academic units recommended:* 4 mathematics, 3 science, (3 science labs), 3 social studies.

Financial Aid

Students should submit: FAFSA, institution's own financial aid form, state aid form, noncustodial PROFILE, business/farm supplement. Regular filing deadline is 3/15. The Princeton Review suggests that all financial aid forms be submitted as soon as possible after January 1. *Need-based scholarships/grants offered:* Federal Pell, SEOG, state scholarships/grants, private scholarships, the school's own gift aid. *Loan aid offered:* FFEL Subsidized Stafford, FFEL Unsubsidized Stafford, FFEL PLUS, Federal Perkins, college/university loans from institutional funds. Private alternative loans. Applicants will be notified of awards on a rolling basis beginning 2/15. Federal Work-Study Program available. Institutional employment available. Off-campus job opportunities are poor.

The Inside Word

Alfred is a fine university somewhat hampered by its location; it takes a special kind of student to want to spend four years in so remote a location, especially one in which winter can seem endless. Outdoorsy types comfortable in layered clothing are best suited to the challenge. The allure for arts students is obvious—Alfred's programs in the arts are especially well regarded—and as a result competition is fiercest among applicants for these programs. A killer portfolio, even more than great grades and standardized test scores, is your most likely ticket in.

THE SCHOOL SAYS "..."

From The Admissions Office

"The admissions process at Alfred University is the foundation for the personal attention each student can expect during their time at AU. Each applicant is evaluated individually and receives genuine, individual care and consideration.

"The best way to discover all Alfred University has to offer is to come to campus. We truly have something for everyone with over 60 courses of study, 22 intercollegiate athletic teams, and 100 clubs and organizations. You can tour campus; meet current students, faculty, coaches, and staff; attend a class; and eat in our dining hall—experience first hand what life at AU is like.

"Alfred University is a place where students are free to pursue their dreams and interests—all of them—no matter how varied or different. Academics, athletics, study abroad, special interests—they're all part of what makes you who you are and who you are going to become."

For even more information on this school, turn to page 447 of the "Stats" section.

ALLEGHENY COLLEGE

OFFICE OF ADMISSIONS, MEADVILLE, PA 16335 • ADMISSIONS: 800-521-5293
FAX: 814-337-0431 • FINANCIAL AID: 800-835-7780 • E-MAIL: ADMISS@ALLEGHENY.EDU • WEBSITE: WWW.ALLEGHENY.EDU

RATINGS
Quality of Life: 75   Academic: 87   Admissions: 91   Financial Aid: 86

STUDENTS SAY "..."

Academics

Allegheny College challenges students to expand their horizons by immersing themselves in "unusual combinations" of classes and resources. This theme, promoted heavily in the school's literature, isn't just rhetoric—students report that it is evidenced in every aspect of their academic experience. "Fostering students' personal interests even when they are unrelated to their major (e.g. a biology major in the orchestra)... Allegheny allows students to pursue their educations while continuing to develop themselves as strong people and contributors to society." Or, to put it more simply, "our school is about doing what you want to do and following your interests and passions." All students at Allegheny must complete both a major and a minor. In conjunction with a mandatory senior project and a battery of required communications classes, this means that "the academics are challenging; you spend a lot of time in class and even more time studying, but it's worth it," and though "there will be times, more often then not, that you may want to pull your hair out." That said, come graduation time, membership has its privileges. The school has "a very good reputation in western Pennsylvania and eastern Ohio and good alumni relations in those areas, so job placement and graduate school connections are excellent there." The curriculum is "very strong in writing (no matter what the major is) and speaking in public due to the large amounts of papers and presentations," and also "strong in research, whether for a thesis paper or in the lab, as we are exposed to it early and often."

> **SURVEY SAYS . . .**
> Small classes
> Lab facilities are great
> Athletic facilities are great
> Career services are great
> Students are friendly
> Students are happy
> Lots of beer drinking

Life

"Class work can dominate your life if you are not careful," so students here "need to find a balance among schoolwork, extra-curricular activities, and your social life." This balance is readily available through the bounty of opportunities the school offers. As one student explains, there are "more clubs then I can name, a slew of intramural sports, and the college always has some sort of programming going on," such as "comedians, paint-your-own-pottery, and other fun, non-alcoholic events." For those so inclined, "Weekends are the real 'party hard' time." However, students also spend their time off "doing community service, participating in athletic events, and raising awareness of global concerns." Hometown Meadville offers "good, small places to eat" along with "little shops," "a bowling alley," and "a movie theater," but it's hardly cosmopolitan, leading some to opine that "If Allegheny could pick itself up out of Meadville and relocate itself somewhere warmer and more exciting, this school could be perfect."

Student Body

The typical Allegheny student has "varied interests." "Each student interacts with a large number of groups each day, [for instance] they may be a political science major but also be involved in the theater program, all before attending their service fraternity at night." The fact that "seemingly everyone has different interests, beliefs, and personal backgrounds" helps offset the fact that Allegheny "is not an extremely ethnically diverse school." Students also tell us that Greek life "only makes up about 25 percent of the student population so anyone is free to have Greek or independent friends and not worry about one or the other dominating the social scene." While undergrads insist they're "not your cookie cutter students" and that "atypical is typical," you can still expect to see a lot of "North Face fleeces and Ugg boots" as you traverse the campus.

THE PRINCETON REVIEW SAYS

Admissions

Very important factors considered include: Class rank, academic GPA, rigor of secondary school record. *Important factors considered include:* Recommendation(s), standardized test scores, character/personal qualities, extracurricular activities, interview. *Other factors considered include:* Application essay, alumni/ae relation, first generation, geographical residence, level of applicant's interest, racial/ethnic status, talent/ability, volunteer work, work experience. SAT or ACT required; ACT with Writing component recommended. TOEFL required of all international applicants. High school diploma is required and GED is accepted. *Academic units required:* 4 English, 3 mathematics, 3 science, 2 foreign language, 3 social studies, 1 academic elective.

Financial Aid

Students should submit: FAFSA. The Princeton Review suggests that all financial aid forms be submitted as soon as possible after January 1. *Need-based scholarships/grants offered:* Federal Pell, SEOG, state scholarships/grants, private scholarships, the school's own gift aid, Federal Academic Competitiveness Grant, National SMART Grant, Veterans Educational Benefits. *Loan aid offered:* FFEL Subsidized Stafford, FFEL Unsubsidized Stafford, FFEL PLUS, Federal Perkins, Private loans from commercial lenders. Applicants will be notified of awards on a rolling basis beginning 3/1. Federal Work-Study Program available. Institutional employment available. Off-campus job opportunities are excellent.

The Inside Word

Academic promise plays a large role in the admissions process at Allegheny. The college looks for students who go beyond their high school's minimum requirements, particularly those who pursue honors and Advanced Placement courses. Admissions officers are known for their individualized approach. While standardized test scores and class rank factor significantly in their decisions, consideration is also given to personal character and extracurricular activities.

THE SCHOOL SAYS "..."

From The Admissions Office

"We're proud of Allegheny's beautiful campus and cutting-edge technologies,. and we know that our professors are leading scholars who pride themselves even more on being among the best teachers in the United States. Yet it's our students who make Allegheny the unique and special place that it is.

"Allegheny attracts students with unusual combinations of interests, skills, and talents. How do we characterize them? Although it's impossible to label our students, they do share some common characteristics. You'll find an abiding passion for learning and life, a spirit of camaraderie, and shared inquiry that spans across individuals as well as areas of study. You'll see over and over again such a variety of interests and passions and skills that, after a while, those unusual combinations don't seem so unusual at all.

"Allegheny is not for everybody. If you find labels reassuring, if you're looking for a narrow technical training, if you're in search of the shortest distance between point A and point B, then perhaps another college will be better for you.

"But, if you recognize that everything you experience between points A and B will make you appreciate point B that much more; if you've noticed that when life gives you a choice between two things, you're tempted to answer both or simply yes; if you start to get excited because you sense there is a college willing to echo the resounding yes, then we look forward to meeting you.

"Applicants for Fall 2008 are required to take either the new SAT or ACT (the new ACT Writing section is recommended but not required). If both tests are taken, we will use the better score of the two. The Writing score of both the SAT and ACT will be reviewed but will not be a major factor in admission decisions."

For even more information on this school, turn to page 448 of the "Stats" section.

AMERICAN UNIVERSITY

4400 Massachusetts Avenue, Northwest, Washington, DC 20016-8001 • Admissions: 202-885-6000
Fax: 202-885-1025 • Financial Aid: 202-885-6100 • E-mail: afa@american.edu • Website: www.american.edu

RATINGS
Quality of Life: 98   **Academic:** 86   **Admissions:** 93   **Financial Aid:** 83

STUDENTS SAY "..."

Academics

American University in Washington, DC boasts a "rigorous" and "very challenging" academic experience that offers students all the benefits of its location close to the political center of the country. The School of Public Affairs is nationally renowned, and "The international studies program is one of the best in the world." There's a "strong business school" too. "Aside from its location," "The best thing about American University is its ability to offer the course catalog of a midsized university while maintaining the feel of a small liberal arts college." "Small classes" ensure that "discussion flows freely." "Extremely accessible" professors "love to teach" and "look forward to speaking with students and helping them in their academic careers." It's not uncommon for an AU faculty member to "have real-world experience with a major corporation, government agency, or international organization." The "amazing" Career Center helps students to find "good jobs" and brings big-time recruiters to campus. "Volunteering with a nonprofit organization" is also a common student activity. Though the AU campus is "completely wireless," "a few buildings are in need of repair," and many students think that the library could use some improvement. "The science facilities don't need any TLC," but only because "No one is using them," one student says.

Life

"The best thing about AU is if you want to do it, it's here for you; if not, it won't bother you." A club exists "for just about every type of person you can think of." Parties "are big on the weekends, but they don't dominate campus life," and "The nightlife on and off campus is always active." AU is located "a little ways outside of the downtown area," but virtually everything is "just a short Metro ride away." "There's so much to do for fun in DC, it's stunning," asserts a sophomore. "Midnight trips to the national monuments" are popular, as are "touring the Smithsonian Museums for free, sampling ethnic food in Adams Morgan, and visiting trendy coffee shops" near Dupont Circle. Attending "protests" is big, too, if that's your bag. Back on campus, AU provides a plethora of speakers. Recent invitees have included Bob Dole, John Kerry, and "former presidents of several countries." Of course, because of the school's location, politics "infect the campus": "Watching CNN" and "working on the Hill" are everyday activities for many students. "Social justice and community-service groups" are also "very popular." "This school lives, breathes, eats, and sleeps politics," explains one student. "When William Rehnquist died, I was at a fraternity party, and when we heard about it over half the party left to go watch the news."

Student Body

American is not really a place for the "college-y college experience," asserts one undergrad, though "It can be if that's what you want." "The atypical student is the norm": The "passionate" and highly "eclectic" student population here runs the gamut from "hippies to hard-core young Republicans." There are "pretty-boy frat guys looking for their next keg to conquer" and "political enthusiasts who love to debate the hottest issues." There are "bookish students" and "pseudo-serious intellectuals." You'll find students of every socioeconomic level and "a good number of minorities." One student says that "for every person who pops his collar, there is someone with blue hair." AU boasts a throng of international students, "a large gay population," and lots of women: "Our female/male ratio is 60/40. I would not complain if we had more guys on campus," laments a frustrated female. Not surprisingly, the biggest differences among students involve politics. "There is a huge amount of contention between the liberals and conservatives on campus," observes a sophomore. "The conservatives walk around like high and mighty warriors of truth, and the liberals walk around like they're saving the world from the conservatives."

THE PRINCETON REVIEW SAYS
Admissions
Very important factors considered include: Rigor of secondary school record, standardized test scores, level of applicant's interest. *Important factors considered include:* Application essay, academic GPA, recommendation(s), extracurricular activities, volunteer work. *Other factors considered include:* Class rank, alumni/ae relation, character/personal qualities, first generation, geographical residence, racial/ethnic status, talent/ability, work experience. SAT Subject Tests recommended; SAT or ACT required; ACT with Writing component required. TOEFL required of all international applicants. High school diploma is required and GED is accepted. *Academic units required:* 4 English, 3 mathematics, 3 science, (2 science labs), 2 foreign language, 2 social studies, 3 academic electives. *Academic units recommended:* 4 English, 4 mathematics, 4 science, 3 foreign language, 4 social studies, 4 academic electives.

Financial Aid
Students should submit: FAFSA, institution's own financial aid form. Regular filing deadline is 2/15. The Princeton Review suggests that all financial aid forms be submitted as soon as possible after January 1. *Need-based scholarships/grants offered:* Federal Pell, SEOG, state scholarships/grants, private scholarships, the school's own gift aid, Academic merit scholarships: Presidential Scholarships, Dean's Scholarships, Leadership Scholarships, Phi Theta Kappa Scholarships (transfers only), Tuition Exchange Scholarships, United Methodist Scholarships, and other private/restricted scholarships are awarded by the Undergraduate Admissions Office. Most scholarships do not require a separate application and are renewable for up to three years if certain criteria are met. *Loan aid offered:* Direct Subsidized Stafford, Direct Unsubsidized Stafford, Direct PLUS, FFEL PLUS, Federal Perkins, college/university loans from institutional funds. Applicants will be notified of awards on or about 4/1. Federal Work-Study Program available. Institutional employment available. Off-campus job opportunities are excellent.

The Inside Word
While DC is a popular locale for undergrads, it also has its fair share of top-notch universities. For that reason, American must compete for students with a number of area schools, so its admissions stats are relatively relaxed for applicants who have strong academic records. Nonetheless, American is a solid option, especially for those interested in government and international relations. Candidates with leadership experience are particularly appealing to Admissions Officers at AU.

THE SCHOOL SAYS "..."
From The Admissions Office
"Ideas, action, and service—at AU, you interact regularly with decision makers and leaders in every profession and corner of the globe. You'll be academically challenged in a rich multicultural environment. Our expert teaching faculty provide a strong liberal arts education, characterized by small classes, the use of cutting-edge technology, and an interdisciplinary curriculum in the arts, education, humanities, social sciences, and sciences. Not just a political town, Washington, DC offers a variety of research, internship, and community-service opportunities in every field. Our AU Abroad Program, with over 80 international locations, lets you expand your studies into international settings. The Princeton Review selected AU for the 2005 edition of America's Best Value Colleges. AU was one of 77 schools, and the only one from DC, selected as a 'best value' for its combination of outstanding academics, moderate tuition, and financial aid packages.

"AU requires all applicants graduating from high school in, or after, 2006 to take the new SAT or the ACT with the Writing section. Fall 2008 applicants are allowed to submit scores from the old versions of both tests as their best scores will be used in making admissions decisions."

For even more information on this school, turn to page 448 of the "Stats" section.

AMHERST COLLEGE

CAMPUS BOX 2231, PO BOX 5000, AMHERST, MA 01002 • ADMISSIONS: 413-542-2328
FAX: 413-542-2040 • FINANCIAL AID: 413-542-2296 • E-MAIL: ADMISSIONS@AMHERST.EDU • WEBSITE: WWW.AMHERST.EDU

RATINGS
Quality of Life: 94   **Academic:** 94   **Admissions:** 98   **Financial Aid:** 92

STUDENTS SAY ". . ."

Academics

At Amherst College, a small, elite liberal arts school in western Massachusetts, "The academic experience is well balanced, comprehensive, and tailored to the desires and needs of each individual student." Students truly get exactly what they want because "There are no core requirements. Every person in every class . . . is enthusiastic about

> **SURVEY SAYS . . .**
> *Large classes*
> *No one cheats*
> *Campus feels safe*
> *Students are happy*

the subject and wants to learn." Students love this set-up, telling us that "the open curriculum guarantees that every student in every class really wants to be there, which makes a huge difference in the liveliness of discussion." Academics "are extremely challenging without being overly burdensome," in part because support networks are so strong. Students "really develop personal relationships with professors, which makes classes that much more enjoyable." Students also appreciate that they "get all the things [they] need and want (services, advice, etc.) when [they] need and want them." As one student puts it, "Amherst College is a small family. Everyone here wants you to succeed; however, it's up to you to reach out for that guidance. If you knock, Amherst shall respond." Professors "all have a great sense of humor" and "are engaging and eclectic." As one student writes, "Even in introductory courses, professors literally bounce off the walls with enthusiasm for the subject." The results tell the story: Nearly three-quarters of all Amherst alumni proceed to postgraduate study within 5 years of graduation.

Life

"Life is usually busy" at Amherst, where "People are generally pretty involved." Academics are demanding, but fortunately "Everyone is here for the same reason: to learn. We learn as much from each other as we do in the classroom because everyone is just so different and has a story to tell. I stay up till the wee hours of the morning with some of my dorm-mates sharing stories and ordering Antonio's Pizza." When they're not working, students "are often playing sports" or "engaging in some other activity." Undergrads "love the academic culture of the Five Colleges area. You can go to music performances, plays, or poetry readings any night of the week." As one student reports, "Events are happening all the time, and there is always something going on . . . concerts, talks about Brazilian economics, West African dance shows, etc. Life here is comfortable and exciting." A "free bus to get to other colleges and towns" makes it easy to access these events, even without a car. It's not only about personal enrichment here, though; while students "work hard throughout the week," they "party on Thursday and Saturday." Why not on Friday? "Because nearly one-third of the student body [are] athletes, parties are often thrown by various teams, but open to all. As a result, Friday nights are pretty dead, since all the athletes are resting up for their games."

Student Body

"It seems like there are many of your typical White, private school students from the New England area" at Amherst, but "Then there are [also] students from all over the United States and from other countries who are so diverse." Most of these "typically well-rounded and motivated" undergraduates "played some sort of sport in high school, and a very large percentage play club or varsity sports at college." These students are "witty, friendly, thoughtful, non-competitive, self-effacing, and know how to have a good time."

Nearly everyone agrees that "Amherst is amazing because of its small size. It's a really close-knit community where everyone is extremely open-minded and considerate." According to another student, "I love that [Amherst's] students are politically aware and serious students but also willing to have a good time. The first thing that struck me about my school is how nice everyone is. The school has a reputation for being stuck-up, but I have not experienced that in the least."

THE PRINCETON REVIEW SAYS

Admissions

Very important factors considered include: Application essay, academic GPA, recommendation(s), rigor of secondary school record, standardized test scores, character/personal qualities, extracurricular activities, first generation, talent/ability. *Important factors considered include:* Class rank, alumni/ae relation, volunteer work. *Other factors considered include:* Geographical residence, state residency, work experience. SAT and SAT Subject Tests or ACT required; ACT with Writing component recommended. High school diploma or equivalent is not required. *Academic units recommended:* 4 English, 4 mathematics, 3 science, (1 science labs), 4 foreign language, 2 social studies, 2 history.

Financial Aid

Students should submit: FAFSA, CSS/Financial Aid PROFILE, noncustodial PROFILE, business/farm supplement. Income documentation submitted through College. The Princeton Review suggests that all financial aid forms be submitted as soon as possible after January 1. *Need-based scholarships/grants offered:* Federal Pell, SEOG, state scholarships/grants, private scholarships, the school's own gift aid. *Loan aid offered:* Direct Subsidized Stafford, Direct Unsubsidized Stafford, Direct PLUS, Federal Perkins, college/university loans from institutional funds. Applicants will be notified of awards on or about 4/5. Federal Work-Study Program available. Institutional employment available. Off-campus job opportunities are excellent.

The Inside Word

A $1 billion endowment allows Amherst to provide admitted students with generous financial aid packages. The school is deeply committed to economic diversity in the student body, increasing the number of working-class and low-income students in the Class of 2010 from 15 percent to 20 percent (New York Times, September 19, 2006). The school is also considering scaling back, or even doing away with, early decision admissions, which are believed to favor upper-income students.

THE SCHOOL SAYS ". . ."

From The Admissions Office

"Amherst College looks, above all, for men and women of intellectual promise who have demonstrated qualities of mind and character that will enable them to take full advantage of the college's curriculum. . . . Admission decisions aim to select from among the many qualified applicants those possessing the intellectual talent, mental discipline, and imagination that will allow them most fully to benefit from the curriculum and contribute to the life of the college and of society. Whatever the form of academic experience—lecture course, seminar, conference, studio, laboratory, independent study at various levels—intellectual competence and awareness of problems and methods are the goals of the Amherst program, rather than the direct preparation for a profession.

"Applicants must submit scores from the new SAT plus two SAT Subject Tests, or the old SAT plus three SAT Subject Tests. Students may substitute the ACT with the Writing component (as of Spring 2005) or without Writing if the test was taken prior to Spring 2005."

For even more information on this school, turn to page 449 of the "Stats" section.

ARCADIA UNIVERSITY

450 SOUTH EASTON ROAD, GLENSIDE, PA 19038 • ADMISSIONS: 215-572-2910 • FAX: 215-572-4049
E-MAIL: ADMISS@ARCADIA.EDU • WEBSITE: WWW.ARCADIA.EDU

RATINGS
Quality of Life: 74   Academic: 77   Admissions: 79   Financial Aid: 78

STUDENTS SAY ". . ."

Academics

Arcadia University near Philadelphia is "a gem in suburbia" that offers "a global learning experience." "Arcadia's all about study abroad" and the program is "huge." Regardless of major, "almost everyone at Arcadia" spends some time globe-

> **SURVEY SAYS . . .**
> *Great library*
> *Frats and sororities are unpopular or nonexistent*

trotting. Destinations for "semesters, summers, or even community service trips" include China, Equatorial Guinea, New Zealand, Ireland, and South Korea. Also, "freshman preview is an amazing, once-in-a-lifetime opportunity" that allows first-year students to spend a week in England, Scotland, or Spain. (Preview for transfer students is in Italy). Back on campus, "there are small class sizes, which make learning so easy." The "usually accessible" professors "genuinely care about their students and the subject that they teach." A host of excellent majors includes a "very hands-on" education program. Arcadia is "a good art school," too. Theater is particularly strong. Some students say that Arcadia is "good for science majors." Others disagree. "Arcadia is okay for science majors," they say, "but not a great place."

Life

This campus "in the suburbs of Philadelphia" is "beautiful." "Arcadia has a friggin' castle," observes a senior. "Enough said." Socially, "everyone knows everyone" and the "unnecessary drama" can occasionally feel like "a glorified high school." Cultural events are abundant. "The dance club (Knight Club) is very popular." "In the fall, we have Mr. Beaver, which is a male mock beauty pageant," explains a senior. It's "always fun." Thursday nights are the big party nights and "as big as a Friday or Saturday night" at other places. On the whole, though, "Arcadia is fairly low key" and "very far from a party school." There's no Greek system and the festivities that do occur "don't get very rowdy." Ordering pizza and watching movies is a "favorite pastime." Many students love the social scene. "This is exactly what I wanted from my school," declares a junior. Others complain about "weekend nothingness." They note that Arcadia has a large commuter population and a reputation as "a suitcase college." Of course, that term has a slightly different connotation here. "There are a huge number of students who are studying abroad," relates a sophomore. "At Arcadia, you get your typical college party life overseas." Also, the train station is "right down the street" from campus. The "20-minute train ride into Philly" is "great for weekend trips or anything fun."

Student Body

"Most students" here are "pretty friendly" and come from middleclass backgrounds. There are also "a good number of international students." Commuter students make up more than a third of the population, and women noticeably outnumber men. "There are more squirrels than boys on campus," laments one female. "If you run into a guy, he is most likely a jock or gay." Indeed, Arcadia boasts "a highly tolerant campus" and a "very strong" gay community. There are also lots of "artsy" types who are "very outside the social norm." Other students are "ridiculously nerdy." Of course, there are plenty of perfectly normal people here, too. "You know: the ones that throw on sweats and leave their hair elegantly disheveled because that's the look these days." For the most part, though, "everyone has their own style." "There seems to be a higher ratio of weird people here at Arcadia than in the regular world."

Admissions

Very important factors considered include: Academic GPA, rigor of secondary school record. *Important factors considered include:* Class rank, application essay, recommendation(s), standardized test scores, extracurricular activities. *Other factors considered include:* Alumni/ae relation, character/personal qualities, interview, talent/ability, volunteer work, work experience. SAT or ACT required; ACT with Writing component required. TOEFL required of all international applicants. High school diploma is required and GED is accepted. *Academic units recommended:* 4 English, 3 mathematics, 3 science, (3 science labs), 2 foreign language, 2 social studies, 2 history,

Finanancial Aid

The Princeton Review suggests that all financial aid forms be submitted as soon as possible after January 1. Off-campus job opportunities are good.

The Inside Word

Solid grades and test scores should get you admitted to Arcadia without much of a problem. Don't miss the campus interview, though, and don't take the process lightly. The admissions staff takes the time to pore over each application. Note that you have to audition if you want to major in acting and submit a portfolio for art programs.

THE SCHOOL SAYS " . . . "

From The Admissions Office

"Arcadia University is a top-ranked private university in metropolitan Philadelphia and a national leader in study abroad. The 2007 Open Doors report ranks Arcadia University 2nd in the nation among master's university in the percentage of undergraduate students studying abroad. U.S. News & World Report ranks Arcadia University among the top 25 master's universities in the North and recognizes it as one of the top 20 study abroad programs in the nation. Arcadia University promises a distinctively global, integrative and personal learning experience that prepares students to contribute and prosper in a diverse and dynamic world. As a student at Arcadia University, your education expands beyond the classroom. Our study abroad programs, international faculty, and global vision of education combine to create an environment that affords you a world of opportunities. Our Center for Education Abroad is study abroad programs are top ranked, and students have the opportunity to study at 100 programs in 14 countries, including England, Equatorial Guinea, France, Scotland, Wales, Ireland, Northern Ireland, Australia, China, Greece, Korea, India, Italy, South Africa, Spain, Tanzania, and New Zealand.

"Freshmen at Arcadia have the unique opportunity to spend spring break in London or Scotland for $495. The London/Scotland Preview Program introduces students to overseas study and travel. Students may choose from more than 45 different undergraduate programs and 15 graduate degrees. Our 13:1 student/faculty ratio enables students to work closely with faculty for academic advising, research, and publication activities."

For even more information on this school, turn to page 449 of the "Stats" section.

The Art Institute of Boston at Lesley University

700 Beacon Street, Boston, MA 02215-2598 • Admissions: 617-585-6700 • Fax: 617-437-1226
E-mail: admissions@aiboston.edu • Website: www.aiboston.edu

RATINGS
Quality of Life: 73   Academic: 85   Admissions: 81   Financial Aid: 66

STUDENTS SAY "..."

Academics

The Art Institute of Boston at Lesley University is a small, private, and "very hands-on" school that offers majors in fine art, illustration, photography, graphic design, animation, and art history. The sophisticated facilities here include a well-stocked printmaking studio, a clay lab with several kilns, a wood shop, an impressive collection of photography equipment, and computer labs for design and animation.

Graduation requirements include a wide array of liberal arts requirements and a sequence of foundational art courses. Art-related courses are reportedly "very long and intense." Students here greatly appreciate that "Every professor at AIB is a working professional." And though "teaching methods can be haphazard at times," the faculty is generally full of "enthusiastic" and "insanely talented" artists who "have a love for their craft." As one student explains, "They teach artists how to improve their art and how to ready themselves for the real world." "One-on-one interaction" is common thanks to an "intimate environment" that "fosters close relationships and connections to job opportunities after graduation." "Some things like registration are confusing," though, and the administration can be hit-or-miss, ranging from "always having its doors open" to needing "to get it together."

Life

The facilities on AIB's tiny campus are "open well past regular hours" and students here, as you might expect, spend a pretty good chunk of their time making art. Traditional clubs and extracurricular activities are very sparse. Students "use the city as their campus." Boston is "a great environment for art students" and, really, every other kind of student. It would be hard to find a better college town anywhere. "The area is packed with students," observes a junior. "AIB practically sits in the backyard of Fenway Park." The location allows students here to take full advantage of the city without the hassle of a car. Cheap restaurants are everywhere. "Bars and music venues are extremely popular." Drinking is certainly possible. Drugs are here, too, but "heavy users never last." "The lifestyle is what you choose it to be," explains a sophomore. "There are plenty of kids who want to party and there are plenty of kids who want to sit in and watch movies in pajamas."

Student Body

With a description like "smoke-loving," it seems fair to say that tobacco is in anything but short supply here. Otherwise, "the only thing every student shares in common is a passion for the visual arts and a desire to create it." The budding professional artists at AIB are "a nice eclectic mix of strangeness and normality." There are "creative and rebellious types." You'll find "the suffering artist" and "pretentious art school stereotypes who think pictures of empty places are really deep and important." "Some of us have tons of piercings," says a freshman. Others dress very fashionably. One student calls AIB "scenester heaven." "Most people are comfortable expressing their individuality and being who they are" and "everyone seems to get along just fine." However, "people generally stick to the friends they made freshman year in their own major and very rarely are able to branch out."

THE PRINCETON REVIEW SAYS

Admissions

Very important factors considered include: Academic GPA, rigor of secondary school record, your portfolio evaluation. *Important factors considered include:* Class rank, application essay, recommendation(s), standardized test scores, character/personal qualities, extracurricular activities, interview, talent/ability. *Other factors considered include:* Alumni/ae relation, first generation, geographical residence, level of applicant's interest, racial/ethnic status, volunteer work, work experience. SAT or ACT required; ACT with Writing component required. TOEFL required of all international applicants. High school diploma is required and GED is accepted. *Academic units required:* 4 English. *Academic units recommended:* 4 English, 1 mathematics, 1 science, 1 foreign language, 2 social studies, 2 history, 2 academic electives, 2 studio art.

Finanancial Aid

Students should submit: FAFSA, institution's own financial aid form. The Princeton Review suggests that all financial aid forms be submitted as soon as possible after January 1. *Need-based scholarships/grants offered:* Federal Pell, SEOG, state scholarships/grants, private scholarships, the school's own gift aid. *Loan aid offered:* FFEL Subsidized Stafford, FFEL Unsubsidized Stafford, FFEL PLUS, Federal Perkins, state loans Applicants will be notified of awards on a rolling basis beginning 2/15. Federal Work-Study Program available. Institutional employment available. Off-campus job opportunities are excellent.

The Inside Word

High school grades are important at AIB. Keep in mind that you'll have to take several general education courses here. Your standardized test scores will be considered as well. However, this is an art school, so the portfolio that you submit is most likely the thing that is going to make or break your application.

THE SCHOOL SAYS " . . . "

From The Admissions Office

"At AIB, art is it. We have all gravitated here because of AIB's creative energy.

"At AIB, you really do join a community of serious artists. You will find a close-knit group who will push and prod and sometimes annoy you to get you to do your best. That's AIB, intimate, supportive, populated by students and teachers who will tell you when your work is phenomenal or especially when your perspective is flat or your concept is trite. To become a working artist you need that honesty.

"AIB's teachers are good. They know how to cajole and push you into fulfilling all your wild potential. Our teachers truly want to be at AIB—for its positive energy and its inquisitive, imaginative students. Both great artists and great teachers, AIB faculty are working professionals, successful artists, designers, and innovators.

"Though AIB is an art school through and through, it is also one of four schools within Lesley University, a multi-site liberal arts university based in Cambridge. Located just across the Charles River from Boston, AIB and Lesley College students live in residence halls and join clubs/activities together. Unlike at most independent art schools, Lesley University opens up the world of liberal arts to AIB students and offers the many benefits a large, urban university has to offer (your parents will be reassured).

"AIB graduates go out into the real world with the skills needed to get a job in their field. With an AIB degree, your opportunities will be limitless."

For even more information on this school, turn to page 450 of the "Stats" section.

ASSUMPTION COLLEGE

500 SALISBURY STREET, WORCESTER, MA 01609-1296 • ADMISSIONS: 888-882-7786 • FAX: 508-799-4412
E-MAIL: ADMISS@ASSUMPTION.EDU • WEBSITE: WWW.ASSUMPTION.EDU

RATINGS
Quality of Life: 73   Academic: 81   Admissions: 77   Financial Aid: 76

STUDENTS SAY ". . ."

Academics

Assumption College is a Catholic school in the greater Boston area, offering liberal arts and pre-professional majors to a small student population of just over 2,000 undergraduates. Relying on both practical instruction and academic expertise, "the professors at Assumption College are very qualified individuals whose goal is to educate students and prepare them for the future. They are not just trying to feed students information but also stimulate thought and discussion." Expectations are high, and "academics can be challenging, but are mostly manageable as long as you put in the time." Fortunately, "the size of the school allows for a large amount of personal attention," and professors, "go above and beyond the call of duty to make sure you get the best education they can offer." Undergrads admit that there are some professors whose courses are less interesting than others; however, they universally praise the faculty's commitment to its students. A freshman details, "The professors, at least 80% of the time, are excellent lecturers. There are almost no lectures, which are not accompanied by productive discussions."

> **SURVEY SAYS . . .**
> Large classes
> Lab facilities are great
> Great computer facilities
> Frats and sororities are unpopular or nonexistent
> Lots of beer drinking
> Hard liquor is popular

Life

Assumption is a Catholic school, so "religion is prominent and there are good programs for religious students. However, if you are not religious it isn't shoved down your throat or forced on you." A largely residential campus, "there is a good sense of community here, especially within the residence halls and clubs." Off-campus, in the surrounding town of Worcester, you'll find "a lot of restaurants and bars that students frequent, as well as a lot of good shopping." While freshmen cannot have cars on campus, "the school has a deal with YellowCab called 'safe ride.' As long as you have your school ID you can get a ride back to campus for $4 only after dark." Students admit, "Drinking is definitely a large part of the culture here." However, they also reassure us that "many people don't drink." For those who prefer a mellower social schedule, "bingo is a favorite activity on campus, and many students are involved in Campus Ministry." In addition, students spend time at "sporting events, comedians, open mic nights, bingo, or just hanging out in a friend's room."

Student Body

A studious, friendly, and social group, Assumption students are generally described as "hard workers, committed, driven, and smart." Outside of their studies, "the typical student gets involved, whether it be sports, student government, academic clubs, or an on-campus job." The majority of Assumption students come from "a suburban, white, upper-middle-class background. There aren't many who deviate from this norm, but those who do manage to fit in well enough." In addition, Assumption students seem to partake in an unwritten preppy dress code. A junior chides "Assumption was once described to me as a walking J. Crew ad, which is basically true." However, students reassure us that Assumption is committed to acceptance; "If you are a minority or not into preppy clothing, you are treated the same and respected for your differences."

THE PRINCETON REVIEW SAYS

Admissions

Very important factors considered include: Application essay, academic GPA, standardized test scores. *Important factors considered include:* Recommendation(s), rigor of secondary school record, interview, level of applicant's interest, volunteer work. *Other factors considered include:* Class rank, alumni/ae relation, character/personal qualities, extracurricular activities, first generation, racial/ethnic status, talent/ability, SAT or ACT required; high school diploma is required and GED is accepted. *Academic units required:* 4 English, 3 mathematics, 2 science, 2 foreign language, 2 history, 5 academic electives.

Finanancial Aid

Students should submit: FAFSA. Regular filing deadline is 2/1. The Princeton Review suggests that all financial aid forms be submitted as soon as possible after January 1. *Need-based scholarships/grants offered:* Federal Pell, SEOG, state scholarships/grants, private scholarships, the school's own gift aid. *Loan aid offered:* FFEL Subsidized Stafford, FFEL Unsubsidized Stafford, FFEL PLUS, Federal Perkins, state loans, college/university loans from institutional funds. Applicants will be notified of awards on a rolling basis beginning 2/16. Federal Work-Study Program available. Institutional employment available. Off-campus job opportunities are good.

The Inside Word

Assumption takes the "personal qualities" of its applicants into consideration, looking closely at candidates' co-curricular activities, leadership experiences, and commitment to community service. Essays and letters of recommendation, both required, are also considered important indicators of character. Spend some extra time on the non-academic part of your application, and choose your recommenders carefully.

THE SCHOOL SAYS " . . . "

From The Admissions Office

"Assumption College, founded in 1904, is the fourth-oldest Catholic college in New England. Assumption combines academically rigorous programs in the liberal arts, the sciences and professional studies grounded in the Catholic intellectual tradition. These programs enable students to cultivate the academic skills and personal values they need to meet the demands of a constantly changing world.

"At Assumption, we believe that a college education should develop and enrich the formation of the spirit and heart as well as the intellect. We value those moments of transformation that make our students more insightful and enlightened – moments that occur not only in the classroom or the lab, but also on the playing field or the stage, in a residence hall, or volunteering in the community.

"We believe that each of our students has the ability to make a positive difference in the world. To that end, our faculty and staff instruct, counsel and inspire students to help them become compassionate leaders, effective problem solvers, and fulfilled, productive adults.

"Assumption's 185-acre campus in Worcester, Massachusetts, combines easy access to New England's second largest city with the beauty, comfort, and security of a residential neighborhood. The college offers a state-of-the-art Science Center, a new Information Technology Center, a new multi-sport athletic field, and guarantees on-campus housing options (including four new residence halls opened since 2000) for all four years."

For even more information on this school, turn to page 450 of the "Stats" section.

Babson College

Mustard Hall, Babson Park, MA 02457-0310 • Admissions: 800-488-3696 • Fax: 781-239-4006
Financial Aid: 781-239-4219 • E-mail: ugradadmission@babson.edu • Website: www.babson.edu

RATINGS

Quality of Life: 82   **Academic:** 88   **Admissions:** 93   **Financial Aid:** 87

STUDENTS SAY ". . ."

Academics

If you already know anything about Babson, you probably know that at this small school in the suburbs of Boston, "everything is related to business. So if you don't like business, you should not even think about coming here." Indeed, Babson has one of the best known and most respected undergraduate business programs in the country. It begins with the Foundations of Management and Entrepreneurship (FME) freshman year, during which students work in groups to conceive and launch a (hopefully) profitable small business. This

> **SURVEY SAYS . . .**
> *Small classes*
> *Great computer facilities*
> *Great library*
> *Career services are great*
> *Diverse student types on campus*
> *Campus feels safe*
> *Lots of beer drinking*

segues into the sophomore year in which students participate in an integrated experience that includes instruction in core business disciplines like accounting, marketing, and finance, among others. By nearly all accounts the curriculum is extremely challenging, and the severe grade curve based on an average of 2.7 comes as a shock to some. But most students feel that although "the homework tends to be a lot compared to most of my friends at other business schools . . . we receive a better education." In large part that's because "Many of the professors have started or still run very successful companies," and they share their invaluable "industry experience" in the classroom. At least business professors do. "The liberal arts teachers vary a lot more in quality." By and large, the administration receives average marks, but most students don't focus on any administrative shortcomings. "At the end of the day, if you want to be a successful entrepreneur or business person, Babson is the best place for you."

Life

The "business boot camp" that is Babson is not known for its social life. During the week, "People are consumed by work, and are constantly concentrating on their future. On the weekends people socialize a lot because they need a break from the stress of the week." The student body splinters into distinct factions when it's time to unwind: "American kids typically party on campus more often, the athletes will party together, frats do their thing, and the international rich kids go in town and are scarce on the weekends since they live at the clubs in Boston." Some undergrads cross-pollinate groups, of course, but these are generally where the lines are drawn. Students who choose to party on campus, however, are well aware that "the campus police [referred to locally as 'Babo'] and Office of Campus Life take a strong stance against parties and alcohol" and that Babo is quite adept at breaking up unauthorized get-togethers. School-sanctioned on-campus activities include "'Knight Parties' on one Saturday night during each month (a club-like atmosphere with a DJ, dancing, and lots of free food and drinks, and beer for 21-year-olds)." Additionally, "The on-campus pub is fun and a common hangout for upperclassmen." For those who feel the lure of Boston, a car definitely makes getting there easier, but "The school also offers a bus that runs into Boston on the weekends for students."

Student Body

At this small business school where "Professionalism is a part of your grade," a "typical student is pretty well off, dressed well no matter what their style is, and pretty intelligent on business and similar subjects." Given its business focus, some students speculate that "Babson is probably the only school in Massachusetts where Republicans are in the majority." Noticeable cliques include the BISOs (Babson International Students), the athletes, and the Greeks, but regardless of the groups students fall into, nearly all of them "constantly think about the next great business idea, internship, or great job at firms like Lehman Brothers, KPMG, Ernst & Young, etc." It should come as no surprise, then, that "we are short on hippies, punks, and extreme liberals. If you fall into those categories, people will still accept you, but eventually you'll probably want to strangle the rest of us and will transfer." No matter what you start out as, the consensus seems to be that 4 years of "Babson will transform you from a driven/motivated individual into a lethal business machine."

THE PRINCETON REVIEW SAYS

Admissions

Very important factors considered include: Application essay, academic GPA, recommendation(s), rigor of secondary school record, standardized test scores, character/personal qualities. *Important factors considered include:* Class rank, extracurricular activities. *Other factors considered include:* Alumni/ae relation, first generation, geographical residence, interview, level of applicant's interest, racial/ethnic status, state residency, talent/ability, volunteer work, work experience. SAT or ACT required; SAT and SAT Subject Tests or ACT recommended; ACT with Writing component required. TOEFL required of all international applicants. High school diploma is required and GED is accepted. *Academic units recommended:* 4 English, 4 mathematics, 4 science, (3 science labs), 4 foreign language, 2 social studies, 2 history, 1 Pre-Calculus.

Financial Aid

Students should submit: FAFSA, CSS/Financial Aid PROFILE, noncustodial PROFILE, business/farm supplement. Federal tax returns, W-2s, and Verification Worksheet. Regular filing deadline is 2/15. The Princeton Review suggests that all financial aid forms be submitted as soon as possible after January 1. *Need-based scholarships/grants offered:* Federal Pell, SEOG, state scholarships/grants, the school's own gift aid. *Loan aid offered:* FFEL Subsidized Stafford, FFEL Unsubsidized Stafford, FFEL PLUS, Federal Perkins, state loans Applicants will be notified of awards on or about 4/1. Federal Work-Study Program available. Institutional employment available. Off-campus job opportunities are good.

The Inside Word

Though Babson offers a unique educational opportunity, their admissions practices are as traditional as they come. Personal qualities and extracurricular activities are taken into consideration, but the best way to impress a Babson Admissions Officer is through strong academic performance. Both scholastic rigor and the demonstration of intellectual curiosity are extremely important. Additionally, applicants will want to focus on their essay—writing ability is viewed as vital at Babson.

THE SCHOOL SAYS ". . ."

From The Admissions Office

"In addition to theoretical knowledge, Babson College is dedicated to providing its students with hands-on business experience. The Foundations of Management and Entrepreneurship (FME) and Management Consulting Field Experience (MCFE) are two prime examples of this commitment. During the FME, all freshmen are placed into groups of 30 and actually create their own businesses that they operate until the end of the academic year. The profits of each FME business are then donated to the charity of each group's choice.

"MCFE offers upperclassmen the unique and exciting opportunity to work as actual consultants for private companies and/or nonprofit organizations in small groups of three to five. Students receive academic credit for their work as well as invaluable experience in the field of consulting. FME and MCFE are just two of the ways Babson strives to produce business leaders with both theoretical knowledge and practical experience.

"Babson College requires freshmen applicants to submit scores from either the new SAT or the ACT with Writing component. The school recommends that students also submit results from SAT Subject Tests."

For even more information on this school, turn to page 451 of the "Stats" section.

BARD COLLEGE

OFFICE OF ADMISSIONS, ANNANDALE-ON-HUDSON, NY 12504 • ADMISSIONS: 845-758-7472
FAX: 845-758-5208 • FINANCIAL AID: 845-758-7526 • E-MAIL: ADMISSION@BARD.EDU • WEBSITE: WWW.BARD.EDU

RATINGS
Quality of Life: 66   Academic: 92   Admissions: 96   Financial Aid: 87

STUDENTS SAY "..."

Academics

Bard College, a small school that excels in the liberal and fine arts, takes a "progressive approach" to academics, allowing students "the opportunity to control your own education and learn more than you would at most other academic institutions." It doesn't make for a walk in the park, though; students claim that the workload can get heavy, "But if you're passionate about your classes, as most people here are, time often goes quickly as you study. This is not the place for anyone who is not intellectually motivated." A "relaxed, pressure-free environment" makes Bard "a great place to learn" and takes some of the stress out of the hard work, as do the "great professors, who are passionate about the subjects they teach and have often just written a book about the material in a class they are currently teaching." Bard doesn't do as much hand-holding as do comparable liberal arts schools; here "The academics rely heavily on the motivation of the individual student," although "Once you begin coming up with your own special projects and supplementing the required reading, professors bend over backward to help you." The relaxed atmosphere does have its downside, though; students claim that "things are extremely disorganized, and you can easily find yourself being told five different things from five different people."

> **SURVEY SAYS . . .**
> *Lots of liberal students*
> *Small classes*
> *No one cheats*
> *Students aren't religious*
> *Campus feels safe*
> *Frats and sororities are unpopular or nonexistent*
> *Political activism is popular*
> *Lots of beer drinking*
> *(Almost) everyone smokes*

LIFE

"People are really involved, both inside and outside of the classroom" at Bard, where "There is a really active club life. We have everything from the International Student Organization to the Surrealist Training Circus and the Children's Expressive Arts Project. There are always dance, theater, music, and art events every weekend," and "The shows are really popular, both those that are student-run and those put on by professionals." Bard undergrads also indulge in "a lot of after-hours discussion about what we're all doing in classes. My friends and I talk about experiments, theories, literature, and various artistic/scientific installations." The Bard campus "is gorgeous, so some people take advantage of amazing hiking and outdoor sports. Other people enjoy Blithewood, a hill that overlooks the Catskills, in a more passive fashion, sunbathing or lounging with friends." Students tell us that they "always feel safe here, even walking in the middle of the night." Bard's party scene is primarily confined to weekends; one student explains, "People party a lot on the weekends but during the week everyone seems to be working." The quaint towns that surround Bard appeal to some, but many prefer "the 2-hour train ride to New York City. It's convenient when you have nothing else to do on the weekend."

Student Body

"Hippies, hipsters, and geek chic" are common sights on the Bard campus, as are "people who have that 'I'm on the cutting edge of underground fashion' look." However, while Bard might appear to be "all about tight designer jeans, indie rock, and everything else NYC or LA," the reality is "There are really a lot of normal college kids here—people seem to think everyone here was a social outcast in high school, but most people here are friendly, social, and pretty normal (although certainly a bit cerebral)." Undergrads tend to be "politically conscious and left-wing-activist types." One student notes, "If you're uncreative or conservative you probably wouldn't fit in. Other than that, just about anything works." Another agrees, "A large percentage of people are extremely talented and creative and express themselves best through creative writing, music, art, dance, or theater." In short, Bard is about "a lot of kids being different together."

THE PRINCETON REVIEW SAYS

Admissions

Very important factors considered include: Application essay, academic GPA, recommendation(s), rigor of secondary school record, character/personal qualities, extracurricular activities, talent/ability. *Important factors considered include:* Volunteer work, work experience. *Other factors considered include:* Class rank, standardized test scores, alumni/ae relation, first generation, geographical residence, interview, level of applicant's interest, racial/ethnic status, religious affiliation/commitment, state residency, TOEFL required of all international applicants. High school diploma is required and GED is accepted. *Academic units recommended:* 4 English, 4 mathematics, 4 science, (3 science labs), 4 foreign language, 4 social studies, 4 history.

Financial Aid

Students should submit: FAFSA, CSS/Financial Aid PROFILE, state aid form, noncustodial PROFILE, business/farm supplement. Regular filing deadline is 2/15. The Princeton Review suggests that all financial aid forms be submitted as soon as possible after January 1. *Need-based scholarships/grants offered:* Federal Pell, SEOG, state scholarships/grants, private scholarships, the school's own gift aid. *Loan aid offered:* FFEL Subsidized Stafford, FFEL Unsubsidized Stafford, FFEL PLUS, Federal Perkins, Loans from institutional funds (for international students only). Applicants will be notified of awards on or about 4/1. Federal Work-Study Program available. Institutional employment available. Off-campus job opportunities are good.

The Inside Word

Because Bard boasts healthy application numbers, it is in a position to concentrate on matchmaking. To that end, Admissions Officers seek students with independent and inquisitive spirits. Applicants who exhibit academic ambition while extending their intellectual curiosity beyond the realm of the classroom are particularly appealing. Successful candidates typically have several honors and Advanced Placement courses on their transcripts, as well as strong letters of recommendation and well-written personal statements.

THE SCHOOL SAYS ". . ."

From The Admissions Office

"An alliance with Rockefeller University, the renowned graduate scientific research institution, gives Bardians access to Rockefeller's professors and laboratories and to places in Rockefeller's Summer Research Fellows Program. Almost all our math and science graduates pursue graduate or professional studies; 90 percent of our applicants to medical and health professional schools are accepted.

"The Globalization and International Affairs (BGIA) Program is a residential program in the heart of New York City that offers undergraduates a unique opportunity to undertake specialized study with leading practitioners and scholars in international affairs and to gain internship experience with international-affairs organizations. Topics in the curriculum include human rights, international economics, global environmental issues, international justice, managing international risk, and writing on international affairs, among others. Internships/tutorials are tailored to students' particular fields of study.

"Student dormitory and classroom facilities are in Bard Hall, 410 West Fifty-eighth Street, a newly renovated 11-story building near the Lincoln Center District in New York City.

"Bard College does not require SAT scores, new or old, to be submitted for admissions consideration. Students may choose to submit scores, and, if submitted, we will consider them in the context of the overall application."

For even more information on this school, turn to page 451 of the "Stats" section.

BARNARD COLLEGE

3009 BROADWAY, NEW YORK, NY 10027 • ADMISSIONS: 212-854-2014 • FAX: 212-854-6220
FINANCIAL AID: 212-854-2154 • E-MAIL: ADMISSIONS@BARNARD.EDU • WEBSITE: WWW.BARNARD.EDU

RATINGS

Quality of Life: 98   Academic: 93   Admissions: 97   Financial Aid: 94

STUDENTS SAY ". . ."

Academics

Life is lived in the fast lane at Barnard, an all-women's liberal arts college affiliated with Columbia University that
incorporates "a small school feel with big school resources
and incorporates both campus and city life." Nestled in the
Morningside Heights neighborhood of Manhattan on a
gated (main) campus, the school maintains an "independent spirit" while providing a "nurturing environment,"
and its partnership with a larger research university gives it

> **SURVEY SAYS . . .**
> *No one cheats*
> *Great library*
> *Career services are great*
> *Students love New York, NY*
> *Great off-campus food*
> *Campus feels safe*

the "best of both worlds" and affords its students the opportunities, course options, and resources that many
colleges don't have.

The academic experience at Barnard is simply "wonderful," according to the students. Teachers here are
"experts in their field" and "value their positions as both teachers and mentors," to the point where "they make
you want to stay on Barnard's campus for class and not take classes at Columbia." "I've never been in an environment where there is such a reciprocal relationship between students wanting to learn and be challenged and
professors wanting to teach and help," says a junior. Though underclassmen typically aren't able to get into as
many of the small classes (the process of which "is a nightmare"), one student claims that "some of the best
classes I've had have been in large lecture halls." The administration gets thumbs up (nearly) across the board
for their accessibility and compassion for students; says one, "Every time there is an issue on campus that students care about or an event that has happened, we get e-mails and town-hall meetings devoted to discussing
the issues." Deans are always available to students wanting to meet, and the alumni network and career serv-
ices are singled out for their efficacy. "Barnard is New York—busy, exciting, full of opportunity, and impersonal," says one student symbolically.

Life

Not much goes on around campus, to the chagrin of a few, but as one freshman puts it, "Why stay on campus
when you're in New York?" Students take good advantage of the resources available to them in New York City,
from Broadway shows and Central Park to museums and restaurants; "the possibilities are endless," and "make
it impossible to stick to a budget." People go out a fair amount, either to campus parties at Columbia or the local
bar scene (if they have a fake ID, which many do), and "dancing is huge." Theater and a capella are also very
big here, and many students are involved with clubs and organizations at Columbia, sometimes even dominating them. There are some complaints that facilities and dorms are "crumbling," but the new student activities building (called the Nexus) should help alleviate building woes when it's completed in August of 2009.
According to one junior, "Life at Barnard is probably 60–75% academic, and around 25–40% free."

Student Body

Even though it's all women here, Barnard is "the anti-women's college," as "very, very few students are here
for the single-sex education"—they're here for the academics and New York. There's a definite liberal slant on
campus, and these "usually politically savvy," "very cultured," "energetic and motivated" girls are "ambitious
and opinionated" and have career goals and leadership at the top of their agenda. "Barnard students are not
lazy" and have no problems booking their days full of study and activities; most here learn to "fit into the mad
rush" very quickly and take advantage of their four short years. Although quite a few students are from the tristate area and the majority are white, "there is still a sense of diversity" thanks to a variety of different backgrounds, both cultural and geographical; there's also a "tiny gay community" that is easily accepted.

THE PRINCETON REVIEW SAYS

Admissions

Very important factors considered include: Application essay, academic GPA, recommendation(s), rigor of secondary school record, character/personal qualities, extracurricular activities. *Important factors considered include:* Class rank, standardized test scores, talent/ability, volunteer work. *Other factors considered include:* Alumni/ae relation, first generation, geographical residence, interview, level of applicant's interest, racial/ethnic status, work experience. SAT and SAT Subject Tests or ACT required; ACT with Writing component required. High school diploma or equivalent is not required. *Academic units recommended:* 4 English, 3 mathematics, 3 science, (2 science labs), 3 foreign language.

Financial Aid

Students should submit: FAFSA, institution's own financial aid form, CSS/Financial Aid PROFILE, state aid form, noncustodial PROFILE, business/farm supplement, federal income tax returns. Regular filing deadline is 2/1. The Princeton Review suggests that all financial aid forms be submitted as soon as possible after January 1. *Need-based scholarships/grants offered:* Federal Pell, SEOG, state scholarships/grants, private scholarships, the school's own gift aid. *Loan aid offered:* FFEL Subsidized Stafford, FFEL Unsubsidized Stafford, FFEL PLUS, Federal Perkins, state loans, college/university loans from institutional funds. Applicants will be notified of awards on or about 3/31. Federal Work-Study Program available. Institutional employment available. Off-campus job opportunities are excellent.

The Inside Word

As at many top colleges, early decision applications have increased at Barnard—although the admissions standards are virtually the same as for their regular admissions cycle. The college's Admissions Staff is open and accessible, which is not always the case at highly selective colleges with as long and impressive a tradition of excellence. The Admissions Committee's expectations are high, but their attitude reflects a true interest in who you are and what's on your mind. Students have a much better experience throughout the admissions process when treated with sincerity and respect—perhaps this is why Barnard continues to attract and enroll some of the best students in the country.

THE SCHOOL SAYS "..."

From The Admissions Office

"Barnard College is a small, distinguished liberal arts college for women that is affiliated with Columbia University and located in the heart of New York City. The college enrolls women from all over the United States, Puerto Rico, and the Caribbean. More than 30 countries, including France, England, Hong Kong, and Greece, are also represented in the student body. Students pursue their academic studies in over 40 majors and are able to cross register at Columbia University.

"Applicants for the Fall 2008 entering class must submit scores from the SAT Reasoning Test and two SAT Subject Tests of their choice, or the ACT with the Writing component."

For even more information on this school, turn to page 452 of the "Stats" section.

BATES COLLEGE

23 CAMPUS AVENUE, LEWISTON, ME 04240-9917 • ADMISSIONS: 207-786-6000 • FAX: 207-786-6025
FINANCIAL AID: 207-786-6096 • E-MAIL: ADMISSIONS@BATES.EDU • WEBSITE: WWW.BATES.EDU

RATINGS
Quality of Life: 86   Academic: 94   Admissions: 95   Financial Aid: 92

STUDENTS SAY ". . ."

Academics

"You will not find it hard to gain access to resources" at Bates College, a small school in Maine that "tries to be unique in the homogeneous world of New England's small liberal arts colleges by weaving together academics with real world experience." First-year seminars, mandatory senior theses, service-learning, and a range of interdisciplinary majors are part of the academic experience. About two-thirds of the students here study abroad at some point before graduation.

> **SURVEY SAYS . . .**
> Small classes
> Great library
> Students are friendly
> Frats and sororities are unpopular
> or nonexistent
> Lots of beer drinking

"Research and internship opportunities" are absurdly abundant. A fairly unusual 4-4-1 calendar includes two traditional semesters and an "incredible" five-week spring term that provides really cool opportunities. Examples include studying marine biology on the Maine coast, Shakespearean drama in England, or economics in China and Taiwan. The "brilliant, accessible, and friendly" faculty does "whatever it takes to actually teach you the material instead of just lecturing and leaving." "The professors at Bates are here because they are passionate about their field and want to be teaching," explains a politics major. "I have never met so many professors who are willing to dedicate endless time outside of class to their students," gushes a psychology major. Course selection can be sparse but the "regularly available" administration is "responsive to student concerns" as well.

Life

"The library is the place to be during the week because everyone is there." The academic workload is reportedly substantial but "it is entirely manageable and does not restrict you from participating in athletics, clubs, or just having some down time." Parties are common on the weekends and students "stand mashed up against everyone else in the keg line." There's a great college radio station—91.5 on your FM dial—and many students get involved. "Bates also has a lot of traditions that students get excited about." In the winter during Puddle Jump, just for instance, Batesies who feel especially courageous can take the plunge into the frigid water of Lake Andrews. Otherwise, "dances, comedians, and trivia challenges are shockingly well attended because there's not a whole lot else to do." The biggest social complaint here centers on the surrounding area. It's the kind of place where "you wouldn't want to be walking alone at three in the morning." Also, relations between Batesies and local residents are reportedly strained. "The interaction between the town and college is relatively minimal," relates a junior. When students feel they just have to get away, they can "hit up the nearby ski slopes." The great outdoors is another option. Bates rents "tents, sleeping bags, kayaks, climbing gear, stoves, vans—really anything you want for outdoor fun." Also, Boston and some smaller cities such as Freeport and Portland are easily accessible.

Student Body

Students tell us that "Bates needs to improve its ethnic diversity." Most of the students here are white. "Your typical Batesie owns at least two flannel shirts" and "likes to have fun on the weekends." There are "a lot of jocks" and some "take the sports teams here way too seriously." Students here call themselves "down to earth" yet "intellectually driven." They enjoy "participating in academics, sports, and clubs." They "love the outdoors." However, this campus is "eclectic" and "Bates students are by no means monolithic in character." "We have everyone from the prep-school spoiled brat to the hippie environmentalist, from people with all different gender and sexual preferences and orientations to the former or current goth," observes a junior. "There are dorks and brains and goof-offs and class clowns." There are "plenty of kids who apparently haven't found the dorm showers," too. "There are few, if any, cliques on campus." "Crossing boundaries" is quite common. "There are different groups but none of them are exclusive in any way." "Even those who do not fit into any specific social group are widely accepted" (with the possible exception of the people who "plain suck").

THE PRINCETON REVIEW SAYS

Admissions

Very important factors considered include: Class rank, application essay, academic GPA, recommendation(s), rigor of secondary school record, character/personal qualities, extracurricular activities, interview, level of applicant's interest, talent/ability. *Other factors considered include:* Standardized test scores, alumni/ae relation, first generation, geographical residence, racial/ethnic status, state residency, volunteer work, work experience. TOEFL required of all international applicants. High school diploma is required and GED is not accepted. *Academic units required:* 4 English, 3 mathematics, 3 science, (2 science labs), 2 foreign language, 3 social studies. *Academic units recommended:* 4 English, 4 mathematics, 4 science, (3 science labs), 4 foreign language, 4 social studies.

Financial Aid

Students should submit: FAFSA, CSS/Financial Aid PROFILE, noncustodial PROFILE, business/farm supplement. Regular filing deadline is 2/1. The Princeton Review suggests that all financial aid forms be submitted as soon as possible after January 1. *Need-based scholarships/grants offered:* Federal Pell, SEOG, state scholarships/grants, private scholarships, the school's own gift aid. *Loan aid offered:* FFEL Subsidized Stafford, FFEL Unsubsidized Stafford, FFEL PLUS, Federal Perkins, state loans Applicants will be notified of awards on or about 4/1. Federal Work-Study Program available. Institutional employment available. Off-campus job opportunities are good.

The Inside Word

While holding its applicants to lofty standards, Bates strives to adopt a personal approach to the admissions process. Officers favor qualitative information and focus more on academic rigor, essays, and recommendations than GPA and test scores. They seek students who look for challenges and take advantage of opportunities in the classroom and beyond. Interviews are strongly encouraged—candidates who opt out may place themselves at a disadvantage.

THE SCHOOL SAYS "..."

From The Admissions Office

"Bates College is widely recognized as one of the finest liberal arts colleges in the nation. The curriculum and faculty challenge students to develop the essential skills of critical assessment, analysis, expression, aesthetic sensibility, and independent thought. Founded by abolitionists in 1855, Bates graduates have always included men and women from diverse ethnic and religious backgrounds. Bates highly values its study abroad programs, unique calendar (4-4-1), and the many opportunities available for one-on-one collaboration with faculty through seminars, research, service-learning, and the capstone experience of senior thesis.

"Co-curricular life at Bates is rich; most students participate in club or varsity sports; many participate in performing arts; and almost all students participate in one of more than 100 student-run clubs and organizations. More than two-thirds of alumni enroll in graduate study within 10 years.

"The Bates College Admissions Staff reads applications very carefully; the high school record and the quality of writing are of particular importance. Applicants are strongly encouraged to have a personal interview, either on campus or with an alumni representative. Students who choose not to interview may place themselves at a disadvantage in the selection process. Bates offers tours, interviews and information sessions throughout the summer and fall. Drop-ins are welcome for tours and information sessions. Please call ahead to schedule an interview.

"At Bates, the submission of standardized testing (the SAT, SAT Subject Tests, and the ACT) is not required for admission. After two decades of optional testing, our research shows no differences in academic performance and graduation rates between submitters and nonsubmitters."

For even more information on this school, turn to page 452 of the "Stats" section.

BENNINGTON COLLEGE

OFFICE OF ADMISSIONS AND FINANCIAL AID, BENNINGTON, VT 05201 • ADMISSIONS: 800-833-6845
FAX: 802-440-4320 • FINANCIAL AID: 802-440-4325 • E-MAIL: ADMISSIONS@BENNINGTON.EDU • WEBSITE: WWW.BENNINGTON.EDU

RATINGS

Quality of Life: 78   Academic: 95   Admissions: 88   Financial Aid: 73

STUDENTS SAY ". . ."

Academics

"I chose Bennington because it was everything high school wasn't," one undergrad writes, neatly summing up what makes this small school with a no distribution-requirements curriculum so appealing to many. Bennington students don't declare majors; rather, they formulate an interdisciplinary academic plan in consultation with faculty advisors. The system makes Bennington a great place "for motivated self-starters who may not know exactly what they want from school but who will thrive if they have control of their education." Prospective students should be forewarned that "it is truly up to the student to decide whether they wish to make their education demanding. Although no one will be allowed to slip by through our plan process, motivation is a must to be extremely

> **SURVEY SAYS . . .**
> Class discussions encouraged
> Small classes
> No one cheats
> Students aren't religious
> Dorms are like palaces
> Campus feels safe
> Intercollegiate sports are unpopular
> or nonexistent
> Frats and sororities are unpopular
> or nonexistent
> Theater is popular

successful." Bennington is strongest in the arts; students love their work in writing, visual arts, and theater. In these and all disciplines, professors "are all active participants in their fields, so literature classes are taught by writers, painting classes by painters, dancing classes by dancers, and so on. This ensures that all faculty members are knowledgeable and have personal experiences that are of use to students. As an added bonus, it is not infrequent that a professor will ask for the help of students in big, exciting projects." Bennington is a small school, and that naturally creates some limitations. Several students in our survey wished for an Art History Department, for example.

Life

Undergraduates at Bennington "work really, really hard and play with the same intensity. In fact, if you were going to describe Bennington in one word, you would call it 'intense.'" Daily life consists of "a mix of independent work and cooperative work. Everyone is working on a project that they are excited about, stressed out about, etc." As one student explains, "A Bennington student reflects the passion that burns in their interests, and the way that they express these interests is by not creating boundaries between work and play. Our lives are our passions. You will be living, working, and playing with dedicated students, supportive and motivated faculty, and a diverse curriculum." When they take a work break, "People here like to hang out a lot, watch movies or just chill and talk, or attend on-campus activities, bands, sponsored parties, theater events, and art openings." The school organizes a lot of "extracurricular opportunities. The campus activities board tries really hard to have things going on all the time for students, and if there isn't something to your liking it isn't very hard to get away to New York or Boston for the weekend." The ease of visiting these cities is a good thing, because there's not much happening immediately off campus; Bennington "is so secluded" that "it's possible to be completely cut off from the world outside if you don't make an attempt to watch/read the news. The closest big city is Albany (a 40- to 50-minute drive), and that's not saying much."

Student Body

"Most of the students enjoy going against the grain" at Bennington. These "really interesting, crazy, creative, brilliant people . . . try to 'out-different' each other: Who can be the most eccentric? Everyone, no matter how nerdy, will not only be super cool here, but have a group of friends just like them." Although they insist that "there is no typical Bennington student," most students would concede that their peers "are usually creative, self-motivated, smart, and hilarious. The only students who don't feel like they fit in are those unwilling to work or take charge of their own college experience." Bennington "is racially very homogenous," but, one student says, "Racial diversity doesn't guarantee diversity of experience or ideals, anyway. Among students here, there is a wide variety of social backgrounds, religious upbringings, intended academic concentrations, and motivations. Politically, though, we are quite limited—the vast majority of students are very liberal."

THE PRINCETON REVIEW SAYS

Admissions

Very important factors considered include: Class rank, application essay, academic GPA, recommendation(s), rigor of secondary school record, character/personal qualities, extracurricular activities, interview, talent/ability. *Other factors considered include:* Standardized test scores, alumni/ae relation, first generation, geographical residence, level of applicant's interest, racial/ethnic status, volunteer work, work experience. TOEFL required of all international applicants. High school diploma is required and GED is accepted. *Academic units recommended:* 4 English, 4 mathematics, 3 science, 2 foreign language, 4 social studies, 4 history.

Financial Aid

Students should submit: FAFSA, institution's own financial aid form, CSS/Financial Aid PROFILE, noncustodial PROFILE, Student and Parent Federal Tax Returns and W-2s. The Princeton Review suggests that all financial aid forms be submitted as soon as possible after January 1. *Need-based scholarships/grants offered:* Federal Pell, SEOG, state scholarships/grants, private scholarships, the school's own gift aid. *Loan aid offered:* FFEL Subsidized Stafford, FFEL Unsubsidized Stafford, FFEL PLUS, college/university loans from institutional funds. NOTE: College/university loans from institutional funds for International students only. Applicants will be notified of awards on or about 4/1. Federal Work-Study Program available. Institutional employment available. Off-campus job opportunities are good.

The Inside Word

Given the freedom and flexibility inherent in a Bennington education, ideal prospective applicants tend to be motivated and independent students. The college hopes to learn as much about each applicant as possible in the admissions process and tries to have a conversation with each applicant in person or via telephone or email. Applicants may (and should!) use their personal statements and interviews to distinguish themselves.

THE SCHOOL SAYS ". . ."

From The Admissions Office

"The educational philosophy of Bennington is rooted in an abiding faith in the talent, imagination, and responsibility of the individual; thus, the principle of learning by practice underlies every major feature of a Bennington education. We believe that a college education should not merely provide preparation for graduate school or a career, but should be an experience valuable in itself and the model for lifelong learning. Faculty, staff, and students at Bennington work together in a collaborative environment based upon respect for each other and the power of ideas to make a difference in the world. We are looking for intellectually curious students who have a passion for learning, are willing to take risks, and are open to making connections.

"Submission of standardized test scores (the SAT, SAT Subject Tests, or the ACT) is recommended, but not required."

For even more information on this school, turn to page 453 of the "Stats" section.

BENTLEY COLLEGE

175 FOREST STREET, WALTHAM, MA 02452-4705 • ADMISSIONS: 781-891-2244 • FAX: 781-891-3414
FINANCIAL AID: 781-891-3441 • E-MAIL: UGADMISSION@BENTLEY.EDU • WEBSITE: WWW.BENTLEY.EDU

RATINGS
Quality of Life: 88   Academic: 82   Admissions: 91   Financial Aid: 80

STUDENTS SAY "..."

Academics

Bentley College, an institution dedicated to creating "business and business-technical leaders," combines a winning location with an intense focus on technology to produce "the business moguls of tomorrow." Students say that the "Resources here are second to none, if you need help scheduling classes, choosing a major, creating a resume . . . anything at all, then there is an entire office of people ready and willing to help you in any way possible." Some of Bentley's perks include "a state-of-the-art trading room that would be

> **SURVEY SAYS . . .**
> *Lab facilities are great*
> *Great computer facilities*
> *Great library*
> *Career services are great*
> *Campus feels safe*
> *Lots of beer drinking*
> *Hard liquor is popular*

used in the case of an emergency on Wall Street," a "superbly wired campus," and a brand-new library that "has all the resources a student could need, with quite a few significant, (not so necessary) extras" (such as a "large flat-panel TV monitors in each of its 20-some odd study rooms"). Bentley doesn't just flash the hardware, though; it also teaches students how to "integrate the newest technological resources into the business environment" by "embedding them into [your] courses. This is important, because technology "is key to success in the business world, whatever profession you are interested in." Bentley's proximity to Boston "makes this a very special place," helping students find meaningful internships and, after graduation, meaningful jobs. Academics here "are challenging but not overwhelming," and most of the classes "weigh class participation in the overall grade, which motivates [you] to complete the readings and assignments in a timely manner." Professors typically have "previous real-life experience in the business world. They like to incorporate that in the classroom."

Life

Life is "very hectic" at Bentley, where "Students tend to crack down during the weekdays and really get their work done. By Thursday [we're] ready for the weekend to start." Bentley's "beautiful campus" has "tons to offer" when it comes to finding activities outside of class, including "Greek life, sports organizations" and "tons of bars, restaurants, sports events, and concerts" so that "it's hard to be bored." Intramural sports "are also very popular, as is exercising in general. Being fit and working out are definitely the 'in' things to do." There are also plenty of parties; "Registered parties are allowed (with regulations) where of-age students can have keg parties in their room," but "There is also substance-free housing available if that's not your fancy." Students across the board agree that "Boston is Bentley's main attraction." Fortunately the city "is easily accessible via the school's shuttle service." Students love to head for Cambridge, the North End, Quincy Market, and other city destinations on the weekend "just to see a show, eat at a restaurant, shop, or just walk around," although some prefer to hang out on campus because the city can be "pretty expensive."

Students

The typical Bentley undergrad is "rich, foreign, and smart." Check that, they're "usually two out of the three: rich and foreign, rich and smart, or smart and foreign." Internationals make up a conspicuous subpopulation, "which is interesting" because you get to "learn from other cultures." One student writes, "Venture through any apartment complex to be greeted to the smells of Indian, Creole, Chinese, South American, and European foods. Diversity is greatly appreciated, as is evidenced by the fact that one of the events with the largest attendance each year is the Festival of Colors, an international extravaganza." The exception to the rule, we're told, is that students from Europe "hail from very big money" and "very rarely interact with domestic students." Most here, unsurprisingly, "are typical business students, usually quite driven and business oriented. They are fairly fun loving as well," the sort who are "studious during the week, rowdy on weekends." Overall, students tend to be "preppy collar-poppin' kids" who can "talk the talk" and "take pride [in] attending Bentley."

THE PRINCETON REVIEW SAYS

Admissions

Very important factors considered include: Academic GPA, rigor of secondary school record, standardized test scores. *Important factors considered include:* Class rank, application essay, recommendation(s), character/personal qualities, extracurricular activities, volunteer work, work experience. *Other factors considered include:* Alumni/ae relation, first generation, geographical residence, interview, level of applicant's interest, racial/ethnic status, state residency, talent/ability, SAT or ACT required; ACT with Writing component required. TOEFL required of all international applicants. High school diploma is required and GED is accepted. *Academic units recommended:* 4 English, 4 mathematics, 3 science, (3 science labs), 3 foreign language, 3 history, 2 additional English, mathematics, social or lab science, foreign language, speech.

Financial Aid

Students should submit: FAFSA, CSS/Financial Aid PROFILE, noncustodial PROFILE, business/farm supplement. Federal Tax Returns, including all schedules for parents and student. Regular filing deadline is 2/1. The Princeton Review suggests that all financial aid forms be submitted as soon as possible after January 1. *Need-based scholarships/grants offered:* Federal Pell, SEOG, state scholarships/grants, private scholarships, the school's own gift aid. *Loan aid offered:* FFEL Subsidized Stafford, FFEL Unsubsidized Stafford, FFEL PLUS, Federal Perkins, state loans Applicants will be notified of awards on a rolling basis beginning 3/25. Federal Work-Study Program available. Institutional employment available. Off-campus job opportunities are good.

The Inside Word

If you've got a bunch of electives available to you senior year, you may think that choosing business classes is the best way to impress the Bentley Admissions Office. Not so; the school would prefer you take a broad range of challenging classes—preferably at the AP level—in English, history/social sciences, math, lab sciences, and foreign language. The school enjoys a sizable applicant pool, so you'll need solid grades and test scores to gain admission.

THE SCHOOL SAYS ". . ."

From The Admissions Office

"Bentley is a national leader in business education. Centered on education and research in business and related professions, Bentley blends the breadth and technological strength of a university with the values and student focus of a small college. A Bentley education combines an unparalleled array of business courses with hands-on technology experience, and a strong foundation in liberal arts. Half of all required courses are in the arts and sciences. In addition, students have the opportunity to pursue a double major in business and liberal studies. The result is that students gain expertise for a competitive edge in today's economy and broad-based skills essential for success in all areas of life. An average class size of 25 students and a student/faculty ratio of 12:1 allow for personal attention and meaningful class discussion. Concepts and theories that students learn in the classroom come alive in several hands-on, high-tech learning laboratories like the Financial Trading Room, Center for Marketing Technology, and Media and Culture Labs and Studio. Outside the classroom, students choose from a number of athletic, social, and cultural opportunities." Ethics and social responsibility are woven throughout the school's curriculum; the Bentley Service-Learning Program is ranked among the top in the United States. Students also choose from 27 countries to study abroad. Students develop skills and build their resume thanks to internships with leading companies." State-of-the-art athletic and recreation facilities complement the 23 varsity teams in Division I and II, and the extensive intramural and recreational sports programs. Boston and Cambridge, just minutes from campus, are accessible via the school's free shuttle. Both cities are great resources for internships, job opportunities, cultural events, and social life. Students applying for freshman admission are required to take the SAT or the ACT with the Writing section. SAT Subject Tests are not required."

For even more information on this school, turn to page 453 of the "Stats" section.

BOSTON COLLEGE

140 Commonwealth Avenue, Devlin Hall 208, Chestnut Hill, MA 02467-3809 • Admissions: 617-552-3100
Fax: 617-552-0798 • Financial Aid: 800-294-0294 • E-mail: ugadmis@bc.edu • Website: www.bc.edu

RATINGS
Quality of Life: 93   Academic: 88   Admissions: 97   Financial Aid: 93

STUDENTS SAY "..."

SURVEY SAYS . . .
Great library
Students love Chestnut Hill, MA
Campus feels safe
Everyone loves the Eagles
Frats and sororities are unpopular
or nonexistent
Lots of beer drinking

Academics
Students praise the strong academics, the competitive athletic teams, the lively social scene, and the premium location that all combine to create a remarkable all-around college experience at Boston College. For many, though, BC's greatest asset is the "strong spiritual presence [that] shows how positive an influence religion can have on one's life." Don't worry; "They don't try to make anybody be Catholic" here. Rather, the school "simply reflects the Jesuit ideals of community, spirituality, and social justice," and these ideals pervade both the curriculum and the academic community. True to the Jesuit ideal of "educating the entire person," BC requires a thorough core curriculum "including philosophy, theology, and language requirements," rounded out by "strong [but optional] programs, such as internships and studying abroad." Beyond the core curriculum, "BC offers something for everyone. If you go here, you are with business students, nursing students, education majors, and arts and science majors." Even though this is a fairly large school, students insist that "you never feel like a number here. Yes, you have to be independent and seek out your professors. But when you do seek them out, you get incredible individualized attention." One undergrad sums it up like this: "BC's strength is a mix of everything. It may not be an Ivy League school in academics or win national championships everywhere in NCAA athletics, but it is a 'jack of all trades' when it comes to academics, athletics, art, and social activity."

Life
There is a "real spirit of volunteerism and giving back to the community [that] is one of BC's greatest strengths," many students here tell us, reporting that "there are about a million volunteer groups on campus, as well as a bunch of immersion trips to different places, the most renowned of which is the Appalachia group trip." Students here "really care about the world outside of Chestnut Hill. In a way, even the notion of studying abroad has turned into a question of 'How can I help people while there?' BC's Jesuit mission is contagious." Not all extracurricular life at BC is so altruistic, however; students here love to have fun in "the greatest location of any college ever! We are on the T [train], so we can get into the city of Boston whenever we like, but we are in suburbia so we can relax without all of the gimmicks of city life." Undergrads love to explore Boston, a city with "tons of great museums, historical sights, restaurants, and a lot of great concerts," that also happens to be "such a big college town. It's easy to meet kids that go to BU, Harvard, Emerson, Northeastern, or any of the other universities in the area." Closer to campus, BC has "great sports. Our football team has won six bowl games in a row and basketball is, at this writing, playing Georgetown in the men's NCAA Tournament. The ice hockey team is consistently ranked high nationally," and students turn out to support their Eagles in both men's and women's athletics.

Student Body
Boston magazine once described the BC student body as "a J. Crew catalogue with a slight hangover," and while students protest that "there are a number of students who do not conform to such a vision of the student body," they also admit that "there are a lot of preppy people at our school. Girls usually wear skirts and Uggs (unless it's freezing out, but it has to be very, very cold), and boys usually wear jeans and t-shirts or collared cotton shirts." And yes, "the typical BC student is White, Catholic, usually from the Northeast, who probably had family who went to BC," but with 9,000 undergrads, "We have students from all sorts of backgrounds, religions, sexual orientations." BC students tend to be extremely ambitious; they are "those super-involved people in high school who were three-season team captains, class president, and straight-A students. [They] have carried over that focus and determination into college."

THE PRINCETON REVIEW SAYS

Admissions

Very important factors considered include: Academic GPA, rigor of secondary school record, standardized test scores. *Important factors considered include:* Class rank, application essay, recommendation(s), alumni/ae relation, character/personal qualities, religious affiliation/commitment, talent/ability, volunteer work. *Other factors considered include:* Extracurricular activities, first generation, racial/ethnic status, work experience. SAT and SAT Subject Tests or ACT required; ACT with Writing component required. TOEFL required of all international applicants. High school diploma is required and GED is accepted. *Academic units recommended:* 4 English, 4 mathematics, 4 science, (4 science labs), 4 foreign language, 4 social studies.

Financial Aid

The Princeton Review suggests that all financial aid forms be submitted as soon as possible after January 1. Federal Work-Study Program available. Institutional employment available. Off-campus job opportunities are excellent.

The Inside Word

BC is one of many selective schools that eschew set admissions formulae. While a challenging high school curriculum and strong test scores are essential for any serious candidate, the college seeks students who are passionate and make connections between academic pursuits and extracurricular activities. The application process should reveal a distinct, mature voice and a student whose interest in education goes beyond the simple desire to earn an A.

THE SCHOOL SAYS ". . ."

From The Admissions Office

"Boston College students achieve at the highest levels with honors including two Rhodes scholarship winners, nine Fulbrights, and one each for Marshall, Goldwater, Madison, and Truman Postgraduate Fellowship Programs. Junior Year Abroad and Scholar of the College Program offer students flexibility within the curriculum. Facilities opened in the past 10 years include: the Merkert Chemistry Center, Higgins Hall (housing the Biology and Physics departments), three new residence halls, the Yawkey Athletics Center, the Vanderslice Commons Dining Hall, the Hillside Cafe, and a state-of-the-art library. Students enjoy the vibrant location in Chestnut Hill with easy access to the cultural and historical richness of Boston.

"Boston College requires freshman applicants to take the SAT with writing (or the ACT with the writing exam required). Two SAT Subject Tests are required; students are encouraged to take Subject Tests in fields in which they excel."

For even more information on this school, turn to page 454 of the "Stats" section.

BOSTON UNIVERSITY

121 BAY STATE ROAD, BOSTON, MA 02215 • ADMISSIONS: 617-353-2300 • FAX: 617-353-9695
FINANCIAL AID: 617-353-2965 • E-MAIL: ADMISSIONS@BU.EDU • WEBSITE: WWW.BU.EDU

RATINGS
Quality of Life: 82   **Academic:** 84   **Admissions:** 94   **Financial Aid:** 82

STUDENTS SAY ". . ."

Academics

Boston University's greatest strengths, students tell us, lie in "the choices students are granted. Do you want to be an alterna-teen or a jock? Do you want to drink or go to shows? Do you want to study ballet, bio, or film? Do you want a scenic riverside location or an energetic urban one? You can have all of the above at BU, which is both over-whelming and exciting." A "top-notch educational institu-

> SURVEY SAYS . . .
> *Athletic facilities are great*
> *Students love Boston, MA*
> *Great off-campus food*
> *Campus feels safe*
> *Student publications are popular*

tion in the middle of one of the best college cities in the world," BU is the perfect place for independent students anxious to explore all options. As one student puts it, "BU not only allowed me access to over 65 majors in my school, the College of Arts and Sciences (I tried out astronomy, international relations, psychology, and anthro-pology before deciding on anthro/religion and French), but also majors in other schools (I took two drama classes in the College of Fine Arts)." Many are drawn here by the "top-notch pre-professional programs" that include "an excellent communications program," a "great management program," and "a great biology pro-gram." Students note that "BU fosters independence: Students can do whatever they want; they just have to have the motivation." Academics "are very, very rigorous," with more than a few students hypothesizing the existence of an unwritten "grade deflation" policy, which, understandably, they regard as unfair.

Life

BU "doesn't have a campus in a traditional sense, and that takes some getting used to. It also means that most of your social life isn't centered on the university," but more on the city itself. To many here, "Boston is the per-fect city. Easy to walk around; not as big and crazy as NYC; and plenty to do on the weekends besides party," such as "walking all the way downtown, passing through all the big entertainment areas, or walking over to Cambridge and Central Square or down the river and over the footbridge to Harvard Square . . . A short T-ride puts you in the North End with its Italian food heaven. If you can't find what you're looking for within 20 min-utes of campus, you just haven't looked hard enough." Parties typically occur off campus "since the university has a fairly strict alcohol and drug policy which RAs monitor closely. The off-campus parties are typically big (100-plus) and, of course, have beer and cheap liquor more than accessible. The bar and club scene is also big, with Lansdowne Street only a few blocks away, so going out to drink and dance on the weekends is also pret-ty common. . . . Because cabs are everywhere, getting around the city, even when [you are] drunk and [it is] late at night, is pretty simple." For those who prefer to stick with school activities, "The school makes a real effort to get students involved and to provide activities for us, albeit through our yearly undergraduate student fee. They have comedy clubs, student concerts, several interesting lectures for every interest imaginable, etc."

Student Body

The undergraduate student body at BU is 16,000 strong, so "there is no 'typical' BU student." Students here "tend to be liberal and politically aware, but other than that, one of the most desirable aspects of BU is that there are no 'types.' Because BU has strong athletics, as well as strong programs in the arts, there is a nice mix . . . and everyone seems to get along well enough. This diversity . . . adds an amazing dynamic to class discussions. This is one of the most valuable aspects of a BU education." That said, many here tell us that "a solid majority of peo-ple are very rich, well dressed, and reasonably snobby." New England prep-school grads are well represented, but so, too, are a broad array of states and nations.

Admissions

Very important factors considered include: Rigor of secondary school record. *Important factors considered include:* Class rank, application essay, academic GPA, recommendation(s), standardized test scores. *Other factors considered include:* Alumni/ae relation, character/personal qualities, extracurricular activities, first generation, geographical residence, level of applicant's interest, racial/ethnic status, state residency, volunteer work, work experience. SAT and SAT Subject Tests or ACT required; ACT with Writing component required. TOEFL required of all international applicants. High school diploma is required and GED is accepted. *Academic units required:* 4 English, 3 mathematics, 3 science, (3 science labs), 2 foreign language, 3 social studies. *Academic units recommended:* 4 English, 4 mathematics, 4 science, (4 science labs), 4 foreign language, 4 social studies.

Financial Aid

Students should submit: FAFSA, CSS/Financial Aid PROFILE, state aid form, noncustodial PROFILE, business/farm supplement. Regular filing deadline is 2/15. The Princeton Review suggests that all financial aid forms be submitted as soon as possible after January 1. *Need-based scholarships/grants offered:* Federal Pell, SEOG, state scholarships/grants, private scholarships, the school's own gift aid. *Loan aid offered:* Direct Subsidized Stafford, Direct Unsubsidized Stafford, Direct PLUS, Federal Perkins, state loans Applicants will be notified of awards on a rolling basis beginning in early April.

The Inside Word

BU has grown more selective over the years; the school added SAT subject exams to its admissions requirements in 2005, a solid indicator that the school is now looking for more ways to eliminate applicants from its pool. Requirements and admissions standards are somewhat more lenient for the College of General Studies, a 2-year program that takes students right up to the point at which they declare a major and enter one of the university's 8 other undergraduate schools. Students in the College of General Studies are admitted as four-year degree candidates and continue as juniors in one of the other schools or colleges, with no new application required.

THE SCHOOL SAYS "..."

From The Admissions Office

"Boston University (BU) is a private teaching and research institution with a strong emphasis on undergraduate education. We are committed to providing the highest level of teaching excellence, and fulfillment of this pledge is our highest priority. Boston University has 10 undergraduate schools and colleges offering more than 250 major and minor areas of concentration. Students may choose from programs of study in areas as diverse as biochemistry, theater, physical therapy, elementary education, broadcast journalism, international relations, business, and computer engineering. BU has an international student body, with students from every state and more than 100 countries. In addition, opportunities to study abroad exist through over 70 semester-long programs, spanning 33 cities and 22 countries on six continents.

"BU requires freshman applicants for Fall 2008 to take the SAT, and two SAT Subject Tests. Students are encouraged to take subject tests in fields in which they excel. Students may submit the results of the ACT (with the Writing section) in lieu of the SAT and SAT Subject Tests."

For even more information on this school, turn to page 454 of the "Stats" section.

BOWDOIN COLLEGE

5000 COLLEGE STATION, BRUNSWICK, ME 04011-8441 • ADMISSIONS: 207-725-3100 • FAX: 207-725-3101
FINANCIAL AID: 207-725-3273 • E-MAIL: ADMISSIONS@BOWDOIN.EDU • WEBSITE: WWW.BOWDOIN.EDU

RATINGS
Quality of Life: 99   Academic: 97   Admissions: 99   Financial Aid: 98

STUDENTS SAY "..."

Academics

Highly selective Bowdoin College is all about providing an "excellent liberal arts education in a supportive, small community" in "a beautiful part of the country." Undergrads cite Bowdoin's "intelligent" and "diverse" student body, "absolutely top-notch" professors, and "challenging, fascinating

academic program that allows you to explore all your areas of interest" as particularly deserving of praise. Students here reap the benefits of "a close-knit community of learners, teachers, and leaders pursuing academics, athletics, music, art, clubs, and fun with relentless positive enthusiasm" in "a very nurturing and safe environment, [where] you can develop without worrying about stuff you don't need to worry about, such as money, food, housing, etc." Standout programs include environmental studies, neuroscience, foreign language, and the English and education departments which students describe as "excellent, bar none." The workload at Bowdoin "is just a few steps shy from unmanageable, which is good" because it forces you to "not only do your work," but "to do it carefully." Students also appreciate a faculty that is "truly interested in learning everyone's name," and "will stay hours after review sessions" until the students grasp the concepts. "They challenge you, and push you to go beyond just the books." Great facilities include the Career Planning Center, Writing Center, Baldwin Center for Academic Development, Counseling Center, and administrative offices. The cherry on the sundae? "Excellent alumni networking."

Life

Students love how Bowdoin "embraces the intellectual experience in a balanced, healthy way, so that its students are generally very happy. There is an awareness that in college, learning comes from everywhere, so there is a real effort by the Bowdoin administration as well as Bowdoin students to bring speakers, events, and entertainment to the campus so that students can learn in every way possible." Extracurriculars are part of the constant learning; students here "are always doing at least one if not 10 things at a time." Physical activity is part of the mix; many students participate in Outing Club events, hiking, whitewater kayaking, and rafting at nearby parks, and "It seems like almost everyone is on a sports team, so during the week most people find a release there." Students tell us that "on the weekends, there is a lot of partying (and with that comes a lot of alcohol)," but "It's not excessive." Plus, the "alcohol policies are also pretty sweet—as long as everyone can be responsible and things are not out of control, security does not want to get anyone in trouble," and "a safe ride system" provides free rides home to intoxicated students for free. Those who don't drink tell us "There is plenty of music at night" and "Brunswick is great for a concert, coffee shop, or bowling." Gourmands, take note: "Bowdoin food is the best!"

Student Body

While "a fair amount of preppy kids" congregate on Bowdoin's campus, "There are all types of people here, providing an interesting mix of personalities, backgrounds, and interactions." Personality types "range from typical straight-out-of-prep-school preppy individuals to crusty hippies to jocks to artsy kids." "Bowdoin students either wear Chacos or Polos with their collars popped. Some even alternate between these two personalities." They also tend to be "multifaceted and multilayered; they are great intellectuals, as well as athletes, political activists, dancers, and community leaders. No one here is involved in just academic activities." Students say everyone here is "down to earth and very passionate about something—the environment, politics, science, the welfare of goats in Chile, etc." Despite being "extremely intelligent" and "highly motivated," Bowdoin undergrads "are not fiercely competitive or grade-grubby," and "Everyone gets along well."

THE PRINCETON REVIEW SAYS

Admissions

Very important factors considered include: Class rank, application essay, academic GPA, recommendation(s), rigor of secondary school record, character/personal qualities, extracurricular activities, talent/ability. *Important factors considered include:* Standardized test scores, alumni/ae relation, first generation. *Other factors considered include:* Geographical residence, interview, racial/ethnic status, state residency, High school diploma is required and GED is not accepted. *Academic units recommended:* 4 English, 4 mathematics, 4 science, (3 science labs), 4 foreign language, 4 social studies.

Financial Aid

Students should submit: FAFSA, CSS/Financial Aid PROFILE, noncustodial PROFILE, business/farm supplement. Regular filing deadline is 2/15. The Princeton Review suggests that all financial aid forms be submitted as soon as possible after January 1. *Need-based scholarships/grants offered:* Federal Pell, SEOG, state scholarships/grants, private scholarships, the school's own gift aid. *Loan aid offered:* FFEL Subsidized Stafford, FFEL Unsubsidized Stafford, FFEL PLUS, Federal Perkins, state loans. Bowdoin will replace loans with grants for all students beginning in Fall 2008. Applicants will be notified of awards on or about 4/5. Federal Work-Study Program available. Institutional employment available. Off-campus job opportunities are good.

The Inside Word

Standardized test scores are optional at Bowdoin, but if you aced the SAT or ACT you should definitely report your scores. The school will almost certainly look at them; in the spring of 2006, the Dean of Admissions at Bowdoin said as much to The New York Times, explaining that he considers test scores helpful. He noted that high school transcripts are difficult to compare, especially in light of grade inflation at many schools, and that the provenance of student essays is often uncertain.

THE SCHOOL SAYS "..."

From The Admissions Office

"A liberal arts education at Bowdoin isn't about being small and safe—it's about having the support to take surprising risks. That means caring more about the questions than giving the right answers. Discovering you're good at something you didn't think was your strength. Making connections where none appears to exist. Bowdoin's curriculum offers a bold blueprint for liberal education designed to inspire students to become world citizens with acute sensitivity to the social and natural worlds. Its interdisciplinary focus encourages students to make connections among subjects, to discover disciplines that excite their imaginations, and to develop keen skills for addressing the challenges of a changing world.

"A Bowdoin education is best summed up by 'The Offer of The College':"

> To be at home in all lands and all ages;
> To count Nature a familiar acquaintance,
> And Art an intimate friend;
> To gain a standard for the appreciation of others' work
> And the criticism of your own;
> To carry the keys of the world's library in your pocket,
> And feel its resources behind you in whatever task you undertake;
> To make hosts of friends...
> Who are to be leaders in all walks of life;
> To lose yourself in generous enthusiasms
> And cooperate with others for common ends —
> This is the offer of the college for the best four years of your life."

Adapted from the original 'Offer of the College'

by William DeWitt Hyde

President of Bowdoin College 1885–1917"

For even more information on this school, turn to page 455 of the "Stats" section.

BRANDEIS UNIVERSITY

415 South Street, MS003, Waltham, MA 02454 • Admissions: 781-736-3500 • Fax: 781-736-3536
Financial Aid: 781-736-3700 • E-mail: sendinfo@brandeis.edu • Website: www.brandeis.edu

RATINGS
Quality of Life: 80   Academic: 88   Admissions: 97   Financial Aid: 81

STUDENTS SAY ". . ."
Academics
Home to "lots of 'pre-somethings' trying to figure out if that 'something' is right for them," Brandeis University is "a good jumping-off point for those looking to go into medicine or law." Boasting "a very good liberal arts education," Brandeis also provides plenty of alternatives to those who start down the "pre-something" path only to find that it's not for them. Even those who stay the course appreciate the "large variety of options"; as one student explains,

"Brandeis is very academically stimulating and has many interesting courses, professors who make themselves available outside of class, and teaching assistants who are very helpful." Aspiring doctors are drawn here by a "stellar" neuroscience department that gives undergraduates "the experience of graduate students as far as research is concerned," in addition to "a very high acceptance rate at medical schools." Other strong programs include psychology, music, economics, political science, and history. Students agree that most professors are "passionate about what they teach." Classes "are generally small, which puts pressure on you to come prepared," and there is "a fair amount of class discussion, which can be great or awful." Students are ready to be engaged in class, as they are typically "friendly and talkative. An intense philosophical discussion is more common at Brandeis than drunken boorishness."

Life
Brandeis boasts "plenty of performance-based clubs (theater, musical, improv comedy, sketch comedy, dance), community-service organizations, activist clubs, ethnic clubs, religious clubs, political clubs, independent sports clubs, and also clubs just for fun, like the hookah club. There are so many opportunities to be involved here," and students "take [their] extracurriculars just as seriously as [their] studies, and tend to excel in both." Students also love their access to Boston, noting that "a free shuttle runs us to and from the city Thursdays through Sundays, and the commuter rail stop on campus." The proximity of Boston helps offset the fact that "there is really nothing to do in Waltham. There is a movie theater, and some restaurants, and bars, but that is about it. Proximity to [Boston College] and Bentley is nice, however." Students say the social scene at Brandeis "is somewhat lacking. If you are looking for big sporting events with lots of spirit or parties with lots of people, you won't like Brandeis." Parties "don't ever fall into your lap at Brandeis; you have to look for them." For some, this is a plus; as one student writes, "I like the school because if you want a quiet Friday night with board games and old movies, it's very easy to do. People won't judge you or pressure you into drinking. But on Saturday when you're ready for some fun, you have to do a little digging."

Student Body
Brandeis has long been a popular destination for Jewish students. About 40 percent of the student population (undergrad and grad) is Jewish, and undergrads tell us that "there are a lot of orthodox Jews here, more than at your average college. Yet, there are also a lot of non-religious students, observant Muslims, and Christians. So the school just teaches us to recognize each others' religions," and "You never feel like your fellow students are judging you." A "nice-sized international community" also "helps diversify the school." Many here tend to be "pretty socially awkward, and kind of an overachiever, but generally well-intentioned and sweet." One student told us that students tend to be "quirky, prone to traditionally nerdy pursuits, and very friendly. At Brandeis, weird is normal." Everyone works hard here "because they want to do well," and students "spend most of their time studying."

THE PRINCETON REVIEW SAYS

Admissions

Very important factors considered include: Class rank, academic GPA, rigor of secondary school record, standardized test scores, character/personal qualities, level of applicant's interest. *Important factors considered include:* Application essay, recommendation(s), extracurricular activities, first generation, talent/ability, volunteer work, work experience. *Other factors considered include:* alumni/ae relation, geographical residence, interview, racial/ethnic status, SAT or ACT required; ACT with Writing component required. TOEFL required of all international applicants. High school diploma is required and GED is accepted. *Academic units recommended:* 4 English, 3 mathematics, 1 science, (1 science labs), 3 foreign language, 1 history, 4 academic electives.

Financial Aid

Students should submit: CSS/Financial Aid PROFILE, FAFSA, noncustodial PROFILE, business/farm supplement. The Princeton Review suggests that all financial aid forms be submitted as soon as possible after January 1. *Need-based scholarships/grants offered:* Federal Pell, SEOG, state scholarships/grants, private scholarships, the school's own gift aid. *Loan aid offered:* Direct Subsidized Stafford, Direct Unsubsidized Stafford, Direct PLUS, Federal Perkins, state loans, college/university loans from institutional funds. Federal Work-Study Program available. Off-campus job opportunities are fair.

The Inside Word

Brandeis requires one of two combinations of standardized test scores: the SAT or the ACT with Writing component. Most students choose the ACT with Writing option, but if you've already taken all your SATs and aced them, submit those scores instead. Brandeis is often looked at as a safety school for students applying to Ivies; as the Ivies now routinely reject many highly qualified applicants, admission to Brandeis is extremely competitive despite its safety school reputation.

THE SCHOOL SAYS ". . ."

From The Admissions Office

"Education at Brandeis is personal, combining the intimacy of a small liberal arts college and the intellectual power of a large research university. Classes are small and are taught by professors, 98 percent of whom hold the highest degree in their fields. They give students personal attention in state-of-the-art resources, giving them the tools to succeed in a variety of postgraduate endeavors.

"This vibrant, freethinking, intellectual university was founded in 1948. Brandeis University reflects the values of the first Jewish Supreme Court Justice Louis Brandeis, which are passion for learning, commitment to social justice, respect for creativity and diversity, and concern for the world.

"Brandeis has an ideal location on the commuter rail nine miles west of Boston; state-of-the-art sports facilities; and internships that complement interests in law, medicine, government, finance, business, and the arts. Brandeis offers generous university scholarships and need-based financial aid that can be renewed for 4 years.

"Brandeis requires that students send official scores for the new SAT or ACT with Writing in place of all SATs. Students for whom English is not their first language should take the TOEFL (Test of English as a Foreign Language)."

For even more information on this school, turn to page 455 of the "Stats" section.

BROWN UNIVERSITY

PO Box 1876, 45 Prospect Street, Providence, RI 02912 • Admissions: 401-863-2378 • Fax: 401-863-9300
Financial Aid: 401-863-2721 • E-mail: admission_undergraduate@brown.edu • Website: www.brown.edu

RATINGS
Quality of Life: 97   Academic: 91   Admissions: 99   Financial Aid: 95

STUDENTS SAY "..."

Academics

Known for its somewhat unconventional (but still highly-regarded) approaches to life and learning, Brown University remains the slightly odd man out of the Ivy League, and wouldn't have it any other way. The school's willingness to employ and support different, untested methods such as the shopping period, the first two weeks of the semester where anyone can drop into any class in order to "find out if it's something they're interested in enrolling in," or the Critical Review, a student publication that produces reviews of courses based on evaluations from students who have completed the course, is designed to treat students "like an adult" through "freedom and choice." This open-minded environment allows them "to practice passion without shame or fear of judgment," the hallmark of a Brown education. Even if a student does find themselves exploring the wrong off-the-beaten path, "there are multitudes of built-in support measures to help you succeed despite any odds." Even grades are a non-issue here, "except amongst paranoid premeds."

> **SURVEY SAYS . . .**
> *No one cheats*
> *Students are friendly*
> *Great off-campus food*
> *Students are happy*

Professors are mostly hit with a few misses, but there are "amazing professors in every department, and they're not hard to find," it's just "up to students to find the teaching styles that work for them." "Academics at Brown are what you make of them," and even though students are diligent in their academic pursuits and feel assured they're "getting a wonderful education with the professors," most agree that their education is "really more about the unique student body and learning through active participation in other activities." The administration gets cautiously decent reviews for their accessibility and general running of the school, but scolded for getting "distracted by the long term." The president, however, is absolutely loved by students for being "an incredible person with a great vision for the school."

Life

Thinking—yes, thinking—and discussing take up a great deal of time of time at Brown. "People think about life, politics, society at large, global affairs, the state of the economy, developing countries, animals, plants, rocket science, math, poker, each other, sex, sexuality, the human experience, gender studies, what to do with our lives, etc.," says a senior anthropology major. "Most people here don't go home that often," and like any school, "there are people who go out five nights a week and people who go out five nights a semester." "Alcohol and weed are pretty embedded in campus life," and most parties are dorm room events, even though partying "never gets in the way of academics or friendship. If you don't drink/smoke, that's totally cool." There's also plenty of cultural activities, such as indie bands, student performances, jazz, swing dancing, and speakers. Themed housing (Art House, Tech House, Interfaith House) and co-ops are also popular social mediators.

Student Body

It's a pretty unique crowd here, where "athletes, preps, nerds, and everyone in between come together" because they "love learning for the sake of learning, and love Brown equally as much." "The 'mainstream' is full of people who are atypical in sense of fashion, taste in music, and academic interests," says a junior. Unsurprisingly, everyone here's "very smart," as well as "very quirky and often funny," and "a great amount are brilliant and passionate about their interests"; "Most have interesting stories to tell." People here are "curious and open about many things," which is perhaps why sexual diversity is a "strong theme" among Brown interactions and events. The overall culture "is pretty laid-back and casual" and "most of the students are friendly and mesh well with everyone."

THE PRINCETON REVIEW SAYS

Admissions

Very important factors considered include: Rigor of secondary school record, character/personal qualities, level of applicant's interest, talent/ability. *Important factors considered include:* Class rank, application essay, academic GPA, recommendation(s), standardized test scores, extracurricular activities. *Other factors considered include:* Alumni/ae relation, first generation, geographical residence, interview, racial/ethnic status, state residency, volunteer work, work experience. SAT and SAT Subject Tests or ACT required; ACT with Writing component required. TOEFL required of all international applicants. High school diploma is required and GED is not accepted. *Academic units required:* 4 English, 3 mathematics, 3 science, (2 science labs), 3 foreign language, 2 history, 1 academic elective. *Academic units recommended:* 4 English, 4 mathematics, 4 science, (3 science labs), 4 foreign language, 2 history, 1 visual/performing arts, 1 academic elective.

Financial Aid

Students should submit: FAFSA, CSS/Financial Aid PROFILE, noncustodial PROFILE, business/farm supplement. Regular filing deadline is 2/1. The Princeton Review suggests that all financial aid forms be submitted as soon as possible after January 1. *Need-based scholarships/grants offered:* Federal Pell, SEOG, state scholarships/grants, private scholarships, the school's own gift aid. *Loan aid offered:* Direct Subsidized Stafford, Direct Unsubsidized Stafford, Direct PLUS, Federal Perkins, college/university loans from institutional funds. Applicants will be notified of awards on or about 4/1. Federal Work-Study Program available. Institutional employment available. Off-campus job opportunities are excellent.

The Inside Word

The cream of just about every crop applies to Brown. Gaining admission requires more than just a superior academic profile from high school. Some candidates, such as the sons and daughters of Brown graduates (who are admitted at virtually double the usual acceptance rate), have a better chance for admission than most others. Minority students benefit from some courtship, particularly once admitted. Ivies like to share the wealth and distribute offers of admission across a wide range of constituencies. Candidates from states that are overrepresented in the applicant pool, such as New York, have to be particularly distinguished in order to have the best chance at admission. So do those who attend high schools with many seniors applying to Brown, as it is rare for several students from any one school to be offered admission.

THE SCHOOL SAYS "..."

From The Admissions Office

"Founded in 1764, Brown is a private, coeducational, Ivy League university in which the intellectual development of undergraduate students is fostered by a dedicated faculty on a traditional New England campus.

"Applicants will be required to submit results of the SAT Reasoning Test and any two SAT Subject Tests (except for the SAT Subject Test Writing). Students may substitute any SAT tests with the ACT with the Writing component."

For even more information on this school, turn to page 456 of the "Stats" section.

BRYANT UNIVERSITY

1150 Douglas Pike, Smithfield, RI 02917 • Admissions: 401-232-6100 • Fax: 401-232-6741
Financial Aid: 401-232-6020 • E-mail: admissions@bryant.edu • Website: www.bryant.edu

RATINGS
Quality of Life: 83   Academic: 78   Admissions: 90   Financial Aid: 93

STUDENTS SAY ". . ."

Academics

There are liberal arts programs at Bryant University, but business is the top draw here. A wealth of programs in accounting, finance, marketing, and management has earned Bryant a reputation far and wide as "a business-driven institution that blends the academic and the real world." The placement rate for internships and meaningful jobs after graduation is "very high," thanks to a loyal alumni base and an "excellent" career center that offers a ton of personalized services. "During interview season, I had interviews every day, which led to second interviews, which led to multiple job offers,"

> **SURVEY SAYS . . .**
> Small classes
> Great computer facilities
> Great library
> Athletic facilities are great
> Career services are great
> Campus feels safe
> Lots of beer drinking
> Hard liquor is popular

boasts an accounting major. Students also rave about their cutting-edge campus technology. Academically, we hear students complain about "too many PowerPoint presentations" and "an excessive amount of group work" but "classes are always small" and professors are "always available." Many professors are "obsessed with their jobs" and "pride themselves on seeing their students succeed." They are "good at teaching but even better at providing real working knowledge and examples." Others, however, could definitely improve "when it comes to the fundamentals of teaching and being able to effectively communicate the subject matter." The part-time faculty is especially "hit or miss." Despite some complaints about registration and limited course offerings, Bryant's "very friendly" and "approachable" administration generally ensures that things "flow smoothly." Red tape is rare.

Life

"Life at Bryant is the typical college experience." Most undergrads choose to live on this clean, "beautiful," and modern campus "all four years" and there's "a great sense of community." The "intense" academic workload means that weekdays can be "stressful." Nevertheless, students at Bryant are "very involved" in "massive amounts of extracurriculars." "The athletic facilities are great" and many students participate in both intramurals and varsity sports. Students are in charge of most of the activities on campus and they put on a lot of events. The "fun social scene" typically begins on Thursday. "Parties are generally all on campus" and "most people get really drunk on the weekends." An assortment of harder stimulants is also popular. "If you want to do drugs, you will be able to find them," suggests one student. "At the same time, if you want nothing to do with drugs, you will never see them." The surrounding town of Smithfield "has nothing to do" but "a short drive into Providence" leads to "great food, bars, clubs, and shopping." For more serious urban life, students can always head up to Boston as well.

Student Body

"Students at Bryant are very similar, with similar goals and objectives in mind." There's kind of a "common mold" here of "health-conscious" suburbanites "from the Northeast" who have "aspirations to make good sums of money after entering the job market." "The administrators and teachers are pretty much the most liberal people on campus," explains a senior. "We are a relatively conservative school." During the week, these "competitive" (occasionally "cutthroat") "business leaders of tomorrow" are "hardworking and diligent." Preppy attire dominates and "clothes often seem to be a big deal." "It is not unusual to see students in suits," but only "when they have presentations or interviews, not just for the hell of it." On the weekends, students tend to be "typical party kids." "There definitely are students who deviate" from the norm but there aren't many and they "don't fit in as well." Some students contend that this place is "diverse economically." Others tell us that "the typical student is white, middle to upper middle class." Ethnic diversity is "rather low" and minority students "tend to stick together." International students do, too. In fact, the whole campus is "very cliquey." "If you're not involved in a sport, or Greek life, or another huge group, then your social life will be limited to your small group of friends."

THE PRINCETON REVIEW SAYS

Admissions

Very important factors considered include: Academic GPA, rigor of secondary school record. *Important factors considered include:* Class rank, application essay, recommendation(s), standardized test scores. *Other factors considered include:* Alumni/ae relation, character/personal qualities, extracurricular activities, first generation, geographical residence, interview, level of applicant's interest, racial/ethnic status, state residency, talent/ability, volunteer work, work experience. SAT or ACT required; TOEFL required of all international applicants. High school diploma is required and GED is accepted. *Academic units required:* 4 English, 4 mathematics, 2 science, (2 science labs), 2 foreign language, 2 history. *Academic units recommended:* 4 English, 4 mathematics, 3 science, (2 science labs), 3 foreign language, 3 history.

Financial Aid

Students should submit: FAFSA Regular filing deadline is 2/15. The Princeton Review suggests that all financial aid forms be submitted as soon as possible after January 1. *Need-based scholarships/grants offered:* Federal Pell, SEOG, state scholarships/grants, private scholarships, the school's own gift aid. *Loan aid offered:* Direct Subsidized Stafford, Direct Unsubsidized Stafford, FFEL PLUS, Federal Perkins Applicants will be notified of awards on or about 3/24. Federal Work-Study Program available. Institutional employment available. Off-campus job opportunities are fair.

The Inside Word

If you're a solid student you should meet little trouble getting into Bryant. The university's admissions effort has brought in qualified applicants from across the country, but the heaviest draw remains from New England. Students attending Bryant will receive a solid business education as well as precious connections in the corporate worlds of Providence and Boston.

THE SCHOOL SAYS ". . ."

From The Admissions Office

"Bryant is a four-year, private university in New England where students build knowledge, develop character, and achieve success—as they define it. In addition to a first-class faculty, state-of-the-art facilities, and advanced technology, Bryant offers stimulating classroom dynamics; internship opportunities at more than 350 companies; 70-plus student clubs and organizations; varsity, intramural, and club sports for men and women; and many opportunities for community service and leadership development. Bryant is the choice for individuals seeking the best integration of business and liberal arts, utilizing state-of-the-art technology. Bryant offers degrees in actuarial mathematics, applied mathematics and statistics, applied economics, applied psychology, business administration, communication, global studies, history, information technology, international business, literary and cultural studies, politics and law, and sociology.

"A cross-disciplinary academic approach teaches students the skills they need to successfully compete in a complex, global environment. Students can pursue one of 27 minors in business and liberal arts, and 80 areas of study. Bryant's rigorous academic standards have been recognized and accredited by NEASC and AACSB International. Bryant's international business program is a member of CUIBE, the Consortium for Undergraduate International Business Education. Technology is a fundamental component of the learning process at Bryant. Every entering freshman is provided with a Thinkpad® laptop for personal use. Students exchange their laptop for a new one in their junior year, which they will own upon graduation.

"Bryant University is situated on a beautiful 420-acre campus in Smithfield, Rhode Island. The campus is only 15 minutes away from the state capital, Providence; 45 minutes from Boston; and 3 hours from New York City.

"Bryant requires that students enrolling in Fall 2008 take the new SAT with the Writing component, or the ACT (writing section not required)."

For even more information on this school, turn to page 456 of the "Stats" section.

BRYN MAWR COLLEGE

101 NORTH MERION AVENUE, BRYN MAWR, PA 19010-2899 • ADMISSIONS: 610-526-5152
FAX: 610-526-7471 • FINANCIAL AID: 610-526-5245 • E-MAIL: ADMISSIONS@BRYNMAWR.EDU • WEBSITE: WWW.BRYNMAWR.EDU

RATINGS
Quality of Life: 96   **Academic:** 94   **Admissions:** 95   **Financial Aid:** 97

STUDENTS SAY "..."

Academics

Tiny Bryn Mawr College is "a community of women scholars" that offers "an amazing, intense, multifaceted," and
"pretty tough" academic experience. Coursework "can be
stressful, especially around midterms and final times, but
in the end it's worth it." The faculty is mostly stellar. "One
of the main things I love about Bryn Mawr is the personal

> **SURVEY SAYS ...**
> *Small classes*
> *Dorms are like palaces*
> *Frats and sororities are unpopular*
> *or nonexistent*

relationships formed over the years with the professors," boasts a chemistry major. "Anywhere you go to school
you will have some bad teachers and some boring classes, and Bryn Mawr is no exception," relates a junior, "but
overall I have been extremely impressed with and challenged by the classes I have taken at my college." The
highly popular administration is "here for the students' success." "Bryn Mawr is an extremely autonomous
place where students are given a lot of freedom to do as they please." "If you need something and you go to the
right people, you can pretty much make it happen." Additionally, students can take courses at nearby
Haverford, Swarthmore, and Penn. And upon graduation, Mawrters can take advantage of a loyal network of
alumnae who "are doing amazing things and have a really strong connection to the school."

Life

Bryn Mawr's "absolutely beautiful" campus is "ensconced in collegiate Gothic arches." The dorms are gorgeous
and the food is "delicious." It's all a little slice of heaven—except for the "bleak" athletic facilities. Neat traditions at Bryn Mawr include Hell Week, which allows first-year students to bond with everyone else, and May
Day, an entire day of catered picnics, live music, and hanging out on the greens, which always involves a
Maypole dance, a Robin Hood play, and a late-night screening of The Philadelphia Story (starring BMC alum
Katherine Hepburn). "These traditions are unique, intimate experiences that bring the whole school together
and make you feel proud to be a Mawrter," explains a junior. When students aren't basking in the warm glow
of ritual, they "love to study, study, study," but other activities are plentiful. "There is always something to do
on campus, whether it's a student theatre production, an a cappella concert, an improv group show, movies
being shown, outside groups coming to perform, speakers coming to campus, you name it," says a senior.
Sports and dance are big extracurricular activities, too. Mawrters drink "more than you'd think for an alleged-
ly quiet, nerdy women's college," but "Bryn Mawr's party scene is more of an intimate-friends-over-to-your-
room type of deal." Trips to Swarthmore, Villanova, or Haverford provide "plenty of chances to interact with
the opposite sex, if that's what you're after." "There are tons of great restaurants, music venues, galleries, and
shopping all within minutes of campus" as well, and nearby Philadelphia offers more urban recreation.

Student Body

Many students say that diversity "is one of the things that makes Bryn Mawr stand out." Others say that students looking for diversity "may not find it here." Whatever the case, "Bryn Mawr is a bunch of brilliant
women." They are "nerdy, ambitious, driven, talented" people who "can occasionally be over-competitive" and
are "swamped with work yet thriving on it." "We all came into Bryn Mawr with a background in leadership,
and all intend to leave Bryn Mawr as future leaders in our respective fields," asserts a junior. It's definitely a
left-leaning crowd. "A lot of students at Bryn Mawr are adamant about being politically correct to the point that
it begins to become annoying." "Contrary to popular belief, Bryn Mawr isn't a haven for lesbians," though
"homosexuality is common and visible." Socially, "the campus is very stratified along group lines." "There is a
variety of types of people at the school—from awkward, socially uncomfortable people to very outgoing, social
butterflies" to "mud-splattered" rugby players. "Some of us fly that freak flag high and proud," declares a senior. However, "there are plenty of average girls who look at Cosmo," too.

THE PRINCETON REVIEW SAYS

Admissions

Very important factors considered include: Recommendation(s), rigor of secondary school record. *Important factors considered include:* Application essay, academic GPA, character/personal qualities, extracurricular activities. *Other factors considered include:* Class rank, standardized test scores, alumni/ae relation, first generation, geographical residence, interview, racial/ethnic status, talent/ability, volunteer work, work experience. SAT and SAT Subject Tests or ACT required; TOEFL is required of international applicants unless: a) English has been the primary language of instruction for the past four years or, b) if student's first language is English. High school diploma or its equivalent is accepted. *Academic units required:* 2 academic electives. *Academic units recommended:* 4 English, 3 mathematics, 2 science, (1 science labs), 3 foreign language, 2 social studies, 2 history.

Financial Aid

Students should submit: FAFSA, CSS PROFILE, signed copies of parents' and students' federal income tax information with all forms and schedules attached. Additional forms may be requested. International *Students should submit:* International Students Financial Aid Form and a statement of earnings from each parent's employer. Bryn Mawr strongly encourages students to file by 2/5. All forms and information must be received no later than 3/1. The Princeton Review suggests that all financial aid forms be submitted as soon as possible after January 1. *Need-based scholarships/grants offered:* Federal Pell, SEOG, state scholarships/grants, the school's own gift aid. Federal Academic Competitiveness Grant (ACG), Federal National Science and Mathematics to Retain Talent Grant (SMART). *Loan aid offered:* FFEL Subsidized Stafford, FFEL Unsubsidized Stafford, FFEL PLUS, Federal Perkins Applicants will be notified of awards on or about 3/23.

The Inside Word

Do not be deceived by Bryn Mawr's admission rate; its student body is among the academically best in the nation. Outstanding preparation for graduate study draws an applicant pool that is well prepared and intellectually curious. The Admissions Committee includes eight faculty members and four seniors. Each applicant is reviewed by four readers, including at least one faculty member and one student.

THE SCHOOL SAYS "..."

From The Admissions Office

"Bryn Mawr is one of the nation's most distinctive, distinguished colleges. Every year 1,300 women from around the world gather on the College's historic campus to study with leading scholars, conduct advanced research, and expand the boundaries of what's possible. A Bryn Mawr woman is defined by a rare combination of personal characteristics: an intense intellectual commitment; a purposeful vision of her life; and a desire to make a meaningful contribution to the world. Consistently producing outstanding scholars, Bryn Mawr is ranked among the top ten of all colleges and universities in percentage of graduates who go on to earn a Ph.D., and is considered excellent preparation for the nation's top law, medical and business schools. More than 500 students collaborate with faculty on independent projects every year; and to augment an already strong curriculum, students may choose from more than 5,000 courses offered through nearby Haverford and Swarthmore Colleges, as well as the University of Pennsylvania. Committed to recruiting a diverse student body, more than a third of Bryn Mawr students are women of color and international students. Furthermore, more than 33% of all students opt to study overseas. Minutes outside of Philadelphia and only two hours by train from New York City and Washington, D.C., Bryn Mawr is recognized by many as one of the most stunning college campuses in the United States. Its mixture of collegiate Gothic architecture and post-modern buildings owe much of their beauty to the original campus plan that was created and executed by Fredrick Law Olmsted and Calvert Vaux, landscape architects and the designers of New York's Central Park."

For even more information on this school, turn to page 457 of the "Stats" section.

Bucknell University

Freas Hall, Lewisburg, PA 17837 • Admissions: 570-577-1101 • Fax: 570-577-3538
Financial Aid: 570-577-1331 • E-mail: admissions@bucknell.edu • Website: www.bucknell.edu

RATINGS
Quality of Life: 81 **Academic:** 91 **Admissions:** 96 **Financial Aid:** 96

STUDENTS SAY "..."

Academics

Bucknell University, "a liberal arts school with a top engineering program," is "a typical Patriot League school where students somehow find a way to balance studying and partying" while remaining "ambitious about their studies, extremely friendly and caring in nature, and bound to succeed." "Small class sizes, a beautiful campus, friendly students and faculty, and amazing facilities" all conspire to justify the premium price tag on a Bucknell education; $31 million in annual financial aid means about half the students don't have to foot the entire bill. "The courses are tough, and the workload is heavy" here, "but the academic experience is a wonderful one," with professors who "are passionate and energetic and convey their love for their field to their students. They give us their home phone numbers and e-mail addresses and tell us to come to their offices just to say hello. They want to teach us, but also want to be our friends." Bucknell offers more than 50 majors and 60 minors, an impressive array for a school of this size; business and engineering majors are most popular, while premeds benefit from numerous opportunities to get involved in research. It's the kind of school that inspires lifelong loyalty; as one undergrad sums up, "Bucknell boasts a tight-knit community where most people are friends with most other people and 99 percent of varsity athletes graduate in four years. Bucknell is a community of scholars as well as social [beings], with many students possessing both qualities. Few students regret their choice and remain involved in campus affairs for lifetimes."

> **SURVEY SAYS . . .**
> Small classes
> Great library
> Athletic facilities are great
> Campus feels safe
> Frats and sororities dominate social scene
> Lots of beer drinking

Life

"Life at Bucknell is centered on a social structure," and "While students do work hard at their academics, they party equally as hard." Indeed, according to some, "On weekends, you have a few choices: dorms or downtown, beer or hard liquor, drugs or alcohol. Partying is it, though." This perception is reinforced by the fact that hometown Lewisburg is very small and very quiet. Greek organizations play a huge role on campus; one reluctant fraternity member writes, "I never thought I would join a fraternity, and the prevalence of Greek life was one of the downsides of coming here originally, but I found a group of guys where I fit in quite well, so I spend a lot of time on fraternity activities. But that's really my choice because I enjoy it." Many here will tell you that there are options "that do not revolve around the party scene, such as the outing club, the nationally known Conservatives Club," and a number of religious- and service-related organizations such as Catholic Campus Ministry and Student Emergency Response Volunteers. Bucknell competes in the Patriot League against the likes of Army, Navy, Lehigh, and Lafayette; "The basketball team has been very good lately, so they're a lot of fun."

Student Body

"A lot of people are preppy—super preppy" on the Bucknell campus, many students tell us, observing that "the sheer number of student-owned luxury cars on this campus is astounding." An adamant minority insists that "Bucknell has a reputation for being a preppy school, but in my experience that reputation is overblown." Most everyone agrees that 'preppy' doesn't have to mean boring; the student body includes "plenty of interesting and different people to hang out with if you look for them." Undergrads tend to be "energetic" and "involved in many things on campus. Students try their best at everything they do." Students typically "come from Pennsylvania, New Jersey, or New York. There are a lot from New England also, and Maryland's probably next."

THE PRINCETON REVIEW SAYS

Admissions

*Very important factors considered include:*Academic GPA, rigor of secondary school record, standardized test scores, character/personal qualities, talent/ability, application essay. *Important factors considered include:* Recommendation(s), extracurricular activities, level of applicant's interest, volunteer work, work experience. *Other factors considered include:* Alumni/ae relation, first generation, geographical residence, interview, racial/ethnic status, religious affiliation/commitment, SAT or ACT with Writing component required. TOEFL required of all international applicants. High school diploma is required and GED is accepted. *Academic units required:* 4 English, 3 mathematics, 2 science, 2 foreign language, 2 social studies, 2 history, 1 academic elective. *Academic units recommended:* 4 English, 4 mathematics, 3 science, 4 foreign language, 2 social studies, 2 history, 1 academic elective.

Financial Aid

Students should submit: FAFSA, CSS/Financial Aid PROFILE, noncustodial PROFILE. Regular filing deadline is 1/1. The Princeton Review suggests that all financial aid forms be submitted as soon as possible after January 1. *Need-based scholarships/grants offered:* Federal Pell, SEOG, state scholarships/grants, private scholarships, the school's own gift aid, Federal ACG Grant, Federal SMART. *Loan aid offered:* FFEL Subsidized Stafford, FFEL Unsubsidized Stafford, FFEL PLUS, Federal Perkins Applicants will be notified of awards on or about 4/1. Federal Work-Study Program available. Institutional employment available. Off-campus job opportunities are poor.

The Inside Word

Admissions rates vary by intended major at Bucknell. The school receives applications from more prospective business majors than the school can handle; as a result, only about 23 percent were admitted to the class of 2010. Admit rates are higher among populations that tend to be self-selecting, including science majors, computer science majors, and engineers. Those listing "undecided" as prospective major made up about 17 percent of admitted applicants; 33 percent of such applicants were admitted. You certainly don't hurt yourself by listing "undecided" as your intended major.

THE SCHOOL SAYS ". . ."

From The Admissions Office

"Bucknell combines the personal experience of a small liberal arts college with the breadth and opportunity typically found at larger research universities. With a low student/faculty ratio, students gain exceptional hands-on experience, working closely with faculty in an environment enhanced by first-class academic, residential, and athletic facilities. Together, the College of Arts and Sciences and the College of Engineering offer 53 majors and 64 minors. Learning opportunities permeate campus life in and out of the classroom and across the disciplines. For example, engineering students participate in music ensembles, theater productions, and poetry readings, while arts and sciences students take engineering courses, conduct scientific research in the field, and produce distinctive creative works. Students also pursue their interests in more than 150 organizations and through athletic competition in the prestigious Division I Patriot League. These activities constitute a comprehensive approach to learning that teaches students how to think critically and develop their leadership skills so that they are prepared to make a difference locally, nationally, and globally."

For even more information on this school, turn to page 457 of the "Stats" section.

CALIFORNIA UNIVERSITY OF PENNSYLVANIA

250 UNIVERSITY AVENUE, CALIFORNIA, PA 15419 • ADMISSIONS: 724-938-4404 • FAX: 724-938-4564
FINANCIAL AID: 724-938-4415 • E-MAIL: INQUIRY@CUP.EDU • WEBSITE: WWW.CUP.EDU

RATINGS
Quality of Life: 74   Academic: 70   Admissions: 74   Financial Aid: 76

STUDENTS SAY ". . ."
Academics

California University of Pennsylvania is a "welcoming" and "affordable" medium-sized school "in a small town setting." Students laud the nursing program and the "strong art department." "This school is big on education majors," reports one student. However, "Professors and academic experience at Cal seem to vary by department." "The professors in my major are knowledgeable and car-

> **SURVEY SAYS . . .**
> Large classes
> Great computer facilities
> Dorms are like palaces
> Lots of beer drinking
> (Almost) everyone smokes

ing," says a satisfied graphic design major. Other happy students describe their profs as "genuinely fascinating people" who are "extremely dedicated" and "very approachable." Some warn that certain faculty members are "not good teachers," while others are "just plain uninteresting." "My professors are, on the whole, really good," sums up a history major, "though I have had some crappy ones who I'd like to forget." The administration is "highly ambitious" and "a majority of the school's staff will remember you on a first name basis." However, some find that the administration "doesn't seem to have a realistic handle on things," and students universal-ly agree that "registering for classes in a real pain." "Classes are almost impossible to get into unless a student is in honors, band, sports, or a senior," notes a student.

Life

Cal U's "small" campus is "surrounded by lush woods" and "gives a feeling of relaxation." The "absolutely amazing" residence halls are "nicer than hotels." "The food needs to be better" though, and parking is a "night-mare." Athletics are "huge." "Intramural sports are fun and the gym is nice," explains one student. "There are several house parties off-campus" during the week but this place is "mostly" a commuter school. Many under-grads "go home on Fridays," leaving the campus "virtually dead on weekends." "If you live on campus, things are pretty boring unless you are into the Greek life and partying," says one student. "If you are of age and stay in town, you go to one of three bars" in the "quaint" but "run down" surrounding hamlet. If you have a car handy, shopping awaits at "three big malls close by." Also, Pittsburgh is less than an hour away and it provides "nightlife and city atmosphere."

Student Body

There's little in the way of ethnic diversity and the typical student is "like any normal student at any other uni-versity." Cal U is full of "middleclass people working toward a degree." "Most of us are here because we could not pay for a better school even if we did get into those schools," says a senior. "A lot of students are from the Pittsburgh area" or from somewhere else in western Pennsylvania. Nontraditional students abound and there's "a ton of commuters." The student body is "a mix of different types." There are "jocks." There's "the art crowd." There are the "nonconformists who actually are conforming to the other nonconformists." "There are a lot of hicks," too. Students report that everyone is "down to earth" and the different cliques on campus interact well. "You'll see football players hanging out with art majors and computer science people," says one student. "The people are a lot friendlier than at the bigger schools I visited," observes a sophomore. "I've kind of grown attached to it."

THE PRINCETON REVIEW SAYS

Admissions

Very important factors considered include: Class rank, rigor of secondary school record, standardized test scores. *Other factors considered include:* Application essay, recommendation(s), extracurricular activities, interview, talent/ability, work experience. SAT or ACT required; high school diploma is required and GED is accepted. *Academic units required:* 4 English, 3 mathematics, 1 science, (1 science labs), 2 social studies, 2 history, 6 academic electives, 1 Arts and Humanities. *Academic units recommended:* 4 English, 3 mathematics, 1 science, (1 science labs), 2 foreign language, 2 social studies, 2 history, 6 academic electives, 1 Arts and Humanities.

Finanancial Aid

Students should submit: FAFSA. The Princeton Review suggests that all financial aid forms be submitted as soon as possible after January 1. *Need-based scholarships/grants offered:* Federal Pell, SEOG, state scholarships/grants, private scholarships, the school's own gift aid. *Loan aid offered:* FFEL Subsidized Stafford, FFEL Unsubsidized Stafford, FFEL PLUS, Federal Perkins Applicants will be notified of awards on a rolling basis beginning 4/1. Federal Work-Study Program available. Institutional employment available. Off-campus job opportunities are good.

The Inside Word

It's not difficult to get admitted to Cal U. If you have standardized test scores at or slightly below average and decent high school grades, you shouldn't have a problem. It's worth noting that you don't need test scores if you've been out of high school for at least two years.

THE SCHOOL SAYS " . . . "

From The Admissions Office

"California University, a proud member of the Pennsylvania State System of Higher Education, has a mission to build character and careers. Character education is a part of every classroom, lived in every residence hall and on every playing field. Career building is an ongoing, 4-year process. Students participate in hands-on learning and research, and gain invaluable real-world experience through co-ops and internships. Cal U's unique Career Advantage Program provides a checklist for career success beginning with the freshman year and continuing through graduation.

"Each bachelor's degree requires a minimum of 120 semester hours of credit including a general education requirement of 51 credits. An honors program provides an opportunity for an enhanced educational experience to students who meet the criteria.

"All classes are taught by teaching faculty members. The student/faculty ratio is 20:1. Doctorates are held by more than 74 percent of the full-time faculty.

"Cal U is recognized as a leader in providing premiere student living options. Two locations, the lower and the upper campus, provide students with the Suite Life, a whole new experience in university living."

For even more information on this school, turn to page 458 of the "Stats" section.

CARNEGIE MELLON UNIVERSITY

5000 FORBES AVENUE, PITTSBURGH, PA 15213 • ADMISSIONS: 412-268-2082 • FAX: 412-268-7838
FINANCIAL AID: 412-268-2068 • E-MAIL: UNDERGRADUATE-ADMISSIONS@ANDREW.CMU.EDU • WEBSITE: WWW.CMU.EDU

RATINGS
Quality of Life: 70   Academic: 99   Admissions: 97   Financial Aid: 78

STUDENTS SAY "..."

Academics

Carnegie Mellon University is "all about technology. Whether it be engineering, music, theater, robotics, science, or psychology; it's about learning by breaking things down to find out how they work." With nearly half the students engaged in computer- and engineering-related disciplines, Carnegie Mellon can seem to be the domain of number-

crunchers, but in fact the school also excels in music, theater, design, architecture, all the hard sciences, business, and economics; it is truly "a place where nerds of all kinds can thrive." One student observes, "Carnegie Mellon is strong in so many different fields. I wasn't sure what I wanted to do, but I wanted to be in a place where I could find out early in a hands-on way, and switch to an equally great program if I wanted." Those who choose Carnegie Mellon should prepare for academic demands that can "overwhelm you with work and stress in order to weed out the weak from the strong." To help students cope, the school offers "tons of academic resources to get extra help, from peer tutoring to office hours to student-led review sessions. Still, it's incredibly important to stay on top of assignments, or they really pile up." Hard work "prepares Carnegie Mellon students for post-undergraduate success," students agree, and when you reach that stage you'll be assisted by "a great career center" that draws "constant job recruiting on campus" and maintains "fantastic alumni connections," though this is somewhat dependent on a student's major.

Life

"Work hard, then work harder" might be the mantra of some Carnegie Mellon students; among them is the undergrad who tells us: "I go to class, I study in the library, and I work out. The day is so long that generally by the time I get home, I eat and am ready for bed because most of the time it's 11:00 or 12:00 at night already." Others tell us, however, that "if you are a social person, you can and will find other social people that you can have fun with." The weekend, or Friday night and Saturday—"Sunday will of course be spent doing work"— is the time to cut loose. Greek life and movies are the big on-campus draws: "Every Friday, Saturday, and Sunday night a just-released movie from the main theaters plays on campus; you can get a ticket, popcorn, and a drink for under three dollars." A good deal of students, though, prefer to have their fun in the city. Pittsburgh "offers a wide variety of things to do off-campus and the Port Authority bus system (free with a Carnegie Mellon ID) does a decent job of transporting students wherever they want to go." There's "always a gallery show to go see" in Pittsburgh, and professional sports, "great restaurants, shopping centers, and malls" are also a draw. The city "has a pretty big bar and club scene, but you must be 21." One student writes, "You can do virtually anything within a reasonable distance, including a trip to a ski mountain."

Student Body

The workload at Carnegie Mellon can be pretty daunting, so it's no surprise that the typical undergrad here "is extremely studious and serious about academics." In terms of priorities, "Extracurricular activities and a social life are far behind academics. Socially, people can be awkward." Even so, "For every recluse or extroverted musical theater major that you'd expect at Carnegie Mellon, there is a polar opposite. People here feel a need to define themselves some way, to defy established stereotypes." Carnegie Mellon draws "a very diverse student body where most people, regardless of race, ethnicity, or gender, tend to get along. Occasionally some cliques form on campus (for example, a certain set of international students, or students from a particular major), but most of the time everyone is friendly."

THE PRINCETON REVIEW SAYS

Admissions

Very important factors considered include: Academic GPA, rigor of secondary school record. *Important factors considered include:* Class rank, application essay, recommendation(s), standardized test scores. *Other factors considered include:* Alumni/ae relation, character/personal qualities, extracurricular activities, first generation, geographical residence, interview, racial/ethnic status, talent/ability, volunteer work, work experience. SAT or ACT required; ACT with Writing component required. High school diploma is required and GED is accepted. *Academic units required:* 4 English, 4 mathematics, 3 science, (3 science labs), 2 foreign language, 3 academic electives. *Academic units recommended:* 4 English, 4 mathematics, 3 science, (3 science labs), 2 foreign language, 4 academic electives.

Financial Aid

Students should submit: FAFSA, institution's own financial aid form, Parent and student Federal Tax Returns. Parent W2 Forms. Regular filing deadline is 5/1. The Princeton Review suggests that all financial aid forms be submitted as soon as possible after January 1. *Need-based scholarships/grants offered:* Federal Pell, SEOG, state scholarships/grants, private scholarships, the school's own gift aid. *Loan aid offered:* FFEL Subsidized Stafford, FFEL Unsubsidized Stafford, FFEL PLUS, Federal Perkins, Gate Student Loan. Applicants will be notified of awards on or about 3/15. Federal Work-Study Program available. Institutional employment available. Off-campus job opportunities are good.

The Inside Word

Don't be misled by Carnegie Mellon's acceptance rate. Although relatively high for a university of this caliber, the applicant pool is fairly self-selecting. If you haven't loaded up on demanding courses in high school, you are not likely to be a serious contender. The Admissions Office explicitly states that it doesn't use formulas in making admissions decisions. That said, a record of strong academic performance in the area of your intended major is key.

THE SCHOOL SAYS ". . ."

From The Admissions Office

"Carnegie Mellon is a private, coeducational university with approximately 5,300 undergraduates; 4,400 graduate students; and 1,200 full-time faculty members. The university's 144-acre campus is located in the Oakland area of Pittsburgh, five miles from downtown. The university is composed of seven colleges: the Carnegie Institute of Technology (engineering), the College of Fine Arts, the College of Humanities and Social Sciences (combining liberal arts education with professional specializations), the Tepper School of Business (undergraduate business and industrial management), the Mellon College of Science, the School of Computer Science, and the H. John Heinz III School of Public Policy and Management.

"Freshman applicants for Fall 2008 must take the SAT plus two SAT Subject Tests, depending on their major interest. Students may take the ACT with Writing in lieu of the SAT. An applicant's best scores will be used in admissions decision-making.

"Carnegie Mellon has campuses in the Silicon Valley, California, and Qatar in the Arabian Gulf."

For even more information on this school, turn to page 458 of the "Stats" section.

THE CATHOLIC UNIVERSITY OF AMERICA

CARDINAL STATION, WASHINGTON, DC 20064 • ADMISSIONS: 202-319-5305 • FAX: 202-319-6533
FINANCIAL AID: 202-319-5307 • E-MAIL: CUA-ADMISSIONS@CUA.EDU • WEBSITE: WWW.CUA.EDU

RATINGS
Quality of Life: 67   **Academic:** 75   **Admissions:** 84   **Financial Aid:** 85

STUDENTS SAY ". . ."

Academics

You'll receive "an education heavy in philosophy and theology" at the Catholic University of America, "a beautiful college campus located in the heart of our nation's capital." That's because every student at CUA completes a core curriculum with an "emphasis on philosophy and religion. Students are required to take a series of both. Unless you are planning on making a career out of either, when else in life will you study these in depth than college?" For a school of just over 3,000 students, CUA has a remarkable

number of strong disciplines. Undergrads laud the "incredibly strong" nursing program, a "wonderful music program" that's ideal for students who "don't want conservatory straight out of high school but still want a challenging program," "the best education in architecture in the DC area," and a "very strong" drama department. While liberal arts and science programs aren't as highly regarded, students appreciate that "Professors are helpful and always available," and point out that political studies are greatly abetted by the school's location. Of DC, one student observes that the school's location in the nation's provides, "easy access to internships, government, and seemingly endless other political opportunities." The school also offers an honors program that "challenges students to push [to] the edge of their abilities."

Life

CUA's Washington, DC address "is absolutely one of the great strengths of the school. A student can get on the Metro and go basically wherever they want, and get whatever it is that they need." Indeed, students "have DC, a storied and cosmopolitan city," at their fingertips, "with plenty of concert venues, movie theaters, play houses, shopping districts, landmarks, and museums to visit on the weekends." Undergrads "go to Starbucks and have study sessions . . . on Sundays, or go and visit friends at George Washington or Georgetown on the weekends." "Chinatown, Dupont Circle, and Union Station" are also popular destinations for "fun times." As one student sums up, "We are in the nation's capital, we have plenty to do." Students tell us that "almost everyone on this campus likes to drink," and while "The school tries really hard to offer nonalcoholic alternatives on the weekends," their efforts "aren't quite enticing enough to lure us away from the neighborhood bars." Drinking generally takes place in the bars, as "House parties are almost nonexistent" on campus. However, students also tell us that "if you don't feel like drinking on the weekends, there is always some option for you" including campus ministry events which provide "students [with] a healthy environment and people to be around as an alternative to drinking."

Student Body

The typical student at CUA "is from the Mid-Atlantic states, White, and went to a Catholic high school"; "fairly conservative," and looks like a "page out of an Abercrombie & Fitch ad." "Everyone wears flip-flops, polo shirts, and khakis. People only wear jeans during the wintertime." Exceptions to the rule include "the very vocal minority groups" who work to make sure "Diversity is highlighted" on campus, "people of other religious backgrounds," and the many "musical theater students" including a large number of "gay men, which is pretty surprising at a Catholic university." Many students are devout and "very open about their faith," but "Very few people will force religion down your throat." Atypical students are "generally welcomed and accepted by these 'typical' students with little or no friction due to religion, sexual orientation, race, socioeconomic class."

THE PRINCETON REVIEW SAYS

Admissions

Very important factors considered include: Academic GPA, recommendation(s), rigor of secondary school record, standardized test scores, character/personal qualities, level of applicant's interest, volunteer work. *Important factors considered include:* Application essay, extracurricular activities, first generation, interview, talent/ability. *Other factors considered include:* Class rank, alumni/ae relation, racial/ethnic status, work experience. SAT Subject Tests recommended; SAT or ACT required; ACT with Writing component required. TOEFL required of all international applicants. High school diploma is required and GED is accepted. *Academic units recommended:* 4 English, 3 mathematics, 3 science, (1 science labs), 2 foreign language, 4 social studies, 1 fine arts or humanities.

Financial Aid

Students should submit: FAFSA, Alumni and Parish Scholarship Applications if appropriate. The Princeton Review suggests that all financial aid forms be submitted as soon as possible after January 1. *Need-based scholarships/grants offered:* Federal Pell, SEOG, state scholarships/grants, private scholarships, the school's own gift aid, Federal Nursing Scholarships. *Loan aid offered:* FFEL Subsidized Stafford, FFEL Unsubsidized Stafford, FFEL PLUS, Federal Perkins, Federal Nursing, college/university loans from institutional funds, commericial Loans. Applicants will be notified of awards on or about 4/1. Federal Work-Study Program available. Institutional employment available. Off-campus job opportunities are good.

The Inside Word

The Catholic University of America is a conservative school that adopts a very traditional approach to higher education. Your application should demonstrate an appreciation for the school's unique qualities and educational philosophy. Present your strongest case by showing solid grades in a demanding curriculum, backed by above average test scores, and you should have little trouble gaining admission. CUA now accepts the Common Application.

THE SCHOOL SAYS ". . ."

From The Admissions Office

"The Catholic University of America's friendly atmosphere, rigorous academic programs, and emphasis on time-honored values attract students from all 50 states and more than 95 foreign countries. Its 193-acre, tree-lined campus is only 10 minutes from the nation's capital. Distinguished as the national university of the Catholic Church in the United States, CUA is the only institution of higher education established by the U.S. Catholic bishops; however, students from all religious traditions are welcome.

"CUA offers undergraduate degrees in more than 80 major areas in seven schools of study. Students enroll into the School of Arts and Sciences, Architecture, Nursing, Engineering, Metropolitan College, Music, or Philosophy. Additionally, CUA students can concentrate in areas of preprofessional study including law, dentistry, medicine, or veterinary studies.

"With Capitol Hill, the Smithsonian Institution, NASA, the Kennedy Center, and the National Institutes of Health among the places students obtain internships, firsthand experience is a valuable piece of the experience that CUA offers. Numerous students also take the opportunity in their junior year to study abroad at one of Catholic's 17 country program sites. Political science majors even have the opportunity to do a Parliamentary Internship in either England or Ireland. With the campus just minutes away from downtown via the Metrorail rapid transit system, students enjoy a residential campus in an exciting city of historical monuments, theaters, festivals, ethnic restaurants, and parks.

"Freshman applicants for Fall 2008 must take the new SAT or ACT. Additionally, students may submit scores from the old SAT, and the best scores from either test will be used. Matriculating students should submit the SAT Subject Test: Foreign Language exam if they plan to continue studying that language at CUA."

For even more information on this school, turn to page 459 of the "Stats" section.

CENTRAL CONNECTICUT STATE UNIVERSITY

1615 STANLEY STREET, NEW BRITAIN, CT 06050 • ADMISSIONS: 800-832-3200 • FAX: 862-832-2295
E-MAIL: ADMISSIONS@CCSU.EDU • WEBSITE: WWW.CCSU.EDU

RATINGS
Quality of Life: 66   **Academic:** 65   **Admissions:** 70   **Financial Aid:** 66

STUDENTS SAY ". . ."
Academics

Central Connecticut State University is an "affordable," medium-sized school with a host of "good academic programs." The school of education is particularly notable. There are solid study abroad options. Opportunities for undergraduate research are ample, "especially in the sciences." CCSU's campus is "beautifully landscaped" but "a few of the buildings need overhauling." The library in particular "could use an aesthetic lift." One student also suggests that "desks should be thrown into Long Island Sound." The faculty receives mixed reviews. "We have some great professors," says an education major. "There are also some that are not so great." "My professors are excellent," says a music education major. "They really know their subject." Other professors "have cool jobs" and bring real world experience to night classes. Some profs "are just here for the benefits," though. Foreign professors with thick accents in math, science, and tech classes also cause "misunderstanding and confusion." The small class sizes at CCSU "make it easier to have one-to-one communication" with professors. Many faculty members are "very accessible" and "may even allow you to make house calls if necessary." Others are "not that reachable." A few students laud the top brass. To others, the administration seems "distant" and "mostly disorganized." "Each department is very different," observes a sophomore.

> **SURVEY SAYS . . .**
> *Great computer facilities*
> *Great library*
> *Diverse student types on campus*
> *Lots of beer drinking*
> *(Almost) everyone smokes*

Life

"The campus at CCSU is a nice size. It's not too big but not too small either." "The cafeteria food is disgusting," though. "I refuse to eat in the dining hall most days," says a junior. Socially, CCSU is "really a commuter school." "For fun, people either go to the student center to hang out or go out with friends to either other dorm rooms or apartments nearby," says a freshman. "There are movie nights on Wednesdays and activity nights every Thursday in the student center." Thursday is also the "big party night." After that, a whole lot of students head home for the weekend. If you stick around, "weekends are awful." "If you're thinking of coming here and are from out of state, I would reconsider unless you're pretty outgoing," cautions a junior. Students who stick around "tend to go off campus to do stuff." Without question, "having a car helps." Surrounding towns and the bright lights of nearby Hartford provide some decent options for weekend fun.

Student Body

"The typical student is a commuter." "Most students are middleclass Connecticut residents who are coming here because it's cheap and nearby," says a junior. There is "a wide range of minority students" on campus. "The diversity is great," enthuses a sophomore. "It's a very welcoming atmosphere." "Everyone fits in one way or another" but cliques are common. "Generally, the athletes hang out with the athletes; minorities hang out with minorities; etc." A lot of students have "many things aside from classes going on, like a job." CCSU is also something of a haven for nontraditional and older students. "It is very appropriate for working professionals."

Admissions

Very important factors considered include: Rigor of secondary school record. *Important factors considered include:* Class rank, standardized test scores. *Other factors considered include:* Application essay, recommendation(s), extracurricular activities, interview, racial/ethnic status, state residency, talent/ability, SAT required; TOEFL required of all international applicants. High school diploma is required and GED is accepted. *Academic units required:* 4 English, 3 mathematics, 2 science, (1 science labs), 2 social studies, 1 history. *Academic units recommended:* 1 mathematics, 3 foreign language.

Finanancial Aid

Students should submit: FAFSA. Regular filing deadline is 9/15. The Princeton Review suggests that all financial aid forms be submitted as soon as possible after January 1. *Need-based scholarships/grants offered:* Federal Pell, SEOG, state scholarships/grants, the school's own gift aid. *Loan aid offered:* Direct Subsidized Stafford, Direct Unsubsidized Stafford, Direct PLUS, FFEL PLUS, Federal Perkins Applicants will be notified of awards on a rolling basis beginning 3/15. Federal Work-Study Program available. Institutional employment available. Off-campus job opportunities are good.

The Inside Word

The admissions process at CCSU is extraordinarily straightforward. If your SAT scores approach average and your high school grades in serious coursework aren't atrocious, you should be fine.

THE SCHOOL SAYS " . . . "

From The Admissions Office

"Selected as one of the 'Great Colleges for the Real World' and honored as a 'Leadership Institution' by the Association of American Colleges and Universities, CCSU stands as a national example of quality undergraduate education. Offering more than 100 majors in 82 fields of study in its four schools, CCSU also provides a wide array of special curricular opportunities to enrich learning.

"As exemplified in the university's slogan, 'Start with a dream. Finish with a future!' CCSU is committed to preparing students for success in whatever field they choose. The Offices of Career Services and Cooperative Education provide interesting career-related work experience plus opportunities to make connections with hundreds of participating employers. Nearly 70 percent of participating students are offered permanent, career-starting positions with their co-op employers upon graduation.

"CCSU's campus is attractive, with new and renovated buildings adding to the classic collegiate 'look' of its historical architecture. Academic buildings feature state-of-the-art, fully networked 'smart classrooms.' A newly renovated and expanded student center provides lounges, conference and game rooms, dining and information services, a bookstore, and a range of other support services. With 120 student clubs and organizations covering a broad spectrum of interests, there is a wealth of opportunities to meet new people, broaden horizons, and develop leadership skills. Athletics are a big part of campus life, and students enjoy a state-of-the-art fitness center with training rooms, a swimming pool, a track, and tennis and basketball courts. And CCSU's 18 Division I sports teams provide exciting opportunities to play or watch."

For even more information on this school, turn to page 459 of the "Stats" section.

CHATHAM UNIVERSITY

WOODLAND ROAD, PITTSBURGH, PA 15232 • ADMISSIONS: 412-365-1290 • FAX: 412-365-1609
E-MAIL: ADMISSIONS@CHATHAM.EDU • WEBSITE: WWW.CHATHAM.EDU

RATINGS

Quality of Life: 97   **Academic:** 81   **Admissions:** 77   **Financial Aid:** 88

STUDENTS SAY ". . ."

Academics

A small, all-women's college within a university of 1,800 students, Chatham University seeks to create "an empowering environment for women who strive to be leaders in today's world," and, according to most students, the school accomplishes its mission. With 600-plus undergraduates, the school is "so small it's really easy to get to know every-

one. Not only do you feel personally connected to campus, but it opens a lot of doors. If there's something that you want to add, attend, dislike, etc., you feel very comfortable asking faculty, staff, students or administration to make changes!" These small class sizes also allow "tons of faculty-student interaction. I had a meltdown where I got really behind in classes and my profs found me, talked me through it and helped me make a plan for getting back on track. I didn't even ask for their help, they just cared enough to do that." The administration could definitely "use a little bit of an improvement" in terms of asking for and implementing student input, but are respected by students for the most part. That said, many students here appreciate that the Chatham experience culminates in a thesis project that "affords an excellent opportunity to truly develop ourselves in a more mature academic format."

Life

Chatham is located in Pittsburgh's Shadyside neighborhood, "a residential area where mansions and trees surround most of the campus." The campus offers "a break from the city" without being "completely secluded from the bulk of things" because "Chatham is just a block away from Walnut Street in Shadyside, where all the fun shopping and dining is," as well as "Squirrel Hill on the other side of campus, which is a great place to browse." Best of all, the college "is located near a lot of major universities" that provide "great things to get involved with off-campus with other area college students. If partying is what you're interested in, it's easy to find, but for those of us who don't party, we have our fun, too." Non-party options include "an abundance of organizations to get involved with and activities to partake in." As well as concerts, "hanging out at one another's apartments, going to gallery crawls, and going to on campus events or events at other nearby campuses." Many students also hold jobs off-campus.

Student Body

Chatham caters to women primarily from the Western Pennsylvania region, but within that distinction, there's plenty of room for diversity on all fronts, as "the student body really is kind of a potpourri." Chatham has "lots of foreign students who are on top of all of their work, and a good solid section of leftist, queer, or queer friendly students to keep things interesting"; indeed, there is a wide range of nationality and sexual orientation represented here, and the "open-minded" crowd is "loud and like to fight for equal rights." That diversity extends to students' interests: "Walking around campus you will find people who are really interested in art, but they are best friends with someone interested in politics and math. Everyone just fits in." Students here tend to be "politically, environmentally, and socially conscious" women who "care about gender, race, and sexual-orientation issues."

THE PRINCETON REVIEW SAYS
Admissions

Very important factors considered include: Rigor of secondary school record. *Important factors considered include:* Application essay, academic GPA. *Other factors considered include:* Class rank, recommendation(s), standardized test scores, alumni/ae relation, character/personal qualities, extracurricular activities, interview, level of applicant's interest, talent/ability, volunteer work, work experience. TOEFL required of all international applicants. High school diploma is required and GED is accepted. *Academic units required:* 4 English, 2 mathematics, 2 science, 3 Social Science. *Academic units recommended:* 4 English, 3 mathematics, 3 science, 2 foreign language, 3 social science.

Finanancial Aid

Students should submit: FAFSA. The Princeton Review suggests that all financial aid forms be submitted as soon as possible after January 1. *Need-based scholarships/grants offered:* Federal Pell, SEOG, state scholarships/grants, private scholarships, the school's own gift aid, United Negro College Fund. *Loan aid offered:* FFEL Subsidized Stafford, FFEL Unsubsidized Stafford, FFEL PLUS, Federal Perkins Applicants will be notified of awards on a rolling basis beginning 2/15. Federal Work-Study Program available. Institutional employment available. Off-campus job opportunities are good.

The Inside Word

Chatham's single-sex demographic turns off some potential undergraduates. As a result, Chatham presents women a unique opportunity for admittance to a fine liberal arts college. The location has its benefits as well. Cooperative learning programs provide access to nine colleges and universities in Pittsburgh, including UPitt and Carnegie Mellon.

THE SCHOOL SAYS " . . . "
From The Admissions Office

"A Chatham College education emphasizes the environment, global issues, and women's leadership. The First-Year Student Sequence introduces students to the college community and culture and provides opportunities to access regional resources and study issues of concern to women. Seniors complete a year-long independent research project known as the Senior Tutorial. Eighty-five percent of Chatham students take advantage of internship opportunities, with most students participating in at least two. Chatham Abroad is a multiweek travel experience during which students and faculty travel to and study in different countries each year, such as Belize, Egypt, Spain, Costa Rica, Ireland, Russia, and the Netherlands.

"All first-year students receive HP tablet computers, which are integrated into course work, with access to a wireless campus network. Chatham's student/faculty ratio is 10:1, which ensures greater interaction between students and faculty.

"Undergraduate students may earn both their bachelor's and master's degrees from Chatham in as few as 5 years through the Five-Year Master's Program, or through a partnership with Carnegie Mellon University's H. John Heinz III School of Public Policy. Chatham's 24 graduate degree programs are open to women and men."

For even more information on this school, turn to page 460 of the "Stats" section.

CHESTNUT HILL COLLEGE

9601 GERMANTOWN AVENUE, PHILADELPHIA, PA 19118-2693 • ADMISSIONS: 215-248-7001 • FAX: 215-248-7082
FINANCIAL AID: 215-248-7182 • E-MAIL: CHCAPPLY@CHC.EDU • WEBSITE: WWW.CHC.EDU

RATINGS

Quality of Life: 81   Academic: 84   Admissions: 60*   Financial Aid: 67

STUDENTS SAY ". . ."

Academics

Based on the "principles of the Sisters of St. Joseph," who founded the school, the purpose of attending Chestnut Hill College is "receiving a 'holistic education.'" That is, students are expected to "to grow in knowledge and in spirituality" during their tenure here. To that end, students are exposed to a wide range of subjects through a core curriculum. Students have mixed feelings about these core classes.

Whereas some students believe that the core classes really make them "well rounded individuals," others complain that that roundedness comes at a cost: "In core classes/general education courses, the teachers are less knowledgeable than other professors and are often first-year teachers and stumble on their own words." Still, overall, students feel "the full-time profs here are excellent." "They actually remember your name and genuinely care about you. To them you are their student and not just a name on the roster sheet." However, "Sometimes the adjuncts aren't too good." Concerning how hard they are expected to work, students feel that "It's not a competitive school, but the academics are challenging." As far as the administration goes, students don't offer very many kind words. Some say that "The registrar is sometimes not quite on the ball," and others "wish financial aid was run more efficiently." Other students offer more generalized critiques: The "administration is inept, unaccountable, and seem to be blind-folded half the time"; "They basically give you a run around. "

Life

"Chestnut Hill College is located on the border of Philadelphia, so there is plenty to do when you step off campus." You can catch "either the Chestnut Hill west or east train into Center City. From there, you can get anywhere. You can also catch the R5 in Ambler (5 miles away) and go up towards Doylestown. You have this safe country, old time feel with the Chestnut Hill area, but you are minutes from anything you could ever want for entertainment." Within the Chestnut Hill area itself students go "down Germantown Ave. for fun. There are a lot of great shops and places to eat on the avenue." "There is also a mall and a movie theater nearby and many campus organizations hold events on campus." The social crossroads of campus is the piazza, where students are almost always hanging out "regardless of how cold it is, and joking around." Because of the school's strict alcohol policies, students also "go off campus to parties whether at a different college or someone's house." The general vibe amongst undergraduates is that there is a time for work and a time for play: "On weeknights, we have heavy workloads, but on Thursday to Sunday we have fun." Students' biggest complaint about living conditions at Chestnut Hill concerns the on-campus fare. Simply put, "the caf food is horrible."

Student Body

The typical student at Chestnut Hill is "between the ages of 18–23," "middle-class," and from the East Coast, most probably from "from the tri-state area." He or she is "goal-oriented" and "focused," but also "very outgoing, friendly and willing to help just about anybody." This person is "involved in campus affairs" and "does a lot of volunteer work," but "could be of any ethnicity." Because of the small size of the school, "everyone knows everyone." In general, the school has a "laid back atmosphere; you can wear sweatpants and a hoodie and not worry" that you will be judged for your sartorial slovenliness. "There are a few atypical students but there does not seem to be any prejudice or discrimination towards them."

THE PRINCETON REVIEW SAYS

Admissions

Very important factors considered include: Application essay, rigor of secondary school record. *Important factors considered include:* Academic GPA, recommendation(s), standardized test scores, character/personal qualities, extracurricular activities, interview. *Other factors considered include:* Class rank, alumni/ae relation, level of applicant's interest, talent/ability, volunteer work, work experience. SAT or ACT required; TOEFL required of all international applicants. High school diploma is required and GED is accepted. *Academic units recommended:* 4 English, 3 mathematics, 3 science, 2 foreign language, 4 social studies.

Finanancial Aid

Students should submit: FAFSA. Regular filing deadline is 4/15. The Princeton Review suggests that all financial aid forms be submitted as soon as possible after January 1. *Need-based scholarships/grants offered:* Federal Pell, SEOG, state scholarships/grants, private scholarships, the school's own gift aid. *Loan aid offered:* FFEL Subsidized Stafford, FFEL Unsubsidized Stafford, FFEL PLUS, Federal Perkins Applicants will be notified of awards on a rolling basis beginning 1/31. Federal Work-Study Program available. Off-campus job opportunities are good.

The Inside Word

Admissions officers rank high school transcript and personal essays as the most important factors in determining who gets into Chestnut Hill. Some extra sweat invested into those personal essays could help an applicant overcome less-than-impressive standardized test scores. A good interview can also help a lot here.

THE SCHOOL SAYS " . . . "

From The Admissions Office

"Chestnut Hill College provides students with an opportunity for the highest quality education needed to achieve personal and professional success. We offer 30 majors and 39 minors that can lead to countless career opportunities. Over 82 percent of our faculty possess the highest degree in their field. They are professors who share a love for learning and readily make themselves available outside of class. There are also opportunities to study abroad and create individualized majors.

"College is much more than declaring a major or cramming for finals. Joining others who share your passion is an ideal way to expand your horizons and build on your classroom education. At Chestnut Hill College there are over 25 organizations devoted to a variety of student interests—everything from the biology club to Amnesty International. There are also 14 NCAA Division II teams, with plans to expand the number of sports offered. If your sports pursuits are of an individual nature, you can go horseback riding, mountain biking in Fairmount Park, or Rollerblading from the Philadelphia suburbs to the art museum.

"At Chestnut Hill College, we pride ourselves on our philosophy of holistic education. We believe that a curriculum should go beyond the lecture hall, off the reading list, and out of the library. It should emphasize growth of the whole person not only through a liberal arts education but also through an exciting social life, a healthy spiritual life, and a well-rounded active life, therefore exposing students to the best college has to offer."

For even more information on this school, turn to page 460 of the "Stats" section.

CITY UNIVERSITY OF NEW YORK—BARUCH COLLEGE

UNDERGRADUATE ADMISSIONS, ONE BERNARD BARUCH WAY BOX H-0720, NEW YORK, NY 10010
ADMISSIONS: 646-312-1400 • FAX: 646-312-1361 • E-MAIL: ADMISSIONS@BARUCH.CUNY.EDU • WEBSITE: WWW.BARUCH.CUNY.EDU

RATINGS
Quality of Life: 74   Academic: 73   Admissions: 88   Financial Aid: 70

STUDENTS SAY ". . ."

Academics

Baruch College consists of three schools, and although its School of Arts and Sciences and School of Public Affairs are both fine, it's the Zicklin School of Business that garners nearly all the attention here (as well over three-quarters of the student body). Zicklin offers a "very demanding business-oriented program that provides a great education in an overcrowded environment" where "it's very easy to get

> **SURVEY SAYS . . .**
> *Great computer facilities*
> *Great library*
> *Diverse student types on campus*
> *Students love New York, NY*
> *Very little drug use*

lost," but just as easy for go-getters to access "unparalleled internships, career, and networking opportunities to major global companies' headquarters." Because New York City is a worldwide finance capital, Baruch's connections and internships provide "a gateway to the world of finance," and it is for this reason—as well as for the fact that "tuition is about one-fourth what it is at NYU," making it "the best college value in New York City"—that students flock to Baruch. Students warn that you must be willing to "put 110 percent into your studies and take advantage of the NYC network and Starr Career Development Center" to reap all available benefits here. Those who make the effort will discover a career office that "works tirelessly to prepare its students for the working world. Not only do they offer workshops on how to make yourself an attractive candidate, they also offer counseling and even resume reviews to make sure your resume is perfect, as well as mock interviews that help you analyze your strengths and weaknesses as an interviewer."

Life

Baruch has no campus, just a collection of six buildings scattered over four city blocks. Most of the action centers around the 17-story Newman Vertical Campus facility, which is "beautiful" but "does not offer a lot of things to do" between classes. Furthermore, the mostly residential area surrounding the school offers "few places you can hang out at, especially when you have huge breaks between classes." Although the building is fairly new, "the escalators almost never work" and the elevators "are always as packed as the commute on the train." Many here grumpily opt for the stairway. School-related extracurriculars are hampered by the lack of a "real campus" and by the fact that many students are commuters who work part-time. Some get involved in community service and/or major-related clubs and organizations, but anyone coming here for a traditional college experience will be sorely disappointed. Access to New York City, for most, more than compensates for this drawback.

Student Body

The "hard-working" student body at Baruch could well be "the most diverse university in the country." It's the sort of place where "You can eat samosas on Tuesday, mooncakes on Wednesday, and falafel on Thursdays for free because of all the cultural events that are held." Students brag that "hundreds of countries are represented in our student body" and note that "The one common thread would be we are mostly business-oriented and have jobs/internships outside of school." While students get along well in class, outside the classroom they can be "very cliquey." One student explains, "If you know people from your high school, you stick with them; if you're a foreign student you stick with others from your home country. Otherwise you get the cold shoulder." Because "the school puts tremendous pressure on grades," most here are "extremely stressed."

THE PRINCETON REVIEW SAYS

Admissions

Very important factors considered include: Rigor of secondary school record, Academic GPA, Standardized test scores. *Important factors considered include:* Application Essay, Recommendation(s). *Other factors considered include:* Class rank, Interview, Extracurricular activities, Talent/ability, Character/personal qualities, Alumni/ae relation, Work experience. SAT or ACT required. TOEFL required of all international applicants. High school diploma is required and GED is accepted. *Academic units required:* 4 English, 3 mathematics, 2 science, (2 science labs), 2 foreign language, 4 social studies. *Academic units recommended:* 4 mathematics, 3 foreign language, 1 academic elective.

Financial Aid

Students should submit: FAFSA. The Princeton Review suggests that all financial aid forms be submitted as soon as possible after January 1. *Need-based scholarships/grants offered:* Federal Pell, SEOG, state scholarships/grants, private scholarships, the school's own gift aid, City merit scholarships. *Loan aid offered:* Federal Perkins. Applicants will be notified of awards on a rolling basis beginning 4/30. Federal Work-Study Program available. Institutional employment available. Off-campus job opportunities are excellent.

The Inside Word

In 2001, Baruch opened its new state-of-the-art business school building, greatly upgrading the school's profile in its hallmark academic field. Admissions have grown steadily more competitive since, especially for students seeking undergraduate business degrees. Today, Baruch receives nearly 10 applications for every slot in its freshman class. Your math scores on standardized tests count more heavily here than verbal scores.

THE SCHOOL SAYS ". . ."

From The Admissions Office

"Baruch College is in the heart of New York City. As an undergraduate, you will join a vibrant learning community of students and scholars in the middle of an exhilarating city full of possibilities. Baruch is a place where theory meets practice. You can network with city leaders; secure business, cultural, and nonprofit internships; access the music, art, and business scene; and meet experts who visit our campus. You will take classes that bridge business, arts, science, and social policy, learning from professors who are among the best in their fields.

"Baruch offers 23 majors and 62 minors in three schools: the School of Public Affairs, the Weissman School of Arts and Science and the Zicklin School of Business. Highly qualified undergraduates may apply to the Baruch College Honors program, which offers scholarships, small seminars and honors courses. Students may also study abroad through programs in 100 countries.

"Our seventeen-floor Newman Vertical Campus serves as the college's hub. Here you will find the atmosphere and resources of a traditional college campus, but in a lively urban setting. Our classrooms have state-of-the-art technology, and our library was named the top college library in the nation. Baruch also has a simulated trading floor for students who are interested in Wall Street. You can also enjoy a three-level Athletics and Recreation Complex, which features a 25 meter indoor pool as well as a performing arts complex.

"Baruch's selective admission standards, strong academic programs, and top national honors make it an exceptional educational value."

For even more information on this school, turn to page 460 of the "Stats" section.

CITY UNIVERSITY OF NEW YORK—BROOKLYN COLLEGE

2900 BEDFORD AVENUE, BROOKLYN, NY 11210 • ADMISSIONS: 718-951-5001
FINANCIAL AID: 718-951-5051 • E-MAIL: ADMINGRY@BROOKLYN.CUNY.EDU • WEBSITE: WWW.BROOKLYN.CUNY.EDU

RATINGS
Quality of Life: 64   **Academic:** 64   **Admissions:** 80   **Financial Aid:** 93

STUDENTS SAY ". . ."

Academics

Brooklyn College of the City University of New York, "the poor people's Harvard," provides "a great education for an unbelievable cost." Students here can take advantage of more than 70 undergraduate programs as well as "the infinite resources" of the CUNY system. "Brooklyn College is the kind of place where anything you want is at your finger tips should you choose to seek it out." The "technologically advanced" library "is a great place to study and do research," and there are enough sections of courses in most majors "for even the most time-limited student." All students must complete a broad core curriculum that consists of about a dozen arts and sciences courses and a foreign language requirement. Some students tell us the core is "challenging and engaging." Others disagree. "Many of the core courses—though they have lots of potential—are organized and conducted in a completely uninspired and un-ambitious manner," argues one less-than-thrilled student. "The faculty here seems really invested in the idea of providing quality higher education to students who otherwise might not be able to afford it" but professors are a mixed bag in the classroom. There are "dedicated and knowledgeable professors." And then there are other profs who "are nuts" or "severely lacking" in teaching skills. The administration is generally "uncoordinated and disorganized." "The staff in the offices has the worst attitude ever," grouses an irate first-year student.

> **SURVEY SAYS . . .**
> *Small classes*
> *Great computer facilities*
> *Great library*
> *Diverse student types on campus*
> *Very little drug use*

Life

Brooklyn College's "clean" and "very beautiful" urban campus boasts sprawling lawns and some gorgeous buildings. It's a "very serene, New England-looking place to escape to and learn." "There are no dorms," though, which is something of an inconvenience according to many, and the expensive cafeteria food is "average at best." BC is home to hoards of clubs and organizations, and the school tries hard to get people involved, but students here "aren't really that into social life." "Students often have long commutes to the school from other boroughs" and once classes end, many "rush to get home or to work." "There is no school pride or engagement with others in any constructive way," observes a sophomore. "Few involve themselves in any activities, and those who do are unenthusiastic." On the other hand, why bother with this campus or any campus when the whole of the Big Apple is at your feet? Brooklyn and all of New York City "is in many ways a part of the experience." The immediate neighborhood of Midwood is quiet and unhip, but "tons of places to eat and cool places to shop" are minutes away, and, of course, the even brighter lights of Manhattan are always available.

Student Body

Politically, it's fair to say that BC leans left, but you'll find "conservative political thinkers" as well. Students here are "serious about learning." They are "mostly working students, which means that they are not stuck-up and take nothing for granted." Diversity at Brooklyn College is fabulous. "Students at Brooklyn College are as diverse as the New York City population," proudly boasts a senior. You'll find students of many, many ethnicities, religions, and cultures here. There are people of all ages, too. You've got your "child prodigies." "You have your baby-faced freshman straight from high school and then your older gentleman who could pass for a history professor with his suit and tie." "Brooklyn College is about opportunity for students of all ages, for whenever they have the time, to be able to get their degrees and feel accomplished, without the burden of any kind of community on campus." Students largely lead their own lives in the city, though, and they "don't seem to really mix with each other." There are "many iPod holders who keep to themselves."

THE PRINCETON REVIEW SAYS

Admissions

Very important factors considered include: Academic GPA, rigor of secondary school record, standardized test scores. *Other factors considered include:* Recommendation(s), SAT or ACT required; TOEFL required of all international applicants. High school diploma is required and GED is accepted. *Academic units recommended:* 4 English, 3 mathematics, 3 science, 3 foreign language, 4 social studies, 4 academic electives.

Financial Aid

Students should submit: FAFSA, state aid form The Princeton Review suggests that all financial aid forms be submitted as soon as possible after January 1. *Need-based scholarships/grants offered:* Federal Pell, SEOG, state scholarships/grants, private scholarships, the school's own gift aid. *Loan aid offered:* Direct Subsidized Stafford, Direct Unsubsidized Stafford, Direct PLUS, Federal Perkins Applicants will be notified of awards on a rolling basis beginning 5/1. Federal Work-Study Program available. Institutional employment available. Off-campus job opportunities are excellent.

The Inside Word

Like other CUNY schools, Brooklyn College provides easy access to a college education for students who want one. Brooklyn raises the bar, however, with superior offerings in the arts and sciences. You don't have to have a spotless academic record to get into Brooklyn College, but once there you will receive a solid and respected education.

THE SCHOOL SAYS ". . ."

From The Admissions Office

"Brooklyn College, a premier public liberal arts college founded in 1930, ranked sixth this year in The Princeton Review's America's Best Value Colleges. In the 2003 edition of The Princeton Review's The Best 351 Colleges the college ranked first in the country for its "Beautiful Campus" and fifth for providing the "Best Academic Bang for Your Buck" and for its friendly diversity on the "Students from Different Backgrounds Interact" list. It again placed among the top five in the guide's 2004 edition.

"Brooklyn College's 15,000 undergraduate and graduate students represent the ethnic and cultural diversity of the borough. And the college's accessibility by subway or bus allows students to further enrich their educational experience through New York City's many cultural events and institutions.

"The college continues on an ambitious program of expansion and renewal. The dazzling new library is the most technologically advanced educational and research facility in the CUNY system. A state-of-the-art student services and physical education building, currently under construction, is scheduled to be completed in 2009.

"Respected nationally for its rigorous academic standards, the college takes pride in such innovative programs as its award-winning Freshman Year College; the Honors Academy, which houses nine programs for high achievers; and the core curriculum. Brooklyn College's strong academic reputation has attracted an outstanding faculty of nationally renowned teachers and scholars. Among the awards they have won are Pulitzers, Guggenheims, Fulbrights, and National Institutes of Health grants. Brooklyn College students also receive such prestigious honors as Fulbright Scholarships, the Beinecke Memorial Scholarship, and the Paul and Daisy Soros Fellowships for New Americans.

"Brooklyn College only factors in the Critical Reading and Math components of the current SAT."

For even more information on this school, turn to page 461 of the "Stats" section.

CITY UNIVERSITY OF NEW YORK—HUNTER COLLEGE

695 PARK AVENUE, NEW YORK, NY 10021 • ADMISSIONS: 212-772-4000 • FAX: 212-650-3336
FINANCIAL AID: 212-772-4820 • E-MAIL: ADMISSIONS@HUNTER.CUNY.EDU • WEBSITE: WWW.HUNTER.CUNY.EDU

RATINGS
Quality of Life: 67   **Academic:** 70   **Admissions:** 85   **Financial Aid:** 84

STUDENTS SAY "..."

Academics

Prospective students for looking for an academic "bang for the buck" in New York City should take a long look at Hunter College, the largest (in terms of enrollment) and most selective of the CUNY colleges. Physically, Hunter is a reflection of its hometown; with nearly 16,000 under-graduates attending classes in four buildings on three blocks of the Upper East Side, the "halls of Hunter College

are extremely crowded." There are figurative similarities to the city, too. Like the Big Apple itself, Hunter has a ton to offer academically, but it's not just handed to you: "The academic experience can be inspiring or painfully dull, depending on one's interests, motivation, and desire to be challenged intellectually, as well as luck." Take professors, for example. "Many professors are accomplished and respected," are "often winners of the highest awards in their chosen profession[s], work as professionals in New York City, and are excellent contacts for further academic pursuits or for work after college." Others are "graduate students with limited experience or time" for students. Moreover, "Dealing with administrative matters at this school is not for the faint of heart," and "run of the mill transactions (processing of financial aid paperwork, registering for classes)" can "devour hours of your life." But students assure us that "if you are self-motivated you'll be fine." Registration is tough "because everyone is competing against each other for classes," but on the upside, "Hunter's class schedule is very accommodating to people who work either part- or full-time" and "Evening classes are abundant."

Life

As a commuter school, "There isn't as much campus life as you would find in other schools." Only about 600 of Hunter's 16,000 undergraduates live in the college's lone residence hall, and of the vast majority of students who are commuters, many simply "have too much going on outside of school to try to experience all that college life has to offer." But that's not to say that school unity is totally lacking. In lieu of residence life bonding experiences, "Clubs are very good at connecting people with similar interests." Plus, during the school day, "There's plenty of places [around campus] to just lounge with friends." Off campus—the question is, what isn't there? For those who like to unwind outside, "The school is close to Central Park." For the more urban-minded, "There are concerts, Broadway plays, and comedy shows." There are "movies," "great restaurants, bars, nightclubs, and shopping." And let's not forget that this is New York City; "just walking down the street can be a very entertaining experience."

Student Body

The typical Hunter student "is from one of the five boroughs and commutes to school every day." That's pretty much where generalizations of the student body end. Hunter College has made repeated appearances on this publication's "Diverse Student Population" top 20 ranking list, and for good reason. "In terms of socioeconomic status, immigrants, languages, cultures, religion, race, ethnicity, age . . . Hunter has it all." "Students range in age from newly graduated high schoolers to retirees." And "There really doesn't seem to be [a] dominant ethnic group." It's the kind of place where "nothing seems too out of the ordinary," "everyone fits in fine," and where it won't surprise you to see a "White punk rock girl having a friendly conversation with a Muslim girl in the full head-to-toe [garb]." If you must generalize, it's easier to say what most Hunter students are not. This list is short: "out-of-state students" who are "not liberal."

THE PRINCETON REVIEW SAYS

Admissions

Very important factors considered include: Application essay, academic GPA, rigor of secondary school record, standardized test scores, SAT or ACT required; High school diploma is required and GED is accepted. *Academic units required:* 2 English, 2 mathematics, 1 science, (1 science labs). *Academic units recommended:* 4 English, 3 mathematics, 2 science, 2 foreign language, 4 social studies, 1 visual/performing arts, 1 academic elective.

Financial Aid

Students should submit: FAFSA, state aid form The Princeton Review suggests that all financial aid forms be submitted as soon as possible after January 1. *Need-based scholarships/grants offered:* Federal Pell, state scholarships/grants, the school's own gift aid. *Loan aid offered:* Direct Subsidized Stafford, Direct Unsubsidized Stafford, Direct PLUS, Federal Perkins, state loans, college/university loans from institutional funds. , CUNY Student Assistance Program(CUSTA), Aide for Part-Time-Study (APTS), SEEK . Applicants will be notified of awards on a rolling basis beginning 5/15.

The Inside Word

In terms of statistics, Hunter College is the most selective of the CUNY undergraduate colleges, but this doesn't mean that you have to be an academic superstar in high school to be admitted. Hunter is, after all, first and foremost a CUNY, dedicated to educating the citizens of New York City. But given an applicant pool comprised mainly of New York City residents, high school grades and test scores are the main factors separating those admitted from those who are not. If you are planning to apply to Hunter's Honors College, note that applications are due December 15, rather than on the regular application deadline of March 15.

THE SCHOOL SAYS "..."

From The Admissions Office

"Located in the heart of Manhattan, Hunter offers students the stimulating learning environment and career-building opportunities you might expect from a college that's been a part of the world's most exciting city since 1870. The largest college in the City University of New York, Hunter pulses with energy. Hunter's vitality stems from a large, highly diverse faculty and student body. Its schools—Arts and Sciences, Education, the Health Professions, and Social Work—provide an affordable first-rate education. Undergraduates have extraordinary opportunities to conduct high-level research under renowned faculty, and many opt for credit-bearing internships in such exciting fields as media, the arts, and government. The college's high standards and special programs ensure a challenging education. The Block Program for first-year students keeps classmates together as they pursue courses in the liberal arts, pre-health science, pre-nursing, premed, or honors. A range of honors programs is available for students with strong academic records, including the highly competitive tuition-free Hunter CUNY Honors College for entering freshmen and the Thomas Hunter Honors Program, which emphasizes small classes with personalized mentoring by outstanding faculty. Qualified students also benefit from Hunter's participation in minority science research and training programs, the prestigious Andrew W. Mellon Minority Undergraduate Program, and many other passports to professional success.

"Applicants for the Fall 2008 entering class are required to take either the SAT or the ACT. We will accept scores from the new SAT and scores from the old (prior to March 2005) version of the SAT. We will use the student's best scores from any of these tests."

For even more information on this school, turn to page 461 of the "Stats" section.

CITY UNIVERSITY OF NEW YORK—QUEENS COLLEGE

65-30 KISSENA BOULEVARD, FLUSHING, NY 11367 • ADMISSIONS: 718-997-5000 • FAX: 718-997-5617
FINANCIAL AID: 718-997-5101 • E-MAIL: ADMISSIONS@QC.EDU • WEBSITE: WWW.QC.EDU

RATINGS
Quality of Life: 67   Academic: 72   Admissions: 60*   Financial Aid: 64

STUDENTS SAY ". . ."

Academics

New York state residents can get "a great education for a cheap price" at Queens College, one of the premier campuses of the City University of New York system. The school's affordable tuition "gives many students a chance to get a higher education." Some here go so far as to call QC "the Harvard of the CUNY system," although students at Baruch, Hunter, City College, and Brooklyn College would probably beg to differ. Regardless of its relative status in the CUNY system, QC undoubtedly provides "great and challenging programs" that are "unique and comprehensive, and are compatible [with one's objectives]." With no residence halls on or near the campus, QC serves a commuter population focused on "building career opportunities" by "getting an education in service of your future profession (and maybe having some fun)." Accounting, psychology, health sciences, and sociology are among the most popular majors here; QC is also home to a competitive school of music. Students at QC tell us that "the administration is okay—comparable to any other out there," and that teachers here are surprisingly "easy to talk to and very helpful, not at all intimidating. You're not afraid to express yourself in class." Students say "smaller classes" and "more students in campus involvement" would be nice, but overall they are satisfied with the college's "multicultural feast sprinkled with a quasi-intellectual environment."

> **SURVEY SAYS . . .**
> *Large classes*
> *Great library*
> *Diverse student types on campus*
> *Students love Flushing, NY*
> *Dorms are like dungeons*
> *Students are happy*
> *Very little drug use*

Life

Queens College "is a commuter school, so campus life is not very lively." Its students "are primarily education- and career-oriented." Many "Students work part-time jobs so they really do not have much time left for other activities." Even so, "Queens has a strong community that is diverse and conducive to positive social interactions and communication." The campus is home to tons of "clubs and organizations," and those with the time to do so report that "joining a club helps make the experience at Queens College worthwhile." One student writes, "Political clubs are pretty popular. A lot of times there are club fairs on the grass. Also, anyone can play club sports. The girls could join the soccer club with the boys if they wanted to." While few students stick around campus once their final classes for the day are done, "Between classes students lounge around in the cafeterias or Student Union to talk with friends." Undergrads tell us that there are events to go to "almost every day of the week," in part because the school's New York City location allows it to attract some prominent speakers. The QC campus is surprisingly large and sports a surprisingly large expanse of green for an urban campus. Hometown Queens is a truly international borough and the area surrounding QC is no exception; right outside the campus gates students will find restaurants serving everything from kosher to Korean, from pizza to pita sandwiches.

Student Body

"There is no typical student at Queens College, and that's what's great about the student body," say the students who belong to this "diverse and dedicated community." "Every racial background imaginable is represented and has a group [on campus], and every religious background is apparent." QC is a place where "Everywhere you turn people are able to speak more than one language." There's also plenty of diversity in personality types, although all students tend to be "very focused." Expect "some very religious students" and some nonbelievers as well; "Most students are very different and that makes it easy for everybody to fit in." In short, "Everyone is unique" here, but students across the board "work hard, and are eager to learn," and "This is something that bonds people together."

THE PRINCETON REVIEW SAYS

Admissions

Very important factors considered include: Academic GPA, rigor of secondary school record, standardized test scores, SAT or ACT required; TOEFL required of all international applicants. High school diploma is required and GED is accepted. *Academic units required:* 4 English, 3 mathematics, 2 science, (2 science labs), 3 foreign language, 4 social studies. *Academic units recommended:* 3 science, (3 science labs).

Financial Aid

Students should submit: FAFSA, and New York state application The Princeton Review suggests that all financial aid forms be submitted as soon as possible after January 1. *Need-based scholarships/grants offered:* Federal Pell, SEOG, ACG and SMART grants, state and city scholarships/grants, private scholarships, the school's own gift aid. *Loan aid offered:* Direct Subsidized Stafford, Direct Unsubsidized Stafford, Direct PLUS, Federal Perkins, and Graduate PLUS. Applicants will be notified of awards on a rolling basis beginning 3/1. Federal Work-Study Program available. Institutional employment available. Off-campus job opportunities are good.

The Inside Word

Minority enrollment has declined at CUNY in the past 7 years, partially as a result of changes to admissions criteria and stiffer competition for minority applicants. The school would love to boost its numbers, meaning that qualified minority students could be able to finagle a pretty sweet financial aid package here, making an already economical education even more affordable.

THE SCHOOL SAYS ". . ."

From The Admissions Office

"Often called "the jewel of the City University of New York," Queens College boasts an award-winning faculty committed to scholarship and teaching, as well as students from more than 140 nations. Combined with our fast-growing student-life program, this creates an exceptionally dynamic learning environment.

"Queens expects to open the doors of its first on-campus residence hall in time for the fall '098 semester. The college boasts a beautifully landscaped, 77-acre campus and a traditional quad facing the Manhattan skyline. Powdermaker Hall, our major classroom building, features state-of-the-art technology throughout. Queens College is also the only CUNY college to participate in Division II sports.

"Consistently included in the Princeton Review America's Best Value Colleges, Queens College offers nationally recognized programs in many fields, including the Aaron Copland School of Music. Recently added degrees include a Bachelor of Business Administration with majors in finance, international business, and actuarial studies, and a Bachelor of Science in Graphic Design. Queens College is the ideal choice for aspiring teachers, preparing more educators than any college in the tristate area through its innovative programs. Would-be teachers admitted to the University Teacher Academy receive free tuition while working towards a degree in math or science. The college also participates in the Macaulay Honors College and offers qualified students its own honors programs in the arts and humanities, sciences, and social sciences.

"Applicants for Fall 2008 should submit the SAT comprising Critical Reading, Writing, and Math. Pending further research on the merits of the Writing section, students will continue to be assessed based on their highest Math and Critical Reading scores."

For even more information on this school, turn to page 462 of the "Stats" section.

CLARK UNIVERSITY

950 MAIN STREET, WORCESTER, MA 01610 • ADMISSIONS: 508-793-7431 • FAX: 508-793-8821
FINANCIAL AID: 508-793-7478 • E-MAIL: ADMISSIONS@CLARKU.EDU • WEBSITE: WWW.CLARKU.EDU

RATINGS
Quality of Life: 72   **Academic:** 83   **Admissions:** 89   **Financial Aid:** 90

STUDENTS SAY ". . ."

Academics

Clark University is a "vibrant," "left-wing" liberal arts school in Worcester, Massachusetts. There are "good research opportunities" and standout offerings in psychology, geography, and the hard sciences. Clark also offers an accelerated, one-year Master's program in several majors at no extra charge. Coursework is "hard but doable." "I am challenged but not burned out," reports an English major. "Overall, you'll get a lot

> **SURVEY SAYS . . .**
> *Large classes*
> *Students are friendly*
> *Frats and sororities are unpopular*
> *or nonexistent*
> *Political activism is popular*

out of Clark if you're willing to work for it." "The small size is very comfortable and welcoming" and "Class discussions are often interesting and enlightening." Professors are generally "committed to facilitating their students' education." "Most get very enthusiastic when teaching." "I've never had a class here with a sage on a stage who just stands behind a lectern and reads from their lecture notes without making eye contact," reports a government major. "My professors have always been available outside of class for help," adds a business major. However, there are also some "utter bores" who "really don't seem to know what they are teaching." The range of classes is "limited" as well. "There is not much variety" and popular courses "fill up fast." Views of the administration are very mixed. Some students call management "nondescript." Others contend that Clark's bureaucracy "rivals some small countries." Still others insist that the brass is "very visible and accessible" and "tries to listen to what the students want."

Life

Some buildings on Clark's "pretty compact" campus are "falling apart." Some classrooms are "kind of crappy." "The food leaves something to be desired," too. "Please send frozen dinners," begs a sophomore. Socially, there's a community feel. Many students are involved in community service and various kinds of activism. "Politics play a huge role." "Every student here believes strongly in something, which makes for an interesting campus." "There aren't big turnouts" at athletic events. "Students are actually more likely to attend a lecture on refugees from Rwanda than a basketball game," predicts a senior. "Many students hang out in small groups in their dorms, suites, or apartments." "There's a substance-free scene." There's also "plenty of weed and alcohol with dabbles here and there into harder drugs." "There is the huge kegger like once a month." "Clark isn't a major party school," though. "People here like to be mellow." "The area around the school isn't the greatest" but some students tell us that Worcester is "a perfectly good place to go to school." "Nightlife off campus is fun," they say, and "there are so many restaurants, it's ridiculous." Also, the "extremely active" Colleges of Worcester Consortium allows students to attend classes and events at several nearby schools. Others students complain that "the city of Worcester is depressing and gloomy at best." "It's unfortunate that Clark is where it is," laments one Clarkie. When students want to escape, Boston isn't too far.

Student Body

"If you couldn't find your niche in high school, you will probably find it at Clark," advises a junior. "It is kind of a haven for the awkward and slightly awkward." Clarkies are an "eclectic" "collection of independent minds." "There's a little of everything." "You can carve your own path here without being a loner." Conservatives are "accepted with curiosity" but most students are "socially conscious" types who "scream their bleeding liberal hearts out at any given cause of the week." Clark also "has an artsy feel." "Hipsteresque" "groovy people" who "dress sloppily in expensive clothes" are numerous. Jocks are here but they are "in the vast minority." "The closet-rich hippie" is not uncommon. However, many students tell us that Clark's flower-power reputation is unwarranted. "Sure, there are maybe a token five students who don't wear shoes, don't shower as often as most people would like, and own bongos," asserts a sophomore, "but three of them are posers anyway." You'll find "various sexual orientations" at Clark but ethnic diversity is pretty paltry. There is a strong contingent of Jewish students and a large population of "filthy rich" international students but little in the way of traditionally underrepresented minorities.

THE PRINCETON REVIEW SAYS

Admissions

Very important factors considered include: Academic GPA, recommendation(s), rigor of secondary school record, standardized test scores, character/personal qualities. *Important factors considered include:* Application essay, extracurricular activities, talent/ability, volunteer work. *Other factors considered include:* Class rank, alumni/ae relation, first generation, geographical residence, interview, level of applicant's interest, racial/ethnic status, work experience. SAT or ACT required; TOEFL required of all international applicants. High school diploma is required and GED is accepted. *Academic units recommended:* 4 English, 3 mathematics, 3 science, (2 science labs), 2 foreign language, 2 social studies, 2 history.

Financial Aid

Students should submit: FAFSA, CSS/Financial Aid PROFILE Regular filing deadline is 2/1. The Princeton Review suggests that all financial aid forms be submitted as soon as possible after January 1. *Need-based scholarships/grants offered:* Federal Pell, SEOG, state scholarships/grants, the school's own gift aid. *Loan aid offered:* FFEL Subsidized Stafford, FFEL Unsubsidized Stafford, FFEL PLUS, Federal Perkins, state loans Applicants will be notified of awards on or about 3/31. Federal Work-Study Program available. Institutional employment available. Off-campus job opportunities are good.

The Inside Word

Clark is surrounded by formidable competitors, and its selectivity suffers because of it. Most B students will encounter little difficulty gaining admission. Given the university's solid academic environment and access to other member colleges in the Worcester Consortium, it can be a terrific choice for students who are not up to the ultra-competitive admission expectations of "top-tier" universities.

THE SCHOOL SAYS "..."

From The Admissions Office

"Challenge Convention, Change Our World" isn't just a motto at Clark University. It's a long tradition that our students and faculty continue in their work—inside and outside the classroom—every day. At Clark, students and faculty are encouraged to follow their intellectual curiosity, seek innovative solutions to real-world problems and create positive change in the world.

"Clark's vibrant intellectual environment is built upon learning through inquiry, making a difference and experiencing diverse cultures. These key elements of a Clark education permeate campus life through courses, independent projects, internships, and other learning opportunities; through research and social action, both locally and globally; through the diverse, urban campus community; through interactions with members of the Clark community, and study-abroad experiences.

"Clark as an institution and its faculty and students have an obligation and a rare opportunity to make our world a better place. Whether in science and technology, international development or business, students who apply to Clark want to be in an environment that will challenge their assumptions and encourage them to understand the ways in which their work as adults will make a difference.

"Clark requires that students submit scores from the SAT. Students will be judged by their performance in Critical Reading and Math. Pending further analysis of the new Writing section, writing aptitude is evaluated as part of the application review process."

For even more information on this school, turn to page 462 of the "Stats" section.

CLARKSON UNIVERSITY

PO Box 5605, Potsdam, NY 13699 • Admissions: 315-268-6479 • Fax: 315-268-7647
Financial Aid: 315-268-7699 • E-mail: admissions@clarkson.edu • Website: www.clarkson.edu

RATINGS
Quality of Life: 62   Academic: 70   Admissions: 86   Financial Aid: 63

STUDENTS SAY "..."

Academics

A "demanding," "hands-on," and "absolutely innovative" academic environment is the big draw at tech-heavy Clarkson University in the "frozen wasteland" of northern New York. Opportunities "for co-ops, internships, and jobs" are another great feature. "Companies love to hire future employees" here. The hard sciences and other fields "are growing," but Clarkson basically remains an "engineering school with some business classes." For engineers, "Clarkson is all about preparing you for the ridiculous amount of work you will get in the real world by giving you an even more ridiculous amount of work." Outstanding programs for business majors include entrepreneurship and supply chain management. Classroom discussion is generally rare here and the faculty gets wildly mixed reviews, which is pretty normal wherever techies congregate. Some professors are "super friendly," and "willing to meet outside of their office hours." "Others couldn't teach at elementary schools" and are "more interested in their own research than their classes." Opinions concerning the administration also vary. Some students call management "very visible" and "truly concerned about student life." Others strongly disagree." "I feel like they market to get students in," vents a senior, "and then really drop the ball." We would be remiss if we did not also add that Clarkson's library is "worthless."

Life

"There's nothing to do" in "extremely rural" Potsdam. "Don't come here if you like the city," advises a senior. "There is a bittersweet relationship between the students and Clarkson," adds a freshman. The "dreary" campus is full of "atrocious" "concrete buildings." The food is "horrible." The "overcrowded" dorms "could use some updating." Winters are "cold and desolate." On the plus side, the students here are "fairly tight knit." "It's a small campus with small classes in a small town" explains a junior, "so people get a chance to develop meaningful relationships." Also, the Adirondack Mountains are "very close" and "a lot of the students" are into the outdoors. If you like ice hockey, it's "the most popular thing on campus." The team here is a Division I powerhouse and home games "bring the whole school together" "We show so much school spirit it's like the other team's fans aren't there," vaunts a first-year student. Business majors (and others) reportedly have "copious amounts of free time." For the engineers, though, grading can be "merciless" and "downtime is a luxury." It's "very hard to achieve good grades but rewarding when you do." Weekend life at Clarkson "gets rowdy." "Greek life is pretty popular" and "stoners and drunks" are abundant. However students "just stay in their dorms" "all day and night" playing "way too many videogames."

Student Body

"It's mostly white males and Asians" "looking to get managerial and high-end engineering jobs" here. "There are many athletes" and plenty of business majors with "gelled hair." Overall, though, Clarkson students are "something of a nerdy crowd." "The typical student is a nerdy white guy," observes a senior. "The only people I have my nerdy classes with are other nerdy white guys." "Pretty much everyone looks the same from an outsider's view," agrees a sophomore. "Diversity has a different meaning at Clarkson," adds a junior. "What type of a techie are you?" Students describe themselves as "very smart," "hardworking," and "generally ambitious." A large contingent is "friendly" and outgoing. The "socially awkward" "quiet kid in high school" who "doesn't understand hygiene" is also here in spades. Clarkson's "horrible ratio of men to women" makes for a "miserable sausage fest," at least according to many males. Meanwhile, women have their own complaints. "It's hard to find a good looking guy," laments a senior. "There is a saying: 'although the odds are good, the goods are odd.'" "If you take out most of the antisocial engineering boys, the ratio becomes closer to 50:50." Other students claim that the ratio is "improving" and note that "SUNY Potsdam isn't far."

> **SURVEY SAYS . . .**
> *Career services are great*
> *Students are friendly*
> *Low cost of living*
> *Everyone loves the Golden Knights*
> *Lots of beer drinking*
> *Hard liquor is popular*

THE PRINCETON REVIEW SAYS

Admissions

Very important factors considered include: Academic GPA, rigor of secondary school record, interview. *Important factors considered include:* Class rank, recommendation(s), standardized test scores, extracurricular activities, volunteer work. *Other factors considered include:* Application essay, alumni/ae relation, character/personal qualities, first generation, level of applicant's interest, talent/ability, work experience. SAT Subject Tests recommended; SAT or ACT required; TOEFL required of all international applicants. High school diploma is required and GED is accepted. *Academic units required:* 4 English, 3 mathematics, 2 science. *Academic units recommended:* 4 mathematics, 3 science.

Financial Aid

Students should submit: FAFSA, institution's own financial aid form, state aid form. The Princeton Review suggests that all financial aid forms be submitted as soon as possible after January 1. *Need-based scholarships/grants offered:* Federal Pell, SEOG, state scholarships/grants, private scholarships, the school's own gift aid, HEOP. *Loan aid offered:* Direct Subsidized Stafford, Direct Unsubsidized Stafford, Direct PLUS, FFEL Subsidized Stafford, FFEL Unsubsidized Stafford, FFEL PLUS, Federal Perkins, college/university loans from institutional funds. , Private/alternative loans. Applicants will be notified of awards on or about 3/19. Federal Work-Study Program available. Institutional employment available. Off-campus job opportunities are excellent.

The Inside Word

Clarkson's acceptance rate is too high for solid applicants to lose much sleep about gaining admission. Serious candidates should interview anyway. If you are particularly solid and really want to come here, it could help you get some scholarship money. Women and minorities will encounter an especially friendly Admissions Committee.

THE SCHOOL SAYS ". . ."

From The Admissions Office

"Clarkson University, a private, nationally ranked research university located in Potsdam, New York, is the institution of choice for 3,000 enterprising, high-ability scholars from diverse backgrounds who embrace challenge and thrive in a rigorous, highly collaborative learning environment.

"Clarkson's programs in engineering, business, the sciences, liberal arts, and health sciences emphasize team-based learning as well as creative problem solving and leadership skills. Clarkson is also on the leading edge of today's emerging technologies and fields of study offering innovative, boundary-spanning degree programs in engineering and management, digital arts and sciences, and environmental science and policy, among others.

"At Clarkson, students and faculty work closely together in a supportive, friendly environment. Students are encouraged to participate in faculty-mentored research projects from their first year, and to take advantage of co-ops and study abroad programs. Our collaborative approach to education translates into graduates in high demand; our placement rates are among the highest in the country. Alumni experience accelerated career growth. One in seven alumni is already a CEO, president, or vice president of a company.

"Recent awards and honors include: Among the Top 100 engineering schools (U.S. News & World Report 2007); ranked number 10 in the nation in 'Supply Chain Management' (U.S. News & World Report 2007); top 25 in the nation in Innovation and Entrepreneurship' (The Princeton Review/Entrepreneur magazine); and among the 'Top 20 Most Wired Colleges' (The Princeton Review/PC magazine 2007). Applicants for Fall 2008 are required to take the ACT with Writing section optional, or the new version of the SAT. We will allow students to submit scores from the old (prior to March 2005) version of the SAT (or ACT) as well, and will use the student's best scores from either test. SAT Subject Tests are recommended but not required."

For even more information on this school, turn to page 463 of the "Stats" section.

COLBY COLLEGE

4800 MAYFLOWER HILL, WATERVILLE, ME 04901-8848 • ADMISSIONS: 207-872-3168 • FAX: 207-872-3474
FINANCIAL AID: 207-872-3168 • E-MAIL: ADMISSIONS@COLBY.EDU • WEBSITE: WWW.COLBY.EDU

RATINGS
Quality of Life: 83   Academic: 91   Admissions: 96   Financial Aid: 94

STUDENTS SAY "..."

Academics

This small, close-knit liberal arts college draws praise from students for its rigorous but caring approach to academics. It's a place where devoted professors "invite students to dinner" and learning happens "for learning's sake." Small classes are one of Colby's biggest draws. "Professors are always willing to go the extra mile," one student says. A senior adds, "Over the course of my time at Colby I've been

> **SURVEY SAYS ...**
> Small classes
> Great food on campus
> Frats and sororities are unpopular
> or nonexistent
> Lots of beer drinking

to at least six different professors' houses for departmental events, class dinners, and group discussions." Professors get high grades for their teaching and accessibility, which together foster a "love for learning" in undergraduates. As one student dryly notes, "Waterville, Maine is not the country's academic capital, so the professors that choose to be at Colby are here to teach, not to use the facilities." This dedication to academics can make Colby an intense place to go to school, and students here aren't "afraid to work hard and study." In addition, students must not only complete their major requirements but also fulfill a hefty load of distribution requirements to graduate. The popular "Jan Plan" lets students take an extra month-long term of focused or independent study in January, sometimes accompanied by an internship. While the administration "works hard to keep students happy and entertained," some feel that their needs are "occasionally ignored in favor of the everlasting quest to turn Colby into a small Ivy."

Life

"Friends and a sense of community drive life at Colby," one senior writes. Students live together in coed, mixed-class dorms. Everything centers around the campus, which is "constructed on a gorgeous wooded hill near the Kennebec River in Central Maine." Since "There isn't a ridiculous amount to do" in these self-contained envirions, "Colby works hard to fill the day with countless events, lectures, discussions, and concerts. People can study hard, party, take advantage of the beautiful outdoors, and most do all three." A student notes that "the size of the school is perfect: On any given day, I could see five friends or acquaintances (and countless familiar faces!) on my way to class." This makes for a friendly atmosphere as "it's easy to start up a conversation with pretty much anyone. When the great outdoors beckons, students answer the call by hiking in autumn and spring, skiing in winter, and participating in traditional outdoor sports like football. A senior explains, "People like to unwind after our incredibly stressful weeks with movies, skiing, and partying." The "alcohol-centered social scene" usually takes place at small dorm parties or at the few local pubs.

Student Body

While the prototypical Colby student may be "White and from 20 minutes outside of Boston," undergrads are quick to point out that their "campus is very open to diversity and ready to embrace it." Students single out the administration for "doing a great job of bringing in a more diverse student population." One student explains that "more and more international students and urban kids are coming through programs like the Posse Scholarship." A junior adds, "We have students here that dress in business suits and bow ties while others walk around in capes." Most students, however, settle for the more general description of "preppy students who enjoy the outdoors and enjoy having a good time." That said, students report that "there's pretty much a place for everyone somewhere at Colby; chances are you'll find people both very similar to you in interests, background, etc. and people who are completely the opposite." One student elaborates, explaining that despite all differences, "The one word I'd use to describe a Colby student is friendly."

THE PRINCETON REVIEW SAYS

Admissions

Very important factors considered include: Rigor of secondary school record, character/personal qualities. *Important factors considered include:* Class rank, application essay, academic GPA, recommendation(s), standardized test scores, extracurricular activities, interview, racial/ethnic status, talent/ability. *Other factors considered include:* Alumni/ae relation, first generation, geographical residence, level of applicant's interest, state residency, volunteer work, work experience. SAT or ACT required; TOEFL required of all international applicants. High school diploma or equivalent is not required. *Academic units recommended:* 4 English, 3 mathematics, 2 science, (2 science labs), 3 foreign language, 2 social studies, 2 academic electives.

Financial Aid

Students should submit: FAFSA and CSS Profile. Regular filing deadline is 2/1. The Princeton Review suggests that all financial aid forms be submitted as soon as possible after January 1. *Need-based scholarships/grants offered:* Federal Pell, SEOG, state scholarships/grants, private scholarships, the school's own gift aid. *Loan aid offered:* Direct Subsidized Stafford, Direct Unsubsidized Stafford, Direct PLUS, FFEL Subsidized Stafford, FFEL Unsubsidized Stafford, FFEL PLUS, Federal Perkins, state loans, college/university loans from institutional funds, alternative loans. Applicants will be notified of awards on or about 4/1. Federal Work-Study Program available. Institutional employment available. Off-campus job opportunities are poor. Colby does not include loans in any of its financial aid packages.

The Inside Word

Colby continues to be both very selective and successful in converting admits to enrollees, which makes for a perpetually challenging admissions process. Currently, only 33 percent of applicants are accepted, so hit those books and ace those exams to stand a fighting chance. One thing that could set you apart from the pack? An interest in travel. Two-thirds of Colby students study abroad—in fact, for some degrees it's required.

THE SCHOOL SAYS ". . ."

From The Admissions Office

"Colby is one of only a handful of liberal arts colleges that offer world-class academic programs, leadership in internationalism, an active community life, and rich opportunities after graduation. Set in Maine on one of the nation's most beautiful campuses, Colby provides students a host of opportunities for active engagement, in Waterville or around the world. The Goldfarb Center for Public Affairs and Civic Engagement connects teaching and research with current political, economic, and social issues at home and abroad. Beginning in 2008-09 Colby replaced loans in its financial aid packages with grants, which don't have to be repaid, making it possible for students to graduate without college-loan debt.

"Students' access to Colby's outstanding faculty is extraordinary, and the college is a leader in undergraduate research and project-based learning. The college has won awards for sustainable environmental practices as well as one of the first Senator Paul Simon Awards for Internationalizing the Campus.

"The challenging academic experience at the heart of Colby's programs is complemented by a vibrant community life and campus atmosphere featuring more than 100 student-run organizations, more than 50 athletic and recreational choices, and numerous leadership and volunteer opportunities.

"Colby graduates succeed, finding their places at the finest medical and other graduate schools, top Wall Street firms, and in the arts, government service, social service, education, and nonprofit organizations.

"Applicants must submit scores from the SAT or the ACT. The optional ACT Writing Test is recommended."

For even more information on this school, turn to page 463 of the "Stats" section.

COLGATE UNIVERSITY

13 OAK DRIVE, HAMILTON, NY 13346 • ADMISSIONS: 315-228-7401 • FAX: 315-228-7544
FINANCIAL AID: 315-228-7431 • E-MAIL: ADMISSION@MAIL.COLGATE.EDU • WEBSITE: WWW.COLGATE.EDU

RATINGS

Quality of Life: 89   Academic: 92   Admissions: 96   Financial Aid: 98

STUDENTS SAY "..."

Academics

Colgate University, "the epitome of a work hard, play hard school," provides "a rigorous academic environment, an outstanding student and faculty population, and an abundance of social opportunities" to its "preppy," "intelligent-but-not-nerdy" student body. Students report that "Colgate is academically strong in the humanities, such as political science, English, psychology, and economics" and "also has good natural sciences programs that are enhanced by the new science building," a $56.3 million structure that houses 40

> **SURVEY SAYS ...**
> *Large classes*
> *Lab facilities are great*
> *Great computer facilities*
> *Great library*
> *Students are happy*
> *Lots of beer drinking*
> *Hard liquor is popular*

research labs, 13 teaching labs, and a teaching/research greenhouse. All students here must complete a set of general education requirements that "force you to look beyond your major work," sometimes leading to discovery of new, unanticipated areas of interest. "It is not uncommon for students to double major in two vastly different departments" as a result of their gen-ed experiences, students tell us. Colgate's size and location foster community-building; the "administration and faculty don't just work at Colgate, but live Colgate. In this way, they are dedicated to your education and create a passionate, hands-on, and inspiring place to learn," translating into "great opportunities to research with great professors and be in leadership positions." The workload is tough here; "At the end of a semester you may have four final exams and 80 pages of writing to do, but that absolutely won't stop you from going out on Friday night. (Saturday night too. And Wednesday night. Maybe Monday also.)"

Life

Colgate University, "the epitome of a work hard, play hard school," provides "a rigorous academic environment, an outstanding student and faculty population, and an abundance of social opportunities" to its "preppy," "intelligent-but-not-nerdy" student body. Students report that "Colgate is academically strong in the humanities, such as political science, English, psychology, and economics" and "also has good natural sciences programs that are enhanced by the new science building," a $56.3 million structure that houses 40 research labs, 13 teaching labs, and a teaching/research greenhouse. All students here must complete a set of general education requirements that "force you to look beyond your major work," sometimes leading to discovery of new, unanticipated areas of interest. "It is not uncommon for students to double major in two vastly different departments" as a result of their gen-ed experiences, students tell us. Colgate's size and location foster community-building; the "administration and faculty don't just work at Colgate, but live Colgate. In this way, they are dedicated to your education and create a passionate, hands-on, and inspiring place to learn," translating into "great opportunities to research with great professors and be in leadership positions." The workload is tough here; "At the end of a semester you may have four final exams and 80 pages of writing to do, but that absolutely won't stop you from going out on Friday night. (Saturday night too. And Wednesday night. Maybe Monday also.)"

Student Body

"When looking from the surface, Colgate students don't appear diverse" because of the "undeniable majority of white students all in Uggs and Oxfords," but "Although most students dress alike, there are great discussions in and out of the classroom because each Colgate student is actually very different from the next once you have the opportunity to talk to them." Even so, just about everyone here concedes that "This is a very preppy campus." Students tend to be "very laid back, but in that perfectly groomed, 'I just rolled out of bed looking this good' kind of way." They are also "passionate about something. Everyone has her own thing to enjoy. It could be a recreational club, a dance group, a community service group, an academic or research project, a student club, etc. You find that a lot of Colgate students are active members in one way or another."

THE PRINCETON REVIEW SAYS

Admissions

Very important factors considered include: Class rank, academic GPA, rigor of secondary school record. *Important factors considered include:* Application essay, recommendation(s), standardized test scores, character/personal qualities, extracurricular activities, talent/ability. *Other factors considered include:* Alumni/ae relation, first generation, geographical residence, racial/ethnic status, volunteer work, work experience. SAT or ACT required; TOEFL required of all international applicants. High school diploma is required and GED is accepted. *Academic units required:* 4 English, 3 mathematics, 3 science, (2 science labs), 3 foreign language, 3 social studies. *Academic units recommended:* 4 English, 4 mathematics, 4 science, (3 science labs), 4 foreign language, 4 social studies.

Financial Aid

Students should submit: FAFSA, CSS/Financial Aid PROFILE, noncustodial PROFILE, business/farm supplement. Regular filing deadline is 1/15. The Princeton Review suggests that all financial aid forms be submitted as soon as possible after January 1. *Need-based scholarships/grants offered:* Federal Pell, SEOG, state scholarships/grants, the school's own gift aid. *Loan aid offered:* FFEL Subsidized Stafford, FFEL Unsubsidized Stafford, FFEL PLUS, Federal Perkins Applicants will be notified of awards on or about 4/1. Federal Work-Study Program available. Institutional employment available. Off-campus job opportunities are fair.

The Inside Word

As at many colleges, Colgate admissions caters to some long-established special interests. Athletes, minorities, and legacies (children of alumni) are among those who benefit from more favorable review. Wait-listed students, take note—less than one percent of students on the waitlist wind up admitted to the school.

THE SCHOOL SAYS ". . ."

From The Admissions Office

"Students and faculty alike are drawn to Colgate by the quality of its academic programs. Faculty initiative has given the university a rich mix of learning opportunities that includes a liberal arts core, 51 academic concentrations, and a wealth of Colgate faculty-led, off-campus study programs in the United States and abroad. But there is more to Colgate than academic life, including more than 160 student organizations, athletics and recreation at all levels, and a full complement of living options set within a campus described as one of the most beautiful in the country. A new center for community service builds upon the tradition of Colgate students interacting with the surrounding community in meaningful ways. Colgate students become extraordinarily devoted alumni, contributing significantly to career networking and exploration programs on and off campus. For students in search of a busy and varied campus life, Colgate is a place to learn and grow."

For even more information on this school, turn to page 464 of the "Stats" section.

COLLEGE OF THE ATLANTIC

105 EDEN STREET, BAR HARBOR, ME 04609 • ADMISSIONS: 800-528-0025 • FAX: 207-288-4126
FINANCIAL AID: 207-288-5015 • E-MAIL: INQUIRY@ECOLOGY.COA.EDU • WEBSITE: WWW.COA.EDU

RATINGS
Quality of Life: 93   **Academic:** 93   **Admissions:** 88   **Financial Aid:** 84

STUDENTS SAY "..."

Academics

Every undergraduate at the tiny College of the Atlantic majors in human ecology. More than a course of study, human ecology is an approach to education that is interdisciplinary, in which all areas of study are seen in relationship to each other. In choosing an area of concentration, students can opt for one of the traditional sub-disciplines such as marine biology or public policy, or they can design their own concentration in another area working on an extensive collection of poetry that incorporates ornithological field-

> ### SURVEY SAYS . . .
> *Small classes*
> *No one cheats*
> *Campus feels safe*
> *Intercollegiate sports are unpopular or nonexistent*
> *Frats and sororities are unpopular or nonexistent*

work, a book-length piece of creative non-fiction that features a student's pre-veterinary internship, or writing a full-fledged green business plan. This leaves students—bonded by a common major—stoked that they still "have the opportunity to shape their own educations. Students who are self-motivated and enthusiastic can have an awesome experience here." Whereas some schools offer a more prescribed program, COA calls on students to arrive inspired to take an active part in carving their own path to graduation. Also setting the school apart is the fact that it doesn't offer tenure to its teachers. Consequently, you'll find only the most dedicated professors at the head of these classrooms. "The professors at our school take a pay cut to work here. They truly love what it is they do, and their classes are incredible." With only 320 students total, it's no wonder that "by the end of your first year, most professors know you even if you haven't taken their classes." Concerning the "optional grades" policy, one sophomore warns prospective students that "just because we have optional grades doesn't mean that you can slack in a class. Evaluations are given at the end of each class. The evaluations give you a whole lot more feedback than a letter grade and make the academic experience a whole lot more personal."

Life

Bar Harbor, Maine, is "a small tourist town, [that's] beautiful in spring and summer, extremely cold and boring in winter." To fill the hole left by the closing of the seasonal Bar Harbor shops and restaurants, students take advantage of a variety of alternative activities. "There are coffeehouses, open mics, guest speakers, dance presentations, puppet shows, talent shows, bands, traveling drama performances, etc. It's wonderful! There will also be discussion groups that will get together. Professors will have their students over for meals. Students living off campus will always cook food together." In town, there's "a great movie theater" called Reel Pizza that serves pizza and beer. For outdoor enthusiasts, COA is a paradise, as it is located literally across the street from Acadia National Park. What's more, the college caters to activities that such a situation lends itself to, with "kayaks and canoes to take out. Many of us share the common passion for hiking. During the snow season, we throw a winter carnival and we also go skiing" and snowshoeing. Since only about a third of the student body resides on campus, "off-campus parties are popular, though there aren't many good ones." That's because "At COA, six people is a big party." In the fall of 2008, COA will open its new Kathryn W. Davis Student Residence Village, green housing with ocean views.

Student Body

"The typical COA student is very self-driven. (You have to be in a curriculum that is so open.) We are also very environmentally friendly. There is a lot of emphasis put on sustainability at the school. We take pride in our organic produce and our hippie ways." If you aren't a hippie when you come to COA, there is a pretty good chance that you'll start developing some of those tendencies before too long, just from pure exposure to the culture. Carnivores can take heart that "there are still meat eaters among our vegetarian population," though "it would be hard to find a right-wing Republican here." While leaning decidedly left on matters political, "People here tend to be accepting, curious, and open-minded, so I think it's hard to be an outcast." For such a small school, COA's student body includes a remarkably high percentage of international students; foreigners account for about one-fifth of the school's undergraduate population, "probably making it one the most diverse places in Maine."

Admissions

Very important factors considered include: Application essay, recommendation(s), rigor of secondary school record. *Important factors considered include:* Class rank, academic GPA, character/personal qualities, extracurricular activities, interview, talent/ability, volunteer work, work experience. *Other factors considered include:* Standardized test scores, alumni/ae relation, first generation, geographical residence, level of applicant's interest, racial/ethnic status, state residency, TOEFL required of all international applicants. High school diploma is required and GED is accepted. *Academic units required:* 4 English, 3 mathematics, 2 science, (2 science labs), 2 social studies. *Academic units recommended:* 4 mathematics, 3 science, 2 foreign language, 2 history, 1 academic elective.

Financial Aid

Students should submit: FAFSA, institution's own financial aid form, noncustodial PROFILE, business/farm supplement. Regular filing deadline is 2/15. The Princeton Review suggests that all financial aid forms be submitted as soon as possible after January 1. *Need-based scholarships/grants offered:* Federal Pell, SEOG, state scholarships/grants, private scholarships, the school's own gift aid. *Loan aid offered:* FFEL Subsidized Stafford, FFEL Unsubsidized Stafford, FFEL PLUS, Federal Perkins Applicants will be notified of awards on or about 4/1. Federal Work-Study Program available. Off-campus job opportunities are good.

The Inside Word

As applicants might expect, admissions standards at College of the Atlantic are somewhat atypical. The school covets students who carve their own intellectual course rather than follow a conventional academic path. Students at COA are expected to bring strong ideas and values to the classroom and applicants are assessed accordingly. Essays and interviews are where candidates make their mark. Of course, the college's integrated approach also means that applicants should have a well-rounded secondary school record. Candidates should also demonstrate a kinship with the philosophy of human ecology.

THE SCHOOL SAYS ". . ."

From The Admissions Office

"College of the Atlantic is a small, intellectually challenging college on Mount Desert Island, Maine. We look for students seeking a rigorous, hands-on, self-directed academic experience. Come for a visit and you will begin to understand that COA's unique approach to education, governance and community life extends throughout its structure. . Resolutely value centered and interdisciplinary—there are no departments and no majors, COA sees its mission as preparing people to become independent thinkers, to challenge conventional wisdom, to deal with pressing global change—both environmental and social—and to be passionately engaged in transforming the world around them into a better place.

"College of the Atlantic does not require standardized testing as part of the application process. Learning and intelligence can be gauged in many ways; standardized test scores are just one of many measures. If an applicant chooses to submit standardized test scores for consideration, the SAT (either version), SAT Subject Tests, or ACT scores are all acceptable."

For even more information on this school, turn to page 464 of the "Stats" section.

COLLEGE OF THE HOLY CROSS

ADMISSIONS OFFICE, ONE COLLEGE STREET, WORCESTER, MA 01610-2395 • ADMISSIONS: 508-793-2443
FAX: 508-793-3888 • FINANCIAL AID: 508-793-2265 • E-MAIL: ADMISSIONS@HOLYCROSS.EDU • WEBSITE: WWW.HOLYCROSS.EDU

RATINGS
Quality of Life: 70   **Academic:** 98   **Admissions:** 96   **Financial Aid:** 92

STUDENTS SAY "..."

Academics

Located in Worcester, the second-largest city in Massachusetts, Holy Cross offers an academic atmosphere that is "always challenging, never boring" thanks to professors who are "genuinely interested in getting their students to think critically about the world." Many students agree that "while it is hard to do well, the professors and overall state of mind here will push you to your maximum potential in every way." With an administration dedicated

> **SURVEY SAYS . . .**
> Small classes
> Great library
> Frats and sororities are unpopular
> or nonexistent
> Lots of beer drinking
> Hard liquor is popular

to making sure that "students are represented on virtually every administrative council at the college," and a system of departmental "student advisory councils which voice student opinion on professors who are up for tenure," it's no wonder the administration "is widely appreciated for its awesome accessibility." This accessibility carries over to the classroom where small class sizes allow for "a lot of faculty-student interaction." As one student explains, "There are no TAs at Holy Cross," which makes it easier for "students who are trying to form relationships" with their "accessible and interested professors." Be warned, however, that if you ever miss a class "Your professor will call to see where you were." Students here enjoy many opportunities for "independent research, study abroad, and intellectual enrichment," including "great internship programs" with "successful Holy Cross alumni" all designed to help them "learn and succeed."

Life

The mantra you might hear repeated often among students at Holy Cross is "work hard, party hard." As one student explains, "Based on all the partying that is done here, you can imagine how hard we work." The school's rigorous academic standards are offset by a lively social scene where the most popular relaxation activities come with a bar tab: "Beer is huge, particularly because our workload here is so intense." Some students boast that they "have a bar for each day of the week" and "theme parties" each weekend. Everyone here is "always active," taking time off from studying to participate in "a varsity team, intramurals, student government, clubs, the newspaper, theater, or music." Holy Cross goes out of its way to "create many on-campus opportunities as well as encourage students to explore off-campus opportunities." "Countless restaurants and bars in Worcester" as well as in nearby Boston and Providence, create "a lively social scene off campus." Physically getting off campus, however, can prove difficult, as "Students cannot have cars until their third year."

Student Body

The typical Holy Cross student is "hardworking, and loves to have fun." With a "general atmosphere of friendliness and acceptance" on campus, most students find it hard to "feel lonely or bored." While the majority of Holy Cross students are "White, Irish Catholics" from "upper-middle-class families," the school's administration has "done a lot of work toward becoming a more diverse and inclusive place." As one student explains, "Most all faculty and administrators are exceptionally welcoming of diversity." Although a Jesuit college, "Religion is not a major issue" here. "Most students do not go to mass though they consider themselves Catholic," and non-Catholics can, if they wish, attend "nondenominational masses" offered on campus. Regardless of their beliefs, Holy Cross students are "very conscious about affairs outside of the college" and "involved in working to better the community." "Devoted to excellence in academics" first and foremost, the typical Holy Cross student "is not afraid to meet new people, go out on the weekends, and have a great time."

Admissions

Very important factors considered include: Class rank, academic GPA, rigor of secondary school record. *Important factors considered include:* Application essay, recommendation(s), alumni/ae relation, character/personal qualities, extracurricular activities, interview. *Other factors considered include:* Standardized test scores, first generation, geographical residence, level of applicant's interest, racial/ethnic status, talent/ability, volunteer work, work experience. TOEFL required of all international applicants. High school diploma is required and GED is accepted. *Academic units recommended:* 4 English, 4 mathematics, 4 science, 3 foreign language, 2 social studies, 2 history, 1 academic elective.

Financial Aid

Students should submit: FAFSA, CSS/Financial Aid PROFILE, noncustodial PROFILE, business/farm supplement, parent and student federal tax returns. Regular filing deadline is 2/1. The Princeton Review suggests that all financial aid forms be submitted as soon as possible after January 1. *Need-based scholarships/grants offered:* Federal Pell, SEOG, state scholarships/grants, private scholarships, the school's own gift aid. *Loan aid offered:* FFEL Subsidized Stafford, FFEL Unsubsidized Stafford, FFEL PLUS, Federal Perkins, MDFA. Applicants will be notified of awards on or about 4/1. Federal Work-Study Program available. Institutional employment available. Off-campus job opportunities are fair.

The Inside Word

Admission to Holy Cross is competitive; therefore, a demanding high school course load is required to be a viable candidate. The college values effective communication skills—it thoroughly evaluates each applicant's personal statement and short essay responses. Interviews are important, especially for those applying early decision. Students who graduate from a Catholic high school might find themselves at a slight advantage.

THE SCHOOL SAYS ". . ."

From The Admissions Office

"When applying to Holy Cross, two areas deserve particular attention. First, the essay should be developed thoughtfully, with correct language and syntax in mind. That essay reflects for the Board of Admissions how you think and how you can express yourself. Second, activity beyond the classroom should be clearly defined. Since Holy Cross [has only] 2,800 students, the chance for involvement/participation is exceptional. The board reviews many applications for academically qualified students. A key difference in being accepted is the extent to which a candidate participates in-depth beyond the classroom—don't be modest; define who you are.

"Standardized test scores (i.e., SAT, SAT Subject Tests, and ACT) are optional. Students may submit their scores if they believe the results paint a fuller picture of their achievements and potential, but those who don't submit scores will not be at a disadvantage in admissions decisions."

For even more information on this school, turn to page 465 of the "Stats" section.

THE COLLEGE OF NEW JERSEY

PO Box 7718, Ewing, NJ 08628-0718 • Admissions: 609-771-2131 • Fax: 609-637-5174
Financial Aid: 609-771-2211 • E-mail: admiss@vm.tcnj.edu • Website: www.tcnj.edu

RATINGS
Quality of Life: 94   Academic: 87   Admissions: 93   Financial Aid: 71

STUDENTS SAY "..."

Academics

Students at The College of New Jersey believe they've found "the best way to get private school education for public school cost." To hear them tell it, The College of New Jersey "is the total package," with "a beautiful campus, great location, top-notch faculty, the newest technology, an interested student body, and competitive sports teams." TCNJ students benefit from their small-school setting, which makes for lots of "interaction between students and professors. The classes are generally 15 to 20 students, enabling greater relationships

> **SURVEY SAYS ...**
> Small classes
> Lab facilities are great
> Great computer facilities
> Great library
> Students are friendly
> Campus feels safe
> Students are happy

between students and their professors." Those relationships yield substantial dividends "when it comes to getting recommendations, taking advantage of internship opportunities, and landing jobs in the 'real world,'" we're told. Of course, first they have to graduate, no small task given that "the classes aren't a joke. They're difficult and a lot of work, but at the end of your 4 years you'll be prepared because the professors know what they're talking about and want to make sure that you do well." Students appreciate that "professors and advisors will go out of their way to help you, whether it is with your schoolwork, your resume, or your career plans. Not only is the caliber of students high, but the professors are willing to work hard for you so you are willing to work hard for them, too!" What students appreciate most is "the affordable price" of a TCNJ education: "You get a great education and it will cost less than $20,000 a year for in-state residents and only a little over for out-of-state students."

Life

The TCNJ campus "is gorgeous, with tree-lined paths and brick buildings in the Georgian Colonial style," though some students wonder whether construction will ever end. Extracurricular options are varied here. Those involved in the Greek scene say it's "always available and fun"; the Greeks and the sports houses are the location of many off-campus parties, we're told. Tuesday, aka "Tuesday Booze Day," is one of the big party nights here, by the way—that's because "The school doesn't offer a lot of classes on Wednesday." There's "always something planned by the college that is announced in the newspaper (e.g., concerts, art exhibits, guest speakers)," and the school's proximity to New York and Philadelphia helps it draw some big names, including, recently, "John Leguizamo, Blessid Union of Souls, the cast of Whose Line is it Anyway?, and Wynton Marsalis." Of course, location also allows for "constant trips running to New York City and other off-campus destinations. Honestly, sometimes it's hard to say no to some of the stuff going on in order to get some work done." Students note that "on [any] given weekend, about half of the population empties out. Most of these students go home, to work, or to visit friends at other schools," but add that "people think everyone goes home on the weekends, and some people do, but for those of us who stay there are fun parties, bars, things to do."

Student Body

TCNJ draws primarily "from New Jersey middle-class suburbia," which "makes for fun 'arguments,' such as: Which is better, North or South Jersey? Is it 'jimmies' or 'sprinkles'? A 'hoagie' or a 'sub'?" A "decent number of students from other backgrounds, states, and countries" supplements the population and adds diversity. Students tend to be "hardworking, diligent, and very bright," and they are "able to balance their 18-credit workload and still have time to blow some steam off on the weekends. They're leaders, both in and out of the classrooms. Our 150-plus student organizations are a testament to that." The school attracts a reasonable cross-section of personality types; one student explains, "There are many different groups at TCNJ. There are athletes, artists, Greeks, and the few who are found playing with swords on Medieval Day out on the lawn. Everyone basically does their own thing, and it's generally just accepted."

THE PRINCETON REVIEW SAYS

Admissions

Very important factors considered include: Class rank, application essay, rigor of secondary school record, standardized test scores, character/personal qualities, extracurricular activities, talent/ability. *Important factors considered include:* Recommendation(s), volunteer work. *Other factors considered include:* Academic GPA, alumni/ae relation, first generation, geographical residence, interview, racial/ethnic status, state residency, work experience. SAT or ACT required; TOEFL required of all international applicants. High school diploma is required and GED is accepted. *Academic units required:* 4 English, 3 mathematics, 3 science, (2 science labs), 2 foreign language, 2 social studies. *Academic units recommended:* 4 English, 3 mathematics, 3 science, (3 science labs), 3 foreign language, 3 social studies.

Financial Aid

Students should submit: FAFSA. The Princeton Review suggests that all financial aid forms be submitted as soon as possible after January 1. *Need-based scholarships/grants offered:* Federal Pell, SEOG, state scholarships/grants, private scholarships, the school's own gift aid. *Loan aid offered:* FFEL Subsidized Stafford, FFEL Unsubsidized Stafford, FFEL PLUS, Federal Perkins, Federal Nursing Applicants will be notified of awards on a rolling basis beginning 6/1. Federal Work-Study Program available. Institutional employment available. Off-campus job opportunities are excellent.

The Inside Word

Don't be deceived by the relatively high acceptance rate at The College of New Jersey. The school boasts a number of rigorous and respected academic programs. Applicants cannot slack off in high school and expect to be handed an acceptance letter—or a favorable first-semester transcript. Those who have succeeded in demanding classes will have the opportunity to receive a stellar education at this lovely public institution and at bargain prices no less.

THE SCHOOL SAYS "..."

From The Admissions Office

"The College of New Jersey is one of the United States' great higher education success stories. With a long history as New Jersey's preeminent teacher of teachers, the college has grown into a new role as educator of the state's best students in a wide range of fields. The College of New Jersey has created a culture of constant questioning—a place where knowledge is not merely received but reconfigured. In small classes, students and faculty members collaborate in a rewarding process: As they seek to understand fundamental principles, apply key concepts, reveal new problems, and pursue new lines of inquiry, students gain a fluency of thought in their disciplines. The college's 289-acre tree-lined campus is a union of vision, engineering, beauty, and functionality. Neoclassical Georgian Colonial architecture, meticulous landscaping, and thoughtful design merge in a dynamic system, constantly evolving to meet the needs of TCNJ students. About 50 percent of TCNJ's 2004 entering class will be academic scholars, with large numbers of National Merit finalists and semifinalists. More than 400 students in the class received awards from New Jersey's Outstanding Student Recruitment Program. The College of New Jersey is bringing together the best ideas from around the nation and building a new model for public undergraduate education on one campus . . . in New Jersey!

"The College of New Jersey will accept both the new and old SAT (administered prior to March 2005 and without a Writing component), as well as the ACT with or without the Writing component."

For even more information on this school, turn to page 465 of the "Stats" section.

COLUMBIA UNIVERSITY

535 WEST 116TH STREET, NEW YORK, NY 10027 • ADMISSIONS: 212-854-2521 • FAX: 212-894-1209
FINANCIAL AID: 212-854-3711 • E-MAIL: UGRAD-ADMISS@COLUMBIA.EDU • WEBSITE: WWW.STUDENTAFFAIRS.COLUMBIA.EDU/

RATINGS
Quality of Life: 93   Academic: 96   Admissions: 99   Financial Aid: 96

STUDENTS SAY "..."

Academics

> SURVEY SAYS . . .
> *Great library*
> *Diverse student types on campus*
> *Students love New York, NY*
> *Great off-campus food*
> *Campus feels safe*
> *Students are happy*

Located on the upper west side of Manhattan, "Columbia University provides an exceptional education, fusing the chaos of New York City" with "the rigors of the Ivy League." The course work here "can be tremendously grueling." Expect to do a lot of studying and "thinking about the world in ways that are new and occasionally uncomfortable." Columbia's "inspiring" professors are "leaders in their fields" who are "brilliant (and don't hide the fact that they, too, think so)." They are "obsessed with what they study" and their "Enthusiasm is contagious." A few professors "have that certain scholarly air of arrogance" and can be tough graders. However, "The professors who are known to grade harshly and give hard tests are usually the ones who teach the best." Central to the academic experience here is the "eye-opening, thought-provoking" core curriculum, a sequence that immerses students in Western philosophy, literature, and fine arts. "Columbia's core prepares you to excel in any field," explains one first-year student. Taking core classes also helps "when you're first trying to make new friends" because "Everyone is dealing with the same classes." Most students feel that the administration here "listens to students" and "generally gets the job done," but can be "bureaucratic" at times. Be warned, however, that "advising is definitely not the strong point of Columbia." It's easy to feel "alone in the big city" on occasion. The resources are there, of course, but "People here don't treat you like a baby."

Life

Students on this "beautiful" campus "in the middle of Manhattan" say that they "study really hard during the week and party really hard on weekends." There's always something to do in the "chic, cultured city of opportunity" that is their home. "It's New York City," boasts one student, "the greatest city in the universe," where "Everything is only a subway ride away." As another student explains, "There is no one activity that dominates the social scene. Instead, everything is at our disposal." Options range from "a trip to the Met [and] shopping on Fifth Avenue" to "movies, clubs, theater, ice skating, and restaurants." Students can go to "art museums, comedy clubs, [and] jazz clubs." The bar scene is also popular. As one student explains, "[Lots of students get] a fake ID the first semester of their freshman year to give them access to New York City's nightlife." Students who plan on experiencing all the "glitzy things you hear about in NYC" should "make sure [they] have money to shell out," advises one cost-conscious student. "Even student tickets can add up and dining out is expensive." Students on a budget can do "plenty of other things around town that don't cost more than the subway fare." While Columbia students are "hardly bound by the campus gates," the university offers "as much of a campus life," including "frat parties or dorm parties," "various activity groups," and a popular "annual musical theater production" that "everyone goes to see."

Student Body

"Columbia is a microcosm of New York," sums up one student. The people here are a "mix of everything." Columbia's "very well-rounded" students "are very passionate about their interests." As one student explains, "You can find conversations about everything from the relationship between gods and mortals in Virgil's Aeneid to the latest hipster music group." On campus, you'll find "a great mix of ethnicities" as well as ample diversity of "religions, socioeconomic backgrounds, national heritage, sexual orientations, political beliefs, and geographic roots." These "smart, motivated, independent, and intellectually curious" students describe themselves as "hardworking, continuously busy," and "not very religious." One student warns, however, that "many students are book smart but not very worldly" and can be "very full of" themselves. Politically, left-liberalism is "raging" on campus, though Columbia is "not as crazy liberal as it used to be."

THE PRINCETON REVIEW SAYS

Admissions

Very important factors considered include: Rigor of secondary school record, class rank, application essay, academic GPA, recommendation (s), standardized test scores, extracurricular activities, talent/ability, character/personal qualities. *Other factors considered include:* Alumni/ae relation, geographical residence, interview, racial/ethnic status, volunteer work, work experience. SAT or ACT and SAT Subject Tests required; ACT with Writing component required. TOEFL required of some international applicants. High school diploma is required and GED is accepted. *Academic units recommended:* 4 English, 4 mathematics, 4 science, (4 science labs), 4 foreign language, 4 history, 4 academic electives.

Financial Aid

Students should submit: FAFSA, CSS/Financial Aid PROFILE, noncustodial PROFILE, Parent and student income tax forms. Regular filing deadline is 3/1. The Princeton Review suggests that all financial aid forms be submitted as soon as possible after January 1. *Need-based scholarships/grants offered:* Federal Pell, SEOG, state scholarships/grants, private scholarships, the school's own gift aid. *Loan aid offered:* FFEL Subsidized Stafford, FFEL Unsubsidized Stafford, FFEL PLUS, Federal Perkins, Alternative loans. Applicants will be notified of awards on or about 4/1. Federal Work-Study Program available. Institutional employment available. Off-campus job opportunities are excellent.

The Inside Word

Earning an acceptance letter from Columbia is no easy feat. Applications to the university continue to rise and many great candidates are rejected each year. Admissions officers take a holistic approach to evaluating applications; there's no magic formula or pattern to guide students seeking admission. One common denominator among applicants is stellar grades in rigorous classes and personal accomplishments in non-academic activities. Admissions Officers are looking to build a diverse class that will greatly contribute to the university.

THE SCHOOL SAYS ". . ."

From The Admissions Office

"Columbia maintains an intimate college campus within one of the world's most vibrant cities. After a day exploring New York City you come home to a traditional college campus within an intimate neighborhood. Nobel Prize–winning professors will challenge you in class discussions and meet one-on-one afterward. The core curriculum attracts intensely free-minded scholars, and connects all undergraduates. Science and engineering students pursue cutting-edge research in world-class laboratories with faculty members at the forefront of scientific discovery. Classroom discussions are only the beginning of your education. Ideas spill out from the classrooms, electrifying the campus and Morningside Heights. Friendships formed in the residence halls solidify during a game of Frisbee on the South Lawn or over bagels on the steps of Low Library. From your first day on campus, you will be part of our diverse community.

"Columbia offers extensive need-based financial aid and meets the full need of every student admitted as a first-year with grants instead of loans. Parents with calculated incomes below $60,000 are not expected to contribute any income or assets to tuition, room, board and mandatory fees and families with calculated incomes between $60,000 and $100,000 and with typical assets have a significantly reduced contribution. To support students pursuing study abroad, research, internships and community service opportunities, Columbia offers additional funding and exemptions from academic year and summer work expectations. A commitment to diversity—of every kind—is a long-standing Columbia hallmark. We believe cost should not be a barrier to pursuing your educational dreams."

For even more information on this school, turn to page 466 of the "Stats" section.

CONNECTICUT COLLEGE

270 Mohegan Avenue, New London, CT 06320 • Admissions: 860-439-2200 • Fax: 860-439-4301
Financial Aid: 860-439-2200• E-mail: admit@conncoll.edu • Website: www.conncoll.edu

RATINGS
Quality of Life: 81   Academic: 91   Admissions: 95   Financial Aid: 94

STUDENTS SAY ". . ."

Academics

A "small liberal arts school with excellent academic standards" and an "interdisciplinary focus," Connecticut College provides its students with "a wide range of academic programs." The "enthusiastic," "approachable and involved" professors here are "great teachers" who regularly "meet with students outside of class to address any concerns." One student gushes, "I can honestly tell you that my professors have been some of the most inspiring, thought-provoking people I've ever met." Perhaps most important, "There are no teaching assistants, ever." The administration "can get a little exasperating," but most of the top brass is "readily available" and dedicated to "making the college run smoothly." Top programs include dance, chemistry, biological sciences, psychology, and international relations. Over half of all students study abroad during their 4 years here. The Career Center and internship programs receive solid praise as well: "A paid internship during the summer" after junior year is yours for the taking "if you complete all career services workshops," says one student. The "student-adjudicated" honor code "is also huge." "We wrote it; we enforce it," explains one student. "It applies to noise in the dorms, cheating on tests, self-scheduled exams, and tolerance of sexual orientations."

Life

Connecticut College's attractive and "very social" campus is its own little "close-knit" universe, complete with "a wide range of activities" and "a beautiful view of Long Island Sound and the ocean." Without question, students here "have a lot of fun." "Keg parties" are abundant, and "Small room parties are also popular." Dances "are quite popular" as well. "Thursday and Saturday nights are the big going-out nights," and there are "live bands every Friday." "If you aren't a party person, you can feel like an outsider," observes a first-year student. "But at the same time, academics are extremely important" to Connecticut College students. Because the school doesn't have Greek organizations, "It's important to make friends and be involved" in students organizations like "activism groups" and intramural and intercollegiate sports. Students tell us that athletics could use "more money," though, and "The fitness center and dorms need to be updated," which the college is planning to complete by fall 2009. As far as off-campus life goes, the surrounding town of New London is not particularly accessible. "It's hard or at least inconvenient to get off campus if you don't have a car," advises one student. If you do have a car—or if you take the train—"You can go to Boston or Providence or New York City for the weekend."

Student Body

Students here describe themselves as "open-minded, active, optimistic," and "not overly competitive." There is "a wide range of personalities" and "a good mix of hippies, jocks, book nerds, gamers, and conservatives." A notable international student population exists as well. "Conn says that it has a very diverse campus, but that's only if you've lived in a small New England town your whole life," asserts a jaded first-year student. "There is some diversity and the diversity that exists is fully embraced, but there isn't a huge variety of backgrounds." "A 'typical' student at Conn is involved in three to four extracurricular activities," including an intercollegiate athletic team. The typical student might also be "very rich," "preppy," and "from New England." Such students "look like they walked off the pages of a J. Crew catalog," comments one undergrad. Students are quick to emphasize, however, that stereotypes are often inaccurate: "We are not all trust-fund babies," a sophomore explains. "More students are on financial aid than it may seem." "There is a lot of wealth on this campus," another student asserts, "but one thing I like about this college is that people don't show their wealth off and everyone is able to get along with each other." "Atypical students" do "tend to stick together," though.

THE PRINCETON REVIEW SAYS

Admissions

TOEFL required of all international applicants. High school diploma is required and GED is accepted.

Financial Aid

Students should submit: FAFSA, CSS/Financial Aid PROFILE, noncustodial PROFILE, business/farm supplement, federal tax returns; personal, partnership, Federal W2 statements. Regular filing deadline is 2/1. The Princeton Review suggests that all financial aid forms be submitted as soon as possible after January 1. *Need-based scholarships/grants offered:* Federal Pell, SEOG, state scholarships/grants, ACG, SMART, the school's own gift aid. *Loan aid offered:* FFEL Subsidized Stafford, FFEL Unsubsidized Stafford, FFEL PLUS, Federal Perkins Federal Work-Study Program available. Institutional employment available. Off-campus job opportunities are good.

The Inside Word

Connecticut College is the archetypal selective New England college, and Admissions Officers are judicious in their decisions. Competitive applicants will have pursued a demanding course load in high school. Admissions Officers look for students who are curious and who thrive in challenging academic environments. Since Connecticut College has a close-knit community, personal qualities are also closely evaluated, and interviews are important.

THE SCHOOL SAYS ". . ."

From The Admissions Office

"Distinguishing characteristics of the diverse student body at this small, highly selective college are honor and tolerance. Student leadership is pronounced in all aspects of the college's administration from exclusive jurisdiction of the honor code and dorm life to active representation on the president's academic and administrative cabinets. Differences of opinion are respected and celebrated as legitimate avenues to new understanding. Students come to Connecticut College seeking opportunities for independence and initiative and find them in abundance.

"Applicants must submit the results of either two SAT Subject Tests or the ACT. For candidates who choose to submit an ACT score, we will accept either the old or the new version, with or without the optional Writing component. Submission of SAT scores in addition to the required testing is optional."

For even more information on this school, turn to page 466 of the "Stats" section.

THE COOPER UNION FOR THE ADVANCEMENT OF SCIENCE AND ART

30 COOPER SQUARE, NEW YORK, NY 10003 • ADMISSIONS: 212-353-4120 • FAX: 212-353-4342
FINANCIAL AID: 212-353-4130 • E-MAIL: ADMISSIONS@COOPER.EDU • WEBSITE: WWW.COOPER.EDU

RATINGS
Quality of Life: 79   Academic: 88   Admissions: 98   Financial Aid: 92

STUDENTS SAY ". . ."

Academics

One of the coolest things about The Copper Union is that there is no tuition. The school "offers a full-tuition scholarship to everyone who is accepted." We hasten to add, though, that room and board (in New York City), books and supplies, and various fees add up to quite a bit each year. There is a mandatory core curriculum here in the humanities but, so far as majors go, programs in engineering, art,

> **SURVEY SAYS . . .**
> *Students are friendly*
> *Diverse student types on campus*
> *Students love New York, NY*
> *Great off-campus food*
> *(Almost) everyone smokes*

and architecture are the only options on the menu. Cooper is "one of the best schools for what it does in the country." "It is a school where the students can really go crazy and learn a lot." "Classes are small" and "professors are more than willing to give extra help outside of class." However, it's "not for the weak of heart." The "very visceral and involving" academic experience is "hell." It's "exhaustive and murderous." "Cooper Union: where your best just isn't good enough," muses a civil engineering major. Cooper is about "hours of study, neglect of personal life," and generally "working your ass off." And "the work you put in does not necessarily reflect in your grades." "I have never worked so hard in my life and probably never will," speculates a junior. All of this "kind of sucks at times" but "as long as you can get through it, you're set for life." Complaints among students here include "worthless" adjunct professors. Some lab equipment "could be upgraded," too. "The administration is sometimes difficult to approach" and "scheduling is always weird." Nonetheless, management "mostly meets the students' needs, with minor mishaps."

Life

"There is no meal plan" at Cooper and the lodging situation is harsh. "There is only housing guaranteed for first-year students and since Manhattan is a very expensive place to live, it becomes a problem after freshman year." "Everyone is extraordinarily busy," comments a fine art major. "School is life and there's no way around it." For the architecture students, life is "nothing except architecture in radical explorations and expressions." For engineers, "Cooper is about selling your soul for four years." Art students sometimes "take time off because it's hard to be creative every minute." "The intense workload gives little break for fun." There are "many extracurricular programs" but the urban fare of New York City consumes most free time. The surrounding East Village is full of funky shops, cheap eateries, theaters, bars, and live music venues; subways can whisk students throughout the five boroughs at any time of day. "Drinking with friends is a great and sometimes necessary way to decompress" but for most students, "ruthlessly sucking on booze" is a very occasional thing. "We are not a party school," says a sophomore. "We get to campus in the morning, and leave late night." "Cooper isn't for everybody," advises a senior. "If you need excessive guidance, or prefer an exclusive, well-defined campus structure, you won't be happy here."

Student Body

Diversity here is simply dreamy. Cooper's overwhelming male population is exceptionally ethnically diverse and "everyone is very different from everyone else." "The student body is teeming with sensitive and excitable minds, which caters to an unbridled sense of adventure and exploration." These "really ridiculously smart" students have "incredible, raw talent." Personalities "range from your seemingly typical frat jock to your genius who knows everything but how to socialize." Cooper students are very often "hardcore" and come in three stereotypes. "The art kids all wear the same 'unique' clothing and smoke a lot." They're "definitely more free-spirit, social people." "The engineers are either playing video games or saying sad jokes that only other engineers would understand." And "the architecture students can be a mixture of both, or anywhere in between, but they are hard to catch because all they do is work all the time." These three groups of students "don't mix so much" and sometimes there are rivalries. "The battle is like the Cold War, mostly sent in written messages on bathroom walls but no direct actions. It's benign in nature and just for amusement."

THE PRINCETON REVIEW SAYS

Admissions

Very important factors considered include: Academic GPA, rigor of secondary school record, standardized test scores, level of applicant's interest, talent/ability. *Important factors considered include:* Application essay, character/personal qualities, extracurricular activities. *Other factors considered include:* Class rank, recommendation(s), first generation, interview, racial/ethnic status, volunteer work, work experience. SAT or ACT required; ACT with Writing component recommended. TOEFL required of all international applicants. High school diploma is required and GED is accepted. *Academic units required:* 4 English, 1 mathematics, 1 science, 1 social studies, 1 history, 8 academic electives. *Academic units recommended:* 4 English, 4 mathematics, 4 science, (3 science labs), 2 foreign language, 4 social studies.

Financial Aid

Students should submit: FAFSA, CSS/Financial Aid PROFILE Regular filing deadline is 6/1. The Princeton Review suggests that all financial aid forms be submitted as soon as possible after January 1. *Need-based scholarships/grants offered:* Federal Pell, SEOG, state scholarships/grants, private scholarships, the school's own gift aid. *Loan aid offered:* FFEL Subsidized Stafford, FFEL Unsubsidized Stafford, FFEL PLUS, Federal Perkins, college/university loans from institutional funds. Applicants will be notified of awards on or about 6/1. Federal Work-Study Program available. Institutional employment available. Off-campus job opportunities are excellent.

The Inside Word

It's ultra-tough to get into The Cooper Union. There are typically over 2500 applicants vying for fewer than 300 slots. Not only do students need to have top academic accomplishments, but also they need to be a good fit for Cooper's offbeat milieu.

THE SCHOOL SAYS ". . ."

From The Admissions Office

"Each of Cooper Union's three schools, architecture, art, and engineering, adheres strongly to preparation for its profession and is committed to a problem-solving philosophy of education in a unique, scholarly environment. A rigorous curriculum and group projects reinforce this unique atmosphere in higher education and contribute to a strong sense of community and identity in each school. With McSorley's Ale House and the Joseph Papp Public Theatre nearby, Cooper Union remains at the heart of the city's tradition of free speech, enlightenment, and entertainment. Cooper's Great Hall has hosted national leaders, from Abraham Lincoln to Booker T. Washington, from Mark Twain to Samuel Gompers, from Susan B. Anthony to Betty Friedan, and more recently, President Bill Clinton and Senator Barack Obama

"In addition, we eagerly await the arrival of our new academic building slated to open in 2009. Designed by Pritzker Prize–winning architect, Thom Mayne, the new building is expected to enhance and encourage more interaction between students in all three schools.

"We're seeking students who have a passion to study our professional programs. Cooper Union students are independent thinkers, following the beat of their own drum. Many of our graduates become world-class leaders in the disciplines of architecture, fine arts, design, and engineering.

"For art and architecture applicants, SAT scores are considered after the home test and portfolio work. For engineering applicants than high school grades, the SAT and SAT Subject Test scores are the most important factors considered in admissions decisions. Currently, we do not use the Writing section of the SAT to assist in making admissions decisions. We expect to reconsider that policy as more data is available in the near future."

For even more information on this school, turn to page 467 of the "Stats" section.

CORNELL UNIVERSITY

410 THURSTON AVENUE, ITHACA, NY 14850 • ADMISSIONS: 607-255-5241 • FAX: 607-255-0659
FINANCIAL AID: 607-255-5145 • E-MAIL: ADMISSIONS@CORNELL.EDU • WEBSITE: WWW.CORNELL.EDU

RATINGS
Quality of Life: 88   **Academic:** 89   **Admissions:** 98   **Financial Aid:** 95

STUDENTS SAY ". . ."

Academics

"A large, diverse university offering a huge variety of courses and majors," Cornell University seems intent on putting
the "universe" in "university." Students tell us that "all the
academic programs are strong, so no matter what you want
to study, Cornell has the resources." But just in case Cornell's
standout undergraduate departments in engineering, business, biology, industrial and labor relations, hotel administration, food science, animal science, and natural resources
don't get you going, "You can [always] design your own

> **SURVEY SAYS . . .**
> *Great computer facilities*
> *Great library*
> *Great food on campus*
> *Frats and sororities dominate*
> *social scene*
> *Student publications are popular*
> *Lots of beer drinking*

major." Cornell offers "a mix of anything and everything, with more opportunities than you could ever want."
Undergrads point out that "Cornell is a great place for people who know what they want to do in life and want to
get things done sooner rather than later, because each major program is very focused and concentrated right from
the beginning." Academics here "are hard, extremely tough." "We don't all have 4.0s, but we work harder than students at the other Ivy League schools. Cornell is the easiest Ivy to get into, and the hardest to graduate from. Grade
inflation doesn't exist here." The school does its best to help students navigate the academic challenges, offering
"enough help so that even the most lost student can find his/her way to a good, deserving grade." Professors "are
available anytime you need them and are more than happy to lend you a helping hand," while both your "peer
advisor and faculty advisor" are "easily accessible." The administration does a great job "running the school
smoothly" and "makes the effort to keep lines of communication open." Students tell us that "undergraduates are
offered unbelievable research opportunities and instruction from those who are at the top of their respective fields."
And when it's time to find a job, "Cornell has a really good alumni network" and a "helpful Career Services" Office.

Life

Cornell is located in remote Ithaca, "on the top of a hill in the middle of a beautiful and cold nowhere."
"Beautiful gorges" and "unrivaled" outdoor activities—"Everything from kayaking to pumpkin picking is just
a small trip away either by foot or by bus." "There really isn't anything you can't do when it comes to nature at
Cornell," but there is not much in the way of urban diversion. As a result, many "Students exist strictly within
the Cornell bubble." They "have no escape from the stress of school and everything they do revolves around
school." For many, weekend options consist of "bars in Collegetown and house parties," along with some on-
campus "concerts, activities, and student-led initiatives." Lots of students "participate in intramural sports or
one of the many clubs." One student observes, "Being in a small town like Ithaca means that most people do
one thing for fun: drink. At the same time, some of the dorms—i.e. the ones with fewer drinkers—are still up
on the weekends playing poker or GameCube or something like that. Nevertheless, the lack of a big city around
you means that sometimes you can get pretty bored"—but then, there is always schoolwork to attend to.

Student Body

Cornell's student body "is diverse, and not just in the racial or ethnic sense. There are so many different courses
of study at Cornell that a wide range of personalities and interests are represented. Every day, architects, engineers, hotel school students, and dairy farm majors sit down to lunch together." Furthermore, "Because Cornell is
half private and half public, the students come from diverse economic backgrounds." Pressed to provide a general description of their peers, students tell us that "the student body is divided into about three groups: The well-
off, stylish-if-conservatively dressed 'practical majors' (most frat members, premeds, pre-laws, sorority girls,
hotelies, aggies); the study-a-holics (engineers, applied sciences, some of the premeds); and the Euro-acting, blaz-
er-and-hoodie wearing, always-thin hipsters (English, comparative literature, philosophy, film, theater, etc.)."

THE PRINCETON REVIEW SAYS

Admissions

Very important factors considered include: Application essay, academic GPA, recommendation(s), rigor of secondary school record, standardized test scores, extracurricular activities, talent/ability. *Important factors considered include:* Class rank. *Other factors considered include:* alumni/ae relation, character/personal qualities, first generation, geographical residence, interview, racial/ethnic status, state residency, volunteer work, work experience. SAT or ACT required; ACT with Writing component required. High school diploma or equivalent is not required. *Academic units required:* 4 English, 3 mathematics. *Academic units recommended:* 3 science, (3 science labs), 3 foreign language, 3 social studies, 3 history.

Financial Aid

Students should submit: FAFSA, institution's own financial aid form, CSS/Financial Aid PROFILE, noncustodial PROFILE, business/farm supplement, prior year tax returns. Regular filing deadline is 2/11. The Princeton Review suggests that all financial aid forms be submitted as soon as possible after January 1. *Need-based scholarships/grants offered:* Federal Pell, SEOG, state scholarships/grants, private scholarships, the school's own gift aid. *Loan aid offered:* Direct Subsidized Stafford, Direct Unsubsidized Stafford, Direct PLUS, FFEL Subsidized Stafford, FFEL Unsubsidized Stafford, FFEL PLUS, Federal Perkins, college/university loans from institutional funds. , Key Bank Alternative Loan.. Applicants will be notified of awards on or about 4/1. Federal Work-Study Program available. Institutional employment available. Off-campus job opportunities are fair.

The Inside Word

Gaining admission to Cornell is a tough coup regardless of your intended field of study, but some of the university's seven schools are more competitive than others. If you're thinking of trying to 'backdoor' your way into one of the most competitive schools—by gaining admission to one, then transferring after one year—be aware that you will have to resubmit the entire application and provide a statement outlining your academic plans. It's not impossible to accomplish, but Cornell works hard to discourage this sort of maneuvering.

THE SCHOOL SAYS ". . ."

From The Admissions Office

"Cornell University, an Ivy League school and land-grant college located in the scenic Finger Lakes region of central New York, provides an outstanding education to students in seven small to midsize undergraduate colleges: Agriculture and Life Sciences; Architecture, Art, and Planning; Arts and Sciences; Engineering; Hotel Administration; Human Ecology; and Industrial and Labor Relations. Cornellians come from all 50 states and more than 100 countries, and they pursue their academic goals in more than 100 departments. The College of Arts and Sciences, one of the smallest liberal arts schools in the Ivy League, offers more than 40 majors, most of which rank near the top nationwide. Applied programs in the other six colleges also rank among the best in the world.

"Other special features of the university include a world-renowned faculty; 4,000 courses available to all students; an extensive undergraduate research program; superb research, teaching, and library facilities; a large, diverse study abroad program; and more than 700 student organizations and 36 varsity sports. Cornell's campus is one of the most beautiful in the country; students pass streams, rocky gorges, and waterfalls on their way to class. First-year students make their home on North Campus, a living-learning community that features a special advising center, faculty-in-residence, a fitness center, and traditional residence halls as well as theme-centered buildings such as Ecology House. Cornell University invites applications from all interested students and uses the Common Application exclusively with a short required Cornell Supplement. Students applying for admissions will submit scores from the SAT or ACT (with writing). We also require SAT Subject Tests. Subject test requirements are college-specific."

For even more information on this school, turn to page 467 of the "Stats" section.

DARTMOUTH COLLEGE

6016 McNUTT HALL, HANOVER, NH 03755 • ADMISSIONS: 603-646-2875 • FAX: 603-646-1216
FINANCIAL AID: 603-646-2451 • E-MAIL: ADMISSIONS.OFFICE@DARTMOUTH.EDU • WEBSITE: WWW.DARTMOUTH.EDU

RATINGS
Quality of Life: 91   **Academic:** 96   **Admissions:** 98   **Financial Aid:** 92

STUDENTS SAY "..."

Academics

Dartmouth College "has a reputation of being like summer camp, and it's true: Students take their academic work very seriously, but they're also all extremely happy to be here, and they have a lot of fun, no matter what their idea of fun is." A school that is small "without being suffocating or lacking opportunities, challenging but not too competitive, has good academics and access to professors, and has its own ski hill" obviously has a lot to offer; how else could it

> **SURVEY SAYS ...**
> Great computer facilities
> Great library
> Campus feels safe
> Frats and sororities dominate social scene
> Lots of beer drinking

entice "artists, athletes, musicians, and future leaders to all gather together in the middle of nowhere?" Students love that Dartmouth is "very undergraduate-focused, unlike the other Ivies that neglect their undergrads to only concentrate on research." They also love the D-Plan, which divides the academic year into four 10-week terms in order to provide maximum flexibility and study abroad opportunities ("Many students use the D-Plan to study abroad up to three times"). On the downside, it "makes being friends with members of other classes difficult," since "D-Plan means consistently being on campus . . . is tricky." Dartmouth professors "are some of the greatest minds in the country, and they're almost all willing to just sit and chat if you feel like it. I've had at least one professor each year who's invited the whole class to her/his house for dinner and discussion (sometimes with famous guests). It's a great way to learn information that is above and beyond what you're learning in the classroom." No wonder "everyone is happy here."

Life

Dartmouth's greatest strength, students tell us, "is its incredible sense of community and tradition," traditions that include "singing the Alma Mater, dancing the Salty Dog Rag, and running 100-plus laps around a 40-foot bonfire." One undergrad notes, "[Students] have a ton of school spirit," and "From the first day on campus, students are learning all about what it means to be a Dartmouth student." Situated in the Upper Connecticut River Valley, Dartmouth has "a great location for skiing and outdoor activities," and it's a place "where the student body is very active, both outdoors (i.e., hiking, biking, rock climbing, ice climbing, and skiing) as well as indoors partying. Whatever you want to do, you can find it here." That is, unless what you want is constant big-city entertainment; hometown Hanover is a "very small town," and "Boston and Montreal, though available, are rarely sought." Students are more likely to flock to the campus' popular Greek scene: "Most people like to go drink at frats on weekends and attend parties. I think like 20 percent of the student population abstains from drinking, but everyone else is pretty into it." Students are also "very involved in on campus organizations and sports teams." As one junior explains, "There's always more to do than can ever be done, and the hardest thing is making time for sleep along with classes, clubs, and friends."

Student Body

The typical Dartmouth student "is hard to define. If I mashed them all up into one person, it'd be a kid from Jersey driving a Lexus with a kayak on the top. His collar popped but his pants torn. In his bag there'd be the works of Marx next to those of Friedman. We're all so different, but at the same time, we're just all here to learn, to love, and to live." Dartmouth "strives to create a world of very different people," and its reputation allows it to cherry-pick top students from all around the globe. The school has a reputation for political conservatism that some argue is overblown: "There are very liberal students at Dartmouth, and there are very conservative student s. . ., but most tend to fall in between." Also, while the school "has a stereotype of being a big party school full of jocks," it's "not really that way" and "That should be more recognized." Across the board students tend to be "well-balanced" and "outgoing," and everyone from the "sweet frat dude to the library dweller all find a place to fit in."

THE PRINCETON REVIEW SAYS

Admissions

Very important factors considered include: Class rank, application essay, academic GPA, recommendation(s), rigor of secondary school record, standardized test scores, character/personal qualities, extracurricular activities. *Important factors considered include:* Talent/ability, volunteer work. *Other factors considered include:* Alumni/ae relation, first generation, geographical residence, interview, racial/ethnic status, SAT; ACT with Writing component and any two SAT II Subject Tests required. TOEFL required of all international applicants. High school diploma or equivalent is not required. *Academic units recommended:* 4 English, 4 mathematics, 34 science, 3 social studies, 3 history.

Financial Aid

Students should submit: FAFSA, CSS/Financial Aid PROFILE, noncustodial PROFILE, business/farm supplement, current W2 or Federal Tax Returns. Regular filing deadline is 2/1. The Princeton Review suggests that all financial aid forms be submitted as soon as possible after January 1. *Need-based scholarships/grants offered:* Federal Pell, SEOG, state scholarships/grants, private scholarships, the school's own gift aid. *Loan aid offered:* FFEL Subsidized Stafford, FFEL Unsubsidized Stafford, FFEL PLUS, Federal Perkins, state loans, college/university loans from institutional funds. Applicants will be notified of awards on or about 4/2. Federal Work-Study Program available. Institutional employment available. Off-campus job opportunities are excellent.

The Inside Word

Like other elite schools, Dartmouth is swamped with more applications from qualified students than it can accommodate. Dartmouth's 2007–2008 admission rate of 13.3 percent was the lowest in the school's history. That wasn't because the applicant pool was less competitive; it's because more kids are applying to Dartmouth every year. Give this your best shot, and don't take it personally if you don't get in; unfortunately, many great candidates don't.

THE SCHOOL SAYS ". . ."

From The Admissions Office

""Dartmouth's mission is to endow students with the knowledge and wisdom needed to make creative and positive contributions to society. The College brings together a breadth of cultures, traditions, and ideas to create a campus that is alive with ongoing debate and exploration. From student-initiated round-table discussions that attempt to make sense of world events to the late-night exchanges in a dormitory lounge, Dartmouth students take advantage of their opportunities to learn from each other. The unique benefits of sharing in this interchange are accompanied by a great sense of responsibility. Each individual's commitment to the College's 'Principles of Community' ensures the vitality of this learning environment, and Dartmouth's size enhances the quality of the experience for all involved.

"To help all Dartmouth students take full advantage of the 'Dartmouth Experience,' the College has eliminated loans from its financial aid packages. Beginning with the Class of 2012, students from families with incomes under $75,000 will receive free tuition to the College.

"All applicants, including those who apply from foreign countries, are required to take the SAT (or ACT) and any two SAT Subject Tests. All testing must be completed by January of the senior year in high school. If standardized testing is repeated, the Admissions Committee only considers highest scores."

For even more information on this school, turn to page 468 of the "Stats" section.

DELAWARE VALLEY COLLEGE

700 EAST BUTLER AVENUE, DOYLESTOWN, PA 18901-2697 • ADMISSIONS: 215-489-2211
FAX: 215-230-2968 • E-MAIL: ADMITME@DEVALCOL.EDU • WEBSITE: WWW.DEVALCOL.EDU

RATINGS
Quality of Life: 73   Academic: 74   Admissions: 78   Financial Aid: 73

STUDENTS SAY "..."

Academics

Delaware Valley College is a small Pennsylvania school that offers an array of majors, predominantly in the agricultural and animal sciences. As one undergraduate puts it, "We know animals and the environment. If a person wants to get into the farming business, [conduct] lab work, or [do] just about anything to do with working or training animals, this is the place to go. We have two barns of horses on campus, cows, sheep, llamas, a small animal facility that has

> **SURVEY SAYS . . .**
> *Small classes*
> *Students are friendly*
> *Students love Doylestown, PA*
> *Everyone loves the Aggies*
> *Lots of beer drinking*
> *(Almost) everyone smokes*

mice, rats, guinea pigs, hamsters, gerbils, lizards, snakes, fish, and dogs and our own greenhouse on campus. We also have connections with the Philadelphia Zoo that allows students internships and jobs." Undergraduates extol professors who "are very proficient in their subjects and are willing to help out students who are struggling and willing to work hard to get the grade." They especially appreciate the fact that "professors have had years [of experience] in the business, so they can offer real-world information and not just what is in books." "Due to our small class sizes, our professors are able to be more personal and hands-on with us than [are professors] at larger schools." For many undergrads, one of the "greatest strengths of Delaware Valley is the hands-on experience that all majors get. The required employment program lets students work in their fields of study."

Life

"Delaware Valley College is basically an agricultural school located in a small, higher-class town." As many students hail from the surrounding counties of Pennsylvania, "People mostly go home on the weekends. A lot of people have jobs back at their houses, whether on the farm or at another kind of business. They live close enough to home that every weekend, they are able to leave. If one does decide to stay at school for the weekend, the Septa [Philadelphia and the surrounding region's rail system] can take him or her right into Philly." On campus, "There are always activities available to students." In addition, "There is a lot of open space for games of football, Ultimate Frisbee, catch, and soccer." People "watch movies, go down to the barns, go to the gym, or just hang out" in their spare time. Hometown Doylestown has "numerous shopping opportunities" and "is a very interesting place to visit and walk around in for a day." Since the campus empties out on Fridays, "Thursdays are a very popular night to socialize with friends." On Thirsty Thursdays, "most of the campus goes out and parties and drinks."

Student Body

Because of DelVal's focus on agricultural and animal sciences, "Many students grew up with agricultural or animal backgrounds," but students report that there are also a lot of students from urban backgrounds here, too—specifically, there are many students "from the city of Philadelphia." "Because our school is so small," one undergrad claims, "it seems very high school-ish at times, and cliques tend to form easily." Another observes: "The cliques are obvious: There are the Southern farmers, the Northern farmers, the future vets, the horse girls, and everyone else who is here to play football." Regardless of their cliques or where they hail from, most DelVal students "love to be outdoors," and a large percentage plan to go on to veterinary school. Concerning ethnic diversity, students report a "very homogenous student body" that is "predominantly White." They also note that there is "very little tolerance or acceptance of minority groups and homosexuals" among the student body. Most DelVal students think their peers possess a good measure of both street smarts and country common sense: "To sum up, students here can differentiate a Jersey cow from a Brown Swiss, then give directions to a hot spot in Philly."

THE PRINCETON REVIEW SAYS

Admissions

Very important factors considered include: academic GPA, standardized test scores. *Important factors considered include:* Class rank, rigor of secondary school record, interview, *Other factors considered include:* application essay, recommendation(s), alumni/ae relation, character/personal qualities, extracurricular activities, level of applicant's interest, talent/ability, volunteer work, work experience. SAT or ACT required; ACT with Writing component recommended. High school diploma is required and GED is accepted. *Academic units required:* 3 English, 2 mathematics, 2 science, (1 science labs), 2 social studies, 6 academic electives,

Finanancial Aid

Students should submit: FAFSA, state aid form The Princeton Review suggests that all financial aid forms be submitted as soon as possible after January 1. *Need-based scholarships/grants offered:* Federal Pell, SEOG, state scholarships/grants, private scholarships, the school's own gift aid *Loan aid offered:* FFEL Subsidized Stafford, FFEL Unsubsidized Stafford, FFEL PLUS, Federal Perkins, Alternative Loans. Applicants will be notified of awards on a rolling basis beginning 2/1. Federal Work-Study Program available. Institutional employment available.

The Inside Word

Delaware Valley considers a variety of factors when making admissions decisions, chief among them are GPA and standardized scores. The school has a rolling admissions policy so students are advised to apply as early as possible, especially those considering the more popular majors. Candidates interested in Del Val's strong agricultural program should bring solid science marks to the table.

For even more information on this school, turn to page 468 of the "Stats" section.

DICKINSON COLLEGE

PO Box 1773, CARLISLE, PA 17013-2896 • ADMISSIONS: 717-245-1231 • FAX: 717-245-1442
FINANCIAL AID: 717-245-1308 • E-MAIL: ADMIT@DICKINSON.EDU • WEBSITE: WWW.DICKINSON.EDU

RATINGS
Quality of Life: 79   Academic: 89   Admissions: 93   Financial Aid: 91

STUDENTS SAY ". . ."

Academics

Dickinson College is a "quintessential small liberal arts school" in a "small town in central Pennsylvania." The big draw here is an "aggressive" global focus. "Dickinson has completely followed through on all of their promises of a campus that supports international experiences," says a sociology major. Courses "have a strong focus on international issues." Studying abroad "fits seamlessly into the curriculum" and is "a huge deal." "Dickinson has exceptional study abroad programs everywhere in the world." The administration is sometimes "preoccupied with rising in the ranks and improving superficial perceptions" of the school but Dickinson's president is insanely popular. He "has weekly office hours." "From the president down, the faculty and administrators make themselves available." "Any complaint is heard and listened to, not just brushed off." The academic atmosphere here is "difficult but doable." Classes are small. "Students do not often skip, as professors do take note." The "completely accommodating" faculty receives high marks. "They are good teachers, passionate about their subjects, and it is very easy for students to develop strong out-of-the-classroom relationships with their professors," says an international business major. "I can honestly say I've only had one professor who I didn't consider high quality," adds one junior.

> SURVEY SAYS . . .
> *Large classes*
> *Great computer facilities*
> *Great library*
> *Lots of beer drinking*

Life

"The campus is beautiful," observes a senior at Dickinson. "On a nice day, it can take your breath away." It's also "overloaded with clubs and organizations." During the week, "there is a lot to do if you're willing to do it and a lot of it is college sponsored." There is a "consistently full schedule of lectures." There are plenty of arts-related events. "All the different cultural clubs have a dinner every semester." "Intramural sports are a big deal." "The gym is in constant use." "Greek life is really big at Dickinson" as well. "The social scene revolves around frat parties," and "it is difficult to maintain a social life in this school if you are not involved in some kind of fraternity or sorority." "On the weekends, the majority of people get nice and drunk." "Dickinson did not get the name Drinkinson for nothing." Drugs are not uncommon, either. Students who don't party are here too, "trying desperately to make their own fun." There's also "a lot of drama" on campus. "We like to call it Dickinson High," one student admits. The "dull" surrounding town is "not a social mecca." "I love art museums, live music, and cultural diversity," says a senior. "Carlisle does not have any of that." "There is nothing to do in Carlisle unless you are 21 and can get into the bars, where the most exciting thing to do is drink and maybe dance with a nice townie." "If you don't mind small towns, you'll be fine," advises a junior, "but big city people should look elsewhere for their college experience unless they're tired of the rat race."

Student Body

"The most glaring trait of the student body is that it is mostly white." "There are tons of international students," and the "growing" Posse program brings poor minority kids to campus. Still, as a first-year student relates, "the school is not as diverse as some of us would want it to be." Overall, "there is a lot of homogeneity." Most students here are "socially oriented" and come from somewhere on the east coast or in the mid-atlantic states. "Many students are very rich and have no problem spending copious amounts of money." "The parking lots are filled with Jeep Grand Cherokees, Saabs, and BMWs." Other students receive "sweet financial aid deals," though. Academically, Dickinsonians "range anywhere from overzealous to apathetic" but the vast majority "can usually balance a full academic load with an active and rich social life." "The typical student at Dickinson is very preppy. The girls are gorgeous and the guys look like they are straight out of a J. Crew catalog, and everyone is also really athletic." "Finding the oddballs can be difficult." Cliques are common and "the campus is quite split between Greek life and non-Greek life."

THE PRINCETON REVIEW SAYS

Admissions

Very important factors considered include: Academic GPA, rigor of secondary school record, extracurricular activities, talent/ability, volunteer work. *Important factors considered include:* Class rank, recommendation(s), standardized test scores, alumni/ae relation, work experience. *Other factors considered include:* Application essay, character/personal qualities, first generation, geographical residence, interview, level of applicant's interest, racial/ethnic status, state residency, SAT or ACT recommended; TOEFL required of all international applicants. High school diploma is required and GED is accepted. *Academic units required:* 4 English, 3 mathematics, 3 science, (2 science labs), 2 foreign language, 2 social studies, 2 academic electives. *Academic units recommended:* 3 foreign language.

Financial Aid

Students should submit: FAFSA, CSS/Financial Aid PROFILE, state aid form, noncustodial PROFILE, business/farm supplement. Regular filing deadline is 2/1. The Princeton Review suggests that all financial aid forms be submitted as soon as possible after January 1. *Need-based scholarships/grants offered:* Federal Pell, SEOG, state scholarships/grants, private scholarships, the school's own gift aid. *Loan aid offered:* FFEL Subsidized Stafford, FFEL Unsubsidized Stafford, FFEL PLUS, Federal Perkins, college/university loans from institutional funds. Applicants will be notified of awards on or about 3/31. Federal Work-Study Program available. Institutional employment available. Off-campus job opportunities are good.

The Inside Word

Dickinson's admissions process is typical of most small liberal arts colleges. The best candidates for such a place are those with solid grades and broad extracurricular involvement—the stereotypical "well-rounded student." Admissions selectivity is kept in check by a strong group of competitor colleges that fight tooth and nail for their cross-applicants.

THE SCHOOL SAYS ". . ."

From The Admissions Office

"College is more than a collection of courses. It is about crossing traditional boundaries, about seeing the interrelationships among different subjects, about learning a paradigm for solving problems, about developing critical thinking and communication skills, and about speaking out on issues that matter. Dickinson was intended as an alternative to the 15 colleges that existed in the U.S. at the time of its founding; its aim, then as now, was to provide a "useful" education whereby students would 'learn by doing' through hands-on experience and engagement with the community, the region, the nation, and the world. And this is truer today than ever, with workshop science courses replacing traditional lectures, fieldwork experiences in community studies in which students take oral histories, and 12 study centers abroad in nontourist cities where students, under the guidance of a Dickinson faculty director, experience a true international culture. Almost 55 percent of the student body study abroad and a total of 58 percent study off campus, preparing them to compete and succeed in a complex global world.

"Applicants wishing to be considered for academic scholarships are required to submit scores from either the SAT or ACT, but Dickinson does not require results from either test for admission into the 2008 entering class."

For even more information on this school, turn to page 468 of the "Stats" section.

DREW UNIVERSITY

36 MADISON AVENUE, MADISON, NJ 07940-1493 • ADMISSIONS: 973-408-3739 • FAX: 973-408-3068
FINANCIAL AID: 973-408-3112 • E-MAIL: CADM@DREW.EDU • WEBSITE: WWW.DREW.EDU

RATINGS

Quality of Life: 77   Academic: 84   Admissions: 87   Financial Aid: 79

STUDENTS SAY "..."

Academics

For fifteen years, Drew University was practically synony-
mous with Tom Kean, the popular university president
who had previously served as Governor of New Jersey.
Kean's prominence brought lots of regional and national
attention to this small school, to the great benefit of students and the university alike. His departure was bound to
ruffle some feathers, and sure enough there are some here

> **SURVEY SAYS . . .**
> *Large classes*
> *Frats and sororities are unpopular*
> *or nonexistent*
> *Theater is popular*
> *Lots of beer drinking*

who simply can't abide the school's new direction, which includes plans for expansion (plans that, incidentally, were made during Kean's tenure). Fortunately, Drew seems to have weathered the transition well; the vast
majority of students here continue to extol this "small school with a beautiful campus and prime location" near
New York City. The school's location allows students to take advantage of "programs such as Wall Street
Semester and United Nations Semester, as well as field trips to theaters on Broadway and Art museums." They
also tell us that location affords "awesome job opportunities in the surrounding areas." Students praise the curriculum's liberal art focus that ensures "that everyone gets exposed to at least a little bit of every other subject
before they leave." Drew's "small class sizes allow for the difficulty of the classes to be manageable" and students say "every professor wants to know your name by the end of the semester." While students acknowledge
that "Drew is a school that's in the midst of finding and creating its unique identity," they also don't feel any
imperative to rush the process. In fact, they tell us that Drew is "one of the best schools in New Jersey when it
comes to education," just as it is.

Life

Drew's small size, coupled with the fact that "there are so many clubs, organizations, and sports teams to join"
encourages student participation in extracurricular activities. One student opines: "With a school so small, I
doubt that anyone who graduates does not have a leadership position in something." An active performing arts
program means that there is "lots of involvement in the arts," among students including theater, musical performances, a capella, and student art exhibits." Drew "is not a party school per se" but "for people who do like
to party, it's very easy because the alcohol policy is like the world's most un-enforced thing." More often, when
students want a wild night they "simply hop on the train a block away and head for Morristown or New York
for an evening or weekend" or "when the weather is conducive" they might "take a trip with a few friends
down to the beach." Hometown Madison is "adorable" with "a small-town atmosphere." On the downside,
"there isn't much to do in town," but with New York City "right around the corner," that's hardly a make-or-
break problem.

Student Body

Drew "caters to a lot of wealthy kids from Dirty Jerz (New Jersey)," students who "live within a few hours of
campus and have the opportunity to travel home if they choose to, although it does not at all feel like a 'suitcase school.'" Despite this trend, "There is a very wide variety of students at Drew—all different races, ethnicities, and backgrounds." The student body includes "tons of theatre kids" as well as "your typical jocks." (One
student observes that "there is definitely a division between jocks and everyone else at this school—not that our
sports teams are even good.") Students tell us that "Drew is a reach school for some and a safety for others, so
there are very, very brilliant students here, while others...not so much." Women outnumber men by a healthy
3-to-2 ratio.

Admissions

Very important factors considered include: Academic GPA, rigor of secondary school record, talent/ability. *Important factors considered include:* Application essay, recommendation(s), extracurricular activities, interview, level of applicant's interest. *Other factors considered include:* Class rank, standardized test scores, alumni/ae relation, character/personal qualities, first generation, geographical residence, racial/ethnic status, volunteer work, work experience. ACT with Writing component recommended. TOEFL required of all international applicants. High school diploma or equivalent is not required. *Academic units recommended:* 4 English, 3 mathematics, 2 science, 2 foreign language, 2 social studies, 2 history, 3 academic electives.

Financial Aid

Students should submit: FAFSA, CSS/Financial Aid PROFILE. Regular filing deadline is 2/15. The Princeton Review suggests that all financial aid forms be submitted as soon as possible after January 1. *Need-based scholarships/grants offered:* Federal Pell, SEOG, state scholarships/grants, private scholarships, the school's own gift aid. *Loan aid offered:* FFEL Subsidized Stafford, FFEL Unsubsidized Stafford, FFEL PLUS, Federal Perkins, state loans Applicants will be notified of awards on or about 4/1. Federal Work-Study Program available. Institutional employment available. Off-campus job opportunities are excellent.

The Inside Word

Since 2005, Drew University has given applicants the option of submitting a graded writing sample in place of standardized test scores. If the goal was to attract more applicants, all we can say is: mission accomplished. Drew drew over 4,500 applicants last year, an increase of about 50 percent over applicants during the 2003–04 admissions season. The profile of the average admitted student, oddly, hasn't changed; instead, Drew seems to be attracting more applications from those who see the school as a safety.

THE SCHOOL SAYS "..."

From The Admissions Office

"At Drew, great teachers are transforming the undergraduate learning experience. With a commitment to teaching, Drew professors have made educating undergraduates their top priority. With a spirit of innovation, they have brought the most advanced technology and distinctive modes of experiential learning into the Drew classroom. The result is a stimulating and challenging education that connects the traditional liberal arts and sciences to the workplace and to the world.

"Drew University will require applicants for the 2008–2009 academic year to take either the new SAT or the ACT. The Selection Committee will consider the highest Verbal, Math, and Writing scores individually in its evaluation of candidates for admission."

For even more information on this school, turn to page 469 of the "Stats" section.

DREXEL UNIVERSITY

3141 CHESTNUT STREET, PHILADELPHIA, PA 19104 • ADMISSIONS: 215-895-2400 • FAX: 215-895-5939
FINANCIAL AID: 215-895-2535 • E-MAIL: ENROLL@DREXEL.EDU • WEBSITE: WWW.DREXEL.EDU

RATINGS
Quality of Life: 65   **Academic:** 73   **Admissions:** 87   **Financial Aid:** 62

STUDENTS SAY ". . ."
Academics

Drexel University "is a lot of work squarely aimed at integration into the professional world," whether that world involves the school's popular majors in engineering, technology, and business, or less-known offerings like the school's programs in the music industry or hospitality management. Drexel has a growing digital media program, making it "one of the only schools in the area with a developed program" in the field. Central to the Drexel experience is the "extremely beneficial" co-op program, which many agree is "the best thing about Drexel." Co-op pro-

> **SURVEY SAYS . . .**
> *Great computer facilities*
> *Career services are great*
> *Diverse student types on campus*
> *Students love Philadelphia, PA*
> *Great off-campus food*
> *Lots of beer drinking*
> *Hard liquor is popular*
> *(Almost) everyone smokes*

vides 18 months of professional experience during the 5-year undergraduate program. One student writes, "You will learn as much in the first couple of months of working in the real world as you did in any college. Drexel gives you all of that knowledge before you're even out of school and gives you the preparation necessary to succeed in the real world." The school's location in Philadelphia, "a source of endless fun and opportunity," helps co-op considerably. "Engineering dominates" at Drexel, but the school "has a variety of programs fit for almost anyone," with "a lot of classes run with web-based resources. Lectures are posted online in WebCT, as well as course syllabi and assignments. This makes it easy to access information. Teachers are easy to get in touch with via e-mail and are very accessible to meet with as needed." Administrative tasks are not so convenient; students warn of "lots of red tape," adding that "most issues require visits to at least three different offices, sometimes on opposite ends of campus." Fortunately, the campus isn't that large.

Life

Campus life at Drexel must compete with the temptations offered by Philadelphia, one of the nation's largest cities. Philly provides "so many things to do (if you have the money) that it can be hard to know where to begin." Students tell us that "museums are great. Lots of kids go to concerts, and there are all sorts, all the time. First Fridays in Center City is also popular." The area immediately surrounding the school has plenty of "great bars, food, and dancing." Drexel is close to the UPenn campus, "and students often go into their parties, which are extraordinary." On campus, "There are numerous fraternities and societies you can join." Intercollegiate sports "aren't incredibly popular here," but "The basketball team is really taking off and is always sold out." Drexel's grounds, once an unbroken sea of brick and concrete, have been renovated; today "There are plenty of green grassy areas for students to hang out and relax," as well as "a new beautiful amphitheater and some nice tree-lined walkways with benches and tables."

Student Body

There "are no real typical students at Drexel. [It's] is a pretty diverse school, with students involved in different kinds of activities, dressing differently, and motivated differently." The school "is a melting pot" with "many, many international and minority students." One student notes, "Drexel's common factor seems to be not race or economic background, but a sense of personal drive. Drexel students work hard—it's a requirement to keep afloat—and that self-propulsion seems to be the tie that binds the student body together." If undergrads "seem to fit in well together," that may be because "Students here are very casual and easygoing." Some have quirky senses of humor; take the one who reports that "the students tend to be of the human variety, with genders varying from male to female. Everyone has their clique, and it takes quite a bit of effort to be excluded from them all."

THE PRINCETON REVIEW SAYS

Admissions

Very important factors considered include: Class rank, academic GPA, rigor of secondary school record, standardized test scores. *Important factors considered include:* Application essay, recommendation(s), character/personal qualities. *Other factors considered include:* Alumni/ae relation, extracurricular activities, first generation, interview, level of applicant's interest, talent/ability, volunteer work, work experience. SAT or ACT required; TOEFL required of all international applicants. High school diploma is required and GED is accepted. *Academic units required:* 3 mathematics, 1 science, (1 science labs). *Academic units recommended:* 1 foreign language.

Financial Aid

Students should submit: FAFSA. The Princeton Review suggests that all financial aid forms be submitted as soon as possible after January 1. *Need-based scholarships/grants offered:* Federal Pell, SEOG, state scholarships/grants, private scholarships, the school's own gift aid, United Negro College Fund. *Loan aid offered:* FFEL Subsidized Stafford, FFEL Unsubsidized Stafford, FFEL PLUS, Federal Perkins, Federal Nursing, college/university loans from institutional funds. Applicants will be notified of awards on a rolling basis beginning 3/15. Federal Work-Study Program available.

The Inside Word

Drexel operates on a rolling admissions basis, meaning that admissions decisions are made relatively quickly after all application materials reach the school. Rolling admissions tend to favor those who apply early in the process, when schools are still worried about whether they will be able to fill their incoming classes. Regardless of when you apply, you shouldn't have too much trouble here if your application establishes you as firmly above average.

THE SCHOOL SAYS ". . ."

From The Admissions Office

"Drexel has gained a reputation for academic excellence since its founding in 1891. In 2006, Drexel became the first top-ranked doctoral university in more than 25 years to open a law school. Its main campus is a 10-minute walk from Center City Philadelphia. Students prepare for successful careers through Drexel's prestigious experiential education program—The Drexel Co-op. Alternating periods of full-time professional employment with periods of classroom study, students can earn an average of $14,000 per 6-month co-op. At any one time, about 2,000 full-time undergraduates are on co-op assignments.

"Drexel integrates science and technology into all 70 undergraduate majors. Students looking for a special challenge can apply to one of 14 accelerated degree programs including the BS/MBA in business; BA/BS/MD in medicine; BA/BS/JD in law; BS/MS or BS/PhD in engineering; BS/MS in information technology; and BS/DPT in physical therapy.

"Pennoni Honors College offers high achievers unique opportunities. Students Tackling Advanced Research (STAR) allows qualified undergraduates to participate in a paid summer research project, and the Center for Civic Engagement matches students with community service opportunities. Students in any major can take dance, music, and theater classes offered through Drexel's performing arts programs.

"Drexel's study abroad program allows students to spend a term or more earning credits while gaining international experience. Adventurous students can also enjoy co-op abroad. Locations include London, Costa Rica, Prague, Rome, and Paris. The Admissions Office invites prospective students to schedule a campus visit for a first-hand look at all Drexel offers.

"Drexel University is currently exploring how to use the new Writing component in admission and placement decisions."

"Students who plan to enter in Fall 2008 will be one of the first classes to take the new SAT for college admissions. Drexel is exploring ways in which the additional Writing component can be used in admissions or placement decisions."

For even more information on this school, turn to page 469 of the "Stats" section.

DUQUESNE UNIVERSITY

600 FORBES AVENUE, PITTSBURGH, PA 15282 • ADMISSIONS: 412-396-5000 • FAX: 412-396-5644
FINANCIAL AID: 412-396-6607 • E-MAIL: ADMISSIONS@DUQ.EDU • WEBSITE: WWW.DUQ.EDU

RATINGS

Quality of Life: 79   Academic: 76   Admissions: 84   Financial Aid: 85

STUDENTS SAY "..."

Academics

Located in a great town for both career networking and college fun, Pittsburgh's Duquesne University offers a prestigious private school education to a "smart, ambitious, and very goal-oriented" student body that "prides itself on its 'Catholic' tradition." DU is perhaps best known for its health sciences programs; students laud the "rigorous pharmacy curriculum," the "wonderful" physical therapy program and "great" nursing, occupational, and athletic training programs, all of which benefit from "great access to all the hospitals in the area." The music program at Duquesne is "amazing," and students say "The employment rate of students that have graduated from the music education program is phenomenal. I'm almost positive every senior that graduated was placed at a job already." Students in many of these areas pursue DUs accelerated bachelor's/graduate degree programs. Regardless of what they study, all DU students must complete a core curriculum that stresses broad general knowledge; students have mixed feelings about the core, warning that these classes are "harder than other courses" and are especially labor intensive. Throughout the school, "Most classes are lecture-driven courses" with relatively large class sizes at the lower levels. The majority of professors are "excellent teachers and very knowledgeable of their respective fields," although, as anywhere, "There are a few awful ones." Nearly all "make themselves available to help you anytime you need. . . . If you are not good at a particular subject, they . . . have tutors available to help you."

> **SURVEY SAYS . . .**
> *Large classes*
> *Students love Pittsburgh, PA*
> *Great off-campus food*
> *Lots of beer drinking*
> *(Almost) everyone smokes*

Life

Student life at Duquesne "is lots of fun," although students say that has more to do with hometown Pittsburgh than with the DU campus. True, the campus offers numerous diversions, including "movies and crafts and sports and tons of organizations," in addition to weekend frat parties which are quite popular with the Greek crowd and underclassmen. However, most students find city life more tempting, reporting that they "like to go downtown to shop, or to the South Side, or to the Waterfront." Oakland is really close by, with "lots of bars, restaurants," and "other colleges." One student explains, "There's always something going on in Pittsburgh, whether it's free concerts, cultural events, or art exhibits, many of which you are admitted into for free or reduced price with a Duquesne ID." The only downside is the weather: "If you're looking for fun, be prepared to bundle up in the winter and to travel by bus or taxi," one student warns. The "beautiful" DU campus features "lots of fountains and grassy areas and stuff." Location is another plus, as the campus is in the middle of Pittsburgh but still has a very private feel. "We have the opportunities of the city but we are secluded on the bluff."

Student Body

The typical Duquesne undergrad is either "well put together" or "cares too much about the way they look"—it's all a matter of perspective. Since most here are the "dress for success" type, the former viewpoint is more popular than the latter, although the "wearing-sweats-and-being-comfortable crowd" make up "about a third" of the campus, so they're hardly a tiny minority. Because "many students at Duquesne went to high school together," the school tends to be quite clique-y. Undergrads also tend to self-segregate by major. As one music student writes, "The typical music major is completely different from the typical student. The majority of music majors have somewhat eclectic taste in fashion, clothing, hobbies . . . which reflects in our personalities. We also talk about stuff we're doing in class outside of school, which isn't very common among other majors." While most students here are Catholic, "There are also people of different religions," and the school "doesn't impose religion" on anyone.

THE PRINCETON REVIEW SAYS

Admissions

Very important factors considered include: Application essay, academic GPA, recommendation(s), rigor of secondary school record, standardized test scores. *Important factors considered include:* Class rank, extracurricular activities, interview, talent/ability, volunteer work. *Other factors considered include:* Alumni/ae relation, first generation, level of applicant's interest, racial/ethnic status, work experience. SAT or ACT required; ACT with Writing component required. High school diploma is required and GED is accepted. *Academic units required:* 4 English, 2 mathematics, 2 science, 2 foreign language, 2 social studies, 4 academic electives.

Financial Aid

Students should submit: FAFSA, institution's own financial aid form Regular filing deadline is 5/1. The Princeton Review suggests that all financial aid forms be submitted as soon as possible after January 1. *Need-based scholarships/grants offered:* Federal Pell, SEOG, state scholarships/grants, private scholarships, the school's own gift aid, United Negro College Fund *Loan aid offered:* FFEL Subsidized Stafford, FFEL Unsubsidized Stafford, FFEL PLUS, Federal Perkins, Federal Nursing, Private Alternative Loans. Applicants will be notified of awards on a rolling basis beginning 3/1. Federal Work-Study Program available. Institutional employment available. Off-campus job opportunities are good.

The Inside Word

Duquesne's overall high admit rate masks the competitiveness of its top programs. Applicants seeking admission to programs in pharmacy, physical therapy, physician's assistant, and forensic science should expect a rigorous review. Others should have little difficulty getting through the door provided they present a respectable complement of transcripts and test scores.

THE SCHOOL SAYS ". . ."

From The Admissions Office

"Duquesne University was founded in 1878 by the Holy Ghost Fathers. Although it is a private, Roman Catholic institution, Duquesne is proud of its ecumenical reputation. The total university enrollment is 10,296. Duquesne University's attractive and secluded campus is set on a 48-acre hilltop ('the bluff') overlooking the large corporate metropolis of Pittsburgh's Golden Triangle. It offers a wide variety of educational opportunities, from the liberal arts to modern professional training. Duquesne is a medium-sized university striving to offer personal attention to its students in addition to the versatility and opportunities of a true university. A deep sense of tradition is combined with innovation and flexibility to make the Duquesne experience both challenging and rewarding. The Palumbo Convocation/Recreation Complex features a 6,300-seat arena, home court to the university's Division I basketball teams; racquetball and handball courts, weight rooms, and saunas. Extracurricular activities are recognized as an essential part of college life, complementing academics in the process of total student development. Students are involved in nearly 100 university-sponsored activities, and Duquesne's location gives students the opportunity to enjoy sports and cultural events both on campus and in the city. There are six residence halls with the capacity to house 3,511 students.

"Although SAT Writing scores will not affect admissions decisions, all freshman applicants are required to take the new SAT (or the ACT with the Writing section). Applicants may choose to submit scores from the old (prior to March 2005) version of the SAT (or ACT) as well, and we will use the student's best scores from either test."

For even more information on this school, turn to page 470 of the "Stats" section.

EASTERN CONNECTICUT STATE UNIVERSITY

83 WINDHAM STREET, WILLIMANTIC, CT 06226 ADMISSIONS: 860-465-5286 • FAX: 860-465-5544
FINANCIAL AID: 860-465-5205 • E-MAIL: ADMISSIONS@EASTERNCT.EDU • WEBSITE: WWW.EASTERNCT.EDU

RATINGS
Quality of Life: 63   Academic: 70   Admissions: 69   Financial Aid: 68

STUDENTS SAY ". . ."

Academics

Wallflowers beware: "If you want to be another face in the crowd . . . Eastern Connecticut State University is not for you." The Nutmeg State's "very affordable" "public liberal arts" university offers "small classes" and the "learning environment of a private college at a lower cost." Expect a challenge as every student here must fulfill "lots and lots" of liberal arts requirements. There are no teaching assistants, and "Almost every class is under 30 students." Thanks

to all this, Eastern has the "best education program in the state." Professors "get to know you and remember your name" and are always "available outside of the classroom." In the words of one sophomore, "I have never had such open, helpful teachers." However, opinions on the administration are split right down the middle between those who say that it "really cares about the students" to those finding it "overly bureaucratic."

Life

Eastern boasts "some of the best dorm rooms ever seen" (including many "singles with kitchens"). The campus is "starting to expand" with "very noisy" but much-needed construction—which has been especially welcomed by commuters who lament the lack of "sufficient parking." There's no shortage of things to do with 60 extracurricular clubs on campus, but many wish for "more school spirit" and "more funding and attention to athletics programs," though there is a baseball team which "is the main core" of campus activity. You might want to leave your toga at home as "There isn't any Greek life." Students report that while Eastern is a "dry campus" with "strict rules concerning alcohol and drug use," there are "a few bars" near campus, and students see "their fair share of parties." Many rely on "concerts, movies, and intramurals" for fun, as Willimantic "offers little to do." That said, those in search of a larger city vibe should take note that "Hartford and Manchester are close."

Student Body

Students agree that "there are many different types of people at Eastern." "The ethnicity is quite mixed," though a typical student, according to some, "wears sweats to class," "lives nearby," and "goes home a lot." These largely "suburban" students are "laid-back and very casual." All in all, it's an independent bunch, as "Everyone does their own thing and has their own cliques." That said, with "all these kinds of people," "no one really has a problem fitting in." Students range from "ambitious, overstudious, or slacking" to a fair amount of "older people getting their degrees." While there are those who "would typically be part of a frat or sorority in any other school," most agree that they have "noticed athletes more than anything."

THE PRINCETON REVIEW SAYS

Admissions

TOEFL required of all international applicants.

Finanancial Aid

The Princeton Review suggests that all financial aid forms be submitted as soon as possible after January 1. Federal Work-Study Program available. Institutional employment available. Off-campus job opportunities are excellent.

The Inside Word

Eastern is a destination for in-state students with above-average grades and SAT scores. That said, prospective students should take note the school rejects about one-third of all applicants, so competition can be fierce if you're on the borderline. When applying, take special care with the essay, interview, and recommendation aspects of the application process. Here's a bonus for all you Northeasterners—residents of New England states are eligible for reduced tuition and fees for a handful of majors.

THE SCHOOL SAYS " . . . "

From The Admissions Office

"Eastern's Admissions Staff encourages motivated students who are interested in a quality, affordable liberal arts education to apply for admission. Eastern's Admission Committee evaluates all applications under the same criteria with emphasis placed on the applicant's prior academic performance in high school and demonstrated commitment to community service and active engagement. Admission decisions are made on a rolling basis. Students are encouraged to apply as early as possible but no later than May 1 for the fall semester. Information sessions and campus tours are offered daily. Prospective students are strongly encouraged to visit to learn firsthand why Eastern is recognized as the best public liberal arts university in Connecticut."

For even more information on this school, turn to page 470 of the "Stats" section.

ELIZABETHTOWN COLLEGE

LEFFLER HOUSE, ONE ALPHA DRIVE, ELIZABETHTOWN, PA 17022 • ADMISSIONS: 717-361-1400
FAX: 717-361-1365 • E-MAIL: ADMISSIONS@ETOWN.EDU • WEBSITE: WWW.ETOWN.EDU

RATINGS
Quality of Life: 88   **Academic:** 85   **Admissions:** 88   **Financial Aid:** 81

STUDENTS SAY "..."

Academics

Elizabethtown College in central Pennsylvania offers a broad core curriculum and "very small" classes. "This semester I have class sizes ranging from five to 23 people," comments a biotechnology major. "It's really nice to hear your professors call you by name during class, or even if they

> **SURVEY SAYS . . .**
> *Students are friendly*
> *Low cost of living*
> *Frats and sororities are unpopular or nonexistent*

see you on campus." Study abroad programs in more than two dozen countries are popular as well. "I have studied abroad in Australia and China," brags a senior. On Etown's "aesthetically appealing campus," "most professors are very good teachers. As you will find everywhere, some are not the greatest, but the tutors [in the Learning Services department] can help with those courses." "I've taken courses in various departments and they are all fabulous instructors and just great people in general," gloats a happy psychology major. "They really take an interest not just in your school work, but are eager to know about your personal life and are willing to do anything to help you succeed." Some students call the management "arrogant and aloof." Others aren't so harsh. "Overall, the administration is incompetent even though they mean well," proposes a senior.

Life

"Etown is a nice place," says a senior. "The intimacy of the college really stands out." It's also "very safe." There's an "integrity policy" that students take seriously. You can leave your valuables most anywhere and "they will be there when you return." Also, Elizabethtown's motto is "Educate for Service" and a laudable amount of volunteerism goes on. Many students think "the dorms could be improved," though. There is also disagreement about the quality of student life. "I would warn people to prepare to have a car and go off campus on weekends if they want something interesting to do," advises a dissatisfied junior. Other students contend that extracurricular involvement is high. Student-run organizations "really put a lot of effort into making sure there are on-campus activities," they say. "Life at Etown is never dull. There are always things to do on the weekend or during the week —everyone is very involved in activities on and off campus." "The students who are disappointed with their time here are those who expect the *Animal House*, large state-school experience." Though drinking definitely happens on this campus, the atmosphere is "rarely thrust in your face." There are no fraternities or sororities. Instead, athletic teams "basically sustain the social life" with house parties. Road trips to Harrisburg and Lancaster are frequent and Hershey is only a few miles north. When the wind is right, the campus "sometimes smells like chocolate."

Student Body

"To sum it up quite simply," says a senior, "Etowners are nice people." They are "down to earth" kids "with diverse interests and spunk." "Geographically, most students are from the Mid-Atlantic area, especially Pennsylvania and New Jersey." They tend to come from a "Christian background." The school is "affiliated with the Church of the Brethren" (which is sort of comparable to the Quaker and Mennonite churches). "You don't see a lot of religious activity on campus, though." Elizabethtown is home to "very typical 18–22 year olds" "from the suburbs." "Most students are a little on the preppy side." "There aren't too many rebels" and "there are barely any atypical students." The gay population is "freakishly small." A solid smattering of international students "adds a diverse element" but ethnic minorities are scarce. "Looking around, you will see mostly white students." "I wish we had more diversity here," hankers a freshman.

THE PRINCETON REVIEW SAYS

Admissions

Very important factors considered include: Rigor of secondary school record. *Important factors considered include:* Class rank, recommendation(s), standardized test scores, interview, racial/ethnic status, volunteer work. *Other factors considered include:* Application essay, alumni/ae relation, character/personal qualities, extracurricular activities, geographical residence, religious affiliation/commitment, state residency, talent/ability, work experience. SAT or ACT required; TOEFL required of all international applicants. High school diploma is required and GED is accepted. *Academic units required:* 4 English, 3 mathematics, 2 science, (2 science labs), 2 foreign language, 2 social studies, 2 history. *Academic units recommended:* 4 English, 4 mathematics, 4 science, (3 science labs), 2 foreign language, 2 social studies, 2 history, 2 academic electives.

Finanancial Aid

Students should submit: FAFSA, institution's own financial aid form, Federal Tax Records. The Princeton Review suggests that all financial aid forms be submitted as soon as possible after January 1. *Need-based scholarships/grants offered:* Federal Pell, SEOG, state scholarships/grants, private scholarships, the school's own gift aid. *Loan aid offered:* FFEL Subsidized Stafford, FFEL Unsubsidized Stafford, FFEL PLUS, Federal Perkins, state loans Applicants will be notified of awards on a rolling basis beginning 3/1.

The Inside Word

The Admissions Office at Elizabethtown strongly encourages you to tell "what experiences are uniquely yours and how [they] will distinguish you from other applicants." The popular occupational therapy and allied health programs fill quickly, so if you are interested in these options, apply early.

THE SCHOOL SAYS " . . . "

From The Admissions Office

"The most important aspect of the admissions program is to admit graduates of Elizabethtown. The entire focus of the admissions process is determining if a student is a good fit for Elizabethtown and if Elizabethtown is a good fit for the student. We pride ourselves on our 'conversational interviews' as a way to set students at ease so that we can discover their potential to contribute to our community. Applicants are assessed in three areas: academic fit, co-curricular fit, and social fit. Integrity, diversity, academic excellence, and a commitment to services are qualities that are highly valued.

"Elizabethtown distinguishes its educational experience by blending a high standard of scholarship with four signature attributes: educating students in a relationship-centered learning community, fostering in students international and cross-cultural perspectives, complementing classroom instruction with experiential-learning opportunities, and preparing students for purposeful lives and meaningful work. This year, the college will graduate two NCAA Postgrad scholars. The college is also one of a few small, regional colleges to have recently graduated a Rhodes Scholar. The campus visit will set Elizabethtown apart from other places as you experience the beautiful campus and new buildings for business and science, mathematics and engineering, and newly renovated athletic facility."

For even more information on this school, turn to page 471 of the "Stats" section.

ELMIRA COLLEGE

ONE PARK PLACE, ELMIRA, NY 14901 • ADMISSIONS: 607-735-1724 • FAX: 607-735-1718
E-MAIL: ADMISSIONS@ELMIRA.EDU • WEBSITE: WWW.ELMIRA.EDU

RATINGS

Quality of Life: 65   **Academic:** 81   **Admissions:** 86   **Financial Aid:** 76

STUDENTS SAY ". . ."

Academics

"Elmira College is all about school spirit," students agree, pointing to the ubiquitous octagons (the official school shape) and purple everything ("Our school color is everywhere: the rugs, the walkways, the soap in the bathrooms, the rock salt in winter... the punch for special occasions"), a fact that many here find appealing and a few feel is "a little ridiculous." Undoubtedly the school is best suited to those who long to immerse themselves in community-building traditions. It also helps if they enjoy co-curricular requirements like the Encore Program (students must attend eight performing arts productions each term during freshman and sophomore years) and community service (60 hours during freshman year). Other unique curricular features here include a required Saturday morning writing class for freshmen (generally resented, although some appreciate how it keeps freshmen from going home on weekends) and a six-week short term in April and May (called Term III, it's "devoted to travel, field experience, research, independent study, and innovative courses"; students call it "the best thing ever"). Elmira "is best known for its nursing and education programs." Business and the sciences are also popular.

> **SURVEY SAYS . . .**
> *Large classes*
> *Low cost of living*
> *Everyone loves the Soaring Eagles*
> *Frats and sororities are unpopular or nonexistent*
> *Lots of beer drinking*
> *Hard liquor is popular*

Life

The city of Elmira "does not give too much to the students. Sure, there are places to eat, mini-malls, and bigger malls, but that can get old. How many times can a college student go out to eat? We're not made of money and can't afford that every week, never mind every night!" Worse still, some here feel the city is "sketchy and unsafe" (others counter that "The idea that Elmira is 'sketchy' depends on where your hometown is. My hometown is a big city, so this area seems really tame to me."). Fortunately, "Elmira College knows this" about its hometown and compensates; "Every weekend they set up some comedian or band to come and play." In addition, campus life provides "athletic events all week and movies every weekend, usually ones that were in theaters and are very popular! All in all, there's a lot to do for a small college." Although EC "does not have any fraternities or sororities, people still find lots of ways to get connected. Partying on weekends is common, but it's not rampant. You can choose not to take part in it and avoid it easily."

Student Body

"There are a lot more females than males at Elmira College," but students tell us that "that is slowly changing" as the school pursues diversity more aggressively. Similarly, "the black community is on the rise" here although it still remains quite small; minority representation arrives mostly in the form of "a rather large international student population." Elmira "loves collecting valedictorians and salutatorians, giving them huge financial aid so they can brag about the ridiculous percentages," so many here were high achievers in high school. "About half of the population participates in sports of some kind at some level, be it varsity, junior varsity, or intramural." There is also "a large gay community" on campus, and students report the environment is "GLBT friendly."

Admissions

Very important factors considered include: Class rank, academic GPA, rigor of secondary school record, character/personal qualities. *Important factors considered include:* Application essay, recommendation(s), standardized test scores, extracurricular activities. *Other factors considered include:* Alumni/ae relation, first generation, geographical residence, interview, level of applicant's interest, racial/ethnic status, talent/ability, volunteer work, work experience. SAT or ACT required; TOEFL required of all international applicants. High school diploma is required and GED is accepted. *Academic units required:* 4 English, 3 mathematics, 3 science, (2 science labs), 3 social studies, 1 history, 2 academic electives. *Academic units recommended:* 2 foreign language.

Finanancial Aid

Students should submit: FAFSA, state aid form. State aid forms if applicable (NY, VT, RI). Regular filing deadline is 6/30. The Princeton Review suggests that all financial aid forms be submitted as soon as possible after January 1. *Need-based scholarships/grants offered:* Federal Pell, SEOG, state scholarships/grants, private scholarships, the school's own gift aid. *Loan aid offered:* FFEL Subsidized Stafford, FFEL Unsubsidized Stafford, FFEL PLUS, Federal Perkins, college/university loans from institutional funds. GATE Student Loan; Private Alternative Loans. Applicants will be notified of awards on a rolling basis beginning 2/1. Federal Work-Study Program available. Institutional employment available. Off-campus job opportunities are good.

The Inside Word

Matchmaking is an important factor in Elmira admissions; the staff has a good idea of who will succeed here and attempts to fashion incoming classes accordingly. Enthusiasm for Elmira is a big part of the equation, meaning an overnight campus visit can impact your chances quite positively.

THE SCHOOL SAYS " . . . "

From The Admissions Office

"Elmira College remains rooted in the liberal arts and sciences, enriching its students' inquiry and analysis of their world, communication skills, and civic and ethical responsibility. The college also requires every student to complete a career-related internship, knowing that this hands-on experience helps 98 percent of June graduates to secure jobs in their desired field of employment or enter graduate or professional school by Labor Day each year. More than one-third of the student body studies abroad with Elmira College professors during the 6-week spring term. The college's 12:1 student/faculty ratio allows the academic experience to be both rigorous and individualized. No classes are taught by teaching assistants. Committed to the residential college experience, on-campus housing is guaranteed all 4 years for undergraduates. Elmira College alumni are loyal, offering internships for students and demonstrating unwavering commitment through giving generously of their time, professional expertise, and financial resources."

For even more information on this school, turn to page 471 of the "Stats" section.

EMERSON COLLEGE

120 BOYLSTON STREET, BOSTON, MA 02116-4624 • ADMISSIONS: 617-824-8600 • FAX: 617-824-8609
FINANCIAL AID: 617-824-8655 • E-MAIL: ADMISSION@EMERSON.EDU • WEBSITE: WWW.EMERSON.EDU

RATINGS
Quality of Life: 90   **Academic:** 82   **Admissions:** 92   **Financial Aid:** 83

STUDENTS SAY "..."

Academics

God help the future Wall Streeter who somehow finds themselves a member of the student body at Emerson, a big happy group of "creative people" who come together to share their passions ("whether it be on the stage, the page, the big screen or the small") and learn more about their own mediums of self-expressions via collaboration with diverse individuals. The focus on the more creative

side of communication and the arts feeds on itself, providing "a community that (usually) understands what an artist needs to thrive and grow." "People come to Emerson knowing exactly what they want to do, and then do that thing all out for four years," says a sophomore. According to its students, Emerson "brings creativity and ingenuity to the arts and communication unlike any other school in the country," and although those that attend the school are more than aware that most of their fellow students might be "part of the next generation of America's starving artists (unless you're a marketing or CSD major)," the school does a tremendous job of offering each a "specialized career-oriented experience," no matter how non-traditional the career path.

The excellent student-teacher ratio means personal attention that goes beyond just office hours, which translates into a lot of time spent with people that are "practicing professionals in their respective fields." The largest classroom at Emerson can only accommodate about 70 students, so lectures (if a student even has any) "are only about 50 students large," and one must "be prepared to do most of your learning outside of the classroom in projects." Design and technology majors in particular get a good deal of hands-on experience. While there can be "a little too much red tape around some of the administrative aspects of Emerson," one student claims that "there is no other school I have encountered where one would feel more easily acknowledged and listened to by their professors."

Life

The drive to succeed in such competitive industries means "a majority of students are busier than the average professional" and "don't really sleep," which is not surprising, considering all of the rehearsals, film shoots, concerts, and organization meetings seemingly required of Emerson life. The school is located right in the heart of downtown Boston, and many admit that it can be hard to concentrate with Boston Common right across the street and the realization that "you live in a city, not a campus bubble." After sophomore year "most people live off-campus," which is where most parties are also hosted; although there's a fair share of partying for those that are interested, "students are more inclined to have an 80s costume and dance party than a frat bash." For those that resist the lure of the cafés, theaters, bars, and performances, plain old-fashioned silliness in the dorms seems equally as exciting, "like coloring or old video games or children's books—everyone just wants to have fun."

Student Body

Around Boston, "an Emerson student can be spotted from a mile away," not because they all look alike, but because they all look so different (although "if you wanted to peg Emerson students as the artsy young adults with an offbeat fashion forward style and a cigarette in one hand and Starbucks in the other, it wouldn't be horribly inaccurate"). Almost all students find a common thread in a love of the arts, which often results in a unifying ambition amongst "people wanting to 'make it' in their field." One film student remarks that Emerson is filled with what she refers to as "my 'type' of people." This "friendly, eclectic and fun" group of students leans pretty far to the left politically, and there is a large gay community at Emerson. There seems to be one student in every class that "can be pretentious and annoying," but these souls are in the minority. Overall, Emersonians are a "very accepting community" of driven individuals.

THE PRINCETON REVIEW SAYS

Admissions

Very important factors considered include: Academic GPA, standardized test scores. *Important factors considered include:* Class rank, application essay, recommendation(s), rigor of secondary school record, character/personal qualities, extracurricular activities, talent/ability. *Other factors considered include:* Alumni/ae relation, first generation, geographical residence, racial/ethnic status, volunteer work, work experience. SAT or ACT required; ACT with Writing component required. TOEFL required of all international applicants. High school diploma is required and GED is accepted. *Academic units required:* 4 English, 3 mathematics, 3 science, 3 foreign language, 3 social studies. *Academic units recommended:* 4 English, 3 mathematics, 3 science, 3 foreign language, 3 social studies, 4 academic electives.

Financial Aid

Students should submit: FAFSA, CSS/Financial Aid PROFILE, noncustodial PROFILE, business/farm supplement, tax Returns, non-custodial statement. The Princeton Review suggests that all financial aid forms be submitted as soon as possible after January 1. *Need-based scholarships/grants offered:* Federal Pell, SEOG, state scholarships/grants, private scholarships, the school's own gift aid. *Loan aid offered:* FFEL Subsidized Stafford, FFEL Unsubsidized Stafford, FFEL PLUS, Federal Perkins, state loans Applicants will be notified of awards on or about 4/1. Federal Work-Study Program available. Institutional employment available. Off-campus job opportunities are excellent.

The Inside Word

Expect your living situation to be made easier by recent developments on Emerson's campus. The Max Mutchnick Campus Center, named in recognition of the substantial gift made by the Emerson alumnus and co-creator/executive producer of Will & Grace, is an 185,000-square-foot building that features a gym, offices, and residence hall. This facility, combined with the recent acquisition of the Colonial Theatre (which will also feature dorm rooms), means nearly three quarters of the students will be able to live on-campus and indulge in affordable rent.

THE SCHOOL SAYS "..."

From The Admissions Office

"Founded in 1880, Emerson is one of the premier colleges in the United States for communication and the arts. Students may choose from more than two-dozen undergraduate and graduate programs supported by state-of-the-art facilities and a nationally renowned faculty. The campus is home to WERS-FM, the first noncommercial station in Boston; the historic 1,200-seat Cutler Majestic Theatre; and Ploughshares, the award-winning literary journal for new writing.

"Located on Boston Common in the heart of the city's Theatre District, Emerson is walking distance from the Massachusetts State House, Chinatown, and historic Freedom Trail. 1,300 students reside on-campus, some in special learning communities such as the Writers' Block and Digital Culture Floor. There is also a fitness center, athletic field, and new gymnasium and campus center.

"Emerson's 3,000 undergraduates come from across the United States and 50 countries. There are more than 60 student organizations and performance groups, 15 NCAA teams, student publications, and honor societies. The College also sponsors programs in Los Angeles; study abroad in the Netherlands, Taiwan, and Czech Republic; and cross-registration with the six-member Boston ProArts Consortium.

"Emerson has the highest quality visual and media arts equipment, including sound-treated television studios, digital editing labs, audio post-production suites with analog and digital peripherals, and a professional marketing suite/focus group room. There are seven on-campus programs to observe speech and hearing therapy, an integrated digital newsroom for aspiring journalists, and an 11-story performance and production center housing rehearsal space, a theatre design/technology center, makeup lab, and costume shop."

For even more information on this school, turn to page 472 of the "Stats" section.

EUGENE LANG COLLEGE—THE NEW SCHOOL FOR LIBERAL ARTS

65 WEST ELEVENTH STREET, NEW YORK, NY 10011 • ADMISSIONS: 212-229-5665 • FAX: 212-229-5355
FINANCIAL AID: 212-229-8930 • E-MAIL: LANG@NEWSCHOOL.EDU • WEBSITE: WWW.LANG.EDU

RATINGS
Quality of Life: 71   **Academic:** 86   **Admissions:** 85   **Financial Aid:** 75

STUDENTS SAY "..."

Academics

Eugene Lang College is an "unconventional," highly urban school with few academic requirements where courses have "really long poetic titles" and professors "go by their first names." "Lang is about small classes in a big city," summarizes a writing major. There's a "rich intellectual tradition" here and, no matter what your major, an "interdisciplinary curriculum." "At Eugene Lang, you have the freedom to pursue your artistic or intellectual direction with absolute freedom," says a philosophy major. However, "students who are uncomfortable in a city and who are not excited about learning for learning's sake should not come to this school." Lang's "clueless," "incredibly bureaucratic" administration is hugely unpopular. The "approachable" and monolithically "radical" faculty is a mixed bag. "75 percent of the professors are pure gold, but the 25 percent who are not really are awful." "Lang's greatest strength (other than location) is its seminar style of teaching," explains a first-year student. "I've yet to be in a class with more then 15 people." Students say their class discussions are phenomenal. "The students, however, at times can be somewhat draining." "All the teachers are highly susceptible to being led off on long tangents" and some "are too gentle and not comfortable shutting down wandering or irrelevant conversation." Juniors and seniors can take classes at several schools within the larger university (including Parsons The New School for Design and Mannes College The New School for Music). "So if Lang's ultra-liberal, writing-intensive seminars are too much," notes an urban studies major, "you can always take a break." Internships all over Manhattan are common, too.

> ### SURVEY SAYS . . .
> *Class discussions encouraged*
> *Athletic facilities need improving*
> *Students aren't religious*
> *Students love New York, NY*
> *Great off-campus food*

Life

There are "great talks given on campus every week by a wide variety of academics on almost every social issue imaginable." Otherwise, "Lang is the anti-college experience." "There is very little community" on this speck of a campus on the northern end of Greenwich Village. "Space and facilities are limited." "There is no safe haven in the form of a communal student space" except for "a courtyard of a million cigarette butts." Certainly, "you aren't going to have the traditional college fun" here. On the other hand, few students anywhere else enjoy this glorious level of independence. "Life at Eugene Lang is integrated completely with living in New York City," and "you have the entire city at your fingertips." When you walk out of class, "you walk out into a city of nine million people." There are dorms here but "most students have apartments," especially after freshman year. For fun, Lang students sometimes "hang around other students' apartments and smoke pot." Many "thoroughly enjoy the club scene." Mostly though, "people band into small groups and then go out adventuring in the city" where "there is always something to do that you've never done, or even heard of, before."

Student Body

"Lang offers the kids with dreadlocks and piercings an alternative place to gather, smoke, and write pretentious essays." It's "overrun with rabid hipsters." "Cool hair" and "avant-garde" attitudes proliferate. So do "tight pants." "Every student at Lang thinks they are an atypical student." "There is a running joke that all Lang students were 'that kid' in high school," says a senior. "Shock is very popular around here," and "everyone fits in as long as they are not too mainstream." "It's the normal ones who have the trouble," suggests a sophomore. "But once they take up smoking and embrace their inner hipster, everything's cool." "There are a lot of queer students, who seem to be comfortable." "We're really not all that ethnically diverse," admits a first-year student. There are "less affluent kids due to great financial aid," and there is a strong contingent of "trust fund babies" and "over-privileged communists from Connecticut." "Most students are wealthy but won't admit it," says a senior. "To be from a rich family and have it be apparent is a cardinal sin." "Most students are extremely liberal and on the same wavelength politically." "Conservative kids are the freaks at our school. Left is in. But having a Republican in class is so exciting," suggest a senior. "We can finally have a debate."

THE PRINCETON REVIEW SAYS

Admissions

Very important factors considered include: Application essay, academic GPA, recommendation(s), rigor of secondary school record. *Important factors considered include:* Standardized test scores, character/personal qualities, interview, level of applicant's interest, volunteer work. *Other factors considered include:* Class rank, alumni/ae relation, extracurricular activities, first generation, geographical residence, work experience. SAT or ACT required; TOEFL required of all international applicants. High school diploma is required and GED is accepted. *Academic units required:* 4 English. *Academic units recommended:* 3 mathematics, 3 science, 2 foreign language, 3 social studies, 2 history.

Financial Aid

Students should submit: FAFSA, state aid form. The Princeton Review suggests that all financial aid forms be submitted as soon as possible after January 1. *Need-based scholarships/grants offered:* Federal Pell, SEOG, state scholarships/grants, private scholarships, the school's own gift aid. *Loan aid offered:* FFEL Subsidized Stafford, FFEL Unsubsidized Stafford, Federal Perkins, college/university loans from institutional funds. Applicants will be notified of awards on a rolling basis beginning 3/1. Federal Work-Study Program available. Institutional employment available.

The Inside Word

The college draws a very self-selected and intellectually curious pool. Those who demonstrate little self-motivation will find themselves denied. It would be a terrible idea to blow off the interview here.

THE SCHOOL SAYS ". . ."

From The Admissions Office

"Eugene Lang College offers students of diverse backgrounds an innovative and creative approach to a liberal arts education, combining the stimulating classroom activity of a small, intimate college with the rich resources of a dynamic, urban university—The New School. The curriculum at Lang is challenging and flexible. Small classes, limited in size to 18 students, promote energetic and thoughtful discussions, and writing is an essential component of all classes. Students can earn a bachelor's degree in Liberal Arts by designing their own program of study within one of 14 interdisciplinary areas in the arts, social sciences, and humanities. Lang also offers bachelor's degrees in the Arts (pending New York State approval), Culture and Media, Economics, Education Studies, Environmental Studies (pending New York State approval), History (pending New York State approval), Philosophy, and Psychology. Students have the opportunity to pursue a five year BA/BFA or BA/MA with other programs offered at the university. Lang's Greenwich Village location puts many of city's cultural treasures—museums, libraries, music venues, theaters, and more—at your doorstep."

For even more information on this school, turn to page 472 of the "Stats" section.

FAIRFIELD UNIVERSITY

1073 NORTH BENSON ROAD, FAIRFIELD, CT 06824 • ADMISSIONS: 203-254-4100 • FAX: 203-254-4199
FINANCIAL AID: 203-254-4125 • E-MAIL: ADMIS@MAIL.FAIRFIELD.EDU • WEBSITE: WWW.FAIRFIELD.EDU

RATINGS
Quality of Life: 75 **Academic:** 82 **Admissions:** 89 **Financial Aid:** 78

STUDENTS SAY "..."

Academics

Study amongst the trees of the "breathtaking campus" at Fairfield University, a competitive mid-sized school with a Division I basketball team and Jesuit ideals. A stalwart of the preppy New England college scene, the school has wealth and is definitely "image conscious," but financial aid packages are said to be super for students in need; several of the large scholarships also "entitle you to preferred registration for small classes." Fairfield's extremely rigorous and time-consuming core courses ensure that students receive a well-rounded education, and the small enrollment assures students small class sizes once they move beyond the mandatory curriculum. The school's Connecticut location is just an hour away from New York City, which provides a plethora of work study and internship possibilities for the students. This is especially convenient for students in Fairfield's notably strong nursing and business programs, the latter of which is taught by a faculty mostly comprised of current and ex-professionals.

> **SURVEY SAYS ...**
> *Large classes*
> *Great library*
> *Diversity lacking on campus*
> *Great off-campus food*
> *Frats and sororities are unpopular or nonexistent*
> *Lots of beer drinking*
> *Hard liquor is popular*

Though students are generally happy here, thanks to an involved student government and a high quality of life, many wish that there was "more school spirit" amongst the student body. The "Leviathan" administration has not curried much favor with students, with the Registrar, Career Planning, and the Division of Student Affairs receiving singular complaints. Complaints of inefficacy and bureaucracy abound, and the various offices "act in distinct bubbles, with one hand not knowing what the other is doing." Opinions of professors are at the opposite end of the spectrum, as most find almost all their teachers "extremely engaging" and "wonderful people." "They actually read your essays and provide constructive criticism," says a student. "Professors have been amazing, inspiring, accessible, and have defined my time at Fairfield," says another.

Life

Not surprising for a school with an "ideal party location on the beaches of the Long Island Sound, only an hour north of New York City by train," students here like to drink. Although all go to "most of the classes," they know that they "must leave time for going out on Tuesdays, Thursdays and the weekend," making Fairfield "the opposite of a suitcase school." "Weekends are usually for partying, whether it's a townhouse party or a party down at the beach. Once you turn 21 there are some great bars in town too." This isn't to say that hedonism completely rules the school; many students remain very active in student activities and service organizations, and for those who don't want to party, the late night programming "offers tons of activities and trips almost every Thursday, Friday, and Saturday night." The student government organizes many of these events, as well as trips into the city for Broadway performances, comedy shows, and sporting events.

Student Body

Almost everyone hails from the northeast at this "homogenous, preppy school" with "generally very intelligent" students. Pockets run pretty deep amongst students, which leads some of this "Ugg wearing, blond haired, Seven for All Mankind-wearing" crowd to "think they're God's gift to mankind." There are plenty of "more mellow, normal folks" here, and even though "it doesn't take much" to be considered an atypical student, those that are usually "find their own niche and have no problems living their lives the way they wish." With the rising enrollment, the school is attempting to increase this diversity, and there's a "growing Gay and Lesbian population."

THE PRINCETON REVIEW SAYS

Admissions

Very important factors considered include: Application essay, academic GPA, recommendation(s), rigor of secondary school record. *Important factors considered include:* Standardized test scores, character/personal qualities, extracurricular activities, first generation, talent/ability, volunteer work, work experience. *Other factors considered include:* Class rank, alumni/ae relation, geographical residence, interview, racial/ethnic status, SAT or ACT required; TOEFL required of all international applicants. High school diploma is required and GED is not accepted. *Academic units required:* 4 English, 3 mathematics, 2 science, (2 science labs), 2 foreign language, 2 social studies, 2 history, 1 academic elective. *Academic units recommended:* 4 English, 4 mathematics, 3 science, (2 science labs), 4 foreign language, 2 social studies, 2 history, 1 academic elective.

Financial Aid

Students should submit: FAFSA, CSS/Financial Aid PROFILE, business/farm supplement. Regular filing deadline is 2/15. The Princeton Review suggests that all financial aid forms be submitted as soon as possible after January 1. *Need-based scholarships/grants offered:* Federal Pell, SEOG, state scholarships/grants, private scholarships, the school's own gift aid, United Negro College Fund. *Loan aid offered:* FFEL Subsidized Stafford, FFEL Unsubsidized Stafford, FFEL PLUS, Federal Perkins, Federal Nursing, Grad Plus, Alternative Loans. Applicants will be notified of awards on or about 4/1. Federal Work-Study Program available. Institutional employment available. Off-campus job opportunities are good.

The Inside Word

Steady increases in the number of admission applications has nicely increased selectivity in recent years. Fairfield's campus and central location, combined with improvements to the library, campus center, classrooms, athletic facilities, and campus residences, make this a campus worth seeing.

THE SCHOOL SAYS ". . ."

From The Admissions Office

"Fairfield University's primary objectives are to develop the creative intellectual potential of its students and to foster in them ethical values and a sense of social responsibility. Towards this end, the application review process is holistic, including not just a student's academic credentials, but their extracurricular pursuits and outside interests. Our students are challenged to be creative and active members of a community in which diversity is not simply accepted, but encouraged and honored. Students learn in a supportive environment with faculty committed to individual development and personal enrichment. As a key to the lifelong process of learning, Fairfield has developed a core curriculum to introduce all students to the broad range of liberal learning. Students choose from 34 majors and 19 interdisciplinary minors. They also have outstanding internship opportunities in Fairfield County and New York City. Additionally, 35 percent of Fairfield's students take advantage of an extensive study abroad program. Fairfield graduates wishing to continue their education are highly successful in gaining graduate and professional school admission, while others pursue extensive job opportunities throughout the region. Thirty-nine Fairfield students have been tapped as Fulbright scholars since 1993.

"Applicants to Fairfield University for Fall 2008 may submit the results from either the SAT or the ACT. We will consider the student's best scores in the application process. Fairfield does not require any SAT Subject Tests."

For even more information on this school, turn to page 473 of the "Stats" section.

FORDHAM UNIVERSITY

441 EAST FORDHAM ROAD, THEBAUD HALL, NEW YORK, NY 10458 • ADMISSIONS: 718-817-4000
FAX: 718-367-9404 • FINANCIAL AID: 718-817-3800 • E-MAIL: ENROLL@FORDHAM.EDU • WEBSITE: WWW.FORDHAM.EDU

RATINGS
Quality of Life: 75   **Academic:** 81   **Admissions:** 92   **Financial Aid:** 73

STUDENTS SAY ". . ."

Academics

Like Certs breath mints, Fordham University is two schools in one. First, there's the school's long-established campus in the Rose Hill section of the Bronx, which might best be regarded as Fordham's 'conventional' undergraduate site. Then there's the newer campus at Manhattan's Lincoln Center, which is "very small and geared toward theater and dance students [though the school says the largest number of majors is liberal arts]." Students are adamant that "they are two different schools going in different directions with different student bodies and different academic focuses." The campuses do share a number of common

> **SURVEY SAYS . . .**
> *Great library*
> *Great off-campus food*
> *Campus feels safe*
> *Students are happy*
> *Frats and sororities are unpopular or nonexistent*
> *Lots of beer drinking*
> *Hard liquor is popular*
> *(Almost) everyone smokes*

traits, however. Each is a Jesuit school "with really big core requirements" that provide undergrads with "a strong background in a broad area of academics before actually specializing in one area, thereby educating the whole mind." The Jesuit influence is also seen in the way each school "promotes social awareness, caring for others, and expanding one's knowledge of the world and helping find one's contribution to it." Each school, of course, benefits from a city location that provides near limitless opportunities for networking, internships, and enriching extracurricular experiences. Rose Hill's students praise Fordham's College of Business ("the school for business professionals"), its pre-law and premedical programs, and its psychology program; undergrads at Lincoln Center boast of "one of the best Theater Departments in the country" and "a great dance program."

Life

Fordham's Rose Hill Campus "is truly beautiful, and the location is pretty much the best of both worlds—the city as well as plenty of green." Here, "life centers around the weekends. Most people go out to local bars, leaving no one on campus on a Tuesday, Friday, or Saturday night. . . . There are numerous events going on on campus all the time, although many of these events are based in religion or politics." Students are also "very involved . . . in intramural sports teams as well as performing arts groups." There's also the city, of course; you can reach it in 15 minutes by Metro North train, or you can save a few bucks and ride the subway. Expect the trip downtown to take about 30 minutes. Closer by is Arthur Avenue, the Bronx's own (and, many say, much better) version of Manhattan's Little Italy. Life at Lincoln Center is understandably less campus-centric; no campus can compete with all that downtown New York City has to offer. One student explains, "The bar and restaurant scene at Lincoln Center is very popular because of the variety of places to go in Manhattan. Dorm parties are not as usual as I would imagine them to be at other colleges. Students from all . . . of Fordham come to Lincoln Center to set out for their various night activities because of the campus's proximity to everything . . . I try to take advantage of the incredible amount of things to do here that one isn't able to do in most other places, but things are very expensive." Lincoln Center dorms "are like apartments, which I know is a definite attraction for many students."

Student Body

Students on the Rose Hill campus tend to be "from an upper-class home in New Jersey, Connecticut, or Long Island . . . [and] wear sandals and jeans and polos, with some popped collars sprinkled in. . . . Off campus (in the Bronx) they stick out like a sore thumb." Many are business and communications majors who favor conservative politics and a businesslike approach to academics. Students at Lincoln Center are more diverse; one writes, "There is no such thing as a typical student at Lincoln Center. Most students who choose to go here are liberal and artsy (writers, dancers, actors). Students tend to be very creative in their clothing choices." The majority of students here are women, and "Most of the boys are gay."

THE PRINCETON REVIEW SAYS

Admissions

Very important factors considered include: Class rank, rigor of secondary school record, standardized test scores. *Important factors considered include:* Application essay, recommendation(s), character/personal qualities, extracurricular activities, talent/ability. *Other factors considered include:* Alumni/ae relation, first generation, geographical residence, racial/ethnic status, volunteer work, work experience. SAT Subject Tests recommended; SAT or ACT required; ACT with Writing component recommended. TOEFL required of all international applicants. High school diploma is required and GED is accepted. *Academic units required:* 4 English, 3 mathematics, 3 science, 2 foreign language, 2 social studies, 2 history, 6 academic electives. *Academic units recommended:* 4 English, 4 mathematics, 4 science, 3 foreign language, 2 social studies, 2 history, 6 academic electives.

Financial Aid

Students should submit: FAFSA, CSS/Financial Aid PROFILE, noncustodial PROFILE, business/farm supplement. Regular filing deadline is 2/1. The Princeton Review suggests that all financial aid forms be submitted as soon as possible after January 1. *Need-based scholarships/grants offered:* Federal Pell, SEOG, state scholarships/grants, private scholarships, the school's own gift aid. *Loan aid offered:* FFEL Subsidized Stafford, FFEL Unsubsidized Stafford, FFEL PLUS, Federal Perkins Applicants will be notified of awards on or about 4/1.

The Inside Word

Applicants to Fordham are required to indicate whether they are applying to Fordham College—Rose Hill, Fordham College—Lincoln Center, or the College of Business Administration. Admissions criteria vary by school, but all are very competitive. Graduation from one of the area's many prestigious Catholic high schools is certainly a plus.

THE SCHOOL SAYS ". . ."

From The Admissions Office

"Fordham University offers a distinctive, values-centered educational experience that is rooted in the Jesuit tradition of intellectual rigor and personal attention. Located in New York City, Fordham offers to students the unparalleled educational, cultural, and recreational advantages of one of the world's greatest cities. Fordham has two residential campuses in New York—the tree-lined, 85-acre Rose Hill in the Bronx, and the cosmopolitan Lincoln Center campus in the heart of Manhattan's performing arts center. The university's state-of-the-art facilities and buildings include one of the most technologically advanced libraries in the country. Fordham offers a variety of majors, concentrations, and programs that can be combined with an extensive career planning and placement program. More than 2,600 organizations in the New York metropolitan area offer students internships that provide hands-on experience and valuable networking opportunities in fields such as business, communications, medicine, law, and education.

"Applicants are required to take SAT or the ACT with or without the Writing section. SAT IIs are recommended but not required."

For even more information on this school, turn to page 473 of the "Stats" section.

FRANKLIN & MARSHALL COLLEGE

PO Box 3003, Lancaster, PA 17604-3003 • Admissions: 717-291-3953 • Fax: 717-291-4381
Financial Aid: 717-291-3991 • E-mail: admission@fandm.edu • Website: www.fandm.edu

RATINGS
Quality of Life: 72   Academic: 88   Admissions: 95   Financial Aid: 81

STUDENTS SAY ". . ."

Academics

Franklin and Marshall is widely regarded as a school that "prepares students well for law school and medical school," along with retaining "a stellar reputation in graduate school admissions departments," but there's more to F&M than a bunch of high-strung future doctors and lawyers. True, the school has earned a reputation as a preprofessional powerhouse through its "intense workload"

and "very difficult grading structure," conditions that some see as necessary in order to provide "an environment for intense personal and academic growth, and development of the skills necessary to achieve well-rounded success in life." However, students deem the workload "far too academically demanding for an average liberal arts college." But F&M also boasts "amazing departments in German, economics, history, government…and geology/environmental science," among others. And in all areas—not just in the high-profile sciences and business—the school ensures that "independent research, especially for upperclassmen, is a vital part of the academic experience," and that "there are enough resources that can be accessed to make good grades more easily attainable," the "demanding" workload notwithstanding. Close student-teacher relationships help make the experience; professors here "are by far the greatest thing about this school. If you're interested in doing something, you can always find a professor or other staff member who would love to help you."

Life

"There is a grind at F&M" during the week, "not a bad one, but you have to be ready for it. Everyone takes his role as a student here very seriously: class, library, meetings, more class, more library, extracurriculars, most students follow this itinerary during the week." Weeknight respites come in the form of "concerts, movies, amazing lectures and other things to break up the schedule." For most, weekends "are a good time to relax and drink and forget about all of the work that has been done and still needs to be done in the week to come," so "most students like to go to one or more of the numerous fraternity parties or they may go to a party in someone's room or apartment." And "If you aren't into the drinking scene or the partying scene on campus"—and contrary to the school's reputation, some students here aren't—"you can go to Ben's Underground, which is an alcohol-free, student-run club. Students can go to play pool or see comedians. It's really a nice facility to use and open all week." Also, "Athletics are fairly popular for a division three school, and the orchestra draws as well." Hometown Lancaster offers "a bunch of art galleries, really good cafés, an old opera house that has great plays, and a concert venue that has pretty big name bands play." However, by the time most students are juniors, "Lancaster and the frat scene get old, so older students take to the local bars and sometimes take road trips to…Philadelphia or Washington DC."

Student Body

F&M is "an extremely preppy school and many designers are flashed all around campus. Students are not afraid to show that they have money, but they are never in your face about it." Not everyone here is a slave to fashion. "You have students that do not get all dressed up for class that just wear sweats and sweatshirt," says a student. Along with those students "from boarding schools or expensive private schools," you'll find "a handful of international students, a smaller handful of minority students, and a few 'townies.' Everyone finds a niche, though." The small campus sometimes feels smaller because students can be cliquish; undergrads here "can be broken into many groups: frats, sororities, specific athletic groups, similar interests (arts, music, etc)."

THE PRINCETON REVIEW SAYS

Admissions

Very important factors considered include: Class rank, academic GPA, rigor of secondary school record, character/personal qualities. *Important factors considered include:* Application essay, recommendation(s), standardized test scores, extracurricular activities, interview, talent/ability, volunteer work. *Other factors considered include:* Alumni/ae relation, geographical residence, level of applicant's interest, racial/ethnic status, work experience. TOEFL required of all international applicants. High school diploma is required and GED is accepted. *Academic units required:* 4 English, 3 mathematics, 2 science, (2 science labs), 2 foreign language, 1 social studies, 2 history, 1 visual/performing arts. *Academic units recommended:* 4 mathematics, 3 science, (3 science labs), 4 foreign language, 3 social studies, 3 history.

Financial Aid

Students should submit: FAFSA, institution's own financial aid form, CSS/Financial Aid PROFILE, noncustodial PROFILE, business/farm supplement. Regular filing deadline is 3/1. The Princeton Review suggests that all financial aid forms be submitted as soon as possible after January 1. *Need-based scholarships/grants offered:* Federal Pell, SEOG, state scholarships/grants, private scholarships, the school's own gift aid. *Loan aid offered:* FFEL Subsidized Stafford, FFEL Unsubsidized Stafford, FFEL PLUS, Federal Perkins, college/university loans from institutional funds. Applicants will be notified of awards on or about 3/15. Federal Work-Study Program available.

The Inside Word

Applicants who feel that their standardized test scores do not accurately reflect their abilities may opt to omit them from their applications, in which case they must instead include two recent (junior or senior year) graded papers, preferably from a humanities or social science course. Since F&M is a school that requires tons of writing from its students, there could hardly be a better way to demonstrate your qualifications to attend than with the written word. Make sure to let F&M know if the school is your first choice. The school loses lots of applicants to 'prestige schools' and will review your application more favorably if you indicate a commitment to attending.

THE SCHOOL SAYS ". . ."

From The Admissions Office

"Franklin & Marshall students choose from a variety of fields of study, traditional and interdisciplinary, that typify liberal learning. Professors in all of these fields are committed to a common purpose, which is to teach students to think, speak, and write with clarity and confidence. Whether the course is in theater or in physics, the class will be small, engagement will be high, and discussion will dominate over lecture. Thus, throughout their 4 years, beginning with the First-Year Seminar, students at Franklin & Marshall are repeatedly invited to active participation in intellectual play at high levels. Our graduates consistently testify to the high quality of an F&M education as a mental preparation for life.

"Beginning with the Fall 2007 incoming class, the school offers an SAT option policy to all students."

For even more information on this school, turn to page 474 of the "Stats" section.

FRANKLIN W. OLIN COLLEGE OF ENGINEERING

OLIN WAY, NEEDHAM, MA 02492-1245 • ADMISSIONS: 781-292-2222 • FAX: 781-292-2210
FINANCIAL AID: 781-292-2364 • E-MAIL: INFO@OLIN.EDU • WEBSITE: WWW.OLIN.EDU

RATINGS

Quality of Life: 99   Academic: 99   Admissions: 99   Financial Aid: 99

STUDENTS SAY ". . ."

Academics

An "innovative," "exceptional" "project-based" curriculum attracts the country's math and science whiz kids to Franklin W. Olin College of Engineering. The school's "small size" and "open atmosphere that's supportive of everyone" are very appealing to the approximately 300 undergraduates on campus. But the piece de resistance—the thing that has students choosing this place over schools like MIT and Cal Tech—has got to be the "free tuition." "Academics-wise, the school kicks people's [butts] right and left. It takes the best and the brightest and breaks them, pushing them when they likely have never had to work hard before. Around here,

everyone is smart, and professors assume that, so the classes are taken to that level; there is no such thing as an easy class." One might describe professors here as "grown up Olin kids" insofar as they "are geniuses," but also "young" and just "generally awesome people." "They love teaching," and are "mostly on [a] first-name basis" with undergrads, professors bend over backwards to make themselves accessible, either in person or over e-mail, which means "that they always seem to be available." In terms of how smoothly things run, keep in mind that Olin is "an experiment, so you never really know what's going to happen," which "tends to lead to some chaos." That doesn't mean that the administration isn't trying—it's actually trying all the time. There is a "constant dialogue of feedback between the students, staff, and faculty" and the administration "always has open doors to everyone." "You can sit down and eat lunch [in the dining hall] with the president if you want to." Feedback drives a "continual reassessment" of the institution with the aim of constant "improvement in all departments."

Life

A popular saying used to describe student life at Olin goes like this: "Choose two: work, sleep, fun." The majority of students choose the first and the last because "An Oliner at rest is an unhappy Oliner." The "Entrepreneurial spirit is strong" here, leading many people to choose to spend what little free time they have "working on cool projects" like "hacking the thermostat in their room" and "playing with lasers and circuits." Not everyone engages in genius science "geek" endeavors in their free time. Instead many do plain-Jane, run-of-the-mill, vanilla geek activities like "playing DDR" and "video gaming." Still, normal college student stuff happens here, too. "There are definitely typical college parties with drinking games," and "Clubs and student organizations put on a lot of activities." Plenty of students also get heavily involved "with local service groups (FIRST Robotics and Habitat for Humanity are particularly active)." And as it is at every one of the gazillion colleges in the greater Beantown area, "going into Boston for events" is a popular pastime here too. Concerning the more mundane details of day-to-day life on campus, students are pleased. The dorms are "nice and warm," and "The food is amazing."

Student Body

Picture this: "Engineers with social skills." Yes, they really do exist, and about 300 of them live and learn happily together at this small college on the outskirts of Boston. These folks "are all extremely intelligent and very high-achieving." "There are students here that have held patents since high school, [and others] who have worked for NASA." Perhaps because people like this—people who have "already made incredible, insane contributions to the world"—are not in short supply, "The majority [of students] don't seem to feel like they're especially smart." So there's little threat of being smothered by peers' egos if one enrolls here. "Olin has a very diverse student body with regard to everything except race." "The full-tuition scholarship allows for students from less wealthy backgrounds" to attend, and a "strong group of very religious students" coexists peacefully with a "decent number of people who express alternative sexualities." In sum, a live-and-let-live philosophy is pervasive. "People are allowed to have their own passions and opinions so long as they have passions and opinions."

THE PRINCETON REVIEW SAYS

Admissions

Very important factors considered include: Rigor of secondary school record, Academic GPA, Application Essay, Recommendation(s), Extracurricular activities, Talent/ability, Character/personal qualities, Level of applicant's interest. *Important factors considered include:* Volunteer work, Class rank, Standardized test scores *Other factors considered include:* Interview, First Generation, Geographical residence, State residency, Racial/ethnic status, Work experience.

Financial Aid

The Princeton Review suggests that all financial aid forms be submitted as soon as possible after January 1.

The Inside Word

Not many colleges can boast that they are filled with students who turned down offers from the likes of MIT, Cal Tech, and Carnegie Mellon, but Olin can. Olin is unique among engineering schools in that the Admissions Office really looks for more than just brains. Things like social skills and eloquence are taken extremely seriously here, so reclusive geniuses seeking 4 years of technical monasticism will be at a disadvantage in the application process.

THE SCHOOL SAYS ". . ."

From The Admissions Office

"Every admitted student at Olin College receives a $130,000 4-year full-tuition scholarship. The endowment to support these scholarships, as well as the funds to build a brand new state-of-the-art campus, was provided by the F. W. Olin Foundation. This commitment, in excess of $460 million, is among the largest grants in the history of U.S. higher education. It is the intention of the founders that this scholarship will be offered in perpetuity.

"The selection process at Olin College is unique to college admission. Each year a highly self-selecting pool of approximately 800 applications is reviewed on traditional selection criteria. Approximately 180 finalists are invited to one of two Candidates' Weekends in February and March. These candidates are grouped into five-person teams for a weekend of design-and-build exercises, group discussions, and interviews with Olin students, faculty, and alumni. Written evaluations and recommendations for each candidate are prepared by all Olin participants and submitted to the faculty Admission Committee. The committee admits about 100 candidates to yield a freshman class of 75. The result is that the freshman class is ultimately chosen on the strength of personal attributes such as leadership, cooperation, creativity, communication, and their enthusiasm for Olin College.

"A waiting list of approximately 20 is also established. Some wait list candidates who are not offered a spot in the class may defer enrollment for 1 year—with the guarantee of the Olin Scholarship. Wait list students are strongly encouraged do something unusual, exciting, and productive during their sabbatical year.

"Students applying for admission in the Fall of 2007 are required to take the SAT (or the ACT with the writing section). Olin College also requires scores from two SAT Subject Tests: Math (level 1 or 2), and a Science of the student's choice."

For even more information on this school, turn to page 474 of the "Stats" section.

THE GEORGE WASHINGTON UNIVERSITY

2121 I Street Northwest, Suite 201, Washington, DC 20052 • Admissions: 202-994-6040
Fax: 202-994-0325 • Financial Aid: 202-994-6620 • E-mail: gwadm@gwis2.circ.gwu.edu • Website: www.gwu.edu

RATINGS
Quality of Life: 94   Academic: 86   Admissions: 96   Financial Aid: 88

STUDENTS SAY ". . ."

Academics

At George Washington University, it's all about "being in the center of the most powerful city in the world and deciding where to make your mark," where students can tap "the nation's capital, whether [for] sports, science and medicine, politics, or psychology." Politics are the primary drawing card; the stellar Elliot School of International Affairs trains tomorrow's diplomats, while solid programs in political science and political communication benefit from heavyweight guest speakers (one student writes, "DeeDee Myers came to my Washington Reporters class, and I got to go interview Bob Siegel of NPR—it's experiences like that that

> **SURVEY SAYS . . .**
> Athletic facilities are great
> Students love Washington, DC
> Great off-campus food
> Dorms are like palaces
> Campus feels safe
> Students are happy
> Student publications are popular
> Student government is popular
> Political activism is popular

make GW special"), and access to incredible internships; as one student puts it, "GW is government's largest source of slave labor. It isn't uncommon . . . [to] see people from your different classes in the halls of Capital Hill." GW doesn't begin and end with government though; the school also has "a wonderful business program with an abundance of internship opportunities," a "computer security and information assurance" program "that's one of the best in the world and is actually one of only a handful accredited by the National Security Agency," and numerous other strengths. GW's administration seems geared toward training future government workers; students describe it as very "bureaucratic." The school maintains a large adjunct faculty; while some love that the adjuncts "have other projects or jobs on the side that can give students firsthand experience with real issues," others complain that "we lose many great adjunct professors every year" and that the large turnover "would be avoided if we just shelled out a little more money [to take on more full-time faculty]."

Life

"Whether it's going to the Kennedy Center, [to] the 9:30 Club, or [for] a midnight monument tour . . . DC is at the center of a GW student's experience." Undergrads boast that "of all DC universities, GW is the best situated. Where else can you party, get drunk, stumble your way to the steps of the Lincoln [Memorial], and attempt to hurry back to get enough sleep to function at your internship on the Hill?" Being in DC "makes it easy to always have something to do, from the monuments to the museums . . . from just hanging out on campus [to] going to sporting events." Speaking of sports, GW basketball "is huge. However than that, we're not much of a sports school. Students are much more interested in joining the College Democrats or the College Republicans." Many are also interested in partying, but a junior stresses that she'd "never call GW a party school. It's definitely there if you want it, but it's not pressured on you at all. Same thing with frats and sororities: Those who want to be in Greek life can be, and those who don't, don't have to [be] in order to have a fulfilling college experience."

Student Body

GW attracts "a lot of wealthy students" (its tuition is among the nation's highest), but there is also "a sense of diversity on campus." Jewish students make up about one-quarter of the undergraduate population; there are also "a lot of international students," "students from each of the 50 states," and, sprinkled among the wealthy, "plenty of middle-class students." At GW, undergrads say, you'll find "people that have disabilities, and people from every race, religion, sexual orientation, and ideology." (While all ideologies are represented, it should be noted that "most students characterize themselves as Democrats.") Students tell us that GW isn't as much "a melting pot as a tossed salad, where people from different backgrounds, frats, and student org[anizations] all blend together and taste pretty darn good." Undergrads here tend to be "very driven, constantly thinking about what their next internship is going to be, and how they're going to get out into Washington more and things like that."

THE PRINCETON REVIEW SAYS

Admissions

Very important factors considered include: Academic GPA, rigor of secondary school record. *Important factors considered include:* Class rank, application essay, recommendation(s), standardized test scores, extracurricular activities, interview, talent/ability, volunteer work. *Other factors considered include:* Alumni/ae relation, character/personal qualities, first generation, geographical residence, level of applicant's interest, racial/ethnic status, work experience. SAT or ACT required; High school diploma is required and GED is not accepted. *Academic units required:* 4 English, 2 mathematics, 2 science, (1 science labs), 2 foreign language, 2 social studies. *Academic units recommended:* 4 English, 4 mathematics, 4 science, 4 foreign language, 4 social studies.

Financial Aid

Students should submit: FAFSA, CSS/Financial Aid PROFILE Regular filing deadline is 2/1. The Princeton Review suggests that all financial aid forms be submitted as soon as possible after January 1. *Need-based scholarships/grants offered:* Federal Pell, SEOG, state scholarships/grants, the school's own gift aid. *Loan aid offered:* FFEL Subsidized Stafford, FFEL Unsubsidized Stafford, FFEL PLUS, Federal Perkins Federal Work-Study Program available. Institutional employment available. Off-campus job opportunities are excellent.

The Inside Word

With over 20,000 applications to process annually, GW would be forgiven if it gave student essays only a perfunctory glance. However, the school considers essays carefully; a school Admissions Officer recently told the Washington Times that student essays represent "the student's voice in the application," adding that the school's low admit rate means that "everything (in the application) takes on significance."

THE SCHOOL SAYS "..."

From The Admissions Office

"At GW, we welcome students who show a measure of impatience with the limitations of traditional education. At many universities, the edge of campus is the real world, but not at GW, where our campus and Washington, DC are seamless. We look for bold, bright students who are ambitious, energetic, and self-motivated. Here, where we are so close to the centers of thought and action in every field we offer, we easily integrate our outstanding academic tradition and faculty connections with the best internship and job opportunities of Washington, DC. A generous scholarship and financial assistance program attracts top students from all parts of the country and the world.

"Students applying for Fall 2008 may send either an old or revised SAT score. Regardless of the version of the SAT submitted, we will use those scores that best work to the student's advantage. Applicants to the BA/MD, IEMP, and BA/JD programs are required to submit SAT Subject Tests. "

For even more information on this school, turn to page 474 of the "Stats" section.

GEORGETOWN UNIVERSITY

THIRTY-SEVENTH AND P STREETS NORTHWEST, WASHINGTON, DC 20057 • ADMISSIONS: 202-687-3600 • FAX: 202-687-5084
FINANCIAL AID: 202-687-4547 • WEBSITE: WWW.GEORGETOWN.EDU

RATINGS
Quality of Life: 84   **Academic:** 92   **Admissions:** 98   **Financial Aid:** 93

STUDENTS SAY ". . ."

Academics

This moderately-sized elite academic establishment stays true to its Jesuit foundations by educating its students with the idea of Cura Personalis, or "care for the whole person." The "well-informed" student body perpetuates upon itself, creating an atmosphere full of vibrant intellectual life, but "also balanced with extra-curricular learning and development." "Georgetown is…a place where people work very, very hard without feeling like they are in direct competition," says an international politics major.   Located in

> **SURVEY SAYS . . .**
> Students love Washington, DC
> Great off-campus food
> Students are happy
> Frats and sororities are unpopular
> or nonexistent
> Political activism is popular
> Lots of beer drinking

Washington, D.C., there's a noted School of Foreign Service here, and the access to internships is a huge perk for those in political or government programs. In addition, the proximity to the nation's capital fetches "high-profile guest speakers," with many of the most powerful people in global politics speaking regularly, as well as a large number of adjunct professors who either are currently working in the government as a day job, or have retired from high level positions.

Georgetown has on offer a "great selection of very knowledgeable professors, split with a good proportion of those who are experienced in realms outside of academia (such as former government officials) and career academics," though there are a few superstars who might be "somewhat less than totally collegial." Professors tend to be "fantastic scholars and teachers" and are "generally available to students," as well as often being "interested in getting to know you as a person (if you put forth the effort to talk to them and go to office hours)." Though Georgetown has a policy of grade deflation, meaning "A's are hard to come by," there are "a ton of interesting courses available" and TAs are used only for optional discussion sessions and help with grading. The academics "can be challenging or they can be not so much (not that they are ever really easy, just easier)"; it all depends on the courses you choose and how much you actually do the work. The school administration is well-meaning and "usually willing to talk and compromise with students," but the process of planning activities can be full of headaches and bureaucracy, and the administration itself "sometimes is overstretched or has trouble transmitting its message." Nevertheless, "a motivated student can get done what he or she wants."

Life

Students are "extremely well aware of the world around them," from government to environment, social to economic, and "Georgetown is the only place where an argument over politics, history, and philosophy is preceded by a keg stand." Hoyas like to have a good time on weekends, and parties at campus and off-campus apartments and townhouses "are generally open to all comers and tend to have a somewhat networking atmosphere; meeting people you don't know is a constant theme." With such a motivated group on such a high-energy campus, "people are always headed somewhere, it seems—to rehearsal, athletic practice, a guest speaker, to the gym." Community service and political activism are particularly popular, as is basketball. Everything near Georgetown is in walking distance, including the world of DC's museums, restaurants, and stores, and "grabbing or ordering late night food is a popular option."

Student Body

There are "a lot of wealthy students on campus," and preppy-casual is the fashion de rigueur; this is "definitely not a 'granola' school," but students from diverse backgrounds are typically welcomed by people wanting to learn about different experiences. Indeed, everyone here is well-traveled and well-educated, and there are "a ton of international students." "You better have at least some interest in politics or you will feel out-of-place," says a student. The school can also be "a bit cliquish, with athletes at the top," but there are "plenty of groups for everybody to fit into and find their niche," and "there is much crossover between groups."

THE PRINCETON REVIEW SAYS

Admissions

Very important factors considered include: Class rank, application essay, academic GPA, recommendation(s), rigor of secondary school record, standardized test scores, character/personal qualities, talent/ability. *Important factors considered include:* Extracurricular activities, interview, volunteer work. *Other factors considered include:* Alumni/ae relation, geographical residence, racial/ethnic status, state residency, work experience. SAT Subject Tests recommended; SAT or ACT required; High school diploma is required and GED is accepted. *Academic units recommended:* 4 English, 2 mathematics, 1 science, 2 foreign language, 2 social studies, 2 history.

Financial Aid

Students should submit: FAFSA, CSS/Financial Aid PROFILE, noncustodial PROFILE, business/farm supplement, tax returns. Regular filing deadline is 2/1. The Princeton Review suggests that all financial aid forms be submitted as soon as possible after January 1. *Need-based scholarships/grants offered:* Federal Pell, SEOG, state scholarships/grants, private scholarships, the school's own gift aid. *Loan aid offered:* FFEL Subsidized Stafford, FFEL Unsubsidized Stafford, FFEL PLUS, Federal Perkins, Federal Nursing, Alternative loans. Applicants will be notified of awards on or about 4/1. Federal Work-Study Program available. Institutional employment available. Off-campus job opportunities are excellent.

The Inside Word

It was always tough to get admitted to Georgetown, but in the early 1980s Patrick Ewing and the Hoyas created a basketball sensation that catapulted the place into position as one of the most selective universities in the nation. There has been no turning back since. GU gets almost 10 applications for every space in the entering class, and the academic strength of the pool is impressive. Virtually 50 percent of the entire student body took AP courses in high school. Candidates who are wait listed should hold little hope for an offer of admission; over the past several years Georgetown has taken very few off their lists.

THE SCHOOL SAYS ". . ."

From The Admissions Office

"Georgetown was founded in 1789 by John Carroll, who concurred with his contemporaries Benjamin Franklin and Thomas Jefferson in believing that the success of the young democracy depended upon an educated and virtuous citizenry. Carroll founded the school with the dynamic Jesuit tradition of education, characterized by humanism and committed to the assumption of responsibility and action. Georgetown is a national and international university, enrolling students from all 50 states and over 100 foreign countries. Undergraduate students are enrolled in one of four undergraduate schools: the College of Arts and Sciences, School of Foreign Service, Georgetown School of Business, and Georgetown School of Nursing and Health Studies. All students share a common liberal arts core and have access to the entire university curriculum.

"Applicants who graduate from high school in 2008 have the option of submitting scores from either the new or existing version of the SAT. Only the Verbal and Math portions of the new SAT will be considered. The student's best composite score will be used in the admission process."

For even more information on this school, turn to page 475 of the "Stats" section.

GETTYSBURG COLLEGE

ADMISSIONS OFFICE, EISENHOWER HOUSE, GETTYSBURG, PA 17325-1484 • ADMISSIONS: 717-337-6100 • FAX: 717-337-6145
FINANCIAL AID: 717-337-6611 • E-MAIL: ADMISS@GETTYSBURG.EDU • WEBSITE: WWW.GETTYSBURG.EDU

RATINGS
Quality of Life: 86   **Academic:** 91   **Admissions:** 95   **Financial Aid:** 98

STUDENTS SAY ". . ."

Academics

Gettysburg College is a quintessential small liberal arts college, a place where "You can be challenged academically in an intimate environment of smaller class sizes and a smaller student-to-faculty ratio," enabling "students to develop a close rapport with peers and professors." Students here speak glowingly of the "welcoming community with limitless opportunities" to get involved and "grow in and out of the classroom." Those opportunities include "strong study abroad programs, community service activities, internships, and externships." Academically, "Gettysburg isn't a walk in the park. Your professors have expectations of you whether you are a first-year in a 101 class or a senior looking into a research proposal." Help is available to those in danger of falling behind; one student writes, "The offices are there to help you from Calc-Aid [tutors], biology [reviews], and the Writing Center . . . There is so much available; you just need to go take advantage of it." The school's strongest disciplines include political science, music, biology, environmental studies, and (unsurprisingly) Civil War–era studies. Gettysburg also "has a great management department for a small liberal arts school."

> **SURVEY SAYS . . .**
> Large classes
> Great computer facilities
> Great library
> Frats and sororities dominate
> social scene
> Lots of beer drinking

Life

"Greek life is where the majority of social life is centered" at Gettysburg, with nearly half of all male students joining a fraternity, "But that's not to say that there are not options beyond that." True, "Greek life is huge at Gettysburg, and for a male who chooses not to 'go Greek' life can be hard socially." It's not as big a deal for females, because "Gettysburg does not have sorority houses." The Greek scene as a whole is "not exclusive"—everyone "goes to the frats." Moreover, "The college doesn't allow rush to take place until second year, so hopefully students have made friends before making the choice to branch out into other social groups such as the frats." "Most everyone makes a conscious effort to get involved on campus in lots of different activities," so the Greeks, while big, aren't the only game in town. The school "does a lot of extras for the students, such as themed dinners, concerts, and special events," and "The Activity Board also brings bands and movies on weekends so there are other things to do." College sports teams "are very strong, both men's and women's," and "lots of students play intramurals or work out." Hometown Gettysburg, with its battlefield and 'ghost tours,' is great for history buffs and has a lot of "small town charm"; others may prefer to "take day trips" to DC and Baltimore for fun, although each requires a 90-minute drive.

Student Body

Gettysburg students tend to be "smart, outgoing, preppy, and determined," the kind of folks who "work real hard during the week and then have fun on the weekend," but also find time to "volunteer and [get] involved in extracurriculars, clubs, and athletics." Students admit that "there is very little diversity on campus, but the majority of the students come from high schools with the same situation," so many "don't notice the lack of diversity, though this can make you stand out if you're different." Students who don't fit the mold tell us they are comfortable here; one writes, "Gettysburg students tend to come from families who are mid- to upper-class, [and] there is a high percentage of legacy students on campus." Quite frequently students show their wealth "in the form of clothing or cars," but "Money isn't the only thing that matters here." While it may be plentiful, "Even if you don't wear Lily Pulitzer or Burberry you will be just fine as long as flip-flops are your favorite footwear!" Students tend to be politically conservative, although the "The Frisbee team is one niche of politically liberal people" on campus.

THE PRINCETON REVIEW SAYS

Admissions

Very important factors considered include: Class rank, academic GPA, recommendation(s), rigor of secondary school record. *Important factors considered include:* Application essay, standardized test scores, character/personal qualities, extracurricular activities, interview, talent/ability, volunteer work. *Other factors considered include:* Alumni/ae relation, first generation, geographical residence, level of applicant's interest, racial/ethnic status, work experience. SAT or ACT required; TOEFL required of all international applicants. High school diploma is required and GED is accepted. *Academic units required:* 4 English, 3 mathematics, 3 science, (3 science labs), 3 foreign language, 3 social studies, 3 history. *Academic units recommended:* 4 English, 4 mathematics, 4 science, (4 science labs), 4 foreign language, 4 social studies, 4 history.

Financial Aid

Students should submit: FAFSA, CSS/Financial Aid PROFILE, business/farm supplement. Regular filing deadline is 2/15. The Princeton Review suggests that all financial aid forms be submitted as soon as possible after January 1. *Need-based scholarships/grants offered:* Federal Pell, SEOG, state scholarships/grants, private scholarships, the school's own gift aid. *Loan aid offered:* FFEL Subsidized Stafford, FFEL Unsubsidized Stafford, FFEL PLUS, Federal Perkins, college/university loans from institutional funds. Applicants will be notified of awards on or about 3/26. Federal Work-Study Program available. Institutional employment available. Off-campus job opportunities are excellent.

The Inside Word

Expect a thorough and highly personalized review of your application at Gettysburg College. Excellent students with relatively weak standardized test scores, take note: Gettysburg no longer requires test scores as part of its application package. The goal of this new policy is to "enrich the classroom environment by encouraging students with a high secondary school grade point average (GPA) and other creative talents who do not perform well on standardized tests to apply for admission." The effect should be to open Gettysburg's doors to capable students who might otherwise not have been previously admitted.

THE SCHOOL SAYS ". . ."

From The Admissions Office

"Four major goals of Gettysburg College to best prepare students to enter the twenty-first century, include: first, to accelerate the intellectual development of our first-year students by integrating them more quickly into the intellectual life of the campus; second, to use interdisciplinary courses combining the intellectual approaches of various fields; third, to encourage students to develop an international perspective through course work, study abroad, association with international faculty, and a variety of extracurricular activities; and fourth, to encourage students to develop (1) a capacity for independent study by ensuring that all students work closely with individual faculty members on an extensive project during their undergraduate years and (2) the ability to work with their peers by making the small group a central feature in college life.

"Gettysburg College requires that freshman applicants submit scores from the old or new SAT. Students may also choose to submit scores from the ACT (with or without the Writing component) in lieu of the SAT."

For even more information on this school, turn to page 475 of the "Stats" section.

GORDON COLLEGE

255 GRAPEVINE ROAD, WENHAM, MA 01984-1899 • ADMISSIONS: 866-464-6736 • FAX: 978-867-4682
E-MAIL: ADMISSIONS@HOPE.GORDON.EDU • WEBSITE: WWW.GORDON.EDU

RATINGS

Quality of Life: 94   Academic: 85   Admissions: 86   Financial Aid: 72

STUDENTS SAY "..."

Academics

SURVEY SAYS . . .
Campus feels safe
Frats and sororities are unpopular or nonexistent
Very little drug use

The motto of Gordon College is "Freedom within a frame-work of faith." For the uninitiated, that translates to "a liberal arts education through a Christian perspective." It's delivered through "engaging professors who share the same passion for Christ and change in the world" that the students here have. In addition to being "great teachers," professors are also "highly skilled, intelligent, accessible, and caring." "Even in big lecture classes, they invite you to have lunch with them and try to learn all their students' names. If a professor's office hours aren't accessible for a student, they are happy to make time for him or her, and they are always available via e-mail." "The teachers expect much out of you, but when you are done with a class you are a master in the field. Even the core curriculum is incredibly straining, but intellectually rewarding." One caveat: "Some of the adjunct teachers are not really that great." "Gordon's administration runs a tight ship, but does not always listen to the opinions of the students when making decisions." That's just fine with many students, though, who coo that "Our administrators are really invested in Gordon's mission, and they really care about students." "Facilities could be better, but they are building new structures, like our new science center, to improve the quality." Several academic programs have their promoters here, but the music department is the object of special praise.

Life

"Life here is fairly quiet." "The week consists mostly of going to class, studying, the gym, and occasional movies and Bible studies." Weekends can also be slow. "We usually manage to entertain ourselves fairly well, though. There are plenty of movies going on all around campus in people's rooms." When they want to get off-campus for fun, "people often go into Boston as we are quite close." "There are numerous museums, exhibits, shows, concerts, restaurants, and games to see there. Many people also enjoy going to one of the many beaches that surround our campus." "There is a lot of school spirit around the sports teams, especially because there are several other rival colleges nearby that we play against often." There are also "a wide variety of extra-curricular activities" for students to join. "There are some party people but not many." "Unfortunately, the 'party group' and the 'Bible group' don't connect much." Not surprisingly, given the religious affiliation of the school, a spiritual vibe pervades the campus, "we enjoy worshipping and getting into deep intellectual conversations about God and existence." "The cafeteria food could be improved," and "Some of the older dorms could be remodeled." Students would also like the school to expend some more resources "providing more ways for students without cars to get off campus."

Student Body

The typical Gordon College student is a "white," "preppy," "middle class, evangelical Christian." She grew up in a "suburban" setting, and is "most likely from the New England area." She was "either home-schooled or went to a private Christian school." Temperamentally, she is "academically focused and hard-working," "involved with either athletics or music," and she "loves the Lord." It is not out of the ordinary for students to "meet their future spouse on campus and get married their senior year." There are "not many international students, or students with different ethnic backgrounds," which leads one student to sum up the student body in both a positive and negative sense, depending on your perspective (i.e., whether the term "Good Shepherd" has meaning for you): "The word sheep sometimes comes to mind—white, fluffy, followers."

Admissions

Very important factors considered include: Class rank, application essay, recommendation(s), rigor of secondary school record, standardized test scores, character/personal qualities, extracurricular activities, interview, religious affiliation/commitment. *Important factors considered include:* Academic GPA, talent/ability. *Other factors considered include:* Alumni/ae relation, racial/ethnic status, volunteer work, work experience. SAT or ACT required; ACT with Writing component required. High school diploma is required and GED is accepted. *Academic units required:* 4 English, 2 mathematics, 2 science, (1 science labs), 2 foreign language, 2 social studies, 5 academic electives. *Academic units recommended:* 3 mathematics, 3 science, (3 science labs), 4 foreign language, 3 social studies.

Finanancial Aid

Students should submit: FAFSA, state aid form Regular filing deadline is 3/1. The Princeton Review suggests that all financial aid forms be submitted as soon as possible after January 1. *Need-based scholarships/grants offered:* Federal Pell, SEOG, state scholarships/grants, private scholarships, the school's own gift aid. *Loan aid offered:* FFEL Subsidized Stafford, FFEL Unsubsidized Stafford, FFEL PLUS, Federal Perkins, state loans, college/university loans from institutional funds. Applicants will be notified of awards on a rolling basis beginning 4/15. Federal Work-Study Program available. Off-campus job opportunities are good.

The Inside Word

Interviews are required at Gordon, presumably so admissions officers can gauge candidates' readiness for the rigorous curriculum and high level of religious commitment. Students interested in studying social work must meet a second, more rigorous set of admissions requirements in addition to general requirements. Prospective music and theater majors must audition as part of their application, and prospective art majors must submit a portfolio for faculty review. The high admit rate here is somewhat misleading, as a look at the high yield percentage and the lifestyle expectations of the college should make clear.

For even more information on this school, turn to page 476 of the "Stats" section.

GOUCHER COLLEGE

1021 DULANEY VALLEY ROAD, BALTIMORE, MD 21204-2794 • ADMISSIONS: 410-337-6100
FAX: 410-337-6354 • FINANCIAL AID: 410-337-6141 • E-MAIL: ADMISSIONS@GOUCHER.EDU • WEBSITE: WWW.GOUCHER.EDU

RATINGS
Quality of Life: 78   Academic: 85   Admissions: 85   Financial Aid: 78

STUDENTS SAY ". . ."

Academics

Goucher College, a "delightfully odd" school at which "Everybody is quirky in some way," offers a surprising number of first-rate programs for a school of its size. The performing and creative arts are big here, and students tout the dance program as "the best non-conservatory program in the country." Goucher's broad "liberal arts education" ensures that all students get to experience "a little bit of everything" academically. Students praise a "great sci-

SURVEY SAYS . . .
Large classes
No one cheats
Students are friendly
Frats and sororities are unpopular
or nonexistent
(Almost) everyone smokes

ence/premed program," "good writing and theater programs," and a riding program bolstered by "stables right on campus." Goucher's growing international relations program reflects the school's "education without boundaries" philosophy, and includes an "innovative and exciting" study abroad requirement. Most students love this requirement, citing it as a primary reason for choosing Goucher; a few naysayers complain that the program "can add up financially" (despite the $1,200 voucher students receive to help offset costs) and that "there are not many options." There's no disagreement about Goucher's professors, however, whom students describe as "amazing people and great mentors." They expect a lot from you, "but in the end [you] accomplish more than [you] ever thought possible, and they are willing to help you every step of the way." Goucher also offers "very good academic support services for students with learning disabilities."

Life

"Goucher students spend lots of time in class and studying hard," but when it's time to take a break, there is always something to do on campus. "A lot of students are very involved in stereotypically feminine activities like painting, horseback riding, and dancing," while others participate in "various clubs and organizations" on campus. Students "often travel into downtown Baltimore on the weekends, and like to hang out at the local cafes and farmer's markets, and see shows." Inner Harbor is "also a frequent destination for fun." Goucher runs "a free college shuttle that picks students up and drops them off at other area universities (Johns Hopkins, Loyola, College of Notre Dame, Towson University) as well as at Penn Station," from which students can easily access downtown Washington, DC, and the Inner Harbor. Hometown Towson, a satellite of Baltimore, provides "cute restaurants and stores," but little in the way of collegiate nightlife. On campus, undergrads can choose from "100 student clubs and activities, and "Anyone can start a new club (it is really easy)." Many here feel that "the lack of Greek societies [on campus] limits a lot of social life," which "isn't to say that drinking doesn't go on here. It does, but it happens quietly and [is] low-key in dorms." Dating "is pretty difficult" due to the lopsided male-female ratio. "The few straight boys are usually taken or they are extremely awkward. It's not uncommon to walk into any boys' dorm and find Magic cards and posters of Lord of the Rings all over."

Student Body

Goucher has "many of the staple groups, such as jocks," but also "a lot of atypical students" including "pirates [there is a Goucher Pirate Alliance], people who play zombies [regular combatants in Humans vs. Zombies, a game played with Nerf guns]," and "lots of aspiring artists and writers who think they are the cream of the crop." In fact, many here tell us that the atypical student in high school is the typical Goucher undergrad, the kid "who was not very popular in high school but rather the creative type, often existing on the periphery." The "only thing that makes Goucher students similar is their acceptance of other students' weirdness." Students also tend to be "laid-back people who enjoy getting an education rather than competing for one." Undergrads report that "there is a strong Jewish community here, but Christian groups are also present." Although "The student body is very friendly as a whole," conservatives warn that "someone with less-than-liberal views is not exactly welcome [on campus]."

Admissions

Very important factors considered include: Academic GPA, rigor of secondary school record. *Important factors considered include:* Application essay, recommendation(s), talent/ability. *Other factors considered include:* Class rank, standardized test scores, alumni/ae relation, character/personal qualities, extracurricular activities, first generation, interview, level of applicant's interest, racial/ethnic status, volunteer work, work experience. TOEFL required of all international applicants. High school diploma is required and GED is accepted. *Academic units required:* 4 English, 3 mathematics, 2 science, 2 foreign language, 3 social studies, 2 academic electives. *Academic units recommended:* 4 English, 4 mathematics, 3 science, 4 foreign language, 3 social studies, 2 academic electives.

Financial Aid

Students should submit: FAFSA, CSS/Financial Aid PROFILE, noncustodial PROFILE, business/farm supplement. Regular filing deadline is 2/15. The Princeton Review suggests that all financial aid forms be submitted as soon as possible after January 1. *Need-based scholarships/grants offered:* Federal Pell, SEOG, state scholarships/grants, private scholarships, the school's own gift aid. *Loan aid offered:* FFEL Subsidized Stafford, FFEL Unsubsidized Stafford, FFEL PLUS, Federal Perkins, college/university loans from institutional funds. Applicants will be notified of awards on a rolling basis beginning 4/1. Federal Work-Study Program available. Institutional employment available. Off-campus job opportunities are excellent.

The Inside Word

Goucher accepts the ACT with Writing in lieu of the new SAT and SAT Subject Tests; for most students, the ACT is the better option. Goucher's high admit rate masks a self-selecting applicant pool; you cannot gain acceptance here without a solid high school transcript and test scores.

THE SCHOOL SAYS ". . ."

From The Admissions Office

"Through a broad-based arts and sciences curriculum and a groundbreaking approach to study abroad, Goucher College gives students a sweeping view of the world. Goucher is an independent, coeducational institution dedicated to both the interdisciplinary traditions of the liberal arts and a truly international perspective on education. The first college in the nation to pair required study abroad with a special travel stipend of $1,200 for every undergraduate, Goucher believes in complementing its strong majors and rigorous curriculum with abundant opportunities for hands-on experience. In addition to participating in the college's many study abroad programs (including innovative 3-week intensive courses abroad alongside traditional semester and academic year offerings), many students also complete internships and service-learning projects that further enhance their learning.

"The college's 1,350 undergraduate students live and learn on a tree-lined campus of 287 acres just north of Baltimore, Maryland. Goucher boasts a student/faculty ratio of just 10:1, and professors routinely collaborate with students on major research projects—often for publication, and sometimes as early as students' first or second years. The curriculum emphasizes international and intercultural awareness throughout, and students are encouraged to explore their academic interests from a variety of perspectives beyond their major disciplines.

"A Goucher College education encompasses a multitude of experiences that ultimately converge into one cohesive academic program that can truly change lives. Students grow in dramatic and surprising ways here. They graduate with a strong sense of direction and self-confidence, ready to engage the world—and succeed—as true global citizens.

"Freshman applicants to Goucher College are required to submit scores from either the new SAT or ACT (with the Writing component)."

For even more information on this school, turn to page 476 of the "Stats" section.

GROVE CITY COLLEGE

100 CAMPUS DRIVE, GROVE CITY, PA 16127-2104 • ADMISSIONS: 724-458-2100 • FAX: 724-458-3395
FINANCIAL AID: 724-458-2163 • E-MAIL: ADMISSIONS@GCC.EDU • WEBSITE: WWW.GCC.EDU

RATINGS
Quality of Life: 78   **Academic:** 82   **Admissions:** 93   **Financial Aid:** 64

STUDENTS SAY "..."

Academics

A small, private liberal arts school dedicated to "cohesive Christian education through academic rigor and integrity," Grove City College provides its students with "a challenging education in a thoroughly Christian environment." In fact, the word challenge is frequently used by respondents; says one, "Students here work their butts off." With a course load that many students describe as "insane," "There is a lot of work to be done and not much time to do it. Most of the work, however, is very beneficial." Students credit the school's "high academic standards" as one of the main reasons GCC enjoys "a fantastic job placement rate and reputation in the professional world." And although the professors assign plenty of homework, they are also "friendly and accessible. Professors give you their home phone numbers so that you can call them if you don't understand something after office hours." What's more, they "are interested mainly in teaching students, not publishing books or conducting research." Finally, undergrads appreciate the fact that professors "are also excellent Christian role models" who give their students a "sound moral foundation." All this is available at bargain-basement prices; the tuition at GCC is "incredibly reasonable," at less than half that of many other private colleges.

> **SURVEY SAYS . . .**
> *Small classes*
> *No one cheats*
> *Career services are great*
> *Students are very religious*
> *Low cost of living*
> *Intramural sports are popular*
> *Very little drug use*

Life

At GCC, "people are very focused on God. Many are involved in campus ministry groups, and almost everyone attends church on Sundays." As one might suspect at such a place, the kind of fun most students go in for here is of the "good, clean" variety. Since "off-campus life is virtually nonexistent," students looking for fun "go to on-campus events, like coffeehouses, dances, plays, and movies," or play intramural sports. However, funding for these activities and clubs can be limited, students complain, because the school's low tuition necessitates a tight activities budget. The dorms at GCC are single sex, but "Intervis (Dorm Intervisitation) is pretty popular." Intervisitation rules are pretty strict; in the words of one student, "Members of the opposite sex can only come to our rooms to hang out during allotted hours on weekends, provided the door is propped open and the lights are on." Alcohol is forbidden on campus, and for those students who want to party off campus, "You have to be careful. Grove City is technically a dry town, and there are not many places that sell alcohol." Students caught drinking on campus, "whether they're 18 or 35," face strict penalties; the school administration "doesn't take that stuff lightly." Undergrads advise prospective students that at GCC, "There is pressure to find a mate by your senior year, so the opposite sex is often on one's mind." As one student puts it, the school's mission is "to provide a thorough education in a Christian environment (and hopefully get you married in the process)."

Student Body

Students at GCC are the first to point out that "Our school is pretty homogenous." The typical student is "an intelligent, studious, straight-edge Protestant" who "got straight A's in high school and has been pretty much a model person for most of his or her life." Ethnically and economically, undergrads are mainly "White and from middle- to upper-class families." One undergrad notes, "There are not too many atypical students, and everyone knows who those students are." Such atypical "Grovers" include "liberal students" who "face much opposition to their political views, but don't suffer discrimination," and the "very few minorities" on campus. While some students wish that the school would "reach out to minorities and people of different backgrounds more," others feel that the fact that GCC does "not try to be like other colleges is what makes it so unique."

Admissions

Very important factors considered include: Application essay, rigor of secondary school record, standardized test scores, character/personal qualities, extracurricular activities, interview, religious affiliation/commitment. *Important factors considered include:* Recommendation(s), talent/ability. *Other factors considered include:* Class rank, alumni/ae relation, geographical residence, racial/ethnic status, state residency, volunteer work, work experience. SAT or ACT required; TOEFL required of all international applicants. High school diploma is required and GED is accepted. *Academic units recommended:* 4 English, 3 mathematics, 3 science, (2 science labs), 3 foreign language, 2 social studies, 2 history.

Financial Aid

Students should submit: institution's own financial aid form. Regular filing deadline is 4/15. The Princeton Review suggests that all financial aid forms be submitted as soon as possible after January 1. *Need-based scholarships/grants offered:* state scholarships/grants, private scholarships, the school's own gift aid, private, alternative loans. Applicants will be notified of awards on a rolling basis beginning 3/20. Institutional employment available. Off-campus job opportunities are good.

The Inside Word

Admission to Grove City has become very competitive, and any serious contender will need to hit the books. While a rigorous class schedule is a given, Admissions Officers also closely assess character and personal qualities. GCC is steeped in Christian values, and the school seeks students who will be comfortable in such an environment. As such, interviews and recommendations hold significant weight.

THE SCHOOL SAYS "..."

From The Admissions Office

"A good college education doesn't have to cost a fortune. For decades, Grove City College has offered a quality education at costs among the lowest nationally. Since the 1990s, increased national academic acclaim has come to Grove City College. Grove City College is a place where professors teach. You will not see graduate assistants or teacher's aides in the classroom. Our professors are also active in the total life of the campus. More than 100 student organizations on campus afford opportunity for a wide variety of cocurricular activities. Outstanding scholars and leaders in education, science, and international affairs visit the campus each year. The environment at GCC is friendly, secure, and dedicated to high standards. Character-building is emphasized and traditional Christian values are supported.

"There is a fresh spiritual vitality on campus that touches every aspect of your college life. In the classroom we don't shy away from discussing all points of view, however we adhere to Christ's teaching as relevant guidance for living. Come and visit and learn more."

For even more information on this school, turn to page 477 of the "Stats" section.

HAMILTON COLLEGE

198 COLLEGE HILL ROAD, CLINTON, NY 13323 • ADMISSIONS: 800-843-2655 • FAX: 315-859-4457
FINANCIAL AID: 800-859-4413 • E-MAIL: ADMISSION@HAMILTON.EDU • WEBSITE: WWW.HAMILTON.EDU

RATINGS
Quality of Life: 80   **Academic:** 95   **Admissions:** 96   **Financial Aid:** 98

STUDENTS SAY ". . ."

Academics

"Cold winters, close friends, and great professors who care" are what make Hamilton "the true liberal arts experience." Indeed, "Its small student population, intelligent and accessible professors, and campus size make Hamilton the ideal small liberal arts college." Students praise the dedication and intellectual caliber of professors, who are more "interested in their students' success" than in "the next research grant." Small class sizes bring personal attention and increased responsibility for one's own learning; one student notes, "It is rarely the case for a professor to lecture for the entire class without engaging the students in the discussion. This way, students interact not only with the professor but [also] with each other, listening to each other and building off other students' ideas." Even "In 'big' lectures (50 students is huge for Hamilton), discussion is strongly encouraged." "Extremely knowledgeable" professors demand a lot of their students, and Hamilton's culture of "grade deflation" means that there are no easy A's at this school; one student observes, "Sometimes you're fighting for a B. The classes are that difficult." "I feel very challenged," says another, adding, "but I am learning so much!" Students who feel too challenged, however, can easily get help; the school offers "free tutoring at the Writing Center and the Quantitative Literacy Center," and the "Career Center is always asking you to come visit, even as a freshman." Those looking for international experience also appreciate the fact that the "school makes it so easy to go abroad."

> **SURVEY SAYS . . .**
> Small classes
> No one cheats
> Lab facilities are great
> Great computer facilities
> Great library
> Lots of beer drinking
> Hard liquor is popular

Life

"Work hard, play hard" is the motto among Hamilton students. "Every weekend, without fail, there is at least one party (often three or four) held in one of the social spaces provided by the campus, generally funded by one of Hamilton's many Greek organizations." Off-campus parties are also popular. To wet your whistle closer to home, the college has its own pub, where professors and students (those over 21, that is) are often seen sharing a pint together. While some students complain that drinking draws too great a focus, there are plenty of options for the straight-edge crowd, including substance-free dorms. Those looking for nonalcoholic fun gather at "Cafe Opus, our own little coffee place, and sit and talk for a while." For the "intellectual population," "all kinds of student-run discussion groups" address "topics ranging from politics to religion to psychology," and "We get great name speakers, ranging from B. B. King to Clinton or Nader." Intrepid Hamiltonians brave upstate New York weather to make the most of their bucolic surroundings: "The glen behind campus is great for running, skiing, or other escapades, and cheering on the perpetually bad football team and the much better soccer and hockey teams is a must." Hometown Clinton's "outdoorsy environment, including extensive acres of hiking/cross-country skiing trails and a ropes course make the college often seem more like camp than school when there is no snow." In the words of one student, "It's small, it's isolated, but Hamilton rock 'n' rolls like nowhere else on earth!"

Student Body

"There is a general impression that many students come from places like Fairfield County [Connecticut]," claims one student, but "While there is certainly a healthy representation, their pink polo shirts and yellow shorts probably just make them more conspicuous. We have students from most states, many countries, and just about every ethnic background. There are all kinds of people here, and they generally associate with everyone else." Another states, "Everyone here is different. That's what makes Hamilton so wonderful." Politically, "The student body seems more moderate than most selective Eastern schools and certainly more tolerant of conservatives than most. Still, many seem nostalgic for Clinton." Whatever their political or social differences, Hamilton students unequivocally characterize themselves as friendly and accepting: "Incredible warmth emanates from all people, regardless of age or status, and despite the snow."

THE PRINCETON REVIEW SAYS

Admissions

Very important factors considered include: Class rank, academic GPA, rigor of secondary school record. *Important factors considered include:* Application essay, recommendation(s), standardized test scores, character/personal qualities, extracurricular activities, interview. *Other factors considered include:* Alumni/ae relation, first generation, geographical residence, level of applicant's interest, racial/ethnic status, talent/ability, volunteer work, work experience. TOEFL required of all international applicants. High school diploma is required and GED is accepted. *Academic units recommended:* 4 English, 3 mathematics, 3 science, 3 foreign language, 3 social studies.

Financial Aid

Students should submit: FAFSA, institution's own financial aid form, CSS/Financial Aid PROFILE, state aid form, noncustodial PROFILE, business/farm supplement. Regular filing deadline is 2/8. The Princeton Review suggests that all financial aid forms be submitted as soon as possible after January 1. *Need-based scholarships/grants offered:* Federal Pell, SEOG, state scholarships/grants, private scholarships, the school's own gift aid. *Loan aid offered:* FFEL Subsidized Stafford, FFEL Unsubsidized Stafford, FFEL PLUS, Federal Perkins Applicants will be notified of awards on or about 4/1. Federal Work-Study Program available. Institutional employment available.

The Inside Word

Similar to many prestigious liberal arts schools, Hamilton takes a well-rounded, personal approach to admissions. Academic achievement and intellectual promise are of first importance, but Admissions Officers also put great weight on leadership and diversity. The college strives to attain a complete, accurate profile of each applicant and relies heavily upon interviews either on or off campus with alumni volunteers. Students who decline to interview put themselves at a competitive disadvantage.

THE SCHOOL SAYS "..."

From The Admissions Office

"As a national leader for teaching students to write effectively, learn from one another, and think for themselves, Hamilton produces graduates who have the knowledge, skills, and confidence to make their own voices heard on issues of importance to them and their communities.

"A key component of the Hamilton experience is the college's open, yet rigorous, liberal arts curriculum. In place of distribution requirements that are common at most colleges, Hamilton gives its students freedom to choose the courses that reflect their unique interests and plans. Faculty advisors assist students in planning a coherent and highly individualized academic program. In fact, close student-faculty relationships at Hamilton are a distinguishing characteristic of the college, but ultimately students at Hamilton take responsibility for their own future. Part of that future includes a lifelong relationship with the college. Hamilton alumni are exceptionally loyal and passionate supporters of their alma mater. That support manifests itself through internships, speaking engagements, job-shadowing opportunities, and financial donations.

"The intellectual maturity that distinguishes a Hamilton education extends to the application process. Students are free to choose which standardized tests to submit, based on a specified set of options, so that those who do not test well on the SAT or ACT may decide to submit the results of their AP or SAT Subject Tests. The approach allows students the freedom to decide how to present themselves best to the Committee on Admission."

For even more information on this school, turn to page 477 of the "Stats" section.

HAMPSHIRE COLLEGE

ADMISSIONS OFFICE, 893 WEST STREET, AMHERST, MA 01002 • ADMISSIONS: 413-559-5471
FAX: 413-559-5631 • FINANCIAL AID: 413-559-5484 • E-MAIL: ADMISSIONS@HAMPSHIRE.EDU • WEBSITE: WWW.HAMPSHIRE.EDU

RATINGS
Quality of Life: 84   **Academic:** 88   **Admissions:** 89   **Financial Aid:** 91

STUDENTS SAY ". . ."

Academics

Hampshire College presents a "do-it-yourself, do-it-as-yourself" approach to education, offering students "a self-designed curriculum" facilitated by "close relationships with professors, small classes, and the great combination of communal living and individualism that a true Hampshire student embodies." Here's how it works: "In class, students learn as a group in discussions or hands-on activities (few lectures, no tests), while outside of class one focuses on inde-

> **SURVEY SAYS . . .**
> *Lots of liberal students*
> *Small classes*
> *No one cheats*
> *Great off-campus food*
> *Frats and sororities are unpopular*
> *or nonexistent*

pendent projects (research, reading, writing, art-making)." The experience culminates in a 'Division III,' an all-consuming year-long senior thesis project "that allows students to become excited and completely invested" while "producing a unique product at the end of the year." Students "receive evaluations instead of grades, which we feel is a much more productive system." The goal is a "hands-on, interdisciplinary education, with the option to incorporate internships and experience abroad," and many here say that's exactly what they accomplish. Undergrads see Hampshire as the "embodiment of academic freedom, personal vision, and self-motivation," a place for students "who can handle the huge responsibility that comes with great opportunities" and "great freedom." Hampshire "is very small," which might limit students' choices; fortunately, "It belongs to the Five College[s] consortium," a group that includes the massive University of Massachusetts—Amherst. With the course offerings of five colleges available to them, Hampshire students can "take any course we could dream of."

Life

Hampshire students enjoy domestic pleasures: At this "very community-based school," undergrads "live together in mods, on-campus, apartment-style housing where they can cook together and share a living space while having their own room." "Potlucks are abundant since most people cook for themselves." Students tell us, "We take our class discussions to our dinner tables. We have a lot of passionate people who infect everybody else with their passion." Hampshire students also enjoy "playing music together" and "chilling out and watching a movie or just having some coffee together." Every weekend students can find plenty of parties, which "generally consist of 50 people or fewer—never the roaring, dangerously wild parties that are often found at other colleges." Overall, undergrads describe it as "a very chill campus. There is no Greek life, and the Frisbee team is the closest thing we have to jocks." The surrounding area provides opportunities "for water sports, biking, hikes," or "bonfires in the woods," and "the nearby towns of Amherst and Northampton aren't too bad," offering "lots of art galleries and live music." Of course, the school's proximity to numerous other colleges provides ample opportunities for those who grow bored with the Hampshire campus.

Student Body

As befits their school's curriculum, "Hampshire students tend to be very self-motivated people who would rather invent their own approach to knowledge than follow a pre-established track." This independent bent means that "we were maybe the 'black sheep' of our high schools, the outcasts, the ones looking for more of a challenge, more say in what they were learning or what they were expected to do with their lives." Students here are "usually good at improvising and, because of the emphasis on class discussion and writing papers, very verbal." They also tend to be "socially conscious, left-wing, and artistic. We are fond of do-it-yourself philosophies, from 'zines to music and film production to designing ecologically sustainable communities. We like a wide variety of music, and like to have parties in cramped mods at which we play this music at high volume. We are comfortable with smoking, drinking, and drug use, in a laissez-faire sort of way. We may be vegetarian, vegan, or meat eaters, but we like to cook, and we love to complain about the dining hall."

THE PRINCETON REVIEW SAYS

Admissions

Very important factors considered include: Application essay, character/personal qualities. *Important factors considered include:* Recommendation(s), rigor of secondary school record, extracurricular activities, level of applicant's interest, talent/ability. *Other factors considered include:* Class rank, academic GPA, standardized test scores, alumni/ae relation, interview, racial/ethnic status, volunteer work, work experience. TOEFL required of all international applicants. High school diploma is required and GED is accepted. *Academic units required:* 4 English, 4 mathematics, 4 science, (2 science labs), 3 foreign language, 2 social studies, 2 history.

Financial Aid

Students should submit: FAFSA, CSS/Financial Aid PROFILE, noncustodial PROFILE. The Princeton Review suggests that all financial aid forms be submitted as soon as possible after January 1. *Need-based scholarships/grants offered:* Federal Pell, SEOG, state scholarships/grants, private scholarships, the school's own gift aid. *Loan aid offered:* Direct Subsidized Stafford, Direct Unsubsidized Stafford, FFEL PLUS, Federal Perkins Applicants will be notified of awards on a rolling basis beginning 4/1. Federal Work-Study Program available.

The Inside Word

As some prospective students have probably deduced, Hampshire's admissions policies are the antithesis of formula-based practices. Officers want to know the individual behind the transcript, and so personal characteristics hold substantial weight. Demonstrating discipline and an independent and inquisitive spirit may just carry more weight than a perfect 4.0. Writing is seen as pivotal to a Hampshire education, and applicants must put considerable thought into their personal statements.

THE SCHOOL SAYS "..."

From The Admissions Office

"Students tell us they like our application. It is less derivative and more open-ended than most. Rather than assigning an essay topic, we ask to learn more about you as an individual and invite your ideas. Instead of just asking for lists of activities, we ask you how those activities (and academic or other endeavors) have shown some of the traits that lead to success at Hampshire (initiative, independence, persistence, for example). This approach parallels the work you will do at Hampshire, defining the questions you will ask and the courses and experiences that will help you to answer them, and integrating your interests.

"Hampshire College requires freshman applicants to submit scores from the old or new SAT. Students may also choose to submit scores from the ACT (with or without the Writing component) in lieu of the SAT."

For even more information on this school, turn to page 478 of the "Stats" section.

HARTWICK COLLEGE

PO Box 4020, Oneonta, NY 13820-4020 • Admissions: 888-427-8925 • Fax: 607-431-4138
E-mail: admissions@hartwick.edu • Website: www.hartwick.edu

RATINGS
Quality of Life: 69   Academic: 77   Admissions: 71   Financial Aid: 78

STUDENTS SAY ". . ."

Academics

Hartwick College is a small liberal arts school in upstate New York with a broad core curriculum, notable offerings in nursing and music education, and "a very strong biology program." Another highlight is the Pine Lake Environmental Campus, "a natural classroom of wood-

lands" that is "an amazing retreat to either relax or study in." Hartwick also boasts a January term, aka "one month of intense study" for internships and "very interesting" classes. "Study abroad opportunities for J-Term are pretty great" as well, and tons of students spend their Januaries in places "all around the world." "Small class sizes are a plus" and "students can do double or even triple majors if they are so inclined." Professors are "easily approachable." As far as teaching goes, "some professors are wonderful, some are horrible." Most students agree that despite a few bad apples, there are some "amazing teachers" here. "They really try to interact with the students and make sure they are learning," says a political science major. The administration is can be "iffy," but for the most part it's "very friendly and involved." Hassles are few. "Things get done so much faster here than at bigger schools," notes an economics major.

Life

Hartwick's campus in the foothills of the Catskill Mountains boasts "great scenery," but it's extremely hilly. The stairs that students must climb to get to class are reportedly "awful." Many students also complain about the grub. "The food here is so bad that fast-food quickly becomes a delicacy," gripes a sophomore. Socially, this campus is "close-knit." "Hartwick is often referred to as Hartwick High School because of how small the school is and how much drama goes on," confides a senior. Student organizations are abundant and "really easy" to start. Many students participate in various musical groups. "A large portion of the student population participates in either varsity or intramural sports," and the "highly respected" men's soccer team is "a big thing around here." "The school puts on a lot of clean-fun type of activities each week," notes a senior. "Attendance is moderate, but it's nice to have the option." Alternatively, "there are always parties." While the Greek system is "not as glorified as it is at other colleges," frats still dictate "much of the social scene." Also, "Oneonta is a bar town" and there is no lack of drinking establishments. Otherwise, though, Oneonta is "just in the middle of nowhere" and has little to offer. "I was hoping for a cuter, artsier town," laments a freshman.

Student Body

The vast majority of student population is from the state of New York and virtually everyone here receives at least some financial aid. Nevertheless, students report that "upper-middle class yuppie offspring" and "unfriendly, rich snobs" who "do little work and party often" make up a sizeable contingent. Also, "jock-types" are "overwhelming" in numbers. In this mix you'll also find some "free spirits," "nature lovers," "tech kids," and "a lot of academics" as well. "Fitting in is not hard for most people." "There are many social circles and it's not hard to find your own little niche." However, "the jocks and the eccentrics" often don't mix well and "Hartwick students tend to stay in cliques."

Admissions

Very important factors considered include: Rigor of secondary school record. *Important factors considered include:* Class rank, academic GPA, recommendation(s). *Other factors considered include:* Application essay, standardized test scores, alumni/ae relation, character/personal qualities, extracurricular activities, first generation, geographical residence, interview, level of applicant's interest, racial/ethnic status, state residency, talent/ability, volunteer work, work experience. TOEFL required of all international applicants. High school diploma is required and GED is accepted. *Academic units recommended:* 4 English, 3 mathematics, 3 science, (2 science labs), 3 foreign language, 2 social studies, 2 history.

Finanancial Aid

Students should submit: FAFSA. The Princeton Review suggests that all financial aid forms be submitted as soon as possible after January 1. *Need-based scholarships/grants offered:* Federal Pell, SEOG, state scholarships/grants, private scholarships, the school's own gift aid. *Loan aid offered:* FFEL Subsidized Stafford, FFEL Unsubsidized Stafford, FFEL PLUS, Federal Perkins, Federal Nursing Applicants will be notified of awards on a rolling basis beginning 3/15. Federal Work-Study Program available. Institutional employment available. Off-campus job opportunities are good.

The Inside Word

The acceptance rate is high at Hartwick and students with average grades and test scores will have no problem gaining admission. If you're serious about Hartwick and your grades and test scores are mediocre or worse, opting for an interview is a really good idea.

THE SCHOOL SAYS " . . . "

From The Admissions Office

"The foundation of a Hartwick education is learning by doing. Students are actively involved in learning, whether it's managing a 'virtual' business, engaging in transcultural nursing in Jamaica, or designing and building environmentally friendly houses on the college's Pine Lake campus. Many Hartwick students conduct research with their professors, sometimes resulting in students coauthoring articles for journals in their disciplines. This hands-on learning helps 96 percent of graduating seniors find jobs or enter graduate or professional school within 6 months of graduation. Another program unique to Hartwick that leads to the high placement rate is MetroLink. This award-winning annual program takes students to New York, Boston, and Washington, DC for a week-long experience in 'shadowing' professionals in those cities. Established Metrolink sites include the Boston Red Sox, Saatchi & Saatchi advertising, the Bronx Zoo, the FBI, and the Smithsonian Institution. Recent full-semester internships have included the National Baseball Hall of Fame, the New York Mets, John Hancock Insurance, the U.S. Congress, and many others."

For even more information on this school, turn to page 478 of the "Stats" section.

HARVARD COLLEGE

BYERLY HALL, 8 GARDEN STREET, CAMBRIDGE, MA 02318 • ADMISSIONS: 617-495-1551 • FAX: 617-495-8821
FINANCIAL AID: 617-495-1581 • E-MAIL: COLLEGE@FAS.HARVARD.EDU • WEBSITE: WWW.FAS.HARVARD.EDU

RATINGS
Quality of Life: 88   **Academic:** 99   **Admissions:** 99   **Financial Aid:** 99

STUDENTS SAY ". . ."

Academics

Those who are lucky enough to attend this legendarily "beautiful, fun, historic and academically alive place" in Cambridge, Massachusetts find a "dynamic universe" that has the ability to both inspire and intimidate, and to open up a portal to an "amazing irresistible hell," plus about a billion opportunities beyond that. Needless to say, it's "very difficult academically," but the school "does a good job of watching over its freshmen through extensive advising programs." Those that are not willing to go after what they want—classes, positions in extracurriculars, jobs, etc—do not gain access to the vast resources of the university. With such a definitive grouping of intelligent people, there does tend to be "latent competition"; nobody is cutthroat in classes, but "people find ways to make everything (especially clubs and even partying) competitive." Still, this is a good thing, and one student claims his experience to be "rewarding beyond anything else I've ever done." "It is impossible to 'get the most out of Harvard' because Harvard offers so much," says another. As at any school, "some professors are better than others," but for the most part, the "the brightest minds in the world" here are "incredible" and "every so often, fantastic," and "the level of achievement is unbelievable." says a student. Harvard employs a lot of Teaching Fellows (TFs) for the larger lecture classes, so "you do have to go to office hours to get to know your big lecture class professors on a personal level," but "this is not a deterrent." The administration can be "waaaaay out of touch with students" and "reticent to change," and there are more than a few claims of bureaucracy, but many agree it has the students' best interests at heart.

Life

Most students have resolved their study habits by the time they get to Harvard, so "studying becomes routine and there is a vibrant social atmosphere on campus, and between students and the local community." In Cambridge and Boston, there's always something to do, whether it's "go see a play, a concert, hit up a party, go to the movies, or dine out." The new pub on campus is an excellent place to hang out and see people, "especially if you want to play a game of pool or have a reasonably priced drink"; drinking also occurs on weekends at parties or at Harvard's Finals clubs, though it is by no means a prevalent part of social life here (partly due to the university's less-than-lax alcohol policies). In addition to school-sponsored events such as panels and film screenings, the number of student organizations is staggering. "Basically, if you want to do it, Harvard either has it or has the money to give to you so you can start it," says a student. "Boredom does not exist here. There are endless opportunities and endless passionate people to do them with." During freshman year, the school organizes a lot of holiday/special event parties for people to get to know one another, and conversations are rarely surface-level and "often incorporate some sort of debate or interesting/important topic."

Student Body

Everyone is here to achieve, and this makes for a very common, if broad mold of a typical student. As one junior computer science major succinctly puts it: "Works really hard. Doesn't sleep. Involved in a million extracurriculars." People here have nothing but the highest opinion of their fellow students, and the when it comes to finding the lowest common denominator, it's that "everyone is great for one reason or another." However, all of these virtuosos are down to earth and there are also a lot of well-rounded kids "who aren't geniuses but are pretty good at most things." Admitting the best of the best makes for quite a diverse campus, and "there is a lot of tolerance and acceptance at Harvard for individuals of all races, religions, socio-economic backgrounds, life styles, etc."

> **SURVEY SAYS . . .**
> *Lab facilities are great*
> *Great computer facilities*
> *Great library*
> *Diverse student types on campus*
> *Students love Cambridge, MA*
> *Student publications are popular*
> *Political activism is popular*

Admissions

Other factors considered include: Application essay, academic GPA, recommendation(s), rigor of secondary school record, standardized test scores, alumni/ae relation, character/personal qualities, extracurricular activities, first generation, geographical residence, interview, racial/ethni SAT Subject Tests required; SAT or ACT required; ACT with Writing component required. High school diploma or equivalent is not required. *Academic units recommended:* 4 English, 4 mathematics, 4 science, 4 foreign language, 3 social studies, 2 history.

Financial Aid

Students should submit: FAFSA, CSS/Financial Aid PROFILE, noncustodial PROFILE, business/farm supplement, tax forms through IDOC. Regular filing deadline is 2/1. The Princeton Review suggests that all financial aid forms be submitted as soon as possible after January 1. *Need-based scholarships/grants offered:* Federal Pell, SEOG, state scholarships/grants, private scholarships, the school's own gift aid. *Loan aid offered:* Direct Subsidized Stafford, Direct Unsubsidized Stafford, Direct PLUS, Federal Perkins, state loans, college/university loans from institutional funds. Applicants will be notified of awards on or about 4/1. Federal Work-Study Program available. Institutional employment available. Off-campus job opportunities are excellent.

The Inside Word

It just doesn't get any tougher than this. Candidates to Harvard face dual obstacles—an awe-inspiring applicant pool and, as a result, admissions standards that defy explanation in quantifiable terms. Harvard denies admission to the vast majority, and virtually all of them are top students. It all boils down to splitting hairs, which is quite hard to explain and even harder for candidates to understand. Rather than being as detailed and direct as possible about the selection process and criteria, Harvard keeps things close to the vest—before, during, and after. They even refuse to admit that being from South Dakota is an advantage. Thus the admissions process does more to intimidate candidates than to empower them. Moving to a common application seemed to be a small step in the right direction, but with the current explosion of early decision applicants and a super-high yield of enrollees, things are not likely to change dramatically.

THE SCHOOL SAYS "..."

From The Admissions Office

"The Admissions Committee looks for energy, ambition, and the capacity to make the most of opportunities. Academic ability and preparation are important, and so is intellectual curiosity—but many of the strongest applicants have significant non-academic interests and accomplishments as well. There is no formula for admission, and applicants are considered carefully, with attention to future promise.

"Freshman applicants for Fall 2008 may submit either the old SAT taken before March 2005, or the new SAT. The ACT with Writing component is also accepted. All students must also submit three SAT Subject Tests of their choosing."

For even more information on this school, turn to page 479 of the "Stats" section.

HAVERFORD COLLEGE

370 West Lancaster Avenue, Haverford, PA 19041 • ADMISSIONS: 610-896-1350 • FAX: 610-896-1338
FINANCIAL AID: 610-896-1350 • E-MAIL: ADMITME@HAVERFORD.EDU • WEBSITE: WWW.HAVERFORD.EDU

RATINGS
Quality of Life: 88   **Academic:** 99   **Admissions:** 99   **Financial Aid:** 99

STUDENTS SAY "..."

Academics

Any fitting description of academic life at Haverford College should start with "two words: honor code!" Here "Students are allowed a great deal of freedom and self-governance," and the "honor code holds the students responsible for their learning, and trusts them to have both concern and respect for their fellow students. That is why our school has both unscheduled and unproctored final exams." As one student puts it, "The success of the institu-

> **SURVEY SAYS . . .**
> *No one cheats*
> *Lab facilities are great*
> *Athletic facilities are great*
> *Campus feels safe*
> *Frats and sororities are unpopular or nonexistent*

tion is dependent upon a body of students who are actively concerned and engaged." Equally concerned and engaged are members of the faculty: "Despite the fact that professors here do incredible research and publish regularly, it is evident that they have come to Haverford to teach. Students are their first priority, and they absolutely make themselves available to discuss anything." In the classroom, professors "are funny and interesting, and lead very good discussions. Class discussions even run overtime every so often, and the students voluntarily stay late to continue the discussions." "If you take one small step toward a Haverford professor," attests one student, "that professor will take a giant leap toward you. Our professors like teaching students and developing personal relationships with us." Like professors here, the administration also draws almost exclusively rave reviews: "Only at a school like Haverford would we have something called 'First Thursdays,' where the entire student community is invited to have an open-forum discussion with the president. Even he makes time for student opinions." Proximity to other great colleges means that Haverford students also have the "opportunity to take classes at Bryn Mawr, Swarthmore, or Penn."

Life

Haverford is "a place where people like to study hard and play hard. During the week students are very hardworking, but on the weekends we like to let our hair down and enjoy ourselves, [by] going into Philly, watching an a cappella group perform, or hanging out with friends. We know how to keep ourselves happy. Since we do not have any Greek life, everyone is part of the social life on campus." Another notes, "The lack of Greek life (which goes against the inclusive nature of Haverford's Quaker roots) on campus is a really strong point." Indeed, "Clubs and organizations are always sponsoring events, like dinners, dances, and parties. The hardest thing to do on weekends is to decide what your plans are for the night." Parties on campus "are open to everyone, and "While many students drink," undergrads say, "it is not necessary to do so to have a good time." If you want to stay in, that's okay, too; Haverford's small size means that "everyone knows everyone else by sophomore year, so it's not like you'll really meet anyone new by going out."

Student Body

Undergrads frequently use the term "closet nerd" to describe their peers. One student defines the term as "someone who is very smart and works very hard but also pursues other interests and has fun." Someone who is "a bit awkward," but "often athletic in some way." Another student sums up Haverfordians in this way: "The typical Haverford student is friendly but not bubbly, self-motivated but not obsessive, smart but not obnoxious, slightly eccentric but not truly weird, nerdy but not socially hopeless. We mill around the edges of the liberal arts stereotypes without quite embodying them." In his or her interactions with others, the Haverfordian is "academically honest and socially respectful, and hopes to make a real difference in the world. There's a variety of personalities, but we're all basically geeks"—"idealist geeks who want to change the world."

THE PRINCETON REVIEW SAYS

Admissions

Very important factors considered include: Application essay, academic GPA, rigor of secondary school record, standardized test scores, character/personal qualities. *Important factors considered include:* Class rank, recommendation(s), extracurricular activities, talent/ability, volunteer work, work experience. *Other factors considered include:* Alumni/ae relation, first generation, geographical residence, interview, level of applicant's interest, racial/ethnic status, ACT with Writing component required. TOEFL required of all international applicants. High school diploma or equivalent is not required. *Academic units required:* 4 English, 3 mathematics, 1 science, (1 science labs), 3 foreign language, 2 social studies. *Academic units recommended:* 4 mathematics, 2 science.

Financial Aid

Students should submit: FAFSA, CSS/Financial Aid PROFILE, business/farm supplement, CSS College Board Noncustodial Parents' Statement is required-not the Noncustodial supplement. Regular filing deadline is 1/31. The Princeton Review suggests that all financial aid forms be submitted as soon as possible after January 1. *Need-based scholarships/grants offered:* Federal Pell, SEOG, state scholarships/grants, the school's own gift aid. *Loan aid offered:* FFEL Subsidized Stafford, FFEL Unsubsidized Stafford, FFEL PLUS, Federal Perkins Applicants will be notified of awards on or about 4/1. Federal Work-Study Program available. Institutional employment available. Off-campus job opportunities are good.

The Inside Word

Haverford's applicant pool is an impressive and competitive lot. Intellectual curiosity is paramount, and applicants are expected to keep a demanding academic schedule in high school. Additionally, the college places a high value on ethics, as evidenced by its honor code. The Admissions Office seeks students who will reflect and promote Haverford's ideals.

THE SCHOOL SAYS ". . ."

From The Admissions Office

"Haverford strives to be a college in which integrity, honesty, and concern for others are dominant forces. The college does not have many formal rules; rather, it offers an opportunity for students to govern their affairs and conduct themselves with respect and concern for others. Each student is expected to adhere to the honor code as it is adopted each year by the Students' Association. Haverford's Quaker roots show most clearly in the relationship of faculty and students, in the emphasis on integrity, in the interaction of the individual and the community, and through the college's concern for the uses to which its students put their expanding knowledge. Haverford's 1,100 students represent a wide diversity of interests, backgrounds, and talents. They come from public, parochial, and independent schools across the United States, Puerto Rico, and 28 foreign countries. Students of color are an important part of the Haverford community.

"Haverford College requires that all applicants submit the results of the new three-part SAT exam or the ACT with the optional writing test. Two SAT Subject Tests are required."

For even more information on this school, turn to page 479 of the "Stats" section.

HOBART AND WILLIAM SMITH COLLEGES

639 SOUTH MAIN STREET, GENEVA, NY 14456 • ADMISSIONS: 315-781-3472 • FAX: 315-781-3471
FINANCIAL AID: 315-781-3315 • E-MAIL: HOADM@HWS.EDU • WEBSITE: WWW.HWS.EDU

RATINGS
Quality of Life: 70   **Academic:** 87   **Admissions:** 88   **Financial Aid:** 91

STUDENTS SAY ". . ."

Academics

"Students come before all else" at tiny upstate Hobart and William Smith, a pair of associated single-sex colleges that share a campus, faculty, and administration, yet remain very distinct in their identities, combining to make the academic and social lives of the students as varied and interesting as possible. While "there aren't always tons of options" for classes, "there are lots of interesting choices

offered for such a small school," and this "liberal arts education with a flair" places a strong emphasis on study abroad as a part of a student's education. There is quite a bit of money in the student body, so tuition can be a workout for some (there are many grants offered, though), but even the brokest of students is enthralled with the school, from the "beautiful, green campus" offering "a small slice of New England stuck in upstate New York" to the "unrivalled experience."

The "vibrant" professors have "diverse viewpoints," and though "you have to learn to adapt to different teaching styles," they treat students with complete respect, so that "the academic experience is more in the vein of colleagues." Everyone here is happy with their academic experience, and even though there's an occasional dud, "for every professor that seems mediocre, there's two more who are absolute gems of teaching ability." "I have had professors invite me to office hours, send me internship opportunities, discuss my career goals, and even invite me to their house for dinner," says another. As for higher up, the raves are similar; the administration works very hard to accommodate everyone on campus and "is usually successful at it," partly due to the coordinate system, which allows for separate deans for both William Smith and Hobart, granting "more individual attention to the students." They will "get to know you and will stop on the sidewalk and have a chat whenever they see you." However, students do wish the administration was a little less strict in its policies and enforcement.

Life

Life in general is pretty hectic, but students are "very good at balancing school and socializing"; most kids always stay busy with their school work, but "really let loose on the weekends." Bars, frat parties, and campus parties can all occur in the same night, and the school offers "a very positive program" in Safe Rides, which provides late night van rides. Geneva is a beautiful town, but it's no NYC; the cold winter months can be endless, and the rural location means students "make their own fun here," whether through tray sledding, barbequing, or skinny-dipping, and it "kind of works out better." On nice days, the quad acts as a hub of student life, when students "bring horse shoes, Frisbees, footballs, baseballs, and blankets and just spend the day together." There's also skiing, malls and outlets for shopping, and a wildlife refuge not too far away. Without a nearby big urban center, students are "continuously immersed in campus life and happenings," and most are very happy with the offerings from the school and campus groups. Community service is very popular here, as well.

Student Body

"Preppy white person" seems to encapsulate most everyone's perception of the student body, with "Polo, LL Bean, Lily Pulitzer & Lacoste...everywhere." A lot of students come from affluent backgrounds, but in recent years, thanks to scholarships and opportunity programs, there's a significant number of international students and minority students and "they blend in seamlessly." "Rich kids and alternative types melting all together in a pretty good harmony," sums up a student. People "usually get along with each other regardless of being typical or not," partially due to the rampant involvement in student organizations and groups. With fewer than two thousand people in the student body, there's not much mystery left after a couple of years, when "you can walk to class and recognize at 90% of the people you see," but the general pervading friendliness of the school as a whole means that "there is a happy niche here for everyone."

Admissions

Very important factors considered include: Rigor of secondary school record. *Important factors considered include:* Class rank, application essay, academic GPA, recommendation(s), standardized test scores, character/personal qualities, extracurricular activities, volunteer work, work experience. *Other factors considered include:* Alumni/ae relation, first generation, geographical residence, interview, level of applicant's interest, racial/ethnic status, talent/ability, SAT or ACT required; ACT with Writing component required. TOEFL required of all international applicants. High school diploma is required and GED is accepted. *Academic units required:* 4 English, 3 mathematics, 3 science, (2 science labs), 2 foreign language, 2 social studies, 2 history, 2 academic electives. *Academic units recommended:* 3 foreign language, 3 social studies, 4 academic electives.

Financial Aid

Students should submit: FAFSA, CSS/Financial Aid PROFILE, state aid form, noncustodial PROFILE, parent's and student's tax return. Regular filing deadline is 2/1. The Princeton Review suggests that all financial aid forms be submitted as soon as possible after January 1. *Need-based scholarships/grants offered:* Federal Pell, SEOG, state scholarships/grants, private scholarships, the school's own gift aid. *Loan aid offered:* FFEL Subsidized Stafford, FFEL Unsubsidized Stafford, FFEL PLUS, Federal Perkins Applicants will be notified of awards on or about 4/1. Federal Work-Study Program available. Institutional employment available. Off-campus job opportunities are good.

The Inside Word

Applicants to the academic side of Seneca Lake's scenic shore should know that HSW likes to see a student who embraces a challenge. They recommend that hopefuls prepare themselves for a rigorous college curriculum by taking at least two years of a foreign language and a couple of AP courses for good measure. Some good news for people who don't like tests: HSW doesn't require standardized test scores.

THE SCHOOL SAYS ". . ."

From The Admissions Office

"Hobart and William Smith Colleges seek students with a sense of adventure and a commitment to the life of the mind. Inside the classroom, students find the academic climate to be rigorous, with a faculty that is deeply involved in teaching and working with them. Outside, they discover a supportive community that helps to cultivate a balance and hopes to foster an integration among academics, extracurricular activities, and social life. Hobart and William Smith, as coordinate colleges, have an awareness of gender differences and equality and are committed to respect and a celebration of diversity.

"Freshman applicants for Fall 2008 class are required to take either the ACT (old or new, with or without the optional Writing portion) or either version of the SAT. Their highest composite score will be used in admissions decisions. Students are encouraged to submit results of any SAT Subject Test they have taken."

For even more information on this school, turn to page 480 of the "Stats" section.

HOFSTRA UNIVERSITY

ADMISSIONS CENTER, BERNON HALL, HEMPSTEAD, NY 11549 • ADMISSIONS: 516-463-6700
FAX: 516-463-5100 • FINANCIAL AID: 516-463-6680 • E-MAIL: HOFSTRA@HOFSTRA.EDU • WEBSITE: WWW.HOFSTRA.EDU

RATINGS
Quality of Life: 62   **Academic:** 77   **Admissions:** 85   **Financial Aid:** 65

STUDENTS SAY ". . ."

Academics

To experience "Long Island in a nutshell," consider Hofstra University, a school that "is dedicated to preparing its students for successful careers." Nearly one-third of the student body are business majors; Hofstra's "great finance program" benefits from "the number-one college Financial Trading Room in the country," while the marketing program supports the Hofstra American Marketing Cub, "which won 'Business Club of the Year.'" Hofstra is also "a

> **SURVEY SAYS . . .**
> *Large classes*
> *Great computer facilities*
> *Great library*
> *Lots of beer drinking*
> *Hard liquor is popular*
> *(Almost) everyone smokes*

great place for accounting majors." Students tell us that the Communications Department is "amazing," with "a state-of-the art radio station" that "offers a large variety of ways to get involved, whether it's having a show or being behind the scenes." It also plays "a large variety of music," from "rap to rock to Irish." Hofstra's education program is also highly regarded, boasting "one of the best music education programs in the country." In all areas, students laud "real-world experience on real-world equipment" and great opportunities for internships. In fact, "There are more internships available than there are people, so we are always informed of new opportunities in our majors as they emerge. Our location [relative] to the city presents many summer and winter internships in Manhattan, especially for communications and business majors." Hofstra is a big university, meaning students can't wait for someone to tell them what to do; one student writes, "If you want to get something done, you definitely can't wait for it to happen. You have to put yourself out there and meet with teachers and join clubs."

Life

Those who live on or near campus tell us that "there is plenty to do here, but you have to have a car to really do it, [because] walking in the area isn't that safe." There are a "ton of malls, movie theaters, and restaurants right around campus." Hofstra "is known as a bar school," and students have many venues to choose from in Hempstead and "cute little surrounding towns" like Mineola and Garden City. On campus, "Interest in [intercollegiate] athletics has grown dramatically"; even so, "Many students don't advantage of the free or discounted activities offered at the campus." But enthusiasts say this just forces students "to be more creative" when it comes to finding fun. "With Manhattan only 45 minutes away via the Long Island Railroad," lots of "people also go into New York City for fun, whether it is to shop, see shows, or go to nightclubs." Hofstra makes it easy for students to take regular trips into the city, offering a "free bus from campus that takes students to the train station."

Student Body

Long Island is a pretty diverse place, and Hofstra University reflects that diversity reasonably well. One student writes, "My first roommate was a White Orthodox Jew, very serious about school; my second set of roommates were White Greek and Italian Christians, loud partiers who played beer pong every night," and "my third roommate is White, Catholic, and gay," and "is the nicest person I know." Undergrads tell us that "there are two types of students at Hofstra University: The kind that work hard, study and succeed, and the other kind who carelessly roll into class 25 minutes late (if they even go at all) with their Chanel sunglasses and Ugg boots, talking on their cell phones to their friends about their fabulous night out." The latter group is sometimes referred to derisively as "the Long Island kids," and some students describe them as "materialistic" and "apathetic" about school. While there might be lot of "stereotypical Long Island kids" on campus, the school also has "a large minority population," and "It's not hard to find someone here who is interested in the same things you are." Over 50% of the class entering in fall 2007 were from out of state.

THE PRINCETON REVIEW SAYS

Admissions

Very important factors considered include: Rigor of secondary school record, Class rank, Academic GPA, Standardized test scores, Application Essay, Recommendation(s) *Important factors considered include:* Interview, Extracurricular activities, Talent/ability, Character/personal qualities. *Other factors considered include:* Alumni/ae relation, Geographical residence, Racial/ethnic status, Volunteer work, Work experience, Level of applicant's interest.

Financial Aid

The Princeton Review suggests that all financial aid forms be submitted as soon as possible after January 1. Federal Work-Study Program available. Institutional employment available. Off-campus job opportunities are excellent.

The Inside Word

This is not your father's Hofstra; the school reports that admission requirements have grown tougher over the years. Average GPAs and standardized test scores of admitted students have gone up, and this has been accompanied by a rise in rejection rates among applicants. Expect an especially thorough review if you indicate communications as your intended field of study.

THE SCHOOL SAYS "..."

From The Admissions Office

"Hofstra is a university on the rise. When you step onto campus you feel the energy and sense the momentum of a university building a national reputation as a center for academic excellence.

"At Hofstra, you'll find an outstanding faculty dedicated to teaching, and small classes, averaging just 22 students. Outside the classroom, you'll find a multitude of study abroad options, a vibrant extracurricular life, and amazing internship opportunities and cultural experiences in nearby New York City.

"The Hofstra campus—so beautiful it is recognized as an arboretum—features new and cutting-edge teaching facilities. At Hofstra, you will share your classrooms and residence halls with students from nearly every U.S. state and 65 countries.

"Hofstra also offers new and unique educational opportunities: During the fall 2008 semester students can participate in Educate '08, a series of programs and events leading up to the third and final presidential debate, which will be held at Hofstra in October 15, 2008. His Holiness the 14th Dalai Lama, the inaugural winner of the Hofstra University's Guru Nanak Interfaith Prize, is expected to visit campus in 2009. In addition, the university plans to establish the nation's newest medical school in partnership with the North Shore-LIJ Health System, subject to preliminary accreditation, and hopes to admit the first medical school class in 2011.

"Students applying for admission may submit either SAT or ACT scores, and an essay is required. The admission team at Hofstra realizes that each applicant is unique and gives each one individual attention."

For even more information on this school, turn to page 480 of the "Stats" section.

HOOD COLLEGE

401 ROSEMONT AVENUE, FREDERICK, MD 21701 • ADMISSIONS: 301-696-3400 • FAX: 301-696-3819
E-MAIL: ADMISSIONS@HOOD.EDU • WEBSITE: WWW.HOOD.EDU

RATINGS
Quality of Life: 85   **Academic:** 84   **Admissions:** 81   **Financial Aid:** 86

STUDENTS SAY "..."

Academics

Students enjoy "a broad and productive education combined with a relaxed and fun campus life" at Hood College, a small private liberal arts college featured on many 'best college bargains' lists (including The Princeton Review's). "Known for its education major," as well as for strong programs in biolo-

> **SURVEY SAYS . . .**
> *Large classes*
> *Students love Frederick, MD*
> *Frats and sororities are unpopular or nonexistent*

gy, economics, and mathematics, Hood features "great overall academics" reinforced by small class sizes that facilitate a "wonderful" learning environment and the "easy flow" of discussion. Students caution that "Most of the classes are moderately difficult and the level of conversation and debate is usually top-notch. If you like to reason, debate, and create well-rounded arguments, this is the place for you." Professors "will go as far as inviting you over for dinner to discuss a project, mourn a loss, or just to give advice," and administrators are "engaging and enjoyable." One student exclaims, "They are the reason I call my college 'my Hood, my home.' The administration will go as far as hugging a homesick freshman or making us all breakfast-for-dinner the night before finals!" On the downside, "Classes that are required for graduation aren't always offered when they are needed," a common problem at small schools.

Life

Hood is located in Frederick, a town of 60,000 "near Washington DC, Baltimore, and Annapolis, which all provide great urban environments for having fun." Downtown Frederick is "right off campus" and "provides good food, shopping, and socializing" as well as opportunities to "explore old historic buildings." The one drawback is that "Frederick still shuts down pretty early at night, so must of us have to get inventive if we want to have fun after 9 P.M. off campus. We'll end up playing flashlight tag or going on scavenger hunts through town in the dark." On campus "the school always provides something for us to do," including "New York day trips, movie night when they pay for our tickets to see the movie of our choice, and tons of free activities for weekend fun." There are also traditions "such as Pergola Party, Policies for Dollars, Handel's Messiah with the United States Naval Academy, Spring Parties weekend, Hood Ball, Vespers, and Holiday Dinner just to name a few," all of which "are an important part of what makes Hood so special." Even so, many students "leave for the weekend, so usually by lunchtime on Friday it's pretty empty here."

Student Body

"Nobody is the same at Hood," one student reports, but "if you had to pinpoint a 'typical' student it would probably either be a white, politically moderate girl majoring in psychology or a tall, jock-like guy who's majoring in biology or chemistry. But really, even they are only a small percentage of our population." Another agrees that Hood students "are a small but very diverse group. There are students who have every possible religious, political, racial and sexual affiliation." Hood is home to "a lot of foreign exchange students and a lot of special-needs.... They make Hood such a rich environment...we're like a big family."

THE PRINCETON REVIEW SAYS

Admissions

Very important factors considered include: Academic GPA, rigor of secondary school record. *Important factors considered include:* Class rank, standardized test scores, alumni/ae relation, character/personal qualities, extracurricular activities, level of applicant's interest, talent/ability. *Other factors considered include:* Application essay, recommendation(s), interview, racial/ethnic status, volunteer work, work experience. SAT or ACT required; TOEFL required of all international applicants. High school diploma is required and GED is accepted. *Academic units recommended:* 4 English, 3 mathematics, 3 science, (2 science labs), 2 foreign language, 3 social studies, 1 academic electives.

Financial Aid

Students should submit: FAFSA. The Princeton Review suggests that all financial aid forms be submitted as soon as possible after January 1. *Need-based scholarships/grants offered:* Federal Pell, SEOG, state scholarships/grants, private scholarships, the school's own gift aid. *Loan aid offered:* Direct Subsidized Stafford, Direct Unsubsidized Stafford, Direct PLUS, FFEL Subsidized Stafford, FFEL Unsubsidized Stafford, FFEL PLUS, Federal Perkins Applicants will be notified of awards on a rolling basis beginning 2/15. Federal Work-Study Program available. Institutional employment available. Off-campus job opportunities are good.

The Inside Word

After years of growth in its applicant pool (subsequent to going fully coed in 2003), the numbers have finally started to level off at Hood College. Despite a lopsided male-female ratio, the male minority receives no preferential treatment here; applicants of both genders were admitted to the Class of 2011 at an identical rate.

THE SCHOOL SAYS ". . ."

From The Admissions Office

"Hood College has experienced several changes in recent years. In 2003, men were enrolled as residential students for the first time (men attended as commuters in the undergraduate and graduate programs since 1973). While some campus traditions have changed to reflect the new student body, the transition to coeducation has been smooth. Student enrollment has increased in recent years, yet classes remain small and students have ample opportunity to meet with faculty outside of class for advising, discussion, and individual research projects. The college opened its new science and technology center in 2002, with state-of-the-art laboratories designed specifically for biology, biochemistry, chemistry, and environmental science. Both the classroom (average class size is 14) and the extracurricular environment focus on active student learning. Hood students also develop and practice critical-thinking skills in every class and every campus activity. Along with the obvious social and cultural advantages of Hood's proximity to Washington, DC and Baltimore, students have an abundant array of internships in government and industry. On campus, students have the opportunity to get involved in numerous clubs, activities, and organizations from community service, literary, and artistic groups to intramurals and NCAA Division III intercollegiate sports. About one-third of Hood's students compete in 17 varsity athletic teams, and several Hood teams are multiyear champions in their respective sports. Hood's lively and involved student body is diverse, including more than one-fifth who are students of color."

For even more information on this school, turn to page 481 of the "Stats" section.

Houghton College

PO Box 128, Houghton, NY 14744 • Admissions: 800-777-2556 • Fax: 585-567-9522
E-mail: admissions@houghton.edu • Website: www.houghton.edu

RATINGS
Quality of Life: 87   **Academic:** 83   **Admissions:** 82   **Financial Aid:** 75

STUDENTS SAY "..."

Academics

Houghton College, "a small Christian liberal arts school" that is "a particularly good choice for those looking into music, the sciences, and ministry," offers students "an academically-challenging experience complemented by a Christian atmosphere and dedication to creating scholar servants." A small student body and a remote location mean that the entire community is "connected through so

many activities and classes.... We get to know our professors as well as our fellow students." It also "allows for quite a bit of discussion in class (the average class size is 21 students). This is a valuable part of my education, since I have learned so much not just from professors' lectures but also from fellow students as we digest information and discuss its application to life and faith." Outstanding disciplines here include biology (featuring "impressive equipment for a small college" and allows many professors to "design their own labs for students, sometimes writing a lab book solely for use at Houghton"), a "great equestrian program," and solid programs in music and education. Students report that "many juniors and seniors take advantage of independent study options, where they can pursue an academic interest one-on-one with a professor." Study abroad programs also attract many students who, as a result of their experiences, become "very interested in going out and getting involved in global issues affecting the world's population."

Life

Houghton is located in a remote area that, depending on your perspective, is either "beautiful...with many things going on" or "boring, insipid, dull." Some simply appreciate how the seclusion leaves them "able to concentrate on school and not worry about going shopping or partying." Others note that "Houghton offers a wide variety of groups and organizations to be involved with, ranging from rock climbing and paddle sports to Student Government and Evangelicals for Social Activism to Gadfly. Life at Houghton is never dull and there are always people around willing to talk over a cup of coffee or try anything fun, crazy, and exciting." Undergrads also "play a lot of sports, go to sporting events, watch movies, and come up with random ways to have fun." "A lot of our out-of-class time, however, is spent doing homework," says a student. Whatever 'typical' party scene exists here is "hidden from the general population" because "alcohol, illegal drugs, and sexual promiscuity" are all banned (and could result in expulsion). In fact, even social dancing is currently prohibited on campus, although "the policy is under review," so don't hang those blue suede shoes up just yet.

Student Body

"Houghton is made up mostly of white Protestant students," reports a student, with over "10 percent...having lived a majority of their lives overseas." Many are "the stereotypical born-again Christians" who "grew up in the church; many with parents who worked in some capacity with in the church." Most are "from New York or Pennsylvania," and "as a result they can go home any weekend that they want," leaving "students from father away...feeling stranded on an isolated campus." Locals are "used to the weather" (i.e. cold winters), while "other students may not be so content with the location." At a nearly two-to-one clip, "Houghton has more females than males."

Admissions

Very important factors considered include: Academic GPA, character/personal qualities, religious affiliation/commitment. *Important factors considered include:* Class rank, application essay, recommendation(s), rigor of secondary school record, standardized test scores. *Other factors considered include:* Alumni/ae relation, extracurricular activities, interview, level of applicant's interest, racial/ethnic status, talent/ability, volunteer work, work experience. SAT or ACT required; TOEFL required of all international applicants. High school diploma is required and GED is accepted. *Academic units recommended:* 4 English, 3 mathematics, 2 science, (2 science labs), 2 foreign language, 1 social studies, 2 history.

Financial Aid

Students should submit: FAFSA. The Princeton Review suggests that all financial aid forms be submitted as soon as possible after January 1. *Need-based scholarships/grants offered:* Federal Pell, SEOG, state scholarships/grants, private scholarships, the school's own gift aid. *Loan aid offered:* FFEL Subsidized Stafford, FFEL Unsubsidized Stafford, FFEL PLUS, Federal Perkins Applicants will be notified of awards on a rolling basis beginning 3/15. Federal Work-Study Program available. Institutional employment available. Off-campus job opportunities are poor.

The Inside Word

Houghton is not for everyone. The curriculum and the student body are deeply committed to evangelical Christianity, and anyone not 100 percent on board with this won't likely feel comfortable here. Admissions officers know this and will block the applications of those who, in their view, are "bad fits" for the college.

THE SCHOOL SAYS ". . ."

From The Admissions Office

"Since 1883, Houghton College has provided a residential educational experience that integrates high-quality academic instruction with the Christian faith. Houghton is selective in admission, attracting a very capable student body from 25 countries and 40 states. The college receives widespread national recognition for the quality of its student profile, faculty, and facilities. Enrolling 1,200 full-time students, Houghton is located on a beautiful 1,300-acre campus in western New York. The college's campus includes a 386-acre equestrian center as well as cross-country and downhill ski trails. Houghton's campus combines classic-style architecture with state-of-the-art technology and facilities, including a campus-wide computer network and wireless Internet access. All incoming students and transfers receive laptop computers and printers, which are included in the cost of tuition. Houghton's traditional liberal arts curriculum offers more than 40 majors and programs. Numerous study abroad programs are available, including Houghton's own offerings in the Adirondack Mountains, Tanzania, Australia, Eastern Europe, and London. The First-Year Honors Program offers highly qualified students the opportunity to study in England or Central Europe during the second semester of their first year with 25 of their peers and two Houghton faculty members. There is a strong pre-professional orientation, with 30 to 35 percent of graduates moving on to graduate or professional school upon graduation. Houghton alumni can be found teaching at 175 colleges and universities around the United States and abroad."

For even more information on this school, turn to page 481 of the "Stats" section.

HOWARD UNIVERSITY

2400 SIXTH STREET NORTHWEST, WASHINGTON, DC 20059 • ADMISSIONS: 202-806-2700 • FAX: 202-806-4462
FINANCIAL AID: 202-806-2800 • E-MAIL: ADMISSION@HOWARD.EDU • WEBSITE: WWW.HOWARD.EDU

RATINGS

Quality of Life: 65   **Academic:** 80   **Admissions:** 87   **Financial Aid:** 67

STUDENTS SAY ". . ."

Academics

Howard University, which students proclaim "the Mecca of black education," parlays a storied history and an excellent location (ideal for students seeking internships and post-graduation job placements) to "prepare students for the future through academic integrity and social enterprise." Recruiters flock to the Howard campus, in part because "academically, Howard is very strong," in part because "the university has connections all over the country and Howard does a great job of bringing those connec-

> **SURVEY SAYS . . .**
> Small classes
> Students are happy
> Frats and sororities dominate social scene
> Musical organizations are popular
> Student publications are popular
> Student government is popular

tions to campus," and in part because of the perception that "organizations are forced to come here to employ their minority quotas." Undergrads here report that "The academic experience largely depends on what you major in. If you're going for African-American studies, business or dentistry you'll get what you've paid for." The presence of a College of Medicine (and its affiliated hospital) bolsters offerings in life sciences and pre-medical studies as well. Other disciplines can present "a challenging and somewhat unfulfilling college experience," students warn. They also caution that "facilities are outdated and need a major technological and physical update" and that "The administration needs some work. There are great, qualified people in places of high authority. However, the people that you have to go through to get to the people who actually care are usually horrible. They never move with a sense of urgency. If it's not their problem, its not a problem, and they usually talk to you like you are 12."

Life

"We always, always, always have something going on" on the "very active" Howard campus. There are "hundreds of organizations that tailor to any needs you can think of," and students are "very active politically and socially, so there are rallies and there are parties. Each and every extreme is met with its opposite here." There's "always somewhere to go" on campus, "whether it be the Punchout Cafe to hang with your friends, Power Hall to relax, study and work with your friends, to 'the yard' to chill and people watch, [or] to the gym to work out…. If you are isolated on Howard's campus it is because you choose to be." The world awaiting off campus is even more active; as one student explains, "There is so much to do in the Washington, DC area that there is rarely any room for boredom. Georgetown, Chinatown, and Pentagon City are just a few of the places that students go." Adams Morgan is another popular destination. No need to bring a car here; "Everything we would want to go to is Metro accessible so there's no problem moving about DC as if we've lived here our whole lives." Fun is typically confined to weekends, as "Many of us work very hard during the week. Sunday through Thursday, we stay on campus and focus on getting schoolwork done and attending any organizational meetings/events."

Student Body

The typical Howard student "is African American with a deep desire toward success." Undergrads are "extremely serious about their career goals and their academic achievement" and "very involved in political activism, campus organizations, and community." They also tend to be "very fashion-conscious and dwell a lot on others perceptions of us, although many of us profess to be strong individuals." Although nearly all black, the student population "is extremely diverse. I sit in classes with people from Spain, England, Trinidad and Tobago, South Africa, Nigeria, Alaska, etc." Students "come from all walks of life. You can find people with different religious beliefs, ethnic origins, and sexual preferences. There are students with interests in every field imaginable. Howard represents the black world."

THE PRINCETON REVIEW SAYS

Admissions

Very important factors considered include: Class rank, rigor of secondary school record, standardized test scores. *Important factors considered include:* Recommendation(s), character/personal qualities. *Other factors considered include:* Application essay, alumni/ae relation, extracurricular activities, talent/ability, volunteer work, work experience. SAT or ACT required; ACT with Writing component required. TOEFL required of all international applicants. High school diploma is required and GED is accepted. *Academic units required:* 4 English, 2 mathematics, 2 science, 2 foreign language, 2 social studies, 2 history. *Academic units recommended:* 4 English, 3 mathematics, 4 science, (2 science labs), 2 foreign language, 2 social studies, 2 history, 4 any other academic courses counted toward graduation.

Financial Aid

Students should submit: FAFSA. Regular filing deadline is 8/15. The Princeton Review suggests that all financial aid forms be submitted as soon as possible after January 1. *Need-based scholarships/grants offered:* Federal Pell, SEOG, state scholarships/grants, private scholarships, the school's own gift aid, Federal Nursing Scholarships. *Loan aid offered:* Direct Subsidized Stafford, Direct Unsubsidized Stafford, Direct PLUS, Federal Perkins, Federal Nursing Applicants will be notified of awards on a rolling basis beginning 4/1. Federal Work-Study Program available. Institutional employment available. Off-campus job opportunities are excellent.

The Inside Word

A large applicant pool and solid yield of acceptees who enroll is a combination that adds up to selectivity at Howard. The school is willing to give applicants a pass on standardized test scores if their high school records indicate seriousness about, and the ability to handle, advanced study.

THE SCHOOL SAYS ". . ."

From The Admissions Office

"Since its founding, Howard has stood among the few institutions of higher learning where African Americans and other minorities have participated freely in a truly comprehensive university experience. Thus, Howard has assumed a special responsibility to prepare its students to exercise leadership wherever their interest and commitments take them. Howard has issued approximately 99,318 degrees, diplomas, and certificates to men and women in the professions, the arts and sciences, and the humanities. The university has produced and continues to produce a high percentage of the nation's African American professionals in the fields of medicine, dentistry, pharmacy, engineering, nursing, architecture, religion, law, music, social work, education, and business. There are more than 8,906 students from across the nation and approximately 85 countries and territories attending the university. Their varied customs, cultures, ideas, and interests contribute to Howard's international character and vitality. More than 1,598 faculty members represent the largest concentration of African American scholars in any single institution of higher education.

"Beginning with the entering class of Fall 2008 all applicants who have never been to college will be required to submit scores from either the new SAT or the ACT (with the Writing component)."

For even more information on this school, turn to page 482 of the "Stats" section.

Indiana University of Pennsylvania

216 Pratt Hall, Indiana, PA 15705 • Admissions: 724-357-2230 • Fax: 724-357-6281
Financial Aid: 415-357-2218 • E-mail: admissions_inquiry@grove.iup.edu • Website: www.iup.edu

RATINGS
Quality of Life: 66   **Academic:** 70   **Admissions:** 66   **Financial Aid:** 71

STUDENTS SAY ". . ."

Academics

Named not for the state, but for the actual town in which the school is located, Indiana University of Pennsylvania (IUP) is "academically challenging but not impossible if you make an honest effort." Students enjoy "awesome professors" who are "concerned with their welfare and academic growth," and find their teachers "ridiculously easy to get into contact with—no need to make an appointment." Thanks to "strong educators" and "small class sizes" students are "pushed to think critically," and those who want even more of a challenge can take part in "excellent honors classes and programs." In recent years, the administration has gone through several changes, leaving some students feeling that it is "often out of touch with the real world." That said, students enjoy an "equal say in the policies that form the foundation of their education" through the University Senate, and "can always access [the administration] when in need." While some students have experienced "scheduling problems" in certain departments, students feel, overall, that they get more for less at IUP: "Anyone attending can achieve the same education as another student at an Ivy League school" as long as "They are truly interested in learning and willing to put forth the effort."

Life

Indiana, Pennsylvania, is the kind of town John Mellencamp would sing about—small, working-class, but not without its charms or bars. As one student explains, "socializing is a large part of IUP life." Since the school is located "in a backwoods kind of area," most students "go to parties for fun," and most but "not all parties involve a keg." While many students "go to fraternities and house parties and drink" there are options available for students "who want no alcohol/drugs involved in their college life whatsoever." For non-partiers, "Life usually consists of movies and games" and "outdoor activities when the weather is nice." The school also boasts a "good selection of clubs" that provides a quick way "to meet people." While "Going to a grocery store or a mall would be much easier" if you "get a car," most students take advantage of the "free bus system" to get to town. There, students enjoy "a pool hall, two bowling alleys, a local theater that shows current, old, and foreign films," as well as "tons of restaurants and bars" and some "great coffeehouses." If you need a taste of city life, "Pittsburgh is an hour and a half away."

Student Body

According to one student, IUP is "more diverse" than the local "predominantly White area," but "less diverse than U.S. Census percentage numbers." As a "public university" the "student body is very mixed," and students have "the opportunity to interact with more people" than they would at "many other colleges," from the "very conservative" to the "extremely unique." As one student explains, "No matter what your interest is, it wouldn't be too hard to find someone that you can share this interest with." While fraternities and sororities are "popular," there is "a place for everyone" on campus. In other words, "No matter who you are, if you go to this college you are going to have a damn good time." Students view themselves as "down to earth" and adept at "balancing academics" with "social outlets." The dorms help instill "a strong feeling of community" as do the honors courses, which provide "a bonding experience without the drinking" for students.

> SURVEY SAYS . . .
> Small classes
> Frats and sororities dominate social scene
> Student publications are popular
> Lots of beer drinking
> Hard liquor is popular
> (Almost) everyone smokes

THE PRINCETON REVIEW SAYS

Admissions

Very important factors considered include: Academic GPA, standardized test scores. *Important factors considered include:* Rigor of secondary school record. *Other factors considered include:* Class rank, application essay, recommendation(s), extracurricular activities, SAT or ACT required; TOEFL required of all international applicants. High school diploma is required and GED is accepted. *Academic units recommended:* 3 English, 3 mathematics, 3 science, 2 foreign language, 3 social studies.

Financial Aid

Students should submit: FAFSA. The Princeton Review suggests that all financial aid forms be submitted as soon as possible after January 1. *Need-based scholarships/grants offered:* Federal Pell, SEOG, state scholarships/grants, private scholarships, the school's own gift aid, United Negro College Fund. *Loan aid offered:* FFEL Subsidized Stafford, FFEL Unsubsidized Stafford, FFEL PLUS, Federal Perkins, Private Alternative Loans. Applicants will be notified of awards on a rolling basis beginning 3/15. Federal Work-Study Program available. Institutional employment available. Off-campus job opportunities are good.

The Inside Word

Indiana University of Pennsylvania offers an academic environment unique among most public universities: undergraduate classes taught solely by professors. Pennsylvania residents will find it especially worthwhile to investigate this school as it offers a solid education at an affordable price to state residents. The admissions process should not give much trouble to students with an above-average secondary school record.

THE SCHOOL SAYS "..."

From The Admissions Office

"At IUP, we look at each applicant as an individual, not as a number. That means we'll review your application materials very carefully. When reviewing applications, the Admissions Committee's primary focus is on the student's high school record and SAT scores. In addition, the committee often reviews the optional personal essay and letters of recommendations submitted by the student to help aid in the decision-making process. We're always happy to speak with prospective students. Call us toll-free at 800-422-6830 or 724-357-2230 or e-mail us at admissions-inquiry@iup.edu.

"Students applying for admission into the Fall 2008 entering class are required to take the new version of the SAT. Students will be allowed to submit scores from the old (prior to March 2005) version of the SAT (or ACT) as well, and we will use the student's best scores from either test."

For even more information on this school, turn to page 482 of the "Stats" section.

IONA COLLEGE

715 NORTH AVENUE, NEW ROCHELLE, NY 10801 • ADMISSIONS: 914-633-2502 • FAX: 914-633-2642
E-MAIL: ADMISSIONS@IONA.EDU • WEBSITE: WWW.IONA.EDU

RATINGS
Quality of Life: 73   **Academic:** 74   **Admissions:** 86   **Financial Aid:** 63

STUDENTS SAY "..."

Academics

Students looking for a liberal arts or business education at a school that provides "an easy adjustment from high school" may find Iona College to be a good fit. Students here report that professors are "extremely accessible, friendly, and eager to help." "I had a teacher once who noticed my grades dropped a little, and e-mailed me asking if I was okay and if she [could] help," one satisfied student writes. Iona's "amazing" Honors Degree Program offers students special classes "with just honors students" and "special professors" who "seem to be a step above." Be warned, however: "Teachers take attendance like in high school," and "Attendance counts [toward] your grade." This irks students who feel that sometimes "you can learn [the material] on your own." The administration, while well meaning, is not easy to deal with. "Financial aid is where most people have the most trouble," a senior reports. On the upside, Iona is "located conveniently close to New York City," which makes it "ideal for interning."

Life

Situated just 20 minutes north of Manhattan in Westchester County, Iona offers great proximity to a world-class metropolis. "The train station is super close" and getting to "the city" is less than "a 30-minute event," students tell us. Manhattan "is very expensive" for a student budget, however, so the majority of the time "students stay nearby." Within Iona's New Rochelle environs, students frequent New Roc City, a complex that features "restaurants, shopping, a movie theater," "bowling, ice skating," "pool," and "mini golf." Other than that, students report, "There is not that much to do in New Rochelle for fun" as "Most of the bars around town have been shut down because of underage drinking." Off-campus house parties hosted by Greek organizations and sports teams help fill the void, as do trips to "bars in the Bronx." Back on campus, "Football, basketball, and soccer games are popular," and "Many students just hang out with their friends in the dorm rooms." "On-campus clubs," on the other hand, "are not particularly popular, nor are the campus-organized activities, except among students who don't drink." Because of the large commuter population "It gets really quiet" on weekends when "a lot of people go home."

Student Body

Students at Iona report that their peers are "mostly Caucasian" and of "Irish or Italian background," though they point out that, "in recent years, the Hispanic and Black populations [have] been increasing." While "Most students are from the Tristate Area," a sanguine undergrad informs us that "the athletic students come from all over the globe! We have athletes from Kenya, Uganda, England, Ireland, Central and South America, and all across the United States." Regardless of background, "Everyone seems to have at least one tight-knit group of friends that they socialize with." In fact, "cliques are formed even before school starts through Facebook.com and orientation," and "living in the dorms is definitely a must in order to make good friends and keep them," a sophomore advises. Physical descriptions of the typical Iona student involve measures of urbanity, materialism, and locomotion: "A large percentage of the students walk around with their cell phone in one hand," a freshman writes, and "The girls seem to walk around looking very rich." "Balance" is a catchphrase on campus. As one accounting major explains, "The typical student at Iona College is well rounded," someone who "strives to do well academically and also has a good social life and good friends."

Admissions

Very important factors considered include: Academic GPA, rigor of secondary school record. *Important factors considered include:* Class rank, application essay, standardized test scores, character/personal qualities, interview. *Other factors considered include:* Recommendation(s), alumni/ae relation, extracurricular activities, first generation, geographical residence, level of applicant's interest, talent/ability, volunteer work, work experience. SAT or ACT required; TOEFL required of all international applicants. High school diploma is required and GED is accepted. *Academic units required:* 4 English, 3 mathematics, 2 science, (2 science labs), 2 foreign language, 1 social studies, 1 history, 1 academic electives. *Academic units recommended:* 4 English, 4 mathematics, 3 science, (2 science labs), 2 foreign language, 2 social studies, 2 history, 3 academic electives.

Financial Aid

Students should submit: FAFSA, institution's own financial aid form, state aid form. Regular filing deadline is 4/15. The Princeton Review suggests that all financial aid forms be submitted as soon as possible after January 1. *Need-based scholarships/grants offered:* Federal Pell, SEOG, state scholarships/grants, private scholarships, the school's own gift aid. *Loan aid offered:* FFEL Subsidized Stafford, FFEL Unsubsidized Stafford, FFEL PLUS, Federal Perkins, Alternative Loans. Applicants will be notified of awards on a rolling basis beginning 12/20. Federal Work-Study Program available. Institutional employment available. Off-campus job opportunities are good.

The Inside Word

Students whose credentials exceed Iona's admissions standards may be interested in its Honors Degree Program. In addition to special classes with the school's best professors, students in the honors program enjoy a mentoring program that matches them with an Iona grad, two tuition-free courses per academic year, and priority registration throughout their undergraduate career at Iona.

THE SCHOOL SAYS "..."

From The Admissions Office

"Students appreciate Iona on a number of levels: They find the academic program challenging and supportive; they enjoy the large number of organized and individual activities, and they love being close to New York City for the internships and social opportunities it provides.

"Iona has a beautiful, green, 35-acre campus in New Rochelle, New York, just 20 minutes from Manhattan. Students use mass transportation to take advantage of New York City for social and educational opportunities, including internships at some of the world's most recognized institutions.

"After Iona, our graduates continue to excel: 76 percent of our graduates go on to pursue graduate or professional studies and gain acceptance at the world's most prestigious graduate schools (Harvard, Yale, Johns Hopkins, Oxford, University of Chicago). Iona alumni also excel in the workplace, currently heading global industries as chairman, president, or CEO (New York Stock Exchange, NASDQ, AOL, American Express, Terex, AFL-CIO) and provide our students with a network of internship opportunities and our graduates with employment opportunities.

"Finding and getting into the right college is hard. While this book provides good information, the best way to narrow down your choices is by visiting various schools to see how you fit in. As you go through the admissions process at Iona, we promise to answer your questions honestly and treat you with dignity. While you may not always get the answer you want, we will be as direct and helpful as we can be."

For even more information on this school, turn to page 483 of the "Stats" section.

ITHACA COLLEGE

100 Job Hall, Ithaca, NY 14850-7020 • Admissions: 607-274-3124 • Fax: 607-274-1900
Financial Aid: 607-274-3131 • E-mail: admission@ithaca.edu • Website: www.ithaca.edu

RATINGS
Quality of Life: 79   Academic: 79   Admissions: 83   Financial Aid: 82

STUDENTS SAY "..."

Academics

Ithaca College offers "a wonderful liberal arts experience," and it's "an overall excellent place to study for four years." "A huge variety of majors" includes a "renowned" cinema program and an "amazing" theater program. There are "strong," "in-depth" majors in physical therapy, music education, and communications, too. Courses are discussion-heavy and "reasonably easy to complete if you show up and pay attention." "Some lectures don't even feel like lectures because the professor knows everyone's name,"

> ### SURVEY SAYS . . .
> Great off-campus food
> Frats and sororities are unpopular
> or nonexistent
> Musical organizations are popular
> College radio is popular
> Theater is popular
> Student publications are popular

says a physical therapy major. "You don't feel like just a number." In general, the IC faculty is full of "nice, funny, generally laidback people" with "real world experience." "Some can teach and some can't." Some are "so enthusiastic it's almost scary." A few "can be very opinionated." After class, professors are "readily available" and they take time to get to know their students. "You would be hard pressed to find a person who hasn't had dinner at a professor's house," claims a communications major. Don't expect many dinners with the administration, though. Management is reportedly "hard to get hold of." Students also complain about IC's general enormity. "This campus is huge and there is a lot of walking." "Some of the buildings look ugly and dated" as well. Costs are another big gripe. "The school nickels and dimes us quite a bit," vents a music education major.

Life

A great deal of student life at Ithaca occurs on campus. "When it's warm out, there are always students outside playing Frisbee and reading on the grass." "The school and student-run activities provide a plethora of opportunities." "There are music concerts nearly every night." There is a "very popular" radio station. "Many students also like to support" the athletic teams. The party scene is strong. "If you walk around the dorms, you will find at least someone to have drinking competitions with," promises a sophomore. Getting stoned is a popular pastime as well. "There is a huge population of people who enjoy it almost every day." Winters are hardcore up here and "getting off campus can be hard." "It can be very isolating if you can't drive." The surrounding town is "safe" and there are "tons of shops and restaurants," but Ithacans usually "don't venture into the city." When they do, they often go "across town" to Cornell "for the frat parties since Ithaca has no social fraternities." "Girls have no problem getting into the frats" but guys have a harder time. "There is a lot of nature to bask in" as well, at least when the water isn't "frozen over." Ithaca "is nothing if not gorges." For somewhat more cosmopolitan fare, "the mall in Syracuse is a nice escape."

Student Body

It's an odd mix of people. There are "quirky communications students, jockish exercise science majors, and weird thespians." There are "diva-like" music majors. "There are many gays and lesbians." There are "the super studious students and the ones who are more concerned with social life." There are a lot of hippies and "radical students" with "sort of a crazy fashion sense." "Anyone who comes here can basically find their niche," says a first-year student. Politically, the environment is "extremely liberal." "There is a lot of activism." "The environmentalists are everywhere and are annoying at times," says a junior. "Ithaca College endlessly brags about how diverse it is" but students tell us that the minority population is "minimal." There are students here from around the country but "it does seem like everyone is from wealthy suburbs in the Northeast." Some students insist that class issues are nonexistent. "There are a lot of rich people on campus," they say, "but that doesn't mean that they'll rub it in." "I'm here because it was cheaper to attend Ithaca with my financial aid package than either of the state schools I applied to," adds a senior. "That says a lot." However, others see a lot of snobbery. "To survive at Ithaca College, it is best to not openly talk about any socioeconomic disadvantages," asserts a sophomore, "because it makes all the white students feel uncomfortable and they'll alienate you."

THE PRINCETON REVIEW SAYS

Admissions

Very important factors considered include: Academic GPA, rigor of secondary school record, standardized test scores. *Important factors considered include:* Class rank, application essay, recommendation(s), character/personal qualities, extracurricular activities, talent/ability. *Other factors considered include:* Alumni/ae relation, first generation, level of applicant's interest, volunteer work, work experience. SAT or ACT required; ACT with Writing component required. TOEFL required of all international applicants. High school diploma is required and GED is accepted. *Academic units required:* 4 English, 3 mathematics, 3 science, 2 foreign language, 3 social studies, 1 academic elective.

Financial Aid

Students should submit: FAFSA. The Princeton Review suggests that all financial aid forms be submitted as soon as possible after January 1. *Need-based scholarships/grants offered:* Federal Pell, SEOG, state scholarships/grants, private scholarships, the school's own gift aid. *Loan aid offered:* FFEL Subsidized Stafford, FFEL Unsubsidized Stafford, FFEL PLUS, Federal Perkins, Alternative Loans. Applicants will be notified of awards on a rolling basis beginning 2/15. Federal Work-Study Program available. Institutional employment available. Off-campus job opportunities are good.

The Inside Word

Ithaca has a moderately competitive admissions profile and the annual crop of freshmen typically ranges from solid to spectacular. If you apply, expect thorough consideration of your personal background, talents, and achievements in addition to your academic accomplishments. Programs requiring an audition or portfolio are among the most demanding for admission; the arts have always been particularly strong here.

THE SCHOOL SAYS "..."

From The Admissions Office

"Ithaca College was founded in 1892 as a music conservatory, and it continues that commitment to performance and excellence. Its modern, residential 750-acre campus, equipped with state-of-the-art facilities, is home to the Schools of Business, Communications, Health Sciences and Human Performance, Humanities and Sciences, and Music and our new Division of Interdisciplinary and International Studies. With more than 100 majors—from biochemistry to business administration, journalism to jazz, philosophy to physical therapy, and special programs in Washington, DC, Los Angeles, London, and Australia—students enjoy the curricular choices of a large campus in a personalized, smaller school environment. And Ithaca's students benefit from an education that emphasizes active learning, small classes, collaborative student-faculty research, and development of the whole student. Located in central New York's spectacular Finger Lakes region in what many consider the classic college town, the college has 25 highly competitive varsity teams, more than 130 campus clubs, two radio stations and a television station, as well as hundreds of concerts, recitals, and theater performances annually.

"Students applying for admission must have official scores from either the SAT or the ACT with the Writing section sent to Ithaca College by the testing agency. The college will also consider results of SAT Subject Tests, if submitted."

For even more information on this school, turn to page 483 of the "Stats" section.

JOHNS HOPKINS UNIVERSITY

3400 NORTH CHARLES STREET/140 GARLAND, BALTIMORE, MD 21218 • ADMISSIONS: 410-516-8171
FAX: 410-516-6025 • FINANCIAL AID: 410-516-8028 • E-MAIL: GOTOJHU@JHU.EDU • WEBSITE: WWW.JHU.EDU

RATINGS
Quality of Life: 68   **Academic:** 86   **Admissions:** 98   **Financial Aid:** 93

STUDENTS SAY ". . ."

Academics

Johns Hopkins University is a premed powerhouse and one of the nation's great producers of tomorrow's prominent doctors and medical researchers. Boasting one of the "top research [hospitals] in the country," the country's "number-one undergraduate biomedical engineering program," and "the number-one school for public health studies," it's no wonder JHU draws so many aspiring doctors that students sometimes think "Almost everyone is premed." That mis-

> **SURVEY SAYS . . .**
> Lab facilities are great
> Great computer facilities
> Great library
> Athletic facilities are great
> Diverse student types on campus
> Lots of beer drinking

conception is one of the reasons JHU's many other strengths are often overlooked. Those strengths are many, including "a fantastic international studies program," a highly respected Writing Seminar that "is paving the way for liberal arts on this science-dominated campus," a School of Engineering that offers students "amazing research experience," and "a wonderful relationship with the Peabody Conservatory for those seriously interested in music." No matter what they study, students at JHU inhabit "an intense academic environment that works hard to make us the best applicants we can be for grad school while teaching us how to be a part of a global community." Research is "a big highlight here"; as one student explains, "JHU was the first research university in the U.S.A.," and you'll find "a lot of [research] opportunities" from freshman year on. What you won't find is a lot of hand-holding, since "Hopkins is an institution where students are given a wide range of freedom with their classes and with their social life, but more importantly, it teaches students to be responsible for their own actions and decisions, both academically and socially."

Life

"Johns Hopkins has a reputation for being a living hell; however, it is actually quite nice," students assure us. One explains, "It is true that we have a very rigorous academic program, but that does not prevent us from having fun and enjoying the many activities and enjoyments that are offered by the school and the neighborhood. The frats and sororities are quite active but not ridiculous; there are many trendy areas in Baltimore with good bars, restaurants, and clubs; and there are many events on campus ranging from a cappella concerts to lectures from prominent political figures to concerts by artists like Guster and Talib Kweli." Hometown Baltimore "gets a bad rep" (if you watch HBO's The Wire, you know what that rep is) "but there is a lot to do in and around campus. There is tons of shopping, and lots of really good restaurants to eat at in the city." There's also "a good band scene, as well as really cheap baseball tickets." All in all, "It's a very fun city." For fun on campus, "Students normally go to frat parties." JHU has some "great Division I sports teams"—men's lacrosse and soccer are always highly ranked—and the student body regularly rallies to their support. The "beautiful" campus is a short walk from the Baltimore Museum of Art, a great place to blow off steam when the pressures of school start to build, and "is free for students."

Student Body

JHU students aren't sure "whether there is such a thing as one typical student here, because there is a strong division between engineering and arts and science students." That said, "Most students work hard and play hard." There are "lots of complaints about the workload, but people are secretly proud of the work they do." Many here "are intensely competitive," which is a "reflection of the pressure they feel on campus," but "It is a myth that Hopkins is filled with cut-throat nerds." Though "it is a stressful atmosphere at times because students want to get ahead, most of the students are very helpful and nice." Demographically speaking, "There are all kinds of people here, which means that everyone can fit in. No matter what kind of person someone may appear to be on the outside, you know that if they're at Hopkins they must be pretty nerdy on the inside, so there's a kind of camaraderie there." Most students "are a little of everything, and it seems like everyone here is exceptional at something."

THE PRINCETON REVIEW SAYS

Admissions

Very important factors considered include: Academic GPA, recommendation(s), rigor of secondary school record, character/personal qualities. *Important factors considered include:* Class rank, application essay, standardized test scores, extracurricular activities, talent/ability, volunteer work, work experience. *Other factors considered include:* Alumni/ae relation, first generation, geographical residence, interview, racial/ethnic status, state residency, SAT or ACT required; SAT and SAT Subject Tests or ACT recommended; ACT with Writing component required. High school diploma or equivalent is not required. *Academic units recommended:* 4 English, 4 mathematics, 4 science, 4 foreign language, 2 social studies, 2 history, 2 foreign language for engineering majors.

Financial Aid

Students should submit: FAFSA, CSS/Financial Aid PROFILE, noncustodial PROFILE, business/farm supplement, prior and current year federal tax returns. Regular filing deadline is 2/15. The Princeton Review suggests that all financial aid forms be submitted as soon as possible after January 1. *Need-based scholarships/grants offered:* Federal Pell, SEOG, state scholarships/grants, private scholarships, the school's own gift aid. *Loan aid offered:* Direct Subsidized Stafford, Direct Unsubsidized Stafford, FFEL PLUS, Federal Perkins, college/university loans from institutional funds. Applicants will be notified of awards on or about 4/1. Federal Work-Study Program available. Institutional employment available.

The Inside Word

Top schools like Hopkins receive more and more applications every year and, as a result, grow harder and harder to get into. With nearly 14,000 applicants for the class of 2010, Hopkins had to reject numerous applicants who were thoroughly qualified. Give your application everything you've got, and don't take it personally if you don't get a fat envelope in the mail.

THE SCHOOL SAYS ". . ."

From The Admissions Office

"The Hopkins tradition of preeminent academic excellence naturally attracts the very best students in the nation and from around the world. The Admissions Committee carefully examines each application for evidence of compelling intellectual interest and academic performance as well as strong personal recommendations and meaningful extracurricular contributions. Every applicant who matriculates to Johns Hopkins University was found qualified by the Admissions Committee through a 'whole person' assessment, and every applicant accepted for admission is fully expected to graduate. The Admissions Committee determines whom they believe will take full advantage of the exceptional opportunities offered at Hopkins, contribute the most to the educational process of the institution, and be the most successful in using what they have learned and experienced for the benefit of society.

"Freshman applicants for Fall 2008 may take either the old SAT and three SAT Subject Tests (one must be Writing) or the ACT. Alternatively, students may take either the new SAT or the ACT with Writing component. For those submitting SAT scores, submitting scores from three SAT Subject Tests is recommended."

For even more information on this school, turn to page 484 of the "Stats" section.

JUNIATA COLLEGE

ENROLLMENT OFFICE, 1700 MOORE ST., HUNTINGDON, PA 16652 • ADMISSIONS: 877-586-4282
FAX: 814-641-3100 • FINANCIAL AID: 814-641-3142 • E-MAIL: ADMISSION@JUNIATA.EDU • WEBSITE: WWW.JUNIATA.EDU

RATINGS
Quality of Life: 83   **Academic:** 87   **Admissions:** 89   **Financial Aid:** 80

STUDENTS SAY "..."

Academics

Juniata College has catapulted from regional to national status in the past decade on the strength of its great natural science programs, housed in the 88,000-square-foot state-of-the-art Von Liebig Center for Science (VLCS) that opened its doors in 2002. Students tell us that while Juniata "is centered around a very tough but rewarding science program," science is hardly the only game in town. The "business, theatre, and education departments are strong, too." Another student explains, "Other departments are

> **SURVEY SAYS . . .**
> *Large classes*
> *Lab facilities are great*
> *Students are friendly*
> *Campus feels safe*
> *Low cost of living*
> *Frats and sororities are unpopular or nonexistent*

beginning to receive support from trustees and alumni now that VLCS is complete. Several buildings will be undergoing renovations to allow for the expansion of the humanities and social sciences." Business, in particular, seems likely to receive a lot of attention as it is among the school's most popular disciplines. Undergrads tout JC's "great entrepreneurial program...where all students are encouraged to start their own businesses and some are given start-up cash." Education is also popular. Students appreciate that they are "given a practicum their first semester freshman year," meaning that "if they don't like being in the classroom, they can change their major right away." "At most other schools, you have to wait until your junior year to get some classroom experience," says a student. Other perks of a Juniata education include the prominence of the study abroad program and that "students are afforded the option to create their own major (Program of Emphasis), which allows us to explore many possibilities that would otherwise be restricted by a designated major."

Life

Juniata "is located in Huntingdon, PA, which is a tiny town in the middle of nowhere, thirty minutes south of State College," so "needless to say, there is not a lot to do off-campus." Fortunately, "The Juniata Activities Board (JAB) brings numerous acts to campus: comedians, musicians, hypnotists, magicians." The campus also hosts "various weekend parties, but they normally don't happen until Saturday nights because a large population of the student body is active in athletics and they have games either Friday night or Saturday afternoon." Since Juniata "doesn't have any Greek societies," students compensate by being "active in many clubs, including the Agriculture Club, Health Occupations Students of America, Student Government, the Equine Club, and the Student Alumni Association." Otherwise, quiet fun ("video games and movie watching are very popular") dominates. One student explains, "The people who are dissatisfied with Juniata were definitely expecting something else, usually something more along the lines of Penn State."

Student Body

Juniata "is notoriously middle class and Caucasian" with "very few minority students." Diversity arrives in the form of "a vast number of international students, both in semester and year-long exchange programs and as four year degree-seeking students. The international presence at Juniata does a lot for class debate, and often opens the eyes of otherwise typically American students to the perspectives of those from other nations." Undergrads here "work hard for their grades. They want to excel. Basically, they're motivated and determined to succeed in the real world," to the point that they often "choose to do homework and study above most other activities." Ultimately, "A typical student is really studious and really cares about their education. Everyone is able to find their own clique in which they fit into and feel comfortable."

THE PRINCETON REVIEW SAYS

Admissions

Very important factors considered include: Application essay, academic GPA, recommendation(s), rigor of secondary school record, standardized test scores, character/personal qualities. *Important factors considered include:* Extracurricular activities, first generation, interview, talent/ability, volunteer work. *Other factors considered include:* Alumni/ae relation, geographical residence, level of applicant's interest, state residency, SAT or ACT recommended; TOEFL required of all international applicants. High school diploma is required and GED is accepted. *Academic units required:* 4 English, 3 mathematics, 3 science, (2 science labs), 2 foreign language, 1 social studies, 3 history. *Academic units recommended:* 4 English, 4 mathematics, 4 science, 2 foreign language, 1 social studies, 3 history.

Financial Aid

Students should submit: FAFSA. Regular filing deadline is 3/1. The Princeton Review suggests that all financial aid forms be submitted as soon as possible after January 1. *Need-based scholarships/grants offered:* Federal Pell, SEOG, state scholarships/grants, private scholarships, the school's own gift aid. *Loan aid offered:* FFEL Subsidized Stafford, FFEL Unsubsidized Stafford, FFEL PLUS, Federal Perkins, college/university loans from institutional funds. Applicants will be notified of awards on a rolling basis beginning 2/21. Federal Work-Study Program available. Institutional employment available. Off-campus job opportunities are good.

The Inside Word

As at many traditional liberal arts schools, the admissions process at Juniata is a personal one. Applications are scoured for evidence that the student is committed to attending Juniata and to remaining there for the full four years. The school is best known for its premedical programs, meaning that applicants to these programs will have the highest hurdles to clear.

THE SCHOOL SAYS ". . ."

From The Admissions Office

"Juniata's unique approach to learning has a flexible, student-centered focus. With the help of two advisors, over half of Juniata's students design their own majors (called the "Program of Emphasis" or "POE"). Those who choose a more traditional academic journey still benefit from the assistance of two faculty advisors and interdisciplinary collaboration between multiple academic departments.

"In addition, all students benefit from the recent, significant investments in academic facilities that help students actively learn by doing. For example, the new Halbritter Performing Arts Center houses an innovative theater program where theater professionals work side by side with students; the Sill Business Incubator provides $5,000 in seed capital to students with a desire to start their own business; the LEEDS-certified Shuster Environmental Studies Field Station, located on nearby Raystown Lake, gives unparalleled hands-on study opportunities to students; and the von Liebig Center for Science provides opportunities for student/faculty research surpassing those available at even large universities.

"As the 2003 Middle States Accreditation Team noted, 'Juniata is truly a student-centered college. There is a remarkable cohesiveness in this commitment—faculty, students, trustees, staff, and alumni, each from their own vantage point, describe a community in which the growth of the student is central.' This cohesiveness creates a dynamic learning environment that enables students to think and grow intellectually, to evolve in their academic careers, and to graduate as active, successful participants in the global community.

"Freshman applicants for Fall 2008 may submit either the new SAT (or the ACT with the Writing component) or the old (before March 2005) SAT (or ACT); we will use their best scores from either test. "

For even more information on this school, turn to page 484 of the "Stats" section.

KEENE STATE COLLEGE

229 MAIN STREET, KEENE, NH 03435 • ADMISSIONS: 603-358-2276 • FAX: 603-358-2767
E-MAIL: ADMISSIONS@KEENE.EDU • WEBSITE: WWW.KEENE.EDU

RATINGS
Quality of Life: 80   **Academic:** 72   **Admissions:** 72   **Financial Aid:** 72

STUDENTS SAY ". . ."

Academics

"Keene State College is a great liberal arts school in a picturesque New England town" that is "really great for education majors." There are almost 40 other majors to choose from, though, and "the academic experience as a whole is generally good." "The physical campus is almost entirely new." "Classrooms are spacious, attractive, and comfortable." A few professors are "dull" and "just suck at teaching." However, "the majority of professors love what they do, and that's reflected in their teaching style." Students receive "lots of individual attention." "Here you are a person and not a number," promises a junior. "My professors are all always more than willing to meet with me whenever I need to," gloats an education major. "They are extremely accessible and helpful." "The administration is always there when you have a question" as well. There's "very little bureaucracy" and everything "flows nicely."

> **SURVEY SAYS . . .**
> *Large classes*
> *Great library*
> *Athletic facilities are great*
> *Students love Keene, NH*
> *Great off-campus food*
> *Lots of beer drinking*
> *Hard liquor is popular*
> *(Almost) everyone smokes*

Life

According to students here, the "gorgeous" and "relaxing" campus at Keene State is the perfect size. "The campus is small enough where I can randomly run into my friends, but big enough that if I need space, it's there," says a sophomore. For many students, "life consists of a lot of studying." "A lot of work gets done Sunday through Thursday." If you want, you can "slack off immensely," though, and still get by. Sports are popular and there is a "wide variety" of clubs and activities. There is also a smattering of Greek life. "The weekend party scene is great." Students here have been known to get "drunk and rowdy." The bar scene is lively. "A lot of the sports teams have houses, so they sometimes throw open parties" as well. The "friendly" surrounding hamlet of Keene "is quintessentially New England," complete with an "awesome main street" and several "unique stores and restaurants." Each year, "thousands of jack-o-lanterns" line the streets for the big pumpkin festival in town and there is a big gourd-carving free-for-fall called Pumpkin Lobotomy on the quad. Further afield, there's "Mount Monadnock to climb" and outdoor activities galore.

Student Body

"There is undoubtedly a lack of ethnic diversity here." "A lot of the kids are from New Hampshire" but a significant percentage comes from others states around the region. "Many students at Keene State seem to be from Connecticut." "The typical student at Keene State is white and preppy or a jock." "There are definitely some students who've come here for the school's regional reputation as a party school." There are "some hipster types." "There are very many crunchy, earthy students" as well. "Everyone drinks coffee." KSC is home to "very few bookworms or nerds." You'll occasionally see kids with "funky-colored hair and Mohawks," but it's definitely not the norm. "There's cliques, but there aren't armored walls" between them. "You have your core group of friends, but most groups are totally willing to expand and diversify," notes one student.

THE PRINCETON REVIEW SAYS

Admissions

Very important factors considered include: Rigor of secondary school record. *Important factors considered include:* Application essay, academic GPA, recommendation(s), standardized test scores. *Other factors considered include:* Class rank, alumni/ae relation, character/personal qualities, extracurricular activities, first generation, level of applicant's interest, racial/ethnic status, talent/ability, volunteer work, work experience. SAT or ACT required; ACT with Writing component recommended. TOEFL required of all international applicants. High school diploma is required and GED is accepted. *Academic units required:* 4 English, 3 mathematics, 3 science, 2 social studies, 2 academic electives.

Financial Aid

Students should submit: FAFSA. Regular filing deadline is 3/1. The Princeton Review suggests that all financial aid forms be submitted as soon as possible after January 1. *Need-based scholarships/grants offered:* Federal Pell, SEOG, state scholarships/grants, private scholarships, the school's own gift aid. *Loan aid offered:* FFEL Subsidized Stafford, FFEL Unsubsidized Stafford, FFEL PLUS, Federal Perkins, college/university loans from institutional funds. Applicants will be notified of awards on a rolling basis beginning 12/1. Federal Work-Study Program available. Institutional employment available. Off-campus job opportunities are excellent.

The Inside Word

Keene State is a safety school for many applicants with aspirations of attending flagship universities throughout New England. Keene State takes the time to look at your admissions application, primarily in an effort to justify admitting otherwise substandard candidates. The gatekeepers here want to invite you in; all you have to do is give them a good reason.

THE SCHOOL SAYS ". . ."

From The Admissions Office

"Keene State College is known as a moderately selective school with retention rates that look more like those of a selective school. We are proud that the quality of our applicants continues to increase each year, and we regularly cross applications with competitive flagship universities throughout New England.

"Students considered for admission to Keene State College are expected to have completed a competitive program of study in high school. Our 19% increase in applications in the past two years has given us the opportunity to become more selective and to close applications to nonresident students by March 1 – a month earlier than our usual deadline. The average GPA for a student entering Keene State College has consistently remained slightly above 3.0 (in academic courses) for the past five years. Admission to Keene's college-wide Honors program is more competitive, with a minimum GPA of 3.25 and cumulative SAT scores of 1050.

"Our applicants' average scores on the SAT verbal and math sections show a slight increase this year compared to recent years, with average scores of 508 verbal and 512 math. Also, as our students have mentioned, Keene State College takes pride in developing the fullest potential of students who enter not only as learners but as good citizens. More than 60 percent of our students are involved in community service. The College's recognition with distinction on President Bush's Honor Roll for Service is a tribute to our students' engagement in the world."

For even more information on this school, turn to page 485 of the "Stats" section.

KUTZTOWN UNIVERSITY OF PENNSYLVANIA

ADMISSIONS OFFICE, 15200 KUTZTOWN ROAD, KUTZTOWN, PA 19530-0730 • ADMISSIONS: 610-683-4060
FAX: 610-683-1375 • E-MAIL: ADMISSION@KUTZTOWN.EDU • WEBSITE: WWW.KUTZTOWN.EDU

RATINGS
Quality of Life: 69   Academic: 70   Admissions: 73   Financial Aid: 83

STUDENTS SAY "..."

Academics

Over the years, Kutztown University has developed a reputation as a place where students can receive a small-school education at state-school prices. And while the prices aren't changing much ("It's really inexpensive!" students assure us), the size of the school is. Undergrads tell us that "Kutztown is expanding horrendously quickly. The largest state-school dorm in Pennsylvania is being opened here next fall.... The academic side of campus is straying from the 'classroom' style buildings and starting to be replaced with lecture halls (capacity 175 per room)." Students tell us that "The growth of the school has definitely taken away its appeal," and that "The school is way too big for the town or campus to handle." The situation isn't likely to change. Students inform us that "KU is the only Pennsylvania state college that is not land-locked, so the state is pushing it to expand further." For those who can abide the burgeoning population, Kutztown offers a number of appealing programs. Education programs are strong, as is the College of Visual and Performing Arts. Science and nursing programs are gaining strength, with students informing us that "Interestingly enough, the hard sciences at this 'liberal arts' school are very thorough and the programs prepare the students for great successes in their careers."

> **SURVEY SAYS...**
> *Large classes*
> *Great library*
> *Athletic facilities are great*
> *Diverse student types on campus*
> *Lots of beer drinking*
> *Hard liquor is popular*
> *(Almost) everyone smokes*

Life

"There isn't too much to do" on and around the Kutztown campus, so "it's all about finding your own fun" here. A once-robust party scene in off-campus housing (the KU campus is dry) has been curtailed since the murder of a student in the fall of 2007. Though the perpetrators had nothing to do with the university or the town, the community watch groups formed in the crime's wake have focused largely on student activity and breaking up off-campus parties. Some undergrads feel that the community has "started hating college students because they think we're ruining their precious town that would cease to exist without us." With few social options to keep them on campus, "most people go home on the weekends." One student explains, "KU is what they call a suitcase school. When it comes to 3:00 on Friday afternoon there is traffic backed up throughout the entire campus." During the week (and occasionally on weekends), the school sponsors a slate of activities, including "guest speakers, plays, concerts, comedians, movies, casino nights, bingo, and other fun events." Various organizations sponsor regular trips to New York City and Washington DC, and to professional sporting events in Philadelphia. Students with cars occasionally seek out fun in nearby Reading and Allentown.

Student Body

KU is home to "preppy teachers, laid back students, and crazy art students" who "all get along because we respect each other and always learn something new about other people. It's more fun when everyone is different." Geographically, the campus is not so diverse; KU is "filled with students from the surrounding towns, and nearly everyone knows each other from their high school," although it should be noted that the school's location "near several urban centers" draws "rural, suburban and urban students equally, with the diversity and opportunities anticipated by this mixture of students." The school also has a substantial population of nontraditional (i.e., older) students.

Admissions

Very important factors considered include: Class rank, rigor of secondary school record, standardized test scores. *Other factors considered include:* Academic GPA, recommendation(s), character/personal qualities, extracurricular activities, geographical residence, interview, racial/ethnic status, state residency, talent/ability, volunteer work, work experience. SAT or ACT required; TOEFL required of all international applicants. High school diploma is required and GED is accepted. *Academic units recommended:* 4 English, 3 mathematics, 3 science, 2 foreign language, 4 social studies.

Financial Aid

Students should submit: FAFSA. The Princeton Review suggests that all financial aid forms be submitted as soon as possible after January 1. *Need-based scholarships/grants offered:* Federal Pell, SEOG, state scholarships/grants, private scholarships, the school's own gift aid. *Loan aid offered:* Direct Subsidized Stafford, Direct Unsubsidized Stafford, Direct PLUS, FFEL Subsidized Stafford, FFEL Unsubsidized Stafford, FFEL PLUS, Federal Perkins Applicants will be notified of awards on a rolling basis beginning 3/30. Federal Work-Study Program available. Institutional employment available. Off-campus job opportunities are fair.

The Inside Word

The profile of an incoming class at Kutztown pretty well matches the profile of the average college-bound high school student. Over one-third of incoming students graduated in the bottom half of their class, so it's fair to say that solid candidates should face little challenge gaining entry.

THE SCHOOL SAYS "..."

From The Admissions Office

"In a recent independent survey, 93 percent of students and recent alumni rated their education at Kutztown University as excellent or good in regard to their overall college experience, the quality of instruction they received, and the quality of the faculty. Kutztown offers excellent academic programs through its undergraduate Colleges of Liberal Arts and Sciences, Visual and Performing Arts, Business, and Education and through its graduate studies program. A wide range of student support services complements the high-quality classroom instruction.

"In addition, Kutztown students have the advantage of a well-rounded program of athletic, cultural, and social events. At Kutztown, there are clubs, organizations, and activities to satisfy nearly every taste. Currently, 8,524 full-time and part-time students are enrolled at the university. About half of the full-time undergraduates live in residence halls; the rest live at home or in apartments in nearby communities.

"Kutztown University's attractive 325-acre campus includes a mix of old and new buildings, including stately Old Main, the historic building known to generations of Kutztown's students; Golden Bear Village West, a modern townhouse complex; and the Student Union Building. A new state-of-the-art science facility is set to open in Fall 2003.

"The university's graduate program awards the Master of Science, Master of Art, Master of Education, Master of Business Administration, Master of Library Science, Master of Public Administration, and Master of Social Work degrees."

For even more information on this school, turn to page 485 of the "Stats" section.

LA ROCHE COLLEGE

9000 BABCOCK BOULEVARD, PITTSBURGH, PA 15237 • ADMISSIONS: 412-536-1272 • FAX: 412-536-1820
E-MAIL: ADMISSIONS@LAROCHE.EDU • WEBSITE: WWW.LAROCHE.EDU

RATINGS

Quality of Life: 72   **Academic:** 73   **Admissions:** 70   **Financial Aid:** 89

STUDENTS SAY "..."

Academics

"You really get a personalized education" at La Roche College, a "small" Roman Catholic school just north of downtown Pittsburgh with a "diverse student population" and "suburban atmosphere." La Roche is "well known" for a "fantastic" graphic design program and "the best program in the state for interior design," as well as "good science programs" and a "great dance program and nursing

program." In the words of one student, "The small class size is ideal and has really allowed me to succeed." Another reports, "It is easy to be able to talk to professors, deans," and even "the president of the college." Though "The administration needs to communicate better with the student body in order to run the school better," the "wonderful" professors "really take time to get to know their students" and "will bend over backwards to help." "I love that I can get one-on-one time with my teachers any time I need it and it's no problem," attests one interior-design major. "At most schools, I would just be lost in the crowd."

Life

While nearly all students agree that "the cafeteria food could be a little better," the residence halls are "extremely comfortable." Some students find campus life "sub-par" and say, "You will never have fun unless you go off campus." Other students disagree. "We have a lot of activities on campus so it is not very hard to find something to do," counters one student. "When there's nothing going on, we usually get a group together and have movie marathons or sometimes watch an entire season of *Will & Grace*." Also, good Samaritans find their needs fulfilled since "With the Catholic affiliation, there are many opportunities for community service." The party scene "isn't impressive," but there is "social drinking," though "hardly ever large parties." Students looking for more excitement often "go downtown to a club" or "to parties at Pitt" and other area universities, while others "bond and interact through sports, like soccer." Just "a 15-minute car ride" from campus, "the great city of Pittsburgh" has "awesome things to do."

Student Body

Students tend to be in the middle- to lower-middle socioeconomic range, and came to La Roche because they "wanted a semilocal college." They are "extremely dedicated," "focused," and "eager to learn," and there are "lots of international students" here. "La Roche has a mix of people," explains one student. "Some kids commute from home 5 minutes away; others are from Africa, the Middle East, and the Caribbean." "I am an American and I feel like I'm a minority," notes a junior. Students disagree about how well different groups get along. Many say that the foreign students "mesh with the natives." "My best friends are a Bulgarian, an Indian, an Ohioan, and a Canadian," announces an information technology major. According to others, though, students from other countries tend to "stick to themselves."

Admissions

Very important factors considered include: Academic GPA, rigor of secondary school record, standardized test scores. *Important factors considered include:* Application essay, recommendation(s), talent/ability. *Other factors considered include:* Class rank, alumni/ae relation, character/personal qualities, extracurricular activities, first generation, geographical residence, interview, level of applicant's interest, volunteer work, work experience. SAT or ACT required; High school diploma is required and GED is accepted. *Academic units required:* 4 English, 3 mathematics, 3 science, (2 science labs), 3 social studies, 3 history. *Academic units recommended:* 4 English, 3 mathematics, 3 science, (2 science labs), 2 foreign language, 3 social studies, 3 history.

Financial Aid

Students should submit: FAFSA. Regular filing deadline is 5/1. The Princeton Review suggests that all financial aid forms be submitted as soon as possible after January 1. *Need-based scholarships/grants offered:* Federal Pell, SEOG, state scholarships/grants, private scholarships, the school's own gift aid *Loan aid offered:* FFEL Subsidized Stafford, FFEL Unsubsidized Stafford, FFEL PLUS, Federal Perkins, Private loans. Applicants will be notified of awards on a rolling basis beginning 2/15. Federal Work-Study Program available. Institutional employment available. Off-campus job opportunities are excellent.

The Inside Word

Academically, a student admitted to La Roche is your average student. For incoming freshman, high school GPAs tend to hover around 3.0, and SAT and ACT scores land almost exactly in the middle. While this shouldn't cause much concern for students who meet these requirements, weaker candidates should keep in mind that La Roche takes all factors into consideration—so get those letters of recommendation and extracurricular activities together!

THE SCHOOL SAYS ". . ."

From The Admissions Office

"You have the power to change your world. Choose a college that will help you make the most of the opportunities that lie ahead. Discover how La Roche College's twenty-first-century approach to individualized education will take you exactly where you want to go.

"At La Roche, our faculty prides itself on getting to know you as an individual and understanding the educational goals you have set for yourself. We keep our classes small, allowing for personal attention. We also put the latest technology at your fingertips with our 'smart' classrooms. The SMARTBoard lets your professor play a DVD or browse the Internet by simply touching a screen. When you're ready to select a course of study, you can choose from more than 50 undergraduate degree programs that combine thoughtful, engaging classroom instruction with 'real-world' experiences.

"'Ad Lucem Per Amorem' is Latin for 'To Light Through Love,' and it is also La Roche College's motto. It is a reminder of the college's Catholic heritage. Founded in 1963, La Roche College originally served as an institution of higher learning for women preparing to enter religious life. Today, the college enrolls young men and women from nearly 25 states and more than 20 countries; students come with different ideas about the world, and they become members of a growing global community.

"The La Roche campus is located on 80 acres of rolling hills and is ranked as one of the safest 4-year private college campuses in the nation. Our apartment-style suites offer the comforts of home, including a refrigerator, a microwave, and a bathroom right in your room. The college supports more than 30 student organizations and 10 varsity sports in NCAA Division III. La Roche's proximity to Pittsburgh, Pennsylvania puts you at the doorstep of a world-class city, providing plenty of internship and career opportunities.

"When it comes to financing a quality La Roche education, we have a host of competitive merit-based scholarships and need-based awards. Contact our Admissions Office and find out for yourself how a La Roche education offers *learning that brings your world together.* Call us at 412-536-1272 (toll-free: 800-838-4LRC) or e-mail us at admissions@laroche.edu. You can also visit our website at www.laroche.edu."

For even more information on this school, turn to page 485 of the "Stats" section.

LABORATORY INSTITUTE OF MERCHANDISING

12 EAST FIFTY-THIRD STREET, NEW YORK, NY 10022 • ADMISSIONS: 212-752-1530 • FAX: 212-317-8602
E-MAIL: ADMISSIONS@LIMCOLLEGE.EDU • WEBSITE: WWW.LIMCOLLEGE.EDU

RATINGS

Quality of Life: 70   Academic: 73   Admissions: 72   Financial Aid: 60*

STUDENTS SAY ". . ."

Academics

LIM is "about the business of fashion," undergrads tell us, to the extent that "if you aren't sure you want to be in the fashion industry," you should most likely "go somewhere else." But if fashion is your passion, LIM "is the only college in the country that focuses on the business end of the fashion industry. "A small college," LIM sets you up for success after graduation. You have three internships, many volunteer and work opportunities, and [a] 90 percent job placement after graduation." Professors here are not only "helpful and enthusiastic" but they're also experienced in their field. "It is rare for me to have a professor [who] did not work in the fashion industry or another business industry," a senior reports. "I learn so much at LIM, I actually am very excited to go to my classes," a sanguine freshman adds. Students are less enthusiastic about visits to administrative offices, where, "let's just say, they're trying to work out the kinks." Students clamor for online registration, as currently "You have to register in person with an advisor . . . a huge pain."

> SURVEY SAYS . . .
> *Large classes*
> *Students love New York, NY*
> *Intercollegiate sports are unpopular or nonexistent*
> *Intramural sports are unpopular or nonexistent*
> *Frats and sororities are unpopular or nonexistent*
> *Theater is popular*

Life

"Life in NYC and at LIM is completely different than 'normal' college life," an undergrad here reports, adding that students here "are thrown into real life from the get-go." LIM's campus is a collection of four buildings in Manhattan's Midtown East, and its dorms are scattered around New York City (though all are within a half hour of campus by subway). While there is a sizable contingent of students who "just go to school and go home," most here enjoy an "exciting," if "expensive," life in the big city. One student tells us she's "living the young girl's dream. I'm living in Manhattan with roommates [who] all go to LIM. We have so much fun. New York City is my campus. There is so much to do. I love to go shopping, go to small coffee shops, see bands play, and be a part of NYC's landscape." In her affinity for shopping, she's not alone—at LIM "Everyone pretty much thinks about shopping." Most students here say they're content to "do whatever the day brings." After all, "It's New York City, there are endless possibilities."

Student Body

Perhaps it's no surprise that LIM students describe their peers as "very into looks," "fashion forward," and "career oriented." "For the most part people are from the Tristate Area," with students from New Jersey and Long Island being the most visible. Undergrads report that the typical LIM student is an "affluent" "commuting girl; not very many boys go to LIM." Some here say their peers are "cliquish" and "basically concerned with their own agenda." "If you haven't talked to them starting on the first day then you don't matter," a junior reports, though it may depend on the approach you take. Students here "build . . . their resume by networking themselves," and, to that end, are "willing to work with different types of people in the business world as well as in school."

THE PRINCETON REVIEW SAYS

Admissions

Very important factors considered include: Academic GPA, interview, level of applicant's interest. *Important factors considered include:* Class rank, application essay, recommendation(s), rigor of secondary school record, standardized test scores, extracurricular activities, work experience. *Other factors considered include:* Alumni/ae relation, character/personal qualities, talent/ability, volunteer work, SAT or ACT required; TOEFL required of all international applicants. High school diploma is required and GED is accepted.

Financial Aid

Students should submit: FAFSA, institution's own financial aid form. The Princeton Review suggests that all financial aid forms be submitted as soon as possible after January 1. *Need-based scholarships/grants offered:* Federal Pell, SEOG, state scholarships/grants, private scholarships, the school's own gift aid *Loan aid offered:* Direct Subsidized Stafford, Direct Unsubsidized Stafford, Direct PLUS Applicants will be notified of awards on a rolling basis beginning 2/15. Federal Work-Study Program available. Institutional employment available. Off-campus job opportunities are excellent.

The Inside Word

When assessing applications, LIM looks for a B average in high school course work as well as a combined score of 950–1000 on the Critical Reading and Math sections of the SAT or a 20 on the ACT. It does, however, accept some applicants who don't quite reach those marks. Students in this camp should consider the school's new early action plan; you'll need to get your application materials in by November 15, but you'll get a decision by December 15. More importantly, early action will allow you to demonstrate significant interest in LIM, which is a very important factor in the school's admit decisions.

THE SCHOOL SAYS ". . ."

From The Admissions Office

"LIM College, the College for the Business of Fashion, has been educating leaders in the fashion industry for nearly 70 years. Located in the heart of Manhattan, just steps from Fifth Avenue, LIM takes full advantage of its New York City campus and believes that the most powerful way to learn is to harvest experience from industry professionals. From day one, LIM incorporates real-world experience into a unique hands-on curriculum.

"With four specialized majors in fashion merchandising, marketing, management, and visual merchandising, a 9:1 student/faculty ratio, and an average class size of 19, LIM understands the value of personal attention. LIM is dedicated to preparing its students for the fashion industry and with over 90 percent career placement upon graduation, LIM graduates move forward and upward into exciting careers.

"LIM's highly regarded faculty, a diverse group of industry professionals and educators, bring the business of fashion into LIM's classrooms. An advisory board comprising top-level business executives also counsels the college on the latest fashion business developments in retail, maufacturing, product development, public relations, marketing, publishing, and visual merchandising.

"Early on, LIM students are exposed to the fashion industry through field trips, an active guest lecture series, and two 5-week full-time internships. In their senior year, students complete a co-op, an entire semester of full-time work in the industry along with a capstone project that incorporates aspects of all 4 years of their education."

For even more information on this school, turn to page 486 of the "Stats" section.

LAFAYETTE COLLEGE

118 MARKLE HALL, EASTON, PA 18042 • ADMISSIONS: 610-330-5100 • FAX: 610-330-5355
FINANCIAL AID: 610-330-5055 • E-MAIL: ADMISSIONS@LAFAYETTE.EDU • WEBSITE: WWW.LAFAYETTE.EDU

RATINGS
Quality of Life: 81   **Academic:** 89   **Admissions:** 96   **Financial Aid:** 96

STUDENTS SAY ". . ."

Academics

Lafayette College is "a small liberal arts college" that is "especially strong in engineering and physical sciences." There are "very cool" undergraduate research opportunities. Career services "is also phenomenal" and "an excellent alumni network" provides abundant career and internship opportunities. The "efficient, helpful, and very accessible" administration "generally listens to the comments of the students" and does "a great job of keeping the school running smoothly." The biggest academic complaint at Lafayette is that the range of courses offered in a typical semester is too narrow. The classes that are offered tend to be "small" and "difficult." "You must study," reports an economics major. "Not every professor is the greatest." "There is the occasional professor who makes you want to tear your hair out." On the whole, though, Lafayette's professors are "really knowledgeable and really do care about how you do and what you take out of the class." "I feel like I get a lot of individual attention," says a chemical engineering major. "Professors will explain difficult material until you understand," relates a math major, "not just say it once and look at you like you're stupid if you still don't understand." Outside of class, faculty members typically remain "extremely available" and "beg you to talk to them and meet with them."

> **SURVEY SAYS . . .**
> *Lab facilities are great*
> *Great computer facilities*
> *Great library*
> *Athletic facilities are great*
> *Career services are great*
> *Campus feels safe*

Life

Lafayette is located on a hill above "terrible and disgusting" Easton, Pennsylvania. The "gorgeous," "scenic" campus is full of "picturesque northeastern college-like buildings." A few dorms "are in desperate need of renovation," though, and the "repetitive" food is "not that great tasting." Socially, Lafayette is reportedly "very homey." "At almost any social gathering, there will be people you know." The "amazing" sports center is "a very popular spot." "Lafayette is a very athletic school and most students participate in either varsity athletics or in a club or intramural sport," explains a sophomore. In the fall, "football games are extremely spirited." The annual contest against hated Lehigh "is attended by basically the whole student body." Beyond sports, many students tell us that "there is always something to do on campus." "Everyone is really involved," they say. There are "a capella concerts, comedians, movies, and club-sponsored activities." A "multitude of speakers" visits campus. There's "a broad range" of religious groups. Lafayette also has a "huge" Greek system. Other students contend that "there should be more to do." "I have not experienced the outpouring of entertainment at the school," grumbles a freshman. Whatever the case, "the party scene is really fun." The frats and various sports teams throw parties "Wednesday through Saturday nights" and many students participate. However, many others don't. "Half the campus considers Lafayette a party school and the other half doesn't know what school the first half is talking about," suggests a junior.

Student Body

Lafayette is a haven for "well-rounded," "preppy," "smart jocks," and "your classic white rich kid" "from New York, New Jersey, or Pennsylvania." "There is certainly a mold," admits a senior. "Everyone is pretty similar." "Collar-popping" suburbanites are everywhere. "Crazy colored hair and facial piercings are not really something you see," observes a first-year student. "You will see a lot of smiling and door-holding," though. Students take pride in the "incredibly friendly" vibe at Lafayette. Many students are "hard-partying" types. There are also "the kids who live in the library 20 hours a day." Most students fall somewhere in the middle. "People like to have a good time but they are also serious about their work and are genuinely interested in their area of study." "Both conservatives and liberals" will find soul mates at Lafayette but many students are "almost completely apathetic" when it comes to politics. Some students "have a snobby attitude," but others either don't flaunt their wealth or don't come from money at all. "We're not all running around with iPhones and Fendi bags," says a sophomore. Ethnic diversity is pretty minimal. "There are a few minority and foreign students but they hang out with each other in their own little cliques."

THE PRINCETON REVIEW SAYS

Admissions

Very important factors considered include: Rigor of secondary school record. *Important factors considered include:* Class rank, application essay, recommendation(s), standardized test scores, alumni/ae relation, character/personal qualities, extracurricular activities, racial/ethnic status, talent/ability, volunteer work. *Other factors considered include:* Geographical residence, interview, work experience. SAT or ACT required; ACT with Writing component required. TOEFL required of all international applicants. High school diploma or equivalent is not required. *Academic units recommended:* 4 English, 3 mathematics, 2 science, (2 science labs), 2 foreign language, 5 academic electives.

Financial Aid

Students should submit: FAFSA, CSS/Financial Aid PROFILE, noncustodial PROFILE, business/farm supplement. Regular filing deadline is 2/1. The Princeton Review suggests that all financial aid forms be submitted as soon as possible after January 1. *Need-based scholarships/grants offered:* Federal Pell, SEOG, state scholarships/grants, private scholarships *Loan aid offered:* FFEL Subsidized Stafford, FFEL Unsubsidized Stafford, FFEL PLUS, Federal Perkins, state loans, college/university loans from institutional funds. HELP loans to parents. Applicants will be notified of awards on or about 4/1. Federal Work-Study Program available. Institutional employment available. Off-campus job opportunities are good.

The Inside Word

Applications are reviewed three to five times and evaluated by as many as nine different committee members. In all cases, students who continually seek challenges and are willing to take risks academically win out over those who play it safe to maintain a high GPA.

THE SCHOOL SAYS ". . ."

From The Admissions Office

"We choose students individually, one by one, and we hope that the ones we choose will approach their education the same way, as a highly individual enterprise. Our first-year seminars have enrollments limited to 15 or 16 students each in order to introduce the concept of learning not as passive receipt of information but as an active, participatory process. Our low average class size and 11:1 student/teacher ratio reflect that same philosophy. We also devote substantial resources to our Marquis Scholars Program, to one-on-one faculty-student mentoring relationships, and to other programs in engineering within a liberal arts context, giving Lafayette its distinctive character, articulated in our second-year seminars exploring values in science and technology. Lafayette provides an environment in which its students can discover their own personal capacity for learning, personal growth, and leadership.

"Submission of scores from either the SAT Reasoning Test or American College Testing Program (ACT) is required. If taking the ACT, the optional Writing Section is required. SAT Subject Test results are recommended, but not required. Scores must be submitted directly from the testing agency or via your college counselor on an 'official' high school transcript or testing summary sheet."

For even more information on this school, turn to page 486 of the "Stats" section.

LANCASTER BIBLE COLLEGE

PO Box 83403, 901 Eden Road, Lancaster, PA 17608 • Admissions: 717-560-8271 • Fax: 717-560-8213
E-mail: admissions@lbc.edu • Website: www.lbc.edu

RATINGS
Quality of Life: 87   Academic: 79   Admissions: 77   Financial Aid: 72

STUDENTS SAY ". . ."

Academics

"Lancaster Bible College is all about preparing young men and women to build God-honoring relationship[s] and to serve God and others through professional ministries, church ministries, and everyday life encounters," students here tell us. As its name might suggest, LBC offers a "teaching program with a strong biblical emphasis." Aside from its specialized focus, what sets LBC apart from most schools is the student body's almost unanimous appreciation of the faculty and administration. Professors are "very

educated in their topics and experienced in fields relating to those topics"; they also "really care about the students and are willing to go the extra mile for them." Administrators do "a fabulous job of communicating their vision to the students. They often spend time with students by eating in the cafeteria, attending chapel, or just being readily available." As one satisfied junior writes: "All of the staff and faculty at my school are usually available to help and talk to students outside the classroom. I have a few professors I talk to about personal issues, and I know that they pray for me."

Life

Students at LBC "study toward the goal of knowing God more," and their "lives reflect this devotion to God." "Everyone is involved in some kind of service, whether that is helping a YMCA or interning at a church." Add "classes," "chapel," and, for many, "on-campus jobs," and one might envision a relatively Spartan existence for LBC undergrads. This, however, is not the case: "Most students are very anxious to have fun and enjoy their college years," a sophomore tells us. Fun entails "a lot of active things," such as "tak[ing] walks," "ice skating at Clipper Stadium," "working out in the gym," and "playing intramural sports such as dodgeball and Ultimate Frisbee," or "three-on-three basketball." Students say that "going to sports games to support our teams [is] very popular here, too." When they tire themselves out, undergrads enjoy "just hanging out playing pool and watching movies," and love exploring hometown Lancaster, which "has a wide variety of restaurants and other things to do." Music fans appreciate that "a lot of time on the weekends there will be a concert going on in the chapel"—often by a well-known Christian musician—"and as students we get in free or [at a] discount."

Student Body

"Because students at LBC are all Bible majors along with their specific majors, most have a desire to be in some [type] of church ministry, whether it be full-time or part-time, after their graduation." Undergrads here tend to "come from a conservative background"; are already "familiar with Christianity and the Bible"; and fall somewhere between "moderate" and "zealous in faith and Christian living." They're also typically "Caucasian," though "There are a few African Americans and Asians" on campus. An undergrad describes the situation this way: "There isn't a variety of diversity on our campus, but those of a different background are definitely loved and cared for." Another student adds: "We all share the common bond of Christ and are, therefore, like one big family." While students "who don't seem to care much about Christ" are still "embraced," they are "somewhat separated, possibly because of their own goals."

THE PRINCETON REVIEW SAYS
Admissions
Very important factors considered include: Application essay, recommendation(s), rigor of secondary school record, standardized test scores, character/personal qualities, religious affiliation/commitment. *Important factors considered include:* Extracurricular activities. *Other factors considered include:* Class rank, interview, talent/ability, volunteer work, SAT or ACT required; TOEFL required of all international applicants. High school diploma is required and GED is accepted.

Financial Aid
Students should submit: FAFSA, state aid form. The Princeton Review suggests that all financial aid forms be submitted as soon as possible after January 1. *Need-based scholarships/grants offered:* Federal Pell, SEOG, state scholarships/grants, private scholarships, the school's own gift aid, Office of Vocational Rehabilitation Blindness and Visual Services Awards. *Loan aid offered:* FFEL Subsidized Stafford, FFEL Unsubsidized Stafford, FFEL PLUS, Federal Perkins, Alternative Loans. Applicants will be notified of awards on a rolling basis beginning 3/15. Federal Work-Study Program available. Institutional employment available. Off-campus job opportunities are good.

The Inside Word
LBC works extra hard to make sure that the students it admits are a good fit with its specialized academic and social environment. Applicants are required to write a 500-word autobiography that should touch upon their conversion, church experiences, and reasons for wanting to attend LBC. Of the three required references, one must come from a pastor and another must come from a Christian friend.

THE SCHOOL SAYS ". . ."
From The Admissions Office
At Lancaster Bible College, you'll discover:

- We believe in training ministry leaders. We believe in educating service-minded scholars like you to serve as ministry leaders in professional positions throughout the globe. Our alumni serve as pastors, worship leaders, counselors, business leaders, college presidents, teachers, missionaries, coaches, and school administrators—here and abroad—and we are just warming up.

- We believe in helping students to fulfill their dreams. We believe in making it a reality for young scholars like you to serve at their best through a premier Bible college education, and we back it up with financial aid. Every year we raise more than $1.5 million to help fund our students' educations.

- We believe in community. From your first visit to LBC through graduation day, you will be amazed at how many faculty homes you're invited into, how many one-on-one conversations you'll have, and just how tight this community of care really is. You'll see and feel why campus friendliness finishes at the top of our student surveys.

You see, at LBC, we believe that students who want to serve the Lord are the world's greatest hope. If you're that kind of student, we want you to be a part of this place we call home---because we believe in you!

For even more information on this school, turn to page 487 of the "Stats" section.

LEBANON VALLEY COLLEGE

101 NORTH COLLEGE AVENUE, ANNVILLE, PA 17003-6100 • ADMISSIONS: 717-867-6181
FAX: 717-867-6026 • E-MAIL: ADMISSION@LVC.EDU • WEBSITE: WWW.LVC.EDU

RATINGS
Quality of Life: 79   **Academic:** 81   **Admissions:** 81   **Financial Aid:** 83

STUDENTS SAY "..."

Academics

Undergrads at Lebanon Valley College attribute a great academic experience to "professors that...really get to know you and are very willing to offer advice and guidance." As one freshman expounds, "Professors are not only interested in expanding your knowledge of your particular topic but also of expanding you as a person." LVC students are held to high standards "especially in the science fields,"

> **SURVEY SAYS . . .**
> *Large classes*
> *Great library*
> *Athletic facilities are great*
> *Low cost of living*
> *Musical organizations are popular*

and many agree that this leads to a "challenging but rewarding" education. Students laud the music department stating it "places a great emphasis on personal development as a musician." The vast majority also heap praise on the administration noting they are "very good at listening to the students and helping them to succeed." A number of undergrads are also quick to highlight the fact that even the president "has an open-door policy" and can be seen "frequently walking around campus or eating in the dining hall."

Life

By and large, students agree that "life at Lebanon Valley is pretty laid back." Though it is "set in the country," LVC is "near enough to larger towns and cities so as not to feel isolated." Fortunately, the campus is generally buzzing with activity, be it the "comedians who come on Friday nights" or the regular "Saturday night dances." Additionally, since "music is big" at LVC, "many students participate in the bands/orchestras/choirs and also form their own bands or perform in theater." While undergrads admit there are definitely students "who like to party," one grateful freshman stresses "there is no pressure to drink." Students tend to venture off-campus quite a bit, often heading "to the local cafés or to the diner outside of town to hang out with friends and get a bite to eat." There is also a "small movie theater in town that offers discounts to students." The college itself sponsors a myriad of weekend trips with destinations such as "New York, Washington, and King of Prussia." Finally, for those undergrads who want to indulge their sweet tooth, "Hershey Park is only eight miles away."

Student Body

On the surface, you might easily categorize LVC undergrads. "You have your student athletes, your student band members, and student actors," but many stress that "there is a group for everyone on campus." Indeed, "there are very few loners." Students readily assert that their peers are "very friendly" and always "willing to lend a hand." While the college may not appear "ethnically diverse at a glance," a freshman assures us that "diversity and acceptance are stressed by various on-campus awareness groups." And while "students are fairly similar to each other in many ways, nearly everyone embraces the differences among us, and those who are different have no problem finding others who feel or think similarly to them."

Admissions

Very important factors considered include: Class rank, rigor of secondary school record. *Important factors considered include:* Academic GPA, character/personal qualities, extracurricular activities, interview, level of applicant's interest, talent/ability. *Other factors considered include:* Application essay, recommendation(s), standardized test scores, alumni/ae relation, first generation, geographical residence, racial/ethnic status, state residency, volunteer work, work experience. TOEFL required of all international applicants. High school diploma is required and GED is accepted. *Academic units required:* 4 English, 3 mathematics, 2 science, 2 foreign language, 1 social studies. *Academic units recommended:* 3 science, (2 science labs), 3 foreign language, 2 history.

Financial Aid

Students should submit: FAFSA, institution's own financial aid form. The Princeton Review suggests that all financial aid forms be submitted as soon as possible after January 1. *Need-based scholarships/grants offered:* Federal Pell, SEOG, state scholarships/grants, private scholarships, the school's own gift aid. *Loan aid offered:* FFEL Subsidized Stafford, FFEL Unsubsidized Stafford, FFEL PLUS, Federal Perkins Applicants will be notified of awards on a rolling basis beginning 3/1. Federal Work-Study Program available. Institutional employment available. Off-campus job opportunities are good.

The Inside Word

Lebanon Valley looks primarily at high school grades and curriculum. If you're a B student in the top half of your class, the school's website reports, you have a very good chance of gaining admittance. Students in the top 30 percent of their graduating class are eligible for generous scholarships.

THE SCHOOL SAYS ". . ."
From The Admissions Office

"Lebanon Valley College encourages applications from students who have taken a challenging college-prep program in high school and performed well. Typical successful applicants have had 3 years of science, 3 of math, and 2 of a foreign language, in addition to English and social studies. While high school grading systems vary widely, we look for applicants to have at least a B average and rank in the top half of their class. Our outstanding, nationally recognized scholarship program complements this process. The college offers scholarships worth up to 50 percent of the value of tuition to students accepted for admission who ranked in the top 30 percent of their high school class. The scholarships are based on the class rank decile, with awards of one-quarter tuition going to those in the third decile, one-third to those in the second decile, and one-half to those in the top 10 percent of their class. Standardized test scores give students from high schools that do not provide a class rank access to the scholarships; during the interview process, the college provides an opportunity for students with a minimum combined SAT critical reading and math score of 1100 to apply for these scholarships. Admission decisions for each class are made on a rolling basis beginning in mid-October. Students offered admission are also informed of their scholarship award based on class rank information received on the high school transcript. Students whose class rank improves during their senior year will be considered for an increased award."

For even more information on this school, turn to page 487 of the "Stats" section.

LEHIGH UNIVERSITY

27 MEMORIAL DRIVE WEST, BETHLEHEM, PA 18015 • ADMISSIONS: 610-758-3100 • FAX: 610-758-4361
FINANCIAL AID: 610-758-3181 • E-MAIL: ADMISSIONS@LEHIGH.EDU • WEBSITE: WWW.LEHIGH.EDU

RATINGS
Quality of Life: 71   Academic: 87   Admissions: 97   Financial Aid: 87

STUDENTS SAY ". . ."

Academics

The main thing that students at Lehigh University in Bethelehem, Pennsylvania seem to share is a general love for the school and its entire way of life, as evidenced by the "amazing" alumni base that returns to the school frequently (and provides for good networking). Despite rigorous academics, Lehigh "maintains a substantial social scene," and "work hard, play hard is not just a saying here—it's the lifestyle." Students have "to work for grades, they are not

> **SURVEY SAYS . . .**
> Great library
> Students are happy
> Frats and sororities dominate
> social scene
> Lots of beer drinking
> Hard liquor is popular

just given out," and outside of the classroom, there's a strong emphasis on experiential learning and real-world applications. The engineering and business programs are particularly strong here, and though tuition is dear, new financial aid policies have been put into place and "the school lives up to its academic reputation...you definitely get your money's worth at the end of the day." The level of instruction here is "top-notch," and "the classes aren't necessarily a drag to go to because the teachers easily manifest how much they want us to learn." "Teaching becomes better" as students begin to take more and more upper level classes; instructors "are always available and want to help you out," and they "really try to have a positive relationship with all of the students," though a few professors seem to be more interested in their research than their teachings. "For my Folktales and Fairytales class, we were invited to the professor's house to tell stories around her fireplace," says a senior. The administration "does not take into account student opinion as well as it could," and many students wish it was more transparent in its reasoning for changes (especially concerning the recent crackdown on partying, the surest way to get a Lehigh student up in arms), but most students are satisfied with the level of accessibility.

Life

Unless you have a car, there really isn't much to in the immediate surrounding area, though the school does provide a shuttle to some common off-campus destinations and the town is home to many festivals throughout the year. On campus, studying takes up most weeknights, and though there are events "here and there," "drinking is king at Lehigh" and "Greek life is everything." "It's party hard, work hard. We have all the Ivy League rejects who are crazy competitive combined with crazy parties. What's better?" asks a sophomore. Though the jury is out as to how crucial drinking is to Lehigh social life, "the school provides a lot of alcohol free activities such as game night, comedians, movie nights, etc.," and there is "plenty of socializing" through sports, student organizations, and plain old hanging out. "Even kids who are obsessed with video games won't just sit and play alone in their rooms. They'll find others with the same interest and do so together," says a student. "There are tons of ways to get involved on campus and have a good time, you just have to get creative," says another.

Student Body

It's a "white and preppy" world at Lehigh, where most students come from the northeast and the typical student's economic background can be described as "appreciates the finer things in life." People here "like to look good" and "tend to dress up for classes very often," and the popped collar has a home at Lehigh. There are still "a few splashes of ethnicity" here, and while there used to be a lot of pressure to fit that specific mold, now "there are a lot of different types of students. It's a friendlier campus." The school has actually seen a rise in enrollment by students from underrepresented backgrounds in recent years, and continues to try and build diversity. Socially, there are three types of students at Lehigh: "those who are Greek, those whose friends are Greek, and those who have no friends." The final group is in the extreme minority, as "it isn't hard to find a friend at Lehigh," and even the atypical students "usually just connect with each other." Ever the balanced bunch, Lehigh students "recognize scholastic the opportunity that Lehigh provides but also thrive on the party scene."

THE PRINCETON REVIEW SAYS

Admissions

Very important factors considered include: Recommendation(s), rigor of secondary school record. *Important factors considered include:* Application essay, standardized test scores, character/personal qualities, extracurricular activities, talent/ability, volunteer work. *Other factors considered include:* Class rank, academic GPA, alumni/ae relation, first generation, geographical residence, level of applicant's interest, racial/ethnic status, work experience. SAT or ACT required; ACT with Writing component required. TOEFL required of all international applicants. High school diploma or equivalent is not required. *Academic units required:* 4 English, 3 mathematics, 2 science, (2 science labs), 2 foreign language, 2 social studies, 3 academic electives.

Financial Aid

Students should submit: FAFSA, CSS/Financial Aid PROFILE, noncustodial PROFILE, business/farm supplement. Regular filing deadline is 2/15. The Princeton Review suggests that all financial aid forms be submitted as soon as possible after January 1. *Need-based scholarships/grants offered:* Federal Pell, SEOG, state scholarships/grants, private scholarships, the school's own gift aid, United Negro College Fund. *Loan aid offered:* FFEL Subsidized Stafford, FFEL Unsubsidized Stafford, FFEL PLUS, Federal Perkins, college/university loans from institutional funds, Private Educational Alternative Loans. Applicants will be notified of awards on or about 3/30. Federal Work-Study Program available. Institutional employment available. Off-campus job opportunities are good.

The Inside Word

Lots of work at bolstering Lehigh's public recognition for overall academic quality has paid off—liberal arts candidates will now find the admissions process to be highly selective. Students without solidly impressive academic credentials will have a rough time getting in regardless of their choice of programs, as will unenthusiastic, but academically strong candidates who have clearly chosen Lehigh as a safety.

THE SCHOOL SAYS ". . ."

From The Admissions Office

"Lehigh University is located 50 miles north of Philadelphia and 75 miles southwest of New York City in Bethlehem, Pennsylvania, where a cultural renaissance has taken place with the opening of more than a dozen ethnic restaurants, the addition of several boutiques and galleries, and Lehigh's Campus Square residential/retail complex. Lehigh combines learning opportunities of a large research university with the personal attention of a small, private college, by offering an education that integrates courses from four colleges and dozens of fields of study. Students customize their experience to their interests by tailoring majors and academic programs from more than 2,000 courses, changing majors, carrying a double major, or taking courses outside their college or major field of study. Lehigh offers unique learning opportunities through interdisciplinary programs such as music and engineering and computer science and business (www.lehigh.edu/distinctive programs). The arts are essential to the learning experience and are integrated throughout the curriculum. Students develop their imagination and creativity while acquiring skills that will complement their professional development. Students have access to world-class faculty who offer their time and personal attention to help students learn and succeed. Students gain hands-on, real-world experience and take part in activities that build confidence and help them develop as leaders. Lehigh's vibrant campus life offers many social and extracurricular activities. Choose from 150 and 40 intramural and club sports, in which over 60 percent of undergraduates participate.

"Lehigh requires students to submit scores from the new SAT with the Writing component. Students may also take the ACT with the Writing portion in lieu of the SAT. SAT Subject Tests are recommended but not required."

For even more information on this school, turn to page 488 of the "Stats" section.

LESLEY COLLEGE AT LESLEY UNIVERSITY

LESLEY COLLEGE, 29 EVERETT STREET, CAMBRIDGE, MA 02138 • ADMISSIONS: 617-349-8800
FAX: 617-349-8810 • E-MAIL: LCADMISSIONS@LESLEY.EDU • WEBSITE: WWW.LESLEY.EDU

RATINGS
Quality of Life: 73   **Academic:** 80   **Admissions:** 81   **Financial Aid:** 70

STUDENTS SAY ". . ."

Academics

Lesley College "is going through a ton of change," with a
switch to coeducation ("We've only been co-ed for three
years") and the addition of the Art Institute of Boston. As a
result, the school is "growing in size and expanding a ton,"
yet professors and administrators have managed to maintain "a really personal experience" in the face of expansion.
Required internships mean that the Lesley experience "is all

> **SURVEY SAYS . . .**
> *Large classes*
> *Students love Cambridge, MA*
> *Great off-campus food*
> *Frats and sororities are unpopular or nonexistent*
> *(Almost) everyone smokes*

about hands-on learning and trying out the professional field that you want to work in." Students call this experience "the greatest strength of Lesley." The emphasis on experiential learning suits Lesley's academic strengths
in art therapy, education, psychology, and sociology. The curriculum is "very socially conscious, very human-
services focused," serving well the "artists, activists, athletes, hippies, and oddballs who come to the People's
Republic of Cambridge in a surprising (not perfect) show of unity to engage in left-wing coursework and
extracurricular activities." Undergrads warn us that "The Lesley style is not for everyone. We do papers, and we
have discussions. We write reflectively. This can get old for some seniors and is not a learning style that everyone can appreciate. However, for those of us that chose Lesley for that reason it is a spectacular way to learn, and
it is also very fitting for our people-focused majors."

Life

Lesley is "a really fun school, but not a party school." The school provides "lots of activities on campus to entertain students (comedians, movie nights, dances, and such). Lesley genuinely cares about keeping students entertained." The school's location "in an extremely convenient part of Cambridge…. It is safe and close to both
Harvard Square and Porter Square," which means "Your options are endless, thanks to public transportation!"
Boston offers "clubs and an amazing music scene" as well as political rallies and, of course, "Red Sox and Celtics
and Bruins games." An active intercollegiate athletic program occupies one segment of the student body, while
others immerse themselves in the arts; writes one student in the latter group, "The theatre program is increasing
quite a bit, so we have much more performance arts programs, considering the size of our school." Undergrads
also participate in "a fair amount of political and environmental discussion and concern."

Student Body

"Atypical is typical" at Lesley, where students constitute "a really, really diverse group. Half of Lesley
University is comprised of the Art Institute of Boston. All of the undergrads live together, and everyone seems
to get along really well whether they go to AIB or LC. There are students from different socioeconomic groups,
different sexual orientations; it's a real mix." The school's active athletic program means there are lots of jocks
here, and "The athletes are pretty close because we spend so much time together, but we're definitely not divided from the rest of the student body like at some schools. I feel like we do a really good job mixing it up overall. Pretty much everyone here has a major that involves helping people or changing the world in some way, I
think that brings us together a lot."

THE PRINCETON REVIEW SAYS

Admissions

Very important factors considered include: Academic GPA, rigor of secondary school record. *Important factors considered include:* Class rank, application essay, recommendation(s), standardized test scores, character/personal qualities, extracurricular activities, interview, talent/ability, volunteer work. *Other factors considered include:* Alumni/ae relation, first generation, geographical residence, level of applicant's interest, racial/ethnic status, work experience. SAT or ACT required; ACT with Writing component required. TOEFL required of all international applicants. High school diploma is required and GED is accepted. *Academic units required:* 4 English, 3 mathematics, 3 science, (2 science labs), 1 social studies, 1 history, 4 academic electives. *Academic units recommended:* 4 English, 4 mathematics, 4 science, (2 science labs), 2 foreign language, 2 social studies, 2 history, 2 visual/performing arts from some expressive therapies programs.

Financial Aid

Students should submit: FAFSA, institution's own financial aid form. The Princeton Review suggests that all financial aid forms be submitted as soon as possible after January 1. *Need-based scholarships/grants offered:* Federal Pell, SEOG, state scholarships/grants, private scholarships, the school's own gift aid. *Loan aid offered:* FFEL Subsidized Stafford, FFEL Unsubsidized Stafford, FFEL PLUS, Federal Perkins, state loans Applicants will be notified of awards on a rolling basis beginning 2/15. Federal Work-Study Program available. Institutional employment available. Off-campus job opportunities are excellent.

The Inside Word

Lesley College seeks students who "desire to impact the world around them." Commitment to social justice is at least as important as academic credentials here. You can't just talk a good game; your extracurricular activities should show that you've acted on your principles. Demonstrated success in a college prep high-school curriculum is also important.

THE SCHOOL SAYS "..."

From The Admissions Office

"Lesley College prepares men and women for careers and lives that make a difference, providing students with the skills and knowledge to make a positive difference and create hope. Central to this mission is a commitment to broad liberal arts preparation, career-focused field placements and internships, and true integration of theory and practice.

"Lesley College combines the advantages of an intimate learning community with all of the academic and co-curricular resources of a large university. That includes access to the professionals and programs of the Art Institute of Boston at Lesley, and a wide-ranging array of graduate programs and academic centers. The Lesley campus is steps away from bustling Harvard Square, in the heart of America's premier college town. The exciting cultural and educational resources of the Boston area are not just an added social benefit to college life; involvement in the community is an important aspect of the Lesley undergraduate experience.

"Lesley graduates are creative problem solvers, highly qualified professionals, confident lifelong learners, and engaged citizens, active in their workplaces and communities. They believe individuals, working collaboratively, can make a difference. Whether they choose to enter professional fields or pursue graduate studies, their undergraduate experiences at Lesley prepare them for leadership and success. In classrooms, human service settings, government, nonprofit organizations and corporations, the environment, and the arts, Lesley graduates are working daily to improve the lives of others and the world around them."

For even more information on this school, turn to page 488 of the "Stats" section.

LOYOLA COLLEGE IN MARYLAND

4501 NORTH CHARLES STREET, BALTIMORE, MD 21210 • ADMISSIONS: 410-617-5012 • FAX: 410-617-2176
FINANCIAL AID: 410-617-2576 • WEBSITE: WWW.LOYOLA.EDU

RATINGS
Quality of Life: 91   **Academic:** 84   **Admissions:** 89   **Financial Aid:** 96

STUDENTS SAY "..."

Academics

A Jesuit school in suburban Baltimore, Loyola College in Maryland "seeks to develop the whole person—intellectually, emotionally, socially, and spiritually." Jesuit values are stressed through the school's "well-rounded curriculum, encouraging participation in community service, and teaching values in diversity both on and off campus." Across the

> **SURVEY SAYS . . .**
> *Athletic facilities are great*
> *Dorms are like palaces*
> *Frats and sororities are unpopular*
> *or nonexistent*

board, students say the Loyola faculty is comprised of accomplished scholars and talented teachers. A senior shares, "Professors are the best part about Loyola College. They love their subjects and their students, and make class interesting with their enthusiasm." When it comes to academic or personal matters, "the professors at Loyola are so caring it almost seems unnatural. They will go out of their way to make sure you understand material and always have their door open after class discussions." What's more, the academic experience is characterized by small class sizes and ample discussion. A sophomore offers, "I could not be happier with my academic experience at Loyola. Even the biggest classes are small enough to facilitate close interaction with the professors." Outside the classroom, academic opportunities abound, and "professors encourage us to become part of the department through research or work-study programs." Likewise, the "administration cares deeply about fostering growth outside of the classroom." A senior attests, "As a three-year member of the student government association at Loyola College I have always been impressed with the openness of the administration and their willingness to work for the best interests of the students."

Life

Despite the demands of coursework, you'll get the full college experience at Loyola College in Maryland. Outgoing and social, most Loyola undergraduates are "motivated to achieve a balance between academic success and the social benefits of college." In the admiring words of one junior, "The typical student at Loyola is genius at time management. They find a way to get to the gym at least three times a week, go out at least three times week, and pull off above a 3.0 GPA every semester." However, Loyola students never lose track of their educational priorities, telling us, "The social life is very important here, but in all honesty, academics come first." In addition to hitting the off-campus bars, there are many attractions in the surrounding city of Baltimore. A sophomore reports, "For fun, my friends and I go out to eat in Baltimore, head to Towson mall, and go to the movies or concerts. Baltimore has a lot to offer to the college student." There are also plenty of extracurricular activities, clubs, and organizations at school, and "Loyola goes to great lengths to develop a sense of community across the campus." On that note, day-to-day life is easygoing and pleasant on Loyola's pretty campus. Happily, campus housing is top-notch, and "many students live in suites or apartments, and can thus cook their own food in their own kitchens."

Student Body

Loyola tends to admit outgoing and well-rounded students who want to benefit from all the academic, extracurricular, and social aspects of college life. On the whole, students "care deeply about their education and realize that they are here to learn. But they also enjoy themselves and are not too uptight." Considering the fact that Loyola is a private, Jesuit college on the East Coast, it's not surprising that "the average student comes from the greater Philadelphia, New Jersey, and New York area (although that seems to be changing) and ranges in economic background from middle to upper class." You'll find a shared affinity for Ugg boots and The North Face apparel on the Loyola campus and "the majority of students are preppy." Even so, you can't judge a book by its cover. A sophomore tells us, "Everyone seems like they may be a typical 'Loyola Girl' but when you look deeper, you find that these people are unique and diverse." No matter what your background or interests, "there are enough clubs and a wonderful student life on-campus that atypical students find their place and become as much a part of Loyola as typical students."

Admissions

Very important factors considered include: Academic GPA, rigor of secondary school record. *Important factors considered include:* Standardized test scores. *Other factors considered include:* Class rank, application essay, recommendation(s), alumni/ae relation, character/personal qualities, extracurricular activities, racial/ethnic status, talent/ability, volunteer work, work experience. SAT or ACT required; TOEFL required of all international applicants. High school diploma is required and GED is accepted. *Academic units required:* 4 English, 3 mathematics, 3 science, 2 history. *Academic units recommended:* 4 English, 4 mathematics, 4 science, 3 history.

Financial Aid

Students should submit: FAFSA, CSS/Financial Aid PROFILE, noncustodial PROFILE, business/farm supplement. Regular filing deadline is 2/15. The Princeton Review suggests that all financial aid forms be submitted as soon as possible after January 1. *Need-based scholarships/grants offered:* Federal Pell, SEOG, state scholarships/grants, private scholarships, the school's own gift aid. *Loan aid offered:* Direct Subsidized Stafford, Direct Unsubsidized Stafford, FFEL PLUS, Federal Perkins, college/university loans from institutional funds. Applicants will be notified of awards on or about 4/1. Off-campus job opportunities are good.

The Inside Word

Grades are more important than standardized test scores in the admissions process at Loyola. Your junior and senior grades are particularly critical. The content of the courses you've taken weighs fairly heavily, too. Obviously, harder courses look better. If your standardized test scores aren't awful and your high school GPA is the equivalent of a "B+" or better, it is extremely likely that you will get admitted here. If your GPA is more like a "B," your odds are still pretty good. If your academic profile is a little thin, definitely take advantage of the opportunity to interview.

THE SCHOOL SAYS ". . ."
From The Admissions Office

"To make a wise choice about your college plans, you will need to find out more. We extend to you these invitations. Question-and-answer periods with an Admissions Counselor are helpful to prospective students. An appointment should be made in advance. Admissions office hours are 9:00 a.m. to 5:00 p.m., Monday through Friday. College day programs and Saturday information programs are scheduled during the academic year. These programs include a video about Loyola, a general information session, a discussion of various majors, a campus tour, and lunch. Summer information programs can help high school juniors to get a head start on investigating colleges. These programs feature an introductory presentation about the college and a campus tour.

"Loyola College will continue to accept results of both the former SAT and ACT. In addition, Loyola will continue to combine the highest sub scores from multiple test administrations from both the old and new tests (SAT: Reading/Math scores). Loyola will not explicitly require submission of results from the new SAT."

For even more information on this school, turn to page 489 of the "Stats" section.

LYCOMING COLLEGE

700 COLLEGE PLACE, WILLIAMSPORT, PA 17701 • ADMISSIONS: 570-321-4026 • FAX: 570-321-4317
E-MAIL: ADMISSIONS@LYCOMING.EDU • WEBSITE: WWW.LYCOMING.EDU

RATINGS

Quality of Life: 75   **Academic:** 81   **Admissions:** 78   **Financial Aid:** 75

STUDENTS SAY ". . ."

Academics

Lycoming College is one of the ever-shrinking group of selective undergraduates-only liberal arts and sciences institutions in the United States, which is a fact it touts proudly in its promotional literature. Students recognize the benefits of the school's approach, extolling the "school's focus on a student-centered liberal arts education" and pro-

> **SURVEY SAYS . . .**
> *Great library*
> *Athletic facilities are great*
> *Lots of beer drinking*
> *Hard liquor is popular*

fessors who "truly care about the students and do whatever they can to ensure the students are getting the education they are paying for." Strong programs in biology, chemistry, business, sociology, archaeology, and English stand out among the 34 majors offered. With only 1,500 undergrads and favorable student-teacher ratio, Lycoming can provide "small class sizes, so we really get a chance to develop good relationships with the faculty. All of our professors know us by name, and they are more than willing to help us with the material outside of class. They even invite us to picnics and dinners at their homes! In the labs, we get hands-on experience that isn't possible at a larger school." The school's size also allows administrators to "try to get to know the students, inviting us to meetings where they interview people for new positions (e.g. director of security), to meetings with the mayor, and to talk about the school." Students also appreciate Lycoming's history of "great job placement" and its reputation with graduate schools.

Life

Lycoming College "has a very active student body," with most students involved in sports and/or clubs. "It is almost a guarantee that if you look out your window you will see groups of students on the quad playing ball, reading under the trees, having snowball fights or sledding down the hill on cafeteria trays," one student observes. On the weekends "everyone stays here, and there is always something going on, from sporting events to campus movies," as "The Campus Activities Board (CAB) does a great job of providing entertainment on campus, with prerelease movies every weekend as well as movies on the campus TV station." Five fraternities and sororities mean "There's generally a party if that's what you're into." Many here feel that "Williamsport is a small town and…that there's nothing to do outside of the college," but "This is untrue. Williamsport actually has a relatively active art, music, and entertainment scene (for a small town)."

Student Body

Lycoming may "remind you of one big high school," particularly a "typical preppy, white, middle- to upper-middle-class" high school. As in high school, students tend to break down into predictable social sets; "There are the Greeks, jocks, and artistic groups, and then everyone else finds a group pretty easily." While "Lycoming is extremely uniform in terms of race/social demographics, the student body is quite diverse in terms of interests and personalities. Because Lycoming offers a few unique programs—archaeology, creative writing, and a lacrosse team, to name a few—the school attracts a wide range of students." Most here "are involved in several clubs and sports" and "hold some type of leadership position in at least one."

THE PRINCETON REVIEW SAYS

Admissions

Very important factors considered include: Rigor of secondary school record. *Important factors considered include:* Class rank, application essay, academic GPA, recommendation(s), standardized test scores, interview, racial/ethnic status. *Other factors considered include:* Alumni/ae relation, character/personal qualities, extracurricular activities, first generation, geographical residence, level of applicant's interest, talent/ability, volunteer work, work experience. SAT or ACT required; TOEFL required of all international applicants. High school diploma is required and GED is accepted. *Academic units required:* 4 English, 3 mathematics, 2 science, (2 science labs), 2 foreign language, 4 social studies, 3 history, 2 academic electives. *Academic units recommended:* 4 English, 4 mathematics, 4 science, (2 science labs), 4 foreign language, 4 social studies, 4 history, 2 academic electives.

Financial Aid

Students should submit: FAFSA, institution's own financial aid form. The Princeton Review suggests that all financial aid forms be submitted as soon as possible after January 1. *Need-based scholarships/grants offered:* Federal Pell, SEOG, state scholarships/grants, private scholarships, the school's own gift aid. *Loan aid offered:* FFEL Subsidized Stafford, FFEL Unsubsidized Stafford, FFEL PLUS, Federal Perkins, college/university loans from institutional funds. Applicants will be notified of awards on a rolling basis beginning 3/1. Federal Work-Study Program available. Institutional employment available. Off-campus job opportunities are good.

The Inside Word

Admissions at Lycoming are competitive but hardly cutthroat. High school students with a B average and above-average standardized test scores should clear all admissions hurdles with little difficulty. Athletes, minority students, and others who add diversity and value to the campus will get more slack; so too will marginal applicants who make clear that Lycoming is their first choice. An interview and campus visit are useful in this regard.

THE SCHOOL SAYS ". . ."

From The Admissions Office

"At a time when many colleges have tried to become all things to all people, Lycoming has chosen to remain a traditional, undergraduate, residential, liberal arts college. What makes Lycoming different is the way it chooses to deliver its curriculum—in small classes taught by highly credentialed, well-seasoned, full-time professors. 'It's how we teach, not what we teach that is special here,' says Professor Mel Zimmerman, chair of the faculty. 'It's the way we respond to questions, the comments we write on papers, and the way we interact with students outside the classroom that makes this school so appealing.' Staying true to who we are is the reason we've been in business since 1812."

For even more information on this school, turn to page 489 of the "Stats" section.

MANHATTANVILLE COLLEGE

2900 PURCHASE STREET, ADMISSIONS OFFICE, PURCHASE, NY 10577 • ADMISSIONS: 914-323-5124
FAX: 914-694-1732 • E-MAIL: ADMISSIONS@MVILLE.EDU • WEBSITE: WWW.MVILLE.EDU

RATINGS
Quality of Life: 94   **Academic: 82**   **Admissions: 80**   **Financial Aid: 78**

STUDENTS SAY "..."

Academics

"Qualified and committed" professors, "very involved" administrators, and an "excellent location" near New York City (one still far enough from its "pollution and distractions") all contribute to the "close and supportive community" that is Manhattanville College. Students here have the

> SURVEY SAYS ...
> *Small classes*
> *Great library*
> *Diverse student types on campus*

"unbelievable" opportunity to "exchange ideas" with professors who have "studied in the best universities in the world. There are so many distinguished professors here, ranging from experts in world religions, to former ambassadors in the UN. Almost all of them are well known in their areas of study." Yet regardless of the faculty's impressive credentials, "Each one of them makes you feel comfortable enough to go and see him or her if you need help, and is more than willing to use his or her own time to help you." Getting such help is made easier by the fact that "one-third of professors live on campus." Mville (as it is affectionately called by its students) places a lot of emphasis on experiential learning, and the school's location is an asset in that regard. Not only is Mville close to the myriad internship opportunities of the megalopolis next door, but "We [also] have tons of corporations literally in our neighborhood, like MasterCard, IBM, MBIA, JPMorgan—[these bring] plenty of internships." In addition to internships, the school reportedly "is very successful in finding students interesting jobs in their fields after they graduate." Students praise a "very helpful" administration, and the president is such a hit with students that one goes so far as to say that he "is probably more popular than the star of the basketball team."

Life

Manhattanville's campus "is a quiet place." Students here "generally focus on their academics first and on partying and having fun second." While "There are parties on campus every 2 weeks or so [at which] alcohol is served," the residential directors and RAs "are so strict, the party scene is not so big." Parties are typically "small get-togethers," and "People are usually nervous that they are going to get caught [if they drink]." Such a tame on-campus party scene means that the drinkers here make it a "very big bar school." They take "the Valiant Express [a campus shuttle] to downtown White Plains," where "dozens of bars" can be found. Students can also find "other stuff to do [in White Plains]," such as visiting its "malls, movie theaters, restaurants, and clubs." The "college bus also takes students [to New York City] every Saturday"; people go there to "see Broadway shows or [attend] professional athletic events." For those students seeking more wholesome fun on campus, There are "lots of interest groups and activities that one can join," and "there is also a game room with different things like billiards and Ping-Pong." Finally, "The students here have a lot of school spirit, so there is always a great turnout for games."

Student Body

"The community at Manhattanville is very diverse," with a community that includes students "from 59 different countries around the world." A typical student might even have "lived in more than three countries." Despite the diversity (or perhaps as a natural consequence of it), sometimes "People tend to hang out with the group they feel most comfortable with (i.e., international students hanging out with fellow international students, sport students with fellow sport students, etc.)." Regardless of any cliques, "All of the students at the school are extremely cordial. Since it is such a small school, you get to know everyone's face." "The typical student works hard about half the time," one claims. "There are atypical students who care a lot about their work and do a lot of studying. Some of them stick out, and others fit in fine."

THE PRINCETON REVIEW SAYS

Admissions

Very important factors considered include: Rigor of secondary school record, standardized test scores. *Important factors considered include:* Application essay, recommendation(s), extracurricular activities, interview. *Other factors considered include:* Alumni/ae relation, character/personal qualities, geographical residence, talent/ability, volunteer work, work experience. SAT or ACT required; TOEFL required of all international applicants. High school diploma is required and GED is accepted. *Academic units required:* 4 English, 3 mathematics, 2 science, 2 social studies, 5 academic electives.

Financial Aid

Students should submit: FAFSA, state aid form. The Princeton Review suggests that all financial aid forms be submitted as soon as possible after January 1. *Need-based scholarships/grants offered:* Federal Pell, SEOG, state scholarships/grants, private scholarships, the school's own gift aid. *Loan aid offered:* FFEL Subsidized Stafford, FFEL Unsubsidized Stafford, FFEL PLUS, Federal Perkins Applicants will be notified of awards on a rolling basis beginning 3/1. Federal Work-Study Program available. Institutional employment available. Off-campus job opportunities are excellent.

The Inside Word

Applicants evincing middle-of-the-road academic achievement will most likely find themselves with an acceptance letter from Manhattanville. The college still seeks to achieve greater gender balance, so male candidates enjoy a slightly higher admission rate than female candidates. In addition to meeting regular admissions requirements, students who wish to pursue a degree in fine arts or performing arts must present a portfolio or audition, respectively.

THE SCHOOL SAYS "..."

From The Admissions Office

"Manhattanville's mission—to educate ethically and socially responsible leaders for the global community—is evident throughout the college, from academics to athletics to social and extracurricular activities. With 1,600 undergraduates from 59 nations and 39 states, our diversity spans geographic, cultural, ethnic, religious, socioeconomic, and academic backgrounds. Students are free to express their views in this tight-knit community, where we value the personal as well as the global. Any six students with similar interest can start a club, and most participate in a variety of campus wide programs. Last year, students engaged in more than 23,380 hours of community service and social justice activity. Study abroad opportunities include not only the most desirable international locations, but also a semester-long immersion for living, studying, and working in New York City. In the true liberal arts tradition, students are encouraged to think for themselves and develop new skills—in music, the studio arts, on stage, in the sciences, or on the playing field. With more than 50 areas of study and a popular self-designed major, there is no limit to our academic scope. Our Westchester County location, just 35 miles north of New York City, gives students an edge for jobs and internships. Over the past few years, Manhattanville has been rated among the '100 Most Wired,' the '100 Most Undeservedly Underappreciated,' the '320 Hottest,' and in U.S. News & World Report's first tier. Last year, the men's and women's ice hockey teams were ranked #1 in the nation for Division III.

"As of this book's publication, Manhattanville College did not have information available about their policy regarding the new SAT."

For even more information on this school, turn to page 490 of the "Stats" section.

MARIST COLLEGE

3399 NORTH ROAD, POUGHKEEPSIE, NY 12601-1387 • ADMISSIONS: 845-575-3226 • FAX: 845-575-3215
E-MAIL: ADMISSIONS@MARIST.EDU • WEBSITE: WWW.MARIST.EDU

RATINGS
Quality of Life: 75   **Academic:** 78   **Admissions:** 89   **Financial Aid:** 66

STUDENTS SAY "..."

Academics

Marist College, a "midsized institute that proudly offers competitive academics, career placement, and a well-rounded college experience," is "the perfect size." Students tell us that it's "small enough that professors remember your name and address you as a person, not a number, but large enough that you are not constantly seeing the same people every day." Pre-professional and career-track pro-

> **SURVEY SAYS . . .**
> *Small classes*
> *Great computer facilities*
> *Great library*
> *Lots of beer drinking*
> *Hard liquor is popular*

grams are most popular here; students laud the "great communications program" with its "unique digital media major" and "strong internship connections," the "very good education program," the popular business programs, and the "excellent Chemistry Department, where personal attention is unmatched." Students here keep their eyes on the prize: They sing the praises of the Center for Career Services, noting that "Our career services and internship opportunities are amazing. By the end of your senior year you will most likely complete an internship with a big-name company, either in the local area or in New York City, which we are in close prox-imity to." They also love the Study Abroad Office, which "has connected students with many countries around the world, allowing students to study abroad for a semester, year, or short-term period." Further sweetening the deal are the school's "strong connections to IBM" and "an amazing library that is ranked among the top 20 in the country."

Life

"Classes keep you busy" at Marist College, but not so busy that you can't also enjoy a variety of extracurricu-lar activities. These include "social organizations, religious organizations, academic organizations, to name sim-ply a few" as well as "campus events such as sports, plays, lectures, seminars, and concerts. Marist is not a suit-case campus, as students who live on campus stay on campus over the weekends." The bar scene is big; some here see Marist as "very much a bar school. Kids go out Tuesday, Thursday, Friday, and Saturday. House par-ties happen, but they aren't as popular as the bars. There's tons of nonalcoholic fun, too." While "The city of Poughkeepsie is generally not safe outside of the venues Marist students flock to," the "diverse" area sur-rounding Poughkeepsie "allows outdoor experiences like hiking, kayaking, and swimming." Undergrads appreciate the fact that "the Marist campus is beautiful, with the most amazing views ever"—"The Hudson River can be seen from almost every dorm."

Student Body

Marist seems to draw "lots of kids from Long Island, New Jersey, and Connecticut, many of them White, upper-middle-class, immigrant-descended Catholics." (One student adds, "They shop at Abercrombie.") Another undergrad notes, "While walking through campus, one may notice that Marist is filled with very similar peo-ple." The student body includes "many athletes [Marist fields 10 men's and 11 women's intercollegiate teams] and preppy students. Many are involved in clubs." Students here "are going to school to gain experience, get their degree, and dive into the competitive workforce. They focus on attaining good grades while also being involved in on-campus activities and having a diverse social life. They are fun-loving people." Undergrads are also "extremely friendly and will go out of their way to hold a door for you." All students "fit in well and get along," we're told.

THE PRINCETON REVIEW SAYS

Admissions

Very important factors considered include: Academic GPA, rigor of secondary school record, standardized test scores. *Important factors considered include:* Class rank, application essay, recommendation(s), character/personal qualities, extracurricular activities, geographical residence, state residency, talent/ability, volunteer work, work experience. *Other factors considered include:* Alumni/ae relation, level of applicant's interest, racial/ethnic status, SAT or ACT required; ACT with Writing component required. TOEFL required of all international applicants. High school diploma is required and GED is accepted. *Academic units required:* 4 English, 3 mathematics, 3 science, (2 science labs), 2 foreign language, 2 social studies, 1 history, 2 academic electives. *Academic units recommended:* 4 mathematics, 4 science, (3 science labs), 3 foreign language.

Financial Aid

Students should submit: FAFSA, institution's own financial aid form. Regular filing deadline is 5/1. The Princeton Review suggests that all financial aid forms be submitted as soon as possible after January 1. *Need-based scholarships/grants offered:* Federal Pell, SEOG, state scholarships/grants, private scholarships, the school's own gift aid. *Loan aid offered:* FFEL Subsidized Stafford, FFEL Unsubsidized Stafford, FFEL PLUS, Federal Perkins, Alternative Loans. Applicants will be notified of awards on a rolling basis beginning 3/15. Federal Work-Study Program available. Institutional employment available. Off-campus job opportunities are excellent.

The Inside Word

Marist attracts some solid students, and viable candidates are usually in the top quarter of their class. Additionally, Admissions Counselors tend to favor applicants who have attained leadership roles and contributed to their communities. State residency is also taken into consideration, as Marist aims to maintain a diverse campus.

THE SCHOOL SAYS "..."

From The Admissions Office

"Marist is a 'hot school' among prospective students. We are seeing a record number of applications each year. But the number of seats available for the freshman class remains the same, about 950. Therefore, becoming an accepted applicant is an increasingly competitive process. Our recommendations: keep your grades up, score well on the SAT, participate in community service both in and out of school, and exercise leadership in the classroom, athletics, extracurricular activities, and your place of worship. We encourage a campus visit. When prospective students see Marist—our beautiful location on a scenic stretch of the Hudson River, the quality of our facilities, the interaction between students and faculty, and the fact that everyone really enjoys their time here—they want to become a part of the Marist College community. We'll help you in the transition from high school to college through an innovative first-year program that provides mentors for every student. You'll also learn how to use technology in whatever field you choose. We emphasize three aspects of a true Marist experience: excellence in education, community, and service to others. At Marist, you'll get a premium education, develop your skills, have fun and make lifelong friends, be given the opportunity to gain valuable experience through our great internship and study abroad programs, and be ahead of the competition for graduate school or work.

"Marist requires the SAT with the Writing component. We recommend all students take the test at least twice and the ACT once. Marist will use the best Verbal, Math, and Writing scores from the SAT or the highest composite ACT score."

For even more information on this school, turn to page 490 of the "Stats" section.

MARLBORO COLLEGE

PO Box A, South Road, Marlboro, VT 05344 • Admissions: 802-258-9236 • Fax: 802-257-4154
Financial Aid: 802-257-4333 • E-mail: admissions@marlboro.edu • Website: www.marlboro.edu

RATINGS
Quality of Life: 81   Academic: 98   Admissions: 88   Financial Aid: 89

STUDENTS SAY "..."

Academics

Marlboro College is all about giving students "the freedom to pursue their own interests and study what they want." Here, undergrads design their own junior and senior curricula, then pursue them in one-on-one tutorials with professors. The process, known here simply as 'The Plan,' culminates in a substantial senior thesis. The goal is to "learn how to think critically and find the resources you need in the course of completing a dissertation-level project," and

undergrads here "wouldn't settle for anything less in their academic pursuits." Freshmen and sophomores complete more traditional-style courses, albeit in smaller classrooms and with a greater-than-usual focus on writing and discussion. The size of the school—just over 300 undergraduates attend—is sometimes a hindrance. One student observes that "Since there is generally only one professor per field, it is a bit disappointing to realize that there can only be a limited number of classes offered per semester." "Too often a student will reach the final year when his/her Plan sponsor goes on sabbatical and a replacement is not hired in time or hired at all. This presents a problem: Does the student leave the college until their professor returns? Or does the student switch Plan sponsors, potentially altering the focus of their work so much they dislike what their doing?" Despite these issues, "professors are very receptive and try to accommodate individual interests as best they can." Most here feel these are reasonable costs to bear in order to pursue "independent, difficult, intellectually-stimulating work inside a student-centered and directed curriculum."

Life

Marlboro is "a little school on top of a hill" with Brattleboro, the closest town, "about a half an hour away," so "life is pretty intensely focused on the campus." "While we do make the trip to Brattleboro fairly often, most of our time is spent 'on the hill,'" says one student. Students "study a lot, but there is also a lot of hanging out, mainly in small impromptu ways." They "like to debate about philosophy, politics, and religion" while "smoking a lot of cigarettes and pot." As one student puts it, "Parties are fun because, while we drink and smoke just as much as the next college, we'll also engage in deep intellectual discussions while doing said activities." Otherwise, fun "is found in the 300 acres that surround the college: skiing, hiking, long walks in an apple orchard, broomball (a hippie version of hockey), soccer, etc." Trips to Brattleboro are pleasant because it's "an arts town." Students occasionally travel to Massachusetts college towns Amherst and Northampton for concerts or shopping and "frequently classes take field trips to NYC or Boston." Many get involved in grassroots political organization, both on campus and off.

Students

The typical Marlboro student "wouldn't fit quite right anywhere else: academically driven, maybe a little nerdy, politically vocal, and looking for a laid-back environment. There is no atypical student at Marlboro, because we all would have been atypical someplace else." Personality types run the gamut, including "hippie environmentalists, geeks and gamers, theater kids, artists, and so on and so forth and every combination thereof. We're underrepresented in the jock and beauty queen categories, but that doesn't seem to bother anybody." Everyone here, we're told, "is extremely passionate about their own little academic niche, and furthermore each person is one of the smartest people you will ever meet." The school is home to "a large gay population and a few transgender students," but "there are a lack of minority students, Republicans, and financially lower-class students."

THE PRINCETON REVIEW SAYS

Admissions

Very important factors considered include: Application essay, academic GPA, rigor of secondary school record, character/personal qualities. *Important factors considered include:* Extracurricular activities, interview, talent/ability. *Other factors considered include:* Class rank, recommendation(s), standardized test scores, alumni/ae relation, first generation, geographical residence, level of applicant's interest, state residency, volunteer work, work experience. SAT or ACT required; TOEFL required of all international applicants. High school diploma is required and GED is accepted. *Academic units recommended:* 4 English, 3 mathematics, 3 science, (1 science labs), 3 foreign language, 3 social studies, 3 history, 3 academic electives.

Financial Aid

Students should submit: FAFSA. Regular filing deadline is 3/1. The Princeton Review suggests that all financial aid forms be submitted as soon as possible after January 1. *Need-based scholarships/grants offered:* Federal Pell, SEOG, state scholarships/grants, private scholarships, the school's own gift aid. *Loan aid offered:* FFEL Subsidized Stafford, FFEL Unsubsidized Stafford, FFEL PLUS, state loans, college/university loans from institutional funds. Applicants will be notified of awards on a rolling basis beginning 3/15. Federal Work-Study Program available. Institutional employment available. Off-campus job opportunities are fair.

The Inside Word

Don't be misled by Marlboro's high acceptance rate—this is not the type of school that attracts many applications from students unsure of whether they belong at Marlboro. Most applicants are qualified both in terms of academic achievement and sincere intellectual curiosity. The school seeks candidates "with intellectual promise, a high degree of self-motivation, self-discipline, personal stability, social concern, and the ability and desire to contribute to the College community." These are the qualities you should stress on your application.

THE SCHOOL SAYS ". . ."

From The Admissions Office

"Marlboro College is distinguished by its curriculum, praised in higher education circles as unique; it is known for its self-governing philosophy, in which each student, faculty, and staff has an equal vote on many issues affecting the community; and it is recognized for its 60-year history of offering a rigorous, exciting, self-designed course of study taught in very small classes and individualized study with faculty. Marlboro's size also distinguishes it from most other schools. With 300 students and a student/faculty ratio of 8:1, it is one of the nation's smallest liberal arts colleges. Few other schools offer a program where students have such close interaction with faculty, and where community life is inseparable from academic life. The result, the self-designed, self-directed Plan of Concentration, allows students to develop their own unique academic work by defining a problem, setting clear limits on an area of inquiry, and analyzing, evaluating, and reporting on the outcome of a significant project. A Marlboro education teaches you to think for yourself, articulate your thoughts, express your ideas, believe in yourself, and do it all with the clarity, confidence, and self-reliance necessary for later success, no matter what postgraduate path you take.

"Marlboro College requires all applicants for admission to submit results of either the ACT and ACT Writing Test or SAT Reasoning Test. Students who have previously taken older versions of the ACT or SAT may submit those test results and are not required to retake the 'new' ACT or SAT. We do not require SAT Subject Tests."

For even more information on this school, turn to page 491 of the "Stats" section.

MARYLAND INSTITUTE COLLEGE OF ART

1300 MOUNT ROYAL AVENUE, BALTIMORE, MD 21217 • ADMISSIONS: 410-225-2222 • FAX: 410-225-2337
E-MAIL: ADMISSIONS@MICA.EDU • WEBSITE: WWW.MICA.EDU

RATINGS
Quality of Life: 70   **Academic:** 90   **Admissions:** 90   **Financial Aid:** 73

STUDENTS SAY ". . ."
Academics

The Maryland Institute College of Art "is about making art nonstop" while "learning about [art] history, figuring out what you are about, and then bringing it to the world to influence others." To many here, MICA is "one of the top art schools in the U.S." Traditionally strong in painting, it is developing strengths in numerous fields. Its illustration program, for example, "has improved quite significantly.

The department has expanded enormously into a new building. . . . Senior studio spaces are now breathtakingly huge and available, there is better gallery space, and the department is constantly . . . adding classes and courses." In addition, "The commercial arts and the digital arts are becoming much better programs, offering less broad and rather focused paths. MICA illustrators, graphic designers, and animators are getting due credit." There's a small downside to the recent improvements—they've resulted in "an awkward growth period" during which resources "are rather tight. This will probably be relieved once the expansion is complete." Students warn that "MICA is a challenge. It's a large workload of not just artwork but academic work as well. You have to have wonderful time-management skills to do [it] all. . . . Luckily the faculty at MICA [are] more than willing to help you as you tackle this monstrous workload." The school is also "very accommodating to students who wish to do interdisciplinary studies."

Life

MICA students say they "do way more homework than normal kids." After all, "Art won't do itself," and doing things halfway isn't an option. Even though the school assigns "a lot of work," students "still find time to party. MICA has a ton of parties off campus attended by lower- and upperclassmen," and the campus itself "is always active. There are students and/or faculty in the buildings 24/7." In addition, "There's always something going on" in the city of Baltimore, which "has a really amazing arts community. Lots of musicians and visual artists and video artists and playwrights and writers and fashion designers move here from New York because it's so cheap and because there are so many other awesome people living down here." A vocal minority finds Baltimore "scary," but most here embrace the city (although even they agree that it's a place where you "need a car" "to get around").

Student Body

The typical MICA student "is Caucasian, though there are large populations of Asian and African American students also. Most come from upper-middle-class backgrounds on either the West Coast or the East Coast. Ideologically, they lean strongly to the left but are not very politically active. If you went to all the (upper-middle-class) cultural centers of America and skimmed the people at each high school that were most effective at being 'different' socially, you would have a good representation of MICA." There is a sense among some that "people go so far . . . to be individual and define their own style," it often "seems that everyone just winds up a part of the same unique blob." As one student wryly puts it, "Everyone is different and we are all the same because of it."

Admissions

Very important factors considered include: Academic GPA, rigor of secondary school record, level of applicant's interest, talent/ability. *Important factors considered include:* Class rank, application essay, standardized test scores, extracurricular activities, interview. *Other factors considered include:* Recommendation(s), alumni/ae relation, character/personal qualities, racial/ethnic status, volunteer work, SAT or ACT required; High school diploma is required and GED is accepted. *Academic units required:* 4 English, 2 mathematics, 2 science, (1 science labs), 4 social studies, 3 history, 6 academic electives, 2 Studio Art 2, 4 studio art recommended, 1 Art History recommended. *Academic units recommended:* 4 English, 3 mathematics, 3 science, 4 social studies, 4 history, 5 Studio Art 2, 4 studio art recommended, 1 Art History recommended.

Financial Aid

Students should submit: FAFSA, institution's own financial aid form. Regular filing deadline is 3/1. The Princeton Review suggests that all financial aid forms be submitted as soon as possible after January 1. *Need-based scholarships/grants offered:* Federal Pell, SEOG, state scholarships/grants, private scholarships, the school's own gift aid. *Loan aid offered:* FFEL Subsidized Stafford, FFEL Unsubsidized Stafford, FFEL PLUS, Federal Perkins Applicants will be notified of awards on or about 4/13. Federal Work-Study Program available. Institutional employment available. Off-campus job opportunities are excellent.

The Inside Word

Test scores, transcripts, and letters of recommendation are all taken into consideration here, but your portfolio is the make-or-break piece of the application. A great portfolio can mitigate many other shortcomings; a bad portfolio will torpedo an otherwise exemplary application.

THE SCHOOL SAYS ". . ."

From The Admissions Office

"Maryland Institute College of Art attracts some of the most talented, passionate, and serious visual art and design faculty and students in the world. The college is a universe of artists, designers, and scholars who celebrate the creative process, the majesty of the arts, and the mind-expanding pursuit of knowledge. To maintain this community of artists, admission is highly competitive. Successful applicants are men and women who have made a commitment to art, and demonstrated this commitment by developing a serious portfolio of artwork. In selecting from among the many outstanding applications we receive for a limited number of places, MICA's Admission Committee considers a comprehensive set of factors. Central to our evaluations are the artistic and academic qualifications of our candidates, but we also consider extracurricular activities and achievements, art experience beyond required classroom instruction, and personal qualities. The portfolio is the most meaningful indicator of serious artistic commitment, ability, and potential to succeed in MICA's rigorous studio environment. Your artwork reflects your visual sensitivity, intellectual curiosity and creativity, motivation and self-discipline, and previous experience in the visual arts. Portfolios are evaluated on an individual basis, in the context of the specific educational background and experiences of each applicant. Our evaluation of your academic performance is determined by grades, level of classwork, test scores, and class rank. The required essay is also seriously considered."

For even more information on this school, turn to page 491 of the "Stats" section.

MASSACHUSETTS INSTITUTE OF TECHNOLOGY

77 MASSACHUSETTS AVENUE, CAMBRIDGE, MA 02139 • ADMISSIONS: 617-253-4791
FAX: 617-253-1986 • FINANCIAL AID: 617-253-4971 • E-MAIL: ADMISSIONS@MIT.EDU • WEBSITE: WWW.MIT.EDU

RATINGS
Quality of Life: 87   **Academic:** 97   **Admissions:** 99   **Financial Aid:** 95

STUDENTS SAY "..."

Academics

Massachusetts Institute of Technology, the East Coast mecca of engineering, science, and mathematics, "is the ultimate place for information overload, endless possibilities, and expanding your horizons." The "amazing collection of creative minds" includes enough Nobel laureates to fill a jury box as well as brilliant students who are given substantial control of their educations; one explains, "The administration's attitude towards students is one of respect. As soon as you come on campus, you are bombard-

ed with choices." Students need to be able to manage a workload that "definitely push[es you] beyond your comfort level." A chemical engineering major elaborates: "MIT is different from many schools in that its goal is not to teach you specific facts in each subject. MIT teaches you how to think. Not about opinions, but about problem solving. Facts and memorization are useless unless you know how to approach a tough problem." Professors here range from "excellent teachers who make lectures fun and exciting" to "dull and soporific" ones, but most "make a serious effort to make the material they teach interesting by throwing in jokes and cool demonstrations." "Access to an amazing number of resources, both academic and recreational," "research opportunities for undergrads with some of the nation's leading professors," and a rock-solid alumni network complete the picture. If you ask "MIT alumni where they went to college, most will immediately stick out their hand and show you their 'brass rat' (the MIT ring, the second most recognized ring in the world)."

Life

At MIT "It may seem . . . like there's no life outside problem sets and studying for exams," but "There's always time for extracurricular activities or just relaxing" for those "with good time-management skills" or the "ability to survive on [a] lack of sleep." Options range from "building rides" (recent projects have included a motorized couch and a human-sized hamster wheel) "to partying at fraternities to enjoying the largest collection of science fiction novels in the U.S. at the MIT Science Fiction Library." Students occasionally find time to "pull a hack," which is an ethical prank "like the life-size Wright brothers' plane that appeared on top of the Great Dome for the one-hundredth anniversary of flight." Undergrads tell us that "MIT has great parties—a lot of Wellesley, Harvard, and BU students come to them," but also that "There are tons of things to do other than party" here. "Movies, shopping, museums, and plays are all possible with our location near Boston. There are great restaurants only [blocks] away from campus, too . . . From what I can tell, MIT students have way more fun on the weekends then their Cambridge counterpart[s at] Harvard."

Student Body

"There actually isn't one typical student at MIT," students here assure us, explaining that "Hobbies range from building robots and hacking to getting wasted and partying every weekend. The one thing students all have in common is that they are insanely smart and love to learn. Pretty much anyone can find the perfect group of friends to hang out with at MIT." While "Most students do have some form of 'nerdiness'" (like telling nerdy jokes, being an avid fan of Star Wars, etc.), "Contrary to MIT's stereotype, most MIT students are not geeks who study all the time and have no social skills. The majority of the students here are actually quite 'normal.'" The "stereotypical student [who] looks techy and unkempt . . . only represents about 25 percent of the school." The rest include "multiple-sport standouts, political activists, fraternity and sorority members, hippies, clean-cut business types, LARPers, hackers, musicians, and artisans. There are people who look like they stepped out of an Abercrombie & Fitch catalog and people who dress in all black and carry flashlights and multi-tools. Not everyone relates to everyone else, but most people get along, and it's almost a guarantee that you'll fit in somewhere."

THE PRINCETON REVIEW SAYS

Admissions

Very important factors considered include: Character/personal qualities. *Important factors considered include:* Class rank, academic GPA, recommendation(s), rigor of secondary school record, standardized test scores, extracurricular activities, interview, talent/ability. *Other factors considered include:* Application essay, alumni/ae relation, first generation, geographical residence, level of applicant's interest, racial/ethnic status, volunteer work, work experience. ACT with Writing component required. High school diploma or equivalent is not required. *Academic units recommended:* 4 English, 4 mathematics, 4 science, 2 foreign language, 2 social studies.

Financial Aid

Students should submit: FAFSA, CSS/Financial Aid PROFILE, noncustodial PROFILE, business/farm supplement, parent's complete federal income tax returns from prior year and W2s. Regular filing deadline is 2/15. The Princeton Review suggests that all financial aid forms be submitted as soon as possible after January 1. *Need-based scholarships/grants offered:* Federal Pell, SEOG, state scholarships/grants, private scholarships, the school's own gift aid. *Loan aid offered:* Direct Subsidized Stafford, Direct Unsubsidized Stafford, Direct PLUS, Federal Perkins, college/university loans from institutional funds. Applicants will be notified of awards on or about 4/1. Federal Work-Study Program available. Institutional employment available. Off-campus job opportunities are excellent.

The Inside Word

MIT has one of the nation's most competitive admissions processes. The school's applicant pool is so rich it turns away numerous qualified candidates each year. Put your best foot forward and take consolation in the fact that rejection doesn't necessarily mean that you don't belong at MIT, but only that there wasn't enough room for you the year you applied. Your best chance to get an edge: Find ways to stress your creativity, a quality that MIT's admissions director told USA Today is lacking in many prospective college students.

THE SCHOOL SAYS ". . ."

From The Admissions Office

"The students who come to the Massachusetts Institute of Technology are some of America's—and the world's—best and most creative. As graduates, they leave here to make real contributions—in science, technology, business, education, politics, architecture, and the arts. From any class, many will go on to do work that is historically significant. These young men and women are leaders, achievers, and producers. Helping such students make the most of their talents and dreams would challenge any educational institution. MIT gives them its best advantages: a world-class faculty, unparalleled facilities, and remarkable opportunities. In turn, these students help to make the institute the vital place it is. They bring fresh viewpoints to faculty research: More than three-quarters participate in the Undergraduate Research Opportunities Program. They play on MIT's 41 intercollegiate teams as well as in its 15 musical ensembles. To their classes and to their out-of-class activities, they bring enthusiasm, energy, and individual style.

"For freshman admission, MIT requires scores from either the SAT or the ACT (with or without the optional Writing test). In addition, we require two SAT Subject Tests: one in Math (Level IC or IIC), one in science (Physics, Chemistry, or Biology)."

For even more information on this school, turn to page 492 of the "Stats" section.

MERRIMACK COLLEGE

OFFICE OF ADMISSION, AUSTIN HALL, NORTH ANDOVER, MA 01845 • ADMISSIONS: 978-837-5100
FAX: 978-837-5133 • E-MAIL: ADMISSION@MERRIMACK.EDU • WEBSITE: WWW.MERRIMACK.EDU

RATINGS
Quality of Life: 72   Academic: 76   Admissions: 79   Financial Aid: 86

STUDENTS SAY "..."

Academics

Merrimack students report a "very satisfying" academic
experience, enhanced by "professors that are brilliant, energetic, and easily approachable both in and out of the classroom." One impressed sophomore notes, "My professors
have gotten to know me on a personal level, and some stay
in touch even when I'm no longer enrolled in any of their

> **SURVEY SAYS . . .**
> *Students are friendly*
> *Campus feels safe*
> *Lots of beer drinking*
> *Hard liquor is popular*

classes." Importantly, they "work with you to examine your future goals and guide you on the right path."
Additionally, undergrads applaud the "small class sizes," which encourage "heavy debate with professors and
fellow students." While students are quick to praise their time in the lecture halls, opinions are mixed when it
comes to the administration. Though a junior assures us that "administrators are easy to work with when solving issues and agendas," others claim dealing with them is a "headache" and a "waste." Fortunately, change is
expected as Merrimack recently welcomed the arrival of a new president.

Life

Though Merrimack students must hit the books during the week, they readily push academics aside once the
weekend rolls around. The athletic undergrads "love the sports here at Merrimack" and many are involved in
intramurals such as "flag football and ski club." Social activities tend to focus around dorm life as they are "very
conducive to having people over to hang out and have fun, from having a few drinks to sitting around watching TV to having large parties." And one sophomore adds, "On weekends, most people just go to on-campus parties in the senior apartments." Of course "Merrimack offers a wide range of opportunities for students, and there
is always something to do." These school sponsored activities range from comedians and bands to speakers such
as "the cast members of MTV's *Real World*." Students do complain that hometown "North Andover and the surrounding area is too quiet for someone looking to have fun after 9 P.M. because everything closes down." And
while there are a number of local dining options, "the area is very expensive making it hard to go out to eat."
Those in search of some urban action can take advantage of Merrimack's proximity to Boston, and many students
do take the occasional weekend trip.

Student Body

Many admit that Merrimack isn't the most diverse of colleges, defining the majority as "white, upper-middle
class, and Christian." Indeed, a sophomore boldly states that "Merrimack is a school of Abercrombie & Fitch
models." That said, many undergrads are "friendly and like to get involved on campus." And a knowledgeable
senior promises that his peers are "easy to get along with." Merrimack students like to be active, and athletes
"make up a surprisingly large part of the student body." Despite the school maintaining Catholic affiliation "the
average student is not that spiritually involved." The relatively small student population leads to a strong community feeling, and "by senior year...you have talked to most of the people in your class."

Admissions

Very important factors considered include: Application essay, academic GPA, rigor of secondary school record. *Important factors considered include:* Class rank, recommendation(s), character/personal qualities, talent/ability. *Other factors considered include:* Alumni/ae relation, extracurricular activities, interview, level of applicant's interest, volunteer work, work experience. ACT with Writing component required. TOEFL required of all international applicants. High school diploma is required and GED is accepted. *Academic units required:* 4 English, 3 mathematics, 3 science, (3 science labs), 2 foreign language, 1 social studies, 1 history, 3 academic electives. *Academic units recommended:* 4 English, 4 mathematics, 4 science, (4 science labs), 3 foreign language, 2 social studies, 2 history, 3 academic electives.

Financial Aid

Students should submit: FAFSA, noncustodial PROFILE, business/farm supplement. Sibling Verification. Regular filing deadline is 2/1. The Princeton Review suggests that all financial aid forms be submitted as soon as possible after January 1. *Need-based scholarships/grants offered:* Federal Pell, SEOG, state scholarships/grants, private scholarships, the school's own gift aid. *Loan aid offered:* FFEL Subsidized Stafford, FFEL Unsubsidized Stafford, FFEL PLUS, Federal Perkins, state loans, college/university loans from institutional funds. , Alternative Loans. Applicants will be notified of awards on or about 3/15. Federal Work-Study Program available. Off-campus job opportunities are good.

The Inside Word

Applicants should seriously consider applying to Merrimack through the early action program if they are interested in merit scholarships. It guarantees priority registration and financial aid for those accepted, provides a variety of school-related discounts, and, best of all, is nonbinding.

THE SCHOOL SAYS "..."

From The Admissions Office

"Merrimack College is a 4-year, independent, Catholic college grounded in the liberal arts and guided by the teachings of St. Augustine. Home to the Girard School of Business and International Commerce, the college is one of the few liberal arts Catholic colleges that offers programs both in science and in engineering. Merrimack's contemporary academic approach of fusing liberal arts with professional education means students become engaged and ready to make critical, moral, and informed decisions of thought, communication, and action in their own lives and in service to others. What makes Merrimack distinctive is that 'active learning' is our educational philosophy and a call to action. Students learn by doing—not only in the classroom and the laboratory, but also in the field and in the real world. Located on a suburban setting just 25 miles north of Boston, Massachusetts, Merrimack offers a strong cooperative education program for all majors, undergraduate research opportunities, and extensive service-learning experiences that promote social responsibility. Students at Merrimack have unparalleled opportunities for an education that extends far beyond campus. Merrimack's 2,000 students represent 28 states and 17 countries; nearly 80 percent live on campus."

For even more information on this school, turn to page 492 of the "Stats" section.

MESSIAH COLLEGE

One College Avenue, Grantham, PA 17027 • Admissions: 717-691-6000 • Fax: 717-796-5374
E-mail: admiss@messiah.edu • Website: www.messiah.edu

RATINGS
Quality of Life: 86   Academic: 84   Admissions: 87   Financial Aid: 73

STUDENTS SAY ". . ."

Academics

Messiah College, a small evangelical liberal arts school just outside Harrisburg, "is a place where Christian theology meets real life, individuals encounter true community, intense scholarship is connected to fervent faith, and where students stop 'doing' and start 'becoming.'" Students come here for a "Christ-centered education" but appreciate that "it is not 'cookie cutter Christianity'—you are forced to think outside your comfort zone and the 'box.' Professors stretch you and you have to really think about what you believe and why." This "community of thinkers, not regurgitators" pursues "stringent academics" in nursing, engineering, education, English, and religious studies. Students here also benefit from a "great study abroad program" that is "easily accessible, easy to pursue, and goes to so many countries!" The school also embodies "a strong concern for social justice and environmental issues" that manifests itself in service as well as "discussions of homelessness, poverty, and other injustices" across the campus. Best of all, "There are plenty of resources to help with homework (including tutoring), there are plenty of places to go to do homework, and there are state-of-the-art labs. Messiah has all a student needs."

Life

"Life is pretty laid back" at Messiah "since we live in a rural area," says one student. Most students here are "very outdoors-oriented: Frisbee, especially ultimate Frisbee, football, soccer, recreational sports, hiking, and rock climbing are popular." Men's and women's soccer games pull big crowds here. "Our men's soccer team won the National Championship for the past three years, and both the men and women usually make it to the Final Four," explains one student. Messiah works hard to bring entertainment to campus and over the past few years performers here have included Bob Dylan, Nickel Creek, Feist, Copeland, Regina Spektor, and Jars of Clay. No wonder "Messiah has been called 'the concert Mecca' of central Pennsylvania." But while some here assure us that "There are lots of places to hang out with other students to have fun" such as the new Student Union ("a great place to go with friends to get something to eat and to hang out") and the dorms ("People have fun by getting together to watch movies and play video games with friends."), some urban transplants tell us "this is a very hard adjustment to make. I'm in the boonies and I hate it."

Student Body

Students at Messiah tend to be "socially and environmentally aware or even active—they care about the school and local community, and they seek to be involved in service locally, nationally, and abroad." Most are "white Christians from the Northeast," but "there are also quite a few international students," and even, surprisingly, "a few atheists." As at many religious schools, Messiah offers "a not-very-welcoming environment for students of other sexual orientations. Rather than really confront these issues, they are typically glossed over or ignored." Words like "sheltered" and "naïve" pop up frequently in students' descriptions of their peers, but many report that "there's actually a lot of diversity in terms of how people grew up."

THE PRINCETON REVIEW SAYS

Admissions

Very important factors considered include: Class rank, academic GPA, recommendation(s), rigor of secondary school record, standardized test scores, character/personal qualities, extracurricular activities, religious affiliation/commitment, talent/ability. *Important factors considered include:* Application essay, volunteer work. *Other factors considered include:* Alumni/ae relation, interview, level of applicant's interest, racial/ethnic status, work experience. TOEFL required of all international applicants. High school diploma is required and GED is accepted. *Academic units required:* 4 English, 2 mathematics, 2 science, (2 science labs), 2 foreign language, 2 social studies, 4 academic electives. *Academic units recommended:* 4 English, 3 mathematics, 3 science, (3 science labs), 2 foreign language, 2 social studies, 2 history, 4 academic electives.

Financial Aid

Students should submit: FAFSA. The Princeton Review suggests that all financial aid forms be submitted as soon as possible after January 1. *Need-based scholarships/grants offered:* Federal Pell, SEOG, state scholarships/grants, private scholarships, the school's own gift aid. *Loan aid offered:* Direct Subsidized Stafford, Direct Unsubsidized Stafford, Direct PLUS, Federal Perkins, Federal Nursing Applicants will be notified of awards on a rolling basis beginning 3/15. Federal Work-Study Program available. Institutional employment available. Off-campus job opportunities are good.

The Inside Word

Don't test well? If you're in the top 20 percent of your high school graduating class, you can opt to submit a graded writing sample in place of your standardized test scores. And good news for those schooled outside of school: Messiah is "homeschool friendly," with over 150 students who were homeschooled during their senior year (and many more who were homeschooled at some point in their education).

THE SCHOOL SAYS ". . ."

From The Admissions Office

"Messiah College is a place where education involves a student's intellect, character, and Christian faith. Students receive a superb higher education and also discover a higher calling as they prepare for lives of service, leadership, and reconciliation.

"As a community of learners, Messiah gives academics a high priority. More than 2,900 students from 39 states and 28 countries receive a thorough liberal arts foundation and pursue their choice of more than 50 liberal or applied majors.

"Messiah students learn in many settings. Whether they are involved in student government, a national championship–quality athletic team, or a community-service project, students apply what they have learned. Co-curricular activities and organizations provide a laboratory for testing values and convictions. These opportunities for character development at Messiah are as diverse as the students who bring their gifts and abilities. The 20 intercollegiate athletic teams, academic clubs, student publications, the radio station, music and theater ensembles, and leadership development programs are just a few of the opportunities available.

"For the person of faith, rigorous intellectual study demands a similar response from the heart. Messiah College faculty and administration mentor students toward spiritual maturity. Students explore their faith while asking the difficult questions of life.

"Interested students should visit during their sophomore or junior year of high school either individually or during one of the various open house events. Applications for admission are considered on a rolling basis."

For even more information on this school, turn to page 493 of the "Stats" section.

MIDDLEBURY COLLEGE

THE EMMA WILLARD HOUSE, MIDDLEBURY, VT 05753 • ADMISSIONS: 802-443-3000 • FAX: 802-443-2056
FINANCIAL AID: 802-443-5158 • E-MAIL: ADMISSIONS@MIDDLEBURY.EDU • WEBSITE: WWW.MIDDLEBURY.EDU

RATINGS
Quality of Life: 98   **Academic:** 98   **Admissions:** 99   **Financial Aid:** 93

STUDENTS SAY "..."

Academics

Home to "smart people who enjoy Aristotelian ethics and quantum physics, but aren't too stuck up to go sledding in front of Mead Chapel at midnight," Middlebury College is a small, exclusive liberal arts school with "excellent foreign language programs" as well as standout offerings in

> **SURVEY SAYS . . .**
> *Small classes*
> *Lab facilities are great*
> *Athletic facilities are great*

environmental studies, the sciences, theater, and writing. Distribution requirements and other general requirements ensure that a Middlebury education "is all about providing students with a complete college experience including excellent teaching, exposure to many other cultures, endless opportunities for growth and success, and a challenging (yet relaxed) environment." Its "small class size and friendly yet competitive atmosphere make for the perfect college experience," as do "the best facilities of a small liberal arts college in the country. The new library, science center, athletic complex, arts center, and a number of the dining halls and dorms have been built in the past 10 years." Expect to work hard here; "It's tough, but this is a mini-Ivy, so what should one expect? There is plenty of time to socialize, and due to the collaborative atmosphere here, studying and socializing can often come hand in hand. The goal of many students here is not to get high grades" but rather "learning in its purest form, and that is perhaps this college's most brightly shining aspect." The collaborative atmosphere is abetted by the fact that "Admissions doesn't just bring in geniuses, they bring in people who are leaders and community servants. Think of the guy or girl in your high school whom everybody describes as 'so nice' . . . that's your typical Middlebury student."

Life

"This high level of involvement in everything translates into an amazing campus atmosphere" at Middlebury, where "Most people are very involved. There is a club for just about everything you can imagine, and if you can imagine one that hasn't yet been created, you go ahead and create it yourself." With great skiing and outdoor activity close by, "Almost everyone is athletic in some way. This can translate into anything from varsity sports to intramural hockey (an extremely popular winter pastime!). People are enthusiastic about being active and having fun." Because the school "is set in a very small town, there aren't too many (if any) problems with violence, drugs, [or] crime. It's the ideal college town because of its rural setting, in that there are no real distractions other than those that are provided within the college campus." Of course, the small-town setting also means that "the only real off-campus activity is going out to eat at the town's quaint restaurants or going to the one bar in town," but fortunately "When it comes to on-campus activities, Middlebury provides the student population with tons of great events. Everything from classy music concerts to late-night movies and dance parties can be found as a Midd-supported activity. The student activity board does a fabulous job with entertaining the students virtually every day."

Student Body

"The typical [Middlebury] student is athletic, outdoorsy, and very intelligent." The two most prominent demographics are "very preppy students (popped collars)" and "extreme hippies." One undergrad explains: "The typical students are one of two types: either 'Polo, Nantucket red, pearls, and summers on the Cape,' or 'Birks, wool socks, granola, and suspicious smells about them.' A lot of people break these two molds, but they often fall somewhere on the spectrum between them." There's also "a huge international student population, which is awesome," but some international students, "tend to separate out and end up living in language houses." There's also "a really strong theater/artsy community" here. One student notes, "Other than a few groups, everyone mingles pretty well. We're all too damn friendly and cheerful for our own good."

THE PRINCETON REVIEW SAYS

Admissions

Very important factors considered include: Class rank, academic GPA, rigor of secondary school record, character/personal qualities, extracurricular activities, talent/ability. *Important factors considered include:* Application essay, recommendation(s), standardized test scores, racial/ethnic status. *Other factors considered include:* Alumni/ae relation, first generation, geographical residence, level of applicant's interest, volunteer work, work experience. SAT and SAT Subject Tests or ACT required; High school diploma or equivalent is not required. *Academic units recommended:* 4 English, 4 mathematics, 3 science, (3 science labs), 4 foreign language, 3 social studies, 2 history, 1 academic elective, 1 Fine Arts, Music, or Drama courses recommended.

Financial Aid

Students should submit: FAFSA, CSS/Financial Aid PROFILE, state aid form, noncustodial PROFILE, business/farm supplement. Regular filing deadline is 1/1. The Princeton Review suggests that all financial aid forms be submitted as soon as possible after January 1. *Need-based scholarships/grants offered:* Federal Pell, SEOG, state scholarships/grants, private scholarships, the school's own gift aid. *Loan aid offered:* Direct Subsidized Stafford, Direct Unsubsidized Stafford, Direct PLUS, Federal Perkins, college/university loans from institutional funds. Applicants will be notified of awards on or about 4/1.

The Inside Word

Middlebury gives you options in standardized testing. The school will accept either the SAT or the ACT or three SAT Subject Tests, (the three must be in different subject areas, however). Middlebury is extremely competitive; improve your chances of admission by crafting a standardized test profile that shows you in the best possible light.

THE SCHOOL SAYS ". . ."

From The Admissions Office

"The successful Middlebury candidate excels in a variety of areas including academics, athletics, the arts, leadership, and service to others. These strengths and interests permit students to grow beyond their traditional 'comfort zones' and conventional limits. Our classrooms are as varied as the Green Mountains, the Metropolitan Museum of Art, or the great cities of Russia and Japan. Outside the classroom, students informally interact with professors in activities such as intramural basketball games and community service. At Middlebury, students develop critical-thinking skills, enduring bonds of friendship, and the ability to challenge themselves.

"Middlebury offers majors and programs in 45 different fields, with particular strengths in languages, international studies, environmental studies, literature and creative writing, and the sciences. Opportunities for engaging in individual research with faculty abound at Middlebury.

"Applicants must submit standardized test results in at least three different areas of study. This requirement may be met by any one of the following three options: the ACT (optional Writing Test recommended, but not required), the new SAT, or three tests in different subject areas from the SAT Subject Tests, Advanced Placement, or International Baccalaureate exams."

For even more information on this school, turn to page 493 of the "Stats" section.

MISERICORDIA UNIVERSITY

301 LAKE STREET, DALLAS, PA 18612 • ADMISSIONS: 570-674-6264 • FAX: 570-675-2441
E-MAIL: ADMISS@MISERICORDIA.EDU • WEBSITE: WWW.MISERICORDIA.EDU

RATINGS
Quality of Life: 81   Academic: 81   Admissions: 77   Financial Aid: 77

STUDENTS SAY ". . ."

Academics

SURVEY SAYS . . .
Large classes
Students get along with local community
Campus feels safe
Frats and sororities are unpopular or nonexistent

Misericordia University, a small Roman Catholic school founded by the Sisters of Mercy, "provides a solid education for the outside world while giving excellent opportunities for service." The influence of the Sisters of Mercy is seen in the way that the "Students really do perform a lot of community service," which the school "encourages." Students are also "serious about their studies," as the academics are "very high-level, and all the instructors help you to think above and beyond what is in the books." MU "has very good health major programs" and students in those programs "are known to have great graduation rates" and good prospects for "jobs after graduation." Physical therapy and occupational therapy, in particular, are standout programs. MU also "has a great reputation [in] the field of education" and "the best communications department in the area." A small student body translates into a "personal" experience in which "Teachers are always available for students" and "are always willing to help you out in and out of the classroom." One undergrad sums it up: "It's been hard work, but I know I'm getting a good education and a reputable degree."

Life

Life at Misericordia "is pretty good," though somewhat sparsely populated on the weekends when "the majority of students go home." Low attendance, however, doesn't translate to a lack of activity. Students tell us there's "always something taking place on campus. Student Activities brings in musicians, comedians, bands, and game shows for students." During the week, "RAs plan different programs." MU sporting events are well supported, as are intramurals; "Almost 75 percent of students participate in sports and the other 25 percent did in high school." Community service, strongly encouraged by the school, is also popular. Hometown Dallas "is not exactly thrilling," but "Wilkes-Barre is 15 minutes away and is a huge city. There are clubs, bars, bowling alleys, movie theaters . . . and tons of places to eat. If people put forth the effort, they can find something to do and have fun." Students also enjoy "a lot of outdoor activities, such as shooting skeet" and skiing and sledding in the winter. To indulge in the weekend party scene "Most students either go to a townhouse or lake house."

Student Body

The typical Misericordia undergraduate is White, middle-class, involved in sports, and "in some health-related major." Most come "from small rural towns." While MU is "a Catholic college," undergrads point out that "a lot of students [who] attend are not Catholic." Those here tend to be "overachiever[s]," people who were "very involved in high school and often continue [to be]" in college through the school's "many clubs to get involved in, from service and academia to social clubs like anime." The small campus means that the students tend to know each other "not just by face but by name, and they all seem to get along with each other." Luckily, familiarity doesn't breed contempt—most students "are very nice and sociable" and "everyone accepts everyone." Women outnumber men here by a ratio of nearly 3:1.

THE PRINCETON REVIEW SAYS

Admissions

Very important factors considered include: Academic GPA, rigor of secondary school record. *Important factors considered include:* Class rank, standardized test scores, character/personal qualities, volunteer work. *Other factors considered include:* Application essay, recommendation(s), extracurricular activities, interview, racial/ethnic status, work experience. SAT or ACT required; TOEFL required of all international applicants. High school diploma is required and GED is accepted. *Academic units required:* 4 English, 4 mathematics, 4 science, 4 social studies.

Financial Aid

Students should submit: FAFSA, institution's own financial aid form. Regular filing deadline is 5/1. The Princeton Review suggests that all financial aid forms be submitted as soon as possible after January 1. *Need-based scholarships/grants offered:* Federal Pell, SEOG, state scholarships/grants, private scholarships, the school's own gift aid, Federal Nursing Scholarships. *Loan aid offered:* FFEL Subsidized Stafford, FFEL Unsubsidized Stafford, FFEL PLUS, Federal Perkins, Federal Nursing, state loans applicants will be notified of awards on a rolling basis beginning 3/15. Federal Work-Study Program available. Institutional employment available. Off-campus job opportunities are good.

The Inside Word

Misericordia has a rolling admissions policy, so it's first come, first served. Because the school considers the intended field of study when making admit decisions, popular departments can fill quickly. If you're considering one, it's a good idea to apply as early as possible. Scheduling an interview and taking a tour of the campus are two great ways to signal your serious interest in attending, and it could help your cause.

THE SCHOOL SAYS " . . . "

From The Admissions Office

"From your first day of classes until you graduate, you'll know what Misericordia expects from you—nothing but the best. When you graduate, you'll be prepared to excel in your career, lead others, and serve the community both professionally and personally. Although we're at a record level for undergraduate enrollment, classes are still kept small, often with as few as 10 students in advanced areas. Overall, the student/faculty ratio is 12:1, ensuring personalized attention. Students choose from 30 majors in three colleges. Some of the majors in high-demand careers include nursing, physical therapy, occupational therapy, biology (premed and pre-vet), and speech-language pathology as well as education and sport management.

"We know you'll be challenged here; but at CM, you'll also find a supportive environment, one of the best in the nation. The National Survey of Student Engagement (NSSE) shows that our students perform better academically and are more satisfied. In fact, 91 percent of our freshmen found their overall experience to be good or excellent, so we know you'll feel right at home.

"At Misericordia, education also means socialization. We believe that there is life outside of the classroom and that those experiences are an integral part of a college education. MU has two-dozen clubs and social organizations. The Student Government Association sponsors a multitude of activities throughout the year, focused on student fun and involvement. As a Division III school, Misericordia competes in the Middle Atlantic Corporation (MAC) Freedom Conference. We currently have 20 men's and women's varsity sports."

For even more information on this school, turn to page 494 of the "Stats" section.

MONMOUTH UNIVERSITY

ADMISSION, MONMOUTH UNIVERSITY, 400 CEDAR AVENUE, WEST LONG BRANCH, NJ 07764-1898
ADMISSIONS: 732-571-3456 • FAX: 732-263-5166 • E-MAIL: ADMISSION@MONMOUTH.EDU • WEBSITE: WWW.MONMOUTH.EDU

RATINGS
Quality of Life: 76   **Academic:** 73   **Admissions:** 78   **Financial Aid:** 71

STUDENTS SAY "..."

Academics

Monmouth University is "not a large university, but not a tiny one," the sort of place where you "can hang out with friends one day and meet a whole new crowd the next." It's big enough to qualify as "a diverse school with good academics, recognized extracurriculars, and impressive athletics," yet small enough that "students really get to build great academic relationships with their professors and get

> **SURVEY SAYS . . .**
> *Large classes*
> *Great computer facilities*
> *Great library*
> *Campus feels safe*
> *Lots of beer drinking*

the attention and education that they need and deserve." Standout departments include communications, business (where most of the professors "have worked for companies prior to teaching so they have a lot of insight"), education, music, criminal justice, and premedical sciences. In all disciplines students must complete "an internship program—what we call the experiential education requirement—that really sets up students for life after college. Many of the students get hired by the people for whom they intern." If there's a drawback here, it's that the student body carries too much dead weight, too many students who "have no interest" in anything but the nearby beach and thus threaten to transform the school into "a post-high school country club." However, "for a student willing to commit himself, Monmouth is a great school. At the same time, it is easy for a student to get by doing marginal work. Basically you get out of it what you put into it."

Life

Life at Monmouth University "is a totally unique experience for each person. Some people go home every weekend and hate it; others choose to get involved and love it. Personally, I chose the latter choice and couldn't be happier about it." One student reports, "when I'm not endlessly slaving away over my senior thesis, you can find me (or any student my age, really) spending time on the beach, shopping, enjoying my wonderful apartment in Pier Village, or frequenting any one of the local bars." The party scene is not what it once was here; one student reports that "Monmouth somehow still has the reputation as a 'party school,' which was true around ten years ago, but not anymore." Students warn, "The MU police are extremely strict about alcohol consumption. Most parties on campus are busted by RAs or the police." As a result, "off-campus parties are popular. Not a lot of people go home on the weekends, but a good number go to different schools around here." Alternatively, "there is lots of nightlife around the area: Long Branch, Seaside Park, Sayreville, Red Bank, Belmar, etc. Lots of dance clubs allow girls 18 and over in with a small cover charge on select days of the week." Finally, "students often take weekend trips into the city (either New York or Philadelphia) by train or by car" when they want to get off campus.

Students

There's a lot of conspicuous wealth at Monmouth in the form of "various expensive cars in the parking lots" and "designer clothes and bags." "Vera Bradley is almost a necessity—it is even sold in the book store." Students are typically "very trendy," and "extremely image-conscious," and "beautiful and very materialistic." Students "are very in tune with the latest fashion and technology trends." They tend to come from "New Jersey, Pennsylvania, Staten Island, or Long Island, New York. We are all from the suburbs and probably have the same family income." Monmouth's proximity to the beach attracts "many skaters and surfers" as well as "a lot of relaxed people." With three women to every two men, "the male-female ratio totally works out in the guy's favor."

THE PRINCETON REVIEW SAYS

Admissions

Very important factors considered include: Academic GPA, rigor of secondary school record, standardized test scores, extracurricular activities, volunteer work, work experience. *Other factors considered include:* Application essay, recommendation(s), alumni/ae relation, SAT or ACT required; ACT with Writing component required. TOEFL required of all international applicants. High school diploma is required and GED is accepted. *Academic units required:* 4 English, 3 mathematics, 2 science, (1 science labs), 2 history, 5 academic electives. *Academic units recommended:* 2 foreign language, 2 social studies.

Financial Aid

Students should submit: FAFSA Regular filing deadline is 6/30. The Princeton Review suggests that all financial aid forms be submitted as soon as possible after January 1. *Need-based scholarships/grants offered:* Federal Pell, SEOG, state scholarships/grants, private scholarships, the school's own gift aid, Federal Nursing Scholarships. *Loan aid offered:* Direct Subsidized Stafford, Direct Unsubsidized Stafford, Direct PLUS, FFEL PLUS, Federal Perkins, state loans, college/university loans from institutional funds, Alternative Loans. Applicants will be notified of awards on a rolling basis beginning 2/1. Off-campus job opportunities are good.

Inside Word

"B" students with slightly above average SAT or ACT scores should find little impediment to gaining admission to Monmouth. The school's national stature is on the rise, resulting in a more competitive applicant base, but Monmouth must still compete with many heavy hitters for top regional students.

THE SCHOOL SAYS "..."

From The Admissions Office

"Monmouth University offers a well-rounded but bold academic environment with plenty of opportunities—personal, professional, and social. Monmouth graduates are poised for success and prepared to assume leadership roles in their chosen professions, because the university invests in students beyond the classroom.

"Monmouth emphasizes hands-on learning, while providing exceptional undergraduate and graduate degree programs. There are programs for medical scholars, honors students, marine scientists, software engineers, teachers, musicians, broadcast producers, and more. Faculty members are lively participants in the education of their students. These teacher/scholars, dedicated to excellence, are often recognized experts in their fields. Students may be in a class with no more than 35 students (half of Monmouth's classes have fewer than 21 students) learning from qualified professors who know each student by name.

"Monmouth recognizes its students are the energy of its campus. The Monmouth community celebrates student life with cultural events, festivals, active student clubs, and organizations that reflect its school spirit. Athletics play a big part in campus life. A well-established member of the NCAA Division I, Monmouth athletics is a rising tide supported by some of the best fans in the Northeast.

"The president of Monmouth University, Paul G. Gaffney II, believes the reputation of the university starts with the achievements and successes of its students. At Monmouth, students find the support and guidance needed to make their mark in the world."

For even more information on this school, turn to page 494 of the "Stats" section.

MOORE COLLEGE OF ART & DESIGN

TWENTIETH STREET AND THE PARKWAY, PHILADELPHIA, PA 19103-1179 • ADMISSIONS: 215-965-4014 • FAX: 215-568-3547
E-MAIL: ADMISS@MOORE.EDU • WEBSITE: WWW.MOORE.EDU

RATINGS
Quality of Life: 73   **Academic:** 86   **Admissions:** 60*   **Financial Aid:** 63

STUDENTS SAY "..."

Academics

"Moore is all about giving women in the arts the technical skill and empowerment to lead and succeed in their professional careers," students here say. "The small size of the school" and "the all-women experience" are a big draw, as are "great employment opportunities through the very active career center." While some students say that "academic teachers" "can be hit-or-miss," students almost unanimously agree that their "studio teachers are out of this world." These "real artists" facilitate "hands-on learning," and "go out of their way to write recommendations [and] help find jobs" and "are truly there because they love to teach and enjoy their students." Students warn, however, "The work is hard and if you don't keep up, it's even harder to pull yourself out of the hole." Opinion of the administration is, at best, mixed: "We need a better food service, more studios, nicer classrooms, and tons more, but the administration chooses to ignore it," a piqued sophomore declares. A more even-handed student avers: "Sometimes the administration does not seem to be looking at the student body's best interests; however, when it comes to individual problems or concerns, they are usually very helpful."

> **SURVEY SAYS . . .**
> *Large classes*
> *Students love Philadelphia, PA*
> *Intercollegiate sports are unpopular or nonexistent*
> *Intramural sports are unpopular or nonexistent*
> *Frats and sororities are unpopular or nonexistent*
> *Theater is popular*

Life

"Don't plan on having much of a life during the school year," Moore students warn. Schoolwork looms large in their lives to the point that one has "nightmares about school and unfinished projects." Less-stressed students take a more organic view of their course load: "The work is diverse and challenging," a 3-D design major writes. "Every day I am opening up my creative self and finding out where it is I want to be in the art world." When students don't have homework, which, they caution, is only "10 percent of the time," they "do lots of things: Go out and drink, go to open galleries, go to parties, draw on sidewalks with chalk, and just hang out." There are also "plenty of leisure activities organized by the administration or other students, such as movie nights, relaxation therapy nights (usually toward finals time), trips out and around the Philadelphia area, [and] shopping trips."

Student Body

"The group of women that make up Moore's student body is so diverse for such a small community that I could never pinpoint a stereotypical Moore girl," a sophomore writes. "Each girl is very unique in personality and creativity." Students tell us that there are "many different cultures and sexual orientations represented" on campus. While some say that "you can tell the design students from the art students"—"Most art students dress down to go to class and are ready to get dirty and work into their art," while "The design students usually dress up to go to class and are a bit more trendy and appearance-conscious"—students across the board agree that "it's an art school: We are all atypical." What's the quality that binds Moore students? "They are up for the challenge," a senior writes. A freshman adds: "We are all a little wacky, especially around final[s] and big project times."

THE PRINCETON REVIEW SAYS

Admissions

Very important factors considered include: Academic GPA, rigor of secondary school record, standardized test scores, character/personal qualities, interview, level of applicant's interest, talent/ability. *Important factors considered include:* Application essay, recommendation(s), extracurricular activities. *Other factors considered include:* Class rank, volunteer work, work experience. SAT recommended; SAT or ACT required; TOEFL required of all international applicants. High school diploma is required and GED is accepted.

Financial Aid

Students should submit: FAFSA. The Princeton Review suggests that all financial aid forms be submitted as soon as possible after January 1. *Need-based scholarships/grants offered:* Federal Pell, SEOG, state scholarships/grants, private scholarships, the school's own gift aid, SMART, ACG. *Loan aid offered:* FFEL Subsidized Stafford, FFEL Unsubsidized Stafford, FFEL PLUS, Federal Perkins, Alternative loans. Applicants will be notified of awards on a rolling basis beginning 2/15. Federal Work-Study Program available. Off-campus job opportunities are good.

The Inside Word

In lieu of submitting a traditional portfolio with their application, Moore applicants may attend the school's Summer Art and Design Institute (SADI), a 4-week program in portfolio development and basic art skills, upon completion of their junior or senior year of high school. Applicants who wish to be considered for SADI must submit a sample of their artwork and a written request to the school's Director of Admissions.

THE SCHOOL SAYS "..."

From The Admissions Office

"Moore College of Art & Design offers 10 arts and design majors leading to a Bachelor of Fine Arts degree. Choose to major in textile design, fashion design, fine arts (with a 2D or 3D emphasis), graphic design, illustration, art education, art history, interior design, curatorial studies and photography and digital arts.

"Each BFA program is designed to nurture students' creative talents and give them the hands-on technical and professional skills essential to building a successful career in fine arts, design, art history, and art education.

"Learn from award-winning, professionally active faculty who bring real-world knowledge and expertise into the classroom, and encourage excellence, exploration, and self-expression. Problem solving, critical thinking, self-confidence, risk taking and creativity all are stressed throughout the BFA curriculum, with the goal of preparing students for lifelong learning and leadership in their chosen field.

"We encourage you to call our Admissions Office. We are all very excited to hear from you and to assist you throughout the admissions process. Admissions Counselors are available to speak with you during regular business hours. We invite you to come visit our campus to experience firsthand the uniqueness of an education at Moore College of Art & Design, which is the best way to find out if it is the right place for you."

For even more information on this school, turn to page 495 of the "Stats" section.

MORAVIAN COLLEGE

1200 Main St., Bethlehem, PA 18018 • Admissions: 800-441-3191 • Fax: 610-625-7930
Financial Aid: 610-861-1330 • E-mail: admissions@moravian.edu • Website: www.moravian.edu

RATINGS
Quality of Life: 83   **Academic:** 84   **Admissions:** 79   **Financial Aid:** 75

STUDENTS SAY "..."

Academics

For those students seeking a place where "everybody knows your name," take a look at Moravian College, a tiny school in eastern Pennsylvania that offers the "liberal arts experience," using a "well-rounded education to mold a well-rounded individual." This "outwardly modest institution" disguises a solid academic environment that is "more

> **SURVEY SAYS . . .**
> *Large classes*
> *Great library*
> *Low cost of living*
> *Lots of beer drinking*

geared toward learning rather than just getting good grades on tests," which, combined with the cozy community feel of the surroundings, provides the "perfect peaceful atmosphere for studying and socializing." One student, commenting on the school's relatively low weekend retention rate, describes the school as "Camp Moravian—a lot of people may go home, but those who stay behind have a lot more fun."

For the most part, Moravian's "fairly forgiving" professors "are engaging and provide students with challenging questions concerning the real world." Their availability and willingness to help students understand the material gets praise all around, as does their demeanor; more than one student tells of being invited into a teacher's home for dinner. "Students are able to get the individual attention they need," says one. However, this doesn't mean that there aren't a few points that need to be worked on: "All of my professors are intelligent, but not all of them are meant to be teachers," says one freshman. A few students express some discontent with the administration's level of involvement, but the "college president is a regular fixture on campus" and "can be seen eating in the student café or sitting on a bench outside the academic building." Though most find the registration process "archaic," the academic advising system helps keep students on track in their course selection.

Life

With such a small undergrad enrollment, students get to know each other's business pretty easily and quickly, and most see this as a positive thing, listing "the chance for strong relationships" as one of the school's greatest strengths. Hanging out with friends, video games, and cards seems to be a pretty big part of relaxing at Moravian, and "there are a lot of different groups and clubs on campus that also plan activities for the rest of the student body to be part of." Almost everything necessary to amuse oneself in this "safe and nurturing environment" is "within walking distance," making it easy to go check out the events offered by the school, such as "movies every week and comedians a few times a semester," and Moravian runs Friday mall trips for those needing other supplies. The soccer field and basketball arena are located in the center of the campus "which makes it easy to attend the home games," and the school has such a wonderful music program that "the recitals are worth checking out, even if you're not a music major." A Greek scene is present on campus but not in an overwhelming way, so that "if you are looking for a party, you can find one. If you are not into the party scene, that's fine."

Student Body

"I'm not going to lie, Moravian's a very white school," confesses a student. Most of the students are from "Pennsylvania, New Jersey, or New York" and come from middle to upper-class homes, though "not many people question the economic situations of others." There is, at least, some diversity at Moravian (the "Multicultural Club is one of the best clubs on campus"), and the students that make up this "close knit community" are a "very open group of people" in how they relate to atypical students. Since there is a separate campus devoted to art and music, there tends to be a fair number of "artsy" students on the South campus to balance out the healthy portion of student athletes that populate mainly the North campus.

Admissions

Very important factors considered include: Class rank, academic GPA, rigor of secondary school record, alumni/ae relation, character/personal qualities. *Important factors considered include:* Application essay, recommendation(s), standardized test scores, extracurricular activities, first generation, level of applicant's interest, racial/ethnic status, talent/ability, volunteer work. *Other factors considered include:* Geographical residence, interview, work experience. SAT or ACT required; ACT with Writing component required. TOEFL required of all international applicants. High school diploma is required and GED is accepted. *Academic units required:* 4 English, 3 mathematics, 3 science, (2 science labs), 2 foreign language, 4 social studies. *Academic units recommended:* 4 mathematics, 3 foreign language.

Financial Aid

Students should submit: FAFSA, CSS/Financial Aid PROFILE, noncustodial PROFILE, business/farm supplement, copies of parent and student W2s and 1040s. Regular filing deadline is 3/15. The Princeton Review suggests that all financial aid forms be submitted as soon as possible after January 1. *Need-based scholarships/grants offered:* Federal Pell, SEOG, state scholarships/grants, the school's own gift aid. *Loan aid offered:* FFEL Subsidized Stafford, FFEL Unsubsidized Stafford, FFEL PLUS, Federal Perkins Applicants will be notified of awards on a rolling basis beginning 4/1.

The Inside Word

Moravian is a small liberal arts school with all the bells and whistles. Applicants will find a pretty straightforward admissions process—solid grades and test scores are required. Counselors will look closely to find the extras—community service, extracurricular activities—that make students stand out from the crowd. Moravian has many programs that should not be overlooked, including music, education, and the sciences.

THE SCHOOL SAYS "..."

From The Admissions Office

"Founded in 1742, Moravian is proud of its history as one of the oldest and most respected liberal arts colleges. Students find a supportive environment for self-discovery and academic achievement that nurtures their capacity for leadership, lifelong learning, and positive societal contributions. Moravian enrolls students from a variety of socioeconomic, religious, racial, and ethnic backgrounds. Providing a highly personalized learning experience, the College offers opportunities for students to direct their education toward individual and professional goals. Students are encouraged to collaborate with faculty on original research, pursue honors projects, independent work, internships, and field study. Moravian recently produced 7 Fulbright scholars, a Goldwater scholar, a Rhodes finalist, a Truman Scholarship finalist, and 3 NCAA postgraduate scholars.

"Facilities range from historic to modern, with a $20 million academic complex featuring current educational technology, at the heart of the Main Street Campus. The College is in the process of building a new residence hall on its historic Hurd Campus. The $25 million project will house approximately 230 students, contain classrooms, and other learning spaces that support the academic and co-curricular mission of the College. The Leadership Center fosters student leadership qualities and skills. Moravian encourages the complete college experience for mind, body, and spirit. Its robust varsity sports program, from football to lacrosse, has produced nationally ranked women's softball and track teams, and All-American student athletes—including several Olympic hopefuls—in many sports. Athletes complete on a state-of-the-art synthetic multi-sport field and the eight-lane Olympic track."

For even more information on this school, turn to page 496 of the "Stats" section.

MOUNT HOLYOKE COLLEGE

50 COLLEGE STREET, SOUTH HADLEY, MA 01075 • ADMISSIONS: 413-538-2023 • FAX: 413-538-2409
FINANCIAL AID: 413-538-2291 • E-MAIL: ADMISSIONS@MTHOLYOKE.EDU • WEBSITE: WWW.MTHOLYOKE.EDU

RATINGS
Quality of Life: 90   **Academic:** 94   **Admissions:** 95   **Financial Aid:** 97

STUDENTS SAY ". . ."

Academics

Mount Holyoke "is a rigorous all women's college that prepares its students to become the leaders of tomorrow by
encouraging them to pursue their passions in a safe, comfortable and yet challenging environment," undergrads at
this small, prestigious liberal arts school tell us. Biology,
chemistry, the humanities, and international studies are
among the strong suits of the school; in nearly all disciplines, professors "are highly respected in their fields, many
of them being very prominent figures among their respective

> **SURVEY SAYS . . .**
> Small classes
> Lab facilities are great
> Great library
> Diverse student types on campus
> Campus feels safe
> Frats and sororities are unpopular
> or nonexistent

academic communities" who are also "very kind, excited to impart their knowledge, and very, very accessible
outside of class and willing to spend a lot of time helping individual students." They aren't pushovers, though;
"Despite their overall generosity, they hold every student to a very high academic standard (no grade inflation
here), and the material covered in each course is always challenging and of high academic caliber." Students may
supplement their curricula with classes at other area colleges through the Five College Consortium, but they do
say that the consortium is "very underused."

Life

"People are very focused on their academics, sometimes too much so" at Mount Holyoke, and "Much of our
time is dedicated to class work." Undergrads typically find time for the "fabulous traditions that help to define"
school life, such as "Milk and cookies in the evening (a snack put out by dining services at 9:30 on school nights)
and class colors and mascots." Otherwise, "Mount Holyoke life is what you make of it. We are an all women's
college, but that doesn't mean you are going off to a convent. It is easy to have a social life through the Five
College Consortium, and it is easy to go into Boston or New York." Also, "people are active in clubs and sports,
and they hang out in the common areas or on the green with friends," and "there are many on-campus events,
such as speakers, movie screenings, etc. to keep anyone busy." The campus itself "is so beautiful…between the
foliage, the classic brick buildings and the well kept landscape of the college, I was in love!" Off-campus life
offers "movie theaters and restaurants, as well as parties at the other four colleges." Hometown South Hadley
"is admittedly not the most happening town ever (to put it mildly)," but Amherst and Northhampton—which
are "great for eating, shopping, and anything else imaginable"—"are only a free bus ride away."

Student Body

The Mount Holyoke student body "is extremely diverse, from ethnicity to race to religion to sexual orientation
to individual interests. However, the community works as a whole because of the common interest in academics and openness of the students who attend." If there is a "typical" student, it's one who "is female and academically motivated," undergrads tell us. Students are also typically "very aware of world issues, politically
active, and open-minded," "very concerned about grades and jobs," and, perhaps, "overly politically correct."
Among the subpopulations that stand out, "The most visible opposites are the 'pearls and cardigans,' the
'Carhartts and piercings' types, and the hippies. There are a ton of people, however, who are somewhere in
between those."

THE PRINCETON REVIEW SAYS

Admissions

Very important factors considered include: Class rank, application essay, academic GPA, recommendation(s), rigor of secondary school record. *Important factors considered include:* Character/personal qualities, extracurricular activities, first generation, interview, talent/ability, volunteer work, work experience. *Other factors considered include:* Standardized test scores, alumni/ae relation, geographical residence, level of applicant's interest, racial/ethnic status, TOEFL required of all international applicants. High school diploma is required and GED is accepted. *Academic units recommended:* 4 English, 3 mathematics, 3 science, (3 science labs), 3 foreign language, 3 history, 1 academic elective.

Financial Aid

Students should submit: FAFSA, CSS/Financial Aid PROFILE, noncustodial PROFILE, business/farm supplement, Federal Tax Returns. Regular filing deadline is 3/1. The Princeton Review suggests that all financial aid forms be submitted as soon as possible after January 1. *Need-based scholarships/grants offered:* Federal Pell, SEOG, state scholarships/grants, private scholarships, the school's own gift aid. *Loan aid offered:* Direct Subsidized Stafford, Direct Unsubsidized Stafford, Direct PLUS, Federal Perkins, college/university loans from institutional funds. Applicants will be notified of awards on or about 4/1. Federal Work-Study Program available. Institutional employment available. Off-campus job opportunities are fair.

The Inside Word

Mount Holyoke has seen a 25 percent increase in the size of its applicant pool since the beginning of the decade, allowing what was already a selective institution to become a highly selective one. Matchmaking is a significant factor here; strong academic performance, well-written essays, and an understanding of and appreciation for "the Mount Holyoke experience" will usually carry the day.

THE SCHOOL SAYS ". . ."

From The Admissions Office

"The majority of students who choose Mount Holyoke do so simply because it is an outstanding liberal arts college. After a semester or two, they start to appreciate the fact that Mount Holyoke is a women's college, even though most Mount Holyoke students never thought they'd go to a women's college when they started their college search. Students talk of having 'space' to really figure out who they are. They speak about feeling empowered to excel in traditionally male subjects such as science and technology. They talk about the remarkable array of opportunities—for academic achievement, career exploration, and leadership—and the impressive, creative accomplishments of their peers. If you're looking for a college that will challenge you to be your best, most powerful self and to fulfill potential, Mount Holyoke should be at the top of your list.

"Submission of standardized test scores is optional for most applicants to Mount Holyoke College. However, the TOEFL is required of students for whom English is not their primary language, and the SAT Subject Tests are required for homeschooled students."

For even more information on this school, turn to page 496 of the "Stats" section.

MUHLENBERG COLLEGE

2400 West Chew Street, Allentown, PA 18104-5596 • Admissions: 484-664-3200 • Fax: 484-664-3234
Financial Aid: 484-664-3175 • E-mail: admission@muhlenberg.edu • Website: www.muhlenberg.edu

RATINGS
Quality of Life: 72   Academic: 87   Admissions: 94   Financial Aid: 93

STUDENTS SAY ". . ."

Academics

Muhlenberg bills itself as "the college that cares," and for many students, it more than lives up to that designation. "The small community and small, personal class sizes" allow "professors [to] become friends, mentors, and role models" to students. "They love what they do, they love students, and they love interacting with the students." In addition, professors are "always very approachable. I've become close with many professors and frequently chat with

them outside of class. Professors are often on campus with their families, and some hold parties at their houses at the end of the year." But professors aren't just friendly faces; "They are [also] very knowledgeable in their fields" and "challenge students to achieve more than they thought they were capable of." In addition to excellent professors, the school's size also provides students with numerous "research opportunities." Muhlenberg students "write a lot" because of the individual attention made possible in the "small, discussion-based classes." Among many quality majors, the Premedical, Pre-Law, Education, and Political Science Departments get rave reviews, and students note that "the theater and dance programs are extremely well regarded," as well.

Life

Some students claim that hometown Allentown "is not a vibrant place, and prospective students should be aware of this," while others point to the "two bars, an excellent deli, a famous movie and art theater, as well as restaurants and all the normal everyday places that a student needs" within walking distance of the campus. As far as partying goes, "If you are looking for a school with 15 parties to choose from every night of the week, then stop reading about Muhlenberg right now." The "school does have Greek life, but the administration is cracking down on [fraternities and sororities] more and more," largely through "a very strict alcohol and drug policy." As a result, "People go to house parties [off-campus] or the bars." Besides parties, "There is a pretty decent mall nearby and good restaurants." On campus "There are always school-sponsored events going on: bands, movies, magicians, comedians, the works," although many claim that "students don't generally participate in the on-campus activities." Particularly popular are the school's "community-service programs," which "work very well with Allentown," challenging students to carry the school's reputation for "caring" to their fellow citizens beyond the campus gates. To get away from the Muhlenberg scene altogether for some fresh experiences, "It's not too long a drive to Philadelphia." "Also, there are several other colleges in the area." Students do caution, however, that a "parking problem" makes owning a car on campus a little difficult.

Student Body

Although "'preppy' would be the word to describe most students on this campus, there are others who do not fit this category at all." And many students emphasize that the student body is not cliquey: "Students have groups of friends, but that can be very fluid." Such intermixing is a function of how "amazingly nice" the students here are, regardless of the fact that "most of the students come from fairly wealthy homes." Politically, students have liberal leanings, and students report that most of their classmates seem to "come from the surrounding areas of New Jersey, Pennsylvania, and New York." "Muhlenberg is extremely gay-friendly," but in terms of ethnicity, "There is little diversity," a fact "that the college is interested in changing." On the bright side, "The little bit of ethnic and racial diversity that we have here is celebrated." According to one student, however, regardless of social groups or differences, "The majority of people that I have come into contact with are their own selves, and they pride themselves on that. After all, college is about finding out who you are as a person, not conforming to the majority."

THE PRINCETON REVIEW SAYS
Admissions
Very important factors considered include: Academic GPA, rigor of secondary school record, character/personal qualities, talent/ability. *Important factors considered include:* Extracurricular activities. *Other factors considered include:* Class rank, application essay, recommendation(s), standardized test scores, alumni/ae relation, first generation, interview, level of applicant's interest, racial/ethnic status, volunteer work, work experience. ACT with Writing component required. TOEFL required of all international applicants. High school diploma is required and GED is accepted. *Academic units required:* 4 English, 3 mathematics, 2 science, (2 science labs), 2 foreign language, 1 social studies, 2 history. *Academic units recommended:* 4 mathematics, 4 science, 3 foreign language, 3 history, 2 academic electives.

Financial Aid
Students should submit: FAFSA, institution's own financial aid form, CSS/Financial Aid PROFILE, noncustodial PROFILE. Regular filing deadline is 2/15. The Princeton Review suggests that all financial aid forms be submitted as soon as possible after January 1. *Need-based scholarships/grants offered:* Federal Pell, SEOG, state scholarships/grants, private scholarships, the school's own gift aid. *Loan aid offered:* FFEL Subsidized Stafford, FFEL Unsubsidized Stafford, FFEL PLUS, Federal Perkins, Private. Applicants will be notified of awards on or about 4/1. Federal Work-Study Program available. Institutional employment available. Off-campus job opportunities are excellent.

The Inside Word
Akin to many liberal arts colleges, Muhlenberg doesn't adhere to a set admissions formula. With application numbers on the rise, however, and the school's selectivity increasing, a strong secondary school transcript is necessary. Standardized tests, on the other hand, are optional at Muhlenberg. Those who don't submit scores can provide a graded paper and sit for an interview instead. Prospective students who have determined Muhlenberg to be their top choice will find it advantageous to apply early decision.

THE SCHOOL SAYS ". . ."
From The Admissions Office
"Listening to our own students, we've learned that most picked Muhlenberg mainly because it has a long-standing reputation for being academically demanding on one hand but personally supportive on the other. We expect a lot from our students, but we also expect a lot from ourselves in providing the challenge and support they need to stretch, grow, and succeed. It's not unusual for professors to put their home phone numbers on the course syllabus and encourage students to call them at home with questions. Upperclassmen are helpful to underclassmen. 'We really know about collegiality here,' says an alumna who now works at Muhlenberg. 'It's that kind of place.' The supportive atmosphere and strong work ethic produce lots of successes. The premed and pre-law programs are very strong, as are programs in theater arts, English, psychology, the sciences, business, and accounting. 'When I was a student here,' recalls Dr. Walter Loy, now a professor emeritus of physics, 'we were encouraged to live life to its fullest, to do our best, to be honest, to deal openly with others, and to treat everyone as an individual. Those are important things, and they haven't changed at Muhlenberg.'

"Students have the option of submitting SAT or ACT scores (including the Writing sections on each), or submitting a graded paper with teacher's comments and grade on it from junior or senior year and interviewing with a member of the Admissions Staff. Muhlenberg will accept old or new SAT scores and will use the student's best scores from either test."

For even more information on this school, turn to page 496 of the "Stats" section.

NAZARETH COLLEGE

4245 EAST AVENUE, ROCHESTER, NY 14618-3790 • ADMISSIONS: 585-389-2860 • FAX: 585-389-2826
E-MAIL: ADMISSIONS@NAZ.EDU • WEBSITE: WWW.NAZ.EDU

RATINGS

Quality of Life: 93   **Academic:** 85   **Admissions:** 84   **Financial Aid:** 74

STUDENTS SAY "..."

Academics

Nazareth College is "a very personalized school" in the suburbs, "about 10 miles from downtown Rochester."
"Education is a huge degree program" and there are quite a
few physical therapy and nursing majors. Naz is also great
for theater and music. "All of their productions are always
spectacular," gushes a sophomore. "I constantly feel like I'm
watching a Broadway show whenever I go see one." The
academic pace is reasonable. "I would say that our academic program is rigorous but not mental-illness inducing,"
suggests an English literature major. "I count this as a

> **SURVEY SAYS . . .**
> *Large classes*
> *Students are friendly*
> *Students love Rochester, NY*
> *Great off-campus food*
> *Frats and sororities are unpopular*
> *or nonexistent*
> *Musical organizations are popular*
> *Theater is popular*

strength." "Most of the professors are a lot of fun, and try to make classes interesting. Plus, they take the time to
get to know you personally, which is great." "Professors care about how you are doing," declares a nursing major.
"You are not just a number." Course selection is limited but classes are wonderfully small. "The administration
loves student feedback" and receives generally glowing reviews. Nazareth's president frequently walks around
campus and greets students. "I think Naz is doing a fine job," proffers a sophomore.

Life

Students here enjoy an "absolutely gorgeous" campus. The residence halls "are very comfortable and quite spacious," and they offer free laundry machines. However, the food is another story. "The dining hall is disgusting, dirty, and unsatisfying," gripes a hungry sophomore, though renovations are planned for summer 2008.
Socially, there is no Greek system but the student activities council does a fantastic job of having activities
planned." Some of these activities are "lame events" but many are widely attended. Intramural and varsity
sports are also reasonably big. The surrounding town is a little hamlet right on the Erie Canal "with fun shops
and places to eat." "Pittsford, as a town, is very safe and very nice to walk around in," says one student.
However, if you attend Nazareth, we recommend that you bring a vehicle with you. "Everyone has a car. It's
like a requirement," warns a sophomore. "If you want to find a party, you (usually) can." Older students (and
students with respectable fake IDs) often frequent the bars and clubs of downtown Rochester for fun. However,
"some weekends are slow" and "Nazareth is definitely not a big party school." Road trips are common.
"Nazareth isn't really far from anywhere, which makes other colleges, towns, and locations easy to access."
Some students also go home on more than a few weekends.

Student Body

"The typical student at Nazareth is a white girl from suburbia"—usually somewhere around Buffalo, Rochester,
or Syracuse. Students at Naz are "concerned about their grades." "The same kids you see drunk on Saturday
night at the bars are the kids working hard in the library all Sunday." They are a little on the cliquey side but
"very friendly," too. "There are a few jerks but nobody likes them, anyway," says one student. "Students here
tend to be very liberal." "There are many preppy and sports-oriented people." "There are a lot of artsy and intellectuals," too. "And there are, of course, your weirdoes, but that's normal." There is apparently a notable contingent of gay males as well, "though more straight men are attending as they realize that they have a big sea
to fish in."

THE PRINCETON REVIEW SAYS

Admissions

Very important factors considered include: Class rank, application essay, academic GPA, recommendation(s), rigor of secondary school record. *Important factors considered include:* Character/personal qualities, extracurricular activities, geographical residence, interview, level of applicant's interest, racial/ethnic status, state residency, talent/ability, volunteer work, work experience. *Other factors considered include:* Standardized test scores, alumni/ae relation, first generation, TOEFL required of all international applicants. High school diploma is required and GED is accepted. *Academic units required:* 4 English, 3 mathematics, 3 science, (2 science labs), 3 foreign language, 3 social studies. *Academic units recommended:* 4 English, 4 mathematics, 4 science, 4 foreign language, 4 social studies.

Financial Aid

Students should submit: FAFSA preferred filing deadline is 2/15. The Princeton Review suggests that all financial aid forms be submitted as soon as possible after January 1. *Need-based scholarships/grants offered:* Federal Pell, SEOG, state scholarships/grants, private scholarships, the school's own gift aid. *Loan aid offered:* FFEL Subsidized Stafford, FFEL Unsubsidized Stafford, FFEL PLUS, Federal Perkins Applicants will be notified of awards on a rolling basis beginning 2/20. Federal Work-Study Program available. Institutional employment available. Off-campus job opportunities are excellent.

The Inside Word

Admissions Officers at Nazareth College are looking for candidates who will enhance the college community as a whole. This means that a special talent in athletics, music, the arts, or leadership areas counts; it can be especially helpful to candidates whose academic records are less than exemplary.

THE SCHOOL SAYS "..."

From The Admissions Office

Growing interest in Nazareth—applications have grown 32 percent in five years—is a result of many factors. New facilities have increased and improved academic, performing arts, residential, and athletic spaces. Major offerings now include music/business, international business, communication and rhetoric, and music theatre. Nazareth has worked diligently to keep tuition at $5,000 less than the New York State average for private colleges. Our track record is strong -- retention and graduation rates exceed national averages; 75 percent of our students participate in a career-related internship with 93 percent of them citing this a very worthwhile experience; and 93 percent of our students are employed or in graduate school within one year of graduation. The College has produced 12 Fulbright scholars and six faculty Fulbrights, in the past decade alone, along with two Thomas R. Pickering Graduate Foreign Affairs Fellowships. The Center for International Education has developed more opportunities for our students to study abroad and for international students to study at Nazareth. With civic engagement and service learning as hallmarks of the Nazareth experience, 91 percent of undergrads participate in community service while at Nazareth. A proactive approach to campus security and state-of-the-art emergency notification system places Nazareth ahead of the curve regarding student safety. Student athletes, veterans of conference and national championships, have one of the highest graduation rates among NCAA Division III institutions. The Nazareth College Arts Center brings an international roster of performing art companies to campus, and provides high-quality facilities for student productions."

For even more information on this school, turn to page 497 of the "Stats" section.

NEUMANN COLLEGE

One Neumann Drive, Aston, PA 19014 • Admissions: 610-558-5616 • Fax: 610-558-5652
E-mail: neumann@neumann.edu • Website: www.neumann.edu

RATINGS
Quality of Life: 78   **Academic:** 73   **Admissions:** 74   **Financial Aid:** 85

STUDENTS SAY "..."

Academics

Neumann College, a small Catholic school outside of Philadelphia, specializes in providing undergraduates with "a personalized educational atmosphere based on Christian beliefs and moral values." Most classes "incorporate faith" or "refer back to spirituality in some manner," and students

praise "the service-learning that is stressed because this is a Franciscan school." One undergrad says, "Serving the community as well as we do is definitely one of the top attributes of this school. The volunteer opportunities and events that are held on this campus are remarkable." So, too, are academic offerings in nursing, education, communications, and criminal justice. Unique programs include sports management ("one of the best in the region") and an intelligence analysis certificate program for adults seeking to change careers in a post-9/11 world. No matter what you study here, you're sure to find "a small, friendly school where everyone knows each other, and the students and teachers know each other. Basically, it is great for students who do not want the huge lecture classes" they might find at bigger schools.

Life

A "quiet environment" is what you'll find at Neumann, a place students adamantly agree is "not a party school." "Strict, outdated policies on overnight visitors and drinking" make for "a good but boring campus"—so much so that some report that "even those living on campus leave on the weekends." Occasional events organized by the Student Activities Board or the Black Student Union draw crowds; these include novelty nights, dances, and black-light volleyball. Hockey games are also extremely popular: "There are shuttles to the rink for games," so students don't have to worry about driving or parking. Still, many here feel that "having a car is a must" because "There is not much to do in the immediate area surrounding the college." There is, however, "a lot to do within a 15- to 30-minute drive off campus." Nearby attractions include "three malls, a number of movie theaters, clubs, a lot of bars, a Wal-Mart, and a bowling alley." A car also makes nearby Philadelphia and Wilmington accessible.

Student Body

"Most of Neumann's population"—two-thirds, to be precise—"is girls." That's the same proportion of the school that belongs to the Roman Catholic Church. Men and non-Catholics need not worry about fitting in here, though. Students report that "everyone gets along, and there are no real problems on campus," undergraduates assure us. Non-Catholic students "even have their own gospel choir." A 16 percent minority population and sizable non-traditional group further add to the school's diversity. A friendly vibe pervades the school: It's the kind of place where "Students hold doors open for you. Even if you are steps away from the door, they wait until you get there."

Admissions

Very important factors considered include: Recommendation(s), rigor of secondary school record, extracurricular activities, talent/ability. *Important factors considered include:* Class rank, standardized test scores, alumni/ae relation, character/personal qualities, interview. *Other factors considered include:* Racial/ethnic status, religious affiliation/commitment, volunteer work, SAT or ACT required; TOEFL required of all international applicants. High school diploma is required and GED is accepted. *Academic units required:* 4 English, 2 mathematics, 2 science, 2 foreign language, 2 social studies, 4 academic electives. *Academic units recommended:* 4 English, 2 mathematics, 3 science, 2 foreign language, 2 social studies, 4 academic electives.

Financial Aid

Students should submit: FAFSA. The Princeton Review suggests that all financial aid forms be submitted as soon as possible after January 1. *Need-based scholarships/grants offered:* Federal Pell, SEOG, state scholarships/grants, private scholarships, the school's own gift aid, Federal Nursing Scholarships. *Loan aid offered:* Direct Subsidized Stafford, Direct Unsubsidized Stafford, Direct PLUS, FFEL Subsidized Stafford, FFEL Unsubsidized Stafford, FFEL PLUS, Federal Nursing Applicants will be notified of awards on a rolling basis beginning 3/1. Federal Work-Study Program available. Off-campus job opportunities are good.

The Inside Word

Neumann College delivers an environment that fosters personal and academic development. The Admissions Team seeks students who will take advantage of this setting and tends to favor applicants who demonstrate a high degree of potential. The ideal candidate desires a learning experience based on Catholic tenets.

THE SCHOOL SAYS ". . ."

From The Admissions Office

"Neumann College offers the ideal educational setting. As a small college, it provides students with the personal attention and support they seek. Dedicated faculty teach and assist our students in developing their thinking, writing, communication, and technical skills. As a Catholic college in the Franciscan tradition, Neumann College supports the spiritual, social, and athletic development of students. Neumann College's academic majors most often include experiential components, allowing students to blend classroom study and real work experiences. Neumann College graduates are well on their way to career advancement, having benefited from a tailored curriculum, personal advisement, support, and field experiences that offer them the competitive edge. Freshmen begin career exploration right away through the Academic Resource and Career Counseling Center.

"Campus life is a real strength of Neumann College. Three new suite-style residence halls are home to almost 800 residents. Residence halls are totally wired. Designed to offer the advantage of living in a community while supporting privacy and independence, the living-learning centers combine academic space and recreational, health, and fitness facilities all under one roof. Two modern dining facilities offer a variety of meal plans including a late-night serving at 10:00 P.M.

"There's always plenty to do at Neumann. The advantages of nearby Philadelphia and a variety of on-campus activities and programs fill the student's schedule. Neumann College offers 15 intercollegiate sports (NCAA), 6 performing arts groups, and dozens of student clubs and organizations. Students planning for college are always invited to visit and see Neumann College firsthand."

For even more information on this school, turn to page 497 of the "Stats" section.

NEW JERSEY INSTITUTE OF TECHNOLOGY

UNIVERSITY HEIGHTS, NEWARK, NJ 07102 • ADMISSIONS: 973-596-3300 • FAX: 973-596-3461
FINANCIAL AID: 973-596-3480 • E-MAIL: ADMISSIONS@NJIT.EDU • WEBSITE: WWW.NJIT.EDU

RATINGS
Quality of Life: 61   Academic: 72   Admissions: 81   Financial Aid: 83

STUDENTS SAY ". . ."

Academics

Mathematics, science, technology, and architecture offerings all shine at New Jersey Institute of Technology, a "leader in the field of technology in the Tri-State Area" whose public school pricing allows students to "graduate without the bank owning our first-borns, which is a definite plus." As is the case at many prestigious tech-oriented schools, "The professors are generally hired for research rather than teaching ability, [so] there are some who cannot teach, and they aren't that great at grading assignments or handing back papers either." The demanding undergraduate curriculum means "You have to be serious about studies if you are choosing NJIT. There is no time for fun and games." Students groan about the demands made on them but also recognize the benefits; "NJIT is an intense academic university that allows students to be prepared for the working world," explains one architect. Another plus of studying at NJIT is "how well the students interact, especially during exam time. Seniors help juniors, who help sophomores, who help freshman. It's helpful when someone who has taken the courses you're taking at the moment can put things into perspective, and give you hints about what may be on the test."

> **SURVEY SAYS . . .**
> Small classes
> Registration is a breeze
> Great computer facilities
> Great library
> Diverse student types on campus
> Campus feels safe

Life

NJIT is "not the best school socially, but few engineering schools are," students here concede. Since "a lot of classes give amazing amounts of homework, it is hard to have a normal social life. Most nights are spent doing homework late, then getting a few hours of fun before passing out." Extracurricular life has improved recently with the addition of new recreation facilities; one student notes, "The game room has been improved, with pool tables, bowling, and arcades, and a much-needed pub on campus." The institute also boasts "a pretty good gym to work out in, and a brand-new soccer field." Undergrads note optimistically that "our team sports are all performing better, and the students are starting to feel a sense of competition building. There are plenty of parties on Thursday nights on campus, organized by frats or clubs." And, of course, "Possibilities are endless because New York City is minutes away" by affordable public transportation, opening the door to "major league sports, world-class museums, and theater." Hometown Newark, although much maligned by students and locals, offers "great food and restaurants less than half a mile away from campus, in the Ironbound section." Students do appreciate how the "small classes and campus make a 'small-town' atmosphere during the semester," even though they also acknowledge the school's urban environs.

Student Body

"There are two types of students at NJIT," writes one undergrad, elaborating: "The first are the ones who are involved with athletics, clubs, organizations, and other things. The others are the antisocial ones. These people stay in their dorms and play computer games all day." How many of each category populate this campus? One student offers some pertinent data: "Class attendance dropped 32 percent the day Halo 2 came out." Like the region surrounding it, "NJIT is a total melting pot; the mix of ethnic backgrounds of students is diverse." While many say the various groups interact well, just as many others describe the student body as "clusters of ethnic groups isolated from each other." Because of curricular demands, "Everyone is pretty smart. But you also have the very smart people." When asked in what ways his school could stand to improve, one succinct information technologist wrote "girls!" reflecting a sentiment running through much of the student body. The male/female ratio is about 4:1.

THE PRINCETON REVIEW SAYS

Admissions

Very important factors considered include: Class rank, rigor of secondary school record, standardized test scores. *Important factors considered include:* Academic GPA. *Other factors considered include:* Application essay, recommendation(s), alumni/ae relation, character/personal qualities, extracurricular activities, geographical residence, interview, level of applicant's interest, racial/ethnic status, religious affiliation/commitment, state residency, SAT or ACT required; TOEFL required of all international applicants. High school diploma is required and GED is accepted. *Academic units required:* 4 English, 4 mathematics, 2 science, (2 science labs). *Academic units recommended:* 2 foreign language, 1 social studies, 1 history, 2 academic electives.

Financial Aid

Students should submit: FAFSA. Regular filing deadline is 5/15. The Princeton Review suggests that all financial aid forms be submitted as soon as possible after January 1. *Need-based scholarships/grants offered:* Federal Pell, SEOG, state scholarships/grants, private scholarships, the school's own gift aid. *Loan aid offered:* Direct Subsidized Stafford, Direct Unsubsidized Stafford, Direct PLUS, Federal Perkins, state loans, college/university loans from institutional funds. Applicants will be notified of awards on a rolling basis beginning 3/1. Federal Work-Study Program available. Institutional employment available. Off-campus job opportunities are good.

The Inside Word

NJIT is a great choice for students who aspire to technical careers but don't meet the requirements for better-known and more selective universities. To top it off, it's a pretty good buy.

THE SCHOOL SAYS ". . ."

From The Admissions Office

"Talented high school graduates from across the nation come to NJIT to prepare for leadership roles in architecture, business, engineering, medical, legal, science, and technological fields. Students experience a public research university conducting more than $75 million in research that maintains a small-college atmosphere at a modest cost. Our attractive 45-acre campus is just minutes from New York City and less than an hour from the Jersey shore. Students find an outstanding faculty and a safe, diverse, caring learning and residential community. All dormitory rooms have sprinklers. NJIT's academic environment challenges and prepares students for rewarding careers and full-time advanced study after graduation. The campus is computing-intunsive. For 5 consecutive years, Yahoo! Internet Life ranked NJIT among America's 'Most Wired Universities.'

"Students applying for admission to NJIT for Fall 2008 may provide scores from either version of the SAT, or the ACT. Writing sample scores will be collected but will not be used for admission purposes for 2008. SAT Subject Test scores are not required for any major."

For even more information on this school, turn to page 497 of the "Stats" section.

NEW YORK UNIVERSITY

22 WASHINGTON SQUARE NORTH, NEW YORK, NY 10011 • ADMISSIONS: 212-998-4500 • FAX: 212-995-4902
FINANCIAL AID: 212-998-4444 • E-MAIL: ADMISSIONS@NYU.EDU • WEBSITE: WWW.NYU.EDU

RATINGS
Quality of Life: 75   **Academic:** 83   **Admissions:** 96   **Financial Aid:** 75

STUDENTS SAY "..."

Academics

Located in the heart of Manhattan's Greenwich Village, New York University feeds off its great home city. The school's layout reinforces this relationship; academic buildings and dormitories are scattered around Washington Square Park and are virtually indistinguishable from the private residences, hotels, and restaurants that are its neighbors. Asked to identify the school's greatest asset, so many students respond "location, location, location" that one could be forgiven for thinking that NYU is a training school for real-estate agents. Nonetheless, the school's location "attracts superb professors and well-known researchers and lecturers" and "It's pretty much guaranteed that you'll have a couple good connections in your field when you leave NYU." While at school, you'll find opportunities for "amazing internship possibilities and real-life experiences," and you'll learn the "independence, maturity, and time-management skills" that come with living in an "expensive place where space is limited but you have access to the best of everything." Students note that NYU "offers a great program for nearly anything you want to major in," including a world-renowned arts school, and excellent programs in business, the humanities, and education. The school's weak spot, undergrads agree, is the administration, where "too much red tape" creates an experience reminiscent of "a daily trip to the Department of Motor Vehicles." A relatively small price to pay, most here agree, for the "endless cultural, culinary, musical, artistic, and academic opportunities" that NYU offers.

> **SURVEY SAYS . . .**
> *Great library*
> *Students love New York, NY*
> *Great off-campus food*
> *Hard liquor is popular*
> *(Almost) everyone smokes*

Life

NYU isn't merely located in "the city that never sleeps." It is, in fact, located in one of the city's hottest social and cultural areas, an agora of restaurants, clubs, concert venues, movie theaters, retail shops, and galleries. Village life ain't cheap, however, and students warn that "money is always an issue. Kids are either worried about getting more money out of their parents or managing what money they have. But money seems to be considerably less of an issue when we're all going out on a Friday night. There is any number of ways to entertain yourself—it's New York City!" Inexpensive diversions include many of the city's famous museums, cheap ethnic eats, and the ever-popular pastime of people-watching. There are also "many free/discounted events put on by the university (like concerts, plays, forums, etc)." Don't expect a typical college party scene here, however, as "There are no frat parties at NYU, as Greek life is virtually nonexistent, even frowned upon by many students. Instead, students prefer to go out to bars and clubs on weekends." Dorm and apartment parties also "aren't too abundant, though pre-gaming is very popular." In fact, "NYU doesn't really provide much of an emphasis on campus activities, especially during the weekend. You're basically left to find your own entertainment which, thankfully, is always possible."

Student Body

Students agree that "NYU is just a diverse as the city it is surrounded by," noting that the campus "is a conglomeration of the atypical. If you are looking for a student body wearing J. Crew and discussing the next frat party, this isn't the school for you." Each college has a specific archetype—"The somewhat eccentric theater student in Tisch, the mostly international Stern business students, the Steinhardt musicians reminiscent of the band groups in high school"—but "The vast majority of students are really pretty average, just doing their own thing like everybody else." The community "is known for its acceptance of students of any ethnicity, religion, sexual orientation, gender, or race. We live in New York, so absolutely nothing shocks us, and virtually everything is accepted." The lack of a traditional campus attracts students of an "independent" bent and, on occasion, drives away those who discover they crave a more conventional college experience.

THE PRINCETON REVIEW SAYS
Admissions
Very important factors considered include: Application essay, academic GPA, recommendation(s), rigor of secondary school record, extracurricular activities. *Important factors considered include:* Class rank, standardized test scores, character/personal qualities, talent/ability. *Other factors considered include:* Alumni/ae relation, first generation, level of applicant's interest, racial/ethnic status, volunteer work, work experience. SAT Subject Tests required; SAT or ACT required; ACT with Writing component required. TOEFL required of all international applicants. High school diploma is required and GED is accepted. *Academic units required:* 4 English, 3 mathematics, 3 science, (3 science labs), 2 foreign language, 3 history. *Academic units recommended:* 4 mathematics, 4 science labs, 3 foreign language.

Financial Aid
Students should submit: FAFSA, state aid form. Early Decision applicants may submit an institutional form for an estimated award. Regular filing deadline is 2/15. The Princeton Review suggests that all financial aid forms be submitted as soon as possible after January 1. *Need-based scholarships/grants offered:* Federal Pell, SEOG, state scholarships/grants, private scholarships, the school's own gift aid. *Loan aid offered:* FFEL Subsidized Stafford, FFEL Unsubsidized Stafford, FFEL PLUS, Federal Perkins, Federal Nursing Applicants will be notified of awards on a rolling basis beginning 4/1. Federal Work-Study Program available. Institutional employment available. Off-campus job opportunities are excellent.

The Inside Word
Undergraduate applicants may apply only to one of NYU's undergraduate schools and colleges. Students applying to the Silver School of Social Work, Steinhardt School of Culture, Education, and Human Development, the Tisch School of the Arts, or the School of Continuing and Professional Studies must indicate an intended major (those applying to the College of Arts and Sciences or the Stern School of Business may indicate that they are undecided on their majors). This is different from the application process at most schools and obviously requires some forethought. Remember that this is a highly competitive school; if your application does not reflect a serious interest in your intended area of study, your chances of getting in will be diminished.

THE SCHOOL SAYS "..."
From The Admissions Office
"Located in Greenwich Village, New York University (NYU) is unlike any other U.S. institution of higher education in the United States. When you enter NYU, you become part of a close-knit community that combines the nurturing atmosphere of a small- to medium-sized college with the myriad offerings and research opportunities of a global, urban university. The energy and resources of New York City serve as an extension of our campus, providing unique opportunities for research, internships, and job placement. With thousands of undergraduate course offerings and over 160 areas of study from which to choose, you can explore and develop your intellectual and professional passions from your very first semester. Along with this extraordinary range of courses and programs, each of our schools offers a strong liberal arts foundation, introducing you to the traditions of scholarship and inquiry that are the keys to success at NYU and throughout life. NYU's intellectual climate is fostered by a faculty of world-famous scholars, researchers, and artists who teach both undergraduate and graduate courses. In addition, an integral element of the NYU academic experience is our study abroad programs. NYU offers nine study abroad sites—in Berlin, Buenos Aires, Florence, Ghana, London, Madrid, Paris, Prague, and Shanghai, with a future site planned for Tel Aviv, Israel.

"At NYU, you will become part of one of the most dynamic universities in the country, in one of the most exciting cities in the world, making NYU's tradition of innovation, learning, and success a part of your future."

For even more information on this school, turn to page 498 of the "Stats" section.

NIAGARA UNIVERSITY

BAILO HALL, OFFICE OF ADMISSIONS, NIAGARA UNIVERSITY, NY 14109 • ADMISSIONS: 800-462-2111 • FAX: 716-286-8710
E-MAIL: ADMISSIONS@NIAGARA.EDU • WEBSITE: WWW.NIAGARA.EDU

RATINGS
Quality of Life: 73   Academic: 75   Admissions: 76   Financial Aid: 81

STUDENTS SAY "..."

Academics

Niagara University is "a small Catholic school that not only educates you for your career but also for your life," thanks in part to a "Vincentian tradition" that emphasizes humility and service to the poor. Also contributing are NU's "very strong program in hospitality," which is "nationally ranked and couldn't offer you a better chance to excel"; "excellent education programs" that provide "experience in real class-

rooms in the local school districts as soon as your freshman year"; a "good program for criminal justice majors"; and "a top program in undergraduate social work." Across all disciplines, "The smaller-sized classes that Niagara University offers really let students voice their opinions and ideas." The school is small enough that "everyone is approachable. Professors are around before and after class to talk, and are in their offices whenever they are not in class. They are interested in getting to know you and [finding] the best way to help you learn." One undergrad notes, "My teachers have served as my mentors and advisors, and you can be sure that any recommendations to graduate school or a job are coming from someone who really knows you and your work."

Life

Niagara University's location creates a wide range of extracurricular options. The Canadian border—and its promise of legal drinking for those 19 and older—is just a stone's throw away. Undergrads occasionally road-trip to Toronto for a show or just to shop at the Eaton Center. Closer to home, Niagara Falls has "two or three clubs that everyone goes to every weekend," while Buffalo offers "professional sports, movies, bars, and clubs." The school capitalizes on its location and organizes lots of activities "such as white-water rafting, movie nights, open mic night, and concerts" as well as "trips to Buffalo Bills games, Blue Jays games, Canada's Wonderland, and the Whirlpool Jet Boat Tour." Sports are a big deal here; NU boasts "a great hockey team," and many students "join club sports and intramurals" or simply take advantage of the "top-notch athletic facilities. You don't have to be a varsity athlete to stay in shape here." While "There is a lot of partying" here, "Somehow everyone gets all their homework done."

Student Body

Niagara is a Catholic university, and "A lot of students grew up in the Catholic school system." Even so, "There are many people from different religions who are always invited to attend Mass and other campus ministry events." Many feel that "religion is not really outwardly noticeable" among much of the student body. In terms of race and geography, the school is undeniably homogeneous: "Everyone is from western New York, Rochester, or Syracuse," and "almost everyone is White, athletic, and preppy." Undergrads report that "students who are lesbian, gay, or bisexual are treated normally, equally, and fairly by everyone." Male undergraduates are "outnumbered, and they fit in just fine for that."

SURVEY SAYS . . .
Small classes
Great computer facilities
Everyone loves the Purple Eagles
Lots of beer drinking
Hard liquor is popular

THE PRINCETON REVIEW SAYS

Admissions
Very important factors considered include: Rigor of secondary school record. *Important factors considered include:* Recommendation(s), standardized test scores, interview. *Other factors considered include:* Class rank, application essay, alumni/ae relation, character/personal qualities, extracurricular activities, talent/ability, volunteer work, SAT or ACT required; TOEFL required of all international applicants. High school diploma is required and GED is accepted. *Academic units required:* 4 English, 2 mathematics, 2 science, 2 foreign language, 2 social studies, 4 academic electives.

Financial Aid
Students should submit: FAFSA, state aid form. The Princeton Review suggests that all financial aid forms be submitted as soon as possible after January 1. *Need-based scholarships/grants offered:* Federal Pell, SEOG, state scholarships/grants, private scholarships, the school's own gift aid. *Loan aid offered:* Direct Subsidized Stafford, Direct Unsubsidized Stafford, Direct PLUS, Federal Perkins, Federal Nursing, state loans, college/university loans from institutional funds. Applicants will be notified of awards on a rolling basis beginning 3/1. Federal Work-Study Program available. Off-campus job opportunities are excellent.

The Inside Word
Niagara is a superb option for students interested in a respectable school with a Catholic underpinning. The Admissions Office focuses primarily on academic achievement rather than more subjective criteria. Applicants who are successful in college preparatory classes should get in with relative ease. With a large portion of the student body hailing from upstate New York, officers welcome candidates who would add a little geographic diversity to the campus.

THE SCHOOL SAYS ". . ."

From The Admissions Office
"'A great place to be!' is the way one undergraduate describes his experience at Niagara University (NU), and he isn't alone. Our 2,900 undergraduates find that NU provides over 50 academic, career-oriented, and pre-professional programs housed within the College of Arts and Sciences, College of Business Administration, College of Education, and the College of Hospitality and Tourism Management. In addition, the university offers an undeclared program, academic exploration, and the Higher Educational Opportunity Program. NU students have the opportunity to enrich their programs with internships, co-ops, overseas study, honors, and community-service work. At NU, it is not unusual for students to get involved in an original research project or work with faculty members on special research assignments.

"Best of all, NU combines the diverse academic opportunities usually associated with a larger university with the close personal attention of a smaller institution. With a 17:1 student/faculty ratio and an average class size of 25, students can ask questions in the classroom and develop rapport with faculty members who are accomplished in their fields. NU's faculty is dedicated and accessible. More importantly, NU faculty members genuinely care about the academic and personal growth of their students. Their commitment to teaching is their primary concern.

"To complement academic life on campus, NU offers a variety of academic, social, cultural, or service organizations. Couple these with Division I, intramural, and recreational sports programs, and there is something for everyone to cheer about at NU.

"NU's suburban campus is located a few minutes from the world-famous Niagara Falls and short drives from Buffalo and Toronto. This affords students with the opportunity to take advantage of all the sights and sounds of the area."

For even more information on this school, turn to page 498 of the "Stats" section.

NORTHEASTERN UNIVERSITY

360 HUNTINGTON AVENUE, 150 RICHARDS HALL, BOSTON, MA 02115 • ADMISSIONS: 617-373-2200
FAX: 617-373-8780 • FINANCIAL AID: 617-373-3190 • E-MAIL: ADMISSIONS@NEU.EDU • WEBSITE: WWW.NEU.EDU

RATINGS
Quality of Life: 87   **Academic:** 79   **Admissions:** 91   **Financial Aid:** 70

STUDENTS SAY "..."

Academics

Northeastern "is all about mixing classroom-based instruction with real-world experience" via a robust, justly
renowned co-op program (which places students in real-
life major-related internships and jobs for up to 18 months)
that provides "meaningful work and life experience" to
nearly all undergraduates. While some may quibble that
co-op "isn't the best thing for all majors, only those oriented toward business, journalism, communications, engineering, some sciences, and architecture," most here insist

that "the co-op program is Northeastern's bragging right" and "without any doubt the school's greatest
strength." As one student explains, "Experiences on co-op lead to better discussion and learning in the classroom as professors tackle real-world applications of their subjects with the knowledge that we have been there
before, rather than stay in the theoretical realm." As an added bonus, "Northeastern students have some of the
strongest post-college resumes in the nation" as a result of their co-op experiences. As you might expect,
Northeastern's strengths lie in such solidly pre-professional programs as business, health services, engineering,
and computer and information sciences. Students caution that it's the type of school "where you get in what
you put out...if you sit around and complain about not getting a good job and not having much help from
advisers or professors, it's probably because you didn't try very hard. If you put in the effort, you will find
many, many people are willing to do a great deal to help you succeed and doors will fly open to ensure your
success, and you'll meet a lot of great people (classmates and faculty) and make a lot of friends along the way."

Life

"There is always something to do, either on campus or around the city" at Northeastern, and understandably so;
the school is located in Boston, perhaps the nation's preeminent college town. Boston affords "unlimited amounts
of things to do like shopping, walking around, movies, etc." Boston is especially accommodating to those over 21,
since "there are plenty of bars to enjoy" all over town. For sports fans, "Fenway Park and the TD Banknorth Garden
are a short distance away for athletic games," and "Matthews Arena, home of Husky hockey and the men's basketball team," are nearby. On campus, Greek life "is on the rise," and "Greeks...are extremely involved on campus,
planning service events, educational speakers or fun events, such as bringing former Red Sox players or popular
comedians to campus." Extracurricular clubs "including but not limited to sports, newspaper, religious groups,
social awareness, diversity groups, and more" are widely available to students, and "The campus has much to offer
as far as recreation from an ice rink to multiple gym facilities. It also has a large student center, multiple outdoor
quads, and dorm activities. There is never a dull moment on campus, there is always something to do."

Student Body

"Because of our highly attractive location, there is no 'typical' Northeastern student," undergrads here insist,
informing us that "Students come from the local Boston neighborhoods, ivy towns in Connecticut, countries
around the world and cities across the country." The university's "wide range of courses to study" further
ensures "a wide range of students" on campus. Finally, the school's large population practically ensures a
diverse mix, as evidenced by the "250 or so clubs ranging from anime to the Caribbean Student Organization,
from fraternities to a gay/lesbian/transsexual organization. You find virtually every
race/gender/religious/political type of people here and they all fit in and generally get along." The enticement
of co-op, of course, means that most everyone here is "looking to obtain a solid education and prepare themselves for the working world." You won't find a lot of ivory-tower intellectuals here.

Admissions

Very important factors considered include: Academic GPA, rigor of secondary school record. *Important factors considered include:* Class rank, application essay, recommendation(s), standardized test scores, character/personal qualities, extracurricular activities, first generation, talent/ability. *Other factors considered include:* Alumni/ae relation, geographical residence, racial/ethnic status, state residency, volunteer work, work experience. SAT or ACT required; ACT with Writing component required. TOEFL required of all international applicants. High school diploma is required and GED is accepted. *Academic units required:* 4 English, 3 mathematics, 3 science, (2 science labs), 2 foreign language, 2 social studies, 2 history. *Academic units recommended:* 4 mathematics, 4 science, (4 science labs), 4 foreign language.

Financial Aid

Students should submit: FAFSA, CSS/Financial Aid PROFILE. The Princeton Review suggests that all financial aid forms be submitted as soon as possible after January 1. *Need-based scholarships/grants offered:* Federal Pell, SEOG, state scholarships/grants, private scholarships, the school's own gift aid, Federal Nursing Scholarships. *Loan aid offered:* FFEL Subsidized Stafford, FFEL Unsubsidized Stafford, FFEL PLUS, Federal Perkins, Federal Nursing, state loans, MEFA, TERI, Signature, Mass. No Interest Loan (NIL), CitiAssist. Applicants will be notified of awards on a rolling basis beginning 2/15. Federal Work-Study Program available. Institutional employment available. Off-campus job opportunities are excellent.

The Inside Word

With more than 30,000 applicants each year, Northeastern admissions officers must wade through an ocean of applications in order to select the incoming class. The volume requires that much of the early winnowing be strictly numbers-based; the school has too many applicants with decent test scores and high school grades to bother with substandard candidates. Those who make the first cut should receive a more personalized review that includes a close look at essays, extracurriculars, and recommendations. A campus visit couldn't hurt.

THE SCHOOL SAYS ". . ."

From The Admissions Office

"Northeastern students take charge of their education in a way you'll find nowhere else, because a Northeastern education is like no other. We integrate challenging liberal arts and professional studies with a variety of experiential learning opportunities anchored by the our signature cooperativeeducation program. Northeastern's dynamic of academic excellence and experience means that our students are better prepared to succeed in the lives they choose. On top of that, they experience all of this on a beautifully landscaped, 73-acre campus in the heart of Boston, where culture, commerce, civic pride, and college students from around the globe are all a part of the mix."

For even more information on this school, turn to page 499 of the "Stats" section.

PACE UNIVERSITY

One Pace Plaza, New York, NY 10038 • Admissions: 212-346-1323 • Fax: 212-346-1040
E-mail: infoctr@pace.edu • Website: www.pace.edu

RATINGS
Quality of Life: 69   Academic: 72   Admissions: 77   Financial Aid: 68

STUDENTS SAY ". . ."

Academics

With campuses "located next to Wall Street" and in "Westchester County," Pace University lures undergrads in the Tristate Area with "a really good reputation," "scholarships," "proximity to home," and "its connectedness to the business community in New York City." As you'd expect, its location provides "tremendous internship opportunities" and professors who have "real-world" perspicacity (particularly, students say, ones at the Lubin School of Business). While students report "some adjuncts who can't teach their way out of a paper bag," they rate their "amazing" professors as "very supportive" and "very knowledgeable." In the past, the administration has been characterized by "an unwelcoming corporate vibe," although the school says it has recently restructured the "Office of Student Assistance" to provide one-stop services. Others object to Pace "doing away with the locked-in tuition feature," (which allowed students to pay for each year of their undergraduate education at the freshman-year rate), a move they suspect is being used "to alleviate" the school's "massive debt." Still, students here believe Pace "offers students a chance to receive a great education." A big-picture student sums up the Pace experience thusly: "Big headaches, but great opportunities."

> **SURVEY SAYS . . .**
> Large classes
> Diverse student types on campus
> Students love New York, NY
> Great off-campus food
> Campus feels safe
> (Almost) everyone smokes

Life

Undergraduate life at Pace is a tale of two counties: New York (aka Manhattan) and Westchester. Students describe life at the former as "very fast-paced." "Life revolves around the various museums, restaurants, theaters, and bars the city has to offer," the urbanites say. Many here "go to clubs and bars," but if "[you] are not really into that scene, you can hang out in your dorm without being disturbed" (most dorms have "the feel of an apartment building"). Students at the Pleasantville-Briarcliff campus in suburban Westchester—about 30 miles north of Manhattan—report a different set of experiences. "The pace is slower," they say. "Greek life," once a major factor here, "has gone down," and students most often "party on campus at the townhouses where mostly upperclassmen live." "Many students" here are "involved in sports." "Malls," "a few bars," and "places to eat" can be found "close by." When they're feeling adventurous, Westchester kids check out the haunts of their urban counterparts: "The city is only about a half-hour away."

Student Body

Students report that "Pace University is truly a melting pot." "Many ethnicities, religions, [and] races" are well represented and the majority of students are quick to call this Pace's "greatest strength." The population here runs the gamut from those who "travel internationally [and] drink nice wine" in their leisure time to those who are "paying their way through college by working two or three jobs on top of their [school] work." But don't go looking for national diversity: Undergrads here are "usually from either New York, New Jersey, or Connecticut." "A lot of commuters" attend, which leads some to allude to "a lack of community" while others note that "not all commuters go to school and come directly home." Students are united, however, by a "goal-oriented" approach to their undergrad years. A few epitomize their peers as "more interested in making money than learning," but most are apt to describe the typical student as one who "knows how to have good time but balances fun with responsibility."

THE PRINCETON REVIEW SAYS

Admissions

Very important factors considered include: Rigor of secondary school record, standardized test scores. *Important factors considered include:* Class rank, academic GPA. *Other factors considered include:* Application essay, recommendation(s), alumni/ae relation, character/personal qualities, extracurricular activities, talent/ability, volunteer work, work experience. SAT or ACT required; TOEFL required of all international applicants. High school diploma is required and GED is accepted. *Academic units required:* 4 English, 3 mathematics, 2 science, (2 science labs), 2 foreign language, 1 social studies, 2 history, 2 academic electives. *Academic units recommended:* 4 English, 4 mathematics, 2 science, (2 science labs), 3 foreign language, 2 social studies, 3 history, 2 academic electives.

Financial Aid

Students should submit: FAFSA, state aid form. The Princeton Review suggests that all financial aid forms be submitted as soon as possible after January 1. *Need-based scholarships/grants offered:* Federal Pell, SEOG, state scholarships/grants, private scholarships, the school's own gift aid. *Loan aid offered:* Direct Subsidized Stafford, Direct Unsubsidized Stafford, Direct PLUS, Federal Perkins, Federal Nursing Applicants will be notified of awards on a rolling basis beginning 2/28. Off-campus job opportunities are good.

The Inside Word

At Pace, your choice of major is usually bound with a particular campus. If you're interested in the school's nursing program, for example, you should also consider whether you'd enjoy life in Westchester. In a similar vein, if you want to study acting, you shouldn't be squeamish when it comes to the subway—one of the world's greatest stages after the Globe Theatre.

THE SCHOOL SAYS "..."

From The Admissions Office

"Pace University blends a wide choice of high-quality professional education with a liberal arts curriculum that teaches critical and independent thinking. For more than 100 years, Pace has provided practical experiences that prepare students for significant careers. Pace students thrive on the opportunities and challenges of the New York metropolitan area.

"Pace's 13,000 diverse undergraduate and graduate students from across the U.S. and 123 countries have a choice of campuses four blocks from Wall Street in New York City or in suburban Westchester County. More than 90 percent of first-year students receive financial aid. Classes average 20 students.

"Nearly 40 percent of Pace undergraduates live on campus, participating in 90 clubs and student organizations (and in Westchester, in Division II sports).

"More than 450 companies come to Pace to find their next generation of talent, and the University's co-op and internship program is the largest of its kind in the metropolitan area. Students find work with Fortune 500 companies like IBM, Citigroup, Verizon, Deloitte, Goldman Sachs, and at institutions like the Argonne National Laboratory. More The Pace Career Advisory Network provides connections to 500-plus alumni who want to help others succeed.

"Pace University successfully challenges its students to lift their lives and prospects to new levels. "There is greatness within us all," reads a poster on the downtown New York City campus, "sometimes you just need the right opportunity to find it. Welcome to Pace University."

For even more information on this school, turn to page 499 of the "Stats" section.

PENNSYLVANIA STATE UNIVERSITY—UNIVERSITY PARK

201 SHIELDS BUILDING, UNIVERSITY PARK, PA 16802-3000 • ADMISSIONS: 814-865-5471
FAX: 814-863-7590 • FINANCIAL AID: 814-865-6301 • WEBSITE: WWW.PSU.EDU

RATINGS
Quality of Life: 84   Academic: 74   Admissions: 91   Financial Aid: 66

STUDENTS SAY ". . ."

Academics

At Penn State "You can do anything you want" academically because with "over 160 majors" to choose from,
"There are unlimited opportunities" for every undergraduate. Such vast resources are typical of a sprawling public
flagship university, but it's the personal touches that leave
students "pretty impressed with how such a large school
can run like a small one." For example, "Professors do a lot
to facilitate personal interactions." They are "really easy to
talk to both in and out of class, and they're always accessi-

> **SURVEY SAYS . . .**
> Great library
> Athletic facilities are great
> Everyone loves the Nittany Lions
> Intramural sports are popular
> Student publications are popular
> Lots of beer drinking
> Hard liquor is popular

ble." Unfortunately, it's not always a professor students end up with: "They do use a lot of teaching assistants,
which can get frustrating." Still, professors are "thought-provoking" and "You can tell that a lot of them really
do want to be teaching." If you can manage to get into it, the Schreyer Honors College's "rigorous" curriculum
presents "tremendous opportunities." In addition to more challenging courses, it "offers incredible amounts of
money for study abroad, internships, and faculty co-ops," and its students get perks like "priority registration
for classes." Administratively, "Penn State is a huge machine . . . run with amazing efficiency." Credit is given
to President Graham Spanier, who is praised for not only "holding office hours" and "responding personally to
e-mails," but also for being "very involved in student life." Despite having "created Late-Night Penn State and
the News Readership Program," he also finds time to be the "advisor to the magician's club" and "play the
washboard in a bar downtown." Perhaps the greatest long-term benefit of a Penn State education is "the social
networking." With an alumni association of over 159,000 members and growing, opportunities for success
through networking are "well in your favor" at Penn State.

Life

At a university this size, "you can do anything and everything" in your free time. There are, however, a couple
of common threads. First, "PSU football is a religion." During the fall, "Everyone goes to the football games and
tailgates on Saturdays." Second, is the partying. "People party as hard on the weekends as they study during
the week." "Popular choices" for freshmen and sophomores are "frat or apartment parties," while "For those
over 21, Penn State's College Avenue has a great range of over 20 bars for students to choose from." However,
"If someone is not a partier, there are plenty of activities and organizations" he or she can devote her time to.
For example, "substance-free activities that occur during the weekends at the Student Union (such as movies,
video game tournaments, concerts)" are alternatives for those that decline to imbibe. In terms of extracurriculars, the options are practically endless. According to several students, "with over 700 student clubs and organizations, there's something for everyone" at Penn State, offering "virtually limitless possibilities to carve out
your own corner" and "help students get involved, build a resume, and network."

Student Body

"There is a bit of everything" on this huge campus in the center of the Keystone State. That's why some students find it so difficult to describe their peers succinctly. Rather than a "typical" student at Penn State, for some
survey respondents it makes more sense to describe the school's "multitude of groups of 'atypical' students: frat
boys . . . jocks, internationals, loners, skaters . . . 'jokers, smokers, midnight tokers' . . . city kids, rednecks, country bumpkins, and so on." In this way, "It's like a large high school, where everyone is in their own group." So
"if you come to Penn State, don't worry about finding friends because there is someone up here for everyone."
Yet even "Though there are a lot of differences, everyone wears blue and white on their sleeve." Ultimately, "All
Penn State students . . . love this college."

Admissions

Very important factors considered include: Academic GPA, standardized test scores. *Important factors considered include:* Rigor of secondary school record. *Other factors considered include:* Class rank, application essay, recommendation(s), alumni/ae relation, character/personal qualities, extracurricular activities, talent/ability, volunteer work, work experience. SAT or ACT required; ACT with Writing component required. TOEFL required of all international applicants. High school diploma is required and GED is accepted. *Academic units required:* 4 English, 3 mathematics, 3 science, 2 foreign language, 3 social studies.

Financial Aid

Students should submit: FAFSA. The Princeton Review suggests that all financial aid forms be submitted as soon as possible after January 1. *Need-based scholarships/grants offered:* Federal Pell, SEOG, state scholarships/grants, private scholarships, the school's own gift aid. *Loan aid offered:* FFEL Subsidized Stafford, FFEL Unsubsidized Stafford, FFEL PLUS, Federal Perkins, college/university loans from institutional funds, Private Loans. Applicants will be notified of awards on a rolling basis beginning 3/1. Federal Work-Study Program available. Institutional employment available. Off-campus job opportunities are good.

The Inside Word

Penn State evaluates applications on a rolling basis. As it is the first choice of a lot of students, the Admissions Office's recommended filing date for applications is about the same time as many other schools' early application deadlines—keep this in mind to avoid the cut-off date. In terms of what factors weigh heavily in terms of admissions decisions, Penn State is quite open, though high school GPA is paramount to securing your blue and white bid.

THE SCHOOL SAYS "..."

From The Admissions Office

"Unique among large public universities, Penn State combines the over-35,000-student setting of its University Park campus with 20 academically and administratively integrated undergraduate locations—small-college settings ranging in size from 600 to 3,400 students. Each year, more than 60 percent of incoming freshmen begin their studies at these residential and commuter campuses, while nearly 40 percent begin at the University Park campus. The smaller locations focus on the needs of new students by offering the first 2 years of most Penn State baccalaureate degrees in settings that stress close interaction with faculty. Depending on the major selected, students may choose to complete their degree at University Park or one of the smaller locations. Your application to Penn State qualifies you for review for any of our campuses. Your two choices of location are reviewed in the order given. Entrance difficulty is based, in part, on the demand. Due to its popularity, the University Park campus is the most competitive for admission.

"Freshman applicants for Fall 2008 may submit the results from the current version of the SAT, the current ACT, the new version of the SAT, or the results of the new ACT with Writing test. The Writing portions of these tests will not necessarily be factored into admission decisions."

For even more information on this school, turn to page 500 of the "Stats" section.

POLYTECHNIC UNIVERSITY—BROOKLYN

SIX METROTECH CENTER, BROOKLYN, NY 11201-2999 • ADMISSIONS: 718-260-3100 • FAX: 718-260-3446
E-MAIL: ADMITME@POLY.EDU • WEBSITE: WWW.POLY.EDU

RATINGS
Quality of Life: 65   Academic: 71   Admissions: 84   Financial Aid: 87

STUDENTS SAY "..."

Academics

Polytechnic University—Brooklyn is a private, "commuter-based engineering school in New York City" that boasts "top-notch" engineering, mathematics, and computer science programs. Be warned, though: Poly is hard-core. "Schoolwork and exams are crazy." Many students "transfer after [their] first year" because they can't hack it; only half of the students in most entering classes graduate. On the bright side, if you can handle the "very demanding" curriculum, "You leave Poly prepared for anything." "Professors are hit or miss": "The good professors are awesome" and "experienced in their field"; "The bad ones are really bad." A common complaint regarding the professors at Poly is "You never know whether they'll speak intelligible English or not." Class sizes are "usually small," which means you "have more chances" to ask questions and interact with professors. Students, however, are generally down on the "very unhelpful" administration, saying, "They blow through money" and "It seems like there is always something wrong with your financial aid package."

SURVEY SAYS . . .

Small classes
Diverse student types on campus
Students love Brooklyn, NY
Great off-campus food
Campus feels safe
Very little drug use

Life

While "The campus could be prettier," it has seen steady improvement in recent years. "Dorms are now right on campus" and "the main academic building has been renovated and expanded." It feels a lot like a "brand-new school." Overall, though, "life on campus is not that exciting," primarily because "There is always a lot to study for." It doesn't help that most students "live in the city or commute." For students who live on campus, "There's a fair amount of drinking." ("It's not uncommon to become intoxicated and play video games.") Clubs and organizations "aren't too popular, though each has a faithful following." Of course, "if you want to party" you can, since "Poly is located in New York City." Some students quibble about the exact location of Poly's Brooklyn home, the Metrotech complex. To set the record straight, the campus is within walking distance of the shops and restaurants of Brooklyn Heights. A mere 15-minute stroll leads to the Brooklyn Bridge and great Manhattan neighborhoods like Little Italy and Chinatown.

Student Body

"We are very nerdy and very Asian," proclaims a senior at Poly. While there is quite a large Asian contingent here, the "science- and math-oriented" student population at Poly is "extremely diverse." There are students here from almost 50 countries, but students gripe there are "very few women" from any countries. "I haven't really seen people showing personality very visibly in the way they dress and what they look like," observes a sophomore. "But kids are very diverse, with many interests and different backgrounds . . . as a foreigner, I [feel] like the entire world met in one place." There are "popular and trendy people" who are "involved in lots of activities," but "The average student is semi-social." Some students "are exceptionally smart and dedicated to their work" but "not really amicable because of their workload." Few students can "really balance" social and academic life. "All the students tend to get along, but there is a lot of sticking with one's ethnic group." There is also little social interaction "between commuters and dormers."

THE PRINCETON REVIEW SAYS

Admissions
Very important factors considered include: Rigor of secondary school record, standardized test scores. *Important factors considered include:* Class rank. *Other factors considered include:* Application essay, recommendation(s), interview, SAT or ACT required; TOEFL required of all international applicants. High school diploma is required and GED is accepted. *Academic units required:* 4 English, 4 mathematics, 4 science, 3 social studies, 2 academic electives, *Academic units recommended:* 2 foreign language.

Financial Aid
Students should submit: FAFSA, institution's own financial aid form, CSS/Financial Aid PROFILE, state aid form. The Princeton Review suggests that all financial aid forms be submitted as soon as possible after January 1. *Need-based scholarships/grants offered:* Federal Pell, SEOG, state scholarships/grants, private scholarships, the school's own gift aid, United Negro College Fund. *Loan aid offered:* FFEL Subsidized Stafford, FFEL Unsubsidized Stafford, FFEL PLUS, Federal Perkins, college/university loans from institutional funds. Alternative Loans. Applicants will be notified of awards on a rolling basis beginning 2/15. Off-campus job opportunities are excellent.

The Inside Word
Most successful applicants to Polytechnic boast strong standardized test scores and a challenging secondary school transcript chock-full of math and science classes. Poly promises a demanding 4 years but makes it worth your while—all graduates are guaranteed a job within 6 months of graduation.

For even more information on this school, turn to page 500 of the "Stats" section.

PRINCETON UNIVERSITY

PO BOX 430, ADMISSION OFFICE, PRINCETON, NJ 08544-0430 • ADMISSIONS: 609-258-3060
FAX: 609-258-6743 • FINANCIAL AID: 609-258-3330 • WEBSITE: WWW.PRINCETON.EDU

RATINGS
Quality of Life: 99   Academic: 98   Admissions: 99   Financial Aid: 99

STUDENTS SAY "..."

Academics

Perhaps you might have heard something about Princeton, a "little suburban oasis in New Jersey" proffering a storied history, a high profile academic curriculum, and stellar financial aid policies, all of which combine to provide "an experience and a network that will transform your life." Or, as one student puts it, "A Princeton education is worth its weight in

gold, especially if you didn't have to pay anything." The undergraduate focus (there are no law, med, or business schools here) gives students access to tremendous resources, and everyone enrolled is granted access not just to classes but to a "scholarly community"; in the math department, for instance, tea is open to everyone. "The school has plenty of funding to put toward your research, and it is amazing to work on something that is completely yours," says a senior history major. With one of the nation's largest endowments, the school is happy to share the wealth, as well. "If you have something reasonable you want to do over the summer, for example, you can do it regardless of your financial situation. Princeton has paid for me to study abroad, work abroad, go on a class trip abroad, and compete internationally at a variety of wonderful locales abroad," says a junior. The rigorous admission process brings together some of the top young adults in America to "study seriously, to party seriously, or to pursue a job seriously, or a combination of the three," and the school has "very high expectations...you have to work extremely hard to succeed." Since "Princeton students rarely do things half-way," the learning here is "demanding and competitive, but enlightening." Professors, "even the famous ones," are very down-to-earth and "love talking to students one-on-one about their goals and ideas," but "they have to be sought out; they won't come to you." The administration "is remarkably cooperative," and have done an "excellent job of incorporating student opinions into actual decisions," with, of course, "the notable exception of grade deflation."

Life

People at Princeton really use the 'work hard, play hard' logic. "Academic discipline is on everyone's mind," but on any given day, "there are soo many interesting events being coordinated by students and the university" that everyone here is "always running from one commitment to the next, and studying in between," but students make plenty of time on weekends for fun, "often at the expense of studying or sleeping." Princeton has a relatively small, "gorgeous campus," and "everyone lives on campus and close to one another." The bulk of students don't have class on Fridays, which is good, because there's "never a dull moment," thanks to lectures, concerts, sporting events, performances, and movies. Most people belong to or go out to the eating clubs, which are a unique Princeton institution that acts as a coed frat/dining hall that provide upper-class students with both meals and social events (such as DJ's and theme nights), and offers "great ways to drink and dance in a safe environment, only with other Princeton students." "Princeton is a lifestyle, not a school," says a junior. "The best of everything is here...you're at the center of the world in a very real sense."

Student Body

Everyone at Princeton "has a nerdy streak in them" and there's a fair share of "hyper-ambitious kids who spend all their time studying," but it's a "pretty friendly environment" and people here are "always ready to have fun." These "driven" students are "all over the map in terms of ethnicity, beliefs, passions, and priorities," though students are all very focused on their future careers. "Your average Princetonian wants to run the world, not change it," says a student. While there are still plenty of people fulfilling the "clean-cut, preppy, and well-dressed" stereotype, this is one that Princetonians "are very aware of and hardly take seriously, even when they conform to it"; most "invariably come from different backgrounds and have different pursuits," anyway. There are fringe groups, but "they do not have a large presence." You will still find kids with mohawks here, and "they're often even more treasured by the student community for their exoticness." The small campus means that "everyone is somehow interconnected," but it's also "big enough that you are always meeting new people."

THE PRINCETON REVIEW SAYS

Admissions

Very important factors considered include: Class rank, application essay, academic GPA, recommendation(s), rigor of secondary school record, standardized test scores, character/personal qualities, extracurricular activities, first generation, talent/ability. *Important factors considered include:* Alumni/ae relation. *Other factors considered include:* Geographical residence, interview, level of applicant's interest, racial/ethnic status, volunteer work, work experience. SAT Subject Tests required; SAT or ACT required; ACT with Writing component recommended. TOEFL required of all international applicants. High school diploma or equivalent is not required. *Academic units recommended:* 4 English, 4 mathematics, 4 science, (2 science labs), 4 foreign language, 2 history.

Financial Aid

Students should submit: FAFSA, institution's own financial aid form, Institutional Noncustodial Parent's Form. The Princeton Review suggests that all financial aid forms be submitted as soon as possible after January 1. *Need-based scholarships/grants offered:* Federal Pell, SEOG, state scholarships/grants, the school's own gift aid. *Loan aid offered:* FFEL Subsidized Stafford, FFEL Unsubsidized Stafford, FFEL PLUS, Federal Perkins, college/university loans from institutional funds. Applicants will be notified of awards on or about 4/1. Federal Work-Study Program available. Institutional employment available. Off-campus job opportunities are good.

The Inside Word

Princeton is much more open about the admissions process than the rest of their Ivy compatriots. The Admissions Staff evaluates candidates' credentials using a 1–5 rating scale, common among highly selective colleges. Princeton's recommendation to interview should be considered a requirement, given the ultracompetitive nature of the applicant pool. In addition, three SAT Subject Tests are required.

THE SCHOOL SAYS ". . ."

From The Admissions Office

"Methods of instruction [at Princeton] vary widely, but common to all areas is a strong emphasis on individual responsibility and the free interchange of ideas. This is displayed most notably in the wide use of preceptorials and seminars, in the provision of independent study for all upperclass students and qualified underclass students, and in the availability of a series of special programs to meet a range of individual interests. The undergraduate college encourages the student to be an independent seeker of information and to assume responsibility for gaining both knowledge and judgment that will strengthen later contributions to society.

Princeton offers a distinctive financial aid program that provides grants, which do not have to be repaid, rather than loans. Princeton meets the full demonstrated financial need of all students—domestic and international—offered admission. More than half of Princeton's undergraduates receive financial aid.

"All applicants must submit results of either the new or old SAT, as well as SAT Subject Tests in three different subject areas. Students applying for the Class of 2010 and beyond will be required to submit results from the new version of the SAT."

For even more information on this school, turn to page 501 of the "Stats" section.

PROVIDENCE COLLEGE

River Avenue and Eaton Street, Providence, RI 02918 • Admissions: 401-865-2535 • Fax: 401-865-2826
Financial Aid: 401-865-2286 • E-mail: pcadmiss@providence.edu • Website: www.providence.edu

RATINGS
Quality of Life: 68   Academic: 80   Admissions: 93   Financial Aid: 73

STUDENTS SAY "..."

Academics

Providence College, "a solid, respectable school with a reputation for having fun," appeals both to those who seek an "intense curriculum" ("especially the Development of Western Civilization course" that can be "stressful and time-consuming" though "It offers a great liberal arts background") and to those who simply want "challenging classes" in an atmosphere that balances "academic and personal growth with an incredibly fun social scene." The centerpiece of the PC experience is "the four-semester Civ program, through which the school truly molds the mind with classical training and gives us a basic understanding of how our civilization came to be where it is today." While some students dismiss the sequence as "unnecessary to our success in the future," others appreciate the forced immersion in philosophy, history, art, and theology, noting "I am happy that I am forced to take Civ because I would not have enrolled into any other courses that deal with the topics introduced in Civ." PC academics are "demanding," but "The school has great support systems for academics" "even outside the classroom stuff. The library has lots of different resources and there's always someone around to help." Undergrads also appreciate how "Being in a smaller school, there are more opportunities to excel in one's chosen field, whether it's getting an internship in a biology lab, writing for the newspaper, or starring in a theatrical production."

> SURVEY SAYS . . .
> Diversity lacking on campus
> Everyone loves the Friars
> Intramural sports are popular
> Frats and sororities are unpopular
> or nonexistent
> Lots of beer drinking
> Hard liquor is popular

Life

Social life at Providence College "revolves around the off-campus bars and the off-campus houses. While there are other activities to participate in, the main focus is drinking." One undergrad reports, "Kids work hard from Sunday night to Thursday afternoon; then the weekend starts, and everyone hits the bars." However, it would be remiss to assume students here do nothing but study and drink—on the contrary, there is "a huge focus on extracurriculars," so much so that students always try to "balance and manage" their time between "schoolwork and a social life." Intercollegiate athletics "are extremely popular (all the hockey games are packed) and bring a great atmosphere to the campus," and intramurals "are lots of fun. There's even a noncompetitive division for students who only want to have fun." Community service "is also really popular. Students are always busy donating their time to different groups." Downtown Providence has a lot more to offer than bars; it has "a great music scene, theater, and lots of art venues. The restaurants are good too." Students can access the city easily as "public transportation is free for us. It's only 5 minutes to downtown, and the bus runs right through campus."

Student Body

Though Providence students "are not the most diverse group," "The administration is really emphasizing our need for people who are different" from what some perceive to be the usual "cookie-cutter" student. That said, students report, by and large, that they are "all comfortable with one another and it is easy to fit in," noting a "strong sense of community." The typical student here "is a White, upper-middle class kid who went to a private/Catholic prep school in New England" and "looks as though he stepped of the pages of the Hollister/Abercrombie catalogue." Students who do not fit the mold "seem to form their own peer groups for the most part. Interaction between atypical and typical students is not a problem." One student says that "Everyone is working together to try to come up with ways to make our student population more diverse, both ethnically and economically." Most here are "friendly and hardworking and are very involved in various organizations, from Student Government to intramural sports to the Board of Multicultural Student Affairs . . . we are proud of our school."

THE PRINCETON REVIEW SAYS

Admissions

Very important factors considered include: Academic GPA, recommendation(s), rigor of secondary school record. *Important factors considered include:* Application essay, character/personal qualities, extracurricular activities. *Other factors considered include:* Class rank, standardized test scores, alumni/ae relation, first generation, geographical residence, level of applicant's interest, racial/ethnic status, talent/ability, volunteer work, work experience. ACT with Writing component required. TOEFL required of all international applicants. High school diploma is required and GED is not accepted. *Academic units required:* 4 English, 4 mathematics, 3 science, (2 science labs), 3 foreign language, 2 social studies, 2 history. *Academic units recommended:* 4 English, 4 mathematics, 4 science, (2 science labs), 3 foreign language, 2 social studies, 2 history.

Financial Aid

Students should submit: FAFSA, CSS/Financial Aid PROFILE, business/farm supplement. Regular filing deadline is 2/1. The Princeton Review suggests that all financial aid forms be submitted as soon as possible after January 1. *Need-based scholarships/grants offered:* Federal Pell, SEOG, state scholarships/grants, private scholarships, the school's own gift aid, Federal Academic Competitive Grant/Smart Grant. *Loan aid offered:* Direct Subsidized Stafford, Direct Unsubsidized Stafford, Direct PLUS, FFEL Subsidized Stafford, FFEL Unsubsidized Stafford, FFEL PLUS, Federal Perkins Applicants will be notified of awards on or about 4/1. Federal Work-Study Program available. Institutional employment available. Off-campus job opportunities are good.

The Inside Word

Few schools can claim a more transparent admissions process than Providence College. The admissions section of the school's website includes a voluminous blog authored by the school's senior Admissions Counselor. Surf on over to http://blogs.targetx.com/providence/ScottSeseske and learn everything you could possibly want to know about the how, what, when, and why of admissions decisions at Providence.

THE SCHOOL SAYS ". . ."

From The Admissions Office

"Infused with the history, tradition, and learning of a 700-year-old Catholic teaching order, the Dominican Friars, Providence College offers a value-affirming environment where students are enriched through spiritual, social, physical, and cultural growth as well as through intellectual development. Providence College offers over 51 programs of study leading to baccalaureate degrees in business, education, the sciences, arts, and humanities. Our faculty is noted for a strong commitment to teaching. A close student/faculty relationship allows for in-depth classwork, independent research projects, and detailed career exploration. While noted for the physical facilities and academic opportunities associated with larger universities, Providence also fosters personal growth through a small, spirited, family-like atmosphere that encourages involvement in student activities and athletics.

"Submission of standardized test scores is optional for students applying for admission. This policy change allows each student to decide whether they wish to have their standardized test results considered as part of their application for admission. Students who choose not to submit SAT or ACT test scores will not be penalized in the review for admission. Additional details about the test-optional policy can be found on our website at Providence.edu/testoptionalpolicy."

For even more information on this school, turn to page 501 of the "Stats" section.

QUINNIPIAC UNIVERSITY

Mount Carmel Avenue, 275 Mount Carmel Avenue, Hamden, CT 06518 • Admissions: 203-582-8600
Fax: 203-582-8906 • E-mail: admissions@quinnipiac.edu • Website: www.quinnipiac.edu

RATINGS
Quality of Life: 78   Academic: 82   Admissions: 88   Financial Aid: 68

STUDENTS SAY "..."

Academics

The physical beauty of Quinnipiac University is a particularly appealing attribute. The "beautiful campus with Sleeping Giant Mountain in the background" boasts many a picturesque vista, both natural and man-made. As far as the latter is concerned, the library "is gorgeous, with huge three-story windows and leather armchairs everywhere!" Quinnipiac's "great" academics manage to draw students away from the windows and into the classrooms. Undergraduate academics at Quinnipiac are divided into five schools (and one new Division of Education), with the School of Health Sciences offering especially outstanding majors. Among these is a 6.5-year physical therapy program that leads to a Doctor of Physical Therapy degree. Students appreciate the fact that "classes here at Quinnipiac are small, with generally less than 30 students," that "not one class in the university is taught by a teacher's assistant" and that professors "have so much experience in the 'real world' with the subject they teach." They warn, however, that "sometimes you can have a little bit of trouble with the adjuncts." Regardless of how good they are as teachers and lecturers, professors "all seem to be willing to help outside of the class time and communicate rapidly through e-mail."

Life

According to students, life at Quinnipiac outside of class follows a regular schedule to it. "Thursday night everyone goes to the clubs in New Haven. Friday night everyone parties on campus. Saturday night most people go to Toad's (a popular New Haven nightclub)." And if you have "no transportation, no problem. Quinnipiac shuttles will take you into New Haven to the clubs." "However, if partying is not your thing, don't worry because Quinnipiac sends out e-mails every week with the [school-sponsored] weekend events. These events include comedians, movies, game room nights, and much more." For outdoorsy types, miles of hiking trails lie right across the street, and "climbing the Sleeping Giant" is a popular pastime here, weather permitting. When it's "nice out," students take full advantage of their gorgeous surroundings: "You will always see kids with their towels lying on the Quad doing work. Others also enjoy playing Frisbee on the beautiful grass." "Support for the athletic teams," however, "is so-so. Men's ice hockey draws the best. Students also support the men's basketball team pretty well."

Student Body

To get a picture of what students here look like, just grab the nearest name-brand clothing catalog: "J. Crew, Ralph Lauren, and the North Face could do a magazine shoot here. [There are lots of] very preppy-looking, clean-cut kids." If their clothes aren't enough to give you a sense of the socioeconomic background from which most QU students come, take a stroll through "the student parking lot, [which] is full of Mercedes, Lexus, BMW, and Acura cars." Intellectually, "Most students don't seem to be their high school class president or their high school overachiever," but respondents emphasize that QU students are "hard workers." Given QU's location, it's not completely shocking to learn that "Many of the students come from surrounding New England states as well as New York and New Jersey." Many respondents lament the female/male ratio (about 3:2), and the fact that there are "very, very, very few minorities"—"but with each entering freshman class the diversity does grow slightly." And regardless of their backgrounds, friendly students make Quinnipiac "a comfortable, enjoyable place to live. The students are understanding of one another."

> **SURVEY SAYS . . .**
> Small classes
> Great computer facilities
> Great library
> Campus feels safe
> Lots of beer drinking
> Hard liquor is popular

THE PRINCETON REVIEW SAYS

Admissions

Very important factors considered include: Rigor of secondary school record. *Important factors considered include:* Class rank, application essay, academic GPA, standardized test scores. *Other factors considered include:* Recommendation(s), alumni/ae relation, character/personal qualities, extracurricular activities, interview, level of applicant's interest, racial/ethnic status, talent/ability, volunteer work, work experience. SAT or ACT required; TOEFL required of all international applicants. High school diploma is required and GED is accepted. *Academic units required:* 4 English, 3 mathematics, 3 science, (2 science labs), 2 foreign language, 2 social studies, 4 4 years of Science and Math req. in PT, OT, Nursing, and PA. *Academic units recommended:* 4 English, 4 mathematics, 4 science, (3 science labs), 2 foreign language, 3 social studies.

Financial Aid

Students should submit: FAFSA. The Princeton Review suggests that all financial aid forms be submitted as soon as possible after January 1. *Need-based scholarships/grants offered:* Federal Pell, SEOG, state scholarships/grants, private scholarships, the school's own gift aid, Federal Nursing Scholarships. *Loan aid offered:* FFEL Subsidized Stafford, FFEL Unsubsidized Stafford, FFEL PLUS, Federal Perkins, Federal Nursing, state loans Applicants will be notified of awards on a rolling basis beginning 2/15. Federal Work-Study Program available. Institutional employment available. Off-campus job opportunities are excellent.

The Inside Word

Applicants with solid grades and test scores won't have much trouble gaining admission to Quinnipiac as long as they apply early in their senior year. Competition grows fiercer, however, as D-Day approaches. With the recent spike in applications, Admissions Officers have established the wait list in January. Students interested in either physical therapy or physician assistant should be aware that they face more stringent requirements.

THE SCHOOL SAYS ". . ."

From The Admissions Office

"The appeal of Quinnipiac University continues to grow each year. Our students come from a variety of states and backgrounds. Seventy-five percent of the freshman class is from out of state. Students come from 25 states and 18 countries. Nearly 30 percent of current undergraduates plan to stay at Quinnipiac to complete their graduate degrees. As admission becomes more competitive and our enrollment remains stable, the university continues to focus on its mission: to provide outstanding academic programs in a student-oriented environment on a campus with a strong sense of community. The development of an honors program, a highly regarded emerging leaders student-life program, and a 'writing across the curriculum' initiative in academic affairs, form the foundation for excellence in business, communications, health sciences, education, liberal arts, and law. The university has a fully digital high-definition production studio in the School of Communications; the Terry Goodwin '67 Financial Technology Center which provides a high-tech simulated trading floor in the School of Business; and a critical care lab for our nursing and physician assistant majors. All incoming students purchase a university-recommended laptop with wireless capabilities supported by a campus wide network. More than 70 student organizations, 21 Division I teams, recreation and intramurals, community service, student publications, and a strong student government offer a variety of outside-of-class experiences. There are many clubs that get students involved in campus life. Multicultural awareness is supported through the Black Student Union, Asian/Pacific Islander Association, Latino Cultural Society, and GLASS. An active alumni association reflects the strong connection Quinnipiac has with its graduates, and they give the faculty high marks for career preparation. Students are encouraged to apply early in the fall of their senior year and can access our online application or the Common Application easily from our website. We use the best individual scores on the SAT Reasoning Test (no Subject Tests required), or the ACT composite. We begin notifying students of our decisions in early January."

For even more information on this school, turn to page 502 of the "Stats" section.

RAMAPO COLLEGE OF NEW JERSEY

505 RAMAPO VALLEY ROAD, MAHWAH, NJ 07430 • ADMISSIONS: 201-684-7300 • FAX: 201-684-7964
E-MAIL: ADMISSIONS@RAMAPO.EDU • WEBSITE: WWW.RAMAPO.EDU

RATINGS
Quality of Life: 79   Academic: 75   Admissions: 89   Financial Aid: 70

STUDENTS SAY "..."

Academics

Ramapo College of New Jersey is a smallish, public, career-oriented liberal arts school on the fringes of northern New Jersey's suburban sprawl. "The classes are small" and students call Ramapo "a great bargain." Business programs are particularly "excellent." Some students like the "hands-on experience" they gain from the required experiential learning components of the curriculum. Other students call experiential learning "a big waste of time and effort." "While watching movies or attending seminars may seem nice to fulfill the requirement, the forced nature of it has irritated many a student," explains an accounting major. The faculty at RCNJ is all over the place. Some professors "have a passion for teaching." They're "dedicated to their students" and "very accessible." "The great professors will blow you away," promises a business major. However, other professors are "dull and incomprehensible." Student opinion really varies when it comes to the administration. "Ramapo runs fairly smoothly," contends an education major. Others disagree. "The school's administration is slightly lacking in terms of service towards their students, but I would assume that is the case in most schools."

> **SURVEY SAYS . . .**
> *Great computer facilities*
> *Athletic facilities are great*
> *Dorms are like palaces*
> *Lots of beer drinking*

Life

Ramapo's campus is "very clean" and "in a beautiful and quiet location." "The gym is really nice" and the rooms in the newer residence halls are "huge" and "extremely comfortable." There are "many extracurricular options" and the school "does try to plan things." However, "school spirit is definitely lacking" and "unless you join a club or activity early on, it is very hard to get to know people." The basic problem is that "too many people go home on the weekends." "It's a suitcase college," laments a junior. "It is completely empty here on a Saturday night." Greek life provides an outlet for students who join frats and sororities but "the college goes a little overboard" with "ridiculously strict and severe" alcohol and drug policies. As a result, it's "hard to have fun and party like a normal college kid." Surrounding Mahwah is a "grim town" and "having a car on campus is essential to avoid feeling cut off from the world." If you have wheels, a handful of malls are "within 20 minutes" and there's "an absolutely gorgeous hiking area" just down the road. If you enjoy more urban pursuits, New York City is also reasonably close. "I go often," proclaims a sophomore.

Student Body

Except for the solid contingent of international students, virtually everyone here is "New Jersey born and bred." Many students are "preppy" and most "come off as put-together," and are "white, upper middle-class suburbans." Commuters, nontraditional students, and "transfers from community college" make up a good percentage of the student population. Though there are a few girls with "the latest Ugg boots," wearing "Hollister," "make-up and sidebangs," it's mostly "lots of jeans and hoodies" and "hats with pre-frayed brims" at Ramapo, and many students describe themselves as "laid back." The campus tends to be "very clique oriented." "Eating in the cafeteria is almost like eating in a high school cafeteria all over again," observes a junior.

THE PRINCETON REVIEW SAYS

Admissions

Very important factors considered include: Class rank, academic GPA, rigor of secondary school record, standardized test scores. *Important factors considered include:* Application essay, recommendation(s), character/personal qualities, extracurricular activities, talent/ability. *Other factors considered include:* Alumni/ae relation, geographical residence, state residency, volunteer work, work experience. SAT required; TOEFL required of all international applicants. High school diploma is required and GED is accepted. *Academic units required:* 4 English, 3 mathematics, 3 science, (3 science labs), 2 foreign language, 3 social studies, 3 academic electives.

Financial Aid

Students should submit: FAFSA. The Princeton Review suggests that all financial aid forms be submitted as soon as possible after January 1. *Need-based scholarships/grants offered:* Federal Pell, SEOG, state scholarships/grants, private scholarships, the school's own gift aid, Federal Nursing Scholarships. *Loan aid offered:* Direct Subsidized Stafford, Direct Unsubsidized Stafford, Direct PLUS, Federal Perkins, state loans Applicants will be notified of awards on a rolling basis beginning 4/1. Federal Work-Study Program available. Institutional employment available. Off-campus job opportunities are good.

The Inside Word

Ramapo's location in North Jersey and proximity to New York City is a perfect combination for many students. Virtually all the students here graduated in the top half of their high school classes and admission is moderately competitive. If you haven't slacked off in college prep courses and your standardized test scores are decent, you shouldn't have much of a problem gaining entry.

THE SCHOOL SAYS "..."

From The Admissions Office

"Students admitted to Ramapo College for Fall 2007 had an average SAT score of 1160 and ranked in the top 20 percent of their graduating class. Applications to the freshman class were the highest in the history of the college; admission was offered to fewer than half (45 percent) of the freshman applicants. Ramapo students come from all 21 counties in New Jersey as well as 17 states and more than 52 countries. Ninety percent of freshmen and about 60 percent of all full-time students live on campus, for a total of 2,929 residential students.

"Ranked a top pick, regional Top Public Universities, Ramapo College of New Jersey is sometimes mistaken for a private college. This is, in part, due to its unique interdisciplinary academic structure, its size of around 5,700 students, and its pastoral setting. Ramapo offers bachelor's degrees in the arts, business, humanities, social sciences, and the sciences as well as in professional studies, which include pre-law, premed, nursing, and social work. In addition, the college offers courses that make students eligible to obtain teacher certification at the elementary and secondary school levels.

"Undergraduate students choose to concentrate their studies in one of five schools: Anisfield School of Business; American and International Studies; Contemporary Arts; Theoretical and Applied Science; and Social Science and Human Services. Of the 700 course offerings and 40 academic programs, the most popular are business administration, communication arts, psychology, nursing, and biology."

For even more information on this school, turn to page 502 of the "Stats" section.

REGIS COLLEGE

235 WELLESLEY STREET, WESTON, MA 02493-1571 • ADMISSIONS: 781-768-7100 • FAX: 781-768-7071
E-MAIL: ADMISSION@REGISCOLLEGE.EDU • WEBSITE: WWW.REGISCOLLEGE.EDU

RATINGS
Quality of Life: 71　　**Academic:** 76　　**Admissions:** 67　　**Financial Aid:** 68

STUDENTS SAY ". . ."

Academics

Regis College is "a small, Catholic liberal arts college" in the suburbs of Boston. The highlights of this "terrific institution" include "rigorous academics," "small classes," and a "close-knit" and "very diverse" student population. The "excellent nursing program" is "very popular." The "wel-

coming" administration is "always available." "Here at Regis, if you have a problem, there is always someone that can help you," promises a senior. The "extremely supportive and encouraging" professors are "very knowledgeable in their subject areas." "As with anywhere, you will have your teachers who suck" but most professors "really care about their students" and "really enjoy getting to know each student on a personal level." "I have been blessed to have met several very inspiring professors," says a happy junior. "They give you so much attention in and out of the classroom." Regis has been going through something of a transition since going coed, though "The typical student is female because it was an all-women's college until recently."

Life

Regis boasts a "quiet," "calm," and "beautiful" campus "in a great area" 12 miles from Boston. It's "small enough so everyone knows everyone else" and there is a real sense of community. "The students value that community and are sentimental about school traditions." "A lot of students participate in some type of sport." Student organizations "try very hard to hold activities on weekends that appeal to students," though most "go home," which can make for a "low-fun atmosphere." Otherwise, "Students spend time with friends during the week while attending classes" and there's a "nice swimming pool." One student notes that "Regis has become almost a commuter school." "The campus is deserted on the weekend." A shuttle is available for students who want to venture off campus, but "Having a car is almost necessary." "For fun many people leave campus and go to other schools for parties." Of course, "the city of Boston" provides an endless array of things to do.

Student Body

"Almost anyone can fit in and have a wonderful experience at Regis," reports a junior. "Regis has been trying hard to diversify its student population, and that shows here on campus." "A wide variety" of "social, ethnic, and socioeconomic groups" call this campus home. "There is a huge range of ethnic groups," says a student. While there are "people from all over the world who speak many different languages," the "typical student is your 'typical' student." The undergrads at Regis report that they are "friendly," "talkative," "intelligent," "hardworking," "goal-oriented," and "easy to get along with." They are also "energetic, outspoken, and generous." "Most aren't that into partying and just like to have fun with friends."

THE PRINCETON REVIEW SAYS

Admissions

Very important factors considered include: Application essay, academic GPA, recommendation(s), rigor of secondary school record, character/personal qualities. *Important factors considered include:* Class rank, standardized test scores, extracurricular activities, interview, talent/ability, volunteer work, work experience. *Other factors considered include:* Alumni/ae relation, first generation, level of applicant's interest, SAT or ACT required; TOEFL required of all international applicants. High school diploma is required and GED is accepted. *Academic units required:* 4 English, 3 mathematics, 2 science, (1 science labs), 2 foreign language, 2 social studies, 3 academic electives.

Financial Aid

Students should submit: FAFSA, institution's own financial aid form. The Princeton Review suggests that all financial aid forms be submitted as soon as possible after January 1. *Need-based scholarships/grants offered:* Federal Pell, SEOG, state scholarships/grants, private scholarships, the school's own gift aid. *Loan aid offered:* FFEL Subsidized Stafford, FFEL Unsubsidized Stafford, FFEL PLUS, Federal Perkins, state loans Applicants will be notified of awards on a rolling basis beginning 3/15. Federal Work-Study Program available. Institutional employment available. Off-campus job opportunities are poor.

The Inside Word

In the words of one student, Regis is "a pretty easy school to get into." There are no cutoffs when it comes to standardized test scores. Decent grades in a solid college-prep curriculum ought to be enough to get you admitted without much of a problem. If you seek admission into the 3-year accelerated nursing program, though, you need a high school GPA of at least 3.4 and an 1100 or better on the Math and Critical Reading sections of the SAT.

THE SCHOOL SAYS ". . ."

From The Admissions Office

"Founded in 1927 by the Sisters of St. Joseph of Boston, Regis College is a 4-year, coeducational, private liberal arts college. Regis College offers a place for young men and women to become individuals, through an innovative personal approach in the classroom and a strong spirit of friendship throughout the campus community. Regis students are educated to succeed in their careers and in their lives. From the start, they are encouraged to take a leadership role in their education. The college is uniquely designed to offer students academic support and flexibility as they complete their studies. As of Fall 2007, Regis College will admit undergraduate men for the first time in its 80-year history.

"Regis is located in Weston, Massachusetts, a residential community just 12 miles from metropolitan Boston. Our picturesque 132-acre campus has the best of both worlds: a suburban setting with quick and easy access to the cultural and social activities of the Boston area, as well as a multitude of internships and job opportunities. Our diverse student body benefits from a low student/faculty ratio, studies abroad in countless locations, and competes in NCAA Division III athletics.

"Whether participating in internships, cultivating academic partnerships that promote intellectual and social growth, or exploring the many attractions of the New England area, students will thrive in the 'Community of Learning' that is Regis College."

For even more information on this school, turn to page 503 of the "Stats" section.

RENSSELAER POLYTECHNIC INSTITUTE

110 EIGHTH STREET, TROY, NY 12180-3590 • ADMISSIONS: 518-276-6216 • FAX: 518-276-4072
FINANCIAL AID: 518-276-6813 • E-MAIL: ADMISSIONS@RPI.EDU • WEBSITE: WWW.RPI.EDU

RATINGS
Quality of Life: 68   **Academic:** 79   **Admissions:** 93   **Financial Aid:** 86

STUDENTS SAY "..."

Academics

Rensselaer Polytechnic Institute, which proud students declare "a small research institute making a large impact on the world," is "essentially a hard-core technical school; heavily oriented towards engineering in the sciences, although it is trying to expand its offerings" in the humanities and arts. The school has already made some headway in that area; as one student points out, "There are a lot of students who are dedicated to their single major in a science or technology field here, which leads to a somewhat narrow-minded type of person...but RPI's saving grace is that it also offers rigorous degrees in architecture and the arts that make this technical institution more like a liberal arts college, as opposed to a strict technical college." Students in all disciplines face "rigorous course loads" that provide "a lesson in perseverance and innovation to overcome future challenges." Most programs incorporate "a hands-on studio-based method" supplemented by "top-of-the-line facilities...and numerous resources for all students to use." RPI's identity as a research center helps here; according to one undergrad, "The greatest resource for students at RPI are the researchers. It's easy to go to any top-ranked school and take hard classes. It's much harder to find as many professors who are on the cutting edge of their disciplines and actively taking undergraduate students into their labs. RPI excels in this, and any RPI student who wants a research position can usually find one." RPI's co-op program and Career Development Center "are also outstanding, leading to a high placement rate in excellent jobs," although of the latter some warn that "many engineering firms are familiar with Rensselaer, but employers in other fields still have yet to learn of the students available."

Life

"The academics are challenging" at RPI, making life "stressful, but in a good way. Time management is a key to success here." A few students have trouble walking away from the books, but most "enjoy relaxing through various clubs and intramural sports" available to all. The Greek scene is popular, but it's not your stereotypical Animal House variety; sure, "There are definitely a bunch of parties every weekend if you're into that," but "they're all pretty much very responsible with sober bartenders and sober drivers." RPI's Greek organizations also "do a lot of community service in the area and philanthropy events on campus." Greek or not, many here agree that "One of the greatest things to do for fun is to head up to the field house on a Friday or Saturday night and watch some Division 1 men's hockey." For those who want something a little more active, "Intramural and inter-fraternity sports are a great way to unwind as well as just hanging out in our student-run union." Hometown Troy "is not the best town to live in, although it has a few cool things to do. But, Albany is only a 20-minute drive away (and the bus is free) and there's always something to do there."

Student Body

"There are a lot of very, very nerdy kids here at RPI, as can be imagined at a school with primarily engineering students," but "There are a large number of 'normal' people as well, and each year, the percent of females in each incoming class increases." While the gender gap may be narrowing, it's still pretty wide, meaning that "there is only one typical student at RPI: a white male. They might be into sports, video games, drinking, Greek life, computers, RPG, or whatever, but they're an overwhelming aspect of campus." The minority population includes "many Asian and Indian students." Nearly everyone "comes from the top of their classes so they are all very intelligent people" who are "driven and hardworking, and think on a global level."

THE PRINCETON REVIEW SAYS

Admissions

Very important factors considered include: Class rank, academic GPA, rigor of secondary school record, standardized test scores. *Important factors considered include:* Application essay, recommendation(s), character/personal qualities, extracurricular activities. *Other factors considered include:* Alumni/ae relation, geographical residence, level of applicant's interest, racial/ethnic status, talent/ability, volunteer work, work experience. SAT or ACT required; ACT with Writing component required. TOEFL required of all international applicants. High school diploma is required and GED is accepted. *Academic units required:* 4 English, 4 mathematics, 3 science, 2 social studies. *Academic units recommended:* 4 science, 3 social studies.

Financial Aid

Students should submit: FAFSA, CSS/Financial Aid PROFILE. The Princeton Review suggests that all financial aid forms be submitted as soon as possible after January 1. *Need-based scholarships/grants offered:* Federal Pell, SEOG, state scholarships/grants, private scholarships, the school's own gift aid, Gates Millennium Scholarship, ACG, Smart Grants. *Loan aid offered:* FFEL Subsidized Stafford, FFEL Unsubsidized Stafford, FFEL PLUS, Federal Perkins, state loans, college/university loans from institutional funds. Applicants will be notified of awards on or about 3/25. Federal Work-Study Program available. Institutional employment available. Off-campus job opportunities are good.

The Inside Word

Outstanding test scores and grades are pretty much a must for any applicant hopeful of impressing the RPI Admissions Committee. Underrepresented minorities and women—two demographics the school would like to augment—will get a little more leeway here than others, but in all cases the school is unlikely to admit anyone who lacks the skills and background to survive here. RPI offers many students January admission in order to allow them to pursue productive activities (work, travel, volunteering) in the fall semester following high school graduation.

THE SCHOOL SAYS "..."

From The Admissions Office

"The oldest degree-granting technological research university in North America, Rensselaer was founded in 1824 to instruct students to apply 'science to the common purposes of life.' Rensselaer offers more than 100 programs and 1,000 courses leading to bachelor's, master's, and doctoral degrees. Undergraduates pursue studies in architecture, engineering, humanities and social sciences, management and technology, science, and information technology (IT). A pioneer in interactive learning, Rensselaer provides real-world, hands-on educational opportunities that cut across academic disciplines. Students have ready access to laboratories and attend classes involving lively discussion, problem solving, and faculty mentoring. New programs and facilities are enriching the student experience. The Office of First-Year Experience provides programs for students and their primary support persons that begin even before students arrive on campus. The new $80-million Biotechnology and Interdisciplinary Studies Center offers space for scientific research and discovery, while newly renovated residence halls, wireless computing network, and studio classrooms create a fertile environment for study and learning. The Experimental Media and Performing Arts Center opening in 2008 will encourage students to explore and create at the intersection of engineering and the arts. Rensselaer offers recreational and fitness facilities plus numerous student-run organizations and activities, including fraternities and sororities, a newspaper, a radio station, drama and musical groups, and more than 160 clubs. In addition to intramural sports, NCAA varsity sports include Division I men's and women's ice hockey teams and 21 Division III men's and women's teams in 13 sports. Applicants may submit scores from either SAT (Critical Reading, Math, and Writing) or ACT (which must include optional Writing component). Applicants to the accelerated program must either take the ACT or submit Math and Science scores from SAT Subject Tests."

For even more information on this school, turn to page 503 of the "Stats" section.

THE RICHARD STOCKTON COLLEGE OF NEW JERSEY

Jim Leeds Road, PO Box 195, Pomona, NJ 08240 • Admissions: 609-652-4261 • Fax: 609-748-5541
E-mail: admissions@stockton.edu • Website: www.stockton.edu

RATINGS

Quality of Life: 73   **Academic:** 73   **Admissions:** 81   **Financial Aid:** 78

STUDENTS SAY ". . ."

Academics

The Richard Stockton College of New Jersey is a midsized, "extremely affordable," "transfer-friendly" public school that "provides a very well-rounded liberal arts education." Classes are typically quite small and students tell us that the business programs here are excellent. There are also outstanding programs in marine science and solid programs

> **SURVEY SAYS . . .**
> Great library
> Campus feels safe
> Lots of beer drinking
> (Almost) everyone smokes

in the visual and performing arts. The academic atmosphere at Stockton is different for different students. "If you want to receive a good education you can," says a math major, "but if you want to skate through, you can also do that." Professors come in "a huge variety." "Most of the professors are great teachers, prefer discussion-oriented classes instead of straight lecture, and are more than willing to help students succeed in and out of the classroom," says a computer science major. However, "there are a few" other faculty members that are "horrible." Registration at Stockton can be a pain. Some classes are reportedly "never available." Some students say that management is "very accessible and in touch." Others call the administration "cumbersome" and "generally a mess."

Life

"You need a strong stomach for campus food" and the parking situation is reportedly "pretty bad." Also, students say that the campus is located "in the sticks." However, an immediate benefit of that is that "the campus itself is right on the edge of New Jersey's Pine Barrens and it is absolutely gorgeous." Socially, "Stockton is a suitcase school that is bustling with commuters and residents during the week but is practically dead on the weekends." "There are plenty of clubs for people to join" and "all the generic stuff people usually do at college" is available here. The Greek system is small but pretty active. Intramural sports are popular and "real competitive." "There isn't much school pride" when it comes to intercollegiate sports, though. For students who stick around on the weekends, "there is the typical college party vibe," but nothing gets too crazy. There isn't a ton to do in the immediate area, but the campus is located "near the beach" and "Atlantic City is right around the corner." Students say that "it's pretty awesome to be so close to such a strong attraction."

Student Body

"There is great ethnic diversity on campus." Stockton has "a good mix" of "small-town kids" from south Jersey and kids from the areas around Philadelphia and New York City. There are lots of commuters. Only about one-third of all undergrads live in residence halls or other campus housing. "You have your hippies, but then you also have you sorority and fraternity members and athletes," observes a first-year student. You "see a lot of skateboarders," and the "Jersey Shore surfer" is pretty common as well. Students call themselves "environmentally-conscious" and "beachy" and tell us they have an "overall laidback demeanor." They are "interested in school but not obsessed with GPAs." Stockton is "somewhat cliquey" but "everyone is very friendly" and "and everyone generally gets along."

THE PRINCETON REVIEW SAYS

Admissions

Very important factors considered include: Class rank, rigor of secondary school record, standardized test scores. *Important factors considered include:* Academic GPA, extracurricular activities. *Other factors considered include:* Application essay, recommendation(s), alumni/ae relation, character/personal qualities, first generation, racial/ethnic status, talent/ability, volunteer work, work experience. SAT or ACT required; TOEFL required of all international applicants. High school diploma is required and GED is accepted. *Academic units required:* 4 English, 3 mathematics, 2 science, (2 science labs), 2 social studies, 2 history, 5 academic electives. *Academic units recommended:* 2 foreign language, 2 social studies, 2 history.

Financial Aid

Students should submit: FAFSA. The Princeton Review suggests that all financial aid forms be submitted as soon as possible after January 1. *Need-based scholarships/grants offered:* Federal Pell, SEOG, state scholarships/grants, the school's own gift aid. *Loan aid offered:* FFEL Subsidized Stafford, FFEL Unsubsidized Stafford, FFEL PLUS, Federal Perkins, state loans Applicants will be notified of awards on a rolling basis beginning 4/1. Federal Work-Study Program available. Institutional employment available. Off-campus job opportunities are excellent.

The Inside Word

Admission at Stockton isn't terrifically competitive. If you can maintain a solid 'B' average in a respectable college-bound high school curriculum and present average SAT scores, you should be fine. Your class rank is something that is very important as well. If your grades and test scores are below par, an on-campus interview is a wise idea.

THE SCHOOL SAYS "..."

From The Admissions Office

"Stockton College of New Jersey offers the atmosphere and rigorous academics of the very finest private institutions, at a surprisingly affordable cost. Stockton's outstanding faculty includes a Pulitzer Prize winner, two Fulbright Scholars, and the recipient of an Academy Award, several Emmy Awards, and a Grammy Award. Awards don't tell the whole story, though. Stockton's faculty is dedicated to teaching excellence and student success.

"Student life at Stockton is second to none. Our sports teams are nationally ranked, including the 2001 National Division III men's soccer champions. We recently opened a state-of-the-art, $17-million sports center that includes a fully equipped fitness center, and there are new arts and science, health science, and student housing buildings. Stockton's beautiful campus was voted one of the state's "Top 10 Architectural Treasures" by *New Jersey Monthly* magazine. Our pristine 1,600 acres are located within the Pinelands national preserves, including four lakes as well as trails for hiking and biking—all within a 10-minute drive to the popular southern New Jersey beach resorts. The numerous attractions of Philadelphia and New York City are easily accessible as well.

"Stockton features small class sizes, professors who are friendly and accessible, and student organizations to serve every interest. For the student seeking a total college experience at the most reasonable cost possible, Stockton College of New Jersey offers the best of both worlds. Stockton truly lives up to its slogan: 'An Environment for Excellence.'"

For even more information on this school, turn to page 504 of the "Stats" section.

RIDER UNIVERSITY

2083 LAWRENCEVILLE ROAD, LAWRENCEVILLE, NJ 08648-3099 • FAX: 609-896-5042
E-MAIL: ADMISSIONS@RIDER.EDU • WEBSITE: WWW.RIDER.EDU

RATINGS
Quality of Life: 70   Academic: 75   Admissions: 75   Financial Aid: 71

STUDENTS SAY "..."

Academics

Rider University is a smallish suburban liberal arts school in New Jersey that offers internships galore and a wide variety of majors. Rider's Westminster Choir College (in nearby Princeton) is worth looking into if you can hum a tune exceptionally well, but the biggest draw here is prob-

> **SURVEY SAYS . . .**
> *Great library*
> *Athletic facilities are great*
> *Lots of beer drinking*
> *(Almost) everyone smokes*

ably the "very good business program." Academically, "the classes aren't too big." "Last semester my biggest class had 17 kids in it," notes a public relations major. Coursework is generally "engaging." A few members of the faculty "should not be teaching," but most professors are "intelligent people with a lot to offer." They're "very interested and involved within their respective fields." "Professors are very easy to contact and are always excited to help answer a question even when you don't have them as a professor anymore," relates an accounting major. "It is easy to build close personal relationships with your professors and that really helps students do well in the classroom." Views of the administration differ pretty radically. Some students call management "very efficient" and "simply wonderful." "Customer service is excellent," they say. Other students say that the staff is "rude and very unhelpful." "It is very hard for me to get a straight answer," gripes an education major.

Life

Rider's main campus is "secluded from town" and full of too many "outdated and jail-like" buildings. Also, some dorms could stand to be "spruced up." The newer residence halls are "great" though, and the gleaming student recreation center is a big hit with many students. There's also a nice on-campus pub. Otherwise, "fun is a touchy topic." Disgruntled students tell us that life at Rider "is not amazingly exciting." It's "a suitcase school," they say, and "a ghost town on the weekends" because so many students "drive home" on Friday night. "Basically there's not a lot to do around here," laments a sophomore. Happier students report an "overwhelming" number of activities and a good amount of free food at weekend events. "One of the biggest perks about staying on the weekend is that you get a really good parking spot," says an optimistic sophomore. Many students who stick around also participate in the Greek system. "A lot of people party," too, but "the alcohol policies are extreme." As a result, there are "numerous parties off campus." Students also frequent "clubs and bars" in the area. While "there's nothing to do anywhere in Lawrenceville without having a car," Rider is situated "directly between" Philadelphia and New York City and those cities are easily accessible.

Student Body

"Mostly, everyone is from New Jersey," but ethnic diversity is pretty laudable at Rider and "students come from many different backgrounds." "It's not too hard to fit in." "There are a lot of students who take their work seriously." "There are the weird people who don't really socialize." There are also "slacker types" with "no sense of the real world" who are "trying to float through college" and "are more concerned with the party scene than academics." There are students "from middleclass homes" and wealthy students "with nice cars." You'll see quite a few women with "skinny jeans, Uggs, and poofy hair." There are "many clone students," too. "Your average student looks like your average kid that you would see in your own town," guesses a junior. "Overall, everyone has a niche" but "you have to join a group to make friends." "There are a lot of cliques," observes a senior. "The athletes stay with the athletes; the Greeks stay with the Greeks; and so on." Many people "stay connected to their high school friends."

THE PRINCETON REVIEW SAYS

Admissions

Very important factors considered include: Application essay, academic GPA, recommendation(s), rigor of secondary school record, standardized test scores. *Important factors considered include:* Class rank, level of applicant's interest. *Other factors considered include:* Alumni/ae relation, character/personal qualities, extracurricular activities, geographical residence, interview, state residency, talent/ability, volunteer work, work experience. SAT or ACT required; High school diploma is required and GED is accepted. *Academic units required:* 4 English, 3 mathematics (including algebra I, II, and geometry). *Academic units recommended:* 4 mathematics, 4 science, (2 science labs), 2 foreign language, 2 social studies, 2 history.

Financial Aid

Students should submit: FAFSA. The Princeton Review suggests that all financial aid forms be submitted as soon as possible after January 1. *Need-based scholarships/grants offered:* Federal Pell, SEOG, state scholarships/grants, private scholarships, the school's own gift aid. *Loan aid offered:* FFEL Subsidized Stafford, FFEL Unsubsidized Stafford, FFEL PLUS, Federal Perkins, state loans, college/university loans from institutional funds, Alternative loans. Applicants will be notified of awards on a rolling basis beginning 3/15. Federal Work-Study Program available. Student employment available.

The Inside Word

In the admissions world there are two all-important mandates: recruit the college's home state, and recruit Jersey! As a school in the Garden State, Rider deserves some special attention for the diverse group of students it brings in each year. Students who wish to attend need to have a solid academic record and good test scores. A few bumps in your academic past, however, shouldn't pose too much of a threat.

THE SCHOOL SAYS "..."

From The Admissions Office

"Rider students are driven by their dreams of a fulfilling career and a desire to have an impact on the world around them. Rider is a place to apply your imagination, talents and aspirations in ways that will make a difference. A Rider education will prepare you as a leader and as a member of a team. When you graduate from Rider, you'll be a different person, confidently ready for your life's challenges and opportunities.

"We invite you to visit and experience Rider firsthand. Open Houses are offered in the fall and late spring, tours are available daily and Information Sessions are offered most weekends. Please see our website (www.rider.edu) for further details.

"Freshmen applicants for Fall 2009 are required to submit the results of either the SAT or ACT exam, the writing component is required for both. The highest scores from either test will be considered for admission."

For even more information on this school, turn to page 504 of the "Stats" section.

ROBERTS WESLEYAN COLLEGE

2301 WESTSIDE DRIVE, ROCHESTER, NY 14624-1997 • ADMISSIONS: 585-594-6400 • FAX: 585-594-6371
E-MAIL: ADMISSIONS@ROBERTS.EDU • WEBSITE: WWW.ROBERTS.EDU

RATINGS
Quality of Life: 78   **Academic:** 76   **Admissions:** 77   **Financial Aid:** 73

STUDENTS SAY ". . ."

Academics

A small, Free Methodist school just outside of Rochester, New York, Roberts Wesleyan College is committed to "shaping students who will go out and impact the world in a positive way." To that end, Roberts employs "extremely friendly" and "very down to earth" professors who "educat[e] the complete person: mind, body, and spirit." Faculty

members "even hand out their home phone numbers if we need help or even a friend to talk to," a freshman gushes. Undergrads are particularly enthusiastic about the school's programs in business, education, music, nursing, and social work. While opinions vary on the difficulty of course work at RWC—some deem it "pretty easy," others rate it "challenging"—students agree that "there are always places to talk and resources to use" for those who want them, and that "motivated student[s] can always take initiative to do more." While a few students gripe that administrators are "not fully in tune with the students," and that "college policies are enforced on a less-than-consistent basis," just as many praise a "great financial [aid] package" and "good scholarship."

Life

Students at Roberts Wesleyan say they have two primary concerns: God and education. Students say, "The focus on education is not negated by our focus on God; rather, it is enhanced [by it]." Undergrads spend considerable time "talk[ing] about and debat[ing] spiritual and ethical issues" with their peers. "I have good grades, but it is easy to choose friends and fun over homework," a marketing major writes. Roberts "does not allow alcohol or drug consumption at all, including cigarettes," and visiting hours "end at 10:00 P.M.," after which "You can't have a [student of the] opposite sex in your room," so "good, clean fun" predominates here. This suits most students just fine. "We are all about service and getting involved in making our school, community, and the world better places," a sophomore writes. "For fun, we get involved in clubs, worship services, intramural sports, community service, and special events such as dances, roller skating, and festivals." Other students feel the Roberts social scene lacks in excitement, "especially on weekends, when the locals go home." These students occasionally head to "downtown Rochester" to blow off steam.

Student Body

Most undergrads at Roberts Wesleyan chose to enroll here because they "wanted to be on a Christian campus, or their parents wanted them to be on a Christian campus." These students, by and large, are "suburban," "White," and "extremely social." Many "have on-campus jobs and are involved in . . . campus organizations, religious or otherwise." Atypical students are those who come to Roberts for a reason other than the Christian environment—such as academics or athletics. These students, while not "discriminate[d] against," are considered either "socially awkward" or "partiers" by the more mainstream students. Many choose to "make their own groups."

THE PRINCETON REVIEW SAYS

Admissions

Very important factors considered include: Application essay, academic GPA, recommendation(s), standardized test scores, character/personal qualities. *Important factors considered include:* Class rank, rigor of secondary school record, religious affiliation/commitment. *Other factors considered include:* Alumni/ae relation, extracurricular activities, interview, level of applicant's interest, talent/ability, volunteer work, work experience. SAT recommended; SAT or ACT required; ACT recommended; ACT with Writing component recommended. TOEFL required of all international applicants. High school diploma is required and GED is accepted. *Academic units required:* 4 English, 3 mathematics, 3 science, (1 science labs), 3 social studies. *Academic units recommended:* (3 science labs), 3 foreign language.

Financial Aid

Students should submit: FAFSA, state aid form. The Princeton Review suggests that all financial aid forms be submitted as soon as possible after January 1. *Need-based scholarships/grants offered:* Federal Pell, SEOG, state scholarships/grants, private scholarships, the school's own gift aid. *Loan aid offered:* FFEL Subsidized Stafford, FFEL Unsubsidized Stafford, FFEL PLUS, Federal Perkins Applicants will be notified of awards on a rolling basis beginning 3/1. Federal Work-Study Program available. Institutional employment available. Off-campus job opportunities are fair.

The Inside Word

Many students who are not a fit with Roberts's strict rules or Christian environment bail before completing a degree here; only about 80 percent of freshmen stick it out. The bottom line? Roberts has a need for transfer students. If you're looking to transfer—and think Roberts would be a good fit for you—the school offers plenty of helpful information on its website, including course comparisons with local community colleges. Students at these schools can see which of their courses will satisfy general and degree requirements at Roberts.

THE SCHOOL SAYS ". . ."

From The Admissions Office

"A Roberts Wesleyan education is beneficial beyond just the first job—Roberts instills in students the knowledge and skills needed for a lifetime of learning and success. At Roberts Wesleyan College, we look for students who are interested in a Christian liberal arts education with plenty of professional opportunities. Students who would benefit from small class sizes, numerous internship options, a close-knit Christian community, and strong academic programs are encouraged to apply.

"Roberts Wesleyan College is a vital part of Rochester, New York's exceptional mix of educational opportunities. With nearly 2,000 students and a tradition of excellence since 1866, Roberts Wesleyan is a dynamic leader among American liberal arts colleges with a Christian worldview.

"Roberts Wesleyan offers over 50 undergraduate programs, with graduate programs in education, school psychology and counseling, social work, management, Nursing Leadership & Administration, and Nursing Education. Roberts also offers undergraduate degree-completion programs for working adults in nursing (classroom-based) and organizational management (classroom and online). Northeastern Seminary on the Roberts campus offers Master of Divinity, Master of Arts in Theology, and Doctor of Ministry degrees.

"Roberts Wesleyan is accredited by the Middle States Association of Colleges and Schools, the National Association of Schools of Music, the National Association of Schools of Art and Design, the National League of Nursing, the Council for Social Work Education, and the International Assembly for Collegiate Business Education (IACBE)."

For even more information on this school, turn to page 505 of the "Stats" section.

ROCHESTER INSTITUTE OF TECHNOLOGY

60 LOMB MEMORIAL DRIVE, ROCHESTER, NY 14623 • ADMISSIONS: 716-475-6631 • FAX: 716-475-7424
FINANCIAL AID: 716-475-2186 • E-MAIL: ADMISSIONS@RIT.EDU • WEBSITE: WWW.RIT.EDU

RATINGS
Quality of Life: 75   Academic: 79   Admissions: 83   Financial Aid: 90

STUDENTS SAY ". . ."

Academics

Rochester Institute of Technology is a "serious, no-non-sense school" "with amazing facilities" and a "unique" cooperative education program which is "very good" at "preparing you to work in the real world." The "great technical education" is a main draw for students. Other "high-quality programs" include animation, design, and the "renowned" College of Business. The National Technical Institute for the Deaf "makes for a diverse population."

> **SURVEY SAYS . . .**
> *Large classes*
> *Lab facilities are great*
> *Great computer facilities*
> *Great library*
> *Athletic facilities are great*
> *Career services are great*

"Hard work" and a "fast pace" define academic life. Courses "go by fast" on RIT's "hard-core" 10-week quarter system. "Classes require a lot of outside work," says a junior. One bonus of attending RIT is that "the best employers in the country hold on-campus interviews frequently." Upon graduation, "Job placement is really high" thanks to RIT's co-op program that "is required for many majors and encouraged for all." Co-op students graduate with "hands-on" experience at firms across the country. The "very passionate" professors here "come to teach, not to do research." "Academic support" is ubiquitous. "Even the worst professors I've had in lecture have been helpful after class," says an engineering major. "If you don't do well, it's your own fault." The "visible" administration is "fairly helpful." Some students wish administrators would "listen to their students a little bit more," but "The dean of your college is just an e-mail and appointment away."

Life

"Everything is made of brick" here and the "freezing" winters can be "very hard to walk through every day." "They should put us in a dome," helpfully suggests a first-year student. The weather notwithstanding, "RIT is a place where you come to work hard and make a lot of money when you graduate," explains a senior. The "competitive academic environment" "makes a lot of the students stress out," and students really "have to study." "On weekends, people tend to relax." "If you're looking for a party school," look elsewhere. "Big parties" are sometimes held "off-campus," but "not like the ones that happen at other schools." "Very intense alcohol-free policies" also stifle the party scene, and Greek organizations "are kept on an annoyingly tight leash." "School spirit" is not the highest, but "There are many different types of activities on campus." "Almost anyone who is looking for something to do can find a place to fit in." Engineering clubs "give students hands-on experience and knowledge that they can apply to both their schoolwork and the career world." The campus "is a great venue for influential speakers" and "The College Activities Board does a great job of getting big acts to come perform." There is also "an amazing gym," and "downtown Rochester is close and has a lot" to offer, including "amazing Indian and sushi restaurants."

Student Body

RIT students are "very hardworking" and "career-motivated." "Grades are taken very seriously." Students say "super-smart" engineering majors and "crazy science students" are typical, as are "ragtag art students, preppy business students, jocks, [and] hippies." Many students "like to fool around with computers." Some students assert that "RIT is a nerd haven." Others complain that RIT has a "reputation of being a dork school when it really isn't." "There is a stereotype that students here are unsocial and like to sit in their room playing video games," complains a senior. Without question, there are "kids who don't come out of their rooms," but those that do leave their confines "are awesome." "The variety of programs offered draws a very diverse group of students that can in no way fit under one general description," explains a junior. "The interaction of these extremely different groups of students is part of what makes life on campus so interesting." That said, RIT is "predominantly male" and many would like to see the male/female ratio improved.

THE PRINCETON REVIEW SAYS
Admissions
Very important factors considered include: Academic GPA, rigor of secondary school record. *Important factors considered include:* Class rank, standardized test scores. *Other factors considered include:* Application essay, recommendation(s), alumni/ae relation, character/personal qualities, extracurricular activities, first generation, geographical residence, interview, level of applicant's interest, racial/ethnic status, talent/ability, volunteer work, SAT or ACT required; High school diploma is required and GED is accepted. *Academic units required:* 4 English, 2 mathematics, 2 science, (1 science labs), 4 social studies, 10 academic electives. *Academic units recommended:* 4 English, 3 mathematics, 3 science, (2 science labs), 3 foreign language, 4 social studies, 5 academic electives.

Financial Aid
Students should submit: FAFSA, state aid form. The Princeton Review suggests that all financial aid forms be submitted as soon as possible after January 1. *Need-based scholarships/grants offered:* Federal Pell, SEOG, state scholarships/grants, private scholarships, the school's own gift aid, NACME. *Loan aid offered:* Direct Subsidized Stafford, Direct Unsubsidized Stafford, Direct PLUS, Federal Perkins, RIT Loan program; Alternative loans. Applicants will be notified of awards on a rolling basis beginning 3/15. Federal Work-Study Program available. Institutional employment available. Off-campus job opportunities are excellent.

The Inside Word
Admission here is nowhere near as cutthroat as it is at other top-tier technical schools on the East Coast. But that doesn't mean admission isn't competitive, since RIT's co-op programs and its tremendous record of job placement with prestigious employers all over the country make it an attractive choice for many academically-talented applicants. The relatively high acceptance rate is somewhat deceiving because the applicant pool is largely self-selecting. The applicant pool is also small enough that RIT can go over your application with the finest-toothed of combs, for better or worse.

THE SCHOOL SAYS ". . ."
From The Admissions Office
"RIT is among the world's leading career-oriented, technological institutions. Ambitious, creative, diverse, and career-oriented students from every state and more than 95 foreign countries find a home in RIT's innovative, vibrant living/learning community.   The university's eight colleges offer undergraduate and graduate programs areas such as engineering, computing, information technology, engineering technology, business, hospitality, science, art, design, photography, biomedical sciences, game design and development, and the liberal arts including psychology, advertising and public relations, and public policy   Distinctive academic offerings include microelectronic and software engineering, imaging science, film and animation, biotechnology, physician assistant, new media, international business, telecommunications, and the programs in the School for American Crafts.   In addition, students may choose from more than seventy different minors to develop personal and professional interests that complement their academic program. As home of the National Technical Institute for the Deaf (NTID), RIT is a leader in providing educational opportunities and access services for deaf and hard-of-hearing students. Experiential learning has been a hallmark of an RIT education since 1912. Every academic program at RIT offers some form of experiential education opportunity which may include cooperative education, internships, study abroad, and undergraduate research. Students work hard, but learning is complemented with plenty of organized and spontaneous events and activities. RIT is a unique blend of rigor and fun, creativity and specialization, intellect and practice that prepares alumni for long-term career success in global society."

For even more information on this school, turn to page 505 of the "Stats" section.

ROGER WILLIAMS UNIVERSITY

ONE OLD FERRY ROAD, BRISTOL, RI 02809 • ADMISSIONS: 401-254-3500 • FAX: 401-254-3557
E-MAIL: ADMIT@RWU.EDU • WEBSITE: WWW.RWU.EDU

RATINGS
Quality of Life: 80   **Academic:** 76   **Admissions:** 80   **Financial Aid:** 85

STUDENTS SAY ". . ."

Academics

Roger Williams University is a "fairly small" private school in a suburban Rhode Island community "right on the water overlooking Mount Hope Bay." The view "can't be beat." There's a nationally renowned program in marine biology. The very demanding architecture program is "really good," too. There are "endless opportunities" for "hands-

on" undergraduate research and study abroad. Some students say the administration is "top notch." Others charge that "registration is a complete pain in the ass" and call management "extremely, unnecessarily bureaucratic." The faculty is generally "wonderful," "except for one or two who are just boring." Most RWU professors are "always trying to engage students" and "approachable." "If they can't teach it to you in class, they will try something different outside of class," one student explains. Classes are small and intimate, too. "I like being in small classes where the professor is on a first-name basis with every student," says an English Literature major. "This school isn't a Harvard or a Caltech," concludes a biology major, "but it seems to serve its place in the education pecking order fairly well."

Life

RWU's "breathtaking" campus is "well kept" and "the new buildings are gorgeous." "The food is *incredible*." "It's healthier than most food at other schools," too. Residence halls are "run down" and "filthy" or "very homey and cozy," presumably depending on where you live. Socially, Roger Williams is "a plethora of fun." "Intramural sports are incredibly popular." "There are nightly programs and guest lectures on campus." A few times each year, the old gym becomes "a nightclub with a theme." There are "tons" of activities—everything from squirrel watching to kayaking. Thanks to the "amazing waterfront location," "many students spend a great deal of time on or near the water." "Kids here love to drink" as well. The festivities start on Thursday (or possibly Wednesday). "Choosing not to be a part of that scene does not condemn you to social death," though. "A lot of students frequent the local bars not necessarily to party or get drunk, but to be social." "Drugs are very popular," too, as are cigarettes. Off-campus, nearby Providence and Newport are "very popular for evening activities" and "it's a reasonably decent drive up to Boston."

Student Body

Nearly 80 percent of the student body ventures to Roger Williams from out-of-state. "The typical student comes from a suburban New England town" or from the Mid-Atlantic region. Many students note that RWU stands for "Rich White Underachievers." "The parking lot is full of BMWs and Volvos" and there is definitely a contingent of "astronomically rich" kids "who slacked off too much in high school" but "there are many middle-class students" as well. These students "are usually preppy" and "dress fashionably." The architecture students consider themselves "a different breed from most of the students on campus" but virtually everyone comes "from the same mold." It's "a sea" of white "but very tan" students. "We need more black people," emphasizes a senior, "Please. I grew up in affluent suburban Connecticut and when I got here I was like 'Wow, it's not very diverse here at all.'" To be sure, "minority students are fully accepted into the college community." It's just that that there aren't many of them. "It's so homogeneous here, it hurts."

THE PRINCETON REVIEW SAYS

Admissions

Very important factors considered include: Application essay, academic GPA, recommendation(s), rigor of secondary school record, standardized test scores. *Important factors considered include:* Class rank, extracurricular activities. *Other factors considered include:* Alumni/ae relation, character/personal qualities, first generation, talent/ability, volunteer work, work experience. SAT or ACT required; ACT with Writing component recommended. High school diploma is required and GED is accepted. *Academic units required:* 4 English, 3 mathematics, 2 science, (2 science labs), 2 social studies, 2 history, 2 academic electives. *Academic units recommended:* 4 English, 4 mathematics, 4 science, (2 science labs), 2 foreign language, 3 social studies, 3 history, 3 academic electives.

Financial Aid

Students should submit: FAFSA, CSS/Financial Aid PROFILE. Regular filing deadline is 2/1. The Princeton Review suggests that all financial aid forms be submitted as soon as possible after January 1. *Need-based scholarships/grants offered:* Federal Pell, SEOG, state scholarships/grants, private scholarships, the school's own gift aid. *Loan aid offered:* FFEL Subsidized Stafford, FFEL Unsubsidized Stafford, FFEL PLUS, Federal Perkins Applicants will be notified of awards on a rolling basis beginning 3/20. Federal Work-Study Program available. Institutional employment available. Off-campus job opportunities are excellent.

The Inside Word

Admission to the school's well-regarded architecture program is competitive; all other programs are much less so. Architecture candidates should apply early and would be well advised to spend considerable effort on their portfolios.

THE SCHOOL SAYS ". . ."

From The Admissions Office

"Located on a beautiful, waterfront campus in historic Bristol, Rhode Island, Roger Williams University is a leading liberal arts university in New England. Our modern, safe, 140-acre campus places you among many nearby resources and attractions. You'll enjoy the region's engaging lifestyles and vibrant cultures. Also, our campus is easily accessible from urban centers such as Providence, Boston, and New York by car or other transportation.

"We offer 35 challenging academic majors through a liberal arts college, five professional schools, graduate programs, and the state's only law school. Accredited by the New England Association of Schools and Colleges, Roger Williams University has 3,300 full-time undergraduates. We're just the right size to offer you the friendliness and attention of a small liberal arts college, but with the professional tracks and research opportunities of a larger university. It's the best of both worlds. You'll also benefit from an array of support services to ease your arrival and make your years here comfortable and enjoyable. We give you what you're looking for—a high-quality education within an ideal academic setting that encompasses excellent facilities, recreation, athletics, and social life. Modern academic and support facilities are within walking distance of residence halls. Students have access to first-rate resources including libraries, state-of-the-art computer centers, and other advantages such as design and art studios. A Roger Williams University education gives you the chance to become a complete person who is successfully able to bridge transitions to a rewarding career and gratifying life."

For even more information on this school, turn to page 506 of the "Stats" section.

ROSEMONT COLLEGE

1400 Montgomery Avenue, Rosemont, PA 19010 • Admissions: 610-526-2966 • Fax: 610-520-4399
E-mail: admissions@rosemont.edu • Website: www.rosemont.edu

RATINGS

Quality of Life: 80   Academic: 79   Admissions: 79   Financial Aid: 75

STUDENTS SAY "..."

Academics

Rosemont College, an "all-female" college just outside of Philadelphia, "is about providing young women the essential tools...to become active, independent, aware and analytical members of society, so that they may be successful in whichever path they choose to pursue." How are those tools conveyed? Reportedly through an "education centered

around personal attention, leadership opportunities, and friendship." "The class sizes are small so there is more discussion in the classroom." "Overall, the professors are excellent, and they are very concerned about their students." One student even describes having "gained confidence as a young woman just because the professors have invested themselves into showing me that they care about my individual success." Additionally, the college's "location and the natural beauty of the campus also help the students to feel safe." Students also really appreciate that the college "provides a lot of financial aid." Academic drawbacks include those typical of a small college: "All classes are only offered once a year, either always in the fall or always in the spring. Or they are offered every two years or only once." So if you are interested in a course, best to take it the first time you see it offered—it might not be offered again.

Life

"Rosemont is known as a 'suitcase college,'" meaning that "most students go home or leave campus for the weekends." Still, "there are activities on campus regularly" during the week, and for those who stick around on weekends. There is "movie night, casino night," and for those looking for a cause to support, "there are many special interest clubs." The Rosemont Activities Council also sponsors dance parties. "The most popular party is the Halloween party because it is the one party that serves free beer to the students who are over 21." And speaking of beer, "Admittedly, people like the bar scene." That common predilection, coupled with the "strict rules and regulations about alcohol" that Rosemont enforces, means that many "students find other colleges and places to have fun." Luckily for them, it's easy to get off campus. "The R5 train a few blocks from campus can take you into Philly or the movies or a grocery store (for real food)." In addition to the taste of city life Philadelphia has to offer, "many students like to go to the King of Prussia mall for shopping."

Student Body

Rosemont is "an all-women's college" where "typically everybody is very friendly...and pretty driven." "They understand that school comes first, but that it is also important to socialize." "They are seriously involved in one or two clubs on campus and may attend a couple of the several campus functions each semester." But beyond these common qualities, the student body is remarkably diverse, consisting "of many different ethnicities and religious backgrounds." "Some wear a hijab, some are running around in a little sundress. Then there are students who are changing their sexual identity." Atypical students are the commuters, who might describe their experience at Rosemont as feeling "a little left out."

THE PRINCETON REVIEW SAYS

Admissions

Very important factors considered include: Class rank, rigor of secondary school record, interview. *Important factors considered include:* Application essay, recommendation(s), standardized test scores, extracurricular activities, talent/ability, volunteer work. *Other factors considered include:* Alumni/ae relation, character/personal qualities, work experience. SAT required; TOEFL required of all international applicants. High school diploma is required and GED is accepted. *Academic units required:* 4 English, 3 mathematics, 3 science, (2 science labs), 1 social studies, 1 history, 7 academic electives. *Academic units recommended:* 4 English, 3 mathematics, 3 science, (2 science labs), 2 foreign language, 2 social studies, 2 history, 4 academic electives.

Financial Aid

Students should submit: FAFSA. The Princeton Review suggests that all financial aid forms be submitted as soon as possible after January 1. *Need-based scholarships/grants offered:* Federal Pell, SEOG, state scholarships/grants, private scholarships, the school's own gift aid. *Loan aid offered:* FFEL Subsidized Stafford, FFEL Unsubsidized Stafford, FFEL PLUS, Federal Perkins, Alternative loans offered, payment plans offered. Applicants will be notified of awards on a rolling basis beginning 2/15. Federal Work-Study Program available. Institutional employment available. Off-campus job opportunities are good.

The Inside Word

Rosemont's Admissions Staff wants to ensure that its students are a perfect fit for both classroom and community. While high school transcript, standardized test scores, and letters of recommendation are all major considerations, pros here strongly suggest a campus visit and admissions interview.

THE SCHOOL SAYS ". . ."

From The Admissions Office

"Current Rosemont students tell us that the college provides them with an excellent education, that their experience is empowering, and that at Rosemont they meet friends they will keep for life. Rosemont has provided a unique educational experience for almost 85 years and continues to seek to enroll women interested in the liberal arts who have the capacity and desire to pursue a rigorous academic program. Students are considered without regard to race, religion, disability, or ethnic or national origin. A candidate for admission must present a satisfactory record of scholastic ability and personal integrity from an accredited high school as well as acceptable scores on the SAT or ACT. The student must have an official copy of her high school transcript sent to Rosemont's Office of Admissions. An applicant's secondary school preparation should include 16 college preparatory courses. Applicants are expected to carry a full academic program during their senior year of high school. Two recommendations are required in support of the student's application. Applications for admission are accepted on a rolling basis. A personal interview with a member of the Admissions Staff is strongly recommended as an important part of the application process. Prospective students are also encouraged to make arrangements to visit classes, meet Rosemont students, and whenever possible, stay overnight.

"To arrange for an interview and a tour, or to receive additional information, students should contact the Office of Admissions."

For even more information on this school, turn to page 506 of the "Stats" section.

ROWAN UNIVERSITY

201 MULLICA HILL ROAD, GLASSBORO, NJ 08028 • ADMISSIONS: 856-256-4200 • FAX: 856-256-4430
E-MAIL: ADMISSIONS@ROWAN.EDU • WEBSITE: WWW.ROWAN.EDU

RATINGS
Quality of Life: 61   Academic: 73   Admissions: 84   Financial Aid: 73

STUDENTS SAY "..."

Academics

A New Jersey state school just southeast of Philadelphia, Rowan University is "dedicated to offering students a high quality education at an affordable price" as well as "a prodigious college experience through its many social, cultural and recreational organizations, events and activities." The school is perhaps best known for its "amazing education program that prepares future teachers in the best way possible," but students here tell us that offerings in engineering, music, business, history, and radio/television/film also shine. Rowan's science departments recently received an upgrade with "newer facilities" that are "very modern and have great equipment." Professors here receive good marks overall, although students warn that there is "too much variation in the quality of a course depending on the professor." "You could end up with great professors who are also tough, but you could also end up with professors whose courses aren't very challenging at all," explains a student. "For me, though, I have found the workload quite sizable and tough at times."

Life

"Campus life during the week tends to be pretty quiet" at Rowan, though most students are active within many of the campus' popular clubs and organizations. Others partake in bowling, shopping, laid back parties, and 50-cent movies (typically "the ones that came out of theaters but have not been released on DVD yet"). There are "plenty of parties to be found on weekends"—but be warned as the weekend starts on "Thursday night, and nearly everyone goes out." Things calm down a bit on Fridays and Saturdays when some students "go home to their families," but those who remain behind "usually end up having a lot of fun." Although drinking is popular, "Most people don't pressure other people into drinking," and nonalcoholic events are available. As one student explains, "There are a lot of options in terms of on-campus jobs, clubs, sports, and other organizations. If Rowan doesn't offer something you're interested in, you can get a few friends and start it on your own!" Many students choose to seek entertainment in nearby Philadelphia; the city is accessible by bus.

Student Body

The Rowan student body is "ethnically-diverse but the majority are Caucasian and familiar with the region of South Jersey." Students are described as "very down-to-earth," "normal," and "average to high-middle class kids just trying to get an education." Many "get involved in several things on campus...have at least one job on-campus or are members of at least one club or organization." "Anyone can find a place to fit in at Rowan University because of the wide variety of students, events and organizations Rowan University offers." Some students "keep to themselves ... [but] overall, students are very friendly and mannered. It's a more mature level of interaction," explains an undergrad.

THE PRINCETON REVIEW SAYS

Admissions

Very important factors considered include: Class rank, academic GPA, rigor of secondary school record, standardized test scores. *Important factors considered include:* Recommendation(s), extracurricular activities, talent/ability. *Other factors considered include:* Character/personal qualities, level of applicant's interest, racial/ethnic status, volunteer work, work experience. SAT or ACT required; TOEFL required of all international applicants. High school diploma is required and GED is accepted. *Academic units required:* 4 English, 3 mathematics, 2 science, (2 science labs), 2 social studies, 5 academic electives.

Financial Aid

Students should submit: FAFSA. The Princeton Review suggests that all financial aid forms be submitted as soon as possible after January 1. *Need-based scholarships/grants offered:* Federal Pell, SEOG, state scholarships/grants, private scholarships, the school's own gift aid. *Loan aid offered:* Direct Subsidized Stafford, Direct Unsubsidized Stafford, Direct PLUS Applicants will be notified of awards on a rolling basis beginning 3/15. Off-campus job opportunities are good.

The Inside Word

Low in-state tuition draws lots of applicants to Rowan, resulting in a pretty high rejection rate. Don't expect too personal an experience during this process. Admissions officers crunch numbers, then consider the balance of the application for marginal applicants, so a good letter of recommendation or an impressive slate of extracurriculars can really help out here. Solid high school students should encounter little difficulty gaining entry, though the school does grow more selective every year as its profile rises.

THE SCHOOL SAYS "..."

From The Admissions Office

"Rowan University is a selective, progressive public university with the funds and public support to transform itself into a top regional university. It is using these resources to improve the academic quality of the university while keeping tuition affordable. Because of its large endowment, the university is able to compete with private colleges and produce direct benefits for students. The university is in the midst of a $530-million 10-year plan to expand the campus, improve facilities, and hire more faculty. By implementing a comprehensive plan for enrollment management, Rowan University will maintain its reputation as a high-quality, moderate-price university.

"These efforts have caught the attention of organizations that evaluate colleges and universities nationwide. *U.S. News & World Report* ranks Rowan University in the 'Top Tier' of Northern Regional Universities. *Kiplinger's* named Rowan University one of the '100 Best Buys in Public Colleges and Universities.'

"At Rowan, students have access to the resources of a large university without sacrificing the personal attention and small class size of a private college. All classes are taught by professors, not teaching assistants. The university enrolls more than 10,000 students among seven colleges (Business, Communication, Education, Engineering, Fine and Performing Arts, Liberal Arts and Sciences, and Professional & Continuing Education). Students can choose from 58 undergraduate majors and 29 graduate programs leading to master's and doctoral degrees."

For even more information on this school, turn to page 506 of the "Stats" section.

RUTGERS, THE STATE UNIVERSITY OF NEW JERSEY—NEW BRUNSWICK

65 DAVIDSON ROAD, PISCATAWAY, NJ 08854-8097 • ADMISSIONS: 732-932-4636 • FAX: 732-445-0237
FINANCIAL AID: 732-932-7057 • E-MAIL: ADMISSIONS@ASB-UGADM.RUTGERS.EDU • WEBSITE: WWW.RUTGERS.EDU

RATINGS
Quality of Life: 63   Academic: 71   Admissions: 87   Financial Aid: 72

STUDENTS SAY "..."

Academics

Rutgers, The State University of New Jersey—New Brunswick, "is the kind of university [at which], if you make the effort to create your niche and find opportunities to succeed, you will have one of the best experiences of your life." With "a great study abroad program, solid academic departments and professors, the vast resources of a large research . . . and lots of scholarship money for honors students," Rutgers "offers boundless opportunity, both educational and professional, but you have to be willing to go out and seek it." Rutgers' immenseness is made more

manageable by its subdivision into 13 colleges, "each with its own unique community and environment, all unified under one entity that can afford all the opportunities of a large university." Even so, the university's bureaucracy is legendary; one student writes, "The school seems to take pride in its web of red tape. The famous 'RU Screw' has become so notorious that the university president had to publicly denounce it." It's a good sign that Rutgers "is progressively changing its administrative policies under the administration of its relatively new president. There is a renewed focus on student service, and the changes are evident." As at many state schools, "Good things will not happen at Rutgers by sitting in the corner and waiting for opportunity to knock. It is a big school, so the more you put yourself out and make yourself known, the more likely you'll be able to find help in academics and administration." For self-starters, the rewards can be great; one writes, "I've had the opportunity to [conduct] my own research in the Rutgers facilities." Indeed, "There is a lot of research going on at Rutgers. The topics are numerous, and there are plenty of spots to fill if you look around well enough."

Life

"Weekdays are busy, and you can find places crowded at any time of the day" on the Rutgers campus, as "There's always something going on: concerts, free movies, talks. It's all about diversity and going out to find what you want to do." Student government "is huge, as is Rock the Vote. . . . There's always voter registration drives, and we even have Tent State University in the spring, during which a bunch of political student groups set up tents on the main courtyard and camp out for a week handing out literature, having fun stuff (concerts, etc.), and talking to people about what they do and how they can get involved." For some, "drinking is a big thing." One student writes, "If there was no such thing as getting inebriated, there would be nothing to do here." Many refute that position, noting that "there are other things you can do as well besides. There are lots of places to eat and drink coffee, . . . stuff like Jazz 'n' Java put on by the Douglass Black Students Caucus, . . . or going to a small discussion group with Jhumpa Lahiri, the Pulitzer Prize–winning writer," to name a few. While weekdays are lively, weekends are another story. One student comments, "Life at Rutgers would feel more college-y if people didn't leave on weekends and it [didn't feel] so deserted."

Student Body

Rutgers "is huge, so there is just about every type of person you could think of here." One undergrad observes, "With so many students, it's hard not to find others with whom you fit in. But the drawback to such a large student body is that you need to go out and make friends; you can't expect them to come to you." Another student adds, "To be fair, sometimes it feels a bit like high school (there are 'skaters' and 'preps' and 'thugs' and all that), but once you're an upperclassmen you kind of learn to ignore it."

THE PRINCETON REVIEW SAYS

Admissions

Very important factors considered include: Class rank, academic GPA, rigor of secondary school record, standardized test scores. *Other factors considered include:* Application essay, recommendation(s), extracurricular activities, first generation, geographical residence, interview, racial/ethnic status, state residency, talent/ability, volunteer work, work experience. SAT or ACT required; High school diploma is required and GED is accepted. *Academic units required:* 4 English, 3 mathematics, 2 science, 2 foreign language, 5 academic electives. *Academic units recommended:* 4 mathematics, 2 foreign language.

Financial Aid

Students should submit: FAFSA. The Princeton Review suggests that all financial aid forms be submitted as soon as possible after January 1. *Need-based scholarships/grants offered:* Federal Pell, SEOG, state scholarships/grants, private scholarships, the school's own gift aid, Outside Scholarships. *Loan aid offered:* Direct Subsidized Stafford, Direct Unsubsidized Stafford, Direct PLUS, Federal Perkins, Federal Nursing, state loans, college/university loans from institutional funds.   Educational Loans. Applicants will be notified of awards on a rolling basis beginning 2/1.

The Inside Word

With a literal mountain of applications to process each admissions season, Rutgers does not have the luxury of time. The school looks at your grades, the quality of your high school curriculum, your standardized test scores, and your essay to decide whether you can make the grade at Rutgers. Although the school grows more competitive each year, solid students should still find little difficulty getting in.

THE SCHOOL SAYS ". . ."

From The Admissions Office

"Rutgers, The State University of New Jersey, one of only 62 members of the Association of American Universities, is a research university that attracts students from across the nation and around the world. What does it take to be accepted for admission to Rutgers University? Our primary emphasis is on your past academic performance as indicated by your high school grades (particularly in required academic subjects), your class rank or cumulative average, the strength of your academic program, your standardized test scores on the SAT or ACT, any special talents you may have, and your participation in school and community activities. We seek students with a broad diversity of talents, interests, and backgrounds. Above all else, we're looking for students who will get the most out of a Rutgers education—students with the intellect, initiative, and motivation to make full use of the opportunities we have to offer.

"Fall 2008 first-year applicants should take the SAT Reasoning Test or the ACT (with Writing component) no later than November 2007 in order to meet our December 1 priority application date. SAT scores from the March 2007 test administration and later are acceptable. Test scores are not required for students who graduated high school more than 2 years ago or have completed more than 12 college credits since graduating."

For even more information on this school, turn to page 507 of the "Stats" section.

SACRED HEART UNIVERSITY

5151 PARK AVENUE, FAIRFIELD, CT 06825 • ADMISSIONS: 203-371-7880 • FAX: 203-365-7607
E-MAIL: ENROLL@SACREDHEART.EDU • WEBSITE: WWW.SACREDHEART.EDU

RATINGS
Quality of Life: 79   Academic: 78   Admissions: 83   Financial Aid: 74

STUDENTS SAY "..."

Academics

Looking for an "excellent education" in Southern New England? Then Sacred Heart University may be the place for you. As one undergrad says, "I feel as though Sacred Heart offers some of the most brilliant professors available in the academic world." High praise, though as another explains, "At SHU, you can really connect with your professors. It is the kind of school where professors know the names of all of their students and remember them after the semester ends." The net result is an academic atmosphere that is "both stimulating and intellectually fulfilling." Learning is enhanced by SHU's "advanced" technology, which means that "the whole campus is wireless and most professors use this to their advantage by putting notes and assignments online, which saves paper and students from arthritis." Some students do complain that some upper-level administrators "seem disconnected." Others note that they would like to see the "registration process improve." But, all in all, if you're willing to suffer a few administrative headaches, you just might discover that "the academic experience is great!"

> ### SURVEY SAYS . . .
> *Large classes*
> *Great computer facilities*
> *Athletic facilities are great*
> *Career services are great*
> *Campus feels safe*
> *Everyone loves the Pioneers*

Life

"If you don't get involved then you don't get the most of the life on campus"—and yes, there's plenty to pick from at SHU. According to one freshman, "There's pretty much a club for anyone, making it easy to become involved. There are also community service projects happening all the time." A classmate adds, "Every day they e-mail us with the 'Events of the Day,' and there's always something going on . . . midnight volleyball, acoustic shows at the Outpost, concerts, sports games, and even Ping-Pong tournaments." Athletics are also a "big part" of student life. "I'm usually at almost every athletic event with my face painted red and a crazy wig on," says an enthusiastic supporter. Though SHU is officially a "dry campus," there are many wet appetites here. "It is a big bar school," explains one student. "There are some parties that go on, but the bars are where people go." To get to the bars in nearby Fairfield or Bridgeport, most students take cabs—"and the cabs are very expensive." There's also "a shuttle that takes everyone to the mall and runs on the hour." Other popular weekend destinations include New Haven, only "20 minutes away," and New York is "an hour" from campus.

Student Body

Your typical SHU student "is either a Yankee or Red Sox fan." In other words, most undergrads hail from the Northeast—"from Massachusetts, New York, and Connecticut," in particular. But if you call some far-off land home, don't worry: "Everyone seems to fit in, even if you're not from these states." A freshman describes her fellow Pioneers as "easily approachable, kind, courteous, respectful, and outgoing." But another first-year says that the four words that best describe your average SHU undergrad are "White, rich, preppy, and Catholic." Look beyond the "average" undergrad and you'll see that "the students at Sacred Heart come in all different shapes and colors, and come from different backgrounds and come from all over the world."

THE PRINCETON REVIEW SAYS

Admissions

Very important factors considered include: Academic GPA, rigor of secondary school record. *Important factors considered include:* Class rank, recommendation(s), standardized test scores, character/personal qualities, extracurricular activities, interview, talent/ability, volunteer work, work experience. *Other factors considered include:* Application essay, alumni/ae relation, first generation, geographical residence, level of applicant's interest, racial/ethnic status, religious affiliation/commitment, state residency, SAT or ACT required; ACT with Writing component required. TOEFL required of all international applicants. High school diploma is required and GED is accepted. *Academic units required:* 4 English, 3 mathematics, 3 science, (1 science labs), 2 foreign language, 3 social studies, 3 history, 3 academic electives. *Academic units recommended:* 4 English, 4 mathematics, 4 science, (2 science labs), 4 foreign language, 4 social studies, 4 history, 4 academic electives.

Financial Aid

Students should submit: FAFSA, CSS/Financial Aid PROFILE, noncustodial PROFILE. The Princeton Review suggests that all financial aid forms be submitted as soon as possible after January 1. *Need-based scholarships/grants offered:* Federal Pell, SEOG, state scholarships/grants, private scholarships, the school's own gift aid, Federal Nursing Scholarships. *Loan aid offered:* FFEL Subsidized Stafford, FFEL Unsubsidized Stafford, FFEL PLUS, Federal Perkins, state loans, Alternative loans. Applicants will be notified of awards on a rolling basis beginning 3/1. Federal Work-Study Program available. Institutional employment available. Off-campus job opportunities are excellent.

The Inside Word

Who's the person behind the application? This is what the Admissions Officers at student-friendly Sacred Heart University want to know. While they place heavy emphasis on traditional academic indicators like high-school curriculum and GPA, they also spend time reading each applicant's admissions essay. If you really want to make an impact, why not head to Sacred Heart for a campus visit? A strong interview can turn many tides to your favor.

THE SCHOOL SAYS ". . ."

From The Admissions Office

"Sacred Heart University, distinguished by the personal attention it provides its students, is a thriving, dynamic university known for its commitment to academic excellence, cutting-edge technology, and community service. The second-largest Catholic university in New England, Sacred Heart continues to be innovative in its offerings to students; recently launched programs include Connecticut's first doctoral program in physical therapy, an MBA program for liberal arts undergraduates at the newly AACSB-accredited John F. Welch College of Business, and a campus in County Kerry, Ireland. The university's commitment to experiential learning incorporates concrete, real-life study for students in all majors. Drawing on the rich resources in New England and New York City, students are connected with research and internship opportunities ranging from co-ops at international advertising agencies to research with faculty on marine life in the Long Island Sound. These experiential learning opportunities are complemented by a rich student life program offering over 80 student organizations including strong music programs, media clubs, and academic honor societies. To help students transition to college life and navigate the many opportunities available, all freshmen are assigned mentors, who work one-on-one to facilitate students' personal development and enhance the learning process both in and out of the classroom. Students applying to Sacred Heart University benefit from a comprehensive, holistic admissions process which takes into account not only applicants' grade point averages and standardized test scores, but also their overall student profiles including strength of college preparatory curricula, leadership and community service experience, character, and extraordinary talents. Either the SAT or the ACT (with Writing component) is required for admission. For students taking the SAT more than once, the highest Math score and the highest Critical Reading score will be evaluated by the Admissions Committee. No current policy exists for the use of the SAT Writing component. "

For even more information on this school, turn to page 507 of the "Stats" section.

SAINT ANSELM COLLEGE

100 SAINT ANSELM DRIVE, MANCHESTER, NH 03102-1310 • ADMISSIONS: 888-4ANSELM
FAX: 603-641-7550 • FINANCIAL AID: FINANCIAL_AID@ANSELM.EDU • WEBSITE: WWW.ANSELM.EDU

RATINGS
Quality of Life: 86   Academic: 84   Admissions: 84   Financial Aid: 79

STUDENTS SAY ". . ."

Academics

If you long for four years of "Catholic faith and hard classes," consider "wonderful, small" Saint Anselm College in
Manchester, New Hampshire. The nursing program is
reportedly "awesome" but Saint Anselm is best known for
providing "a true liberal arts education." In addition to com-

> SURVEY SAYS . . .
> Great library
> Students are friendly
> Lots of beer drinking

prehensive exams in every major, all students must complete three courses each in philosophy and theology, two
English courses, two science courses, a year of foreign language, and four common humanities courses. "Some
people enjoy the humanities program." Others say "the lectures can be absolute torture." Depending on who you
talk to, the administration either "functions smoothly" or is "too Catholic" and "takes its sweet ass time with
everything." Students almost universally gush about their "passionate" professors. "I get tons of individual attention," brags a nursing major. "They are always willing to set a time with you outside of class for help." However,
"essays are numerous," and "classes are very difficult." "The library is always filled." There is something of a "cru-
sade against grade inflation" on this campus as well. "St. A's is known as St. C's," explains a junior. "Despite how
hard you work, you may not see the results you want," warns an English major. Other students tell us that "the
work is not excruciatingly hard." "It's definitely not impossible," says a biochemistry major. "I'm no rocket scien-
tist, and I'm taking in at least two A's this semester," agrees a classics major. "St. A's requires you to work very
hard, but in a warm, friendly, and respectful atmosphere where there are plenty of opportunities to make your college years fantastic," reflects a business major.

Life

This "absolutely gorgeous" campus boasts "spectacular" food. "Internet technology is a joke" though, and the
recreational facilities aren't much. A few students complain that Saint Anselm is "a suitcase school" but others
say that "you can be involved in numerous things." "It is a small, tight-knit school, where if you stick around
on-campus and get involved you will have the best time ever," declares a senior. "Community service is big."
"I've never seen such a giving school," gloats a first-year student. There's Mass every day, and you'll always
find a few Benedictine monks around campus. "The monks are awesome," says a junior. "For students who are
interested, Saint Anselm is a haven for politics." The "really cool" New Hampshire Institute of Politics provides
"a lot of speakers and political candidates," particularly when primary season rolls around. "It's a big deal to
go to the hockey games." "Intramural sports are very popular," too. "The pub is a great place on campus for
juniors and seniors who are 21 to grab a drink and relax." Various campus policies are "strict" though. First year
residence halls are not co-ed and visitation hours for members of the opposite sex are limited. "If you're looking for an intense party scene, Saint Anselm College isn't the place," advises a senior. Nevertheless, "the senior
housing always has something going on" and "drinking is very prevalent" on the weekends, "though students
must be sneaky." Nearby Boston is "a great option for the weekends" as well.

Student Body

The stereotype at Saint Anselm is definitely a "white, Catholic Red Sox fan." "Most students I've met here have
Boston accents, at least half are Irish, and went to a private school," observes a freshman. There's "only a handful of minorities." "The student body is not the most diverse community but most people are very welcoming,"
adds a senior. "Social groups here tend to be well defined and yet somehow still permeable, or at least, amiable
to one another." There are "sheltered, ignorant snobs," but "the majority of students is middle-class and receives
some sort of financial aid." Students at Saint A's describe themselves as "smart, hardworking, involved in community service," and "very preppy." "There are a select few who are rebellious, artsy, and try to stand out but
they generally get along with the preppy kids." "Most kids are on an athletic team of some type." Many are serious about religion, "but many are not." Politically, opinions "are surprisingly varied for a campus that is pretty conservative."

Admissions

Very important factors considered include: Academic GPA, rigor of secondary school record, character/personal qualities. *Important factors considered include:* Class rank, application essay, recommendation(s), standardized test scores, talent/ability. *Other factors considered include:* Alumni/ae relation, extracurricular activities, geographical residence, level of applicant's interest, racial/ethnic status, volunteer work, work experience. SAT or ACT required; TOEFL required of all international applicants. High school diploma is required and GED is accepted. *Academic units required:* 4 English, 3 mathematics, 3 science, (3 science labs), 2 foreign language, 2 social studies, 1 history, 3 academic electives. *Academic units recommended:* 4 mathematics, 4 science, 4 foreign language, 2 history.

Financial Aid

Students should submit: FAFSA, CSS/Financial Aid PROFILE. Regular filing deadline is 3/15. The Princeton Review suggests that all financial aid forms be submitted as soon as possible after January 1. *Need-based scholarships/grants offered:* Federal Pell, SEOG, state scholarships/grants, private scholarships *Loan aid offered:* FFEL Subsidized Stafford, FFEL Unsubsidized Stafford, FFEL PLUS, Federal Perkins, GATE student loans. Applicants will be notified of awards on a rolling basis beginning 3/1. Federal Work-Study Program available. Institutional employment available. Off-campus job opportunities are excellent.

The Inside Word

St. Anselm gets a predominately regional applicant pool, and Massachusetts is one of its biggest suppliers of students. An above-average academic record should be more than adequate to gain admission.

THE SCHOOL SAYS ". . ."

From The Admissions Office

"Why Saint Anselm? The answer lies with our graduates. Not only do our alumni go on to successful careers in medicine, law, human services, and other areas, but they also make connections on campus that last a lifetime. With small classes, professors are accessible and approachable. The Benedictine monks serve not only as founders of the college but as teachers, mentors, and spiritual leaders.

"Saint Anselm is rich in history, but certainly not stuck in a bygone era. In fact, the college has launched a $50-million fund-raising campaign, which will significantly increase funding for financial aid, academic programs, and technology. New initiatives include the New Hampshire Institute of Politics, where the guest list includes every major candidate from the 2000 presidential race, as well as other political movers and shakers. Not a political junkie? No problem. The NHIOP is a diverse undertaking that also involves elements of psychology, history, theology, ethics, and statistics.

"Saint Anselm encourages students to challenge themselves academically and to lead lives that are both creative and generous. On that note, more than 40 percent of our students participate in community service locally and globally. Each year, about 150 students take part in Spring Break Alternative to help those less fortunate across the United States and Latin America. High expectations and lofty goals are hallmarks of a Saint Anselm College education, and each student is encouraged to achieve his/her full potential here. Why Saint Anselm? Accept the challenge and soon you will discover your own answers.

"Freshman applicants for Fall 2008 must take the SAT or the ACT. Students may submit scores from the old or new SAT. The best scores from either test will be used in admissions decisions."

For even more information on this school, turn to page 508 of the "Stats" section.

SAINT JOSEPH'S UNIVERSITY (PA)

5600 CITY AVENUE, PHILADELPHIA, PA 19131 • ADMISSIONS: 888-BE-A-HAWK • FAX: 610-660-1314
E-MAIL: ADMIT@SJU.EDU • WEBSITE: WWW.SJU.EDU

RATINGS
Quality of Life: 78   **Academic:** 82   **Admissions:** 86   **Financial Aid:** 78

STUDENTS SAY ". . ."
Academics

"Saint Joseph's University is a tight-knit Jesuit school," which means that it is dedicated to "cura personalis," that is, "developing the whole person." To that end, students "have to take a number of general ed courses, such as theology and the like." Some students feel they "could definitely do without some of the GERs and have more electives," but others appreciate the more "rounded" academic experience that the general education requirements provide.

Another component of a Jesuit education is a "commitment to social justice," so students are encouraged to provide "service to others." Fortunately, students report, "a lot of our service projects are good." The undergraduate business school, which is "pretty well known," is the standout academic program here. "The study abroad center is also good." As far as professors go, they "make themselves wholly available to students—many give out their home/cell phone numbers—and are generally committed to high standards of personal and professional competence." On balance, the "administration is very polite," and students generally agree that "the president, Father Lannon, is brilliant and so cool." While "Saint Joe's has a gorgeous campus," students complain that some "academic facilities aren't as state-of-the-art as other universities."

Life

To say that school spirit at Saint Joseph's is overflowing is an understatement. "The Hawk will never die!" is not just a school cheer; for many, it's a mantra that captures the very gestalt of the student experience here. What are the main elements of that experience? First, in general, "sporting events are popular," and in particular, "basketball games are insane." Second, "service/volunteering is a big part of student life, and…often people are off building houses in the Appalachia region or tutoring kids in Camden, NJ." Then there are the more typical college pastimes that are also popular at Saint Joseph's. "The bar scene is…very big." "Parties are also a big scene, both during the week and on weekends." "SJU also provides a lot of weekend programming that is geared toward freshmen, but can be enjoyed by the entire student body. The programs are generally free or at a low cost to the students and take them off campus (to a New York Broadway show, a cultural event in the city of Philadelphia, or a concert right at SJU)." "Because SJU is so close to the city and other areas like Manayunk and the Main Line many people go into the city on weekends." "You are literally a five-minute train ride away." In addition, "King of Prussia Mall isn't far away, and neither is the Jersey shore." Students grouse that campus "security and cafeteria food could be a little better."

Student Body

"St. Joe's is heaven on Earth if you are a semi-preppy, middle class student who has school-spirit," are "white," "went to a Catholic high school" "or top public school" in "New Jersey, Pennsylvania, Maryland, New York, or Connecticut," and are "looking for a job." The typical student here "works hard, plays hard, and has most likely done weekly community service." "Although not necessarily devoutly religious, students are, for the most part, somewhat religious." That is, the typical student here "loves the bars and parties on the weekends, then goes to Mass" on Sunday. "There are some minorities, but they still fit the middle-class Catholic school mold." If there is one uniting force for students here, it is that "school spirit is huge. Almost everyone takes a lot of pride in being a Hawk."

Admissions

Very important factors considered include: Academic GPA, rigor of secondary school record. *Important factors considered include:* Application essay, recommendation(s), character/personal qualities. *Other factors considered include:* Class rank, standardized test scores, alumni/ae relation, extracurricular activities, first generation, religious affiliation/commitment, talent/ability, volunteer work, work experience. SAT or ACT required; High school diploma is required and GED is not accepted. *Academic units required:* 4 English, 3 mathematics, 2 science, (2 science labs), 2 foreign language, 1 history. *Academic units recommended:* 4 English, 3 mathematics, 2 science, (2 science labs), 2 foreign language, 1 history.

Financial Aid

Students should submit: FAFSA. The Princeton Review suggests that all financial aid forms be submitted as soon as possible after January 1. *Need-based scholarships/grants offered:* Federal Pell, SEOG, state scholarships/grants, private scholarships, the school's own gift aid. *Loan aid offered:* FFEL Subsidized Stafford, FFEL Unsubsidized Stafford, FFEL PLUS, Federal Perkins Applicants will be notified of awards on a rolling basis beginning 3/1. Federal Work-Study Program available. Institutional employment available. Off-campus job opportunities are excellent.

The Inside Word

Despite a growing applicant pool, the credentials that enrolled students generally bring to the table have not changed much in recent years. Those with GPAs above 3.5 and SAT scores above 1200 should not face many problems gaining admission as long as they take the application process seriously. The Jesuit ideals of educating the whole person and social justice are valued here, so students do well to highlight any community service experience they have during the application process.

THE SCHOOL SAYS ". . ."

From The Admissions Office

"For over 150 years, Saint Joseph's University has advanced the professional and personal ambitions of men and women by providing a rigorous Jesuit education—one that demands high achievement, expands knowledge, deepens understanding, stresses effective reasoning and communication, develops moral and spiritual character, and imparts enduring pride.

"As a Jesuit university, Saint Joseph's believes each student realizes his or her fullest potential through challenging classroom study, hands-on learning opportunities, and a commitment to excellence in all endeavors. The university also reinforces the individual's lifelong engagement with the wider world. Graduates of Saint Joseph's attain success in their careers with the help of an extensive network of alumni who have become leading figures in business, law, medicine, education, the arts, technology, government, and public service.

"A Saint Joseph's education encompasses all aspects of personal growth and development, reflecting the Ignatian credo of *cura personalis*—concern for the individual student. Guided by a faculty committed to both teaching and scholarship, students develop intellectually through an intense liberal arts curriculum and advanced study in a chosen discipline. Students *grow personally* by participating in Saint Joseph's campus life, noted for its rich variety of activities, infectious enthusiasm, and mutual respect. Students grow ethically and spiritually by living their own values in the larger society beyond campus.

"Located on the edge of metropolitan Philadelphia, Saint Joseph's University provides ready access to the vast career opportunities and cultural resources of America's fifth-largest city, while affording students a cohesive and intimate campus experience."

For even more information on this school, turn to page 508 of the "Stats" section.

SAINT MARY'S COLLEGE OF MARYLAND

ADMISSIONS OFFICE, 18952 EAST FISHER ROAD, ST. MARY'S CITY, MD 20686-3001 • ADMISSIONS: 800-492-7181 • FAX: 240-895-5001
FINANCIAL AID: 240-895-3000 • E-MAIL: ADMISSIONS@SMCM.EDU • WEBSITE: WWW.SMCM.EDU

RATINGS
Quality of Life: 93   Academic: 87   Admissions: 90   Financial Aid: 85

STUDENTS SAY ". . ."

Academics

Set on the "beautiful St. Mary's River", St. Mary's College of Maryland is a "humble oasis" that "has all of the intellectual stimulation of a private liberal arts school with none of the academic rivalry." The blissfully content students at SMCM throw around the word "community" like rice at a wedding, and always precede it with some sort of positive lead-in: "small," "open-minded," "social justice minded, environmentally-friendly, hippie-loving, and very diverse and accepting" are just some of the descriptors used. Classes

> **SURVEY SAYS . . .**
> *Large classes*
> *Athletic facilities are great*
> *Students are friendly*
> *Campus feels safe*
> *Students are happy*
> *Frats and sororities are unpopular or nonexistent*

here are "rigorous" and "very engaging, requiring participation and input from all of the students," and the "amazing" professors are lauded for their brilliance, love of the material, and sheer accessibility; students talk of having seen professors "at school events not related to their classes and been invited to class dinners at their houses." Not only does the small size of the school mean that the faculty knows each student's name—"you are NEVER a number"—but "you get to know your professors on a personal level, which is great when it comes time for them to write recommendations for scholarships, graduate school, or future jobs." The administration gets positive reviews with just a few naysayers. The deans are commended for being "everywhere, participating in athletics, music programs, etc." and making it clear " that the students are the first priority," but a few students still say that the administration "can be a little bit withdrawn from the student body." Although there are complaints of too much construction around the campus, most students know that improvements and growth are necessary for the growth of the college, though they do wish to see more immediate changes to the health services, which "need some serious work."

Life

The phrase "summer camp setting" doesn't just refer to the campus' looks; Frisbee golf, sailing, bonfires, sun tanning, and kayaking in the school-provided kayaks are some of the main activities for students taking a break from their studies (which often occur outside). The river seems to be the hub of student life, not only acting as a "tremendous stress reliever"," but a sort of ad hoc campus center. Since the "very outdoorsy" campus is located in a remote location, "most of the fun that happens occurs on campus," and "the cold winter months are often difficult to bear and result in cabin fever." The lack of metropolitan areas (the nearest being Annapolis) means SMCM is "very residential," and "you really develop your own home and nest here with your friends as family." "There is a decent party scene on campus" with "parties on the weekends, studying during the week," but "students are rarely pressured to drink and many don't do it all." The plethora of clubs and other activities mean no one goes home bored. "I couldn't ask for a better college experience," says a junior.

Student Body

The diversity rate here isn't all that high (though it's not expected to be at such a small school), but no one has any real complaints. Most here are very environmentally oriented, "both in terms of their leisure activities and in terms of their political leanings." Some affectionately refer to their "hippie" classmates, but the "very accepting" student body has plenty of "pearl-wearing preps" and jocks in its "big social mosh pit," so "even the non-tree huggers amongst us can find a comfortable niche with little trouble." "It's entirely acceptable to be a bit quirky," says a junior. SMCM "is truly its own place," and this extreme love of the campus and its surroundings creates a sort of communal understanding anyone not contributing to its betterment will find themselves answering to the angry masses. "Word gets around on a small campus, and if you are mean or vandalize or something, people will know and shun you for that bad action."

Admissions

Very important factors considered include: Academic GPA, rigor of secondary school record. *Important factors considered include:* Application essay, recommendation(s), standardized test scores, alumni/ae relation, character/personal qualities, extracurricular activities, first generation, talent/ability, volunteer work. *Other factors considered include:* Class rank, geographical residence, interview, racial/ethnic status, state residency, work experience. SAT or ACT required; High school diploma is required and GED is accepted. *Academic units required:* 4 English, 3 mathematics, 3 science, (2 science labs), 2 foreign language, 2 social studies, 1 history, 3 academic electives. *Academic units recommended:* 4 English, 4 mathematics, 3 science, (2 science labs), 4 foreign language, 2 social studies, 2 history, 3 academic electives.

Financial Aid

Students should submit: FAFSA Regular filing deadline is 3/1. The Princeton Review suggests that all financial aid forms be submitted as soon as possible after January 1. *Need-based scholarships/grants offered:* Federal Pell, SEOG, state scholarships/grants, private scholarships, the school's own gift aid. *Loan aid offered:* FFEL Subsidized Stafford, FFEL Unsubsidized Stafford, FFEL PLUS, Federal Perkins Applicants will be notified of awards on or about 4/1. Federal Work-Study Program available. Institutional employment available. Off-campus job opportunities are good.

The Inside Word

There are few better choices than St. Mary's for better-than-average students who are not likely to get admitted to one of the top 50 or so colleges in the country. It is likely that if funding for public colleges is able to stabilize, or even grow, that this place will soon be joining the ranks of the best. Now is the time to take advantage, before the academic expectations of the Admissions Committee start to soar.

THE SCHOOL SAYS ". . ."

From The Admissions Office

"St. Mary's College of Maryland occupies a distinctive niche and represents a real value in American higher education. It is a public college, dedicated to the ideal of affordable, accessible education but committed to quality teaching and excellent programs for undergraduate students. The result is that St. Mary's offers the small college experience of the same high caliber usually found at prestigious private colleges, but at public college prices. Designated by the state of Maryland as 'a public honors college,' one of only two public colleges in the nation to hold that distinction, St. Mary's has become increasingly attractive to high school students. Admission is very selective.

"For Fall 2008, applicants must take the new version of the SAT, but students may submit scores from the old (prior to March 2005) SAT, and admissions will use the student's best scores from either test. The ACT with the Writing section is also accepted."

For even more information on this school, turn to page 509 of the "Stats" section.

SAINT MICHAEL'S COLLEGE

ONE WINOOSKI PARK, COLCHESTER, VT 05439 • ADMISSIONS: 802-654-3000 • FAX: 802-654-2591
E-MAIL: ADMISSION@SMCVT.EDU • WEBSITE: WWW.SMCVT.EDU

RATINGS
Quality of Life: 98   **Academic:** 84   **Admissions:** 84   **Financial Aid:** 77

STUDENTS SAY ". . ."

Academics

St Michael's College is a Catholic liberal art college that boasts "an absolutely unbeatable location" in the heart of "prime" Vermont ski territory. A reasonably broad set of core course requirements includes two mandatory religion classes. Study abroad is "huge." "Sciences are a very popular." "The education department, in general, is amazing." Coursework at SMC "can be very challenging—by no means

is everything a breeze." However, classes tend to be manageably small. "Rarely do you have a class larger than 30 students which gives you a nice, intimate classroom experience." "The administration and professors at the school are all very open and welcoming to every student," promises a junior. "Like any school, there are the good and the bad teachers." For the most part, though, "professors are really passionate and devoted to the subjects that they teach." They are "available outside of class and open to lots of discussion in the classroom, and always are willing to help." The biggest academic gripe here is probably the "insufficient" course selection, since "The size of the college limits the overall variety of courses."

Life

Saint Mike's is lively. "It's my opinion that you cannot be bored on this campus," asserts one student. "The theater kids, the sports kids, the campus ministry kids, the volunteer program kids, the fire and rescue kids—there are groups for everyone." The community service program is "extremely popular." Rallies and demonstrations are common. "Most people are moderately interested in the outdoors" and the Wilderness Program runs student-led trips each weekend. Socially, SMC is "really close knit." "The big family aspect of Saint Mike's makes it easy to meet people and make friends. That boils down to awesome weekends." "Monday through Thursday, people tend to really focus on classes." Thursday marks the beginning of the weekend, which continues until late Saturday night. Mostly, "people get absolutely hammered in their rooms," then amble around campus to "various parties and get-togethers." There's a drug scene, too, if that's your bag. If you choose not to partake in the festivities, it's fine. However, virtually all students "are required to live on campus all four years," and the "overcrowded" dorms are "a mess." Also, the Internet is "slower than death," and Vermont winters are "brutal." On the plus side, if you ski or snowboard, "several great mountains" are nearby. (Smugglers' Notch offers ridiculously cheap season passes through a special offer to Saint Mike's students.) In warmer weather, "many activities—even parties—happen outside in the beautiful Vermont scenery." For a change of pace, students take the free bus to "artsy," "adorable" Burlington, "a hubbub of fun."

Student Body

"We have little to no ethnic or racial diversity at our school," admits a senior. "For what it's worth, however, the minorities here blend in with the rest of the student body." "A typical student is a solid 'B' student in high school who's really involved" and hails from "20 minutes outside Boston," observes one student. There are plenty of "hockey/rugby player types" and many students are "involved in sports." Quite a few students grew up wealthy. "New, expensive cars" dot the campus. "There is an abundance of preppy kids." You'll know them by their "Ugg boots, North Face fleeces, and Vera Bradley bags." "Hippies" are around, but not pervasive. "St Mike's is painted as more of a hippie college than it really is," reports one student. Politically, there are conservatives, but there are a lot more "left-wing liberals who care too much about the environment." Overall, there's an "open, welcoming" vibe. "Everyone is pretty low key about fitting in." "You can see a hippie hugging a preppie or a Yankees fan and Red Sox fan eating lunch together," swears one student. "Everyone gets along here."

THE PRINCETON REVIEW SAYS

Admissions

Very important factors considered include: Class rank, academic GPA, rigor of secondary school record. *Important factors considered include:* Application essay, recommendation(s), standardized test scores, character/personal qualities, extracurricular activities, talent/ability. *Other factors considered include:* Alumni/ae relation, first generation, geographical residence, level of applicant's interest, racial/ethnic status, state residency, volunteer work, work experience. SAT or ACT required; ACT with Writing component required. TOEFL required of all international applicants. High school diploma is required and GED is accepted. *Academic units required:* 4 English, 3 mathematics, 3 science, (2 science labs), 3 foreign language, 3 social studies. *Academic units recommended:* 4 English, 4 mathematics, 4 science, (3 science labs), 4 foreign language, 4 social studies.

Financial Aid

Students should submit: FAFSA, Signed copies of Parent's 2007 Federal Tax Return, Parent's Federal W-2 forms, Signed copies of Student's 2007 Federal Tax Return, Student's Federal W-2 forms, Dependent 2008-09 Verification Worksheet (Please check the Student Financial Services fo The Princeton Review suggests that all financial aid forms be submitted as soon as possible after January 1. *Need-based scholarships/grants offered:* Federal Pell, SEOG, state scholarships/grants, private scholarships, the school's own gift aid. *Loan aid offered:* Direct Subsidized Stafford, FFEL Subsidized Stafford, FFEL Unsubsidized Stafford, FFEL PLUS, Federal Perkins Applicants will be notified of awards on a rolling basis beginning 1/15. Federal Work-Study Program available. Institutional employment available. Off-campus job opportunities are excellent.

Inside Word

Saint Mike's is a pretty easy admit if you've shown a reasonable level of consistency in solid college prep curriculum. Candidates who goofed around a little too much in high school would be well advised to strongly highlight their extracurricular activities.

THE SCHOOL SAYS "..."

From The Admissions Office

"Saint Michael's is a residential, Catholic, liberal arts college for students who want to make the world a better place.

"A Saint Michael's education will prepare you for life, as each of our 30 majors is grounded in our liberal studies core. Our superb faculty are committed first and foremost to teaching, and are known for really caring about their students while simultaneously challenging them to reach higher than they ever thought possible. Because of our holistic approach, Saint Michael's graduates are prepared for their entire careers, not just their first jobs out of college.

"With nearly 100% of students living on campus, our "24/7" learning environment means exceptional teaching goes beyond the classroom and into the living areas which include three new suite-style residences, townhouse apartments and traditional residence halls. The remarkable sense of community encourages students to get involved, take risks and think differently. A unique passion for social justice issues on campus reflects the heritage of the Edmundite priests who founded Saint Michael's in 1904.

"Saint Michael's is situated just outside of Burlington, Vermont's largest city and a true college town. A unique Cultural Pass program allows students to see an array of music, dance, theater and Broadway productions at the Flynn Center downtown. They also take advantage of some of the best skiing in the East through an agreement with Smugglers' Notch ski resort—an all-access season pass is provided to any Saint Michael's student in good academic standing."

For even more information on this school, turn to page 509 of the "Stats" section.

SALISBURY UNIVERSITY

ADMISSIONS OFFICE, 1101 CAMDEN AVENUE, SALISBURY, MD 21801 • ADMISSIONS: 410-543-6161
FAX: 410-546-6016 • FINANCIAL AID: 410-543-6165 • E-MAIL: ADMISSIONS@SALISBURY.EDU • WEBSITE: WWW.SALISBURY.EDU

RATINGS
Quality of Life: 78   **Academic:** 73   **Admissions:** 86   **Financial Aid:** 70

STUDENTS SAY ". . ."

Academics

Salisbury University has come a long way since it first opened its doors in 1925. Originally a two-year college, Salisbury gradually grew into a four-year BA-conferring school, then added graduate programs in education, business, and nursing. The pace of ascendance has quickened over the past decade, transforming Salisbury from a local school to a regional favorite to, most recently, a university

> **SURVEY SAYS . . .**
> *Lab facilities are great*
> *Great computer facilities*
> *Intramural sports are popular*
> *Lots of beer drinking*
> *Hard liquor is popular*

with some national draw. As one student observes, SU is "rapidly gaining respect and a reputation as a challenging, high-level academic institution." Part of the school's allure has to do with cost; SU is extremely affordable for Maryland residents and not much more expensive for out-of-state students. Scale is another factor at this "laid back, perfectly sized university" small enough to be "your home away from home," but large enough to "offer a top-notch education." Undergraduate business programs are the biggest draw here, attracting nearly 20 percent of all undergrads. Students love that the business curriculum prepares "well-rounded individuals" by "requiring us to have an internship to graduate, which forces one to get some real-world experience." The nursing, education, and communication programs also attract big crowds. In all programs, students enjoy "small class sizes, a compact campus, nice accessible professors, great majors, and fun trips." One student tells us that Salisbury "is about life learning, not just from textbooks and lectures, but from opportunity and diversity." Another adds that the university "is on its way to great things very soon."

Life

Life at SU "depends on what you are looking for. There is a club or organization for everything," and "all kinds of work, volunteer opportunities, and internships available through the school." The Student Office of Activity Programming (SOAP) "brings concerts, comedians, imitations of game shows, and open mic nights to campus and gives us students something fun and constructive to do!" The school's "amazing" Division III sports teams are well supported as well. Even so, many here tell us that life at SU "can get boring a lot of the time though because everything except bars and Taco Bell shuts down early, so many people end up going off-campus or to bars and getting drunk." This does not sit well with the conservative rural locals, and as a result, "We have a bad reputation with the Salisbury community. We are known for being a drinking school." And indeed, "Students do drink here at SU. I mean, we are known to be a party school and it's not a lie. But if you don't do that sort of thing then it's not a big deal. I had a hard time my freshman year first semester because I thought every one on campus went to parties and that's all there was to do. However, I found people who didn't go to parties to be friends with, and I started becoming more active in theatre and the Honors Student Association and I found my niche here at SU." As one student sums up, "Basically anything you want, SU has."

Student Body

SU undergrads are typically "laid back and like to hang out with friends, yet they know how and when to get work done when it needs to be done," although there are some here who "drink too much and complain when they don't get the grades they want even though they've skipped most classes due to hangovers. " Most of the latter are presumably gone by sophomore year. There are "a lot of student athletes" here as well as "a D&D crowd who are really nice. They sort of hang out with other Starnet (SciFi club) members." Insofar as diversity, SU apparently has "a department devoted to it."

THE PRINCETON REVIEW SAYS
Admissions
Very important factors considered include: Academic GPA, rigor of secondary school record, extracurricular activities, talent/ability. *Important factors considered include:* Class rank, standardized test scores, alumni/ae relation, geographical residence, volunteer work. *Other factors considered include:* Application essay, recommendation(s), character/personal qualities, racial/ethnic status, work experience. TOEFL required of all international applicants. High school diploma is required and GED is accepted. *Academic units required:* 4 English, 3 mathematics, 3 science, (2 science labs), 2 foreign language, 3 social studies. *Academic units recommended:* 4 English, 4 mathematics, 4 science, (3 science labs), 3 foreign language, 3 social studies, 3 academic electives.

Financial Aid
Students should submit: FAFSA Regular filing deadline is 12/31. The Princeton Review suggests that all financial aid forms be submitted as soon as possible after January 1. *Need-based scholarships/grants offered:* Federal Pell, SEOG, state scholarships/grants, private scholarships, the school's own gift aid. *Loan aid offered:* Direct Subsidized Stafford, Direct Unsubsidized Stafford, Direct PLUS, Federal Perkins Applicants will be notified of awards on a rolling basis beginning 3/15. Federal Work-Study Program available. Institutional employment available. Off-campus job opportunities are fair.

The Inside Word
Salisbury has increased its undergraduate population by nearly 20 percent since the start of the decade, which hasn't made admission here any easier. On the contrary, the expansion was a reaction to a growing national profile and corresponding increase in the number of applications. Despite the trend, you can still expect a careful, personalized reading of your application here. It's about a lot more than just the numbers at Salisbury; prepare your application accordingly.

THE SCHOOL SAYS ". . ."
From The Admissions Office
"Friendly, convenient, safe, and beautiful are just a few of the words used to describe the campus of Salisbury University. The campus is a compact, self-contained community that offers the full range of student services. Beautiful, traditional-style architecture and impeccably landscaped grounds combine to create an atmosphere that inspires learning and fosters student pride. Located just 30 minutes from the beaches of Ocean City, Maryland, SU students enjoy a year-round resort social life as well as an inside track on summer jobs. Situated less than 2 hours from the urban excitement of Baltimore and Washington, DC, greater Salisbury makes up for its lack of size—its population is about 80,000—by being strategically located. Within easy driving distance of a number of other major cities, including New York City, Philadelphia, and Norfolk, Salisbury is the hub of the Delmarva Peninsula, a mostly rural region flavored by the salty air of the Chesapeake Bay and Atlantic Ocean.

"Submission of SAT and/or ACT scores when applying would be optional to freshman applicants who present a weighted high school grade point average (GPA) of 3.5 or higher on a 4.0 scale. Any student applying with less than a 3.5 would still need to submit a standardized test score to supplement the official high school transcript. Additionally, an applicant may wish to submit a standardized test score subsequent to admission for full scholarship consideration as the majority of the University scholarships include test scores as a requirement."

For even more information on this school, turn to page 510 of the "Stats" section.

SALVE REGINA UNIVERSITY

100 OCHRE POINT AVENUE, NEWPORT, RI 02840-4192 • ADMISSIONS: 401-341-2908 • FAX: 401-848-2823
E-MAIL: SRUADMIS@SALVE.EDU • WEBSITE: WWW.SALVE.EDU

RATINGS

Quality of Life: 76   Academic: 80   Admissions: 87   Financial Aid: 70

STUDENTS SAY "..."

Academics

SURVEY SAYS . . .
Large classes
Students love Newport, RI
Great off-campus food
Frats and sororities are unpopular or nonexistent
Lots of beer drinking

Salve Regina offers "an excellent Catholic education" with a "focus on global issues combined with an unbelievably beautiful setting and small campus" to its 2,000 predominantly female students. The school "does an awesome job of tying the teachings of the Sisters of Mercy into every class" and "emphasizing the importance of community service in conjunction with higher learning in a multitude of areas." Best of all for those outside the Catholic faith, the school is "very supportive and welcoming of other religions." "The nursing and teaching programs are very strong" here, and students in all disciplines receive an "education centered around the classic liberal arts" that helps students "become better speakers, writers, and thinkers." An "extremely accessible faculty and administration" creates "an atmosphere where your teachers really care about you and your classmates become your best friends." "By the time you're a senior here, the professors and dean will know your name, make no doubt about it," one student assures us. Most undergrads here "find the academic experience challenging, but not overwhelming." One student reports that "Even in the honors sector, it seems that the emphasis is placed on more work, like essays and research papers, rather than on open-mindedness and independent projects. But overall, you can tell the teachers try their hardest to make classes fun and interesting."

Life

Located alongside Newport's mansion-lined Cliff Walk, the Salve Regina campus is "an unbelievably beautiful setting." The location—"10 minutes from the beach" with "an ocean view" from student residences ("students get to live in mansions")—is optimal. The city is "easy to get to via the trolley, which runs from downtown Newport to several stops on campus every twenty minutes." Newport "is fun, especially in the early fall and late spring when the stores are open late for tourist season" and it's "also a great place for outdoor activities, like bike riding, hiking, and going to the beach." During the off-season, "Many people go to Providence on weekends because there are a lot of over-18 clubs." Students also point out that "Boston is fairly close and easy to get to." Closer to home, students find that their peers "are very involved in campus activities." "The school is very good about having fun things available to students on campus. There is a movie theatre, there are concerts, and there is also a game area with pool tables." Parties are infrequent due to the school's 'dry campus' policy; "There are not many parties on campus because it is so strict, but there are some in Newport at people's houses," one student explains.

Student Body

"Everyone is pretty much the same: preppy and white," notes one student. Others agree, "The typical student is a white, upper-class female who wears Uggs and Prada sunglasses everyday." There are "a lot of spoiled kids here" but "that is countered with a good amount of genuine, fun, artsy people. You just have to know where to find these people, and in general you will find your niche by sophomore year." "Salve is pretty homogenous," though there are "lots of transfer students" and the international population includes "lots of students from Japan."

THE PRINCETON REVIEW SAYS

Admissions

Very important factors considered include: Class rank, academic GPA, rigor of secondary school record. *Important factors considered include:* Application essay, recommendation(s), standardized test scores. *Other factors considered include:* Alumni/ae relation, character/personal qualities, extracurricular activities, level of applicant's interest, racial/ethnic status, talent/ability, volunteer work, work experience. SAT or ACT required; TOEFL required of all international applicants. High school diploma is required and GED is accepted. *Academic units required:* 4 English, 3 mathematics, 2 science, (2 science labs), 2 foreign language, 1 social studies, 4 academic electives.

Financial Aid

Students should submit: FAFSA, CSS/Financial Aid PROFILE, business/farm supplement. Regular filing deadline is 3/1. The Princeton Review suggests that all financial aid forms be submitted as soon as possible after January 1. *Need-based scholarships/grants offered:* Federal Pell, SEOG, state scholarships/grants, private scholarships, the school's own gift aid. *Loan aid offered:* FFEL Subsidized Stafford, FFEL Unsubsidized Stafford, FFEL PLUS, Federal Perkins, Federal Nursing, state loans, college/university loans from institutional funds, private loans. Applicants will be notified of awards on a rolling basis beginning 2/1. Federal Work-Study Program available. Institutional employment available. Off-campus job opportunities are excellent.

The Inside Word

Salve Regina attracts many more applicants than it can accommodate in its freshman class, explaining why only about 55 percent of applicants are accepted. The school competes with many regional powerhouses for students, and as a result attracts few elite candidates. The profile of a typical admit here is a solid but not outstanding high school student with SAT scores in the mid-500s per section and a B+ grade average. Admission to the university does not guarantee subsequent admission to such popular programs as education.

THE SCHOOL SAYS "..."

From The Admissions Office

"Salve Regina University is a small university with big opportunity. Located on one of the most beautiful campuses in the country, Salve Regina's historic oceanfront campus is a place where students feel at home. Students study and live in historic mansions, yet receive an education that prepares them for modern careers and a lifetime of serving their communities. Salve offers excellent professional and liberal arts programs (most popular are business, education, administration of justice, and biology). The classes are small and are all taught by professors (no grad assistants). Salve's small size also makes it easy for students to get involved on campus with clubs, activities, athletics, or intramurals. At Salve, it is easy to become a leader—even in your first year.

"Newport offers the perfect location for students who love history, sailing, and the outdoors. Students can surf and ocean kayak from First Beach, or bike ride on the famous Ocean Drive. Newport also hosts several festivals throughout the year. All students get a free statewide trolley/bus pass that takes them throughout Newport or to Providence, only 30 minutes away.

"Admission to Salve Regina is competitive. The Admissions Office looks at several factors in reviewing applications. Most important are applicants' day-to-day academic work and the level of the courses they have taken. Recommendation letters and test scores are also reviewed, as are leadership positions and community involvement."

For even more information on this school, turn to page 510 of the "Stats" section.

SARAH LAWRENCE COLLEGE

One Mead Way, Bronxville, NY 10708-5999 • Admissions: 914-395-2510 • Fax: 914-395-2676
Financial Aid: 914-395-2570 • E-mail: slcadmit@mail.slc.edu • Website: www.slc.edu

RATINGS
Quality of Life: 64   **Academic:** 92   **Admissions:** 89   **Financial Aid:** 79

STUDENTS SAY "..."

Academics

Offering a unique approach to liberal arts education, Sarah Lawrence College is a "serious academic and artistic environment where individual passion fuels learning." Through SLC's distinctive curriculum, students are the architects of their own educational experience and the school "places a

> **SURVEY SAYS . . .**
> *Class discussions encouraged*
> *Large classes*
> *No one cheats*

great emphasis on personal research and personal responsibility." In their first year, undergrads meet with their advisors every week to discuss their academic plans, and "besides your don (permanent counselor), you have a slew of people who really want you to be the best that you can be." Of particular note, students benefit from "inordinate amounts of individual time with each professor," who are all "enormously educated, good teachers, and passionate about their subjects." Across disciplines, Sarah Lawrence professors "are generally willing to give over copious amounts of time to undergraduate research papers, projects, ideas, and extracurricular discussion." A student shares this noteworthy story: "I am in a lecture about Epic Poetry but I'm not really interested in poetry, so I talked to the professor and he was totally cool with all my papers being about anthropological elements of the text and not poetic one." Among other innovations, SLC's unusual (but, some say, inefficient) course registration system allows students to interview teachers before signing up for classes. Fortunately, "all of the classes here are excellent, so if one doesn't get into a desired class, it isn't the end of the world." Unfortunately, many students feel SLC's administration can be bureaucratic and out-of-step with the school's dominant philosophy and culture. When discussing these shortcomings, however, students acknowledge that the administration faces many challenges in that the school is "expensive to run" and funds are more limited than at larger colleges.

Life

Whether you enjoy attending "study parties" or playing Frisbee in your underwear, "life at Sarah Lawrence is about as quirky as the college itself." Club meetings and school-sponsored activities are lightly attended; however, poetry readings, artistic pursuits, live music shows, and political organizing are widely popular, and "there is a growing athletic community on campus" as well. On campus, there are occasional dance parties, as well as casual get-togethers; however, on the whole, campus life is fairly subdued. A student claims, "The best way to relax is to get together with a few friends, put on some music, and just hang out. Conversations range from deep political or philosophical debates to discussing cartoons." Located in Bronxville, "everybody enjoys the fact that we're a hop, skip and a jump away from wonderful Manhattan," and a majority of students head to the city on the weekend. For those who stay on campus, "weekends include a lot of wandering around, but mostly just sitting and talking in friends dorm rooms about typical stuff, you know, Nietzsche and the importance of green architecture." In addition, students might be found "playing music together, listening to music, throwing dinner parties, drinking beer, playing board games, playing drinking games, talking about music, going to the city, eating a lot of Chinese and Sushi take-out, [or] playing in the snow."

Student Body

With a motto like "we're different, so are you," it's not surprising that "Sarah Lawrence is like Mecca for creative, proactive, outrageous, and independent students who want ultimate freedom in designing their education." Bohemian attire and alternative music are culturally prevalent, and "writers, artists, eccentrics, musicians, academics, activists, and scientists all call Sarah Lawrence home." In fact, many students say that, "the typical Sarah Lawrence student looks like the atypical student at any mainstream university." Students agree that the SLC "environment is very inclusive of all people and walks of life;" however, many complain that the "indie" or bohemian veneer attracts students who are unfriendly, self-absorbed, or who are "so used to being the "different" ones that they can't deal with the fact that they aren't "special" here." While some would like a warmer and friendlier college atmosphere, students reassure us that "there is a wide spectrum of interests and lifestyles so almost everyone can find a crowd of friends that suits them."

THE PRINCETON REVIEW SAYS

Admissions

Very important factors considered include: Application essay, recommendation(s), rigor of secondary school record. *Important factors considered include:* Academic GPA, character/personal qualities, extracurricular activities, talent/ability. *Other factors considered include:* Class rank, alumni/ae relation, first generation, geographical residence, interview, level of applicant's interest, racial/ethnic status, volunteer work, work experience. High school diploma is required and GED is accepted. *Academic units required:* 4 English, 2 mathematics, 2 science, 2 foreign language, 2 history. *Academic units recommended:* 4 mathematics, 4 science, 4 foreign language, 4 history.

Financial Aid

Students should submit: FAFSA, CSS/Financial Aid PROFILE, state aid form, noncustodial PROFILE. Regular filing deadline is 2/1. The Princeton Review suggests that all financial aid forms be submitted as soon as possible after January 1. *Need-based scholarships/grants offered:* Federal Pell, SEOG, state scholarships/grants, private scholarships, the school's own gift aid. *Loan aid offered:* FFEL Subsidized Stafford, FFEL Unsubsidized Stafford, FFEL PLUS, Federal Perkins Applicants will be notified of awards on or about 4/1.

The Inside Word

In addition to three required essay questions, Sarah Lawrence College requests that candidates submit a graded, academic writing sample. Students say you shouldn't underestimate the importance of this unusual requirement, as SLC's curriculum is writing-based and a good sample can make your application stand out. Sarah Lawrence College doesn't believe that standardized test scores accurately reflect a student's ability to succeed in their academic program, and therefore, they do not review ACT or SAT scores.

THE SCHOOL SAYS ". . ."

From The Admissions Office

"Students who come to Sarah Lawrence are curious about the world, and they have an ardent desire to satisfy that curiosity. Sarah Lawrence offers such students two innovative academic structures: the seminar/conference system and the arts components. Courses in the humanities, social sciences, natural sciences, and mathematics are taught in the seminar/conference style. The seminars enroll an average of 11 students and consist of lecture, discussion, readings, and assigned papers. For each seminar, students also have private tutorials, called conferences, for which they conceive of individualized projects and shape them under the direction of professors. Arts components let students combine history and theory with practice. Painters, printmakers, photographers, sculptors, filmmakers, composers, musicians, choreographers, dancers, actors, and directors work in readily available studios, editing facilities, and darkrooms, guided by accomplished professionals. The secure, wooded campus is 30 minutes from midtown Manhattan, and the diversity of people and ideas at Sarah Lawrence make it an extraordinary educational environment.

"Sarah Lawrence College no longer uses standardized test scores in the admissions process. This decision reflects our conviction that overemphasis on test preparation can distort results and make the application process inordinately stressful, and that academic success is better predicted by the student's course rigor, their grades, recommendations, and writing ability."

For even more information on this school, turn to page 511 of the "Stats" section.

SETON HALL UNIVERSITY

400 South Orange Avenue, South Orange, NJ 07079-2697 • Admissions: 973-761-9332
Fax: 973-275-2040 • Financial Aid: 973-761-9332 • E-mail: thehall@shu.edu • Website: www.admissions.shu.edu

RATINGS
Quality of Life: 70 **Academic:** 77 **Admissions:** 81 **Financial Aid:** 74

STUDENTS SAY "..."

Academics

Named after Saint Elizabeth Ann Seton, Seton Hall is a Catholic university dedicated to "shaping students into servant leaders by enriching the mind, heart, and spirit." Servant leaders are people "who help to change the world" by offering their talents to the improvement of the community, as did the person for whom the university is a namesake. Professors are at the forefront of this intellectual, emotional, and spiritual enrichment, and students say "You won't find better anywhere." "They are always willing to meet with you outside of class and will do anything to help." Professors in the specialty Schools of Diplomacy, Nursing, Education, and Business receive especially high marks. Although students in the honors program "get the best professors" and benefit from "discussion-based classes," all students enjoy "small class sizes" in which "questions are always welcome." Students are much less enthusiastic about the "very conservative" administration, which for many is a "typical bureaucracy that could be improved but could also be much, much worse." Despite the administration's overall conservatism, it has fully embraced certain forms of progress. "One of Seton Hall's greatest strengths is probably its student technology program where every incoming student is issued a laptop that they can use anywhere on campus thanks to wireless Internet."

> **SURVEY SAYS ...**
> *Small classes*
> *Great computer facilities*
> *Great library*
> *Diverse student types on campus*
> *College radio is popular*
> *Student publications are popular*
> *Lots of beer drinking*

Life

As one student explains, "Life in general here is what happens at most colleges." "During the week everyone is stressed and a lot of work gets done." On the weekends, students spend their "free time watching movies, attending on-campus events, going to parties, hanging out, and exploring New York." With fewer than half of the students living on campus, Seton Hall is "very much a commuter school." A lot of students come for class and head home afterwards. Even among resident students, "Seton Hall is a suitcase school," which means "a lot of the Jersey kids go home on the weekends." Still, there are "plenty of things to do for those who stay on campus." "The Greek population is relatively small but is highly visible." Students enjoy "a lot of frat parties on the weekends" as well as "drive-in movies" and "dance lessons." Additionally, "extracurricular activities abound" with many students playing "intramural and intercollegiate sports." Even with all these options, students often "hop on the train" and "go into New York City for fun" which can make the campus feel "deserted on the weekends."

Student Body

While the typical student is "probably Catholic" and from "local towns in New Jersey or New York," diversity is "highly valued" on campus, with many students from "different backgrounds, religious beliefs, sexual orientation, everything." Most students manage to "mix in and feel like they're part of the student body." One student warns, however, that there is "very little tolerance for certain groups," especially gay students who are "targets of active discrimination by the university." While many students think the administration "does not handle GLBT issues well," those who are GLBT have "great support from the rest of the SHU community." Students describe themselves as "friendly" and "pretty motivated," conversant in everything from "political and historical issues to fashion." SHU students concentrate on their "work during the week" and "enjoying themselves on the weekend." As one student sums up, "Most students are just average people" with a "broad variance in personalities and interests."

THE PRINCETON REVIEW SAYS

Admissions

Very important factors considered include: Rigor of secondary school record, Academic GPA, Standardized test scores, Application Essay,Recommendation(s). *Important factors considered include:* Volunteer work, Work experience. *Other factors considered include:* Class rank, Talent/ability, Character/personal qualities.

Financial Aid

Students should submit: FAFSA *Need-based scholarships/grants offered:* Federal Pell, SEOG, State scholarships/grants, Private scholarships, College/university scholarship or grant aid from institutional fund. *Loan aid offered:* FFEL Subsidized Stafford Loans, FFEL Unsubsidized Stafford Loans, FFEL PLUS loans, Federal Perkins Loans, State Loans.

The Inside Word

Students looking for a good school with solid Catholic roots should consider Seton Hall. Decent grades in college preparatory courses coupled with strong recommendations will net an acceptance for most students. Applicants with above-average marks are often recipients of scholarship money. The university's close proximity to New York allows for myriad educational, internship, and entertainment opportunities.

THE SCHOOL SAYS ". . ."

From The Admissions Office

"For more than 150 years, Seton Hall University has been a catalyst for leadership, developing the whole student—mind, heart and spirit. As a Catholic university that embraces students of all races and religions, Seton Hall combines the resources of a large university with the personal attention of a small liberal arts college. The University's attractive suburban campus is only 14 miles by train, bus or car to New York City, with the wealth of employment, internship, cultural and entertainment opportunities the city offers. Outstanding faculty, a technologically advanced campus, and a values-centered curriculum challenge Seton Hall students. Students are exposed to a world of ideas from great scholars, opening their minds to the perspectives, history and achievements of many cultures. Our new core curriculum focuses on the need for our students to have common experiences and encourages them to become thinking, caring, communicative and ethically responsible leaders while emphasizing practical proficiencies and intellectual development Our commitment to our students goes beyond textbooks and homework assignments, though. At Seton Hall, developing servant leaders who will make a difference in the world is a priority. That's why all students take classes in ethics and learn in a community informed by Catholic ideals and universal values. While Seton Hall certainly enjoys a big reputation, our campus community is close-knit and inclusive. Students, faculty and staff come from around the world, bringing with them a kaleidoscope of experiences and perspectives to create a diverse yet unified campus environment."

For even more information on this school, turn to page 511 of the "Stats" section.

SETON HILL UNIVERSITY

ONE SETON HILL DRIVE, GREENSBURG, PA 15601 • ADMISSIONS: 800-826-6234 • FAX: 724-830-1294
E-MAIL: ADMIT@SETONHILL.EDU • WEBSITE: WWW.SETONHILL.EDU

RATINGS
Quality of Life: 70　　**Academic:** 76　　**Admissions:** 82　　**Financial Aid:** 75

STUDENTS SAY "..."

Academics

Seton Hill University is a "tiny" Catholic liberal arts school located, coincidentally enough, "on a hill" "in a rural area" renowned for its "gorgeous" scenery. Until recently, SHU was a women's college, though now there are "more male students" than many would have "expected" thanks to "the new . . . football and wrestling teams." Despite the changes, Seton Hill still offers "a great variety of majors" in addition to "a great liberal arts curriculum." Students single out the "great physician assistant program," as well as the "music and theater" programs. Seton Hill also "offers an adult degree program" on Saturdays. Classes are "intimate" and "challenging," and professors, "for the most part," are "dedicated" and "easily approachable." Opinions on the administration run the gamut from "efficient" and "accessible" to "a mess." Some claim it to be "friendly" and "supportive," while others feel that "it is very hard" to find "office workers that will reply in a timely manner" to their needs.

Life

Seton Hill is located in a "very peaceful" rural town in western Pennsylvania. It's a "cozy atmosphere" and "Students are generally very active in campus life." "A large majority of students" participate in sports. Students also put "a lot of time and effort" into "campus clubs" and "community service." There are "a lot of concerts" and "performances." "On the weekends," SHU gamely offers free activities but life can be "boring." "There are no fraternities or sororities," though "a lot of parties on weekends" seem to fill that void. In theory, SHU is "a dry campus." Nevertheless, "A lot of people get together on the weekends to hang out and drink alcohol." Conversely, "a lot" of other students "go home." "One of the hardest things about SHU is that it's so secluded from the rest of Greensburg." "Parking is always an issue" but it's good to have a car. "Getting around campus is fine" without one, "but trying to get groceries is a bit hard." "For a night in the city," Pittsburgh is "only 40 minutes east."

Student Body

Thanks to this "small campus," "most" students "know each other." "Walking around campus guarantees about five people saying 'hi' to you." Music and art students "often group together." There are plenty of "academically oriented, focused students" and "also many adult students." Some students report "tension" between "student-athletes" and regular students, mostly due to a feeling that the "financial aid" system "favors" sports over those on "the Dean's list." As one student explains, "Seton Hill University is unpleasantly split between those who are attending for academic purposes and those who are attending to play their sport and receive an obscene amount of financial aid." That said, despite "students coming from eclectic backgrounds, there is a great deal of harmony on campus." "Theater and sports people are generally involved in their own activities," reports one, "but everyone is able to cross paths with each other without becoming hostile."

THE PRINCETON REVIEW SAYS

Admissions

Very important factors considered include: Academic GPA, rigor of secondary school record, interview. *Important factors considered include:* Class rank, standardized test scores, character/personal qualities, extracurricular activities, talent/ability. *Other factors considered include:* Application essay, recommendation(s), alumni/ae relation, level of applicant's interest, volunteer work, work experience. SAT or ACT recommended; ACT with Writing component recommended. TOEFL required of all international applicants. High school diploma is required and GED is accepted. *Academic units required:* 4 English, 2 mathematics, 1 science, (1 science labs), 2 social studies, 4 academic electives. *Academic units recommended:* 4 English, 2 mathematics, 1 science, (1 science labs), 2 foreign language, 2 social studies, 4 academic electives.

Financial Aid

Students should submit: FAFSA, institution's own financial aid form. The Princeton Review suggests that all financial aid forms be submitted as soon as possible after January 1. *Need-based scholarships/grants offered:* Federal Pell, SEOG, state scholarships/grants, private scholarships, the school's own gift aid. *Loan aid offered:* FFEL Subsidized Stafford, FFEL Unsubsidized Stafford, FFEL PLUS, Federal Perkins, college/university loans from institutional funds. Applicants will be notified of awards on a rolling basis beginning 11/15. Federal Work-Study Program available. Institutional employment available. Off-campus job opportunities are good.

The Inside Word

Over two-thirds of all applicants get admitted to Seton Hill, largely because it's trying to expand right now; this is good news for marginal candidates. So if you have middling grades and test scores, you should well get through the door. Requirements for the physician assistant program are a bit higher. You need at least a 3.0 GPA (especially for all your science courses) and an SAT score of at least 1100 (or a 24 on the ACT).

THE SCHOOL SAYS ". . ."

From The Admissions Office

"Seton Hill University is an innovative center for learning, offering a variety of educational opportunities to diverse populations within and beyond the Southwestern Pennsylvania region. Seton Hill University produces graduates possessing the values and perspectives inherent in a Catholic education, capable of accomplishment and leadership in the workplace and their communities.

"Undergraduates choose from over 30 areas of study including the sciences, humanities, business, education, and visual and performing arts. At the graduate level, Seton Hill University grants master's degrees in art therapy, inclusive education, special education, writing popular fiction, marriage and family therapy, physician assistant, elementary education, business administration, and instructional design. For working adults, Seton Hill University offers an adult degree program in which students can complete an undergraduate degree in 4 years or less by attending only on Saturdays. In addition, Seton Hill hosts over 50 international students from 20 different countries in both graduate and undergraduate study. It is the aim of Seton Hill University to do everything possible to provide each student with a complete and fulfilling academic experience that will serve as the foundation for a lifetime of learning.

"Seton Hill University offers basketball, cross country, equestrian, field hockey, track and field, golf, lacrosse, soccer, softball, tennis, and volleyball for women and baseball, basketball, cross-country, equestrian, football, golf, lacrosse, soccer, tennis, track and field, and wrestling for men. Scholarship money is available for most sports."

For even more information on this school, turn to page 512 of the "Stats" section.

SIENA COLLEGE

515 LOUDON ROAD, LOUDONVILLE, NY 12211 • ADMISSIONS: 518-783-2423 • FAX: 518-783-2436
FINANCIAL AID: 518-783-2427 • E-MAIL: ADMIT@SIENA.EDU • WEBSITE: WWW.SIENA.EDU

RATINGS
Quality of Life: 80   **Academic:** 80   **Admissions:** 86   **Financial Aid:** 74

STUDENTS SAY ". . ."

> SURVEY SAYS . . .
> *Large classes*
> *Great library*
> *Students love Loudonville, NY*
> *Frats and sororities are unpopular or nonexistent*
> *Lots of beer drinking*

Academics

The Franciscan tradition "is all about community," and, at Siena College, a small school with "a strong Franciscan atmosphere," students benefit from a friendly community in which "there is always someone to lend a helping hand." That someone may be a professor, a tutor, or, on occasion, a Rollerblading friar in robes. No matter whose hand is extended, however, "Every student really has a lot of opportunities to get any amount of personal academic attention or other scholastic opportunities that they want." Biology and other premedical disciplines are highly regarded, and students especially love the Siena College–Albany Medical College Program, a joint acceptance program that focuses on humanities and community service. In addition, the school's many business undergrads feel their program, which is enhanced by a loyal alumni base that helps newly minted grads quickly find jobs, is the school's "greatest strength." Regardless of discipline, Siena "Teachers know who you are and do not just consider you a number, as opposed [how it is at] larger colleges and universities." An honors program offers "even smaller classes, preferential registration, and seminars" to those seeking an extra challenge.

Life

For many students, recreation time at Siena means it's time for a beer or two, and lately that's become a point of contention with the administration. Students tell us that the administration, in its effort to crack down on underage drinking, has instituted security checkpoints at the townhouses (where upperclassmen live and, in previous years, had hosted parties) and limits on the amount of alcohol allowed in the rooms of students over 21. Security can be aggressive, we're told, to the point that more than one undergraduate told us that students sometimes feel "like prisoners." Though this has driven the drinking crowd off campus to nearby clubs and the bars of Albany, on-campus drinking still occurs, but it's more often of the pre-gaming or small-quiet-party variety. The campus still bustles during the week, however, as "Most people are involved in clubs" and at least "one sport, whether intramural or intercollegiate." Other diversions include a school-sponsored bus that takes students to the Crossgates Mall, which "is pretty large and houses a bunch of amazing stores," and "a whole strip of dining-out places." Still, an English major admits, "If you don't drink, I can see where weekends would be boring, especially in the winter." The school does sponsor activities on campus designed "to draw students away from the drinking scene," but "There is often a stigma about the 'coolness' of these events."

Student Body

There "isn't much diversity" on the Siena campus, where it seems just about everyone "is from an upper-middle-class Catholic family from Long Island" or "upstate New York." There are some who don't fit the mold, but not many; students speculate that they're mostly nontraditional or international students. Minority students tend to "stick together, but all seem well-liked." Many students "are involved either in D1 athletics, intramural teams, or clubs and Student Senate activities"; students in these groups tend to party together on the weekends "and generally create a strong group of friends easily." While there's a solid contingent of folks at Siena who "drink, party, and hardly ever study," there are also students, particularly in the sciences, who work hard but "don't socialize much outside of their departments, due to the nature of their program."

THE PRINCETON REVIEW SAYS

Admissions

Very important factors considered include: Academic GPA, rigor of secondary school record. *Important factors considered include:* Recommendation(s), standardized test scores. *Other factors considered include:* Class rank, application essay, alumni/ae relation, character/personal qualities, extracurricular activities, first generation, interview, level of applicant's interest, racial/ethnic status, talent/ability, volunteer work, work experience. SAT or ACT required; ACT with Writing component required. TOEFL required of all international applicants. High school diploma is required and GED is accepted. *Academic units required:* 4 English, 3 mathematics, 3 science, (3 science labs), 1 social studies, 2 history. *Academic units recommended:* 4 English, 4 mathematics, 4 science, (4 science labs), 3 foreign language, 1 social studies, 3 history.

Financial Aid

Students should submit: FAFSA, state aid form. The Princeton Review suggests that all financial aid forms be submitted as soon as possible after January 1. *Need-based scholarships/grants offered:* Federal Pell, SEOG, state scholarships/grants, private scholarships, the school's own gift aid, Siena Grants, St. Francis Community Grants. *Loan aid offered:* FFEL Subsidized Stafford, FFEL Unsubsidized Stafford, FFEL PLUS, Federal Perkins Applicants will be notified of awards on or about 4/1.

The Inside Word

Siena's draw is still primarily regional, with the vast majority of students arriving from in state. Standards aren't especially high; the admit rate says as much about the applicant pool as it does about the school's selectivity. Expect to meet higher standards if you indicate an interest in the School of Science, as it is the gateway to the school's desirable premedical programs. The school does applicants a favor here—substandard students stand little chance of surviving the school's science regimen.

THE SCHOOL SAYS ". . ."

From The Admissions Office

"Siena is a coeducational, independent liberal arts college with a Franciscan tradition. It is a community where the intellectual, personal, and social growth of all students is paramount. Siena's faculty calls forth the best Siena students have to give—and the students do the same for them. Students are competitive, but not at each other's expense. Siena's curriculum includes 23 majors in three schools—liberal arts, science, and business. In addition, there are over a dozen pre-professional and special academic programs. With a student/faculty ratio of 14:1, class size ranges between 15 and 35 students. Siena's 152-acre campus is located in Loudonville, a suburban community within two miles of the New York State seat of government in Albany. With 15 colleges in the area, there is a wide variety of activities on weekends. Regional theater, performances by major concert artists, and professional sports events compete with the activities on the campus. Within 50 miles are the Adirondacks, the Berkshires, and the Catskills, providing outdoor recreation throughout the year. Because the capital region's easy, friendly lifestyle is so appealing, many Siena graduates try to find their first jobs in upstate New York.

"Freshman applicants must submit the SAT or ACT with the Writing component."

For even more information on this school, turn to page 512 of the "Stats" section.

SIMMONS COLLEGE

300 THE FENWAY, BOSTON, MA 02115 • ADMISSIONS: 617-521-2051 • FAX: 617-521-3190
FINANCIAL AID: 617-521-2001 • E-MAIL: UGADM@SIMMONS.EDU • WEBSITE: WWW.SIMMONS.EDU

RATINGS
Quality of Life: 87   Academic: 85   Admissions: 84   Financial Aid: 65

STUDENTS SAY ". . ."

Academics

Simmons College, an "all-women's college located in the Fenway area of Boston," provides students with "lots of opportunities to work closely with faculty and interact with local Boston communities." The school excels in pre-professional programs in nursing and physical therapy, each of which capitalizes on the school's location to "give students opportunities to do internships/clinical placements at world-renowned hospitals that are only a few blocks away (e.g. Children's Hospital Boston, Brigham and Women's, Mass General)." Students also rave about Simmons' offerings in psychology, biology, pre-dental sciences, economics, and management, and they praise the school's "excellent facilities, including an amazing new library" and the "large career resource department." Small classes here "allow great discussions, because those who want to participate have the opportunity to do so," which can be both a blessing and a curse. As one student points out, "Because Simmons is not the most selective school there are some students who don't study very much." The same students add that "If you work hard, you get out of it what you put in." Another drawback is the study abroad program. One undergrad gripes, "There just aren't enough choices! And if there are, they are all usually around the same time, making it quite difficult to choose."

> **SURVEY SAYS . . .**
> Large classes
> Great computer facilities
> Great library
> Students love Boston, MA
> Great off-campus food
> Frats and sororities are unpopular or nonexistent

Life

Life at Simmons College "is more academic in nature: the classes are teaching-based, and life on campus revolves around schoolwork." One student agrees, "Simmons is pretty much where students go to school. We go elsewhere to have fun/party/live." With downtown Boston outside the school's front door, the options are plentiful. There are museums ("great things to do in the area" include "free gallery talks at the Museum of Fine Arts"), "shopping on Newbury Street," and "eating great food on the North End." Public transportation means "getting around is easy and exploring the city is amazing." When students seek a party, they typically "go to other local colleges...like MIT, Harvard, Boston University, and Northeastern." On-campus fun is more subdued. There's "a lot of random friendly girl-time things going on, like decorating our doors for the holidays, making paper chains, or watching television. For entertainment here, you really have to turn to your friends, because almost nothing worth attending happens on campus," a female student notes. Most see this as a boon; writes one student, "What's nice about living at Simmons is that it is a peaceful and nice place to live, but when you want to go to a party, Northeastern and BU are just minutes away. After spending a night there, you realize how thankful you are for clean dorms and the lack of boys."

Student Body

The student body at Simmons is "mostly middle- to upper-class women who hail from all over the United States and many other countries. The school is predominately white, but a range of ethnicities are represented." One student reports that her study group consists of "an orthodox Jew, a Saudi Arabian, an African American, a Cambodian, an Indian, and two Caucasians. The UN could take lessons from us." Politically, "Most students are liberal and involved with their community." Left-leaning politics dominates to the point that "it can be challenging to express conservative viewpoints." Sexual orientation "tends not to be a question, and it is very common for girls to be open about being straight, gay, or bisexual." While "there are a lot of lesbians here," they are "not at all the majority." Simmons hosts a conspicuous butch subculture. As one women explains, "Even though you know going into it that Simmons is an all-women's college, you may be shocked to see some guys walking around attending your classes...until you realize that they are girls! It's great that everyone is cool with everyone else and the people who are narrow-minded stick to themselves."

THE PRINCETON REVIEW SAYS

Admissions

Very important factors considered include: Academic GPA, rigor of secondary school record. *Important factors considered include:* Class rank, application essay, recommendation(s), standardized test scores. *Other factors considered include:* Extracurricular activities, interview, talent/ability, volunteer work, work experience. SAT or ACT required; TOEFL required of all international applicants. High school diploma or equivalent is not required. *Academic units required:* 4 English, 3 mathematics, 3 science, 3 foreign language, 3 social studies, 3 history. *Academic units recommended:* 4 English, 4 mathematics, 3 science, 4 foreign language, 4 social studies, 3 history.

Financial Aid

Students should submit: FAFSA. Regular filing deadline is 3/1. The Princeton Review suggests that all financial aid forms be submitted as soon as possible after January 1. *Need-based scholarships/grants offered:* Federal Pell, SEOG, state scholarships/grants, private scholarships, the school's own gift aid. *Loan aid offered:* FFEL Subsidized Stafford, FFEL Unsubsidized Stafford, FFEL PLUS, Federal Perkins, state loans, college/university loans from institutional funds. Applicants will be notified of awards on a rolling basis beginning 3/15. Federal Work-Study Program available. Institutional employment available. Off-campus job opportunities are excellent.

The Inside Word

Most of the nation's best all-women's colleges are in the Northeast, including those Seven Sister schools (roughly the female equivalent of the formerly all-male Ivies) that remain single-sex institutions. The competition for students is intense, and although Simmons is a solid school, there are at least a half-dozen competitors more appealing to most candidates. Solid high school performers should have little need to worry here. The school's excellent academics and Boston location make Simmons a worthy option for any woman interested in single-sex education.

THE SCHOOL SAYS ". . ."

From The Admissions Office

"Simmons believes passionately in an 'educational contract' that places students first and helps them build successful careers, lead meaningful lives, and realize a powerful return on their investment. Simmons honors this contract by delivering a quality education and measurable success through singular approach to professional preparation, intellectual exploration, and community orientation.

"Simmons is a 100-year-old university in Boston, with a tradition of providing women with a collaborative environment that stimulates dialogue, enhances listening, catalyzes action, and spurs personal and professional growth.

"Simmons College accepts both the ACT and SAT. Students who enroll in September 2007 and thereafter are required to submit the SAT or the ACT with Writing. Additionally, if English is not your native language a TOEFL is required."

For even more information on this school, turn to page 513 of the "Stats" section.

SIMON'S ROCK COLLEGE OF BARD

84 ALFORD ROAD, GREAT BARRINGTON, MA 01230 • ADMISSIONS: 413-528-7312 • FAX: 413-528-7334
FINANCIAL AID: 413-528-7297 • E-MAIL: ADMIT@SIMONS-ROCK.EDU • WEBSITE: WWW.SIMONS-ROCK.EDU

RATINGS
Quality of Life: 86   **Academic:** 97   **Admissions:** 90   **Financial Aid:** 88

STUDENTS SAY "..."
Academics

SURVEY SAYS . . .
Small classes
Athletic facilities are great
Campus feels safe
Frats and sororities are unpopular
or nonexistent
(Almost) everyone smokes

Simon's Rock, "the only college in the country that is specifically designed for students of high school age who are ready for college," offers "brilliant and creative kids a combination of a lot of freedom and a lot of very demanding work so that they can begin college early and move forward with their lives earlier. It's the perfect environment for kids who think outside the box." Students at the Rock are given a challenging curriculum; one student jokingly describes the approach as "do as you please, and also 400 pages of reading." Undergrads report that "the average student spends more than 7 hours on homework a night and writes at least one six- to ten-page paper a week." In return for their hard work, students receive "up-close and personal attention of teachers who care about you and are not afraid to tell you when you've screwed up," and who are also "more than willing to set up tutorials and even arrange courses that match your academic interests, regardless of how off-the-wall they may be." Slightly more than half the students at Simon's Rock stick around for 2 years, long enough to earn an associate's degree, and then transfer to a larger school. Those who remain here enter the Upper College through "a self-selection process that tends to weed out the people who aren't as serious about the work they want to do. While the Lower College students can be, from time to time, indolent pot-smokers, by and large the juniors and seniors are extremely serious students."

Life

Simon's Rock is located "on top of a mountain in the middle-of-nowhere New England," with the closest town "a mile and a half away." Those who make the trek to town are rewarded with "yummy burritos, groceries, thrift-store shopping and a rad toy store." Because of the school's remote locale, "Students have to make their own fun," and they do so in a variety of ways: "Lots of kids meditate. Lots of kids ride bikes, fence, play soccer, go to the rock wall, or otherwise work out." Others "watch lots of movies, hang out with friends, and play intellectual games," and still others "go to one of the many swimming holes around here." Those with cars (or those who have friends with cars) are most likely to be completely satisfied; they point out that "we're only an hour from Northampton, where there's everything from lectures to concerts, and we also get to live in a nice, quiet New England town." They also note that "going to New York City and Boston is a breeze, and that's what most upperclassmen do on the weekends." Those who are campus-bound, however, caution that "if you're not a nature person, you might not be as happy here as [you would be] somewhere more urban."

Student Body

Who attends Simon's Rock? "Those [students] who are frustrated with the social and academic limitations of high school" are the school's target market, and they are mostly the ones who find their way here. One such student explains, "Simon's Rock is an exceptionally self-selecting institution. Most of us are atypical because if we weren't, we would not be at Simon's Rock." Undergrads "are very smart, or at least smart enough to realize the conformity and uselessness of high school" and "are either very studious or very artistic, or caught somewhere in the middle." Some see Simon's Rock as "'nerd camp' all over again. From neon hair to preppy-looking science students, the Simon's Rock type is that there isn't one." Contrary to popular perception, "We're not all communist beat poets majoring in Movement Studies. Yeah, we have lots of vegetarian liberal kids in sandals from Vermont, but they [also] carry 3.3 GPAs and head our Community Counsel and Fencing Club."

THE PRINCETON REVIEW SAYS

Admissions

Very important factors considered include: Application essay, recommendation(s), rigor of secondary school record, character/personal qualities, interview, talent/ability. *Important factors considered include:* Class rank, academic GPA, level of applicant's interest. *Other factors considered include:* Standardized test scores, alumni/ae relation, extracurricular activities, first generation, racial/ethnic status, volunteer work, work experience. TOEFL required of all international applicants. High school diploma or equivalent is not required. *Academic units recommended:* 2 English, 2 mathematics, 2 science, (1 science labs), 2 foreign language, 2 social studies, 2 history.

Financial Aid

Students should submit: FAFSA, CSS/Financial Aid PROFILE, business/farm supplement, Parent and Student Federal Taxes/ Federal Verification Worksheet. The Princeton Review suggests that all financial aid forms be submitted as soon as possible after January 1. *Need-based scholarships/grants offered:* Federal Pell, SEOG, state scholarships/grants, private scholarships, the school's own gift aid. *Loan aid offered:* FFEL Subsidized Stafford, FFEL Unsubsidized Stafford, FFEL PLUS, Federal Perkins, state loans, Alternative Educational Loans. Applicants will be notified of awards on a rolling basis beginning 4/15. Federal Work-Study Program available. Institutional employment available. Off-campus job opportunities are good.

The Inside Word

The application process at Simon's Rock is highly personalized. The school's unique composition calls for Admissions Officers to thoroughly assess candidates and evaluate whether the college will be a good fit. Prospective students must be extremely motivated and thrive in intellectual environments. They also need to demonstrate a high degree of maturity and an ability to work independently. Officers tend to focus on personal statements, recommendations, and interviews.

THE SCHOOL SAYS ". . ."

From The Admissions Office

"Simon's Rock is dedicated to one thing: To allow bright, highly motivated students the opportunity to pursue college work leading to the AA and BA degrees at an age earlier than our national norm.

"Simon's Rock College of Bard will accept either the new SAT or the old SAT (administered prior to March 2005 and without a Writing component), as well as the ACT with or without the Writing component."

For even more information on this school, turn to page 513 of the "Stats" section.

SKIDMORE COLLEGE

815 NORTH BROADWAY, SARATOGA SPRINGS, NY 12866-1632 • ADMISSIONS: 518-580-5570
FAX: 518-580-5584 • FINANCIAL AID: 518-580-5750 • E-MAIL: ADMISSIONS@SKIDMORE.EDU • WEBSITE: WWW.SKIDMORE.EDU

RATINGS
Quality of Life: 88   **Academic:** 90   **Admissions:** 94   **Financial Aid:** 93

STUDENTS SAY ". . ."

Academics

"Creative thought matters" is Skidmore's slogan, and students here echo it frequently enough to convince us that it's more than your standard college hype; nearly one in five undergrads major in the visual or performing arts. Skidmore also boasts "great science programs," a "superb" English Department, and an "excellent" business program. The combined effect produces "a haven for inquisitive, artsy, liberal-minded students looking for a place to get a good education with minimal pretentiousness." Arts students laud the school's "great artistic community, populated by so many musicians, artists, actors, and dancers who are all passionate about what they do. This leads to collaboration in and outside of schoolwork, making it a great place to develop as an artist." Undergrads in more traditional liberal arts and sciences disciplines love the "opportunities for real work"—such as working as a "lab assistant for research projects" or "in local schools"—and "the very enthusiastic professors who are passionate about their work." Those for whom Skidmore is a fit feel it represents the "perfect balance between structure and freedom."

> **SURVEY SAYS . . .**
> *Large classes*
> *Students love Saratoga Springs, NY*
> *Great off-campus food*
> *Dorms are like palaces*
> *Frats and sororities are unpopular*
> *or nonexistent*

Life

Students tell us that Skidmore's Saratoga Springs location is one of the best things about the school. "The town is great," a senior raves. "The nightlife is fantastic, internships and volunteer opportunities abound, you have access to the Adirondacks and all of the best ski sites, it's a great place for friends and family to visit . . . everyone loves the place. Most students end up spending a summer or two in Saratoga just so they can enjoy everything about it without being distracted by studies." On campus, life is "very relaxed, and there is generally little pressure on students to do anything. However, the campus is a very involved one and there are countless extracurricular clubs and events going on at any point." Many students "get drunk and go to parties on the weekend," often at upperclassmen's houses, but "It is really easy to find other activities to participate in if partying isn't your scene. There are tons of events every night and lots of people who don't make partying their number one choice." These activities include "tons of campus concerts, performances, and shows" produced by the campus' glut of artists and performers.

Student Body

"Artistic/liberal kids" and "business major/athletic kids" form the two most conspicuous and readily identifiable populations on the Skidmore campus; one student explains, "You can usually tell who is who by the way they dress." While those two groups do "make a large part of the student body," undergrads point out that "there are all types of students that are not in those categories, or lie somewhere in between the two." For example, "We have kids who double major in business and art, athletes who are in the orchestra—you can be anyone you want to be and be accepted as an individual and as a part of the Skidmore community." Indeed, "The student body as a whole is extremely open-minded to diversity. There are a number of LGBT students who are strongly supported by the student body." "Although there is not a large amount of ethnic diversity," one student reports, "I have never seen a student of a different ethnicity be discriminated against, or even heard another student make any racist statement[s]." Are Skidmore students entirely free of prejudice? No, not entirely; one student explains, "The only discrimination I have seen here is against Republicans. Skidmore is extremely liberal, and I would say it is pretty hard to fit in here with extremely conservative beliefs."

THE PRINCETON REVIEW SAYS

Admissions

Very important factors considered include: Rigor of secondary school record. *Important factors considered include:* Class rank, application essay, academic GPA, recommendation(s), character/personal qualities, extracurricular activities, talent/ability, volunteer work, work experience. *Other factors considered include:* Standardized test scores, alumni/ae relation, first generation, geographical residence, interview, racial/ethnic status, SAT Subject Tests recommended; SAT or ACT required; ACT with Writing component required. TOEFL required of all international applicants. High school diploma is required and GED is accepted. *Academic units recommended:* 4 English, 4 mathematics, 4 science, (3 science labs), 4 foreign language, 4 social studies.

Financial Aid

Students should submit: FAFSA, CSS/Financial Aid PROFILE. Regular filing deadline is 1/15. The Princeton Review suggests that all financial aid forms be submitted as soon as possible after January 1. *Need-based scholarships/grants offered:* Federal Pell, SEOG, state scholarships/grants, the school's own gift aid. *Loan aid offered:* FFEL Subsidized Stafford, FFEL Unsubsidized Stafford, FFEL PLUS, Federal Perkins Applicants will be notified of awards on or about 4/1.

The Inside Word

Skidmore remains a fallback option for Northeastern kids who don't get into their top choices. Admits are very bright kids and a successful applicant must present the Admissions Office with a fairly compelling picture. You'll receive friendly, personalized assistance from the Admissions Office here, especially if you communicate a strong desire to attend Skidmore.

THE SCHOOL SAYS ". . ."

From The Admissions Office

"Launched in 2005, Skidmore's First-Year Experience (FYE) is a year-long academic, co-curricular, and residential initiative that immediately engages each first-year student with a faculty mentor-advisor, with 14 other students in an innovative Scribner Seminar, and with the entire college community through a series of artistic, cultural, and social events. FYE's centerpiece, 50 distinctive seminars—ranging from the human colonization of space to lessons learned from Hurricane Katrina to British national identity—requires each student to participate actively and creatively in his or her own learning. Seminar instructors function as faculty mentor-advisors for their 15 students, and provide curricular and co-curricular perspectives not only on the specific seminar topic but on the liberal arts in general. In most cases, students live in residence halls in close proximity to classmates from their seminar.

"In terms of skills and habits of mind, seminar participants will learn to distinguish among and formulate the types of questions asked by different disciplines; read critically and gather and interpret evidence; consider and address complexities and ambiguities; recognize choices, examine assumptions, and take a skeptical stance; formulate conclusions based upon evidence; and communicate those conclusions orally and in writing. These are the fundamentals for academic excellence.

"The First-Year Experience is just the beginning of the expectation that students will creatively craft an experience leading to intensive work in a major field of study, often via a double major or major and minor, supplemented by a semester abroad, collaborative research with a faculty member, and internships. It is also a singular manifestation of Skidmore's commitment to the belief that 'Creative Thought Matters'—that every life, career, and endeavor is made more profound with creative ability at its core.

"Applicants for Fall 2008 are required to take the SAT or the ACT with the Writing section. We recommend that students provide scores for two SAT Subject Test examinations."

For even more information on this school, turn to page 514 of the "Stats" section.

SLIPPERY ROCK UNIVERSITY OF PENNSYLVANIA

OFFICE OF UNDERGRADUATE ADMISSIONS, SLIPPERY ROCK, PA 16057 • ADMISSIONS: 724-738-2015 OR 800-929-4778
FAX: 724-738-2913 • E-MAIL: ASKTHEROCK@SRU.EDU • WEBSITE: WWW.SRU.EDU

RATINGS
Quality of Life: 76   **Academic:** 71   **Admissions:** 75   **Financial Aid:** 78

STUDENTS SAY "..."

Academics

Slippery Rock University is a medium-sized school Western Pennsylvania that is growing tremendously but remains "fairly small compared to" other schools in the state. SRU has a "wonderful business school" and notable programs in music and physical therapy. The education majors are "excellent" as well. Academics at The Rock are solid but not overly demanding. "I don't feel like I'm wild-

> **SURVEY SAYS . . .**
> *Large classes*
> *Great library*
> *Athletic facilities are great*
> *Lots of beer drinking*
> *(Almost) everyone smokes*

ly intelligent," muses a senior, "but when I hear that people have honest trouble making it through this school, I worry about the future of the country." Many professors are "very good teachers." Once you get into your major, "professors start to care about you." "I have been pleased with the availability of the professors, their willingness to work with students, and their reliability," reflects a senior. SRU's administration "rocks." "They are very personable and take the time to listen to students." However, it's often hard to get into the classes you need.

Life

This "breathtakingly beautiful" campus "in the middle of nowhere" is rather enormous. "It is a hike to get to some classes" and the "hilly layout" doesn't help, particularly in the winter. ("The school is called 'Slippery Rock' for a reason.") The gym is excellent and there are some nice dorms." "I think some of the classrooms and buildings could be fixed up," says a sophomore. "I know that are trying to change the look and feel of the campus and that is great [because] it really is a beautiful place to be." And "parking is atrocious." Clubs and organized activities are abundant. Posters and sidewalk chalk describing various happenings are reportedly every-where. "Intramural sports are huge." "Greek life is big enough to have an impact, but not too big where you can't have a social life without joining one." However, Slippery Rock is basically "a commuter school that is try-ing to become a stay-on-campus school." "Every Friday afternoon, the place clears out." The students who remain "definitely tend to party" but "don't get too extreme." Some students call the surrounding community "quaint." Others say it's "a hick town." Whatever the case, there's "not a lot of action" except for a few bars. Without your own vehicle, "you will be stuck in your dorm or apartment. *A lot.*" With a car, trips to larger near-by towns are possible. "The proximity to Pittsburgh" allows for an easy escape when the urge for a more seri-ous road trip strikes.

Student Body

It's a "blue collar" crowd, "not a bunch of spoiled rich kids." For the most part, "the people here are real peo-ple who have to actually work their way though college." "Most of the students come from the Pittsburgh area, or smaller towns" in the region and they "have a lot in common" with each other. Nontraditional students will find many kindred souls and so will students "straight out of high school." The Rock is "more diverse than a small farm town" but only by a little. "There are some foreign students" and some kids from different ethnic groups, but not many. "There is a variety of personalities on campus," though. "The stereotypical prep or jock" is well represented but "cliques are pretty diverse, ranging from social partying crowds, to study groups, to tree-hugging hippies."

THE PRINCETON REVIEW SAYS

Admissions

Important factors considered include: Class rank, academic GPA, rigor of secondary school record, standardized test scores. *Other factors considered include:* Application essay, recommendation(s), alumni/ae relation, racial/ethnic status, state residency, talent/ability, SAT or ACT required; TOEFL required of all international applicants. High school diploma is required and GED is accepted. *Academic units recommended:* 4 English, 3 mathematics, 3 science, (1 science labs), 2 foreign language, 3 social studies, 3 history.

Financial Aid

Students should submit: FAFSA. The Princeton Review suggests that all financial aid forms be submitted as soon as possible after January 1. *Need-based scholarships/grants offered:* Federal Pell, SEOG, state scholarships/grants, private scholarships, the school's own gift aid. *Loan aid offered:* FFEL Subsidized Stafford, FFEL Unsubsidized Stafford, FFEL PLUS, Federal Perkins Applicants will be notified of awards on a rolling basis beginning 3/15. Federal Work-Study Program available. Institutional employment available. Off-campus job opportunities are good.

The Inside Word

Applicants to The Rock tend to be average high school students with average grades who have the ambition and abilities but couldn't get into the bigger colleges. A 3.0 GPA and either a combined math and critical reading score on the 950 or a 20 on the ACT gets admitted automatically.

THE SCHOOL SAYS ". . ."

From The Admissions Office

"It's a great time to be at Slippery Rock University—Pennsylvania's premier public residential university. The evidence is everywhere. SRU is one of the top five "best value" public universities in America—and has the award to prove it. Enrollment is at a record level. And the campus is beaming with state-of-the-art academic and residence hall facilities.

"Slippery Rock's main campus is located on more than 650 acres in scenic western Pennsylvania, only 50 miles north of Pittsburgh and 35 miles east of Youngstown, Ohio. Founded in 1889, the SRU family is comprised of more than 8,300 students and 890 faculty and staff.

"SRU offers more than 65 undergraduate majors through our colleges of Education; Humanities, Fine and Performing Arts; Business, Information and Behavioral Sciences; and Health, Environment and Science. Our Honor's Program provides academically gifted students an opportunity to study with select faculty in small, highly interactive academic settings both here and abroad.

"The University has an accomplished faculty; 90 percent have an earned doctorate or terminal degree. And, because our most common class size is only 20–29 students, faculty members have time to mentor students and provide the personal attention that has become a hallmark of a Slippery Rock University education.

"Our students do amazing things. Not surprising since SRU is student centered and intentionally combines academic with "hands-on" learning opportunities. At SRU you'll find opportunities to conduct undergraduate research, participate in service learning projects, volunteer or just have fun by participating in one or more of our 100 student organizations, intercollegiate athletics or intramural sports"

For even more information on this school, turn to page 514 of the "Stats" section.

SMITH COLLEGE

SEVEN COLLEGE LANE, NORTHAMPTON, MA 01063 • ADMISSIONS: 413-585-2500 • FAX: 413-585-2527
FINANCIAL AID: 413-585-2530 • E-MAIL: ADMISSIONS@SMITH.EDU • WEBSITE: WWW.SMITH.EDU

RATINGS

Quality of Life: 96   Academic: 94   Admissions: 95   Financial Aid: 96

STUDENTS SAY "..."

Academics

Smith College, one of the nation's most prestigious all-women's undergraduate institutions, empowers "incredible women to discover where there true passions lie while allowing them to develop the confidence and skills needed to really make a difference, while dispelling any self-doubt" about making their way in "a world still dominated by men." Academics are legendarily demanding here. "Life at Smith is

> **SURVEY SAYS . . .**
> *Great off-campus food*
> *Dorms are like palaces*
> *Frats and sororities are unpopular*
> *or nonexistent*
> *Political activism is popular*

dominated by work," notes one student. "If you don't want to study hard and take school seriously, you won't survive here." An open curriculum—no required classes here—motivates students to work hard by allowing them to immerse themselves only in what most intrigues them. As one undergrad explains, "I've never had this much work before, but I've also never been able to choose all my classes. I have a ton of work, but it's all stuff I'm interested in. Plus, Smith professors rarely get busy-work-happy, so it's all relevant work. Smith just expects that all its students can handle an academically rigorous schedule, so they aren't shy about assigning a large volume of work." "Fantastic free tutoring and editing available for every class" also help lighten the load a bit. What makes the Smith experience worth the hard work are the "phenomenal" resources and "tons of opportunities." Chief among Smith's assets is its "friendly and accessible" faculty whose "first priority obviously is teaching." The school also boasts a great Career Development Office and an exceptional alumnae network. "Before the Ivies went co-ed, Smith was the place for women to get educated. Our alumnae connections are insane, and our career development office keeps track of all of them," writes one student. Though small, Smith offers "a great selection of courses," and "If you can't find a class you want on campus, Smith s a part of the Five College Consortium of Amherst, Hampshire, UMass Amherst, and Mount Holyoke, where you can participate in clubs and take classes that you find interesting."

Life

Smith is located in Northampton, "a perfect college town." "The residents love Smithies and vise versa," explains one student. "It doesn't feel like a small town, but it isn't by any means an overwhelming city. The Pleasant Street Theater shows great independent films, and there are plenty of delicious restaurants ranging from fancy cuisines to casual weekend brunches. The music scene in Northampton is also extremely popular. There are about five venues where fantastic musicians often play at." All in all, "It's hard not to immerse yourself in the wide variety of concerts available in Northampton." In the spring and fall, "canoeing and kayaking on Paradise Pond and walking through the surrounding trails" entice many. On campus, "Most people participate in some sort of extracurricular activity, whether they are singing in an a cappella group or part of a play or on a sports team. In terms of weekends, there are at least two parties on most weekends and a number of lectures, performances, movies, and many other activities to attend. Thus, Smith is a place where you do not need to drink to have a good time but that is also available if that's what you want to do. There is something for everyone." Smith parties tend to be more subdued than your average college bash, so those seeking a more conventional college experience trek on over to UMass or Amherst.

Student Body

There is "a wide diversity of types of people at Smith. You'll walk to class and pass by a jock, a cardigan set and pearls-type person, a Dungeon and Dragons addict...there's a niche for everyone. You just have to find it." Smith women are typically "smart, competitive, motivated, and wants to make a difference in her community." Many are "politically liberal, opinionated, pride themselves on being well-informed, and can be overly sensitive and overly politically correct." They also share "a strong acceptance of lesbian/bisexual/same gender loving identities, which usually changes back to 'straight' once people graduate. This is usually referred to as LUGs (Lesbians Until Gradation) or BUGs (Bisexual Until Graduation)."

THE PRINCETON REVIEW SAYS

Admissions

Very important factors considered include: Academic GPA, recommendation(s), rigor of secondary school record, character/personal qualities. *Important factors considered include:* Class rank, application essay, standardized test scores, extracurricular activities, interview, talent/ability. *Other factors considered include:* Alumni/ae relation, first generation, racial/ethnic status, volunteer work, work experience. SAT or ACT required; TOEFL required of all international applicants. High school diploma or equivalent is not required. *Academic units recommended:* 4 English, 4 mathematics, 3 science, (3 science labs), 3 foreign language, 2 history.

Financial Aid

Students should submit: FAFSA, CSS/Financial Aid PROFILE, noncustodial PROFILE, business/farm supplement. Regular filing deadline is 2/1. The Princeton Review suggests that all financial aid forms be submitted as soon as possible after January 1. *Need-based scholarships/grants offered:* Federal Pell, SEOG, state scholarships/grants, the school's own gift aid. *Loan aid offered:* Direct Subsidized Stafford, Direct Unsubsidized Stafford, FFEL PLUS, Federal Perkins, state loans, college/university loans from institutional funds. Applicants will be notified of awards on or about 4/1. Federal Work-Study Program available. Institutional employment available. Off-campus job opportunities are excellent.

The Inside Word

Smith's relatively high acceptance rate results from its self-selecting applicant pool, meaning that students with no chance of getting in here simply don't bother applying. The fact that the school has no intention of admitting men tells you all you need to know about its success in attracting accomplished, highly talented women. Put your best foot forward here and hope for the best.

THE SCHOOL SAYS "..."

From The Admissions Office

"Smith students choose from 1,000 courses in more than 50 areas of study. There are no specific course requirements outside the major; students meet individually with faculty advisers to plan a balanced curriculum. Smith programs offer unique opportunities, including the chance to study abroad, or at another college in the United States, and a semester in Washington, DC. The Ada Comstock Scholars Program encourages women beyond the traditional age to return to college and complete their undergraduate studies. Smith is located in the scenic Connecticut River valley of western Massachusetts near a number of other outstanding educational institutions. Through the Five College Consortium, Smith, Amherst, Hampshire, and Mount Holyoke colleges and the University of Massachusetts enrich their academic, social, and cultural offerings by means of joint faculty appointments, joint courses, student and faculty exchanges, shared facilities, and other cooperative arrangements. Smith is the only women's college to offer an accredited major in engineering; it's also the only college in the country that offers a guaranteed paid internship program ("Praxis")."

"Smith requires either the SAT or the ACT. Scores from older versions of the SAT (pre-March 2005 version) and the ACT are acceptable."

For even more information on this school, turn to page 515 of the "Stats" section.

St. Bonaventure University

PO Box D, Saint Bonaventure, NY 14778 • Admissions: 716-375-2400 • Fax: 716-375-4005
Financial Aid: 716-375-2528 • E-mail: admissions@sbu.edu • Website: www.sbu.edu

RATINGS
Quality of Life: 73   Academic: 76   Admissions: 73   Financial Aid: 80

STUDENTS SAY "..."

Academics

St. Bonaventure is "a small-town university with a lot to offer," including a "simply stellar" journalism and mass communications program that features "an amazing faculty" that "wants you to get the best job possible." SBU's business program is also "very strong," and its education department "has a good reputation"; a new science building, scheduled for completion in the fall of 2008, should bolster the university's small but growing biology, chemistry, and computer science departments. Regardless of major, all students must complete a core curriculum offered through SBU's

> SURVEY SAYS . . .
> Large classes
> Athletic facilities are great
> Students are friendly
> Frats and sororities are unpopular
> or nonexistent
> College radio is popular
> Lots of beer drinking
> Hard liquor is popular

Clare College. While a few here insist that "Clare College is not that bad, and a lot of the classes are interesting," the majority complain that the "required Catholic core curriculum" is "a complete drag and a waste of students' time and effort, in addition to being a GPA reducer." Somewhere in between are those pragmatists who tell us that "Clare College courses are annoying but not over demanding. If you didn't want to learn about Catholic heritage, you shouldn't come to a Catholic school." Amen! While SBU undergrads may not agree on the value of the core curriculum, nearly all concur that professors here "are easy to talk to and are always available after class and outside of class. They make students feel comfortable and want to get to know the students. We are not just numbers." They also agree that their degree provides them access to "great connections with alumni" and that, all things considered, SBU leaves them "as well equipped to take the jobs of their choosing out of college as students at any other college, period."

Life

"When the weekend arrives, the general consensus of the students is one thing: partying. Off campus houses host triple keggers every weekends and the four local bars begin to draw crowds on Wednesday nights." Almost everyone agrees that "Drinking is huge...and so are basketball games"—as one student explains it, "we all love love love basketball games; the entire student population will be at a basketball game on a Saturday night, without fail"—but undergrads add that "there are lots of other things to keep busy" for those outliers to whom neither beer nor hoops appeals. Winter sports such as snowboarding and skiing are quite popular, and students have access to numerous parks and trails for hiking during the warm months. Furthermore, "The radio station and Campus Activities Board work very hard to bring in an up-and-coming band probably once a week." Students add that "The radio station is also great thing to do, it's very easy to get involved in." Finally, the school's many community-spirited undergrads can participate in "the oldest student-run soup kitchen in the country" or "a program called Bona Buddies that matches up students with underprivileged local kids to mentor them."

Student Body

The typical Bona undergrad "is white and Catholic, with a desire to do well and succeed but a stronger desire to have fun while doing so." Most "wear jeans and a North Face jacket or something very similar"; students are "trendy" but casual. A great number "hail from within three hours of the school, mostly in the Rochester and Buffalo area." Western New York is conservative terrain so SBU "has a good number of conservative students." They are typically "involved, whether it be in our soup kitchen or radio station." While the demographic is largely white, "There are more and more minority students every year," and the school offers "a plethora of activities, groups and policies that seem to provide a soaring number of opportunities for minority students."

THE PRINCETON REVIEW SAYS

Admissions

Very important factors considered include: Academic GPA, recommendation(s), rigor of secondary school record, character/personal qualities, interview. *Important factors considered include:* Application essay, standardized test scores, extracurricular activities, level of applicant's interest, talent/ability, volunteer work. *Other factors considered include:* Class rank, alumni/ae relation, first generation, work experience. SAT recommended; SAT or ACT required; ACT recommended; TOEFL required of all international applicants. High school diploma is required and GED is accepted. *Academic units required:* 4 English, 3 mathematics, 3 science, 2 foreign language, 4 social studies. *Academic units recommended:* 4 English, 3 mathematics, 3 science, (3 science labs), 2 foreign language, 4 social studies.

Financial Aid

Students should submit: FAFSA, institution's own financial aid form, state aid form. The Princeton Review suggests that all financial aid forms be submitted as soon as possible after January 1. *Need-based scholarships/grants offered:* Federal Pell, SEOG, state scholarships/grants, private scholarships, the school's own gift aid. *Loan aid offered:* FFEL Subsidized Stafford, FFEL Unsubsidized Stafford, FFEL PLUS, Federal Perkins, college/university loans from institutional funds. Applicants will be notified of awards on a rolling basis beginning 4/1.

The Inside Word

Above average students should meet little resistance from the St. Bonaventure admissions office; nearly nine in ten applicants here are accepted, and the academic profile of the median admitted student is respectable but hardly overwhelming. A personal essay and interview are optional; barring a misstep of catastrophic proportions, they can only improve your chances of getting in.

THE SCHOOL SAYS "..."

From The Admissions Office

"The St. Bonaventure University family has been imparting the Franciscan tradition to men and women of a rich diversity of backgrounds for more than 130 years. This tradition encourages all who become a part of it to face the world confidently, respect the earthly environment, and work for productive change in the world. The charm of our campus and the inspirational beauty of the surrounding hills provide a special place where growth in learning and living is abundantly realized. The Richter Student Fitness Center, scheduled to be completed in 2004, will provide all students with state-of-the-art facilities for athletics and wellness. Academics at St. Bonaventure are challenging. Small classes and personalized attention encourage individual growth and development for students. St. Bonaventure's nationally known Schools of Arts and Sciences, Business Administration, Journalism/Mass Communication, and Education offer majors in 31 disciplines. The School of Graduate Studies also offers several programs leading to the master's degree.

"Applicants for Fall 2008 can submit scores from either the old or new SAT, as well as the ACT. For students who have taken both versions, the best composite score from either the old or new SAT will be used. The Biology Subject Test is required only for students applying to one of our Dual Admission medical programs. "

For even more information on this school, turn to page 515 of the "Stats" section.

ST. JOHN'S COLLEGE (MD)

PO BOX 2800, ANNAPOLIS, MD 21404 • ADMISSIONS: 410-626-2522 • FAX: 410-269-7916
FINANCIAL AID: 410-626-2502 • E-MAIL: ADMISSIONS@SJCA.EDU • WEBSITE: WWW.SJCA.EDU

RATINGS
Quality of Life: 91   Academic: 94   Admissions: 86   Financial Aid: 92

STUDENTS SAY ". . ."

Academics

Tiny St. John's College specializes in the great books. The entire four-year curriculum is an "exhilarating and exhausting" survey of intellectual history, starting with ancient Greece and ending in modern times. Virtually all classes are required. There are no majors. There are no textbooks. And there are no tests, except for "occasional grammar and vocab

> **SURVEY SAYS . . .**
> Class discussions encouraged
> No one cheats
> Frats and sororities are unpopular
> or nonexistent

quizzes" in Ancient Greek and French. Grades are based on papers and class participation. Students here encounter the works of "the greatest minds of Western Civilization" in their original, unadulterated form. While students at others schools may occasionally think outside the box, students at St. John's critically examine "the eternal questions of this world," namely "what it is to be a human." It's "certainly not the best education for everyone (especially students who want to learn certain technical skills)." For these students, though, it is a little slice of heaven. Classes are small—"never larger than 20 students"—and "discussion-based." Professors (called "tutors" here, incidentally) are "deeply intelligent" and "can bounce from Newton to Leibniz to Baudelaire to Bach" with ease. They "do little or no lecturing," favoring instead to "facilitate discussion." Students engage in conversation, "instead of sitting through lectures on other people's interpretations." "There's a wonderful sense of camaraderie that develops in the classroom, as we wrestle with the Great Questions of the ages," enthuses one student.

Life

Despite the "overbearing" workload, "there is an almost snuggly feeling of community here." "The academic atmosphere is immersing and supportive, especially since everyone is in or has had or will have all the same classes." Social life is "alarmingly insular." "We at St. John's are removed from the world to a truly shocking degree," elaborates one student. "The campus feels not like a campus, but a miniature world, which actually is not very much like the real world." Extracurricular activities include "heaps of clubs." "Most everyone attends the Shakespeare plays and classical music concerts." Intramural sports are "incredibly fun" and a big part of Johnnie life. "Skill is optional but enthusiasm is required." "It is a great stress reliever," explains one student. "The books tear your soul apart," but sports here are a way of "pasting it back together." Campus-wide parties on the weekends include "raucous" reality dance parties as well as waltz and swing dancing parties. Drinking is popular. Coffee and cigarettes are big. Johnnies also "sail, watch movies," and play board games. Or they just hang out, "finding adventures where they pop up." Students also talk late into the night "about set theory, socks, art history, Moby Dick, why macaroni is so orange," and pretty much everything except politics. "Johnnies are extraordinarily uninterested in politics." While the food on campus "sucks," students find epicurean delights in "Annapolis, Baltimore, Washington DC, or New York."

Student Body

"St. John's is a unique program, and it takes a unique group of people to keep it going." "The one thing Johnnies have in common is their love of learning and their love for thought," says a junior. "A Johnnie is a bookworm, socially awkward in some fashion, an intense thinker." Eyeglasses are common. "This campus may have the worst collective eyesight in America." "Many students are quite intelligent, and most are highly eccentric." "'Intellectual elitism' can be a problem." "Upperclassmen especially have an esprit de corps and traditionalist spirit that borders on crotchetiness." "Most people here are strange." Many are "brash and freakish." "There is definitely a certain type of person that picks St. John's, but how that quality reveals itself is different for every person," notes one student. "St. John's is entirely made up of atypical students, so none of them fit in, and they don't feel like they need to." Johnnies are "an amazing conglomeration of artists, mathematicians, jocks, role-playing enthusiasts, poets, iconoclasts, activists, and some who are all of these." That said, there's a serious lack of "ethnic diversity." However, intellectual diversity abounds. Students are "willing to assert opinions, and, more importantly, to reconsider them."

THE PRINCETON REVIEW SAYS

Admissions

Very important factors considered include: Application essay. *Important factors considered include:* Recommendation(s), rigor of secondary school record, character/personal qualities. *Other factors considered include:* Class rank, academic GPA, standardized test scores, alumni/ae relation, extracurricular activities, first generation, interview, racial/ethnic status, talent/ability, TOEFL required of all international applicants. High school diploma is required and GED is accepted. *Academic units required:* 3 mathematics, 2 foreign language. *Academic units recommended:* 4 English, 4 mathematics, 3 science, (3 science labs), 4 foreign language, 2 social studies, 2 history.

Financial Aid

Students should submit: FAFSA, CSS/Financial Aid PROFILE, state aid form, noncustodial PROFILE, business/farm supplement. The Princeton Review suggests that all financial aid forms be submitted as soon as possible after January 1. *Need-based scholarships/grants offered:* Federal Pell, SEOG, state scholarships/grants, the school's own gift aid. *Loan aid offered:* FFEL Subsidized Stafford, FFEL Unsubsidized Stafford, FFEL PLUS, Federal Perkins, college/university loans from institutional funds. Applicants will be notified of awards on a rolling basis beginning 12/1. Off-campus job opportunities are good.

The Inside Word

St. John's has one of the most personal admissions processes in the country. The applicant pool is highly self-selected and extremely bright, so don't be fooled by the high acceptance rate—every student who is offered admission deserves to be here. Candidates who don't give serious thought to the kind of match they make with the college and devote serious energy to their essays are not likely to be successful.

THE SCHOOL SAYS ". . ."

From The Admissions Office

"The purpose of the admission process is to determine whether an applicant has the necessary preparation and ability to complete the St. John's program satisfactorily. The essays are designed to enable applicants to give a full account of themselves. They can tell the committee much more than statistical records reveal. Previous academic records show whether an applicant has the habits of study necessary at St. John's. Letters of reference, particularly those of teachers, are carefully read for indications that the applicant has the maturity, self-discipline, ability, energy, and initiative to succeed in the St. John's program. St. John's attaches little importance to 'objective' test scores, and no applicant is accepted or rejected because of such scores.

"St. John's College does not require the results of standardized tests, except in the case of international students, homeschooled students, and those who will not receive a high school diploma. Results of the ACT or SAT are sufficient for these students."

For even more information on this school, turn to page 516 of the "Stats" section.

ST. JOHN'S UNIVERSITY

8000 UTOPIA PARKWAY, JAMAICA, NY 11439 • ADMISSIONS: 718-990-2000 • FAX: 718-990-5728
E-MAIL: ADMISSIONS@STJOHNS.EDU • WEBSITE: WWW.STJOHNS.EDU

RATINGS

Quality of Life: 75   Academic: 71   Admissions: 81   Financial Aid: 70

STUDENTS SAY " . . . "

Academics

Like its hometown of Queens, NY, St. John's moves inex-
orably forward without forgetting its history and traditions. The school's administration is committed to constantly "updating the university's facilities." Recent
improvements include "a state-of-the-art athletic training
facility and revamped cafeterias,"as well as a $20 million

upgrade to science facilities. In addition, the school distributes "brand-new laptops to all incoming students"
and has "done a tremendous job of implementing technology throughout the campus," which "is completely
wireless except for a few athletic fields and parking lots." On the traditions side of the balance, the school
recently built "a beautiful brand-new, free-standing church" and maintains "a lot of policies and politics
opposed by typical college students . . . [such as] the visitor policies in the dorms." Regarding academics, the
university offers some amazing opportunities such as the Institute for Writing Studies and the "Discover the
World" study-abroad program. When it comes to classroom experience, "Professors are professors. Like [at] any
school, some are better than others." Students report that "the experience you have at St. John's really depends
on what you do with it. Don't take a professor just because he/she is easy—chances are that means they suck!
If you are self-motivated . . . you will find challenging professors." Big-picture people will see that St. John's
offers "a quality private education" and, in many instances, a "generous" financial aid package that translates
to an overall "low cost."

Life

Historically, St. John's has been known as "basically a school for commuters." According to many students, it
still is. They argue that because "There aren't many on-campus students," "On the weekends this place is a
ghost town." Others counter that "Recently there has been an amazing effort" by the school's Residence Life
Department "to bring back campus life," an effort which includes posting "weekly calendars informing us
about campus events and activities." For those who prefer off-campus activities in their spare time, the school
helps to make that possible, too. There are "shuttles that can take us into the city [aka Manhattan, to those outside New York City] and on weekends . . . to the mall." In addition, the "school runs programs to see Broadway
shows for free." Even without the school's help, however, New York is at students' fingertips; almost everything
the city has to offer "is just a subway ride away." "Clubs, sports events, parties, restaurants"—you name it,
NYC's got it, and St. John's students sample it. The faithful will be happy to know that "St. John's makes it easy
to incorporate a spiritual life with an academic one." For the altruistic, there are "community-service initiatives
galore."

Student Body

Because it is "located in Queens, the most diverse place on Earth," it's no surprise that St. John's itself is "very,
very diverse." Though "everyone gets along exceptionally well," getting along well doesn't equal total integration. There are "major ethnic lines" at St. John's, and each "ethnic group tends [to] hang around with itself, a
sight typical of New York in general." Yet students' external differences belie intangible similarities. Many students may be the first in their family to attend college, so a strong work ethic is pervasive. Everyone "wants to
achieve something greater than their parents." The second major similarity stems from the first: Students here
generally have many responsibilities outside of their schoolwork."

THE PRINCETON REVIEW SAYS

Admissions

Very important factors considered include: Academic GPA, standardized test scores. *Important factors considered include:* Application essay, recommendation(s), rigor of secondary school record, character/personal qualities, volunteer work. *Other factors considered include:* Class rank, alumni/ae relation, extracurricular activities, interview, level of applicant's interest, work experience. SAT or ACT required; ACT with Writing component recommended. TOEFL required of all international applicants. High school diploma is required and GED is accepted. *Academic units required:* 4 English, 3 mathematics, 3 science, (3 science labs), 2 foreign language, 3 social studies, 5 academic electives.

Financial Aid

Students should submit: FAFSA. The Princeton Review suggests that all financial aid forms be submitted as soon as possible after January 1. *Need-based scholarships/grants offered:* Federal Pell, SEOG, state scholarships/grants, private scholarships, the school's own gift aid. *Loan aid offered:* FFEL Subsidized Stafford, FFEL Unsubsidized Stafford, FFEL PLUS, Federal Perkins Applicants will be notified of awards on a rolling basis beginning 3/15. Federal Work-Study Program available. Institutional employment available. Off-campus job opportunities are good.

The Inside Word

The admissions process at St. John's doesn't include many surprises. High school grades and standardized test scores are undoubtedly the most important factors though volunteer work and extracurricular activities are also highly regarded. What is surprising is that this Catholic university doesn't consider religious affiliation at all when making admissions decisions; there are students of every religious stripe here (see the "Student Body" section).

THE SCHOOL SAYS ". . ."

From The Admissions Office

"Founded by the Vincentian Fathers in 1870, St. John's is a world-class Catholic university that prepares students for leadership in today's global society. St. John's combines a friendly, residential college experience with full access to the resources and opportunities only available in exciting New York City.

"Students pursue more than 100 quality programs in the arts, sciences, business, education, pharmacy and allied health. Professors are internationally respected scholars, 90 % of whom hold a Ph.D. or comparable degree. The 17:1 student-faculty ratio ensures personal attention in the classroom.

"Representing 45 states and 125 foreign countries, students also benefit from these advantages:

- A dynamic freshman year featuring "Learning Communities" – themed clusters of like-minded students sharing classes, activities and residence hall suites.
- Unequaled opportunities to experience the "Big Apple" through unique core courses like Discover New York.
- Wireless laptop computers for entering students, with access to our award-winning campus network.
- Academic Service-Learning – course-related volunteer activities that give students real-world experience while assisting those in need.
- Unique study abroad programs like Discover the World, allowing students to earn 15 credits while living and learning in three foreign cities in a single semester.
- Vibrant campus activities with 180 student clubs and organizations that keep students engaged around the clock.

"St. John's has three residential New York City campuses: a 105-acre flagship campus in Queens, NY; a wooded Staten Island, NY, campus; and an award-winning Manhattan campus. St. John's also has campuses in Oakdale, NY, and Rome, Italy."

For even more information on this school, turn to page 516 of the "Stats" section.

St. Lawrence University

PAYSON HALL, CANTON, NY 13617 • ADMISSIONS: 315-229-5261 • FAX: 315-229-5818
FINANCIAL AID: 315-229-5265 • E-MAIL: ADMISSIONS@STLAW.EDU • WEBSITE: WWW.STLAWU.EDU

RATINGS
Quality of Life: 83   Academic: 88   Admissions: 89   Financial Aid: 88

STUDENTS SAY "..."

Academics

Described by one student as a "hidden jewel tucked away in the tundra of the North Country," St. Lawrence University offers a "unique liberal arts education" to prospective undergraduates. Two things that "really stand out" at this small university are the "study abroad programs and the First-Year Program (FYP)." FYP is one of the oldest living-learning programs in the country and all first-year students are required to participate, which "helps

> **SURVEY SAYS . . .**
> *Small classes*
> *Great computer facilities*
> *Great library*
> *Athletic facilities are great*
> *Everyone loves the Saints*
> *Lots of beer drinking*

strengthen skills and better prepares students for their next 3 years in college." Moreover, nearly 50 percent of the student body "participates in the study abroad programs offered" at some point during their time here. According to one student, "The professors are the best asset of St. Lawrence . . . they are very knowledgeable, and they love what they teach." Classes emphasize "critical thinking and writing," and "Professors are always there for students." Many students "form long-lasting friendships with their professors." Despite the university's small size there are "many class offerings," and students praise a "wonderful president" who leads a "very accessible" administration.

Life

Students at St. Lawrence "work hard [and] play harder!" Most students "socialize frequently" through a variety of outlets, from "theme parties [and] midnight breakfasts" to hanging out at "local bars." Although the surrounding area is "fairly void of cultural experiences," many students participate in "outdoor trips to the accessible Adirondacks or to cosmopolitan Montreal or Ottawa . . . all of which are between 1 to 2 and a half hours away from campus." The university makes "a lot of the accessories for these [outdoor] activities available for little or no upfront price." In addition, "There is always something happening at the student center for those who might prefer a more low-key night, like free movies." Most students "enjoy attending collegiate athletics, especially hockey" with "more than 60 percent of students involved with some sport." All of this contributes to a "very energetic atmosphere" on campus where there is "always an event to watch or participate in." Some students see the relatively isolated location of St. Lawrence as a blessing because it "forces students to form tighter bonds than at schools in cities where there is easy access to many different activities."

Student Body

The typical student at St. Lawrence is "very preppy" and "comes from the New England area." Here, "The guys are called 'Larrys' and the girls are 'Muffies,'" but "Most personalities do not fit the 'snobby preppy' stereotype." Many students qualify as "outdoorsy" types and there are "quite a few jocks." While students acknowledge a "lack of diversity" on campus, they say this is "slowly improving." Even though there are "not many atypical students"—"students all in black or with several piercings"—those who deviate from the "popped collar" and "Vera Bradley bag" trends "fit in regardless." While one student warns that some St. Lawrence students can be "very cliquey" and "difficult to approach," most students describe themselves as "friendly, enthusiastic, and open-minded." Typical or not, an SLU student is primarily "dedicated to academics and is very involved outside of the classroom." "Be it sports or other clubs, SLU students rarely spend time just sitting in their dorm rooms doing nothing."

THE PRINCETON REVIEW SAYS

Admissions

Very important factors considered include: Application essay, academic GPA, recommendation(s), character/personal qualities. *Important factors considered include:* Class rank, rigor of secondary school record, extracurricular activities, interview, racial/ethnic status. *Other factors considered include:* Standardized test scores, alumni/ae relation, first generation, geographical residence, level of applicant's interest, talent/ability, volunteer work, work experience. TOEFL required of international applicants for whom English is a foreign language. High school diploma is required and GED is accepted. *Academic units recommended:* 4 English, 4 mathematics, 4 science, 4 foreign language, 2 social studies, 2 history.

Financial Aid

Students should submit: FAFSA, PROFILE, business/farm supplement, Income Tax Returns/W-2s. Regular filing deadline is 2/1. The Princeton Review suggests that all financial aid forms be submitted as soon as possible after January 1. *Need-based scholarships/grants offered:* Federal Pell, SEOG, ACG, state scholarships/grants, the school's own gift aid. *Loan aid offered:* FFEL Subsidized Stafford, FFEL Unsubsidized Stafford, FFEL PLUS, Federal Perkins, college/university loans from institutional funds. Applicants will be notified of awards on or about 3/30. Federal Work-Study Program available. Institutional employment available. Off-campus job opportunities are poor.

The Inside Word

Despite facing stiff competition from many regional competitors, St. Lawrence University has managed to increase its application numbers over the past several years. Because it's increasingly selective, candidates must post decent grades in challenging courses if they hope to be accepted. The Admissions Committee appreciates the time each student puts into his or her application and recognizes those efforts by having three different counselors read each one. The school is a great choice for students looking to attend a small college in the Northeast.

THE SCHOOL SAYS ". . ."

From The Admissions Office

"In an ideal location, St. Lawrence is a diverse liberal arts learning community of inspiring faculty and talented students guided by tradition and focused on the future. The students who live and learn at St. Lawrence are interesting and interested; they enroll with myriad accomplishments and talents, as well as desire to explore new challenges. Our faculty has chosen St. Lawrence intentionally because they know that there is institutional commitment to support great teaching. They are dedicated to making each student's experience challenging and rewarding. Our graduates make up one of the strongest networks of support among any alumni body and are ready, willing, and able to connect with students and help them succeed.

"Which students are happiest at St. Lawrence? Students who like to be actively involved. Students who are open-minded and interested in meeting people with backgrounds different from their own. Students who value having a voice in decisions that affect them. Students who appreciate all that is available to them and cannot wait to take advantage of both the curriculum and the co-curricular options. Students who want to enjoy their college experience and are able to find joy in working hard.

"You can learn the facts about us from this guidebook: We have about 2,200 students; we offer more than 30 majors; the average class size is 16 students; a great new science center is open as of 2007; close to 50 percent of our students study abroad; and we have an environmental consciousness that fits our natural setting between the Adirondack Mountains and St. Lawrence River. You must visit, meet students and faculty, and sense the energy on campus to begin to understand just how special St. Lawrence University is.

"Beginning with applications for entry in Fall 2006, the submission of standardized test scores (SAT or ACT) is optional. Students must indicate on the St. Lawrence Common Application supplement which scores, if any, they wish to have considered in the application process. "

For even more information on this school, turn to page 517 of the "Stats" section.

STATE UNIVERSITY OF NEW YORK AT BINGHAMTON

PO BOX 6000, BINGHAMTON, NY 13902-6001 • ADMISSIONS: 607-777-2171 • FAX: 607-777-4445
FINANCIAL AID: 607-777-2428 • E-MAIL: ADMIT@BINGHAMTON.EDU • WEBSITE: WWW.BINGHAMTON.EDU

RATINGS
Quality of Life: 74   Academic: 76   Admissions: 94   Financial Aid: 87

STUDENTS SAY "..."

Academics

With fewer than 12,000 undergraduates, Binghamton University is "a decent sized school that doesn't feel that big." It's thanks to this that "you get to know people easily" here. Yet the school is also large enough to accommodate "a great education in a variety of fields, ranging from the liberal arts to engineering to business to education to nursing." Students report that "the school does the best it

> **SURVEY SAYS ...**
> *Great library*
> *Diverse student types on campus*
> *Campus feels safe*
> *Student publications are popular*
> *Lots of beer drinking*

can to prepare its students at an Ivy level. It knows that it does not have the name recognition of others but teaches its students the values of hard work so that they can compete with Ivy students for jobs. Students aim for these jobs and are often successful getting them." Professional programs, which are among the most popular here, are "amazing" and "the connection with alumni is great," not to mention "the career development center is awesome," all huge pluses when it comes time for the job search. And the school accomplishes all this at a very reasonable cost. "Everyone here says value is a huge strength for this school," one student explains. Like most state schools, BU has some problems at the administrative level. Administrators "can sometimes be frustrating to deal with. It seems like if you have a problem you end up getting sent to another office. Once you get to that office you're then directed to yet another office, as though the administration really doesn't know the system.... It can be a wild goose chase." Students also warn that "academic advising is atrocious and unhelpful." When it comes to managing its own bureaucracy, some here feel that "the school is too large for itself to handle."

Life

Students tell us that "campus life is really great" at Binghamton, offering "tons of activities to participate in, including club or intramural sports, student government, fraternities/sororities (both social and professional), student groups, and more." Dorms are "convenient" and "clean" (although "living off-campus is less expensive"), and undergrads are kept busy "trying to balance classes, school work, jobs, volunteer work and sports.... There's never enough time for everything you want to do." Some complain that "The weekends can get pretty dull on campus," which is why they opt for beer-soaked fraternity parties or "the bars downtown that don't check ID." According to the drinking crowd, "The weeks can be stressful with a lot of classes, papers and tests, so students tend to unwind on the weekends. Because there is no major city nearby besides Ithaca—which is an hour away—students are forced to drink in their dorms and then head downtown to one of the many frats. Once the frats run out of alcohol, people generally walk about 10 minutes to the bars." However, the drinking scene is by no means the only weekend alternative. As one student explains, "For people not interested in that, there is Late Night Binghamton," which "shows movies, has hypnotists, magicians, or comedians come, has crafts to do, and it's all free."

Student Body

The typical BU undergrad "is someone who was smart in high school"—they had to be to get in here—but were "well-rounded enough so as to not be only invested in academics. In general, although people are relatively smart, they have other things on their mind than pure academics." The campus is "very ethnically diverse," with "a lot of Jewish students and a lot of Asians" factoring into the mix. Geographically, Long Island and New York City are extremely well represented, "but there are many others from around the country and the world." Class background and local weather conspire to make "The North Face" a conspicuous brand on campus.

THE PRINCETON REVIEW SAYS

Admissions

Very important factors considered include: Academic GPA, rigor of secondary school record, standardized test scores. *Important factors considered include:* Class rank, application essay, recommendation(s), extracurricular activities, first generation, volunteer work. *Other factors considered include:* Alumni/ae relation, character/personal qualities, geographical residence, level of applicant's interest, racial/ethnic status, state residency, talent/ability, work experience. SAT or ACT required; ACT with Writing component required. TOEFL required of all international applicants. High school diploma is required and GED is accepted. *Academic units required:* 4 English, 3 mathematics, 2 science, 3 foreign language, 2 social studies. *Academic units recommended:* 4 mathematics, 4 science, 3 foreign language, 3 history.

Financial Aid

Students should submit: FAFSA, state aid form. The Princeton Review suggests that all financial aid forms be submitted as soon as possible after January 1. *Need-based scholarships/grants offered:* Federal Pell, SEOG, state scholarships/grants, private scholarships, the school's own gift aid. *Loan aid offered:* Direct Subsidized Stafford, Direct Unsubsidized Stafford, Direct PLUS, Federal Perkins, Federal Nursing, college/university loans from institutional funds. Applicants will be notified of awards on a rolling basis beginning 3/17. Federal Work-Study Program available. Institutional employment available. Off-campus job opportunities are excellent.

The Inside Word

Binghamton receives nearly 11 applications for every slot in its freshman class. That's bad news for marginal candidates, who should probably start looking elsewhere in the SUNY system if they have their hearts set on attending one. With competition this stiff, you'll need solid test scores and high school grades just to get past the first winnowing stage.

THE SCHOOL SAYS ". . ."

From The Admissions Office

"SUNY Binghamton has established itself as the premier public university in the Northeast, because of our outstanding undergraduate programs, vibrant campus culture, and committed faculty. Students are academically motivated, but there is a great deal of mutual help as they compete against the standard of a class rather than each other. Faculty and students work side by side in research labs or on artistic pursuits. Achievement, exploration, and leadership are hallmarks of a Binghamton education. Add to that a campus wide commitment to internationalization that includes a robust study abroad program, cultural offerings, languages and international studies, and you have a place where graduates leave prepared for success.

"Students applying for freshman admission for Fall 2008 are required to take the new version of the SAT (or the ACT with the Writing section). SAT Subject Test scores are not required for admission."

For even more information on this school, turn to page 517 of the "Stats" section.

STATE UNIVERSITY OF NEW YORK—THE COLLEGE AT BROCKPORT

350 NEW CAMPUS DRIVE, BROCKPORT, NY 14420 • ADMISSIONS: 585-395-2751 • FAX: 585-395-5452
E-MAIL: ADMIT@BROCKPORT.EDU • WEBSITE: WWW.BROCKPORT.EDU

RATINGS
Quality of Life: 78   **Academic:** 73   **Admissions:** 85   **Financial Aid:** 76

STUDENTS SAY "..."

Academics

The College at Brockport is "a school that specializes in producing nurses, PE teachers, and other teachers," but is still able to "accommodate students with a wide variety of interests." The school "has a unique atmosphere (especially

> **SURVEY SAYS . . .**
> *Great food on campus*
> *Lots of beer drinking*

in the Delta College Program [an interdisciplinary learning community]) in which students are able to come out of their comfort zone and blend with new people." "The professors are diverse," says one student. "Some are excellent teachers, others are simply extremely intelligent individuals. Most or all of them seem concerned that students take something valuable away from their classes." Still, "everyone has the occasional bad professor." Students like that "class sizes are small for the most part" and that the school offers "a great study abroad program." "The administration that has recently come into place at Brockport is clearly trying to change the school for the better," notes one student. "It has put academics first and has aggressively lobbied for, and raised, money to expand programs and encourage positive intellectual growth within the college." Students also appreciate that the president is so visible and involved with the student body. "You will see him around campus a lot, at basketball and football games, and basically anywhere." All in all, Brockport seems a "good education for a good price!"

Life

Hometown Brockport, NY is "a relatively small town" with an "inviting" community. "For entertainment students hang out in the dorms like other colleges, but also peruse the shops, restaurants, and bars of Brockport's quaint and thriving downtown. There is a regular bus schedule that makes rounds to the many malls, museums, cultural events, and landmarks of the Rochester, NY area." "In the village there is a movie theater" that offers "$1 current midnight movies on Fridays," and also a bowling alley, where students enjoy "$1 bowling on Tuesdays and Thursdays." "Sports and fitness are very important here," and students are keen to both support and participate in them. "For the weekends drinking is pretty popular here," says one student. "Drinking starts on Thursday nights and continues throughout the weekend." As "the school has become more academically focused over the last decade," "internships, studying abroad, and other academic experiences are becoming more popular." One on-campus perk several students cite is that "the food is rated number one in all of SUNY schools for the past few years."

Students

While some think "the typical student here is your white, upstate, and western New York jock," others see a bit more diversity. "The student body varies from super athletic to super academic," notes one student. Still, most agree that the typical student here is "middle-class," "Christian," "and pretty moderate politically." And there is no question that there are "a lot of physical education majors as well as nursing majors." One tool for categorizing these students might be the city/suburbs/rural divide. For example, "Some people come from small towns and have that small town something about them. Others come from Long Island, so they are opposite." While there are few atypical students, those that are "can fit in with other people with whom they identify." A student explains, "It can be difficult to find the right crowd for you at first, especially at a smaller school like Brockport, but once you find it, you're golden."

THE PRINCETON REVIEW SAYS

Admissions

Very important factors considered include: Class rank, academic GPA, rigor of secondary school record, standardized test scores. *Important factors considered include:* Application essay, recommendation(s), extracurricular activities, talent/ability. *Other factors considered include:* Character/personal qualities, interview, racial/ethnic status, volunteer work, work experience. SAT or ACT required; ACT with Writing component recommended. TOEFL required of all international applicants. High school diploma is required and GED is accepted. *Academic units required:* 4 English, 3 mathematics, 3 science, (1 science labs), 4 social studies, 3 academic electives. *Academic units recommended:* 3 foreign language.

Financial Aid

Students should submit: FAFSA, state aid form. The Princeton Review suggests that all financial aid forms be submitted as soon as possible after January 1. *Need-based scholarships/grants offered:* Federal Pell, SEOG, state scholarships/grants, private scholarships, the school's own gift aid. *Loan aid offered:* Direct Subsidized Stafford, Direct Unsubsidized Stafford, Direct PLUS, Federal Perkins, Federal Nursing, Alternative Education loans. Applicants will be notified of awards on a rolling basis beginning 4/15. Federal Work-Study Program available. Institutional employment available. Off-campus job opportunities are good.

The Inside Word

Admission to Brockport is competitive, with less than half of all applicants gaining acceptance. Not surprisingly, it bases admissions decisions largely on the applicant's high school academic profile and standardized test results, along with some consideration of leadership, community service, and the like. The school uses the SUNY application, a standardized online application used by 50 of the 64 SUNY campuses. Admissions at Brockport are rolling, so as a general rule, the earlier you apply, the more likely a space in the freshman class will be available for you.

THE SCHOOL SAYS "..."

From The Admissions Office

"The College at Brockport "has the success of its students as its highest priority," asserts the college's mission statement.

"A selective comprehensive liberal arts college that can trace its roots back nearly 175 years to the opening of the Erie Canal, The College at Brockport, State University of New York, offers a multi-dimensional education that prepares students for success—personally and professionally.

"With a wealth of academic programs and co-curricular activities, our students explore their intellectual, creative and athletic potential, and pursue their talents. There are 42 undergraduate majors, 29 graduate programs and 18 areas of teacher certification. The College holds program accreditation in 12 areas. Each student at Brockport receives individual attention from our faculty—leading scholars in their own right—who also are dedicated advisors and mentors. Our students have access to one of the largest Study Abroad programs in the nation, a variety of internships with major corporations, 23 NCAA intercollegiate athletic teams, arts and cultural events and performance, and more than 60 clubs and organizations.

"Nearly 30 percent of undergraduates go on to graduate school, and 92 percent find jobs or are in graduate school within six months of graduation.

"Substantial investments on the 464-acre campus in recent years include renovation of Smith-Lennon Science Center, Hartwell Hall and Seymour College Union. New projects include the 208-bed townhome facility, renovation of Harrison Dining Hall, and plans for a $44-million Special Events Recreation Center.

"The College is located in the historic Village of Brockport, 16 miles west of Rochester with easy access to Buffalo and Lake Ontario. Students enjoy a small college-town atmosphere as well as easy access to Rochester's culture, shopping, professional sports and parks.

"To fully appreciate our outstanding academic programs, our beautiful campus, and our energetic student body, nothing compares to a personal visit. Schedule your visit online."

For even more information on this school, turn to page 518 of the "Stats" section.

STATE UNIVERSITY OF NEW YORK—COLLEGE OF ENVIRONMENTAL SCIENCE AND FORESTRY

OFFICE OF UNDERGRADUATE ADMISSIONS, SUNY-ESF, SYRACUSE, NY 13210 • ADMISSIONS: 315-470-6600 • FAX: 315-470-6933
E-MAIL: ESFINFO@ESF.EDU • WEBSITE: WWW.ESF.EDU

RATINGS
Quality of Life: 84   **Academic:** 60*   **Admissions:** 84   **Financial Aid:** 94

STUDENTS SAY ". . ."

Academics

The motto is "Improve your world" at SUNY's nationally renowned College of Environmental Science and Forestry in Syracuse. In addition to environmental science and a bunch of different specialties in forestry, programs include fisheries science, landscape architecture, construction management, paper engineering, and wildlife science. It's "a small, personal school" (once you get past the often surprisingly large intro

> **SURVEY SAYS . . .**
> *Great computer facilities*
> *Great library*
> *Students are friendly*
> *Great off-campus food*
> *Lots of beer drinking*

courses) with "tough" classes. "The courses here are very challenging but also very interesting and real," says a wildlife science major. "They connect real-life problems to all the course work." "Science is really strong." "Students are often very involved in research." "Field trips are prominent in most classes. There's always the opportunity to be outside." Faculty members are "not always great teachers" but they "can back up their teaching with real experiences" and "professors and students have a good relationship." "Registration is a mess" and there's some useless bureaucracy (this is a SUNY school, after all) but administrators are generally "flexible in their approach" and the "awesome" top brass is "very organized and on top of problems."

Life

"Most activity focuses around the main quad" at ESF. "People are very involved in wildlife organizations and doing community service" "There are a lot of protests." "Winter is brutal because our campus is on a huge hill," notes a senior. Weather permitting, ultimate Frisbee is popular. The woodsmen's team competes in contests using old-fashioned lumberjack techniques with other schools in the Northeast and naturally Canada. "ESF has one of the strictest drug and alcohol policies in the state" but drinking is nevertheless a frequent pastime. "Most of the student body smokes something" as well. Off-campus, "downtown offers lots of culture and a lot of students spend weekends hiking (especially in the Adirondacks)." "No one here ever says no to going out for a hike." Syracuse University is "right next to the ESF campus" and "it easy to get involved there." "You can take their classes, use their facilities, and play their club sports and intramurals."

Student Body

Ethnic diversity at ESF is seriously lacking. It's an overwhelming white group of people from the state of New York. "Students generally don't put a lot of time into dressing for school and are generally very laidback" here. People universally "love the outdoors." To grossly generalize, "there are two loose groups at ESF." The "more populous" group is the "vegan, save-the-world" "tree huggers." For them, "tie-dye and green are the preferred colors to wear." "We're always taking the stairs instead of the elevators (even up to the eighth floor), using Tupperware instead of Styrofoam or plastic, and we love plants," explains a first-year hippie. Not surprisingly, these students "lean more toward the left." The other, smaller group is "fairly conservative" "hunters" and "rednecks" who have "a management view of the environment." "They "often major in forestry resources management, construction management, paper science engineering, or some such thing." "Somehow," members of both groups manage to get along pretty well.

THE PRINCETON REVIEW SAYS

Admissions

Very important factors considered include: Application essay, academic GPA, rigor of secondary school record, standardized test scores, level of applicant's interest. *Important factors considered include:* Class rank, recommendation(s), character/personal qualities, extracurricular activities, talent/ability, volunteer work, work experience. *Other factors considered include:* Alumni/ae relation, first generation, geographical residence, interview, racial/ethnic status, state residency, SAT or ACT required; TOEFL required of all international applicants. High school diploma is required and GED is accepted. *Academic units required:* 4 English, 3 mathematics, 3 science, (3 science labs), 3 social studies. *Academic units recommended:* 4 mathematics, 4 science, (4 science labs), 1 history.

Financial Aid

Students should submit: FAFSA, state aid form. The Princeton Review suggests that all financial aid forms be submitted as soon as possible after January 1. *Need-based scholarships/grants offered:* Federal Pell, SEOG, state scholarships/grants, private scholarships, the school's own gift aid Federal SMART Grants, Federal ACG Grants. *Loan aid offered:* FFEL Subsidized Stafford, FFEL Unsubsidized Stafford, FFEL PLUS, Federal Perkins Applicants will be notified of awards on a rolling basis beginning 3/15. Federal Work-Study Program available. Institutional employment available. Off-campus job opportunities are excellent.

The Inside Word

Due to the highly specialized nature of the programs here, applicants to ESF are a highly self-selected group. Many high school students want to dedicate themselves to natural resources and the environment, so the admission is competitive. Serious candidates will devote thoughtful attention to the required essay.

For even more information on this school, turn to page 518 of the "Stats" section.

STATE UNIVERSITY OF NEW YORK—FREDONIA

178 CENTRAL AVENUE, FREDONIA, NY 14063 • ADMISSIONS: 716-673-3251 • FAX: 716-673-3249
E-MAIL: ADMISSIONS.OFFICE@FREDONIA.EDU • WEBSITE: WWW.FREDONIA.EDU

RATINGS
Quality of Life: 77   **Academic:** 76   **Admissions:** 82   **Financial Aid:** 76

STUDENTS SAY ". . ."

Academics

"Music and art are paramount" at this "beautiful, friendly, welcoming, and accepting," "small, liberal public arts school" in upstate New York. In addition to music and art, SUNY—Fredonia also offers "great degree programs" in "education, theatre, and communications." "Most if not all professors are masters of their craft" and "are welcoming and have open-door policies." "A lot of the professors could realistically be teaching at better schools, but they choose to be at Fredonia because the area is wonderful," says one student. Of course, "like anywhere else, there are always a few professors nobody can stand, but there is usually enough flexibility so you can avoid them when registering for classes if you put the effort into it." "The school's administration is great," agree students. "It really means something when you see President Hefner and other campus administrators walking around campus, eating in our dining halls, and attending nearly every campus event showing support." If there is any complaint about the administration, it's that it has a tendency to play favorites. "The administration focuses mainly on education, acting, and music majors." Still, such favoritism must go only so far, as "a new science building is being built" at this decidedly artsy school.

> **SURVEY SAYS . . .**
> *Large classes*
> *Great library*
> *Theater is popular*
> *Lots of beer drinking*

Life

"Besides attending classes and studying outside of class, life consists of attending various intercollegiate sports events including hockey and soccer," says one undergrad. Well, not entirely. In addition, there are "millions of clubs and organizations, a lot of which do community service," and also many "campus jobs that are not work study, so are open to everyone." As its academic reputation suggests, students also have numerous opportunities to take in "shows put on by the music and theater departments." Those seeking them will find "plenty of frat parties, if that's your idea of fun." Off-campus, "While the town of Fredonia is small and consists of mainly an older population, there is always something to do." For example, there are also "numerous bars in town that admit 18+ to dance." Outdoorsy types appreciate that "there are beautiful parks to go walking around, including the New York State Lake Erie Park." Some "go fishing and take walks along the creek that runs through town." If you seek big-city excitement "you can easily drive to Erie, PA or to Buffalo." "Politics and diversity are strong topics for students at Fredonia."

Student Body

"The typical Fredonia student likes art and indie music and cares about environmental issues," however, there are also "a lot of the typical 'jock' and 'prep' type students." "Everyone at Fredonia parties a lot," says one student, "that includes drinking and drugs." "The average student is white, middle-class, and from upstate New York suburbia" and "is very friendly, outgoing, and has a smile on his or her face." In addition, he or she is "very open-minded." No surprise, then, that "there is a large LGBT population on our campus and they are treated without prejudice." Students are "often spiritual as opposed to religious and most show an appreciation for the arts." Politically, students are "typically left-wing liberal Democrats." As far as fashion goes, "Everyone is exactly the same in the way they try to be different: black clothes, weird hairdos, chains and pajama pants," or some combination thereof.

THE PRINCETON REVIEW SAYS

Admissions

Very important factors considered include: Academic GPA, rigor of secondary school record. *Important factors considered include:* Class rank, recommendation(s), standardized test scores, extracurricular activities. *Other factors considered include:* Application essay, alumni/ae relation, character/personal qualities, first generation, level of applicant's interest, racial/ethnic status, talent/ability, volunteer work, work experience. SAT or ACT required; TOEFL required of all international applicants. High school diploma is required and GED is accepted. *Academic units required:* 4 English, 3 mathematics, 3 science, 3 foreign language, 4 social studies. *Academic units recommended:* 4 English, 4 mathematics, 4 science, 3 foreign language, 4 social studies.

Financial Aid

Students should submit: FAFSA, state aid form. The Princeton Review suggests that all financial aid forms be submitted as soon as possible after January 1. *Need-based scholarships/grants offered:* Federal Pell, SEOG, state scholarships/grants, private scholarships, the school's own gift aid. *Loan aid offered:* FFEL Subsidized Stafford, FFEL Unsubsidized Stafford, FFEL PLUS, Federal Perkins Applicants will be notified of awards on a rolling basis beginning 3/15. Federal Work-Study Program available. Off-campus job opportunities are good.

The Inside Word

Fredonia accepts about half of all applicants, making admission to the school competitive. The average freshman had a high B+ average in high school, an SAT score over 1100, and an ACT score over 24. The school uses the SUNY application, a standardized online application used by 50 of the 64 SUNY campuses. To be considered for scholarships, applicants must complete a supplemental application after submitting the application for admission. Admissions at Fredonia are rolling, so as a general rule, the earlier you apply, the more likely you'll find a spot in the freshman class.

THE SCHOOL SAYS ". . ."

From The Admissions Office

"The State University of New York College of Environmental Science and Forestry (SUNY—ESF) is the oldest and largest college in the nation focused on the science, design, engineering, and management of natural resources and the environment. ESF offers students 22 undergraduate and 28 graduate degree programs to choose from, and is consistently ranked among the nation's top universities based on value, class size, and student engagement in learning.

"Faculty members at ESF come from impressive backgrounds and are working on research that's at the forefront of solving many of the world's environmental problems. Students work side-by-side with faculty on research projects ranging from restoring polluted lakes to developing new sources of biofuels. ESF has more faculty and students engaged in academic programs focused on the environment than any other college in the United States, but our small-college atmosphere guarantees that faculty get to know students on a first-name basis. Outstanding teaching is the top priority for our faculty.

"ESF's special relationship with neighboring Syracuse University provides some truly unique advantages. Students at ESF can take classes at SU while paying SUNY tuition, use library and computing facilities, join more than 300 student organizations, and cheer on the Syracuse Orange sports teams. ESF students live in residence halls and apartments located on the Syracuse University campus, which is directly adjacent to ESF."

For even more information on this school, turn to page 519 of the "Stats" section.

STATE UNIVERSITY OF NEW YORK AT GENESEO

One College Circle, Geneseo, NY 14454-1401 • Admissions: 716-245-5571 • Fax: 716-245-5550
Financial Aid: 716-245-5731 • E-mail: ADMISSIONS@GENESEO.EDU • Website: WWW.GENESEO.EDU

RATINGS

Quality of Life: 81   Academic: 80   Admissions: 94   Financial Aid: 89

STUDENTS SAY "..."

Academics

State University of New York—Geneseo, the school that considers itself the Honors College of the SUNY system, offers "challenging academics in a very home-like atmosphere" where "you don't get lost in the crowd like bigger schools." As one student puts it, "Geneseo is all about the classic college experience: a small town, rigorous academics, and having fun at the same time." One in five students pursues a teaching degree here, leading some to conclude that "Geneseo focuses mainly on training future teachers, but for the rest of us, they are preparing us for our next step into employment or further education." Nearly as many study business and marketing; the "best academic departments are by far the natural sciences," however, where "the students are the brightest, the courses are the toughest, and the professors really know their stuff." Geneseo also provides "great pre-professional (medical, dental, pharmacological) preparation in sciences." Students here enjoy a small-school experience that includes "superior academics, small, intimate classes, and professors who truly care about students and will offer them every opportunity to succeed" as well as "many study abroad options (students are encouraged to explore the world)." They also point out that "Leadership and research are also a great focus at SUNY Geneseo. If a student wants to do individual research, professors are more than willing to help students organize projects and carry them out." For these and other reasons, students describe Geneseo as a school "for the academically inclined non-rich citizen. It's the Harvard of the SUNY system."

Life

"The great thing about Geneseo is that there's always a party to go to if you want, but there's no pressure to go," and "It's perfectly acceptable to stay home and watch movies with friends on the weekends or even study on Saturday nights." Indeed, students tell us that "There is so much more to do than just party. The college always has amazing activities going on in the union. Every weekend there are crafts and games, and sometimes they bring in comedians or performers.... At the Halloween Monster Mash Bash, there is a costume ball and activities as well as a raffle for really great prizes. There are far too many activities to list here!" Intercollegiate hockey games "are a big hit, and lots of students go to them on weekends." There are "also many different organizations you can get involved in, including several volunteer organizations, intramural sports, and different hobbies." Despite all the alternatives, some students tell us that because "the student body isn't all that creative with what they come up with to do on the weekends... most weekends most students just end up drinking themselves stupid." The town of Geneseo is little help; "There is nothing to do in town, and the closest city is a 45-minute drive away (Rochester, NY)."

Student Body

"The typical student here at SUNY Geneseo is much like that of the ordinary New York State public high school," except that "Most of the school is white (the college is making efforts to diversify). Despite the majority being white, there is still a wide diversity of student types, be it that they are from different backgrounds, economic classes, or simply around the nation." Undergrads "spend most of their time studying in Milne Library, and those who choose not to study usually don't make it to graduation." There are "a few minority and gay/lesbian/bisexual students" here, "but they really are the minority and often have difficulty adjusting. Many students feel like outsiders and transfer before graduating." Students tell us that "The two largest minorities are Asian and African American...the different ethnic groups tend to clump together."

> SURVEY SAYS ...
> Lab facilities are great
> Great computer facilities
> Students are friendly
> Campus feels safe
> Low cost of living
> Students are happy
> Lots of beer drinking
> Hard liquor is popular

THE PRINCETON REVIEW SAYS

Admissions

Very important factors considered include: Rigor of secondary school record, standardized test scores. *Important factors considered include:* Application essay, academic GPA, recommendation(s), extracurricular activities, racial/ethnic status, talent/ability. *Other factors considered include:* Class rank, first generation, level of applicant's interest, volunteer work, work experience. SAT or ACT required; TOEFL required of all international applicants. High school diploma is required and GED is accepted. *Academic units recommended:* 4 English, 4 mathematics, 4 science, 4 foreign language, 4 social studies.

Financial Aid

Students should submit: FAFSA, state aid form. Regular filing deadline is 2/15. The Princeton Review suggests that all financial aid forms be submitted as soon as possible after January 1. *Need-based scholarships/grants offered:* Federal Pell, SEOG, state scholarships/grants, private scholarships, the school's own gift aid. *Loan aid offered:* FFEL Subsidized Stafford, FFEL Unsubsidized Stafford, FFEL PLUS, Federal Perkins, state loans, alternative loans. Applicants will be notified of awards on a rolling basis beginning 3/15. Federal Work-Study Program available. Institutional employment available. Off-campus job opportunities are poor.

The Inside Word

Geneseo is the most selective of SUNY's 13 undergraduate colleges and more selective than three of SUNY's university centers. No formulaic approach is used here. Expect a thorough review of your academic accomplishments (over half the student body graduated in the top 10 percent of their class) and your extracurricular/personal side. Admissions standards are tempered only by a somewhat low yield of admits who enroll. The school competes for students with some big-time schools, meaning it must admit many more students than it expects will attend.

THE SCHOOL SAYS ". . ."

From The Admissions Office

"Geneseo has carved a distinctive niche among the nation's premier public liberal arts colleges. The college now competes for students with some of the nation's most selective private colleges, including Colgate, Vassar, Hamilton, and Boston College. Founded in 1871, the college occupies a 220-acre hillside campus in the historic Village of Geneseo, overlooking the scenic Genesee Valley. As a residential campus—with nearly two-thirds of the students living in college residence halls—it provides a rich and varied program of social, cultural, recreational, and scholarly activities. Geneseo is noted for its distinctive core curriculum and the extraordinary opportunities it offers undergraduates to pursue independent study and research with faculty who value close working relationships with talented students. Equally impressive is the remarkable success of its graduates, nearly one-third of whom study at leading graduate and professional schools immediately following graduation.

"For Fall 2008, SUNY Geneseo will use either SAT or ACT test results in the admission selection process. The SAT Writing test result will not be used. SAT Subject Test results are not required but will be considered if the applicant submits the test results."

For even more information on this school, turn to page 519 of the "Stats" section.

STATE UNIVERSITY OF NEW YORK—MARITIME COLLEGE

ADMISSIONS OFFICE, SIX PENNYFIELD AVENUE, THROGGS NECK, NY 10465 • ADMISSIONS: 718-409-7200
FAX: 718-409-7465 • E-MAIL: ADMISSIONS@SUNYMARITIME.EDU • WEBSITE: WWW.SUNYMARITIME.EDU/THE PRINCETON REVIEW SAYS

RATINGS
Quality of Life: 74   **Academic:** 74   **Admissions:** 73   **Financial Aid:** 61

STUDENTS SAY "..."
Academics

"SUNY Maritime College trains and educates merchant mariners for today's commercial and Naval Reserve fleet[s]," and the students who fill the Fort Schuyler campus call it "the best place to learn about going to sea." Students rave about "hands-on" Summer Sea Terms aboard the well-equipped Empire State VI; one engineer says, "If you want to be a part of running a steam propul-

> **SURVEY SAYS . . .**
> Large classes
> Career services are great
> Frats and sororities are unpopular or nonexistent
> Theater is popular
> Very little drug use

sion plant and visit . . . 12 to 15 different countries before you graduate, then this is the place." Teachers of the "licensing classes" are "seasoned mariners," and students describe Maritime's "heavy course load" as a suffer-now, profit-later enterprise: "Although we take a lot more credits than most college students . . . in the end it will be well worth it" because "The average starting salary upon graduating is one of the highest in the country. . . . There is also no obligation to ship out or join the Navy or Merchant Marine Reserves, so if you want a shoreside job upon graduation or . . . internships in lieu of Summer Sea Terms, SUNY—Maritime College will give you the opportunity." The facilities aren't posh: One student likens the restrooms to "truck stop bathrooms" and calls the hallways "dark and dingy." Fortunately, "There are plans to extend our pier and build and upgrade the facilities which will accommodate a larger student population and increase the learning experience while keeping up with the technological advances in the maritime industry."

Life

"Most students take between 17 and 23 credits a semester," generally topping 24 hours of weekly class time in concurrent pursuit of "a normal bachelor's degree" and "a Coast Guard license." Add to this schedule early-morning regimental exercises and weekly room inspections, and it's no surprise that social life is often "bleak" and "monotonous," with free time dedicated to "studying [and] having a clean uniform and room." Nonetheless, most students make time to play intramural or intercollegiate sports, hang out with friends, and "drink on or off campus even though the penalties are tough." Weekday "liberty," or free time, is a privilege that increases in frequency as students ascend the ranks. Students here "really treasure our weekends, since [they are] our only time off," and "run off the campus on Fridays" either "to go home and blow off steam" or to go "out in the Bronx or in Manhattan." As a result, "The campus is a ghost town on the weekends." Although the school isn't in the most hopping section of New York City, students love their "big-city" access. "Public transportation is very easy to use," raves one undergrad, "and, if you're a . . . Yankees fan, you can attend games in dress uniform and get in for free." Opportunities for fun increase dramatically in summer, when brief foreign port calls interrupt the strenuous work shipboard.

Student Body

"Maritime feels like a big fraternity," says one cadet. Students "share a common love for the ocean and ships" and are drawn together by a freshman "year of hardships and training, which brings everyone together and makes them stronger," and by the annual 2 months together at sea. There is, however, a major split between the regimented majority and civilian minority. Civilians, says one cadet, "do not fit in quite as well because we, as cadets, cannot understand what they are doing here." Many of the predominantly "conservative," "middle-class" cadets are Long Islanders who "go . . . home every weekend." "There is also a faction of foreign students." Students say, however, that discrimination is not a problem. Though the regiment is overwhelmingly "White male," "female and minority cadets are accepted by the majority," and, "regardless of race everyone wears a uniform and looks the same."

THE PRINCETON REVIEW SAYS

Admissions

Very important factors considered include: Application essay, academic GPA, rigor of secondary school record. *Important factors considered include:* Character/personal qualities, extracurricular activities, interview, level of applicant's interest, talent/ability, volunteer work, work experience. *Other factors considered include:* Class rank, recommendation(s), standardized test scores, alumni/ae relation, SAT or ACT required; TOEFL required of all international applicants. High school diploma is required and GED is accepted. *Academic units required:* 3 English, 3 mathematics, 3 science, (1 science labs), 3 foreign language, 3 social studies, 3 history. *Academic units recommended:* 4 mathematics, 4 science.

Financial Aid

Students should submit: FAFSA, institution's own financial aid form. Regular filing deadline is 7/15. The Princeton Review suggests that all financial aid forms be submitted as soon as possible after January 1. *Need-based scholarships/grants offered:* Federal Pell, SEOG, state scholarships/grants, private scholarships, the school's own gift aid. *Loan aid offered:* FFEL Subsidized Stafford, FFEL Unsubsidized Stafford, FFEL PLUS, Federal Perkins, state loans Applicants will be notified of awards on a rolling basis beginning 3/15. Federal Work-Study Program available. Institutional employment available. Off-campus job opportunities are excellent.

The Inside Word

Unlike the national military academies, Maritime charges tuition. However, like all SUNY campuses, the school offers low in-state tuition to 15 states along the eastern seaboard and participates in EOP (the Equal Opportunity Program), an economic affirmative action program in which New York State students with lower-than-average GPAs and SATs can be admitted on full scholarship. The school also offers a number of named scholarships and participates in Naval ROTC.

THE SCHOOL SAYS ". . ."

From The Admissions Office

"The world is open for business! In today's global market, SUNY—Maritime College prepares students for success—in the maritime industry, at sea, in the business world, in government—the choice is yours. SUNY—Maritime College undergraduates enjoy the best value of a public education while consistently earning the top undergraduate average starting salaries in the country. Seventy-nine percent of our student body receives financial aid. The average starting salary of our undergraduate Class of 2006 was $58,000. SUNY—Maritime College is nationally recognized as an Accreditation Board for Engineering and Technology (ABET)–accredited institution and home of the National Institute for Leadership and Ethics. We are one of only six colleges in the United States to offer a Naval Architecture degree. In 2007 SUNY—Maritime College received the Andrew Heiskell Award for Innovation in International Education by the Institute for International Education. Are you ready for an exciting 4 years of learning, discovery, and leadership development? To find out if a SUNY—Maritime College education can launch your life, contact our Admissions Office at 718-409-7221 or admissions@sunymaritime.edu, and visit our website at www.sunymaritime.edu."

For even more information on this school, turn to page 520 of the "Stats" section.

STATE UNIVERSITY OF NEW YORK—OSWEGO

211 CULKIN HALL, OSWEGO, NY 13126 • ADMISSIONS: 315-312-2250 • FAX: 315-312-3260
E-MAIL: ADMISS@OSWEGO.EDU • WEBSITE: WWW.OSWEGO.EDU

RATINGS
Quality of Life: 78   Academic: 75   Admissions: 82   Financial Aid: 81

STUDENTS SAY ". . ."

Academics

An "excellent business program," a strong education program, a "successful honors program," and "good study
abroad options" highlight the academic offerings of
SUNY—Oswego. Professors seem focused on creating for
undergraduates a "personal and comfortable learning
environment." Oswego profs are "knowledgeable about
their subject and excited to be in Oswego." And they seem

> **SURVEY SAYS . . .**
> *Great library*
> *Students are friendly*
> *Students are happy*
> *Lots of beer drinking*
> *Hard liquor is popular*

to "really care about what you do and want to help you in every way to make sure you do well." Students also
appreciate that they "have a lot of opportunities to work with professors on research and other projects outside
of the classroom to help build real world experience." That makes sense to many students, as they view an
Oswego education mainly as "preparation for the working world." That said, "Some of the GE (general education) professors are not so great." But all-in-all, it's the "amazing professors" who make an Oswego bachelor's
degree "a great education for the amount of money you pay." The administration gets only fair reviews. While
it "has good intentions at heart," it is "pretty disorganized in many ways." Case in point: advising. "Thanks to
them the majority of Oswego students have to stay 1–2 semesters longer than their expected graduation date
because of Gen Eds that they missed," says one student.

Life

Winter sport enthusiasts be advised, "Oswego offers some awesome winter activities due to the amount of
snow we get." These include "one of the best" ice skating rinks, "so ice skating is always a fun activity." In addition, "snowball fights are a must." And of course, "One of everyone's favorite things is going to the home hockey games (we won the national championship last year [2007])." "When the weather is nice we have bonfires
down by the lake," and "in the summer and spring people will spread out beach towels and get some sun on
the lakeside of campus." In addition, "There are also concerts and performers that come throughout the year to
the school." "Some students go out on the weekends to parties and bars and others see a movie or go bowling,"
says one student. "A large percentage of the student population seems to go home frequently, like every weekend or every other weekend." Some here think that "the city of Oswego has seen better days," finding that
because it is "a small city," it lacks the "excitement of big city life." "The fun things to do in Oswego? Drink. If
there was more to do, there would be more to do!" advises one student. "We need more off-campus activities
that don't involve getting messed up."

Student Body

SUNY—Oswego's student body "consists mostly of middle-class to lower-middle-class students from upstate
New York." That said, there are also many here "from downstate like NYC and Long Island." How do you tell
the difference between upstaters and downstaters? "Upstaters like to hunt a lot, downstaters like to dress up
nice." In addition to permanent residence somewhere in the Empire State, "the majority of students are white."
Temperamentally, "the typical student is usually someone who is studious from Sunday to Wednesday, and parties like a rock star from Thursday to Saturday, being able to separate academics and partying, and sometimes
a job." "There are some atypical students, those who don't go to class, and those who don't party," explains an
undergrad. "They are all accepted by the community and will have friends in different social cliques." "They
normally fit in by finding a club that they enjoy," agrees another.

THE PRINCETON REVIEW SAYS

Admissions

Very important factors considered include: Academic GPA, rigor of secondary school record. *Important factors considered include:* Application essay. *Other factors considered include:* Class rank, recommendation(s), standardized test scores, character/personal qualities, extracurricular activities, interview, racial/ethnic status, talent/ability, volunteer work, work experience. SAT or ACT required; TOEFL required of all international applicants. High school diploma is required and GED is accepted. *Academic units required:* 4 English, 3 mathematics, 3 science, (2 science labs), 2 foreign language, 4 social studies. *Academic units recommended:* 4 English, 4 mathematics, 4 science, (3 science labs), 4 foreign language, 4 social studies.

Financial Aid

Students should submit: FAFSA, state aid form. The Princeton Review suggests that all financial aid forms be submitted as soon as possible after January 1. *Need-based scholarships/grants offered:* Federal Pell, SEOG, state scholarships/grants, private scholarships, the school's own gift aid. *Loan aid offered:* FFEL Subsidized Stafford, FFEL Unsubsidized Stafford, FFEL PLUS, Federal Perkins Applicants will be notified of awards on a rolling basis beginning 3/1.

The Inside Word

About half of all applicants are accepted to Oswego, making admission here competitive. The school uses the SUNY application, a standardized online application used by 50 of the 64 SUNY campuses. However, Oswego does use a supplement to this application to find out more about you as a person, specifically about your extracurricular involvement, including work experience. Basically, the admissions office is interested in more than just numbers, so take this opportunity to shine. Admissions at Oswego are rolling, so as a general rule, the earlier you apply, the more likely a space in the freshman class will be available for you.

THE SCHOOL SAYS ". . ."

From The Admissions Office

"Oswego offers a great higher education value on a beautiful 696-acre lakeside campus in upstate New York, 35 miles northwest of Syracuse. Oswego is small enough to provide a friendly, welcoming environment and big enough to provide wide-ranging academic and social opportunities. The diverse selection of degree programs ranges from accounting to zoology and includes interdisciplinary options like cognitive science and international trade. The schools of education and business have each won the stamp of excellence from the premier accrediting organizations in their field. The weather makes the college popular with future meteorologists—one of Oswego's best-known alumni is the *Today Show*'s Al Roker. Oswego is noted for its honors program, internships, and international study. Ninety percent of students are full-time, one of the highest percentages among public colleges, and all courses are taught by faculty, not graduate assistants. More than $200 million dollars in campus construction is under way, including a $26-million-dollar campus convocation center, which will provide new living accommodations, high-tech classrooms, and recreational facilities. Students participate in 130 clubs and organizations and 24 intercollegiate sports. Over half of all students and 90 percent of freshmen live on campus, which has been named one of the safest in the country. Over $2.5 million in academic merit scholarships are awarded to nearly 30 percent of the entering class in renewable awards worth ranging from $500 to $4,400 per year, and over $65 million in need-based financial aid is awarded. The Oswego Guarantee promises both that room and board costs will not increase during a student's 4 years on campus and that a student can complete a degree in that time."

For even more information on this school, turn to page 520 of the "Stats" section.

STATE UNIVERSITY OF NEW YORK—PURCHASE COLLEGE

ADMISSIONS OFFICE, 735 ANDERSON HILL ROAD, PURCHASE, NY 10577 • ADMISSIONS: 914-251-6300 • FAX: 914-251-6314
FINANCIAL AID: 914-251-6350 • E-MAIL: ADMISSIONS@PURCHASE.EDU • WEBSITE: WWW.PURCHASE.EDU

RATINGS
Quality of Life: 63   Academic: 77   Admissions: 84   Financial Aid: 67

STUDENTS SAY "..."

Academics

Purchase College is the SUNY system's answer to the region's many high-priced conservatories and arts schools set within a public liberal arts and sciences college. While it may not have the cache of Julliard or Rhode Island School of Design, students here don't feel they're getting shorted. On the contrary, they laud the teachers with professional experience (the school's proximity to New York City helps here) who "are caring, inspirational, and focused." They also appreciate the fact that access to Purchase's School of

Liberal Arts and Sciences provides "a diverse curriculum" with a greater liberal arts focus than you'll find at most arts schools. Of course, they also love how they're "paying state tuition for a school full of ex-Ivy League teachers who were all too eccentric for Ivy schools, so now they teach at Purchase!" The school's more conventional liberal arts and science offerings notwithstanding, Purchase is primarily "an artistic community." Peer "work in the dance, music, photography, film, art, and acting conservator[ies] is amazing, and it is wonderful to be able to experience the work of these students." Classes tend to be small "with a heavy emphasis on writing skills." Students "are usually well-read and prepared for discussion," and, because "Class sizes are not too large," they "are able to contribute to both the structure of the class and the content." Outside the creative arts, Purchase excels in psychology, journalism, premed, biology, and creative writing.

Life

"Campus activities are amazing" at Purchase, a result of the art school/proximity-to-New York combo, which helps bring "nationally recognized figures in the arts to speak on a regular basis, including Art Speigelman and Tony Kushner. There are also free shows several days a week performed by excellent indie bands like My Brightest Diamond and Gregory and the Hawk" as well as numerous events featuring student performances, such as "Fall Ball, a major campus event [that] features a drag show performed by students. Given that many people who dance or sing are in one of the conservatories, it's very entertaining." And then there's New York City, "just a 40-minute train ride away" and "the most popular destination for entertainment." When students "plan on doing something special, [they] plan on going there for the weekend." Purchase has the requisite college parties, but "Excessive drinking is probably far less common at Purchase than at a more frat-oriented school." Students tend to keep very busy with schoolwork, especially those in the conservatories, who "spend a great deal of time practicing and studying."

Student Body

At Purchase, "many students who would be stereotyped as 'freaks' are not that freaky." This group includes "the 'artsy' type" who has "green hair" and "piercings" and is "blatantly alternative to pop culture." Such students "comprise a good half of the student population," and, as a result, "they make everyone else considered 'normal' look weird." That being said, the student body here is "extremely diverse." There's "an outspoken gay community and a ton of different ethnicities." Because of the school's "urban feel, racism is virtually obsolete, and there is no hostility towards those of different sexual orientations." "Most everyone finds [his or her] niche at Purchase." In all areas, students "like to dive deep into their interests . . . Purchase is where the dancers, musicians, actors, visual artists, liberal arts and science majors, etc. are all interacting with one another to create a really interesting group of students."

THE PRINCETON REVIEW SAYS

Admissions

Very important factors considered include: Application essay, academic GPA, talent/ability. *Important factors considered include:* Standardized test scores. *Other factors considered include:* Recommendation(s), rigor of secondary school record, character/personal qualities, extracurricular activities, interview, SAT recommended; SAT or ACT required; TOEFL required of all international applicants. High school diploma is required and GED is accepted.

Financial Aid

Students should submit: FAFSA, state aid form. The Princeton Review suggests that all financial aid forms be submitted as soon as possible after January 1. *Need-based scholarships/grants offered:* Federal Pell, SEOG, state scholarships/grants, private scholarships, the school's own gift aid. *Loan aid offered:* FFEL Subsidized Stafford, FFEL Unsubsidized Stafford, FFEL PLUS, Federal Perkins Applicants will be notified of awards on a rolling basis beginning 3/1. Federal Work-Study Program available. Institutional employment available. Off-campus job opportunities are excellent.

The Inside Word

About one-third of Purchase College undergraduates enroll in the School of the Arts. All must undergo some type of audition or portfolio review to gain admission; this is the most important piece of the application. Traditional application components—such as high school transcript, test scores, and personal essay—are also considered, but do not figure as prominently. Applicants to the School of Liberal Arts and Sciences undergo a more conventional application review.

THE SCHOOL SAYS "..."

From The Admissions Office

"At Purchase College, you're encouraged to 'Think Wide Open.' The campus combines the energy and excitement of professional training in the performing and the visual arts with the intellectual traditions and spirit of discovery of the humanities and sciences. A Purchase College education emphasizes creativity, individual accomplishment, openness, and exploration. It culminates in a senior research or creative project that may focus on civic engagement or interdisciplinary work to become an excellent springboard to a career or to graduate or professional school. The Conservatories of Art and Design, Dance, Music, and Theatre Arts and Film that make up the School of the Arts deliver a cohort-based education with apprenticeships and other professional opportunities in nearby New York City.

"You'll find a unique and engaging atmosphere at Purchase, whether you are a student in the arts, humanities, natural sciences, or social sciences. You choose among a wide variety of programs, including arts management, journalism, creative writing, environmental science, new media, dramatic writing, premed, pre-law, and education. You'll attend performances by your friends, see world-renowned artists on stage at the Performing Arts Center, and experience the artworks on display in the Neuberger Museum of Art (one of the largest campus art museums in the country)—all without leaving campus. The new student services building, along with an enhanced student services website, is making Purchase a lot more user-friendly for its students.

"Admissions requirements vary with each program in the college and can include auditions, portfolio reviews, essays, writing samples, and interviews.

"In addition to individual program requirements, Purchase College requires SAT or ACT scores to complete your application. You can apply on line through the college website at www.purchase.edu/admissions."

For even more information on this school, turn to page 521 of the "Stats" section.

STATE UNIVERSITY OF NEW YORK—STONY BROOK UNIVERSITY

Office of Admissions, Stony Brook, NY 11794-1901 • Admissions: 631-632-9898 • Fax: 631-632-9898
Financial Aid: 631-632-6840 • E-mail: UGADMISSIONS@NOTES.CC.SUNYSB.EDU • Website: WWW.STONYBROOK.EDU

RATINGS
Quality of Life: 62   **Academic:** 70   **Admissions:** 60*   **Financial Aid:** 65

STUDENTS SAY "..."

Academics

Stony Brook University "is a great place for ambitious, focused students who actually want to learn something" at a "great research university in which classes are challenging and interesting." Nearly half the undergraduates here pursue traditionally punishing majors such as biology, computer science ("one of the best undergraduate computer science programs," according to at least one student), and engineering. The school also boasts "a strong

> **SURVEY SAYS . . .**
> *Class discussions are rare*
> *Great computer facilities*
> *Great library*
> *Diverse student types on campus*
> *Lots of beer drinking*
> *(Almost) everyone smokes*

marine biology program," a popular undergraduate business program, and a solid selection of liberal arts majors. Students in the science and tech majors describe the school as "challenging but worth it," noting that "the sciences here are amazing. Now that I'm interviewing for medical schools, I'm seeing just how highly they think of Stony Brook's undergraduate science programs!" Professors are accomplished and, while "They can be boring, they know what they're teaching like the back of their hand. They will be very helpful in office hours, as long as you ask questions that show them you're trying." As at similar schools, "The only thing you have to watch out for, occasionally, is getting a professor who does not speak English well; that can cause some problems!" Students have "plenty of research opportunities" here, which is another plus. Stony Brook's administration "may consist of nice people, but it's pretty poorly organized. When there is some sort of paperwork involved, nothing ever goes right the first time around. Also, nothing is convenient, and you'll usually have to go in circles to get something done." Most students find the difficulties worth enduring and focus instead on how the school delivers "a great education for a reasonable price."

Life

"Life at Stony Brook depends on whom you surround yourself with," students tell us. While "a lot of students complain that there's nothing to do on campus," others counter that "the problem is that students aren't willing to put in the effort to find those activities." One undergrad explains, "There are many activities in campus life. However, you won't be aware of them at all if you don't . . . look them up. There are a lot of places where you can go play sports, and most dorms have places to play pool, Ping-Pong, or just watch TV." The school is home to "lots of student clubs with something for everyone" and Division I intercollegiate athletic teams, but "No one goes to athletic games. It's really depressing as a pep band member to play to a dead crowd." Hometown Stony Brook "is basically suburban. It is not the best college town. There are a few clubs and bars in the area that some students go to on Thursday nights. However, you have to have a car to get there. . . . If I want to have fun, I generally have to go into the city [NYC]. The city is about 2 hours away by train."

Student Body

The typical student at Stony Brook University "is a middle-class Long Island or Queens kid of Jewish, East Asian, or Indian background." Minority populations are large across a broad demographic range; the school is home to many who are "either Asian, African American, or Hispanic and very, very liberal." Subpopulations "tends to stick to themselves. . . . The atypical students are probably quite miserable at Stony Brook. There is definitely a very Long Island high school–like atmosphere," in part because of the large commuter population and in part because the student body is so large. One student writes, "All students fit in, but the student body is often impersonal, and it is very difficult to develop lasting friendships and relationships as a result."

THE PRINCETON REVIEW SAYS

Admissions

Very important factors considered include: Rigor of secondary school record, academic GPA, atandardized test scores. *Important factors considered include:* Class rank, application essay, recommendation(s). *Other factors considered include:* Interview, Extracurricular activities, Talent/ability, Character/personal qualities, Alumni/ae relation, State residency, Volunteer work, Work experience, Level of applicant's interest. TOEFL required of all international applicants.

Financial Aid

The Princeton Review suggests that all financial aid forms be submitted as soon as possible after January 1. Off-campus job opportunities are excellent.

The Inside Word

Liberal arts and social science candidates with above-average grades and test scores should encounter little difficulty gaining entry to SUNY Stony Brook. Students in technical fields (engineering, applied mathematics, computer science), in business, and in music must clear some higher hurdles. You can indicate "undecided" for your major on your application, but know that this does not guarantee you entry into these more competitive majors; you'll still have to meet the admissions requirements when you finally declare a major.

THE SCHOOL SAYS ". . ."

From The Admissions Office

"Stony Brook is ranked among the top 2 percent of universities worldwide by the London Times Higher Education Supplement and is a flagship campus of the State University of New York. U.S. News & World Report has ranked Stony Brook among the top 100 best national universities. The Wall Street Journal has ranked us eighth in the nation among public institutions placing students in elite graduate schools in medicine, law, and business. Our graduates include Carolyn Porco, the leader of the Imaging Team for the Cassini mission to Saturn; John Hennessy, the president of Stanford University; and Scott Higham, a Pulitzer Prize-winning investigative journalist for the Washington Post who has come to speak to students at our new School of Journalism.

"Situated on 1,100 wooded acres on the North Shore of Long Island, Stony Brook offers more than 150 majors, minors, and combined-degree programs for undergraduates, including our Fast Track MBA program, a thriving research environment, and a dynamic first-year experience in one of six small undergraduate communities. Stony Brook Southampton is our new residential campus focused on sustainability. Faculty include four members of our School of Marine and Atmospheric Sciences who are recent co-winners of the 2007 Nobel Peace Prize.

"Students enjoy comfortable campus housing, outstanding recreational facilities that include a new stadium, modern student activities center, and indoor sports complex. In addition, the Staller Center for the Arts offers spectacular theatrical and musical performances throughout the year.

"We invite students who possess both intellectual curiosity and academic ability to explore the countless exciting opportunities available at Stony Brook. Freshmen applying for admission to the university for Fall 2008 are required to take the SAT (or the ACT with the Writing section). SAT Subject Test scores are recommended, but not required."

For even more information on this school, turn to page 521 of the "Stats" section.

STATE UNIVERSITY OF NEW YORK—UNIVERSITY AT ALBANY

1400 WASHINGTON AVENUE, ALBANY, NY 12222 • ADMISSIONS: 518-442-5435 • FAX: 518-442-5383
FINANCIAL AID: 518-442-5757 • E-MAIL: UGADMISSIONS@ALBANY.EDU • WEBSITE: WWW.ALBANY.EDU

RATINGS

Quality of Life: 61   Academic: 63   Admissions: 83   Financial Aid: 74

STUDENTS SAY ". . ."

Academics

Is SUNY Albany (UAlbany to those in the know) the per-fect-sized school? Many here think so. Students describe it as "a big school numbers-wise that feels small." Notes one student, "It has a very broad range of quality academic programs, which is very important for an undecided senior in high school." Another adds, "If you know what you want and are motivated, the sky is the limit." The school

> **SURVEY SAYS . . .**
> *Great library*
> *Diverse student types on campus*
> *Lots of beer drinking*
> *Hard liquor is popular*
> *(Almost) everyone smokes*

exploits its location in the state capital to bolster programs in political science, criminal justice, and business, and it "offers internship opportunities to college students that very few schools can." Other standout depart-ments include psychology, Japanese studies, mathematics, and many of the hard sciences. Professors here vary widely in quality, but a surprising number "are receptive, active, and engaging"—in other words, "a lot more accessible than I would have thought for a school this big." Teachers are especially willing to "go out of their way to help students who are interested in learning, come to class regularly, and care about their academic work." The administration, as at most state-run schools, "is basically an over-bloated bureaucracy. Students are sent from department to department in each of their endeavors. It is advisable to avoid [the] administration if at all possible."

Life

There are three distinct social orbits on the Albany campus. Some students take the initiative "by joining one of the many clubs or groups or getting involved with the student government." Others "party for a good time," telling us that "any night of the week you can find people to go out to the bars and clubs with you" and that "the average night ends between 2:30–4:00 a.m." Both of these groups are likely to tell you that "there is a lot to do in Albany and the surrounding area," including "a great arts district, tons of awesome restaurants, muse-ums, [and] a state park." A third, sizable group primarily complains about the cold weather, and asserts that "there's nothing to do in Albany." The school works to excite these students with "fun programs and enter-tainers who come to the campus. We have had a series of comedians, rappers/singers, guests from MTV and VH1, authors, political figures, musical performances, sporting events, spirit events, and many other things around campus." School spirit is on the rise among all groups, we're told. The reason? "This year our basket-ball team began winning, and everyone came out of the woodwork to support them—it was really a great thing to see."

Student Body

Undergrads here believe that the student body is very diverse in terms of ethnicity and also in terms of per-sonality type; one student observes, "You have your motivated students [who] get good grades, are involved, and get amazing jobs in NYC after college. Then you have your unmotivated kids [who] complain, don't go to class, and blame a bad grade on the professor (when really it is because they crammed the night before and did-n't go to class)." Geographically, the school is less diverse. Nearly everyone is a New York State resident, with many coming from "downstate New York"—Long Island, New York City, and Westchester County. There's a fair amount of upstate kids as well, and "a lot of people have certain stereotypes in their heads when they first come to Albany. The Long Islander has his idea about the upstater and vice versa. After a few weeks, though, people see that these aren't always true. I think people from anywhere get along pretty well." The internation-al students, who form a small but noticeable contingent, "tend to keep to themselves," perhaps "due to a cul-ture or language barrier." About one-quarter of the campus population is Jewish.

THE PRINCETON REVIEW SAYS

Admissions

Very important factors considered include: Class rank, academic GPA, recommendation(s), rigor of secondary school record, standardized test scores, character/personal qualities. *Important factors considered include:* Application essay. *Other factors considered include:* Alumni/ae relation, extracurricular activities, first generation, geographical residence, talent/ability, volunteer work, work experience. SAT or ACT required; ACT with Writing component required. TOEFL required of all international applicants. High school diploma is required and GED is accepted. *Academic units required:* 4 English, 2 mathematics, 2 science, (2 science labs), 1 foreign language, 3 social studies, 2 history, 4 academic electives. *Academic units recommended:* 4 mathematics, 3 science, (3 science labs), 3 foreign language.

Financial Aid

Students should submit: FAFSA, NY State residents should apply for TAP on-line at www.tapweb.org. The Princeton Review suggests that all financial aid forms be submitted as soon as possible after January 1. *Need-based scholarships/grants offered:* Federal Pell, SEOG, state scholarships/grants. *Loan aid offered:* FFEL Subsidized Stafford, FFEL Unsubsidized Stafford, FFEL PLUS, Federal Perkins Applicants will be notified of awards on a rolling basis beginning 3/15. Federal Work-Study Program available. Institutional employment available. Off-campus job opportunities are excellent.

The Inside Word

In November 2006, The Wall Street Journal noted a growing trend among students who, in the past, had limited their postsecondary options to high-end private schools: More such students, the paper reported, have broadened their vision to include prestigious state schools such as SUNY Albany. The driving force, unsurprisingly, is economic. In the event of an unlikely decline in the cost of private education, expect admissions at schools like UAlbany to grow more competitive in coming years.

THE SCHOOL SAYS ". . ."

From The Admissions Office

"Increasing numbers of well-prepared students are discovering the benefits of study in UAlbany's nationally ranked programs and are taking advantage of outstanding internship and employment opportunities in Upstate New York's 'Tech Valley.' The already strong undergraduate program is being further enhanced by the recently established Honors College, a university-wide program for ambitious students. Building upon the long-standing success of the University Scholars Program, the Honors College offers enhanced honors courses and co-curricular options including honors housing.

"Ten schools and colleges, including the nation's first College of Nanoscale Science and Engineering, offer bachelor's, master's, and doctoral programs to more than 12,000 undergraduates and 5,000 graduate students. An award-winning advisement program helps students take advantage of all these options by customizing the undergraduate experiences. More than two-thirds of Albany graduates go on for advanced degrees, and acceptance to law and medical school is above the national average.

"Student life on campus includes 200 clubs, honor societies, and other groups, and 19 Division I varsity teams. With 19 other colleges in the region, Albany is a great college town, adjacent to the spectacular natural and recreational centers of New York and New England.

"Freshmen are awarded over $800,000 in merit scholarships each year and nearly three-quarters of our students receive financial aid. Plus, Kiplinger's Personal Finance ranks us in the nation's 'Top 50 for Excellence and Affordability.' All applicants must submit either the new SAT or the ACT with Writing component."

For even more information on this school, turn to page 521 of the "Stats" section.

STATE UNIVERSITY OF NEW YORK—UNIVERSITY AT BUFFALO

15 Capen Hall, Buffalo, NY 14260 • Admissions: 888-UB-ADMIT • Fax: 716-645-6411
Financial Aid: 866-838-7257 • E-mail: ub-admissions@buffalo.edu • Website: www.buffalo.edu

RATINGS
Quality of Life: 74   **Academic:** 71   **Admissions:** 85   **Financial Aid:** 81

STUDENTS SAY ". . ."

Academics

Offering "more academic programs per dollar than any other university in the state," SUNY Buffalo (UB for short) "is about choices. You can choose many different . . . combinations of academics and social activities with the support in place." Students brag that UB's "Programs are all of the highest quality, translating [into] a best-value education for students." The School of Engineering and Applied Science in particular "is well respected" and "works with corporate partners in a variety of ways that range from joint-research ventures to continuing education to co-op work arrangements for our students." Other stand-out offerings include: pharmacy, physical therapy, a popular business and management school "that is ranked highly," "a solid undergrad and grad architecture program," and "one of the top nursing programs in the state." Of course, a school with this much to offer is bound to be large, making it "easy not to attend class and fall through the cracks, so one must be self-motivated to do well." Administrative tasks are occasionally Kafkaesque, with "a lot of red tape to go through to get anything done. I feel like a pebble being kicked around when trying to get support or services," notes one student. Many students point out that support services and contact with professors improves during junior and senior years when students are pursuing their majors and forging stronger relationships within their departments.

Life

UB is divided into two campuses. Traditionally, South Campus in Northeast Buffalo has been where "the parties are," though students say, "It's much less safe than North Campus," which is located in the suburban enclave of Amherst. The recent closing of several bars near South Campus has made it less of a party destination than it was in years past; these days many students report going to downtown Buffalo "to go clubbing." Students living on North Campus describe it as "its own little city. We have food services, our own bus system, a highway, even our own zip codes. If you know how to play, North Campus is just as much fun as Main Street [which runs by South Campus]; you just need to know where to go." The North Campus, which features "a lake and a nice bike path for when you want to escape from the hectic [atmosphere]" of academic life, is the more populous of the two; the inter-campus bus system is "convenient," although a car is preferred. Students tell us that "between all of the clubs and organizations, the Office of Student Life, athletics, and the Student Association, there is always something to do" on campus. The school's Division I sports teams "are a big hit around here. Even if we are the worst in the division, we still cheer hard and go crazy for our guys and girls." Those who explore Buffalo extol its "amazing art and music scene."

Student Body

Because of UB's size, "You can find just about every kind of person there is here. Everyone has a place in this large and diverse student population." As one student notes, "Although the typical student is of traditional college age, there really isn't a 'typical' student—the student body is very diverse in terms of religion, ethnicity, nationality, age, gender, and orientation. 'Atypical' students fit in well because of the diversity of the student population." Another student adds, "There are a lot of foreign and minority students, to the point that the actual 'majority' is the minority here at UB." Geographically, UB draws "from urban areas, rural areas, NYC, Long Island, and most every country in the world." As a state school, "A lot of the students are from New York State, but with differing areas of the state, there are many different types of students."

Admissions

Very important factors considered include: Class rank, rigor of secondary school record, standardized test scores. *Other factors considered include:* Application essay, recommendation(s), character/personal qualities, extracurricular activities, geographical residence, racial/ethnic/economic status, talent/ability, volunteer work, work experience. SAT or ACT required; ACT with Writing component required. TOEFL required of all international applicants. High school diploma is required and GED is accepted. *Academic units recommended:* 4 English, 3 mathematics, 3 science, 3 foreign language, 4 social studies.

Financial Aid

Students should submit: FAFSA. The Princeton Review suggests that all financial aid forms be submitted as soon as possible after January 1. *Need-based scholarships/grants offered:* Federal Pell, SEOG, state scholarships/grants, private scholarships, the school's own gift aid, Federal Nursing Scholarships. *Loan aid offered:* Direct Subsidized Stafford, Direct Unsubsidized Stafford, Direct PLUS, Federal Perkins, Federal Nursing, college/university loans from institutional funds. Applicants will be notified of awards on a rolling basis beginning 2/1.

The Inside Word

As students point out, UB "is famous for its architecture, nursing, and pharmacy school[s]"; as such, it makes sense that "those majors are a harder to get into." In fact, admissions standards at UB have grown more demanding across all programs in recent years. Despite the school's large applicant pool, it takes a close look at applications, searching for evidence of special talents and experiences that will enrich campus life.

THE SCHOOL SAYS ". . ."

From The Admissions Office

"The University at Buffalo (UB) is among the nation's finest public research universities—a learning community where you'll work side by side with world-renowned faculty, including Nobel, Pulitzer, National Medal of Science, and other award winners. As the largest, most comprehensive university center in the State University of New York (SUNY) system, UB offers more undergraduate majors than any public university in New York or New England. Through innovative resources like our Undergraduate Research and Creative Activities, Discovery Seminars, and Undergraduate Academics, you'll be free to chart an academic course that meets your individual goals. At UB you can even design your own major. Our unique University Honors College and University Scholars Program scholarship programs offer an enhanced academic experience, including opportunities for independent study, advanced research, and specialized advisement. The university is committed to providing the latest information technology—and is widely considered to be one of the most wired (and wireless) universities in the country. UB also places a high priority on offering an exciting campus environment. With nonstop festivals, Division I sporting events, concerts, and visiting lecturers, you'll have plenty to do outside of the classroom. We encourage you and your family to visit campus to see UB up close and in person. Our Visit UB campus tours and presentations are offered year-round.

"Freshman applicants for Fall 2008 must take the new SAT (or the ACT with Writing component)."

For even more information on this school, turn to page 522 of the "Stats" section.

STEVENS INSTITUTE OF TECHNOLOGY

CASTLE POINT ON HUDSON, HOBOKEN, NJ 07030 • ADMISSIONS: 800-458-5323 • FAX: 201-216-8348
FINANCIAL AID: 201-216-5194 • E-MAIL: ADMISSIONS@STEVENS-TECH.EDU • WEBSITE: WWW.STEVENS-TECH.EDU

RATINGS
Quality of Life: 77   Academic: 70   Admissions: 93   Financial Aid: 71

STUDENTS SAY ". . ."

Academics

Students at the Stevens Institute of Technology tell us time and again that "Stevens' reputation amongst some of the world's best employers is outstanding." This leads to a "high job placement [rate] and great starting salaries," which, for many, are the primary charms of this small Hoboken school. Engineering disciplines claim about two-thirds of all Stevens undergraduates, and "a huge number participate in the co-op program," which "allows students a break from the theoretical nonsense while putting it to use." In this program, "students spend 5 years getting their

undergraduate degree [while] work[ing] three semesters at a company getting experience and pay." That's three semesters of work on top of a 156-credit program that awards a "Bachelor's of Engineering, not [a] Bachelor's of Science in engineering. (We are one of [fewer] than half a dozen schools in the country to offer [it].)" It's a calendar that is not for the faint of heart, since it means a freshman "can have eight classes in [his or her] first semester." Stevens also delivers in mathematics and the sciences; students in the latter area brag that Stevens "always gets a high percent[age] of students accepted . . . to medical school." As at most tech and science schools, students here complain that, while "The professors are very intelligent," "Sometimes we get professors who are unable to communicate the material." This is often attributed to professors whose first language is not English; some say it's "50/50" whether you'll be able to understand your professor. Even so, most agree that "the juice is worth the squeeze . . . you'll get a good job" if you graduate.

Life

Stevens is situated in the town of Hoboken, NJ, which is "located right on the doorstep of New York City." Hoboken boosters believe that "there is simply no better spot in the world to have a college." In truth, this small town close to the capital of the world pleases multiple tastes: "Those that don't enjoy the city are quite content in Hoboken, [and] the more city-slicker-type students feel very at home with the Manhattan skyline as a backdrop." Because the train to New York City is only "a 7-minute walk from campus," it's easy for students to touch as well as look. Despite its great location, Stevens' "highly demanding" academics play the largest role in student life, which is driven by the ebb and flow—usually the latter—of course work. Nevertheless, "Students are very involved [on] campus. Whether it [is] a sports team or Greek life, the vast majority of students do at least one extracurricular activity." Stevens boasts "a very good Division III athletic program," and its teams "have been getting larger fan turnouts" in recent years. Students tell us that there's also "no lack of parties and alcohol [at] this school. You can count on a party every Thursday." A 3:1 male/female ratio drives some male students off campus in search of companionship.

Student Body

Like most tech schools, Stevens "is a nerd school, no doubt about it." It's home to many students who are "very smart but lacking social skills," preferring to "play World of Warcraft in their rooms or watch anime on a Friday night." Students point out that you'll also find "musicians, theater junkies, sports fanatics, and bookworms" on campus. And "just about everybody here has a secret hobby or talent you would have never thought of." In addition, Stevens also has a substantial number of international students—and "lots of minorities" who boost the diversity factor. On the downside, students tend to be very cliquish and "don't associate with each other outside of class" unless they are part of "the group."

THE PRINCETON REVIEW SAYS

Admissions

Very important factors considered include: Application essay, academic GPA, recommendation(s), rigor of secondary school record, standardized test scores, character/personal qualities, extracurricular activities, interview, volunteer work, work experience. *Important factors considered include:* Class rank, talent/ability. *Other factors considered include:* Alumni/ae relation, SAT or ACT required; TOEFL required of all international applicants. High school diploma is required and GED is not accepted. *Academic units required:* 4 English, 4 mathematics, 3 science, (3 science labs). *Academic units recommended:* 4 science, (4 science labs), 2 foreign language, 2 social studies, 2 history, 4 academic electives.

Financial Aid

Students should submit: FAFSA. The Princeton Review suggests that all financial aid forms be submitted as soon as possible after January 1. *Need-based scholarships/grants offered:* Federal Pell, SEOG, state scholarships/grants, private scholarships, the school's own gift aid. *Loan aid offered:* Direct Subsidized Stafford, Direct Unsubsidized Stafford, Direct PLUS, FFEL Subsidized Stafford, Federal Perkins, state loans, Signature Loans, TERI Loans, NJ CLASS, CitiAssist. Applicants will be notified of awards on a rolling basis beginning 3/30. Federal Work-Study Program available. Off-campus job opportunities are excellent.

The Inside Word

Stevens is among the most desirable "second tier" engineering/science/math schools; its location and cachet with employers guarantee that. It's a good choice for those who can't get through the door at MIT or Caltech but who are nonetheless extremely smart and unafraid of hard work. Such students will find the Stevens Admissions Office quite sympathetic to their applications.

THE SCHOOL SAYS ". . ."

From The Admissions Office

"Founded in 1870 as the first American college to devote itself exclusively to engineering education based on scientific principles, Stevens Institute of Technology is a prestigious independent university for study and research. In 2004, Stevens was ranked by the Princeton Review as one of the nation's 'Most Entrepreneurial Campuses' for having tailored their undergraduate business and technology curricula to encourage young entrepreneurs, providing them with the training and guidance they need to start their own businesses. In 2006, Stevens was ranked among the nation's top-20 'Most Wired Campuses' by PC Magazine and the Princeton Review. In 2007 Stevens' office of Career Development was ranked among the nation's top 20 (#16) by The Princeton Review.

"At the undergraduate level, Stevens' broad-based education leads to prestigious degrees in business, science, computer science, engineering, or humanities. Research activities are vital to the university's educational mission, thus Stevens attracts world-renowned faculty to complement its exceptional on-campus facilities. In addition, Stevens maintains an honor system that has been in existence since 1908. Stevens' more than 2,000 undergraduates come from more than 42 states and 65 countries, creating a diverse, dynamic environment. Stevens also boasts an outstanding campus life—students will find more than 150 student organizations and 25 NCAA Division III athletics teams.

"Stevens requires the SAT or ACT for all applicants. We recommend that all students take SAT Subject Tests to show their strength in English, math, and a science of their choice. Accelerated premed and pre-dentistry applicants must take the SAT as well as two SAT Subject Tests in Math (Level I or II), and Biology or Chemistry. Accelerated law applicants must take two SAT Subject Tests of their choice."

For even more information on this school, turn to page 523 of the "Stats" section.

STONEHILL COLLEGE

320 WASHINGTON STREET, EASTON, MA 02357-5610 • ADMISSIONS: 508-565-1373 • FAX: 508-565-1545
E-MAIL: ADMISSIONS@STONEHILL.EDU • WEBSITE: WWW.STONEHILL.EDU

RATINGS
Quality of Life: 94   **Academic:** 86   **Admissions:** 93   **Financial Aid:** 73

STUDENTS SAY "..."

Academics

"Stonehill is a small liberal arts college" "focused on educating the mind and soul" in the Roman Catholic tradition.
"With a great small, interactive classroom experience" and
"amazing" professors who "will help you no matter what,"
the academic experience here is distinctly "personal." "You
won't be lost in the crowd at Stonehill. Professors know who

> **SURVEY SAYS ...**
> *Students are friendly*
> *Intramural sports are popular*
> *Frats and sororities are unpopular or nonexistent*
> *Student government is popular*

you are and want to help you succeed." (Dare we say they will also notice when you are absent and may call
you to find out why?) But that does not mean professors don't expect students to work hard. To the contrary,
they "challenge you to question. Question your readings, your professors, yourself." The whole point is to teach
you "how to be a critical thinker and to look more in depth on ideas and topics." Faculty and administrators
are extremely accessible; "many give students not only their school e-mail addresses, but their cell phone or
home phone numbers as well as their AIM screen names if they have them!" Students also appreciate the learning opportunities off-campus. "Stonehill has an amazing focus on internships and studying abroad, and is
known for having connections in the working world. The internships and opportunities given to students are
pretty unique."

Life

"Being in the middle of Boston and Providence as well as having over 80 clubs and organizations on campus
that are made to do two events a semester, there is always something to do" at Stonehill. "During the week,
most people are considerate and allow you to get work done." "We have quiet hours at 10 p.m. on the weekday
and 1 A.M. on the weekends." But on the weekends, students cut loose. "For fun, people head into Boston a lot;
the school has a shuttle to take us to the metro T station so it's very accessible if you don't have a car to take you
in." On campus, "Each night of the week there are different events sponsored by different groups on-campus
or by Student Activities. Some of the more widely attended events include our mixers (dances) which are held
at various points throughout the year." "If you're looking for the frat/sorority party school, this isn't the place
for you. It's much more laid-back, with drinking in the dorm rooms or in the 21-plus common rooms." And it
should be noted that alcohol is taken seriously here; many call the school's alcohol policy "way too strict,"
though it's possible to "learn the ways around it." The dorms here "are beautiful and you get to choose your
housing based on a point system. You get points for being active in the school (sports, clubs, attending lectures,
etc.) so the more you participate the better housing you get. You can lose points for misbehavior, so the best
housing goes to the best students, which is a huge plus!"

Student Body

"Stonehill is a pretty homogeneous place." Most students are "Caucasian and from middle class families in New
England." They tend to be "preppy" and "love to party on the weekends." However, they "also know how to
crack down during the week and excel in class." "The typical student at Stonehill is kind, considerate, friendly
and smart. Here at Stonehill we hold doors, sometimes for an akwardly long time," "but the friendly population makes everyone feel welcome." "There are some minorities, but the one thing that does not deviate from
this mold is the expected college 'look.'"

THE PRINCETON REVIEW SAYS

Admissions

Very important factors considered include: Class rank, academic GPA, rigor of secondary school record, volunteer work. *Important factors considered include:* application essay, recommendation(s), alumni/ae relation, character/personal qualities, extracurricular activities, geographical residence, level of applicant's interest, religious affiliation/commitment, talent/ability, work experience. *Other factors considered include:* Standardized test scores, first generation, ACT with Writing component recommended. TOEFL required of all international applicants. High school diploma is required and GED is accepted. *Academic units required:* 4 English, 3 mathematics, 1 science, (1 science labs), 2 foreign language, 4 social studies, 3 history, 3 academic electives. *Academic units recommended:* 4 English, 4 mathematics, 3 science, (2 science labs), 3 foreign language, 4 social studies, 3 history, 3 academic electives.

Financial Aid

Students should submit: FAFSA, CSS/Financial Aid PROFILE, noncustodial PROFILE, business/farm supplement. Regular filing deadline is 2/1. The Princeton Review suggests that all financial aid forms be submitted as soon as possible after January 1. *Need-based scholarships/grants offered:* Federal Pell, SEOG, state scholarships/grants, private scholarships, the school's own gift aid. *Loan aid offered:* Direct Subsidized Stafford, Direct Unsubsidized Stafford, Direct PLUS, Federal Perkins, state loans, Private Education Loans. Applicants will be notified of awards on or about 4/1.

The Inside Word

Though not nearly as selective as some of its fellow Boston-area colleges, Stonehill students are no dummies. Half of them graduated in the top ten percent of their high school classes. Members of ethnic minorities may feel a bit isolated here: Stonehill is about as lily white as it gets.

THE SCHOOL SAYS " . . ."

From The Admissions Office

"Founded in 1948 by the Congregation of Holy Cross, Stonehill's mission is to provide education of the highest caliber, grounded in the liberal arts, comprehensive in nature, and nurtured by Catholic intellectual and moral ideas. Stonehill College is a selective, private, coeducational Catholic college enrolling 2,100 full-time students. Located 22 miles south of Boston on a 375-acre campus with easy access to Boston, we offer 31 challenging majors in the liberal arts, business, and science degree programs. Stonehill also offers students 37 minor programs as well as the opportunity to double major. The college's programs, through an involved and engaging faculty and a commitment to hands-on learning, aim to foster effective communication, critical thinking, and problem-solving skills in all our students. An honors program, undergraduate research opportunities, and area internships enrich the educational experience of many students.

"To gain experience internationally, our students may study abroad, spending 4 to 9 months living and studying in another part of the world. Full-time internships in Dublin, London, Brussels, Paris, Montreal, and Zaragoza, Spain, allow highly motivated students to gain valuable work experience while earning academic credit. On campus, more than 85 percent of our students live in first-rate residence halls that feature large rooms and well-designed layouts. Stonehill's 20 Division II varsity sports, over 60 clubs and organizations, as well as intramural and recreational sports programs provide students with many ways to become involved. Stonehill provides its students with a powerful environment for learning where students are safe, known, and valued."

For even more information on this school, turn to page 523 of the "Stats" section.

SUFFOLK UNIVERSITY

8 ASHBURTON PLACE, BOSTON, MA 02108 • ADMISSIONS: 617-573-8460 • FAX: 617-742-4291
EMAIL: ADMISSION@ADMIN.SUFFLOLK.EDU • WEBSITE: WWW.SUFFLOLK.EDU

RATINGS
Quality of Life: 79   Academic: 73   Admissions: 72   Financial Aid: 68

STUDENTS SAY ". . ."

Academics

"A small classroom university in the heart of a big city," Boston's Suffolk University "is small enough that you actually recognize students from their pictures in the admissions booklets [and] big enough to attract national speakers like George Bush Sr." It's also a school with a huge international component, thanks to its campuses in Madrid, Spain, and Dakar, Senegal and "a unique partnership with Charles University in Prague," all of which "provide students an easy opportunity to study abroad without the usual hassle of all the paperwork." Academic life on the home campus "includes "down-to-earth professors" who "are always available outside of class and are very helpful" and the Balloti Learning Center, which "offers extra help to students who want or need it." Make no mistake: Academics are "incredibly student oriented" here—"The student and [his or her] concerns come first." Top programs include psychology, government, history, and sociology, which "offers concentrations in criminology and justice or health and human services as opposed to just a general major."

> **SURVEY SAYS . . .**
> *Large classes*
> *Great library*
> *Diverse student types on campus*
> *Students love Boston, MA*
> *Great off-campus food*
> *(Almost) everyone smokes*

Life

Suffolk lacks a traditional sprawling suburban campus. Simply put, Suffolk students know they ain't in Kansas any more! The university consists of a collection of buildings located in swanky Beacon Hill, literally steps from Boston Common and the Public Gardens. So, if you're a city lover you my have just found heaven! Suffolk students are quick to point out that their urban existence can make some feel "disconnected" compounded by the fact that many students choose to live off campus. One commuter writes, "It's sometimes difficult for me to join in some of the activities that they have going on at the school." Even so, many here are satisfied with the status quo; they'll skip the conventional campus activities and the rah-rah campus unity, preferring to spend their free time enjoying the city of Boston. "Most people have lots of friends [at] other schools" and the prevalence of fun activities in Boston such as "movies at the Museum of Fine Arts" and "local concerts." Undergrads agree that "drinking is definitely a huge part of Suffolk," and "Being 21 in Boston or having a good fake ID makes it a much better time. What you lose in the lack of campus, you gain with the city."

Student Body

Suffolk's overseas ties draw a large international population to the Boston campus, to the point that "in some classes, almost half of the students are foreign-born. Interacting with students from different backgrounds or cultures isn't an option—it's a daily occurrence. In my international business classes it leads to fascinating discussions because, rather than read about business in different cultures, we have firsthand experiences." Most of the American student body comes from Boston and the surrounding area; while "The majority [are] pretty run-of-the mill products of Massachusetts suburbia, the minority is pretty eclectic." This minority includes "art-school hipsters" and a "relatively large gay community." Each group also features a lot of "rich and preppy" students who use "Boston as their playground." Students report that there "isn't a real strong sense of community, unless you live in the dorms" (about one in five does).

Admissions

Very important factors considered include: Rigor of secondary school record. *Important factors considered include:* Class rank, application essay, academic GPA, standardized test scores. *Other factors considered include:* Recommendation(s), alumni/ae relation, character/personal qualities, extracurricular activities, first generation, geographical residence, interview, level of applicant's interest, talent/ability, volunteer work, work experience. SAT or ACT required; TOEFL required of all international applicants. High school diploma is required and GED is accepted. *Academic units required:* 4 English, 3 mathematics, 2 science, (1 science labs), 2 foreign language, 1 history, 4 academic electives. *Academic units recommended:* 4 mathematics, 3 science, (1 science labs), 3 foreign language, 1 social studies, 1 history, 4 academic electives.

Financial Aid

Students should submit: FAFSA, institution's own financial aid form. Regular filing deadline is 3/1. The Princeton Review suggests that all financial aid forms be submitted as soon as possible after January 1. *Need-based scholarships/grants offered:* Federal Pell, SEOG, state scholarships/grants, private scholarships, the school's own gift aid. *Loan aid offered:* Direct Subsidized Stafford, Direct Unsubsidized Stafford, Direct PLUS, Federal Perkins Applicants will be notified of awards on a rolling basis beginning 2/5. Federal Work-Study Program available. Institutional employment available. Off-campus job opportunities are excellent.

The Inside Word

Suffolk is unapologetic about its mission to provide access and opportunity to college bound students. That said, test scores and high school GPA requirements are average. Applicants who are borderline based on straight numbers should make their case to the Admissions Office directly.

THE SCHOOL SAYS "..."

From The Admissions Office

"Ask any student, and they'll tell you: The best thing about Suffolk is the professors. They go the extra mile to help students to succeed. Suffolk faculty members are noted scholars and experienced professionals, but first and foremost, they are teachers and mentors. Suffolk's faculty is of the highest caliber. Ninety-four percent of the faculty hold PhDs. Suffolk maintains a 13:1 student/faculty ratio with an average class size of 19.

"The university was selected by U.S. News' 2007 edition as one of 'America's Best Colleges.' Career preparation is a high priority at Suffolk. Many students work during the school year in paid internships, co-op jobs, or work-study positions. Suffolk has an excellent job placement record. More than 94 percent of recent graduates are either employed or enrolled in graduate school at the time of graduation.

"The university's academic programs emphasize quality teaching, small class size, real-world career applications, and an international experience. There are more than 50 study abroad sites available to students. The undergraduate academic program offers more than 70 majors and 1,000 courses.

"We require applicants to submit the SAT with the essay score or the ACT taken with the Writing component. Standardized tests are used for both placement and assessment. International students may submit any of the following tests for admission: the TOEFL or ELPT, IELTS, CPE, CAE, and FCE. The role of standardized testing is still a secondary role when considering admission to the university. The candidate's grades and the overall strength of curriculum are primary factors in the admission decision."

For even more information on this school, turn to page 524 of the "Stats" section.

Susquehanna University

514 University Avenue, Selinsgrove, PA 17870 • Admissions: 570-372-4260 • Fax: 570-372-2722
Financial Aid: 570-372-4450 • E-mail: suadmiss@susqu.edu • Website: www.susqu.edu

RATINGS
Quality of Life: 81   **Academic:** 81   **Admissions:** 79   **Financial Aid:** 83

STUDENTS SAY "..."

Academics

Students tell us that Susquehanna University's small size makes it "the perfect university to give students the opportunity to excel in all aspects of school—academics, research, athletics, clubs, and many other activities." Located in rural central Pennsylvania, SU is regarded by students as "an oasis of quirky in the middle of nowhere."

This quirkiness emanates from the school's strong programs in the fine arts (including a "big music program," solid departments in creative writing and graphic design, and an active theatre program). Less quirky and more populous is the school's popular School of Business—one in four students here pursues a business major. Students note that "This is a liberal arts university requiring you to take classes from many areas," meaning that all here receive a well-rounded education. They also point out that "It is understandable that you aren't going to be the best at all of those areas. The professors know this as well and are there to help." Indeed, what students love most about SU is the sense that "It is all about the student here. There are no graduate students teaching the undergraduates, the advisers want to make sure how you are doing, and the relationships formed with professors are priceless."

Life

SU's hometown of Selinsgrove "doesn't have the most exciting night life," but that "doesn't really matter" because students "don't have much money to spend on nightlife anyway" and "there's a ton of free stuff to do on campus." Popular campus options include TRAX, "a place were students can go and dance and have a few drinks if they are 21," and Charlie's Coffeehouse, a venue "that provides entertainment like live bands, movies, or games on Friday and Saturday nights." Students are also kept busy with the "abundance of student organizations and campus activities. Not only does it seem like students at Susquehanna are eager to get involved in probably more things than they realistically have time for, but the staff in our student life and campus activities office are amazing." As one student explains, "SU tries to provide as many options as it can because there is literally nothing to do around Selinsgrove." Well, maybe not exactly nothing. Some here concede that the town provides "close proximity to restaurants and stores" and a "decent-sized mall just a couple miles away, as well as everything else from Wall-Mart to every type of fast food restaurant you could think of, all within five miles of school." When small town life gets to be too much, students take advantage of "one-day bus trips to big cities like New York."

Student Body

While there is "a broad mix of students in the sense that there are those that relish in the fine arts, others that are greatly involved in the sciences, and others that enjoy the analytical business aspect of Susquehanna," SU undergrads concede that the typical student is "white and moderately well-off financially" and that "atypical students fit in because they hang out with other atypical students." Overall, students here are "somewhat preppy, but with their own style" and "are hard-working" individuals "who are involved in a ton of activities and sports, but still go out on the weekends."

THE PRINCETON REVIEW SAYS

Admissions

Very important factors considered include: Academic GPA, rigor of secondary school record. *Important factors considered include:* Class rank, application essay, recommendation(s), standardized test scores, alumni/ae relation, character/personal qualities, extracurricular activities, interview, level of applicant's interest, racial/ethnic status, talent/ability, volunteer work, work. *Other factors considered include:* First generation, geographical residence, religious affiliation/commitment, state residency, TOEFL required of all international applicants. High school diploma is required and GED is accepted. *Academic units required:* 4 English, 3 mathematics, 3 science, (2 science labs), 2 foreign language, 1 social studies, 1 history, 2 academic electives. *Academic units recommended:* 4 English, 4 mathematics, 4 science, (3 science labs), 3 foreign language, 3 social studies, 1 history, 3 academic electives.

Financial Aid

Students should submit: FAFSA, CSS/Financial Aid PROFILE, business/farm supplement. , Prior year Federal tax return. Regular filing deadline is 5/1. The Princeton Review suggests that all financial aid forms be submitted as soon as possible after January 1. *Need-based scholarships/grants offered:* Federal Pell, SEOG, state scholarships/grants, private scholarships, the school's own gift aid. *Loan aid offered:* FFEL Subsidized Stafford, FFEL Unsubsidized Stafford, FFEL PLUS, Federal Perkins, college/university loans from institutional funds. Applicants will be notified of awards on a rolling basis beginning 2/15. Federal Work-Study Program available. Institutional employment available. Off-campus job opportunities are good.

The Inside Word

Susquehanna competes with a number of similar area schools for its student body, and as a result cannot afford to be as selective as it might like, thus creating an opportunity for high school underachievers to attend a challenging and prestigious school. Further improving the odds, Susquehanna does not require standardized test scores of applicants. Those who choose not to submit SAT/ACT scores must instead submit two graded writing samples.

THE SCHOOL SAYS "..."

From The Admissions Office

"Students tell us they are getting a first-rate education and making the connections that will help them be competitive upon graduation. Our size makes it easy for students to customize their 4 years here with self-designed majors, internships, volunteer service, research, leadership opportunities, and rewarding off-campus experiences. Many academic programs are interdisciplinary, meaning that you learn to make connections between different fields of knowledge, which will help make you an educated citizen of the world. A high percentage of students do internships at such sites as Morgan Stanley, Cable News Network, Estee Lauder, and Bristol-Myers Squibb. More than 90 percent of our graduates go on for advanced degrees or get jobs in their chosen field within six months of graduation. There are also more than 100 student organizations on campus, which provide lots of opportunity for leadership and involvement in campus life. The campus is known for its beauty and is a few blocks from downtown Selinsgrove and about a mile from shopping and movie theaters at the Susquehanna Valley Mall.

"Susquehanna will consider a student's top standardized test score (SAT or ACT) when evaluating their application. Students are also encouraged to consider SU's alternative to standardized tests, the Write Option. Under the Write Option, a student may submit two graded writing samples instead of SAT or ACT scores."

For even more information on this school, turn to page 524 of the "Stats" section.

Swarthmore College

500 COLLEGE AVENUE, SWARTHMORE, PA 19081 • ADMISSIONS: 610-328-8300 • FAX: 610-328-8580
FINANCIAL AID: 610-328-8358 • E-MAIL: ADMISSIONS@SWARTHMORE.EDU • WEBSITE: WWW.SWARTHMORE.EDU

RATINGS

Quality of Life: 89   **Academic:** 99   **Admissions:** 99   **Financial Aid:** 98

STUDENTS SAY "..."

Academics

Swarthmore College, a school that is "as intense and stimulating as it claims to be," suits students who prefer "an emphasis on learning because it's fun and interesting rather than learning to get a job." One undergrad writes, "A lot of what unifies its student body is the fact that, whether we're pursuing a degree in engineering or we're planning on writing the next Great American Novel, we're

> **SURVEY SAYS . . .**
> *Small classes*
> *No one cheats*
> *Lab facilities are great*
> *Low cost of living*
> *Political activism is popular*

all passionate and devoted to something." Swatties love that "Swarthmore is amazingly flexible. The requirements are very limited, allowing you to explore whatever you are interested in and change your mind millions of times about your major and career path. If they don't offer a major you want, you can design your own with ease." Professors also earn raves: They're "genuinely interested in giving the students the best academic experience possible" and "challenge students to become knowledgeable in so many areas yet force them to create their own thoughts." Best of all, they come to Swarthmore to teach undergraduates, meaning that "here you can interact with A-list professors straight out of high school. At other universities I'd be lucky to interact one-on-one with professors of similar stature in my third year of graduate school." Students also think you should know that "the school has a lot of money and is very generous with spending it on undergrads, as there isn't anyone else to spend it on."

Life

"There is a misconception that Swarthmore students do nothing but study," students tell us. "While we certainly do a lot of it, we still find many ways to have fun." Though there "isn't a lot to do right in the area surrounding Swarthmore," "With a train station on campus, Philly is very accessible." Most students, however, find no need to leave campus on a regular basis: "The campus provides for us all that we need, and we rarely make it out to Philly," one content freshman writes. On-campus activities "are varied, and there is almost always something to do on the weekend. There are student musical performances, drama performances, movies, speakers, and comedy shows," as well as "several parties every weekend, with and without alcohol, and a lot of pre-partying with friends." For many, things that are the most fun are "the low-key events, just hanging out with friends, talking about classes, or playing in the snow." One student sums up, "While it is tough to generalize on the life of a Swarthmore student, one word definitely applies to us all: busy. All of us are either working on extracurriculars, studying, or fighting sleep to do more work."

Student Body

Students are "not sure if there is a typical Swattie," but suspect that "the defining feature among us is that each person is brilliant at something. Maybe dance, maybe quantum physics, maybe philosophy; each person here has at least one thing that [he or she does] extraordinarily well." There's also "a little bit of a nerd in every one of us—much more in some than in others. The people are all truly genuine, though, and everyone tends to get along well. We're all a little idiosyncratic: When anything that you might call eccentric, or maybe even a little weird at Swat occurs, the typical reaction is, 'That is so Swarthmore!'" A Swattie "tends to have a tremendously hectic life because he or she joins organizations for which he or she holds a passion, and then has 28 hours of work to accomplish in a 24-hour day." Swatties also tend to be "politically left-wing. One says, "If you are not left-wing it is more difficult, but still possible, to fit in—you just have to expect a lot of debate about your political . . . views."

Admissions

Very important factors considered include: Rigor of secondary school record, academic GPA, character/personality qualities, application essay, class rank, recommendations. *Important factors considered include:* Standardized test scores, extracurricular activities. *Other factors considered include:* Alumni/ae relation, first generation, geographical diversity, interview, level of applicant's interest, racial/ethnic identity, talent/ability, volunteer work, work experience. Applicants are required to submit scores for any one of the three following testing scenarios: 1) SAT and any two SAT Subject tests; 2) the ACT with Writing; or 3) SAT and ACT (with or without writing). Prospective engineers are encouraged to take the Mathematics Level 2 Subject Test, regardless of whether they opt for the SAT or ACT. High school diploma or equivalent is not required.

Financial Aid

Students should submit: FAFSA, institution's own financial aid form, CSS/Financial Aid PROFILE, state aid form, noncustodial PROFILE, business/farm supplement. , Federal Tax Return, W2 Statements, Year-end paycheck stub. Regular filing deadline is 2/15. The Princeton Review suggests that all financial aid forms be submitted as soon as possible after January 1. *Need-based scholarships/grants offered:* Federal Pell, SEOG, state scholarships/grants, private scholarships, the school's own gift aid. *Loan aid offered:* Beginning with the 2008-09 academic year all Swarthmore financial aid awards will be loan free. Applicants will be notified of awards on or about 4/1. Federal Work-Study Program available. Institutional employment available. Off-campus job opportunities are good.

The Inside Word

Competition for admission to Swarthmore remains fierce, as the school consistently receives applications from top students across the country. With numerous qualified candidates, prospective students can be assured that every aspect of their applications will be thoroughly evaluated. While there might not be a typical admit, successful applicants have all proven themselves intellectually curious, highly motivated, and creative-minded.

THE SCHOOL SAYS ". . ."

From The Admissions Office

"Swarthmore College, a highly selective college of liberal arts and engineering, celebrates the life of the mind. Since its founding in 1864, Swarthmore has given students of uncommon intellectual ability the knowledge, insight, skills, and experience to become leaders for the common good. The College is private, yet open to all regardless of financial need; American, yet decidedly global in outlook and diversity, drawing students from around the world and all 50 states. So much of what Swarthmore stands for, from its commitment to curricular breadth and rigor to its demonstrated interest in facilitating discovery and fostering ethical intelligence among exceptional young people, lies in the quality and passion of its faculty. A student/faculty ratio of 8:1 ensures that students have close, meaningful engagement with their professors, preparing them to translate the skills and understanding gained at Swarthmore into the mark they want to make on the world. The College's Honors program features small groups of dedicated and accomplished students working closely with faculty; an emphasis on independent learning; students entering into a dialogue with peers, teachers, and examiners; a demanding program of study in major and minor fields; and an examination at the end of two years' study by outside scholars. Located 11 miles southwest of Philadelphia, Swarthmore's idyllic, 357-acre campus is a designated arboretum, complete with rolling lawns, creek, wooded hills, and hiking trails."

For even more information on this school, turn to page 525 of the "Stats" section.

SYRACUSE UNIVERSITY

201 TOLLEY, ADMINISTRATION BUILDING, SYRACUSE, NY 13244 • ADMISSIONS: 315-443-3611
FINANCIAL AID: 315-443-1513 • E-MAIL: ORANGE@SYR.EDU • WEBSITE: WWW.SYRACUSE.EDU

RATINGS
Quality of Life: 63   Academic: 82   Admissions: 92   Financial Aid: 87

STUDENTS SAY "..."

Academics

Syracuse University "is very strong academically" and boasts "some of the nation's top programs" in a broad range of disciplines. Students are especially bullish on the "prestigious" S. I. Newhouse School of Public Communications, which "has some amazing professors who have worked out in the field and are eager to share all of their experiences with their students," as well as the School of Architecture, "an energetic, sleepless journey of collaboration and individuality in an amazingly cool atmosphere." SU's programs

> ### SURVEY SAYS ...
> *Great library*
> *Everyone loves the Orange*
> *Frats and sororities dominate*
> *social scene*
> *Student publications are popular*
> *Lots of beer drinking*
> *Hard liquor is popular*

in advertising, art, business, music, political science, engineering, and the life sciences also earn plaudits from undergraduates. Best of all, students say, SU delivers the benefits of "both large schools and small schools," which means it can offer the ability "to concentrate in an area while also taking a variety of other classes that do not have to be within your major or college," as well as plenty of research faculty who put "SU at the front of [the] material" and "professors who are always available to meet during office hours [or] by appointment." One undergrad sums it up: "SU is big enough to have a wealth of resources but small enough so that you always fit in." Another adds, "SU is about academics and preparing us as best as possible for our future careers, along with a little bit of men's basketball."

Life

Students tell us that "the social life at Syracuse is the epitome of the great American college experience. Local bars, frats, and house parties are all popular. Partying takes place from Thursday through Sunday, and close friendships are easily cultivated during the recovery period in between." However, it's important to note that "the school is great about providing other activities" as well. "You don't need to drink to find something fun to do at night or on weekends." "People climb trees on the quad, go rock climbing on the weekends, [and] take ballet classes. We're notorious for our frat parties, but, at the same time, the library is packed every Saturday night." "The student union also provides free movies on weekends, and there are loads of speakers, concerts, and cultural events throughout the week." Of course, SU sports "are huge"—"Syracuse Basketball is going to win the national championship!" Students are mixed on the city of Syracuse. Some tell us "It's pretty much dead" and "The weather sucks," while others aver that "upstate New York is a great location with lots of outdoor activities, unless you hate sub-Arctic climates."

Student Body

While SU undergrads report that a typical peer would be "fashionable," "wealthy," and "trend-driven," they also point out that "there are also tons of students who don't fit that description." Indeed there are upstate, out-of-state, and international students in addition to an abundance from Long Island and New Jersey. While the student body includes "a large frat/sorority presence," there's also a fair share of "neo-hippies." Although SU's student population appears homogenous to some, other students say "[This] seems to be proven wrong on many occasions. For example, the guy living next to me is from St. Thomas. I have friends from all over the world. . . . All religions, sexual orientations, and ethnic groups are strongly represented."

THE PRINCETON REVIEW SAYS

Admissions

Very important factors include: Rigor of secondary school record, academic GPA, class rank, standardized test scores, application essay, recommendation(s), character/personal qualities, level of applicant's interest. *Important factors considered include:* Interview, extracurricular activities, talent/ability, volunteer work, work experience. *Other factors considered include:* First generation, alumni/ae relation, racial/ethnic status. SAT or ACT required; TOEFL required of all international applicants. High school diploma is required and GED is accepted. *Academic units required:* 4 English, 4 mathematics, 4 science (4 science labs), 3 foreign language, 4 social studies.

Financial Aid

Students should submit: FAFSA, CSS/Financial Aid PROFILE, business/farm supplement. Regular filing deadline is 2/1. The Princeton Review suggests that all financial aid forms be submitted as soon as possible after January 1. *Need-based scholarships/grants offered:* Federal Pell, SEOG, state scholarships/grants, private scholarships, the school's own gift aid. *Loan aid offered:* FFEL Subsidized Stafford, FFEL Unsubsidized Stafford, FFEL PLUS, Federal Perkins Applicants will be notified of awards on or about 4/1. Federal Work-Study Program available. Institutional employment available. Off-campus job opportunities are good.

The Inside Word

Syracuse University is divided into nine colleges, and applicants apply to the college in which they are interested. Some colleges make specific requirements of applicants (for example: a portfolio, an audition, or specific high school course work) in addition to SU's general admissions requirements. Applicants are allowed to indicate a second and third choice—you may still gain admission even if you don't get into your first-choice program.

THE SCHOOL SAYS ". . ."

From The Admissions Office

"Syracuse University provides a dynamic learning environment with a focus on scholarship in action, in which excellence is connected to ideas, problems, and professions in the world. Students at SU focus on interactive, collaborative, and interdisciplinary learning while choosing their course of study from more than 200 options. About half of undergraduates study abroad. SU operates centers in Beijing, Florence, Hong Kong, London, Madrid, Santiago, and Strasbourg. New facilities continue to expand scholarship in action opportunities for students. The Newhouse 3 building houses various facilities for public communications students, including research centers, a high-tech convergence lab, and meeting rooms for student activities. A $107 million Life Sciences Complex will promote interdisciplinary research and education, signaling a new era in scientific research.

"A distinction of the SU education is the breadth of opportunity combined with individualized attention. Average class size is 24 students. Only 3 percent of all classes have more than 100 students. Faculty members are experts in their field, who are dedicated to teaching while conducting research, writing, and experiments they can share with students to aid in the learning process.

"Outside of the classroom, students are encouraged to immerse themselves in organizations and take advantage of the opportunities available in the city of Syracuse. The University community collaborates with city residents, organizations, and businesses in such areas as the arts, entrepreneurship and economic development, and scientific research. The Connective Corridor, a three-mile pedestrian pathway and shuttle bus circuit, links SU and downtown Syracuse's arts institutions, entertainment venues, and public spaces."

For even more information on this school, turn to page 525 of the "Stats" section.

TEMPLE UNIVERSITY

1801 NORTH BROAD STREET, PHILADELPHIA, PA 19122-6096 • ADMISSIONS: 215-204-7200
FAX: 215-204-5694 • FINANCIAL AID: 215-204-8760 • E-MAIL: TUADM@MAIL.TEMPLE.EDU • WEBSITE: WWW.TEMPLE.EDU

RATINGS
Quality of Life: 74   **Academic:** 76   **Admissions:** 83   **Financial Aid:** 79

STUDENTS SAY "..."

Academics

Students find "very broad choices in classes and majors" within Temple's 12 schools offering undergraduate academic programs. They also find various levels of classroom intimacy, as "class sizes range from about five students up to 200 depending on level and honors." These broad options are a consequence of the school's large enrollment. Another consequence is the fact that "most professors here have a huge number of students to take care of," which means "A student can get lost easily in the numbers." Due to that reality, students who take the initiative are the ones

> **SURVEY SAYS . . .**
> Great computer facilities
> Great library
> Athletic facilities are great
> Diverse student types on campus
> Great off-campus food
> Campus feels safe
> Lots of beer drinking
> (Almost) everyone smokes

who do best here: "Temple is a great example of a university where you get out what you put in. If you work hard then you will be recognized and succeed." This is not to say that professors are deaf to their students' needs. On the contrary, "Professors are very accessible and genuinely want to help you learn, but you will be working for that A; don't expect it to be handed to you." The academic environment "is intellectually challenging. Due to the diverse nature of both the faculty and student body, professors usually challenge us to assimilate disparate cultural views and to affirm or change our own views of other cultures."

Administratively, "Every Temple student, at one time, has gotten the 'Temple run-around.' In other words, because the school is so big, sometimes finding the exact person you need to talk to is impossible due to limited office hours and [the fact] that the Temple staff has very limited knowledge of other Temple services." Students appreciate the fact that "the technology is outstanding" at Temple, but complain that the school "needs to build more on-campus housing for students." "After sophomore year you are no longer able to live in dorms," and "The surrounding area is not known for having abundant off-campus housing options."

Life

As you consider Temple, keep in mind its hometown: "This is Philly. There are always things to do. There are plenty of museums and historical tours, there are many places to shop, and the food is so diverse and tasty—there is always something new to try." What's more, "There are subway stops at each end of the campus, so it's a breeze to get to Center City." But you don't have to travel far to socialize: "There are a few college bars just steps away from campus which have gotten extremely popular recently." You don't even have to leave campus if you don't want to. "We go to the bars here (there are two on campus); the SAC has food and the new Student Center has everything you could want," writes one satisfied student. "Frats and sororities are pretty unpopular on the whole," however, so "Temple isn't a bona fide party school."

Student Body

The "student body is so diverse," it often feels to students as if "There is a little of everything at Temple University": "From goth to preppy, from European to Asian, from straight male to transsexual, Temple has it all." "Students come from so many diverse backgrounds; no common denominator among them can really be found." This diversity might be "the reason why all students feel welcome here." It also "makes it a great place to learn and live. It's a full cultural experience." If you absolutely had to describe a typical student, you might say that "most students here care about their grades, and you will find lots of people in the library studying at early hours in the morning at finals time."

THE PRINCETON REVIEW SAYS

Admissions

Very important factors considered include: Academic GPA, rigor of secondary school record. *Important factors considered include:* Class rank, standardized test scores. *Other factors considered include:* Application essay, recommendation(s), alumni/ae relation, character/personal qualities, extracurricular activities, talent/ability, volunteer work, work experience. SAT or ACT required; ACT with Writing component required. TOEFL required of all international applicants. High school diploma is required and GED is accepted. *Academic units required:* 4 English, 3 mathematics, 2 science, (1 science labs), 2 foreign language, 2 social studies, 1 history, 1 academic elective. *Academic units recommended:* 4 English, 4 mathematics, 3 science, (2 science labs), 2 foreign language, 2 social studies, 2 history, 3 academic electives.

Financial Aid

Students should submit: FAFSA. The Princeton Review suggests that all financial aid forms be submitted as soon as possible after January 1. *Need-based scholarships/grants offered:* Federal Pell, SEOG, state scholarships/grants, private scholarships, the school's own gift aid, Federal Nursing Scholarships. *Loan aid offered:* FFEL Subsidized Stafford, FFEL Unsubsidized Stafford, FFEL PLUS, Federal Perkins, Federal Nursing, state loans, college/university loans from institutional funds. Applicants will be notified of awards on a rolling basis beginning 2/15. Federal Work-Study Program available. Institutional employment available. Off-campus job opportunities are excellent.

The Inside Word

Temple's distinguished reputation and urban environment make the university a good choice for many students, especially Pennsylvania residents. Admissions Officers are fairly objective about their approach to application assessment: They tend to focus principally on GPA, class rank, and test scores. There are no minimum requirements, though, so students who show potential in more subjective arenas should make sure they convey their accomplishments in their applications.

THE SCHOOL SAYS "..."

From The Admissions Office

"Temple combines the academic resources and intellectual stimulation of a large research university with the intimacy of a small college. The university experienced record growth in attracting new students from all 50 states and over 125 countries: up 60 percent in 3 years. Students choose from 125 undergraduate majors. Special academic programs include honors, learning communities for first-year undergraduates, co-op education, and study abroad. Temple has seven regional campuses, including Main Campus and the Health Sciences Center in historic Philadelphia, suburban Temple University, Ambler, and overseas campuses in Tokyo and Rome. Main Campus is home to the Tuttleman Learning Center, with 1,000 computer stations linked to Paley Library. Our TECH Center has over 600 computer workstations, 100 laptops, and a Starbucks. The Liacouras Center is a state-of-the-art entertainment, recreation, and sports complex that hosts concerts, plays, trade shows, and college and professional athletics. It also includes the Independence Blue Cross Student Recreation Center, a major fitness facility for students now and in the future. Students can also take advantage of our Student Fieldhouse. The university has constructed two new dorms, built to meet an unprecedented demand for main campus housing.

"Applicants for Fall 2009 are required to take the new version of the SAT (or the ACT with Writing) and will be considered using the 2400 scale. The best Critical Reading, Math and Writing scores from either test will be considered."

For even more information on this school, turn to page 526 of the "Stats" section.

TOWSON UNIVERSITY

8000 YORK ROAD, TOWSON, MD 21252-0001 • ADMISSIONS: 1-888-4TOWSON • FAX: 410-704-3030
E-MAIL: ADMISSIONS@TOWSON.EDU • WEBSITE: WWW.TOWSON.EDU/DISCOVER

RATINGS
Quality of Life: 77   **Academic:** 72   **Admissions:** 80   **Financial Aid:** 71

STUDENTS SAY ". . ."

Academics

Since Towson University offers more than one hundred undergraduate and graduate programs, chances are that any student can find his or her educational niche. The education program is especially popular and of high quality, a fact that isn't surprising given that "Towson was the State Normal School for many years." As is the case at many a school its size, "Some professors really care and some don't, but the ones who do will help you with everything, not just [the material for] their class"; some professors even go so far as to "require private office chats with each student at some time during the semester." In the eyes of the majority of stu-

> **SURVEY SAYS . . .**
> *Small classes*
> *Great computer facilities*
> *Great library*
> *Students love Towson, MD*
> *Great off-campus food*
> *Student publications are popular*
> *Lots of beer drinking*
> *Hard liquor is popular*
> *(Almost) everyone smokes*

dents, "The professors are generally excellent teachers—available outside of class and very concerned for student success and mastery of content." For some students, "The best part of the academic experience at Towson is that professors actually teach the classes; [teachers are] not TAs, like at a lot of other schools."

Life

Towson students report an active social life at their school. There are "lots of things to do in and around campus. Lots of bars downtown, a movie theater, Barnes & Noble, and a huge mall all within walking distance. There are lots of sports activities going on when the weather is nice, as well as outside festivals." "Also, there's a venue in Towson that has a live band almost every night of the week." "On campus, for fun, we go rock climbing (the gym is so nice!) or to other on-campus programs. The lectures and events sponsored by student groups are always worth attending" too. "The city of Baltimore, where there are countless things to do, is just a short cab ride away and a popular Thursday-night destination for underclassmen looking to dance and drink." Many "People go to the Inner Harbor in Baltimore or [to] Fells Point, where there are bars and clubs." "Towson is often referred to as a 'party' school," but a junior clarifies that might be better characterized as a "'bar and club' school." With fewer than a quarter of students living on campus, Towson lives up to its rep as a commuter school, so if you are a residential student, be prepared to watch the campus empty out when the weekend arrives.

Student Body

One Towson student tells us that the student body "reflects today's pop culture: average to above-average intelligence, good work ethic, fairly social. There are always outliers, but most seem well integrated with each other and the majority student body." That's because most "Everyone at Towson is 'nice,' [and] there's no getting around that. However, the population here is incredibly homogenous; it's primarily White, suburban kids interested in clubbing who played lacrosse in high school. There are atypical students who seem to band together, but overall, people here pretty much have the same taste in everything, which can be disenchanting." These descriptions mainly apply to the population of traditional students from the United States. But "There are also many foreigners here, and there is also a large section of older persons who come back to college later in life," and, by most accounts, "They fit in well."

THE PRINCETON REVIEW SAYS

Admissions

Very important factors considered include: academic GPA. *Important factors considered include:* Rigor of secondary school record, standardized test scores. *Other factors considered include:* Class rank, application essay, recommendation(s), first generation, talent/ability, SAT or ACT required; ACT with Writing component required. TOEFL required of all international applicants. High school diploma is required and GED is accepted. *Academic units required:* 4 English, 3 mathematics, 3 science, (2 science labs), 2 foreign language, 3 social studies, 6 academic electives.

Financial Aid

Students should submit: FAFSA. The Princeton Review suggests that all financial aid forms be submitted as soon as possible after January 1. *Need-based scholarships/grants offered:* Federal Pell, SEOG, state scholarships/grants, private scholarships, the school's own gift aid. *Loan aid offered:* Direct Subsidized Stafford, Direct Unsubsidized Stafford, Direct PLUS, Federal Perkins Applicants will be notified of awards on a rolling basis beginning 3/21. Federal Work-Study Program available. Institutional employment available. Off-campus job opportunities are excellent.

The Inside Word

Solid students with modest test scores will find it advantageous to investigate Towson. The school offers an intimate learning environment in a large university setting. Its proximity to both Baltimore and Washington, DC also ensures access to myriad cultural and educational events. Applicants should be advised that secondary school GPA is the primary focus when admissions decisions are made.

THE SCHOOL SAYS " . . ."

From The Admissions Office

"Towson University is one of the most dynamic college communities in the country, offering academic programs that provide a solid liberal arts foundation and preparation for jobs and graduate school. Founded in 1866, Towson University today is nationally recognized for programs in the arts, sciences, business, communications, health professions, and education and computer science. *U.S. News & World Report* names Towson as one of the best regional public universities in the United States. Students choose from more than 60 undergraduate majors and 37 graduate programs. Towson offers a student-centered learning environment with big-school choices and small-school personal attention. We encourage students to pursue learning inside and outside the classroom—through internships, student organizations, extracurricular activities, and research projects with faculty.

"An NCAA Division I program, Towson fields intercollegiate athletic teams in 19 sports. Our 24-acre sports complex includes Johnny Unitas University Stadium, home of Tiger football, field hockey, track, and lacrosse. The Tiger basketball, volleyball, and gymnastics teams compete at the 5,000-seat Towson Center. Athletic and recreation facilities include an NCAA-regulation swimming pool, gymnasiums, a sand volleyball court, tennis courts, a fitness center, a climbing wall, and racquetball and squash courts.

"A member of the University System of Maryland, we enroll more than 18,000 students on our 328-acre campus located just eight miles north of downtown Baltimore. Local attractions include the National Aquarium, Oriole Park at Camden Yards, the Maryland Science Center, the Walters Art Museum, and historic Fells Point. The campus is a 10-minute walk to suburban shops, restaurants, movie theaters, and bookstores."

For even more information on this school, turn to page 526 of the "Stats" section.

TRINITY COLLEGE (CT)

300 SUMMIT STREET, HARTFORD, CT 06016 • ADMISSIONS: 860-297-2180 • FAX: 860-297-2287
FINANCIAL AID: 860-297-2046 • E-MAIL: ADMISSIONS.OFFICE@TRINCOLL.EDU • WEBSITE: WWW.TRINCOLL.EDU

RATINGS
Quality of Life: 61 **Academic:** 90 **Admissions:** 95 **Financial Aid:** 98

STUDENTS SAY "..."

Academics

Connecticut's Trinity College "offers a rare combination of high academic standards, a balanced political climate, intense athletic competitiveness/participation, awesome financial aid" and, last but not least, "a huge party scene," prompting some students to opine that "Trinity offers the most even balance of academics (amazing professors, room to find your niche) and social life" among U.S. colleges.

Here, "Monday through Thursday everyone goes to class, studies, and gets their work done," but, "Come the weekend, people let loose and party just as hard as they study." Weekdays offer "a great learning experience that provides ample opportunities," thanks in part to the school's small size (which means undergraduates have opportunities for research), a faculty staffed by "brilliant and caring" professors who "prioritize teaching above publishing," and a library that is "nothing less than phenomenal." Students also appreciate Trinity's urban setting, noting that "the city of Hartford [is used] as a valuable learning tool" and pointing out that, unlike "the majority of top liberal arts schools . . . [where] internship opportunities are limited, Trinity offered me the opportunity [for] many hands-on experiences." This may be particularly true if your field of interest is politics (Trinity's "location in a capital city means lots of opportunities for political internships," explains one student). Other standout departments include English (both literature and creative writing), Engineering, Theater, French, and the interdisciplinary program in human rights.

Life

For many Trinity undergrads, "The fraternities dominate the weekend social scene," and because these groups can be "fairly elitist" when it comes to allowing people into their late-night soirees, "Sometimes it's hard to find something to do." Other students take a broader view of campus life. Such students tell us that new groups are "gaining social power," among them "The Fred (named after late professor Fred Pfiel)," which hosts "open mic evenings, nonalcoholic competitions, [and] theme nights," among other events. They also call out Trinity's Cinestudio, "one of the best on-campus student-run movie theaters in the country." While campus theater, orchestra, a cappella, and chamber groups have limited participation, their performances are often well attended by the student body. Students note that "everything is available on campus so there is minimal effort to find things off campus." Those who have cars "often travel to nicer parts of Hartford or other Connecticut towns." One student observes, "Hartford, Connecticut is not as bad as people make it out to be. It has a lot to offer as long as you are willing to leave campus. There are some great restaurants and lots of shows to go to. Don't let yourself get stuck on campus every weekend."

Student Body

"Despite admissions' efforts, Trinity is still characterized by the New England boarding-school grad in polos and pink pants," undergrads here tell us, although some assert that "what many see as the typical student is actually a minority." Still, "The picture that immediately comes to mind is a blond, blue-eyed girl buying Coach . . . with daddy's money." Adding some diversity is "a growing population of 'Wesleyan-types,' who probably got rejected from our fellow Connecticut school. There's [been] an influx of intelligent, down-to-earth people at Trinity who are passionate about a lot more than getting wasted Thursday through Sunday." Students tend to be "over-wired" when not in class, attached to a "cell phone, IM, computer, [or] iPod, and therefore socially awkward or impolite. . . . In class, they are overachievers, very articulate and competitive. Most spend an impressive amount of time studying."

THE PRINCETON REVIEW SAYS

Admissions

Very important factors considered include: Rigor of secondary school record. *Important factors considered include:* Class rank, application essay, academic GPA, recommendation(s), standardized test scores, character/personal qualities, extracurricular activities, interview, racial/ethnic status, talent/ability. *Other factors considered include:* Alumni/ae relation, first generation, geographical residence, level of applicant's interest, volunteer work, work experience. SAT or ACT required; ACT with Writing component recommended. High school diploma is required and GED is accepted. *Academic units required:* 4 English, 3 mathematics, 2 science, (2 science labs), 3 foreign language, 2 history.

Financial Aid

Students should submit: FAFSA, CSS/Financial Aid PROFILE, noncustodial PROFILE, business/farm supplement, Federal Income tax returns. Regular filing deadline is 3/1. The Princeton Review suggests that all financial aid forms be submitted as soon as possible after January 1. *Need-based scholarships/grants offered:* Federal Pell, SEOG, state scholarships/grants, private scholarships, the school's own gift aid. *Loan aid offered:* Direct Subsidized Stafford, Direct Unsubsidized Stafford, Direct PLUS, FFEL Subsidized Stafford, FFEL Unsubsidized Stafford, FFEL PLUS, Federal Perkins, college/university loans from institutional funds. Applicants will be notified of awards on or about 4/1. Federal Work-Study Program available. Institutional employment available. Off-campus job opportunities are good.

The Inside Word

Students describe Trinity as "the home of Yale rejects," an appraisal that accurately characterizes the school's rep as an Ivy safety (if not the actual makeup of the student body). The school's high price tag ensures that a large percentage of the student body is made up of wealthy prepsters, but the school does offer generous financial aid packages to top candidates who can't afford the hefty price of attending. The school would love to broaden its student demographic, so competitive minority students should receive a very receptive welcome here.

THE SCHOOL SAYS ". . ."

From The Admissions Office

"An array of distinctive curricular options—including an interdisciplinary neuroscience major and a professionally accredited engineering degree program, a unique Human Rights Program, a Health Fellows Program, and interdisciplinary programs such as the Cities Program, Interdisciplinary Science Program, and InterArts— is one reason record numbers of students are applying to Trinity. In fact, applications are up 80 percent over the past 5 years. In addition, the college has been recognized for its commitment to diversity; students of color have represented approximately 20 percent of the freshman class for the past 4 years, setting Trinity apart from many of its peers. Trinity's capital city location offers students unparalleled 'real-world' learning experiences to complement classroom learning. Students take advantage of extensive opportunities for internships for academic credit and community service, and these opportunities extend to Trinity's global learning sites in cities around the world. Trinity's faculty is a devoted and accomplished group of exceptional teacher-scholars; our 100-acre campus is beautiful; Hartford is an educational asset that differentiates Trinity from other liberal arts colleges; our global connections and foreign study opportunities prepare students to be good citizens of the world; and our graduates go on to excel in virtually every field. We invite you to learn more about why Trinity might be the best choice for you.

"Students applying for admission for the entering class of Fall 2008 may submit the following testing options: SAT, ACT with Writing."

For even more information on this school, turn to page 527 of the "Stats" section.

TUFTS UNIVERSITY

BENDETSON HALL, MEDFORD, MA 02155 • ADMISSIONS: 617-627-3170 • FAX: 617-627-3860
FINANCIAL AID: 617-627-3528 • E-MAIL: ADMISSIONS.INQUIRY@ASE.TUFTS.EDU • WEBSITE: WWW.TUFTS.EDU

RATINGS
Quality of Life: 85   **Academic:** 91   **Admissions:** 97   **Financial Aid:** 94

STUDENTS SAY "..."

Academics

Tufts University boasts a "small-campus feel," a "globally recognized" reputation, and "engaging," "personable" faculty. Professors here "know what they are talking about" and "seem to go out of their way to make themselves accessible." These very same professors, however, "flood" students "with tons of work." Lower-level classes can be huge on occasion, but upper-level classes are "small and well-focused." The "transparent" administration tends "to grapple with technolo-

gy and change" but it is "incredibly helpful" and very well liked, despite "militant political correctness." "President Bacow will generally respond to any e-mail sent to him by a student within about 20 minutes." Academically, while you can choose from a massive number of stellar majors in the liberal arts and engineering, Tufts is probably best known for its "very strong" science programs (especially premeds) and its prestigious international relations programs. "Tufts is internationalism," declares one student. "From the Music Department's ethnomusicology [major] to Political Science and International Relations, every facet of Tufts, both in and out of the classroom, revolves around thinking globally." Studying abroad "is highly encouraged"; about 40 percent of students take advantage of awesome study abroad programs in a host of exotic locales including an "amazing" summer program in the Alps.

Life

At Tufts, the campus is "gorgeous," "The food is incredible," and course work is time-consuming, so it's no surprise that social life is basically centered on campus. Students here "know each other." "It's a nice feeling," an undergrad ventures, but "If you want to be anonymous, Tufts is not for you." The "fabulous extracurricular opportunities" include "a daily paper, a dozen student magazines," and "countless service and activism organizations." In addition, a vast array of large-scale, free campus events helps to keep students entertained. While "Drinking is very popular on the weekends," undergrads report that "there is not always a party guaranteed on a Friday or Saturday night, which is unthinkable at bigger schools." When there is one, it can seem as if "The campus police break everything up." This may be why "As you get older and you meet more people, you begin to go to more parties and social events off of campus," a more seasoned student tells us. Many feel that the surrounding town of Medford leaves a lot to be desired, but fortunately, "You have the greatest college city in the nation a subway ride away" if "you get tired [of] the Tufts scene." It should be noted, however, that public transportation into Boston takes "like an hour (counting waiting)." "We're not in Boston," cautions one student. "Don't let the admissions folks fool you."

Students

Some students tell us that Tuft's reputation as a haven for the "Ivy League reject" is accurate. Others vehemently disagree. "The Tufts Ivy complex is over," argues one student. "Anyone here could get into Cornell!" Students describe themselves as "genuinely nice," "painfully liberal," and "very goal-oriented." They are "laid-back" and only "competitive with themselves." One undergrad asserts, "The typical student here is very intelligent and ambitious, but they don't want you to think that." Another adds, "They get their work done so they can have fun too." Ethnic diversity is notable; traditionally underrepresented minorities on campus have a strong presence. However, "People tend to separate into their little cliques after first semester and rarely interact with other people." "Almost all Tufts students are rich" as well. "The frustrating thing is not the lack of ethnic diversity, but the lack of socioeconomic diversity," an English major writes. This student body features "a lot of smart kids in Lacoste polos who are looking to save the world" (or, at least, "convince others they are looking to save to world") and a lot of "preppy," "Louis V. bag," "North Face fleece," "big sunglasses," "rich kids." There are also "the stoners, the die-hard partiers, the activists, the coffeehouse philosophers," and a slew of "obscenely wealthy international kids."

THE PRINCETON REVIEW SAYS

Admissions

Very important factors considered include: Application essay, academic GPA, rigor of secondary school record, character/personal qualities. *Important factors considered include:* Class rank, recommendation(s), standardized test scores, extracurricular activities, talent/ability, volunteer work, work experience. *Other factors considered include:* Alumni/ae relation, first generation, geographical residence, interview, racial/ethnic status, SAT and SAT Subject Tests or ACT required; ACT with Writing component required. TOEFL required of international applicant s if appropriate. High school diploma is required and GED is accepted. *Academic units recommended:* 4 English, 3 mathematics, 2 science, 3 foreign language, 2 history.

Financial Aid

Students should submit: FAFSA, CSS/Financial Aid PROFILE, noncustodial PROFILE, business/farm supplement, Parent and Student Federal Income Tax Returns. Regular filing deadline is 2/15. The Princeton Review suggests that all financial aid forms be submitted as soon as possible after January 1. *Need-based scholarships/grants offered:* Federal Pell, SEOG, state scholarships/grants, private scholarships, the school's own gift aid. *Loan aid offered:* FFEL Subsidized Stafford, FFEL Unsubsidized Stafford, FFEL PLUS, Federal Perkins, state loans, college/university loans from institutional funds. Applicants will be notified of awards on or about 4/1. Federal Work-Study Program available. Institutional employment available. Off-campus job opportunities are good.

The Inside Word

The admissions process is rigorous. With an acceptance rate hovering not much over 25 percent and average SAT section scores in the low 700s, you'll need to demonstrate fairly extraordinary academic accomplishments and submit a thorough and well-prepared application in order to get admitted to Tufts. On the bright side, Tufts is still a little bit of a safety school for aspiring Ivy Leaguers. Since many applicants who also get into an Ivy League school will pass on Tufts, it has spots for "mere mortals" at the end of the day.

THE SCHOOL SAYS ". . ."

From The Admissions Office

"Tufts University, on the boundary between Medford and Somerville, sits on a hill overlooking Boston, five miles northwest of the city. The campus is a tranquil New England setting within easy access by subway and bus to the cultural, social, and entertainment resources of Boston and Somerville. Since its founding in 1852 by members of the Universalist church, Tufts has grown from a small liberal arts college into a nonsectarian university of over 8,000 students with undergraduate programs in Arts & Sciences and Engineering. By 1900 the college had added a medical school, a dental school, and graduate studies. The university now also includes the Fletcher School of Law and Diplomacy, the Graduate School of Arts and Sciences, the Cummings School of Veterinary Medicine, the Friedman School of Nutrition Science and Policy, the Sackler School of Graduate Biomedical Sciences, and the Gordon Institute of Engineering Management.

"Applicants for Fall 2009 are required to submit scores (including the Writing assessment) from either the SAT or ACT. If an applicant submits the SAT, SAT Subject Tests are also required (candidates for the School of Engineering are encouraged to submit Math and either Chemistry or Physics)."

For even more information on this school, turn to page 527 of the "Stats" section.

UNION COLLEGE (NY)

GRANT HALL, SCHENECTADY, NY 12308 • ADMISSIONS: 518-388-6112 • FAX: 518-388-6986
FINANCIAL AID: 518-388-6123 • E-MAIL: ADMISSIONS@UNION.EDU • WEBSITE: WWW.UNION.EDU

RATINGS

Quality of Life: 63   **Academic:** 88   **Admissions:** 95   **Financial Aid:** 60*

STUDENTS SAY "..."

Academics

Immersing a bunch of engineers and premeds in an accelerated trimester calendar should be a formula for a high-
stress campus, but somehow Union College manages to
keep the situation under control. A highly capable student
body helps, as does, perhaps, the availability of quality liberal arts classes to intersperse among the science- and math-
heavy classes; as one student puts it, "There aren't too many
schools that do a good job combining engineering with liberal arts, [but it's] important if you actually want to commu-

> SURVEY SAYS . . .
> *Large classes*
> *Great library*
> *Athletic facilities are great*
> *Frats and sororities dominate
> social scene*
> *Lots of beer drinking*
> *Hard liquor is popular*

nicate with people." In fact, many students here believe Union is actually an "excellent liberal arts school with a
solid footing in the hard sciences—I wasn't sure exactly what I wanted to do with my life after graduation, [and]
Union gave me a myriad of options." Those options include not only "great Science and Engineering
Department[s]" but also strong programs in economics, political science, and psychology, all taught by top-notch
professors. An economics major writes, "I was really amazed and pleasantly surprised when I saw the caliber of
the professors here. They are all interested in their particular field of research, and their enthusiasm in the classroom rubs off on the students and makes for interesting and fun-filled learning exercises." Students even love
the trimester system, which "allows a normal course load of only three classes a term." Some feel this allows for
"lots of free time." Others caution, "The amount of work is increased, and in addition we must complete courses in only 10 weeks as opposed to the normal 12 to 14. By nature, Union is an accelerated school."

Life

For as long as anyone can remember, the Greeks have dominated the social scene at Union College, and while
the frats are still "a big scene on the weekends (30–40 percent of campus is involved in Greek life)," the school
is increasing attempts to provide more alternatives. The 2004 creation of seven Minerva Houses—each incoming student is assigned to one—represents the most significant effort; the houses are intended "to provide a
nonexclusive (i.e., [non-] Greek) space for students to live and work." It's too early to deem this experiment a
success or failure, although almost everyone here has an opinion one way or another. Some report that the
Minervas are "a great idea" that are "slowly gaining popularity and momentum," while others see them as
"creat[ing] tension over the distribution of funds" or, worse yet, "rapidly becoming small [frat-like] cliques
themselves. For example, almost the entire Ultimate Frisbee team lives in Orange House." There's no disagreement over the city of Schenectady; everyone agrees it is less than ideal, and worse, there is "nothing to do."
General consensus is that fun means "staying on campus and drinking" or "maybe an excursion to Albany (20
minutes away) for a concert." Campus perks up whenever the hockey team plays, as "Hockey games are huge
events here"; football also draws a crowd. While students concede that drinking is big at Union, they also report
that "there are other options for students. Every weekend at least one Minerva has to hold an event, [and] there
are speakers, lecturers, movies, [and] performances. We always have a lot going on!"

Student Body

While "You can find a variety of people at Union," students say there is definitely "a typical Union student,"
who can be described as "preppy, Northeastern, [and] middle- to upper-class." By all accounts, you'll find "a
lot of athletes, a lot of frat boys," and a lot of students who "wear Polo and Abercrombie" here. Atypical students are those who "find their place on campus in the Minerva House activities and clubs such as Women's
Union, Black Student Union, performing arts groups, the college's radio station—WRUC, Ultimate Frisbee, and
others." The "terribly cliquish nature of the social scene makes it difficult to provide a decent analysis of individual students."

THE PRINCETON REVIEW SAYS

Admissions

Very important factors considered include: Academic GPA, rigor of secondary school record. *Important factors considered include:* Class rank, recommendation(s), character/personal qualities, extracurricular activities, talent/ability. *Other factors considered include:* Application essay, standardized test scores, alumni/ae relation, first generation, geographical residence, interview, level of applicant's interest, racial/ethnic status, state residency, volunteer work, work experience. TOEFL required of all international applicants. High school diploma is required and GED is not accepted. *Academic units required:* 4 English, 3 mathematics, 2 science, (2 science labs), 2 foreign language, 1 social studies, 1 history. *Academic units recommended:* 4 English, 4 mathematics, 4 science, (4 science labs), 4 foreign language, 2 social studies, 2 history.

Financial Aid

Students should submit: FAFSA, CSS/Financial Aid PROFILE, state aid form, business/farm supplement, Noncustodial (Divorced/Separated) Parent's Statement. Regular filing deadline is 2/1. The Princeton Review suggests that all financial aid forms be submitted as soon as possible after January 1. *Need-based scholarships/grants offered:* Federal Pell, SEOG, state scholarships/grants, private scholarships, the school's own gift aid. *Loan aid offered:* FFEL Subsidized Stafford, FFEL Unsubsidized Stafford, FFEL PLUS, Federal Perkins, college/university loans from institutional funds. Applicants will be notified of awards on or about 4/1. Federal Work-Study Program available. Institutional employment available. Off-campus job opportunities are good.

The Inside Word

Hoping to produce world-historical progeny some day? Attending Union College may improve your odds; the school is alma mater to Franklin D. Roosevelt's father and Winston Churchill's grandfather. Craft your application package carefully here. Since Union does not require standardized test scores, there is no need to submit these scores unless they strengthen your application.

THE SCHOOL SAYS ". . ."

From The Admissions Office

"'Breadth' and 'flexibility' characterize the Union academic program. Whether the subject is the poetry of ancient Greece or the possibilities of developing fields such as nanotechnology, Union students can choose from among nearly 1,000 courses—a range that is unusual among America's highly selective colleges. Students can major in a single field, combine work in two or more departments, or even create their own organizing-theme major. Undergraduate research is strongly encouraged, and more than half of Union's students take advantage of the college's extensive international study program.

"Admission to Union is merit based and driven by years of academic success. Union seeks students with excellent academic credentials. Those credentials are primarily transcripts. Submission of SAT and ACT scores are optional except for the law and medicine programs. Please check Union.edu/Admissions for details."

For even more information on this school, turn to page 528 of the "Stats" section.

UNITED STATES COAST GUARD ACADEMY

31 MOHEGAN AVENUE, NEW LONDON, CT 06320-8103 • ADMISSIONS: 800-883-8724 • FAX: 860-701-6700
E-MAIL: ADMISSIONS@CGA.USCG.MIL • WEBSITE: WWW.CGA.EDU

RATINGS
Quality of Life: 62   **Academic:** 87   **Admissions:** 96   **Financial Aid:** 60*

STUDENTS SAY ". . ."

Academics

If you're ready to "deal with military rules and discipline along with a rigorous engineering education" so that "in four years you get the job you've always wanted" (provided that job involves military, maritime, or multi-mission humanitarian service), the United States Coast Guard Academy may be the place for you. "Rigorous academics and military training" prepare cadets "for success as junior officers in the [Coast Guard] as ship drivers, pilots, and marine safety officers." The workload is considerable. Students must take a minimum of 19 credits per semester while also handling military training and athletics. Cadets note that this regimen "builds character through intense

> **SURVEY SAYS . . .**
> *Large classes*
> *No one cheats*
> *Career services are great*
> *Campus feels safe*
> *Everyone loves the Bears*
> *Intramural sports are popular*
> *Frats and sororities are unpopular*
> *or nonexistent*
> *Political activism is unpopular or nonexistent*
> *Very little drug use*

physical and mental training," although some opine that "It's like a cup of boiling hot chocolate: It smells good, you know it tastes good, but you have wait a long time to let it cool down in order to enjoy it fully." Others simply say that the demands make USCGA "a great place to be from but not always the greatest place to be." The school offers eight majors, most heavily in Science, Technology, Engineering, and Math, including operations research, management, and government. In all disciplines, "The academic program is extremely difficult, but most instructors are willing to work with you one-on-one if necessary."

Life

Life at USCGA, unsurprisingly, is highly regimented. One student sums it up: "We have to wake up at 0600 every day whether we have class or not. We have to have our doors open whether we're in our rooms or not from 0600 to 1600. They tell us exactly what we can and can't do, and what we can wear and what we can't. We have military training period from 0700 to 0800 and class from 0800 to1600. We all eat lunch together at the same time in a family-style fashion. Sports period is from 1600 to 1800. Military training period from 1900 to 2000. Study hour from 2000 to 2200. We all have to stand duty and play sports and get a certain number of community service hours. We can't drink on base, and we can't leave during the week. We have to make our own fun, which involves some creativity sometimes (and demerits), but our fun wouldn't appeal to most college students because it's silly and doesn't involve alcohol." Cadets warn that "The school can be very rigid with the rules. It hurts to see one of your friends get kicked out after having made a stupid decision, as almost all college students do," but they recognize that "that goes with the territory of being a military institution." Students "can only leave campus on the weekends." When they do "there is a bus system that takes cadets to familiar places in the New London area" as well as "a nearby Amtrak station that takes cadets to New York City or Boston when cadets are allowed to leave the Academy for an extended period of time (rare), usually holiday weekends."

Student Body

Service academies tend to attract students from particular demographics, and the USCGA is no exception. Most here are "fairly conservative," "extremely athletic," "very smart," and "were leaders of their schools while in high school." They tend to be "type A personalities" who are "very disciplined or looking for discipline" in their lives. Students tell us that "Although there are exceptions, almost everyone here is very selfless, willing to take one for the team, or sacrifice to help out a buddy. As the saying goes, 'Ship, shipmates, self.' Along those same lines, everyone is held to a high standard by both comrades and superiors. Both have a low tolerance for slacking."

THE PRINCETON REVIEW SAYS

Admissions

Very important factors considered include: Class rank, academic GPA, rigor of secondary school record, standardized test scores, character/personal qualities, extracurricular activities. *Important factors considered include:* Application essay, recommendation(s), talent/ability. *Other factors considered include:* Alumni/ae relation, interview, level of applicant's interest, volunteer work, work experience. SAT or ACT required; ACT with Writing component required. High school diploma is required and GED is accepted. *Academic units required:* 4 English, 4 mathematics, 3 science, (3 science labs).

Financial Aid

The Princeton Review suggests that all financial aid forms be submitted as soon as possible after January 1.

The Inside Word

Though USCGA has a low level of public recognition, gaining admission is still a steep uphill climb. Candidates must go through the rigorous multi-step admissions process as do their other service-academy peers (although no congressional nomination is required) and will encounter a serious roadblock if they fall short on any step. Those who pass muster join a proud, if somewhat under-recognized, student body, virtually equal in accomplishment to those at other service academies.

THE SCHOOL SAYS ". . ."

From The Admissions Office

"Founded in 1876, the United States Coast Guard Academy enjoys a proud tradition of graduating leaders of character. The academy experience melds academic rigor, leadership development, and athletic participation to prepare you to graduate as a commissioned officer. Character development of cadets is founded on the core values of honor, respect, and devotion to duty. You build friendships that last a lifetime, study with inspiring professors in small classes, and train during the summer aboard America's tall ship Eagle, as well as the service's ships and aircraft. Top performers spend their senior summer traveling on exciting internships around the nation and overseas. Graduates serve for 5 years and have unmatched opportunities to attend flight school and graduate school, all funded by the Coast Guard.

"Appointments to the Academy are based on a selective admissions process; Congressional nominations are not required. Your leadership potential and desire to serve your country are what counts. Our student body reflects the best America has to offer—with all its potential and diversity!

"Applicants for Fall 2008 are required to take the new SAT (or the ACT with the Writing section), but students may submit scores from the old SAT or ACT as well, and will use the student's best scores from either test."

For even more information on this school, turn to page 528 of the "Stats" section.

UNITED STATES MERCHANT MARINE ACADEMY

OFFICE OF ADMISSIONS, KINGS POINT, NY 11024-1699 • ADMISSIONS: 516-773-5391 • FAX: 516-773-5390
EMAIL: ADMISSIONS@USMMA.EDU • WEBSITE: WWW.USMMA.EDU

RATINGS
Quality of Life: 63   **Academic:** 74   **Admissions:** 93   **Financial Aid:** 97

STUDENTS SAY "..."

Academics

"Producing the highest caliber of professional mariners in terms of character and ability" is what it's all about at the federally funded United States Merchant Marine Academy. The USMMA is not a carefree experience; the workload is intense ("17 to 25 hours per week in class," students estimate), because a year spent at sea means students "have to fit four years of college into the three years we are physically on campus." This time spent at sea, however, is "what sets Kings Point [USMMA] apart. Sea year teaches midshipmen how to

> **SURVEY SAYS . . .**
> Small classes
> Career services are great
> Lousy food on campus
> Low cost of living
> Frats and sororities are unpopular or nonexistent
> Political activism is unpopular or nonexistent

study independently and work in an adult environment, and it gives us a global perspective." One midshipman notes, "The training that the students get while out at sea is second to none in learning about engineering, navigation, and business." Another thing that makes the hard work worthwhile is the prospect of "incredible options when you graduate." One student explains, "We can become officers in any branch of the military, including the NOAA [National Oceanic and Atmospheric Administration] and Coast Guard. We can sail merchant ships or go into shore-side engineering and management careers. We can go to grad school with a stipend from the government. And the alumni network is unbelievable. Aside from all of that, we graduate having worked in our chosen field and sailed in almost every sea on Earth," and visited "maybe a dozen different countries." Graduates of USMMA walk away with "one of the top maritime educations that can be found in the world."

Life

Life at USMMA is rugged and highly regimented. It's especially difficult for first-year students (called "plebes"), who "are on lockdown most of the time" and "who clean everything. Rather than having a janitor service for the barracks, the plebes clean, and if cleaning isn't done well, we get in trouble with the upperclassmen." While many underclassmen jokingly compare the plebe experience to being "in jail," they also praise the way the experience of being a plebe molds character; as one student states, "Plebes have horrible lives to begin with. However, the structure and environment develop great leaders and provide a solid foundation for success." All students participate in a daily regimen of reveille, morning inspection, colors, classes, muster, more classes, and drills. Upperclassmen, on the other hand, enjoy "more liberty and spend a lot of time off campus, either in Great Neck (the town nearest us) or in New York City." USMMA midshipmen appreciate "the many opportunities for student leadership; every student is required to be a team leader for a room of plebes [during] sophomore year, every junior is required to hold a petty officer position to a student senior officer for at least a trimester, and every senior holds an officer position for at least half of senior year." Students also praise the way academy life presents "various ways to challenge oneself physically, mentally, and emotionally" and to expand one's horizons. One student sums up, "It's a full schedule, but it's fulfilling. I have personally been to Japan, China, Germany, England, New Zealand, Antarctica, Belgium, and up and down the East and West Coasts of the United States."

Students

The stereotypical USMMA student "is a conservative White male, often—but not always—from a military background." Women and students of color are in the minority at USMMA. Regardless of race or sex, however, all students "share a common love for the United States and a desire to serve it admirably." Beyond love for their country, what ties students together is the shared experience: "At USMMA there is a bond that is formed during Indoc [the 2-week indoctrination program], and there is a sense of pride in being a Kings Pointer." Because of "the close bonds developed, race and geographical origin are nonissues among the student body." Or, as another student puts it, "Shared pain makes most people fit in just fine."

Admissions
Very important factors considered include: Rigor of secondary school record, standardized test scores, character/personal qualities. *Important factors considered include:* Class rank, application essay, academic GPA, recommendation(s), extracurricular activities, geographical residence, talent/ability. *Other factors considered include:* interview, level of applicant's interest, racial/ethnic status, state residency, volunteer work, work experience. SAT or ACT required; TOEFL required of all international applicants. High school diploma is required and GED is accepted. *Academic units required:* 4 English, 3 mathematics, 3 science, (1 science labs), 8 academic electives. *Academic units recommended:* 4 English, 4 mathematics, 4 science, (2 science labs), 2 foreign language, 4 social studies.

Financial Aid
Students should submit: FAFSA, institution's own financial aid form. Regular filing deadline is 5/1. The Princeton Review suggests that all financial aid forms be submitted as soon as possible after January 1. *Need-based scholarships/grants offered:* Federal Pell, private scholarships, Federal SMART Grants & Federal Academic Competitiveness Grants. *Loan aid offered:* FFEL Subsidized Stafford, FFEL Unsubsidized Stafford, FFEL PLUS Applicants will be notified of awards on a rolling basis beginning 1/31. Off-campus job opportunities are poor.

The Inside Word
Prospective midshipmen face demanding admission requirements. The USMMA assesses scholastic achievement, strength of character, and stamina (applicants must meet specific physical standards). Candidates must also be nominated by a proper nominating authority, typically a state representative or senator.

THE SCHOOL SAYS "..."
From The Admissions Office
"What makes the U.S. Merchant Marine Academy different from the other federal service academies? The difference can be summarized in two phrases that appear in our publications. The first: 'The World Is Your Campus.' You will spend a year at sea—a third of your sophomore year and two-thirds of your junior year—teamed with a classmate aboard a U.S. merchant ship. You will visit an average of 18 foreign nations while you work and learn in a mariner's true environment. You will graduate with seafaring experience and as a citizen of the world. The second phrase is 'Options and Opportunities.' Unlike students at the other federal academies, who are required to enter the service connected to their academy, you have the option of working in the seagoing merchant marine and transportation industry or applying for active duty in the Navy, Coast Guard, Marine Corps, Air Force, or Army. Nearly 25 percent of our most recent graduating class entered various branches of the armed forces with an officer rank. As a graduate of the U.S. Merchant Marine Academy, you will receive a Bachelor of Science degree, a government-issued merchant marine officer's license, and a Naval Reserve commission (unless you have been accepted for active military duty). No other service academy offers so attractive a package.

"Freshman applicants for the academic year starting in July 2008 must take the new SAT or the ACT with the Writing component. Students may still submit scores from older SAT or ACT tests that did not include a writing/essay component. For homeschooled students, we recommend they also submit scores from SAT Subject Tests in Chemistry and/or Physics."

For even more information on this school, turn to page 528 of the "Stats" section.

UNITED STATES MILITARY ACADEMY

600 THAYER ROAD, WEST POINT, NY 10996-1797 • ADMISSIONS: 914-938-4041 • FAX: 914-938-3021
FINANCIAL AID: 914-938-3516 • E-MAIL: 8DAD@EXMAIL.USMA.ARMY.MIL • WEBSITE: WWW.USMA.EDU

RATINGS
Quality of Life: 71   **Academic:** 97   **Admissions:** 96   **Financial Aid:** 60*

STUDENTS SAY "..."

Academics

A United States Military Academy education "is not easy and not always fun, but it is a great experience to be proud of," and one that is designed "to educate tomorrow's world leaders." Don't come to West Point expecting the typical college experience. As one student explains, "The military atmosphere makes everything different. Teachers are usually commissioned Army officers and strict discipline is maintained within the classroom at all times. Disciplinary actions ensure that students turn in assignments on time, arrive to class on time, and do not miss class." Also, USMA uses "the Thayer method" of education, under which "Cadets are required to teach themselves the material before

coming to class and then spend class time clarifying what was self-taught the night before." Though some find the system "unrealistic," most agree that "it is not really enjoyable to endure, but it does help foster individual academic responsibility." It also contributes to the sense that USMA "give you 28 hours of things to do in a 24-hour day." Expect to be "busy," but know that "every teacher makes an explicit point of stating that any help that a cadet needs will be given. If you want to do well here and are willing to work for it, the path is available for you to do so." Take heart; though the program "is as grueling as can be for the first 2 years," you'll find that in the final 2 years "You have a lot more time to do what you want to do."

Life

"Life at West Point is very regimented" and "Just about every hour of every day is busy." As one student puts it, "West Point tries to make sure that we have little free time and are always doing something (physical, academic, or military)." Another adds that there is "not much room for fun." "Physical fitness is a big part of every student's life," as "West Point has corps-wide physical testing events. From the APFT (Army Physical Fitness Test) to the infamous and dreaded IOCT (Indoor Obstacle Course Test), this place will make you stay in shape or get rid of you." In order to leave campus overnight, students need a pass. "During the first year, you are only guaranteed one pass to leave a semester, but everyone is allowed to go on trip sections, plebes included. Plebes are also allowed to go to the mall, visit sponsors' houses, play sports, and go to their own club to hang out—all without having to take pass." Also, "Passes are awarded for grades, physical fitness, attitude, special activities, etc." So as long as you are a "good person" and "take care of your business," the school is "more than happy to reward you and let you get off post for the weekend." Cadets love to "go to New York City on the weekend." Fitness doesn't end with the school day as many "enjoy the thrill of the outdoors and taking things to the extreme."

Student Body

Being a military school, it should come as no surprise that things as USMA are "uniform." "Most students are the same," notes a senior. They're "intelligent, athletic, honest, and committed to serving in the Army." And while it is a coed institution, expect a greater number of "male students." Gender aside, students are "very alike as far as life goals and ambitions . . . all are very intellectual and bring their own views to the school." There are "a lot of type-A personalities" here, all "prepared to do anything and everything to be the best." However, some find that the school "still has a long way to go" in terms of "ethnic diversity." But being part of "The Long Gray Line" comes with a "unifying, competitive spirit" that "levels the playing field" for these "soldiers and students."

Admissions

Very important factors considered include: Academic GPA, application essay, character/personal qualities, class rank, extracurricular activities, recommendation(s), rigor of secondary school record, standardized test scores, talent/ability. *Important factors considered include:* Geographical residence, interview, level of applicant's interest, racial/ethnic status, volunteer work. *Other factors considered include:* Alumni/ae relation, state residency, work experience. SAT or ACT required. High school diploma is required, and GED is accepted. *Academic units recommended:* 4 English, 4 math, 4 science (2 science labs), 2 foreign language, 3 social studies, 1 history, 3 academic electives.

Financial Aid

The Princeton Review suggests that all financial aid forms be submitted as soon as possible after January 1. *Need-based scholarships/grants offered:* All cadets are on active duty as members of the United States Army and receive an annual salary of approximately $10,148. Room and board, medical and dental care is provided by the U.S. Army. A one-time deposit of $2,900 is required upon admission.

The Inside Word

America's military academies experienced an increase in applicants after 9/11. They've been experiencing a similar drop in applications as the Iraq War continues, although it should be noted that the academies believe factors other than the war explain the drop. Regardless, fewer applicants means less competition, but it's still plenty tough to get into West Point. You have to begin the process in your junior year in order to get the requisite nomination. You'll need to excel in school to have a prayer; you'll also need to get into great physical condition to survive the vetting process.

THE SCHOOL SAYS ". . ."

From The Admissions Office

"As a young man or woman considering your options for obtaining a quality college education, you may wonder what unique aspects the United States Military Academy has to offer. West Point offers one of the most highly respected, quality education programs in the nation. A West Point cadetship includes a fully funded 4-year college education. Tuition, room, board, medical, and dental care are provided by the U.S. Army. As members of the armed forces, cadets also receive an annual salary of more than $8,880. This pay covers the cost of uniforms, books, a personal computer, and living incidentals. By law, graduates of West Point are appointed on active duty as commissioned officers.

"Since its founding nearly two centuries ago, the Military Academy has accomplished its mission by developing cadets in four critical areas: intellectual, physical, military, and moral-ethical—a 4-year process called the 'West Point Experience.' Specific developmental goals are addressed through several fully coordinated and integrated programs.

"A challenging academic program that consists of a core of 31 courses provides a balanced education in the arts and sciences. This core curriculum establishes the foundation for elective courses that permit cadets to explore in greater depth a field of study or an optional major. All cadets receive a Bachelor of Science degree, which is designed specifically to meet the intellectual requirements of a commissioned officer in today's army.

"The physical program at West Point includes both physical education classes and competitive athletics. Every cadet participates in an intercollegiate, club, or intramural-level sport each semester. This rigorous physical program contributes to the mental and physical fitness that is required for service as an officer in the army.

"Applicants are required to take the new SAT (or the ACT with the Writing component). Students may also submit scores from the old SAT or ACT, and their best scores will be used regardless of test date."

For even more information on this school, turn to page 529 of the "Stats" section.

UNITED STATES NAVAL ACADEMY

117 DECATUR ROAD, ANNAPOLIS, MD 21402 • ADMISSIONS: 410-293-4361 • FAX: 410-295-1815
E-MAIL: WEBMAIL@GWMAIL.USNA.EDU • WEBSITE: WWW.USNA.EDU

RATINGS
Quality of Life: 84   Academic: 91   Admissions: 96   Financial Aid: 60*

STUDENTS SAY "..."

Academics

SURVEY SAYS . . .
Lab facilities are great
Great computer facilities
Great library
Career services are great
Campus feels safe
Everyone loves the Navy

The United States Naval Academy is "a rugged, in-your-face" "leadership laboratory" that "teaches you to think critically and develops your skills as a future combat leader." You'll find "the highest ideals of duty, honor, and loyalty" here. You'll find "unreal" facilities, too. Few colleges can boast a sub-critical nuclear reactor, just for example. All midshipmen get "a full-ride scholarship" that includes tuition, room and board, medical care, and a stipend. And you'll "have a guaranteed job when you graduate" as a Navy or Marine Corps officer. "Classes are extremely small." Academics "pile on fast." Regardless of major, you'll take a ton of core courses in the humanities, the hard sciences, engineering, and naval science and weapons systems. Though the experience is "grueling," the professors at the Academy are "some of the most caring and well educated people in the world." They "are always accessible outside of class," and "they do whatever it takes for the students to understand the material." To put it mildly, the top brass "practices tough love." "Think of Stalin and Hitler having a child, and then that child running your school." On one hand, "the administration has obligations to the military and the United States government" to train future officers. On the other hand, "there are too many stupid policies." While the atmosphere "tends to brew cynicism," major reform is unlikely. "The administration is what it is," muses a chemistry major. "Deal with it."

Life

Ultimately, the Naval Academy "gives you a great education, a job, and financial security, but at the cost of your freedom for four years." "To quote a popular slogan: 'We're here to defend liberty, not enjoy it,'" quips one midshipman. During the summer before classes start, first-year students get indoctrinated with "yelling, physical training," and basic seamanship. The entire first year is a "stressful" "crucible-type experience," and it's "no fun." Older students have it only slightly better. Life is "extremely micromanaged." "Midshipmen are never allowed outside the walls during the week." "Each day begins for every student at 6:30 A.M. and ends well past 11:00 at night." "You have to wear a uniform almost all the time." There are "mandatory meals, formations," and sports and study periods. "Most people work out, watch movies, and play various videogames." "On weekends, you may or may not be allowed to leave for a night or two, depending on which class year you are." Older midshipmen often spend that time soaking up "the great bar scene" in Annapolis. "Catching up on sleep" is also popular. Graduates usually leave here with "at least some degree of spite." "The food will always suck." Nevertheless, a "strong camaraderie" is pervasive. "Even though people complain, there is no place we'd rather be," declares a junior. "Nobody here was drafted."

Student Body

The overwhelmingly male population here represents "every state and a lot of foreign countries." "Everyone is 100 percent equal regardless of gender, race, or religion." "The only intolerance is that open homosexuals are not allowed in the military under federal law." Politically, there's "a fair share of liberals" but the majority is "conservative-minded." "You can usually point out a midshipman in a crowd." Students "are pretty much the same person" because they are "made to conform." "We try to kick out the 'individuals' early on," dryly notes a junior. Many midshipmen were "the best from where they came from." "The school is full of enormous egos." "Fiercely competitive," "type A" personalities proliferate. "Almost everyone was a sports star in high school," and "everyone is in great physical condition." At the same time, "there are many students who play a lot of videogames and are socially awkward." Deep down, "everyone here is a dork or a geek, even the most macho of athletic commandos. They're "resilient," "hardworking," "intellectual," and "pretty straightedge." They have "a good sense of humor and a level head." The average midshipman is also "a little jaded," and, on some days, "a zombie that just tries to make it to the meals."

THE PRINCETON REVIEW SAYS

Admissions

Very important factors considered include: Class rank, application essay, academic GPA, recommendation(s), rigor of secondary school record, standardized test scores, character/personal qualities, extracurricular activities, interview, level of applicant's interest. *Important factors considered include:* Talent/ability. *Other factors considered include:* Alumni/ae relation, first generation, geographical residence, racial/ethnic status, volunteer work, work experience. SAT or ACT required; TOEFL required of all international applicants. High school diploma or equivalent is not required. *Academic units recommended:* 4 English, 4 mathematics, 2 science, (1 science labs), 2 foreign language, 2 history, 1 Introductory computer and typing courses.

Financial Aid

The Princeton Review suggests that all financial aid forms be submitted as soon as possible after January 1.

The Inside Word

It doesn't take a genius to recognize that getting admitted to the USNA requires true strength of character; simply completing the arduous admissions process is an accomplishment worthy of remembrance. Those who have successful candidacies are strong, motivated students, and leaders in both school and community. Perseverance is an important character trait for anyone considering the life of a midshipman—the application process is only the beginning of a truly challenging and demanding experience.

THE SCHOOL SAYS ". . ."

From The Admissions Office

"The Naval Academy offers you a unique opportunity to associate with a broad cross-section of the country's finest young men and women. You will have the opportunity to pursue a 4-year program that develops you mentally, morally, and physically as no civilian college can. As you might expect, this program is demanding, but the opportunities are limitless and more than worth the effort. To receive an appointment to the academy, you need 4 years of high school preparation to develop the strong academic, athletic, and extracurricular background required to compete successfully for admission. You should begin preparing in your freshman year and apply for admission at the end of your junior year. Selection for appointment to the academy comes as a result of a complete evaluation of your admissions package and completion of the nomination process. Complete admissions guidance may be found at www.usna.edu.

"SAT results from tests prior to March 2005 and ACT results from tests prior to February 2005 will be used by the Naval Academy, and no conversion of scores is necessary due to compatibility of old and new scoring systems."

For even more information on this school, turn to page 529 of the "Stats" section.

UNITY COLLEGE

PO Box 532, Unity, ME 04988-0532 • Admissions: 207-948-3131 • Fax: 207-948-6277
E-mail: admissions@unity.edu • Website: www.unity.edu

RATINGS
Quality of Life: 84   Academic: 72   Admissions: 70   Financial Aid: 88

STUDENTS SAY ". . ."

Academics

At Unity College, each student receives a "sound back-ground in environmental awareness" as well as "first-rate instruction in the major of their choice," which, by and large, has an environmental focus. In this regard, the school's "rural location" allows an "emphasis on hands-on, experiential learning" and undergrads love being able to "spend incredible amounts of time in the field." In addition, "many classes and labs are held outside." "There are very few strictly lecture classes," a freshman says. Many here allude to the school's "personal atmosphere," in which administrators and professors "aren't just the people in charge of our education. They are our friends and neighbors who live with us, learn with us, and play with us. By the end of the first week of classes, all students learn to feel comfortable being on a first-name basis with every person they meet on this campus." Professors here "understand the necessity of getting to know the people in your area of study" and "encourage students to make contacts." As a whole, undergrads feel that Unity puts them on track to be the "environmental leaders of the future."

> **SURVEY SAYS . . .**
> *Large classes*
> *Career services are great*
> *Students are friendly*
> *Students get along with local community*
> *Campus feels safe*
> *Students are happy*
> *Frats and sororities are unpopular or nonexistent*

Life

Unity students describe their school as "pretty far away from civilization" (a 20-to-30-minute drive, to be precise), but most appreciate the "laid-back" lifestyle and report "lots to do" on campus and in its immediate environs. Oft-mentioned diversions include "bands in the student center every other week," and "a ton of clubs, such as the outing club, rock-climbing club, martial arts club, [and] indoor soccer." Rural Maine is a haven for outdoor enthusiasts; a senior defines fun as: "ice fishing, snowmobiling, national toboggan races in Camden in winter, hiking, hunting, [regular] fishing, camping, biking, wildlife watching and photography, traveling, sugar maple-ing, paintball, target shooting, and volunteering year-round." The college doesn't feature "a strong nightlife because of the rural area," though "There's usually one party that half the school shows up to," and it usually entails "drinking some beer in someone's room." Those looking for something a little more urban often head to "Waterville (about 25 minutes away) to go to bars and clubs." Nevertheless, students say, "It is a miniscule group of people who show up only for classes and then disappear home. There is too much fun to be had."

Student Body

Students report two distinct Unity types: "The first group is likely to be seen in boots, camouflage pants, a baseball cap, and a Carhartt jacket. They spend their free time after class and studies hunting or fishing, depending on the season. They likely have a large group of friends who will troop out to the parking lot to see the latest catch and grill up venison steaks, no matter what the weather is like." In contrast, the second group "is very different, preferring tie-dye and jeans, vegetarian meals, and activities like Frisbee games, rock climbing, and musical entertainment." "The rest of the student body" falls somewhere between "those two ends of the spectrum." So where does the unity come from at Unity? A freshman ventures: "The one thing everybody has in common is we all love the outdoors and want to protect it." Not everyone, however, endorses the same means to that end: "Beliefs on environmental ethics are wide ranging." Ultimately, though, the school earns its name, as students "are accepting of hunters and vegetarians alike."

THE PRINCETON REVIEW SAYS

Admissions

Very important factors considered include: Application essay, interview, recommendation(s), rigor of secondary school record. *Important factors considered include:* Character/personal qualities, extracurricular activities, talent/ability. *Other factors considered include:* Alumni/ae relation, standardized test scores, volunteer work, work experience. SAT recommended; ACT recommended; TOEFL required of all international applicants. High school diploma is required, and GED is accepted. *Academic units required:* 4 English, 2 science. *Academic units recommended:* 4 math, 4 social studies.

Financial Aid

Students should submit: FAFSA. Regular filing deadline is April 15. The Princeton Review suggests that all financial aid forms be submitted as soon as possible after January 1. *Need-based scholarships/grants offered:* Pell Grant, SEOG, state scholarships/grants, private scholarships, the school's own gift aid. *Loan aid offered:* FFEL Subsidized Stafford, FFEL Unsubsidized Stafford, FFEL PLUS. Applicants will be notified of awards on a rolling basis beginning or about March 15. Federal Work-Study Program available. Off-campus job opportunities are fair.

The Inside Word

In addition to specific academic requirements, which include 2 years of lab science and 3 years of college-prep math, Unity seeks certain qualities in its future students. Among these are prior experience with the natural environment (activities or course work) and a passion for hands-on learning. If a student seems like a good fit with the school's milieu and is keen to be part of an intimate campus environment, average grades and test scores will do the trick.

THE SCHOOL SAYS " . . ."

From The Admissions Office

"At Unity, you will become part of a community of individuals who share your love of nature.

"Because of their common interests in the outdoors, Unity students, faculty, and staff work together closely, both in and out of the classroom.

"If you are looking for an opportunity to study environmental science, natural resource management, or outdoor recreation, and have the opportunity to learn and grow in a small college atmosphere in a distinctly rural setting, then Unity College in Maine may be the right place for you.

"Unity College exists for the student whose passion for the outdoors is reflected in their education and career choices. Unity students typically place a premium on jobs that do not require sitting behind a desk.

"Your education at Unity can be your first step to a position with a state park, wildlife refuge, nature education center, or wilderness recreation organization, so . . . pack your notebook, your hiking boots, and follow your dreams."

For even more information on this school, turn to page 530 of the "Stats" section.

The University of the Arts

320 South Broad Street, Philadelphia, PA 19102 • Admissions: 215-717-6049 • Fax: 215-717-6045
E-mail: admissions@uarts.edu • Website: www.uarts.edu

RATINGS
Quality of Life: 81   Academic: 84   Admissions: 79   Financial Aid: 79

STUDENTS SAY ". . ."

Academics

The "fun," "accessible," and "learned" art professors at The University of the Arts "are all working artists" who "take it to the next level of teaching," infusing classes "with their own unique theories and techniques" and teaching students "what it is like to be a working professional." The "Theater and dance programs are arguably the most successful and popular" here, and dance professors "push you daily to make you a better dancer." In fact, all three colleges—Art and Design, Media and Communication, and Performing Arts—are very strong. "The financial aid and billing office[s]," however, "cause multiple problems for many students" and "have the worst reputation[s] on campus"—perhaps, jokes one student, "because someone assumed they could hire artists to count." Some students say that smaller programs deserve more attention and money—"The Communication Department is the only department in the school without studios for upperclassmen"—and that the school needs "a recreational center, parking lots, new studios, [and] renovated classrooms." The "open," "well-intentioned" "administration is [undergoing] a major change"; respected university president Miguel Angel Corzo just left for California.

Life

Another art fix is always around the corner at UArts, which has "amazing connection[s] to real-life artists and the theater. There is always access to lectures and show openings." Since "Life at school is centered around what it takes to do your art," "Nine times out of ten, a conversation you'll overhear is about a project or production." Fun is disciplinary: Animation majors "watch cartoons with other animation majors," film and TV writers head to "the movies," and musicians "go to concert[s] and jazz clubs" and "get together and have jam sessions." Social divisions by medium are reinforced by the physical separation of the three schools and by unconventional living arrangements: "no real dorms, no meal plan, no 'campus,'" and no "student center." Philly is a more-than-adequate substitute: "The school is located right in the theater district . . . half a block from the Kimmel Center and other state-of-the-art performance halls. The nightlife is great" and the surrounding area is filled with "pool halls," "bars, movie theaters, theaters, South Street . . . it's a great time." Students agree that life here "is much better than the average college situation of going to a frat house and getting wasted." Anyway, partying isn't why UArts students are here. One student sums up the general attitude: "We work for the love of art, and that's fun for us."

Student Body

"All those crazy artists, actors, musicians, dancers, and computer geeks you knew in high school are all here." In fact, "Everyone is very accepted" and "You can act however you want, and nothing is crazy enough." While the typical undergrad is "White and from New Jersey," the African American community is much larger than at most other art schools, and many students are gay, lesbian, or bisexual. Personality types "run from extremely extroverted (the theater kids) to introverted until you get to know them. All are for the most part excited to be here, and while some stay in the cliques of their majors, most have a friends-circle that spans the university." The student body boasts that they are "overall nice people," and "Not only is it easy to find friends that you can relate to but they are [also] great friends that you will have for a long time." Students in all three schools are "very creative" and "focused on . . . career goals," but they "sometimes don't get all their work in on time. . . . They do take classes seriously, though."

THE PRINCETON REVIEW SAYS

Admissions

Very important factors considered include: Rigor of secondary school record, interview, talent/ability. *Important factors considered include:* Class rank, application essay, standardized test scores, character/personal qualities, extracurricular activities. *Other factors considered include:* Recommendation(s), alumni/ae relation, racial/ethnic status, volunteer work, work experience. SAT or ACT required; TOEFL required of all international applicants. High school diploma is required and GED is accepted. *Academic units required:* 4 English. *Academic units recommended:* 3 mathematics, 2 science, 2 foreign language, 2 social studies, 2 history, 2 study in visual art, music, dance, drama, or creative writing.

Financial Aid

Students should submit: FAFSA. Regular filing deadline is 3/1. The Princeton Review suggests that all financial aid forms be submitted as soon as possible after January 1. *Need-based scholarships/grants offered:* Federal Pell, SEOG, state scholarships/grants, private scholarships, the school's own gift aid, merit scholarships. *Loan aid offered:* FFEL Subsidized Stafford, FFEL Unsubsidized Stafford, FFEL PLUS, Federal Perkins, alternative loans. Applicants will be notified of awards on a rolling basis beginning 3/15. Federal Work-Study Program available. Institutional employment available. Off-campus job opportunities are excellent.

The Inside Word

UArts recommends a GPA of 2.0 or better and requires the SAT or ACT, but does not place much emphasis on scores; applicants who received a C or better in a college-level English class can dodge the SAT requirement. The upshot? A selective admissions process that favors budding Picassos and Arbuses who spent more time in the studio than in the library. As at all art schools, the primary emphasis is on applicants' portfolios and auditions. If you are serious about admission to this or any other art college, strongly consider attending a National Portfolio Days event (during which Admissions Officers from various schools will give feedback on your portfolio) and look into intensive precollege summer programs (especially those offered by your school of choice).

THE SCHOOL SAYS " . . . "

From The Admissions Office

"'Art is central to our everyday lives,' says Barbara Elliot, Dean of Enrollment Management at UArts. 'It drives the media we consume, the design of products we use, the form of the buildings we frequent, the layout of cities in which we live, and the channels through which we communicate.' As the only university in the nation dedicated exclusively to the visual, performing, communication, and media arts, UArts is committed to advancing this notion by preparing students to apply their strengths to create a better society.

"Located in the heart of Philadelphia on the Avenue of the Arts, UArts offers 25 majors in a single environment where students inspire each other with their creativity, focus, and drive. UArts students learn through exposure to all the languages of imagination—sound, movement, words, and form. The university offers traditional programs in painting, sculpture, printmaking, and photography as well as state-of-the-art programs in digital video, graphics, and multimedia communication. Its performing arts programs train dancers, musicians, actors, and directors for top jobs in entertainment around the country. At the same time, UArts provides its 2,200 undergraduate students with an education grounded in the liberal arts through core courses in English, history, and others.

"'We help students satisfy their need to create while preparing them to apply their talents and strengths to contribute to society as a whole,' says Elliot. 'These characteristics not only are important to success in the arts but to success in society in general.'"

For even more information on this school, turn to page 530 of the "Stats" section.

UNIVERSITY OF CONNECTICUT

2131 HILLSIDE ROAD, U-3088, STORRS, CT 06268-3088 • ADMISSIONS: 860-486-3137 • FAX: 860-486-1476
FINANCIAL AID: 860-486-2819 • E-MAIL: BEAHUSKY@UCONN.EDU • WEBSITE: WWW.UCONN.EDU

RATINGS

Quality of Life: 74   Academic: 74   Admissions: 89   Financial Aid: 73

STUDENTS SAY ". . ."

Academics

The hardy students of University of Connecticut recognize that a UConn education "is based on a solid foundation of research and academics" and a pedagogical approach that "promotes learning in and out of the classroom," although that's not to say that there's not a contingency that are "all about partying, having a good time, and doing the least amount of studying possible." UConn is large enough to offer "a wide range of great majors," including programs at the "fantastic School of Business," the "well-known Neag

School of Education," and "a solid engineering school with a unique biomedical engineering major." In most areas, UConn "networks to provide students [with] millions of opportunities for students to expand in academics, self, and even careers," including "great internships." The school "does a great job of publicizing these opportunities, as well. We are a big icon of the state, and we keep our prestige." Thanks to the "UConn 2000" and "UConn Twenty-first Century" initiatives, the campus "is improving drastically with a $2.8-billion construction program designated to refurbishing (and adding onto) nearly every building on campus." As is the case at many large state schools, "The success of a UConn student's education is really a matter of personal responsibility. Introductory classes tend to be large and very impersonal, so it is up to the individual to do well." Bureaucratic tasks such as registration "can be a real pain,"and "the class enrollment process is very confusing and difficult to use," but overall, students speak warmly of their interactions with administrators. "While usually you have to go through a middleman to get to the administration, it is possible to voice your concerns," sums up a satisfied student.

Life

UConn is located in Storrs, which "is pretty much in the middle of nowhere." It seems especially so to students without cars, of whom there are quite a few (those with wheels can take advantage of Hartford and, occasionally, Boston). Some students feel this predicament "forces us to go out and party simply because there is nothing better to do." Others point out that "people go out a lot, yeah, and there's often alcohol involved, but there are many interesting and fun things to do here for those who don't like that kind of stuff. For instance, there are UConn Late Nights in Student Union at which students can just hang out, meet new people, play games, and have fun. There are also interesting lectures given by guest speakers at the Dodd Research Center, and movie nights and concerts. Since I've been here I've seen Dave Chappelle, Kanye West, NAS, Busta Rhymes, Lewis Black, and more perform." Those eager to join clubs and organizations will also find many to accommodate them here. And then there are the intercollegiate sports. "Basketball and football games are always a blast!" undergraduates assure us (the men's and women's hoops squads are both perennial national contenders).

Student Body

Students report that the typical UConn undergraduate "is a Connecticut resident"—but after that, "it is so hard to generalize a student population of nearly 15,000." Sure, "A lot of students are very similar in appearance" because "They are from in-state, and a lot of the same trends are prevalent. But there are plenty of students who do not follow this stereotype, and everyone fits in fine." Many feel that UConn is "a fantastic representation of the Northeast in all respects," especially the "actively involved, down-to-earth, [and] pretty friendly" student body. The party animal is a vanishing breed here (though the speed at which he or she is vanishing is open to debate); one student explains, "UConn has had its reputation as a drinking school for many years. And every year, the number of students who come here specifically to party and drink declines."

THE PRINCETON REVIEW SAYS

Admissions

Very important factors considered include: Class rank, academic GPA, rigor of secondary school record, standardized test scores, talent/ability. *Important factors considered include:* Application essay, recommendation(s), character/personal qualities, extracurricular activities, first generation, racial/ethnic status, volunteer work. *Other factors considered include:* Alumni/ae relation, geographical residence, level of applicant's interest, state residency, work experience. SAT or ACT required; ACT with Writing component required. High school diploma is required and GED is accepted. *Academic units required:* 4 English, 3 mathematics, 2 science, (2 science labs), 2 foreign language, 2 social studies, 3 academic electives. *Academic units recommended:* 3 foreign language.

Financial Aid

Students should submit: FAFSA. The Princeton Review suggests that all financial aid forms be submitted as soon as possible after January 1. *Need-based scholarships/grants offered:* Federal Pell, SEOG, ACG, SMART grants, TEACH grants, state scholarships/grants, private scholarships, the school's own gift aid. *Loan aid offered:* FFEL Subsidized Stafford, FFEL Unsubsidized Stafford, FFEL PLUS, Federal Perkins Applicants will be notified of awards on a rolling basis beginning 3/1. Off-campus job opportunities are good.

The Inside Word

Similar to most large, public institutions, UConn focuses primarily on quantifiable data such as grades, class rank, and test scores when making admit decisions. Connecticut residents who demonstrate significant academic achievement stand a good chance of being admitted, though the acceptance rate has decreased significantly over the past few years. Candidates are advised to apply early as the school has a rolling admissions policy and applications are considered on a space-available basis.

THE SCHOOL SAYS ". . ."

From The Admissions Office

"Thanks to a $2.8-billion construction program that is impacting every area of university life, the University of Connecticut provides students a high-quality and personalized education on one of the most attractive and technologically advanced college campuses in the United States. Applications are soaring nationally as an increasing number of high-achieving students from diverse backgrounds are making UConn their school of choice. From award-winning actors to governmental leaders, students enjoy an assortment of fascinating speakers each year, while performances by premier dance, jazz, and rock musicians enliven student life. Our beautiful New England campus is convenient and safe, and most students walk to class or ride university shuttle buses. State-of-the-art residential facilities include interest-based learning communities and honors housing as well as on-campus suite-style and apartment living. Championship Division I athletics have created fervor known as Huskymania among UConn students.

"Freshman applicants seeking admittance for Fall 2008 are required to submit official score reports from the new SAT or ACT with Writing component."

For even more information on this school, turn to page 530 of the "Stats" section.

UNIVERSITY OF DELAWARE

116 HULLIHEN HALL, NEWARK, DE 19716 • ADMISSIONS: 302-831-8123 • FAX: 302-831-6905
FINANCIAL AID: 302-831-8761 • E-MAIL: ADMISSIONS@UDEL.EDU • WEBSITE: WWW.UDEL.EDU/VIEWBOOK

RATINGS
Quality of Life: 75   Academic: 79   Admissions: 93   Financial Aid: 80

STUDENTS SAY ". . ."

Academics

The University of Delaware is in the midst of major institutional changes: A new president took the reins in July
2007, and a new class registration system was implement-
ed in 2006. Regarding the former, students are delighted.
Because the new president is the former Dean of the
Wharton School of Business, undergraduates are hopeful
that he will "do wonders for our prestige." Regarding the
latter, they couldn't be more displeased. "Registration is a

nightmare," making it "near impossible to get the exact schedule you want." Between those two extremes,
respondents to our survey describe a middle-of-the-road academic experience. Take professors, for example.
Some "are experts in their fields and are excellent at teaching," while others "are purely there for research," or
"have no clue how to teach a class." While most may be "genuinely interested in meeting with students and
talking about the class material," "They won't hunt you down" to make sure you're getting it. In other words,
there is a willingness to help "as long as the student takes the initiative." The same can be said of the administration. Students generally consider it to be of "average quality." It "can be a pain with some administrative
tasks (financial aid, anything that involves going to student services), but it's probably par for the course." In a
departure from their typically balanced assessments of UD, undergrads maintain an exceptionally positive view
of their school's "absolutely beautiful" campus and its "phenomenal" study abroad program.

Life

Student life at UD is characterized by the timeless effort "to balance partying and studying." During the week,
which runs from Sunday through Wednesday, "Life usually remains centered around studies." "You will find
the libraries [and] computer labs filled," and "Quiet hours are enforced." For many, working out is part of their
weekday work regimen: "A lot of people enjoy going to the gym." Come Thursday, however, "Those with good
schedules start going out." "Parties are what everyone looks for," especially house parties, and they are reportedly in abundant supply. Those who aren't into drinking but want to stay on campus can take advantage of "a
movie theater right on campus that show[s] fairly current movies for only $3." The SCPAB (Student-Centered
Programming Advisory Board) also "books some pretty good musicians and comedians." Many students "hang
out on Main Street," which "intersects campus" and includes "endless restaurants, the bookstores, a bowling
alley, and a movie theater." Because "the campus is close to Baltimore, DC, and Philly, road trips to museums
and other universities [are] always possible."

Student Body

Budding psychologists take note: Undergrads here report a collective "tunnel vision," and it's focused on "success." According to a junior, "Most of us come from upper-middle-class homes and won't be satisfied with anything less than what we already have." As a means to an end, "Academics are important." But only so much—
course work "won't stop anyone from going out," an international relations major reports. Geographically, students mainly hail "from the New Jersey, Delaware, Maryland, and Pennsylvania region." Sartorially, "People
care what they look like" and those "who have money flaunt it by what they wear." Temperamentally, people
are "relaxed, friendly, and generally very approachable." There are very few categories UD students can be sort-
ed into, but an in-state/out-of-state divide exists. Students "from Delaware are not considered as smart as those
not from Delaware because it is easier for them to get in," and there is also a widespread perception that those
from in-state "are not as well off financially."

THE PRINCETON REVIEW SAYS

Admissions

Very important factors considered include: Academic GPA, rigor of secondary school record, state residency. *Important factors considered include:* Application essay, recommendation(s), standardized test scores, character/personal qualities, extracurricular activities, talent/ability, volunteer work, work experience. *Other factors considered include:* Class rank, alumni/ae relation, first generation, geographical residence, interview, level of applicant's interest, racial/ethnic status, SAT Subject Tests recommended; SAT or ACT required; ACT with Writing component required. TOEFL required of all international applicants. High school diploma is required and GED is accepted. *Academic units required:* 4 English, 3 mathematics, 3 science, (2 science labs), 2 foreign language, 2 social studies, 2 history, 2 academic electives. *Academic units recommended:* 4 English, 4 mathematics, 4 science, (3 science labs), 4 foreign language, 2 social studies, 2 history, 2 academic electives.

Financial Aid

Students should submit: FAFSA. Regular filing deadline is 3/15. The Princeton Review suggests that all financial aid forms be submitted as soon as possible after January 1. *Need-based scholarships/grants offered:* Federal Pell, SEOG, state scholarships/grants, private scholarships, the school's own gift aid. *Loan aid offered:* Direct Subsidized Stafford, Direct Unsubsidized Stafford, Direct PLUS, Federal Perkins, Federal Nursing Applicants will be notified of awards on a rolling basis beginning 3/15. Federal Work-Study Program available. Institutional employment available.

Inside Word

It's rare that a flagship state university enrolls more students from out of state than in state, but the University of Delaware does. It is situated near many more-populous states on the East Coast which makes it a viable and desirable alternative for those states' residents. The school is sensitive to this fact, and in-state students will find admission to UD significantly easier than out-of-state students will.

THE SCHOOL SAYS ". . ."

From The Admissions Office

"The University of Delaware is a major national research university with a long-standing commitment to teaching and serving undergraduates. It is one of only a few universities in the country designated as a land-grant, sea-grant, urban-grant, and space-grant institution. The academic strength of this university is found in its highly selective honors program, nationally recognized Undergraduate Research Program, study abroad opportunities on all seven continents, and its successful alumni, including three Rhodes Scholars since 1998. The University of Delaware offers the wide range of majors and course offerings expected of a university but in spirit remains a small place where you can interact with your professors and feel at home. The beautiful green campus is ideally located at the very center of the East Coast 'megacity' that stretches from New York City to Washington, DC. All of these elements, combined with an endowment approaching $1 billion and a spirited Division I athletics program, make the University of Delaware a tremendous value.

"Freshman applicants for Fall 2008 are required to take the SAT Reasoning Test (or the ACT with the Writing section). If a student takes the new SAT more than once, the best individual scores from each test taken will be combined. Two SAT Subject Tests are recommended for applicants to the University Honors Program."

For even more information on this school, turn to page 531 of the "Stats" section.

THE UNIVERSITY OF MAINE

5713 CHADBOURNE HALL, ORONO, ME 04469-5713 • ADMISSIONS: 207-581-1561 • FAX: 207-581-1213
FINANCIAL AID: 207-581-1324 • E-MAIL: UM-ADMIT@MAINE.EDU • WEBSITE: WWW.UMAINE.EDU

RATINGS
Quality of Life: 74   **Academic:** 74   **Admissions:** 78   **Financial Aid:** 76

STUDENTS SAY ". . ."

Academics
The University of Maine boasts "a phenomenal engineering school" and notable programs in ecology, marine science, and forestry. "The campus is beautiful," says a sophomore, "melding scenery, history, and modernity." "The resources available through the library are quite staggering." There are also some "very fancy new labs." "It can be disheartening to see the beauty and grand scale of the engineering and science buildings, and then walk back to the buildings where most of your classes are held and see the lack of basic upkeep," gripes a history major. The academic atmosphere here is "challenging but not overwhelming." "Classes range in size from 20-200." "Professors can vary noticeably." There are "some rather dull professors." There are also plenty of "intelligent, kind, realistic human beings" on the faculty who are "quite flexible about meeting with and accommodating students." Some students say the top brass is "reasonable," "decently efficient," and "personable." Others see "layers of administration" and "terrible" management.

Life
Prepare for "bitter, arctic-like cold" and "a lot of snow" if you attend UMaine. Prepare for "unhealthy" food, too. "Ninety percent of it is deep fried or covered in a dairy-based something," protests a famished junior. On the bright side, campus life is active. There are "tons of things to do." "Musicians, comedians, and other artists" perform frequently. Sports keep many students busy. "Intramurals are great." The recreation center is "state of the art" and "hugely popular." Naturally, "hockey is crazy." "The campus is usually buzzing on game day," and the arena is "generally packed." Students are probably "too obsessed with the Red Sox" as well. "The party scene isn't too shabby." All in all, "consuming large quantities of cheap beer" is pretty common. There's a decent Greek presence, and, for some students, the frat houses are "the place to go on the weekends." There are also "house parties" and "a few local bars." More intimate get-togethers happen, too. "There's a tremendous amount of small-scale social drinking," notes a junior. The "rural community" of Orono "maintains that remote appeal" but it's "boring." "There is a ton of natural beauty around," though. "The extensive wilderness between campus and Canada" provides hiking, kayaking, and hunting opportunities galore. "Ventures to Sugarloaf are abundant."

Student Body
"Most of the students are Maine natives" or New Englanders. To put it diplomatically, the "minority percentage reflects that of the state." To put it bluntly, "this school is almost all white." "The typical student at UMaine is one who loves the outdoors, embraces the cold, is not too concerned with fashion, and lives in North Face or Patagonia clothes," reflects a sophomore. However, students report that you can find "every type of white person imaginable" on this campus. "There are tons of unique styles and groups that mix together." You've got "Carhartt-wearing, wood-chopping, straight-from-the-sticks, true-blue Mainers." There are "hockey rowdies" and "obnoxious frat boys." "There are a lot of hippies" and people who "care about the environment." There are "rare, wild-looking characters" and nontraditional students as well. The atmosphere is "relaxed" and "laid-back." "People are friendly up here." Some students tell us that "out-of-staters have a really hard time." Others disagree. "The in-state kids will totally accept you," promises a junior. "An out-of-stater can be distinguished from a Mainer fairly easily," explains a junior. "They can't drive, dress inappropriately for the weather, or wonder why school isn't cancelled during a blizzard. But we get used to them, and eventually, just maybe, by the time they graduate, part of them is Mainer, too."

THE PRINCETON REVIEW SAYS

Admissions

Very important factors considered include: Class rank, academic GPA, rigor of secondary school record, standardized test scores. *Important factors considered include:* Application essay, recommendation(s). *Other factors considered include:* Character/personal qualities, extracurricular activities, geographical residence, interview, talent/ability, volunteer work, work experience. SAT or ACT required; High school diploma is required and GED is accepted. *Academic units required:* 4 English, 3 mathematics, 2 science, (2 science labs), 2 foreign language, 2 social studies, 4 academic electives, 1 PE for education majors. *Academic units recommended:* 4 English, 4 mathematics, 4 science, (3 science labs), 2 foreign language, 3 social studies, 1 history, 4 academic electives, 1 PE for education majors.

Financial Aid

Students should submit: FAFSA. The Princeton Review suggests that all financial aid forms be submitted by March 1. *Need-based scholarships/grants offered:* Federal Pell, SEOG, state scholarships/grants, private scholarships, the school's own gift aid. *Loan aid offered:* FFEL Subsidized Stafford, FFEL Unsubsidized Stafford, FFEL PLUS, Federal Perkins, state loans Applicants will be notified of awards on a rolling basis beginning 3/15. Federal Work-Study Program available. Institutional employment available. Off-campus job opportunities are good.

The Inside Word

The University of Maine is much smaller than most public flagship universities, and its admissions process reflects this; it is a much more personal approach than most others use. Candidates are reviewed carefully for fit with their choice of college and major, and the committee will contact students regarding a second choice if the first doesn't seem to be a good match. Prepare your application as if you are applying to a private university.

THE SCHOOL SAYS "..."

From The Admissions Office

"The University of Maine offers you the best of both worlds—the excitement, breadth and depth that are available at a land grant, sea grant, research university with the personal attention and community feel of a smaller college. Five academic colleges and an Honors College offer you the chance to belong to a supportive academic community, while providing the specialization, resources and opportunities for research, internships and scholarly activity you would expect at a major university. Academics are a priority at UMaine; most programs hold the highest level of accreditation possible, setting UMaine apart nationally.

"And at UMaine there is always something to do—there are over 200 clubs and student organizations, lots of volunteer opportunities, an active student government, a new multi-million dollar student recreation center with an busy intramural schedule and Division I varsity athletics to keep you busy. A special First Year Residence Experience (FYRE) will help support your transitions to college—this unique program includes special activities and theme living communities. It is located between the new Student Recreation Center and the newly renovated Hilltop dining complex. Check out our web page to learn more—or better yet—come visit us in person and see the campus for yourself!"

For even more information on this school, turn to page 531 of the "Stats" section.

UNIVERSITY OF MAINE—FORT KENT

23 UNIVERSITY DRIVE, FORT KENT, ME 04743 • ADMISSIONS: 207-834-7500 • FAX: 207-834-7609
E-MAIL: UMFKADM@MAINE.MAINE.EDU • WEBSITE: WWW.UMFK.MAINE.EDU

RATINGS
Quality of Life: 90   Academic: 76   Admissions: 64   Financial Aid: 74

STUDENTS SAY "..."

Academics

"Learning while enjoying the Northern Maine living experience" is what the University of Maine at Fort Kent is all
about. In addition to its "rural location" that gives unlimited opportunities for all things "outdoorsy," UMFK
provides a "small," "close-knit academic community" that
features students and faculty "of varying ideas and
cultures." Standout programs include a "great education
program," a "huge and very successful" nursing program,
and a business program with faculty who have worked "in the field that they teach." Most professors here
"actually like teaching" and "are eager to help students and answer any questions." This translates to plenty of
"one-on-one attention." A junior explains, "The professors do not evoke apathy—you care enough to hate them
or love them. In hindsight, those teachers that you hate are really just pushing you to succeed—they get the best
you have to offer, better than even you knew you had." If a professor gets under a student's skin, Academic
Counseling offers "free tutoring services" and is reportedly "very helpful."

Life

UMFK "is a small campus in a small town" and undergrads "get to know other students quickly." "A large
number of students leave the dorms" in search of excitement, and as a result, "Life in the dorms tends to be a
little boring." Students "study hard and party hard," with many heading into town to "hang out at the local bar
and listen to music." However, those who heed the call of the wild take advantage of UMFK's natural environment. A senior explains: "We live in an area that is . . . rich in outdoor activities. We have skiing, snowshoeing,
skidoos, ice-fishing, hunting, hockey, and skating." In addition, "biathlon events" (skiing and marksmanship)
are held near campus "in a new center developed for these athletes." Fancy something under a roof? Try the "$1
movie night," aka Sunday, "at the local theater." Many people go to Canada "for fun," as it's just "a short jaunt
from the campus." Students truly appreciate the "different restaurants and different culture . . . just across the
border."

Student Body

Most undergrads at UMFK hail from the St. John Valley. The "predominantly Caucasian" student body features
"a few ethnic minorities," but the largest minority groups are Canadians and nontraditional students ("the typical off-campus student" is "a middle-aged, second-career-seeking adult.") Because "Most students are from
local towns," undergrads tell us, "they're very similar. Once in a while we get someone that is obviously from
'away' and they stand out a bit more than the usual person." However, "They fit in well despite their differences."
What qualities does the "usual person" possess? A significant number of students fall under the umbrella of "out-
doorsman." Many are also described as "friendly" and "easy to hang out with." Regardless of one's position in
or out of the mainstream, students say that everyone here "seems to have found their 'place' or group of friends
that they have things in common with."

Admissions

Very important factors considered include: Rigor of secondary school record. *Important factors considered include:* Application essay. *Other factors considered include:* Class rank, recommendation(s), standardized test scores, character/personal qualities, extracurricular activities, interview, talent/ability, volunteer work, work experience. SAT recommended; SAT or ACT recommended; TOEFL required of all international applicants. High school diploma is required and GED is accepted. *Academic units required:* 4 English, 2 mathematics, 2 science, (2 science labs), 2 social studies.

Financial Aid

Students should submit: FAFSA. The Princeton Review suggests that all financial aid forms be submitted as soon as possible after January 1. *Need-based scholarships/grants offered:* Federal Pell, SEOG, state scholarships/grants, private scholarships, the school's own gift aid. *Loan aid offered:* FFEL Subsidized Stafford, FFEL Unsubsidized Stafford, FFEL PLUS, Federal Perkins, state loans Federal Work-Study Program available. Institutional employment available. Off-campus job opportunities are good.

The Inside Word

Applying to colleges got you down? UMFK aims to make the admissions process—and, by extension, attendance—as user-friendly as possible. To that end, visitors to its website can browse scholarships based on their status (freshman, transfer, Maine resident, etc.) or scholarship administrator (UMFK, University of Maine system, third party, etc.). They can also search for scholarships by name.

For even more information on this school, turn to page 532 of the "Stats" section.

UNIVERSITY OF MARYLAND—BALTIMORE COUNTY

1000 HILLTOP CIRCLE, BALTIMORE, MD 21250 • ADMISSIONS: 410-455-2291 • FAX: 410-455-1094
FINANCIAL AID: 410-455-2387 • E-MAIL: ADMISSIONS@UMBC.EDU • WEBSITE: WWW.UMBC.EDU

RATINGS
Quality of Life: 69   Academic: 75   Admissions: 85   Financial Aid: 79

STUDENTS SAY ". . ."

Academics

Students agree that University of Maryland—Baltimore County "is a great school for scientific and information technology people" that boasts "very good programs in biology and mechanical engineering." Undergrads here find themselves immersed in "a science-y environment with some good departments and some not-so-good, but if

> **SURVEY SAYS . . .**
> *Great computer facilities*
> *Great library*
> *Diverse student types on campus*
> *Campus feels safe*

you find the right niche you'll do fantastically." Provided, that is, you can survive the "discouragingly difficult exams" and "very strict and/or too harsh grading of papers and exams" typically encountered in the school's trademark disciplines. Students of political science and government benefit from the fact that "The school is located near Baltimore and is a train ride from DC, which opens up internship and learning opportunities. (One political science professor takes kids to embassies related to the class he's teaching every semester; I've met the Iraqi and Indonesian ambassadors to the USA.)" Students in the liberal arts, on the other hand, complain that "the school has no concern for us. All money in the school only goes to the Science and Tech department," which explains the "amazing technology" undergrads brag about. "There's a lot of focus on research" at UMBC, so "The professors and the library are a great strength" here. Professors "are required to do research in their fields, so they are always up-to-date on that material that they teach. Even if they are mean or difficult, they all know what they are talking about." The library "has a great deal of research assistance and access to a consortium of millions of books."

Life

"For the most part, campus is quiet" because "people take studying seriously," and "during the weekend many students go home." Add the large commuter population and the school's proximity to some attractive social destinations (downtown Baltimore, DC, Columbia) and you begin to understand why "it may seem as if there's nothing going on" on the UMBC campus. Students assure us that, perceptions to the contrary, "someone is usually having a party or get together" on or around campus, most frequently in the apartment-style residences. Undergrads also enjoy about "200 clubs to join such as dancing, bike riding, football and even juggling" as well as "the game room or the Sports Zone if a person just wants to relax." Mostly, though, students find their fun away from school grounds. The school sponsors "shuttle buses to go to the clubs in Baltimore, so it's great that they promote safety in regard to drinking and driving." Fells Point, a bar district near Baltimore's Inner Harbor, is a popular destination, as is the University of Maryland's College Park campus. All in all, this is not a highly social campus; "Everybody really dances to his own beat here," we're told.

Student Body

"There is no typical student" on the "very diverse" UMBC campus. "Everyone varies, from preppy cheerleaders and jocks to antisocial art nerds to normal human beings to religious fanatics to animal rights activists to overachievers to underachievers to foreigners to truly gifted kids to how-did-they-pass-their-SATs kids to druggies to good people and everything in between." The campus is also "full of nontraditional students who are married/engaged, have kids, and work." The Asian population is so large at UMBC that "Some folks describe UMBC as 'U Must Be Chinese,' but the majority are Caucasians, with minority Black/African-Americans, and a noticeable number of Indian/Pakistani ethnic groups." The student body tends to form cliques along lines of background and academic field; this is hardly unusual for a predominantly commuter campus (only about one-third of students live on campus, over half of whom are freshmen).

Admissions

Very important factors considered include: Academic GPA, rigor of secondary school record, standardized test scores. *Important factors considered include:* Application essay, recommendation(s). *Other factors considered include:* Class rank, extracurricular activities, talent/ability, volunteer work, SAT required; SAT or ACT required; ACT required; ACT with Writing component recommended. TOEFL required of all international applicants. High school diploma is required and GED is accepted. *Academic units required:* 4 English, 3 mathematics, 3 science, 2 foreign language, 3 Social Studies & History. *Academic units recommended:* 4 science.

Financial Aid

Students should submit: FAFSA. The Princeton Review suggests that all financial aid forms be submitted as soon as possible after January 1. *Need-based scholarships/grants offered:* Federal Pell, SEOG, state scholarships/grants, private scholarships, the school's own gift aid. *Loan aid offered:* FFEL Subsidized Stafford, FFEL Unsubsidized Stafford, FFEL PLUS, Federal Perkins Applicants will be notified of awards on a rolling basis beginning 4/1. Federal Work-Study Program available. Institutional employment available. Off-campus job opportunities are excellent.

The Inside Word

UMBC is an Honors College within the University of Maryland system; after the College Park campus, it is perhaps the most prestigious state-run undergraduate institution in Maryland. Selectivity is somewhat hampered by the school's inability to accommodate residents; about 70 percent of students commute. Even so, the densely populated Baltimore metropolitan area gives the school plenty of top-flight candidates to choose from. Your high school transcript must show a challenging curriculum (and success in your most demanding courses) if you hope to attend this school.

THE SCHOOL SAYS ". . ."

From The Admissions Office

"When it comes to universities, a midsized school can be just right. Some students want the resources of a large community. Others are looking for the attention found at a smaller one. With an undergraduate population of over 9,000, UMBC can offer the best of both. There are always new people to meet and things to do—from Division I sports to more than 170 student clubs. As a research university, we offer an abundance of programs, technology, and opportunities for hands-on experiences. Yet we are small enough that students don't get lost in the shuffle. More than 80 percent of our classes have fewer than 40 students. Among public research universities, UMBC is recognized for its success in placing students in the most competitive graduate programs and careers. Of course, much of the success of UMBC has to do with the students themselves—highly motivated students who get involved in their education.

"Freshman applicants for Fall 2008 are strongly encouraged to take the new SAT or ACT; however, the Admissions Committee will consider scores from the old SAT or ACT if no new scores are available."

For even more information on this school, turn to page 532 of the "Stats" section.

UNIVERSITY OF MARYLAND—COLLEGE PARK

MITCHELL BUILDING, COLLEGE PARK, MD 20742-5235 • ADMISSIONS: 301-314-8385 • FAX: 301-314-9693
FINANCIAL AID: 301-314-9000 • E-MAIL: UM-ADMIT@UGA.UMD.EDU • WEBSITE: WWW.MARYLAND.EDU

RATINGS

Quality of Life: 69   **Academic:** 75   **Admissions:** 94   **Financial Aid:** 68

STUDENTS SAY "..."

Academics

The University of Maryland—College Park is a major research institution and students see this as a mixed blessing. Undergrads gain exposure to world-class scholars doing cutting-edge work in their fields. Unfortunately, some of those same professors would rather be doing their research or teaching graduate students instead of delivering an introductory lecture to freshmen. One student warns, "These professors are paid to research and told they have to teach. Many of them don't have teaching degrees and obviously have no idea how to teach." While the problem is most pronounced in the sciences and mathematics, it is by no means universal; even in the aforementioned areas, students report some "amazing" teachers among the duds. Still, most here note that, at UMD, "You are responsible for your own education. No one will hold your hand as they did in high school." Some believe this "prepares you for the real world. You are a number, but that make[s] you try harder to stand out." Those hoping for a warmer and fuzzier education need not abandon hope, provided they can gain admission to the "living-learning programs—i.e., Honors, College Park Scholars, [and] Civicus," which all "provide opportunities for smaller classes and meeting people." College Park's many outstanding programs include the "amazing journalism program" and strong departments in education, engineering, political science, criminology, and business.

> **SURVEY SAYS . . .**
> *Great library*
> *Athletic facilities are great*
> *Diverse student types on campus*
> *Everyone loves the Terrapins*
> *Student publications are popular*
> *Lots of beer drinking*

Life

The Big Three of campus life at UMD are "Greek life," "bars and/or house parties," and "football games"—both "tailgating and attending." But with "tons of things to do" here, there's more than just "a lot of parties" at College Park. According to one student, the campus "is like its own little town. We have a movie theater, tons of dorms, a huge gym, athletic fields, convenience stores, many restaurants, a bowling alley—all on campus!" UMD students also enjoy hundreds of student groups and an active intramural scene. While a student could easily fill his or her hours with campus activities, the more adventurous take frequent advantage of the school's proximity to Washington, DC, which students confirm "is not a boring city—it has a fantastic nightlife and a great subway/metro system. It's easy to get around." The city of Baltimore is also easily reached by rail. It's not surprising that many here feel that UMD's "location is a big strength."

Student Body

"The great thing about a big public university is that there's no such thing as the typical student," explains a sophomore. "Lots of Jews, Catholics, African Americans, Muslims—it's a very nice melting pot," confirms a junior. UMD's College Park campus also hosts "a good mix of returning [i.e., nontraditional] students" who "seem to add to the environment." Undergrads here report that "it's common to see students of every race and background in a discussion class." When classes are finished, however, "Many students socialize and interact" only "within their 'clique,' whether it be religious, cultural, etc." While it is impossible to define a typical student on a campus this large, undergrads spot the following trends: Maryland students usually have "tons of Maryland shirts, sweatpants, and hoodies," "were in the top quarter of their high school," and "take classes seriously," but also "love to support the football and basketball teams. They party pretty hard on weekends, but buckle down when Sunday comes."

THE PRINCETON REVIEW SAYS

Admissions

Very important factors considered include: Academic GPA, rigor of secondary school record, standardized test scores. *Important factors considered include:* Class rank, application essay, recommendation(s), first generation, state residency, talent/ability. *Other factors considered include:* Alumni/ae relation, character/personal qualities, extracurricular activities, geographical residence, racial/ethnic status, volunteer work, work experience. SAT or ACT required; ACT with Writing component required. TOEFL required of all international applicants. High school diploma is required and GED is accepted. *Academic units required:* 4 English, 3 mathematics, 3 science, (2 science labs), 2 foreign language, 3 social studies. *Academic units recommended:* 4 mathematics.

Financial Aid

Students should submit: FAFSA. The Princeton Review suggests that all financial aid forms be submitted as soon as possible after January 1. *Need-based scholarships/grants offered:* Federal Pell, SEOG, state scholarships/grants, private scholarships, the school's own gift aid. *Loan aid offered:* FFEL Subsidized Stafford, FFEL Unsubsidized Stafford, FFEL PLUS, Federal Perkins Applicants will be notified of awards on a rolling basis beginning 4/1. Federal Work-Study Program available. Institutional employment available. Off-campus job opportunities are good.

The Inside Word

Many state schools make admissions decisions based on little more than the high school transcript and standardized test scores. University of Maryland is not one of these schools; the College Park Admissions Office also considers (in descending order of importance): essay, extracurricular activities, counselor/teacher recommendations, and responses to its short-answer questions. Don't give any of these application components short shrift; admissions are competitive, and each needs to be strong in order for you to have a decent shot.

THE SCHOOL SAYS ". . ."

From The Admissions Office

"Commitment to excellence, to diversity, to learning—these are the hallmarks of a Maryland education. As the state's flagship campus and one of the nation's leading public universities, Maryland offers students and faculty the opportunity to come together to explore and create knowledge, to debate and discover our similarities and our differences, and to serve as a model of intellectual and cultural excellence for the state and the nation's capital. With leading programs in engineering, business, journalism, architecture, and the sciences, the university offers an outstanding educational value."

For even more information on this school, turn to page 533 of the "Stats" section.

UNIVERSITY OF MASSACHUSETTS—AMHERST

UNIVERSITY ADMISSIONS CENTER, AMHERST, MA 01003 • ADMISSIONS: 413-545-0222
FAX: 413-545-4312 • FINANCIAL AID: 413-545-0801 • E-MAIL: MAIL@ADMISSIONS.UMASS.EDU • WEBSITE: WWW.UMASS.EDU

RATINGS
Quality of Life: 62   **Academic:** 70   **Admissions:** 83   **Financial Aid:** 72

STUDENTS SAY ". . ."

Academics

It's all about "finding out where you fit in" at the large University of Massachusetts Amherst, where students say the experience is "all what you make of it: If you want to party, there is one available to you almost every night. However, it is not difficult to get your work done and be successful." A pre-law student notes, "[You] can just slide by, [but] academics are challenging if [you] wants to get all A's or [are] taking honors courses." Academics are especially demanding in the engineering program, the hard sciences, the sports management program ("one of the oldest and best in the country"), and at the Isenberg School of Management.

As at many big schools, "It is easy to not go to class because they are so large, although many teachers now use PRS [a handheld wireless interactive remote unit] which quizzes you and is a method of [taking] attendance during each class." Unlike many major research institutions, UMass Amherst has a surprising number of professors who "show a passion for teaching. I have yet to see a professor who just teaches for money," a sports management major reports. By all accounts, "More than half of the professors are awesome." Students agree that "UMass Amherst has countless opportunities for one to get involved and improve his or her leadership and responsibilities."

Life

"There is so much to do on campus here that you rarely have to leave the school to find something," students report, pointing out that, in addition to attending one of the school's ubiquitous sporting events, "You can go ice skating on campus, go to a play, see bands play, see a movie, etc." Are you sitting down? "Most of these things are also free of charge, or available for a reduced fee." When the weather permits, "Numerous people are outside doing some sort of activity, whether it's playing catch, playing a sport with a bunch of people, or just laying out in the sun. In the Southwest Residential area, there is a horseshoe that people call Southwest Beach because on nice days it is packed with hundreds of people." If you're into parties, "There is something going on every night of the week somewhere." However, "It is more than possible to stay in on a Friday night, do your laundry, and watch a movie with friends. Parties are available, but not required." To clarify: "Drinking is big here, but not totally out of control like some say. Off campus is an entirely different concept. The townhouses and off-campus apartments have been known to hold parties of over 1,200 people. Those can be a little intense." Hometown Amherst provides "great restaurants and shows." Northampton and Holyoke, both close by, are "good place[s] to go shopping."

Student Body

"There is no such thing as a typical student at UMass Amherst." An undergraduate population of over 20,000 makes that impossible; however, students do seem to fall into a few readily identified groups. There are "plenty of students who are here strictly for academics," "people who are here for the party scene," and "a lot of people who came here for academics but fell into the party scene." Most learn to balance fun and work; those who don't exit long before graduation. Students also "tend to fit the mold of their residence," undergrads tell us. One student writes, "Southwest houses students of mainstream culture. Students there can be seen wearing everything from UMass—Amherst sweats to couture. Students in Central (especially Upper Central) tend to be the 'hippie' or 'scene' type kid[s]. Northeast houses . . . the more reserved types. Orchard Hill typically houses the more quiet types as well. . . . The kids in Sylvan are those who couldn't get into their first-choice dorm and "spend their time . . . wishing that they lived somewhere else."

THE PRINCETON REVIEW SAYS

Admissions

Very important factors considered include: Academic GPA, rigor of secondary school record. *Important factors considered include:* Class rank, standardized test scores. *Other factors considered include:* Application essay, recommendation(s), character/personal qualities, extracurricular activities, first generation, geographical residence, level of applicant's interest, state residency, talent/ability, volunteer work, work experience. SAT or ACT required. TOEFL required of all international applicants. High school diploma is required and GED is accepted. *Academic units required:* 4 English, 3 mathematics, 3 science, (2 science labs), 2 foreign language, 2 social studies, 2 academic electives.

Financial Aid

Students should submit: FAFSA. The Princeton Review suggests that all financial aid forms be submitted as soon as possible after January 1. *Need-based scholarships/grants offered:* Federal Pell, SEOG, ACG, SMART, state scholarships/grants, private scholarships, the school's own gift aid. *Loan aid offered:* Direct Subsidized Stafford, Direct Unsubsidized Stafford, Direct PLUS, Federal Perkins, state loans. Applicants will be notified of awards on a rolling basis beginning 4/1. Federal Work-Study Program available. Institutional employment available.

The Inside Word

University of Massachusetts Amherst requires applicants to identify a first-choice and a second-choice major; admissions standards are tougher in the school's most prestigious programs (such as engineering, business, communications and journalism, economics, computer science, and sports management). It is possible to be admitted for your second-choice major but not your first; it is also possible to be admitted as an "undeclared" student if you fail to gain admission via your chosen majors. You can transfer into either major later, although doing so will require you to excel in your freshman and sophomore classes.

THE SCHOOL SAYS ". . ."

From The Admissions Office

"The University of Massachusetts Amherst is the largest public university in New England, offering its students an almost limitless variety of academic programs and activities. Over 85 majors are offered, including a unique program called Bachelor's Degree with Individual Concentration (BDIC) in which students create their own program of study. (If you are a legal resident of Connecticut, Maine, New Hampshire, Rhode Island or Vermont, and the major you want at UMass Amherst is not available at your public college, you may qualify for reduced tuition through the New England Regional Student Program.)The outstanding full-time faculty of over 1,100 is the best in their fields and they take teaching seriously. Students can take courses through the honors program and sample classes at nearby Amherst, Hampshire, Mount Holyoke, and Smith Colleges at no extra charge. First-year students participate in the Residential First-Year Year Experience with opportunities to explore every possible interest through residential life. The extensive library system is the largest at any public institution in the Northeast. The Center for Student Development brings together more than 200 clubs and organizations, fraternities and sororities, multicultural and religious centers. The campus completes in NCAA Division I sports for men and women, with teams winning national recognition. Award-winning student-operated businesses, the largest college daily newspaper in the region, and an active student government provide hands-on experience. About 5,000 students a year participate in the intramural sports program. The picturesque New England Town of Amherst offers shopping and dining, and the ski slopes of western Massachusetts and southern Vermont are close by. SAT or ACT scores are required for admission to the university. The school takes a holistic view of the student's application package, and considers these scores as only part of the evaluation criteria. Additionally, any Advanced Placement, Honors, and SAT Subject Test scores are considered when reviewing each applicant. Increased applications in recent years have made admission more selective. "

For even more information on this school, turn to page 533 of the "Stats" section.

UNIVERSITY OF MASSACHUSETTS—BOSTON

100 MORRISSEY BOULEVARD, BOSTON, MA 02125-3393 • ADMISSIONS: 617-287-6000 • FAX: 617-287-5999
E-MAIL: ENROLLMENT.INFO@UMB.EDU • WEBSITE: WWW.UMB.EDU

RATINGS
Quality of Life: 72   **Academic:** 78   **Admissions:** 60*   **Financial Aid:** 87

STUDENTS SAY "..."

Academics

The University of Massachusetts—Boston is an "afford-able" and "challenging" "commuter school" "that cares about its students" and provides "a public education to all persons regardless of their walk of life." A "wide variety" of exemplary majors includes a "great nursing program." "At UMass—Boston you get what you put in," explains a

sophomore. "If you put in the effort to get an Ivy League education you can get that, but if you only put in the effort to get a community college education, that's what you'll come away with." The faculty is "accomplished" and "very accessible outside of class." A few "awful" professors "can't teach," but most professors "will blow your mind with their intensity, passion, and commitment to your success." Administratively, "There are a lot of obnoxious bureaucratic obstacles." Class schedules are often "lousy." "If you want more guidance, you need to seek it out," warns a junior. "Otherwise, no one is going to help you." "Things generally sort themselves out," concludes another student. "There is a lot of red tape, but the academics are really great."

Life

UMass—Boston is "mostly" a "commuter campus." The "urban" campus has "a beautiful location," being "pre-cariously close to Boston Harbor." Students lament "the parking situation" and wish that "The buildings could be improved and renovated to look as nice as the Campus Center." Following that, the Campus Center "is a beau-tiful place with great food and places to hang out and study." "There are no residence halls" but "A lot of students live in an apartment complex called Harbor Point, next door to the school." There are "tons" of "fun and unique" organizations and activities here, though since "There are no dorms," "Most of the socializing happens off campus." "Students meet for classes without much interaction after classes." "UMB doesn't have a true stu-dent life," explains a senior. "It is quite possible to go through the day without interacting with other students, and to go through your college career without actually feeling that you are a part of the UMB community." "It's hard to meet people," agrees a nursing major. "They do their time and leave." That said, "There are parties" and "There is always something fun to do" in "the great and famous student city of Boston."

Student Body

"UMass—Boston is the epitome of a diverse school," one student says. "Students come from suburbs and inner-city high schools with a huge range of perspectives." "Everyone brings with them unique experiences," says a junior, "just like the real world." "There are many international students" and "a significant number of older, adult, and elderly students . . . attend the school regularly between full-time and part-time jobs." "No student at the school is the same," so much so that "the only thing most students have in common is that they are from Massachusetts." UMass—Boston is full of "uniquely determined," "individualistic" "career-seeking individu-als." "We are, bar none, the hardest-working college students on the planet," boldly declares a sophomore. "We have to be, because we want to be lawyers, doctors, and leaders." "Except we have to do that and hold down full-time jobs," "raise families," and "run businesses."

THE PRINCETON REVIEW SAYS

Admissions

Very important factors considered include: Academic GPA, rigor of secondary school record, standardized test scores, character/personal qualities. *Important factors considered include:* Application essay, recommendation(s). *Other factors considered include:* Extracurricular activities, first generation, interview, level of applicant's interest, talent/ability, volunteer work, work experience. SAT required; SAT or ACT required; ACT required; TOEFL required of all international applicants. High school diploma is required and GED is accepted. *Academic units required:* 4 English, 3 mathematics, 3 science, (2 science labs), 2 foreign language, 1 social studies, 1 history, 2 academic electives.

Financial Aid

Students should submit: FAFSA. The Princeton Review suggests that all financial aid forms be submitted as soon as possible after January 1. *Need-based scholarships/grants offered:* Federal Pell, SEOG, state scholarships/grants, private scholarships, the school's own gift aid, Federal Nursing Scholarships. *Loan aid offered:* Direct Subsidized Stafford, Direct Unsubsidized Stafford, Direct PLUS, Federal Perkins Applicants will be notified of awards on a rolling basis beginning 3/21. Off-campus job opportunities are excellent.

The Inside Word

Unless you want to be a part of the honors program, admission to UMass—Boston is not terribly difficult. Average high school grades and SAT or ACT scores are usually sufficient (in some cases a GED can be too). If you're an older student, you don't have to submit standardized test scores. Though for all applicants the 500-word essay rings true and plays a vital role in your acceptance, so get typing!

THE SCHOOL SAYS " . . ."

From The Admissions Office

"The best advice we give out to any student considering us is simple: Just come see us for yourself. Visit us either for one of our year-round campus tours and info sessions. Or better yet, join us along with your friends and family for our annual fall Open House for prospective students, held on a Saturday at the end of every October—it's fun, informative, and you'll come away from it with a good idea of what life's like at UMass—Boston.

"No matter when you decide to visit the campus, you'll get the opportunity to talk with one of our Admissions Counselors and current students about UMass—Boston's academic programs, students services, student activities, and the application and financial aid process. Also, you'll get to check out the fitness center, library, computer labs, art gallery, sport facilities, bookstore, game room, food court, cafés, and classrooms. In addition, tours of the two apartment communities—located within steps of campus, where many students opt to live—can also be arranged.

"We also offer monthly Showcase Saturdays during most of the academic year for those who would prefer to visit us on the weekend for an in-depth information session and tour.

"For more about the admissions process, and other aspects of UMass—Boston—including the latest on campus visit options—please go to www.umb.edu/admissions or call 617-287-6000."

For even more information on this school, turn to page 534 of the "Stats" section.

UNIVERSITY OF NEW HAMPSHIRE

FOUR GARRISON AVENUE, DURHAM, NH 03824 • ADMISSIONS: 603-862-1360 • FAX: 603-862-0077
FINANCIAL AID: 603-862-3600 • E-MAIL: ADMISSIONS@UNH.EDU • WEBSITE: WWW.UNH.EDU

RATINGS
Quality of Life: 67   **Academic:** 72   **Admissions:** 81   **Financial Aid:** 74

STUDENTS SAY "..."

Academics

The benefits of going to a large, well-established state school such as the University of New Hampshire are exactly what one expects—its low in-state tuition, firmly established reputation, and place in the system allows it to offer "many resources to help students out in life." Located in tiny, beautiful Durham, the school "emphasizes research in every field, including non-science fields," and a lot of importance is placed "on the outdoors and the environment." The small town really fosters "lots of school spirit," and the laid-back denizens of UNH make it known that "having a good time" is a priority in their lives: "Weekends are for the Warriors."

Most professors "truly care" about the students' learning so that "you never feel like a number at the school but rather a respected student," and they "will get down and dirty when it comes to experiencing what they're teaching first-hand." Though there are definitely complaints that some can be "subpar," a student "just needs to posses the initiative to go to their office hours" and they're more than willing to help. Some of the general education classes "are HUGE," and TA's can be difficult to understand, but for the most part, students report that they've had a "good experience" and their academic career has been "very successful." The Honors program is particularly challenging (in a very positive way) and offers "great seminar/inquiry classes that have about fifteen students so you can really get in depth." Students universally pan the administration, claiming it "is a massive bureaucracy that gets little done," partially due to poor communication, or "the left hand has no idea what the right hand is doing." "The school is way more challenging than I thought it would be because the administration makes things harder than they need to be," says a sophomore.

> **SURVEY SAYS...**
> *Great library*
> *Athletic facilities are great*
> *Frats and sororities dominate*
> *social scene*
> *Lots of beer drinking*
> *Hard liquor is popular*

Life

Located in a town just "fifteen minutes to the beach, one hour to the mountains, and one hour to Boston," the world is a Wildcat's oyster. Partying is big here, and the weekends are crazy; "Everyone goes out pretty much every Thursday, Friday, and Saturday night." The small number of bars in town "makes the age limit pretty well enforced," so there are few underage drinkers at the bars, which means they "go out to the frats or off-campus apartments." After a hard night out, "there are many late night convenience stores and food places to go to." In fact, it can be "difficult to find activities to do on the weekend that don't involve drinking," though UNH does a good job of bringing in "popular comedians, musicians, bands, political figures, etc.," and the school has tons of "amazing" a capella groups, so there is "almost always something to go see." Sports are also big here: "We love our hockey and football," says a student. Though there's a pretty big housing crunch, the oft-used athletic and recreational facilities here are both convenient and excellent, and since everything on this "beautiful" campus is only about ten minutes away, "you walk pretty much everywhere," though public transportation and school-provided buses run often. Students do a lot of socializing over meals at the "eight cafes or in any of the three dining halls"

Student Body

This being New Hampshire, people are "very politically and socially aware." Students here are mostly middle class and hail from New England (especially from New Hampshire, naturally), and a main point of contention among students is that there "is not a lot of ethnic/racial diversity," though the school is working on it. The size of UNH means that "even the most unique individual will find a group of friends if they look," and even the most atypical students "fit in perfectly well." Most of these "laid-back" and "easy to get along with" Wildcats party, and it can be "hard to find one that doesn't." "EVERYONE skis or snowboards," and in the cold weather "Uggs and North Face fleece jackets abound."The Princeton Review Says

THE PRINCETON REVIEW SAYS

Admissions

Very important factors considered include: Class rank, academic GPA, rigor of secondary school record. *Important factors considered include:* Recommendation(s). *Other factors considered include:* Application essay, standardized test scores, alumni/ae relation, character/personal qualities, extracurricular activities, first generation, geographical residence, racial/ethnic status, state residency, talent/ability, volunteer work, work experience. SAT or ACT required; ACT with Writing component required. TOEFL required of all international applicants. High school diploma is required and GED is accepted. *Academic units required:* 4 English, 3 mathematics, 3 science, (2 science labs), 2 foreign language, 3 social studies. *Academic units recommended:* 4 English, 4 mathematics, 4 science, (3 science labs), 3 foreign language, 3 social studies, 1 academic elective.

Financial Aid

Students should submit: FAFSA. Regular filing deadline is 2/1. The Princeton Review suggests that all financial aid forms be submitted as soon as possible after January 1. *Need-based scholarships/grants offered:* Federal Pell, SEOG, state scholarships/grants, private scholarships, the school's own gift aid, Veterans Educational Benefits. *Loan aid offered:* FFEL Subsidized Stafford, FFEL Unsubsidized Stafford, FFEL PLUS, Federal Perkins, state loans, college/university loans from institutional funds. Applicants will be notified of awards on a rolling basis beginning 3/1. Federal Work-Study Program available. Institutional employment available. Off-campus job opportunities are excellent.

The Inside Word

New Hampshire's emphasis on academic accomplishment in the admissions process makes it clear that the Admissions Committee is looking for students who have taken high school seriously. Standardized tests take as much of a backseat here as is possible at a large public university.

THE SCHOOL SAYS ". . ."

From The Admissions Office

"The University of New Hampshire is an institution best defined by the students who take advantage of its opportunities. Enrolled students who are willing to engage in a high quality academic community in some meaningful way, who have a genuine interest in discovering or developing new ideas, and who believe in each person's obligation to improve the community they live in typify the most successful students at UNH. Undergraduate students practice these three basic values in a variety of ways: by undertaking their own, independent research projects, by collaborating in faculty research, and by participating in study abroad, residential communities, community service, and other cultural programs.

"University of New Hampshire will require all high school graduates to submit results from the new SAT or the ACT (with the Writing component). The Writing portions will not be used for admissions decisions during the first 2–3 admissions cycles. Students graduating from high school prior to 2006 can submit results from the 'old' SAT or ACT. The UNH admissions process does not require SAT Subject tests."

For even more information on this school, turn to page 534 of the "Stats" section.

UNIVERSITY OF PENNSYLVANIA

ONE COLLEGE HALL, PHILADELPHIA, PA 19104 • ADMISSIONS: 215-898-7507 • FAX: 215-898-9670
FINANCIAL AID: 215-898-1988 • E-MAIL: INFO@ADMISSIONS.UGAO.UPENN.EDU • WEBSITE: WWW.UPENN.EDU

RATINGS
Quality of Life: 88   **Academic:** 89   **Admissions:** 99   **Financial Aid:** 96

STUDENTS SAY "..."

Academics

At the University of Pennsylvania, everyone shares an intellectual curiosity and top-notch resources, but doesn't "buy into the stigma of being an Ivy League school." Still, no one turns down the opportunity to rave about the school's strong academic reputation or the large alumni network, and students here are also "very passionate about what they do outside the classroom" and the opportunities presented to them through attending UPenn. The university is composed of four undergraduate schools (and "a library for pretty much any topic"), and students tend to focus on what they'll do with their degree pretty early on. Wharton, UPenn's "highly competitive undergraduate business school," creates a "tremendous pre-professional atmosphere" that keeps students competitive and somewhat stressed with their studies during the week, and this "career-oriented" attitude spills over into other factions of the university, leaving some desiring more grounds for creativity and less climbing over each other. "It's when individuals' grades are on the line when the claws come out," says a student.

> **SURVEY SAYS...**
> *Great library*
> *Athletic facilities are great*
> *Great off-campus food*
> *Students are happy*
> *Student publications are popular*
> *Lots of beer drinking*
> *Hard liquor is popular*

Professors can "sometimes seem to be caught up more in their research than their classes," but "there are very few other institutions where you can take every one of your classes with a professor who is setting the bar for research in his or her field." If you are willing to put in the time and effort, your professors "will be happy to reciprocate." In general, the instructors here are "very challenging academically," and one student says that "some of them have been excellent, but all of them have at least been good." The administration is "very professional and efficient" and "truly interested in students' well being." "Academically, I have access to opportunities unparalleled elsewhere," says a student.

Life

Penn kids don't mind getting into intellectual conversations over dinner, but "partying is a much higher priority here than it is at other Ivy League schools." Many students schedule their classes so as to not have class on Fridays, making the weekend "officially" start on Thursday night, and frat parties and Center City bars and clubs are popular destinations. However, when it comes down to midterms and finals, "people get really serious and...buckle down and study." Between weekend jaunts to New York and Philadelphia itself ("a city large enough to answer the needs of any type of person"), students have plenty of access to restaurants, shopping, concerts, and sports games, as well as plain old "hanging out with hallmates playing Mario Kart." The school provides plenty of guest speakers, cultural events, clubs, and organizations for students to channel their energies, and seniors can even attend "Feb Club" in the month of February, which is essentially an event every night. It's a busy life at UPenn, and "people are constantly trying to think about how they can balance getting good grades academically and their weekend plans."

Student Body

This "determined" bunch is very career-oriented, "take their classes pretty seriously," leans to the left, and "personality-wise tends to be Type A." "There is always someone smarter than you are," says a Chemical Biomolecular Engineering major. Everyone has "a strong sense of personal style and his or her own credo," but no group deviates too far from the more mainstream stereotypes, and there's a definite lack of "emos" and hippies. There's "the Career-driven Wharton kid who will stab you in the back to get your interview slot" and "the Nursing kid who's practically non-existent," but on the whole, there is "tremendous school diversity," and whatever kind of person you are, "you will find a group of people like you."

THE PRINCETON REVIEW SAYS

Admissions

Very important factors considered include: Rigor of secondary school record, Academic GPA, Recommendation(s), Talent/ability, Character/personal qualities. *Important factors considered include:* Standardized test scores, Application Essay, Extracurricular activities, First Generation. *Other factors considered include:* Class rank, Interview, Alumni/ae relation, Geographical residence, Racial/ethnic status. *Academic units recommended:*

Financial Aid

The Princeton Review suggests that all financial aid forms be submitted as soon as possible after January 1. Federal Work-Study Program available. Institutional employment available. Off-campus job opportunities are excellent.

The Inside Word

After a small decline four cycles ago, applications are once again climbing at Penn—the fifth increase in 6 years. The competition in the applicant pool is formidable. Applicants can safely assume that they need to be one of the strongest students in their graduating class in order to be successful.

THE SCHOOL SAYS ". . ."

From The Admissions Office

"The nation's first university, the University of Pennsylvania, had its beginnings in 1740, some 36 years before Thomas Jefferson, Benjamin Franklin (Penn's founder), and their fellow revolutionaries went public in Philadelphia with incendiary notions about life, liberty and the pursuit of happiness. Today, Penn continues in the spirit of the Founding Fathers, developing the intellectual, discussion-oriented seminars that comprise the majority of our course offerings, shaping innovative new courses of study, and allowing a remarkable degree of academic flexibility to its undergraduate students.

"Penn is situated on a green, tree-lined, 260-acre urban campus, four blocks west of the Schuylkill River in Philadelphia. The broad lawns that connect Penn's stately halls embody a philosophy of academic freedom within our undergraduate schools. Newly developed interdisciplinary programs fusing classical disciplines with practical, professional options enable Penn to define cutting-edge academia in and out of the classroom. Students are encouraged to partake in study and research that may extend into many of the graduate and professional schools. As part of our College House system, Penn's Faculty Masters engage students in academic and civic experience while leading residential programs that promote an environment where living and learning intersect around the clock.

"Penn students are part of a dynamic community that includes a traditional campus, a lively neighborhood, and a city rich in culture and diversity. Whether your interests include artistic performance, community involvement, student government, athletics, fraternities and sororities, or cultural and religious organizations, you'll find many different options. Most importantly, students at Penn find that their lives in and out of the classroom compliment each other and are full, interesting and busy. We invite you to visit Penn in Philadelphia. You'll enjoy the revolutionary spirit of the campus and city.

"Penn requires either the new SAT plus two SAT Subject Tests (in different fields) or the ACT. Scores from older versions of the SAT (pre-March 2005 version) and the ACT are acceptable. For the old SAT, scores must be submitted with the results of three SAT Subject Tests, one of which must be the writing test."

For even more information on this school, turn to page 535 of the "Stats" section.

UNIVERSITY OF PITTSBURGH—BRADFORD

OFFICE OF ADMISSIONS—HANLEY LIBRARY, 300 CAMPUS DRIVE, BRADFORD, PA 16701 • ADMISSIONS: 814-362-7555 • FAX: 814-362-7578
E-MAIL: ADMISSIONS@WWW.UPB.PITT.EDU • WEBSITE: WWW.UPB.PITT.EDU

RATINGS
Quality of Life: 75   **Academic:** 74   **Admissions:** 71   **Financial Aid:** 77

STUDENTS SAY "..."

Academics

"Academics go way beyond the classroom," at the University of Pittsburgh—Bradford. Professors at this "student-oriented" public school are "willing to stay after class, adjust office hours, and give out home and cell phone numbers." A senior enthuses, "The professors here are your friends. They help you in any way they can." Pitt—Bradford is "well organized" too; one student explains, "My advisor has gone above the call of duty to work with me and my schedule to accomplish my goals." Even the administration is described as "extremely accessible" and the "deans know literally every student on campus." With the "small class sizes," students can "work closely and personally" with their professors. That said, the school is growing, and "with the larger incoming freshman class, it made getting what you want and need more difficult during registration." However, students appreciate that Pitt—Bradford "puts forth a serious effort to offer a diverse and eclectic course catalogue," including "a lot of fun winter sport classes you can take for credit."

> **SURVEY SAYS . . .**
> Large classes
> Great computer facilities
> Athletic facilities are great
> Campus feels safe
> (Almost) everyone smokes

Life

Located in northwestern Pennsylvania, Pitt—Bradford's campus feels "like going to school at a summer cabin." In addition to enjoying the "beauty" of the "outdoor environment," campus residents live in "apartment-style residence halls" that students appreciate for the "privacy" they afford. On the other hand, the food ("all right sometimes but most of the time it isn't") and a need for "increased internet bandwidth in the residence halls" can get students down. Like the academic experience, life at Pitt—Bradford is characterized by the school's "small" size. Students describe Pitt—Bradford as a "friendly, close-knit campus where everyone really has a chance to experience the good things about university life." Students "make their own fun" with "40 student clubs and organizations," and the "Student Activities Counsel likes to have at least one or two different activities a week." In addition, the "Student Government Association here on campus makes it so easy to start your own club and/or organization and get university funding to run it." While the surrounding town of Bradford offers "only a few things to do," students take advantage of the "many opportunities to explore the campus and the nature surrounding the campus." In fall 2008, a new residence hall will open to accomodate the university's growing enrollment.

Student Body

"Life" on campus is "pretty laid-back," and Pitt-Bradford students are generally "hardworking and dedicated to their studies." For being located in a "small town," "The student body is actually quite diverse" and there seems to be "a lot of city kids." The school population is comprised of a "variety of traditional and nontraditional students, which makes a nice overall group of people." Students agree that "everyone seems to get along very well no matter how different they are," and "It's easy to meet like-minded individuals." Since "The campus isn't very big, it's very easy to make a lot of friends." In fact, "You always find someone to hang with even if you don't know them."

Admissions

Very important factors considered include: Level of applicant's interest. *Important factors considered include:* Academic GPA, rigor of secondary school record, standardized test scores, interview. *Other factors considered include:* Class rank, application essay, recommendation(s), character/personal qualities, extracurricular activities, talent/ability, volunteer work, work experience. SAT or ACT required; TOEFL required of all international applicants. High school diploma is required and GED is accepted. *Academic units required:* 4 English, 2 mathematics, 1 science, (1 science labs), 2 foreign language, 1 history, 5 academic electives. *Academic units recommended:* 4 English, 3 mathematics, 2 science, (2 science labs), 2 foreign language, 1 history, 5 academic electives.

Financial Aid

Students should submit: FAFSA. The Princeton Review suggests that all financial aid forms be submitted as soon as possible after January 1. *Need-based scholarships/grants offered:* Federal Pell, SEOG, ACG, SMART, state scholarships/grants, private scholarships, the school's own gift aid. *Loan aid offered:* FFEL Subsidized Stafford, FFEL Unsubsidized Stafford, FFEL PLUS, Federal Perkins Applicants will be notified of awards on a rolling basis beginning 4/1. Federal Work-Study Program available. Institutional employment available. Off-campus job opportunities are fair.

The Inside Word

While the small and intimate environment is the hallmark of a Pitt—Bradford education, the school continues to expand. In October 2002, the college began a $13-million "Complete the Campus" fund-raising campaign designed to create the facilities, technology, financial aid, and academic support needed to support a larger undergraduate community. In 2004, the school opened a new fine arts and communication arts building, including a 500-seat theater, and the future only holds further developments at this up-and-coming university.

THE SCHOOL SAYS " . . . "

From The Admissions Office

"When it comes to picking a college, many students discover that they have to choose between a university where teachers know and care about their students or a world-renowned institution from which they can earn a reputable degree. At Pitt—Bradford, you don't have to choose. You can have both and so much more.

"You can go beyond: Go beyond the classroom by participating in one of the many internships and research opportunities. Go beyond the degree by taking advantage of our robust Career Services Office and our informal alumni network to help you find a satisfying career. Go beyond the typical 9-to-5 day by taking part in an active student life, a friendly residence life environment, and excellent athletic, cultural, and recreational opportunities. Go beyond place by receiving a liberal arts education that will expose you to the world and participating in one of several study abroad opportunities. And go beyond your expectations by receiving a college experience that will transform you.

"At Pitt—Bradford, you will live and learn on a safe, intimate campus where you will receive individual and personalized attention from committed professors who will work side by side with you. And you will earn a degree from the University of Pittsburgh, which commands respect around the world."

For even more information on this school, turn to page 535 of the "Stats" section.

UNIVERSITY OF PITTSBURGH—JOHNSTOWN

450 SCHOOLHOUSE ROAD, 157 BLACKINGTON HALL, JOHNSTOWN, PA 15904 • ADMISSIONS: 814-269-7050
FAX: 814-269-7044 • E-MAIL: UPJADMIT@PITT.EDU • WEBSITE: WWW.UPJ.PITT.EDU

RATINGS

Quality of Life: 73 **Academic:** 71 **Admissions:** 71 **Financial Aid:** 65

STUDENTS SAY " . . ."

Academics

Undergrads tell us that The University of Pittsburgh at Johnstown "is about having a good college experience at a small campus while growing as a student and person." The school offers "an excellent undergraduate campus to explore scientific fields," as well as engineering and education programs that "have a high success rate." Academics focus on practical experience in most disciplines; as one student explains, "My professors have all worked in the field that they are teaching," which not only "adds validity to what they are teaching," but also means that "they can help students get internships and the experience that they need." Profs here "are generally very accessible," but their teaching can be "hit or miss." One student explains, "Some professors at UPJ are sensational, but others can be total bores. The academic experience in Johnstown is what you make of it. If you want to get the most out of it, you can." Those who succeed in doing so insist that UPJ offers "a small school feel with a big university name" that translates into "a very positive employment rate for graduating students."

> **SURVEY SAYS . . .**
> *Large classes*
> *Great library*
> *Campus feels safe*
> *Lots of beer drinking*
> *(Almost) everyone smokes*

Life

"The weekends can get pretty boring sometimes" at UPJ because "there isn't much to do in Johnstown" and "a lot of students go home on the weekends." As one student observes, "It's a rural atmosphere, so the social life reflects that. It's like choosing between living in the city and living in a small town. UPJ is the small-town choice. The safe and pleasant atmosphere compensates for the lack of nightlife." One perk of the location is that "We get a lot of snow, so many students enjoy going to local ski resorts or sled riding on campus." Students tell us that "there are parties every weekend," but "Although there is a majority of students who like to drink alcohol and party, it is easy to find other students that are not interested in those activities. Just because you don't drink, doesn't mean that you're not going to have any friends here." "The movies and bowling" are "always popular places for students" and it's "hard to go to either location without seeing another group of students from the university."

Student Body

UPJ undergrads are "hardworking, fun-loving individuals looking to make a difference on campus on way or another." They are "generally from western Pennsylvania," either "from the Pittsburgh or Johnstown-Somerset area," with many "who live nearby in small towns." The school is predominantly Caucasian "so ethnically, it's not very diverse," but this is something that the school is "working on." Additionally, "Many students here are engineering majors," so some find that the school also lacks diversity in terms of areas of interest. One student observes that "The typical student is a walking advertisement for Hollister. It is very preppy here. There aren't a lot of artsy, goth, or other types of people." That said, the atypical students here "fit in by banding in groups in which they recognize and celebrate each others uniqueness."

THE PRINCETON REVIEW SAYS

Admissions

Very important factors considered include: Class rank, academic GPA, rigor of secondary school record. *Important factors considered include:* Application essay, recommendation(s), standardized test scores, extracurricular activities, interview, level of applicant's interest, talent/ability, volunteer work, work experience. *Other factors considered include:* Character/personal qualities, racial/ethnic status, SAT or ACT required; ACT with Writing component recommended. High school diploma is required and GED is accepted. *Academic units required:* 4 English, 2 mathematics, 2 science, (1 science labs), 2 foreign language, 4 social studies. *Academic units recommended:* 3 mathematics, (2 science labs).

Financial Aid

Students should submit: FAFSA. The Princeton Review suggests that all financial aid forms be submitted as soon as possible after January 1. *Need-based scholarships/grants offered:* Federal Pell, SEOG, state scholarships/grants, private scholarships, the school's own gift aid, Federal Nursing Scholarships. *Loan aid offered:* FFEL Subsidized Stafford, FFEL Unsubsidized Stafford, FFEL PLUS, Federal Perkins Applicants will be notified of awards on a rolling basis beginning 3/15. Federal Work-Study Program available. Institutional employment available. Off-campus job opportunities are good.

The Inside Word

UPJ admits over 93 percent of all applicants. Essentially, the school admits everyone it believes has a chance to succeed in its academic programs. As a result of attrition through failure or transfer, just slightly over half of all students who enroll at UPJ graduate from the school within six years.

THE SCHOOL SAYS " . . ."

From The Admissions Office

"The University of Pittsburgh—Johnstown (UPJ) was established in 1927, one of the first regional campuses of a major university in the United States, and became a 4-year, degree-granting college of the university in 1970. As a regional campus of a public (state-related) university, it has the more affordable costs and the comprehensive range of programs (education, business, engineering technology, etc.) of a public institution. At the same time, it has many of the features found in a private college. It has a good reputation for academic rigor and quality programs. It's a relatively small enrollment (about 3,100 full- and part-time students); most students are full-time and of traditional age (18–24); it's entirely undergraduate—no graduate programs; all teachers are faculty, no graduate teaching assistants; the classes are typically small; the campus is largely residential (more than 60 percent of students reside in campus housing); and the campus itself is very attractive—suburban, wooded, with lots of room, a consistent fieldstone architecture, and peripheral parking.

"Students who choose the University of Pittsburgh—Johnstown feel that it offers a smaller setting and a beautiful campus, combined with most of the advantages of a large university. Students like the fact that most professors and administrators are accessible, and also see UPJ as offering a good variety of challenging classes. There is a strong emphasis on undergraduate research opportunities, a solid internship program, and good career guidance. Students often talk about finding a 'comfort zone' at UPJ."

For even more information on this school, turn to page 536 of the "Stats" section.

UNIVERSITY OF PITTSBURGH—PITTSBURGH CAMPUS

ALUMNI HALL, 4227 FIFTH AVENUE, FIRST FLOOR, PITTSBURGH, PA 15260 • ADMISSIONS: 412-624-7488
FAX: 412-648-8815 • FINANCIAL AID: 412-624-7488 • E-MAIL: OAFA@PITT.EDU • WEBSITE: WWW.PITT.EDU

RATINGS
Quality of Life: 91   Academic: 80   Admissions: 89   Financial Aid: 77

STUDENTS SAY ". . ."

Academics

The University of Pittsburgh "is the perfect-sized institution," a place with "all the benefits of a large urban university, including research, internships, and lots of amazing experiences," but also small enough "that people truly have a chance to make a name for themselves on campus. You can't go five minutes without bumping into someone you know here." Many departments stand out; all medical fields benefit from the school's affiliation with the renowned research-oriented University of Pittsburgh Medical Center; and programs in dentistry, pharmacology, physical therapy, neuroscience, and biology are all considered outstanding. Programs in engineering, business, and the liberal arts are also noteworthy. Students appreciate the fact that "professors here are all very accessible and really want their students to learn and understand their courses. They are willing to work with the students to [help them] achieve better grades and enhance the learning experience." Opportunities to study abroad abound, and undergrads "can often find study-abroad programs that are cheaper for them than their tuition would have been."

> **SURVEY SAYS . . .**
> *Great computer facilities*
> *Great library*
> *Athletic facilities are great*
> *Students are happy*
> *Everyone loves the Panthers*
> *Student publications are popular*
> *Lots of beer drinking*

Life

Pitt is located in Oakland, a "really nice location relative to downtown Pittsburgh and the surrounding neighborhoods." Thanks to "the school's arrangement" with the city of Pittsburgh, "every Pitt student gets free city busing," a perk that allows and encourages undergrads to explore the city. Further such encouragement comes in the form of PittArts, a program that "heavily subsidizes cultural events in the city. When Broadway shows come to Pittsburgh, you can get tickets for $10, a dinner at an Italian restaurant, and free transportation downtown. They also offer free lectures, operas, and symphonies." No wonder students tell us that "Pittsburgh is a college city, one that really caters to students. Bigger cities may offer more renowned acts coming through, or more famous museums, but in Pittsburgh we can actually afford to experience them!" The campus is also busy, with "many campus organizations," "free movies in the Union, student performances on campus, lectures (Maya Angelou came recently)"; these offer students lots of opportunities to socialize. Pitt athletics are also popular, with basketball and football drawing the biggest crowds. All of these options "make socializing easier and less alcohol-centric. While there is a lot of drinking on campus, it is just as easy and socially acceptable to sit down to coffee."

Student Body

A "very diverse population" of 16,796 undergraduates virtually guarantees that "everyone is bound to meet someone whom he or she would have never met staying in his or her hometown." The school has "over 450 organizations, and all those groups provide a place for students to come and be their own people in a group they feel comfortable with." Highly competitive admissions mean that "kids here are definitely intelligent and have a lot going for them." They're not just brainiacs, though—in fact, Pitt students "like to have a good time too, not just going out to parties. Many students really take advantage of the free admission to numerous museums and free city busing to visit the many neighborhoods of Pittsburgh." The most dedicated students here, our respondents report, can be found in the medical sciences (neuroscience, chemistry, and biology) as well as in some of the humanities (writing, literature, philosophy).

THE PRINCETON REVIEW SAYS

Admissions

Very important factors considered include: Academic GPA, rigor of secondary school record. *Important factors considered include:* Standardized test scores. *Other factors considered include:* Class rank, application essay, recommendation(s), character/personal qualities, extracurricular activities, first generation, geographical residence, level of applicant's interest, racial/ethnic status, talent/ability, volunteer work, work experience. SAT or ACT required; High school diploma is required and GED is not accepted. *Academic units required:* 4 English, 3 mathematics, 3 science, (3 science labs), 1 foreign language, 1 social studies, 4 academic electives. *Academic units recommended:* 4 mathematics, 4 science, 3 foreign language, 3 social studies, 2 history, 1 computer science.

Financial Aid

Students should submit: FAFSA, institution's own financial aid form. The Princeton Review suggests that all financial aid forms be submitted as soon as possible after January 1. *Need-based scholarships/grants offered:* Federal Pell, SEOG, state scholarships/grants, private scholarships, the school's own gift aid, Federal Nursing Scholarships. *Loan aid offered:* FFEL Subsidized Stafford, FFEL Unsubsidized Stafford, FFEL PLUS, Federal Perkins, Federal Nursing, college/university loans from institutional funds. Applicants will be notified of awards on a rolling basis beginning 3/15. Federal Work-Study Program available. Off-campus job opportunities are excellent.

The Inside Word

With the overwhelming number of applications Pitt receives, it's no wonder its Admissions Counselors rely on numbers. Comparable to its public university brethren, the school makes admit decisions based mostly on secondary school records and test scores. Applicants who provide transcripts laced with honors classes, Advanced Placement classes, and solid grades should be accepted.

THE SCHOOL SAYS ". . ."

From The Admissions Office

"The University of Pittsburgh is one of 62 members of the Association of American Universities, a prestigious group whose members include the major research universities of North America. There are nearly 400 degree programs available at the 16 Pittsburgh campus schools (two offering only undergraduate degree programs, four offering graduate degree programs, and ten offering both) and four regional campuses, allowing students a wide latitude of choices, both academically and in setting and style, size and pace of campus. Programs ranked nationally include philosophy, history and philosophy of science, chemistry, economics, English, history, physics, political science, and psychology. The University Center for International Studies is ranked one of the exemplary international programs in the country by the Council on Learning.

"Freshman applicants for Fall 2008 are required to submit SAT or ACT test results. All testing should preferably be completed by fall of your senior year for September admission. We strongly recommend that you take the SAT or ACT at least once as a junior and once as a senior."

For even more information on this school, turn to page 536 of the "Stats" section.

UNIVERSITY OF RHODE ISLAND

14 UPPER COLLEGE ROAD, KINGSTON, RI 02881-1391 • ADMISSIONS: 401-874-7000 • FAX: 401-874-5523
FINANCIAL AID: 401-874-9500 • E-MAIL: URIADMIT@ETA1.URI.EDU • WEBSITE: WWW.URI.EDU

RATINGS
Quality of Life: 66   Academic: 70   Admissions: 78   Financial Aid: 71

STUDENTS SAY "..."

Academics

The University of Rhode Island "is a pretty decent middle-sized school in a great location." Notable majors include "nursing, engineering, or anything science." The "excellent" pharmacy program at URI is competitive and nationally recognized. Many classes are "very rigorous." Others are "wicked easy." For both, "there are many resources available to get help." The faculty really runs the gamut. "There are some really good ones, but some are just awful." The good profs "genuinely care about teaching" and "willingly offer their time" outside of class. "All of my teachers

> **SURVEY SAYS . . .**
> *Great library*
> *Great off-campus food*
> *Frats and sororities dominate
> social scene*
> *Student publications are popular*
> *Lots of beer drinking*
> *Hard liquor is popular*
> *(Almost) everyone smokes*

have had considerable experience in their field and bring a lot to the classroom," says an impressed freshman. As for the bad professors, "there are some serious horror stories." Some students think the subpar professors "cancel class almost too much," some bemoan the lack of outside help and the brief periods of time that qualify as office hours, and some have a hard time understanding the accents of foreign professors. URI's administration receives similarly mixed reviews. "I have had very few problems with administration," says one student. "They are happy to sit down and talk with you about any concerns that you have and they will help solve your problems." Other students see "an ardent bureaucracy" "too obsessed with drinking policies to pay attention to what really matters." "These people are tools," remarks one student.

Life

"URI is a gorgeous school—especially in the fall—on a big hill." It's located in a "safe" and "rural" area. "Parking is horrible," though the university has recently opened 1,400 new student parking spaces and set a shuttle bus system into place so as to make pedestrian traffic safer. "Some of the dorm buildings are in very poor condition." For some students, URI is a "suitcase school." "A lot of students do go home on the weekends just because they live so close by." "If you get involved on campus you will love it," says a psychology major. "If not, you will want to transfer." Intramurals and varsity sports are popular. "Basketball is huge; so is hockey" "There are beautiful beaches right down the road from campus where you can surf, swim, or just sit and read," weather permitting. "Greek life is very popular, and if you live on campus it feels like everyone is part of it (but they're not)." The campus is ostensibly dry but the alcohol policy certainly "hasn't stopped URI students from getting wasted." "One thing I didn't know coming to URI was how much of the social life happens off campus," discloses an English major. Parties occur 15 minutes away—"down the line," as students here say. There are "raging house parties every single weekend" in Narragansett by the beach. Narragansett bars are popular, too. "If you are not 21, a fake ID is almost necessary." Students looking for more urban pursuits often travel 30 miles north to Providence.

Student Body

"The University of Rhode Island is an affordable option for in-state students." "Most out-of-state residents are from wealthy families or have scholarships." There are "a lot of generic college kids who go to college for the social aspect." "URI is mostly made up of guys that want to party and drive BMWs and girls that wear North Face jackets, Ugg boots, and big Dior sunglasses," stereotypes one student. Politically, it's a "pretty liberal" but mostly "apathetic" crowd. "However, if you search you can find some cool people who don't fit the mold." "There are many different students here," attests a nutrition major, "from jocks and jockettes to artists to frat boys and sorority girls." Ethnic diversity is not unreasonable but URI is cliquish. "People here do tend to hang out with people who are more similar to them." "Ethnicities mostly do not mix." Rhode Islanders often "stick to" high school friends.

THE PRINCETON REVIEW SAYS

Admissions

Very important factors considered include: Rigor of secondary school record. *Important factors considered include:* Class rank, application essay, academic GPA, standardized test scores. *Other factors considered include:* Recommendation(s), alumni/ae relation, character/personal qualities, extracurricular activities, first generation, geographical residence, level of applicant's interest, racial/ethnic status, state residency, talent/ability, volunteer work, work experienc SAT or ACT required; ACT with Writing component required. TOEFL required of all international applicants. High school diploma is required and GED is accepted. *Academic units required:* 4 English, 3 mathematics, 2 science, (1 science labs), 2 foreign language, 2 social studies, 5 academic electives.

Financial Aid

Students should submit: FAFSA. The Princeton Review suggests that all financial aid forms be submitted as soon as possible after January 1. *Need-based scholarships/grants offered:* Federal Pell, SEOG, state scholarships/grants, private scholarships, the school's own gift aid. *Loan aid offered:* Direct Subsidized Stafford, Direct Unsubsidized Stafford, Direct PLUS, Federal Perkins, Federal Nursing, state loans, college/university loans from institutional funds. Applicants will be notified of awards on a rolling basis beginning 3/31. Federal Work-Study Program available. Institutional employment available. Off-campus job opportunities are good.

The Inside Word

Any candidate with solid grades is likely to find the university's Admissions Committee to be welcoming. The yield of admits who enroll is low and the state's population small. Out-of-state students are attractive to URI because they are sorely needed to fill out the student body. Students who graduate in the top 10 percent of their class are good scholarship bets. If you are a resident of a New England state other then Rhode Island, you get a tuition discount, but only if you enroll in certain degree programs.

THE SCHOOL SAYS ". . ."

From The Admissions Office

"Outstanding freshman candidates for Fall 2009 admission with a minimum SAT score of 1200 (combined Critical Reading and Math) or ACT composite score of 25 who rank in the top quarter of their high school class are eligible to be considered for a Centennial Scholarship. These merit-based scholarships range up to full tuition and are renewable each semester if the student maintains full-time continuous enrollment and a 3.0 average or better. In order to be eligible for consideration, all application materials must be received in the Admission Office by the December 15, 2008 early action deadline. Applications are not considered complete until the application fee, completed application, official high school transcript, list of senior courses, personal essay, and SAT or ACT scores (sent directly from the testing agency) are received.

"If a student is awarded a Centennial Scholarship, and his or her residency status changes from out-of-state to regional or in-state, the amount of the award will be reduced to reflect the reduced tuition rate.

"The SAT Math and Critical Reading scores are used for admission evaluation and Centennial Scholarship consideration. The Writing score is not currently used for admission evaluation or Centennial Scholarship consideration."

For even more information on this school, turn to page 536 of the "Stats" section.

UNIVERSITY OF SCRANTON

800 LINDEN STREET, SCRANTON, PA 18510 • ADMISSIONS: 570-941-7540 • FAX: 570-941-5928
FINANCIAL AID: 570-941-7700 • E-MAIL: ADMISSIONS@SCRANTON.EDU • WEBSITE: WWW.SCRANTON.EDU

RATINGS
Quality of Life: 78   **Academic:** 79   **Admissions:** 86   **Financial Aid:** 70

STUDENTS SAY "..."

Academics

With "an outstanding record for admission to graduate programs, not only in law and medicine but also in several other fields," the University of Scranton is a good fit for ambitious students seeking "a Jesuit school in every sense of the word. If you come here, expect to be challenged to become a better person, to develop a strong concern for the poor and marginalized, and to grow spiritually and intellectually." The school manages to accomplish this without "forcing religion upon you, which is nice." Undergraduates also approve of the mandatory liberal-arts-based curriculum that "forces you to learn about broader things than your own major." Strong majors here include "an amazing occupational therapy program, [an] excellent special education program," business, and biology. "This is a great place for premeds and other sciences," students agree. While the workload can be difficult, "a tutoring center provides free tutoring for any students who may need it, and also provides work-study positions for students who qualify to tutor." Need more help? Professors "are extremely accessible. They will go to any lengths to help you understand material and do well," while administrators "are here for the students, and show that every day inside and outside of the classroom." Community ties here are strong; as one student points out, "The Jesuits live in our dorms, creating an even greater sense of community, because we don't view them as just priests, we view them as real people who can relate on our level."

Life

"There is a whole range of activities to do on the weekends" at University of Scranton, including "frequent trips, dances, and movies that are screened for free." Students tell us that "the school and student organizations provide plenty of options, such as retreats, talent shows, and other various activities." There are also "many intramurals to become involved in, and the varsity sports (specifically the women's) are very successful." Furthermore, "Being a Jesuit school, social justice issues are huge. They are taught in the classroom, and students spend a lot of time volunteering." Hometown Scranton is big enough to provide "movie theaters, two malls, parks, a zoo, a bowling alley, and a skiing/snowboarding mountain." In short, there are plenty of choices for the non-partier at Scranton; the many we heard from in our survey reported busy extracurricular schedules. But those seeking a party won't be disappointed here, either. Scranton undergrads "party a lot, but they balance it with studying. Parties are chances to go out, see people, dance, and drink if you want." You "can find a party any time of day, seven days a week" here, usually with a keg tapped and pouring. Few here feel the party scene is out of hand, however; a typical student writes, "It's very different than at schools with Greek systems. It is a lot more laid-back, and all about everyone having a good time."

Students

While "the typical Scranton student is White, Catholic, and from the suburbs," students hasten to point out that "within this sameness, there is much diversity. There are people who couldn't care at all about religion, and there are people who are deeply religious. Even in the Catholic atmosphere of the school, the school only requires that you learn about Catholicism as it stands. Theology classes . . . are prefaced with the idea that 'You do not have to believe this!'" Undergrads here are generally "friendly and welcoming. Cliques are pretty much nonexistent, and anyone who would be classified as 'popular' is only considered so because they are extremely friendly, outgoing, and seek out friendships with as many people as possible." Students tend to be on the Abercrombie-preppy side, with lots of undergrads of Italian, Irish, and Polish descent.

THE PRINCETON REVIEW SAYS
Admissions
Very important factors considered include: Class rank, academic GPA, rigor of secondary school record, standardized test scores. *Important factors considered include:* extracurricular activities. *Other factors considered include:* Application essay, recommendation(s), alumni/ae relation, character/personal qualities, interview, level of applicant's interest, talent/ability, volunteer work, work experience. SAT or ACT required; TOEFL required of all international applicants. High school diploma is required and GED is accepted. *Academic units required:* 4 English, 3 mathematics, 3 science, (1 science labs), 2 foreign language, 2 social studies, 2 history, 4 academic electives. *Academic units recommended:* 4 English, 4 mathematics, 3 science, (1 science labs), 2 foreign language, 3 social studies, 3 history, 4 academic electives.

Financial Aid
Students should submit: FAFSA. The Princeton Review suggests that all financial aid forms be submitted as soon as possible after January 1. *Need-based scholarships/grants offered:* Federal Pell, SEOG, state scholarships/grants, private scholarships, the school's own gift aid. *Loan aid offered:* FFEL Subsidized Stafford, FFEL Unsubsidized Stafford, FFEL PLUS, Federal Perkins, Federal Nursing Applicants will be notified of awards on a rolling basis beginning 3/15. Federal Work-Study Program available. Institutional employment available. Off-campus job opportunities are good.

The Inside Word
Admission to Scranton gets harder each year. A steady stream of smart kids from the Tristate Area keeps classes full and the admit rate low. Successful applicants will need solid grades and test scores. As with many religiously affiliated schools, students should be a good match philosophically as well.

THE SCHOOL SAYS ". . ."
From The Admissions Office
"A Jesuit institution in Pennsylvania's Pocono Northeast, the University of Scranton is known for its outstanding academics, state-of-the art campus, and exceptional sense of community. Founded in 1888, the university offers more than 80 undergraduate and graduate academic programs of study through four colleges and schools.

"For 13 consecutive years, U.S. News & World Report has named Scranton among the top-10 master's universities in the North. For the past 3 years, Scranton has also been among the 'Great Schools as a Great Price' in the 'Universities—Master's in the North' category. The Princeton Review included Scranton among The Best 361 Colleges in the nation for the past 5 years. For 4 consecutive years, USA Today included Scranton students on its 'All-U.S.A. College Academic Teams' list. In 2005, Scranton was the only college in Pennsylvania and the only Jesuit university to have a student named to the first academic team. In other national recognition, Kaplan counted Scranton among the nation's '369 Most Interesting Colleges' and was also listed among the 247 colleges in the nation included in the ninth edition of Barron's Best Buys in College Education.

"Known for the remarkable success of its graduates, Scranton is listed among the 'Top Producers' of Fulbright awards for American students in the October 20, 2006, issue of The Chronicle of Higher Education.

"Freshman applicants for Fall 2008 are required to take the SAT or ACT exam. The writing scores will not be considered in the admissions decision process. Students are encouraged to apply early for admission and can do so online with no application fee at Scranton.edu/apply."

For even more information on this school, turn to page 537 of the "Stats" section.

UNIVERSITY OF SOUTHERN MAINE

37 COLLEGE AVENUE, GORHAM, ME 04038 • ADMISSIONS: 207-780-5670 • FAX: 207-780-5640
E-MAIL: USMADM@USM.MAINE.EDU • WEBSITE: WWW.USM.MAINE.EDU

RATINGS
Quality of Life: 69   **Academic:** 71   **Admissions:** 72   **Financial Aid:** 74

STUDENTS SAY "..."

Academics

The University of Southern Maine "provides the best bang for your buck for local and nontraditional students." The USM campus, with its hubs in Portland and Gorham, offers residence hall living on its Gorham hub. There are over 50 undergraduate majors here and USM is the largest of the seven campuses in the University of Maine System but it's "not a gigantic university." "Lectures aren't that big" and upper-level courses tend to be pretty small. Some students

> **SURVEY SAYS . . .**
> *Large classes*
> *Great library*
> *Students love Gorham, ME*
> *Great off-campus food*
> *Lots of beer drinking*
> *Hard liquor is popular*

tell us that classroom discussion is solid. Others contend that "the learning atmosphere is not at all lively." Whatever the case, USM's professors are often "passionate about the material" and sometimes "incredibly good." Students report that they are "very accommodating" outside of the classroom as well. The administration, on the other hand, is "fairly secretive" and not as popular. "The college is in desperate need of streamlining basic processes such as financial aid," recommends a computer science major.

Life

In more ways than one, USM is largely "a commuter school." The majority of the "younger, traditional students" here live on the Gorham campus but many classes occur on the Portland campus, some 10 miles away. "It's quite frankly a pain to deal with two campuses," advises a weary senior. "Your freshman and sophomore year you spend a lot of time traveling between them." Also, "aesthetically, the campuses have some big eyesores." "The buildings are mostly old, cold, and outdated," though a state of the art green dorm has just opened and three new buildings forming a "university commons" on the Portland campus be completed by fall 2008. Students also complain about the "nauseating food." Socially, USM offers "a ton of things to do." Intercollegiate sports are strong and there are "dances, concerts, and game nights throughout the week." Quite a bit of social activity takes place in Portland. It's "a very nice city, the biggest in Maine" and it's reportedly "very much an epicenter for the arts, pubs, and eateries." The numerous bars in Portland's cobble-stoned Old Port district afford "the opportunity to get drunk quite often." Also, there are "two ski resorts within an hour away" and "winter sports are pretty much unlimited."

Students

"Most people who go to USM live in Maine or at least the New England area." Ethnic diversity is minimal. "Maine is not very diverse," points out a senior. "The student population reflects the overall population of Maine." Students describe themselves as "very laidback and polite." "Everyone seems to get along pretty well." Nevertheless, "USM lacks a cohesive, unified student body." "Many students work full time" and a sizeable segment of the population is either "slightly above traditional college age" or middle-aged and "in the midst of a total career change." Many nontraditional students are too busy with their own lives to really participate in campus activities. The traditionally college-aged students tend to stick to smaller groups. "It's kind of like high school with all the different clique types you see around campus," says a senior. "The range is from Abercrombie wannabe to eclectic nerd to gothic." There are the "left-wing liberal hippies," "the sorority girls, the frat guys," and the "music and theater kids." There is also "a big homosexual community."

Admissions

Very important factors considered include: Class rank, rigor of secondary school record, standardized test scores. *Important factors considered include:* Application essay, recommendation(s). *Other factors considered include:* Alumni/ae relation, character/personal qualities, extracurricular activities, geographical residence, interview, racial/ethnic status, state residency, talent/ability, volunteer work, work experience. SAT or ACT required; TOEFL required of all international applicants. High school diploma is required and GED is accepted. *Academic units required:* 4 English, 3 mathematics, 2 science, (2 science labs), 2 social studies, 2 history. *Academic units recommended:* 4 mathematics, 3 science, (3 science labs), 2 foreign language, 3 social studies.

Financial Aid

Students should submit: FAFSA The Princeton Review suggests that all financial aid forms be submitted as soon as possible after January 1. *Need-based scholarships/grants offered:* Federal Pell, SEOG, state scholarships/grants, private scholarships, the school's own gift aid. *Loan aid offered:* FFEL Subsidized Stafford, FFEL Unsubsidized Stafford, FFEL PLUS, Federal Perkins, Federal Nursing, state loans Applicants will be notified of awards on a rolling basis beginning 3/15. Federal Work-Study Program available. Off-campus job opportunities are excellent.

The Inside Word

Admission at USM operates on a rolling basis and it's basically uncompetitive. If you get your application in early and have remotely decent grades and standardized scores, you should have no problems getting in. It's also worth noting that applicants don't need to submit test scores if they have been out of high school for three years or have at least 30 hours of college credit.

THE SCHOOL SAYS " . . ."

From The Admissions Office

"At the center of the USM experience is a bustling campus with its hubs—only 12 miles apart—one in downtown Portland and the other in nearby Gorham. Students spend time at both hubs, living the Maine lifestyle to the fullest. The energy of the sophisticated city of Portland on the water, full of shopping, art, music, dining, and career opportunities, offer a living and learning experience that blends seamlessly from the classroom into the city.

"USM offers over 70 areas of study at the undergraduate level, 25 NCAA Division III athletic teams, and over 100 clubs and organizations. Students are given opportunities to uncover their hidden talents, and to take advantage of opportunities to get experience—whether it be through internships, volunteer projects, musical or theater performances, or any variety of experiences.

"USM gives students a motivating learning environment, with classmates whose varied experiences and cultures make discussion stimulating, and professors whose priority is teaching, USM is a place where not only knowledge is gained, but wisdom, too."

For even more information on this school, turn to page 537 of the "Stats" section.

UNIVERSITY OF VERMONT

OFFICE OF ADMISSIONS, 194 S. PROSPECT STREET, BURLINGTON, VT 05401-3596 • ADMISSIONS: 802-656-3370
FAX: 802-656-8611 • FINANCIAL AID: 802-656-3156 • E-MAIL: ADMISSIONS@UVM.EDU • WEBSITE: WWW.UVM.EDU

RATINGS
Quality of Life: 83   Academic: 76   Admissions: 83   Financial Aid: 74

STUDENTS SAY ". . ."

Academics

Quality of life issues are important to most University of Vermont undergrads; when discussing their reasons for choosing UVM, they're as likely to cite the "laid-back environment," the "proximity to skiing facilities," the "great parties," and their "amazing" hometown of Burlington as they are to mention the academics. But, students remind us, "That doesn't mean that there are not strong academics

> **SURVEY SAYS . . .**
> *Students are friendly*
> *Students love Burlington, VT*
> *Great off-campus food*
> *Lots of beer drinking*
> *Hard liquor is popular*

[at UVM]." On the contrary, UVM is made up of several well-established colleges and offers "a wide variety of majors." "You can jump around between majors, and then leave with a recognized diploma in hand for something you love to do." Students single out the business school, the "top-notch" education program, the Psychology Department, premedical sciences, and "the amazing animal science program" for praise, and are especially proud of The Rubenstein School of Natural Resources, home to UVM's environmental science majors; they tell us it "is a great college that feels like it's much smaller, [more] separate, and just cozier than the rest of the school." No matter which discipline, "You get out what you put in." "Teachers are readily available and are willing to help you do well in your classes. They encourage you to get help if you need it and are enthusiastic about what they teach. It's all there; you just have to take advantage of it." The size of the university, we're told, is just right; UVM is "a moderately large school," and it allows undergrads "to feel at home while still offering just about any activity possible."

Life

"UVM is known to be a party school," and "Even though the university has cracked down on drinking (they made it a dry campus this year), it hasn't actually changed much." Indeed, students tell us that one can find "a good balance of having fun and academics" at UVM, "but it's tough, because there's always a party going on somewhere." Students who want to dodge the party scene will find "There is always something" happening in Burlington. The town has "lots of wonderful restaurants, a few movie theaters, a rockin' music scene, several bars, some dancing, and various environmental and social activities downtown." "On campus, there is typically at least one university-sponsored event each night, including interesting lectures, movies, games, or social events." Students love outdoor activities: "When it snows, it's very popular to go to the ski resorts around here and ski or snowboard for the day. When it's still warm out, going to the waterfront and swimming in Lake Champlain is popular too." UVM is an intercollegiate hockey powerhouse, and "In the fall and winter, hockey games are huge social events." They're so popular "that you have to get tickets to them the Monday before the game, or they will be sold out!"

Student Body

There's a "great variety of students" at UVM "because it's a big university," undergrads report, but they also note that "students at UVM are mostly White" and that there's "a lot of money at this school." While the most prevalent UVM archetype is "the guitar-loving, earth-saving, relaxed hippie" who "care[s] strongly about the environment" and "social justice," the student body also includes "your athletic types, your artsy people, and a number of other groups" including "vocal LGBTQ and ALANA populations" who, "though they usually hang out in their own groups," "are also active in all sorts of clubs across campus." Not surprisingly, there are many "New England types," "potheads," and "snow bums." Students report they "pretty much get along well with everyone." They either come here loving the outdoors or learn to love the outdoors by the time they leave.

THE PRINCETON REVIEW SAYS

Admissions

Very important factors considered include: Rigor of secondary school record. *Important factors considered include:* Class rank, application essay, academic GPA, standardized test scores, character/personal qualities, state residency. *Other factors considered include:* Recommendation(s), alumni/ae relation, extracurricular activities, first generation, geographical residence, interview, level of applicant's interest, racial/ethnic status, talent/ability, volunteer work, work experience. SAT or ACT required; ACT with Writing component required. TOEFL required of all international applicants. High school diploma is required and GED is accepted. *Academic units required:* 4 English, 3 mathematics, 2 science, (1 science labs), 2 foreign language, 3 social studies.

Financial Aid

Students should submit: FAFSA. The Princeton Review suggests that all financial aid forms be submitted as soon as possible after January 1. *Need-based scholarships/grants offered:* Federal Pell, SEOG, state scholarships/grants, private scholarships, the school's own gift aid, Federal Nursing Scholarships. *Loan aid offered:* FFEL Subsidized Stafford, FFEL Unsubsidized Stafford, FFEL PLUS, Federal Perkins, Federal Nursing, college/university loans from institutional funds. Applicants will be notified of awards on a rolling basis beginning 3/15. Federal Work-Study Program available. Institutional employment available. Off-campus job opportunities are good.

The Inside Word

UVM is a very popular choice among out-of-state students, whom the school welcomes; over half the student body originates from outside of Vermont. While admissions standards are significantly more rigorous for out-of-staters, solid candidates (B-plus/A-minus average, about a 600 on each section of the SAT) should do fine here. The school assesses applications holistically, meaning students who are weak in one area may be able to make up for it with strengths or distinguishing skills and characteristics in other areas.

THE SCHOOL SAYS ". . ."

From The Admissions Office

"The University of Vermont blends the close faculty-student relationships most commonly found in a small liberal arts college with the dynamic exchange of knowledge associated with a research university. This is not surprising, because UVM is both. A comprehensive research university offering nearly 100 undergraduate majors and extensive offerings through its Graduate College and College of Medicine, UVM is one of the nation's premier public research universities. UVM prides itself on the richness of its undergraduate experience. Distinguished senior faculty teach introductory courses in their fields. They also advise not only juniors and seniors, but also first- and second-year students, and work collaboratively with undergraduates on research initiatives. Students find extensive opportunities to test classroom knowledge in field through practicums, academic internships, and community service. More than 100 student organizations (involving 80 percent of the student body), 20 Division I varsity teams, 15 intercollegiate club and 14 intramural sports programs, and a packed schedule of cultural events fill in where the classroom leaves off.

"Applicants for the entering class of Fall 2008 class and beyond are required to take the new version of the SAT, or the ACT with the Writing section, and must submit official test scores. SAT Subject Tests are neither required nor recommended for the admission application."

For even more information on this school, turn to page 538 of the "Stats" section.

URSINUS COLLEGE

URSINUS COLLEGE, ADMISSIONS OFFICE, COLLEGEVILLE, PA 19426 • ADMISSIONS: 610-409-3200
FAX: 610-409-3662 • FINANCIAL AID: 610-409-3600 • E-MAIL: ADMISSIONS@URSINUS.EDU • WEBSITE: WWW.URSINUS.EDU

RATINGS
Quality of Life: 85   **Academic:** 91   **Admissions:** 89   **Financial Aid:** 89

STUDENTS SAY ". . ."

Academics

Ursinus College, a small liberal arts school in aptly named Collegeville, Pennsylvania, offers a wide array of courses and "has the facilities of a much larger school." "I truly believe that Ursinus is a transformative experience," declares an international relations major. "If you embrace the liberal arts education, this is the institution to be at." "Academic rigor is demanding." A required pair of first-year courses called "the Common Intellectual Experience" "create a bonding experience for the students, and it gets them to think about some extremely important issues." Beyond that, students must complete a host of core requirements in addition to their majors. You'll "do your fair share of 10- to 15-page term papers; usually a couple per semester." "But it pays off in the end." The small size allows for "discussion-based classes" and professors "really try to get students involved." "Some professors are full of themselves," admits a neuroscience major. However, they are "great teachers and certainly know what they're talking about." "I have loved all of my professors," gushes a math major. "They've been friendly, helpful, and knowledgeable. They're eager to get students involved in research." Management is "accessible" as well. The "down-to-earth" administrators "are often seen about the campus attending lectures, concerts, and sporting events." Strong majors here include biology and chemistry. Ursinus boasts an impressive 90-plus percent acceptance rate with medical schools. Students also laud the economics and arts programs.

Life

Ursinus boasts "a very beautiful campus." Some of the older dorms cry out for refurbishing, though, and newer ones are "faintly reminiscent of a hospital." The food isn't great, either. "They stop carting out the good food after the second week," warns a biology major. Also, wireless Internet is spotty. Despite these complaints, students tell us they are extremely happy. "People overall love the school," says a freshman. Ursinus students are proud of their ability to have fun. "There are parties almost every night," especially Thursday through Saturday, as students "ruin their collective liver." The administration tries to crack down, but students persevere and the drinking scene remains rollicking. House parties or suite parties are options but the Greek system "rules campus life." "The keggers held by Greek organizations" are the most widely attended bashes. Not everyone drinks, of course, "not by a long shot." "The cool thing about Ursinus is that regardless of whether you drink or not, you can still go to the parties and have a great time." Some students warn that "Ursinus can be a little dull" if you insist on avoiding the party scene altogether. Others disagree. "There is an incredible availability of activities and clubs on campus," they say. Intramural and varsity athletics are also very popular. Students "love to go to all the food places in Collegeville" as well. It is "difficult" to get too far off campus without a car, though. (And first-year students can't have them.) While "there is no shame inherent in taking the bus" to Philadelphia, few students do.

Students

By and large, while ethnic diversity isn't terrible for a small liberal arts school, Ursinus is "homogenous." "Most people come from wealthier families" and grew up in the comfortable suburbs of "New Jersey, Pennsylvania, and New York." Ursinus students are "very hardworking" and "have similar values." Politically, there's a mildly liberal slant. "Most students on this campus are active and highly involved, although those who do not engage in clubs and activities do seem to find each other." The prototypical Ursinus student is a "somewhat clean-cut, friendly, occasionally drunk," "Hollister-clad, Ugg-wearing" prepster. "Different cliques are evident," though. There are "smart jocks and wonderfully weird nerds." There are "stereotypical frat boys." "There are many weirdoes and there are many average Joes." "Ursinus somehow seems to provide a safe and comfortable environment for people of all different interests," remarks one student.

THE PRINCETON REVIEW SAYS

Admissions

Very important factors considered include: Class rank, rigor of secondary school record, extracurricular activities. *Important factors considered include:* Application essay, academic GPA, recommendation(s), standardized test scores, alumni/ae relation, racial/ethnic status, talent/ability, volunteer work, work experience. *Other factors considered include:* Character/personal qualities, first generation, geographical residence, interview, level of applicant's interest, TOEFL required of all international applicants. High school diploma is required and GED is not accepted. *Academic units required:* 4 English, 3 mathematics, 1 science, (1 science labs), 2 foreign language, 1 social studies, 5 academic electives. *Academic units recommended:* 4 mathematics, 3 science, 4 foreign language, 3 social studies.

Financial Aid

Students should submit: FAFSA, institution's own financial aid form, CSS/Financial Aid PROFILE Regular filing deadline is 2/15. The Princeton Review suggests that all financial aid forms be submitted as soon as possible after January 1. *Need-based scholarships/grants offered:* Federal Pell, SEOG, state scholarships/grants, private scholarships, the school's own gift aid. *Loan aid offered:* FFEL Subsidized Stafford, FFEL Unsubsidized Stafford, FFEL PLUS, Federal Perkins, college/university loans from institutional funds, Ursinus Gate First Marblehead Loans. Applicants will be notified of awards on or about 3/15. Federal Work-Study Program available. Institutional employment available. Off-campus job opportunities are excellent.

The Inside Word

Grades, test scores, and class rank count for more than anything else, and unless you are academically inconsistent, you'll likely get good news. If you are hoping to snag a scholarship, it's really essential that you visit campus and get yourself interviewed. Students in the top 10 percent of their graduating classes aren't required to submit SAT score.

THE SCHOOL SAYS ". . ."

From The Admissions Office

"Located a half-hour from center-city Philadelphia, the college boasts a beautiful 168-acre campus that includes the Residential Village (renovated Victorian-style homes that decorate the Main Street and house our students) and the nationally recognized Berman Museum of Art. Ursinus is a member of the Centennial Conference, competing both in academics and in intercollegiate athletics with institutions such as Dickinson, Franklin & Marshall, Gettysburg, and Muhlenberg. The academic environment is enhanced with such fine programs as a chapter of Phi Beta Kappa, an early assurance program to medical school with the Medical College of Pennsylvania, and myriad student exchanges both at home and abroad. A heavy emphasis is placed on student research—an emphasis that can only be carried out with the one-on-one attention Ursinus students receive from their professors.

"Ursinus will continue to ask applicants for writing samples—both a series of application essays and a graded high school paper. Pending further examination, the Writing portion of the new SAT will not initially affect admissions decisions."

For even more information on this school, turn to page 538 of the "Stats" section.

VASSAR COLLEGE

124 RAYMOND AVENUE, POUGHKEEPSIE, NY 12604 • ADMISSIONS: 845-437-7300 • FAX: 845-437-7063
FINANCIAL AID: 845-437-5320 • E-MAIL: ADMISSIONS@VASSAR.EDU • WEBSITE: WWW.VASSAR.EDU

RATINGS
Quality of Life: 80   Academic: 96   Admissions: 97   Financial Aid: 97

STUDENTS SAY "..."

Academics

Vassar College "is a great place to explore your options" because "There's no real core curriculum. All you need in the way of requirements are one quantitative class and one foreign language credit. Plus, one-quarter of your credits must be outside of your major." This approach, students agree, "really encourages students to think creatively and

> **SURVEY SAYS ...**
> *Small classes*
> *Great library*
> *Frats and sororities are unpopular*
> *or nonexistent*

pursue whatever they're passionate about, whether that be medieval tapestries, neuroscience, or unicycles. Not having a core curriculum is great because it gives students the opportunity to delve into many different interests." So much academic freedom might be a license to goof off at some schools; here, however, students "are passionate learners who participate in both academic and extracurriculars with all their might." Most of these "smart hippies with books in hand discussing feminism and politics and last night" don't need curricular requirements to compel them to take challenging courses. Vassar excels in the visual and performing arts—the "Drama Department is huge" —as well as in English, psychology, history, life sciences, and natural sciences. In all disciplines, "Profs here are mostly great teachers, and they're teachers first. Since there are no grad students here, undergrads are the top priority, and it shows in the one-on-one interactions you have with your teachers."

Life

"Life is campus-centered" at Vassar, in large part because hometown Poughkeepsie "does not offer much in the way of entertainment. The campus provides most of the weekend activities." One undergrad observes, "It's unfortunate but not rare for people to graduate from Vassar knowing nothing about Poughkeepsie other than where the train station to New York City is." The sojourn to New York, alas, is a relatively "expensive endeavor for weekly entertainment; it's about $30 round-trip, and that doesn't include doing stuff once you get there." Fortunately, "There is a huge array of things to do every night on campus. Comedy shows, improv, an incredibly wide array of theater productions"—including "several shows a year and three student groups devoted to drama"—four comedy groups, five a cappella groups," and interesting lectures create numerous opportunities to get out of the dorms at night." Provided you "pay attention to all the events e-mails Vassar sends out, you can usually find something random, fun, and free to do on a slow afternoon or weekday night." Weekends, on the other hand, "are completely different. If you don't drink or like being in situations where drinking/recreational drugs are involved, you'll probably have a dead social life." It's "not a wild, enormous party scene like at a state school" here, but rather one that occurs "earlier in the night, and in smaller groups of people." Vassar's self-contained social scene illustrates "something called the 'Vassar Bubble,' which means that you see the same people every day. You are so cut off from the world that sometimes it's difficult to keep up with current events."

Student Body

"There are common labels that get placed on people at Vassar," including "'hippie,' 'hipster,' and 'pretentious,' and to a degree, the labels are accurate." Vassar is a comfortable respite for "indie-chic students who revel in obscurity, some socially awkward archetypes, and some prep school pin-ups with their collars popped. But the majority of kids on campus are a mix of these people, which is why we mesh pretty well despite the cliques that inevitably form." What nearly everyone shares is "an amazing talent or something that they passionately believe in" and "far-left politics, with no desire or intention to try to understand any political view even slightly left of center. Most of them are pretty nice people, though."

THE PRINCETON REVIEW SAYS

Admissions

Very important factors considered include: Rigor of secondary school record. *Important factors considered include:* Class rank, application essay, academic GPA, recommendation(s), standardized test scores, character/personal qualities, extracurricular activities. *Other factors considered include:* Alumni/ae relation, first generation, geographical residence, interview, level of applicant's interest, racial/ethnic status, talent/ability, volunteer work, work experience. SAT and SAT Subject Tests or ACT required; ACT with Writing component recommended. TOEFL required of all international applicants. High school diploma is required and GED is accepted. *Academic units required:* 4 English, 4 mathematics, 4 science, (3 science labs), 3 foreign language, 2 social studies, 2 history, 4 academic electives. *Academic units recommended:* 4 English, 4 mathematics, 4 science, (3 science labs), 4 foreign language, 4 social studies, 2 history.

Financial Aid

Students should submit: FAFSA, institution's own financial aid form, CSS/Financial Aid PROFILE, state aid form, noncustodial PROFILE, business/farm supplement. Regular filing deadline is 2/1. The Princeton Review suggests that all financial aid forms be submitted as soon as possible after January 1. *Need-based scholarships/grants offered:* Federal Pell, SEOG, state scholarships/grants, private scholarships, the school's own gift aid. *Loan aid offered:* FFEL Subsidized Stafford, FFEL Unsubsidized Stafford, FFEL PLUS, Federal Perkins, Loans for Non-citizens with need. Applicants will be notified of awards on or about 3/30. Federal Work-Study Program available. Institutional employment available. Off-campus job opportunities are fair.

The Inside Word

With acceptance rates hitting record lows, stellar academic credentials are a must for any serious Vassar candidate. Importantly, the college prides itself on selecting students that will add to the vitality of the campus; once Admissions Officers see that you meet their rigorous scholastic standards, they'll closely assess your personal essay, recommendations, and extracurricular activities. Indeed, demonstrating an intellectual curiosity that extends outside the classroom is as important as success within it.

THE SCHOOL SAYS "..."

From The Admissions Office

"Vassar presents a rich variety of social and cultural activities, clubs, sports, living arrangements, and regional attractions. Vassar is a vital, residential college community recognized for its respect for the rights and individuality of others.

"Candidates for admission to the Class of 2012 at Vassar must submit either the SAT Reasoning Test and two SAT Subject Tests taken in different subject fields, or the ACT exam (the optional ACT writing component is recommended)."

For even more information on this school, turn to page 539 of the "Stats" section.

VILLANOVA UNIVERSITY

800 LANCASTER AVENUE, VILLANOVA, PA 19085-1672 • ADMISSIONS: 610-519-4000 • FAX: 610-519-6450
FINANCIAL AID: 610-519-4010 • E-MAIL: GOTOVU@EMAIL.VILLANOVA.EDU • WEBSITE: WWW.VILLANOVA.EDU

RATINGS
Quality of Life: 98   Academic: 88   Admissions: 95   Financial Aid: 71

STUDENTS SAY ". . ."

Academics

"An exceptional and well-known business program" with particular strengths in business attracts nearly a quarter of the undergraduate student body at Villanova University, a prestigious Augustinian school located in the suburbs of Philadelphia. "Employers look to employ Nova graduates" because they know they've studied with "professors who bring real-world experience to the classrooms" and have benefited from "an awesome internship program." Students here are not just business wonks; the school's "rigorous core curriculum" "emphasizes a solid foundation in liberal arts and creative thinking," thereby "developing the whole person through ethical learning." The ethical learning component here "goes far beyond the classroom," as "Participation in service programs (some of the largest in the country), involvement with extracurricular groups, and strong programs established by the university (such as learning communities), are a perfect complement to the excellent development that takes place inside the classroom." Engineering is another area in which Nova students enjoy "an incredible program" with "great facilities." Across the board, "Class sizes are small, and even in a bigger lecture atmosphere, groups are broken up once a week for discussion." Beyond this, "Villanova provides its students with a very high level of technology: access to wireless internet, webmail, and class websites."

> ### SURVEY SAYS . . .
> *Small classes*
> *Career services are great*
> *Students are friendly*
> *Great off-campus food*
> *Campus feels safe*
> *Students are happy*
> *Everyone loves the Wildcats*

Life

At Villanova, "You will work hard Sunday through Wednesday, have fun Thursday through Saturday, and on Sunday you will donate your time to a good cause." Academics, Nova athletics (especially men's basketball), and clubs keep students busy right up until Thursday evening, at which point "People are ready to party, so they either hop on the train to Philly, go to the local bars on the Main Line, or catch a ride to a fraternity party." (Because "There are no frat houses or team houses on campus," all parties "are off campus, and tickets often need to be purchased for as much as $30 the week before. Buses are taken to and from, or you have to know someone to get in. It is a huge hassle for an underclassman, but it's worth the effort.") For many, Sundays are dedicated to church and service. Semester breaks are often also devoted to service: "For fall, winter, and spring break our school runs trips to different parts of the world. Habitat for Humanity trips take place within the United States and allow students to build a house while interacting with the community, strengthening their faith, and creating amazing friendships. Mission trips travel outside of the United States to Mexico, South America, Africa, etc. These trips open the eyes and broaden the minds of those who go on them."

Student Body

"Villanova has the stereotype of White, preppy, private schooled, rich kids." It may be true that, at first glance, what one sees here is "a lot of outgoing, wealthy, well-kept, suburban students who look like they graced the cover of the newest J. Crew magazine and are currently shooting a Crest ad." It's worth noting, however, that "appearances are deceiving. There are plenty of people who do not fit this stereotype." Those schooled in the nuances of Villanova demographics tell us that "there are actually two typical types of students at Villanova. One type consists of preppy, White, rich kids. The other type of student is the one who's interested in community service. There are many students who care a great deal about others and will participate in any activity that allows them to do so." This student is quick to point out, however, that "this is not to say that these groups do not sometimes overlap."

THE PRINCETON REVIEW SAYS

Admissions

Very important factors considered include: Class rank, academic GPA, rigor of secondary school record, standardized test scores. *Important factors considered include:* Application essay, recommendation(s), extracurricular activities, talent/ability, volunteer work, work experience. SAT or ACT required; ACT with Writing component required. TOEFL required of all international applicants. High school diploma is required and GED is accepted. *Academic units required:* 4 English, 4 mathematics, 4 science, (2 science labs), 2 foreign language, 2 academic electives. *Academic units recommended:* 4 English, 4 mathematics, 4 science, (3 science labs), 4 foreign language, 2 academic electives.

Financial Aid

Students should submit: FAFSA, institution's own financial aid form. Regular filing deadline is 2/7. The Princeton Review suggests that all financial aid forms be submitted as soon as possible after January 1. *Need-based scholarships/grants offered:* Federal Pell, SEOG, state scholarships/grants, private scholarships, the school's own gift aid. *Loan aid offered:* FFEL Subsidized Stafford, FFEL Unsubsidized Stafford, FFEL PLUS, Federal Perkins, Federal Nursing Applicants will be notified of awards on or about 4/1. Federal Work-Study Program available. Institutional employment available. Off-campus job opportunities are excellent.

The Inside Word

While not as competitive as some of its Catholic brethren, Villanova's growing reputation makes it a strong choice for capable and accomplished students. The university gives equal weight to most facets of the application, and candidates are expected to do the same. Applicants should be aware that admissions criteria vary slightly among Villanova's schools. Students who opt to apply early action also must contend with more arduous standards.

THE SCHOOL SAYS "..."

From The Admissions Office

"The university is a community of persons of diverse professional, academic, and personal interests who in a spirit of collegiality cooperate to achieve their common goals and objectives in the transmission, the pursuit, and the discovery of knowledge. Villanova attempts to enroll students with diverse social, geographic, economic, and educational backgrounds. Villanova welcomes students who consider it desirable to study within the philosophical framework of Christian Humanism. Finally, this community seeks to reflect the spirit of St. Augustine by the cultivation of knowledge, by respect for individual differences, and by adherence to the principle that mutual love and respect should animate every aspect of university life."

—Villanova University Mission Statement

For even more information on this school, turn to page 539 of the "Stats" section.

WAGNER COLLEGE

ONE CAMPUS ROAD, STATEN ISLAND, NY 10301 • ADMISSIONS: 718-390-3411 • FAX: 718-390-3105
FINANCIAL AID: 718-390-3183 • E-MAIL: ADMISSIONS@WAGNER.EDU • WEBSITE: WWW.WAGNER.EDU

RATINGS
Quality of Life: 78   Academic: 80   Admissions: 88   Financial Aid: 84

STUDENTS SAY "..."

Academics

Wagner College on Staten Island boasts one of the most pastoral campuses New York City has to offer. The college is also a pioneer in "practical liberal arts education." All students here must complete a pretty broad curriculum. Interdisciplinary courses for first-year students focus on a unifying theme and include about 30 hours of course-related fieldwork. Seniors must complete a thesis or a big project within their major. Also, "Wagner requires senior-year internships" and "most" students end up working somewhere pretty cool in Manhattan. Classes "never really exceed 30 people." Some students tell us that "this school is very strong academically." Others say that Wagner's coursework is "absolutely cake." The difficulty level really varies from class to class. There are "very personable" professors who "really know what they're talking about," and there are "terrible ones." "It all depends on who you get." Virtually the entire faculty is "constantly available," though. "The administration, up to the president, is very accessible and conscious of students' needs," relates a biology major. "You can generally walk in without an appointment and get whatever help you need." However, the "mean old women" in the bursar's office are a problem. Also, advising can be hit or miss. "Make sure you get a good adviser," counsels an arts administration major, "because mine blows."

> **SURVEY SAYS . . .**
> Athletic facilities are great
> Students are friendly
> Campus feels safe
> Theater is popular
> Lots of beer drinking
> Hard liquor is popular

Life

Some students at Wagner contend that "the dining hall is excellent." Others disagree. "The food here is terrible," gripes a sophomore. "I hate it." Critics also point out that "there are really no fast food places" near campus. "Some of the facilities are a little out of date," too. "Campus maintenance and upkeep would be my biggest complaint," suggests a first-year student. "If they fixed things like clogged drains and broken lights faster, it would be nice." Also, while it's unquestionably "safe" around campus, that's only because "the overprotective security feels like a Gestapo." On the plus side, students relish their "gorgeous" dorm-room views of the Lower Manhattan skyline. They also love their location. "Wagner represents a unique mix of big city and small town." "Rumors are atrocious and spread quickly," but, on the whole, it's "a friendly and small campus where you pretty much know everyone." "There's always a sporting event of some kind going on." The coffeehouse on campus "is a great place to meet new people and play a game of pool or hear great local bands." Otherwise, "Greek life and the theater program seem to dominate." "Parties are really not too extensive on campus but we get it done," says a sophomore. Local bars and clubs on Staten Island are popular for students who are 21 or who have solid fake ID's. When students tire of the local scene, there's always Manhattan. A free shuttle "runs to the ferry quite often" and "almost all of the students" take advantage frequently. "The city can sometimes be expensive," but "you're never bored."

Student Body

While there is clear and growing diversity in Wagner's numbers, one student notes there are "a lot of Staten Islanders and Jersey people." There are substantially more women than men here, and there's a decent gay population. As a result, "there just aren't that many guys who are actively pursuing girls." Overall, it's a "very cliquey" scene. There are "tanning princess types" and "spoiled rich kids" "who'd rather party than study." Other students "are your average go-to-class, hang-out-with-friends, and study kind of people." The biggest social divide is between thespians and jocks. "There are two main groups of students at Wagner," explains a senior. So expect some show tune humming mixed in with Sports Center recaps—and everything in between. Suprised? Didn't your mom tell ya New York City was a big melting pot?

Admissions

Very important factors considered include: Class rank, academic GPA, rigor of secondary school record. *Important factors considered include:* Application essay, recommendation(s), standardized test scores, extracurricular activities, interview. *Other factors considered include:* Character/personal qualities, geographical residence, level of applicant's interest, talent/ability, volunteer work, work experience. SAT or ACT required; TOEFL required of all international applicants. High school diploma is required and GED is accepted. *Academic units required:* 4 English, 3 mathematics, 2 science, (1 science labs), 2 foreign language, 1 social studies, 3 history, 6 academic electives.

Financial Aid

Students should submit: FAFSA, institution's own financial aid form, state aid form. The Princeton Review suggests that all financial aid forms be submitted as soon as possible after January 1. *Need-based scholarships/grants offered:* Federal Pell, SEOG, state scholarships/grants, private scholarships *Loan aid offered:* FFEL Subsidized Stafford, FFEL Unsubsidized Stafford, FFEL PLUS, Federal Perkins, Federal Nursing Applicants will be notified of awards on a rolling basis beginning 3/1. Federal Work-Study Program available. Institutional employment available. Off-campus job opportunities are good.

The Inside Word

As far as grades and test scores, the profile of the average freshman class at Wagner is solid but not spectacular. Don't take the application process too lightly, though. The admissions staff here is dedicated to finding the right students for their school. An interview is definitely a good idea.

THE SCHOOL SAYS "..."

From The Admissions Office

"At Wagner College, we attract and develop active learners and future leaders. Wagner College has received national acclaim (Time magazine, American Association of Colleges and Universities) for its innovative curriculum, The Wagner Plan for the Practical Liberal Arts. At Wagner, we capitalize on our unique geography; we are a traditional, scenic, residential campus, which happens to sit atop a hill on an island overlooking lower Manhattan. Our location allows us to offer a program that couples required off-campus experiences (experiential learning), with 'learning community' clusters of courses. This program begins in the first semester and continues through the senior capstone experience in the major. Fieldwork and internships, writing-intensive reflective tutorials, connected learning, 'reading, writing, and doing': At Wagner College our students truly discover 'the practical liberal arts in New York City.'

"Applicants for Fall 2008 are required to take the current version of the SAT, or the ACT with the Writing section."

For even more information on this school, turn to page 540 of the "Stats" section.

WASHINGTON COLLEGE

300 WASHINGTON AVENUE, CHESTERTOWN, MD 21620 • ADMISSIONS: 410-778-7700 • FAX: 410-778-7287
E-MAIL: ADM.OFF@WASHCOLL.EDU • WEBSITE: WWW.WASHCOLL.EDU

RATINGS
Quality of Life: 70   Academic: 83   Admissions: 88   Financial Aid: 89

STUDENTS SAY ". . ."

Academics

Washington College is a small, private liberal arts college in eastern Maryland that is "steeped in history." It's the tenth oldest college in the United States. Undergraduate research is commonplace here, and internships are tremendous. Study abroad is "really big" and available in about two dozen destinations around the world. The creative writing

program is "well respected." Other notable majors include business and theater. Course selection "isn't that great," but academics are "challenging." Some classes "have upwards of 50 people in them" but most are pretty intimate. Usually, "there is a great deal of individualized attention," and "there is no hiding in the back of the classroom." Washington College's "caring" professors are "ridiculously eager about their subjects." Most are "willing to meet outside of class or chat through e-mail" and "willing to go the extra mile." "My professors treat me as an individual and more than just the kid they have to grind the information into," relates an English major. Complaints include the library, which isn't much. Some students also grumble about tuition and call WAC "a money pit." The "ambitious" administration "does everything possible to keep students happy in most aspects of life," but the top brass can be "out of touch" and, sometimes, things "just don't run very smoothly."

Life

"The food on campus is usually not very good and sometimes difficult to eat." Also, some dorms are "falling apart," and a host of construction projects has made this campus look like a "war zone" lately. Some students say they like the way Washington College "combines colonial charm with modern facilities." Others disagree. "Concrete plus brick equals ugly," asserts a senior. Socially, WAC is "close-knit." "The general atmosphere is comfortable and laidback." "Pretty much everything happens on campus." "Numerous speakers and musical events" are frequent. There are "strong" athletic programs. Men's lacrosse is especially huge. Fraternities and sororities aren't overwhelming here but they are certainly noticeable. On the weekends, "parties are plentiful." "If you don't drink alcohol, this school isn't for you," advises a junior. The festivities around May Day get especially crazy. Off campus, "there really is nothing to do at all" in "sleepy," "remote," and "very rural" Chestertown. "Many old people live there." "The waterfront area of town is nice." If you want to, you can wakeboard, water ski, and sail to your heart's content. Otherwise, there are a few "little trinket and book shops," but that's about it. "The closet mall is 45 minutes" away. There's "a shuttle that runs to D.C. and Annapolis on the weekends," but "transportation is highly recommended." Many students with cars head to Baltimore and Philadelphia for day trips.

Student Body

"I find this school to be extremely diverse," indicates a first-year student. "Granted, we might have had four black kids in my high school." There's "a fun bunch" of international students and smattering of minorities but "Washington College, embodied in a human would be white." Some students "come from a rural way of life," and there are many middle-class students who "depend on fairly generous scholarships." However, a large contingent of students comes "from private high schools" in "wealthy suburbs" in "Jersey, Maryland, or Pennsylvania." "Most of us are pretty smart, go to class, and participate in extracurriculars," says a junior. There are "meathead athletes and musicians with tweed jackets." There also "tree huggers, rock climbers, wannabe rockers, dramatists, philosophers, future business leaders," and "your average goths and freaks." On the whole, though, the culture is very preppy. "It would be possible to believe that Polo sponsors our students because it is everywhere," explains a sophomore. "The kids are generic." "Cliques" are reportedly noticeable on this campus, and "boundaries are definitely defined." However, "there is a real sense of community" as well. "Everyone knows everyone," says a junior, "so it's very hard to be excluded."

THE PRINCETON REVIEW SAYS

Admissions

Very important factors considered include: Academic GPA, rigor of secondary school record, interview. *Important factors considered include:* Class rank, standardized test scores, level of applicant's interest. *Other factors considered include:* Application essay, recommendation(s), alumni/ae relation, character/personal qualities, extracurricular activities, first generation, geographical residence, racial/ethnic status, state residency, talent/ability, volunteer work, work experience. SAT or ACT required; High school diploma is required and GED is accepted. *Academic units required:* 4 English, 3 mathematics, 3 science, (2 science labs), 2 foreign language, 2 social studies, 2 history. *Academic units recommended:* 4 English, 4 mathematics, 4 science, (3 science labs), 4 foreign language, 4 social studies.

Financial Aid

Students should submit: FAFSA, institution's own financial aid form. The Princeton Review suggests that all financial aid forms be submitted as soon as possible after January 1. *Need-based scholarships/grants offered:* Federal Pell, SEOG, state scholarships/grants, private scholarships, the school's own gift aid. *Loan aid offered:* FFEL Subsidized Stafford, FFEL Unsubsidized Stafford, FFEL PLUS, Federal Perkins, college/university loans from institutional funds. Applicants will be notified of awards on a rolling basis beginning 3/15. Federal Work-Study Program available. Institutional employment available. Off-campus job opportunities are good.

The Inside Word

Though Washington's acceptance rate hovers just under 60 percent, the statistic belies the competitive nature of the applicants. Prospective students who view WC as one of their top choices should do themselves a favor and complete their application ahead of the prescribed deadline. Interviews are also highly recommended and those who decline the opportunity will be putting themselves at a disadvantage.

THE SCHOOL SAYS ". . ."

From The Admissions Office

"We tell our students, 'Your revolution starts here,' because the person who graduates from Washington College is not the same one who matriculated 4 years earlier, and because through your experiences here, you will be empowered and emboldened to change the world. Your education reflects the maxims of our founder, George Washington: The strength of America's democracy depends on the success of students like you to evolve as a critical and independent thinker, to persevere in the face of challenge, to assume the responsibilities and privileges of informed citizenship. That's where we come in, providing a truly personalized education that tests—and stretches—the limits of each student's talents and potentials. We reach beyond the classroom to create challenges and opportunities that expand your brainpower and creativity through collaborative research with faculty, through independent and self-directed study, and through the rigor of creating a senior project that demonstrates the power of a maturing intellect. All this happens in a wonderfully distinct setting—in historic Chestertown, on the Chester River, amid the ecological bounty of Maryland's Chesapeake Bay—that helps define who we are and that will shape your own college experience.

"Washington College requires either SAT or ACT scores. There is no minimum SAT/ACT cut-off score for admission. However, the middle 50 percent of accepted applicants have SAT scores in the 1050 to 1250 range. The average SAT (Critical Reading and Math) score for enrolled freshmen is 1150 (24 for ACT)."

For even more information on this school, turn to page 540 of the "Stats" section.

WASHINGTON & JEFFERSON COLLEGE

60 SOUTH LINCOLN STREET, WASHINGTON, PA 15301 • ADMISSIONS: 724-223-6025 • FAX: 724-223-6534
E-MAIL: ADMISSION@WASHJEFF.EDU • WEBSITE: WWW.WASHJEFF.EDU

RATINGS
Quality of Life: 72   Academic: 85   Admissions: 92   Financial Aid: 72

STUDENTS SAY "..."

Academics

"High academic standards" and small class sizes, coupled with a student body made up of individuals "very serious about their education" leads to a lot of hard work and accountability for the undergrads of Washington & Jefferson College. While many choose the college for its strong programs in the sciences and the liberal arts, every major at W&J is reportedly difficult. The college's friendly professors, administrators, and staff, however, do their best to help students to succeed and "make you feel as comfy as possible." Despite the heavy workload, students describe W&J as a "fun, challenging, and nurturing environment" where students are truly mentored and supported by the faculty and staff. As one freshman writes, "The professors are amazing. They are always there whenever you are struggling, confused, or just want to talk. Even the administration is available to chat!" While the quality of the academic program is undisputed, some students gripe about the high costs of this private school. In particular, students tell us that "the Financial Aid Department needs some work." Commenting on this state of affairs, a freshman jokes that the college might consider changing its motto to "providing the best education possible for the most amount of money."

Life

When considering student life at W&J, a junior offers this 1980s analogy: "It's like a mullet: business in the front, party in the back." Indeed, students say that W&J is the place to go for both a "good education and a good time," as the friendly student body is as social as it is studious. On campus, "People are busy with sports, clubs, and fraternities/sororities"; athletics are also particularly popular with students. A sophomore writes, "Our school is all about education . . . and after education comes sports." During the weekend, the W&J campus comes alive with parties. "After a hard week of stressful classes, most of the people here drink," writes a student. However, undergraduates reassure us that there are "no crazy state school–style parties" at W&J, and most students prioritize books over booze. As one sophomore reports, "I like to drink and party on the weekends, but get my homework done during the week." Whether you like the W&J social life or not, you're stuck with it, as undergraduates are required to live on campus.

Student Body

On the whole, this small campus is home to "nice, studious, involved, and athletic" undergrads, most of whom take their education very seriously. Almost all students claim to be "hard workers" and generally describe their classmates as intelligent and motivated, but the similarities don't end there. A junior reports that "everyone is pretty typical—White, upper-middle-class American. We have very few minorities." Another confesses, "The majority of students are cookie-cutter images of each other. There is very little individuality on this campus." Even so, students claim that their classmates are generally accepting and friendly, even if there are very few students who don't fit in. A junior writes, "Everyone gets along no matter what they look like; a benefit to a small campus." In fact, students insist that W&J, "works like a small community; everyone helps everyone."

> **SURVEY SAYS . . .**
> Small classes
> Great computer facilities
> Everyone loves the Presidents
> Frats and sororities dominate
> social scene
> Lots of beer drinking
> Hard liquor is popular

Admissions

Very important factors considered include: Class rank, application essay, academic GPA, recommendation(s), rigor of secondary school record, interview. *Important factors considered include:* Standardized test scores, character/personal qualities, extracurricular activities. *Other factors considered include:* Alumni/ae relation, geographical residence, level of applicant's interest, racial/ethnic status, state residency, talent/ability, volunteer work, SAT or ACT required; TOEFL required of all international applicants. High school diploma is required and GED is accepted. *Academic units required:* 3 English, 3 mathematics, 2 foreign language, 1 history, 6 academic electives.

Financial Aid

Students should submit: FAFSA. The Princeton Review suggests that all financial aid forms be submitted as soon as possible after January 1. *Need-based scholarships/grants offered:* Federal Pell, SEOG, state scholarships/grants, private scholarships, the school's own gift aid, ACG and SMART Grants. *Loan aid offered:* FFEL Subsidized Stafford, FFEL Unsubsidized Stafford, FFEL PLUS, Federal Perkins, college/university loans from institutional funds. Applicants will be notified of awards on a rolling basis beginning 3/1. Federal Work-Study Program available. Institutional employment available. Off-campus job opportunities are good.

The Inside Word

In a reflection of the students they aim to admit, Washington & Jefferson College takes a well-rounded approach to admissions. Academic record, class rank, personal statement, and extracurricular activities are all thoroughly evaluated. Most prospective students work diligently to secure admittance. The lucky applicants who receive a fat letter in the mail are welcomed into a distinctive community that promises to broaden their horizons and prepare them for a successful future.

THE SCHOOL SAYS ". . ."

From The Admissions Office

"There is a palpable sense of momentum and energy at Washington & Jefferson. Enrollment has grown significantly over the past 5 years. Additional faculty members have been hired, and academic programs have been added and expanded to accommodate the increased enrollment. The student-centered teaching and learning community that has always distinguished W&J remains our top priority. It is no surprise that 100 percent of our graduates who took the bar exam passed in 2006, or that 90 percent of our graduates recommended for medical and law school are admitted. The college has added almost $75 million dollars in new facilities since 2002, including two new residence halls, ten theme-based residential houses, new athletic facilities, a state-of-the-art technology center, and the Howard J. Burnett Center, which houses our programs in accounting, business, economics, education, entrepreneurial studies, and modern languages. Construction on a new $30 million science facility is scheduled to begin within the next 2 years. Despite an almost fourfold increase in applications in this time, the Admission Staff remains committed to reviewing each application individually. Our students are balanced, goal oriented, active, engaged and involved and we look for evidence of these traits in prospective students. We encourage students to use every aspect of the application process to demonstrate that they possess these qualities. If you are looking to become part of an institution that is constantly changing for the better and that will be an even better place by the time you graduate, then we encourage you to consider W&J.

"Students applying for Fall 2009 must submit scores from the SAT (or ACT). It is not required that they take the new version of the SAT (or the ACT with the Writing section). We will allow students to submit scores from either version of the SAT (or ACT) and will use the student's best scores from either test."

For even more information on this school, turn to page 541 of the "Stats" section.

WEBB INSTITUTE

298 CRESCENT BEACH ROAD, OCEAN COVE, NY 11542 • ADMISSIONS: 516-674-9838
FINANCIAL AID: 516-671-2213 • E-MAIL: ADMISSIONS@WEBB-INSTITUTE.EDU • WEBSITE: WWW.WEBB-INSTITUTE.EDU

RATINGS
Quality of Life: 99   **Academic:** 95   **Admissions:** 98   **Financial Aid:** 85

STUDENTS SAY "..."

Academics

Webb Institute on Long Island is a ridiculously small school wholly dedicated to boats. If you feel destined to become one of "America's future ship designers and engineers," enroll here. Every student receives a four-year, full-tuition scholarship. The only costs are books and supplies, room and board, and personal expenses. Everyone majors in naval architecture and marine engineering. "There are no classes to choose," explains a junior. "The curriculum is set for all students." Webbies are exposed to a smattering of

> **SURVEY SAYS . . .**
> *Large classes*
> *Registration is a breeze*
> *Career services are great*
> *Frats and sororities are unpopular*
> *or nonexistent*
> *Political activism is unpopular or nonexistent*
> *Very little drug use*

the liberal arts and a ton of advanced math and physics. Virtually every other course involves ship design. There's also a senior thesis and a "required internship program." In January and February, all students get real, paying jobs in the marine industry. Job prospects are phenomenal. Newly minted Webb graduates enjoy "a 100 percent placement rate in grad schools and careers." Coursework is "rigorous," but the academic atmosphere is very intimate. "A huge plus of Webb's small size is that everyone knows everyone," relates a junior. "You're not just another number." "The administration, professors, and students all work in the same building every day, every week." "The admiral can get carried away when he perceives a problem" but the faculty is "approachable," "always accessible," and "very dedicated to the school and students." "Professors have a great deal of respect for the students and work closely with us to accomplish our goals," says a sophomore. "If you're passionate about architecture and engineering, you cannot hope for a better learning environment."

Life

Webb has a "family-like atmosphere." It's "a tiny student body living, eating, sleeping, and learning ship design in a mansion" "in a residential area overlooking the beautiful Long Island Sound." There's an honor code "that is strictly adhered to by all students." Cheating and stealing just don't happen here. "You can leave your wallet lying in the reception room, and if someone doesn't return it to you just because they know what your wallet looks like compared to the other 90 wallets in the school, it will still be there the next day and even the next week." Life at Webb "revolves around course load and the attempts to find distractions from it." "We average about five to seven hours of homework per night," advises a freshman. "At the end of the semesters, life sucks due to a ton of projects." "People generally think about homework and spend most of their time discussing class assignments." When students find some down time, movies and unorganized sports are common. Not surprisingly, "many people turn to the water" for amusement as well. "Sailing is popular." "The school has a skiff and sailboats, which are frequently used during the warm months," says a sophomore. Annual whitewater rafting and ski trips are well attended. New York City is a little less than an hour away, and "a bunch of people venture into" Manhattan on the weekends. "A lot of spontaneous and off-the-wall things occur" too, and "a fair amount of partying goes on at least once a week." However, Webb is absolutely not a party school.

Student Body

The average Webbie is a "middleclass white male who enjoys engineering and sciences." "There are very few atypical students." "Everyone is motivated and works hard." Basically, you have your bookworms who "don't socialize as much" and your more social students who get their work done but also play sports and "have a good time." "The differences in these two groups are by far the most visible division within the student body." Camaraderie is reportedly easy due to the academic stress and Webb's small size. Everyone interacts with everyone else, regardless of background. With fewer than 100 students, it's "impossible to completely isolate yourself." "There are no social cliques, and everyone is included in anything they'd like to be included in." As at most engineering schools, the ratio between males and females is pretty severely lopsided here. "We want more women!" plead many students.

THE PRINCETON REVIEW SAYS

Admissions

Very important factors considered include: Class rank, academic GPA, rigor of secondary school record, standardized test scores, character/personal qualities, interview, level of applicant's interest. *Important factors considered include:* Recommendation(s), extracurricular activities. *Other factors considered include:* talent/ability, volunteer work, work experience. SAT required; SAT Subject Tests required; High school diploma is required and GED is not accepted. *Academic units required:* 4 English, 4 mathematics, 2 science, (2 science labs), 2 social studies, 4 academic electives.

Financial Aid

Students should submit: FAFSA Regular filing deadline is 7/1. The Princeton Review suggests that all financial aid forms be submitted as soon as possible after January 1. *Need-based scholarships/grants offered:* Federal Pell, state scholarships/grants, private scholarships, the school's own gift aid. *Loan aid offered:* FFEL Subsidized Stafford, FFEL Unsubsidized Stafford, FFEL PLUS Applicants will be notified of awards on or about 8/1. Off-campus job opportunities are fair.

The Inside Word

Let's not mince words; admission to Webb is mega-tough. Webb's Admissions Counselors are out to find the right kid for their curriculum—one that can survive the school's rigorous academics. The applicant pool is highly self-selected because of the focused program of study: naval architecture and marine engineering.

THE SCHOOL SAYS "..."

From The Admissions Office

"Webb, the only college in the country that specializes in the engineering field of naval architecture and marine engineering, seeks young men and women of all races from all over the country who are interested in receiving an excellent engineering education with a full-tuition scholarship. Students don't have to know anything about ships, they just have to be motivated to study how mechanical, civil, structural, and electrical engineering come together with the design elements that make up a ship and all its systems. Being small and private has its major advantages. Every applicant is special and the President will interview all entering students personally. The student/faculty ratio is 8:1, and since there are no teaching assistants, interaction with the faculty occurs daily in class and labs at a level not found at most other colleges. The college provides each student with a high-end laptop computer. The entire campus operates under the Student Organization's honor system that allows unsupervised exams and 24-hour access to the library, every classroom and laboratory, and the shop and gymnasium. Despite a total enrollment of between 70 and 80 students and a demanding workload, Webb manages to field six intercollegiate teams. Currently more than 60 percent of the members of the student body play on one or more intercollegiate teams. Work hard, play hard and the payoff is a job for every student upon graduation. The placement record of the college is 100 percent every year.

"Freshman applicants must take the new SAT. In addition, students may submit scores from the old SAT (before March 2005), and the best scores from either test will be used. We also require scores from two SAT Subject Tests: Math Level I or II and either Physics or Chemistry."

For even more information on this school, turn to page 542 of the "Stats" section.

WELLESLEY COLLEGE

BOARD OF ADMISSION, 106 CENTRAL STREET, WELLESLEY, MA 02481-8203 • ADMISSIONS: 781-283-2270
FAX: 781-283-3678 • FINANCIAL AID: 781-283-2360 • E-MAIL: ADMISSION@WELLESLEY.EDU • WEBSITE: WWW.WELLESLEY.EDU

RATINGS
Quality of Life: 96   Academic: 98   Admissions: 97   Financial Aid: 98

STUDENTS SAY ". . ."

Academics

Wellesley College, "a small liberal arts institution with the intimacy of a family and the academic excellence of a top-rank university," provides its "all-female" student body with "an excellent education to make women independent individuals" while "preparing ambitious women to succeed in the professional world." This elite school located just outside Boston offers "undergraduate research opportunities, close relationships with professors, a suburban environment," and much more. One student explains,

"Wellesley has everything I was looking for. It was a small, liberal arts school in New England with small class sizes, excellent professors, and an amazing reputation. I also appreciated the culture within the student body, the dedicated alumnae network, and the academic challenge." "Class work is rigorous" at Wellesley as teachers here "have incredibly high expectations," "But there are lots of resources available to help you if you need it," not the least of which are professors who "hold a large amount of office hours and even provide you with their home phone numbers and cell phone numbers in case you have any questions, whether about the class, the assignment, or life. The dedication of the Wellesley community is what I find to be stand out about the school." Spending part of junior year abroad is a staple of a Wellesley education. One student reports that "over 50 percent of Wellesley students travel abroad." Indeed, at home or abroad Wellesley offers "unlimited opportunities" and "takes the steps necessary" to help young women "realize [their] potential."

Life

At Wellesley, "the focus is all on academics," especially during the week. "You won't see students partying here on weekdays! Instead, you'll find students attending lectures, or discussing the news or issues on campus and what homework they have." The school's "close-knit atmosphere and location" make for an "unbelievably rich" college experience. While it's true that "there are no males around, at least not to the degree that there would be on a co-ed campus," students see this as a benefit. A freshman says, "This simply makes me focus more on what I'm really at college for: To get the most out of the educational opportunities available to me. In class, I am able to focus whole-heartedly on the subject matter, which is sometimes more difficult to do if there's a cute guy sitting in the class with me who is looking at me or whom I like." When it's time to chill, "Students attend cultural shows and plays on campus but mostly head into Boston." Social connections in this city dictate that eventually "Everyone ends up knowing someone else who goes to school in Boston and from that person, develops an additional social network in the city. This gives students a much-needed break on weekends from the often stressful Wellesley environment."

Students

Students describe the typical Wellesley undergrad (aka "Wendy Wellesley") as "an overachiever balancing two majors, 10 extracurricular activities, and several volunteer jobs." She is "passionate, hardworking, and wants to have an impact on the world around her." One student notes that "strong personalities," "diverse" individuals, and a "large range of interests" do not "allow the existence of absolutely typical students." Though "trends do occur," the "common denominator" among students is their "commitment to academic excellence." Beyond these traits, "Students are extremely diverse—ethnically, geographically, and socioeconomically. Because students come from so many backgrounds, no students are truly in the minority, and it is therefore easy for anyone to fit in."

THE PRINCETON REVIEW SAYS

Admissions

Very important factors considered include: Application essay, academic GPA, recommendation(s), rigor of secondary school record, standardized test scores, character/personal qualities. *Important factors considered include:* Class rank, extracurricular activities. *Other factors considered include:* Alumni/ae relation, first generation, geographical residence, interview, level of applicant's interest, racial/ethnic status, state residency, talent/ability, volunteer work, work experience. SAT and SAT Subject Tests or ACT required; ACT with Writing component required. High school diploma or equivalent is not required. *Academic units recommended:* 4 English, 4 mathematics, 3 science, (2 science labs), 4 foreign language, 4 social studies, 4 history.

Financial Aid

Students should submit: FAFSA, institution's own financial aid form, CSS/Financial Aid PROFILE, noncustodial PROFILE, business/farm supplement, parents' and students' tax returns and W-2s. The Princeton Review suggests that all financial aid forms be submitted as soon as possible after January 1. *Need-based scholarships/grants offered:* Federal Pell, SEOG, state scholarships/grants, the school's own gift aid. *Loan aid offered:* FFEL Subsidized Stafford, FFEL Unsubsidized Stafford, FFEL PLUS, Federal Perkins, state loans, college/university loans from institutional funds. Applicants will be notified of awards on or about 4/1. Federal Work-Study Program available. Institutional employment available. Off-campus job opportunities are excellent.

The Inside Word

As the number of women's colleges diminishes—The New York Times recently reported that the U.S. now has only about 60 all-women's schools, down from over 300 in the 1960s—competition for admission to the remaining single-sex institutions stiffens. Wellesley has always been an elite institution, but it grows ever more so as its number of competitors for top women students shrinks. If you submit your application materials to Wellesley by November 1, the school will provide you with an early evaluation, giving you some idea of your chances for admission.

THE SCHOOL SAYS ". . ."

From The Admissions Office

"Ranked fourth among liberal arts and sciences colleges according to the 2006 U.S. News & World Report survey, and widely acknowledged as the nation's best women's college, Wellesley College provides students with numerous opportunities on campus and beyond. With a long-standing commitment to and established reputation for academic excellence, Wellesley offers more than 1,000 courses in 53 established majors and supports 180 clubs, organizations, and activities for its students. The college is easily accessible to Boston, a great city in which to meet other college students and to experience theater, art, sports, and entertainment. Considered one of the most diverse colleges in the nation, Wellesley students hail from 79 countries and all 50 states.

"As a community, we are looking for students who possess intellectual curiosity: the ability to think independently, ask challenging questions, and grapple with answers. Strong candidates demonstrate both academic achievement and an excitement for learning. They also display leadership, an appreciation for diverse perspectives, and an understanding of the college's mission to educate women who will make a difference in the world.

"SAT and SAT Subject Tests or ACT with Writing component required. Two SAT Subject Tests required, one of which should be quantitative (Math or Science). We strongly recommend that students planning to apply early decision complete the tests before the end of their junior year and no later than October of their senior year."

For even more information on this school, turn to page 542 of the "Stats" section.

WELLS COLLEGE

ROUTE 90, AURORA, NY 13026 • ADMISSIONS: 315-364-3264 • FAX: 315-364-3327
FINANCIAL AID: 315-364-3289 • E-MAIL: ADMISSIONS@WELLS.EDU • WEBSITE: WWW.WELLS.EDU

RATINGS
Quality of Life: 77   Academic: 88   Admissions: 85   Financial Aid: 75

STUDENTS SAY "..."

Academics

Most Wells students enrolled expecting an education designed to "form a strong community and strong female leaders." Not surprisingly, the college's recent decision to admit men and the arrival of its first coed class have left the student body with mixed feelings toward the administration. "The deans and the president are not straightforward in their interaction[s] with students," writes a senior. "They

SURVEY SAYS . . .
Small classes
No one cheats
Students are friendly
Frats and sororities are unpopular
or nonexistent

say one thing but do another, with seemingly little interest as to the desires of the students." A more even-handed student tells us, "Although [the] administration has proven to be not fully trustworthy in the information conveyed to students regarding Wells going coed, they have been accessible for dialogue on the matter, as well as for personal concerns." Students unite in praise of the school's honor code, which rewards responsibility with freedom—"Students are allowed to take exams out of the classroom and leave it in the[ir] professor's office when they're done." They also enjoy "one-on-one relationships" with professors who "are often upset if you don't come to their office hours to bug them" and "will approach you after [class] if they think you did well or saw that you were unprepared." With "highly rigorous" academics, extensive study abroad opportunities, and a "very interesting and very rare" book arts center, we predict Wells will continue to attract students into its coed halls.

Life

The Wells existence "can be summarized in one word: isolation." Hometown Aurora mostly shuts down by 8:00 p.m. One student warns: "If you are from NYC, you may be culture shocked" when you find yourself spending "Friday and Saturday nights doing homework." Besides the farms and barns, "There's a bar where the entire senior class congregates on Fridays, a wickedly expensive inn, and a pizza place." Students tell us that at Wells "The most fun comes from the traditions: The Even/Odd rivalry, Junior Blast, Freshman Elves . . . these are really what give Wells its fabulous life." Civilization, meaning malls and other college students, lies 45 minutes away in Ithaca, but some people prefer to stay put, swimming in Cayuga Lake, sledding down Student Union hill, exploring the local cemetery, and involving themselves with campus organizations. Spontaneous games of "hallway soccer," "wine and Cheez-Its" parties, and trips to the 24-hour Wal-Mart are also common. Students emphasize the luxury of "the safe space we have here. You can walk back to your dorm across campus at 3:00 a.m. alone and your biggest worry is bumping into the campus skunk." However, that might not hold true during dining hours: "I was told I was going to get the 'freshman 15,'" a student writes. "Whoever said that never ate in my school's dining hall."

Student Body

With only about 470 undergrads, "Everyone knows everyone else" at Wells. So it's fortunate that, despite a lingering resentment over the administration's decision to go coed, most students are tolerant of their new male peers. One student explains, "There were a lot of protests over it [two years ago], but the people who were in those protests left that to [two years ago] and they treat the guys great." As a male student was elected freshman class president in 2005–2006, it would seem that male students have been fully integrated into the Wells community. One male student, however, offers a different perspective: "Guys have been discriminated against here, but that's [to be] expected. Over time this will fade. I think there is more anger at the girls who are here because of the guys than anger at the guys themselves!" Regardless of gender, Wells students are outspoken, with "politics, establishing fair trade with poor countries, [and] women's studies" common topics of conversation. The liberal students tend to dominate this discussion: "It's generally assumed that whoever goes to the school is either a feminist or a Democrat."

THE PRINCETON REVIEW SAYS

Admissions

Very important factors considered include: Academic GPA, recommendation(s), rigor of secondary school record, standardized test scores, extracurricular activities. *Important factors considered include:* Application essay, interview. *Other factors considered include:* Class rank, alumni/ae relation, character/personal qualities, level of applicant's interest, talent/ability, volunteer work, work experience. SAT or ACT required; TOEFL required of all international applicants. High school diploma is required and GED is accepted. *Academic units required:* 4 English, 3 mathematics, 2 science, (2 science labs), 1 social studies, 3 history, 2 academic electives. *Academic units recommended:* 4 mathematics, 3 science, (3 science labs), 2 foreign language, 2 social studies, 2 history, 3 academic electives, 2 music, art, computer science.

Financial Aid

Students should submit: FAFSA, CSS/Financial Aid Profile for Early Decision Applicants only. The Princeton Review suggests that all financial aid forms be submitted as soon as possible after January 1. *Need-based scholarships/grants offered:* Federal Pell, SEOG, state scholarships/grants, private scholarships, the school's own gift aid. *Loan aid offered:* FFEL Subsidized Stafford, FFEL Unsubsidized Stafford, FFEL PLUS, Federal Perkins Applicants will be notified of awards on a rolling basis beginning 3/1. Federal Work-Study Program available. Institutional employment available. Off-campus job opportunities are poor.

The Inside Word

Wells is engaged in that age-old admissions game called matchmaking. There are no minimums or cutoffs in the admissions process here. But don't be fooled by the high admit rate. The Admissions Committee will look closely at your academic accomplishments, but also gives attention to your essay, recommendations, and extracurricular pursuits. The committee also recommends an interview; we suggest taking them up on it.

THE SCHOOL SAYS ". . ."

From The Admissions Office

"Wells College believes the twenty-first century needs well-educated individuals with the ability, self-confidence, and vision to contribute to an ever-changing world. Wells offers an outstanding classroom experience and innovative liberal arts curriculum that prepares students for leadership in a variety of fields, including business, government, the arts, sciences, medicine, and education. By directly connecting the liberal arts curriculum to experience and career development through internships, off-campus study, study abroad, research with professors, and community service, each student has an ideal preparation for graduate and professional school as well as for the twenty-first century.

"Wells College requires freshman applicants to submit scores from the old or new SAT. Students may also choose to submit scores from the ACT (with or without the Writing component) in lieu of the SAT."

For even more information on this school, turn to page 542 of the "Stats" section.

WENTWORTH INSTITUTE OF TECHNOLOGY

550 HUNTINGTON AVENUE, ADMISSIONS OFFICE, BOSTON, MA 02115-5998 • ADMISSIONS: 617-989-4000 • FAX: 617-989-4010
E-MAIL: ADMISSIONS@WIT.EDU • WEBSITE: WWW.WIT.EDU

RATINGS
Quality of Life: 75   **Academic:** 79   **Admissions:** 60*   **Financial Aid:** 64

STUDENTS SAY "..."

Academics

Providing engineers, designers, and architects with "a mix of hands-on learning and academics, giving you the best of both worlds and a nice head start for the working world," Wentworth Institute of Technology "is about knowing everything there is to know about your major, then going out in the field [and] doing a co-op to fully understand it." Here, "Two semesters of co-op work are required," and, as a result "Wentworth students are highly regarded in their fields due to [having] real-world job experience upon graduation. Wentworth students also gain technical skills through the hands-on teaching approach and numerous lab requirements." Don't expect a liberal arts approach here; the "learning environment is more geared toward students moving toward becoming young professionals." Many courses are required, and so "The range of electives is small," and students "live at studio. It's not the conventional college experience." WIT professors earn high marks from students; students say that most "genuinely care about the education of the students and do all they can to help them succeed," although they also note that "careful selection of your professors during registration" is highly recommended. The administration "is hard to work with sometimes," and some even go so far as to describe it as "a confused, jumbled, unorganized mess."

> **SURVEY SAYS . . .**
> Large classes
> Students love Boston, MA
> Great off-campus food
> Frats and sororities are unpopular or nonexistent
> Theater is popular

Life

"People are very involved with their studies and turning out good projects" at WIT, and many spend a great deal of their waking hours "in classes, at the dorm, studio, or doing the things one needs to do to live, such as grocery shop. There isn't a ton of free time here." Even so, "Life at school is pretty good. For the most part there is almost always something going on. If not, we are located in Boston (about a 5-minute walk to Fenway, 10-minute walk to the Prudential Center) so there is always something going on around us." Wentworth's location "at the base of Mission Hill places the campus in close proximity to numerous other schools." Students here "tend to have parties with friends (alcohol based or not, depending on the crowd), head out to wander Boston, play video games, watch movies, go to concerts and such, and participate in outdoor sports and other activities."

Student Body

The typical Wentworth student "is a middle-class White male from the Boston area" who "can easily fit into either the jock or the geek stereotype." You'll usually find them dressed in "sneakers or work boots, jeans, and a t-shirt or hoody, sometimes more for the bitterly cold wind that one experiences during a typical Boston winter." Because the student body "tends to be all kids interested in technical/design fields, [it] gives everyone a trait they share. There are always a few kids who are brilliant at what they do, and there are usually a few really creative kids. Pretty much everyone fits in, especially in studio." The school "has a low female student body and a lack of out-of-state students and international students (there are likely more international professors than students)." But while there is "little diversity" on campus, "Those who are different fit in fine."

THE PRINCETON REVIEW SAYS

Admissions

Very important factors considered include: Rigor of secondary school record. *Important factors considered include:* Application essay, recommendation(s), standardized test scores. *Other factors considered include:* Academic GPA, extracurricular activities, interview, level of applicant's interest, volunteer work, work experience. SAT or ACT required; ACT with Writing component required. TOEFL required of all international applicants. High school diploma is required and GED is accepted. *Academic units required:* 4 English, 3 mathematics, 1 science, (1 science labs). *Academic units recommended:* 4 mathematics, 3 science, (2 science labs).

Financial Aid

Students should submit: FAFSA. The Princeton Review suggests that all financial aid forms be submitted as soon as possible after January 1. *Need-based scholarships/grants offered:* Federal Pell, SEOG, state scholarships/grants, the school's own gift aid. *Loan aid offered:* Direct Subsidized Stafford, Direct Unsubsidized Stafford, Direct PLUS, Federal Perkins, state loans Applicants will be notified of awards on a rolling basis beginning 3/15. Federal Work-Study Program available. Institutional employment available. Off-campus job opportunities are good.

The Inside Word

Wentworth admits nearly 80 percent of its applicant pool; a quick look at admitted students' average SAT scores, however, suggests that this high admit rate is more the result of self-selection than of lax admissions standards. Admissions Officers will be looking for a solid high school transcript, with special attention given to math and science classes. Indications of character, such as involvement in community service and athletics, are also considered.

THE SCHOOL SAYS " . . ."

From The Admissions Office

"One of the most affordable colleges in greater Boston, Wentworth Institute of Technology provides the tools today's career-oriented students need to succeed in the marketplace: strong academic programs, cutting-edge labs and studios, and a cooperative education program (co-op) that is one of the largest and most comprehensive of its kind.

"When you join the Wentworth community, you'll find energetic, can-do students from 36 states and 44 countries. You'll find individuals ready to roll up their sleeves and get to work. Most importantly, you'll find fellow students with a strong drive to succeed academically and professionally.

"At Wentworth you get the best of both worlds: small-college comforts and big-city excitement. You'll find a tree-lined quad, a food court cafeteria, traditional and modern residence halls, recreational facilities, and more on our 35-acre campus. You'll also enjoy easy access to Boston's exciting venues and New England's scenic wonders: walk to Fenway Park, the Museum of Fine Arts, or Copley Place; take a ferry to Cape Cod; hike the White Mountains. Whatever your destination, having the 'T' Green Line and the Ruggles Station stop on the commuter rail right beside campus means you can get into—or out of—Boston easily.

"Wentworth is also a member of the Colleges of the Fenway consortium. This consortium offers the benefits of cross registration and access to social events, professional activities, libraries, and campus facilities at six colleges within walking distance of one another. The other Colleges of the Fenway members are Emmanuel College, Massachusetts College of Art, Massachusetts College of Pharmacy and Health Sciences, Simmons College, and Wheelock College."

For even more information on this school, turn to page 543 of the "Stats" section.

WESLEYAN UNIVERSITY

THE STEWART M. REID HOUSE, 70 WYLLYS AVENUE, MIDDLETOWN, CT 06459-0265 • ADMISSIONS: 860-685-3000 • FAX: 860-685-3001
FINANCIAL AID: 860-685-2800 • E-MAIL: ADMISSIONS@WESLEYAN.EDU • WEBSITE: WWW.WESLEYAN.EDU

RATINGS
Quality of Life: 83   Academic: 94   Admissions: 97   Financial Aid: 95

STUDENTS SAY ". . ."

Academics

Students at Wesleyan University relish "the immense amount of freedom the school gives you," both in terms of curricular choices ("because of the lack of core curriculum, you can mold each semester however you want: lots of lecture, lots of discussion, a mix") and in extracurricular life (in other words, "Public Safety rarely bothers the students"). The latter may sound like a recipe for a nonstop

party, but that's hardly the case at Wesleyan; students here don't see the school as a 24/7 kegger, but rather as "a playground for the most opinionated and social-norm-destroying students of our generation to debate issues that really matter to them." If that suggests a school entirely focused on humanities and social sciences, guess again; Wes "has one of the strongest science programs [of] any of the top liberal arts school[s]. One-quarter of the students major in a science. Since we're in a university, but have very few graduate students, there are tons of opportunities for students to get involved in research. As a sophomore, I was highly involved in a $5 million NIH grant. That's pretty unique and amazing." In all disciplines, "Professors are incredible. They are all as available as they could be to us and more willing to help than I ever expected college professors to be." Those who teach "upper level courses are ridiculously passionate about what they teach, and are usually doing research that is very relevant to their field. At Wesleyan, I always get the sense that I am surrounded by many brilliant minds." A "very active student body . . . frequently tries to make changes in the way that the school is run," and "The administration does a good job [of] working with students to ensure that we all have the most positive experience possible."

Life

The Wesleyan campus is a busy one, replete with club and intercollegiate athletics, frat and house parties, and lots of performances and lectures. One student explains, "The Wes social scene is very much what you want to make it. Want to party? We do have frats (though they're a super-small part of campus life) and house parties. Don't want to party? Go to a play, concert, movie, or just hang out. Not everyone here is partying." Indeed, "There is plenty to keep you occupied" at Wesleyan, including campus politics, as "On this campus there is always some issue being fought or demonstrated against." Students take a strong hand in driving campus life, as "Everything is mostly student-run." "If a Wes student wants something that doesn't currently exist on campus, [he or she] make[s] it happen." Hometown Middletown, while "clearly lacking the resources of a large city," "has lots of opportunities to get involved and feel like a member of the community for four years." A junior reports, "Main Street in Middletown has changed tremendously just in the three years I have been here. Lots of new restaurants, bars, and art galleries have opened."

Student Body

"Passionate" is a word that pops up frequently when Wesleyan undergrads describe their peers, as does "intelligent." In fact, Wesleyan is a magnet for kids who value intellect, not only as a means to good grades and a career, but also as an instrument of self-development. "Everyone is excited about something," undergrads report. Students here are engaged in campus life, meaning that "a lot of things on campus are student-run and a lot of learning takes place outside the classroom due to casual interaction between peers." Demographically speaking, there are "two main molds of a Wesleyan student: The preppy New England kid and the kid . . . that [is] some kind of mix between a hipster and a hippie. Outside of that it's an extremely diverse group of kids who come from all over and have a wide range of interests." Most students here "are liberal and 'alternative.'"

THE PRINCETON REVIEW SAYS

Admissions

Very important factors considered include: Rigor of secondary school record. *Important factors considered include:* Class rank, application essay, academic GPA, recommendation(s), standardized test scores, character/personal qualities, first generation, racial/ethnic status, talent/ability. *Other factors considered include:* Alumni/ae relation, extracurricular activities, geographical residence, interview, volunteer work, work experience. SAT and SAT Subject Tests or ACT required; ACT with Writing component recommended. TOEFL required of all international applicants. High school diploma or equivalent is not required. *Academic units recommended:* 4 English, 4 mathematics, 4 science, (3 science labs), 4 foreign language, 4 social studies.

Financial Aid

Students should submit: FAFSA, CSS/Financial Aid PROFILE, noncustodial PROFILE, business/farm supplement. Regular filing deadline is 2/15. The Princeton Review suggests that all financial aid forms be submitted as soon as possible after January 1. *Need-based scholarships/grants offered:* Federal Pell, SEOG, state scholarships/grants, private scholarships, the school's own gift aid. *Loan aid offered:* FFEL Subsidized Stafford, FFEL Unsubsidized Stafford, FFEL PLUS, Federal Perkins, college/university loans from institutional funds. Applicants will be notified of awards on or about 4/1. Federal Work-Study Program available. Institutional employment available. Off-campus job opportunities are good.

The Inside Word

You want the inside word on Wesleyan admissions? Read The Gatekeepers: Inside the Admissions Process at a Premier College, by Jacques Steinberg. The author spent an entire admissions season at the Wesleyan Admissions Office; his book is a wonderfully detailed description of the Wesleyan admissions process (which is quite similar to processes at other private, highly selective colleges and universities).

THE SCHOOL SAYS ". . ."

From The Admissions Office

"Wesleyan faculty believe in an education that is flexible and affords individual freedom and that a strong liberal arts education is the best foundation for success in any endeavor. The broad curriculum focuses on essential communication skills and analytical abilities through course content and teaching methodology, allowing students to pursue their intellectual interests with passion while honing those capabilities. As a result, Wesleyan students achieve a very personalized but broad education. Wesleyan's Dean of Admission and Financial Aid, Nancy Hargrave Meislahn, describes the qualities Wesleyan seeks in its students: 'Our very holistic process seeks to identify academically accomplished and intellectually curious students who can thrive in Wesleyan's rigorous and vibrant academic environment; we look for personal strengths, accomplishments, and potential for real contribution to our diverse community.'

"Applicants will meet standardized testing requirements one of two ways: by taking the new SAT plus two SAT Subject Tests of the student's choice, or by taking the old SAT plus three SAT Subject Tests (one of which must be Writing)."

For even more information on this school, turn to page 543 of the "Stats" section.

WESTMINSTER COLLEGE (PA)

319 SOUTH MARKET STREET, NEW WILMINGTON, PA 16172 • ADMISSIONS: 800-942-8033
FAX: 724-946-7171 • FINANCIAL AID: 724-946-7102 • E-MAIL: ADMIS@WESTMINSTER.EDU • WEBSITE: WWW.WESTMINSTER.EDU

RATINGS
Quality of Life: 88   Academic: 82   Admissions: 79   Financial Aid: 62

STUDENTS SAY ". . ."

Academics

Students choose Westminster College, a small Presbyterian-affiliated liberal arts school north of Pittsburgh, for its cozy atmosphere and well-regarded pre-professional programs. Undergrads describe Westminster as "an extremely small school where everyone pretty much knows each other," where "professors are dedicated to helping students on all levels from the classroom and out-

> **SURVEY SAYS . . .**
> *Career services are great*
> *Students are friendly*
> *Frats and sororities dominate*
> *social scene*
> *Student government is popular*

side of class to calling them up on the weekends at home to discuss coursework," and where the community is like "a family bound together with blue and white pride and a love for the people who are currently attending and those that have moved on." Indeed, "Once you become a part of the Westminster tradition, it lasts for a life-time!" The small class environment "creates opportunities and values diversified learning above focused, by-rote study," facilitated by a "very hands-on" approach from both faculty and administrators. Premedical stud-ies excel here. Students warn that "being a biology major is much harder than some of the other majors, and even if you don't fail a class it is hard to graduate on time." However, this hard work pays off in Westminster's admit rate to medical schools, which is double the national average. Students also love the music, education, and public relations programs here. Other majors are "hit or miss…depending on the staff in the department." Where the school falls shortest, however, is in its facilities. Undergrads tell us that because Westminster is "a very old school that relies on alumni for donations, our building are terribly old and it shows" and that "the libraries are sub-par." Westminster has spent $36 million on renovations in the last few years, however, and cur-rent renovations to McGill Library will be complete in Fall 2008.

Life

Westminster has "a very active Greek life in which the majority of our student population is involved," and "students have integrated Greek life as a positive force and influence in their school careers with many oppor-tunities for leadership roles and future connections leading up to a week-long "Greek Week."" Weekends usu-ally "involve going to the fraternities," which "gets old after a while," but since the school is located "in a very small town located near an Amish community, there isn't much off-campus to do besides go to fraternity hous-es." On-campus alternatives include "weekly events with a musician, comedian, etc. Also, there are two free movies offered each weekend." As one student warns, "If you're into the bar scene, clubs, or big-city life, don't go to Westminster. You'll be disappointed. If you like things more laid-back and prefer a slow-paced life, Westminster is probably going to fit you pretty well." Aesthetes will also find much to enjoy, as "The campus is the most beautiful [place]…. There are so many wide open spaces with pastures, barns, acres of land and the trees are gorgeous in the fall." Among intercollegiate athletics, "Football is a big thing on campus as well as bas-ketball. Many students come out to support their fellow teammates and friends."

Student Body

"Westminster does not have a lot of diversity," as "most students are local," meaning that they tend to be "white and from a middle to upper middle class family." "Of course you have your various groups that have only been moderately refined since high school: the jocks, the gothic kids, the cheerleader types, the hippies that never bathe, etc., but the typical student here would have to be someone who is relatively laid back," explains one stu-dent. "They wear American Eagle jeans, vintage t-shirts, and flip-flops year round. They are moderately aware of the world around them, politically and environmentally. They play ultimate Frisbee and guitar, and have probably started or head some club on campus that is particular to their interests. In their free time they read poems, sing, practice an instrument, watch Family Guy, or catch up with some friends. Many on campus seem apathetic toward just about everything, but a surprising number actually take the responsibility and initiative to make a difference." Politically, the student body leans toward the "conservative."

THE PRINCETON REVIEW SAYS

Admissions

Very important factors considered include: Rigor of secondary school record, standardized test scores, interview. *Important factors considered include:* Class rank, application essay, recommendation(s), character/personal qualities. *Other factors considered include:* Alumni/ae relation, extracurricular activities, racial/ethnic status, talent/ability, volunteer work, work experience. SAT or ACT required; TOEFL required of all international applicants. High school diploma is required and GED is accepted. *Academic units required:* 4 English, 3 mathematics, 2 science, (2 science labs), 2 foreign language, 2 social studies, 1 history, 3 academic electives.

Financial Aid

Students should submit: FAFSA, institution's own financial aid form, F. The Princeton Review suggests that all financial aid forms be submitted as soon as possible after January 1. *Need-based scholarships/grants offered:* Federal Pell, SEOG, state scholarships/grants, private scholarships, the school's own gift aid. *Loan aid offered:* FFEL Subsidized Stafford, FFEL Unsubsidized Stafford, FFEL PLUS, Federal Perkins, Resource Loans. Applicants will be notified of awards on a rolling basis beginning 11/1.

The Inside Word

Westminster College has grown increasingly more selective throughout the decade, the result of a 40+ percent increase in its applicant pool (without any corresponding increase in the size of its freshman class). The school is still less selective than most competitive undergraduate institutions, meaning those with less-than-stellar high school careers may find a home here. The school admits on a rolling basis. Apply early to improve your chances.

THE SCHOOL SAYS "..."

From The Admissions Office

"Since its founding, Westminster has been dedicated to a solid foundation in today's most crucial social, cultural, and ethical issues. Related to the Presbyterian Church (U.S.A.), Westminster is home to people of many faiths. Our students and faculty, tradition of campus, and small-town setting all contribute to an enlightening educational experience.

"For purposes of admission and merit scholarships Westminster College will evaluate applicants for Fall 2008 using the composite score of the Math and Critical Reading sections of the new SAT or the composite score of the ACT. Westminster will collect new Writing section scores and compare with national percentiles for possible inclusion in admission and scholarship criteria for the future."

For even more information on this school, turn to page 544 of the "Stats" section.

WHEATON COLLEGE (MA)

OFFICE OF ADMISSION, NORTON, MA 02766 • ADMISSIONS: 508-286-8251 • FAX: 508-286-8271
FINANCIAL AID: 508-286-8232 • E-MAIL: ADMISSION@WHEATONCOLLEGE.EDU • WEBSITE: WWW.WHEATONCOLLEGE.EDU

RATINGS
Quality of Life: 67   Academic: 92   Admissions: 93   Financial Aid: 89

STUDENTS SAY "..."

Academics

A "small liberal arts school trying to break through and compete with the 'small Ivies' (Williams, Amherst, Colby etc.)," Wheaton College is "a true liberal arts college: People study what they are interested in for the sake of learning it and because it fascinates them" here. The school caters to students with eclectic interests through its Foundations requirements (which require at least one course in non-Western civilization) and its Connections cur-

> **SURVEY SAYS . . .**
> Large classes
> Great library
> Frats and sororities are unpopular
> or nonexistent
> Lots of beer drinking
> Hard liquor is popular

riculum (which requires students to take either two sets of two related courses or one set of three related cours- es across academic categories), leading students to crow that "Wheaton's curriculum is based on providing stu- dents with global awareness. It focuses on trying to get students to understand the dynamics of their own per- sonal actions alongside that of those around the world." Undergrads also love the personal attention ("You can't get lost here—there's always someone you can talk to, your own age or a professor or administrator, if you're having problems. It's a really supportive and safe environment") and the "many opportunities to apply class- room knowledge outside of the class (whether through internships, research projects, fellowships, study abroad, etc.)." Many praise the school's new "absolutely amazing" Kollett Center, which houses "peer mentors, peer tutors for every subject, the academic advising office, and internship/career/job search Filene Center," "the most useful college center on the face of the planet…because they help with you in writing resumes, find- ing internships, and preparing for life after college." Wheaton students also benefit from "a really active" alum- ni network "willing to help in any way they can."

Life

"From Monday through Wednesday, people are reserved and very focused" on the Wheaton campus. Thursday "usually starts the weekend where upperclassmen will head to the bars," while on "Friday and Saturday, most of the school will socialize by drinking at one of the on-campus houses or in groups in the dorms." Students explain that "Because there are no frats, parties are held in houses (either on or off campus) or in dorm rooms." Observes one student, "It's actually a bit pathetic that that's the best they can do." There are also "college dances, which sometimes have free beer for those over 21," but many feel that "The dances are reminiscent of high school, and usually suck except for the free beer." There are also "tons of musical and theatrical perform- ances, club events, lectures, and other great things going on" around campus. Even so, students concede that the campus "gets a little boring at times." Hometown Norton "is very, very, very (did I say very yet?) small," the sort of place where "the biggest decision is whether you want to walk to Walgreen or CVS," so students seeking off-campus diversion must travel further. That's why "A lot of students will go into Boston or Providence for a day on the weekends. Also, there are always home games or away games on the weekends, so many students attend one or the other."

Student Body

Wheaton "is made up of reasonably familiar subgroups. We have our jocks, and our über-nerds, slackers, and artists. There is, however, a large gray area, and most people don't limit themselves to one group." The predomi- nant vibe is "a little bit preppy with a portion of hippie," with "the popped collar and pearls set" coexisting with "plenty of free spirits… Whether they choose to wear boat-shoes or Birks, they've got a place" here. Most students "are well-balanced…academically serious, but school is not the only activity in their lives." They "seem to gener- ally be liberal, but everyone is so apathetic toward current events that it is difficult to inspire student activism." Undergrads estimate that "35 percent of us are varsity athletes"; more than a few of the remaining 65 percent "do not like [the athletes] and feel like they get preferential treatment just because they are athletes."

Admissions
Very important factors considered include: Application essay, academic GPA, rigor of secondary school record, character/personal qualities, extracurricular activities, first generation, talent/ability. *Important factors considered include:* Class rank, recommendation(s), alumni/ae relation, interview, volunteer work, work experience. *Other factors considered include:* Standardized test scores, geographical residence, level of applicant's interest, racial/ethnic status, state residency, TOEFL required of all international applicants. High school diploma is required and GED is accepted. *Academic units recommended:* 4 English, 4 mathematics, 3 science, (2 science labs), 4 foreign language, 3 social studies, 2 history.

Financial Aid
Students should submit: FAFSA, CSS/Financial Aid PROFILE, noncustodial PROFILE, business/farm supplement, Parent and Student Federal Tax Returns and W-2s. Regular filing deadline is 2/1. The Princeton Review suggests that all financial aid forms be submitted as soon as possible after January 1. *Need-based scholarships/grants offered:* Federal Pell, SEOG, state scholarships/grants, private scholarships, the school's own gift aid. *Loan aid offered:* FFEL Subsidized Stafford, FFEL Unsubsidized Stafford, FFEL PLUS, Federal Perkins Applicants will be notified of awards on or about 4/1. Federal Work-Study Program available. Institutional employment available. Off-campus job opportunities are good.

The Inside Word
Wheaton gives applicants the option of not submitting standardized test scores. The school also invites applicants to submit optional personal academic portfolios, collections of completed schoolwork that demonstrates talents the applicant wants to highlight. All applicants should seriously consider this option; for those who do not submit test scores, an academic portfolio is practically imperative, both as an indicator of the applicant's seriousness about Wheaton and as evidence of academic excellence (evidence that standardized test scores might otherwise provide).

THE SCHOOL SAYS ". . ."
From The Admissions Office
"What makes for a 'best college'? Is it merely the hard-to-define notions of prestige or image? We don't think so. We think what makes college 'best' and best for you is a school that will make you a first-rate thinker and writer, a pragmatic professional in your work, and an ethical practitioner in your life. To get you to all these places, Wheaton takes advantage of its great combinations: a beautiful, secluded New England campus combined with access to Boston and Providence; a high quality, classic liberal arts and sciences curriculum combined with award-winning internship, job, and community-service programs; and a campus that respects your individuality in the context of the larger community. What's the 'best' outcome of a Wheaton education? A start on life that combines meaningful work, significant relationships, and a commitment to your local and global community. Far more than for what they've studied or for what they've gone on to do for a living, we're most proud of Wheaton graduates for who they become.

"Wheaton does not require students to submit the results of any standardized testing. The only exception is the TOEFL for students for whom English is a second language. Students who choose to submit standardized testing may use results from the historic SAT, its revised version, or from the ACT."

For even more information on this school, turn to page 544 of the "Stats" section.

WILKES UNIVERSITY

84 WEST SOUTH STREET, WILKES-BARRE, PA 18766 • ADMISSIONS: 570-408-4400 • FAX: 570-408-4904
E-MAIL: ADMISSIONS@WILKES.EDU • WEBSITE: WWW.WILKES.EDU

RATINGS
Quality of Life: 69   Academic: 72   Admissions: 74   Financial Aid: 75

STUDENTS SAY ". . ."

Academics

Students describe Wilkes University as "a science-based school with a strong focus on the individual," and cite the school's excellent programs in premedical sciences, the nursing program, and especially the high-profile pharmacy program. The school's innovative business administration program also draws raves; its curriculum includes a freshman project "in which you actually run a business with peo-

> **SURVEY SAYS . . .**
> *Small classes*
> *Frats and sororities are unpopular or nonexistent*
> *Student publications are popular*
> *Lots of beer drinking*
> *(Almost) everyone smokes*

ple from your own class." In all areas, "The small size of the school is one of its greatest strengths. The campus feels like its own little community, which is important, especially when dealing with professors. They're awesome and part of our community as well." The intimacy of the school fosters great mentorship opportunities: One biology major reports, "My professors have taken me to scientific conferences in Washington, DC, Orlando, and Seattle. If there is one thing Wilkes does well, it is build lasting professor-student relationships." Undergrads here also appreciate the fact that "while some of the professors can be confusing, there are always tutoring sessions available and the professors must have office hours, so you can go in and get whatever help you need on a one-on-one basis."

Life

In the past, students have complained about the lack of activity on and around the Wilkes campus. The school has taken measures to address the problem and now offers "many activities for those of us who commute as well as those who live on campus. We have rock climbing, skip trips, free buses to NYC or the local mall, pool tournaments, or anything else you can think of." One student adds, "The Wilkes University Programming Board puts together some great activities. For example, this past Sunday previous cast members from MTV's *The Real World* spoke in the student center." While the school has apparently started turning the corner, it's still a fact that "many people here cannot wait for the weekends to get home. There is not a lot to do on the weekends, which is why this is a suitcase school." Students are split on the merits of hometown Wilkes-Barre; some complain that "there's not too much to do in town," while others praise the "small city close to the mountains, which is convenient for wintertime fun." According to some, "There are a lot of great restaurants around the campus area. Also, there are a lot of college bars and clubs where everyone goes to hang out."

Student Body

With substantial programs in nursing, premedicine, psychology, and pre-pharmacy, it sometimes seems as though "Most people at Wilkes are on a medical career track." Students in like majors tend to hang together. While "everyone has the potential to interact if they choose," "the differences in workload really prevent you from socializing with other majors." The fact that many students leave campus immediately after Friday classes also doesn't help. Undergrads observe that "neither Wilkes University nor the Wilkes-Barre area is ethnically or racially diverse at all." According to the Admissions office, 10.5% of undergrads are non-Caucasian.

THE PRINCETON REVIEW SAYS

Admissions

Very important factors considered include: Class rank, rigor of secondary school record. *Important factors considered include:* Academic GPA, standardized test scores, character/personal qualities, extracurricular activities. *Other factors considered include:* Recommendation(s), alumni/ae relation, interview, talent/ability, volunteer work, work experience. SAT or ACT required; TOEFL required of all international applicants. High school diploma is required and GED is accepted. *Academic units recommended:* 4 English, 3 mathematics, 3 science, (2 science labs), 2 foreign language, 3 social studies, 1 computer science.

Financial Aid

Students should submit: FAFSA. The Princeton Review suggests that all financial aid forms be submitted as soon as possible after January 1. *Need-based scholarships/grants offered:* Federal Pell, SEOG, state scholarships/grants, private scholarships, the school's own gift aid. *Loan aid offered:* FFEL Subsidized Stafford, FFEL Unsubsidized Stafford, FFEL PLUS, Federal Perkins, Federal Nursing, state loans, college/university loans from institutional funds. Applicants will be notified of awards on a rolling basis beginning 3/1. Federal Work-Study Program available. Institutional employment available. Off-campus job opportunities are good.

The Inside Word

The application process at Wilkes is fairly relaxed. Admissions Officers rely mostly on hard data—essays and recommendations are optional. This allows them to make admit decisions and relay those decisions to applicants in only a few weeks. Wilkes processes applications on a rolling basis so an early application will increase your chances.

THE SCHOOL SAYS " . . ."

From The Admissions Office

"As our students reported, 'People honestly care about [a student's] success at Wilkes.' This is the basis for deep and meaningful relationships between students and faculty members. Students conduct independent research under the direction of active, faculty scholars. Faculty members can be found interacting with their students in the cafeteria, at campus activities and sporting events, and in the hallways of the academic buildings, as well as in their offices and homes.

"These mentoring relationships, which extend from professional guidance to personal direction, blossom over 4 years, but don't end at graduation. Instead, alumni report that they stay in contact with their faculty members throughout their professional careers. Consider this recent event: During winter break, one professor drove two senior students to Boston to visit graduate schools. Upon arrival, they met with a Wilkes alumna, herself a former advisee of this professor, who shared her experiences with them. As our students say, "[Professors] really try to help you; they are here for you.

"In choosing our students, we look for students who want to actively engage in their personal and professional development. To do so, we look at the entire individual: the academic record and strength of curriculum, community service and active extracurricular life, career goals and motivation for success. Successful students are those who want to learn in collaboration with their peers and professors. They also energetically participate in campus life because they know that learning takes place both in and outside the classroom."

For even more information on this school, turn to page 545 of the "Stats" section.

WILLIAMS COLLEGE

33 STETSON COURT, WILLIAMSTOWN, MA 01267 • ADMISSIONS: 413-597-2211 • FAX: 413-597-4052
FINANCIAL AID: 413-597-4181 • E-MAIL: ADMISSIONS@WILLIAMS.EDU • WEBSITE: WWW.WILLIAMS.EDU

RATINGS
Quality of Life: 91   Academic: 98   Admissions: 99   Financial Aid: 98

STUDENTS SAY "..."

Academics

Williams College is a small bastion of the liberal arts "with a fantastic academic reputation." Administrators sometimes "ignore student consensus in their misguided efforts to improve campus life" but they are "incredibly compassionate and accessible" and red tape is virtually unheard of. Financial aid is outrageous. Absolute, "full-ride" assistance with no loans is available to any student who needs it. "Williams students tend to spend a lot of time complaining

> **SURVEY SAYS . . .**
> *Lab facilities are great*
> *Campus feels safe*
> *Everyone loves the Ephs*
> *Frats and sororities are unpopular*
> *or nonexistent*
> *Lots of beer drinking*

about how much work they have" but they say the academic experience is "absolutely incomparable." Classes are "small" and "intense." "The facilities are absolutely top notch in almost everything." Research opportunities are plentiful. A one-month January term offers study abroad programs and a host of short pass/fail courses that are "a college student's dream come true." "The hard science departments are incredible." Economics, art history, and English are equally outstanding. Despite the occasional professor "who should not even be teaching at the high school level," the faculty at Williams is one of the best. Most professors "jump at every opportunity to help you love their subject." "They're here because they want to interact with undergrads." "If you complain about a Williams education then you would complain about education anywhere," wagers an economics major.

Life

Students at Williams enjoy a "stunning campus." "The Berkshire mountains are in the background every day as you walk to class" and opportunities for outdoor activity are numerous. The location is in "the boonies," though, and the surrounding "one-horse college town" is "quaint" at best. "There is no nearby place to buy necessities that is not ridiculously overpriced." Student life happens almost exclusively on campus. Dorm rooms are "large" and "well above par" but the housing system is "very weird." While some students like it, there is a general consensus that its creators "should be slapped and sent back to Amherst." Entertainment options include "lots of" performances, plays, and lectures. Some students are "obsessed with a capella groups." Intramurals are popular, especially broomball ("a sacred tradition involving a hockey rink, sneakers, a rubber ball, and paddles"). Intercollegiate sports are "a huge part of the social scene." For many students, the various varsity teams "are the basic social blocks at Williams." "Everyone for the most part gets along, but the sports teams seem to band together," expplains a sophomore. Booze-laden parties" "and general disorder on weekends" are common. "A lot of people spend their lives between homework and practice and then just get completely smashed on weekends." Nothing gets out of hand, though. "We know how to unwind without being stupid," says a sophomore.

Student Body

The student population at Williams is not the most humble. They describe themselves as "interesting and beautiful" "geniuses of varying interests." They're "quirky, passionate, zany, and fun." They're "athletically awesome." They're "freakishly unique" and at the same time "cookie-cutter amazing." Ethnic diversity is stellar and you'll find all kinds of different students here including "the goth students," "nerdier students," "a ladle of environmentally conscious pseudo-vegetarians," and a few "west coast hippies." However, "a typical student looks like a rich white kid" who grew up "playing field hockey just outside Boston" and spends summers "vacationing on the Cape." Sporty students abound. "There definitely is segregation between the artsy kids and the athlete types but there is also a significant amount of crossover." "Williams is a place where normal social labels tend not to apply," report a junior. "Everyone here got in for a reason. So that football player in your theater class has amazing insight on Chekhov and that outspoken environmental activist also specializes in improv comedy."

Admissions

Very important factors considered include: Application essay, academic GPA, recommendation(s), rigor of secondary school record, standardized test scores. *Important factors considered include:* Class rank, extracurricular activities, talent/ability. *Other factors considered include:* Alumni/ae relation, character/personal qualities, first generation, racial/ethnic status, volunteer work, work experience. SAT or ACT required; SAT and SAT Subject Tests or ACT required; ACT with Writing component required. High school diploma or equivalent is not required. *Academic units recommended:* 4 English, 4 mathematics, 3 science, (3 science labs), 4 foreign language, 3 social studies.

Financial Aid

Students should submit: FAFSA, CSS/Financial Aid PROFILE, noncustodial PROFILE, business/farm supplement, Parent and Student federal taxes and W-2s. Regular filing deadline is 2/1. The Princeton Review suggests that all financial aid forms be submitted as soon as possible after January 1. *Need-based scholarships/grants offered:* Federal Pell, SEOG, state scholarships/grants, private scholarships, the school's own gift aid. *Loan aid offered:* Direct Subsidized Stafford, Direct Unsubsidized Stafford, Direct PLUS, Federal Perkins, college/university loans from institutional funds. Applicants will be notified of awards on or about 4/1. Federal Work-Study Program available. Institutional employment available.

The Inside Word

As is typical of highly selective colleges, at Williams high grades and test scores work more as qualifiers than to determine admissibility. Beyond a strong record of achievement, evidence of intellectual curiosity, noteworthy non-academic talents, and a noncollege family background are some aspects of a candidate's application that might make for an offer of admission. But there are no guarantees—the evaluation process here is rigorous. The Admissions Committee (the entire Admissions Staff) discusses each candidate in comparison to the entire applicant pool. The pool is divided alphabetically for individual reading; after weak candidates are eliminated, those who remain undergo additional evaluations by different members of the staff. Admission decisions must be confirmed by the agreement of a plurality of the committee. Such close scrutiny demands a well-prepared candidate and application.

THE SCHOOL SAYS "..."

From The Admissions Office

"Special course offerings at Williams include Oxford-style tutorials, where students (in teams of two) research and defend ideas, engaging in weekly debate with a faculty tutor. Annually 30 Williams students devote a full year to the tutorial method of study at Oxford; half of Williams students pursue overseas education. Four weeks of Winter Study each January provide time for individualized projects, research, and novel fields of study. Students compete in 32 Division III athletic teams, perform in 25 musical groups, stage 10 theatrical productions, and volunteer in 30 service organizations. The college receives several million dollars annually for undergraduate science research and equipment. The town offers two distinguished art museums, and 2,200 forest acres—complete with a treetop canopy walkway—for environmental research and recreation.

"Students are required to submit either the SAT or the ACT including the optional Writing section. Applicants should also submit scores from any two SAT Subject Tests."

For even more information on this school, turn to page 545 of the "Stats" section.

WORCESTER POLYTECHNIC INSTITUTE

100 INSTITUTE ROAD, WORCESTER, MA 01609 • ADMISSIONS: 508-831-5286 • FAX: 508-831-5875
FINANCIAL AID: 508-831-5469 • E-MAIL: ADMISSIONS@WPI.EDU • WEBSITE: WWW.WPI.EDU

RATINGS
Quality of Life: 86   **Academic:** 87   **Admissions:** 93   **Financial Aid:** 77

STUDENTS SAY "..."

Academics

Worcester Polytechnic Institute, students boast, "is revolutionary with its approach to teaching," employing a "project-based curriculum that stresses the importance of both theory and practice." Students here must complete three projects, "one relating to humanities, one relating to the impact of technology on society, and a final senior project" that is typically a "group project done in cooperation with industry; i.e., not an 'academic' project." The Project Enhanced Curriculum ensures that students get "real-world industry experience before getting into the real world by applying what you learn in the classroom into projects." Students typically travel abroad to complete at least one of their projects, allowing them to "help another community on the other side of the world." As yet another added bonus, "The projects program looks excellent on your resume." Students also love WPI's quarterly academic calendar. One writes, "If I don't like a class but have to get through it, it's only 7 weeks. If I love the material, I can get out in 7 weeks and jump onto the next class!" Students warn that "the terms are pretty intense and go by so quickly that there is little room for error" but add that "it is very easy to get in touch with the professors after class, and they are very willing to help." A lenient grading system—"You can only receive an A, B, C, or an NR"—reduces the pressure somewhat, although it does little to mitigate the "immense workload." Independent students are especially well suited to WPI, which "fosters a can-do attitude that allows students to pave their own ways, create their own degree programs, and arrange their own degree requirement projects."

> **SURVEY SAYS . . .**
> Lab facilities are great
> Great computer facilities
> Career services are great
> Students are happy
> Frats and sororities dominate
> social scene

Life

"During the week [at WPI], most of the attention is focused on school activities, whether it's homework, clubs, or other extracurriculars," while "on the weekends, people try to relax after the week that has just ended and prepare themselves for the upcoming week." The campus enjoys "a strong sense of community, probably because of the campus set-up. The campus is on a hill, so we are separate from the city, and we are our own community with its own issues, and we deal with issues as a whole." Students tell us that "the Greek life on campus holds a big presence, and it is hard to find other activities to occupy your free time without at least socializing with members of the Greek community." Of the intercollegiate sports, "Basketball is big. The men's team made it to the NCAA Division III national tournament in 2005 and 2006." Because "Worcester isn't the greatest town," students tend to stick close to campus for fun, although "We also make trips to Boston and other better cities," including Hartford and Providence.

Student Body

The WPI student body spans two extremes, from "the students who do not come out of their room and are very nerdy," and those who "are very involved and meet everyone and fit in." One student writes, "WPI is an experiment in social interactions the likes of which the world rarely sees. For every typical frat guy and girl, there's a computer nerd or D&D guru who could write this entire response in COBOL coding for you." Nearly everyone here was "an atypical high school student" who "did very well in high school" while also being "really good in X (where X is a sport, club president, highly active student)." Finally, the "One thing that binds everyone at WPI is their love for technology. Within that major division of technology-loving people, the campus is filled with diverse students."

THE PRINCETON REVIEW SAYS

Admissions

Very important factors considered include: Academic GPA, rigor of secondary school record. *Important factors considered include:* Class rank, application essay, recommendation(s), standardized test scores, character/personal qualities, extracurricular activities. *Other factors considered include:* Alumni/ae relation, geographical residence, interview, level of applicant's interest, racial/ethnic status, talent/ability, volunteer work, work experience. SAT or ACT required; TOEFL required of all international applicants. High school diploma is required and GED is accepted. *Academic units required:* 4 English, 4 mathematics, 2 science, (2 science labs). *Academic units recommended:* 4 science, 2 foreign language, 2 social studies, 1 history.

Financial Aid

Students should submit: FAFSA, CSS/Financial Aid PROFILE, noncustodial PROFILE, Parent's and copy of student's prior year Federal Tax Return. Regular filing deadline is 2/1. The Princeton Review suggests that all financial aid forms be submitted as soon as possible after January 1. *Need-based scholarships/grants offered:* Federal Pell, SEOG, state scholarships/grants, private scholarships, the school's own gift aid. *Loan aid offered:* FFEL Subsidized Stafford, FFEL Unsubsidized Stafford, FFEL PLUS, Federal Perkins, state loans, college/university loans from institutional funds. Applicants will be notified of awards on or about 4/1. Federal Work-Study Program available. Institutional employment available. Off-campus job opportunities are good.

The Inside Word

WPI's high admission rate is the result of a self-selecting applicant pool; very few people bother to apply here if they don't think they have a good chance of getting in. The relatively low rate of acceptees attending tells you that WPI is a 'safety' or backup choice for students hoping to get into MIT, CalTech, RPI, Case Western, and other top tech schools.

THE SCHOOL SAYS ". . ."

From The Admissions Office

"Projects and research enrich WPI's academic program. WPI believes that in these times simply passing courses and accumulating theoretical knowledge is not enough to truly educate tomorrow's leaders. Tomorrow's professionals ought to be involved in project work that prepares them today for future challenges. Projects at WPI come as close to professional experience as a college program can possibly achieve. In fact, WPI works with more than 200 companies, government agencies, and private organizations each year. These groups provide opportunities where students get a chance to work in real, professional settings. Students gain invaluable experience in planning, coordinating team efforts, meeting deadlines, writing proposals and reports, making oral presentations, doing cost analyses, and making decisions.

"Applicants for Fall 2008 are required to take either the new SAT or the ACT (the Writing section is optional). We will allow students to submit scores from the old SAT (prior to March 2005) or ACT as well, and will use the student's best scores from either test. Science and Math SAT Subject Tests are recommended."

For even more information on this school, turn to page 546 of the "Stats" section.

WORCESTER STATE COLLEGE

486 CHANDLER STREET, DEPARTMENT OF ADMISSIONS, WORCESTER, MA 01602-2597 • ADMISSIONS: 508-929-8793 • FAX: 508-929-8183
E-MAIL: ADMISSIONS@WORCESTER.EDU • WEBSITE: WWW.WORCESTER.EDU

RATINGS
Quality of Life: 70   **Academic:** 79   **Admissions:** 60*   **Financial Aid:** 79

STUDENTS SAY ". . ."

Academics

At this "small" and "affordable" public school, "Professors are available at almost all times of the day and night. They are devoted to teaching, and they enjoy what they do." Students appreciate that Worcester accommodates those who don't "have a ton of money but still want a good education." A nursing major reports that her peers "study way more than your average student, get up at 4:00 A.M. for clin-

> **SURVEY SAYS . . .**
> *Large classes*
> *Lab facilities are great*
> *Frats and sororities are unpopular or nonexistent*
> *Lots of beer drinking*
> *(Almost) everyone smokes*

icals, and are constantly on the go." She adds, "Our department is great, we love our professors, and we know we're going to have . . . great careers when we get out." Students seem less certain about the administration, which most agree can "be good except during registration time." Some wish that there could be "better communication" between the administration and students. A significant minority are pleased with how the school runs: "The school's administrators, professors, and staff are all very understanding about real-world situations and work with students to make their college experiences the best possible." Despite bureaucratic snafus, nearly all students report that their "overall academic experience has been memorable."

Life

Students at "the Woo" tend to "do as they please and let others do as they please." Many "work full-time"; "It's a big commuter school," so some find that "there isn't a very tight network of students." However, students who live on campus praise "dorm life," which "makes it very easy to make friends. The freshman dorms are set up like traditional dorm buildings, so people are always interacting with each other." "People are always coming and going and stopping by to say hi." Worcester maintains a "dry campus" and "There are not a lot of house or on-campus parties," but "Thursday nights" can get "a little . . . crazy." Party animals can take heart that Worcester is "surrounded by a whole bunch of other colleges" and "local bars like the Irish Times and Funky Murphy's." In addition, "A large number of students that live on campus work in the city, particularly in the bars and restaurants surrounding the college, so it is easy to find employment and there is always a promotion going on to ensure a fun weekend." "The Woo" also has "great" athletics and "a bunch of student clubs to join." For sports fans, the best of all is "that the city of Worcester has multiple . . . colleges in our division, so it is convenient to go to away games."

Student Body

"Typical students," an undergrad says, "are those in hooded Worcester State sweatshirts and jeans, holding cups of coffee, shuffling into class. We typically have tired expressions on our faces, as most of us work several hours at night and attend classes during the day." Most are "friendly" and "have all kinds of interests." Much of the diversity comes from the "older" and "international" students. But all "work hard" and "like to have a good time with their friends." Many students are "paying their own way" and fully "understand the value of their education." There's also a "welcoming" vibe since "Most students are between 18 and 25," though older students "blend into classes" and "All the students benefit greatly from intergenerational perspectives that occur in such a learning environment."

THE PRINCETON REVIEW SAYS

Admissions

Very important factors considered include: Academic GPA, rigor of secondary school record, standardized test scores. *Other factors considered include:* Application essay, recommendation(s), extracurricular activities, interview, talent/ability, SAT or ACT required; TOEFL required of all international applicants. High school diploma is required and GED is accepted. *Academic units required:* 4 English, 3 mathematics, 3 science, (2 science labs), 2 foreign language, 1 social studies, 1 history, 2 academic electives.

Financial Aid

Students should submit: FAFSA, institution's own financial aid form. The Princeton Review suggests that all financial aid forms be submitted as soon as possible after January 1. *Need-based scholarships/grants offered:* Federal Pell, SEOG, state scholarships/grants, private scholarships, the school's own gift aid. *Loan aid offered:* FFEL Subsidized Stafford, FFEL Unsubsidized Stafford, FFEL PLUS, Federal Perkins, state loans Applicants will be notified of awards on a rolling basis beginning 3/1. Federal Work-Study Program available. Institutional employment available. Off-campus job opportunities are good.

The Inside Word

There's an essay. There are some special requirements for certain majors (e.g., education and occupational therapy). However, high school grades are most important. If your grade-point average in serious academic courses is a 3.0 or higher, you should be pretty automatic. If your GPA is lower than a 3.0, there is a sliding scale involving standardized test scores. With a GPA between 2.5 and 3.0, for example, you need something like a combined 920 on the SAT Math and Critical Reading. With a 2.3 GPA, you need a combined 1000 or so.

THE SCHOOL SAYS " . . ."

From The Admissions Office

"Worcester State College, a public institution located on 58 acres of rolling wooded land in central Massachusetts, offers a wide variety of majors in the areas of liberal arts and sciences, business, teacher education, and the health professions. The college is dedicated to offering affordable undergraduate and graduate programs and to promoting lifelong intellectual growth and career opportunities, and is accredited by the New England Association of Schools and Colleges. The Worcester State College campus is a completely wireless network environment, and the number of online courses has increased by 200 percent since 2003. Student housing is safely set in the back of campus on a hill that commands a spectacular view of the entire campus. Applications for admission are evaluated on a rolling basis with an application deadline of June 1. Student-guided tours of campus are offered on a weekly basis, and two open houses are held in the fall for prospective students and their families. Financial Assistance is offered in the form of grants, loans, and campus work. For more information about Worcester State College contact the Office of Admission or visit the college's website at www.worcester.edu."

For even more information on this school, turn to page 546 of the "Stats" section.

YALE UNIVERSITY

PO Box 208234, New Haven, CT 06520-8234 • Admissions: 203-432-9316 • Fax: 203-432-9392
Financial Aid: 203-432-2700 • E-mail: student.questions@yale.edu • Website: www.yale.edu/admit

RATINGS
Quality of Life: 95   Academic: 96   Admissions: 99   Financial Aid: 96

STUDENTS SAY ". . ."

Academics

Listening to Yale students wax rhapsodic about their school, one can be forgiven for wondering whether they aren't actually describing the Platonic form of the university. By their own account, students here benefit not only from

> SURVEY SAYS . . .
> *Great library*
> *Student publications are popular*

"amazing academics and extensive resources" that provide "phenomenal in- and out-of-class education," but also from participation in "a student body that is committed to learning and to each other." Unlike some other prestigious prominent research universities, Yale "places unparalleled focus on undergraduate education," requiring all professors to teach at least one undergraduate course each year "so [you know] the professors actually love teaching, because if they just wanted to do their research, they could have easily gone elsewhere." A residential college system further personalizes the experience. Each residential college "has a Dean and a Master, each of which is only responsible for 300 to 500 students, so administrative attention is highly specialized and widely available." Students further enjoy access to "a seemingly never-ending supply of resources (they really just love throwing money at us)" that includes "the 12 million volumes in our libraries." In short, "The opportunities are truly endless." "The experiences that you have here and the people that you meet will change your life and strengthen your dreams," says ones student. Looking for the flip side to all this? "If the weather were a bit nicer, that would be excellent," one student offers. Guess that will have to do.

Life

Yale is, of course, extremely challenging academically, but students assure us that "Aside from the stress of midterms and finals, life at Yale is relatively carefree." Work doesn't keep undergrads from participating in "a huge variety of activities for fun. There are over 300 student groups, including singing, dancing, juggling fire, theater...the list goes on. Because of all of these groups, there are shows on-campus all the time, which are a lot of fun and usually free or less than $5. On top of that, there are parties and events on-campus and off-campus, as well as many subsidized trips to New York City and Boston." Many here "are politically active (or at least politically aware)" and "a very large number of students either volunteer or try to get involved in some sort of organization to make a difference in the world." When the weekend comes around, "There are always parties to go to, whether at the frats or in rooms, but there's definitely no pressure to drink if you don't want to. A good friend of mine pledged a frat without drinking and that's definitely not unheard of (but still not common)." The relationship between Yale and the city of New Haven "sometimes leaves a little to be desired, but overall it's a great place to be for four years."

Student Body

A typical Yalie is "tough to define because so much of what makes Yale special is the unique convergence of different students to form one cohesive entity. Nonetheless, the one common characteristic of Yale students is passion—each Yalie is driven and dedicated to what he or she loves most, and it creates a palpable atmosphere of enthusiasm on campus." True enough, the student body represents a wide variety of ethnic, religious, economic, and academic backgrounds, but they all "thrive on learning, whether it be in a class, from a book, or from a conversation with a new friend." Students here also "tend to do a lot." "Everyone has many activities that they are a part of, which in turn fosters the closely connected feel of the campus." Undergrads tend to lean to the left politically, but for "those whose political views aren't as liberal as the rest of the campus...there are several campus organizations that cater to them."

THE PRINCETON REVIEW SAYS

Admissions

Very important factors considered include: Class rank, application essay, academic GPA, recommendation(s), rigor of secondary school record, standardized test scores, character/personal qualities, extracurricular activities, talent/ability. *Other factors considered include:* Alumni/ae relation, first generation, geographical residence, interview, level of applicant's interest, racial/ethnic status, state residency, volunteer work, work experience. SAT and SAT Subject Tests or ACT Writing component required. TOEFL required of all international applicants. High school diploma or equivalent is not required.

Financial Aid

Students should submit: FAFSA, CSS/Financial Aid PROFILE, noncustodial PROFILE, business/farm supplement, Parent Tax returns. Regular filing deadline is 3/1. The Princeton Review suggests that all financial aid forms be submitted as soon as possible after January 1. *Need-based scholarships/grants offered:* Federal Pell, SEOG, state scholarships/grants, private scholarships, the school's own gift aid, United Negro College Fund. *Loan aid offered:* FFEL Subsidized Stafford, FFEL Unsubsidized Stafford, FFEL PLUS, Federal Perkins, state loans, college/university loans from institutional funds. Applicants will be notified of awards on or about 4/1.

The Inside Word

Yale estimates that over three-quarters of all its applicants are qualified to attend the university, but less than ten percent get in. That adds up to a lot of broken hearts among kids who, if admitted, could probably handle the academic program. With so many qualified applicants to choose from, Yale can winnow to build an incoming class that is balanced in terms of income level, racial/ethnic background, geographic origin, and academic interest. For all but the most qualified, getting in typically hinges on offering just what an admissions officer is looking for to fill a specific slot. Legacies (descendents of Yale grads) gain some advantage—they're admitted at a 30 percent rate.

THE SCHOOL SAYS ". . ."

From The Admissions Office

"The most important questions the Admissions Committee must resolve are 'Who is likely to make the most of Yale's resources?' and 'Who will contribute significantly to the Yale community?' These questions suggest an approach to evaluating applicants that is more complex than whether Yale would rather admit well-rounded people or those with specialized talents. In selecting a class of 1,300 from over 20,000 applicants, the Admissions Committee looks for academic ability and achievement combined with such personal characteristics as motivation, curiosity, energy, and leadership ability. The nature of these qualities is such that there is no simple profile of grades, scores, interests, and activities that will assure admission. Diversity within the student population is important, and the Admissions Committee selects a class of able and contributing individuals from a variety of backgrounds and with a broad range of interests and skills.

"Applicants for the entering class of Fall 2009 may take either version of the SAT. In addition, applicants will be required to take two SAT Subject Tests of their choice. Applicants may take the ACT, with the Writing component, as an alternative to the SAT and SAT Subject Tests."

For even more information on this school, turn to page 547 of the "Stats" section.

YORK COLLEGE OF PENNSYLVANIA

ADMISSIONS OFFICE, 441 COUNTRY CLUB ROAD, YORK, PA 17403-3651 • ADMISSIONS: 717-849-1600 OR 800-455-8018
FAX: 717-849-1607 • FINANCIAL AID: 717-815-1282 • WEBSITE: WWW.YCP.EDU/

RATINGS
Quality of Life: 62   **Academic:** 71   **Admissions:** 79   **Financial Aid:** 75

STUDENTS SAY ". . ."

Academics

York College's "beautiful campus" "is a nice size, easy to get around. . . . Actually, if you want to avoid someone, it's almost difficult [to]." This "intimate" size translates into small classes and extremely accessible professors. One student writes, "I came to this school not expecting much, and have been completely blown away by the professors' dedication to their students." Many distribute personal "cell phone numbers or even home phone numbers in case we have a question that we want or need to have answered right away." Students say that "the criminal justice professors are excellent," the unique "professional writing program is awesome," and "the greatest strengths of York College are its athletic programs, nursing programs, and other health-field programs." However, the college could "offer more diverse classes, especially in languages (i.e., advanced Italian)." Academic help is always available: "The Learning Resource Center is amazing; there are tutors for just about every subject. They are always willing to help and make sure you get it!" One undergrad says, "I always wanted a college [that would] 'hold my hand' when I needed help, since I don't always know what to do. The professors and administrators have 'carried me' along the way."

> **SURVEY SAYS . . .**
> *Large classes*
> *Great library*
> *Athletic facilities are great*
> *Lots of beer drinking*
> *(Almost) everyone smokes*

Life

Students rave about the "outstanding," "beautiful" new Grumbacher Sport and Fitness Center, which one student calls "probably my favorite building on campus." "The pool at night looks awesome, because it is all lit up," and the gym "hosts lots of activities." Undergrads here have a definite athletic streak and "can always be seen playing sports outside on their own time or . . . between classes." York has no intercollegiate football team, but "Basketball is huge, and soccer is pretty big as well." "There are a lot of clubs on campus and many events to attend for entertainment and class credit," as well. Campus is officially "dry," which puts the many students who feel that "it is not so safe to go out [in York] at night by yourself" in a bind. Most partiers go out to Jackson Street (the fraternity row, "a very short walk [from] campus"), York bars and clubs, and even Baltimore. The typical "weekend night starts at a warm-up house party [with] tons of people crammed into a tiny off-campus basement . . . drinking keg beer. [Then the] party moves on to one of the local bars within walking distance, [usually] Murph's Study Hall. [The] night usually ends with a huge line of students outside [the] local pizzeria (best pizza in the world!)."

Student Body

Students describe the typical Joe or Jane York as an "upper-middle-class" "White . . . Republican between the ages of 18 and 25" from the Mid-Atlantic. He or she is friendly and pretty "average"—not "too popular or too geeky," not "too smart or too stupid," and never "believing he [or] she is better than someone else." It's theorized that York has the social groups characteristic of a "stereotypical high school," including "homosexuals," "sorority and fraternity" types, "athletes," and "drama and musical" enthusiasts. Unlike high school, however, "Everyone [here] accepts everyone else and shows a genuine concern for fellow students." The student body also includes a sizable faction of commuters and "older students coming back to college to get their degree, especially in night classes." Living on a tiny campus unites diverse groups, but commuters "miss out on a lot of the bonding that goes on on campus. . . . But even [they] aren't that shafted." One commuting freshman confirms: "I am always invited out, and many groups have tried to get me to join."

Admissions

Very important factors considered include: Rigor of secondary school record. *Important factors considered include:* Class rank, standardized test scores, character/personal qualities. *Other factors considered include:* Application essay, recommendation(s), alumni/ae relation, extracurricular activities, interview, talent/ability, volunteer work, work experience. SAT or ACT required; ACT with Writing component required. TOEFL required of all international applicants. High school diploma is required and GED is accepted. *Academic units required:* 4 English, 3 mathematics, 3 science, 2 foreign language, 3 social studies. *Academic units recommended:* 4 mathematics.

Financial Aid

Students should submit: FAFSA The Princeton Review suggests that all financial aid forms be submitted as soon as possible after January 1. *Need-based scholarships/grants offered:* Federal Pell, SEOG, state scholarships/grants, private scholarships, the school's own gift aid. *Loan aid offered:* Direct Subsidized Stafford, Direct Unsubsidized Stafford, Direct PLUS, FFEL Subsidized Stafford, FFEL Unsubsidized Stafford, FFEL PLUS, Federal Perkins, Federal Nursing, state loans, college/university loans from institutional funds. Applicants will be notified of awards on a rolling basis beginning 2/15. Federal Work-Study Program available. Institutional employment available. Off-campus job opportunities are good.

The Inside Word

York courts top students with AP score credit, half-tuition packages for valedictorians and salutatorians (a tool with the convenient secondary effect of boosting economic and geographic diversity), and an honors program that requires a combined score of 1210 on the Math and Reading sections of the SAT. Here, as elsewhere, an imbalanced gender ratio (approximately 59 percent female, 41 percent male) likely gives male applicants a leg up.

THE SCHOOL SAYS " . . . "
From The Admissions Office

"York College of Pennsylvania is a comprehensive college of liberal arts and professions. With 4,600 full-time students, York is a rare breed: an ideally sized private college.

"But does size really make a difference? Incoming freshman think so: It's their number-one reason for choosing York. York is small enough to maintain its strong student focus. Classes are small. Students build close relationships with faculty and enjoy one-on-one advising and counseling. You won't find that at a big state school, certainly not at the undergraduate level. Yet York is large enough to provide far more extensive resources than you find at most small colleges. Our campus facilities are fantastic—come see for yourself. You'll also find that York offers a breadth of extracurricular activities that small colleges rarely provide.

"We're also a private institution, so we enjoy the independence to seize opportunities whenever they happen. As a result York College has been transformed and is transforming still. We have built new state-of-the-art facilities like the Grumbacher Sport and Fitness Center and our new Performing Arts Center. New construction is also transforming facilities for English and Humanities, and Social Sciences and Engineering. Additional student residences are being built on West Campus, and more projects are in the works.

"Most people agree that first impressions matter. If you are ready, York College offers you a world of opportunities in an environment where you are challenged and supported, and where your accomplishments are recognized and valued. Visit York College and your first impression will be 'Wow!'"

For even more information on this school, turn to page 547 of the "Stats" section.

PART 3: THE STATS

ADELPHI UNIVERSITY

CAMPUS LIFE
Fire Safety Rating	**99**
Green Rating	**73**
Type of school	private
Environment	metropolis

STUDENTS
Total undergrad enrollment	4,973
% male/female	28/72
% from out of state	8
% from public high school	75
% live on campus	23
% in (# of) fraternities	7 (2)
% in (# of) sororities	4 (5)
% African American	14
% Asian	6
% Caucasian	50
% Hispanic	8
% international	4
# of countries represented	56

ACADEMICS
Calendar	semester
Profs interesting rating	76
Profs accessible rating	76
Student/faculty ratio	9:1
Most common	
reg class size	20–29 students
Most common lab size	10–19 students

MOST POPULAR MAJORS
education
nursing, other
business/commerce

SELECTIVITY
# of applicants	6,165
% of applicants accepted	69
% of acceptees attending	21

FRESHMAN PROFILE
Range SAT Critical Reading	480–580
Range SAT Math	490–590
Range SAT Writing	480–580
Range ACT Composite	20–24
Minimum paper TOEFL	550
Minimum computer TOEFL	213
Average HS GPA	3.3
% graduated top 10% of class	19.7
% graduated top 25% of class	47.6
% graduated top 50% of class	85.6

DEADLINES
Early action	
Deadline	12/1
Notification	12/31
Notification	rolling
Nonfall registration?	yes

FINANCIAL FACTS
Annual tuition	$21,000
Room and board	$9,900
Required fees	$1,200
Books and supplies	$1,000
% frosh rec. need-based	
scholarship or grant aid	58
% UG rec. need-based	
scholarship or grant aid	54
% frosh rec. non-need-based	
scholarship or grant aid	34
% UG rec. non-need-based	
scholarship or grant aid	33
% frosh rec. need-based self-help aid	60
% UG rec. need-based self-help aid	57
% frosh rec. athletic scholarships	2
% UG rec. athletic scholarships	1
% frosh rec. any financial aid	93
% UG rec. any financial aid	88

ALBRIGHT COLLEGE

CAMPUS LIFE
Fire Safety Rating	**60***
Green Rating	**60***
Type of school	private
Affiliation	Methodist
Environment	city

STUDENTS
Total undergrad enrollment	2,074
% male/female	42/58
% from out of state	33
% from public high school	77
% live on campus	61
% in (# of) fraternities	25 (4)
% in (# of) sororities	30 (3)
% African American	9
% Asian	2
% Caucasian	78
% Hispanic	4
% international	3
# of countries represented	26

ACADEMICS
Calendar	4/1/4
Profs interesting rating	87
Profs accessible rating	87

Student/faculty ratio	14:1
Most common	
reg class size	10–19 students
Most common lab size	10–19 students

MOST POPULAR MAJORS
sociology
business/commerce

SELECTIVITY
# of applicants	3,013
% of applicants accepted	71
% of acceptees attending	21

FRESHMAN PROFILE
Range SAT Critical Reading	470–580
Range SAT Math	460–570
Average HS GPA	3.3
% graduated top 10% of class	23
% graduated top 25% of class	48
% graduated top 50% of class	79

DEADLINES
Regular	
Priority	3/1
Notification	rolling
Nonfall registration?	yes

FINANCIAL FACTS
Annual tuition	$25,232
Room and board	$7,888
Required fees	$800
Books and supplies	$800
% frosh rec. need-based	
scholarship or grant aid	81
% UG rec. need-based	
scholarship or grant aid	68
% frosh rec. non-need-based	
scholarship or grant aid	11
% UG rec. non-need-based	
scholarship or grant aid	9
% frosh rec. need-based self-help aid	67
% UG rec. need-based self-help aid	59
% frosh rec. any financial aid	95
% UG rec. any financial aid	94
% UG borrow to pay for school	88
Average cumulative indebtedness	$24,671

ALFRED UNIVERSITY

CAMPUS LIFE
Fire Safety Rating	**60***
Green Rating	**60***
Type of school	private
Environment	rural

STUDENTS

Total undergrad enrollment	2,030
% male/female	49/51
% from out of state	35
% live on campus	67
% African American	4
% Asian	2
% Caucasian	63
% Hispanic	2.5
% international	1

ACADEMICS

Calendar	semester
Student/faculty ratio	12:1
Profs interesting rating	85
Profs accessible rating	84
Most common reg class size	10–19 students
Most common lab size	fewer than 10 students

MOST POPULAR MAJORS
fine/studio arts
ceramic sciences and engineering
business/commerce

SELECTIVITY

# of applicants	2,355
% of applicants accepted	74
% of acceptees attending	30
# of early decision applicants	53
% accepted early decision	83

FRESHMAN PROFILE

Range SAT Critical Reading	490–610
Range SAT Math	500–620
Range ACT Composite	22–27
Minimum paper TOEFL	550
Minimum computer TOEFL	213
% graduated top 10% of class	18
% graduated top 25% of class	46
% graduated top 50% of class	85

DEADLINES

Early decision	
Deadline	12/1
Notification	12/15
Regular	
Priority	2/1
Notification	rolling
Nonfall registration?	yes

FINANCIAL FACTS

Annual tuition	$23,428
Room and board	$10,796
Required fees	$850
Books and supplies	$900
% frosh rec. need-based scholarship or grant aid	74
% UG rec. need-based scholarship or grant aid	73
% frosh rec. non-need-based scholarship or grant aid	44
% UG rec. non-need-based scholarship or grant aid	39
% frosh rec. need-based self-help aid	66
% UG rec. need-based self-help aid	66
% frosh rec. any financial aid	92
% UG rec. any financial aid	90
% UG borrow to pay for school	82.5
Average cumulative indebtedness	$23,292

ALLEGHENY COLLEGE

CAMPUS LIFE

Fire Safety Rating	79
Green Rating	93
Type of school	private
Environment	town

STUDENTS

Total undergrad enrollment	2,163
% male/female	44/56
% from out of state	37
% from public high school	83
% live on campus	77
% in (# of) fraternities	20 (5)
% in (# of) sororities	28 (4)
% African American	2
% Asian	3
% Caucasian	92
% Hispanic	2
% international	1
# of countries represented	32

ACADEMICS

Calendar	semester
Student/faculty ratio	14:1
Profs interesting rating	91
Profs accessible rating	89
Most common reg class size	10–19 students
Most common lab size	10–19 students

MOST POPULAR MAJORS
psychology
biology/biological sciences
economics

SELECTIVITY

# of applicants	4,354
% of applicants accepted	57
% of acceptees attending	23
# accepting a place on wait list	509
% admitted from wait list	4
# of early decision applicants	90
% accepted early decision	71

FRESHMAN PROFILE

Range SAT Critical Reading	560–660
Range SAT Math	555–650
Range ACT Composite	24–28
Minimum paper TOEFL	550
Minimum computer TOEFL	213
Average HS GPA	3.8
% graduated top 10% of class	46
% graduated top 25% of class	77
% graduated top 50% of class	97

DEADLINES

Early decision	
Deadline	11/15
Notification	12/15
Regular	
Deadline	2/15
Notification	4/1
Nonfall registration?	yes

FINANCIAL FACTS

Annual tuition	$31,680
Room and board	$8,000
Required fees	$320
Books and supplies	$900
% frosh rec. need-based scholarship or grant aid	69
% UG rec. need-based scholarship or grant aid	68
% frosh rec. non-need-based scholarship or grant aid	13
% UG rec. non-need-based scholarship or grant aid	11
% frosh rec. need-based self-help aid	57
% UG rec. need-based self-help aid	58
% frosh rec. any financial aid	98
% UG rec. any financial aid	98

AMERICAN UNIVERSITY

CAMPUS LIFE

Fire Safety Rating	94
Green Rating	75
Type of school	private
Affiliation	Methodist
Environment	metropolis

STUDENTS

Total undergrad enrollment	5,824
% male/female	37/63
% from out of state	79
% live on campus	75

% in (# of) fraternities	14 (11)
% in (# of) sororities	16 (12)
% African American	5
% Asian	5
% Caucasian	63
% Hispanic	5
% international	6
# of countries represented	137

ACADEMICS

Calendar	semester
Student/faculty ratio	14:1
Profs interesting rating	86
Profs accessible rating	84
Most common	
reg class size	10–19 students

MOST POPULAR MAJORS
international relations and affairs
business/commerce
mass communication/media studies

SELECTIVITY

# of applicants	15,847
% of applicants accepted	53
% of acceptees attending	15
# of early decision applicants	370
% accepted early decision	55

FRESHMAN PROFILE

Range SAT Critical Reading	590–690
Range SAT Math	580–670
Range SAT Writing	580–690
Range ACT Composite	25–30
Minimum paper TOEFL	610
Minimum computer TOEFL	263
Minimum web-based TOEFL	101
% graduated top 10% of class	50
% graduated top 25% of class	83
% graduated top 50% of class	99

DEADLINES

Early decision	
Deadline	11/15
Notification	12/31
Regular	
Deadline	1/15
Notification	4/1
Nonfall registration?	yes

FINANCIAL FACTS

Annual tuition	$32,816
Room and board	$12,418
Required fees	$467
Books and supplies	$600
% frosh rec. need-based	
scholarship or grant aid	34
% UG rec. need-based	
scholarship or grant aid	34
% frosh rec. non-need-based	
scholarship or grant aid	14
% UG rec. non-need-based	
scholarship or grant aid	11
% frosh rec. need-based	
self-help aid	39
% UG rec. need-based	
self-help aid	40
% frosh rec. athletic scholarships	3
% UG rec. athletic scholarships	2
% frosh rec. any financial aid	82
% UG rec. any financial aid	69
% UG borrow to pay for school	50

AMHERST COLLEGE

CAMPUS LIFE

Fire Safety Rating	**60***
Green Rating	**60***
Type of school	private
Environment	town

STUDENTS

Total undergrad enrollment	1,683
% male/female	50/50
% from out of state	88
% live on campus	98
% African American	10
% Asian	12
% Caucasian	44
% Hispanic	32
% Native American	3
% international	7
# of countries represented	39

ACADEMICS

Calendar	semester
Student/faculty ratio	8:1
Profs interesting rating	86
Profs accessible rating	93
Most common	
reg class size	10–19 students
Most common	
lab size	fewer than 10 students

MOST POPULAR MAJORS
political science and government
psychology
biology/biological sciences

SELECTIVITY

# of applicants	6,680
% of applicants accepted	18
% of acceptees attending	40
# accepting a place on wait list	574
# of early decision applicants	350
% accepted early decision	39

FRESHMAN PROFILE

Range SAT Critical Reading	670–770
Range SAT Math	660–760
Range SAT Writing	670–760
Range ACT Composite	29–34
% graduated top 10% of class	85
% graduated top 25% of class	95
% graduated top 50% of class	100

DEADLINES

Early decision	
Deadline	11/15
Notification	12/15
Regular	
Deadline	1/1
Notification	4/5
Nonfall registration?	no

FINANCIAL FACTS

Annual tuition	$35,580
Room and board	$9,420
Required fees	$652
Books and supplies	$1,000
% frosh rec. need-based	
scholarship or grant aid	51
% UG rec. need-based	
scholarship or grant aid	52
% frosh rec. need-based	
self-help aid	45
% UG rec. need-based	
self-help aid	46
% frosh rec. any financial aid	53
% UG rec. any financial aid	51
% UG borrow to pay for school	43
Average cumulative	
indebtedness	$11,655

ARCADIA UNIVERSITY

CAMPUS LIFE

Fire Safety Rating	**60***
Green Rating	**60***
Type of school	private
Affiliation	none
Environment	town

STUDENTS

Total undergrad enrollment	2,075
% male/female	26/74
% from out of state	42
% from public high school	59
% live on campus	67

% African American	7
% Asian	3
% Caucasian	83
% Hispanic	3
% international	2
# of countries represented	10

ACADEMICS

Calendar	semester
Profs interesting rating	78
Profs accessible rating	75
Student/faculty ratio	13:1
Most common reg class size	10–19 students
Most common lab size	10–19 students

MOST POPULAR MAJORS
education
psychology
business/commerce

SELECTIVITY

# of applicants	4,75
% of applicants accepted	67
% of acceptees attending	20

FRESHMAN PROFILE

Range SAT Critical Reading	510–610
Range SAT Math	500–590
Range SAT Writing	510–610
Range ACT Composite	21–27
Minimum paper TOEFL	530
Minimum computer TOEFL	70
% graduated top 10% of class	31
% graduated top 25% of class	62
% graduated top 50% of class	93

DEADLINES

Regular	
Priority	1/15
Deadline	3/1
Notification	rolling
Nonfall registration?	yes

FINANCIAL FACTS

Annual tuition	$29,340
Room and board	$10,280
Required fees	$360
Books and supplies	$1,000
% frosh rec. any financial aid	98

THE ART INSTITUTE OF BOSTON AT LESLEY UNIVERSITY

CAMPUS LIFE

Fire Safety Rating	**88**
Green Rating	**72**
Type of school	private
Environment	metropolis

STUDENTS

Total undergrad enrollment	1,225
% male/female	25/75
% from out of state	42
% from public high school	84
% live on campus	53
% African American	5
% Asian	4
% Caucasian	65
% Hispanic	5
% international	2
# of countries represented	15

ACADEMICS

Calendar	semester
Profs interesting rating	90
Profs accessible rating	73
Student/faculty ratio	9:1
Most common reg class size	10–19 students

MOST POPULAR MAJORS
graphic design
illustration
photography

SELECTIVITY

# of applicants	1,568
% of applicants accepted	86
% of acceptees attending	26

FRESHMAN PROFILE

Range SAT Critical Reading	450–600
Range SAT Math	460–560
Range SAT Writing	480–580
Range ACT Composite	20–26
Minimum paper TOEFL	500
Minimum computer TOEFL	173
Average HS GPA	3
% graduated top 10% of class	15
% graduated top 25% of class	25
% graduated top 50% of class	84

DEADLINES

Early action	
Deadline	12/1
Notification	12/31

Regular	
Priority	2/15
Notification	rolling
Nonfall registration?	yes

FINANCIAL FACTS

Annual tuition	$24,825
Room and board	$12,000
Required fees	$810
Books and supplies	$1,575
% frosh rec. need-based scholarship or grant aid	71
% UG rec. need-based scholarship or grant aid	64
% frosh rec. non-need-based scholarship or grant aid	18
% UG rec. non-need-based scholarship or grant aid	18
% frosh rec. need-based self-help aid	60
% UG rec. need-based self-help aid	55
% frosh rec. any financial aid	70
% UG rec. any financial aid	70
% UG borrow to pay for school	91
Average cumulative indebtedness	$15,000

ASSUMPTION COLLEGE

CAMPUS LIFE

Fire Safety Rating	**82**
Green Rating	**67**
Type of school	private
Affiliation	Roman Catholic
Environment	city

STUDENTS

Total undergrad enrollment	2,172
% male/female	41/59
% from out of state	31
% live on campus	89
% African American	2
% Asian	1
% Caucasian	79
% Hispanic	3
# of countries represented	8

ACADEMICS

Calendar	semester
Profs interesting rating	84
Profs accessible rating	85
Student/faculty ratio	12:1
Most common reg class size	20–29 students
Most common lab size	10–19 students

MOST POPULAR MAJORS
English language and literature
psychology
marketing/marketing management

SELECTIVITY

# of applicants	3,899
% of applicants accepted	67
% of acceptees attending	23
# accepting a place on wait list	240
% admitted from wait list	70

FRESHMAN PROFILE

Range SAT Critical Reading	490–570
Range SAT Math	490–570
Range ACT Composite	20–24
Average HS GPA	3.39
% graduated top 10% of class	11.7
% graduated top 25% of class	35.1
% graduated top 50% of class	80.8

DEADLINES

Early action	
Deadline	11/15
Notification	12/15
Regular	
Deadline	2/15
Nonfall registration?	yes

FINANCIAL FACTS

Annual tuition	$27,320
Room and board	$9,492
Required fees	$165
Books and supplies	$850
% frosh rec. need-based scholarship or grant aid	74
% UG rec. need-based scholarship or grant aid	69
% frosh rec. non-need-based scholarship or grant aid	9
% UG rec. non-need-based scholarship or grant aid	7
% frosh rec. need-based self-help aid	63
% UG rec. need-based self-help aid	61
% frosh rec. athletic scholarships	1
% UG rec. athletic scholarships	1
% frosh rec. any financial aid	86
% UG rec. any financial aid	90
% UG borrow to pay for school	80
Average cumulative indebtedness	$32,900

BABSON COLLEGE

CAMPUS LIFE

Fire Safety Rating	**86**
Green Rating	**60***
Type of school	private
Environment	village

STUDENTS

Total undergrad enrollment	1,799
% male/female	59/41

% from out of state	46
% from public high school	50
% live on campus	84
% in (# of) fraternities	13 (4)
% in (# of) sororities	15 (3)
% African American	4
% Asian	11
% Caucasian	44
% Hispanic	8
% international	18
# of countries represented	60

ACADEMICS

Calendar	semester
Student/faculty ratio	16:1
Profs interesting rating	88
Profs accessible rating	87
Most common reg class size	30–39 students

MOST POPULAR MAJORS

accounting
entrepreneurial and small business operations
finance

SELECTIVITY

# of applicants	3,530
% of applicants accepted	38
% of acceptees attending	34
# accepting a place on wait list	159
% admitted from wait list	13
# of early decision applicants	235
% accepted early decision	55

FRESHMAN PROFILE

Range SAT Critical Reading	560–640
Range SAT Math	590–680
Range SAT Writing	570–650
Range ACT Composite	25–29
Minimum paper TOEFL	600
Minimum computer TOEFL	250
Minimum web-based TOEFL	100
% graduated top 10% of class	22
% graduated top 25% of class	17
% graduated top 50% of class	99

DEADLINES

Early decision	
Deadline	11/15
Notification	12/15
Early action	
Deadline	11/15
Notification	1/1
Regular	
Priority	11/15
Deadline	1/15
Notification	4/1
Nonfall registration?	no

FINANCIAL FACTS

Annual tuition	$36,096
% frosh rec. need-based scholarship or grant aid	40
% UG rec. need-based scholarship or grant aid	38
% frosh rec. non-need-based scholarship or grant aid	6
% UG rec. non-need-based scholarship or grant aid	6
% frosh rec. need-based self-help aid	44
% UG rec. need-based self-help aid	41
% frosh rec. any financial aid	44
% UG rec. any financial aid	42
% UG borrow to pay for school	51
Average cumulative indebtedness	$28,902

BARD COLLEGE

CAMPUS LIFE

Fire Safety Rating	**78**
Green Rating	**90**
Type of school	private
Environment	rural

STUDENTS

Total undergrad enrollment	1,737
% male/female	44/56
% from out of state	70
% from public high school	64
% live on campus	77
% African American	2
% Asian	3
% Caucasian	75
% Hispanic	3
% Native American	1
% international	9
# of countries represented	48

ACADEMICS

Calendar	semester
Student/faculty ratio	9:1
Profs interesting rating	88
Profs accessible rating	86
Most common reg class size	10–19 students

MOST POPULAR MAJORS

English language and literature
social sciences
visual and performing arts

SELECTIVITY

# of applicants	4,980
% of applicants accepted	27
% of acceptees attending	36

# accepting a place on wait list	279
% admitted from wait list	8

FRESHMAN PROFILE

Range SAT Critical Reading	680–740
Range SAT Math	640–690
Minimum paper TOEFL	600
Minimum computer TOEFL	250
Average HS GPA	3.5
% graduated top 10% of class	63
% graduated top 25% of class	85
% graduated top 50% of class	100

DEADLINES

Early action	
Deadline	11/1
Notification	1/1
Regular	
Deadline	1/15
Notification	4/1
Nonfall registration?	no

FINANCIAL FACTS

Annual tuition	$37,574
Books and supplies	$850
% frosh rec. need-based scholarship or grant aid	56
% UG rec. need-based scholarship or grant aid	53
% frosh rec. need-based self-help aid	52
% UG rec. need-based self-help aid	49
% frosh rec. any financial aid	64
% UG rec. any financial aid	65
% UG borrow to pay for school	65
Average cumulative indebtedness	$19,507

BARNARD COLLEGE

CAMPUS LIFE

Fire Safety Rating	**69**
Green Rating	**86**
Type of school	private
Environment	metropolis

STUDENTS

Total undergrad enrollment	2,346
% male/female	/100
% from out of state	68
% live on campus	90
% African American	5
% Asian	16
% Caucasian	66
% Hispanic	9

% international	4
# of countries represented	32

ACADEMICS

Calendar	semester
Student/faculty ratio	10:1
Profs interesting rating	94
Profs accessible rating	89
Most common reg class size	10–19 students
Most common lab size	fewer than 10 students

MOST POPULAR MAJORS
English language and literature
psychology
economics

SELECTIVITY

# of applicants	4,574
% of applicants accepted	29
% of acceptees attending	43
# accepting a place on wait list	457
% admitted from wait list	3
# of early decision applicants	432
% accepted early decision	42

FRESHMAN PROFILE

Range SAT Critical Reading	640–740
Range SAT Math	620–700
Range SAT Writing	650–730
Range ACT Composite	29–31
Average HS GPA	3.91
% graduated top 10% of class	75
% graduated top 25% of class	94
% graduated top 50% of class	100

DEADLINES

Early decision	
Deadline	11/15
Notification	12/15
Regular	
Deadline	1/1
Notification	4/1
Nonfall registration?	no

FINANCIAL FACTS

Annual tuition	$35,972
% frosh rec. need-based scholarship or grant aid	41
% UG rec. need-based scholarship or grant aid	42
% frosh rec. need-based self-help aid	44
% UG rec. need-based self-help aid	44
% frosh rec. any financial aid	44
% UG rec. any financial aid	43
% UG borrow to pay for school	44

Average cumulative indebtedness	$17,630

BATES COLLEGE

CAMPUS LIFE

Fire Safety Rating	**93**
Green Rating	**99**
Type of school	private
Environment	town

STUDENTS

Total undergrad enrollment	1,660
% male/female	48/52
% from out of state	89
% from public high school	56
% live on campus	92
% African American	3
% Asian	6
% Caucasian	81
% Hispanic	2
% international	5
# of countries represented	70

ACADEMICS

Calendar	4-4-1
Student/faculty ratio	10:1
Profs interesting rating	89
Profs accessible rating	94
Most common reg class size	10–19 students
Most common lab size	10–19 students

MOST POPULAR MAJORS
political science and government
economics
psychology

SELECTIVITY

# of applicants	4,434
% of applicants accepted	30
% of acceptees attending	34

FRESHMAN PROFILE

Range SAT Critical Reading	635–710
Range SAT Math	630–700
% graduated top 10% of class	55
% graduated top 25% of class	86
% graduated top 50% of class	99

DEADLINES

Early decision	
Deadline	11/15
Notification	12/20
Regular	
Deadline	1/1
Notification	3/31
Nonfall registration?	yes

FINANCIAL FACTS

Comprehensive fee	$46,800
Books and supplies	$1,150
% frosh rec. need-based	
scholarship or grant aid	41
% UG rec. need-based	
scholarship or grant aid	38
% frosh rec. need-based	
self-help aid	39
% UG rec. need-based	
self-help aid	38
% frosh rec. any financial aid	43
% UG rec. any financial aid	40
% UG borrow to pay for school	48.1
Average cumulative	
indebtedness	$13,947

BENNINGTON COLLEGE

CAMPUS LIFE

Fire Safety Rating	**81**
Green Rating	**88**
Type of school	private
Environment	town

STUDENTS

Total undergrad enrollment	583
% male/female	32/68
% from out of state	96
% live on campus	99
% African American	2
% Asian	2
% Caucasian	84
% Hispanic	2
% international	3
# of countries represented	15

ACADEMICS

Calendar	15 Wk Fall Spring, 7 Wk Winter Work Term
Student/faculty ratio	8:1
Profs interesting rating	97
Profs accessible rating	96
% classes taught by TAs	0
Most common	
reg class size	10–19 students

MOST POPULAR MAJORS
visual and performing arts
English language and literature
drama and dramatics/theatre arts

SELECTIVITY

# of applicants	1,011
% of applicants accepted	63
% of acceptees attending	32
# accepting a place on wait list	10
# of early decision applicants	73
% accepted early decision	73

FRESHMAN PROFILE

Range SAT Critical Reading	580–700
Range SAT Math	540–630
Range SAT Writing	580–690
Range ACT Composite	24–30
Minimum paper TOEFL	577
Minimum computer TOEFL	233
Minimum web-based TOEFL	90–91
Average HS GPA	3.4
% graduated top 10% of class	28
% graduated top 25% of class	70
% graduated top 50% of class	95

DEADLINES

Early decision	
Deadline	11/15
Notification	12/15
Regular	
Deadline	1/3
Notification	4/1
Nonfall registration?	yes

FINANCIAL FACTS

Annual tuition	$37,280
Room and board	$10,680
Books and supplies	$800
Required Fees	$990
% frosh rec. need-based	
scholarship or grant aid	71
% UG rec. need-based	
scholarship or grant aid	67
% frosh rec. non-need-based	
scholarship or grant aid	4
% UG rec. non-need-based	
scholarship or grant aid	2
% frosh rec. need-based	
self-help aid	64
% UG rec. need-based	
self-help aid	64
% frosh rec. any financial aid	81
% UG rec. any financial aid	77
% UG borrow to pay for school	72
Average cumulative	
indebtedness	$20,936

BENTLEY COLLEGE

CAMPUS LIFE

Fire Safety Rating	**99**
Green Rating	**95**
Type of school	private
Environment	town

STUDENTS

Total undergrad enrollment	4,148
% male/female	60/40
% from out of state	50

% from public high school	75
% live on campus	79
% in (# of) fraternities	9 (6)
% in (# of) sororities	12 (4)
% African American	3
% Asian	8
% Caucasian	66
% Hispanic	4
% international	7
# of countries represented	77

ACADEMICS

Calendar	semester
Student/faculty ratio	12:1
Profs interesting rating	82
Profs accessible rating	85
Most common	
reg class size	20–29 students

MOST POPULAR MAJORS
marketing/marketing management
finance
business administration and
management

SELECTIVITY

# of applicants	6,689
% of applicants accepted	38
% of acceptees attending	37
# accepting a place on wait list	425
# of early decision applicants	210
% accepted early decision	60

FRESHMAN PROFILE

Range SAT Critical Reading	550–630
Range SAT Math	600–680
Range SAT Writing	550–640
Range ACT Composite	24–29
Minimum paper TOEFL	550
Minimum computer TOEFL	213
Minimum web-based TOEFL	80
% graduated top 10% of class	42.1
% graduated top 25% of class	80.5
% graduated top 50% of class	97.4

DEADLINES

Early decision	
Deadline	11/15
Notification	12/15
Early action	
Deadline	11/15
Notification	1/15
Regular	
Deadline	1/15
Notification	4/1
Nonfall registration?	yes

FINANCIAL FACTS

Annual tuition	$31,450

Room and board | $10,940
Required fees | $1,446
Books and supplies | $1,000
% frosh rec. need-based
 scholarship or grant aid | 46
% UG rec. need-based
 scholarship or grant aid | 42
% frosh rec. non-need-based
 scholarship or grant aid | 26
% UG rec. non-need-based
 scholarship or grant aid | 13
% frosh rec. need-based
 self-help aid | 49
% UG rec. need-based
 self-help aid | 47
% frosh rec. athletic scholarships | 1
% UG rec. athletic scholarships | 1
% frosh rec. any financial aid | 79
% UG rec. any financial aid | 73
% UG borrow to pay for school | 63
Average cumulative
 indebtedness | $31,665

BOSTON COLLEGE

CAMPUS LIFE
Fire Safety Rating | **92**
Green Rating | **88**
Type of school | private
Affiliation | Roman Catholic
Environment | city

STUDENTS
Total undergrad enrollment | 9,081
% male/female | 48/52
% from out of state | 71
% from public high school | 53
% live on campus | 82
% African American | 6
% Asian | 10
% Caucasian | 71
% Hispanic | 8
% international | 2
# of countries represented | 84

ACADEMICS
Calendar | semester
Student/faculty ratio | 13:1
Profs interesting rating | 83
Profs accessible rating | 82
Most common
 reg class size | 10–19 students
MOST POPULAR MAJORS
English language and literature
finance

SELECTIVITY
of applicants | 28,850
% of applicants accepted | 27
% of acceptees attending | 29
# accepting a place on wait list | 2,000
% admitted from wait list | 5

FRESHMAN PROFILE
Range SAT Critical Reading | 610–710
Range SAT Math | 630–720
Range SAT Writing | 620–710
Minimum paper TOEFL | 600
Minimum computer TOEFL | 250
% graduated top 10% of class | 80
% graduated top 25% of class | 95
% graduated top 50% of class | 99

DEADLINES
Early action
 Deadline | 11/1
 Notification | 12/25
Regular
 Deadline | 1/1
 Notification | 4/15
Nonfall registration? | yes

FINANCIAL FACTS
Annual tuition | $37,410
Room and board | $11,610
Required fees | $540
Books and supplies | $750
% frosh rec. any financial aid | 70
% UG rec. any financial aid | 70

BOSTON UNIVERSITY

CAMPUS LIFE
Fire Safety Rating | **60***
Green Rating | **60***
Type of school | private
Environment | metropolis

STUDENTS
Total undergrad enrollment | 16,673
% male/female | 40/60
% from out of state | 77
% from public high school | 70
% live on campus | 65
% in (# of) fraternities | 3 (8)
% in (# of) sororities | 5 (9)
% African American | 3
% Asian | 13
% Caucasian | 56
% Hispanic | 7
% international | 6
# of countries represented | 101

ACADEMICS
Calendar | semester
Student/faculty ratio | 14:1
Profs interesting rating | 78
Profs accessible rating | 78
% classes taught by TAs | 7
Most common
 reg class size | 10–19 students
Most common
 lab size | 20–29 students
MOST POPULAR MAJORS
psychology
international relations
business/marketing
communications/journalism

SELECTIVITY
of applicants | 33,390
% of applicants accepted | 56
% of acceptees attending | 22
# accepting a place on wait list | 1,944
% admitted from wait list | 59
# of early decision applicants | 1,074
% accepted early decision | 37

FRESHMAN PROFILE
Range SAT Critical Reading | 580–680
Range SAT Math | 590–690
Range SAT Writing | 590–670
Range ACT Composite | 25–30
Minimum paper TOEFL | 550
Minimum computer TOEFL | 215
Average HS GPA | 3.45
% graduated top 10% of class | 51
% graduated top 25% of class | 85
% graduated top 50% of class | 100

DEADLINES
Early decision
 Deadline | 11/1
 Notification | 12/15
Regular
 Deadline | 1/1
Nonfall registration? | yes

FINANCIAL FACTS
Annual tuition | $36,450
Room and board | $11,418
Required fees | $510
Books and supplies | $860
% frosh rec. need-based
 scholarship or grant aid | 41
% UG rec. need-based
 scholarship or grant aid | 39
% frosh rec. non-need-based
 scholarship or grant aid | 17
% UG rec. non-need-based
 scholarship or grant aid | 11

% frosh rec. need-based
self-help aid   40
% UG rec. need-based
self-help aid   38
% frosh rec. athletic scholarships   2
% UG rec. athletic scholarships   2
% frosh rec. any financial aid   46
% UG rec. any financial aid   42
% UG borrow to pay for school   60
Average cumulative
indebtedness $24,939

BOWDOIN COLLEGE

CAMPUS LIFE
Fire Safety Rating   **95**
Green Rating   **94**
Type of school   private
Environment   village

STUDENTS
Total undergrad enrollment   1,710
% male/female   48/52
% from out of state   88
% live on campus   92
% African American   6
% Asian   13
% Caucasian   68
% Hispanic   7
% Native American   1
% international   3
# of countries represented   30

ACADEMICS
Calendar   semester
Student/faculty ratio   10:1
Profs interesting rating   95
Profs accessible rating   97
Most common
reg class size   10–19 students
Most common
lab size   10–19 students

MOST POPULAR MAJORS
economics
political science and government
history

SELECTIVITY
of applicants   4,434
% of applicants accepted   30
% of acceptees attending   34

FRESHMAN PROFILE
Range SAT Critical Reading   635–710
Range SAT Math   630–700
% graduated top 10% of class   55
% graduated top 25% of class   86
% graduated top 50% of class   99

DEADLINES
Early decision
Deadline   11/15
Notification   12/20
Regular
Deadline   1/1
Notification   3/31
Nonfall registration?   yes

FINANCIAL FACTS
Comprehensive fee $46,800
Books and supplies $1,150
% frosh rec. need-based
scholarship or grant aid   41
% UG rec. need-based
scholarship or grant aid   38
% frosh rec. need-based
self-help aid   39
% UG rec. need-based
self-help aid   38
% frosh rec. any financial aid   43
% UG rec. any financial aid   40
% UG borrow to pay for school   48.1
Average cumulative
indebtedness $13,947

BRANDEIS UNIVERSITY

CAMPUS LIFE
Fire Safety Rating   **60***
Green Rating   **60***
Type of school   private
Environment   city

STUDENTS
Total undergrad enrollment   3,203
% male/female   44/56
% from out of state   75
% from public high school   72
% live on campus   77
% African American   3
% Asian   9
% Caucasian   57
% Hispanic   4
% international   7
# of countries represented   55

ACADEMICS
Calendar   semester
Student/faculty ratio   8:1
Profs interesting rating   82
Profs accessible rating   82
Most common
reg class size   10–19 students

MOST POPULAR MAJORS
biology/biological sciences
psychology
economics

SELECTIVITY
of applicants   7,562
% of applicants accepted   34
% of acceptees attending   27
# accepting a place on wait list   414
% admitted from wait list   25
# of early decision applicants   359
% accepted early decision   57

FRESHMAN PROFILE
Range SAT Critical Reading   630–720
Range SAT Math   650–740
Range ACT Composite   28–32
Minimum paper TOEFL   600
Minimum computer TOEFL   250
Minimum web-based TOEFL   100
Average HS GPA   3.8
% graduated top 10% of class   71
% graduated top 25% of class   96
% graduated top 50% of class   100

DEADLINES
Early decision I
Deadline   11/15
Notification   12/15
Early decision II
Deadline   1/1
Notification   2/1
Regular
Deadline   1/15
Notification   4/1
Nonfall registration?   yes

FINANCIAL FACTS
Annual tuition $34,566
Room and board $9,908
Required fees $1,136
Books and supplies $700
% frosh rec. need-based
scholarship or grant aid   52
% UG rec. need-based
scholarship or grant aid   45
% frosh rec. non-need-based
scholarship or grant aid   8
% UG rec. non-need-based
scholarship or grant aid   5
% frosh rec. need-based
self-help aid   41
% UG rec. need-based
self-help aid   40
% frosh rec. any financial aid   53
% UG rec. any financial aid   47
% UG borrow to pay for school   74
Average cumulative
indebtedness $22,381

BROWN UNIVERSITY

CAMPUS LIFE
Fire Safety Rating	**86**
Green Rating	**93**
Type of school	private
Environment	city

STUDENTS
Total undergrad enrollment	5,813
% male/female	48/52
% from out of state	95
% from public high school	60
% live on campus	80
% in (# of) fraternities	10 (8)
% in (# of) sororities	7 (2)
% African American	7
% Asian	15
% Caucasian	49
% Hispanic	8
% Native American	1
% international	7
# of countries represented	93

ACADEMICS
Calendar	semester
Student/faculty ratio	9:1
Profs interesting rating	88
Profs accessible rating	89
Most common	
reg class size	10–19 students

MOST POPULAR MAJORS
biology/biological sciences
history
international relations and affairs

SELECTIVITY
# of applicants	19,097
% of applicants accepted	14
% of acceptees attending	56
# accepting a place on wait list	450
% admitted from wait list	16
# of early decision applicants	2,324
% accepted early decision	23

FRESHMAN PROFILE
Range SAT Critical Reading	660–760
Range SAT Math	670–770
Range SAT Writing	660–760
Range ACT Composite	28–33
Minimum paper TOEFL	600
Minimum computer TOEFL	250
Minimum web-based TOEFL	100
% graduated top 10% of class	92
% graduated top 25% of class	99
% graduated top 50% of class	100

DEADLINES
Early decision	
Deadline	11/1
Notification	12/1
Regular	
Deadline	1/1
Notification	4/1
Nonfall registration?	no

FINANCIAL FACTS
Annual tuition	$35,584
% frosh rec. need-based	
scholarship or grant aid	44
% UG rec. need-based	
scholarship or grant aid	42
% frosh rec. need-based	
self-help aid	35
% UG rec. need-based	
self-help aid	39
% frosh rec. any financial aid	45
% UG rec. any financial aid	44
% UG borrow to pay for school	46
Average cumulative	
indebtedness	$18,610

BRYANT UNIVERSITY

CAMPUS LIFE
Fire Safety Rating	**91**
Green Rating	**83**
Type of school	private
Environment	town

STUDENTS
Total undergrad enrollment	3,369
% male/female	58/42
% from out of state	84
% live on campus	83
% in (# of) fraternities	5 (5)
% in (# of) sororities	3 (4)
% African American	3
% Asian	3
% Caucasian	84
% Hispanic	4
% international	3
# of countries represented	45

ACADEMICS
Calendar	semester
Student/faculty ratio	17:1
Profs interesting rating	78
Profs accessible rating	82
Most common	
reg class size	30–39 students
Most common	
lab size	20–29 students

MOST POPULAR MAJORS
marketing/marketing management
accounting
finance

SELECTIVITY
# of applicants	5,649
% of applicants accepted	44
% of acceptees attending	35
# accepting a place on wait list	563
% admitted from wait list	12
# of early decision applicants	190
% accepted early decision	55

FRESHMAN PROFILE
Range SAT Critical Reading	520–600
Range SAT Math	550–630
Range SAT Writing	520–600
Range ACT Composite	22–26
Minimum paper TOEFL	550
Minimum computer TOEFL	213
Minimum web-based TOEFL	80
Average HS GPA	3.42
% graduated top 10% of class	25
% graduated top 25% of class	64
% graduated top 50% of class	95

DEADLINES
Early decision	
Deadline	11/15
Notification	12/15
Regular	
Deadline	2/1
Notification	3/21
Nonfall registration?	yes

FINANCIAL FACTS
Annual tuition	$27,639
Room and board	$10,715
Books and supplies	$1,200
% frosh rec. need-based	
scholarship or grant aid	53
% UG rec. need-based	
scholarship or grant aid	56
% frosh rec. non-need-based	
scholarship or grant aid	51
% UG rec. non-need-based	
scholarship or grant aid	32
% frosh rec. need-based	
self-help aid	60
% UG rec. need-based	
self-help aid	60
% frosh rec. athletic scholarships	2
% UG rec. athletic scholarships	2
% frosh rec. any financial aid	67
% UG rec. any financial aid	66
% UG borrow to pay for school	48

Average cumulative
indebtedness $29,128

BRYN MAWR COLLEGE

CAMPUS LIFE
Fire Safety Rating **74**
Green Rating **85**
Type of school private
Environment metropolis

STUDENTS
Total undergrad enrollment 1,275
% male/female /100
% from out of state 82
% from public high school 66
% live on campus 95
% African American 6
% Asian 12
% Caucasian 47
% Hispanic 3
% international 7
# of countries represented 43

ACADEMICS
Calendar semester
Student/faculty ratio 8:1
Profs interesting rating 91
Profs accessible rating 91
Most common
reg class size 10–19 students
MOST POPULAR MAJORS
mathematics
English language and literature
psychology

SELECTIVITY
of applicants 2,106
% of applicants accepted 45
% of acceptees attending 37
# accepting a place on wait list 200
% admitted from wait list 10
# of early decision applicants 146
% accepted early decision 52

FRESHMAN PROFILE
Range SAT Critical Reading 620–730
Range SAT Math 580–690
Range SAT Writing 620–720
Range ACT Composite 26–30
Minimum paper TOEFL 600
Minimum computer TOEFL 250
Minimum web-based TOEFL 100
% graduated top 10% of class 62
% graduated top 25% of class 91
% graduated top 50% of class 100

DEADLINES
Early decision I
Deadline 11/15
Notification 12/15
Early decision II
Deadline 1/1
Notification 2/1
Regular
Deadline 1/15
Notification 4/15
Nonfall registration? no

FINANCIAL FACTS
Annual tuition $35,700
% frosh rec. need-based
scholarship or grant aid 50
% UG rec. need-based
scholarship or grant aid 53
% frosh rec. non-need-based
scholarship or grant aid 11
% UG rec. non-need-based
scholarship or grant aid 6
% frosh rec. need-based
self-help aid 45
% UG rec. need-based
self-help aid 51
% frosh rec. any financial aid 50
% UG rec. any financial aid 59
% UG borrow to pay for school 61
Average cumulative
indebtedness $19,049

BUCKNELL UNIVERSITY

CAMPUS LIFE
Fire Safety Rating **87**
Green Rating **83**
Type of school private
Environment village

STUDENTS
Total undergrad enrollment 3,495
% male/female 49/51
% from out of state 73
% from public high school 70
% live on campus 87
% in (# of) fraternities 39 (13)
% in (# of) sororities 40 (6)
% African American 3
% Asian 7
% Caucasian 80
% Hispanic 3
% international 3
# of countries represented 42

ACADEMICS
Calendar semester
Student/faculty ratio 11:1
Profs interesting rating 88
Profs accessible rating 89
Most common
reg class size 10–19 students
Most common
lab size 10–19 students
MOST POPULAR MAJORS
business administration and
management
economics
English language and literature

SELECTIVITY
of applicants 8,943
% of applicants accepted 30
% of acceptees attending 33
# accepting a place on wait list 1,046
% admitted from wait list 1
# of early decision applicants 639
% accepted early decision 56

FRESHMAN PROFILE
Range SAT Critical Reading 600–690
Range SAT Math 630–710
Range SAT Writing 600–690
Range ACT Composite 27–31
Minimum paper TOEFL 550
Minimum computer TOEFL 213
% graduated top 10% of class 72
% graduated top 25% of class 93
% graduated top 50% of class 100

DEADLINES
Early decision
Deadline 11/15
Notification 12/15
Regular
Deadline 1/15
Notification 4/1
Nonfall registration? no

FINANCIAL FACTS
Annual tuition $39,434
Room and board $8,728
Required fees $218
Books and supplies $870
% frosh rec. need-based
scholarship or grant aid 48
% UG rec. need-based
scholarship or grant aid 45
% frosh rec. non-need-based
scholarship or grant aid 6
% UG rec. non-need-based
scholarship or grant aid 3
% frosh rec. need-based
self-help aid 48
% UG rec. need-based
self-help aid 47

% frosh rec. athletic scholarships	1
% UG rec. athletic scholarships	1
% frosh rec. any financial aid	62
% UG rec. any financial aid	64
% UG borrow to pay for school	64
Average cumulative	
indebtedness	$17,700

CALIFORNIA UNIVERSITY OF PENNSYLVANIA

CAMPUS LIFE

Fire Safety Rating	**95**
Green Rating	**99**
Type of school	public
Environment	village

STUDENTS

Total undergrad enrollment	6,199
% male/female	48/52
% from out of state	6
% live on campus	34
% in (# of) fraternities	10 (6)
% in (# of) sororities	10 (7)
% African American	6
% Caucasian	67
% Hispanic	1
% international	1
# of countries represented	18

ACADEMICS

Calendar	semester
Profs interesting rating	72
Profs accessible rating	67
Student/faculty ratio	19:1
Most common	
reg class size	20–29 students
Most common	
lab size	20–29 students

MOST POPULAR MAJORS
elementary education and teaching
criminal justice/safety studies
business administration and management

SELECTIVITY

# of applicants	3,849
% of applicants accepted	68
% of acceptees attending	51

FRESHMAN PROFILE

Range SAT Critical Reading	460–536
Range SAT Math	460–540
Average HS GPA	3.3
% graduated top 10% of class	7
% graduated top 25% of class	28
% graduated top 50% of class	65

DEADLINES

Regular	
Priority	5/1
Nonfall registration?	yes

FINANCIAL FACTS

Annual in-state tuition	$5,178
Annual out-of-state tuition	$8,284
Room and board	$8,466
Required fees	$1,673
Books and supplies	$875
% frosh rec. need-based	
scholarship or grant aid	45
% UG rec. need-based	
scholarship or grant aid	49
% frosh rec. non-need-based	
scholarship or grant aid	21
% UG rec. non-need-based	
scholarship or grant aid	13
% frosh rec. need-based self-help aid	55
% UG rec. need-based self-help aid	60
% frosh rec. athletic scholarships	2
% UG rec. athletic scholarships	3
% frosh rec. any financial aid	76
% UG rec. any financial aid	72
% UG borrow to pay for school	83
Average cumulative indebtedness	$21,860

CARNEGIE MELLON UNIVERSITY

CAMPUS LIFE

Fire Safety Rating	**77**
Green Rating	**60***
Type of school	private
Environment	metropolis

STUDENTS

Total undergrad enrollment	5,580
% male/female	61/39
% from out of state	76
% live on campus	66
% in (# of) fraternities	8 (17)
% in (# of) sororities	9 (8)
% African American	5
% Asian	24
% Caucasian	40
% Hispanic	5
% Native American	1
% international	13
# of countries represented	95

ACADEMICS

Calendar	semester
Student/faculty ratio	10:1
Profs interesting rating	70
Profs accessible rating	76

Most common	
reg class size	fewer than 10 students
Most common	
lab size	20–29 students

MOST POPULAR MAJORS
computer science
computer engineering
liberal arts and sciences/liberal studies

SELECTIVITY

# of applicants	18,864
% of applicants accepted	34
% of acceptees attending	22
# accepting a place on wait list	319
% admitted from wait list	18
# of early decision applicants	813
% accepted early decision	35

FRESHMAN PROFILE

Range SAT Critical Reading	610–710
Range SAT Math	690–780
Range SAT Writing	610–700
Range ACT Composite	28–32
Average HS GPA	3.61
% graduated top 10% of class	75
% graduated top 25% of class	95
% graduated top 50% of class	100

DEADLINES

Early decision	
Deadline	11/1
Notification	12/15
Regular	
Deadline	1/1
Notification	4/15
Nonfall registration?	no

FINANCIAL FACTS

Annual tuition	$35,580
Room and board	$9,350
Required fees	$404
Books and supplies	$966
% frosh rec. need-based	
scholarship or grant aid	49
% UG rec. need-based	
scholarship or grant aid	46
% frosh rec. non-need-based	
scholarship or grant aid	18
% UG rec. non-need-based	
scholarship or grant aid	22
% frosh rec. need-based	
self-help aid	49
% UG rec. need-based	
self-help aid	47
% frosh rec. any financial aid	68
% UG rec. any financial aid	66
% UG borrow to pay for school	52

Average cumulative
  indebtedness $27,395

THE CATHOLIC UNIVERSITY
OF AMERICA

CAMPUS LIFE
Fire Safety Rating **85**
Green Rating **69**
Type of school private
Affiliation Roman Catholic
Environment metropolis

STUDENTS
Total undergrad enrollment 3,245
% male/female 46/54
% from out of state 94
% from public high school 49
% live on campus 68
% in (# of) fraternities 1 (1)
% in (# of) sororities 1 (1)
% African American 5
% Asian 3
% Caucasian 69
% Hispanic 6
% international 2
# of countries represented 76

ACADEMICS
Calendar semester
Student/faculty ratio 10:1
Profs interesting rating 73
Profs accessible rating 75
% classes taught by TAs 9
Most common
  reg class size 10–19 students
Most common
  lab size 10–19 students
MOST POPULAR MAJORS
political science and government
architecture (barch, ba/bs, march, ma/ms,
phd)
nursing/registered nurse
(RN, ASN, BSN, MSN)

SELECTIVITY
of applicants 4,911
% of applicants accepted 80
% of acceptees attending 22

FRESHMAN PROFILE
Range SAT Critical Reading 520–620
Range SAT Math 510–610
Range SAT Writing 520–610
Range ACT Composite 22–26
Minimum paper TOEFL 560
Minimum computer TOEFL 220

Minimum web-based TOEFL 80
Average HS GPA 3.26
% graduated top 10% of class 18
% graduated top 25% of class 57
% graduated top 50% of class 87

DEADLINES
Early action
  Deadline 11/15
  Notification 12/15
Regular
  Deadline 2/15
  Notification 3/15
Nonfall registration? yes

FINANCIAL FACTS
Annual tuition $30,520
% frosh rec. need-based
  scholarship or grant aid 58
% UG rec. need-based
  scholarship or grant aid 50
% frosh rec. need-based
  self-help aid 54
% UG rec. need-based
  self-help aid 45
% frosh rec. any financial aid 99
% UG rec. any financial aid 92

CENTRAL CONNECTICUT
STATE UNIVERSITY

CAMPUS LIFE
Fire Safety Rating **81**
Green Rating **60***
Type of school public
Environment town

STUDENTS
Total undergrad enrollment 9,161
% male/female 50/50
% from out of state 5
% from public high school 93
% live on campus 23
% in (# of) fraternities 1 (NR)
% in (# of) sororities 1 (1)
% African American 6
% Asian 2
% Caucasian 74
% Hispanic 4
% international 1
# of countries represented 64

ACADEMICS
Calendar semester
Profs interesting rating 66
Profs accessible rating 64
Student/faculty ratio 16:1

Most common
  reg class size 20–29 students
Most common
  lab size less than 10 students
MOST POPULAR MAJORS
psychology
accounting
marketing/marketing management

SELECTIVITY
of applicants 5,665
% of applicants accepted 61
% of acceptees attending 42

FRESHMAN PROFILE
Range SAT Critical Reading 460–540
Range SAT Math 460–560
Range SAT Writing 460–540
Minimum paper TOEFL 500
% graduated top 10% of class 6
% graduated top 25% of class 25
% graduated top 50% of class 66

DEADLINES
Regular
  Priority 10/1
  Deadline 6/1
  Notification rolling
Nonfall registration? yes

FINANCIAL FACTS
Annual in-state tuition $3,346
Annual out-of-state tuition $10,831
Room and board $8,350
Required fees $3,388
Books and supplies $1,010
% frosh rec. need-based
  scholarship or grant aid 36
% UG rec. need-based
  scholarship or grant aid 36
% frosh rec. non-need-based
  scholarship or grant aid 8
% UG rec. non-need-based
  scholarship or grant aid 8
% frosh rec. need-based self-help aid 32
% UG rec. need-based self-help aid 43
% frosh rec. athletic scholarships 3
% UG rec. athletic scholarships 3
% frosh rec. any financial aid 39
% UG rec. any financial aid 51
% UG borrow to pay for school 28
Average cumulative indebtedness $17,875

CHATHAM COLLEGE

CAMPUS LIFE
Fire Safety Rating	**65**
Green Rating	**89**
Type of school	private
Environment	metropolis

STUDENTS
Total undergrad enrollment	651
% male/female	1/99
% from out of state	19
% live on campus	61
% African American	10
% Asian	2
% Caucasian	66
% Hispanic	2
% international	6
# of countries represented	17

ACADEMICS
Calendar	Chatham uses a 4-4-1 calendar
Profs interesting rating	89
Profs accessible rating	86
Student/faculty ratio	8:1
Most common reg class size	less than 10 students
Most common lab size	10–19 students

MOST POPULAR MAJORS
English language and literature
biology/biological sciences
psychology

SELECTIVITY
# of applicants	600
% of applicants accepted	76
% of acceptees attending	39

FRESHMAN PROFILE
Range SAT Critical Reading	480–583
Range SAT Math	440–563
Range ACT Composite	21–26
Minimum paper TOEFL	550
Minimum computer TOEFL	210
Minimum web-based TOEFL	79
Average HS GPA	3.33
% graduated top 10% of class	18
% graduated top 25% of class	41
% graduated top 50% of class	74

DEADLINES
Regular	
Priority	3/15
Deadline	8/1
Notification	rolling
Nonfall registration?	yes

FINANCIAL FACTS
Annual tuition	$25,216
Room and board	$7,892
Required fees	$900
Books and supplies	$860
% frosh rec. need-based scholarship or grant aid	77
% UG rec. need-based scholarship or grant aid	57
% frosh rec. non-need-based scholarship or grant aid	45
% UG rec. non-need-based scholarship or grant aid	54
% frosh rec. need-based self-help aid	77
% UG rec. need-based self-help aid	69
% frosh rec. any financial aid	99
% UG rec. any financial aid	99

CHESTNUT HILL COLLEGE

CAMPUS LIFE
Fire Safety Rating	**83**
Green Rating	**68**
Type of school	private
Affiliation	Roman Catholic
Environment	metropolis

STUDENTS
Total undergrad enrollment	1,248
% male/female	32/68
% from out of state	32
% live on campus	69
% African American	37
% Asian	2
% Caucasian	51
% Hispanic	6
% international	1
# of countries represented	3

ACADEMICS
Calendar	semester
Profs interesting rating	83
Profs accessible rating	86
Student/faculty ratio	11:1
Most common reg class size	10–19 students
Most common lab size	10–19 students

MOST POPULAR MAJORS
business administration and management
human services
criminal justice/
law enforcement administration

SELECTIVITY
# of applicants	1,387
% of applicants accepted	86
% of acceptees attending	19

FRESHMAN PROFILE
Range SAT Critical Reading	440–550
Range SAT Math	420–530
Range SAT Writing	440–540
Range ACT Composite	17–21
Minimum paper TOEFL	500
Average HS GPA	3.04

DEADLINES
Early decision	
Deadline	12/10
Notification	12/15
Regular	
Priority	1/20
Notification	rolling
Nonfall registration?	yes

FINANCIAL FACTS
Annual tuition	$26,000
Room and board	$8,550
Books and supplies	$1,200
% frosh rec. need-based scholarship or grant aid	78
% UG rec. need-based scholarship or grant aid	77
% frosh rec. non-need-based scholarship or grant aid	6
% UG rec. non-need-based scholarship or grant aid	6
% frosh rec. need-based self-help aid	72
% UG rec. need-based self-help aid	72
% frosh rec. athletic scholarships	2
% UG rec. athletic scholarships	2
% frosh rec. any financial aid	80
% UG rec. any financial aid	82

CITY UNIVERSITY OF NEW YORK—BARUCH COLLEGE

CAMPUS LIFE
Fire Safety Rating	**60***
Green Rating	**66**
Type of school	public
Environment	metropolis

STUDENTS
Total undergrad enrollment	12,626
% male/female	48/52
% from out of state	3
% in (# of) fraternities	10 (9)
% in (# of) sororities	10 (7)
% African American	11
% Asian	30
% Caucasian	30
% Hispanic	17

% international	13
# of countries represented	151

ACADEMICS

Calendar	semester
Student/faculty ratio	19:1
Profs interesting rating	64
Profs accessible rating	64
Most common reg class size	20–29 students
Most common lab size	10–19 students

MOST POPULAR MAJORS
accounting
finance

SELECTIVITY

# of applicants	17,114
% of applicants accepted	26
% of acceptees attending	34

FRESHMAN PROFILE

Range SAT Critical Reading	480–580
Range SAT Math	540–650
Minimum paper TOEFL	620
Minimum computer TOEFL	260
Average HS GPA	3.0
% graduated top 10% of class	37
% graduated top 25% of class	67
% graduated top 50% of class	93

DEADLINES

Regular	
Deadline	2/1
Notification	rolling
Nonfall registration?	yes

APPLICANTS ALSO LOOK AT AND OFTEN PREFER
City University of New York—
Hunter College

FINANCIAL FACTS

Annual in-state tuition	$4,000
Annual out-of-state tuition	$8,640
Required fees	$320
Books and supplies	$1,016
% frosh rec. need-based scholarship or grant aid	50
% UG rec. need-based scholarship or grant aid	59
% frosh rec. non-need-based scholarship or grant aid	69
% UG rec. non-need-based scholarship or grant aid	18
% frosh rec. need-based self-help aid	21
% UG rec. need-based self-help aid	20

% frosh rec. any financial aid	72
% UG rec. any financial aid	57
% UG borrow to pay for school	19
Average cumulative indebtedness	$14,159

CITY UNIVERSITY OF NEW YORK—BROOKLYN COLLEGE

CAMPUS LIFE

Fire Safety Rating	**60***
Green Rating	**77**
Type of school	public
Environment	metropolis

STUDENTS

Total undergrad enrollment	11,923
% male/female	40/60
% from out of state	2
% in fraternities	2
% in sororities	2
% African American	27
% Asian	14
% Caucasian	41
% Hispanic	12
% international	6

ACADEMICS

Calendar	semester
Student/faculty ratio	16:1
Profs interesting rating	63
Profs accessible rating	63
Most common reg class size	20–29 students

SELECTIVITY

# of applicants	14,754
% of applicants accepted	40
% of acceptees attending	22

FRESHMAN PROFILE

Range SAT Critical Reading	450–560
Range SAT Math	490–590
Minimum paper TOEFL	509
Minimum computer TOEFL	545
% graduated top 10% of class	14
% graduated top 25% of class	48
% graduated top 50% of class	77

DEADLINES

Regular	
Priority	3/1
Notification	rolling
Nonfall registration?	yes

FINANCIAL FACTS

Annual in-state tuition	$4,000
Annual out-of-state tuition	$10,800

Required fees	$381
% frosh rec. need-based scholarship or grant aid	76
% UG rec. need-based scholarship or grant aid	67
% frosh rec. non-need-based scholarship or grant aid	24
% UG rec. non-need-based scholarship or grant aid	21
% frosh rec. need-based self-help aid	71
% UG rec. need-based self-help aid	70
% frosh rec. any financial aid	80
% UG rec. any financial aid	64
% UG borrow to pay for school	36
Average cumulative indebtedness	$15,500

CITY UNIVERSITY OF NEW YORK—HUNTER COLLEGE

CAMPUS LIFE

Fire Safety Rating	**93**
Green Rating	**76**
Type of school	public
Environment	metropolis

STUDENTS

Total undergrad enrollment	14,573
% male/female	32/68
% from out of state	4
% in (# of) fraternities	1 (2)
% in (# of) sororities	NR (2)
% African American	12
% Asian	18
% Caucasian	40
% Hispanic	19
% international	10

ACADEMICS

Calendar	semester
Student/faculty ratio	15:1
Profs interesting rating	66
Profs accessible rating	62
Most common reg class size	20–29 students

SELECTIVITY

# of applicants	24,701
% of applicants accepted	30
% of acceptees attending	26

FRESHMAN PROFILE

Range SAT Critical Reading	480–550
Range SAT Math	490–560

DEADLINES

Regular
Deadline	3/15
Notification	rolling
Nonfall registration?	yes

FINANCIAL FACTS

Annual in-state tuition	$4,000
Annual out-of-state tuition	$10,800
Room and board	$3,276
Required fees	$329
% frosh rec. need-based scholarship or grant aid	60
% UG rec. need-based scholarship or grant aid	6
% frosh rec. non-need-based scholarship or grant aid	43
% UG rec. non-need-based scholarship or grant aid	2
% frosh rec. need-based self-help aid	13
% UG rec. need-based self-help aid	2
% UG borrow to pay for school	38
Average cumulative indebtedness	$7,124

CITY UNIVERSITY OF NEW YORK—QUEENS COLLEGE

CAMPUS LIFE

Fire Safety Rating	**60***
Green Rating	**60***
Type of school	public
Environment	metropolis

STUDENTS

Total undergrad enrollment	14,610
% male/female	40/60
% from out of state	1
% from public high school	55
% in (# of) fraternities	1 (4)
% in (# of) sororities	1 (3)
% African American	9
% Asian	20
% Caucasian	46
% Hispanic	18
% international	7
# of countries represented	140

ACADEMICS

Calendar	semester
Student/faculty ratio	17:1
Profs interesting rating	65
Profs accessible rating	63
% classes taught by TAs	1

Most common reg class size	20–29 students

MOST POPULAR MAJORS

accounting
psychology
sociology

SELECTIVITY

# of applicants	14,436
% of applicants accepted	40
% of acceptees attending	30

FRESHMAN PROFILE

Range SAT Critical Reading	450–550
Range SAT Math	480–580
Range SAT Writing	490–550
Minimum paper TOEFL	500
Minimum computer TOEFL	173
Minimum web-based TOEFL	62

DEADLINES

Regular
Priority	1/1
Notification	rolling
Nonfall registration?	yes

FINANCIAL FACTS

Annual in-state tuition	$4,000
Annual out-of-state tuition	$8,640
Required fees	$377
% frosh rec. need-based scholarship or grant aid	34
% UG rec. need-based scholarship or grant aid	45
% frosh rec. non-need-based scholarship or grant aid	25
% UG rec. non-need-based scholarship or grant aid	10
% frosh rec. need-based self-help aid	20
% UG rec. need-based self-help aid	15
% frosh rec. athletic scholarships	2
% UG rec. athletic scholarships	1
% frosh rec. any financial aid	55
% UG rec. any financial aid	58
% UG borrow to pay for school	41
Average cumulative indebtedness	$18,000

CLARK UNIVERSITY

CAMPUS LIFE

Fire Safety Rating	**97**
Green Rating	**73**
Type of school	private
Environment	city

STUDENTS

Total undergrad enrollment	2,217
% male/female	39/61
% from out of state	64
% from public high school	58
% live on campus	76
% African American	2
% Asian	4
% Caucasian	67
% Hispanic	2
% international	8
# of countries represented	63

ACADEMICS

Calendar	semester
Student/faculty ratio	10:1
Profs interesting rating	83
Profs accessible rating	84
Most common reg class size	10–19 students
Most common lab size	10–19 students

MOST POPULAR MAJORS

biology/biological sciences
psychology
political science and government

SELECTIVITY

# of applicants	5,201
% of applicants accepted	56
% of acceptees attending	20
# accepting a place on wait list	28
% admitted from wait list	25
# of early decision applicants	90
% accepted early decision	84

FRESHMAN PROFILE

Range SAT Critical Reading	553–660
Range SAT Math	543–650
Range ACT Composite	24–28
Minimum paper TOEFL	577
Minimum computer TOEFL	233
Minimum web-based TOEFL	90–91
Average HS GPA	3.47
% graduated top 10% of class	32
% graduated top 25% of class	74
% graduated top 50% of class	98

DEADLINES

Early decision
Deadline	11/15
Notification	12/15

Regular
Deadline	1/15
Notification	4/1
Nonfall registration?	yes

FINANCIAL FACTS

Annual tuition	$33,900
Room and board	$6,650
Required fees	$320
Books and supplies	$800
% frosh rec. need-based scholarship or grant aid	52
% UG rec. need-based scholarship or grant aid	52
% frosh rec. non-need-based scholarship or grant aid	31
% UG rec. non-need-based scholarship or grant aid	31
% frosh rec. need-based self-help aid	45
% UG rec. need-based self-help aid	45
% frosh rec. any financial aid	78
% UG rec. any financial aid	81
% UG borrow to pay for school	99
Average cumulative indebtedness	$21,100

CLARKSON UNIVERSITY

CAMPUS LIFE

Fire Safety Rating	**76**
Green Rating	**95**
Type of school	private
Environment	village

STUDENTS

Total undergrad enrollment	2,521
% male/female	74/26
% from out of state	28
% live on campus	83
% in (# of) fraternities	13 (10)
% in (# of) sororities	14 (3)
% African American	3
% Asian	3
% Caucasian	90
% Hispanic	2
% international	2
# of countries represented	43

ACADEMICS

Calendar	semester
Student/faculty ratio	15:1
Profs interesting rating	64
Profs accessible rating	72
% classes taught by TAs	1
Most common reg class size	fewer than 10 students
Most common lab size	20–29 students

MOST POPULAR MAJORS
engineering
biology/biological sciences
business/commerce

SELECTIVITY

# of applicants	2,983
% of applicants accepted	81
% of acceptees attending	28
# accepting a place on wait list	23
% admitted from wait list	83
# of early decision applicants	98
% accepted early decision	97

FRESHMAN PROFILE

Range SAT Critical Reading	510–610
Range SAT Math	560–670
Range SAT Writing	500–630
Range ACT Composite	23–29
Minimum paper TOEFL	550
Minimum computer TOEFL	213
Average HS GPA	3.52
% graduated top 10% of class	39.5
% graduated top 25% of class	73
% graduated top 50% of class	96

DEADLINES

Early decision	
Deadline	12/1
Notification	1/1
Regular	
Deadline	1/15
Nonfall registration?	yes

FINANCIAL FACTS

Annual tuition	$30,320
Room and board	$10,612
Required fees	$690
Books and supplies	$1,100
% frosh rec. need-based scholarship or grant aid	61
% UG rec. need-based scholarship or grant aid	64
% frosh rec. non-need-based scholarship or grant aid	11
% UG rec. non-need-based scholarship or grant aid	9
% frosh rec. need-based self-help aid	53
% UG rec. need-based self-help aid	69
% frosh rec. athletic scholarships	2
% UG rec. athletic scholarships	1
% frosh rec. any financial aid	95
% UG rec. any financial aid	91
% UG borrow to pay for school	87
Average cumulative indebtedness	$33,774

COLBY COLLEGE

CAMPUS LIFE

Fire Safety Rating	**95**
Green Rating	**95**
Type of school	private
Environment	village

STUDENTS

Total undergrad enrollment	1,867
% male/female	45/55
% from out of state	90
% from public high school	54
% live on campus	94
% African American	2
% Asian	8
% Caucasian	75
% Hispanic	3
% international	6
# of countries represented	50

ACADEMICS

Calendar	4/1/4
Student/faculty ratio	10:1
Profs interesting rating	91
Profs accessible rating	87
Most common reg class size	10–19 students
Most common lab size	10–19 students

MOST POPULAR MAJORS
Biology/biological sciences
economics
government

SELECTIVITY

# of applicants	4,679
% of applicants accepted	32
% of acceptees attending	31
# accepting a place on wait list	397
% admitted from wait list	11
# of early decision applicants	453
% accepted early decision	42

FRESHMAN PROFILE

Range SAT Critical Reading	640–720
Range SAT Math	640–720
Range SAT Writing	630–710
Range ACT Composite	28–31
Minimum paper TOEFL	600
Minimum computer TOEFL	240
% graduated top 10% of class	60
% graduated top 25% of class	90
% graduated top 50% of class	98

DEADLINES

Early decision

Deadline	1/1
Notification	2/1

Regular

Deadline	1/1
Notification	4/1
Nonfall registration?	yes

FINANCIAL FACTS

Comprehensive fee	$48/520
Books and supplies	$700
% frosh rec. need-based scholarship or grant aid	39
% UG rec. need-based scholarship or grant aid	39
% frosh rec. need-based self-help aid	34
% UG rec. need-based self-help aid	33
% frosh rec. any financial aid	41
% UG rec. any financial aid	37
% UG borrow to pay for school	44
Average cumulative indebtedness	$19,222

COLGATE UNIVERSITY

CAMPUS LIFE

Fire Safety Rating	**78**
Green Rating	**86**
Type of school	private
Environment	rural

STUDENTS

Total undergrad enrollment	2,750
% male/female	47/53
% from out of state	71
% from public high school	65
% live on campus	93
% in (# of) fraternities	28 (6)
% in (# of) sororities	34 (4)
% African American	5
% Asian	7
% Caucasian	75
% Hispanic	5
% Native American	1
% international	5
# of countries represented	36

ACADEMICS

Calendar	semester
Student/faculty ratio	10:1
Profs interesting rating	94
Profs accessible rating	97
Most common reg class size	10–19 students

Most common

lab size	10–19 students

MOST POPULAR MAJORS

English language and literature
economics
history

SELECTIVITY

# of applicants	8,759
% of applicants accepted	26
% of acceptees attending	33
# accepting a place on wait list	469
% admitted from wait list	44
# of early decision applicants	730
% accepted early decision	50

FRESHMAN PROFILE

Range SAT Critical Reading	620–720
Range SAT Math	630–710
Range ACT Composite	29–32
Average HS GPA	3.7
% graduated top 10% of class	64
% graduated top 25% of class	83
% graduated top 50% of class	100

DEADLINES

Early decision

Deadline	11/15
Notification	12/15

Regular

Deadline	1/15
Notification	4/1
Nonfall registration?	no

FINANCIAL FACTS

Annual tuition	$37,405
Room and board	$9,170
Required fees	$255
Books and supplies	$1,880
% frosh rec. need-based scholarship or grant aid	29
% UG rec. need-based scholarship or grant aid	33
% frosh rec. need-based self-help aid	23
% UG rec. need-based self-help aid	28
% frosh rec. athletic scholarships	5
% UG rec. athletic scholarships	6
% frosh rec. any financial aid	35
% UG rec. any financial aid	46
% UG borrow to pay for school	36
Average cumulative indebtedness	$16,666

COLLEGE OF THE ATLANTIC

CAMPUS LIFE

Fire Safety Rating	**88**
Green Rating	**99**
Type of school	private
Environment	rural

STUDENTS

Total undergrad enrollment	327
% male/female	36/64
% from out of state	80
% from public high school	71
% live on campus	40
% Asian	1
% Caucasian	24
% Hispanic	1
% international	13
# of countries represented	36

ACADEMICS

Calendar	trimester
Student/faculty ratio	11:1
Profs interesting rating	95
Profs accessible rating	98
Most common reg class size	10–19 students
Most common lab size	fewer than 10 students

MOST POPULAR MAJORS

education
biology/biological sciences
ecology

SELECTIVITY

# of applicants	305
% of applicants accepted	77
% of acceptees attending	36
# of early decision applicants	31
% accepted early decision	90

FRESHMAN PROFILE

Range SAT Critical Reading	590–690
Range SAT Math	540–640
Range SAT Writing	570–670
Range ACT Composite	24–30
Minimum paper TOEFL	567
Minimum computer TOEFL	227
Average HS GPA	3.49
% graduated top 10% of class	33
% graduated top 25% of class	52
% graduated top 50% of class	89

DEADLINES

Early decision

Deadline	12/1
Notification	12/15

Regular
Priority 2/15
Deadline 2/15
Notification 4/1
Nonfall registration? yes

FINANCIAL FACTS

Annual tuition $30,990
Room and board $8,490
Required fees $480
Books and supplies $600
% frosh rec. need-based
scholarship or grant aid 79
% UG rec. need-based
scholarship or grant aid 78
% frosh rec. need-based
self-help aid 81
% UG rec. need-based
self-help aid 81
% frosh rec. any financial aid 85
% UG rec. any financial aid 87
% UG borrow to pay for school 63
Average cumulative
indebtedness $19,692

COLLEGE OF THE HOLY CROSS

CAMPUS LIFE
Fire Safety Rating **95**
Green Rating **94**
Type of school private
Affiliation Roman Catholic
Environment city

STUDENTS
Total undergrad enrollment 2,817
% male/female 44/56
% from out of state 61
% from public high school 51
% live on campus 90
% African American 4
% Asian 5
% Caucasian 71
% Hispanic 5
% international 1
# of countries represented 13

ACADEMICS
Calendar semester
Student/faculty ratio 11:1
Profs interesting rating 92
Profs accessible rating 92
Most common
reg class size 10–19 students
Most common
lab size fewer than 10 students

MOST POPULAR MAJORS
economics
psychology
history

SELECTIVITY
of applicants 7,066
% of applicants accepted 33
% of acceptees attending 31
# accepting a place on wait list 296
% admitted from wait list 15
# of early decision applicants 469
% accepted early decision 54

FRESHMAN PROFILE
Range SAT Critical Reading 590–690
Range SAT Math 620–690
Minimum paper TOEFL 550
Minimum computer TOEFL 213
Minimum web-based TOEFL 79
% graduated top 10% of class 65
% graduated top 25% of class 97
% graduated top 50% of class 100

DEADLINES
Early decision
Deadline 12/15
Notification 1/15
Regular
Deadline 1/15
Notification 4/1
Nonfall registration? yes

FINANCIAL FACTS
Annual tuition $36,710
Room and board $10,260
Required fees $532
Books and supplies $700
% frosh rec. need-based
scholarship or grant aid 46
% UG rec. need-based
scholarship or grant aid 46
% frosh rec. non-need-based
scholarship or grant aid 1
% UG rec. non-need-based
scholarship or grant aid 2
% frosh rec. need-based
self-help aid 43
% UG rec. need-based
self-help aid 42
% frosh rec. athletic scholarships 1
% UG rec. athletic scholarships 1
% frosh rec. any financial aid 61
% UG rec. any financial aid 58
Average cumulative
indebtedness $17,000

THE COLLEGE OF NEW JERSEY

CAMPUS LIFE
Fire Safety Rating **96**
Green Rating **91**
Type of school public
Environment village

STUDENTS
Total undergrad enrollment 6,164
% male/female 42/58
% from out of state 5
% from public high school 65
% live on campus 48
% in (# of) fraternities 12 (11)
% in (# of) sororities 11 (15)
% African American 6
% Asian 8
% Caucasian 73
% Hispanic 8
# of countries represented 20

ACADEMICS
Calendar semester
Student/faculty ratio 13:1
Profs interesting rating 89
Profs accessible rating 86
Most common
reg class size 20–29 students
Most common
lab size 10–19 students

MOST POPULAR MAJORS
business administration and
management
elementary education and teaching
psychology

SELECTIVITY
of applicants 8,607
% of applicants accepted 47
% of acceptees attending 32
# accepting a place on wait list 547
% admitted from wait list 27
# of early decision applicants 532
% accepted early decision 42

FRESHMAN PROFILE
Range SAT Critical Reading 560–650
Range SAT Math 580–680
Range SAT Writing 560–660
Minimum paper TOEFL 550
Minimum computer TOEFL 213
% graduated top 10% of class 66
% graduated top 25% of class 87
% graduated top 50% of class 99

DEADLINES

Early decision

Deadline	11/15
Notification	12/15

Regular

Deadline	2/15
Notification	rolling
Nonfall registration?	yes

FINANCIAL FACTS

Annual in-state tuition	$8,072
Annual out-of-state tuition	$15,295
Room and board	$9,242
Required fees	$3,235
Books and supplies	$1,000
% frosh rec. need-based scholarship or grant aid	17
% UG rec. need-based scholarship or grant aid	16
% frosh rec. non-need-based scholarship or grant aid	16
% UG rec. non-need-based scholarship or grant aid	16
% frosh rec. need-based self-help aid	28
% UG rec. need-based self-help aid	31
% UG borrow to pay for school	55
Average cumulative indebtedness	$20,056

COLUMBIA UNIVERSITY

CAMPUS LIFE

Fire Safety Rating	**60***
Green Rating	**60***
Type of school	private
Environment	metropolis

STUDENTS

Total undergrad enrollment	5,602
% male/female	53/47
% from out of state	75
% from public high school	59
% live on campus	95
% in (# of) fraternities	15 (17)
% in (# of) sororities	10 (11)
% African American	9
% Asian	18
% Caucasian	42
% Hispanic	10
% Native American	1
% international	9
# of countries represented	87

ACADEMICS

Calendar	semester
Student/faculty ratio	6:1

Profs interesting rating	77
Profs accessible rating	74
Most common reg class size	10–19 students

MOST POPULAR MAJORS
political science
English
engineering

SELECTIVITY

# of applicants	21,342
% of applicants accepted	10
% of acceptees attending	64
# of early decision applicants	2,429
% accepted early decision	24

FRESHMAN PROFILE

Range SAT Critical Reading	680–760
Range SAT Math	680–780
Range SAT Writing	670–760
Range ACT Composite	28–33
Minimum paper TOEFL	600
Minimum computer TOEFL	250
Average HS GPA	3.9
% graduated top 10% of class	94
% graduated top 25% of class	98
% graduated top 50% of class	99

DEADLINES

Early decision

Deadline	11/1
Notification	12/15

Regular

Deadline	1/2
Notification	4/1
Nonfall registration?	no

FINANCIAL FACTS

Annual tuition	$35,516
% frosh rec. need-based scholarship or grant aid	49
% UG rec. need-based scholarship or grant aid	46
% frosh rec. need-based self-help aid	43
% UG rec. need-based self-help aid	43
% frosh rec. any financial aid	61
% UG rec. any financial aid	56

CONNECTICUT COLLEGE

CAMPUS LIFE

Fire Safety Rating	**81**
Green Rating	**80**
Type of school	private
Environment	town

STUDENTS

Total undergrad enrollment	1,746
% male/female	41/59
% from out of state	85
% from public high school	55
% live on campus	99
% African American	4
% Asian	4
% Caucasian	75
% Hispanic	5
% international	4
# of countries represented	74

ACADEMICS

Calendar	semester
Student/faculty ratio	9:1
Profs interesting rating	87
Profs accessible rating	93

MOST POPULAR MAJORS
English language and literature
psychology
political science and government

SELECTIVITY

# of applicants	4,742
% of applicants accepted	35
% of acceptees attending	30
# accepting a place on wait list	433
% admitted from wait list	7
# of early decision applicants	313
% accepted early decision	67

FRESHMAN PROFILE

Range SAT Critical Reading	630–720
Range SAT Math	610–690
Range SAT Writing	630–720
Range ACT Composite	25–29
Minimum paper TOEFL	600
Minimum computer TOEFL	250
Minimum web-based TOEFL	100
% graduated top 10% of class	60
% graduated top 25% of class	93
% graduated top 50% of class	100

DEADLINES

Early decision

Deadline	11/15
Notification	12/15

Regular

Deadline	1/1
Notification	3/31
Nonfall registration?	no

FINANCIAL FACTS

Comprehensive fee	$49,385
Books and supplies	$1,000
% frosh rec. need-based scholarship or grant aid	39

% UG rec. need-based
scholarship or grant aid — 38
% frosh rec. need-based
self-help aid — 37
% UG rec. need-based
self-help aid — 37
% frosh rec. any financial aid — 45
% UG borrow to pay for school — 38
Average cumulative
indebtedness — $23,488

COOPER UNION

CAMPUS LIFE
Fire Safety Rating — **98**
Green Rating — **80**
Type of school — private
Environment — metropolis

STUDENTS
Total undergrad enrollment — 906
% male/female — 63/37
% from out of state — 40
% from public high school — 65
% live on campus — 20
% in (# of) fraternities — 10 (2)
% in (# of) sororities — 5 (1)
% African American — 6
% Asian — 26
% Caucasian — 47
% Hispanic — 9
% international — 14

ACADEMICS
Calendar — semester
Student/faculty ratio — 8:1
Profs interesting rating — 64
Profs accessible rating — 64
Most common
reg class size — 10–19 students
Most common
lab size — fewer than 10 students

MOST POPULAR MAJORS
electrical, electronics and communications
engineering
fine arts and art studies
mechanical engineering

SELECTIVITY
of applicants — 2,551
% of applicants accepted — 11
% of acceptees attending — 74
# accepting a place on wait list — 60
% admitted from wait list — 5
# of early decision applicants — 380
% accepted early decision — 20

FRESHMAN PROFILE
Range SAT Critical Reading — 610–700
Range SAT Math — 640–770
Range ACT Composite — 29–33
Minimum paper TOEFL — 600
Minimum computer TOEFL — 250
Minimum web-based TOEFL — 100
Average HS GPA — 3.6
% graduated top 10% of class — 93
% graduated top 25% of class — 98
% graduated top 50% of class — 99

DEADLINES
Early decision
Deadline — 12/1
Notification — 12/23
Regular
Priority — 12/1
Deadline — 1/1
Notification — 4/1
Nonfall registration? — no

FINANCIAL FACTS
Annual tuition — $31,500
Room and board — $13,500
Required fees — $1,600
Books and supplies — $1,800
% frosh rec. need-based
scholarship or grant aid — 35
% UG rec. need-based
scholarship or grant aid — 31
% frosh rec. non-need-based
scholarship or grant aid — 35
% UG rec. non-need-based
scholarship or grant aid — 31
% frosh rec. need-based
self-help aid — 22
% UG rec. need-based
self-help aid — 22
% frosh rec. any financial aid — 100
% UG rec. any financial aid — 100
% UG borrow to pay for school — 29

CORNELL UNIVERSITY

CAMPUS LIFE
Fire Safety Rating — **72**
Green Rating — **92**
Type of school — private
Environment — town

STUDENTS
Total undergrad enrollment — 13,455
% male/female — 51/49
% from out of state — 62
% live on campus — 44
% in (# of) fraternities — NR (49)

% in (# of) sororities — NR (22)
% African American — 5
% Asian — 16
% Caucasian — 50
% Hispanic — 6
% Native American — 1
% international — 8
# of countries represented — 76

ACADEMICS
Calendar — semester
Student/faculty ratio — 9:1
Profs interesting rating — 74
Profs accessible rating — 78
Most common
reg class size — 10–19 students
Most common
lab size — 10–19 students

MOST POPULAR MAJORS
labor and industrial relations
biology/biological sciences
agribusiness/agricultural business operations

SELECTIVITY
of applicants — 30,383
% of applicants accepted — 21
% of acceptees attending — 47
# accepting a place on wait list — 1,976
% admitted from wait list — 14
# of early decision applicants — 3,015
% accepted early decision — 37

FRESHMAN PROFILE
Range SAT Critical Reading — 630–770
Range SAT Math — 660–730
Range ACT Composite — 28–32
% graduated top 10% of class — 87
% graduated top 25% of class — 98
% graduated top 50% of class — 100

DEADLINES
Early decision
Deadline — 11/1
Notification — 12/15
Regular
Deadline — 1/1
Notification — 4/1
Nonfall registration? — no

FINANCIAL FACTS
Annual tuition — $34,600
Room and board — $11,190
Required fees — $181
Books and supplies — $720
% frosh rec. need-based
scholarship or grant aid — 40
% UG rec. need-based
scholarship or grant aid — 38

% frosh rec. need-based	
self-help aid	39
% UG rec. need-based	
self-help aid	39
% frosh rec. any financial aid	44
% UG rec. any financial aid	42
% UG borrow to pay for school	54
Average cumulative	
indebtedness	$23,936

DARTMOUTH COLLEGE

CAMPUS LIFE

Fire Safety Rating	**60***
Green Rating	**60***
Type of school	private
Environment	village

STUDENTS

Total undergrad enrollment	4,164
% male/female	50/50
% from out of state	97
% live on campus	86
% in (# of) fraternities	43 (14)
% in (# of) sororities	40 (6)
% African American	7
% Asian	14
% Caucasian	57
% Hispanic	6
% Native American	4
% international	7

ACADEMICS

Calendar	quarter
Student/faculty ratio	8:1
Profs interesting rating	78
Profs accessible rating	82
Most common	
reg class size	10–19 students

MOST POPULAR MAJORS
economics
psychology
political science and government

SELECTIVITY

# of applicants	14,176
% of applicants accepted	15
% of acceptees attending	52
# accepting a place on wait list	797
# of early decision applicants	1,285
% accepted early decision	29

FRESHMAN PROFILE

Range SAT Critical Reading	660–770
Range SAT Math	670–780
Range SAT Writing	660–770
Range ACT Composite	29–34
Minimum paper TOEFL	550

Minimum computer TOEFL	213
Minimum web-based TOEFL	79
% graduated top 10% of class	91
% graduated top 50% of class	100

DEADLINES
Early decision

Deadline	11/1
Notification	12/15
Regular	
Deadline	1/1
Notification	4/1
Nonfall registration?	no

FINANCIAL FACTS

Annual tuition	$36,915
Room and board	$10,930
Required fees	$213
Books and supplies	$1,412
% frosh rec. need-based	
scholarship or grant aid	48
% UG rec. need-based	
scholarship or grant aid	49
% frosh rec. need-based	
self-help aid	48
% UG rec. need-based	
self-help aid	48
% frosh rec. any financial aid	48
% UG rec. any financial aid	50
% UG borrow to pay for school	51
Average cumulative	
indebtedness	$20,926

DELAWARE VALLEY COLLEGE

CAMPUS LIFE

Fire Safety Rating	**73**
Green Rating	**81**
Type of school	private
Environment	village

STUDENTS

Total undergrad enrollment	1,851
% male/female	42/58
% from out of state	38
% live on campus	58
% in (# of) fraternities	4 (5)
% in (# of) sororities	5 (3)
% African American	3
% Asian	1
% Caucasian	85
% Hispanic	2
# of countries represented	4

ACADEMICS

Calendar	semester
Profs interesting rating	72
Profs accessible rating	81

Student/faculty ratio	15:1
Most common	
reg class size	10–19 students
Most common	
lab size	10–19 students

MOST POPULAR MAJORS
animal sciences, other
animal sciences
business administration and management

SELECTIVITY

# of applicants	1,932
% of applicants accepted	66
% of acceptees attending	37

FRESHMAN PROFILE

Range SAT Critical Reading	460–560
Range SAT Math	460–560
Range SAT Writing	450–550
Range ACT Composite	20–25
Average HS GPA	3.491
% graduated top 10% of class	14
% graduated top 25% of class	38
% graduated top 50% of class	78

DEADLINES
Regular

Priority	5/1
Notification	rolling
Nonfall registration?	yes

FINANCIAL FACTS

Annual tuition	$23,110
Books and supplies	$1,000
% frosh rec. need-based	
scholarship or grant aid	78
% UG rec. need-based	
scholarship or grant aid	74
% frosh rec. non-need-based	
scholarship or grant aid	20
% UG rec. non-need-based	
scholarship or grant aid	22
% frosh rec. need-based self-help aid	63
% UG rec. need-based self-help aid	62
% frosh rec. any financial aid	98
% UG rec. any financial aid	91
% UG borrow to pay for school	60
Average cumulative indebtedness	$21,461

DICKINSON COLLEGE

CAMPUS LIFE

Fire Safety Rating	**75**
Green Rating	**89**
Type of school	private
Environment	city

STUDENTS

Total undergrad enrollment	2,349
% male/female	45/55
% from out of state	75
% from public high school	62
% live on campus	92
% in (# of) fraternities	16 (5)
% in (# of) sororities	28 (5)
% African American	4
% Asian	5
% Caucasian	78
% Hispanic	5
% international	6
# of countries represented	46

ACADEMICS

Calendar	semester
Student/faculty ratio	11:1
Profs interesting rating	86
Profs accessible rating	89
Most common	
reg class size	10–19 students

MOST POPULAR MAJORS
international business/trade/
commerce
political science and government
English language and literature

SELECTIVITY

# of applicants	5,844
% of applicants accepted	42
% of acceptees attending	25
# accepting a place on wait list	456
% admitted from wait list	6
# of early decision applicants	425
% accepted early decision	67

FRESHMAN PROFILE

Range SAT Critical Reading	600–690
Range SAT Math	590–680
Range ACT Composite	27–30
Minimum paper TOEFL	600
Minimum computer TOEFL	250
Minimum web-based TOEFL	100
% graduated top 10% of class	48
% graduated top 25% of class	79
% graduated top 50% of class	95

DEADLINES

Early decision	
Deadline	11/15
Notification	12/15
Early action	
Deadline	12/1
Notification	1/15
Regular	
Deadline	2/1
Notification	3/31
Nonfall registration?	no

FINANCIAL FACTS

Annual tuition	$37,900
Room and board	$9,600
Required fees	$334
Books and supplies	$1,000
% frosh rec. need-based scholarship or grant aid	44
% UG rec. need-based scholarship or grant aid	41
% frosh rec. non-need-based scholarship or grant aid	6
% UG rec. non-need-based scholarship or grant aid	5
% frosh rec. need-based self-help aid	42
% UG rec. need-based self-help aid	39
% frosh rec. any financial aid	48
% UG rec. any financial aid	44
% UG borrow to pay for school	54
Average cumulative indebtedness	$22,853

DREW UNIVERSITY

CAMPUS LIFE

Fire Safety Rating	**98**
Green Rating	**74**
Type of school	private
Affiliation	Methodist
Environment	village

STUDENTS

Total undergrad enrollment	1,620
% male/female	39/61
% from out of state	39
% from public high school	65
% live on campus	86
% African American	6
% Asian	5
% Caucasian	65
% Hispanic	8
% international	2
# of countries represented	11

ACADEMICS

Calendar	semester
Student/faculty ratio	11:1
Profs interesting rating	87
Profs accessible rating	85
Most common	
reg class size	10–19 students
Most common	
lab size	10–19 students

MOST POPULAR MAJORS
psychology
economics
political science and government

SELECTIVITY

# of applicants	3,816
% of applicants accepted	77
% of acceptees attending	16
# of early decision applicants	36
% accepted early decision	86

FRESHMAN PROFILE

Range SAT Critical Reading	520–650
Range SAT Math	510–630
Range SAT Writing	530–650
Range ACT Composite	20–25
Minimum paper TOEFL	550
Minimum computer TOEFL	213
Average HS GPA	3.35
% graduated top 10% of class	28.1
% graduated top 25% of class	64.3
% graduated top 50% of class	90.3

DEADLINES

Early decision	
Deadline	12/1
Notification	12/24
Regular	
Deadline	2/15
Notification	3/21
Nonfall registration?	yes

FINANCIAL FACTS

Annual tuition	$2,850
% UG rec. need-based scholarship or grant aid	49
% UG rec. non-need-based scholarship or grant aid	7
% UG rec. need-based self-help aid	42
% frosh rec. any financial aid	90
% UG rec. any financial aid	82
% UG borrow to pay for school	61.9
Average cumulative indebtedness	$16,777

DREXEL UNIVERSITY

CAMPUS LIFE

Fire Safety Rating	**75**
Green Rating	**98**
Type of school	private
Environment	metropolis

STUDENTS

Total undergrad enrollment	12,722
% male/female	56/44
% from out of state	48
% from public high school	70
% live on campus	25
% in (# of) fraternities	3 (12)
% in (# of) sororities	3 (11)
% African American	8
% Asian	12
% Caucasian	63
% Hispanic	3
% international	7
# of countries represented	104

ACADEMICS

Calendar	Quarter for most, Semester for College of Medicine
Student/faculty ratio	9:1
Profs interesting rating	62
Profs accessible rating	62
Most common reg class size	10–19 students

MOST POPULAR MAJORS
information science/studies
mechanical engineering
biology/biological sciences

SELECTIVITY

# of applicants	16,867
% of applicants accepted	72
% of acceptees attending	20

FRESHMAN PROFILE

Range SAT Critical Reading	530–630
Range SAT Math	560–670
Range ACT Composite	23–28
Minimum paper TOEFL	550
Minimum computer TOEFL	213
Average HS GPA	3.47
% graduated top 10% of class	30
% graduated top 25% of class	60
% graduated top 50% of class	86

DEADLINES

Regular Deadline	3/1
Nonfall registration?	yes

FINANCIAL FACTS

Annual tuition	$28,500
Room and board	$12,135
Required fees	$1,940
Books and supplies	$1,800
% UG rec. need-based scholarship or grant aid	38
% UG rec. need-based self-help aid	40
% frosh rec. any financial aid	94
% UG rec. any financial aid	89
% UG borrow to pay for school	75
Average cumulative indebtedness	$31,333

DUQUESNE UNIVERSITY

CAMPUS LIFE

Fire Safety Rating	**88**
Green Rating	**84**
Type of school	private
Affiliation	Roman Catholic
Environment	metropolis

STUDENTS

Total undergrad enrollment	5,562
% male/female	42/58
% from out of state	18
% live on campus	57
% in (# of) fraternities	8 (10)
% in (# of) sororities	11 (9)
% African American	3
% Asian	2
% Caucasian	81
% Hispanic	1
% international	2
# of countries represented	82

ACADEMICS

Calendar	semester
Student/faculty ratio	15:1
Profs interesting rating	72
Profs accessible rating	76
Most common reg class size	10–19 students
Most common lab size	20–29 students

MOST POPULAR MAJORS
nursing/registered nurse
(RN, ASN, BSN, MSN)
pharmacy (pharmd [usa], pharmd or
bs/bpharm [canada])
psychology

SELECTIVITY

# of applicants	5,374
% of applicants accepted	74
% of acceptees attending	34
# of early decision applicants	76
% accepted early decision	78

FRESHMAN PROFILE

Range SAT Critical Reading	510–600
Range SAT Math	510–610
Range SAT Writing	510–600
Range ACT Composite	22–26
Average HS GPA	3.65
% graduated top 10% of class	26
% graduated top 25% of class	56
% graduated top 50% of class	88

DEADLINES

Early decision Deadline	11/1
Notification	12/15
Early action Deadline	12/1
Notification	1/15
Regular Priority	11/1
Deadline	7/1
Notification	rolling
Nonfall registration?	yes

FINANCIAL FACTS

Annual tuition	$22,054
Room and board	$8,546
Required fees	$1,896
Books and supplies	$600
% frosh rec. need-based scholarship or grant aid	70
% UG rec. need-based scholarship or grant aid	64
% frosh rec. non-need-based scholarship or grant aid	68
% UG rec. non-need-based scholarship or grant aid	53
% frosh rec. need-based self-help aid	59
% UG rec. need-based self-help aid	56
% frosh rec. athletic scholarships	5
% UG rec. athletic scholarships	5
% frosh rec. any financial aid	93
% UG rec. any financial aid	85
% UG borrow to pay for school	80
Average cumulative indebtedness	$27,080

EASTERN CONNECTICUT STATE UNIVERSITY

CAMPUS LIFE

Fire Safety Rating	**84**
Green Rating	**60***
Environment	village

STUDENTS

Total undergrad enrollment	4,704
% male/female	45/55
% from out of state	7
% live on campus	52

% African American	7
% Asian	2
% Caucasian	79
% Hispanic	6
% international	1
# of countries represented	37

ACADEMICS

Profs interesting rating	71
Profs accessible rating	66

MOST POPULAR MAJORS
business/commerce
psychology
social sciences

FRESHMAN PROFILE

Minimum paper TOEFL	550
Minimum computer TOEFL	213

FINANCIAL FACTS

Comprehensive fee	$10,831
Room and board	$8,377
Required fees	$3,615
Books and supplies	$1,168
% frosh rec. any financial aid	58
% UG rec. any financial aid	58

ELIZABETHTOWN COLLEGE

CAMPUS LIFE

Fire Safety Rating	60*
Green Rating	60*
Type of school	private
Affiliation	Church of Brethren
Environment	village

STUDENTS

Total undergrad enrollment	2,096
% male/female	35/65
% from out of state	34
% from public high school	80
% live on campus	85
% African American	1
% Asian	2
% Caucasian	82
% Hispanic	1
% international	2
# of countries represented	17

ACADEMICS

Calendar	semester
Profs interesting rating	83
Profs accessible rating	83
Student/faculty ratio	13:1
Most common	
reg class size	10–19 students
Most common	
lab size	10–19 students

MOST POPULAR MAJORS
business/commerce

SELECTIVITY

# of applicants	2,923
% of applicants accepted	64
% of acceptees attending	29

FRESHMAN PROFILE

Range SAT Critical Reading	510–610
Range SAT Math	510–630
Range ACT Composite	21–26
Minimum paper TOEFL	525
Minimum computer TOEFL	200
Average HS GPA	3.64
% graduated top 10% of class	30
% graduated top 25% of class	65
% graduated top 50% of class	93

DEADLINES

Notification	rolling
Nonfall registration?	yes

FINANCIAL FACTS

Annual tuition	$26,950
Room and board	$7,300
Books and supplies	$700
% frosh rec. need-based	
scholarship or grant aid	71
% UG rec. need-based	
scholarship or grant aid	71
% frosh rec. non-need-based	
scholarship or grant aid	14
% UG rec. non-need-based	
scholarship or grant aid	9
% frosh rec. need-based self-help aid	59
% UG rec. need-based self-help aid	61
% frosh rec. any financial aid	96
% UG rec. any financial aid	94
% UG borrow to pay for school	78
Average cumulative indebtedness	$25,545

ELMIRA COLLEGE

CAMPUS LIFE

Fire Safety Rating	60*
Green Rating	60*
Type of school	private
Environment	town

STUDENTS

Total undergrad enrollment	1,363
% male/female	29/71
% from out of state	51
% from public high school	65
% live on campus	92
% African American	1
% Asian	1

% Caucasian	67
% Hispanic	1
% international	5
# of countries represented	20

ACADEMICS

Calendar	
Profs interesting rating	72
Profs accessible rating	77
Student/faculty ratio	12:1
Most common	
reg class size	10–19 students
Most common	
lab size	10–19 students

MOST POPULAR MAJORS
elementary education and teaching
psychology
business/commerce

SELECTIVITY

# of applicants	2,118
% of applicants accepted	68
% of acceptees attending	25
# accepting a place on wait list	55
% admitted from wait list	4
# of early decision applicants	108
% accepted early decision	62

FRESHMAN PROFILE

Range SAT Critical Reading	480–600
Range SAT Math	480–590
Range ACT Composite	19–26
Minimum paper TOEFL	500
Minimum computer TOEFL	173
Average HS GPA	3.4
% graduated top 10% of class	30
% graduated top 25% of class	65
% graduated top 50% of class	98

DEADLINES

Early decision	
Deadline	11/15
Notification	12/15
Regular	
Priority	2/1
Deadline	3/1
Notification	rolling
Nonfall registration?	yes

FINANCIAL FACTS

Annual tuition	$29,000
Room and board	$9,100
Required fees	$1,050
Books and supplies	$450
% frosh rec. need-based	
scholarship or grant aid	82
% UG rec. need-based	
scholarship or grant aid	78

% frosh rec. non-need-based scholarship or grant aid	10
% UG rec. non-need-based scholarship or grant aid	9
% frosh rec. need-based self-help aid	69
% UG rec. need-based self-help aid	65
% frosh rec. any financial aid	80
% UG rec. any financial aid	80
% UG borrow to pay for school	69
Average cumulative indebtedness	$25,347

EMERSON COLLEGE

CAMPUS LIFE
Fire Safety Rating	**74**
Green Rating	**76**
Type of school	private
Environment	metropolis

STUDENTS
Total undergrad enrollment	3,293
% male/female	45/55
% from out of state	74
% from public high school	75
% live on campus	49
% in (# of) fraternities	3 (4)
% in (# of) sororities	3 (3)
% African American	3
% Asian	5
% Caucasian	76
% Hispanic	7
% Native American	1
% international	2
# of countries represented	50

ACADEMICS
Calendar	semester
Student/faculty ratio	14:1
Profs interesting rating	80
Profs accessible rating	77
% classes taught by TAs	3
Most common reg class size	10–19 students
Most common lab size	10–19 students

MOST POPULAR MAJORS
theater
creative writing
cinematography and film/
video production

SELECTIVITY
# of applicants	4,981
% of applicants accepted	45
% of acceptees attending	38
# accepting a place on wait list	281
% admitted from wait list	1

FRESHMAN PROFILE
Range SAT Critical Reading	590–680
Range SAT Math	550–650
Range SAT Writing	580–670
Range ACT Composite	25–29
Minimum paper TOEFL	550
Minimum computer TOEFL	213
Minimum web-based TOEFL	80
Average HS GPA	3.62
% graduated top 10% of class	42.4
% graduated top 25% of class	78.6
% graduated top 50% of class	98.3

DEADLINES
Early action	
Deadline	11/1
Notification	12/15
Regular	
Deadline	1/5
Notification	4/1
Nonfall registration?	yes

FINANCIAL FACTS
Annual tuition	$28,352
Room and board	$11,832
Required fees	$522
Books and supplies	$720
% frosh rec. need-based scholarship or grant aid	44
% UG rec. need-based scholarship or grant aid	40
% frosh rec. non-need-based scholarship or grant aid	8
% UG rec. non-need-based scholarship or grant aid	6
% frosh rec. need-based self-help aid	51
% UG rec. need-based self-help aid	48
% frosh rec. any financial aid	73.3
% UG rec. any financial aid	64.4

EUGENE LANG COLLEGE

CAMPUS LIFE
Fire Safety Rating	**60***
Green Rating	**60***
Type of school	private
Environment	metropolis

STUDENTS
Total undergrad enrollment	1,294
% male/female	31/69
% from out of state	68
% live on campus	27
% African American	4
% Asian	5

% Caucasian	61
% Hispanic	6
% Native American	1
% international	3
# of countries represented	36

ACADEMICS
Calendar	semester
Student/faculty ratio	15:1
Profs interesting rating	81
Profs accessible rating	78
Most common reg class size	10–19 students
Most common lab size	20–29 students

SELECTIVITY
# of applicants	1,670
% of applicants accepted	63
% of acceptees attending	30
# accepting a place on wait list	39
% admitted from wait list	18

FRESHMAN PROFILE
Range SAT Critical Reading	555–665
Range SAT Math	490–610
Range SAT Writing	560–660
Range ACT Composite	23–28
Minimum paper TOEFL	600
Minimum computer TOEFL	250
Minimum web-based TOEFL	100
Average HS GPA	3.19

DEADLINES
Early decision	
Deadline	11/15
Notification	12/15
Regular	
Deadline	2/1
Notification	rolling
Nonfall registration?	yes

FINANCIAL FACTS
Annual tuition	$30,660
Room and board	$11,750
Required fees	$650
Books and supplies	$2,050
% frosh rec. need-based scholarship or grant aid	50
% UG rec. need-based scholarship or grant aid	49
% frosh rec. non-need-based scholarship or grant aid	18
% UG rec. non-need-based scholarship or grant aid	16
% frosh rec. need-based self-help aid	51

FAIRFIELD UNIVERSITY

CAMPUS LIFE

Fire Safety Rating	**92**
Green Rating	**84**
Type of school	private
Affiliation	Roman Catholic/Jesuit
Environment	town

STUDENTS

Total undergrad enrollment	3,893
% male/female	42/58
% from out of state	77
% from public high school	55
% live on campus	78
% African American	2
% Asian	3
% Caucasian	78
% Hispanic	5
% international	1
# of countries represented	45

ACADEMICS

Calendar	semester
Student/faculty ratio	13:1
Profs interesting rating	85
Profs accessible rating	82
Most common	
reg class size	20–29 students

MOST POPULAR MAJORS
communication studies/speech communication and rhetoric
nursing/registered nurse (bsn, msn)
marketing/marketing management

SELECTIVITY

# of applicants	8,557
% of applicants accepted	55
% of acceptees attending	18
# accepting a place on wait list	1,196
% admitted from wait list	8

FRESHMAN PROFILE

Range SAT Critical Reading	530–620
Range SAT Math	550–640
Range ACT Composite	23–28
Minimum paper TOEFL	550
Minimum computer TOEFL	213
Average HS GPA	3.4
% graduated top 10% of class	36
% graduated top 25% of class	76
% graduated top 50% of class	96

DEADLINES

Early action	
Deadline	11/15
Notification	1/1
Regular	
Deadline	1/15
Notification	4/1
Nonfall registration?	no

FINANCIAL FACTS

Annual tuition	$33,340
Room and board	$10,430
Required fees	$565
Books and supplies	$900
% frosh rec. need-based	
scholarship or grant aid	46
% UG rec. need-based	
scholarship or grant aid	46
% frosh rec. non-need-based	
scholarship or grant aid	18
% UG rec. non-need-based	
scholarship or grant aid	20
% frosh rec. need-based	
self-help aid	45
% UG rec. need-based	
self-help aid	43
% frosh rec. athletic scholarships	8
% UG rec. athletic scholarships	6
% frosh rec. any financial aid	59
% UG rec. any financial aid	59
% UG borrow to pay for school	60
Average cumulative	
indebtedness	$31,984

FORDHAM UNIVERSITY

CAMPUS LIFE

Fire Safety Rating	**60***
Green Rating	**60***
Type of school	private
Affiliation	Roman Catholic
Environment	metropolis

STUDENTS

Total undergrad enrollment	7,652
% male/female	43/57
% from out of state	46
% from public high school	47
% live on campus	56
% African American	5.6
% Asian	6.4
% Caucasian	56
% Hispanic	12.3
% international	2
# of countries represented	58

ACADEMICS

Calendar	semester
Student/faculty ratio	12:1
Profs interesting rating	71
Profs accessible rating	73
Most common	
reg class size	10–19 students
Most common	
lab size	10–19 students

MOST POPULAR MAJORS
social sciences
business/commerce

SELECTIVITY

# of applicants	22,035
% of applicants accepted	42.1
% of acceptees attending	19.2
# accepting a place on wait list	1,189
% admitted from wait list	10

FRESHMAN PROFILE

Range SAT Critical Reading	570–670
Range SAT Math	560–660
Range SAT Writing	560–660
Range ACT Composite	25–29
Minimum paper TOEFL	575
Minimum computer TOEFL	231
Average HS GPA	3.7
% graduated top 10% of class	42.5
% graduated top 25% of class	73
% graduated top 50% of class	96

DEADLINES

Early action	
Deadline	11/1
Notification	12/25
Priority	
Deadline	1/15
Notification	4/1
Nonfall registration?	yes

FINANCIAL FACTS

Annual tuition	$30,000
Room and board	$11,780
Required fees	$730
Books and supplies	$800
% frosh rec. need-based	
scholarship or grant aid	66
% UG rec. need-based	
scholarship or grant aid	62
% frosh rec. non-need-based	
scholarship or grant aid	8
% UG rec. non-need-based	
scholarship or grant aid	5
% frosh rec. need-based	
self-help aid	51
% UG rec. need-based	
self-help aid	52

% frosh rec. athletic scholarships	2
% UG rec. athletic scholarships	2
% frosh rec. any financial aid	67
% UG rec. any financial aid	62

FRANKLIN & MARSHALL COLLEGE

CAMPUS LIFE

Fire Safety Rating	**60***
Green Rating	**78**
Type of school	private
Environment	town

STUDENTS

Total undergrad enrollment	2,059
% male/female	51/49
% from out of state	66
% from public high school	58
% live on campus	80
% in (# of) fraternities	26 (7)
% in (# of) sororities	12 (2)
% African American	4
% Asian	4
% Caucasian	72
% Hispanic	4
% international	8
# of countries represented	64

ACADEMICS

Calendar	semester
Student/faculty ratio	10:1
Profs interesting rating	89
Profs accessible rating	94
Most common reg class size	20–29 students
Most common lab size	10–19 students

MOST POPULAR MAJORS
economics
political science and government
business/commerce

SELECTIVITY

# of applicants	5,018
% of applicants accepted	37
% of acceptees attending	30
# accepting a place on wait list	511
% admitted from wait list	10
# of early decision applicants	471
% accepted early decision	68

FRESHMAN PROFILE

Range SAT Critical Reading	600–690
Range SAT Math	610–690
Minimum paper TOEFL	600
Minimum computer TOEFL	250

Average HS GPA	3.57
% graduated top 10% of class	57
% graduated top 25% of class	87
% graduated top 50% of class	99

DEADLINES

Early decision	
Deadline	11/15
Notification	12/15
Regular	
Deadline	2/1
Notification	4/1
Nonfall registration?	yes

FINANCIAL FACTS

Annual tuition	$36,430
Room and board	$9,174
Required fees	$50
Books and supplies	$650
% frosh rec. need-based scholarship or grant aid	44
% UG rec. need-based scholarship or grant aid	43
% frosh rec. non-need-based scholarship or grant aid	4
% UG rec. non-need-based scholarship or grant aid	3
% frosh rec. need-based self-help aid	45
% UG rec. need-based self-help aid	41
% frosh rec. any financial aid	69
% UG rec. any financial aid	70
% UG borrow to pay for school	58
Average cumulative indebtedness	$24,752

FRANKLIN W. OLIN COLLEGE OF ENGINEERING

CAMPUS LIFE

Fire Safety Rating	**98**
Green Rating	**60***
Type of school	private
Environment	town

STUDENTS

Total undergrad enrollment	296
% male/female	58/42
% from out of state	92
% from public high school	71
% live on campus	98
# of countries represented	8

ACADEMICS

Profs interesting rating	99
Profs accessible rating	98

MOST POPULAR MAJORS
engineering
mechanical engineering
electrical, electronics and communications engineering

SELECTIVITY

# of applicants	1,054
% of applicants accepted	11
% of acceptees attending	71

FRESHMAN PROFILE

Range SAT Critical Reading	700–790
Range SAT Math	740–800
Range ACT Composite	32–35
% graduated top 10% of class	94
% graduated top 25% of class	100
% graduated top 50% of class	100

DEADLINES

Regular	12/01
Nonfall registration?	No

FINANCIAL FACTS

Comprehensive fee	$33,600
Room and board	$11,800
Required fees	$175
Books and supplies	$750
% frosh rec. need-based scholarship or grant aid	12
% UG rec. need-based scholarship or grant aid	12
% frosh rec. non-need-based scholarship or grant aid	10
% UG rec. non-need-based scholarship or grant aid	3
% frosh rec. any financial aid	100
% UG rec. any financial aid	100
% UG borrow to pay for school	2
Average cumulative indebtedness	$4,525

THE GEORGE WASHINGTON UNIVERSITY

CAMPUS LIFE

Fire Safety Rating	**60***
Green Rating	**60***
Type of school	private
Environment	metropolis

STUDENTS

Total undergrad enrollment	10,370
% male/female	45/55
% from out of state	98
% live on campus	64
% in (# of) fraternities	19 (12)

% in (# of) sororities	18 (9)
% African American	6
% Asian	10
% Caucasian	62
% Hispanic	6
% international	4
# of countries represented	101

ACADEMICS

Calendar	semester
Student/faculty ratio	13:1
Profs interesting rating	77
Profs accessible rating	75
% classes taught by TAs	3
Most common	
reg class size	10–19 students
Most common	
lab size	20–29 students

SELECTIVITY

# of applicants	19,606
% of applicants accepted	37
% of acceptees attending	30
# accepting a place on wait list	702
% admitted from wait list	22

FRESHMAN PROFILE

Range SAT Critical Reading	600–690
Range SAT Math	600–690
Range SAT Writing	600–690
Range ACT Composite	26–29
% graduated top 10% of class	66
% graduated top 25% of class	90
% graduated top 50% of class	100

DEADLINES

Early decision	
Deadline	11/10
Notification	12/15
Regular	
Priority	12/1
Deadline	1/10
Notification	4/1
Nonfall registration?	yes

FINANCIAL FACTS

Annual tuition	$38,500
Room and board	$12,155
Required fees	$30
Books and supplies	$1,000
% frosh rec. need-based	
scholarship or grant aid	35
% UG rec. need-based	
scholarship or grant aid	39
% frosh rec. non-need-based	
scholarship or grant aid	11
% UG rec. non-need-based	
scholarship or grant aid	11

% frosh rec. need-based	
self-help aid	31
% UG rec. need-based	
self-help aid	34
% frosh rec. athletic scholarships	1
% UG rec. athletic scholarships	2
% UG borrow to pay for school	49
Average cumulative	
indebtedness	$30,817

GEORGETOWN UNIVERSITY

CAMPUS LIFE

Fire Safety Rating	**91**
Green Rating	**95**
Type of school	private
Affiliation	Roman Catholic
Environment	metropolis

STUDENTS

Total undergrad enrollment	6,623
% male/female	45/55
% from out of state	98
% live on campus	71
% African American	7
% Asian	9
% Caucasian	67
% Hispanic	7
% international	5
# of countries represented	138

ACADEMICS

Calendar	semester
Student/faculty ratio	11:1
Profs interesting rating	82
Profs accessible rating	80
% classes taught by TAs	8

MOST POPULAR MAJORS
political science and government
international relations and affairs
English language and literature

SELECTIVITY

# of applicants	16,163
% of applicants accepted	21
% of acceptees attending	47
# accepting a place on wait list	1,035
% admitted from wait list	4

FRESHMAN PROFILE

Range SAT Critical Reading	650–750
Range SAT Math	650–740
% graduated top 10% of class	90
% graduated top 25% of class	96
% graduated top 50% of class	99

DEADLINES

Early action	
Deadline	11/1
Notification	12/15
Regular	
Deadline	1/10
Notification	4/1
Nonfall registration?	no

FINANCIAL FACTS

Annual tuition	$35,568
Room and board	$12,146
Required fees	$396
Books and supplies	$1,060
% frosh rec. need-based	
scholarship or grant aid	40
% UG rec. need-based	
scholarship or grant aid	37
% frosh rec. non-need-based	
scholarship or grant aid	1
% frosh rec. need-based	
self-help aid	32
% UG rec. need-based	
self-help aid	34
% frosh rec. athletic scholarships	3
% UG rec. athletic scholarships	3
% frosh rec. any financial aid	40
% UG rec. any financial aid	39
% UG borrow to pay for school	46
Average cumulative	
indebtedness	$27,117

GETTYSBURG COLLEGE

CAMPUS LIFE

Fire Safety Rating	**85**
Green Rating	**87**
Type of school	private
Affiliation	Lutheran
Environment	village

STUDENTS

Total undergrad enrollment	2,491
% male/female	48/52
% from out of state	74
% from public high school	80
% live on campus	94
% in (# of) fraternities	40 (10)
% in (# of) sororities	26 (6)
% African American	4
% Asian	2
% Caucasian	87
% Hispanic	2
% international	2
# of countries represented	27

ACADEMICS

Calendar	semester
Student/faculty ratio	11:1
Profs interesting rating	85
Profs accessible rating	88
Most common	
reg class size	10–19 students

MOST POPULAR MAJORS
psychology
political science and government
business/commerce

SELECTIVITY

# of applicants	6,126
% of applicants accepted	36
% of acceptees attending	32
# accepting a place on wait list	805
# of early decision applicants	484
% accepted early decision	65

FRESHMAN PROFILE

Range SAT Critical Reading	610–690
Range SAT Math	610–670
Minimum paper TOEFL	525
Minimum computer TOEFL	200
% graduated top 10% of class	66
% graduated top 25% of class	89
% graduated top 50% of class	100

DEADLINES

Early decision	
Deadline	11/15
Notification	12/15
Regular	
Deadline	2/1
Notification	4/1
Nonfall registration?	yes

FINANCIAL FACTS

Annual tuition	$33,700
Room and board	$8,260
Required fees	$250
Books and supplies	$500
% frosh rec. need-based	
scholarship or grant aid	52
% UG rec. need-based	
scholarship or grant aid	54
% frosh rec. non-need-based	
scholarship or grant aid	31
% UG rec. non-need-based	
scholarship or grant aid	27
% frosh rec. need-based	
self-help aid	43
% UG rec. need-based	
self-help aid	47
% frosh rec. any financial aid	70
% UG rec. any financial aid	70
% UG borrow to pay for school	63

Average cumulative	
indebtedness	$27,440

GORDON COLLEGE

CAMPUS LIFE

Fire Safety Rating	**85**
Green Rating	**60***
Type of school	private
Affiliation	Protestant
Environment	village

STUDENTS

Total undergrad enrollment	1,523
% male/female	36/64
% from out of state	71
% live on campus	89
% African American	2
% Asian	2
% Caucasian	88
% Hispanic	3
% international	2
# of countries represented	23

ACADEMICS

Calendar	semester
Profs interesting rating	86
Profs accessible rating	82
Student/faculty ratio	14:1
Most common	
reg class size	10–19 students
Most common	
lab size	10–19 students

MOST POPULAR MAJORS
English language and literature
psychology
business/commerce

SELECTIVITY

# of applicants	986
% of applicants accepted	83
% of acceptees attending	47
# of early decision applicants	74
% accepted early decision	88

FRESHMAN PROFILE

Range SAT Critical Reading	540–650
Range SAT Math	530–640
Range SAT Writing	540–640
Range ACT Composite	23–28
Average HS GPA	3.6
% graduated top 10% of class	34
% graduated top 25% of class	60
% graduated top 50% of class	88

DEADLINES

Early decision	
Deadline	11/15
Notification	12/15
Early action	
Deadline	12/1
Notification	1/1
Regular	
Priority	3/1
Notification	rolling
Nonfall registration?	yes

FINANCIAL FACTS

Annual tuition	$24,652
Room and board	$6,906
Required fees	$1,096
Books and supplies	$800
% frosh rec. need-based	
scholarship or grant aid	66
% UG rec. need-based	
scholarship or grant aid	62
% frosh rec. non-need-based	
scholarship or grant aid	10
% UG rec. non-need-based	
scholarship or grant aid	6
% frosh rec. need-based self-help aid	56
% UG rec. need-based self-help aid	57
% frosh rec. any financial aid	93
% UG rec. any financial aid	90
% UG borrow to pay for school	86.2
Average cumulative indebtedness	$30,115

GOUCHER COLLEGE

CAMPUS LIFE

Fire Safety Rating	**80**
Green Rating	**97**
Type of school	private
Environment	city

STUDENTS

Total undergrad enrollment	1,462
% male/female	33/67
% from out of state	71
% from public high school	67
% live on campus	80
% African American	5
% Asian	3
% Caucasian	71
% Hispanic	3
# of countries represented	22

ACADEMICS

Calendar	semester
Student/faculty ratio	9:1
Profs interesting rating	87
Profs accessible rating	82

Most common

   reg class size   10–19 students

MOST POPULAR MAJORS
English language and literature
psychology
mass communication/media studies

SELECTIVITY

# of applicants	3,563
% of applicants accepted	66
% of acceptees attending	17
# accepting a place on wait list	213
% admitted from wait list	23

FRESHMAN PROFILE

Range SAT Critical Reading	540–670
Range SAT Math	510–620
Range SAT Writing	540–650
Minimum paper TOEFL	550
Minimum computer TOEFL	213
Minimum web-based TOEFL	79-80
Average HS GPA	3.2
% graduated top 10% of class	16.94
% graduated top 25% of class	58.06
% graduated top 50% of class	94.35

DEADLINES

Early action	
Deadline	12/1
Notification	2/15
Regular	
Priority	2/1
Deadline	2/1
Notification	4/1
Nonfall registration?	yes

FINANCIAL FACTS

Annual tuition	$30,363
Room and board	$9,478
Required fees	$446
Books and supplies	$800
% frosh rec. need-based	
scholarship or grant aid	53
% UG rec. need-based	
scholarship or grant aid	52
% frosh rec. non-need-based	
scholarship or grant aid	7
% UG rec. non-need-based	
scholarship or grant aid	6
% frosh rec. need-based	
self-help aid	52
% UG rec. need-based	
self-help aid	49
% frosh rec. any financial aid	80
% UG rec. any financial aid	85
% UG borrow to pay for school	58
Average cumulative	
indebtedness	$14,221

GROVE CITY COLLEGE

CAMPUS LIFE

Fire Safety Rating	**83**
Green Rating	**63**
Type of school	private
Affiliation	Presbyterian
Environment	rural

STUDENTS

Total undergrad enrollment	2,490
% male/female	51/49
% from out of state	53
% from public high school	75
% live on campus	93
% in (# of) fraternities	17 (8)
% in (# of) sororities	28 (8)
% African American	1
% Asian	2
% Caucasian	94
% Hispanic	1
% international	1
# of countries represented	11

ACADEMICS

Calendar	semester
Student/faculty ratio	15:1
Profs interesting rating	77
Profs accessible rating	88
Most common	
reg class size	10–19 students
Most common	
lab size	10–19 students

MOST POPULAR MAJORS
mechanical engineering
elementary education and teaching
English language and literature

SELECTIVITY

# of applicants	1,916
% of applicants accepted	55
% of acceptees attending	62
# accepting a place on wait list	236
% admitted from wait list	7
# of early decision applicants	630
% accepted early decision	51

FRESHMAN PROFILE

Range SAT Critical Reading	566–702
Range SAT Math	574–691
Range ACT Composite	25–30
Minimum paper TOEFL	550
Minimum computer TOEFL	213
Average HS GPA	3.71
% graduated top 10% of class	52
% graduated top 25% of class	83
% graduated top 50% of class	97

DEADLINES

Early decision	
Deadline	11/15
Notification	12/15
Regular	
Deadline	2/1
Notification	3/15
Nonfall registration?	yes

FINANCIAL FACTS

Annual tuition	$12,074
Room and board	$6,134
Books and supplies	$900
% frosh rec. need-based	
scholarship or grant aid	41
% UG rec. need-based	
scholarship or grant aid	33
% frosh rec. non-need-based	
scholarship or grant aid	7
% UG rec. non-need-based	
scholarship or grant aid	4
% frosh rec. need-based	
self-help aid	18
% UG rec. need-based	
self-help aid	19
% frosh rec.	
any financial aid	42
% UG rec. any financial aid	35
% UG borrow to pay for school	62
Average cumulative	
indebtedness	$24,721

HAMILTON COLLEGE

CAMPUS LIFE

Fire Safety Rating	**79**
Green Rating	**95**
Type of school	private
Environment	town

STUDENTS

Total undergrad enrollment	1,810
% male/female	48/52
% from out of state	66
% from public high school	60
% live on campus	98
% in (# of) fraternities	29 (7)
% in (# of) sororities	19 (3)
% African American	4
% Asian	7
% Caucasian	69
% Hispanic	5
% Native American	1
% international	5
# of countries represented	42

ACADEMICS

Calendar	semester
Student/faculty ratio	10:1
Profs interesting rating	96
Profs accessible rating	97
Most common	
reg class size	10–19 students
Most common	
lab size	10–19 students

MOST POPULAR MAJORS
economics
government
mathematics
psychology

SELECTIVITY

# of applicants	4,962
% of applicants accepted	28
% of acceptees attending	34
# accepting a place on wait list	248
% admitted from wait list	10
# of early decision applicants	640
% accepted early decision	36

FRESHMAN PROFILE

Range SAT Critical Reading	640–740
Range SAT Math	640–720
Minimum paper TOEFL	600
Minimum computer TOEFL	250
% graduated top 10% of class	74
% graduated top 25% of class	90
% graduated top 50% of class	99

DEADLINES

Early decision	
Deadline	11/15
Notification	12/15
Regular	
Deadline	1/1
Notification	4/1
Nonfall registration?	yes

FINANCIAL FACTS

Annual tuition	$36,500
Room and board	$9,350
Required fees	$360
Books and supplies	$1,300
% frosh rec. need-based	
scholarship or grant aid	43
% UG rec. need-based	
scholarship or grant aid	47
% frosh rec.	
non-need-based scholarship or grant aid	3
% UG rec. non-need-based	
scholarship or grant aid	4
% frosh rec. need-based	
self-help aid	34
% UG rec. need-based	
self-help aid	38
% UG borrow to pay for school	48
Average cumulative	
indebtedness	$16,808

HAMPSHIRE COLLEGE

CAMPUS LIFE

Fire Safety Rating	**60***
Green Rating	**79**
Type of school	private
Environment	town

STUDENTS

Total undergrad enrollment	1,412
% male/female	43/57
% from out of state	83
% from public high school	49
% live on campus	89
% African American	4
% Asian	4
% Caucasian	72
% Hispanic	5
% Native American	1
% international	3
# of countries represented	27

ACADEMICS

Calendar	4/1/4
Student/faculty ratio	12:1
Profs interesting rating	86
Profs accessible rating	81
Most common	
reg class size	10–19 students

MOST POPULAR MAJORS
English language and literature
social sciences
cinematography and film/video production

SELECTIVITY

# of applicants	2,571
% of applicants accepted	55
% of acceptees attending	28
# accepting a place on wait list	102
% admitted from wait list	23
# of early decision applicants	74
% accepted early decision	72

FRESHMAN PROFILE

Range SAT Critical Reading	610–710
Range SAT Math	540–660
Range SAT Writing	590–700
Range ACT Composite	25–30
Minimum paper TOEFL	577
Minimum computer TOEFL	233
Average HS GPA	3.45
% graduated top 10% of class	28
% graduated top 25% of class	58
% graduated top 50% of class	88

DEADLINES

Early decision	
Deadline	11/15
Notification	12/15
Early action	
Deadline	12/1
Notification	2/1
Regular	
Priority	11/15
Deadline	1/15
Notification	4/1
Nonfall registration?	yes

FINANCIAL FACTS

Annual tuition	$37,789
Books and supplies	$500
% frosh rec. need-based	
scholarship or grant aid	57
% UG rec. need-based	
scholarship or grant aid	55
% frosh rec. non-need-based	
scholarship or grant aid	38
% UG rec. non-need-based	
scholarship or grant aid	29
% frosh rec. need-based	
self-help aid	57
% UG rec. need-based	
self-help aid	52
% frosh rec.	
any financial aid	61
% UG rec. any financial aid	71
% UG borrow to pay for school	56
Average cumulative	
indebtedness	$20,300

HARTWICK COLLEGE

CAMPUS LIFE

Fire Safety Rating	**85**
Green Rating	**72**
Type of school	private
Environment	village

STUDENTS

Total undergrad enrollment	1,513
% male/female	44/56
% from out of state	37
% from public high school	84
% live on campus	83
% in (# of) fraternities	15 (3)
% in (# of) sororities	13 (3)
% African American	5
% Asian	2
% Caucasian	62

% Hispanic 4
% international 3

ACADEMICS
Calendar 4/1/4
Profs interesting rating 84
Profs accessible rating 83
Student/faculty ratio 12:1
Most common
  reg class size 10–19 students

MOST POPULAR MAJORS
psychology
nursing/registered nurse (rn, asn, bsn, msn)
business/commerce

SELECTIVITY
of applicants 2,422
% of applicants accepted 84
% of acceptees attending 22
# accepting a place on wait list 138
% admitted from wait list 8
# of early decision applicants 129
% accepted early decision 91

FRESHMAN PROFILE
Range SAT Critical Reading 480–600
Range SAT Math 510–595
Range SAT Writing 480–590
Range ACT Composite 21–26
Minimum paper TOEFL 550
Minimum computer TOEFL 213
Average HS GPA 86.3
% graduated top 10% of class 18
% graduated top 25% of class 45
% graduated top 50% of class 77

DEADLINES
Early decision
  Deadline 11/15
  Notification 12/1
Regular
  Deadline 2/15
  Notification 3/7
Nonfall registration? yes

FINANCIAL FACTS
Annual tuition $30,125
Books and supplies $700
% frosh rec. need-based
  scholarship or grant aid 73
% UG rec. need-based
  scholarship or grant aid 70
% frosh rec. non-need-based
  scholarship or grant aid 8
% UG rec. non-need-based
  scholarship or grant aid 5
% frosh rec. need-based self-help aid 65
% UG rec. need-based self-help aid 67

% UG rec. athletic scholarships 1
% frosh rec. any financial aid 87
% UG rec. any financial aid 82.7
% UG borrow to pay for school 70
Average cumulative indebtedness $25,044

HARVARD COLLEGE

CAMPUS LIFE
Fire Safety Rating **60***
Green Rating **99**
Type of school private
Environment city

STUDENTS
Total undergrad enrollment 6,648
% male/female 50/50
% from out of state 81
% African American 8
% Asian 16
% Caucasian 45
% Hispanic 7
% Native American 1
% international 10
# of countries represented 97

ACADEMICS
Calendar semester
Student/faculty ratio 7:1
Profs interesting rating 74
Profs accessible rating 69

MOST POPULAR MAJORS
psychology
economics
political science and government

SELECTIVITY
of applicants 22,955
% of applicants accepted 9
% of acceptees attending 79

FRESHMAN PROFILE
Range SAT Critical Reading 700–800
Range SAT Math 700–790
Range SAT Writing 690–790
Range ACT Composite 31–35
% graduated top 10% of class 95
% graduated top 25% of class 100
% graduated top 50% of class 100

DEADLINES
Regular
  Priority 12/1
  Deadline 1/1
  Notification 4/1
Nonfall registration? no

FINANCIAL FACTS
Annual tuition $32,557
Books and supplies $1,000
% frosh rec. need-based
  scholarship or grant aid 55
% UG rec. need-based
  scholarship or grant aid 51
% frosh rec. need-based
  self-help aid 39
% UG rec. need-based
  self-help aid 44
% frosh rec.
  any financial aid 70
% UG rec. any financial aid 70
% UG borrow to pay for school 46
Average cumulative
  indebtedness $9,290

HAVERFORD COLLEGE

CAMPUS LIFE
Fire Safety Rating **70**
Green Rating **60***
Type of school private
Environment town

STUDENTS
Total undergrad enrollment 1,168
% male/female 47/53
% from out of state 86
% from public high school 55
% live on campus 99
% African American 8
% Asian 11
% Caucasian 69
% Hispanic 7
% Native American 1
% international 4
# of countries represented 47

ACADEMICS
Calendar semester
Student/faculty ratio 8:1
Profs interesting rating 88
Profs accessible rating 95
Most common
  reg class size fewer than 10 students
Most common
  lab size fewer than 10 students

MOST POPULAR MAJORS
English language and literature
biology/biological sciences
economics

SELECTIVITY
of applicants 3,351
% of applicants accepted 26
% of acceptees attending 36

# accepting a place on wait list	312
% admitted from wait list	17
# of early decision applicants	235
% accepted early decision	42

FRESHMAN PROFILE

Range SAT Critical Reading	640–760
Range SAT Math	650–740
Minimum paper TOEFL	600
Minimum computer TOEFL	250
% graduated top 10% of class	88
% graduated top 25% of class	97
% graduated top 50% of class	100

DEADLINES

Early decision	
Deadline	11/15
Notification	12/15
Regular	
Deadline	1/15
Notification	4/15
Nonfall registration?	no

FINANCIAL FACTS

Annual tuition	$33,394
Room and board	$10,390
Required fees	$316
Books and supplies	$1,194
% frosh rec. need-based	
scholarship or grant aid	39
% UG rec. need-based	
scholarship or grant aid	40
% frosh rec. need-based	
self-help aid	37
% UG rec. need-based	
self-help aid	38
% frosh rec.	
any financial aid	41
% UG rec. any financial aid	42
% UG borrow to pay for school	39
Average cumulative	
indebtedness	$15,875

HOBART AND WILLIAM SMITH COLLEGES

CAMPUS LIFE

Fire Safety Rating	60*
Green Rating	60*
Type of school	private
Environment	village

STUDENTS

Total undergrad enrollment	1,855
% male/female	46/54
% from out of state	55
% from public high school	65

% live on campus	90
% in (# of) fraternities	15 (5)
% African American	4
% Asian	2
% Caucasian	88
% Hispanic	4
% international	2
# of countries represented	18

ACADEMICS

Calendar	semester
Student/faculty ratio	11:1
Profs interesting rating	87
Profs accessible rating	90
Most common	
reg class size	10–19 students

MOST POPULAR MAJORS

English language and literature
economics
history

SELECTIVITY

# of applicants	3,410
% of applicants accepted	65
% of acceptees attending	25
# accepting a place on wait list	194
% admitted from wait list	16

FRESHMAN PROFILE

Range SAT Critical Reading	530–640
Range SAT Math	540–630
Range ACT Composite	24–27
Minimum paper TOEFL	550
Minimum computer TOEFL	220
Average HS GPA	3.22
% graduated top 10% of class	33
% graduated top 25% of class	67
% graduated top 50% of class	95

DEADLINES

Early decision	
Deadline	11/15
Notification	12/15
Regular	
Deadline	2/1
Notification	4/1
Nonfall registration?	no

FINANCIAL FACTS

Annual tuition	$31,850
Room and board	$8,386
Required fees	$887
Books and supplies	$850
% frosh rec. need-based	
scholarship or grant aid	58
% UG rec. need-based	
scholarship or grant aid	60

% frosh rec. non-need-based	
scholarship or grant aid	10
% UG rec. non-need-based	
scholarship or grant aid	7
% frosh rec. need-based	
self-help aid	48
% UG rec. need-based	
self-help aid	53
% frosh rec.	
any financial aid	74
% UG rec. any financial aid	64
% UG borrow to pay for school	65
Average cumulative	
indebtedness	$21,545

HOFSTRA UNIVERSITY

CAMPUS LIFE

Fire Safety Rating	92
Green Rating	83
Type of school	private
Environment	city

STUDENTS

Total undergrad enrollment	8,298
% male/female	47/53
% from out of state	50
% live on campus	80
% in (# of) fraternities	9 (19)
% in (# of) sororities	9 (15)
% African American	9
% Asian	5
% Caucasian	62
% Hispanic	8
% Native American	1
% international	1
# of countries represented	67

ACADEMICS

Calendar	4/1/4
Student/faculty ratio	14:1
Profs interesting rating	72
Profs accessible rating	69

MOST POPULAR MAJORS

psychology
accounting
marketing/marketing management

SELECTIVITY

# of applicants	18,471
% of applicants accepted	54
% of acceptees attending	17

FRESHMAN PROFILE

Range SAT Critical Reading	540–630
Range SAT Math	550–630
Range ACT Composite	23–26
Average HS GPA	3.4

% graduated top 10% of class	26
% graduated top 25% of class	56
% graduated top 50% of class	85

DEADLINES

Nonfall registration?	Yes

FINANCIAL FACTS

Annual tuition	$25,700
Room and board	$10,300
Required fees	$1,030
Books and supplies	$1,000
% frosh rec. need-based scholarship or grant aid	53
% UG rec. need-based scholarship or grant aid	49
% frosh rec. non-need-based scholarship or grant aid	6
% UG rec. non-need-based scholarship or grant aid	4
% frosh rec. need-based self-help aid	51
% UG rec. need-based self-help aid	49
% frosh rec. athletic scholarships	1
% UG rec. athletic scholarships	1
% frosh rec. any financial aid	90
% UG rec. any financial aid	84
% UG borrow to pay for school	57

HOOD COLLEGE

CAMPUS LIFE

Fire Safety Rating	**85**
Green Rating	**68**
Type of school	private
Environment	town

STUDENTS

Total undergrad enrollment	1,380
% male/female	29/71
% from out of state	19
% from public high school	82
% live on campus	51
% African American	9
% Asian	3
% Caucasian	75
% Hispanic	3
% international	2
# of countries represented	41

ACADEMICS

Calendar	semester
Profs interesting rating	92
Profs accessible rating	88
Student/faculty ratio	13:1
Most common reg class size	10–19 students

Most common lab size	10–19 students

MOST POPULAR MAJORS
psychology
business administration and management
history

SELECTIVITY

# of applicants	1,719
% of applicants accepted	71
% of acceptees attending	24

FRESHMAN PROFILE

Range SAT Critical Reading	490–610
Range SAT Math	410–590
Range SAT Writing	490–590
Range ACT Composite	20–26
Minimum paper TOEFL	550
Minimum computer TOEFL	215
Average HS GPA	3.54
% graduated top 10% of class	22
% graduated top 25% of class	51
% graduated top 50% of class	83

DEADLINES

Early action	
Deadline	12/1
Notification	12/15
Regular	
Priority	2/15
Notification	rolling
Nonfall registration?	yes

FINANCIAL FACTS

Annual tuition	$33,600
% frosh rec. need-based scholarship or grant aid	68
% UG rec. need-based scholarship or grant aid	75
% frosh rec. non-need-based scholarship or grant aid	18
% UG rec. non-need-based scholarship or grant aid	17
% frosh rec. need-based self-help aid	49
% UG rec. need-based self-help aid	55
% frosh rec. any financial aid	97
% UG rec. any financial aid	98
% UG borrow to pay for school	76
Average cumulative indebtedness	$19,890

HOUGHTON COLLEGE

CAMPUS LIFE

Fire Safety Rating	**73**
Green Rating	**73**
Type of school	private
Affiliation	Wesleyan
Environment	rural

STUDENTS

Total undergrad enrollment	1,324
% male/female	36/64
% from out of state	37
% from public high school	67
% live on campus	82
% African American	2
% Asian	2
% Caucasian	90
% Hispanic	1
% international	3
# of countries represented	22

ACADEMICS

Calendar	semester
Profs interesting rating	88
Profs accessible rating	89
Student/faculty ratio	14:1
Most common reg class size	10–19 students
Most common lab size	10–19 students

MOST POPULAR MAJORS
elementary education and teaching
biology/biological sciences
business administration and management

SELECTIVITY

# of applicants	1,005
% of applicants accepted	84
% of acceptees attending	31

FRESHMAN PROFILE

Range SAT Critical Reading	510–640
Range SAT Math	490–620
Range SAT Writing	510–630
Range ACT Composite	21–28
Minimum paper TOEFL	550
Minimum computer TOEFL	213
Average HS GPA	3.5
% graduated top 10% of class	33
% graduated top 25% of class	64
% graduated top 50% of class	94

DEADLINES

Early action	
Deadline	11/15
Notification	1/1
Notification	rolling
Nonfall registration?	yes

FINANCIAL FACTS

Annual tuition	$21,620
Room and board	$6,860
Books and supplies	$750
% frosh rec. need-based scholarship or grant aid	80

% UG rec. need-based scholarship or grant aid	79	
% frosh rec. non-need-based scholarship or grant aid	17	
% UG rec. non-need-based scholarship or grant aid	14	
% frosh rec. need-based self-help aid	74	
% UG rec. need-based self-help aid	74	
% frosh rec. athletic scholarships	12	
% UG rec. athletic scholarships	9	
% frosh rec. any financial aid	99	
% UG rec. any financial aid	97	
% UG borrow to pay for school	75	
Average cumulative indebtedness	$28,515	

HOWARD UNIVERSITY

CAMPUS LIFE

Fire Safety Rating	**97**
Green Rating	**60***
Type of school	private
Environment	metropolis

STUDENTS

Total undergrad enrollment	6,963
% male/female	33/67
% from out of state	77
% from public high school	80
% live on campus	55
% in (# of) fraternities	2 (10)
% in (# of) sororities	1 (8)
% African American	67
% Asian	1
% international	5
# of countries represented	86

ACADEMICS

Calendar	semester
Student/faculty ratio	8:1
Profs interesting rating	65
Profs accessible rating	63
Most common reg class size	fewer than 10 students
Most common lab size	10–19 students

MOST POPULAR MAJORS
biology/biological sciences

SELECTIVITY

# of applicants	7,603
% of applicants accepted	54
% of acceptees attending	36

FRESHMAN PROFILE

Range SAT Critical Reading	460–660
Range SAT Math	440–650
Range SAT Writing	410–650
Range ACT Composite	20–28
Minimum paper TOEFL	550

Minimum computer TOEFL	213
Average HS GPA	3.2
% graduated top 10% of class	23
% graduated top 25% of class	49
% graduated top 50% of class	82

DEADLINES

Early decision	
Deadline	11/1
Notification	12/24
Early action	
Deadline	11/1
Notification	12/24
Regular	
Priority	11/1
Deadline	2/15
Nonfall registration?	yes

FINANCIAL FACTS

Annual tuition	$13,215
Room and board	$6,976
Required fees	$805
Books and supplies	$1,300
% frosh rec. need-based scholarship or grant aid	35
% UG rec. need-based scholarship or grant aid	35
% frosh rec. non-need-based scholarship or grant aid	63
% UG rec. non-need-based scholarship or grant aid	63
% frosh rec. need-based self-help aid	18
% UG rec. need-based self-help aid	25
% frosh rec. athletic scholarships	40
% UG rec. athletic scholarships	33
% frosh rec. any financial aid	96
% UG rec. any financial aid	96
% UG borrow to pay for school	80
Average cumulative indebtedness	$16,473

INDIANA UNIVERSITY OF PENNSYLVANIA

CAMPUS LIFE

Fire Safety Rating	**94**
Green Rating	**60***
Type of school	public
Environment	village

STUDENTS

Total undergrad enrollment	11,724
% male/female	45/55
% from out of state	4
% from public high school	95
% live on campus	31
% in (# of) fraternities	9 (19)
% in (# of) sororities	9 (14)
% African American	11
% Asian	1
% Caucasian	76
% Hispanic	2
% international	2
# of countries represented	56

ACADEMICS

Calendar	semester
Student/faculty ratio	16:1
Profs interesting rating	75
Profs accessible rating	76
Most common reg class size	20–29 students
Most common lab size	10–19 students

MOST POPULAR MAJORS
criminology
nursing/registered nurse
(rn, asn, bsn, msn)
management

SELECTIVITY

# of applicants	10,116
% of applicants accepted	59
% of acceptees attending	42

FRESHMAN PROFILE

Range SAT Critical Reading	430–530
Range SAT Math	430–540
Range SAT Writing	420–520
Minimum paper TOEFL	500
Minimum computer TOEFL	173
% graduated top 10% of class	8.6
% graduated top 25% of class	27.8
% graduated top 50% of class	62

DEADLINES

Notification	rolling
Nonfall registration?	yes

FINANCIAL FACTS

Annual in-state tuition	$5,178
Annual out-of-state tuition	$12,944
Room and board	$5,436
Required fees	$1,517
Books and supplies	$1,000
% frosh rec. need-based scholarship or grant aid	47

% UG rec. need-based scholarship or grant aid	46
% frosh rec. non-need-based scholarship or grant aid	22
% UG rec. non-need-based scholarship or grant aid	14
% frosh rec. need-based self-help aid	63
% UG rec. need-based self-help aid	58
% frosh rec. athletic scholarships	3
% UG rec. athletic scholarships	2
% frosh rec. any financial aid	81
% UG rec. any financial aid	81
% UG borrow to pay for school	81
Average cumulative indebtedness	$22,431

IONA COLLEGE

CAMPUS LIFE

Fire Safety Rating	**86**
Green Rating	**83**
Type of school	private
Affiliation	Roman Catholic
Environment	city

STUDENTS

Total undergrad enrollment	3,480
% male/female	46/54
% from out of state	20
% from public high school	55
% live on campus	30
% in (# of) fraternities	4 (4)
% in (# of) sororities	6 (6)
% African American	6
% Asian	2
% Caucasian	68
% Hispanic	11
% international	1
# of countries represented	32

ACADEMICS

Calendar	semester
Profs interesting rating	75
Profs accessible rating	72
Student/faculty ratio	13:1
Most common reg class size	20–29 students
Most common lab size	10–19 students

MOST POPULAR MAJORS
mass communication/media studies
finance
psychology

SELECTIVITY

# of applicants	6,017
% of applicants accepted	59
% of acceptees attending	26
# accepting a place on wait list	187
% admitted from wait list	42

FRESHMAN PROFILE

Range SAT Critical Reading	530–640
Range SAT Math	550–660
Minimum paper TOEFL	550
Minimum computer TOEFL	213
Average HS GPA	3.4
% graduated top 10% of class	31
% graduated top 25% of class	54
% graduated top 50% of class	93

DEADLINES

Early action	
Deadline	12/1
Notification	12/21
Regular	
Deadline	2/15
Notification	3/20
Nonfall registration?	yes

FINANCIAL FACTS

Annual tuition	$24,406
Room and board	$10,800
Required fees	$1,800
Books and supplies	$1,500
% frosh rec. need-based scholarship or grant aid	58
% UG rec. need-based scholarship or grant aid	40
% frosh rec. non-need-based scholarship or grant aid	75
% UG rec. non-need-based scholarship or grant aid	71
% frosh rec. need-based self-help aid	58
% UG rec. need-based self-help aid	57
% frosh rec. athletic scholarships	8
% UG rec. athletic scholarships	7
% frosh rec. any financial aid	98
% UG rec. any financial aid	89
% UG borrow to pay for school	67
Average cumulative indebtedness	$19,451

ITHACA COLLEGE

CAMPUS LIFE

Fire Safety Rating	**75**
Green Rating	**91**
Type of school	private
Environment	town

STUDENTS

Total undergrad enrollment	6,185
% male/female	45/55
% from out of state	54
% from public high school	75
% live on campus	70
% in (# of) fraternities	1 (4)
% in (# of) sororities	1 (1)
% African American	3
% Asian	4
% Caucasian	80
% Hispanic	4
% international	2
# of countries represented	67

ACADEMICS

Calendar	semester
Student/faculty ratio	12:1
Profs interesting rating	81
Profs accessible rating	80
% classes taught by TAs	1
Most common reg class size	10–19 students

MOST POPULAR MAJORS
business/commerce

SELECTIVITY

# of applicants	11,235
% of applicants accepted	74
% of acceptees attending	22

FRESHMAN PROFILE

Range SAT Critical Reading	530–630
Range SAT Math	540–630
Minimum paper TOEFL	550
Minimum computer TOEFL	213
Minimum web-based TOEFL	80
% graduated top 10% of class	29.5
% graduated top 25% of class	65.7
% graduated top 50% of class	93.4

DEADLINES

Regular	
Deadline	2/1
Notification	rolling
Nonfall registration?	yes

FINANCIAL FACTS

Annual tuition	$30,606
Room and board	$11,162
Books and supplies	$1,130
% frosh rec. need-based scholarship or grant aid	66
% UG rec. need-based scholarship or grant aid	58
% frosh rec. non-need-based scholarship or grant aid	20

% UG rec. non-need-based	
scholarship or grant aid	14
% frosh rec. need-based	
self-help aid	60
% UG rec. need-based	
self-help aid	57
% frosh rec.	
any financial aid	90
% UG rec. any financial aid	85

JOHNS HOPKINS UNIVERSITY

CAMPUS LIFE

Fire Safety Rating	**70**
Green Rating	**60***
Type of school	private
Environment	metropolis

STUDENTS

Total undergrad enrollment	4,578
% male/female	52/48
% from out of state	85
% live on campus	60
% in (# of) fraternities	21 (11)
% in (# of) sororities	22 (7)
% African American	6
% Asian	25
% Caucasian	46
% Hispanic	7
% Native American	1
% international	5
# of countries represented	71

ACADEMICS

Calendar	4/1/4
Profs interesting rating	61
Profs accessible rating	68
Most common	
reg class size	10–19 students
Most common	
lab size	10–19 students

MOST POPULAR MAJORS
biomedical/medical engineering
economics
international relations and affairs

SELECTIVITY

# of applicants	14,848
% of applicants accepted	24
% of acceptees attending	33
# accepting a place on wait list	1,319
% admitted from wait list	3
# of early decision applicants	997
% accepted early decision	45

FRESHMAN PROFILE

Range SAT Critical Reading	630–730
Range SAT Math	660–770

Range SAT Writing	630–730
Range ACT Composite	28–33
Average HS GPA	3.7
% graduated top 10% of class	82
% graduated top 25% of class	97
% graduated top 50% of class	100

DEADLINES

Early decision	
Deadline	11/1
Notification	12/15
Regular	
Deadline	1/1
Notification	4/1
Nonfall registration?	no

FINANCIAL FACTS

Annual tuition	$33,000
% frosh rec.	
any financial aid	47
% UG rec. any financial aid	46

JUNIATA COLLEGE

CAMPUS LIFE

Fire Safety Rating	**77**
Green Rating	**85**
Type of school	private
Environment	village

STUDENTS

Total undergrad enrollment	1,410
% male/female	46/54
% from out of state	32
% from public high school	85
% live on campus	85
% African American	1
% Asian	2
% Caucasian	89
% Hispanic	1
% international	5
# of countries represented	34

ACADEMICS

Calendar	semester
Student/faculty ratio	13:1
Profs interesting rating	84
Profs accessible rating	88
Most common	
reg class size	10–19 students
Most common	
lab size	10–19 students

MOST POPULAR MAJORS
biology/biological sciences
business/commerce
education

SELECTIVITY

# of applicants	1,958
% of applicants accepted	67
% of acceptees attending	29
# of early decision applicants	33
% accepted early decision	94

FRESHMAN PROFILE

Range SAT Critical Reading	525–630
Range SAT Math	540–630
Minimum paper TOEFL	550
Minimum computer TOEFL	213
Average HS GPA	3.78
% graduated top 10% of class	36
% graduated top 25% of class	77
% graduated top 50% of class	99

DEADLINES

Early decision	
Deadline	12/1
Notification	12/31
Early action	
Deadline	1/1
Notification	1/31
Regular	
Priority	12/1
Deadline	3/15
Notification	2/28
Nonfall registration?	yes

FINANCIAL FACTS

Annual tuition	$29,610
Room and board	$8,420
Required fees	$670
Books and supplies	$600
% frosh rec. need-based	
scholarship or grant aid	72
% UG rec. need-based	
scholarship or grant aid	71
% frosh rec. non-need-based	
scholarship or grant aid	71
% UG rec. non-need-based	
scholarship or grant aid	64
% frosh rec. need-based	
self-help aid	59
% UG rec. need-based	
self-help aid	62
% frosh rec.	
any financial aid	99
% UG rec. any financial aid	99
% UG borrow to pay for school	83.75
Average cumulative	
indebtedness	$21,426

KEENE STATE COLLEGE

CAMPUS LIFE

Fire Safety Rating	**97**
Green Rating	**87**
Type of school	public
Environment	village

STUDENTS

Total undergrad enrollment	4,658
% male/female	42/58
% from out of state	46
% live on campus	60
% in (# of) fraternities	3 (2)
% in (# of) sororities	3 (4)
% African American	1
% Caucasian	95
% Hispanic	1
# of countries represented	7

ACADEMICS

Calendar	semester
Profs interesting rating	73
Profs accessible rating	76
Student/faculty ratio	18:1
Most common	
reg class size	10–19 students

MOST POPULAR MAJORS
elementary education
occupational safety and health
business administration and management
clinical psychology
sociology

SELECTIVITY

# of applicants	4,676
% of applicants accepted	73
% of acceptees attending	38

FRESHMAN PROFILE

Range SAT Critical Reading	440–540
Range SAT Math	440–540
Range SAT Writing	440–540
Minimum paper TOEFL	500
Minimum computer TOEFL	173
Minimum web-based TOEFL	61
Average HS GPA	2.99
% graduated top 10% of class	4
% graduated top 25% of class	20
% graduated top 50% of class	62

DEADLINES

Regular	
Deadline	4/1
Nonfall registration?	yes

FINANCIAL FACTS

Books and supplies	$800
% frosh rec. need-based	
scholarship or grant aid	37
% UG rec. need-based	
scholarship or grant aid	34
% frosh rec. non-need-based	
scholarship or grant aid	12
% UG rec. non-need-based	
scholarship or grant aid	12
% frosh rec. need-based self-help aid	53
% UG rec. need-based self-help aid	49
% UG borrow to pay for school	79
Average cumulative indebtedness	$23,775

KUTZTOWN UNIVERSITY OF PENNSYLVANIA

CAMPUS LIFE

Fire Safety Rating	**60***
Green Rating	**60***
Type of school	public
Environment	rural

STUDENTS

Total undergrad enrollment	8,768
% male/female	42/58
% from out of state	10
% from public high school	99
% live on campus	48
% in (# of) fraternities	1 (8)
% in (# of) sororities	13 (9)
% African American	7
% Asian	1
% Caucasian	85
% Hispanic	4
% international	1
# of countries represented	64

ACADEMICS

Calendar	semester
Profs interesting rating	70
Profs accessible rating	75
Student/faculty ratio	19:1
Most common	
reg class size	20–29 students
Most common	
lab size	less than 10 students

MOST POPULAR MAJORS
business administration and management
criminal justice/safety studies
psychology

SELECTIVITY

# of applicants	9,002
% of applicants accepted	65
% of acceptees attending	32

FRESHMAN PROFILE

Range SAT Critical Reading	440–530
Range SAT Math	440–540
Range SAT Writing	430–520
Range ACT Composite	17–21
Minimum paper TOEFL	500
Minimum computer TOEFL	173
Minimum web-based TOEFL	70
Average HS GPA	3.04
% graduated top 10% of class	6.2
% graduated top 25% of class	28.3
% graduated top 50% of class	67.2

DEADLINES

Regular	
Priority	1/1
Notification	rolling
Nonfall registration?	yes

FINANCIAL FACTS

Annual in-state tuition	$5,177
Annual out-of-state tuition	$12,944
Room and board	$6,960
Required fees	$1,696
Books and supplies	$1,100
% frosh rec. need-based	
scholarship or grant aid	42
% UG rec. need-based	
scholarship or grant aid	40
% frosh rec. non-need-based	
scholarship or grant aid	2
% UG rec. non-need-based	
scholarship or grant aid	2
% frosh rec. need-based self-help aid	51
% UG rec. need-based self-help aid	48
% frosh rec. athletic scholarships	2
% UG rec. athletic scholarships	2
% frosh rec. any financial aid	81
% UG rec. any financial aid	81
% UG borrow to pay for school	82
Average cumulative indebtedness	$16,954

LA ROCHE COLLEGE

CAMPUS LIFE

Fire Safety Rating	**90**
Green Rating	**60***
Type of school	private
Affiliation	Roman Catholic
Environment	city

STUDENTS

Total undergrad enrollment	1,306
% male/female	34/66
% from out of state	5
% from public high school	79
% live on campus	36

% African American	5
% Asian	1
% Caucasian	74
% Hispanic	1
% Native American	1
% international	12
# of countries represented	38

ACADEMICS
Calendar	semester
Profs interesting rating	76
Profs accessible rating	74
Student/faculty ratio	12:1
Most common reg class size	10–19 students
Most common lab size	less than 10 students

MOST POPULAR MAJORS
design and visual communications
elementary education and teaching
interior architecture

SELECTIVITY
# of applicants	944
% of applicants accepted	73
% of acceptees attending	43

FRESHMAN PROFILE
Range SAT Critical Reading	410–510
Range SAT Math	410–510
Range SAT Writing	430–510
Range ACT Composite	15–19
Average HS GPA	3.106
% graduated top 10% of class	8
% graduated top 25% of class	24
% graduated top 50% of class	62

DEADLINES
Notification	rolling
Nonfall registration?	yes

FINANCIAL FACTS
Annual tuition	$18,600
	$18,600
Room and board	$7,942
Required fees	$652
Books and supplies	$800
% frosh rec. need-based scholarship or grant aid	56
% UG rec. need-based scholarship or grant aid	51
% frosh rec. non-need-based scholarship or grant aid	96
% UG rec. non-need-based scholarship or grant aid	98
% frosh rec. need-based self-help aid	60
% UG rec. need-based self-help aid	60
% frosh rec. any financial aid	95

% UG rec. any financial aid	90
% UG borrow to pay for school	84
Average cumulative indebtedness	$18,750

LABORATORY INSTITUTE OF MERCHANDISING

CAMPUS LIFE
Fire Safety Rating	**60***
Green Rating	**60***
Type of school	proprietary
Environment	metropolis

STUDENTS
Total undergrad enrollment	1,107
% male/female	5/95
% from out of state	58
% from public high school	73
% live on campus	32
% African American	9
% Asian	6
% Caucasian	68
% Hispanic	16
% international	1
# of countries represented	18

ACADEMICS
Calendar	semester
Profs interesting rating	75
Profs accessible rating	70
Student/faculty ratio	17:1
Most common reg class size	10–19 students

MOST POPULAR MAJORS
marketing/marketing management
fashion merchandising

SELECTIVITY
# of applicants	837
% of applicants accepted	63
% of acceptees attending	54

FRESHMAN PROFILE
Range SAT Critical Reading	430–503
Range SAT Math	420–500
Range ACT Composite	17–23
Minimum paper TOEFL	550
Minimum computer TOEFL	213
Average HS GPA	2.83
% graduated top 10% of class	5
% graduated top 25% of class	17
% graduated top 50% of class	54

DEADLINES
Early action	
Deadline	11/15
Notification	12/15

Regular	
Priority	11/15
Nonfall registration?	yes

FINANCIAL FACTS
Annual tuition	$19,300
Room and board	$18,700
Required fees	$525
Books and supplies	$1,100
% frosh rec. need-based scholarship or grant aid	38
% UG rec. need-based scholarship or grant aid	43
% frosh rec. non-need-based scholarship or grant aid	15
% UG rec. non-need-based scholarship or grant aid	10
% frosh rec. need-based self-help aid	44
% UG rec. need-based self-help aid	51
% frosh rec. any financial aid	85
% UG rec. any financial aid	85
% UG borrow to pay for school	91
Average cumulative indebtedness	$19,593

LAFAYETTE COLLEGE

CAMPUS LIFE
Fire Safety Rating	**60***
Green Rating	**95**
Type of school	private
Affiliation	Presbyterian
Environment	village

STUDENTS
Total undergrad enrollment	2,381
% male/female	52/48
% from out of state	70
% from public high school	68
% live on campus	96
% in (# of) fraternities	26 (7)
% in (# of) sororities	45 (6)
% African American	5
% Asian	3
% Caucasian	80
% Hispanic	5
% international	6
# of countries represented	46

ACADEMICS
Calendar	semester
Student/faculty ratio	11:1
Profs interesting rating	87
Profs accessible rating	88
Most common reg class size	10–19 students
Most common lab size	10–19 students

SELECTIVITY

# of applicants	5,875
% of applicants accepted	37
% of acceptees attending	29
# accepting a place on wait list	636
% admitted from wait list	9
# of early decision applicants	395
% accepted early decision	68

FRESHMAN PROFILE

Range SAT Critical Reading	580–670
Range SAT Math	620–710
Range SAT Writing	580–670
Range ACT Composite	24–29
Minimum paper TOEFL	550
Average HS GPA	3.78
% graduated top 10% of class	62
% graduated top 25% of class	92
% graduated top 50% of class	100

DEADLINES

Early decision	
Deadline	2/15
Notification	12/1
Regular	
Priority	1/1
Deadline	1/1
Notification	4/1
Nonfall registration?	yes

FINANCIAL FACTS

Annual tuition	$33,634
Room and board	$10,377
Required fees	$177
Books and supplies	$600
% frosh rec. need-based scholarship or grant aid	48
% UG rec. need-based scholarship or grant aid	48
% frosh rec. non-need-based scholarship or grant aid	13
% UG rec. non-need-based scholarship or grant aid	7
% frosh rec. need-based self-help aid	32
% UG rec. need-based self-help aid	38
% UG borrow to pay for school	49
Average cumulative indebtedness	$17,576

LANCASTER BIBLE COLLEGE

CAMPUS LIFE

Fire Safety Rating	**60***
Green Rating	**60***
Type of school	private
Environment	village

STUDENTS

Total undergrad enrollment	640
% male/female	50/50
% from out of state	23
% from public high school	60
% live on campus	48
% African American	3
% Asian	1
% Caucasian	65
% Hispanic	1
% international	1

ACADEMICS

Calendar	semester
Profs interesting rating	87
Profs accessible rating	88
Student/faculty ratio	17:1
Most common reg class size	less than 10 students
Most common lab size	10–19 students

MOST POPULAR MAJORS
elementary education and teaching
bible/biblical studies
theology and religious vocations, other

SELECTIVITY

# of applicants	239
% of applicants accepted	67
% of acceptees attending	68

FRESHMAN PROFILE

Range SAT Critical Reading	480–580
Range SAT Math	460–570
Range ACT Composite	17–23
Minimum paper TOEFL	550
Minimum computer TOEFL	213
Average HS GPA	3.25
% graduated top 10% of class	15
% graduated top 25% of class	32
% graduated top 50% of class	82

DEADLINES

Regular	
Priority	8/1
Notification	rolling
Nonfall registration?	yes

FINANCIAL FACTS

Annual tuition	$13,920
Room and board	$6,170
Required fees	$600
% frosh rec. need-based scholarship or grant aid	53
% UG rec. need-based scholarship or grant aid	51
% frosh rec. non-need-based scholarship or grant aid	69
% UG rec. non-need-based scholarship or grant aid	58
% frosh rec. need-based self-help aid	69
% UG rec. need-based self-help aid	65
% UG borrow to pay for school	10
Average cumulative indebtedness	$14,621

LEBANON VALLEY COLLEGE

CAMPUS LIFE

Fire Safety Rating	**77**
Green Rating	**65**
Type of school	private
Affiliation	Methodist
Environment	rural

STUDENTS

Total undergrad enrollment	1,705
% male/female	45/55
% from out of state	21
% from public high school	95
% live on campus	74
% in (# of) fraternities	19 (4)
% in (# of) sororities	13 (3)
% African American	1
% Asian	2
% Caucasian	89
% Hispanic	3
# of countries represented	5

ACADEMICS

Calendar	semester
Profs interesting rating	74
Profs accessible rating	85
Student/faculty ratio	13:1
Most common reg class size	10–19 students
Most common lab size	10–19 students

MOST POPULAR MAJORS
elementary education and teaching
psychology
business/commerce

SELECTIVITY

# of applicants	2,131
% of applicants accepted	71
% of acceptees attending	30

FRESHMAN PROFILE

Range SAT Critical Reading	480–600

Range SAT Math	490–620
Range SAT Writing	480–600
Range ACT Composite	20–26
Minimum paper TOEFL	550
Minimum computer TOEFL	213
Minimum web-based TOEFL	80
% graduated top 10% of class	36
% graduated top 25% of class	71
% graduated top 50% of class	95

DEADLINES

Notification	rolling
Nonfall registration?	yes

FINANCIAL FACTS

Annual tuition	$27,125
Room and board	$7,430
Required fees	$675
Books and supplies	$900
% frosh rec. need-based scholarship or grant aid	83
% UG rec. need-based scholarship or grant aid	77
% frosh rec. non-need-based scholarship or grant aid	13
% UG rec. non-need-based scholarship or grant aid	9
% frosh rec. need-based self-help aid	68
% UG rec. need-based self-help aid	65
% frosh rec. any financial aid	98
% UG rec. any financial aid	98
% UG borrow to pay for school	81
Average cumulative indebtedness	$27,566

LEHIGH UNIVERSITY

CAMPUS LIFE

Fire Safety Rating	**60***
Green Rating	**84**
Type of school	private
Environment	city

STUDENTS

Total undergrad enrollment	4,732
% male/female	59/41
% from out of state	76
% live on campus	71
% in (# of) fraternities	35 (21)
% in (# of) sororities	38 (8)
% African American	3
% Asian	6
% Caucasian	77
% Hispanic	4
% international	2
# of countries represented	44

ACADEMICS

Calendar	semester
Student/faculty ratio	9:1
Profs interesting rating	78
Profs accessible rating	85

MOST POPULAR MAJORS
mechanical engineering
finance
accounting

SELECTIVITY

# of applicants	12,155
% of applicants accepted	32
% of acceptees attending	30
# accepting a place on wait list	1,096
% admitted from wait list	7
# of early decision applicants	827
% accepted early decision	58

FRESHMAN PROFILE

Range SAT Critical Reading	600–680
Range SAT Math	640–710
Minimum paper TOEFL	570
Minimum computer TOEFL	230
% graduated top 10% of class	93
% graduated top 25% of class	99
% graduated top 50% of class	100

DEADLINES

Early decision	
Deadline	11/15
Notification	12/15
Regular	
Deadline	1/1
Nonfall registration?	yes

FINANCIAL FACTS

Annual tuition	$37,250
% frosh rec. need-based scholarship or grant aid	40
% UG rec. need-based scholarship or grant aid	43
% frosh rec. non-need-based scholarship or grant aid	5
% UG rec. non-need-based scholarship or grant aid	7
% frosh rec. need-based self-help aid	39
% UG rec. need-based self-help aid	42
% frosh rec. athletic scholarships	1
% frosh rec. any financial aid	65
% UG rec. any financial aid	60
% UG borrow to pay for school	53
Average cumulative indebtedness	$26,768

LESLEY COLLEGE

CAMPUS LIFE

Fire Safety Rating	**85**
Green Rating	**72**
Type of school	private
Environment	metropolis

STUDENTS

Total undergrad enrollment	1,225
% male/female	25/75
% from out of state	42
% from public high school	83
% live on campus	53
% African American	5
% Asian	4
% Caucasian	65
% Hispanic	5
% international	2
# of countries represented	30

ACADEMICS

Calendar	semester
Profs interesting rating	77
Profs accessible rating	80
Student/faculty ratio	9:1
Most common reg class size	10–19 students

MOST POPULAR MAJORS
elementary education and teaching
counseling psychology
marketing/marketing management

SELECTIVITY

# of applicants	1,568
% of applicants accepted	86
% of acceptees attending	26
# accepting a place on wait list	33
% admitted from wait list	18

FRESHMAN PROFILE

Range SAT Critical Reading	450–600
Range SAT Math	460–560
Range SAT Writing	480–580
Range ACT Composite	20–26
Minimum paper TOEFL	500
Minimum computer TOEFL	173
Average HS GPA	2.98
% graduated top 10% of class	15
% graduated top 25% of class	25
% graduated top 50% of class	84

DEADLINES

Early action	
Deadline	12/1
Notification	12/31

Regular
Priority 2/15
Notification rolling
Nonfall registration? yes

FINANCIAL FACTS

Annual tuition	$27,200
Room and board	$12,000
Required fees	$310
Books and supplies	$700
% frosh rec. need-based scholarship or grant aid	71
% UG rec. need-based scholarship or grant aid	64
% frosh rec. non-need-based scholarship or grant aid	18
% UG rec. non-need-based scholarship or grant aid	18
% frosh rec. need-based self-help aid	60
% UG rec. need-based self-help aid	55
% frosh rec. any financial aid	70
% UG rec. any financial aid	70
% UG borrow to pay for school	91
Average cumulative indebtedness	$15,000

LOYOLA COLLEGE IN MARYLAND

CAMPUS LIFE

Fire Safety Rating	**78**
Green Rating	**60***
Type of school	private
Affiliation	Roman Catholic
Environment	village

STUDENTS

Total undergrad enrollment	3,580
% male/female	42/58
% from out of state	82
% from public high school	60
% live on campus	78
% African American	5
% Asian	3
% Caucasian	85
% Hispanic	3
% international	1
# of countries represented	31

ACADEMICS

Calendar	semester
Student/faculty ratio	12:1
Profs interesting rating	96
Profs accessible rating	93
Most common reg class size	20–29 students
Most common lab size	10–19 students

MOST POPULAR MAJORS
business
communications
biology

SELECTIVITY

# of applicants	8,594
% of applicants accepted	60
% of acceptees attending	19

FRESHMAN PROFILE

Range SAT Critical Reading	560–650
Range SAT Math	560–660
Minimum paper TOEFL	550
Minimum computer TOEFL	213
Average HS GPA	3.5
% graduated top 10% of class	37
% graduated top 25% of class	75
% graduated top 50% of class	96

DEADLINES
Regular
Priority	1/15
Deadline	1/15
Notification	4/1
Nonfall registration?	yes

FINANCIAL FACTS

Annual tuition	$35,140
Room and board	$9,740
Required fees	$1,265
Books and supplies	$1,010
% frosh rec. need-based scholarship or grant aid	37
% UG rec. need-based scholarship or grant aid	36
% frosh rec. non-need-based scholarship or grant aid	19
% UG rec. non-need-based scholarship or grant aid	16
% frosh rec. need-based self-help aid	44
% UG rec. need-based self-help aid	42
% frosh rec. athletic scholarships	3
% UG rec. athletic scholarships	3
% frosh rec. any financial aid	66
% UG rec. any financial aid	71
% UG borrow to pay for school	72
Average cumulative indebtedness	$19,730

LYCOMING COLLEGE

CAMPUS LIFE

Fire Safety Rating	**60***
Green Rating	**78**
Type of school	private
Affiliation	Methodist
Environment	town

STUDENTS

Total undergrad enrollment	1,402
% male/female	45/55
% from out of state	32
% from public high school	90
% live on campus	85
% in (# of) fraternities	8 (5)
% in (# of) sororities	12 (5)
% African American	2
% Asian	1
% Caucasian	95
% Hispanic	1
% international	1
# of countries represented	9

ACADEMICS

Calendar	semester
Profs interesting rating	81
Profs accessible rating	83
Student/faculty ratio	14:1
Most common reg class size	10–19 students
Most common lab size	10–19 students

MOST POPULAR MAJORS
psychology
biology/biological sciences
business administration and management

SELECTIVITY

# of applicants	1,585
% of applicants accepted	78
% of acceptees attending	32

FRESHMAN PROFILE

Range SAT Critical Reading	460–570
Range SAT Math	470–580
Range SAT Writing	450–560
Range ACT Composite	20–25
Minimum paper TOEFL	500
Minimum computer TOEFL	173
% graduated top 10% of class	19
% graduated top 25% of class	43
% graduated top 50% of class	75

DEADLINES

Regular	
Priority	4/1
Deadline	7/1
Notification	rolling
Nonfall registration?	yes

FINANCIAL FACTS

Annual tuition	$28,224
Room and board	$7,672
Required fees	$540
Books and supplies	$800
% frosh rec. need-based scholarship or grant aid	80
% UG rec. need-based scholarship or grant aid	82
% frosh rec. non-need-based scholarship or grant aid	11
% UG rec. non-need-based scholarship or grant aid	8
% frosh rec. need-based self-help aid	66
% UG rec. need-based self-help aid	72
% frosh rec. any financial aid	95
% UG rec. any financial aid	95
% UG borrow to pay for school	85
Average cumulative indebtedness	$26,538

MANHATTANVILLE COLLEGE

CAMPUS LIFE

Fire Safety Rating	**60***
Green Rating	**88**
Type of school	private
Environment	town

STUDENTS

Total undergrad enrollment	1,752
% male/female	33/67
% from out of state	36
% live on campus	80
% African American	7
% Asian	2
% Caucasian	56
% Hispanic	16
% Native American	1
% international	9
# of countries represented	59

ACADEMICS

Calendar	semester
Student/faculty ratio	11:1
Profs interesting rating	83
Profs accessible rating	86
Most common reg class size	10–19 students

MOST POPULAR MAJORS

psychology
visual and performing arts
business/commerce

SELECTIVITY

# of applicants	3,927
% of applicants accepted	50
% of acceptees attending	27

FRESHMAN PROFILE

Range SAT Critical Reading	500–620
Range SAT Math	500–610
Range ACT Composite	20–25
Minimum paper TOEFL	550
Minimum computer TOEFL	217
% graduated top 10% of class	22
% graduated top 25% of class	47
% graduated top 50% of class	80

DEADLINES

Early decision	
Deadline	12/1
Notification	12/31
Regular	
Priority	3/1
Deadline	3/1
Notification	rolling
Nonfall registration?	yes

FINANCIAL FACTS

Annual tuition	$30,400
Room and board	$13,040
Required fees	$1,220
Books and supplies	$800
% frosh rec. need-based scholarship or grant aid	62
% UG rec. need-based scholarship or grant aid	57
% frosh rec. non-need-based scholarship or grant aid	59
% UG rec. non-need-based scholarship or grant aid	57
% frosh rec. need-based self-help aid	58
% UG rec. need-based self-help aid	54
% frosh rec. any financial aid	75
% UG rec. any financial aid	70
% UG borrow to pay for school	67
Average cumulative indebtedness	$23,253

MARIST COLLEGE

CAMPUS LIFE

Fire Safety Rating	**80**
Green Rating	**81**
Type of school	private
Environment	town

STUDENTS

Total undergrad enrollment	4,769
% male/female	43/57
% from out of state	41
% from public high school	72
% live on campus	72
% in (# of) fraternities	1 (3)
% in (# of) sororities	3 (4)
% African American	3
% Asian	2
% Caucasian	77
% Hispanic	5
# of countries represented	11

ACADEMICS

Calendar	semester
Student/faculty ratio	15:1
Profs interesting rating	75
Profs accessible rating	76
Most common reg class size	10–19 students
Most common lab size	20–29 students

MOST POPULAR MAJORS

special education and teaching
business administration and management
communication & media studies

SELECTIVITY

# of applicants	8,328
% of applicants accepted	42
% of acceptees attending	29
# accepting a place on wait list	731
% admitted from wait list	8
# of early decision applicants	102
% accepted early decision	83

FRESHMAN PROFILE

Range SAT Critical Reading	520–620
Range SAT Math	540–630
Range SAT Writing	530–630
Range ACT Composite	22–27
Minimum paper TOEFL	550
Minimum computer TOEFL	213
Minimum web-based TOEFL	79
Average HS GPA	3.3
% graduated top 10% of class	29
% graduated top 25% of class	75
% graduated top 50% of class	94

DEADLINES

Early decision

Deadline	11/15
Notification	12/15

Early action

Deadline	12/1
Notification	1/30

Regular

Deadline	2/15
Notification	3/15
Nonfall registration?	yes

FINANCIAL FACTS

Annual tuition	$23,560
Room and board	$10,250
Required fees	$480
Books and supplies	$1,230
% frosh rec. need-based scholarship or grant aid	59
% UG rec. need-based scholarship or grant aid	57
% frosh rec. non-need-based scholarship or grant aid	43
% UG rec. non-need-based scholarship or grant aid	33
% frosh rec. need-based self-help aid	47
% UG rec. need-based self-help aid	50
% frosh rec. athletic scholarships	8
% UG rec. athletic scholarships	6
% frosh rec. any financial aid	92
% UG rec. any financial aid	86
% UG borrow to pay for school	68
Average cumulative indebtedness	$28,374

MARLBORO COLLEGE

CAMPUS LIFE

Fire Safety Rating	**66**
Green Rating	**72**
Type of school	private
Environment	rural

STUDENTS

Total undergrad enrollment	324
% male/female	47/53
% from out of state	88
% from public high school	70
% live on campus	80
% Asian	2
% Caucasian	67
% Hispanic	2

% Native American	1
# of countries represented	3

ACADEMICS

Calendar	semester
Student/faculty ratio	8:1
Profs interesting rating	97
Profs accessible rating	91
Most common reg class size	fewer than 10 students
Most common lab size	fewer than 10 students

MOST POPULAR MAJORS
English language and literature
social sciences
visual and performing arts

SELECTIVITY

# of applicants	459
% of applicants accepted	68
% of acceptees attending	30
# of early decision applicants	19
% accepted early decision	68

FRESHMAN PROFILE

Range SAT Critical Reading	590–690
Range SAT Math	510–650
Range SAT Writing	640–720
Range ACT Composite	24–32
Minimum paper TOEFL	550
Minimum computer TOEFL	213
Minimum web-based TOEFL	80
Average HS GPA	3.2
% graduated top 10% of class	40
% graduated top 25% of class	60
% graduated top 50% of class	95

DEADLINES

Early decision

Deadline	12/1
Notification	12/15

Early action

Deadline	2/1
Notification	2/15

Regular

Priority	1/15
Deadline	2/15
Notification	rolling
Nonfall registration?	yes

FINANCIAL FACTS

Annual tuition	$31,140
Room and board	$9,040
Required fees	$1,040
Books and supplies	$1,000
% frosh rec. need-based scholarship or grant aid	70

% UG rec. need-based scholarship or grant aid	74
% frosh rec. non-need-based scholarship or grant aid	49
% UG rec. non-need-based scholarship or grant aid	16
% frosh rec. need-based self-help aid	75
% UG rec. need-based self-help aid	72
% frosh rec. any financial aid	77
% UG rec. any financial aid	84
% UG borrow to pay for school	84
Average cumulative indebtedness	$19,758

MARYLAND INSTITUTE COLLEGE OF ART

CAMPUS LIFE

Fire Safety Rating	**88**
Green Rating	**65**
Type of school	private
Environment	metropolis

STUDENTS

Total undergrad enrollment	1,672
% male/female	34/66
% from out of state	80
% live on campus	88
% African American	4
% Asian	10
% Caucasian	67
% Hispanic	4
% international	4
# of countries represented	48

ACADEMICS

Calendar	semester
Profs interesting rating	85
Profs accessible rating	70
Student/faculty ratio	10:1
Most common reg class size	10–19 students

MOST POPULAR MAJORS
painting
illustration
intermedia/multimedia (GFA)
graphic design

SELECTIVITY

# of applicants	2,602
% of applicants accepted	37
% of acceptees attending	41

FRESHMAN PROFILE

Range SAT Critical Reading	530–660
Range SAT Math	500–620
Range SAT Writing	490–630
Average HS GPA	3.43
% graduated top 10% of class	31
% graduated top 25% of class	61
% graduated top 50% of class	89

DEADLINES

Early decision	
Deadline	11/15
Notification	12/15
Regular	
Deadline	2/15
Notification	3/15
Nonfall registration?	yes

FINANCIAL FACTS

Annual tuition	$29,700
Room and board	$8,390
Required fees	$980
Books and supplies	$1,400

MASSACHUSETTS INSTITUTE OF TECHNOLOGY

CAMPUS LIFE

Fire Safety Rating	75
Green Rating	85
Type of school	private
Environment	city

STUDENTS

Total undergrad enrollment	4,163
% male/female	55/45
% from out of state	90
% from public high school	69
% live on campus	90
% in (# of) fraternities	49 (27)
% in (# of) sororities	26 (5)
% African American	7
% Asian	26
% Caucasian	37
% Hispanic	12
% Native American	1
% international	8
# of countries represented	89

ACADEMICS

Calendar	4/1/4
Student/faculty ratio	6:1
Profs interesting rating	70
Profs accessible rating	76
Most common	
reg class size	fewer than 10 students

Most common	
lab size	10–19 students

MOST POPULAR MAJORS
computer science
chemical engineering
mechanical engineering

SELECTIVITY

# of applicants	12,445
% of applicants accepted	12
% of acceptees attending	69
# accepting a place on wait list	443
% admitted from wait list	5

FRESHMAN PROFILE

Range SAT Critical Reading	660–760
Range SAT Math	720–800
Range SAT Writing	660–750
Range ACT Composite	31–34
Minimum paper TOEFL	577
Minimum computer TOEFL	233
Minimum web-based TOEFL	90
% graduated top 10% of class	97
% graduated top 25% of class	100
% graduated top 50% of class	100

DEADLINES

Early action	
Deadline	11/1
Notification	12/15
Regular	
Deadline	1/1
Notification	3/20
Nonfall registration?	no

FINANCIAL FACTS

Annual tuition	$34,750
Room and board	$10,400
Required fees	$236
Books and supplies	$1,114
% frosh rec. need-based scholarship or grant aid	63
% UG rec. need-based scholarship or grant aid	60
% frosh rec. need-based self-help aid	51
% UG rec. need-based self-help aid	53
% frosh rec. any financial aid	79
% UG rec. any financial aid	71
% UG borrow to pay for school	41
Average cumulative indebtedness	$15,051

MERRIMACK COLLEGE

CAMPUS LIFE

Fire Safety Rating	60*
Green Rating	60*
Type of school	private
Affiliation	Roman Catholic
Environment	town

STUDENTS

Total undergrad enrollment	2,093
% male/female	49/51
% from out of state	35
% from public high school	65
% live on campus	80
% in (# of) fraternities	3 (3)
% in (# of) sororities	7 (3)
% African American	2
% Asian	3
% Caucasian	78
% Hispanic	4
% international	1
# of countries represented	14

ACADEMICS

Calendar	semester
Profs interesting rating	77
Profs accessible rating	80
Student/faculty ratio	13:1
Most common reg class size	20–29 students
Most common lab size	10–19 students

MOST POPULAR MAJORS
education
psychology
business/commerce

SELECTIVITY

# of applicants	3,870
% of applicants accepted	70
% of acceptees attending	23

FRESHMAN PROFILE

Range SAT Critical Reading	520–580
Range SAT Math	530–590
Range ACT Composite	21–26
Minimum paper TOEFL	550
Minimum computer TOEFL	230
Average HS GPA	3.3
% graduated top 10% of class	15
% graduated top 25% of class	45
% graduated top 50% of class	88

DEADLINES

Early action	
Deadline	11/15
Notification	12/20

Regular
Deadline — 2/1
Notification — 4/1
Nonfall registration? — yes

FINANCIAL FACTS

Annual tuition	$29,310
Room and board	$10,190
Required fees	$700
Books and supplies	$800
% frosh rec. need-based scholarship or grant aid	82
% UG rec. need-based scholarship or grant aid	64
% frosh rec. non-need-based scholarship or grant aid	5
% UG rec. non-need-based scholarship or grant aid	15
% frosh rec. need-based self-help aid	82
% UG rec. need-based self-help aid	62
% frosh rec. athletic scholarships	6
% UG rec. athletic scholarships	12
% frosh rec. any financial aid	86
% UG rec. any financial aid	70
% UG borrow to pay for school	72
Average cumulative indebtedness	$25,000

MESSIAH COLLEGE

CAMPUS LIFE

Fire Safety Rating	**75**
Green Rating	**85**
Type of school	private
Environment	village

STUDENTS

Total undergrad enrollment	2,798
% male/female	37/63
% from out of state	45
% from public high school	75
% live on campus	86
% African American	2
% Asian	2
% Caucasian	87
% Hispanic	1
% international	2
# of countries represented	25

ACADEMICS

Calendar	semester
Profs interesting rating	81
Profs accessible rating	86
Student/faculty ratio	13:1
Most common reg class size	10–19 students

MOST POPULAR MAJORS

elementary education and teaching
psychology
nursing/registered nurse (rn, asn, bsn, msn)

SELECTIVITY

# of applicants	2,496
% of applicants accepted	79
% of acceptees attending	37

FRESHMAN PROFILE

Range SAT Critical Reading	520–640
Range SAT Math	520–640
Range SAT Writing	510–630
Range ACT Composite	22–27
Minimum paper TOEFL	550
Minimum computer TOEFL	213
Minimum web-based TOEFL	80
Average HS GPA	3.71
% graduated top 10% of class	35
% graduated top 25% of class	67
% graduated top 50% of class	90

DEADLINES

Regular
Priority — 5/1
Notification — rolling
Nonfall registration? — yes

FINANCIAL FACTS

Annual tuition	$23,710
Room and board	$7,340
Required fees	$710
Books and supplies	$900
% frosh rec. need-based scholarship or grant aid	71
% UG rec. need-based scholarship or grant aid	69
% frosh rec. non-need-based scholarship or grant aid	10
% UG rec. non-need-based scholarship or grant aid	7
% frosh rec. need-based self-help aid	56
% UG rec. need-based self-help aid	56
% frosh rec. any financial aid	99
% UG rec. any financial aid	97
% UG borrow to pay for school	73
Average cumulative indebtedness	$33,283

MIDDLEBURY COLLEGE

CAMPUS LIFE

Fire Safety Rating	**60***
Green Rating	**60***
Type of school	private
Environment	village

STUDENTS

Total undergrad enrollment	2,475
% male/female	49/51
% from out of state	93
% from public high school	52
% live on campus	97
% African American	3
% Asian	8
% Caucasian	67
% Hispanic	6
% international	10
# of countries represented	75

ACADEMICS

Calendar	4/1/4
Student/faculty ratio	9:1
Profs interesting rating	99
Profs accessible rating	96
Most common reg class size	10–19 students

MOST POPULAR MAJORS

English language and literature
psychology
economics

SELECTIVITY

# of applicants	7,180
% of applicants accepted	21
% of acceptees attending	44
# accepting a place on wait list	603
# of early decision applicants	1,011
% accepted early decision	25

FRESHMAN PROFILE

Range SAT Critical Reading	650–750
Range SAT Math	650–740
Range SAT Writing	650–730
Range ACT Composite	29–33
Average HS GPA	4
% graduated top 10% of class	82
% graduated top 25% of class	97
% graduated top 50% of class	100

DEADLINES

Early decision
Deadline — 11/1
Notification — 12/15
Regular
Deadline — 1/1
Notification — 4/1
Nonfall registration? — yes

FINANCIAL FACTS

Comprehensive fee	$46,910
Books and supplies	$750
% frosh rec. need-based scholarship or grant aid	45

% UG rec. need-based scholarship or grant aid	41
% frosh rec. need-based self-help aid	43
% UG rec. need-based self-help aid	38
% UG borrow to pay for school	39.2
Average cumulative indebtedness	$20,808

MISERICORDIA UNIVERSITY

CAMPUS LIFE

Fire Safety Rating	**66**
Green Rating	**60***
Type of school	private
Affiliation	Roman Catholic
Environment	town

STUDENTS

Total undergrad enrollment	2,003
% male/female	26/74
% from out of state	17
% from public high school	85
% live on campus	38
% African American	1
% Asian	1
% Caucasian	96
% Hispanic	1
% Native American	1
# of countries represented	1

ACADEMICS

Calendar	semester
Profs interesting rating	92
Profs accessible rating	84
Student/faculty ratio	12:1
Most common reg class size	10–19 students
Most common lab size	10–19 students

MOST POPULAR MAJORS
nursing/registered nurse (rn, asn, bsn, msn)
physical therapy/therapist
business/commerce

SELECTIVITY

# of applicants	1,289
% of applicants accepted	74
% of acceptees attending	39
# accepting a place on wait list	30
% admitted from wait list	20

FRESHMAN PROFILE

Range SAT Critical Reading	455–550
Range SAT Math	460–560
Range ACT Composite	19–24
Minimum paper TOEFL	500

Minimum computer TOEFL	75
Average HS GPA	3.21
% graduated top 10% of class	16
% graduated top 25% of class	53
% graduated top 50% of class	77

DEADLINES

Notification	rolling
Nonfall registration?	yes

FINANCIAL FACTS

Annual tuition	$21,990
Room and board	$9,650
Required fees	$1,120
Books and supplies	$850
% frosh rec. need-based scholarship or grant aid	84
% UG rec. need-based scholarship or grant aid	82
% frosh rec. non-need-based scholarship or grant aid	12
% UG rec. non-need-based scholarship or grant aid	13
% frosh rec. need-based self-help aid	70
% UG rec. need-based self-help aid	69
% frosh rec. any financial aid	99
% UG rec. any financial aid	98
% UG borrow to pay for school	77
Average cumulative indebtedness	$20,006

MONMOUTH UNIVERSITY

CAMPUS LIFE

Fire Safety Rating	**87**
Green Rating	**75**
Type of school	private
Environment	village

STUDENTS

Total undergrad enrollment	4,694
% male/female	42/58
% from out of state	10
% from public high school	86
% live on campus	44
% in (# of) fraternities	9 (7)
% in (# of) sororities	11 (6)
% African American	4
% Asian	2
% Caucasian	75
% Hispanic	5
# of countries represented	14

ACADEMICS

Calendar	semester
Student/faculty ratio	16:1
Profs interesting rating	74
Profs accessible rating	75

Most common reg class size	20–29 students

MOST POPULAR MAJORS
education
business administration and management
communication studies/speech communication and rhetoric

SELECTIVITY

# of applicants	6,982
% of applicants accepted	57
% of acceptees attending	24

FRESHMAN PROFILE

Range SAT Critical Reading	490–560
Range SAT Math	500–580
Range SAT Writing	480–570
Range ACT Composite	21–24
Minimum paper TOEFL	550
Minimum computer TOEFL	213
Minimum web-based TOEFL	79
Average HS GPA	3.17
% graduated top 10% of class	11
% graduated top 25% of class	39
% graduated top 50% of class	72

DEADLINES

Early action	
Deadline	12/1
Notification	1/15
Regular	
Priority	12/1
Deadline	3/1
Nonfall registration?	yes

FINANCIAL FACTS

Annual tuition	$22,406
Room and board	$8,904
Required fees	$628
Books and supplies	$1,000
% frosh rec. need-based scholarship or grant aid	21
% UG rec. need-based scholarship or grant aid	28
% frosh rec. non-need-based scholarship or grant aid	56
% UG rec. non-need-based scholarship or grant aid	53
% frosh rec. need-based self-help aid	48
% UG rec. need-based self-help aid	49
% frosh rec. athletic scholarships	3
% UG rec. athletic scholarships	3
% frosh rec. any financial aid	65

% UG rec. any financial aid 92
% UG borrow to pay for school 76
Average cumulative
   indebtedness $34,484

MOORE COLLEGE OF ART & DESIGN

CAMPUS LIFE
Fire Safety Rating **60***
Green Rating **60***
Type of school private
Environment metropolis

STUDENTS
Total undergrad enrollment 507
% male/female /100
% from out of state 38
% from public high school 72
% live on campus 23
% African American 7
% Asian 4
% Caucasian 71
% Hispanic 5
% Native American 1
% international 2
# of countries represented 10

ACADEMICS
Calendar semester
Profs interesting rating 84
Profs accessible rating 62
Student/faculty ratio 8:1
Most common
   reg class size 10–19 students

MOST POPULAR MAJORS
fashion/apparel design
graphic design
fine/studio arts

SELECTIVITY
of applicants 461
% of applicants accepted 65
% of acceptees attending 42

FRESHMAN PROFILE
Minimum paper TOEFL 527
Minimum computer TOEFL 197
Average HS GPA 3.08

DEADLINES
Early decision
   Deadline 11/15
   Notification 12/1

Regular
   Priority 3/1
   Deadline 9/15
   Notification rolling
Nonfall registration? yes

FINANCIAL FACTS
Annual tuition $22,858
Room and board $9,346
Required fees $816
Books and supplies $2,160
% frosh rec. need-based
   scholarship or grant aid 78
% UG rec. need-based
   scholarship or grant aid 78
% frosh rec. non-need-based
   scholarship or grant aid 2
% UG rec. non-need-based
   scholarship or grant aid 2
% frosh rec. need-based self-help aid 72
% UG rec. need-based self-help aid 74
% UG rec. any financial aid 97
% UG borrow to pay for school 35
Average cumulative indebtedness $36,778

MORAVIAN COLLEGE

CAMPUS LIFE
Fire Safety Rating 82
Green Rating 78
Type of school private
Affiliation Moravian
Environment city

STUDENTS
Total undergrad enrollment 1,784
% male/female 42/58
% from out of state 43
% from public high school 73
% live on campus 71
% in (# of) fraternities 13 (3)
% in (# of) sororities 20 (4)
% African American 2
% Asian 2
% Caucasian 90
% Hispanic 3
% international 1
# of countries represented 15

ACADEMICS
Calendar semester
Student/faculty ratio 11:1
Profs interesting rating 83
Profs accessible rating 85
Most common
   reg class size 10–19 students
Most common
   lab size 10–19 students

MOST POPULAR MAJORS
psychology
sociology
business/commerce

SELECTIVITY
of applicants 2,189
% of applicants accepted 64
% of acceptees attending 29
# accepting a place on wait list 122
% admitted from wait list 25
# of early decision applicants 210
% accepted early decision 72

FRESHMAN PROFILE
Range SAT Critical Reading 500–600
Range SAT Math 500–610
Range SAT Writing 490–590
Minimum paper TOEFL 550
Minimum computer TOEFL 213
% graduated top 10% of class 29
% graduated top 25% of class 54
% graduated top 50% of class 87

DEADLINES
Early decision
   Deadline 2/1
Regular
   Deadline 3/1
Nonfall registration? yes

FINANCIAL FACTS
Annual tuition $29,547
Room and board $8,312
Required fees $515
Books and supplies $900
% frosh rec. need-based
   scholarship or grant aid 75
% UG rec. need-based
   scholarship or grant aid 74
% frosh rec. non-need-based
   scholarship or grant aid 6
% UG rec. non-need-based
   scholarship or grant aid 6
% frosh rec. need-based
   self-help aid 69
% UG rec. need-based
   self-help aid 68
% frosh rec.
   any financial aid 95
% UG rec. any financial aid 94

MOUNT HOLYOKE COLLEGE

CAMPUS LIFE

Fire Safety Rating	**80**
Green Rating	**82**
Type of school	private
Environment	village

STUDENTS

Total undergrad enrollment	2,185
% male/female	/100
% from out of state	75
% from public high school	61
% live on campus	93
% African American	5
% Asian	12
% Caucasian	50
% Hispanic	5
% Native American	1
% international	16
# of countries represented	64

ACADEMICS

Calendar	semester
Student/faculty ratio	10:1
Profs interesting rating	97
Profs accessible rating	93
Most common reg class size	10–19 students
Most common lab size	10–19 students

MOST POPULAR MAJORS
English language and literature
psychology
political science and government

SELECTIVITY

# of applicants	3,194
% of applicants accepted	52
% of acceptees attending	31
# accepting a place on wait list	178
# of early decision applicants	225
% accepted early decision	53

FRESHMAN PROFILE

Range SAT Critical Reading	640–730
Range SAT Math	590–690
Range SAT Writing	630–710
Range ACT Composite	26–30
Minimum paper TOEFL	600
Minimum computer TOEFL	250
Average HS GPA	3.67
% graduated top 10% of class	55
% graduated top 25% of class	86
% graduated top 50% of class	99

DEADLINES

Early decision	
Deadline	11/15
Notification	1/1
Regular	
Deadline	1/15
Notification	4/1
Nonfall registration?	yes

FINANCIAL FACTS

Annual tuition	$37,480
% frosh rec. need-based scholarship or grant aid	60
% UG rec. need-based scholarship or grant aid	63
% frosh rec. non-need-based scholarship or grant aid	55
% UG rec. non-need-based scholarship or grant aid	60
% frosh rec. need-based self-help aid	58
% UG rec. need-based self-help aid	60
% frosh rec. any financial aid	67
% UG rec. any financial aid	69
% UG borrow to pay for school	67
Average cumulative indebtedness	$22,270

MUHLENBERG COLLEGE

CAMPUS LIFE

Fire Safety Rating	**89**
Green Rating	**75**
Type of school	private
Affiliation	Lutheran
Environment	city

STUDENTS

Total undergrad enrollment	2,324
% male/female	42/58
% from out of state	70
% from public high school	70
% live on campus	92
% in (# of) fraternities	14 (4)
% in (# of) sororities	17 (4)
% African American	2
% Asian	2
% Caucasian	89
% Hispanic	4
# of countries represented	5

ACADEMICS

Calendar	semester
Student/faculty ratio	12:1
Profs interesting rating	84
Profs accessible rating	88
Most common reg class size	10–19 students
Most common lab size	10–19 students

MOST POPULAR MAJORS
psychology
drama and dramatics/theatre arts
business/commerce

SELECTIVITY

# of applicants	4,703
% of applicants accepted	37
% of acceptees attending	31
# accepting a place on wait list	541
% admitted from wait list	8
# of early decision applicants	420
% accepted early decision	67

FRESHMAN PROFILE

Range SAT Critical Reading	550–650
Range SAT Math	560–660
Range SAT Writing	560–660
Range ACT Composite	24–29
Minimum paper TOEFL	550
Minimum computer TOEFL	213
Average HS GPA	3.41
% graduated top 10% of class	47
% graduated top 25% of class	80
% graduated top 50% of class	98

DEADLINES

Early decision	
Deadline	2/1
Regular	
Deadline	2/15
Nonfall registration?	yes

FINANCIAL FACTS

Annual tuition	$32,850
Room and board	$7,790
Required fees	$240
Books and supplies	$800
% frosh rec. need-based scholarship or grant aid	41
% UG rec. need-based scholarship or grant aid	42
% frosh rec. non-need-based scholarship or grant aid	11
% UG rec. non-need-based scholarship or grant aid	10
% frosh rec. need-based self-help aid	30
% UG rec. need-based self-help aid	31
% frosh rec. any financial aid	73.8
% UG rec. any financial aid	72.1

% UG borrow to pay for school 81
Average cumulative
  indebtedness $18,052

NAZARETH COLLEGE

CAMPUS LIFE
Fire Safety Rating **60***
Green Rating **60***
Type of school private
Environment village

STUDENTS
Total undergrad enrollment 2,120
% male/female 25/75
% from out of state 5
% from public high school 90
% live on campus 55
% African American 5
% Asian 2
% Caucasian 84
% Hispanic 3
% international 1
# of countries represented 8

ACADEMICS
Calendar semester
Student/faculty ratio 12:1
Profs interesting rating 89
Profs accessible rating 88
Most common
  reg class size 10–19 students
Most common
  lab size 10–19 students

SELECTIVITY
of applicants 2,076
% of applicants accepted 74
% of acceptees attending 30
# of early decision applicants 33
% accepted early decision 94

FRESHMAN PROFILE
Range SAT Critical Reading 530–630
Range SAT Math 530–630
Range SAT Writing 510–610
Range ACT Composite 23–27
Minimum paper TOEFL 550
Minimum computer TOEFL 213
Average HS GPA 3.31
% graduated top 10% of class 30
% graduated top 25% of class 69

DEADLINES
Early decision
  Deadline 11/15
  Notification 12/15
Early action
  Deadline 12/15
  Notification 1/15
Regular
  Priority 12/15
  Deadline 2/15
  Notification 3/1
Nonfall registration? yes

FINANCIAL FACTS
Annual tuition $21,900
Room and board $9,500
Required fees $980
Books and supplies $900
% frosh rec. need-based
  scholarship or grant aid 76
% UG rec. need-based
  scholarship or grant aid 77
% frosh rec. non-need-based
  scholarship or grant aid 14
% UG rec. non-need-based
  scholarship or grant aid 10
% frosh rec. need-based
  self-help aid 60
% UG rec. need-based
  self-help aid 65
% UG borrow to pay for school 77
Average cumulative
  indebtedness $26,795

NEUMANN COLLEGE

CAMPUS LIFE
Fire Safety Rating **99**
Green Rating **60***
Type of school private
Affiliation Roman Catholic
Environment town

STUDENTS
Total undergrad enrollment 2,499
% male/female 35/65
% from out of state 29
% from public high school 60
% live on campus 46
% African American 13
% Asian 1
% Caucasian 64
% Hispanic 2
% international 2
# of countries represented 7

ACADEMICS
Calendar semester
Profs interesting rating 76
Profs accessible rating 77
Student/faculty ratio 14:1

Most common
  reg class size 20–29 students
Most common
  lab size 10–19 students

MOST POPULAR MAJORS
elementary education and teaching
criminal justice/law enforcement administration
nursing/registered nurse (rn, asn, bsn, msn)

SELECTIVITY
of applicants 2,490
% of applicants accepted 95
% of acceptees attending 23

FRESHMAN PROFILE
Range SAT Critical Reading 400–490
Range SAT Math 400–490
Minimum paper TOEFL 550
Minimum computer TOEFL 213
Average HS GPA 3.25
% graduated top 10% of class 30
% graduated top 25% of class 50
% graduated top 50% of class 90

DEADLINES
Nonfall registration? yes

FINANCIAL FACTS
Annual tuition $18,846
Room and board $8,838
Required fees $640
Books and supplies $1,500
% frosh rec. need-based
  scholarship or grant aid 77
% UG rec. need-based
  scholarship or grant aid 74
% frosh rec. need-based self-help aid 77
% UG rec. need-based self-help aid 74
% frosh rec. any financial aid 95
% UG rec. any financial aid 90
% UG borrow to pay for school 70
Average cumulative indebtedness $25,000

NEW JERSEY INSTITUTE OF TECHNOLOGY

CAMPUS LIFE
Fire Safety Rating **91**
Green Rating **60***
Type of school public
Environment metropolis

STUDENTS
Total undergrad enrollment 4,967
% male/female 81/19
% from out of state 8

% from public high school	80
% live on campus	25
% in (# of) fraternities	7 (17)
% in (# of) sororities	5 (8)
% African American	3
% Asian	5
% Caucasian	10
% Hispanic	5
% international	1
# of countries represented	98

ACADEMICS

Calendar	semester
Student/faculty ratio	12:1
Profs interesting rating	61
Profs accessible rating	61
Most common	
reg class size	20–29 students

MOST POPULAR MAJORS
information technology
mechanical engineering

SELECTIVITY

# of applicants	3,027
% of applicants accepted	64
% of acceptees attending	38

FRESHMAN PROFILE

Range SAT Critical Reading	480–580
Range SAT Math	550–650
Range SAT Writing	470–570
Minimum paper TOEFL	550
Minimum computer TOEFL	213
% graduated top 10% of class	28
% graduated top 25% of class	56
% graduated top 50% of class	83

DEADLINES

Regular	
Deadline	4/1
Notification	rolling
Nonfall registration?	yes

FINANCIAL FACTS

Annual in-state tuition	$9,700
Annual out-of-state tuition	$18,432
Room and board	$9,264
Required fees	$1,650
Books and supplies	$1,200
% frosh rec. need-based	
scholarship or grant aid	51
% UG rec. need-based	
scholarship or grant aid	42
% frosh rec. non-need-based	
scholarship or grant aid	25
% UG rec. non-need-based	
scholarship or grant aid	18

% frosh rec. need-based	
self-help aid	38
% UG rec. need-based	
self-help aid	34
% frosh rec.	
athletic scholarships	3
% UG rec. athletic scholarships	2
% frosh rec.	
any financial aid	70
% UG rec. any financial aid	70
Average cumulative	
indebtedness	$16,000

NEW YORK UNIVERSITY

CAMPUS LIFE

Fire Safety Rating	**74**
Green Rating	**96**
Type of school	private
Environment	metropolis

STUDENTS

Total undergrad enrollment	21,327
% male/female	38/62
% from out of state	64
% from public high school	71
% live on campus	53
% in (# of) fraternities	1 (15)
% in (# of) sororities	2 (10)
% African American	4
% Asian	19
% Caucasian	50
% Hispanic	8
% international	6
# of countries represented	127

ACADEMICS

Calendar	semester
Student/faculty ratio	11:1
Profs interesting rating	65
Profs accessible rating	62
Most common	
reg class size	10–19 students
Most common	
lab size	10–19 students

MOST POPULAR MAJORS
liberal arts and sciences/liberal
studies
drama and dramatics/theatre arts
finance

SELECTIVITY

# of applicants	34,389
% of applicants accepted	37
% of acceptees attending	39
# of early decision applicants	2,990
% accepted early decision	35

FRESHMAN PROFILE

Range SAT Critical Reading	620–710
Range SAT Math	620–720
Range SAT Writing	620–710
Range ACT Composite	28–31
Average HS GPA	3.6
% graduated top 10% of class	66
% graduated top 25% of class	93
% graduated top 50% of class	99

DEADLINES

Early decision	
Deadline	11/1
Notification	12/15
Regular	
Deadline	1/1
Notification	4/1
Nonfall registration?	yes

FINANCIAL FACTS

Annual tuition	$35,230
% frosh rec. need-based	
scholarship or grant aid	50
% UG rec. need-based	
scholarship or grant aid	48
% frosh rec. need-based	
self-help aid	50
% UG rec. need-based	
self-help aid	47
% frosh rec.	
any financial aid	60
% UG rec. any financial aid	74
% UG borrow to pay for school	58
Average cumulative	
indebtedness	$33,637

NIAGARA UNIVERSITY

CAMPUS LIFE

Fire Safety Rating	**60***
Green Rating	**60***
Type of school	private
Affiliation	Roman Catholic
Environment	town

STUDENTS

Total undergrad enrollment	3,259
% male/female	38/62
% from out of state	7
% live on campus	52
% in (# of) fraternities	4 (3)
% in (# of) sororities	2 (2)
% African American	4
% Asian	1
% Caucasian	72
% Hispanic	2

% international	12
# of countries represented	12

ACADEMICS
Calendar	semester
Profs interesting rating	81
Profs accessible rating	83
Student/faculty ratio	14:1
Most common reg class size	10–19 students
Most common lab size	10–19 students

MOST POPULAR MAJORS
teacher education, multiple levels
criminal justice/
law enforcement administration
commerce
hotel planning
psychology

SELECTIVITY
# of applicants	3,078
% of applicants accepted	77
% of acceptees attending	31

FRESHMAN PROFILE
Range SAT Critical Reading	480–590
Range SAT Math	470–570
Range ACT Composite	19–25
Minimum paper TOEFL	500
Minimum computer TOEFL	173
Average HS GPA	3.3
% graduated top 10% of class	14
% graduated top 25% of class	42
% graduated top 50% of class	77

DEADLINES
Early action	
Deadline	12/10
Regular	
Deadline	8/1
Nonfall registration?	yes

FINANCIAL FACTS
Annual tuition	$22,500
Room and board	$9,750
Required fees	$950
Books and supplies	$900
% frosh rec. need-based scholarship or grant aid	81
% UG rec. need-based scholarship or grant aid	70
% frosh rec. non-need-based scholarship or grant aid	22
% UG rec. non-need-based scholarship or grant aid	19
% frosh rec. need-based self-help aid	80
% UG rec. need-based self-help aid	64
% frosh rec. athletic scholarships	9

% UG rec. athletic scholarships	5
% frosh rec. any financial aid	82
% UG rec. any financial aid	79
% UG borrow to pay for school	82
Average cumulative indebtedness	$23,267

NORTHEASTERN UNIVERSITY

CAMPUS LIFE
Fire Safety Rating	**87**
Green Rating	**87**
Type of school	private
Environment	metropolis

STUDENTS
Total undergrad enrollment	15,339
% male/female	49/51
% from out of state	65
% live on campus	48
% in (# of) fraternities	4 (9)
% in (# of) sororities	4 (8)
% African American	6
% Asian	8
% Caucasian	61
% Hispanic	5
% international	5
# of countries represented	94

ACADEMICS
Calendar	semester
Student/faculty ratio	16:1
Profs interesting rating	67
Profs accessible rating	75
Most common reg class size	10–19 students

MOST POPULAR MAJORS
engineering
health services/allied health/health sciences
business/commerce

SELECTIVITY
# of applicants	30,349
% of applicants accepted	39
% of acceptees attending	24
# accepting a place on wait list	1,342
% admitted from wait list	27

FRESHMAN PROFILE
Range SAT Critical Reading	570–660
Range SAT Math	600–680
Range ACT Composite	25–29
Minimum paper TOEFL	550
Minimum computer TOEFL	213
% graduated top 10% of class	42
% graduated top 25% of class	77
% graduated top 50% of class	96

DEADLINES
Early action	
Deadline	11/15
Notification	12/31
Regular	
Deadline	1/15
Nonfall registration?	yes

FINANCIAL FACTS
Annual tuition	$31,500
Room and board	$11,420
Required fees	$399
Books and supplies	$900
% frosh rec. need-based scholarship or grant aid	55
% UG rec. need-based scholarship or grant aid	52
% frosh rec. non-need-based scholarship or grant aid	9
% UG rec. non-need-based scholarship or grant aid	5
% frosh rec. need-based self-help aid	47
% UG rec. need-based self-help aid	48
% frosh rec. athletic scholarships	2
% UG rec. athletic scholarships	2
% frosh rec. any financial aid	90
% UG rec. any financial aid	83

PACE UNIVERSITY

CAMPUS LIFE
Fire Safety Rating	**82**
Green Rating	**71**
Type of school	private
Environment	metropolis

STUDENTS
Total undergrad enrollment	7,178
% male/female	40/60
% from out of state	35
% from public high school	70
% live on campus	34
% in (# of) fraternities	5 (11)
% in (# of) sororities	5 (8)
% African American	9
% Asian	8
% Caucasian	41
% Hispanic	9
% international	3
# of countries represented	102

ACADEMICS

Calendar	semester
Profs interesting rating	70
Profs accessible rating	68
Student/faculty ratio	14:1
Most common	
reg class size	10–19 students
Most common	
lab size	10–19 students

MOST POPULAR MAJORS
finance
accounting
nursing/registered nurse (rn, asn, bsn, msn)

SELECTIVITY

# of applicants	7,444
% of applicants accepted	78
% of acceptees attending	27

FRESHMAN PROFILE

Range SAT Critical Reading	480–580
Range SAT Math	490–590
Range ACT Composite	20–26
Minimum paper TOEFL	570
Minimum computer TOEFL	230
Average HS GPA	3.3
% graduated top 10% of class	12
% graduated top 25% of class	38
% graduated top 50% of class	74

DEADLINES

Early action	
Deadline	11/30
Notification	1/1
Regular	
Priority	3/1
Notification	rolling
Nonfall registration?	yes

FINANCIAL FACTS

Annual tuition	$30,632
Room and board	$11,180
Required fees	$743
Books and supplies	$800
% frosh rec. need-based	
scholarship or grant aid	73
% UG rec. need-based	
scholarship or grant aid	64
% frosh rec. non-need-based	
scholarship or grant aid	4
% UG rec. non-need-based	
scholarship or grant aid	3
% frosh rec. need-based self-help aid	65
% UG rec. need-based self-help aid	60
% frosh rec. any financial aid	87
% UG rec. any financial aid	79
% UG borrow to pay for school	70
Average cumulative indebtedness	$27,016

PENNSYLVANIA STATE UNIVERSITY— UNIVERSITY PARK

CAMPUS LIFE

Fire Safety Rating	**94**
Green Rating	**97**
Type of school	public
Environment	town

STUDENTS

Total undergrad enrollment	35,876
% male/female	55/45
% from out of state	24
% live on campus	36
% in (# of) fraternities	12 (53)
% in (# of) sororities	11 (34)
% African American	4
% Asian	5
% Caucasian	84
% Hispanic	4
% international	2
# of countries represented	121

ACADEMICS

Calendar	semester
Student/faculty ratio	17:1
Profs interesting rating	65
Profs accessible rating	65
Most common	
reg class size	20–29 students
Most common	
lab size	20–29 students

MOST POPULAR MAJORS
engineering
business administration and
management

SELECTIVITY

# of applicants	39,551
% of applicants accepted	51
% of acceptees attending	32
# accepting a place on wait list	1,704
% admitted from wait list	80

FRESHMAN PROFILE

Range SAT Critical Reading	530–630
Range SAT Math	560–670
Minimum paper TOEFL	550
Minimum computer TOEFL	213
Minimum web-based TOEFL	80
Average HS GPA	3.58
% graduated top 10% of class	44.65
% graduated top 25% of class	81.3
% graduated top 50% of class	97.44

DEADLINES

Regular	
Priority	11/30
Notification	rolling
Nonfall registration?	yes

FINANCIAL FACTS

Annual in-state tuition	$12,284
Annual out-of-state tuition	$23,152
Room and board	$7,180
Required fees	$560
Books and supplies	$1,168
% frosh rec. need-based	
scholarship or grant aid	24
% UG rec. need-based	
scholarship or grant aid	30
% frosh rec. non-need-based	
scholarship or grant aid	20
% UG rec. non-need-based	
scholarship or grant aid	17
% frosh rec. need-based	
self-help aid	37
% UG rec. need-based	
self-help aid	42
% frosh rec.	
athletic scholarships	2
% UG rec. athletic scholarships	2
% frosh rec.	
any financial aid	75
% UG rec. any financial aid	73
% UG borrow to pay for school	67
Average cumulative	
indebtedness	$26,300

POLYTECHNIC UNIVERSITY— BROOKLYN

CAMPUS LIFE

Fire Safety Rating	**60***
Green Rating	**60***
Type of school	private
Environment	metropolis

STUDENTS

Total undergrad enrollment	1,467
% male/female	81/19
% from out of state	7
% from public high school	82
% live on campus	20
% in (# of) fraternities	4 (3)
% in (# of) sororities	2 (1)
% African American	12
% Asian	30
% Caucasian	27
% Hispanic	12

% international 13
# of countries represented 45

ACADEMICS

Calendar   semester
Profs interesting rating   64
Profs accessible rating   65
Student/faculty ratio   13:1
Most common
  reg class size   20–29 students
Most common
  lab size   10–19 students

MOST POPULAR MAJORS

computer and information sciences
computer engineering
electrical, electronics and communications
engineering

SELECTIVITY

of applicants   1,484
% of applicants accepted   72
% of acceptees attending   31

FRESHMAN PROFILE

Range SAT Critical Reading   470–600
Range SAT Math   560–675
Minimum paper TOEFL   550
Minimum computer TOEFL   217
Average HS GPA   3.3
% graduated top 10% of class   31
% graduated top 25% of class   61
% graduated top 50% of class   89

DEADLINES

Nonfall registration?   yes

FINANCIAL FACTS

Annual tuition $31,538
% frosh rec. need-based
  scholarship or grant aid   63
% UG rec. need-based
  scholarship or grant aid   66
% frosh rec. non-need-based
  scholarship or grant aid   69
% UG rec. non-need-based
  scholarship or grant aid   61
% frosh rec. need-based self-help aid   67
% UG rec. need-based self-help aid   69
% frosh rec. any financial aid   99
% UG rec. any financial aid   92
% UG borrow to pay for school   75.4
Average cumulative indebtedness $25,012

PRINCETON UNIVERSITY

CAMPUS LIFE

Fire Safety Rating   **60***
Green Rating   **94**
Type of school   private
Environment   town

STUDENTS

Total undergrad enrollment   4,833
% male/female   53/47
% from out of state   84
% from public high school   58
% live on campus   98
% African American   9
% Asian   14
% Caucasian   52
% Hispanic   8
% Native American   1
% international   9

ACADEMICS

Calendar   semester
Student/faculty ratio   8:1
Profs interesting rating   87
Profs accessible rating   96
Most common
  reg class size   10–19 students
Most common
  lab size   10–19 students

MOST POPULAR MAJORS

economics
political science and government
history

SELECTIVITY

of applicants   18,942
% of applicants accepted   10
% of acceptees attending   68
# accepting a place on wait list   483
% admitted from wait list   10

FRESHMAN PROFILE

Range SAT Critical Reading   690–790
Range SAT Math   700–790
Range SAT Writing   690–780
Range ACT Composite   30–34
Minimum paper TOEFL   600
Minimum computer TOEFL   250
Average HS GPA   3.87
% graduated top 10% of class   96
% graduated top 25% of class   99
% graduated top 50% of class   100

DEADLINES

Regular
  Deadline   1/1
  Notification   4/1
Nonfall registration?   no

FINANCIAL FACTS

Annual tuition $34,290
Room and board $11,405
Books and supplies $1,200
% frosh rec. need-based
  scholarship or grant aid   55
% UG rec. need-based
  scholarship or grant aid   52
% frosh rec. need-based
  self-help aid   55
% UG rec. need-based
  self-help aid   52
% frosh rec.
  any financial aid   55
% UG rec. any financial aid   53
% UG borrow to pay for school   22
Average cumulative
  indebtedness $5,592

PROVIDENCE COLLEGE

CAMPUS LIFE

Fire Safety Rating   **97**
Green Rating   **75**
Type of school   private
Affiliation   Roman Catholic
Environment   city

STUDENTS

Total undergrad enrollment   3,959
% male/female   44/56
% from out of state   87
% from public high school   55
% live on campus   78
% African American   2
% Asian   2
% Caucasian   83
% Hispanic   2
% international   1
# of countries represented   14

ACADEMICS

Calendar   semester
Student/faculty ratio   12:1
Profs interesting rating   72
Profs accessible rating   78
Most common
  reg class size   20–29 students
Most common
  lab size   10–19 students

MOST POPULAR MAJORS
business administration and management
marketing/marketing management
biology/biological sciences

SELECTIVITY
# of applicants	9,802
% of applicants accepted	41
% of acceptees attending	24
# accepting a place on wait list	879
% admitted from wait list	13

FRESHMAN PROFILE
Range SAT Critical Reading	530–630
Range SAT Math	540–640
Range SAT Writing	540–650
Range ACT Composite	23–28
Minimum paper TOEFL	550
Minimum computer TOEFL	213
Minimum web-based TOEFL	79
Average HS GPA	3.47
% graduated top 10% of class	45
% graduated top 25% of class	83
% graduated top 50% of class	98

DEADLINES
Early action	
Deadline	11/1
Notification	1/1
Regular	
Deadline	1/15
Notification	4/1
Nonfall registration?	yes

FINANCIAL FACTS
Annual tuition	$28,920
Room and board	$10,335
Required fees	$579
Books and supplies	$800
% frosh rec. need-based scholarship or grant aid	49
% UG rec. need-based scholarship or grant aid	47
% frosh rec. non-need-based scholarship or grant aid	8
% UG rec. non-need-based scholarship or grant aid	8
% frosh rec. need-based self-help aid	54
% UG rec. need-based self-help aid	49
% frosh rec. athletic scholarships	4
% UG rec. athletic scholarships	5
% frosh rec. any financial aid	70
% UG rec. any financial aid	66
% UG borrow to pay for school	72

Average cumulative indebtedness	$35,216

QUINNIPIAC UNIVERSITY

CAMPUS LIFE
Fire Safety Rating	**86**
Green Rating	**60***
Type of school	private
Environment	town

STUDENTS
Total undergrad enrollment	5,650
% male/female	38/62
% from out of state	70
% from public high school	70
% live on campus	75
% in (# of) fraternities	6 (2)
% in (# of) sororities	8 (3)
% African American	3
% Asian	2
% Caucasian	80
% Hispanic	5
% international	1
# of countries represented	23

ACADEMICS
Calendar	semester
Student/faculty ratio	14:1
Profs interesting rating	76
Profs accessible rating	74
Most common reg class size	10–19 students
Most common lab size	10–19 students

MOST POPULAR MAJORS
psychology
physical therapy/therapist
business/commerce

SELECTIVITY
# of applicants	12,060
% of applicants accepted	47
% of acceptees attending	24
# accepting a place on wait list	562
% admitted from wait list	10

FRESHMAN PROFILE
Range SAT Critical Reading	540–610
Range SAT Math	560–630
Range ACT Composite	23–27
Minimum paper TOEFL	550
Minimum computer TOEFL	213
Minimum web-based TOEFL	77
Average HS GPA	3.4
% graduated top 10% of class	25
% graduated top 25% of class	66
% graduated top 50% of class	95

DEADLINES
Regular	
Priority	2/1
Notification	rolling
Nonfall registration?	yes

FINANCIAL FACTS
Annual tuition	$29,700
Room and board	$12,200
Required fees	$1,200
Books and supplies	$800
% frosh rec. need-based scholarship or grant aid	55
% UG rec. need-based scholarship or grant aid	56
% frosh rec. non-need-based scholarship or grant aid	26
% UG rec. non-need-based scholarship or grant aid	21
% frosh rec. need-based self-help aid	46
% UG rec. need-based self-help aid	50
% frosh rec. athletic scholarships	4
% UG rec. athletic scholarships	4
% frosh rec. any financial aid	70
% UG rec. any financial aid	68
% UG borrow to pay for school	71
Average cumulative indebtedness	$35,086

RAMAPO COLLEGE OF NEW JERSEY

CAMPUS LIFE
Fire Safety Rating	**90**
Green Rating	**72**
Type of school	public
Environment	town

STUDENTS
Total undergrad enrollment	5,131
% male/female	53/47
% from out of state	6
% live on campus	62
% in (# of) fraternities	5 (9)
% in (# of) sororities	8 (10)
% African American	6
% Asian	4
% Caucasian	78
% Hispanic	9
% international	3
# of countries represented	52

ACADEMICS

Calendar	semester
Profs interesting rating	71
Profs accessible rating	71
Student/faculty ratio	18:1
Most common	
reg class size	20–29 students
Most common	
lab size	10–19 students

MOST POPULAR MAJORS
psychology
business administration and management
nursing science (ms, phd)

SELECTIVITY

# of applicants	4,983
% of applicants accepted	49
% of acceptees attending	37
# accepting a place on wait list	198
% admitted from wait list	87

FRESHMAN PROFILE

Range SAT Critical Reading	520–620
Range SAT Math	540–630
Range SAT Writing	530–620
Minimum paper TOEFL	550
Minimum computer TOEFL	213
Minimum web-based TOEFL	90
Average HS GPA	3.5
% graduated top 10% of class	35
% graduated top 25% of class	67
% graduated top 50% of class	96

DEADLINES

Early action	
Deadline	11/15
Notification	12/15
Regular	
Deadline	3/1
Nonfall registration?	yes

FINANCIAL FACTS

Annual in-state tuition	$6,904
Annual out-of-state tuition	$12,475
Room and board	$10,310
Required fees	$3,061
Books and supplies	$1,200
% frosh rec. need-based	
scholarship or grant aid	24
% UG rec. need-based	
scholarship or grant aid	25
% frosh rec. non-need-based	
scholarship or grant aid	19
% UG rec. non-need-based	
scholarship or grant aid	14
% frosh rec. need-based self-help aid	43
% UG rec. need-based self-help aid	43
% frosh rec. any financial aid	79
% UG rec. any financial aid	72
% UG borrow to pay for school	55
Average cumulative indebtedness	$20,513

REGIS COLLEGE

CAMPUS LIFE

Fire Safety Rating	**83**
Green Rating	**60***
Type of school	private
Affiliation	Roman Catholic
Environment	village

STUDENTS

Total undergrad enrollment	934
% male/female	9/91
% from out of state	10
% from public high school	71
% live on campus	48
% African American	19
% Asian	6
% Caucasian	37
% Hispanic	9
% international	1
# of countries represented	34

ACADEMICS

Calendar	semester
Profs interesting rating	78
Profs accessible rating	67
Student/faculty ratio	14:1
Most common	
reg class size	10–19 students
Most common	
lab size	10–19 students

MOST POPULAR MAJORS
biology/biological sciences
nursing/registered nurse (rn, asn, bsn, msn)
communication studies/speech communication and rhetoric

SELECTIVITY

# of applicants	1,283
% of applicants accepted	77
% of acceptees attending	27

FRESHMAN PROFILE

Range SAT Critical Reading	400–500
Range SAT Math	400–500
Range SAT Writing	400–510
Range ACT Composite	16–20
Minimum paper TOEFL	550
Minimum computer TOEFL	213
Minimum web-based TOEFL	79–80
Average HS GPA	2.77
% graduated top 10% of class	3
% graduated top 25% of class	24
% graduated top 50% of class	67

DEADLINES

Regular	
Priority	2/15
Notification	rolling
Nonfall registration?	yes

FINANCIAL FACTS

Annual tuition	$27,800
% frosh rec. need-based	
scholarship or grant aid	78
% UG rec. need-based	
scholarship or grant aid	75
% frosh rec. non-need-based	
scholarship or grant aid	41
% UG rec. non-need-based	
scholarship or grant aid	42
% frosh rec. need-based self-help aid	81
% UG rec. need-based self-help aid	79
% frosh rec. any financial aid	84
% UG rec. any financial aid	81
% UG borrow to pay for school	85
Average cumulative indebtedness	$29,794

RENSSELAER POLYTECHNIC INSTITUTE

CAMPUS LIFE

Fire Safety Rating	**73**
Green Rating	**88**
Type of school	private
Environment	city

STUDENTS

Total undergrad enrollment	5,119
% male/female	73/27
% from out of state	57
% from public high school	78
% live on campus	53
% in (# of) fraternities	25 (32)
% in (# of) sororities	18 (5)
% African American	4
% Asian	10
% Caucasian	75
% Hispanic	6
% international	2
# of countries represented	62

ACADEMICS

Academic Rating	**79**
Calendar	semester
Student/faculty ratio	14:1
Profs interesting rating	61
Profs accessible rating	73
Most common	
reg class size	20–29 students
Most common	
lab size	20–29 students

MOST POPULAR MAJORS
computer engineering
electrical, electronics and communications
engineering
business/commerce

RICHARD STOCKTON
COLLEGE OF NEW JERSEY

CAMPUS LIFE
Fire Safety Rating **89**
Green Rating **60***
Type of school public
Environment town

STUDENTS
Total undergrad enrollment 6,600
% male/female 41/59
% from out of state 1
% from public high school 74
% live on campus 31
% in (# of) fraternities 5 (11)
% in (# of) sororities 5 (10)
% African American 8
% Asian 5
% Caucasian 78
% Hispanic 6
# of countries represented 10

ACADEMICS
Calendar semester
Profs interesting rating 76
Profs accessible rating 73
Student/faculty ratio 19:1
Most common
reg class size 20–29 students
Most common
lab size less than 10 students
MOST POPULAR MAJORS
psychology
criminology
business administration and management

SELECTIVITY
of applicants 3,962
% of applicants accepted 54
% of acceptees attending 37

FRESHMAN PROFILE
Range SAT Critical Reading 480–570
Range SAT Math 500–580
Range SAT Writing 471–560
Range ACT Composite 18–21
Minimum paper TOEFL 550
Minimum computer TOEFL 217
% graduated top 10% of class 18

% graduated top 25% of class 48
% graduated top 50% of class 93

DEADLINES
Early action
Deadline 2/1
Notification 3/1
Regular
Priority 2/1
Deadline 5/1
Notification rolling
Nonfall registration? yes

FINANCIAL FACTS
Annual in-state tuition $5,956
Annual out-of-state tuition $10,550
Room and board $9,077
Required fees $3,135
Books and supplies $1,200
% frosh rec. need-based
scholarship or grant aid 31
% UG rec. need-based
scholarship or grant aid 29
% frosh rec. non-need-based
scholarship or grant aid 21
% UG rec. non-need-based
scholarship or grant aid 11
% frosh rec. need-based self-help aid 48
% UG rec. need-based self-help aid 47
% frosh rec. any financial aid 82
% UG rec. any financial aid 71

RIDER UNIVERSITY

CAMPUS LIFE
Fire Safety Rating **60***
Green Rating **71**
Type of school private
Environment village

STUDENTS
Total undergrad enrollment 4,733
% male/female 40/60
% from out of state 22
% live on campus 65
% in (# of) fraternities 8 (5)
% in (# of) sororities 9 (8)
% African American 9
% Asian 3
% Caucasian 73
% Hispanic 5
% international 3
# of countries represented 50

ACADEMICS
Calendar semester
Student/faculty ratio 13:1
Profs interesting rating 76

Profs accessible rating 75
Most common
reg class size 10–19 students
Most common
lab size 10–19 students
MOST POPULAR MAJORS
elementary education and teaching
business/commerce
accounting
psychology
communication

SELECTIVITY
of applicants 6,213
% of applicants accepted 75
% of acceptees attending 21
# accepting a place on wait list 93
% admitted from wait list 12

FRESHMAN PROFILE
Range SAT Critical Reading 470–570
Range SAT Math 480–590
Range SAT Writing 470–570
Range ACT Composite 20–24
Average HS GPA 3.24
% graduated top 10% of class 12
% graduated top 25% of class 38
% graduated top 50% of class 75

DEADLINES
Early decision
Deadline 11/15
Notification 12/15
Early action
Deadline 12/15
Notification 1/15
Regular
Notification rolling
Nonfall registration? yes

FINANCIAL FACTS
Annual tuition $25,650
% frosh rec. need-based
scholarship or grant aid 66
% UG rec. need-based
scholarship or grant aid 62
% frosh rec. non-need-based
scholarship or grant aid 9
% UG rec. non-need-based
scholarship or grant aid 8
% frosh rec. need-based
self-help aid 51
% UG rec. need-based
self-help aid 48
% frosh rec.
athletic scholarships 8
% UG rec. athletic scholarships 6

% frosh rec.	
any financial aid	85
% UG rec. any financial aid	66
% UG borrow to pay for school	76
Average cumulative indebtedness	$32,132

ROBERTS WESLEYAN COLLEGE

CAMPUS LIFE

Fire Safety Rating	**60***
Green Rating	**60***
Type of school	private
Affiliation	Free Methodist
Environment	city

STUDENTS

Total undergrad enrollment	1,312
% male/female	31/69
% from out of state	8
% live on campus	65
% African American	8
% Caucasian	77
% Hispanic	1
% international	2

ACADEMICS

Calendar	semester
Profs interesting rating	80
Profs accessible rating	79
Student/faculty ratio	14:1
Most common reg class size	10–19 students
Most common lab size	10–19 students

SELECTIVITY

# of applicants	1,531
% of applicants accepted	63
% of acceptees attending	27

FRESHMAN PROFILE

Range SAT Critical Reading	470–590
Range SAT Math	450–570
Range SAT Writing	460–580
Range ACT Composite	20–25
Minimum paper TOEFL	550
Minimum computer TOEFL	213
Average HS GPA	3.2
% graduated top 10% of class	23
% graduated top 25% of class	44
% graduated top 50% of class	86

DEADLINES

Regular	
Priority	2/1
Notification	rolling
Nonfall registration?	yes

FINANCIAL FACTS

Annual tuition	$21,766
Room and board	$8,228
Required fees	$1,156
Books and supplies	$1,000
% frosh rec. need-based scholarship or grant aid	92
% UG rec. need-based scholarship or grant aid	93
% frosh rec. non-need-based scholarship or grant aid	10
% UG rec. non-need-based scholarship or grant aid	5
% frosh rec. need-based self-help aid	85
% UG rec. need-based self-help aid	86
% frosh rec. athletic scholarships	3
% UG rec. athletic scholarships	3
% frosh rec. any financial aid	91
% UG rec. any financial aid	93
% UG borrow to pay for school	92
Average cumulative indebtedness	$16,489

ROCHESTER INSTITUTE OF TECHNOLOGY

CAMPUS LIFE

Fire Safety Rating	**60***
Green Rating	**60***
Type of school	private
Environment	city

STUDENTS

Total undergrad enrollment	12,779
% male/female	68/32
% from out of state	45
% live on campus	67
% in (# of) fraternities	5 (19)
% in (# of) sororities	5 (10)
# of countries represented	95

ACADEMICS

Calendar	quarter
Student/faculty ratio	14:1
Profs interesting rating	73
Profs accessible rating	78
Most common reg class size	10–19 students
Most common lab size	10–19 students

MOST POPULAR MAJORS

information technology
photography
business/commerce

SELECTIVITY

# of applicants	11,012
% of applicants accepted	65
% of acceptees attending	35
# accepting a place on wait list	174
% admitted from wait list	36
# of early decision applicants	1,130
% accepted early decision	69

FRESHMAN PROFILE

Range SAT Critical Reading	530–630
Range SAT Math	560–670
Range ACT Composite	24–29
% graduated top 10% of class	26
% graduated top 25% of class	59
% graduated top 50% of class	88

DEADLINES

Early decision	
Deadline	12/1
Notification	1/15
Regular	
Deadline	2/1
Notification	rolling
Nonfall registration?	yes

FINANCIAL FACTS

Annual tuition	$27,624
Room and board	$9,381
Required fees	$411
Books and supplies	$900
% frosh rec. need-based scholarship or grant aid	69
% UG rec. need-based scholarship or grant aid	64
% frosh rec. non-need-based scholarship or grant aid	20
% UG rec. non-need-based scholarship or grant aid	21
% frosh rec. need-based self-help aid	65
% UG rec. need-based self-help aid	60
% frosh rec. any financial aid	88
% UG rec. any financial aid	77
% UG borrow to pay for school	77
Average cumulative indebtedness	$22,000

ROGER WILLIAMS UNIVERSITY

CAMPUS LIFE
Fire Safety Rating	**89**
Green Rating	**60***
Type of school	private
Environment	town

STUDENTS
Total undergrad enrollment	4,347
% male/female	51/49
% from out of state	82
% from public high school	85
% live on campus	78
% African American	1
% Asian	1
% Caucasian	76
% Hispanic	2
% international	2
# of countries represented	41

ACADEMICS
Calendar	semester
Profs interesting rating	73
Profs accessible rating	75
Student/faculty ratio	13:1
Most common reg class size	10–19 students
Most common lab size	10–19 students

MOST POPULAR MAJORS
architecture (barch, ba/bs, march, ma/ms, phd)
psychology
business/commerce

SELECTIVITY
# of applicants	7,335
% of applicants accepted	68
% of acceptees attending	21

FRESHMAN PROFILE
Range SAT Critical Reading	490–580
Range SAT Math	510–600
Range ACT Composite	21–25
Average HS GPA	3.16
% graduated top 10% of class	14
% graduated top 25% of class	37
% graduated top 50% of class	77

DEADLINES
Early decision
Deadline	11/1
Notification	12/15

Early action
Deadline	11/15
Notification	1/15

Regular
Deadline	2/1
Notification	3/15
Nonfall registration?	yes

FINANCIAL FACTS
Annual tuition	$24,312
Room and board	$11,490
Required fees	$1,630
Books and supplies	$900
% frosh rec. need-based scholarship or grant aid	39
% UG rec. need-based scholarship or grant aid	38
% frosh rec. non-need-based scholarship or grant aid	34
% UG rec. non-need-based scholarship or grant aid	29
% frosh rec. need-based self-help aid	56
% UG rec. need-based self-help aid	54
% frosh rec. any financial aid	85
% UG rec. any financial aid	79
% UG borrow to pay for school	69
Average cumulative indebtedness	$31,400

ROSEMONT COLLEGE

CAMPUS LIFE
Fire Safety Rating	**82**
Green Rating	**79**
Type of school	private
Affiliation	Roman Catholic
Environment	village

STUDENTS
Total undergrad enrollment	551
% male/female	5/95
% from out of state	35
% from public high school	61
% live on campus	70
% in (# of) sororities	2 (NR)
% African American	36
% Asian	6
% Caucasian	42
% Hispanic	8
% international	1
# of countries represented	13

ACADEMICS
Calendar	semester
Profs interesting rating	83
Profs accessible rating	88
Student/faculty ratio	8:1
Most common reg class size	10–19 students

MOST POPULAR MAJORS
English language and literature
psychology
social sciences

SELECTIVITY
# of applicants	367
% of applicants accepted	60
% of acceptees attending	31

FRESHMAN PROFILE
Range SAT Critical Reading	410–500
Range SAT Math	415–500
Range SAT Writing	410–505
Minimum paper TOEFL	500
Minimum computer TOEFL	173
Average HS GPA	3
% graduated top 10% of class	24
% graduated top 25% of class	46
% graduated top 50% of class	71

DEADLINES
Regular
Deadline	8/1
Notification	rolling
Nonfall registration?	yes

FINANCIAL FACTS
Annual tuition	$26,476
% frosh rec. need-based scholarship or grant aid	73
% UG rec. need-based scholarship or grant aid	77
% frosh rec. non-need-based scholarship or grant aid	9
% UG rec. non-need-based scholarship or grant aid	13
% frosh rec. need-based self-help aid	56
% UG rec. need-based self-help aid	60
% UG borrow to pay for school	70
Average cumulative indebtedness	$27,941

ROWAN UNIVERSITY

CAMPUS LIFE
Fire Safety Rating	**87**
Green Rating	**87**
Type of school	public
Environment	town

STUDENTS
Total undergrad enrollment	8,912
% male/female	47/53
% from out of state	5
% live on campus	34
% in (# of) fraternities	15
% in (# of) sororities	14
% African American	9

% Asian 3
% Caucasian 78
% Hispanic 7
% Native American 1
# of countries represented 30

ACADEMICS

Calendar semester
Profs interesting rating 69
Profs accessible rating 68
Student/faculty ratio 15:1
Most common
  reg class size 20–29 students

MOST POPULAR MAJORS
elementary education and teaching
communications
business
engineering
biology

SELECTIVITY

of applicants 8,088
% of applicants accepted 52
% of acceptees attending 34
# accepting a place on wait list 140
% admitted from wait list 50

FRESHMAN PROFILE

Range SAT Critical Reading 530–620
Range SAT Math 440–650
Minimum paper TOEFL 550
Minimum computer TOEFL 213
Average HS GPA 3.6
% graduated top 10% of class 18
% graduated top 25% of class 47
% graduated top 50% of class 86

DEADLINES

Regular
  Deadline 3/1
  Notification 10/15–4/15
Nonfall registration? yes

FINANCIAL FACTS

Annual in-state tuition $7,308
Annual out-of-state tuition $14,616
Room and board $9,242
Required fees $2,760
Books and supplies $900
% frosh rec. need-based
  scholarship or grant aid 53
% UG rec. need-based
  scholarship or grant aid 44
% frosh rec. non-need-based
  scholarship or grant aid 52
% UG rec. non-need-based
  scholarship or grant aid 39

% frosh rec. need-based self-help aid 44
% UG rec. need-based self-help aid 51

RUTGERS, THE STATE UNIVERSITY OF NEW JERSEY—NEW BRUNSWICK

CAMPUS LIFE

Fire Safety Rating **81**
Green Rating **60***
Type of school public
Environment town

STUDENTS

Total undergrad enrollment 26,479
% male/female 51/49
% from out of state 7
% live on campus 49
% in (# of) fraternities NR (29)
% in (# of) sororities NR (15)
% African American 9
% Asian 24
% Caucasian 52
% Hispanic 8
% international 2
# of countries represented 117

ACADEMICS

Calendar semester
Student/faculty ratio 14:1
Profs interesting rating 61
Profs accessible rating 61
% classes taught by TAs 20

MOST POPULAR MAJORS
engineering
biology/biological sciences

SELECTIVITY

of applicants 28,208
% of applicants accepted 56
% of acceptees attending 35

FRESHMAN PROFILE

Range SAT Critical Reading 530–630
Range SAT Math 560–670
% graduated top 10% of class 40
% graduated top 25% of class 81
% graduated top 50% of class 99

DEADLINES

Regular
  Priority 12/1
  Notification 3/1
Nonfall registration? yes

FINANCIAL FACTS

Annual tuition $8,541
% frosh rec. need-based
  scholarship or grant aid 31
% UG rec. need-based
  scholarship or grant aid 32
% frosh rec. non-need-based
  scholarship or grant aid 30
% UG rec. non-need-based
  scholarship or grant aid 25
% frosh rec. need-based
  self-help aid 44
% UG rec. need-based
  self-help aid 44
% frosh rec.
  athletic scholarships 1
% UG rec. athletic scholarships 1
% frosh rec.
  any financial aid 67
% UG rec. any financial aid 69
% UG borrow to pay for school 65
Average cumulative
  indebtedness $16,283

SACRED HEART UNIVERSITY

CAMPUS LIFE

Fire Safety Rating **82**
Green Rating **70**
Type of school private
Affiliation Roman Catholic
Environment town

STUDENTS

Total undergrad enrollment 4,188
% male/female 39/61
% from out of state 69
% from public high school 70
% live on campus 66
% in (# of) fraternities 5 (3)
% in (# of) sororities 5 (6)
% African American 4
% Asian 2
% Caucasian 85
% Hispanic 6
% international 1
# of countries represented 40

ACADEMICS

Calendar semester
Student/faculty ratio 13:1
Profs interesting rating 79
Profs accessible rating 80
Most common
  reg class size 10–19 students

MOST POPULAR MAJORS
kinesiology and exercise science
psychology
business/commerce

SELECTIVITY
# of applicants	7,532
% of applicants accepted	62
% of acceptees attending	21
# of early decision applicants	359
% accepted early decision	47

FRESHMAN PROFILE
Range SAT Critical Reading	490–570
Range SAT Math	500–580
Range ACT Composite	21–25
Minimum paper TOEFL	500
Minimum computer TOEFL	70
Average HS GPA	3.3
% graduated top 10% of class	14
% graduated top 25% of class	45
% graduated top 50% of class	85

DEADLINES
Early decision	
Deadline	11/15
Notification	12/15
Regular	
Priority	2/1
Notification	rolling
Nonfall registration?	yes

FINANCIAL FACTS
Annual tuition	$26,950
Room and board	$10,816
Required fees	$200
Books and supplies	$700
% frosh rec. need-based scholarship or grant aid	66
% UG rec. need-based scholarship or grant aid	64
% frosh rec. non-need-based scholarship or grant aid	21
% UG rec. non-need-based scholarship or grant aid	20
% frosh rec. need-based self-help aid	57
% UG rec. need-based self-help aid	56
% frosh rec. athletic scholarships	5
% UG rec. athletic scholarships	5
% frosh rec. any financial aid	87
% UG rec. any financial aid	91
% UG borrow to pay for school	94
Average cumulative indebtedness	$25,505

SAINT ANSELM COLLEGE

CAMPUS LIFE
Fire Safety Rating	60*
Green Rating	60*
Type of school	private
Affiliation	Roman Catholic
Environment	city

STUDENTS
Total undergrad enrollment	1,936
% male/female	43/57
% from out of state	78
% from public high school	45
% live on campus	89
% African American	1
% Asian	1
% Caucasian	77
% Hispanic	1
% Native American	1
# of countries represented	18

ACADEMICS
Calendar	semester
Student/faculty ratio	12:1
Profs interesting rating	89
Profs accessible rating	86
Most common reg class size	10–19 students
Most common lab size	10–19 students

SELECTIVITY
# of applicants	3,521
% of applicants accepted	69
% of acceptees attending	23
# accepting a place on wait list	368
# of early decision applicants	106
% accepted early decision	77

FRESHMAN PROFILE
Range SAT Critical Reading	510–600
Range SAT Math	510–600
Range SAT Writing	510–610
Range ACT Composite	22–26
Minimum paper TOEFL	550
Minimum computer TOEFL	213
Minimum web-based TOEFL	80
Average HS GPA	3.15
% graduated top 10% of class	21
% graduated top 25% of class	53
% graduated top 50% of class	87

DEADLINES
Early decision	
Deadline	11/15
Notification	12/1

Regular
Priority	3/1
Notification	rolling
Nonfall registration?	yes

FINANCIAL FACTS
Annual tuition	$26,960
Room and board	$10,200
Required fees	$750
Books and supplies	$750
% frosh rec. need-based scholarship or grant aid	67
% UG rec. need-based scholarship or grant aid	67
% frosh rec. non-need-based scholarship or grant aid	41
% UG rec. non-need-based scholarship or grant aid	39
% frosh rec. need-based self-help aid	60
% UG rec. need-based self-help aid	62
% frosh rec. athletic scholarships	1
% UG rec. athletic scholarships	1
% UG borrow to pay for school	81.69
Average cumulative indebtedness	$33,656

SAINT BONAVENTURE UNIVERSITY

CAMPUS LIFE
Fire Safety Rating	60*
Green Rating	60*
Type of school	private
Affiliation	Roman Catholic
Environment	village

STUDENTS
Total undergrad enrollment	2,072
% male/female	51/49
% from out of state	24
% from public high school	70
% live on campus	77
# of countries represented	24

ACADEMICS
Calendar	semester
Student/faculty ratio	15:1
Profs interesting rating	81
Profs accessible rating	82
Most common reg class size	10–19 students
Most common lab size	10–19 students

MOST POPULAR MAJORS
elementary education and teaching
business/commerce

SELECTIVITY
# of applicants	1,730
% of applicants accepted	86
% of acceptees attending	32

FRESHMAN PROFILE
Range SAT Critical Reading	480–570
Range SAT Math	470–570
Range ACT Composite	19–23
Minimum paper TOEFL	550
Minimum computer TOEFL	213
Average HS GPA	3.13
% graduated top 10% of class	11
% graduated top 25% of class	31
% graduated top 50% of class	68

DEADLINES
Regular	
Priority	2/1
Deadline	4/15
Notification	rolling
Nonfall registration?	yes

FINANCIAL FACTS
Annual tuition	$21,650
Room and board	$7,760
Required fees	$865
Books and supplies	$650
% frosh rec. need-based scholarship or grant aid	73
% UG rec. need-based scholarship or grant aid	71
% frosh rec. non-need-based scholarship or grant aid	13
% UG rec. non-need-based scholarship or grant aid	12
% frosh rec. need-based self-help aid	60
% UG rec. need-based self-help aid	59
% frosh rec. athletic scholarships	3
% UG rec. athletic scholarships	4
% UG borrow to pay for school	72
Average cumulative indebtedness	$16,900

SAINT JOHN'S COLLEGE (MD)

CAMPUS LIFE
Fire Safety Rating	**84**
Green Rating	**78**
Type of school	private
Environment	town

STUDENTS
Total undergrad enrollment	481
% male/female	53/47
% from out of state	83
% from public high school	53
% live on campus	73
% African American	1
% Asian	3
% Caucasian	90
% Hispanic	3
# of countries represented	12

ACADEMICS
Calendar	semester
Student/faculty ratio	87:1
Profs interesting rating	98
Profs accessible rating	97
Most common reg class size	10–19 students

MOST POPULAR MAJORS
liberal arts and sciences studies
and humanities

SELECTIVITY
# of applicants	441
% of applicants accepted	81
% of acceptees attending	40

FRESHMAN PROFILE
Range SAT Critical Reading	660–770
Range SAT Math	580–680
Minimum paper TOEFL	600
Minimum computer TOEFL	270
% graduated top 10% of class	32
% graduated top 25% of class	65
% graduated top 50% of class	87

DEADLINES
Regular	Rolling
Priority	3/1
Nonfall registration?	yes

FINANCIAL FACTS
Annual tuition	$36,346
Room and board	$8,684
Required fees	$250
Books and supplies	$280
% frosh rec. need-based scholarship or grant aid	56
% UG rec. need-based scholarship or grant aid	77
% frosh rec. need-based self-help aid	62
% UG rec. need-based self-help aid	85
% frosh rec. any financial aid	76
% UG rec. any financial aid	52

SAINT JOHN'S UNIVERSITY— QUEENS

CAMPUS LIFE
Fire Safety Rating	**92**
Green Rating	**89**
Type of school	private
Affiliation	Roman Catholic
Environment	metropolis

STUDENTS
Total undergrad enrollment	12,178
% male/female	45/55
% from out of state	15
% from public high school	64
% live on campus	19
% in (# of) fraternities	3 (22)
% in (# of) sororities	2 (24)
% African American	16
% Asian	16
% Caucasian	38
% Hispanic	14
% international	4
# of countries represented	125

ACADEMICS
Calendar	semester
Student/faculty ratio	17:1
Profs interesting rating	63
Profs accessible rating	61
Most common reg class size	10-19 students
Most common lab size	10-19 students

MOST POPULAR MAJORS
biology/biological sciences
psychology
pharmacy (pharmd [USA], pharmd or
bs/bpharm [Canada])

SELECTIVITY
# of applicants	27,754
% of applicants accepted	56
% of acceptees attending	21
# accepting a place on wait list	63

FRESHMAN PROFILE
Range SAT Critical Reading	480–580
Range SAT Math	480–600
Minimum paper TOEFL	500
Minimum computer TOEFL	173
Minimum web-based TOEFL	61
Average HS GPA	3.2
% graduated top 10% of class	22
% graduated top 25% of class	44
% graduated top 50% of class	67

DEADLINES

Notification	rolling
Nonfall registration?	yes

FINANCIAL FACTS

Annual tuition	$26,200
Room and board	$12,070
Required fees	$690
Books and supplies	$1,000
% frosh rec. need-based scholarship or grant aid	74
% UG rec. need-based scholarship or grant aid	69
% frosh rec. non-need-based scholarship or grant aid	75
% UG rec. non-need-based scholarship or grant aid	66
% frosh rec. need-based self-help aid	58
% UG rec. need-based self-help aid	70
% frosh rec. athletic scholarships	2
% UG rec. athletic scholarships	2
% frosh rec. any financial aid	97
% UG rec. any financial aid	98
% UG borrow to pay for school	74
Average cumulative indebtedness	$28,010

SAINT JOSEPH'S UNIVERSITY (PA)

CAMPUS LIFE

Fire Safety Rating	**92**
Green Rating	**78**
Type of school	private
Affiliation	Roman Catholic-Jesuit
Environment	metropolis

STUDENTS

Total undergrad enrollment	4,825
% male/female	48/52
% from out of state	49
% live on campus	59
% in (# of) fraternities	7 (3)
% in (# of) sororities	13 (4)
% African American	8
% Asian	3
% Caucasian	81
% Hispanic	3
% international	2
# of countries represented	54

ACADEMICS

Calendar	semester
Profs interesting rating	85
Profs accessible rating	87
Student/faculty ratio	13:1
Most common reg class size	10–19 students
Most common lab size	10–19 students

MOST POPULAR MAJORS
accounting
marketing/marketing management
general merchandising, sales, and related
marketing operations, other

SELECTIVITY

# of applicants	8,779
% of applicants accepted	62
% of acceptees attending	20
# accepting a place on wait list	683
% admitted from wait list	37

FRESHMAN PROFILE

Range SAT Critical Reading	530–620
Range SAT Math	540–630
Range ACT Composite	23–28
Average HS GPA	3.32

DEADLINES

Early action	
Deadline	11/15
Notification	1/15
Regular	
Deadline	2/1
Notification	3/1
Nonfall registration?	no

FINANCIAL FACTS

Annual tuition	$32,710
% frosh rec. need-based scholarship or grant aid	50
% UG rec. need-based scholarship or grant aid	42
% frosh rec. non-need-based scholarship or grant aid	48
% UG rec. non-need-based scholarship or grant aid	40
% frosh rec. need-based self-help aid	46
% UG rec. need-based self-help aid	39
% frosh rec. athletic scholarships	3
% UG rec. athletic scholarships	4
% frosh rec. any financial aid	94
% UG rec. any financial aid	95

SAINT LAWRENCE UNIVERSITY

CAMPUS LIFE

Fire Safety Rating	**68**
Green Rating	**87**
Type of school	private
Environment	village

STUDENTS

Total undergrad enrollment	2,198
% male/female	46/54
% from out of state	52
% from public high school	70
% live on campus	99
% in (# of) fraternities	3 (1)
% in (# of) sororities	19 (4)
% African American	3
% Asian	2
% Caucasian	71
% Hispanic	3
% Native American	1
% international	5
# of countries represented	42

ACADEMICS

Calendar	semester
Student/faculty ratio	11:1
Profs interesting rating	92
Profs accessible rating	88
Most common reg class size	10–19 students
Most common lab size	10–19 students

MOST POPULAR MAJORS
psychology
economics
government

SELECTIVITY

# of applicants	4,645
% of applicants accepted	44
% of acceptees attending	31
# accepting a place on wait list	151
# of early decision applicants	209
% accepted early decision	79

FRESHMAN PROFILE

Range SAT Critical Reading	560–640
Range SAT Math	560–640
Range SAT Writing	560–640
Range ACT Composite	25–29
Minimum paper TOEFL	600
Minimum computer TOEFL	250
Average HS GPA	3.49
% graduated top 10% of class	35

% graduated top 25% of class 74
% graduated top 50% of class 96

DEADLINES
Early decision
  Deadline 11/15
  Notification 12/15
Regular
  Deadline 2/1
  Notification 3/30
Nonfall registration? yes

FINANCIAL FACTS
Annual tuition $33,690
% frosh rec. need-based
  scholarship or grant aid 61
% UG rec. need-based
  scholarship or grant aid 63
% frosh rec. non-need-based
  scholarship or grant aid 11
% UG rec. non-need-based
  scholarship or grant aid 8
% frosh rec. need-based
  self-help aid 58
% UG rec. need-based
  self-help aid 59
% frosh rec.
  athletic scholarships 1
% UG rec. athletic scholarships 2
% frosh rec.
  any financial aid 81
% UG rec. any financial aid 82
% UG borrow to pay for school 74
Average cumulative
  indebtedness $28,776

SAINT MARY'S COLLEGE OF MARYLAND

CAMPUS LIFE
Fire Safety Rating **79**
Green Rating **84**
Type of school public
Environment rural

STUDENTS
Total undergrad enrollment 1,922
% male/female 43/57
% from out of state 16
% live on campus 84
% African American 8
% Asian 4
% Caucasian 76
% Hispanic 5
% Native American 1

% international 2
# of countries represented 37

ACADEMICS
Calendar semester
Student/faculty ratio 12:1
Profs interesting rating 96
Profs accessible rating 96
Most common
  reg class size 10–19 students
Most common
  lab size 10–19 students

MOST POPULAR MAJORS
economics
English language and literature
biology/biological sciences

SELECTIVITY
of applicants 2,351
% of applicants accepted 55
% of acceptees attending 36
# accepting a place on wait list 132
% admitted from wait list 8
# of early decision applicants 307
% accepted early decision 47

FRESHMAN PROFILE
Range SAT Critical Reading 570–670
Range SAT Math 560–660
Range SAT Writing 560–670
Average HS GPA 3.47
% graduated top 10% of class 42
% graduated top 25% of class 76
% graduated top 50% of class 95

DEADLINES
Early decision
  Deadline 12/1
  Notification 1/1
Regular
  Deadline 1/15
  Notification 4/1
Nonfall registration? yes

FINANCIAL FACTS
Annual in-state tuition $10,472
Annual out-of-state tuition $21,322
Room and board $9,225
Required fees $2,132
Books and supplies $1,000
% frosh rec. need-based
  scholarship or grant aid 18
% UG rec. need-based
  scholarship or grant aid 19
% frosh rec. non-need-based
  scholarship or grant aid 18
% UG rec. non-need-based
  scholarship or grant aid 19

% frosh rec. need-based
  self-help aid 18
% UG rec. need-based
  self-help aid 19
% frosh rec.
  any financial aid 59
% UG rec. any financial aid 61
% UG borrow to pay for school 69
Average cumulative
  indebtedness $17,125

SAINT MICHAEL'S COLLEGE

CAMPUS LIFE
Fire Safety Rating **74**
Green Rating **89**
Type of school private
Affiliation Roman Catholic
Environment city

STUDENTS
Total undergrad enrollment 1,980
% male/female 47/53
% from out of state 80
% from public high school 66
% live on campus 98
% African American 1
% Asian 1
% Caucasian 94
% Hispanic 1
% international 1
# of countries represented 30

ACADEMICS
Calendar semester
Student/faculty ratio 12:1
Profs interesting rating 89
Profs accessible rating 92
Most common
  reg class size 10–19 students
Most common
  lab size 10–19 students

MOST POPULAR MAJORS
English language and literature
psychology
business/commerce

SELECTIVITY
of applicants 3,504
% of applicants accepted 69
% of acceptees attending 22
# accepting a place on wait list 203
% admitted from wait list 17

FRESHMAN PROFILE
Range SAT Critical Reading 520–620
Range SAT Math 520–610
Range SAT Writing 520–620

Range ACT Composite	22–26
Minimum paper TOEFL	550
Minimum computer TOEFL	213
Minimum web-based TOEFL	79-80
Average HS GPA	3.4
% graduated top 10% of class	23
% graduated top 25% of class	50
% graduated top 50% of class	86

DEADLINES
Early action
Deadline	11/1
Notification	1/1

Regular
Priority	11/1
Deadline	2/1
Notification	4/1
Nonfall registration?	yes

FINANCIAL FACTS
Annual tuition	$31,675
Room and board	$7,960
Required fees	$265
Books and supplies	$1,200
% frosh rec. need-based scholarship or grant aid	53
% UG rec. need-based scholarship or grant aid	61
% frosh rec. non-need-based scholarship or grant aid	8
% UG rec. non-need-based scholarship or grant aid	7
% frosh rec. need-based self-help aid	47
% UG rec. need-based self-help aid	55
% frosh rec. athletic scholarships	1
% UG rec. athletic scholarships	1
% frosh rec. any financial aid	90.7
% UG rec. any financial aid	89.8
% UG borrow to pay for school	75
Average cumulative indebtedness	$24,451

SALISBURY UNIVERSITY

CAMPUS LIFE
Fire Safety Rating	**72**
Green Rating	**77**
Type of school	public
Environment	town

STUDENTS
Total undergrad enrollment	6,726
% male/female	45/55

% from out of state	14
% from public high school	85
% live on campus	40
% in (# of) fraternities	5 (6)
% in (# of) sororities	6 (5)
% African American	11
% Asian	3
% Caucasian	81
% Hispanic	2
% Native American	1
% international	1
# of countries represented	60

ACADEMICS
Calendar	4/1/4
Student/faculty ratio	18:1
Profs interesting rating	72
Profs accessible rating	76
% classes taught by TAs	2
Most common reg class size	20–29 students
Most common lab size	20–29 students

MOST POPULAR MAJORS
elementary education and teaching
business administration and management

SELECTIVITY
# of applicants	6,593
% of applicants accepted	56
% of acceptees attending	31

FRESHMAN PROFILE
Range SAT Critical Reading	510–590
Range SAT Math	520–610
Range SAT Writing	520–589
Range ACT Composite	20–24
Minimum paper TOEFL	550
Minimum computer TOEFL	213
Average HS GPA	3.5
% graduated top 10% of class	23.4
% graduated top 25% of class	60.9
% graduated top 50% of class	91.7

DEADLINES
Early action
Deadline	12/1
Notification	1/15

Regular
Priority	12/1
Notification	3/15
Nonfall registration?	yes

FINANCIAL FACTS
Annual tuition	$4,814
Books and supplies	$100

% frosh rec. need-based scholarship or grant aid	34
% UG rec. need-based scholarship or grant aid	28
% frosh rec. need-based self-help aid	31
% UG rec. need-based self-help aid	32
% frosh rec. any financial aid	73
% UG rec. any financial aid	67
% UG borrow to pay for school	52
Average cumulative indebtedness	$17,669

SALVE REGINA UNIVERSITY

CAMPUS LIFE
Fire Safety Rating	**87**
Green Rating	**80**
Type of school	private
Affiliation	Roman Catholic
Environment	town

STUDENTS
Total undergrad enrollment	2,109
% male/female	31/69
% from out of state	85
% from public high school	60
% live on campus	59
% African American	1
% Asian	1
% Caucasian	82
% Hispanic	3
% international	2
# of countries represented	17

ACADEMICS
Calendar	semester
Profs interesting rating	71
Profs accessible rating	78
Student/faculty ratio	14:1
Most common reg class size	10–19 students
Most common lab size	20–29 students

MOST POPULAR MAJORS
criminal justice/law enforcement administration
elementary education and teaching
business studies

SELECTIVITY
# of applicants	5,801
% of applicants accepted	54
% of acceptees attending	18

# accepting a place on wait list	225
% admitted from wait list	15

FRESHMAN PROFILE
Range SAT Critical Reading	510–600
Range SAT Math	510–590
Range SAT Writing	510–600
Range ACT Composite	22–26
Minimum paper TOEFL	500
Minimum computer TOEFL	173
Minimum web-based TOEFL	63
Average HS GPA	3.32
% graduated top 10% of class	15
% graduated top 25% of class	52
% graduated top 50% of class	87

DEADLINES
Early action	
Deadline	11/1
Notification	12/15
Regular	
Priority	2/1
Notification	rolling
Nonfall registration?	yes

FINANCIAL FACTS
Annual tuition	$26,750
Room and board	$10,200
Required fees	$200
Books and supplies	$900
% frosh rec. need-based scholarship or grant aid	61
% UG rec. need-based scholarship or grant aid	62
% frosh rec. non-need-based scholarship or grant aid	2
% UG rec. non-need-based scholarship or grant aid	2
% frosh rec. need-based self-help aid	62
% UG rec. need-based self-help aid	63
% frosh rec. any financial aid	65
% UG rec. any financial aid	67
% UG borrow to pay for school	77.44
Average cumulative indebtedness	$30,752

SARAH LAWRENCE COLLEGE

CAMPUS LIFE
Fire Safety Rating	**81**
Green Rating	**86**
Type of school	private
Environment	metropolis

STUDENTS
Total undergrad enrollment	1,383
% male/female	26/74
% from out of state	77

% live on campus	85
% African American	4
% Asian	5
% Caucasian	63
% Hispanic	5
% Native American	1
% international	2
# of countries represented	32

ACADEMICS
Calendar	semester
Student/faculty ratio	6:1
Profs interesting rating	98
Profs accessible rating	89
Most common reg class size	10–19 students

SELECTIVITY
# of applicants	2,801
% of applicants accepted	44
% of acceptees attending	29
# accepting a place on wait list	271
% admitted from wait list	31
# of early decision applicants	164
% accepted early decision	48

FRESHMAN PROFILE
Average HS GPA	3.6
% graduated top 10% of class	37
% graduated top 25% of class	84
% graduated top 50% of class	98

DEADLINES
Early decision	
Deadline	11/15
Notification	12/15
Regular	
Deadline	1/1
Notification	4/1
Nonfall registration?	no

FINANCIAL FACTS
Annual tuition	$39,450
Room and board	$13,104
Required fees	$960
% frosh rec. need-based scholarship or grant aid	44
% UG rec. need-based scholarship or grant aid	48
% frosh rec. non-need-based scholarship or grant aid	1
% UG rec. non-need-based scholarship or grant aid	1
% frosh rec. need-based self-help aid	43
% UG rec. need-based self-help aid	49

% frosh rec. any financial aid	48
% UG rec. any financial aid	54
% UG borrow to pay for school	61
Average cumulative indebtedness	$16,332

SETON HALL UNIVERSITY

CAMPUS LIFE
Fire Safety Rating	**84**
Green Rating	**60***
Type of school	private
Environment	city

STUDENTS
Total undergrad enrollment	4,896
% male/female	44/56
% from out of state	26
% live on campus	46
% African American	12
% Asian	6
% Caucasian	52
% Hispanic	11
% international	2
# of countries represented	43

ACADEMICS
Student/faculty ratio	14:1
Profs interesting rating	76
Profs accessible rating	74

MOST POPULAR MAJORS
Communication Studies/Speech
Nursing/Registered Nurse
Diplomacy Finance

SELECTIVITY
Admissions Rating	**81**
# of applicants	6,626
% of applicants accepted	72
% of acceptees attending	27

FRESHMAN PROFILE
Range SAT Critical Reading	470–580
Range SAT Math	480–590
Average HS GPA	3.2
% graduated top 10% of class	21
% graduated top 25% of class	49
% graduated top 50% of class	80

DEADLINES
Priority	03/01
Nonfall registration?	Yes

FINANCIAL FACTS
Annual tuition	$27,680
Room and board	$11,360
Required fees	$2,250.00
Books and supplies	$1,300

% frosh rec. need-based scholarship or grant aid	70
% UG rec. need-based scholarship or grant aid	51
% frosh rec. non-need-based scholarship or grant aid	46
% UG rec. non-need-based scholarship or grant aid	36
% frosh rec. need-based self-help aid	41
% UG rec. need-based self-help aid	43
% frosh rec. athletic scholarships	5
% UG rec. athletic scholarships	4
% frosh rec. any financial aid	79
% UG rec. any financial aid	69
% UG borrow to pay for school	6
Average cumulative indebtedness	$16,566

SETON HILL UNIVERSITY

CAMPUS LIFE

Fire Safety Rating	**79**
Green Rating	**61**
Type of school	private
Affiliation	Roman Catholic
Environment	town

STUDENTS

Total undergrad enrollment	1,535
% male/female	38/62
% from out of state	21
% live on campus	50
% African American	8
% Asian	1
% Caucasian	79
% Hispanic	2
% international	2
# of countries represented	21

ACADEMICS

Calendar	semester
Profs interesting rating	74
Profs accessible rating	71
Student/faculty ratio	14:1
Most common reg class size	10–19 students

MOST POPULAR MAJORS
psychology
fine/studio arts
business/commerce

SELECTIVITY

# of applicants	1,701
% of applicants accepted	63
% of acceptees attending	30

FRESHMAN PROFILE

Range SAT Critical Reading	450–550
Range SAT Math	450–570
Minimum paper TOEFL	550
Minimum computer TOEFL	213
Average HS GPA	3.33
% graduated top 10% of class	23
% graduated top 25% of class	49
% graduated top 50% of class	74

DEADLINES

Regular	
Priority	5/1
Deadline	8/15
Notification	rolling
Nonfall registration?	yes

FINANCIAL FACTS

Annual tuition	$24,806
% frosh rec. need-based scholarship or grant aid	84
% UG rec. need-based scholarship or grant aid	81
% frosh rec. non-need-based scholarship or grant aid	14
% UG rec. non-need-based scholarship or grant aid	9
% frosh rec. need-based self-help aid	70
% UG rec. need-based self-help aid	69
% frosh rec. athletic scholarships	10
% UG rec. athletic scholarships	6
% frosh rec. any financial aid	97
% UG rec. any financial aid	83
% UG borrow to pay for school	84
Average cumulative indebtedness	$26,872

SIENA COLLEGE

CAMPUS LIFE

Fire Safety Rating	**60***
Green Rating	**60***
Type of school	private
Affiliation	Roman Catholic
Environment	town

STUDENTS

Total undergrad enrollment	3,151
% male/female	44/56
% from out of state	13
% live on campus	74
% African American	2
% Asian	4
% Caucasian	84
% Hispanic	4
# of countries represented	6

ACADEMICS

Calendar	semester
Student/faculty ratio	13:1
Profs interesting rating	80
Profs accessible rating	84
Most common reg class size	20–29 students
Most common lab size	10–19 students

MOST POPULAR MAJORS
marketing/marketing management
psychology
accounting

SELECTIVITY

# of applicants	5,792
% of applicants accepted	54
% of acceptees attending	25
# accepting a place on wait list	318
% admitted from wait list	5
# of early decision applicants	130
% accepted early decision	33

FRESHMAN PROFILE

Range SAT Critical Reading	500–590
Range SAT Math	520–620
Range SAT Writing	490–590
Range ACT Composite	20–24
Minimum paper TOEFL	550
Minimum web-based TOEFL	79
Average HS GPA	89.4
% graduated top 10% of class	21
% graduated top 25% of class	57
% graduated top 50% of class	91

DEADLINES

Early decision	
Deadline	12/1
Notification	12/15
Early action	
Deadline	12/1
Notification	1/1
Regular	
Priority	3/1
Deadline	3/1
Notification	3/15
Nonfall registration?	yes

FINANCIAL FACTS

Annual tuition	$22,510
Room and board	$8,875
Required fees	$175
Books and supplies	$930
% frosh rec. need-based scholarship or grant aid	69
% UG rec. need-based scholarship or grant aid	66
% frosh rec. non-need-based scholarship or grant aid	6

% UG rec. non-need-based
  scholarship or grant aid — 4
% frosh rec. need-based
  self-help aid — 57
% UG rec. need-based
  self-help aid — 55
% frosh rec.
  athletic scholarships — 9
% UG rec. athletic scholarships — 8
% frosh rec.
  any financial aid — 96.1
% UG rec. any financial aid — 95.3
% UG borrow to pay for school — 77
Average cumulative
  indebtedness — $21,800

SIMMONS COLLEGE

CAMPUS LIFE
Fire Safety Rating — **89**
Green Rating — **90**
Type of school — private
Environment — city

STUDENTS
Total undergrad enrollment — 2,069
% male/female — /100
% from out of state — 40
% live on campus — 56
# of countries represented — 45

ACADEMICS
Calendar — semester
Student/faculty ratio — 13:1
Profs interesting rating — 83
Profs accessible rating — 83
Most common
  reg class size — 10–19 students
MOST POPULAR MAJORS
psychology
nursing/registered nurse
(RN, ASN, BSN, MSN)

SELECTIVITY
of applicants — 2,937
% of applicants accepted — 57
% of acceptees attending — 28
# accepting a place on wait list — 22
% admitted from wait list — 5

FRESHMAN PROFILE
Range SAT Critical Reading — 500–600
Range SAT Math — 480–590
Range SAT Writing — 510–610
Range ACT Composite — 21–26
Minimum paper TOEFL — 560
Minimum computer TOEFL — 220
Minimum web-based TOEFL — 83

Average HS GPA — 3.17
% graduated top 10% of class — 18
% graduated top 25% of class — 58
% graduated top 50% of class — 92

DEADLINES
Early action
  Deadline — 12/1
  Notification — 1/20
Regular
  Priority — 2/1
  Deadline — 2/1
  Notification — 4/15
Nonfall registration? — yes

FINANCIAL FACTS
Annual tuition — $27,468
Room and board — $11,138
Required fees — $834
Books and supplies — $800
% frosh rec. need-based
  scholarship or grant aid — 63
% UG rec. need-based
  scholarship or grant aid — 67
% frosh rec. non-need-based
  scholarship or grant aid — 4
% UG rec. non-need-based
  scholarship or grant aid — 2
% frosh rec. need-based
  self-help aid — 60
% UG rec. need-based
  self-help aid — 65
% frosh rec.
  any financial aid — 72
% UG rec. any financial aid — 70
% UG borrow to pay for school — 82
Average cumulative
  indebtedness — $34,940

SIMON'S ROCK COLLEGE OF BARD

CAMPUS LIFE
Fire Safety Rating — **60***
Green Rating — **60***
Type of school — private
Environment — village

STUDENTS
Total undergrad enrollment — 368
% male/female — 43/57
% from out of state — 80
% live on campus — 85
% African American — 7
% Asian — 4
% Caucasian — 58

% Hispanic — 6
% Native American — 1
% international — 4

ACADEMICS
Calendar — semester
Student/faculty ratio — 8:1
Profs interesting rating — 99
Profs accessible rating — 97
Most common
  reg class size — 10–19 students
Most common
  lab size — 10–19 students
MOST POPULAR MAJORS
creative writing
cell/cellular biology and histology
psychology

SELECTIVITY
of applicants — 204
% of applicants accepted — 84
% of acceptees attending — 74

FRESHMAN PROFILE
Range SAT Critical Reading — 560–690
Range SAT Math — 530–680
Range ACT Composite — 25–30
Minimum paper TOEFL — 550
Minimum computer TOEFL — 200
Average HS GPA — 3.36
% graduated top 10% of class — 60
% graduated top 25% of class — 82
% graduated top 50% of class — 94

DEADLINES
Regular
  Priority — 4/15
  Deadline — 5/31
  Notification — rolling
Nonfall registration? — yes

FINANCIAL FACTS
Annual tuition — $34,804
Room and board — $9,260
Required fees — $530
Books and supplies — $1,000
% frosh rec. need-based
  scholarship or grant aid — 51
% UG rec. need-based
  scholarship or grant aid — 39
% frosh rec. non-need-based
  scholarship or grant aid — 50
% UG rec. non-need-based
  scholarship or grant aid — 33
% frosh rec. need-based
  self-help aid — 47
% UG rec. need-based
  self-help aid — 43

% frosh rec.
any financial aid 78
% UG rec. any financial aid 71
% UG borrow to pay for school 70
Average cumulative
indebtedness $15,000

SKIDMORE COLLEGE

CAMPUS LIFE
Fire Safety Rating **60***
Green Rating **60***
Type of school private
Environment town

STUDENTS
Total undergrad enrollment 2,771
% male/female 40/60
% from out of state 68
% from public high school 63
% live on campus 85
% African American 4
% Asian 7
% Caucasian 66
% Hispanic 5
% Native American 1
% international 3
# of countries represented 41

ACADEMICS
Calendar semester
Student/faculty ratio 9:1
Profs interesting rating 86
Profs accessible rating 91
Most common
reg class size 10–19 students
Most common
lab size 10–19 students
MOST POPULAR MAJORS
English language and literature
fine arts and art studies
business/commerce

SELECTIVITY
of applicants 6,768
% of applicants accepted 37
% of acceptees attending 28
# accepting a place on wait list 522
% admitted from wait list 11
# of early decision applicants 418
% accepted early decision 64

FRESHMAN PROFILE
Range SAT Critical Reading 580–680
Range SAT Math 580–670
Range SAT Writing 590–690
Range ACT Composite 26–30
Minimum paper TOEFL 590

Minimum computer TOEFL 243
Average HS GPA 3.335
% graduated top 10% of class 38.8
% graduated top 25% of class 79.8
% graduated top 50% of class 96.8

DEADLINES
Early decision
Deadline 11/15
Notification 12/15
Regular
Deadline 1/15
Notification 4/1
Nonfall registration? no

FINANCIAL FACTS
Annual tuition $36,126
Room and board $9,836
Required fees $734
Books and supplies $1,000
% frosh rec. need-based
scholarship or grant aid 40
% UG rec. need-based
scholarship or grant aid 41
% frosh rec. non-need-based
scholarship or grant aid 2
% UG rec. non-need-based
scholarship or grant aid 2
% frosh rec. need-based
self-help aid 49
% UG rec. need-based
self-help aid 50
% frosh rec.
any financial aid 49
% UG rec. any financial aid 50
% UG borrow to pay for school 47
Average cumulative
indebtedness $16,078

SLIPPERY ROCK UNIVERSITY OF PENNSYLVANIA

CAMPUS LIFE
Fire Safety Rating **95**
Green Rating **84**
Type of school public
Environment rural

STUDENTS
Total undergrad enrollment 7,521
% male/female 44/56
% from out of state 7
% from public high school 80
% live on campus 33
% in (# of) fraternities 5 (7)
% in (# of) sororities 5 (8)

% African American 5
% Asian 1
% Caucasian 87
% Hispanic 1
% international 1
# of countries represented 39

ACADEMICS
Calendar semester
Profs interesting rating 69
Profs accessible rating 73
Student/faculty ratio 20:1
Most common
reg class size 20–29 students
Most common
lab size 20–29 students
MOST POPULAR MAJORS
elementary education and teaching
athletic training/trainer
business administration and management

SELECTIVITY
of applicants 4,736
% of applicants accepted 70
% of acceptees attending 45
# accepting a place on wait list 533
% admitted from wait list 87

FRESHMAN PROFILE
Range SAT Critical Reading 450–530
Range SAT Math 460–550
Range ACT Composite 19–23
Minimum paper TOEFL 500
Minimum computer TOEFL 173
Average HS GPA 3.26
% graduated top 10% of class 10
% graduated top 25% of class 35
% graduated top 50% of class 72

DEADLINES
Nonfall registration? yes

FINANCIAL FACTS
Annual in-state tuition $5,178
Annual out-of-state tuition $7,767
Room and board $7,862
Required fees $1,493
Books and supplies $1,278
% frosh rec. need-based
scholarship or grant aid 45
% UG rec. need-based
scholarship or grant aid 44
% frosh rec. non-need-based
scholarship or grant aid 25
% UG rec. non-need-based
scholarship or grant aid 16
% frosh rec. need-based self-help aid 61
% UG rec. need-based self-help aid 58

% frosh rec. athletic scholarships	5
% UG rec. athletic scholarships	4
% frosh rec. any financial aid	89
% UG rec. any financial aid	83
% UG borrow to pay for school	80
Average cumulative indebtedness	$21,680

SMITH COLLEGE

CAMPUS LIFE
Fire Safety Rating	**74**
Green Rating	**96**
Type of school	private
Environment	town

STUDENTS
Total undergrad enrollment	2,598
% male/female	/100
% from out of state	78
% from public high school	67
% live on campus	88
% African American	7
% Asian	12
% Caucasian	50
% Hispanic	7
% Native American	1
% international	7
# of countries represented	56

ACADEMICS
Calendar	semester
Profs interesting rating	93
Profs accessible rating	88
Most common	
reg class size	10–19 students

MOST POPULAR MAJORS
psychology
political science and government

SELECTIVITY
# of applicants	3,427
% of applicants accepted	53
% of acceptees attending	37
# accepting a place on wait list	286
% admitted from wait list	6
# of early decision applicants	212
% accepted early decision	78

FRESHMAN PROFILE
Range SAT Critical Reading	580–700
Range SAT Math	560–670
Range SAT Writing	640–730
Range ACT Composite	25–29
Minimum paper TOEFL	600
Minimum computer TOEFL	250
Average HS GPA	4
% graduated top 10% of class	61
% graduated top 25% of class	91

% graduated top 50% of class	100

DEADLINES
Early decision	
Deadline	11/15
Notification	12/15
Regular	
Deadline	1/15
Notification	4/1
Nonfall registration?	no

FINANCIAL FACTS
Annual tuition	$32,320
Room and board	$10,880
Required fees	$238
Books and supplies	$600
% frosh rec. need-based scholarship or grant aid	59
% UG rec. need-based scholarship or grant aid	59
% frosh rec. need-based self-help aid	58
% UG rec. need-based self-help aid	58
% frosh rec. any financial aid	66
% UG rec. any financial aid	65
% UG borrow to pay for school	71
Average cumulative indebtedness	$19,760

STATE UNIVERSITY OF NEW YORK—BINGHAMTON

CAMPUS LIFE
Fire Safety Rating	**72**
Green Rating	**99**
Type of school	public
Environment	town

STUDENTS
Total undergrad enrollment	11,435
% male/female	52/48
% from out of state	7
% from public high school	87
% live on campus	56
% in (# of) fraternities	8 (22)
% in (# of) sororities	9 (18)
% African American	5
% Asian	13
% Caucasian	45
% Hispanic	7
% international	8
# of countries represented	91

ACADEMICS
Calendar	semester
Student/faculty ratio	20:1
Profs interesting rating	64
Profs accessible rating	69
% classes taught by TAs	9
Most common	
reg class size	20–29 students
Most common	
lab size	20–29 students

MOST POPULAR MAJORS
business administration and management
psychology
English language and literature

SELECTIVITY
# of applicants	25,242
% of applicants accepted	39
% of acceptees attending	24
# accepting a place on wait list	664
% admitted from wait list	15

FRESHMAN PROFILE
Range SAT Critical Reading	570–660
Range SAT Math	610–690
Range ACT Composite	25–29
Minimum paper TOEFL	550
Minimum computer TOEFL	213
Minimum web-based TOEFL	80
Average HS GPA	3.7
% graduated top 10% of class	49
% graduated top 25% of class	85
% graduated top 50% of class	99

DEADLINES
Early action	
Deadline	11/15
Notification	1/1
Regular	
Priority	12/1
Notification	4/1
Nonfall registration?	yes

FINANCIAL FACTS
Annual in-state tuition	$4,350
Annual out-of-state tuition	$10,610
Room and board	$9,188
Required fees	$1,662
Books and supplies	$800
% frosh rec. need-based scholarship or grant aid	35
% UG rec. need-based scholarship or grant aid	39
% frosh rec. non-need-based scholarship or grant aid	13
% UG rec. non-need-based scholarship or grant aid	10

% frosh rec. need-based self-help aid	40
% UG rec. need-based self-help aid	42
% frosh rec. athletic scholarships	4
% UG rec. athletic scholarships	2
% frosh rec. any financial aid	78
% UG rec. any financial aid	68
% UG borrow to pay for school	56
Average cumulative indebtedness	$14,530

STATE UNIVERSITY OF NEW YORK—THE COLLEGE AT BROCKPORT

CAMPUS LIFE
Fire Safety Rating	**79**
Green Rating	**87**
Type of school	public
Environment	village

STUDENTS
Total undergrad enrollment	6,841
% male/female	43/57
% from out of state	1
% live on campus	40
% in (# of) fraternities	1 (5)
% in (# of) sororities	1 (3)
% African American	6
% Asian	1
% Caucasian	75
% Hispanic	3
% international	1
# of countries represented	20

ACADEMICS
Calendar	semester
Profs interesting rating	70
Profs accessible rating	70
Student/faculty ratio	18:1
Most common reg class size	20–29 students
Most common lab size	10–19 students

MOST POPULAR MAJORS
business administration and management
physical education teaching and coaching
criminal justice/safety studies

SELECTIVITY
# of applicants	8,522
% of applicants accepted	42
% of acceptees attending	29

FRESHMAN PROFILE
Range SAT Critical Reading	500–600
Range SAT Math	480–580
Range SAT Writing	460–560
Range ACT Composite	21–25
Minimum paper TOEFL	530
Minimum computer TOEFL	197
Average HS GPA	3.47
% graduated top 10% of class	14.22
% graduated top 25% of class	52.33
% graduated top 50% of class	89.13

DEADLINES
Nonfall registration?	yes

FINANCIAL FACTS
Annual in-state tuition	$4,350
Annual out-of-state tuition	$10,610
Room and board	$8,190
Required fees	$1,056
Books and supplies	$1,000
% frosh rec. need-based scholarship or grant aid	60
% UG rec. need-based scholarship or grant aid	54
% frosh rec. non-need-based scholarship or grant aid	20
% UG rec. non-need-based scholarship or grant aid	11
% frosh rec. need-based self-help aid	56
% UG rec. need-based self-help aid	52
% frosh rec. any financial aid	90
% UG rec. any financial aid	82
% UG borrow to pay for school	82
Average cumulative indebtedness	$22,575

STATE UNIVERSITY OF NEW YORK—COLLEGE OF ENVIRONMENTAL SCIENCE AND FORESTRY

CAMPUS LIFE
Fire Safety Rating	**60***
Green Rating	**97**
Type of school	public
Environment	city

STUDENTS
Total undergrad enrollment	1,456
% male/female	63/37
% from out of state	9
% live on campus	33
% in (# of) fraternities	5 (26)
% in (# of) sororities	5 (21)
% African American	1

% Asian	3
% Caucasian	91
% Hispanic	3
% Native American	1
% international	1

ACADEMICS
Calendar	semester
Profs interesting rating	78
Profs accessible rating	80
Most common reg class size	10–19 students
Most common lab size	less than 10 students

MOST POPULAR MAJORS
environmental science
landscape architecture (bs, bsla, bla, msla, mla, phd)
environmental biology

SELECTIVITY
# of applicants	1,349
% of applicants accepted	51
% of acceptees attending	36
# accepting a place on wait list	42
% admitted from wait list	24

FRESHMAN PROFILE
Range SAT Critical Reading	510–610
Range SAT Math	530–610
Range ACT Composite	22–27
Minimum paper TOEFL	550
Minimum computer TOEFL	213
Minimum web-based TOEFL	79
% graduated top 10% of class	24
% graduated top 25% of class	55
% graduated top 50% of class	91

DEADLINES
Early action Deadline	12/1
Notification	1/1
Regular Priority	12/1
Notification	rolling
Nonfall registration?	yes

FINANCIAL FACTS
Annual in-state tuition	$4,350
Annual out-of-state tuition	$10,610
Room and board	$11,320
Required fees	$750
Books and supplies	$1,200
% frosh rec. need-based scholarship or grant aid	74
% UG rec. need-based scholarship or grant aid	61
% frosh rec. non-need-based scholarship or grant aid	31

% UG rec. non-need-based scholarship or grant aid	118
% frosh rec. need-based self-help aid	74
% UG rec. need-based self-help aid	61
% frosh rec. any financial aid	100
% UG rec. any financial aid	82
% UG borrow to pay for school	80

STATE UNIVERSITY OF NEW YORK—FREDONIA

CAMPUS LIFE

Fire Safety Rating	**77**
Green Rating	**60***
Type of school	public
Environment	village

STUDENTS

Total undergrad enrollment	5,067
% male/female	44/56
% from out of state	2
% from public high school	75
% live on campus	52
% in (# of) fraternities	3 (3)
% in (# of) sororities	3 (3)
% African American	3
% Asian	2
% Caucasian	86
% Hispanic	3
% Native American	1
# of countries represented	8

ACADEMICS

Calendar	semester
Profs interesting rating	69
Profs accessible rating	71
Student/faculty ratio	17:1
Most common reg class size	10–19 students
Most common lab size	20–29 students

MOST POPULAR MAJORS
elementary education and teaching
music, other
business/commerce

SELECTIVITY

# of applicants	5,893
% of applicants accepted	56
% of acceptees attending	32
# of early decision applicants	82
% accepted early decision	65

FRESHMAN PROFILE

Range SAT Critical Reading	500–590
Range SAT Math	510–600
Range ACT Composite	21–26
Minimum paper TOEFL	500
Minimum computer TOEFL	177
Minimum web-based TOEFL	62
Average HS GPA	3.45
% graduated top 10% of class	16.1
% graduated top 25% of class	44.8
% graduated top 50% of class	87.4

DEADLINES

Early decision Deadline	11/1
Notification	rolling
Nonfall registration?	yes

FINANCIAL FACTS

Annual in-state tuition	$4,350
Annual out-of-state tuition	$10,610
Room and board	$8,380
Required fees	$1,192
Books and supplies	$1,000
% frosh rec. need-based scholarship or grant aid	59
% UG rec. need-based scholarship or grant aid	60
% frosh rec. non-need-based scholarship or grant aid	20
% UG rec. non-need-based scholarship or grant aid	12
% frosh rec. need-based self-help aid	54
% UG rec. need-based self-help aid	55
% frosh rec. any financial aid	81
% UG rec. any financial aid	85
% UG borrow to pay for school	81
Average cumulative indebtedness	$19,341

STATE UNIVERSITY OF NEW YORK—GENESEO

CAMPUS LIFE

Fire Safety Rating	**84**
Green Rating	**77**
Type of school	public
Environment	village

STUDENTS

Total undergrad enrollment	5,376
% male/female	42/58
% from out of state	1
% from public high school	81
% live on campus	56
% in (# of) fraternities	9 (9)
% in (# of) sororities	11 (11)
% African American	2
% Asian	6
% Caucasian	73
% Hispanic	3
% international	2
# of countries represented	30

ACADEMICS

Calendar	semester
Student/faculty ratio	19:1
Profs interesting rating	73
Profs accessible rating	79
Most common reg class size	10–19 students

MOST POPULAR MAJORS
elementary education and teaching
biology/biological sciences
business/commerce

SELECTIVITY

# of applicants	10,274
% of applicants accepted	36
% of acceptees attending	28
# accepting a place on wait list	320
# of early decision applicants	323
% accepted early decision	42

FRESHMAN PROFILE

Range SAT Critical Reading	600–690
Range SAT Math	620–690
Range ACT Composite	28–30
Minimum paper TOEFL	525
Minimum computer TOEFL	197
Average HS GPA	3.8
% graduated top 10% of class	57
% graduated top 25% of class	88
% graduated top 50% of class	99

DEADLINES

Early decision Deadline	11/15
Notification	12/15
Regular Deadline	1/1
Notification	3/1
Nonfall registration?	yes

FINANCIAL FACTS

Annual in-state tuition	$4,350
Annual out-of-state tuition	$10,610
Room and board	$8,550
Required fees	$1,266
Books and supplies	$800
% frosh rec. need-based scholarship or grant aid	25
% UG rec. need-based scholarship or grant aid	43
% frosh rec. non-need-based scholarship or grant aid	27
% UG rec. non-need-based scholarship or grant aid	8

% frosh rec. need-based self-help aid	20
% UG rec. need-based self-help aid	37
% frosh rec. any financial aid	68
% UG rec. any financial aid	75
% UG borrow to pay for school	65
Average cumulative indebtedness	$18,300

STATE UNIVERSITY OF NEW YORK—MARITIME COLLEGE

CAMPUS LIFE
Fire Safety Rating	**81**
Green Rating	**74**
Type of school	public
Environment	metropolis

STUDENTS
Total undergrad enrollment	1,327
% male/female	90/10
% from out of state	27
% live on campus	87
% African American	5
% Asian	4
% Caucasian	72
% Hispanic	10
% international	8

ACADEMICS
Calendar	semester
Profs interesting rating	71
Profs accessible rating	75
Student/faculty ratio	15:1
Most common reg class size	20–29 students
Most common lab size	20–29 students

MOST POPULAR MAJORS
engineering
transportation/transportation management

SELECTIVITY
# of applicants	1,158
% of applicants accepted	70
% of acceptees attending	50

FRESHMAN PROFILE
Range SAT Critical Reading	460–560
Range SAT Math	490–590
Range ACT Composite	18–22
Minimum paper TOEFL	500
Minimum computer TOEFL	213
Average HS GPA	2.85
% graduated top 10% of class	4

% graduated top 25% of class	29
% graduated top 50% of class	82

DEADLINES
Early decision	
Deadline	11/15
Notification	12/15
Nonfall registration?	yes

FINANCIAL FACTS
Annual in-state tuition	$4,350
Annual out-of-state tuition	$10,610
Room and board	$9,380
Required fees	$2,742
Books and supplies	$928
% frosh rec. need-based scholarship or grant aid	40
% UG rec. need-based scholarship or grant aid	40
% frosh rec. non-need-based scholarship or grant aid	2
% UG rec. non-need-based scholarship or grant aid	4
% frosh rec. need-based self-help aid	42
% UG rec. need-based self-help aid	41
% UG borrow to pay for school	43
Average cumulative indebtedness	$9,017

STATE UNIVERSITY OF NEW YORK—OSWEGO

CAMPUS LIFE
Fire Safety Rating	**67**
Green Rating	**70**
Type of school	public
Environment	village

STUDENTS
Total undergrad enrollment	6,962
% male/female	46/54
% from out of state	2
% live on campus	58
% in (# of) fraternities	7 (11)
% in (# of) sororities	6 (9)
% African American	4
% Asian	2
% Caucasian	88
% Hispanic	4
% Native American	1
% international	1
# of countries represented	13

ACADEMICS
Calendar	semester
Profs interesting rating	72
Profs accessible rating	72
Student/faculty ratio	18:1

Most common reg class size	10–19 students
Most common lab size	20-29 students

MOST POPULAR MAJORS
elementary education and teaching
business/commerce

SELECTIVITY
# of applicants	9,400
% of applicants accepted	50
% of acceptees attending	30
# of early decision applicants	160
% accepted early decision	53

FRESHMAN PROFILE
Range SAT Critical Reading	510–590
Range SAT Math	520–580
Range ACT Composite	21–25
Minimum paper TOEFL	550
Minimum computer TOEFL	213
Minimum web-based TOEFL	80
Average HS GPA	3.29
% graduated top 10% of class	13
% graduated top 25% of class	51
% graduated top 50% of class	85

DEADLINES
Early decision	
Deadline	11/15
Notification	12/15
Regular	
Priority	1/15
Notification	rolling
Nonfall registration?	yes

FINANCIAL FACTS
Annual in-state tuition	$4,350
Annual out-of-state tuition	$10,610
Room and board	$9,470
Required fees	$1,584
Books and supplies	$800
% frosh rec. need-based scholarship or grant aid	56
% UG rec. need-based scholarship or grant aid	57
% frosh rec. non-need-based scholarship or grant aid	25
% UG rec. non-need-based scholarship or grant aid	14
% frosh rec. need-based self-help aid	52
% UG rec. need-based self-help aid	55
% frosh rec. any financial aid	62
% UG rec. any financial aid	64
% UG borrow to pay for school	84
Average cumulative indebtedness	$21,845

STATE UNIVERSITY OF NEW YORK—PURCHASE COLLEGE

CAMPUS LIFE
Fire Safety Rating	**60***
Green Rating	**60***
Type of school	public
Environment	town

STUDENTS
Total undergrad enrollment	3,480
% male/female	47/53
% from out of state	20
% live on campus	69
% African American	9
% Asian	4
% Caucasian	57
% Hispanic	10
% international	2
# of countries represented	21

ACADEMICS
Calendar	semester
Student/faculty ratio	15:1
Profs interesting rating	77
Profs accessible rating	65
% classes taught by TAs	1
Most common reg class size	fewer than 10 students
Most common lab size	10–19 students

MOST POPULAR MAJORS
liberal arts and sciences/liberal studies
psychology

SELECTIVITY
# of applicants	7,388
% of applicants accepted	30
% of acceptees attending	31
# of early decision applicants	11
% accepted early decision	73

FRESHMAN PROFILE
Range SAT Critical Reading	510–620
Range SAT Math	480–590
Minimum paper TOEFL	550
Minimum computer TOEFL	213
Average HS GPA	3.04
% graduated top 10% of class	10
% graduated top 25% of class	32
% graduated top 50% of class	72

DEADLINES
Early decision Deadline	11/1
Notification	12/5
Regular Priority	3/1
Deadline	7/15
Notification	5/1
Nonfall registration?	yes

FINANCIAL FACTS
Annual in-state tuition	$4,350
Annual out-of-state tuition	$10,610
Room and board	$9,028
Required fees	$1,359
Books and supplies	$1,500
% frosh rec. any financial aid	78
% UG rec. any financial aid	77
% UG borrow to pay for school	78
Average cumulative indebtedness	$20,222

STATE UNIVERSITY OF NEW YORK—STONY BROOK UNIVERSITY

CAMPUS LIFE
Fire Safety Rating	**60***
Green Rating	**84**
Type of school	public
Environment	town

STUDENTS
Total undergrad enrollment	15,222
% male/female	50/50
% from out of state	5
% from public high school	90
% live on campus	52
% in (# of) fraternities	1 (17)
% in (# of) sororities	1 (17)
% African American	9
% Asian	22
% Caucasian	35
% Hispanic	8
% international	6
# of countries represented	86

ACADEMICS
Calendar	semester
Student/faculty ratio	18:1
Profs interesting rating	62
Profs accessible rating	61

MOST POPULAR MAJORS
psychology
biology/biological sciences
health professions and related clinical sciences

SELECTIVITY
# of applicants	24,060
% of applicants accepted	43
% of acceptees attending	27

FRESHMAN PROFILE
Range SAT Critical Reading	520–620
Range SAT Math	560–660
Minimum paper TOEFL	550
Minimum computer TOEFL	213
Minimum web-based TOEFL	80

DEADLINES
Regular	12/01
Nonfall registration?	Yes

FINANCIAL FACTS
Annual in-state tuition	$4,350
Annual out-of-state tuition	$10,610
Room and board	$9,170
Required fees	$1,480
Books and supplies	$900
% frosh rec. need-based scholarship or grant aid	51
% UG rec. need-based scholarship or grant aid	51
% frosh rec. non-need-based scholarship or grant aid	5
% UG rec. non-need-based scholarship or grant aid	5
% frosh rec. need-based self-help aid	37
% UG rec. need-based self-help aid	40
% frosh rec. athletic scholarships	2
% UG rec. athletic scholarships	1
% frosh rec. any financial aid	74
% UG rec. any financial aid	67
% UG borrow to pay for school	71
Average cumulative indebtedness	$15,076

STATE UNIVERSITY OF NEW YORK—UNIVERSITY AT ALBANY

CAMPUS LIFE
Fire Safety Rating	**60***
Green Rating	**88**
Type of school	public
Environment	city

STUDENTS
Total undergrad enrollment	12,449
% male/female	51/49

% from out of state	5
% live on campus	57
% in (# of) fraternities	4 (11)
% in (# of) sororities	5 (18)
% African American	9
% Asian	6
% Caucasian	58
% Hispanic	7
% international	2
# of countries represented	91

ACADEMICS

Calendar	semester
Student/faculty ratio	19:1
Profs interesting rating	61
Profs accessible rating	61
% classes taught by TAs	7
Most common	
reg class size	20–29 students
Most common	
lab size	10–19 students

MOST POPULAR MAJORS
English language and literature
psychology
business/commerce

SELECTIVITY

# of applicants	20,249
% of applicants accepted	52
% of acceptees attending	24

FRESHMAN PROFILE

Range SAT Critical Reading	520–600
Range SAT Math	540–620
Range ACT Composite	23–26
Minimum paper TOEFL	550
Minimum computer TOEFL	213
Average HS GPA	3.4
% graduated top 10% of class	15
% graduated top 25% of class	49
% graduated top 50% of class	90

DEADLINES

Early action	
Deadline	11/15
Notification	1/1
Regular	
Priority	1/15
Deadline	3/1
Notification	rolling
Nonfall registration?	yes

FINANCIAL FACTS

Annual in-state tuition	$4,350
Annual out-of-state tuition	$10,610
Room and board	$9,032
Required fees	$1,668
Books and supplies	$1,000

% frosh rec. need-based	
scholarship or grant aid	50
% UG rec. need-based	
scholarship or grant aid	49
% frosh rec. non-need-based	
scholarship or grant aid	2
% UG rec. non-need-based	
scholarship or grant aid	2
% frosh rec. need-based	
self-help aid	48
% UG rec. need-based	
self-help aid	46
% frosh rec.	
athletic scholarships	1
% UG rec. athletic scholarships	1
% frosh rec.	
any financial aid	61
% UG rec. any financial aid	60
% UG borrow to pay for school	85
Average cumulative	
indebtedness	$13,842

STATE UNIVERSITY OF NEW YORK—UNIVERSITY AT BUFFALO

CAMPUS LIFE

Fire Safety Rating	**60***
Green Rating	**60***
Type of school	public
Environment	metropolis

STUDENTS

Total undergrad enrollment	18,779
% male/female	54/46
% from out of state	4
% live on campus	40
% in (# of) fraternities	2 (19)
% in (# of) sororities	4 (14)
% African American	7
% Asian	9
% Caucasian	60
% Hispanic	4
% international	10
# of countries represented	113

ACADEMICS

Calendar	semester
Student/faculty ratio	16:1
Profs interesting rating	62
Profs accessible rating	67
% classes taught by TAs	12
Most common	
reg class size	20–29 students

Most common	
lab size	20–29 students

MOST POPULAR MAJORS
engineering
psychology
business/commerce

SELECTIVITY

# of applicants	19,831
% of applicants accepted	52
% of acceptees attending	32
# accepting a place on wait list	344
% admitted from wait list	80
# of early decision applicants	512
% accepted early decision	69

FRESHMAN PROFILE

Range SAT Critical Reading	500–610
Range SAT Math	540–650
Range ACT Composite	23–27
Minimum paper TOEFL	550
Minimum computer TOEFL	213
Average HS GPA	3.2
% graduated top 10% of class	24
% graduated top 25% of class	62
% graduated top 50% of class	93

DEADLINES

Early decision	
Deadline	11/1
Notification	12/15
Regular	
Priority	11/1
Notification	rolling
Nonfall registration?	yes

FINANCIAL FACTS

Annual in-state tuition	$4,350
Annual out-of-state tuition	$10,610
Room and board	$9,132
Required fees	$1,867
Books and supplies	$947
% frosh rec. need-based	
scholarship or grant aid	35
% UG rec. need-based	
scholarship or grant aid	33
% frosh rec. non-need-based	
scholarship or grant aid	21
% UG rec. non-need-based	
scholarship or grant aid	11
% frosh rec. need-based	
self-help aid	52
% UG rec. need-based	
self-help aid	50
% frosh rec. athletic scholarships	1
% UG rec. athletic scholarships	1
% frosh rec. any financial aid	67
% UG rec. any financial aid	75

% UG borrow to pay for school	69
Average cumulative indebtedness	$17,657

STEVENS INSTITUTE OF TECHNOLOGY

CAMPUS LIFE

Fire Safety Rating	**60***
Green Rating	**60***
Type of school	private
Environment	town

STUDENTS

Total undergrad enrollment	2,044
% male/female	75/25
% from out of state	32
% from public high school	80
% live on campus	67
% in (# of) fraternities	25 (10)
% in (# of) sororities	23 (3)
% African American	4
% Asian	12
% Caucasian	52
% Hispanic	9
% international	5
# of countries represented	65

ACADEMICS

Calendar	semester
Student/faculty ratio	8:1
Profs interesting rating	61
Profs accessible rating	62
Most common reg class size	20–29 students
Most common lab size	10–19 students

MOST POPULAR MAJORS
computer and information sciences
mechanical engineering
business & technology

SELECTIVITY

# of applicants	3,058
% of applicants accepted	49
% of acceptees attending	38
# accepting a place on wait list	328
% admitted from wait list	17
# of early decision applicants	277
% accepted early decision	79

FRESHMAN PROFILE

Range SAT Critical Reading	550–650
Range SAT Math	620–710
Minimum paper TOEFL	550
Minimum computer TOEFL	213
Average HS GPA	3.7

% graduated top 10% of class	49
% graduated top 25% of class	86
% graduated top 50% of class	97

DEADLINES

Early decision I	
Deadline	11/15
Notification	12/15
Early decision II	
Deadline	1/15
Notification	2/15
Regular	
Priority	11/15
Deadline	2/1
Notification	4/1
Nonfall registration?	no

FINANCIAL FACTS

Annual tuition	$34,900
Room and board	$11,000
Required fees	$1,800
Books and supplies	$900
% frosh rec. need-based scholarship or grant aid	58
% UG rec. need-based scholarship or grant aid	54
% frosh rec. non-need-based scholarship or grant aid	59
% UG rec. non-need-based scholarship or grant aid	50
% frosh rec. need-based self-help aid	57
% UG rec. need-based self-help aid	56
% frosh rec. any financial aid	83
% UG rec. any financial aid	76
% UG borrow to pay for school	68
Average cumulative indebtedness	$14,700

STONEHILL COLLEGE

CAMPUS LIFE

Fire Safety Rating	**60***
Green Rating	**60***
Type of school	private
Affiliation	Roman Catholic
Environment	village

STUDENTS

Total undergrad enrollment	2,413
% male/female	39/61
% from out of state	43
% from public high school	67
% live on campus	87
% African American	2
% Asian	2

% Caucasian	92
% Hispanic	4
# of countries represented	10

ACADEMICS

Calendar	semester
Profs interesting rating	93
Profs accessible rating	88
Student/faculty ratio	13:1
Most common reg class size	20–29 students
Most common lab size	10–19 students

MOST POPULAR MAJORS
English language and literature
biology/biological sciences
psychology

SELECTIVITY

# of applicants	5,704
% of applicants accepted	52
% of acceptees attending	22
# accepting a place on wait list	496
% admitted from wait list	5
# of early decision applicants	43
% accepted early decision	65

FRESHMAN PROFILE

Range SAT Critical Reading	540–630
Range SAT Math	550–640
Range ACT Composite	24–27
Minimum paper TOEFL	550
Minimum computer TOEFL	213
Average HS GPA	3.57
% graduated top 10% of class	49
% graduated top 25% of class	89
% graduated top 50% of class	99.5

DEADLINES

Early decision	
Deadline	11/1
Notification	12/15
Early action	
Deadline	11/1
Notification	1/15
Regular	
Deadline	1/15
Notification	4/1
Nonfall registration?	yes

FINANCIAL FACTS

Annual tuition	$28,440
% frosh rec. any financial aid	93
% UG rec. any financial aid	89
% UG borrow to pay for school	76.84
Average cumulative indebtedness	$16,661

SUFFOLK UNIVERSITY

CAMPUS LIFE

Fire Safety Rating	**99**
Green Rating	**91**
Type of school	private
Environment	metropolis

STUDENTS

Total undergrad enrollment	5,289
% male/female	44/56
% from out of state	27
% from public high school	67
% live on campus	16
% in (# of) fraternities	NR (1)
% in (# of) sororities	NR (1)
% African American	3
% Asian	6
% Caucasian	62
% Hispanic	5
% international	9
# of countries represented	94

ACADEMICS

Calendar	semester
Student/faculty ratio	12:1
Profs interesting rating	73
Profs accessible rating	72
% classes taught by TAs	1
Most common reg class size	20–29 students
Most common lab size	10–19 students

MOST POPULAR MAJORS
sociology
interior design
business/corporate communications

SELECTIVITY

# of applicants	8,044
% of applicants accepted	80
% of acceptees attending	21
# accepting a place on wait list	391
% admitted from wait list	25

FRESHMAN PROFILE

Range SAT Critical Reading	460–560
Range SAT Math	450–570
Range SAT Writing	460–560
Range ACT Composite	20–24
Minimum paper TOEFL	525
Minimum computer TOEFL	197
Average HS GPA	2.95
% graduated top 10% of class	9
% graduated top 25% of class	31
% graduated top 50% of class	68

DEADLINES

Early action	
Deadline	11/20
Notification	12/20
Regular	
Deadline	3/1
Notification	modified
Nonfall registration?	yes

FINANCIAL FACTS

Annual tuition	$25,850
% frosh rec. need-based scholarship or grant aid	64
% UG rec. need-based scholarship or grant aid	68
% frosh rec. non-need-based scholarship or grant aid	17
% UG rec. non-need-based scholarship or grant aid	16
% frosh rec. need-based self-help aid	72
% UG rec. need-based self-help aid	77
% frosh rec. any financial aid	63
% UG rec. any financial aid	62

SUSQUEHANNA UNIVERSITY

CAMPUS LIFE

Fire Safety Rating	**84**
Green Rating	**79**
Type of school	private
Affiliation	Lutheran
Environment	town

STUDENTS

Total undergrad enrollment	1,976
% male/female	46/54
% from out of state	43
% from public high school	85
% live on campus	77
% in (# of) fraternities	20 (4)
% in (# of) sororities	25 (5)
% African American	3
% Asian	2
% Caucasian	91
% Hispanic	2
% international	1
# of countries represented	8

ACADEMICS

Calendar	semester
Student/faculty ratio	14:1
Profs interesting rating	81
Profs accessible rating	87
Most common reg class size	10–19 students
Most common lab size	10–19 students

SELECTIVITY

# of applicants	2,373
% of applicants accepted	86
% of acceptees attending	29
# accepting a place on wait list	68
% admitted from wait list	21
# of early decision applicants	212
% accepted early decision	62

FRESHMAN PROFILE

Range SAT Critical Reading	520–610
Range SAT Math	530–610
Range SAT Writing	510–610
Range ACT Composite	22–27
Minimum paper TOEFL	550
Minimum computer TOEFL	213
% graduated top 10% of class	34.3
% graduated top 25% of class	60.5
% graduated top 50% of class	90.5

DEADLINES

Early decision	
Deadline	11/15
Notification	12/1
Regular	
Priority	3/1
Deadline	8/1
Notification	rolling
Nonfall registration?	yes

FINANCIAL FACTS

Annual tuition	$31,080
Books and supplies	$750
% frosh rec. need-based scholarship or grant aid	58
% UG rec. need-based scholarship or grant aid	57
% frosh rec. non-need-based scholarship or grant aid	9
% UG rec. non-need-based scholarship or grant aid	7
% frosh rec. need-based self-help aid	53
% UG rec. need-based self-help aid	54
% frosh rec. any financial aid	92
% UG rec. any financial aid	92
% UG borrow to pay for school	82
Average cumulative indebtedness	$16,863

SWARTHMORE COLLEGE

CAMPUS LIFE
Fire Safety Rating **88**
Green Rating **83**
Type of school   private
Environment   village

STUDENTS
Total undergrad enrollment   1,480
% male/female   48/52
% from out of state   87
% from public high school   59
% live on campus   95
% in (# of) fraternities   7 (2)
% African American   8
% Asian   17
% Caucasian   43
% Hispanic   10
% Native American   1
% international   7
# of countries represented   35

ACADEMICS
Calendar   semester
Student/faculty ratio   8:1
Profs interesting rating   97
Profs accessible rating   95
Most common
   reg class size   fewer than 10
                                 students
Most common
   lab size   fewer than 10 students

MOST POPULAR MAJORS
economics
political science and government
biology/biological sciences

SELECTIVITY
of applicants   5,242
% of applicants accepted   18
% of acceptees attending   39
# of early decision applicants   424
% accepted early decision   36

FRESHMAN PROFILE
Range SAT Critical Reading   680–780
Range SAT Math   680–760
Range SAT Writing   680–760
Range ACT Composite   27–33
% graduated top 10% of class   90.5
% graduated top 25% of class   96.3
% graduated top 50% of class   100

DEADLINES
Early decision
   Deadline   11/15
   Notification   12/15

Regular
   Deadline   1/2
   Notification   4/1
Nonfall registration?   no

FINANCIAL FACTS
Annual tuition $34,564
Room and board $10,816
Required fees $320
Books and supplies $1,080
% frosh rec. need-based
   scholarship or grant aid   48
% UG rec. need-based
   scholarship or grant aid   48
% frosh rec. need-based
   self-help aid   46
% UG rec. need-based
   self-help aid   47
% frosh rec. any financial aid   48
% UG rec. any financial aid   50
% UG borrow to pay for school   30

SYRACUSE UNIVERSITY

CAMPUS LIFE
Fire Safety Rating **60***
Green Rating **89**
Type of school   private
Environment   metropolis

STUDENTS
Total undergrad enrollment   11,794
% male/female   45/55
% from out of state   56
% from public high school   75
% live on campus   75
% in (# of) fraternities   18 (27)
% in (# of) sororities   21 (18)
% African American   7
% Asian   9
% Caucasian   64
% Hispanic   6
% Native American   1
% international   4
# of countries represented   115

ACADEMICS
Calendar   semester
Student/faculty ratio   15:1
Profs interesting rating   70
Profs accessible rating   73
% classes taught by TAs   6
Most common
   reg class size   10–19 students
Most common
   lab size   20–29 students

MOST POPULAR MAJORS
commercial and advertising art
radio, television, and digital
communication
business administration and
management

SELECTIVITY
of applicants   21,219
% of applicants accepted   51
% of acceptees attending   29
# accepting a place on wait list   1,761
% admitted from wait list   11
# of early decision applicants   757
% accepted early decision   80

FRESHMAN PROFILE
Range SAT Critical Reading   540–650
Range SAT Math   570–680
Range ACT Composite   24–29
Minimum paper TOEFL   560
Minimum computer TOEFL   213
Minimum web-based TOEFL   80
Average HS GPA   3.6
% graduated top 10% of class   42
% graduated top 25% of class   70
% graduated top 50% of class   94

DEADLINES
Early decision
   Deadline   11/15
   Notification   12/15
Regular
   Deadline   1/1
   Notification   3/15
Nonfall registration?   yes

FINANCIAL FACTS
Annual tuition $30,470
Room and board $10,940
Required fees $1,216
Books and supplies $1,230
% frosh rec. need-based
   scholarship or grant aid   54
% UG rec. need-based
   scholarship or grant aid   53
% frosh rec. non-need-based
   scholarship or grant aid   3
% UG rec. non-need-based
   scholarship or grant aid   2
% frosh rec. need-based
   self-help aid   53
% UG rec. need-based
   self-help aid   51
% frosh rec. athletic scholarships 3
% UG rec. athletic scholarships   3
% frosh rec. any financial aid   79
% UG rec. any financial aid   78

% UG borrow to pay for school 63
Average cumulative
indebtedness $27,152

TEMPLE UNIVERSITY

CAMPUS LIFE
Fire Safety Rating **85**
Green Rating **75**
Type of school public
Environment metropolis

STUDENTS
Total undergrad enrollment 24,861
% male/female 45/55
% from out of state 22
% from public high school 76.5
% live on campus 20
% in (# of) fraternities 1 (14)
% in (# of) sororities 1 (9)
% African American 17
% Asian 10
% Caucasian 58
% Hispanic 3
% international 3
# of countries represented 133

ACADEMICS
Calendar semester
Student/faculty ratio 17:1
Profs interesting rating 67
Profs accessible rating 71
Most common
  reg class size 10–19 students
Most common
  lab size 20–29 students
MOST POPULAR MAJORS
psychology
elementary education and teaching
marketing/marketing management

SELECTIVITY
of applicants 16,659
% of applicants accepted 63
% of acceptees attending 39
# accepting a place on wait list 250
% admitted from wait list 4

FRESHMAN PROFILE
Range SAT Critical Reading 490–590
Range SAT Math 490–590
Range ACT Composite 20–25
Minimum paper TOEFL 550
Minimum computer TOEFL 213
Minimum web-based TOEFL 79
Average HS GPA 3.35
% graduated top 10% of class 19
% graduated top 25% of class 52

% graduated top 50% of class 89

DEADLINES
Regular
  Deadline 3/1
  Notification rolling
Nonfall registration? yes

FINANCIAL FACTS
Annual in-state tuition $10,252
Annual out-of-state tuition $18,770
Room and board $8,518
Required fees $550
Books and supplies $1,000
% frosh rec. need-based
  scholarship or grant aid 68
% UG rec. need-based
  scholarship or grant aid 63
% frosh rec. non-need-based
  scholarship or grant aid 41
% UG rec. non-need-based
  scholarship or grant aid 32
% frosh rec. need-based
  self-help aid 58
% UG rec. need-based
  self-help aid 54
% frosh rec. athletic scholarships 1
% UG rec. athletic scholarships 1
% frosh rec. any financial aid 86
% UG rec. any financial aid 89
% UG borrow to pay for school 75
Average cumulative
  indebtedness $29,046

TOWSON UNIVERSITY

CAMPUS LIFE
Fire Safety Rating **95**
Green Rating **79**
Type of school public
Environment metropolis

STUDENTS
Total undergrad enrollment 15,488
% male/female 40/60
% from out of state 17
% live on campus 22
% in (# of) fraternities 7 (12)
% in (# of) sororities 7 (10)
% African American 11
% Asian 4
% Caucasian 70
% Hispanic 2
% international 3
# of countries represented 101

ACADEMICS
Calendar semester
Profs interesting rating 74
Profs accessible rating 71
Student/faculty ratio 18:1
Most common
  reg class size 20–29 students
Most common
  lab size 10–19 students
MOST POPULAR MAJORS
psychology
mass communication/media studies

SELECTIVITY
of applicants 15,464
% of applicants accepted 60
% of acceptees attending 29
# accepting a place on wait list 2,678
% admitted from wait list 26

FRESHMAN PROFILE
Range SAT Critical Reading 490–580
Range SAT Math 500–590
Range SAT Writing 500–580
Range ACT Composite 20–24
Minimum paper TOEFL 500
Minimum computer TOEFL 173
Average HS GPA 3.46
% graduated top 10% of class 18
% graduated top 25% of class 44
% graduated top 50% of class 79

DEADLINES
Regular
  Priority 12/1
  Deadline 2/15
  Notification rolling
Nonfall registration? yes

FINANCIAL FACTS
Annual in-state tuition $5,180
Annual out-of-state tuition $15,120
Room and board $7,986
Required fees $2,054
Books and supplies $948
% frosh rec. need-based
  scholarship or grant aid 32
% UG rec. need-based
  scholarship or grant aid 28
% frosh rec. non-need-based
  scholarship or grant aid 21
% UG rec. non-need-based
  scholarship or grant aid 13
% frosh rec. need-based self-help aid 29
% UG rec. need-based self-help aid 29
% frosh rec. athletic scholarships 1
% UG rec. athletic scholarships 1
% frosh rec. any financial aid 65

% UG rec. any financial aid 72
% UG borrow to pay for school 51
Average cumulative indebtedness $11,844

TRINITY COLLEGE (CT)

CAMPUS LIFE
Fire Safety Rating **86**
Green Rating **60***
Type of school private
Environment metropolis

STUDENTS
Total undergrad enrollment 2,375
% male/female 50/50
% from out of state 83
% from public high school 44
% live on campus 95
% in (# of) fraternities 20 (7)
% in (# of) sororities 16 (3)
% African American 7
% Asian 5
% Caucasian 61
% Hispanic 6
% international 4
# of countries represented 30

ACADEMICS
Calendar semester
Student/faculty ratio 10:1
Profs interesting rating 82
Profs accessible rating 81
Most common
 reg class size 10–19 students
Most common
 lab size 10–19 students
MOST POPULAR MAJORS
economics
political science and government
history

SELECTIVITY
of applicants 5,950
% of applicants accepted 34
% of acceptees attending 28
# accepting a place on wait list 460
% admitted from wait list 37
# of early decision applicants 412
% accepted early decision 69

FRESHMAN PROFILE
Range SAT Critical Reading 600–690
Range SAT Math 610–690
Range SAT Writing 608–700
Range ACT Composite 26–29
% graduated top 10% of class 61
% graduated top 25% of class 88
% graduated top 50% of class 96

DEADLINES
Early decision
 Deadline 11/15
 Notification 12/15
Regular
 Deadline 1/1
 Notification 4/1
Nonfall registration? no

FINANCIAL FACTS
Annual tuition $35,110
Room and board $9,420
Required fees $1,760
Books and supplies $900
% frosh rec. need-based
 scholarship or grant aid 35
% UG rec. need-based
 scholarship or grant aid 36
% frosh rec. non-need-based
 scholarship or grant aid 11
% UG rec. non-need-based
 scholarship or grant aid 9
% frosh rec. need-based
 self-help aid 28
% UG rec. need-based
 self-help aid 31
% frosh rec. any financial aid 39
% UG rec. any financial aid 40
% UG borrow to pay for school 43
Average cumulative
 indebtedness $19,835

TUFTS UNIVERSITY

CAMPUS LIFE
Fire Safety Rating **96**
Green Rating **94**
Type of school private
Environment town

STUDENTS
Total undergrad enrollment 5,015
% male/female 49/51
% from out of state 75
% from public high school 62
% live on campus 75
% in (# of) fraternities 10 (11)
% in (# of) sororities 4 (3)
% African American 7
% Asian 12
% Caucasian 57
% Hispanic 6
% international 6
# of countries represented 93

ACADEMICS
Calendar semester
Student/faculty ratio 7:1

Profs interesting rating 83
Profs accessible rating 80
% classes taught by TAs 1
Most common
 reg class size 10–19 students
Most common
 lab size 10–19 students
MOST POPULAR MAJORS
English language and literature
economics
international relations and affairs

SELECTIVITY
of applicants 15,380
% of applicants accepted 28
% of acceptees attending 32
# of early decision applicants 1,321
% accepted early decision 32

FRESHMAN PROFILE
Range SAT Critical Reading 670–750
Range SAT Math 670–740
Range SAT Writing 670–740
Range ACT Composite 30–32
Minimum paper TOEFL 300
Minimum computer TOEFL 100
% graduated top 10% of class 80
% graduated top 25% of class 96
% graduated top 50% of class 99

DEADLINES
Early decision
 Deadline 11/1
 Notification 12/15
Regular
 Deadline 1/1
 Notification 4/1
Nonfall registration? no

FINANCIAL FACTS
Annual tuition $38,840
% frosh rec. need-based
 scholarship or grant aid 38
% UG rec. need-based
 scholarship or grant aid 35
% frosh rec. non-need-based
 scholarship or grant aid 1
% UG rec. non-need-based
 scholarship or grant aid 1
% frosh rec. need-based
 self-help aid 38
% UG rec. need-based
 self-help aid 35
% frosh rec. any financial aid 42
% UG rec. any financial aid 38
% UG borrow to pay for school 42
Average cumulative
 indebtedness $14,200

UNION COLLEGE (NY)

CAMPUS LIFE
Fire Safety Rating	**83**
Green Rating	**85**
Type of school	private
Environment	town

STUDENTS
Total undergrad enrollment	2,134
% male/female	52/48
% from out of state	60
% from public high school	69
% live on campus	89
% in (# of) fraternities	30 (7)
% in (# of) sororities	32 (3)
% African American	3
% Asian	6
% Caucasian	84
% Hispanic	4
% international	2
# of countries represented	26

ACADEMICS
Calendar	trimester
Student/faculty ratio	10:1
Profs interesting rating	85
Profs accessible rating	86
Most common reg class size	10–19 students
Most common lab size	10–19 students

MOST POPULAR MAJORS
psychology
economics
political science and government

SELECTIVITY
# of applicants	4,837
% of applicants accepted	43
% of acceptees attending	27
# accepting a place on wait list	183
% admitted from wait list	23
# of early decision applicants	259
% accepted early decision	83

FRESHMAN PROFILE
Range SAT Critical Reading	560–660
Range SAT Math	590–680
Range SAT Writing	570–670
Range ACT Composite	25–29
Minimum paper TOEFL	600
Minimum computer TOEFL	250
Minimum web-based TOEFL	90
Average HS GPA	3.5
% graduated top 10% of class	64
% graduated top 25% of class	87
% graduated top 50% of class	97

DEADLINES
Early decision	
Deadline	11/15
Notification	12/15
Regular	
Deadline	1/15
Notification	4/1
Nonfall registration?	no

FINANCIAL FACTS
Comprehensive fee	$46,245
Books and supplies	$450
% frosh rec. need-based scholarship or grant aid	35
% UG rec. need-based scholarship or grant aid	48
% frosh rec. non-need-based scholarship or grant aid	1
% UG rec. non-need-based scholarship or grant aid	2
% frosh rec. need-based self-help aid	35
% UG rec. need-based self-help aid	42
% frosh rec. any financial aid	67
% UG rec. any financial aid	65
% UG borrow to pay for school	54
Average cumulative indebtedness	$24,100

UNITED STATES COAST GUARD ACADEMY

CAMPUS LIFE
Fire Safety Rating	**77**
Green Rating	**77**
Type of school	public
Environment	city

STUDENTS
Total undergrad enrollment	996
% male/female	72/28
% from out of state	94
% live on campus	100
% African American	3
% Asian	5
% Caucasian	86
% Hispanic	5
% Native American	1
% international	1
# of countries represented	9

ACADEMICS
Calendar	semester
Student/faculty ratio	9:1
Profs interesting rating	68
Profs accessible rating	96
Most common reg class size	10–19 students
Most common lab size	10–19 students

MOST POPULAR MAJORS
engineering
marine science
government

SELECTIVITY
# of applicants	1,633
% of applicants accepted	24
% of acceptees attending	70

FRESHMAN PROFILE
Range SAT Critical Reading	570–670
Range SAT Math	610–680
Range ACT Composite	25–29
Average HS GPA	3.76
% graduated top 10% of class	50
% graduated top 25% of class	90
% graduated top 50% of class	99

DEADLINES
Early action	
Deadline	11/1
Notification	12/15
Regular	
Priority	12/15
Deadline	3/1
Notification	rolling
Nonfall registration?	no

FINANCIAL FACTS
Annual in-state tuition	$0*
Annual out-of-state tuition	$0*

*Tuition covered by full scholarship.

UNITED STATES MERCHANT MARINE ACADEMY

CAMPUS LIFE
Fire Safety Rating	**60***
Green Rating	**60***
Type of school	public
Environment	village

STUDENTS
Total undergrad enrollment	995
% male/female	88/12
% from out of state	87
% from public high school	71
% live on campus	100
% international	2
# of countries represented	5

ACADEMICS
Calendar	trimester

Student/faculty ratio	11:1
Profs interesting rating	61
Profs accessible rating	69
Most common	
reg class size	10–19 students
Most common	
lab size	10–19 students

MOST POPULAR MAJORS
engineering
naval architecture and
marine engineering
transportation and materials moving

SELECTIVITY
# of applicants	1,754
% of applicants accepted	26
% of acceptees attending	60

FRESHMAN PROFILE
Range SAT Critical Reading	540–633
Range SAT Math	588–669
Range ACT Composite	26–29
Minimum paper TOEFL	533
Minimum computer TOEFL	200
Minimum web-based TOEFL	73
Average HS GPA	3.6
% graduated top 10% of class	21
% graduated top 25% of class	53
% graduated top 50% of class	89

DEADLINES
Early decision	
Deadline	11/1
Notification	12/31
Regular	
Deadline	3/1
Notification	rolling
Nonfall registration?	no

FINANCIAL FACTS
Required fees	$2,843
% frosh rec. need-based	
scholarship or grant aid	15
% UG rec. need-based	
scholarship or grant aid	5
% frosh rec. non-need-based	
scholarship or grant aid	27
% UG rec. non-need-based	
scholarship or grant aid	13
% frosh rec. need-based	
self-help aid	15
% UG rec. need-based	
self-help aid	8
% UG borrow to pay for school	18
Average cumulative	
indebtedness	$10,497

UNITED STATES MILITARY ACADEMY

CAMPUS LIFE
Fire Safety Rating	**86**
Green Rating	**60***
Type of school	public
Environment	village

STUDENTS
Total undergrad enrollment	4,231
% male/female	85/15
% from out of state	92
% from public high school	86
% live on campus	100
% African American	6
% Asian	7
% Caucasian	77
% Hispanic	7
% Native American	1
% international	1
# of countries represented	35

ACADEMICS
Calendar	semester
Student/faculty ratio	7:1
Profs interesting rating	89
Profs accessible rating	99
% profs teaching	
UG courses	100
% classes taught by TAs	0
Most common	
lab size	10–19 students
Most common	
reg class size	10–19 students

MOST POPULAR MAJORS
economics
history
political science and government

SELECTIVITY
# of applicants	10,778
% of applicants accepted	14
% of acceptees attending	77

FRESHMAN PROFILE
Range SAT Critical Reading	570–670
Range SAT Math	600–690
Range ACT Composite	21–36
Average HS GPA	3.75
% graduated top 10% of class	48
% graduated top 25% of class	77
% graduated top 50% of class	94

DEADLINES
Regular application deadline	2/28
Regular notification	rolling
Nonfall registration?	no

FINANCIAL FACTS
Annual in-state tuition	$0*
Annual out-of-state tuition	$0*

*Tuition covered by full scholarship.

UNITED STATES NAVAL ACADEMY

CAMPUS LIFE
Fire Safety Rating	**60***
Green Rating	**60***
Type of school	public
Environment	town

STUDENTS
Total undergrad enrollment	4,443
% male/female	79/21
% from out of state	95
% from public high school	60
% live on campus	100
% African American	4
% Asian	3
% Caucasian	76
% Hispanic	10
% Native American	1
% international	1
# of countries represented	24

ACADEMICS
Calendar	semester
Student/faculty ratio	8:1
Profs interesting rating	81
Profs accessible rating	99
Most common	
reg class size	10–19 students

MOST POPULAR MAJORS
systems engineering
economics
political science and government

SELECTIVITY
# of applicants	12,003
% of applicants accepted	12
% of acceptees attending	85
# accepting a place on wait list	70
% admitted from wait list	21

FRESHMAN PROFILE
Range SAT Critical Reading	560–660
Range SAT Math	600–690
Minimum paper TOEFL	200
% graduated top 10% of class	56
% graduated top 25% of class	81
% graduated top 50% of class	96

DEADLINES

Regular

Deadline 1/31

Notification rolling

Nonfall registration? no

FINANCIAL FACTS

Annual in-state tuition $0*

Annual out-of-state tuition $0*

Books and supplies $1,000

*Tuition covered by full scholarship.

UNITY COLLEGE

CAMPUS LIFE

Fire Safety Rating 60*

Green Rating 98

Type of school private

Environment rural

STUDENTS

Total undergrad enrollment 512

% male/female 69/31

% from out of state 64

% from public high school 98

% live on campus 80

% African American 1

% Caucasian 98

% international 1

ACADEMICS

Calendar semester

Student/faculty ratio 14:1

Profs interesting rating 88

Profs accessible rating 84

% profs teaching UG courses 100

% classes taught by TAs 0

SELECTIVITY

of applicants 500

% of applicants accepted 92

% of acceptees attending 34

FRESHMAN PROFILE

Range SAT Critical Reading 480–500

Range SAT Math 500–510

Minimum Paper TOEFL 500

Minimum Computer Based TOEFL 1

Average HS GPA 2.7

% graduated top 10% of class 3

% graduated top 25% of class 13

% graduated top 50% of class 48

DEADLINES

Regular notification rolling

Nonfall registration? yes

FINANCIAL FACTS

Annual tuition $12,330

Room & Board $5,300

Books and supplies $450

Required fees $560

% frosh rec. need-based

scholarship or grant aid 75

% UG rec. need-based

scholarship or grant aid 67

% frosh rec. need-based self-help aid 78

% UG rec. need-based self-help aid 74

UNIVERSITY OF THE ARTS

CAMPUS LIFE

Fire Safety Rating 60*

Green Rating 60*

Type of school private

Environment metropolis

STUDENTS

Total undergrad enrollment 2,100

% male/female 46/54

% from out of state 62

% from public high school 85

% live on campus 35

% African American 11

% Asian 3

% Caucasian 65

% Hispanic 4

% international 3

# of countries represented 40

ACADEMICS

Calendar semester

Profs interesting rating 90

Profs accessible rating 65

Student/faculty ratio 9:1

Most common

reg class size 10–19 students

MOST POPULAR MAJORS

graphic design

drama and dramatics/theatre arts

photography

SELECTIVITY

of applicants 2,349

% of applicants accepted 49

% of acceptees attending 49

accepting a place on wait list 22

% admitted from wait list 27

FRESHMAN PROFILE

Range SAT Critical Reading 470–580

Range SAT Math 450–570

Range SAT Writing 460–580

Range ACT Composite 19–26

Minimum paper TOEFL 500

Minimum computer TOEFL 173

Average HS GPA 2.88

% graduated top 10% of class 10

% graduated top 25% of class 32

% graduated top 50% of class 66

DEADLINES

Regular

Priority 3/1

Notification rolling

Nonfall registration? yes

FINANCIAL FACTS

Annual tuition $23,380

Room and board $7,800

Required fees $950

Books and supplies $2,000

% frosh rec. need-based

scholarship or grant aid 43

% UG rec. need-based

scholarship or grant aid 40

% frosh rec. non-need-based

scholarship or grant aid 65

% UG rec. non-need-based

scholarship or grant aid 90

% frosh rec. need-based self-help aid 65

% UG rec. need-based self-help aid 90

% frosh rec. any financial aid 87

% UG rec. any financial aid 90

% UG borrow to pay for school 85

Average cumulative indebtedness $17,500

UNIVERSITY OF CONNECTICUT

CAMPUS LIFE

Fire Safety Rating 86

Green Rating 88

Type of school public

Environment town

STUDENTS

Total undergrad enrollment 16,036

% male/female 49/51

% from out of state 23

% live on campus 68

% in (# of) fraternities 8 (14)

% in (# of) sororities 8 (12)

% African American 5

% Asian 7

% Caucasian 67

% Hispanic 5

% international 1

# of countries represented 109

ACADEMICS

Calendar semester

Student/faculty ratio 17:1

Profs interesting rating 65

Profs accessible rating 71
% classes taught by TAs 23
Most common
  reg class size 10–19 students
Most common
  lab size 10–19 students

MOST POPULAR MAJORS
business
political science
psychology, general

SELECTIVITY
of applicants 21,105
% of applicants accepted 49
% of acceptees attending 30
# accepting a place on wait list 1,373
% admitted from wait list 27

FRESHMAN PROFILE
Range SAT Critical Reading 530–630
Range SAT Math 560–660
Range SAT Writing 540–640
Range ACT Composite 23–28
% graduated top 10% of class 40
% graduated top 25% of class 81
% graduated top 50% of class 98

DEADLINES
Early action
  Deadline 12/1
  Notification 2/1
Regular
  Deadline 2/1
  Notification rolling
Nonfall registration? yes

FINANCIAL FACTS
Annual in-state tuition $7,200
Annual out-of-state tuition $21,912
Room and board $9,300
Required fees $2,138
Books and supplies $800
% frosh rec. need-based
  scholarship or grant aid 41
% UG rec. need-based
  scholarship or grant aid 36
% frosh rec. non-need-based
  scholarship or grant aid 32
% UG rec. non-need-based
  scholarship or grant aid 22
% frosh rec. need-based
  self-help aid 37
% UG rec. need-based
  self-help aid 38
% frosh rec. athletic scholarships 3
% UG rec. athletic scholarships 2
% frosh rec. any financial aid 50
% UG rec. any financial aid 48

% UG borrow to pay for school 61
Average cumulative
  indebtedness $20,658

UNIVERSITY OF DELAWARE

CAMPUS LIFE
Fire Safety Rating **93**
Green Rating **81**
Type of school public
Environment town

STUDENTS
Total undergrad enrollment 15,211
% male/female 42/58
% from out of state 60
% from public high school 80
% live on campus 47
% in (# of) fraternities 12 (15)
% in (# of) sororities 12 (15)
% African American 5
% Asian 4
% Caucasian 83
% Hispanic 4
% international 1
# of countries represented 100

ACADEMICS
Calendar 4/1/4
Student/faculty ratio 12:1
Profs interesting rating 73
Profs accessible rating 77
% classes taught by TAs 5
Most common
  reg class size 10–19 students
Most common
  lab size 10–19 students

MOST POPULAR MAJORS
elementary education and teaching
biology/biological sciences
psychology

SELECTIVITY
of applicants 21,930
% of applicants accepted 47
% of acceptees attending 31
# accepting a place on wait list 1,237
% admitted from wait list 48

FRESHMAN PROFILE
Range SAT Critical Reading 540–640
Range SAT Math 560–660
Range SAT Writing 540–650
Range ACT Composite 23–28
Minimum paper TOEFL 550
Minimum computer TOEFL 213
Average HS GPA 3.6
% graduated top 10% of class 39

% graduated top 25% of class 80
% graduated top 50% of class 98

DEADLINES
Regular
  Priority 12/1
  Deadline 1/15
  Notification 3/15
Nonfall registration? yes

FINANCIAL FACTS
Annual in-state tuition $7,340
Annual out-of-state tuition $18,590
Room and board $7,948
Required fees $810
Books and supplies $800
% frosh rec. need-based
  scholarship or grant aid 26
% UG rec. need-based
  scholarship or grant aid 24
% frosh rec. non-need-based
  scholarship or grant aid 20
% UG rec. non-need-based
  scholarship or grant aid 11
% frosh rec. need-based
  self-help aid 29
% UG rec. need-based
  self-help aid 28
% frosh rec. athletic scholarships 3
% UG rec. athletic scholarships 3
% UG borrow to pay for school 44
Average cumulative
  indebtedness $17,200

UNIVERSITY OF MAINE

CAMPUS LIFE
Fire Safety Rating **73**
Green Rating **93**
Type of school public
Environment village

STUDENTS
Total undergrad enrollment 8,777
% male/female 50/50
% from out of state 16
% live on campus 42
% in (# of) fraternities NR (13)
% in (# of) sororities NR (6)
% African American 1
% Asian 1
% Caucasian 94
% Hispanic 1
% Native American 2
% international 2
# of countries represented 67

ACADEMICS

Calendar	semester
Student/faculty ratio	16:1
Profs interesting rating	68
Profs accessible rating	70
% classes taught by TAs	17
Most common reg class size	10–19 students
Most common lab size	10–19 students

MOST POPULAR MAJORS
education
engineering
business/commerce

SELECTIVITY

# of applicants	6,958
% of applicants accepted	77
% of acceptees attending	36

FRESHMAN PROFILE

Range SAT Critical Reading	480–580
Range SAT Math	480–600
Range SAT Writing	470–570
Range ACT Composite	19–25
Average HS GPA	3.12
% graduated top 10% of class	21
% graduated top 25% of class	52
% graduated top 50% of class	86

DEADLINES

Early action	
Deadline	12/15
Notification	1/31
Regular	
Priority	2/1
Notification	rolling
Nonfall registration?	yes

FINANCIAL FACTS

Annual in-state tuition	$6,690
Annual out-of-state tuition	$18,960
Room and board	$7,484
Required fees	$1,790
Books and supplies	$600
% frosh rec. need-based scholarship or grant aid	53
% UG rec. need-based scholarship or grant aid	46
% frosh rec. non-need-based scholarship or grant aid	4
% UG rec. non-need-based scholarship or grant aid	3
% frosh rec. need-based self-help aid	52
% UG rec. need-based self-help aid	52
% frosh rec. any financial aid	76
% UG rec. any financial aid	93
% UG borrow to pay for school	76
Average cumulative indebtedness	$22,630

UNIVERSITY OF MAINE— FORT KENT

CAMPUS LIFE

Fire Safety Rating	**60***
Green Rating	**60***
Type of school	public
Environment	rural

STUDENTS

Total undergrad enrollment	926
% male/female	36/64
% from out of state	31
% from public high school	96
% live on campus	13
% in (# of) fraternities	5 (NR)
% in (# of) sororities	2 (1)
% Caucasian	8
% international	3

ACADEMICS

Calendar	semester
Profs interesting rating	84
Profs accessible rating	85
Student/faculty ratio	18:1
Most common reg class size	10–19 students

MOST POPULAR MAJORS
elementary education and teaching
nursing/registered nurse (rn, asn, bsn, msn)
business/commerce

SELECTIVITY

# of applicants	260
% of applicants accepted	93
% of acceptees attending	54

FRESHMAN PROFILE

Minimum paper TOEFL	500
Average HS GPA	2.72
% graduated top 10% of class	11
% graduated top 25% of class	25
% graduated top 50% of class	59

DEADLINES

Nonfall registration?	yes

FINANCIAL FACTS

Annual in-state tuition	$5,100
Annual out-of-state tuition	$12,780
Room and board	$6,620
Required fees	$653
Books and supplies	$1,030
% UG borrow to pay for school	81
Average cumulative indebtedness	$10,483

UNIVERSITY OF MARYLAND— BALTIMORE COUNTY

CAMPUS LIFE

Fire Safety Rating	**85**
Green Rating	**76**
Type of school	public
Environment	metropolis

STUDENTS

Total undergrad enrollment	9,304
% male/female	54/46
% from out of state	7
% live on campus	34
% in (# of) fraternities	4 (9)
% in (# of) sororities	4 (8)
% African American	16
% Asian	21
% Caucasian	53
% Hispanic	4
% Native American	1
% international	4
# of countries represented	95

ACADEMICS

Calendar	4/1/4
Student/faculty ratio	18:1
Profs interesting rating	68
Profs accessible rating	67
% classes taught by TAs	2
Most common reg class size	10–19 students
Most common lab size	10–19 students

MOST POPULAR MAJORS
computer and information sciences
biology/biological sciences
psychology

SELECTIVITY

# of applicants	5,836
% of applicants accepted	69
% of acceptees attending	36
# accepting a place on wait list	263
% admitted from wait list	48

FRESHMAN PROFILE

Range SAT Critical Reading	520–640
Range SAT Math	560–660
Range SAT Writing	520–630
Range ACT Composite	22–27

Minimum paper TOEFL	550
Minimum computer TOEFL	220
Minimum web-based TOEFL	80
Average HS GPA	3.6
% graduated top 10% of class	28.3
% graduated top 25% of class	58.6
% graduated top 50% of class	86.1

DEADLINES

Early action	
Deadline	11/1
Notification	12/15
Regular	
Priority	11/1
Deadline	2/1
Notification	rolling
Nonfall registration?	yes

FINANCIAL FACTS

Annual in-state tuition	$8,707
% frosh rec. need-based	
scholarship or grant aid	39
% UG rec. need-based	
scholarship or grant aid	37
% frosh rec. non-need-based	
scholarship or grant aid	8
% UG rec. non-need-based	
scholarship or grant aid	4
% frosh rec. need-based	
self-help aid	41
% UG rec. need-based	
self-help aid	42
% frosh rec. athletic scholarships	6
% UG rec. athletic scholarships	5
% frosh rec. any financial aid	87
% UG rec. any financial aid	73
% UG borrow to pay for school	53
Average cumulative	
indebtedness	$20,572

UNIVERSITY OF MARYLAND— COLLEGE PARK

CAMPUS LIFE

Fire Safety Rating	**83**
Green Rating	**94**
Type of school	public
Environment	metropolis

STUDENTS

Total undergrad enrollment	25,251
% male/female	52/48
% from out of state	23
% live on campus	41
% in (# of) fraternities	9 (31)
% in (# of) sororities	10 (25)

% African American	13
% Asian	14
% Caucasian	57
% Hispanic	6
% international	2
# of countries represented	149

ACADEMICS

Calendar	semester
Student/faculty ratio	18:1
Profs interesting rating	71
Profs accessible rating	68
% classes taught by TAs	15
Most common	
reg class size	20–29 students
Most common	
lab size	20–29 students

MOST POPULAR MAJORS
economics
criminology
political science and government

SELECTIVITY

# of applicants	24,176
% of applicants accepted	47
% of acceptees attending	37

FRESHMAN PROFILE

Range SAT Critical Reading	570–680
Range SAT Math	600–700
Minimum paper TOEFL	575
Minimum computer TOEFL	232
Average HS GPA	3.90
% graduated top 10% of class	56
% graduated top 25% of class	89
% graduated top 50% of class	99

DEADLINES

Early action	
Deadline	12/1
Notification	2/15
Regular	
Priority	12/1
Deadline	1/20
Notification	4/1
Nonfall registration?	yes

FINANCIAL FACTS

Annual in-state tuition	$6,566
Annual out-of-state tuition	$20,805
Room and board	$8,854
Required fees	$1,403
Books and supplies	$1,025
% frosh rec. need-based	
scholarship or grant aid	29
% UG rec. need-based	
scholarship or grant aid	27
% frosh rec. non-need-based	

scholarship or grant aid	24
% UG rec. non-need-based	
scholarship or grant aid	14
% frosh rec. need-based	
self-help aid	23
% UG rec. need-based	
self-help aid	26
% frosh rec. athletic scholarships	1
% UG rec. athletic scholarships	1
% frosh rec. any financial aid	67.8
% UG rec. any financial aid	59.5
% UG borrow to pay for school	42
Average cumulative indebtedness	$18,958

UNIVERSITY OF MASSACHUSETTS—AMHERST

CAMPUS LIFE

Fire Safety Rating	**73**
Green Rating	**82**
Type of school	public
Environment	town

STUDENTS

Total undergrad enrollment	20,114
% male/female	50/50
% from out of state	20
% live on campus	60
% in (# of) fraternities	4 (19)
% in (# of) sororities	4 (15)
% African American	5
% Asian	8
% Caucasian	73
% Hispanic	4
% international	1
# of countries represented	28

ACADEMICS

Calendar	semester
Student/faculty ratio	17:1
Profs interesting rating	63
Profs accessible rating	62
% classes taught by TAs	14
Most common	
reg class size	10–19 students
Most common	
lab size	20–29 students

MOST POPULAR MAJORS
psychology
biological and physical sciences
English language and literature

SELECTIVITY

# of applicants	27,138
% of applicants accepted	66
% of acceptees attending	24

# accepting a place on wait list	426
% admitted from wait list	54

FRESHMAN PROFILE
Range SAT Critical Reading	510–610
Range SAT Math	520–630
Minimum paper TOEFL	550
Minimum computer TOEFL	213
Average HS GPA	3.48
% graduated top 10% of class	22
% graduated top 25% of class	58
% graduated top 50% of class	94

DEADLINES
Early action	
Deadline	11/1
Notification	12/15
Regular	
Deadline	1/15
Notification	rolling
Nonfall registration?	yes

FINANCIAL FACTS
Annual in-state tuition	$9,921
Books and supplies	$1,000
% frosh rec. need-based	
scholarship or grant aid	45
% UG rec. need-based	
scholarship or grant aid	39
% frosh rec. non-need-based	
scholarship or grant aid	4
% UG rec. non-need-based	
scholarship or grant aid	2
% frosh rec. need-based	
self-help aid	45
% UG rec. need-based	
self-help aid	46
% frosh rec. athletic scholarships	1
% UG rec. athletic scholarships	1
% frosh rec. any financial aid	84
% UG rec. any financial aid	78
% UG borrow to pay for school	56
Average cumulative	
indebtedness	$12,062

UNIVERSITY OF
MASSACHUSETTS—BOSTON

CAMPUS LIFE
Fire Safety Rating	60*
Green Rating	98
Type of school	public
Environment	metropolis

STUDENTS
Total undergrad enrollment	8,999
% male/female	42/58

% from out of state	5
% African American	16
% Asian	13
% Caucasian	48
% Hispanic	8
% international	3
# of countries represented	133

ACADEMICS
Calendar	semester
Profs interesting rating	77
Profs accessible rating	69
Student/faculty ratio	16:1
Most common	
reg class size	20–29 students
Most common	
lab size	less than 10 students

MOST POPULAR MAJORS
psychology
nursing/registered nurse (rn, asn, bsn, msn)
management science

SELECTIVITY
# of applicants	4,213
% of applicants accepted	61
% of acceptees attending	39

FRESHMAN PROFILE
Range SAT Critical Reading	460–570
Range SAT Math	480–580
Minimum paper TOEFL	550
Minimum computer TOEFL	213
Average HS GPA	3

DEADLINES
Regular	
Priority	3/1
Deadline	6/1
Nonfall registration?	yes

FINANCIAL FACTS
Annual in-state tuition	$1,714
Annual out-of-state tuition	$9,758
Required fees	$7,397
% frosh rec. need-based	
scholarship or grant aid	59
% UG rec. need-based	
scholarship or grant aid	53
% frosh rec. non-need-based	
scholarship or grant aid	2
% UG rec. non-need-based	
scholarship or grant aid	1
% frosh rec. need-based self-help aid	58
% UG rec. need-based self-help aid	59
% UG borrow to pay for school	47
Average cumulative indebtedness	$17,772

UNIVERSITY OF NEW
HAMPSHIRE

CAMPUS LIFE
Fire Safety Rating	96
Green Rating	99
Type of school	public
Environment	village

STUDENTS
Total undergrad enrollment	11,622
% male/female	44/56
% from out of state	45
% from public high school	84
% live on campus	55
% in (# of) fraternities	2 (9)
% in (# of) sororities	7 (6)
% African American	1
% Asian	2
% Caucasian	82
% Hispanic	2
% international	1
# of countries represented	39

ACADEMICS
Calendar	semester
Student/faculty ratio	18:1
Profs interesting rating	62
Profs accessible rating	62
% classes taught by TAs	1
Most common	
reg class size	10–19 students
Most common	
lab size	20–29 students

MOST POPULAR MAJORS
psychology
business administration and management
communication, journalism, and related programs

SELECTIVITY
# of applicants	14,382
% of applicants accepted	59
% of acceptees attending	31

FRESHMAN PROFILE
Range SAT Critical Reading	500–610
Range SAT Math	510–620
Minimum paper TOEFL	550
Minimum computer TOEFL	213
Minimum web-based TOEFL	80
% graduated top 10% of class	24
% graduated top 25% of class	66
% graduated top 50% of class	98

DEADLINES
Early action
  Deadline 11/1
  Notification 1/1
Regular
  Deadline 2/1
  Notification 4/15
Nonfall registration? yes

FINANCIAL FACTS
Annual in-state tuition $8,810
Annual out-of-state tuition $21,770
Room and board $8,168
Required fees $2,260
Books and supplies $1,400
% frosh rec. need-based
  scholarship or grant aid 55
% UG rec. need-based
  scholarship or grant aid 63
% frosh rec. non-need-based
  scholarship or grant aid 44
% UG rec. non-need-based
  scholarship or grant aid 40
% frosh rec. need-based
  self-help aid 54
% UG rec. need-based
  self-help aid 62
% frosh rec. athletic scholarships 2
% UG rec. athletic scholarships 2
% frosh rec. any financial aid 83
% UG rec. any financial aid 80
% UG borrow to pay for school 75
Average cumulative
  indebtedness $25,145

UNIVERSITY OF PENNSYLVANIA

CAMPUS LIFE
Fire Safety Rating **71**
Green Rating **93**
Type of school private
Environment metropolis

STUDENTS
Total undergrad enrollment 9,687
% male/female 51/49
% from out of state 81
% live on campus 64
% in (# of) fraternities 30 (32)
% in (# of) sororities 26 (16)
% African American 8
% Asian 17
% Caucasian 45
% Hispanic 6

% international 10
# of countries represented 111

ACADEMICS
Student/faculty ratio 6:1
Profs interesting rating 74
Profs accessible rating 80
% classes taught by TAs 5
MOST POPULAR MAJORS
business administration and management
finance
nursing/registered nurse
(RN, ASN, BSN, MSN)

SELECTIVITY
# of applicants 22,645
% of applicants accepted 16
% of acceptees attending 66

FRESHMAN PROFILE
Range SAT Critical Reading 650–750
Range SAT Math 680–770
Range ACT Composite 29–33
Average HS GPA 3.8
% graduated top 10% of class 96
% graduated top 25% of class 99
% graduated top 50% of class 100

DEADLINES
Regular
  Priority 01/01
Nonfall registration? No

FINANCIAL FACTS
Annual tuition $35,916
Room and board $10,621
Required fees $3,925
Books and supplies $1,043
% frosh rec. any financial aid 60
% UG rec. any financial aid 55

UNIVERSITY OF PITTSBURGH AT BRADFORD

CAMPUS LIFE
Fire Safety Rating **80**
Green Rating **77**
Type of school public
Environment village

STUDENTS
Total undergrad enrollment 1,407
% male/female 42/58
% from out of state 15
% live on campus 52
% in (# of) fraternities 2 (3)
% in (# of) sororities 2 (3)
% African American 4

% Asian 2
% Caucasian 83
% Hispanic 1
# of countries represented 9

ACADEMICS
Calendar semester
Profs interesting rating 78
Profs accessible rating 69
Student/faculty ratio 14:1
Most common
  reg class size 10–19 students
Most common
  lab size 10–19 students
MOST POPULAR MAJORS
criminal justice/law enforcement
administration
nursing/registered nurse (rn, asn, bsn, msn)
business/commerce

SELECTIVITY
# of applicants 737
% of applicants accepted 84
% of acceptees attending 52
# accepting a place on wait list 5
% admitted from wait list 100

FRESHMAN PROFILE
Range SAT Critical Reading 420–530
Range SAT Math 440–560
Range SAT Writing 430–510
Range ACT Composite 17–22
Minimum paper TOEFL 550
Minimum computer TOEFL 213
Minimum web-based TOEFL 79–80
Average HS GPA 3.1
% graduated top 10% of class 6
% graduated top 25% of class 30
% graduated top 50% of class 70

DEADLINES
Regular
  Priority 5/1
  Notification rolling
Nonfall registration? yes

FINANCIAL FACTS
Annual in-state tuition $10,590
Annual out-of-state tuition $20,170
Room and board $6,850
Required fees $710
Books and supplies $1,000
% frosh rec. need-based
  scholarship or grant aid 63
% UG rec. need-based
  scholarship or grant aid 58
% frosh rec. non-need-based
  scholarship or grant aid 64

% UG rec. non-need-based scholarship or grant aid	54
% frosh rec. need based self-help aid	82
% UG rec. need-based self-help aid	73
% frosh rec. any financial aid	88
% UG rec. any financial aid	83
% UG borrow to pay for school	90
Average cumulative indebtedness	$24,910

UNIVERSITY OF PITTSBURGH AT JOHNSTOWN

CAMPUS LIFE

Fire Safety Rating	**60***
Green Rating	**60***
Type of school	public
Environment	city

STUDENTS

Total undergrad enrollment	3,116
% male/female	53/47
% from out of state	1
% live on campus	61
% in (# of) fraternities	5 (5)
% in (# of) sororities	5 (3)
% African American	2
% Asian	1
% Caucasian	94
% Hispanic	1

ACADEMICS

Calendar	semester
Profs interesting rating	77
Profs accessible rating	77
Student/faculty ratio	19:1
Most common reg class size	20–29 students
Most common lab size	10–19 students

MOST POPULAR MAJORS

SELECTIVITY

# of applicants	1,749
% of applicants accepted	88
% of acceptees attending	55

FRESHMAN PROFILE

Range SAT Critical Reading	450–540
Range SAT Math	470–560
Range SAT Writing	460–540
Range ACT Composite	18–22
Average HS GPA	3.33
% graduated top 10% of class	11
% graduated top 25% of class	35
% graduated top 50% of class	73

DEADLINES

Notification	rolling
Nonfall registration?	yes

FINANCIAL FACTS

% frosh rec. need-based scholarship or grant aid	53
% UG rec. need-based scholarship or grant aid	50
% frosh rec. non-need-based scholarship or grant aid	29
% UG rec. non-need-based scholarship or grant aid	23
% frosh rec. need-based self-help aid	71
% UG rec. need-based self-help aid	63
% frosh rec. athletic scholarships	2
% UG rec. athletic scholarships	3
% frosh rec. any financial aid	75
% UG rec. any financial aid	75
% UG borrow to pay for school	86
Average cumulative indebtedness	$23,412

UNIVERSITY OF PITTSBURGH—PITTSBURGH

CAMPUS LIFE

Fire Safety Rating	**85**
Green Rating	**78**
Type of school	public
Environment	city

STUDENTS

Total undergrad enrollment	16,798
% male/female	49/51
% from out of state	17
% live on campus	45
% in (# of) fraternities	8 (22)
% in (# of) sororities	8 (16)
% African American	9
% Asian	5
% Caucasian	83
% Hispanic	1
% international	1
# of countries represented	43

ACADEMICS

Calendar	semester
Student/faculty ratio	16:1
Profs interesting rating	71
Profs accessible rating	81
Most common reg class size	10–19 students
Most common lab size	20–29 students

MOST POPULAR MAJORS
psychology
speech and rhetorical studies
marketing/marketing management

SELECTIVITY

# of applicants	19,056
% of applicants accepted	56
% of acceptees attending	32
# accepting a place on wait list	310
% admitted from wait list	12

FRESHMAN PROFILE

Range SAT Critical Reading	570–670
Range SAT Math	580–670
Range ACT Composite	24–30
% graduated top 10% of class	48
% graduated top 25% of class	81
% graduated top 50% of class	98

DEADLINES

Regular Notification	rolling
Nonfall registration?	yes

FINANCIAL FACTS

Annual in-state tuition	$12,876
% frosh rec. need-based scholarship or grant aid	43
% UG rec. need-based scholarship or grant aid	40
% frosh rec. non-need-based scholarship or grant aid	25
% UG rec. non-need-based scholarship or grant aid	17
% frosh rec. need-based self-help aid	42
% UG rec. need-based self-help aid	44
% frosh rec. athletic scholarships	3
% UG rec. athletic scholarships	2

UNIVERSITY OF RHODE ISLAND

CAMPUS LIFE

Fire Safety Rating	**80**
Green Rating	**60***
Type of school	public
Environment	village

STUDENTS

Total undergrad enrollment	12,268
% male/female	44/56
% from out of state	39
% live on campus	45
% in (# of) fraternities	12 (11)
% in (# of) sororities	15 (9)

% African American 5
% Asian 2
% Caucasian 72
% Hispanic 5
# of countries represented 64

ACADEMICS
Calendar semester
Student/faculty ratio 19:1
Profs interesting rating 62
Profs accessible rating 62
Most common
  reg class size 20–29 students
Most common
  lab size 10–19 students

MOST POPULAR MAJORS
nursing/registered nurse
(RN, ASN, BSN, MSN)
communication studies/speech communication and rhetoric
psychology
Pharm. D.

SELECTIVITY
of applicants 14,272
% of applicants accepted 79
% of acceptees attending 28

FRESHMAN PROFILE
Range SAT Critical Reading 490–590
Range SAT Math 500–600
Minimum web-based TOEFL 79
Average HS GPA 3.12
% graduated top 10% of class 12

DEADLINES
Early action
  Deadline 12/15
  Notification 1/31
Regular
  Deadline 2/1
  Notification rolling
Nonfall registration? yes

FINANCIAL FACTS
Annual in-state tuition $6,440
Annual out-of-state tuition $21,294
Room and board $8,732
Required fees $1,744
Books and supplies $1,000
% frosh rec. need-based
  scholarship or grant aid 52
% UG rec. need-based
  scholarship or grant aid 53
% frosh rec. non-need-based
  scholarship or grant aid 7
% UG rec. non-need-based
  scholarship or grant aid 5

% frosh rec. need-based
  self-help aid 51
% UG rec. need-based
  self-help aid 52
% frosh rec. any financial aid 52
% UG rec. any financial aid 54
% UG borrow to pay for school 64
Average cumulative
  indebtedness $21,125

UNIVERSITY OF SCRANTON

CAMPUS LIFE
Fire Safety Rating **73**
Green Rating **60***
Type of school private
Affiliation Roman Catholic/Jesuit
Environment city

STUDENTS
Total undergrad enrollment 3,994
% male/female 43/57
% from out of state 52
% live on campus 53
% African American 1
% Asian 2
% Caucasian 80
% Hispanic 5
# of countries represented 27

ACADEMICS
Calendar semester
Student/faculty ratio 11:1
Profs interesting rating 77
Profs accessible rating 81
Most common
  reg class size 10–19 students
Most common
  lab size 10–19 students

MOST POPULAR MAJORS
elementary education and teaching
marketing/marketing management
biology/biological sciences

SELECTIVITY
of applicants 7,609
% of applicants accepted 66
% of acceptees attending 20
# accepting a place on wait list 481
% admitted from wait list 4

FRESHMAN PROFILE
Range SAT Critical Reading 510–600
Range SAT Math 520–620
Minimum paper TOEFL 500
Minimum computer TOEFL 173
Average HS GPA 3.36
% graduated top 10% of class 27

% graduated top 25% of class 63
% graduated top 50% of class 92

DEADLINES
Early action
  Deadline 11/15
  Notification 12/15
Regular
  Deadline 3/1
  Notification rolling
Nonfall registration? yes

FINANCIAL FACTS
Annual tuition $27,604
% frosh rec. need-based
  scholarship or grant aid 67
% UG rec. need-based
  scholarship or grant aid 63
% frosh rec. non-need-based
  scholarship or grant aid 6
% UG rec. non-need-based
  scholarship or grant aid 4
% frosh rec. need-based
  self-help aid 59
% UG rec. need-based
  self-help aid 56
% frosh rec. any financial aid 85
% UG rec. any financial aid 82
% UG borrow to pay for school 76
Average cumulative
  indebtedness $26,169

UNIVERSITY OF SOUTHERN MAINE

CAMPUS LIFE
Fire Safety Rating **60***
Green Rating **60***
Type of school public
Environment town

STUDENTS
Total undergrad enrollment 6,603
% male/female 42/58
% from out of state 9
% live on campus 19
% in (# of) fraternities 2 (4)
% in (# of) sororities 2 (4)
% African American 2
% Asian 2
% Caucasian 93
% Hispanic 1
% Native American 1
# of countries represented 40

ACADEMICS

Calendar	semester
Profs interesting rating	70
Profs accessible rating	63
Student/faculty ratio	13:1
Most common	
reg class size	10–19 students
Most common	
lab size	less than 10 students

MOST POPULAR MAJORS
psychology
perioperative/operating room and surgical
nurse/nursing

SELECTIVITY

# of applicants	4,016
% of applicants accepted	80
% of acceptees attending	30

FRESHMAN PROFILE

Range SAT Critical Reading	440–550
Range SAT Math	430–540
Range SAT Writing	440–540
Range ACT Composite	20–25
Minimum paper TOEFL	550
Minimum computer TOEFL	213
Average HS GPA	2.83
% graduated top 10% of class	10
% graduated top 25% of class	33
% graduated top 50% of class	71

DEADLINES

Regular	
Priority	2/15
Notification	rolling
Nonfall registration?	yes

FINANCIAL FACTS

Annual in-state tuition	$5,940
Annual out-of-state tuition	$16,410
Room and board	$8,038
Required fees	$927
Books and supplies	$900
% frosh rec. need-based	
scholarship or grant aid	57
% UG rec. need-based	
scholarship or grant aid	54
% frosh rec. non-need-based	
scholarship or grant aid	2
% UG rec. non-need-based	
scholarship or grant aid	2
% frosh rec. need-based self-help aid	59
% UG rec. need-based self-help aid	60
% frosh rec. any financial aid	70
% UG rec. any financial aid	79

UNIVERSITY OF VERMONT

CAMPUS LIFE

Fire Safety Rating	**78**
Green Rating	**96**
Type of school	public
Environment	city

STUDENTS

Total undergrad enrollment	9,454
% male/female	45/55
% from out of state	65
% from public high school	70
% live on campus	54
% in (# of) fraternities	6 (8)
% in (# of) sororities	5 (5)
% African American	1
% Asian	2
% Caucasian	93
% Hispanic	2
# of countries represented	46

ACADEMICS

Calendar	semester
Student/faculty ratio	16:1
Profs interesting rating	75
Profs accessible rating	77
% classes taught by TAs	2
Most common	
reg class size	10–19 students
Most common	
lab size	10–19 students

MOST POPULAR MAJORS
English language and literature
psychology
business administration and
management

SELECTIVITY

# of applicants	18,814
% of applicants accepted	70
% of acceptees attending	19
# accepting a place on wait list	1,261

FRESHMAN PROFILE

Range SAT Critical Reading	540–630
Range SAT Math	540–640
Range SAT Writing	530–630
Range ACT Composite	23–28
Minimum paper TOEFL	550
Minimum computer TOEFL	213
% graduated top 10% of class	23
% graduated top 25% of class	61
% graduated top 50% of class	97

DEADLINES

Early action	
Deadline	11/1
Notification	12/15
Regular	
Deadline	1/15
Notification	3/31
Nonfall registration?	yes

FINANCIAL FACTS

Annual in-state tuition	$10,422
Annual out-of-state tuition	$26,306
Room and board	$8,024
Required fees	$1,632
Books and supplies	$936
% frosh rec. need-based	
scholarship or grant aid	50
% UG rec. need-based	
scholarship or grant aid	49
% frosh rec. non-need-based	
scholarship or grant aid	4
% UG rec. non-need-based	
scholarship or grant aid	3
% frosh rec. need-based	
self-help aid	45
% UG rec. need-based	
self-help aid	46
% frosh rec. athletic scholarships	2
% UG rec. athletic scholarships	1
% frosh rec. any financial aid	90
% UG rec. any financial aid	78
% UG borrow to pay for school	61
Average cumulative	
indebtedness	$23,567

URSINUS COLLEGE

CAMPUS LIFE

Fire Safety Rating	**89**
Green Rating	**91**
Type of school	private
Environment	metropolis

STUDENTS

Total undergrad enrollment	1,563
% male/female	48/52
% from out of state	39
% from public high school	61
% live on campus	95
% in (# of) fraternities	18 (7)
% in (# of) sororities	28 (7)
% African American	6
% Asian	5
% Caucasian	75
% Hispanic	3
% international	1
# of countries represented	13

ACADEMICS

Calendar	semester
Student/faculty ratio	12:1
Profs interesting rating	85
Profs accessible rating	86
Most common reg class size	fewer than 10 students
Most common lab size	10–19 students

MOST POPULAR MAJORS

biology/biological sciences
psychology
economics

SELECTIVITY

# of applicants	5,141
% of applicants accepted	53
% of acceptees attending	17
# accepting a place on wait list	210
% admitted from wait list	29
# of early decision applicants	232
% accepted early decision	59

FRESHMAN PROFILE

Range SAT Critical Reading	550–660
Range SAT Math	560–660
Range SAT Writing	550–660
Range ACT Composite	22–29
Minimum paper TOEFL	500
Minimum computer TOEFL	173
% graduated top 10% of class	40
% graduated top 25% of class	74
% graduated top 50% of class	96

DEADLINES

Early decision	
Deadline	1/15
Notification	2/15
Early action	
Deadline	12/15
Notification	1/15
Regular	
Deadline	2/15
Notification	4/1
Nonfall registration?	yes

FINANCIAL FACTS

Annual tuition	$36,750
Room and board	$8,800
Required fees	$160
Books and supplies	$1,000
% frosh rec. need-based scholarship or grant aid	64
% UG rec. need-based scholarship or grant aid	68

% frosh rec. non-need-based scholarship or grant aid	13
% UG rec. non-need-based scholarship or grant aid	14
% frosh rec. need-based self-help aid	65
% UG rec. need-based self-help aid	70
% frosh rec. any financial aid	78
% UG rec. any financial aid	83
% UG borrow to pay for school	75
Average cumulative indebtedness	$18,509

VASSAR COLLEGE

CAMPUS LIFE

Fire Safety Rating	**81**
Green Rating	**60***
Type of school	private
Environment	town

STUDENTS

Total undergrad enrollment	2,409
% male/female	40/60
% from out of state	74
% from public high school	65
% live on campus	95
% African American	5
% Asian	10
% Caucasian	72
% Hispanic	7
% international	6
# of countries represented	43

ACADEMICS

Calendar	semester
Student/faculty ratio	8:1
Profs interesting rating	90
Profs accessible rating	89
Most common reg class size	10–19 students
Most common lab size	10–19 students

MOST POPULAR MAJORS

English language and literature
psychology
political science and government

SELECTIVITY

# of applicants	6,393
% of applicants accepted	29
% of acceptees attending	37
# accepting a place on wait list	430
# of early decision applicants	534
% accepted early decision	48

FRESHMAN PROFILE

Range SAT Critical Reading	660–750
Range SAT Math	640–710
Range SAT Writing	650–740
Range ACT Composite	29–32
Minimum paper TOEFL	600
Minimum computer TOEFL	250
Average HS GPA	3.76
% graduated top 10% of class	69
% graduated top 25% of class	95
% graduated top 50% of class	100

DEADLINES

Early decision	
Deadline	11/15
Notification	12/15
Regular	
Deadline	1/1
Notification	4/1
Nonfall registration?	no

FINANCIAL FACTS

Annual tuition	$37,570
Room and board	$8,570
Required fees	$545
Books and supplies	$860
% frosh rec. need-based scholarship or grant aid	53
% UG rec. need-based scholarship or grant aid	51
% frosh rec. need-based self-help aid	53
% UG rec. need-based self-help aid	51
% frosh rec. any financial aid	54
% UG rec. any financial aid	52
% UG borrow to pay for school	54
Average cumulative indebtedness	$20,589

VILLANOVA UNIVERSITY

CAMPUS LIFE

Fire Safety Rating	**89**
Green Rating	**81**
Type of school	private
Affiliation	Roman Catholic
Environment	village

STUDENTS

Total undergrad enrollment	6,949
% male/female	49/51
% from out of state	71
% from public high school	56
% live on campus	72
% in (# of) fraternities	20 (9)
% in (# of) sororities	28 (9)

% African American	4
% Asian	6
% Caucasian	78
% Hispanic	6
% international	2

ACADEMICS

Calendar	semester
Student/faculty ratio	13:1
Profs interesting rating	86
Profs accessible rating	92
Most common reg class size	10–19 students
Most common lab size	20–29 students

MOST POPULAR MAJORS
biological and physical sciences
nursing/registered nurse
(RN, ASN, BSN, MSN)
finance

SELECTIVITY

# of applicants	15,088
% of applicants accepted	37
% of acceptees attending	28
# accepting a place on wait list	2,300
% admitted from wait list	10

FRESHMAN PROFILE

Range SAT Critical Reading	580–680
Range SAT Math	610–700
Range SAT Writing	590–680
Range ACT Composite	27–31
Minimum paper TOEFL	550
Minimum computer TOEFL	213
Average HS GPA	3.76
% graduated top 10% of class	54
% graduated top 25% of class	96
% graduated top 50% of class	98

DEADLINES

Early action	
Deadline	11/1
Notification	12/20
Regular	
Deadline	1/7
Notification	4/1
Nonfall registration?	no

FINANCIAL FACTS

Annual tuition	$34,320
Room and board	$9,810
Required fees	$300
Books and supplies	$950
...ant aid	39

% frosh rec. non-need-based scholarship or grant aid	11
% UG rec. non-need-based scholarship or grant aid	11
% frosh rec. need-based self-help aid	45
% UG rec. need-based self-help aid	40
% frosh rec. athletic scholarships	2
% UG rec. athletic scholarships	2
% frosh rec. any financial aid	64
% UG rec. any financial aid	68
% UG borrow to pay for school	56
Average cumulative indebtedness	$28,107

WAGNER COLLEGE

CAMPUS LIFE

Fire Safety Rating	85
Green Rating	60*
Type of school	private
Affiliation	Lutheran
Environment	metropolis

STUDENTS

Total undergrad enrollment	1,926
% male/female	37/63
% from out of state	58
% live on campus	72
% in (# of) fraternities	6 (5)
% in (# of) sororities	8 (4)
% African American	5
% Asian	2
% Caucasian	76
% Hispanic	5
% international	1
# of countries represented	18

ACADEMICS

Calendar	semester
Student/faculty ratio	13:1
Profs interesting rating	75
Profs accessible rating	79
Most common reg class size	10–19 students
Most common lab size	fewer than 10 students

MOST POPULAR MAJORS
biology/biological sciences
psychology
business/commerce

SELECTIVITY

# of applicants	2,842
% of applicants accepted	60
% of acceptees attending	31
# accepting a place on wait list	72

% admitted from wait list	4
# of early decision applicants	130
% accepted early decision	59

FRESHMAN PROFILE

Range SAT Critical Reading	530–640
Range SAT Math	540–650
Range SAT Writing	530–640
Range ACT Composite	24–28
Minimum paper TOEFL	550
Minimum computer TOEFL	217
Average HS GPA	3.52
% graduated top 10% of class	18
% graduated top 25% of class	68
% graduated top 50% of class	92

DEADLINES

Early decision	
Deadline	1/1
Notification	2/1
Regular	
Priority	2/15
Deadline	3/1
Notification	3/1
Nonfall registration?	yes

FINANCIAL FACTS

Annual tuition	$29,400
Room and board	$8,900
Books and supplies	$725
% frosh rec. need-based scholarship or grant aid	62
% UG rec. need-based scholarship or grant aid	56
% frosh rec. non-need-based scholarship or grant aid	14
% UG rec. non-need-based scholarship or grant aid	11
% frosh rec. need-based self-help aid	48
% UG rec. need-based self-help aid	42
% frosh rec. athletic scholarships	5
% UG rec. athletic scholarships	5
% frosh rec. any financial aid	95
% UG rec. any financial aid	87
% UG borrow to pay for school	44
Average cumulative indebtedness	$35,717

WASHINGTON COLLEGE

CAMPUS LIFE

Fire Safety Rating	97
Green Rating	60*
Type of school	private
Environment	rural

STUDENTS

Total undergrad enrollment	1,269
% male/female	39/61
% from out of state	47
% from public high school	67
% live on campus	77
% in (# of) fraternities	18 (3)
% in (# of) sororities	20 (3)
% African American	4
% Asian	1
% Caucasian	84
% Hispanic	1
% international	3
# of countries represented	34

ACADEMICS

Calendar	semester
Student/faculty ratio	10:1
Profs interesting rating	88
Profs accessible rating	87
Most common reg class size	10–19 students
Most common lab size	10–19 students

MOST POPULAR MAJORS
English language and literature
psychology
business/commerce

SELECTIVITY

# of applicants	2,167
% of applicants accepted	64
% of acceptees attending	24
# accepting a place on wait list	218
% admitted from wait list	33
# of early decision applicants	40
% accepted early decision	75

FRESHMAN PROFILE

Range SAT Critical Reading	520–630
Range SAT Math	520–610
Range SAT Writing	520–610
Range ACT Composite	21–27
Average HS GPA	3.34
% graduated top 10% of class	32
% graduated top 25% of class	68
% graduated top 50% of class	92

DEADLINES

Early decision	
Deadline	11/1
Notification	12/1
Early action	
Deadline	11/15
Notification	12/15
Regular	
Priority	2/1
Deadline	3/1
Notification	rolling
Nonfall registration?	yes

FINANCIAL FACTS

Annual tuition	$33,385
Room and board	$7,180
Required fees	$620
Books and supplies	$1,000
% frosh rec. need-based scholarship or grant aid	36
% UG rec. need-based scholarship or grant aid	43
% frosh rec. non-need-based scholarship or grant aid	26
% UG rec. non-need-based scholarship or grant aid	32
% frosh rec. need-based self-help aid	27
% UG rec. need-based self-help aid	32
% frosh rec. any financial aid	79
% UG rec. any financial aid	85
% UG borrow to pay for school	60
Average cumulative indebtedness	$20,483

WASHINGTON & JEFFERSON COLLEGE

CAMPUS LIFE

Fire Safety Rating	**85**
Green Rating	**85**
Type of school	private
Environment	village

STUDENTS

Total undergrad enrollment	1,514
% male/female	53/47
% from out of state	24
% from public high school	84
% live on campus	94
% in (# of) fraternities	30 (6)
% in (# of) sororities	33 (4)
% African American	3
% Asian	1
% Caucasian	89
% Hispanic	1
# of countries represented	7

ACADEMICS

Calendar	4/1/4
Student/faculty ratio	12:1
Profs interesting rating	86
Profs accessible rating	88
Most common reg class size	10–19 students
Most common lab size	10–19 students

MOST POPULAR MAJORS
business/commerce
English language and literature
psychology

SELECTIVITY

# of applicants	7,377
% of applicants accepted	34
% of acceptees attending	16
# accepting a place on wait list	98
% admitted from wait list	28
# of early decision applicants	12
% accepted early decision	50

FRESHMAN PROFILE

Range SAT Critical Reading	520–620
Range SAT Math	530–640
Range ACT Composite	23–27
Minimum paper TOEFL	500
Minimum computer TOEFL	267
Average HS GPA	3.46
% graduated top 10% of class	37
% graduated top 25% of class	76
% graduated top 50% of class	98

DEADLINES

Early decision	
Deadline	12/1
Notification	12/15
Early action	
Deadline	1/1
Notification	1/15
Regular	
Priority	1/15
Deadline	3/1
Notification	rolling
Nonfall registration?	yes

FINANCIAL FACTS

Annual tuition	$29,532
Books and supplies	$800
% frosh rec. need-based scholarship or grant aid	64
% UG rec. need-based scholarship or grant aid	62
% frosh rec. non-need-based scholarship or grant aid	69
% UG rec. non-need-based scholarship or grant aid	60
% frosh rec. need-based self-help aid	70
% UG rec. need-based self-help aid	64
% frosh rec. any financial aid	99

% UG rec. any financial aid 96
% UG borrow to pay for school 75
Average cumulative
  indebtedness $20,000

WEBB INSTITUTE

CAMPUS LIFE
Fire Safety Rating **65**
Green Rating **60***
Type of school private
Environment village

STUDENTS
Total undergrad enrollment 91
% male/female 78/22
% from out of state 82
% from public high school 91
% live on campus 100
% Asian 2
% Caucasian 95
% Hispanic 2

ACADEMICS
Calendar semester
Student/faculty ratio 12:1
Profs interesting rating 89
Profs accessible rating 99
Most common
  reg class size 20–29 students

SELECTIVITY
of applicants 95
% of applicants accepted 31
% of acceptees attending 79
# of early decision applicants 31
% accepted early decision 39

FRESHMAN PROFILE
Range SAT Critical Reading 620–700
Range SAT Math 680–740
Range SAT Writing 600–710
Average HS GPA 3.9
% graduated top 10% of class 83
% graduated top 25% of class 100
% graduated top 50% of class 100

DEADLINES
Early decision
  Deadline 10/15
  Notification 12/15
Regular
  Priority 10/15
  Deadline 2/15
  Notification rolling
Nonfall registration? no

FINANCIAL FACTS
Room and board $9,500
Books and supplies $750
% frosh rec. need-based
  scholarship or grant aid 8
% UG rec. need-based
  scholarship or grant aid 14
% frosh rec. non-need-based
  scholarship or grant aid 4
% UG rec. non-need-based
  scholarship or grant aid 10
% frosh rec. need-based
  self-help aid 21
% UG rec. need-based
  self-help aid 11
% frosh rec. any financial aid 25
% UG rec. any financial aid 20
% UG borrow to pay for school 20
Average cumulative
  indebtedness $7,303

WELLESLEY COLLEGE

CAMPUS LIFE
Fire Safety Rating **86**
Green Rating **87**
Type of school private
Environment town

STUDENTS
Total undergrad enrollment 2,247
% male/female /100
% from out of state 83
% from public high school 66
% live on campus 97
% African American 6
% Asian 28
% Caucasian 45
% Hispanic 7
% international 8
# of countries represented 70

ACADEMICS
Calendar semester
Student/faculty ratio 9:1
Profs interesting rating 99
Profs accessible rating 98
Most common
  reg class size 10–19 students
Most common
  lab size 10–19 students

MOST POPULAR MAJORS
economics
psychology
political science and government

SELECTIVITY
of applicants 4,017
% of applicants accepted 36
% of acceptees attending 41
# accepting a place on wait list 381
% admitted from wait list 3
# of early decision applicants 236
% accepted early decision 55

FRESHMAN PROFILE
Range SAT Critical Reading 660–750
Range SAT Math 640–730
Range SAT Writing 660–730
Range ACT Composite 29–32
% graduated top 10% of class 78
% graduated top 25% of class 98
% graduated top 50% of class 100

DEADLINES
Early decision
  Deadline 11/1
  Notification 12/15
Regular
  Deadline 1/15
  Notification 4/1
Nonfall registration? no

FINANCIAL FACTS
Annual tuition $34,994
% frosh rec. need-based
  scholarship or grant aid 53
% UG rec. need-based
  scholarship or grant aid 56
% frosh rec. need-based
  self-help aid 50
% UG rec. need-based
  self-help aid 53
% frosh rec. any financial aid 55
% UG rec. any financial aid 59
% UG borrow to pay for school 52
Average cumulative
  indebtedness $11,902

WELLS COLLEGE

CAMPUS LIFE
Fire Safety Rating **84**
Green Rating **81**
Type of school private
Environment rural

STUDENTS
Total undergrad enrollment 544
% male/female 23/77
% from out of state 31
% from public high school 88
% live on campus 86
% African American 5

% Asian	2
% Caucasian	68
% Hispanic	4
% Native American	1
% international	2
# of countries represented	13

ACADEMICS

Calendar	semester
Student/faculty ratio	9:1
Profs interesting rating	94
Profs accessible rating	93
Most common	
reg class size	10–19 students

MOST POPULAR MAJORS
English language and literature
psychology
history

SELECTIVITY

# of applicants	1,148
% of applicants accepted	64
% of acceptees attending	24
# of early decision applicants	16
% accepted early decision	63

FRESHMAN PROFILE

Range SAT Critical Reading	510–640
Range SAT Math	490–590
Range ACT Composite	23–27
Minimum paper TOEFL	550
Minimum computer TOEFL	213
Average HS GPA	3.5
% graduated top 10% of class	25
% graduated top 25% of class	60
% graduated top 50% of class	92

DEADLINES

Early decision	
Deadline	12/15
Notification	1/15
Early action	
Deadline	12/15
Notification	2/1
Regular	
Priority	12/15
Deadline	3/1
Notification	4/1
Nonfall registration?	no

FINANCIAL FACTS

Annual tuition	$17,580
Room and board	$8,420
Required fees	$1,900
Books and supplies	$800
% frosh rec. need-based	
scholarship or grant aid	71

% UG rec. need-based	
scholarship or grant aid	76
% frosh rec. non-need-based	
scholarship or grant aid	37
% UG rec. non-need-based	
scholarship or grant aid	34
% frosh rec. need-based	
self-help aid	71
% UG rec. need-based	
self-help aid	75
% frosh rec. any financial aid	71
% UG rec. any financial aid	76
% UG borrow to pay for school	77
Average cumulative	
indebtedness	$20,355

WENTWORTH INSTITUTE OF TECHNOLOGY

CAMPUS LIFE

Fire Safety Rating	**60***
Green Rating	**60***
Type of school	private
Environment	metropolis

STUDENTS

Total undergrad enrollment	3,613
% male/female	80/20
% from out of state	40
% live on campus	60
% African American	4
% Asian	5
% Caucasian	77
% Hispanic	3
% international	3
# of countries represented	51

ACADEMICS

Calendar	semester
Profs interesting rating	70
Profs accessible rating	73
Student/faculty ratio	15:1
Most common	
reg class size	20–29 students
Most common	
lab size	10–19 students

MOST POPULAR MAJORS
Architecture
construction Management
mechanical engineering technology
interior design
civil engineering technology

SELECTIVITY

# of applicants	2,704
% of applicants accepted	80
% of acceptees attending	50

FRESHMAN PROFILE

Range SAT Critical Reading	470–510
Range SAT Math	560–600
Range ACT Composite	21–25
Minimum paper TOEFL	525
Minimum computer TOEFL	197
Average HS GPA	3

DEADLINES

Regular	
Priority	5/1
Notification	rolling
Nonfall registration?	yes

FINANCIAL FACTS

Annual tuition	$21,000
Room and board	$10,000
Books and supplies	$1,000
% frosh rec. need-based	
scholarship or grant aid	17
% UG rec. need-based	
scholarship or grant aid	11
% frosh rec. non-need-based	
scholarship or grant aid	61
% UG rec. non-need-based	
scholarship or grant aid	45
% frosh rec. need-based self-help aid	57
% UG rec. need-based self-help aid	47
% frosh rec. any financial aid	78
% UG rec. any financial aid	78
% UG borrow to pay for school	80
Average cumulative indebtedness	$22,000

WESLEYAN UNIVERSITY

CAMPUS LIFE

Fire Safety Rating	**86**
Green Rating	**92**
Type of school	private
Environment	town

STUDENTS

Total undergrad enrollment	2,787
% male/female	50/50
% from out of state	92
% from public high school	57
% live on campus	99
% in (# of) fraternities	2 (9)
% in (# of) sororities	NR (4)
% African American	7
% Asian	11
% Caucasian	61
% Hispanic	8
% Native American	1
% international	6
# of countries represented	48

ACADEMICS

Calendar	semester
Student/faculty ratio	9:1
Profs interesting rating	89
Profs accessible rating	83
Most common	
reg class size	10–19 students
Most common	
lab size	20–29 students

MOST POPULAR MAJORS
English language and literature
psychology
political science and government

SELECTIVITY

# of applicants	7,750
% of applicants accepted	27
% of acceptees attending	35
# accepting a place on wait list	441
% admitted from wait list	22
# of early decision applicants	665
% accepted early decision	43

FRESHMAN PROFILE

Range SAT Critical Reading	650–750
Range SAT Math	650–740
Range SAT Writing	650–740
Range ACT Composite	27–32
Minimum paper TOEFL	600
Minimum computer TOEFL	250
Minimum web-based TOEFL	100
Average HS GPA	3.77
% graduated top 10% of class	71
% graduated top 25% of class	93
% graduated top 50% of class	100

DEADLINES

Early decision	
Deadline	11/15
Notification	12/15
Regular	
Deadline	1/1
Notification	4/1
Nonfall registration?	no

FINANCIAL FACTS

Annual tuition	$36,806
% frosh rec. need-based	
scholarship or grant aid	40
% UG rec. need-based	
scholarship or grant aid	43
% frosh rec. need-based	
self-help aid	44
% UG rec. need-based	
self-help aid	47
% frosh rec. any financial aid	43
% UG rec. any financial aid	44

% UG borrow to pay for school	45
Average cumulative	
indebtedness	$21,464

WESTMINSTER COLLEGE (PA)

CAMPUS LIFE

Fire Safety Rating	**98**
Green Rating	**60***
Type of school	private
Affiliation	Presbyterian
Environment	village

STUDENTS

Total undergrad enrollment	1,387
% male/female	36/64
% from out of state	21
% from public high school	90
% live on campus	78
% in (# of) fraternities	33 (5)
% in (# of) sororities	34 (5)
% African American	3
% Caucasian	80
% Hispanic	1
# of countries represented	1

ACADEMICS

Calendar	semester
Student/faculty ratio	12:1
Profs interesting rating	89
Profs accessible rating	87
Most common	
reg class size	10–19 students
Most common	
lab size	10–19 students

MOST POPULAR MAJORS
education
biology/biological sciences
business/commerce

SELECTIVITY

# of applicants	1,368
% of applicants accepted	71
% of acceptees attending	32

FRESHMAN PROFILE

Range SAT Critical Reading	480–592
Range SAT Math	480–590
Range ACT Composite	20–25
Minimum paper TOEFL	550
Minimum computer TOEFL	213
Average HS GPA	3.4
% graduated top 10% of class	20
% graduated top 25% of class	55
% graduated top 50% of class	87

DEADLINES

Early action	
Deadline	11/15
Regular	
Deadline	4/15
Notification	rolling
Nonfall registration?	no

FINANCIAL FACTS

Annual tuition	$25,900
Room and board	$8,110
Required fees	$1,100
Books and supplies	$1,000
% frosh rec. need-based	
scholarship or grant aid	81
% UG rec. need-based	
scholarship or grant aid	79
% frosh rec. non-need-based	
scholarship or grant aid	80
% UG rec. non-need-based	
scholarship or grant aid	71
% frosh rec. need-based	
self-help aid	68
% UG rec. need-based	
self-help aid	65
% UG borrow to pay for school	73
Average cumulative	
indebtedness	$17,930

WHEATON COLLEGE (MA)

CAMPUS LIFE

Fire Safety Rating	**83**
Green Rating	**86**
Type of school	private
Environment	village

STUDENTS

Total undergrad enrollment	1,551
% male/female	40/60
% from out of state	65
% from public high school	63
% live on campus	93
% African American	5
% Asian	3
% Caucasian	77
% Hispanic	3
% international	3
# of countries represented	39

ACADEMICS

Calendar	semester
Student/faculty ratio	10:1
Profs interesting rating	88
Profs accessible rating	87
Most common	
reg class size	10–19 students

Most common
lab size 10–19 students
MOST POPULAR MAJORS
psychology
English language and literature
economics

SELECTIVITY
# of applicants	3,833
% of applicants accepted	37
% of acceptees attending	30
# accepting a place on wait list	283
% admitted from wait list	6
# of early decision applicants	259
% accepted early decision	75

FRESHMAN PROFILE
Range SAT Critical Reading	580–670
Range SAT Math	560–650
Range ACT Composite	25–28
Minimum paper TOEFL	580
Minimum computer TOEFL	243
Average HS GPA	3.5
% graduated top 10% of class	44
% graduated top 25% of class	70
% graduated top 50% of class	94

DEADLINES
Early decision	
Deadline	11/1
Notification	12/15
Regular	
Deadline	1/15
Notification	4/1
Nonfall registration?	yes

FINANCIAL FACTS
Annual tuition	$36,430
Room and board	$8,640
Required fees	$260
Books and supplies	$940
% frosh rec. need-based scholarship or grant aid	51
% UG rec. need-based scholarship or grant aid	47
% frosh rec. need-based self-help aid	53
% UG rec. need-based self-help aid	48
% frosh rec. any financial aid	70
% UG rec. any financial aid	64
% UG borrow to pay for school	58
Average cumulative indebtedness	$23,222

WILKES UNIVERSITY

CAMPUS LIFE
Fire Safety Rating	**60***
Green Rating	**72**
Type of school	private
Environment	city

STUDENTS
Total undergrad enrollment	2,257
% male/female	50/50
% from out of state	19
% live on campus	42
% African American	3
% Asian	2
% Caucasian	88
% Hispanic	2
% international	2
# of countries represented	10

ACADEMICS
Calendar	semester
Profs interesting rating	73
Profs accessible rating	75
Student/faculty ratio	15:1
Most common reg class size	20–29 students
Most common lab size	10–19 students

MOST POPULAR MAJORS
business administration and management
nursing/registered nurse (rn, asn, bsn, msn)
elementary education and teaching

SELECTIVITY
# of applicants	2,668
% of applicants accepted	79
% of acceptees attending	30

FRESHMAN PROFILE
Range SAT Critical Reading	460–560
Range SAT Math	470–600
Range SAT Writing	440–560
Minimum paper TOEFL	500
Minimum computer TOEFL	183
% graduated top 10% of class	24
% graduated top 25% of class	48
% graduated top 50% of class	82

DEADLINES
Notification	rolling
Nonfall registration?	yes

FINANCIAL FACTS
Annual tuition	$22,820
Room and board	$10,310
Required fees	$1,260
Books and supplies	$1,050

% frosh rec. need-based scholarship or grant aid	73
% UG rec. need-based scholarship or grant aid	65
% frosh rec. non-need-based scholarship or grant aid	63
% UG rec. non-need-based scholarship or grant aid	50
% frosh rec. need-based self-help aid	82
% UG rec. need-based self-help aid	76
% frosh rec. any financial aid	97
% UG rec. any financial aid	96
% UG borrow to pay for school	88
Average cumulative indebtedness	$29,478

WILLIAMS COLLEGE

CAMPUS LIFE
Fire Safety Rating	**60***
Green Rating	**60***
Type of school	private
Environment	village

STUDENTS
Total undergrad enrollment	1,962
% male/female	50/50
% from out of state	86
% from public high school	58
% live on campus	93
% African American	10
% Asian	11
% Caucasian	64
% Hispanic	9
% international	7
# of countries represented	61

ACADEMICS
Calendar	4/1/4
Student/faculty ratio	7:1
Profs interesting rating	94
Profs accessible rating	99
Most common reg class size	fewer than 10 students
Most common lab size	10–19 students

MOST POPULAR MAJORS
economics
visual and performing arts
English language and literature/
letters

SELECTIVITY
# of applicants	7,500
% of applicants accepted	18
% of acceptees attending	45
# accepting a place on wait list	682
% admitted from wait list	10

# of early decision applicants	537
% accepted early decision	40

FRESHMAN PROFILE

Range SAT Critical Reading	670–760
Range SAT Math	670–760
Range ACT Composite	29–33
% graduated top 10% of class	89
% graduated top 25% of class	100
% graduated top 50% of class	100

DEADLINES

Early decision	
Deadline	11/10
Notification	12/15
Regular	
Deadline	1/1
Notification	4/1
Nonfall registration?	no

FINANCIAL FACTS

Annual tuition	$35,438
Room and board	$9,470
Required fees	$232
Books and supplies	$800
% frosh rec. need-based scholarship or grant aid	51
% UG rec. need-based scholarship or grant aid	46
% frosh rec. need-based self-help aid	51
% UG rec. need-based self-help aid	47
% frosh rec. any financial aid	51
% UG rec. any financial aid	47
% UG borrow to pay for school	45
Average cumulative indebtedness	$9,727

WORCESTER POLYTECHNIC INSTITUTE

CAMPUS LIFE

Fire Safety Rating	**84**
Green Rating	**60***
Type of school	private
Environment	city

STUDENTS

Total undergrad enrollment	2,857
% male/female	74/26
% from out of state	50
% from public high school	66
% live on campus	59
% in (# of) fraternities	29 (11)
% in (# of) sororities	31 (3)
% African American	2

% Asian	6
% Caucasian	79
% Hispanic	4
% international	7
# of countries represented	81

ACADEMICS

Calendar	quarter
Student/faculty ratio	13:1
Profs interesting rating	76
Profs accessible rating	89
Most common reg class size	fewer than 10 students
Most common lab size	20–29 students

MOST POPULAR MAJORS
computer science
electrical, electronics and communications engineering
mechanical engineering

SELECTIVITY

# of applicants	4,931
% of applicants accepted	67
% of acceptees attending	24
# accepting a place on wait list	174
% admitted from wait list	16

FRESHMAN PROFILE

Range SAT Critical Reading	560–670
Range SAT Math	640–720
Range SAT Writing	550–640
Range ACT Composite	25–30
Minimum paper TOEFL	550
Minimum computer TOEFL	213
Minimum web-based TOEFL	79
Average HS GPA	3.7
% graduated top 10% of class	53
% graduated top 25% of class	83
% graduated top 50% of class	99

DEADLINES

Early action	
Deadline	1/1
Notification	12/15
Regular	
Deadline	2/1
Notification	4/1
Nonfall registration?	yes

FINANCIAL FACTS

Annual tuition	$34,830
Comprehensive fee	$45,240
Books and supplies	$1,000
% frosh rec. need-based scholarship or grant aid	76

% UG rec. need-based scholarship or grant aid	67
% frosh rec. non-need-based scholarship or grant aid	23
% UG rec. non-need-based scholarship or grant aid	16
% frosh rec. need-based self-help aid	51
% UG rec. need-based self-help aid	54
% frosh rec. any financial aid	96
% UG rec. any financial aid	94
% UG borrow to pay for school	82.4
Average cumulative indebtedness	$34,409

WORCESTER STATE COLLEGE

CAMPUS LIFE

Fire Safety Rating	**90**
Green Rating	**79**
Type of school	public
Environment	city

STUDENTS

Total undergrad enrollment	4,020
% male/female	42/58
% from out of state	3
% live on campus	25
% African American	4
% Asian	3
% Caucasian	80
% Hispanic	5
% international	2
# of countries represented	27

ACADEMICS

Calendar	semester
Profs interesting rating	74
Profs accessible rating	67
Student/faculty ratio	15:1
Most common reg class size	20–29 students
Most common lab size	10–19 students

MOST POPULAR MAJORS
business administration and management
psychology
criminal justice/safety studies

SELECTIVITY

# of applicants	3,810
% of applicants accepted	53
% of acceptees attending	34
# accepting a place on wait list	57

FRESHMAN PROFILE

Range SAT Critical Reading	450–540
Range SAT Math	460–560
Range ACT Composite	20–24
Minimum paper TOEFL	550
Minimum computer TOEFL	213
Minimum web-based TOEFL	79
Average HS GPA	3

DEADLINES

Regular	
Priority	3/15
Deadline	6/1
Notification	rolling
Nonfall registration?	yes

FINANCIAL FACTS

% frosh rec. need-based scholarship or grant aid	48
% UG rec. need-based scholarship or grant aid	36
% frosh rec. non-need-based scholarship or grant aid	25
% UG rec. non-need-based scholarship or grant aid	14
% frosh rec. need-based self-help aid	52
% UG rec. need-based self-help aid	43
% frosh rec. any financial aid	55
% UG rec. any financial aid	51
% UG borrow to pay for school	41
Average cumulative indebtedness	$17,985

YALE UNIVERSITY

CAMPUS LIFE

Fire Safety Rating	**60***
Green Rating	**99**
Type of school	private
Environment	city

STUDENTS

Total undergrad enrollment	5,311
% male/female	51/49
% from out of state	93
% from public high school	55
% live on campus	88
% African American	8
% Asian	13
% Caucasian	50
% Hispanic	8
% Native American	1
% international	8
# of countries represented	108

ACADEMICS

Calendar	semester
Profs interesting rating	83
Profs accessible rating	83

Most common reg class size	10–19 students

MOST POPULAR MAJORS

economics
political science and government
history

SELECTIVITY

# of applicants	19,323
% of applicants accepted	9
% of acceptees attending	71

FRESHMAN PROFILE

Range SAT Critical Reading	700–800
Range SAT Math	700–790
Range ACT Composite	30–34
Minimum paper TOEFL	600
Minimum computer TOEFL	250
% graduated top 10% of class	97
% graduated top 25% of class	100
% graduated top 50% of class	100

DEADLINES

Early action	
Deadline	11/1
Notification	12/15
Regular	
Deadline	12/31
Notification	4/1
Nonfall registration?	no

FINANCIAL FACTS

Annual tuition	$34,530
Room and board	$10,470
Books and supplies	$2,700
% frosh rec. need-based scholarship or grant aid	42
% UG rec. need-based scholarship or grant aid	42
% frosh rec. need-based self-help aid	43
% UG rec. need-based self-help aid	43
% UG borrow to pay for school	32
Average cumulative indebtedness	$13,344

YORK COLLEGE OF PENNSYLVANIA

CAMPUS LIFE

Fire Safety Rating	**92**
Green Rating	**60***
Type of school	private
Environment	village

STUDENTS

Total undergrad enrollment	5,219
% male/female	44/56
% from out of state	43
% from public high school	80
% live on campus	44
% in (# of) fraternities	7 (9)
% in (# of) sororities	9 (7)
# of countries represented	35

ACADEMICS

Calendar	semester
Profs interesting rating	74
Profs accessible rating	71
Student/faculty ratio	12:1
Most common reg class size	20–29 students
Most common lab size	less than 10 students

MOST POPULAR MAJORS

nursing/registered nurse (rn, asn, bsn, msn)
criminal justice/law enforcement administration
elementary education and teaching

SELECTIVITY

# of applicants	7,009
% of applicants accepted	64
% of acceptees attending	27

FRESHMAN PROFILE

Range SAT Critical Reading	490–580
Range SAT Math	500–600
Range SAT Writing	480–570
Range ACT Composite	19–24
Minimum paper TOEFL	530
Minimum computer TOEFL	200
Average HS GPA	3.5
% graduated top 10% of class	12
% graduated top 25% of class	36
% graduated top 50% of class	76

DEADLINES

Notification	rolling
Nonfall registration?	yes

FINANCIAL FACTS

Annual tuition	$12,320
Room and board	$7,800
Required fees	$1,360
Books and supplies	$1,000
% frosh rec. need-based scholarship or grant aid	42
% UG rec. need-based scholarship or grant aid	37
% frosh rec. non-need-based scholarship or grant aid	26

% UG rec. non-need-based
   scholarship or grant aid   16
% frosh rec. need-based self-help aid   50
% UG rec. need-based self-help aid   50
% frosh rec. any financial aid   86
% UG rec. any financial aid   74
% UG borrow to pay for school   69
Average cumulative indebtedness $20,625

PART 4: INDEX
ALPHABETICAL INDEX

INDEX BY LOCATION

INDEX BY COST

Paying For College 101

It's not a long shot to bet that you're reading this book because you're thinking of going to college. We're near psychic, right?! The odds are also good that you understand if you want to get into the college of your choice, you need the grades and the scores, and you need to demonstrate the things you dig outside the four walls of your classroom.

Positioning yourself for college admissions is not gambling; it's an investment. You've been investing your time and effort to be the best candidate for your prospective colleges and now, you've invested a little bit of money—right now by buying and reading this book! We applaud you for it!

But what else do you need to know to go to college?

If you answered, How am I going to pay for it? Then you're not alone and you're solidly on the right track to figuring it out. We think we can help.

Your college education is an investment in your future, and paying for college is a big part of that investment. In the next pages you'll find lots of basic information on that big scary subject—financial aid. While we tried to stick to "need to know" nuggets, the information you'll read about here is powerful because it diffuses frenzy around the aid process and equips you with the knowledge to navigate the process as an educated consumer. We ask that you take a little bit of time right now to learn about what it takes to afford yourself an excellent education.

WHAT ARE THE COSTS INVOLVED?

The first thing that comes to mind when you think about how much it costs to go to school is tuition, right? Well, tuition may be the first thing, but don't make the mistake of thinking that's it. The total cost of a year at college involves more than just the tuition amount that the school lists.

Let's break it down:

- Tuition and fees
- Room and board
- Books and supplies
- Personal expenses
- Travel expenses

All of these things together make up the total cost of attendance (COA) for a year at a particular college. So your tuition might be $20,000, but add on room and board, the cost of books, lab fees, not to mention the cost of travel back and forth for breaks, and miscellaneous personal expenses (you will need to buy toothpaste occasionally), and your COA could be as much as $30,000—that's a big difference.

According to a study by The College Board, during the 2006–2007 school year, the cost of attending a four-year private college for that year averaged approximately $30,367. The same study found that the total cost of attending a public university for that year was, on average, $12,796.

Paying for college is hard, yes; just about everyone needs some kind of financial assistance. More than 17 million students attend college each year—and only 20 percent manage to pay for it without some kind of financial aid package. That means almost 14 million students receive help.

WHATS IN A FINANCIAL AID PACKAGE?

A typical financial aid package contains money, from the school, federal government, or state, in various forms: grants, scholarships, work-study programs, and loans.

Grants

Grants are essentially gifts—free money given to you by the federal government, state agencies, and an individual college. They are usually need-based, and you are not required to pay them back.

Some states have grant programs established specifically to help financially needy students, usually to attend schools within that state. Different states have different standards and application requirements.

Scholarships

Scholarships are also free money, but unlike grants, they are merit-based. Some are also based on your financial need; others are based on different qualifications, and are often need-blind.

Scholarships can be based on anything: academic achievement or test scores (the National Merit Scholarship is a well-known one), athletic achievements, musical or artistic talent, religious affiliations or ethnicity, and so on.

They don't have to come from colleges, either. Corporations, churches, volunteer organizations, unions, advocacy groups, and many other organizations offer merit-based, need-based, or simply existence-based scholarships.

When considering outside scholarships, make sure you know how the college(s) you're applying to treat them. Some schools (but not all!) will count any money you receive from outside sources as income, and reduce the amount of any aid package accordingly.

Work-Study Programs

The federal government subsidizes a nationwide program that provides part-time, on-campus jobs to students who need financial aid to attend school. Work-study participants can work in academic departments, deans' offices, libraries, and so on. You get a paycheck, like you would at any job, and you can spend the money however you like—but it's meant for tuition, books, and food.

My Family Doesn't Have $30,000 Lying Around!

You and your family are not alone. In many cases, a school's financial aid package doesn't cover all of your costs, and you might not have the resources to make up the difference. When a school doesn't offer enough in the way of aid to cover the cost of attendance, many families turn to loans.

Let's start with the biggest source of student loans—the federal government.

Federal student aid is intended to bridge the gap between what college costs and what you and your family can actually afford to pay. The government does this in two ways: It makes money available to colleges, which then, through their financial aid offices, make the money available to students in the form of aid packages; and it helps students get affordable loans themselves, through guarantees to loan lenders and other ways (which we'll discuss in a minute).

How Does the Government Decide How Much to Give Me?

When you're applying for financial aid, you'll be filling out a lot of forms. The most important of those forms will be the Free Application for Federal Student Aid (FAFSA). Basically, the FAFSA will want to know the following information:

- Your parents' available income
- Your parents' available assets
- Your available income
- Your available assets

The federal government will take all this information and apply a complex formula to determine what your family's expected contribution should be.

What Is This "Expected Contribution"?

This is how much of your and your family's income and assets the government thinks you can afford to put toward the cost of attending college. This amount is called the Expected Family Contribution, or EFC.

Your financial need (i.e., the money you need in order to attend college) is defined as the difference between the school's total cost of attendance (tuition, room and board, books, etc.) and your expected family contribution. Or, to put it another way:

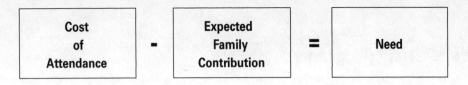

| Cost of Attendance | − | Expected Family Contribution | = | Need |

When you are accepted to a college, the school's financial aid office will then put together an aid package that, hopefully, will make up this difference and cover the cost of your need.

What Do You Mean, "Hopefully"?

The idea is that your EFC will be the same for every school, regardless of the cost of the school. This means that if your EFC is determined to be $9,500, that is the amount you would be expected to pay if you go to State U., where the COA is $14,000, or if you go to Private U., where the COA is $37,000. Ideally, the school will then provide you with a financial aid package that makes up the difference—$4,500 in the case of State U., $27,500 for Private U.

Ideally?

Yes, in a perfect world, where a school offers to meet 100% of your need, you and your family would pay no more than your EFC, and your EFC would always be exactly what you and your family believe you can afford.

In reality, this doesn't happen nearly as often as we'd like. Some schools have larger endowments for financial aid and can meet your need 100%. Other schools may not.

When that happens, you and your family may want to investigate student loans.

LOANS

The federal government and private commercial lenders offer educational loans to students. Federally-guaranteed loans are usually the "first resort" for borrowers because many are subsidized by the federal government and offer capped interest rates. Private loans, on the other hand, have fewer restrictions or borrowing limits, but may have higher interest rates and more stringent credit-based qualification process—but not always, as we'll see later on.

Federal Loans

For many students seeking financial aid, the Stafford loan is the typical place to start. The federal Stafford loan program features a low capped interest rate and yearly caps on the maximum amount a student can borrow. Stafford loans can either be subsidized (the government pays the interest while you're in school) or unsubsidized (you are responsible for the interest that accrues while in school). Most students who get Stafford loans will end up with a combination of the two. Stafford loans do not have to be repaid until you've graduated or dropped below part-time status.

Here's the thing you might not know about Stafford loans:

Many people assumed that the government sets the rate on student loans, and that that rate is locked in stone. That's not true. The government merely sets the maximum rate lenders can charge (which is 6.8% as of 2007). Lenders are free to charge less than that if they want to.

Historically, however, most lenders have charged the maximum rate because Stafford loans are distributed via colleges' financial aid offices, which maintain preferred lender lists of a limited number of lenders to choose from. Reduced numbers of lenders meant little competition for borrowers, which meant the lenders had very little incentive to offer more competitive rates.

In the last few years, though, a lot has changed. More students now know that they are not required to take a loan from a lender on a preferred lender list. And there are more lenders now willing to compete on price. It's vital that you, as the person making this important and, frankly, expensive investment in your future, educate yourself fully as to all your options when it comes to student loans.

Know Your Rights

You have the right to shop for and secure the best rates possible for your student loans. You have the right to choose the lending institution you prefer. You do not have to use the lenders recommended by your college. All your college must do—and all it is legally allowed to do—is to certify for the lending institution of your choice that you are indeed enrolled and the amount you are eligible to receive.

Private Loans

Student loans from private lenders can make it possible to cover the costs of higher education when other sources of funding have been exhausted.

When you apply for a private loan, the lending institution will check your credit score and determine your capacity to pay back the money you borrow. For individuals whose credit history is less than positive, or if you have no credit history, lenders may require a co-borrower: a credit-worthy individual—often a parent—who also agrees to be accountable to the terms of the loan. While private loans do have annual borrowing limits, they are usually higher than government loans, around $40,000; they also have higher interest rates and have floating rate caps, not fixed as in federal loans.

Do Your Research

All student loan lenders are not created equal, so investigate all your options, and look for lenders that are offering loans at rates less than the federally mandated maximum (remember, that's 6.1% for subsidized Staffords, and 6.8% for unsubsidized as of July 2008).

One lending institution that's been in the news lately is MyRichUncle. MyRichUncle offers federal loans, including subsidized and unsubsidized Stafford loans and private loans. However, MyRichUncle has re-membered that the government sets the maximum interest rate for Stafford loans, and has chosen to discount the rate upon repayment. Those discounts will not disappear, like they may with other lenders, unless you default on the loan.

So, Why MyRichUncle?

Well, we here at The Princeton Review think it's important that you have all the information when you're figuring out how to pay for college, and we think MyRichUncle is doing something different—and helpful—with their approach to student loans.

They know that getting a student loan can be a complicated and intimidating process. They believe, as does The Princeton Review, that students should have access to the best education even if they don't yet have a credit history, or at least an opportunity to prove they can be credit-worthy borrowers. They also believe student loan debt can be a serious problem so your loans should be about getting the tools necessary for the best education possible that will position you for the most opportunities when you graduate.

Something else to remember: Your student loan will, ultimately, be your responsibility. When you enter into a loan agreement, you're entering into a long-term relationship with your lender—10 to 15 years, on average. The right student loan, from the right lender, can help you avoid years of unnecessary fees and payments.

MyRichUncle was featured in *FastCompany* magazine's Fast 50 and *BusinessWeek*'s Top Tech Entrepreneurs. MyRichUncle and its parent company, MRU Holdings, are financed by a number of leading investment banks and venture capitalists, including subsidiaries of Merrill Lynch, Lehman Brothers, and Battery Ventures

For more information, check out

THE BOTTOM LINE

College is expensive, period. But if you're reading this book, you're already invested in getting the best education that you can. You owe it to yourself and your future to invest just as much in learning about all your financial options—and opportunities—as well.

IS THIS BOOK JUST LIKE YOUR COURSE?

Since the book came out, many students and teachers have asked us, "Is this book just like your course?" The short answer is no.

It isn't easy to raise SAT scores. Our course is more than 50 hours long and requires class participation, quizzes, homework, four practice examinations, and possibly additional tutoring.

We like to think that this book is fun, informative, and well written, but no book can capture the magic of our instructors and course structure. Each Princeton Review instructor has attended a top college and has excelled on the SAT. Moreover, each of our instructors undergoes rigorous training.

While this book contains many of the techniques we teach in our course, some of our techniques are too difficult to include in a book without a trained and experienced Princeton Review teacher to explain and demonstrate them. Moreover, this book is written for the average student. Each class in our course is tailored so that we can gear our techniques to each student's level.

We're Flattered, But…

Some tutors and schools use this book to run their own "Princeton Review course." While we are flattered, we are also concerned.

It has taken us many years of teaching tens of thousands of students across the country to develop our SAT program, and we're still learning. Many teachers think that our course is simply a collection of techniques that can be taught by anyone. It isn't that easy.

We train each Princeton Review instructor for many hours for every hour he or she will teach class. Each of the instructors is monitored, evaluated, and supervised throughout the course.

Another concern is that many of our techniques conflict with traditional math and English techniques as taught in high school. For example, in the Math section, we tell our students to avoid setting up algebraic equations. Can you imagine your math teacher telling you that? And in the Critical Reading section, we tell our students not to read the passage too carefully. Can you imagine your English teacher telling you that?

While we also teach traditional math and English in our course, some teachers may not completely agree with some of our approaches.

Beware of Princeton Review Clones

We have nothing against people who use our techniques, but we do object to tutors or high schools who claim to "teach The Princeton Review method." If you want to find out whether your teacher has been trained by The Princeton Review or whether you're taking an official Princeton Review course, call us toll-free at 1-800-2REVIEW.

If You'd Like More Information

Princeton Review sites are in hundreds of cities around the country. For the office nearest you, call 1-800-2REVIEW.

ABOUT THE AUTHORS

Robert Franek is a graduate of Drew University and has been a member of The Princeton Review staff for four years. Robert comes to The Princeton Review with an extensive admissions background, most recently at Wagner College in Staten Island, New York. In addition, he owns a walking tour business and leads historically driven, yet not boring, tours of his home town.

Tom Meltzer is a graduate of Columbia University. He has taught for The Princeton Review since 1986 and is the author or co-author of seven TPR titles, the most recent of which is *Illustrated Word Smart*, which Tom co-wrote with his wife, Lisa. He is also a professional musician and songwriter. A native of Baltimore, Tom now lives in Hillsborough, North Carolina.

Christopher Maier is a graduate of Dickinson College. During the past five years, he's lived variously in New York City, coastal Maine, western Oregon, central Pennsylvania, and eastern England. Now he's at an oasis somewhere in the Midwestern cornfields—the University of Illinois—where he's earning his MFA in fiction. Aside from writing for magazines, newspapers, and The Princeton Review, he's worked as a radio disc jockey, a helping hand in a bakery, and a laborer on a highway construction crew. He's trying to avoid highway construction these days.

Julie Doherty is a freelance writer, Web designer, and preschool teacher. She lives in Mexico City.

Andrew Friedman graduated in 2003 from Stanford University where he was a President's Scholar. He lives in New York City.

Our Books Help You Navigate the College Admissions Process

Find the Right School

Best 368 Colleges, 2009 Edition
978-0-375-42872-2 • $21.95/C$25.00
Previous Edition: 978-0-375-76621-3

Complete Book of Colleges, 2009 Edition
978-0-375-42874-6 • $26.95/C$32.00

College Navigator
978-0-375-76583-4 • $12.95/C$16.00

**America's Best Value Colleges,
2008 Edition**
978-0-375-76601-5 • $18.95/C$24.95

Guide to College Visits
978-0-375-76600-8 • $20.00/C$25.00

Get In

Cracking the SAT, 2009 Edition
978-0-375-42856-2 • $19.95/C$22.95

**Cracking the SAT with DVD,
2009 Edition**
978-0-375-42857-9 • $33.95/C$37.95

Math Workout for the SAT
978-0-375-76433-2 • $16.00/C$23.00

**Reading and Writing Workout
for the SAT**
978-0-375-76431-8 • $16.00/C$23.00

**11 Practice Tests for the SAT and PSAT,
2009 Edition**
978-0-375-42860-9 • $19.95/C$22.95

12 Practice Tests for the AP Exams
978-0-375-76584-1 • $19.95/C$24.95

Cracking the ACT, 2008 Edition
978-0-375-76634-3 • $19.95/C$22.95

**Cracking the ACT with DVD,
2008 Edition**
978-0-375-76635-0 • $31.95/C$35.95

Crash Course for the ACT, 3rd Edition
978-0-375-76587-2 • $9.95/C$12.95

Get Help Paying For It

**Paying for College Without
Going Broke, 2009 Edition**
978-0-375-42883-8 • $20.00/C$23.00
Previous Edition: 978-0-375-76630-5

Available at Bookstores Everywhere
www.PrincetonReview.com

AP Exams

Cracking the AP Biology Exam, 2008 Edition
978-0-375-76640-4 • $18.00/C$22.00

Cracking the AP Calculus AB & BC Exams, 2008 Edition
978-0-375-76641-1 • $19.00/C$23.00

Cracking the AP Chemistry Exam, 2008 Edition
978-0-375-76642-8 • $18.00/C$22.00

Cracking the AP Computer Science A & AB Exams, 2006–2007 Edition
978-0-375-76528-5 • $19.00/C$27.00

Cracking the AP Economics Macro & Micro Exams, 2008 Edition
978-0-375-42841-8 • $18.00/C$22.00

Cracking the AP English Language & Composition Exam, 2008 Edition
978-0-375-42842-5 • $18.00/C$21.00

Cracking the AP English Literature Exam, 2008 Edition
978-0-375-42843-2 • $18.00/C$22.00

Cracking the AP Environmental Science Exam, 2008 Edition
978-0-375-42844-9 • $18.00/C$22.00

Cracking the AP European History Exam, 2008 Edition
978-0-375-42845-6 • $18.00/C$22.00

Cracking the AP Physics B Exam, 2008 Edition
978-0-375-42846-3 • $18.00/C$21.00

Cracking the AP Physics C Exam, 2008 Edition
978-0-375-42854-8 • $18.00/C$21.00

Cracking the AP Psychology Exam, 2008 Edition
978-0-375-42847-0 • $18.00/C$22.00

Cracking the AP Spanish Exam, 2006–2007 Edition
978-0-375-76530-8 • $17.00/C$24.00

Cracking the AP Statistics Exam, 2008 Edition
978-0-375-42849-4 • $19.00/C$23.00

Cracking the AP U.S. Government & Politics Exam, 2008 Edition
978-0-375-42850-0 • $18.00/C$22.00

Cracking the AP U.S. History Exam, 2008 Edition
978-0-375-42851-7 • $18.00/C$21.00

Cracking the AP World History Exam, 2008 Edition
978-0-375-42852-4 • $18.00/C$22.00

SAT Subject Tests

Cracking the SAT Biology E/M Subject Test, 2007–2008 Edition
978-0-375-76588-9 • $19.00/C$25.00

Cracking the SAT Chemistry Subject Test, 2007–2008 Edition
978-0-375-76589-6 • $18.00/C$22.00

Cracking the SAT French Subject Test, 2007–2008 Edition
978-0-375-76590-2 • $18.00/C$22.00

Cracking the SAT Literature Subject Test, 2007–2008 Edition
978-0-375-76592-6 • $18.00/C$22.00

Cracking the SAT Math 1 and 2 Subject Tests, 2007–2008 Edition
978-0-375-76593-3 • $19.00/C$25.00

Cracking the SAT Physics Subject Test, 2007–2008 Edition
978-0-375-76594-0 • $19.00/C$25.00

Cracking the SAT Spanish Subject Test, 2007–2008 Edition
978-0-375-76595-7 • $18.00/C$22.00

Cracking the SAT U.S. & World History Subject Tests, 2007–2008 Edition
978-0-375-76591-9 • $19.00/C$25.00

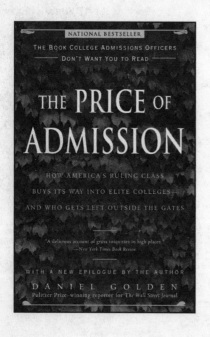
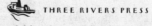